ROUTLEDGE HANDBOOK OF SOCIAL AND SUSTAINABLE FINANCE

Routledge Handbook of Social and Sustainable Finance brings together an international cast of leading authorities to map out and display the disparate voices, traditions, and professional communities engaged in social finance activity.

With a clear societal or environmental mission, foundations, individual and group investors, as well as public bodies around the world have become increasingly eager to finance and support innovative forms of doing business. Together, founders and established businesses alike are embracing new sustainable business models with a distinct stakeholder approach to tackle social or environmental problems in what they see as a failed economic system in crisis. As a result, the topic of social and sustainable finance is at the forefront of financial economic thought.

This handbook is divided up into three parts. The first, "The Landscape of Social and Sustainable Finance and Investments," comprises of chapters from a multitude of perspectives in an effort to grasp the entirety of the landscape. The second, "Challenges, Suggestions, Critiques, and Debates," focuses on areas ranging from sociological underpinnings to critical takes on markets, and the identification of specialized business models. Among ethical considerations, topics include the scaling of impact, an analysis of sustainability as risk prevention, and comparative analyses of various methods of justification and measurement. In the final section, "Markets and Institutions," contributions range from various perspectives on sustainable banking to environmental marketplaces, and finally on to practical cases and country-specific observations.

This volume is essential reading for both students and academics in economics and finance. It is also of interest to those who study environmental economics, microeconomics, and banking.

Othmar M. Lehner is a full Professor of Finance and Risk and a leading researcher in the field of social finance and impact investment. With a professional background as a bank manager, he now dedicates his academic career to the advancement of the field through research publications, advisory services, conferences, and lecturing in MBA and doctoral programs.

ROUTLEDGE HANDBOOK OF SOCIAL AND SUSTAINABLE FINANCE

Edited by Othmar M. Lehner

LONDON AND NEW YORK

First published 2017
by Routledge
2 Park Square, Milton Park, Abingdon, Oxon OX14 4RN

and by Routledge
711 Third Avenue, New York, NY 10017

First issued in paperback 2018

Routledge is an imprint of the Taylor & Francis Group, an informa business

British Library Cataloguing in Publication Data
A catalogue record for this book is available from the British Library

Library of Congress Cataloging in Publication Data
Names: Lehner, Othmar M., editor.
Title: Routledge handbook of social and sustainable finance / edited by Prof. Dr. Othmar M. Lehner.
Description: Abingdon, Oxon ; New York, NY : Routledge, 2016. | Includes index.
Identifiers: LCCN 2015049234| ISBN 9781138777545 (hardback) | ISBN 9781315772578 (ebook)
Subjects: LCSH: Finance—Social aspects. | Finance—Environmental aspects. | Investments—Environmental aspects. | Investments—Social aspects. | Sustainable development.
Classification: LCC HG101 .R68 2016 | DDC 332—dc23
LC record available at http://lccn.loc.gov/2015049234

ISBN 13: 978-1-138-34377-1 (pbk)
ISBN 13: 978-1-138-77754-5 (hbk)

Typeset in Bembo
by Book Now Ltd, London

CONTENTS

FIGURES

TABLES

CONTRIBUTORS

Lauryn Agnew, Seal Cove Financial, United States. With nearly three decades of experience in developing and implementing strategies in the institutional investment industry, Lauryn Agnew serves as a resource to non-profit organizations for investment consulting services and provides fiduciary education and trustee training for public fund and non-profit board and committee members. She is the founder of the Bay Area Impact Investing Initiative (baiii.org), developing in-depth research papers into customized regional Impact Investing model portfolios across all asset classes for mission alignment under fiduciary standards of due diligence and performance expectations.

Lauryn has served as a trustee and Board Chair for a public pension plan as well as for several non-profit organizations in the San Francisco Bay Area.

Belinda Bell, Social Incubator East, United Kingdom, is Programme Director of Social Incubator East, an incubator that provides specialist support for social ventures, and Fellow of Social Innovation at Cambridge Judge Business School.

She is a social entrepreneur herself having established a range of social ventures over the last decade including those focusing on finance, aging, and young people. She has acted as a mentor, advisor and supporter to many more social entrepreneurs and as such has developed a broad knowledge of business models for social innovation.

Her specific research interest is in the social finance market and leveraging capital for social impact. She was Founder and first Chief Executive of Foundation East, a ground-breaking community finance organization where she remains a Director.

Belinda holds a Master's degree in Community Enterprise from the University of Cambridge and a Bachelor's degree in Social Anthropology from Goldsmiths College, University of London.

Emmanuel Olatunbosun Benjamin, Technische Universität München, Germany, Olatunbosun Benjamin majored in economics and graduated from the Bergische University of Wuppertal, Germany. He is a researcher in the Department of Agriculture and Food Economics at Technische Universität München, Germany. His research in development and agricultural economics includes issues related to smallholder sustainable production, climate change mitigation and agricultural financing in Sub-Saharan Africa. He focuses on the socioeconomic (co)benefits of agri-environmental schemes involving agroforestry to participating smallholder farmers which includes improving productivity, access to financial and emission trading markets as well as human and social capital development. He has published in a number of international journals including the *Journal of Sustainable Finance and Investment* as well as *Enterprise Development & Microfinance*.

Saeed Binmahfouz, Salem Independent researcher in Islamic Finance and Investments, is an independent researcher in Islamic Finance and Investments, who graduated from Durham University. His research focuses on Islamic and Socially Responsible Investments, which are published in a number of international journals and edited books. Also, he is interested in critically reviewing and re-examining the Sharia issues related to Islamic finance and Investments.

Andrea Bonoldi, University of Trento, Italy, studied Political Economy and Economic and Social History in Trento, Vienna and Milan. He received his PhD in Economic and Social History from the University "L. Bocconi" in Milan. He is an associate professor and teaches Economic History at the University of Trent. His research interests center on economic relationships and development processes in Alpine regions in pre-modern and modern times. He has published numerous works in Italian, German, and English.

Mariana Bozesan, AQAL Investing and AQAL Capital, is an integral Impact Investor, serial entrepreneur, philanthropist, author, and academic researcher. Based on Ken Wilber's integral theory, she developed the Theta model and successfully implemented parity between people, planet, and profit in early stage investing through the integration of financial, ecological, and social sustainability with cultural, behavioral, and human consciousness factors. She is a full international member of the Club of Rome and serves as a strategic advisor on integral finance and sustainability to various funds, businesses, and governmental organizations. Educated at Stanford University and Karlsruhe Institute of Technology (KIT), Dr. Bozesan holds an MS degree in Artificial Intelligence from KIT and a PhD from the Institute for Transpersonal Psychology (ITP), Palo Alto.

Lisa Brandstetter, Deloitte & Touche GmbH Wirtschaftsprüfungsgesellschaft, is a graduate of the master program "Accounting, Controlling and Financial Management" at the University of Applied Sciences, Upper Austria located in Steyr. In the course of her studies, her interest for alternative investment philosophies awakened. Fascinated by the basic concept of impact investing, her research focuses on impact portfolios, while engaging in the broad field of Corporate Finance in her daily work at a consulting firm in Vienna. Enthusiastic about sports and nature, Lisa enjoys spending time in the Austrian Alps.

Eleonora Broccardo, University of Trento, Italy, is Senior Lecturer in Finance at the University of Trento, where she teaches Advanced Corporate Finance. She achieved her PhD in markets and financial intermediaries at the Catholic University of Milan. Her main interests include small corporate finance, securitization, credit derivatives and a bank's risk management.

Gertrud Buchenrieder, Technische Universität München, Germany, received her doctoral degree (1994) from the University of Hohenheim, Germany, researching the interrelationship of food security and rural finance in Cameroon. For her "Second Book" (in 2000), she analyzed the financial market transformation in Central and Eastern Europe. She then became a member of the directorate at the Leibniz Institute of Agricultural Development in Transition Economies (2006–2010) in Halle (Saale) and an adjunct professor in Agricultural and Development Policy at the Martin-Luther-University Halle-Wittenberg. Presently, she is

Head of Department and acts as chair in Agricultural and Food Economics at the TUM School of Life Sciences, Weihenstephan. Broadly speaking, she is interested in socio-economic issues of rural development.

Marija Buzevska, University of Technology Sydney, Australia, graduated from the University of Technology, Sydney in 2014 and currently holds a BBus degree with a honors in finance. Her particular interest in the broader field of sustainable finance, led her to extend her studies for an additional year to allow for further research into the structure of the Australian carbon trading market. Marija's curiosity remains in ongoing developments in both Australian and global sustainability practices in finance.

Qihai Cai, Chinese University of Hong Kong, is a doctoral student of Public Policy and Management at the Chinese University of Hong Kong and focuses on Social Entrepreneurship and Social Finance.

Rosella Carè, Magna Graecia University of Catanzaro, Italy, received a PhD in Health Care Management and Economics from the University Magna Graecia of Catanzaro and a PhD in "Sciences de Gestion" from the Conservatoire National des Arts et Metiers of Paris in March 2014 with a dissertation that focused on the sustainability of public expenditure. During 2012 and 2013, she was a visiting PhD student at the ESCP Europe of Paris. Currently, she teaches "Problem Solving and Decision Making", "Financial Markets and Instruments", and "Economics of Financial Markets" at the University Magna Graecia of Catanzaro. Her research interests are: Social and Sustainable Finance; Impact Investing; Alternative Finance and Sustainability; Reputational risk and reputational crisis in the banking sector.

Guillermo Casasnovas, University of Oxford, United Kingdom, is a doctoral student in Management at Saïd Business School, University of Oxford. His dissertation looks at the formation of the UK social investment market, and his research interests include the study of new ventures and nascent markets, both at the organizational and institutional levels, especially in the contexts of social entrepreneurship and social finance.

Before joining Oxford, Guillermo worked at the Corporate Finance division of Deloitte and at ESADE's Institute for Social Innovation in Barcelona (Spain), and as a lecturer and consultant at the Universidad Centroamericana in Managua (Nicaragua). He has a BS and MS in Business Administration from ESADE Business School.

Andrew James (Jim) Clifford, MSc OBE, City University, United Kingdom, is Head of Advisory and Impact at leading charity and social enterprise lawyers Bates Wells Braithwaite, where he develops social investment instruments, including Social Impact Bonds. He co-developed, with social sector leaders It's All About Me, the UK Adoption Bond, the first SIB wholly created by the social sector. He jointly chaired the European Commission's GECES sub-group on social impact measurement, also serving on the G8 equivalent, and was lead author of the EU standards (2014). Now a full GECES member advising the Commission on social business, his research work is undertaken at Cass Business School, where he teaches social impact measurement and investment.

Ericka Costa, University of Trento, Italy, (PhD in Business Economics, University of Udine, Italy) is Assistant Professor of Business Administration and Accounting, University of Trento and Research Fellow in the European Research Institute on Cooperatives and social enterprise based in Trento. In 2011 she spent a visiting period of three months at the Centre for Social and Environmental Accounting Research (CSEAR) based in St. Andrews (Scotland), and in November 2012 she spent a week as a visiting professor at the Center of Excellence in Accounting and Reporting for Co-operatives—SOBEY Business School, St. Mary University (Canada). She is member of the CSEAR, European Business Ethics, and ACCOOP (International Research Network on Accounting for Cooperatives and Mutual Entities) networks and from 2012 she has been an International Associate of CSEAR UK. She represents Italy in the CSEAR. She is a reviewer for *Accounting, Auditing and Accountability Journal, Journal of Management and Governance, Social and Environmental and Accountability Journal, and Review of International Co-operation.*

Her research interests are aimed at investigating Sustainability Accounting and Corporate Social Responsibility both for profit and non-profit organizations. She has written a number of chapters in books and articles and papers that have been accepted for national and international journals and conferences. Together with these research interests, she has matured her professional experience as a consultant and executive educator on accounting and performance measurement both for profit and non-profit organizations.

Deborah Cotton, University of Technology Sydney, Australia, is a lecturer at the University of Technology Sydney and has a PhD in applied finance. She previously worked in stock broking before becoming an academic. Her teaching is in the UTS Business School and she specializes in corporate finance and ethics and sustainability in finance. Her research is on emissions trading and sustainable finance, with a particular interest in Sustainable Investing and gender diversity. Recently she has been working with business on Impact Investing for social good.

Jess Daggers, Said Business School, University of Oxford, is a London-based consultant, researcher, and PhD student. Her doctoral studies employ critical theory in examining the development of the social investment market in the UK. Jess works on a freelance basis with a range of social enterprises and charities, supporting them to develop measurement strategies for evidencing social impact. Previous projects include producing an impact report for Citizens UK and evaluating the first two years of UnLtd's Big Venture Challenge. As well as her work with the Saïd Business School at the University of Oxford, she has produced research for several social sector organizations in the UK, including Big Society Capital and New Philanthropy Capital.

Pascal Dey, University of St. Gallen, Switzerland, is a senior research fellow at the Institute for Business Ethics, University of St. Gallen, Switzerland. Much of Pascal's work, which is chiefly informed by critical sociological and philosophical theories, has focused on the intersection of entrepreneurship, politics and society. Pascal's most recent interest lies in issues pertaining to fantasy, willful ignorance or prefigurative praxis. He is in the process of co-editing two books, *Critical Perspectives on Social Entrepreneurship* (Edward Elgar) and *Critical Entrepreneurship Studies* (Routledge), respectively, which are both geared toward establishing critical perspectives as a new frontier of theorizing in the realm of entrepreneurship studies.

Mehmet Hasan Eken, Istanbul Commerce University, Turkey, was born to Mahmut and Latife Eken in Silopi, located in the southeast of Turkey, in 1965. He received his BA in economics from Anadolu University, his MPhil in finance from the University of Exeter in 1992, and his PhD in banking from Marmara University in 1999. Having started his career as a banker, Dr. Eken worked for several banks in Turkey during the period 1992–2003.

Before joining academia and terminating his professional banking career, he also served as the board member of several banks in Turkey and Romania. He is the author and co-author of several finance and banking-related academic books and articles written in Turkish and English, and he is also the author of two novels and a storybook. Specializing in the area of asset/liability management in commercial banks, he teaches portfolio theory, bank management, and other banking and finance-related courses. Before joining Kirklareli University as full professor of banking and finance in 2015, Dr. Eken worked as the Director of the Institute of Social Sciences first at Kadir Has University and then at Istanbul Commerce University. Dr. Eken is fluent in Kurdish, Turkish, and English. He is married with one child.

Luca Erzegovesi, University of Trento, Italy, is a finance professor at the University of Trento. His research interests are mainly in credit risk management, financial planning models, and the financial communication of SMEs. He has been a consultant to the Bank of Italy and the Italian Ministry of Economic Development. He participates actively in the debate on credit policies in Italy through his personal blog aleablog.net. He is the author of numerous works on financial markets, risk management in banks, and small business finance.

Clelia Fiondella, Second University of Naples, Italy, is Assistant Professor in Accounting at the Second University of Naples (Italy), and her research interests cover the areas of risk disclosure, risk management, management accounting and accounting history, and ethics in finance.

Noriko Fujiwara, Center of European Policy Studies, is Associate Research Fellow at the Centre for European Policy Studies in Brussels. She has undertaken research on climate change and energy policies at international, EU, and country levels, focusing on topics such as the EU emissions trading scheme and international carbon markets.

In addition, she is Research Fellow at the China Insurance and Social Security Research Center, Fudan University, Shanghai, and Adjunct Researcher at the Research Institute for the Environment and Trade, Waseda University, Tokyo.

She has a DPhil in International Relations from the University of Sussex, MPhil in Development Studies from the University of Cambridge, and Master of Law (International Political Economy) from Hitotsubashi University in Tokyo.

Scott Fullwiler, University of Missouri-Kansas City, United States, holds the James A. Leach Chair in Banking and Monetary Economics and is Co-director of the Social Entrepreneurship Program at Wartburg College in Iowa, United States. He is also a research scholar at the Binzagr Institute for Sustainable Prosperity at Denison University in Ohio and serves as an adjunct faculty in Presidio Graduate School's sustainable MBA program in San Francisco. Fullwiler publishes and presents research regularly on the interactions of banks, central banks, and government treasuries in financial markets; macroeconomic theory and policy; systems theory-based approaches to policy analysis; and sustainable finance.

Sean Geobey, Waterloo Institute for Social Innovation and Resilience, Canada, is Assistant Professor of Social Entrepreneurship and Social Innovation at the University of Waterloo's School of Environment, Enterprise and Development. His research looks at financial tools that can support social innovation including crowdfunding, Impact Investing, and the role of credit unions. He holds a PhD specialized in social innovation from the University of Waterloo and is the Director of Academic Programs at the Waterloo Institute for Social Innovation and Resilience (WISIR).

Philippe Gillet, University Paris-Sud, France, is a tenured professor at Paris-Saclay University (University of Paris-Sud, RITM Laboratory). Its main research topics are related to Financial Market Efficiency, Asset Management, Performance and Risk Measurement, and Socially Responsible Investments. He also teaches at Paris-Dauphine University; he is an independent consultant, and he was formerly Head of Performance and Risk Management at Fortis Investment, among other experiences.

Gunnar Glänzel, Heidelberg University, Germany, has been working the Centre for Social Investment since 2008 in research projects on hybrid organizations, social impact in the field of education, social innovation, and social entrepreneurship. His research and publication interests particularly lie in the fields of organizational hybridity, Impact Investment, and social innovation. Gunnar holds a Master's degree in international business administration and a diploma in sociology, economics and philosophy. He is working on a PhD thesis on Social Impact Investing.

Lisa M. Hanley, Marie Zeppelin University, Germany, is a research fellow at the Civil Society Center at Zeppelin University where she coordinates the International Research Network on Social Economic Empowerment funded by the Siemens Stiftung. She has worked in the field of international development and urban studies and her research interests focus on the public–private debate and the role of social enterprises in the delivery of services, with particularly their role in the social economy. She holds a PhD in City and Regional Planning from Cornell University. She is also the recipient of a Ford Foundation Social Science Research fellowship and a Fulbright fellowship.

Jennifer L. Harrison, Southern Cross University, Australia, is a senior lecturer in the School of Business and Tourism, Southern Cross University, Gold Coast, Australia. Jennifer has taught in the areas of accounting, finance, economics, and research methods in undergraduate and postgraduate programs for over 15 years. She has also been actively involved in consulting projects across a variety of industries including banking, agriculture, software development, and sport and fitness and for organizations such as Microsoft. Her research interests include voluntary financial disclosures and ethical and sustainable investments and financing.

Helen Haugh, University of Cambridge, United Kingdom, is a senior lecturer at Cambridge Judge Business School; Director of the Masters in Innovation, Strategy, and Organizations, and Research Director for the Centre for Social Innovation. Helen's research interests focus on social and community entrepreneurship, family business, and Corporate Social Responsibility. Her research in the social economy has examined community-led regeneration in rural communities, cross-sector collaboration, and innovations in governance. Her work has been published in the *Academy of Management Learning and Education*, *Organization Studies*, *Entrepreneurship Theory and Practice*, *Journal of Business Ethics*, *Cambridge Journal of Economics*, and *Entrepreneurship* and *Regional Development*.

Tobias Jung, University of St. Andrews, United Kingdom, is a senior lecturer at the University of St Andrews' School of Management and a founding member of the Centre for Charitable Giving and Philanthropy at Cass Business School. His research focuses on philanthropy, non-profit organizations, and evidence-based policy and practice, and he is the lead editor of *The Routledge Companion to Philanthropy*, the first critical international handbook in the field.

Suleyman Kale, Kırklareli University, Turkey, is an assistant professor at the Banking and Finance Department of Kırklareli University. He received his BSc degree in Petroleum Engineering from Middle East Technical University in 1992. After a year of education at the Banking School of Ziraat Bankası, he started his career at the treasury department of the bank. He was then appointed to different managerial positions at various domestic and international departments, and subsidiaries. In parallel to his banking career, he received his Master's and PhD degrees in Banking and Finance, and in 2015 he became a full-time professor at Kırklareli University. His research interests include data envelopment analysis, financial markets, and fixed-income securities. He is the father of Öykü and Umut.

Arne Kroeger, Leibniz University of Hannover, Germany, works and researches at the Leibniz University of Hanover. His research interests are in the field of social entrepreneurship, in particular social impact measurement and Impact Investment. He consults the Social Venture Fund in Munich on the impact assessment of its potential and current investments and holds a PhD from the Leibniz University of Hanover. His research has appeared in *The Academy of Management Review* and others.

Aline Margaux Laucke, Zeppelin University, Germany, is a PhD candidate in Strategic Organization and Finance at Zeppelin University (Germany) and holds a scholarship from Siemens Stiftung to conduct research on social enterprises in healthcare in Colombia, Mexico, Kenya, and South Africa. Her research interests focus on strategic paradoxes, hybrid organizations, and the Base of the Pyramid. She has served as a consultant for Corporate Responsibility, Social Enterprise, and Social Financing for several years and has worked at the Grameen Creative Lab, a think tank and accelerator for social businesses initiated by Muhammad Yunus.

Linne Marie Lauesen, Vand og Affald, Denmark, is a postdoctoral fellow at Copenhagen Business School at the Department of Intercultural Communication and Management, Centre for Corporate Social Responsibility. Linne has over 15 years of experience as a practitioner in the water sector in Denmark, and left academia 5 years ago to do research in Corporate Social Responsibility, Sustainability, Social Entrepreneurship and the like. Her area covers aspects of economic, social, and environmental fields within finance and the governance of sustainability in various businesses. Linne has published a range of papers, book chapters, and the book *Sustainable Governance in Hybrid Organizations*.

Tommi Lehtonen, University of Vaasa, Finland, is a professor of Applied Philosophy at the University of Vaasa, Finland. He specializes in social ethics and cultural philosophy. His current research focuses on multi-attractedness in decision making, values and ethics of governance, and Socially Responsible Investment. He is the author of *After Secularization* (2012) and *Punishment, Atonement and Merit* (1999). He is the editor of *Perspectives on Culture, Values, and Justice* (2015) and has published widely in philosophical journals.

Andrea Leonardi, University of Trento, Italy, is Full Professor of Economic History in the Department of Economics and Management at the University of Trento. He has been a visiting professor at the University of Innsbruck and Milan. His research was initially focused on the analysis of development trajectories in the Alpine regions. He then devoted his studies to the modernization process in the Habsburg Monarchy between the eighteenth-century and World War I. He also examined specific aspects of the financial history of twentieth-century

Italy and the dynamics in activating new paths of technological innovation. His research has produced more than 200 publications, both in the form of monographs (18) and essays in collected volumes and historical and economic journals.

Fergus Lyon, Middlesex University, United Kingdom, leads research on social enterprise and alternative investment models at Middlesex University in London. He is the Deputy Director of the Centre for the Understanding of Sustainable Prosperity, a £6-million program of research funded by the UK Economic and Social Research Council. He has published widely on entrepreneurship, social enterprise, and sustainability in the UK, Africa and South Asia.

Marco Maffei, University of Naples Federico II, Italy, is Associate Professor in Accounting at the University of Naples "Federico II" (Italy), and his research interests cover the areas of risk disclosure and risk management, financial accounting and management accounting, and ethics in finance.

Daniela Majerčáková, Comenius University, Slovakia, is part of the team of teachers and young scientists of the Faculty of Management of Comenius University in Bratislava, Slovakia. She lectures on the topics from financial management, banking, and investing. She cooperates with several universities in Slovakia and also abroad in the areas of research and is an active lecturer in various selected topics of financial management and investing. Her research priorities are specifics of non-European banking systems, impact investing, and applications of managerial models in social services. She combines theoretical models with the practical aspects of impact investing in the area of Vysegrad countries.

Laurent Marti, University of St. Gallen, Switzerland, is a PhD candidate in organization studies at the University of St. Gallen, Switzerland, and a visiting researcher at RMIT University, Melbourne, Australia. Mainly building on process-relational ontologies, his research focuses on entrepreneurial processes and strategies in the creative industries. He has conducted several case studies on creative industry enterprises, from large technology companies to experimental arts collectives—applying (video) ethnographic methods. Among others, Laurent is particularly interested in the innovation and performativity of resourcing practices as well as the various modes of prototyping emerging ventures.

Maximilian Martin, Impact Economy, Switzerland, is the Founder and CEO of Impact Economy. His investment and advisory work as well as more than 100 articles have helped define the trajectory of market-based solutions and the impact revolution in finance, business, and philanthropy. Dr. Martin created Europe's first global philanthropic services and Impact Investing department for UBS and the UBS Philanthropy Forum, as well as the first university course on social entrepreneurship in Europe at the University of Geneva. In 2013, he wrote the primer on Impact Investing "Status of the Social Impact Investing Market" for the UK G8 policy makers' conference.

Ainulashikin Marzuki, University Sains Islam, Malaysia, is a senior lecturer in the Faculty of Economics and Muamalat at Universiti Sains Islam Malaysia. She holds a Bachelor of Accountancy with honors and a Master in Business Administration from Universiti Teknologi MARA and obtained her doctorate from the Griffith University in 2013. Her thesis focuses on three main themes; the comparative performance of Islamic and conventionally managed funds, the impact of screening intensity on performance and the behavior of both Islamic and conventionally managed fund investors. Her current research interest is in the fields of Islamic Finance, managed funds, social responsibility, wealth management, and household finance.

Christopher Mason, Swinburne University of Technology, Australia, is Senior Research Fellow at the Centre for Social Impact Swinburne. His research interests cover social enterprise, policy development, governance and discourse. Chris works at centers on developing collaborative projects with civil society and public and private organizations, generating novel insights into the social impact of their operations. Chris plays a developmental role for social enterprise in Australia, raising awareness of their work through high quality research. Chris's work has an international focus, and has been published in the *Journal of Business Ethics*, the *Journal of Services Marketing*, *Business Ethics: A European Review*, and the *Journal of Social Entrepreneurship*.

Maria Mazzuca, University of Calabria, Italy, has been an associate professor in banking and finance at the University of Calabria (Italy) since 2014 and an assistant professor since 2007. She teaches courses on Financial System and Financial Institutions Management. Her research interests concern topics related to financial institutions regulation, disclosure by banks, Corporate Social Responsibility in banks, securitization, and credit derivatives. Her publications include several articles in *The European Journal of Finance*, *Corporate Social Responsibility and Environmental Management*, *Journal of Economics and Business*, *The Journal of Risk Finance*, *Sustainable Development*, *Business Ethics: A European Review*, and *Journal of Financial Regulation and Compliance*.

Maria Cristina Migliazza, Magna Graecia University of Catanzaro, received her PhD in Healthcare Management and Economics from the University Magna Graecia of Catanzaro (UMG). Her research interests are: Social and Sustainable Finance, Corporate Social Responsibility and Irresponsibility in the financial and banking sector, Financial Services and Instruments for Healthcare and Public Sector.

Scott J. Niblock, Southern Cross University, Australia, is a lecturer of finance in the School of Business and Tourism, Southern Cross University, Gold Coast, Australia. He has been involved in undergraduate and postgraduate programs for over eight years, teaching courses such as security analysis, portfolio management, derivatives, international finance, and corporate finance. Scott's research interests include carbon trading, Socially Responsible Investment, capital market efficiency, asset pricing, superannuation, and options strategies. He has also worked as a private client advisor in the stockbroking industry, gaining high-level Australian equities and derivatives accreditation.

Alex Nicholls, Said Business School, University of Oxford, is Professor of Social Entrepreneurship within the Skoll Centre for social entrepreneurship at Saïd Business School, University of Oxford. His research interests range across several key areas within social entrepreneurship and social innovation, including: the nexus of relationships between accounting, accountability, and governance; public and social policy contexts; Impact Investing; and Fair Trade. As the first staff member of the Skoll Centre for social entrepreneurship in 2004, Nicholls has helped the Centre develop a global profile in researching and teaching social entrepreneurship. Alex is the editor of *Social Entrepreneurship: New Models of Sustainable Social Change* (2006), the first book to present a wide-ranging, internationally-focused collection of key social entrepreneurship work from leading academics, policy makers, and practitioners.

Tamaki Onishi, University of North Carolina at Greensboro, United States, is Assistant Professor of Political Science at the University of North Carolina at Greensboro. She received her PhD in philanthropic studies with a minor in entrepreneurship and organizational theory from Indiana University. Her research explores social entrepreneurship, social investment, non-profit fundraising, and philanthropy primarily through entrepreneurial and institutional theories and/or a comparative perspective. Formally trained as a classical pianist and musicologist, she also conducted research on arts entrepreneurship. Her work has been presented at major conferences, such as Academy of Management Annual Meetings, and published within prominent research journals.

Adeboye Oyegunle, University of Waterloo, Canada, is a graduate research candidate for the Masters of Environmental Studies in Sustainability Management at the University of Waterloo. He spent over 6 years in the Nigerian banking sector, with the key function of developing and integrating environmental and social processes in banks. He was a member of the Strategic Sustainability Working Group, which drafted the Nigerian Sustainable Banking Principles (NSBP), and a member of the NSBP steering committee. His research interests are in the development and integration of environmental and social governance in financial institutions and the impacts of environmental and social considerations on financial institutions' lending processes.

Aaron Z. Pitluck, Illinois State University, United States, is Associate Professor of Sociology at Illinois State University, and a visiting scholar at the Department of Sociology at the University of Chicago (2015–2016). He is completing a multi-year research project that investigates Islamic Finance as a case study for understanding the possibilities and limitations of radical reform of financial markets. He has also conducted research on the behavior of professional investors in emerging markets; most recently he published "Watching foreigners: How counterparties enable herds, crowds, and generate liquidity in financial markets," *Socio-Economic Review, 12*(1): 5–31. This article was showcased in Bloomberg Businessweek and is available at SSRN.

Julia M. Puaschunder, The New School for Social Research, Austria, studied Philosophy/Psychology (MPhil), Business (MBA), Public Administration (MPA), Social and Economic Sciences (Doctor), Natural Sciences (Doctor), and Law and Economics (pending). Julia M. Puaschunder has launched and administered research projects in Australia, Austria, Canada, China, Germany, Indonesia, Switzerland, and the US. After having captured social responsibility in corporate and financial markets in Europe and North America with attention to Financial Social Responsibility and Socially Responsible Investment, she currently pursues the idea of Eternal Equity—responding to Western world intergenerational equity constraints regarding climate justice, overindebtedness, and pension reform.

Sven Remer, Institute of Social Banking, Germany, is the founder and manager of impact.capital, an online forum to gather, share, and discuss information on sustainable finance. He is also on the board of the Institute for Social Banking, a charitable association founded by European social banks to further the development of social banking through training and research. Previously, Sven was Associate Professor "Social Banking and Social Finance" at Alanus University in Alfter, Germany, and management consultant with KPMG. He holds an MSc in Biology/Ecology (LMU Munich) and an MBA and a PhD in Finance (both CASS Business School, London).

Gadaf Rexhepi, South East European University, Macedonia, is an assistant professor at South-East European University, Republic of Macedonia, in the the management field at undergraduate and postgraduate levels. His research interests include Management, Strategic Management and

Finance. He is the author of more than 40 research papers in different peer and refereed journals. He is also the author of several text books, on Game Theory, TQM, Introduction to Business, etc., and has had many book chapters published by Springer, Elsevier, Taylor & Francis, etc. He is also involved as a consultant to the minister of economy, consultant at SEE University, consultant for development at Alma-M, one of the biggest companies in Macedonia.

Alessandro Rizzello, Magna Graecia University of Catanzaro, Italy, is a PhD Student at the University "Magna Graecia" of Catanzaro (Italy). His research focuses on Social Impact Investing, Social Impact Bond, Social and Sustainable Finance and Social Enterprise Financing. Currently, he teaches "Social & Sustainable Finance" at the University Magna Graecia of Catanzaro. Before he worked as Head of Financial Office in the Italian public administration. He received his master's degree in Economics from the LUISS University in Rome.

Carol Royal, The University of New South Wales, Australia, (BA, MCom, PhD, UNSW), is the Director of the Master of Technology and Innovation Management and an academic at the UNSW Business School at the University of New South Wales in Sydney, Australia. Dr. Royal is Honorary Visiting Fellow at Cass Business School, City University, London, and a member of the Australian Institute of Company Directors, Australia Human Resources Institute, and the American Academy of Management. Her research work evaluates publicly listed companies through human capital analysis and its links to corporate performance, and she provides research/advisory services to Investment Management, Investment Banking, and Stock broking industries in the International Equity Markets (UK, USA, Australia) on Human Capital Intangibles and Management Quality. Prior to her academic and consulting roles, she held senior-line human resource management positions with the manufacturing and retail sectors.

Julie Salaber-Ayton, Westminster Business School, United Kingdom, has 10 years of teaching and research experience in the fields of asset pricing, behavioral finance, corporate finance, investments, mergers and acquisitions, banking, and macroeconomics. She is currently Senior Lecturer in Finance at the University of Westminster in London, and before that she was working at the American International University in London and at the University of Bath. She has recently published in the *European Journal of Finance*, *International Business Review*, *International Journal of the Economics of Business*, *Research in International Business and Finance*, and *European Journal of Political Economy*.

Björn Schmitz, Philiomondo, Germany, is founder and owner of Philiomondo, a consulting firm in the field of innovation, business modeling, sustainability, and organizational development in Heidelberg, Germany. He is also responsible for cooperation and business development at the Schmid Foundation in Heidelberg. Schmid Stiftung is providing pro bono support in the field of organizational development. Formerly he worked as a project manager and researcher for the Centre for Social Investment at the University of Heidelberg and as a consultant at SAP. He studied business administration in Mannheim, and sociology, philosophy, and psychology in Heidelberg.

Hüseyin Selimler, Ziraat Bankası, Turkey, was born to Hamdi and Ruhiye Selimler in Akhisar/Manisa in 1967. He received his BA in public finance from Marmara University, his MA in public finance from the İstanbul University in 1996, and his PhD in banking from Marmara University in 2006. Dr. Selimler started his career as Emlak Bank's board inspector and continued as regional manager the marketing and retail banking departments at Ziraat Bank in Turkey. He is the author and co-author of several finance and banking-related academic books and articles written in Turkish and English. He teaches credit management, banking accounts and other banking and finance related courses. He is married to Özlem and has one child called Meriç.

Archana Shah, Pace University, United States, is the Associate Director of the Helene and Grant Wilson Center for Social Entrepreneurship at Pace University. Prior to that, she worked in the financial services industry for over 18 years, initially at JP Morgan and then at Morgan Stanley from where she retired as a senior executive director in the Emerging Markets Derivative Sales Group in 2012. She has served as chair of the New York Chapter of Women Advancing Microfinance, and Director of Development at Grameen America. Ms. Shah earned her BA in Finance and French from the University of Pennsylvania, and her Master's degree in Economic Development from New York University.

John Simmons, University of Liverpool, United Kingdom, teaches on postgraduate and undergraduate HRM programs in the Management School at the University of Liverpool, UK. Prior to this he was Head of the HRM Group at Liverpool John Moores University, UK. His doctorate is in performance management and his work has been published in a range of academic journals, including *Management Decision, Employee Relations*, and the *Journal of Business Ethics*. He has a longstanding involvement in quality assurance roles with the UK Chartered Institute of Personnel and Development and is currently researching in the areas of whistleblowing and business ethics.

Rosanna Spanò, University of Naples Federico II, holds a PhD in economics and management in healthcare from the Magna Graecia University of Catanzaro and is postdoctoral fellow in accounting at the Department of Economics, Management, Institutions of the University of Naples Federico II, where she actively collaborates for teaching activities and advises students of the Master's degree in accounting and management accounting. She has a long-settled experience in qualitative methodologies for management accounting research. She has managed as principal author a good number of research projects on accounting, management accounting, ethics and public health, co-authored with both Italian and international researchers, published in national and international peer-reviewed journals, and accepted to international conferences. Rosanna owns good personal and professional relationships with Italian academics that resulted in a number of co-authored research projects with social and environmental impact. Rosanna has excellent and long-settled cooperation with international academics and has been visiting scholar at the University of South Australia and at the Royal Holloway University of London.

Rebecca Tekula, Pace University, United States, is Assistant Professor of Public Administration in Pace University's Dyson College of Arts and Sciences. She also serves as the Executive Director of the Helene and Grant Wilson Center for Social Entrepreneurship. Dr. Tekula received her PhD in Economics and Public Management at the University of Lugano, Switzerland. Her doctoral research was funded by the Swiss National Science Foundation and the Swiss Public Administration Network. She earned her BA in English literature from Vassar College, her MPA in Non-profit Management from Pace University, and her MBA from the University of Oxford. She is the author of numerous articles and reports on topics related to social enterprise, non-profit economics and governance, and non-profit management education.

Daniel Tischer, Manchester Business School, United Kingdom, is Lecturer in Political Economy and Organization Studies at the University of Manchester where he wrote his PhD on "The Embeddedness of Ethical Banking in the UK." He has been a fellow at the Social Science Centre in Berlin and has been a Research Officer at the Center for Mutual and Employee-owned Business at the University of Oxford. Daniel's research interests evolve around the study of (global) finance and banking from a critical perspective, including social network studies of financial derivatives and ethical banking, retail banking studies, and a wider engagement with the mutual and cooperative banking sectors.

Annarita Trotta, Magna Graecia University of Catanzaro, Italy, is a professor of Banking and Finance at University Magna Graecia (UMG) of Catanzaro (Italy). She holds a PhD in Business Administration from the University Federico II of Naples (Italy), where she was an assistant Professor of Banking on the Faculty of Economics from 1995 to 2001. From 2001 to 2006, she was an associate professor at the University of Catanzaro. Since 2006, she has been a professor of Economics and Management of Financial Institutions and Markets at UMG, where she teaches Banking, Financial Markets, and Corporate Finance. Over her 20-year academic career, Trotta has authored (or co-authored) more than 50 scientific publications and four books. Her primary areas of research are Social and Sustainable Finance; Impact Investing; Alternative Finance and Sustainability; Reputational risk and reputational crisis in the banking sector; Corporate Social Responsibility in the banking sector; Subprime crisis and Credit Rating Agencies; Local banking and information asymmetries; Credit risk; Small business, Venture Capital and Informal Venture Capital; Bank-small business relationships; and Finance and Medicine.

Marc J. Ventresca, University of Oxford, United Kingdom, joined the university in 2004, on faculty at the Saïd Business School and as a Governing Body Fellow of Wolfson College. He is also Senior Research Fellow at the Technology and Management for Development Centre at Queen Elizabeth House. Marc's research and teaching focus on innovation, institutions and infrastructure, with particular empirical projects at the intersection of organizational strategy and economic sociology in nascent markets. He is Academic Lead for the "Ideas to Impact" (I2I) initiative, a collaboration with the Oxford Sciences and Engineering Division in support of innovation and enterprise. He earned undergraduate and graduate degrees at Stanford University in politics and political philosophy, education policy, and sociology. He previously served on faculty at Northwestern University/Kellogg Graduate School of Management and the US Naval Postgraduate School; he was visiting faculty at the Stanford University School of Engineering, the University of California, Irvine, and the University of Illinois, Urbana-Champaign, as well as Copenhagen Business School and the Mediterranean Business School in Tunis.

Christiana Weber, Leibniz University Hannover, Germany, holds the chair for Management and Organization Theory at the Leibniz University of Hanover, Germany. She researches and consults at the intersection of (social) entrepreneurship/sustainability, innovation management, and social network theory.

Christiana Weber studied Social and Business Communications in Berlin, Germany (MSc), and in Grenoble, France, as well as Management Science in Berlin and in Berkeley, United States. She holds her PhD in sociology from the Social Science Research Center, Berlin (WZB). Christiana is the author of over 30 articles and book chapters. Her research has appeared in such journals as *AMR*, *JBV*, *JET-M*, *SJM*, *IJEV* and others.

Olaf Weber, University of Waterloo, Canada, a professor in the School of Environment, Enterprise and Development, is Export Development Canada Chair in Environmental Finance. As far as he knows, he is the only such chair anywhere in the world. As such, he is helping pioneer global thought and policy on the interactions between environment, social justice, and finance.

Weber is currently working on developing guidelines to integrate environmental and social factors into project financing decisions, so banks can assess whether investing in a mine, for example, will result in locals getting jobs—or being forcibly displaced. More generally, Weber researches how financial institutions can support sustainable development. "Green" funds, for instance, can influence the share price of companies whose activities may have a positive effect on the environment. On the flip side, people who buy into traditional mutual funds can end up supporting companies whose practices they dislike.

Tim Weiss, Zeppelin University, Germany, MA, is a research fellow and doctoral candidate in the Department for Strategic Organization and Finance at Zeppelin University (Germany). He has several years of work experience in Kenya and Ethiopia and was a visiting PhD student at the Management and Organizations Department at the Kellogg School of Management, Northwestern University, United States. His research focuses on the economic, cultural, and social underpinnings governing the interaction between Kenyan technology entrepreneurs and international venture capital, private equity, and incubator and accelerator models. He engaged in an intensive investigation of Kenya's ICT ecosystem in 2014 and is the co-editor of the forthcoming book *Digital Kenya: The New Generation of Entrepreneurs*.

G. Sampath S. Windsor, University of New South Wales, Australia, obtained his PhD from the School of Management at the Australian School of Business, University of New South Wales, Australia. With 15 years of experience within the ICT sector, he has served Optus and IBM Australia as a senior manager. Academically he holds BEng (Information Systems) honors from the University of Sydney, Master of Technology Management from the University of New South Wales, and an MBA from the University of New England, Armidale. His research interests include Human Capital, Corporate Sustainability, ICT, and Corporate Social Responsibility synergies within ICT for sustainable development.

Andrew C. Worthington, Griffith University, Australia, is Professor of Finance in the Department of Accounting, Finance, and Economics at Griffith University. He holds Master's degrees from the University of New South Wales and the University of New England and obtained his doctorate from the University of Queensland. His previous career appointments comprise the University of New England, Queensland University of Technology, and the University of Wollongong His published research includes financial and commodity markets, alternative investments, Islamic Finance, and household finance. He is the editor of the contributed volume *Contemporary Issues in Islamic Finance: Principles, Progress, and Prospects* (2014).

Claudia Zagaria, Second University of Naples, Italy, is a postdoctoral researcher in accounting at the Second University of Naples (Italy). Her research interests cover the areas of social and environmental disclosure, risk reporting and risk management systems, management accounting, and business ethics.

FOREWORD

As is so often noted in the media and elsewhere, finance and the global financial services industry seems to many to be an insiders' game played by a few to their advantage, as opposed to the advantage of us all. The clarion call for change in the principles and practices of finance has been taken up around the world, underlined, no doubt, by the costs and consequences of turmoil in developed and developing financial markets. Critics of finance are many and varied—from Nobel Prize winners in economics through to the "occupy Wall Street" movement. Indeed, there is a veritable academic industry developing around the shortcomings of finance as an academic field and as a global industry. This is not lost on leading finance professors and professionals.

This is also a welcome development. In response, professional accreditation bodies have begun new programs in responsible finance, ESG, sustainability, and the like. As well, leading universities are introducing related courses and programs so as to cater for the curiosity of a new generation of well-trained students not content with the status quo. If we are to capitalize on these developments, the field of social and sustainable finance must surely put its own academic house in order. In particular, there is an urgent need to clarify what is meant by Social and Sustainable Finance, provide analytical and methodological tools through which to give expression to a commitment to sustainability, and develop the models and metrics necessary to integrate Social and Sustainable Finance with the practice of finance as investment. As such, this handbook is a welcome addition to the field.

It seems unlikely that Social and Sustainable Finance will be content with being assimilated or co-opted with mainstream theories and methods. In part, this reflects a wider sense of unease about the plausibility of inherited theories and concepts. There is a rising tide of academic thought that discounts the central pillars of finance as an academic discipline. So, for example, many mainstream economists now dispute the plausibility of rational expectations, the efficient markets hypothesis, and the rational economic agent. There were, of course, voices raised many years ago against the plausibility of these central pillars of finance. But, they were lost in the rush toward crowning the hegemony of a simple, indeed simplistic, idea. Now, there is room for many voices and many ideas. We need to take advantage of this moment in intellectual history.

Here, I would challenge my colleagues to find ways of organizing disparate voices and ideas around a common theme or themes so as to deepen our academic endeavors. As well, we need to find ways of harnessing the energy of critique so as to develop the field. Again, this handbook can make a significant contribution on both counts.

We must take very seriously indeed the issue of sustainability. This is the challenge of the twenty-first century. Ironically, this may well mean that we need to strengthen a core function of finance: intermediation—mobilizing savings for investment and a sustainable future. If we are to have an environmentally sustainable future, it is vital that ways are found of speeding long-term economic and technological transformation. Without long-term investment in alternative sources of energy and in more efficient ways of using, recycling, and sustaining the environment, climate change will wreak havoc upon many regions of the world. The disruption and degradation of human life on this scale can only result in the impoverishment of future generations. Surprisingly, mainstream finance has not yet grasped this opportunity. This handbook is a way of charting such a future.

Gordon L. Clark

PREFACE

An epiphany of Social and Sustainable Finance

Othmar M. Lehner

Undoubtedly, the topic of Social and Sustainable Finance is timely and of high relevance. Foundations, individual and group investors, a globally minded internet-based crowd, and public bodies around the world have become increasingly interested and eager to finance and support innovative forms of doing business with a clear societal or environmental mission that are well embedded in all "three pillars" of sustainability (environmental, social, and economic). At the same time, founders and established businesses alike are increasingly embracing new sustainable business models with a distinct stakeholder approach to tackle social or environmental problems in what they see as a failed economic system in crisis.

A strong positive focus on environment, social, and governance (ESG) factors in the respective business strategy seems to be one way to develop and nurture such a model, yet more radical approaches even put the societal "impact" first (Brandstetter & Lehner, 2015) at the expense of economic sustainability and financial returns.

Recent developments such as ongoing currency fluctuations and rising state debts, long-lasting regional economic crises, severe cutbacks on welfare spending, and bailouts of large banks with taxpayers' money both manifest and foster the sentiment for alternative business models even further—thus creating legitimacy in the eyes of the people for public and private investments into such innovative businesses (Frydrich, Bock, & Kinder, 2014; Lehner & Nicholls, 2014).

While at first this may look like a timely matched supply and demand, in reality it quickly becomes clear that the philosophical underpinnings of the involved players are not always compatible. The spectrum ranges from a more radical and systemic agenda of societal (social and environmental) impact in businesses first, via the welcome embrace of ESG factors to increase sustainability in ethical businesses, to the alleged "greenwashing" efforts of large corporations that otherwise do not intend to change their activities. Not only the logics but also the terminology used differs very much between these agendas; so it is no wonder that at the present stage of development there seems to be no rational, efficient, and global market—more a network of supply, demand, and intermediary groups linking capital and diverse projects with various rational underpinnings and policies. On a brighter note, involved parties continuously express their strong belief in a more promising future for social finance and Impact Investing, with their potential to revolutionize how we think about investing itself (Salamon, 2014).

When I was asked to assume the editorship of the T&F *Routledge Handbook of Social and Sustainable Finance*, I felt first and foremost exceedingly honored, because personally I very much believe in the promise of this field. My immediate concerns, however, were whether we could succeed in actually combining the rather distinct logics of "social" and "sustainable" into one handbook. After much talking and debating with my academic colleagues and peers in the industry, I realized that the distinction between social and sustainable may well be only theoretically sustained, because in everyday discourse within the field both terms are used interchangeably, and sometimes one even seems to encompass the premises of the other—and vice versa. In addition, looking at the differences and similarities between these two logics may also hold the promise of a better understanding of the fundamental motivational underpinnings of the various players in the field. The purposes of the handbook are thus as follows:

- To clarify the concepts of social finance and sustainable finance and to delineate their boundaries;
- To map out, display, and scale the disparate voices, critiques, traditions, and public and professional communities engaged in social finance and sustainable finance;
- To develop a range of analytical approaches, theoretical constructs, and metrics for decision making.

Following the thoughts as previously laid out, it was important for me to give voice to the various and often disparate players in the market with the aim of providing a rich and multi-perspective description of the contexts in which Social and Sustainable Finance is currently of relevance. I feared that a predefined and more narrow research agenda at this stage may well have encouraged just one particular side through the writings and neglected and diminished the future perspectives and approaches of others through a "reflexive isomorphism" (Nicholls, 2010).

The handbook is divided into three main parts:

- The Landscape of Social and Sustainable Finance and Investments
- Challenges, Suggestions, Critiques, and Debates
- Markets and Institutions.

The first part, "The Landscape of Social and Sustainable Finance and Investments" comprises chapters from a multitude of perspectives in an effort to grasp the entirety of the landscape of Social and Sustainable Finance. Because of the many and sometimes even disparate voices, there will undoubtedly be contradictions and overlap, but I am personally convinced that it may be important for the reader to understand how and why the market ticks. Authors in this part provide background and information on the institutional field emergence, on instruments and architecture of social finance—for example, by looking at crowdfunding and Social Impact Bonds—and on the interplay between social ventures, social investors, and other finance providers. What is prominent in this part are the well-carved-out future research agendas which many of the authors provide, stemming from their specific perspectives—appropriate to the handbook's promise to examine the status quo but also take a peek into the future of the field.

As a result, the handbook provides solid background information on the "whatness" of Social and Sustainable Finance or—as James Joyce would call it (by embracing Thomas Aquinas's three concepts of aesthetics)—on their "epiphany":

> *Claritas is quidditas. After the analysis which discovers the second quality the mind makes the only logically possible synthesis and discovers the third quality. This is the moment which I call epiphany. First we recognise that the object is one integral thing, then we recognise that it is an organised composite structure, a thing in fact: finally, when the relation of the parts is exquisite,*

> *when the parts are adjusted to the special point, we recognise that it is that thing which it is. Its soul, its whatness, leaps to us from the vestment of its appearance. The soul of the commonest object, the structure of which is so adjusted, seems to us radiant. The object achieves its epiphany.*
> *(James Joyce,* Stephen Hero*, p. 213)*

Ample room has been provided for "Challenges, Suggestions, Critiques, and Debates" in the following part. The first subsection of this part deals with the concept of social responsibility (SR) in finance from various perspectives. Looking at financial SR from the standpoint of religion (in Islamic Finance) is so far an almost undiscovered land in literature; yet many people are inevitably encouraged to do the "ethical thing" by their religious beliefs, and such insights should help to further understand the underlying motivations. An overall consideration of social origins theory (Salamon & Anheiner, 1998), connected to Weber's protestant ethics and embracing more sociological inquiries, may well be a way forward in the field.

Identifying SR as a risk prevention activity, and examining the change of the underpinnings of SR due to the financial crises of recent years, are but a few more angles from which authors in this subsection approach the topic of SR. Without the necessary reflexivity and SR in the investment decision-making process, social or sustainable finance would probably not exist. As such, the concept of SR can be seen as an important worldview within which many of the assumptions of the following chapters are rooted.

The second subsection of the "Challenges" part includes critical perspectives on markets, institutions, and ideology. A deeper look at who pays for the scaling of social ventures, to the interplay between social investments and fiduciary duties, illustrates the range of fascinating insights that the respective authors are providing. A sociological turn on the convergence paradox between Islamic and social finance again looks at the ideological background of social finance as a movement.

In the third subsection of this part, looking at business models and measurements, a more functionalist debate takes place. Discussing hybrid value creation of social as well as financial returns, looking at organizational hybridity, and finally a lengthy discussion by several authors on how to evaluate and include these additional social returns in investment decisions—for example, through various metrics and a new portfolio approach—provide great insights into how the players in the field could move forward in accounting for and justifying their activities. Such evaluation and justification needs to be different from the traditional strands in finance, yet, so far, approaches such as social return on investment, while fundamentally sound, have failed to be embraced by the field. This subsection thus discusses various other methods and their merits and shortcomings.

The final part, "Markets and Institutions," first looks at the banking industry, from cooperative banks with a long tradition to relatively new dedicated social banks with an impact mission, and finally on to traditional banks and the recent regulatory changes such as Basel III. Sustainability in banking seems like a major issue, although it is still poorly understood—especially given the recent turmoil and necessary bailouts in the financial sector and the political failure to address the underlying causes.

Leaving the financial sector, the second subsection of this part looks specifically at environmental marketplaces, especially carbon emission markets. Besides current insights and critical approaches to emissions trading, an interesting case study on emission-certified agroforestry will enlighten the reader with a fresh look at possible environmental Impact Investments with public–private guarantees.

The final subsection in the "Markets and Institutions" part provides sufficient room for country-specific case studies and perspectives. Besides the institutional and structural barriers inhibiting a fully functioning market, cultural and national contexts paint a very different picture of what Social and Sustainable Finance is and could be. Therefore, I invited the foremost experts and practitioners in the field to provide insights from their often focused view on one country, region, or venture. Although one cannot and should by no means generalize from these, the lesson is clear—that investors will need to listen carefully to understand the various contexts and ecosystems in which social ventures around the world develop and scale.

This handbook is the result of numerous talks with academics and practitioners, the outcome of a dedicated conference, various panel discussions, and of course the result of the great work and dedication of the authors and reviewers.

From my own observations, the discourse taking place in the field of Social and Sustainable Finance can by no means be understood by one paradigm only. Applying the framework of four paradigms or worldviews by Burrell and Morgan (1979), "Social and Sustainable Finance" as a term and implicit research agenda in this handbook seems to be a structurally loaded "rallying call" for two very different factions.

On one side are a group of researchers with a "radical-structuralist" worldview and agenda, who seek a change in the classic capitalistic world order and want to understand the new contexts in which society as a whole can profit from investments. The implicit agenda here may well be the development of a kind of capitalism 2.0 or "sharing economy" with great respect for the environment. Piketty's book with his famous turn on "inequality" may well be a vanguard of this movement, fueled by the difficult economic situation of a large portion of society and misguided globalization efforts with serious ecological implications.

On the other side, a group with a strong "functionalist" approach can be identified that seek new opportunities by embracing ESG criteria in their investment decisions, for example through investing in innovative environmental tech, and are looking for evidence of a lower financial risk through a focus on governance and sustainability in the business models. Far from radically changing the existing system, their approach nevertheless incorporates ethical considerations (e.g., through "negative" ESG screenings) and stakeholder-oriented investment decision making to cater for legitimacy and reputational risks. These investors are often externally motivated by public opinion and fear of reputational risks.

Between these logics, a whole spectrum of investment philosophies can be identified, as depicted in Figure P.1. The clashing logics of the extreme expressions, however, may negatively impact the finding of a common ground in the near future because both groups claim sovereignty of the rationale of "Social and Sustainable Finance" and are unreceptive to each other. The long-term future will see whether there can be a reconciliation of these worldviews or whether the two streams will remain separate in theory and practice.

Both the left as well as the right extreme positions in Figure P.1 have already seen exhaustive inquiries in the literature. A traditional financial return orientation with its focus on portfolios maximizing financial returns for accepted risks, on the one hand, and philanthropy as part of the larger non-profit stream, on the other, both have their own sound theories and narrations.

As discussed before, even traditional investors more and more embrace a "don't invest in evil" perspective with a negative ESG screening of assets. Despite this welcome approach, by most working definitions such negative screening and selection does not lead to true Impact Investments.

Impact Investments as discussed in this handbook are typically found to be attached to one of two core selection logics. The first one looks out for financially attractive (either higher returns or lower risks) investment opportunities based on innovation within a market that addresses environmental and social problems. The second, which was dubbed "visionary" by the authors of Figure P.1, puts the social and environmental problem solving first (mission driven), with the

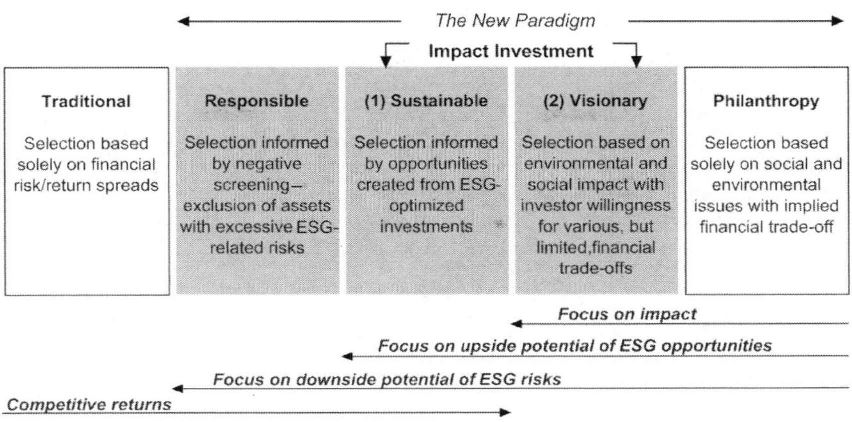

Figure P.1 Investment philosophies

Source: Brandstetter and Lehner (2015). Based on Nicklin (2012), with contributions from Clara Barby, Bridges Ventures UK.

willingness of investors to accept either sub-par returns compared to the accepted risks or even a minor loss of capital as long as the societal returns are delivered.

What is currently underresearched, apart from early adaptions by Brandstetter and Lehner (2015) and Moore, Westley, and Nicholls (2012), is the topic of "social risk." Social risk has not been fully conceptualized at present; it ranges from negative societal impacts despite the well-intended investment motives, to opportunity costs because of an adverse selection of impact projects that fail to deliver. Future research will certainly need to look into this further; otherwise rational decision making may remain problematic, which severely impairs the creation of a functioning global market of Social and Sustainable Finance.

Coming to an end, I now invite you to enjoy reading the various thoughts and fascinating insights from some of the foremost experts in the field and sincerely hope this handbook with its carefully selected chapters fulfills its purposes and provides great value to you, to the field, and to society as a whole.

Acknowledgments

The editor would like to express his deepest gratitude to all the authors and reviewers of this handbook for their wonderful gift of time and devotion. A big thank you also to the people at the Skoll Centre of the Saïd Business School and the Smith School of Enterprise and the Environment, both at Oxford University, and to the ACRN Oxford Research Centre, for providing such an inspiring and supporting infrastructure. Several individuals have especially inspired the formation of this handbook, and so I would like to thank Prof. Alex Nicholls, Prof. Gordon Clark, Prof. Jill Kickul, and Prof. Olaf Weber for their stimulating discussions, great opportunities for networking, and valuable feedback. Thank you also to the people at Taylor and Francis Routledge, specifically to our contact Laura Johnson. She was always open to our questions and assisted us greatly in all aspects. Last but not least, I want to extend a heartfelt thank you to my editorial assistant Susanne Baumann for her incredible support and dedication and for numerous hours of focused work in making this handbook possible.

Othmar M. Lehner

References

Brandstetter, L., & Lehner, O. M. (2015). Opening the market for impact investments: The need for adapted portfolio tools. *Entrepreneurship Research Journal, 5*(3), 87–107. doi:10.1515/erj-2015-0003

Burrell, G., & Morgan, G. (1979). *Sociological paradigms and organisational analysis*. London, England: Heinemann.

Frydrich, D., Bock, A. J., & Kinder, T. (2014). exploring entrepreneurial legitimacy in reward-based crowdfunding. *Venture Capital, 16*(3), 249–269.

Lehner, O. M., & Nicholls, A. (2014). Social finance and crowdfunding for social enterprises: A public–private case study providing legitimacy and leverage. *Venture Capital, 16*(3), 271–286. doi:10.1080/13691066.2014.925305

Moore, M.-L., Westley, F. R., & Nicholls, A. (2012). The social finance and social innovation nexus. *Journal of Social Entrepreneurship, 3*(2), 115–132. doi:10.1080/19420676.2012.725824

Nicholls, A. (2010). The legitimacy of social entrepreneurship: Reflexive isomorphism in a pre-paradigmatic field. *Entrepreneurship Theory and Practice, 34*(4), 611–633.

Nicklin, S. (2012). *The power of advice in the UK sustainable and impact investment market*. Retrieved August 25, 2015, from http://bridgesventures.com/wp-content/uploads/2014/07/BV001_Bridges_Ventures_report_final.pdf

Salamon, L. M. (2014). *New frontiers of philanthropy: A guide to the new tools and new actors that are reshaping global philanthropy and social investing*. New York, NY: Oxford University Press.

Salamon, L. M., & Anheiner, H. K. (1998). Social origins of civil society: Explaining the nonprofit sector cross-nationally. *VOLUNTAS: International Journal of Voluntary and Nonprofit Organizations, 9*(3), 213–248.

PART I

The Landscape of Social and Sustainable Finance and Investments

I.1
Introducing Social and Sustainable Finance

1
THE LANDSCAPE AND SCALE OF SOCIAL AND SUSTAINABLE FINANCE

Linne Marie Lauesen

Social and Sustainable Finance has been a popular topic within multiple books and journals during the last decade (Lauesen, 2013). Although the financial crisis has diminished the investment pace in Social and Sustainable Finance, this crisis has shown what happens when the market is exploited beyond its limits: the global recession, which we have seen during the last nine years. This malicious event—although not outstanding, because financial crisis has historically had a tendency to occur in circles (Galbraith, 1994)—has witnessed that Social and Sustainable Investing equals investing in the future for the welfare and security of future generations.

This chapter focuses on the large events of Social and Sustainable Finance in a broad perspective. It not only looks at the financial sector or social enterprises within this sector but also examines the role of traditional private companies and public sectors in the landscape of Social and Sustainable Finance. It is built on the idea that our future is based on investments in people, planet, and profit (e.g., Jeucken, 2010; Schaper, 2010).

Not only will this chapter show the positive outcome of different actors' successes in the landscape of Social and Sustainable Finance: in order to balance the view, this chapter will also show examples of the negative outcomes that have impacted it. The latter concerns the major events leading to the financial crisis (see, e.g., Hellwig, 2009; Kindleberger & Aliber, 2011); the contemporary continuity of high-risk financing (Heyde & Neyer, 2010); and the fallacies or the unintentional backlashes of expected positive investments in Social and Sustainable Finance (Banerjee, Duflo, Glennerster, & Kinnan, 2013) on a global level from micro to macro.

The chapter is structured as follows. First comes a short historical review of Social and Sustainable Financing, including the major events that have caused financial turmoil, settlement, or expansion. Next comes an overview of the financial crisis in 2008 and its impact upon the landscape of Social and sustainable finance. Finally, the contemporary landscape of Social and Sustainable Finance is described with concrete examples.

Social and Sustainable Financing: An historical review

Social and Sustainable Finance is today known under names such as microfinance, social enterprises, Social Impact Bonds, social funding, sustainable funding, or social enterprise lending. Although these relatively new names (and issues) suggest that Social and Sustainable Financing is a young movement into social and environmental spheres, it is not quite so: what is new is rather the concepts built around how to fund or finance social improvements and sustainability, and the actors investing in it.

In many nations, the state is responsible of taking care of social funding for marginalized groups and communities that are unable to finance their own living. The state also co-funds various environmental issues and regulates and sets rules for businesses about their responsibilities. Typically states and governments use part of their general tax income to fund these areas. In liberal market economies, for instance the Anglo Saxon nations in which the tax burden typically is lower than in welfare states, the social welfare systems are typically less extensive than in welfare states as well. The neoliberal philosophy is that the state should intervene in business conduct as little as possible. In such social welfare systems, it is typically up to each family to finance their own health insurances in order to be able to fund their health-related issues. Often there are differences between public and private institutions in relation to the quality of services, depending on the price each family is capable of paying privately on top of the public funding of different social issues. In welfare states such as the Scandinavian nations, the tax levels are generally higher, and these states' welfare models include most of the social welfare program: education, hospitalization, elder care, partially childcare, etc. It means that many public services are financed through the tax system and require no or only partial user payment.

Despite different market economies and social welfare systems, it has during the last 30 years become necessary and therefore desirable to engage business in co-funding certain social and sustainability issues worldwide, especially regarding environmental protection, emission of greenhouse gases, and social responsibilities toward the stakeholders—both locally and globally. As a benefit for business to enter the sphere of social and sustainable funding, businesses have seen a potential to combine this with financial and marketing/branding fortunes related to competitive global markets. Customers and investors are becoming more concerned about businesses' social and sustainability responsibilities and make demands for goods to be more consciously produced.[1]

The historical review of this development begins in the early days of Social and Sustainable Finance related to business engagement. The earliest movements of sustainability are detectable back to the early 1970s, after the Stockholm Conference on the Human Environment in 1972 and later the World Conservation Strategy of the International Union for the Conservation of Nature in 1980, in which world leaders realized the need for a worldwide and intergovernmental organization to raise awareness of the need for social and sustainable development.

In 1974, the Gaia Hypothesis, coined by James Lovelock and Lynn Margulis, was set forth. This hypothesis claimed that the biosphere of the planet Earth formed a complex interacting system as a whole organism, where the biosphere has a regulatory effect (homeostasis) on the Earth's environment with a limited capacity (Lovelock, 2006, cited from Lauesen, 2014, pp. 246–247). This hypothesis suggested that nature will and can adapt to certain environmental changes in order to sustain it. However, rainforest reduction, depletion of natural resources and biodiversity, and the addition of greenhouse gases to the atmosphere are, according to Lovelock, the planet's natural reaction to human impact. Although the devastating impact of human and business development consisting of more and more exploitation of natural and human resources had been recognized, the events only began to take more speed when the World Commission on Environment and Development with the Brundtland Commission was established with a mission to unite governments toward sustainable development.

The Brundtland Report (1989) recognized that the delimiting tendencies were getting out of control and defined sustainable development as "development that meets the needs of the present without compromising the ability of future generations to meet their own needs" (1989, p. 43, cited from Lauesen, 2014, p. 247). The leaders of the developed countries were now becoming more aware about social and environmental impacts stemming from the industrialization and growth within especially the Western world. The developing countries were, on the other hand, becoming discouraged about this tendency, because they were not able to reach the higher levels of economic growth and could not see how they could contribute to this reduction of harmful impacts. They had enough issues concerning economic stagnation, poverty, and thereof derived social issues to deal with. For the developing countries to reach the level of the industrialized countries, they felt pushed to use efficient technologies and cheap labor in order to keep up the momentum of growth. This, however, meant that impacts against the environment and the working force in the developing countries were not sound. Therefore, it was a pending issue for the world leaders to come up with suggestions that benefited both the industrialized as well as the developing countries, so that the technological and social development could go hand in hand with less social and environmental impact.

The UN formed the Global Compact in the late 1990s (Annan, 1999), and the OECD Guidelines, which has a history back to 1976, began with the ILO[2] to frame their intergovernmental understandings of what social and sustainable business conduct were meant to comprise both politically, governmentally, and for business practice (Lauesen, 2014, p. 247). In 2001 the UN defined the Global Compact, and the OECD adopted these principles into its Guidelines. The UN Global Compact defines specific principles covering human rights, labor, environment, sustainable behavior, and anti-corruption. These headlines were made because of the rising sweatshop activities (the use of child labor) in the factories in the supply chains of the multinational companies—typically in the developing world; women's rights violations; and the major environmental disasters such as the oil spills and exploitations in Third World countries during the 1990s (Lauesen, 2014, p. 247). Critics say that although businesses are being made more aware of social and sustainability issues in contemporary times, they still misuse these terms only for reputation management, also called "greenwashing" and "window dressing." Social and Sustainable Finance have according to these critics not gained the prominence and excellence suggested by their ethical intentions, and the intergovernmental organizations have not managed to make things better, because they have no regulating power (e.g., Letnar Cernic, 2008).

Despite this critique, many small as well as large and multinational companies are committed to do good things for society, and they strive to combine social, environmental, and financial sustainability (see, e.g., Haigh & Hoffman, 2012; Lauesen, 2014, p. 248). The rising awareness of issues within Social and Sustainable Financing has led to new ventures within microfinance, social entrepreneurship, and businesses that have seen the potential to work with sustainability. These businesses have recognized that depreciation of natural capital cannot go on endlessly (Lovins, Lovins, & Hawken, 1999, p. 146, cited in Dyllick & Hockerts, 2002, p. 133, cited in Lauesen, 2014, p. 33). Some natural capital such as wood, fish, and culturally grown seed is renewable, while others such as fossil fuels and biodiversity are non-renewable.

A good society needs certain services for the people in terms of granting them access to a good educational system, care system, infrastructural system, and culturally supportive system (Dyllick & Hockerts, 2002, p. 134, cited in Lauesen, 2014, p. 33). Social enterprises, which offer microfinance to poorer communities, can help these people with economic capital in order to substitute some natural and social capital due to technological innovations. This does not mean, however, that all natural capital can be substituted by economic capital due to the irreversibility of natural depletion or climate change (Lauesen, 2014, p. 33). Therefore, social enterprises have become aware of their need to support social development alongside environmental and financial development for the people they support as well as for themselves as capital funds.

The inventions of cheap banking systems in remote rural areas, for instance in India and Africa, have improved the transfer of money between people mobilized by cell phone technology. This means that remote populations do not have to carry physical money to a physical bank in a city far away, risking being robbed during the travel. Now they can make their monetary transactions through their cell phone connections to their bank accounts (Kumar, McKay, & Rotman, 2010). This invention has thus meant that microbusinesses can be sustained and improve the life of small families that may have borrowed funds from social enterprises in order to initiate, carry on with, or develop their local businesses. The social enterprises, on the other hand, depend on dividends from their investments, but since they often spread their risks in multiple small businesses, they have often managed to succeed financially, environmentally, and socially with this relatively new market area (see also Goldberg & Palladini, 2010).

The 2008 financial crisis and its impact upon the landscape of Social and Sustainable Finance

The latest financial crisis erupting in 2008 has had a tremendous negative impact upon the business world as well as the general increased poverty at a global scale. This impact has not been seen at the same scale since the Depression in the 1930s. Large financial sector institutions were touted responsible for the financial bubble. Most of these companies, for instance the Lehman Brothers, Bear Stearns, Merrill Lynch, Freddie Mac, and Fannie Mae, no longer exist in their former realm. Others have succeeded in surviving the financial collapse, such as Goldman Sachs, Morgan Stanley, and CitiGroup, despite the harsh critique of the entire banking and investment sector on a global scale for creating the current recession (e.g., Hellwig, 2009; Herzig & Moon, 2013; Lauesen, 2013, 2014, p. 194; Reinhart & Rogoff, 2008, 2009; White, 2008).

The story about the 2008 financial crisis began much earlier and can be dated back to the early 1990s with the invention of ways for investment companies and banks to delineate and spread the risks from loans they gave to other businesses (Lauesen, 2013, 2014; White, 2008). JP Morgan was among the earliest to learn from the agricultural sectors about how they spread their risks of bad harvests by planting various different seeds in order for some fields to deliver a better harvest than others. This was an idea that easily could be used in the financial sector, especially if they could pool different kinds of risks—high-risk loans with low-risk loans, JP thought. Through this the investment banks could be guaranteed a profit and minimize their losses ultimately. Thus a new product called Credit Default Swaps (CDS) was created in order for investment companies like JP Morgan to continue their business and invest in high-risk loans. They combined their high-risk investments with more secure low-risk investments and sent these conglomerates to the global investment markets for others—multiples—to share the risks and the potential earnings as well (Lauesen, 2013). This idea worked well in times of growth, and as long as investment companies made sure to merge risks cleverly having trustworthy evaluations of the CDSs, this kind of business was sound within the banking and investment world.

However, JP Morgan could not have foreseen the explosiveness of their initial idea. Soon after the new conglomerates entered the market, other investment companies began to diffuse much more high-risk products to the markets such as Mortgage-Backed Securities, Asset-Backed Securities, and Collateralized Debt Obligations (Lauesen, 2013; see also Hellwig, 2009 and Schwarcz, 2008 for further explanation of these financial instruments). Banks and investment companies were taking more risks to pool with the fewer and fewer low-risk products contained in the opaque conglomerates.

This negative development began to concern especially the American federal regulators, which in the late 1990s felt that the financial bubble and the rapid growth of investment conglomerates were at stake. They feared the financial risks connected with the more complex and intractable products. However, a massive financial lobby argued to the then American leading politician Alan Greenspan that deregulation was the way forward, because the financial sector could secure some of the promises that President Bill Clinton had stated before the public. Clinton had stated relatively soon after his inauguration that every American was entitled to own a house (White House, 1995). Therefore, the lobby argued that banks and investment companies should be able to enter the mortgage market as well in order to make this promise effective. If the financial sector was regulated as stated in the Glass-Steagal Act, which came after the Depression in the 1930s in order to prevent another financial meltdown from happening, the political promises would never be fulfilled, the lobby argued (Lauesen, 2013). Alan Greenspan saw the potential in letting the financial sector develop their ideas and enter the mortgage markets and pleaded for deregulation of the financial sector. This resulted in a new market moving not only into the business-related risk areas but now also the consumer-related risk areas and especially the high-risk subprime mortgage market. Banks were now allowed to engage in all kinds of investments, and make riskier loans both for businesses and private families, which was stated in the then new Gramm-Leach-Bliley Act in 1999 that liberalized the financial market (White, 2008). Politically, the president's promises toward the public were fulfilled. However, insolvent loan takers too were offered finance for houses on promises they could never fulfill. The growing house market made banks and investment companies ensure that the new assets easily could be resold at a much higher price than the initial loan given (Lauesen, 2013; Partnoy, 2009).

This development in the American financial sector soon diffused to other parts of the world (Vives, 2001). In the EU, the liberalization created a massive market for investment banks such as the German IKB Bank, Credit Suisse, and others. Even the smallest banks in small countries wanted to be part of the new money party. Every bank and investment company began more or less aggressively to speculate in the subprime mortgage derivatives. The bubble burst happened in late 2007 in America and in 2008 for the rest of the world (Lauesen, 2013; Partnoy, 2009). Bankruptcies, families that had to leave their houses and live in tents on public spaces, family businesses that could not renew their loans, and businesses that downscaled rapidly left the world in one of the worst recessions seen since the 1930s, where politicians at that time promised each other that this should never happen again (Galbraith, 1994).

How did these events affect the landscape or markets for Social and Sustainable Finance?

Since it is well known that economic growth has been the mantra among governments on a global scale since World War II, which has superseded environmental and social concerns, the 2008 financial crisis showed that this strategy had severe backlashes especially on the latter (Schneider, Kallis, & Martinez-Alier, 2010). Many scholars have written about this for more than half a century. Schneider et al. found that despite the financial crisis in 2008 and the financial growth in China, India, and Indonesia, the increased emission of CO_2 up to 3 percent is now reversed. Instead a reduction about 3 percent has been recognized because of economic degrowth (Schneider et al., 2010, p. 515). The same pattern is seen according to these scholars with the reduction of forestation in the Brazilian rainforest.

> It is likely that the reduction of natural resource extraction and CO_2 emissions is larger than the de-growth rate of the economy because in times of economic shrinking it seems (at least in the present crisis) that material and energy intensive industries are

> heavily affected, leading to an actual decoupling. For instance, the cement output has decreased faster than the overall economy in many countries; in Spain in the first four months of 2009, cement demand dropped by about 45% [49]. If well targeted "green Keynesianism" rather than "public works Keynesianism" and "car subsidy Keynesianism" had been applied, the dematerialization of the economy could have advanced further in the economic crisis of 2008–09.
>
> *(Schneider et al., 2010, pp. 515–516)*

Despite the seemingly positive outcome in regard to reduced climate impact and resource extraction, the financial crisis had a social downside leading to social catastrophes in some nations—for instance, in the Mediterranean countries in Europe, among other places (Lauesen, 2013, 2014).

Another approach to Social and Sustainable Finance has been initiated because of the repeatedly minor or major financial crisis during the last half century. Social entrepreneurship, microfinance, Islamic banking models, and other ways to delegate money for social and sustainable purposes with beneficial conditions for both borrower and lender have been proved viable also prior to the global financial crisis in 2008. For instance, the Grameen Bank in Bangladesh, which emphasizes the finance of projects in rural areas in order for borrowers to finance self-employance, has shown how Social and Sustainable Finance can survive a major economic disaster such as a financial crisis (Chapra, 2008, p. 19).

However, as to whether "respectable rates of return and low default rates" are fair, which the research adviser at the Islamic Research and Training Institute of the Islamic Development Bank, M. Umer Chapra, writes (p. 19), is a good question. Microfinance institutions (MFIs) charge annual interest rates from 30 percent to 70 percent compared to other kinds of bank loans. Annual interest rates for mortgages range down below 5 percent in the richer parts of the Western world (Andriotis, October 2014[3]). The huge difference between traditional banking with favorable mortgage interests in the West and the microfinancial entrepreneurship investment banks in poorer areas of the world is, of course, the *risk* that is attached to these kinds of loans. People who have assets, jobs, and secure incomes are in the traditional banking world entitled to beneficial mortgage loans with extremely low interests. Whereas people who have nothing and just want to create a living for themselves and their families are regarded as high-risk borrowers. They can only engage with microfinance institutions, which take on higher risks to lose money to micro projects that may not succeed eventually. It is hard to be fair talking about fairness when dealing with different kinds of risks in the financial sector. Nevertheless the rise of microfinance has with no doubt meant a decrease of poverty in many poor areas around the world, thanks to these new possibilities for poor populations to get access to loans and investors willing to fund their local projects.

The 2008 financial crisis also had an impact on microfinance institutions, although many of them have managed to survive it. At the Global Microcredit Summit 2011, Adrian Gonzales, a lead researcher from the Microfinance Information Exchange (MIX), provided an overview of the consequences of the financial crisis on microfinance. Gonzales (2011, p. 3) explained that some of the impacts, which were enforced or intensified by the 2008 financial crisis on microfinance, actually had their roots before the crisis. This includes, according to Gonzales, a saturated market for microfinance, deficient credit policies, deficient governance structures, negative policy interventions, and poor adaptability to dealing with crises ultimately (Gonzales, 2011). In 2009, Gonzales reports, developing countries in Eastern Europe and Central Asia (ECA) and Latin America and the Carribean (LAC) were among those countries that were affected most by the recession, whereas those in South Asia were almost untouched.

> Of the 58 developing countries with more than four MFIs reporting to MIX in the period 2008–2009, 17 experienced a contraction in gross domestic product (GDP) in 2009 ... 15 of these were located in ECA and LAC.
>
> *(Gonzales, 2011, pp. 3–4)*

Gonzales explains the impact on MFIs in terms of Liquidity and Credit Crunches, which means "less funding is available for all financial institutions, including MFIs" (Gonzales, 2011, p. 4). For MFIs this problem is, according to Gonzales, more harmful, because it *a priori* is more difficult for MFIs to attract funding for social and sustainable purposes. However, the MIX institution reports that economic contraction in MFIs was not as severe as many expected in terms of growing debts, because 40 percent of MFIs experienced a reduction in debt in 2009 versus 36 percent in 2008. As a consequence of the financial crisis, many MFIs actually increased their funding, and more than half of the 374 MFIs experienced a decrease of costs of funds, while the rest reported minor increases of costs of funds (below 2 percent) with only 10 percent reporting an increase of more than 2 percent (Gonzales, 2011).

Gonzales mentions other impacts of the financial crisis on MFIs such as high inflation periods, where salaries and consumer prices go up, including food and fuel prices, which affect the costs for MFIs in general. However, it may be more severe in times of global financial crises. This is also part of the causes for economic contraction, which MFIs cannot necessarily be resilient to (Gonzales, 2011, p. 5). Other impacts include currency devaluations, high unemployment rates, demands for higher priced goods and services, low remittances, less savings, and reduced demands for production besides the general low trust in financial systems in general (2011, p. 6). MIX has reported the following potential effects on MFIs (2011, pp. 7–8):

- Reduction in borrower repayment
- Higher costs and interest rates for borrowers
- Reduced growth due to liquidity crunch (less funding available on the supply side), reduced demands for loans, and deposit withdrawal due to derived food and fuel crises
- Increased foreign exchange losses due to currency depreciation from inappropriate asset liability management
- Deterioration of microcredit repayment due to arrears in the general financial system, political intervention, and competition from other financial institutions more tolerant to arrears and defaults.

These risks were apparent even before the 2008 financial crisis. However, they have been more apparent during the current recession among general financial institutions including MFIs. This has made them consider policies of how to become more resilient to such impacts in the future alongside national governments considering how to strengthen regulation of financial institutions in order to avoid runaway financial bubbles in the future (Lauesen, 2013).

The contemporary landscape of Social and Sustainable Finance

Inter-organizational institutions have regarded the 2008 financial crisis as a springboard for introducing new policies for member nations and businesses in general, including the financial sector, in order to avoid further economic contractions and new financial crises, and in order to stabilize growth and recovery from the current recession. The OECD and UN have been exposed to much criticism due to "soft law" impacts showing their vague role in guarding the world from hazardous behaviors. This is both from business-related behavior in general but also from financial speculations leading to economic collapses (Lauesen, 2013; Letnar Cernic, 2008).

The OECD has established a new forum called the "Global Forum on Responsible Business Conduct." This forum concerns the 2011 OECD Guidelines for Multinational Enterprises and the 2011 UN Guiding Principles for Business and Human Rights. They want to advance the common understanding and expectations of how business should avoid and address risks and how governments can support and promote responsible business behavior.[4] The issues debated in this new forum are social and sustainable management in general, which indirectly includes behavioral and financial issues. The main agenda for the conference held at Paris on June 26–27, 2014 was improving the business climate to address the downside risks to global recovery with business responsibility, accountability, and transparency, so that markets can function well (Global Forum, 2014, p. 5). One of the issues of the conference was the Rana Plaza aftermath and how to make supply chains in the textiles and garment sector more responsible; stakeholder engagement and due diligence in the extraction sector (oil, gas, water, natural resources); problems in the agricultural sector regarding quality and environmental and social care; and finally responsible business conduct in the financial sector restoring public trust and improving governance in this sector.

The April 24, 2013 Rana Plaza disaster in Sava, 25 km from Dhaka in Bangladesh, showed how poor construction facilities and working environment made a nine-story fashion factory building collapse, killing more than 1,130 people.[5] Soon after, a global critique of multinational fashion companies, who had clothes and garments fabricated in Rana Plaza, aroused, and some of the largest companies came together and supported financially the new Rana Plaza Donors Trust Fund.[6] Despite the branding value for multinational companies supporting a trust fund to help survivors and relatives as well as the reestablishment of the factory, financial support cannot improve the conditions of garment workers in the developing world alone. According to the OECD Global Forum for Responsible Business Conduct, multiple initiatives have been made in order to avoid similar catastrophes in the fashion industry:

> The Bangladesh Tripartite National Action Plan; the Sustainability Compact for Bangladesh launched by the European Union, the United States, the ILO and Bangladesh; the Accord on Fire and Building Safety in Bangladesh and the Alliance for Bangladesh Worker Safety; the work of the ILO, such as the Better Work Programme in Bangladesh; the in depth reports of the NCPs of France and Italy on the implementation of the OECD Guidelines in the textile and garment sector; and the initiatives of Belgium, Canada, Denmark, Germany, the Netherlands, Sweden, the United Kingdom and the United States.
>
> *(Global Forum, 2014, p. 11)*

Regarding the future of Social and Sustainable Finance and the lessons learned from the 2008 financial crisis, the OECD Global Forum suggests that the principal goal of the financial sector in general is the creation of long-term values. This is the typical goal of microfinance institutions, but this should be broadened up to include the entire financial sector in general. The Global Forum recommended that it should be supported by regulation, standardization, and internalization of external costs in order to secure the long-term values. These long-term values should include natural capital, human capital, social capital, manufactured capital, and intellectual capital, as well as financial capital (Global Forum, 2014, p. 17). The panelists from the Global Forum suggested that it should be a fiduciary duty in the financial sector to include environmental and social due diligence in their general risk management systems. Although markets have been stabilized, growth is detectable, and unemployment on its way down, the need for social and sustainable funding for several countries is still crucial.

Beyond microfinance institutions, Social and Sustainable Finance comes from many other financial resources—for instance, from companies wanting to become sustainable and socially responsible in their business conduct. Although sustainability and social responsibility for private companies typically are tailored to the specific production and whereabouts of company interests, many—especially multinational companies—are massively investing in order to sustain their market positions, their brands, and their allowances in the areas in which their productions take place. One of the most popular market places, where multinational companies in all industries compete for conscious investors, is the Dow Jones Sustainability Indices (DJSI). This index was launched in 1999, and in 2014 it had 3,395 invited companies, of which they have analyzed 1,813[7] according to their economic, environmental, and social performances. The DJSI only invites the best companies in the world, according to their sustainability performance criteria, to compete on their index. Out of this pool, 800 of the largest companies are located in the emerging markets in 23 countries,[8] of which 10 percent of the best companies are selected for the indices plus a buffer of an additional 15 percent—in total 86 companies are represented in this category.

One of the companies on the DJSI is the beverage company Coca-Cola,[9] which has a large production site in India. This particular site has received much criticism,[10] and Coca-Cola as a response has improved their social and sustainable co-financial activities for the locals in India. Coca-Cola has established a foundation—the Anandana—The Coca-Cola India Foundation, with a mission to mitigate water stress, the use of renewable energy, promoting active and healthy lifestyles, and contributing to social advance locally.[11]

> In order to promote the Foundation's objectives, monetary grants and other assistance are provided to civil society members, beneficiary organizations, cooperatives, philanthropic organizations and such others who can be suitable partners in implementing projects for social welfare across the country.
>
> *(Coca-Cola India, Environmental Report, 2012, p. 9)*

Despite the branding, this foundation has spent 33,444,106 INR (US$ 611,072) on sustainable and social funding for the community, benefiting 33,660 people in the areas they operate in 2012.

Another example is the Danish shipping company Maersk with its foundation, the A.P. Moller Relief Foundation, which together with their employees and the Maersk Group donated US$ 256,050 to the Red Cross in the Philippines to help the survivors find relatives, get food, and re-establish a new home after the typhoon Haiyan hit the Central Philippines in November 2013.[12]

Conclusion

Although Social and Sustainable Finance are often thought of in terms of monetary help in order to mitigate poverty among half of the world, who live on below US$ 2 per day, the scope of this field is much wider and impossible to fully map. Although the 2008 financial crisis had a severe impact on all industries in the world, it seems that the world of microfinance as well as the entire business world is recovering pretty well, which means that Social and Sustainable Finance has a sustainable future itself continuing to help the poorest parts of the world to grow out of poverty eventually. With the help of the media, the investors' growing interest, and intergovernmental intervention and interaction in communicating and setting Social and sustainable finance at the top of the agenda, Social and Sustainable Finance is a "growing industry," which attracts more and more investors and agents.

Future research in Social and Sustainable Finance, however, could benefit from looking more into the "gray areas" of combined effects between Social and Sustainable Finance—for instance, the impact of climate changes in terms of how this affects the mitigation of poverty. With the release of the fifth assessment report (AR5) on October 31, 2014, the future risks of flooding and drought and melting of ice caps as a result of greenhouse emissions will rise to even further heights than earlier expected within this century (IPCC, 2014). What impacts do these negative effects have on those who live on below US$ 2 per day? Who is going to help these people diminish the risks they face? Social and Sustainable Finance is an area of such importance that its scope naturally must go beyond financial perspectives and business management, so that the impacts, effects, and responsibilities of multiple business agents in this field are correlated with the hazards on nature created by human and business impact on the planet and the people who live here.

Notes

1 Retrieved August 20, 2015, from http://en.wikipedia.org/wiki/Socially_responsible_investing
2 International Labour Organization.
3 Retrieved August 20, 2015, from http://online.wsj.com/articles/mortgage-rates-tumble-1414079815
4 Retrieved August 20, 2015, from http://mneguidelines.oecd.org/globalforumonresponsiblebusinessconduct/2014GFRBC_Summary.pdf
5 Retrieved August 20, 2015, from http://www.bbc.com/news/world-asia-27107860
6 Retrieved August 20, 2015, from http://www.cleanclothes.org/ranaplaza/who-needs-to-pay-up
7 Retrieved August 18, 2015, from http://www.sustainability-indices.com/images/DJSI_Review_Presentation_09_2014_final.pdf
8 Brazil, Chile, China, Colombia, Czech Republic, Egypt, Greece, Hungary, India, Indonesia, Malaysia, Mexico, Morocco, Peru, the Philippines, Poland, Qatar, Russia, South Africa, Taiwan, Thailand, Turkey, and the United Arab Emirates.
9 Retrieved August 18, 2015, from http://yearbook.robecosam.com/companies.html
10 See the NGO India Resource Center's webpage. Retrieved August 18, 2015, from http://www.indiaresource.org/campaigns/coke
11 Retrieved February 26, 2016, from http://www.coca-colaindia.com/wp-content/themes/73002/includes/pdf/sustainabilityReports/environment_Report_2012.pdf
12 Retrieved August 18, 2015, from http://www.maersk.com/en/the-maersk-group/sustainability/~/media/97169B32CA46458897FAE47C780CF69F.ashx

References

Annan, K. (1999, January 31). Business and the UN: A global compact of shared values and principles. *Proceedings from World Economic Forum, Davos, Switzerland.* Reprinted in *Vital Speeches of the Day, 65*(9), 260–261.

Banerjee, A. V., Duflo, E., Glennerster, R., & Kinnan, C. (2013, May). The miracle of microfinance? Evidence from a randomized evaluation. *NBER Working Paper Series.* doi:10.3386/w18950

Brundtland Report. (1989). *World Commission on Environment and Development (WCED). Our common future.* Oxford: Oxford University Press.

Chapra, M. U. (2008, October). *The global financial crisis: Can Islamic finance help minimize the severity and frequency of such a crisis in the future?* Paper presented at the Forum on the Global Financial Crisis at the Islamic Development Bank (Vol. 25).

Dyllick, T., & Hockerts, K. (2002). Beyond the business case for corporate sustainability. *Business Strategy and the Environment, 11*(2), 130–141. doi:10.1002/bse.323

Galbraith, J. K. (1994). *A short history of financial euphoria.* New York: Penguin Books.

Global Forum. (2014, June 26–27). *Global forum: On responsible business conduct* (Summary report). OECD Conference Centre, Paris, France. Retrieved August 18, 2015, from https://mneguidelines.oecd.org/globalforumonresponsiblebusinessconduct/2014GFRBC_Summary.pdf

Goldberg, M., & Palladini, E. (2010). *Managing risk and creating value with microfinance* (No. 189). Washington, DC: World Bank Publications.

Gonzales, A. (2011, November 14–17). *An empirical review of the actual impact of financial crisis and recessions on MFIs, and other factors explaining recent microfinance crisis.* Commissioned Workshop Paper, Global Microcredit Summit, Valladolid, Spain.

Haigh, N., & Hoffman, A. J. (2012). Hybrid organizations: The next chapter of sustainable business. *Organizational Dynamics, 41,* 126–134.

Hellwig, M. F. (2009). Systemic risk in the financial sector: An analysis of the subprime-mortgage financial crisis. *De Economist, 157*(2), 129–207. doi:10.1007/s10645-009-9110-0

Herzig, C., & Moon, J. (2013). Discourses on corporate social ir/responsibility in the financial sector. *Journal of Business Research, 66*(10), 1870–1880. doi:10.1016/j.jbusres.2013.02.008

Heyde, F., & Neyer, U. (2010). Credit default swaps and the stability of the banking sector. *International Review of Finance, 10*(1), 27–61. doi:10.1111/j.1468-2443.2010.01104.x

IPCC. (2014). *Climate Change 2014: Impacts, adaption and vulnerability.* Report published from *Working Group II, the Intergovernmental Panel on Climate Change.* Retrieved August 18, 2015, from http://www.ipcc.ch/report/ar5/wg2/

Jeucken, M. (2010). *Sustainable finance and banking: The financial sector and the future of the planet.* London, UK: Routledge.

Kindleberger, C. P., & Aliber, R. Z. (2011). *Manias, panics and crashes: A history of financial crises.* London, UK: Palgrave Macmillan.

Kumar, K., McKay, C., & Rotman, S. (2010, July). Microfinance and mobile banking: The story so far. *Focus Note, 62.* Retrieved August 18, 2015, from http://www.cgap.org/sites/default/files/CGAP-Focus-Note-Microfinance-and-Mobile-Banking-The-Story-So-Far-Jul-2010.pdf

Lauesen, L. M. (2013). CSR in the aftermath of the financial crisis. *Social Responsibility Journal, 9*(4), 641–663. doi:10.1108/SRJ-11-2012-0140

Lauesen, L. M. (2014). *Corporate social responsibility in the water sector: How material and physical practices and their symbolic meanings form a colonising logic* (PhD thesis). Doctoral School in Organisation and Management Studies. Copenhagen: Copenhagen Business School.

Letnar Cernic, J. (2008). Corporate responsibility for human rights: A critical analysis of the OECD guidelines for multinational enterprises. *Hanse Law Review, 4*(1), 71–100.

Lovelock, J. (2006). *The revenge of Gaia: Why the Earth is fighting back—and how we can still save humanity.* London, UK: Allen Lane.

Lovins, A. B., Lovins, L. H., & Hawken, P. (1999). A road map for natural capitalism. *Harvard Business Review,* 77(3), 145–158.

Margulis, L., & Lovelock, J. E. (1974). Biological modulation of the Earth's atmosphere. *Icarus, 21*(4), 471–489. doi:10.1016/0019-1035(74)90150-X

Partnoy, F. (2009). Historical perspectives on the financial crisis: Ivar Krueger, the credit-rating agencies, and two theories about the function, and dysfunction, of markets. *Essay,* no. 26, Yale J. on Reg. 431. Retrieved August 18, 2015, from http://heinonline.org/HOL/LandingPage?collection=journals&handle=hein.journals/yjor26&div=18&id=&page=

Reinhart, C. M., & Rogoff, K. S. (2008). Is the 2007 U.S. sub-prime financial crisis so different? An international historical comparison. *NBER working papers, prepared for the American Economic Review Papers and Proceedings.* Reinhart: School of Public Policy and Department of Economics, 4105 Van Munching Hall, University of Maryland, College Park, Maryland 20742.

Reinhart, C. M., & Rogoff, K. S. (2009). *This time is different: Eight centuries of financial folly.* New Jersey: Princeton University Press.

Schaper, M. (Ed.). (2010). *Making ecopreneurs: Developing sustainable entrepreneurship.* London, UK: Gower Publishing, Ltd.

Schneider, F., Kallis, G., & Martinez-Alier, J. (2010). Crisis or opportunity? Economic degrowth for social equity and ecological sustainability. Introduction to this special issue. *Journal of Cleaner Production, 18*(6), 511–518. doi:10.1016/j.jclepro.2010.01.014

Schwarcz, S. L. (2008). *Protecting financial markets: Lessons from the subprime mortgage meltdown* (American Law and Economics Association Annual Meetings, Paper 19). Retrieved January 14, 2013, from http://law.bepress.com/cgi/viewcontent.cgi?article=2664&context=alea

Vives, X. (2001). Competition in the changing world of banking. *Oxford Review of Economic Policy, 17*(4), 535–547. doi:10.1093/oxrep/17.4.535

White House. (1995, August). *The national homeowner strategy: Partners in the American dream* (Message of the President (Bill Clinton). Urban Policy Brief, No. 2). Retrieved September 23, 2013, from http://www.huduser.org/publications/txt/hdbrf2.txt

White, L. H. (2008, November 18). *How did we get into this financial mess?* (Cato Institute Briefing Paper, No. 110). Retrieved January 14, 2013, from http://www.icpcolombia.org/archivos/publicaciones/cato1.pdf

2

SUSTAINABLE FINANCE

Building a more general theory of finance

Scott Fullwiler

John Maynard Keynes titled his best known work *The General Theory of Employment, Interest, and Money* because he believed he had developed a *general* theory that could explain macroeconomic cycles while relying upon fewer restrictive assumptions than the Classical economists. He argued that the generally accepted framework developed by the Classicals was merely a *special case*—that is, it was applicable only to a fully employed macroeconomy—due to its simplifying assumptions that essentially assumed away the possibility of aggregate demand-led, prolonged recessions such as the Great Depression.

This chapter argues that sustainable finance has the potential to contribute similarly to a more general theory of finance. Traditional financial theory is based upon restrictive assumptions regarding values and investment outcomes, limiting both to financial gains/losses and their risks. sustainable finance instead recognizes both a greater range of potential values—including financial return, risk aversion, altruism for current and future generations, and concern for ecological resilience—and a larger potential set of returns or losses, both financial and otherwise.

Because the *general theory* framework has fewer restrictive assumptions and broader applicability, it is a more appropriate starting point for analysis. It is counterproductive to use a theory of macroeconomics that largely ignores the possibility of financial crises and large macroeconomic downturns to understand a world in which such events have repeatedly happened. It is similarly backward to begin financial analysis with traditional financial theory when it is known that financial gains and losses are necessarily intertwined with human values beyond financial returns, resilience of ecological systems, and the well-being of others within and beyond the current generation. To that end, this chapter discusses several potential components of a new theory of sustainable finance that are building blocks for a more general theory of finance.

Sustainable finance, blended values, and blended returns

Muhammad Yunus (2008) writes that an important problem with traditional economic theory is its view that individuals are purely self-interested when it is quite evident that an individual in fact is driven by a blend of self-interest and altruism. For more than two decades, Jed Emerson (e.g., Emerson, 2003) has preached the concept of "blended value," which recognizes that no company or organization is purely "good" or "bad" but rather generates a "blend" of social, environmental, and financial returns (which can be positive or negative). A world in which investors have a blend of altruistic and self-interested values, and where all companies generate blended returns, should not look like the received dichotomy of investing 90 percent of one's wealth for self-interested financial return, completely divorced from philanthropic, altruistic giving of the other 10 percent. As RSF social finance's Don Shaffer put it,

> We're in the midst of a transition from a very 20th Century mentality—which can be described as a wealth now, philanthropy later way of compartmentalizing the two and getting wealthy before you can get into charitable and philanthropic activities.
>
> What it seems to be transitioning into with younger generations is a blending of those two buckets—investing/wealth and philanthropy. Instead of looking at it in a compartmentalized way, they see it as a spectrum, especially when it comes to rate of return on investment. You could have plus 15 percent on the high end, and negative 100 percent on the other end—which is to give money away—and a whole range in between with a lot of territory in it.
>
> *(Waggoner, 2010)*

While not new—"socially responsible investing" (hereafter SRI) dates back at least to the practice of screening out South African investments from portfolios in the 1980s due to apartheid—the current momentum for integrating environmental, social, and governance (hereafter ESG) criteria into investment decisions represents an opportunity to build investment practice *and theory* on the principles of blended values and blended returns.

Instead of the traditional investing/philanthropy dichotomy, Emerson and Freundlich (2012, p. 4) refer to a "unified investor" who invests across three broad categories to align his/her blended values with a blend of investment and impact returns:

1 Capital that is intentionally structured to generate a blend of social and financial returns, requiring a minimum of a market rate risk-adjusted financial return.
2 Capital that is structured to create a blend of social and financial returns, but accepts financial returns lower than the risk-adjusted market rate in exchange for greater social returns.
3 Capital that generates a core mission-aligned social return, but no financial return to the investor other than tax deduction value.

Unified portfolios of blended value/blended return investments can incorporate all traditional asset classes—public equities, private equity, fixed income, deposit accounts and CDs, real estate, real assets, hedge funds, philanthropy, etc. (e.g., Bridges Ventures, 2010; Emerson, 2012, p. 8; Emerson & Freundlich, 2012; Humphreys, Solomon, & Electris, 2012). Opportunities continue to emerge for still greater alignment with unified investing goals for blended values/returns, for instance in community food systems, community development, ecotourism, sustainable agriculture in developing economies, water markets, carbon markets and offsets, carbon-reducing projects (e.g., climate bonds), and conservation finance.

Practitioners are already creating new approaches to building portfolios based on blended values of their clients as a result of ESG criteria applied to traditional investments, financial instruments, and even asset classes emerging from sustainable finance, ESG-based indexes, and benchmarks. Within public equities (and often fixed income), there are two main approaches, albeit with several sub-variations:

- The exclusionary or negative screening approach of traditional SRI, where undesirable investments—fossil fuels, tobacco, industrial agriculture, national defense, companies with poor ESG ratings—are omitted either by individual investors or by fund managers (such as TIAA-CREF's Social Choice fund).
- The positive screening approach, which screens better ESG performing companies into the portfolio, either to (a) replace lower ESG performers (e.g., Humphreys et al., 2012; Kiernan, 2009), often within the same industry, in order to maintain desired diversification against a benchmark, or (b) to "tilt" the portfolio to weighting the higher ESG-rated companies higher while lower rated companies remain at lower weights, consistent with the view that no company is "all good" or "all bad," while suggesting that there remain diversification benefits to keeping the lower rated companies in the portfolio (e.g., Herman, 2010).

Both groups also engage in investor activism in an attempt to shape the behavior of companies and increasingly improve their ESG performance. Blended value investors (even the negative screeners) may maintain investments in even very low ESG performing companies in order to file shareholder resolutions or otherwise engage with management as owners. Shareholder resolutions are usually non-binding, but they can impact company policies in various ways, for example by generating public attention (even when unsuccessful) or encouraging management to negotiate to avoid such attention. These strategies further align blended returns of unified portfolios with blended values (e.g., Digitale, 2014; Emerson & Freundlich, 2012; Humphreys et al., 2012).

The strict focus on financial returns of investments and self-interest of investors is a special case of a more general theory of finance. The more general case of sustainable finance is to build a theory of unified portfolios by recognizing that (1) investors possess blended values, and that (2) every investment generates a blend of financial and non-financial returns.

Sustainable finance and financial risk

There is growing evidence that risk-adjusted returns from ESG-based investing could outperform traditional diversified portfolios. Mercer (2011b), for instance, found that in 30 of 36 studies the relationship between ESG factors and return was neutral or positive. In a much heralded and comprehensive study published by Deutsche Bank, Fulton, Kahn, and Sharpies (2012) reviewed 58 academic studies evaluating ESG-based portfolios and found that ESG factors were strongly associated with reduced cost of capital and market based or accounting-based outperformance. Edmans, Li, and Zhang (2014) reported that employee satisfaction is associated with risk-adjusted abnormally high returns in countries with flexible labor markets. Ghoul, Guedhami, Kwok, and Mishra (2012) also reported that companies with higher ratings for employee relations and environmental responsibility had lower *ex ante* implied costs of equity even after accounting for industry, asset value, market beta, and leverage. Their more recent research found evidence for lower costs of equity among higher ESG-rated firms in manufacturing industries across 30 countries (Ghoul, Guedhami, Kwok, & Mishra, 2014). Looking at market indices, Murtha and Hamilton (2012) report that the Dow Jones Sustainability World Total Return Index persistently outperformed the MSCI World Total Return Index during 2001–2010.

There are a few commonly cited explanations for why ESG investments might outperform. First, managers who manage ESG factors better may in fact be better managers. It is well known that manager quality is the key driver of business value; ESG performance could be an *ex ante* indicator of higher quality management (e.g., Herman, 2010; Kiernan, 2009). Second, the risks and opportunities presented by ESG-related issues are seen as the future, if not current, operating environment of business in general (e.g., De Boer & van Bergen, 2012; Lubber, 2010). Consequently, ESG factors are now often viewed as material to business value and thus also to company reporting (e.g., Bonner et al., 2012; Hespenheide & Koehler, 2013). The logical outcome is increasing investor demand for greater ESG transparency and standards for mandatory reporting of ESG-related outcomes and managerial practices.

But if ESG factors that in some cases are already publicly available are related to higher risk-adjusted returns, why has the market not priced these factors in already? Leaving aside the issue of whether capital markets are efficient (in the efficient markets hypothesis sense), from the perspective of a more general theory of finance, it follows that an asset pricing model in which ESG factors have systematic properties could in fact be a better model (e.g., Jussa et al., 2013). At the same time, the majority view in capital markets (and in academic finance) continues to be that ESG factors are *not* systematic, and therefore explicitly integrating them into portfolio building results in a *reduced* reward-to-risk balance (e.g., Forbes, 2013; Kiernan, 2009). In other words, if the true or at least better model is one in which ESG factors reduce risk systematically, and if market participants on average are using an asset pricing model that does not incorporate ESG factors, then there could by definition be alpha (excess risk free return) associated with ESG-based investing (e.g., Harold, Spitzer, & Emerson, 2007).

The doubts of many investors and finance academics notwithstanding, there are many reasons to believe that ESG factors could become essential systematic factors of portfolios of the future (again, if they are not already), such as the following:

- The future interaction of climate and biodiversity-related risks/opportunities with new technologies and the extent of policy responses will form the context of investing, risks, and returns, according to Mercer (2011a). Strategic allocations among different asset classes, and among higher versus lower ESG rated within and across these asset classes, will matter in many reasonable scenarios (Mercer, 2011a).
- Some argue forcefully that even current fossil fuel reserves are "unburnable" given imminent climate legislation, which would mean that existing assets of the respective firms are grossly overvalued already based on cash flows that can reasonably be forecast from these assets (e.g., Leaton, 2014).
- Some newer ESG-related asset classes—such as sustainable agriculture or Social Impact Bonds—could have low correlations with traditional investments and thus could provide benefits to diversification (e.g., Barby & Pedersen, 2014; McGrath & Lai, 2014).
- ESG ratings have been found to be related to lower cost of debt among publicly held corporations (e.g., Principles for Responsible Investment, 2013), while anecdotal evidence suggests that ESG ratings for municipal bonds may predict state and local government defaults (Gerlach, Herman, Hecker, & Bernhardt, 2013).

Of course, this is not to suggest that ESG investments will always outperform "traditional" investments. Even those publishing such studies find the favorable results tend to be related to specific characteristics of portfolios or firms. For instance, the results of Fulton et al. (2012) were most strongly associated with the "G" or governance part of ESG and with portfolios built from positive rather than negative screens typical of traditional SRI investing. Krosinsky (2014) reminds us that a portfolio constructed from Sustainalytics' "10 Companies to Watch in 2014" would have been "an unmitigated short-term disaster, dramatically underperforming benchmarks"; he warns that while Sustainalytics' evaluations are likely correct and in general represent a high quality of analysis and detail, ESG factors become material only if companies are held accountable by policy, markets, or both. Referring to his own research, Krosinsky confirms the Fulton et al. result that positive screens can be associated with outperformance, while negative screens rarely are.

The question, of course, is which positive screens are appropriate. There are too many approaches to discuss or even name here for aligning ESG ratings and financial return, but the overarching themes tend to be building portfolios of companies that are (a) best at managing the opportunities and risks of environmental factors in their own operations, in their supply chains, and in terms of potential regulatory changes, and (b) best at managing a range of stakeholders from employees to communities to customers. (See, for instance, the various chapters in Krosinsky (2012) or Jussa et al. (2013) for examples and discussions of ESG portfolio building, many of which blend ESG analysis with traditional financial and competitive advantage analysis.) More recently, Khan, Serafeim, and Yoon (2015) draw a distinction between material and non-material ESG issues, finding that better performance on material ESG issues has been the driver of ESG outperformance.

For building a more general theory of finance, the growing evidence of how financial risk, financial return, and ESG factors are related suggests that traditional single- or even multi-factor models of the risk/return relationship are overly simplistic. Instead, sustainable finance provides the impetus to do analysis that more explicitly integrates context—that is, a company's sustainability policy, employee relations, community relations, board diversity, exposure to regulatory risks, ESG disclosure, and so on are economically significant for determining materiality and systematic risks. A theory of finance that omits or otherwise downplays this context is a special case, not a general one.

Sustainable finance and financial innovation

Through the deliberate blend of altruism and self-interest, traditional financial tools are used to build financial innovations to solve social and environmental problems where blended returns can be aligned with blended values. One of the most notable characteristics of sustainable finance to this point is the large amount of financial innovation it has catalyzed. At least five of these innovations are now well known:

- Microfinance proved that the very poor in developing countries can be very good credit risks. A key innovation was "community collateral" in which loans are made and paid back by groups of people in the community (usually women).
- Carbon rights trading markets (and earlier sulfur dioxide trading markets) enable the internalizing of one of the most important environmental externalities.
- Social Impact Bonds allow financial return to be explicitly tied to impact thresholds.
- Crowdfunding platforms enable direct, often (but not necessarily) very small donations or investments for small businesses, non-profits, and impact-related projects to be pooled together.
- Payments for ecosystem services enable internalizing externalities—this time positive externalities provided from protecting ecological systems—while also providing payments to investors and/or inhabitants or owners who often happen to be poor in developing countries.

None of these has been without difficulties—legal, press-related, development of necessary infrastructure, etc.—but each shows the potential for a more general approach to finance that integrates blended returns and blended values to integrate traditional tools of finance with social and environmental impact.

All five examples have also directly or indirectly encouraged even more innovation. Investment carbon funds, for example, raise public or private capital to purchase carbon credits in primary markets in bulk earned by emissions-reducing projects, conservation, community development, etc., and sell the credits into retail secondary markets at a spread above the bulk price. Microfinance and crowdfunding platforms are blended together by Kiva, Vittana, and others for traditional financing of small business loans and education loans in developing countries; crowdfunding also serves as a platform used by SparkFund to finance low-cost energy efficiency improvements in communities across the United States. Social Impact Bonds—already being attempted in public healthcare, education, and anti-recidivism initiatives—have the potential to serve as a model for Environmental Impact Bonds (Nicola, 2013) and Development Impact Bonds, and could further expand beyond the public sector as an initiator into more traditional grant-making foundations that have impact-driven missions like the public sector. Finally, ecosystem services payments can be integrated with numerous other financial instruments and markets, such as carbon markets via carbon offsets, water markets, and conservation finance.

Microfinance loans, sales of agricultural goods by developing nation farmers, and sharing economy assets are each now legitimate collateral for asset-backed financing. Based themselves on "community collateral," microfinance loans have proven to be securitizable in a way similar to loans from banks and credit cards. They can thereby serve as sources of ongoing, growing financial resources for microfinance institutions (Emerson & Spitzer, 2006; Jayadev & Rao, 2012). Root Capital—which lends to farmers and small businesses that are generally too large for microfinance and too small for traditional banks (the so-called "missing middle")—utilizes the purchase orders received by its borrowers as collateral for loans it makes; the buyers of the goods then pay Root Capital directly, and Root Capital then sends the payment net of principal and interest to the borrower (Milder, 2010). Though also not without challenges, residential solar power leases (e.g., Solarcity) and Zipcar fleets have likewise proven to be securitizable assets. Some think negawatts (a unit measuring electricity *saved*) might have properties consistent with marketable securities issued for solar and wind power purchase agreements (Equilibrium Capital, 2010). A Seattle utility and investors in energy efficiency upgrades are now testing the negawatt model; utilities in New York, California, and other states may follow (Bank, 2014).

Capital structure innovations can similarly enhance and embed a sustainability mission. For instance:

- Venture philanthropy fund Acumen's approach yields deals that establish below-market returns in investments in entrepreneurs with a possibility of making significant, replicable impact in education, healthcare, or sanitation in the developing world. Acumen has labeled its approach "patient capital"; it might also be referred to as purchasing a long-term European call option on impact, where—unlike traditional venture capital—entrepreneurs have flexibility and time to make mistakes and adjust business models in search of one that might solve social problems in a replicable and/or scalable way.
- When Good Capital invested in Better World Books (BWB), there was concern that BWB's practice of regular donations to its literacy partners as a percent of profits (originally a percent of sales, but then changed) might not survive if the company were purchased. The solution was ultimately to vest the literacy partners with ownership in BWB, providing them with the opportunity to take a substantial payday in an acquisition or own a percent of the profits as it was doing prior to vesting (Jones, 2009). Good Capital also dealt with a typical difficulty of private impact investing—exits—in its BWB deal by creating a put option with a strike at a pre-agreed multiple of sales that was exercisable after a period of years; the effect was to enable Good Capital to exit whether or not a liquidity event occurred, allowing BWB the choice of using cash, issuing equity, or issuing debt to pay for the put if it were exercised (Jones, 2009).

Though this section has only scratched the surface of ongoing innovations in sustainable finance, the fact that innovation *has* had such a significant role within sustainable finance is unsurprising. Blended values and blended returns are *themselves* innovative ideas from a traditional finance view; combining business models and finance where motivations for both go beyond traditional financial returns almost by definition should result in new forms of capital structure, financial asset classes, market infrastructure, and so forth. This is precisely why a more general theory of finance is necessary—the appropriate, more general framework for innovation that helps build a sustainable, equitable economy is one that considers blended values and blended returns from the outset.

Infrastructure for sustainable finance

The ability to develop scale ESG-based investing—whether from approaches based on blended values, competitive returns, or outperformance of benchmarks—requires a financial infrastructure that enables this. If anything, this infrastructure is more important to creating financial innovations in sustainable finance. In a more general sense, building the infrastructure for sustainable finance illustrates the inherent embeddedness of the financial system within a broader socio-ecological context. In other words, markets—financial markets as much as any—are necessarily social constructs as are market prices.

One could argue that there are few things that have been more important to the evolution of business and finance than double-entry accounting (e.g., Most & Enzensberger, 1972; Previts & Merino, 1998; Sombart, 1924). Whereas traditional accounting evolved over centuries, growing concern that ESG-related factors are material and the increasing demand by investors for ESG reporting mean that the era of accounting and financial reporting for a world of blended values and blended returns is already here. The ability to further scale ESG investing and ESG-based financial innovations relies crucially on the ability to create transparency in the ESG factors for evaluating and valuing risks and returns required for price discovery (Chen, 2011). In turn, transparency requires agreed-upon approaches to measuring/accounting and reporting standards.

While at an early stage, the infrastructure in accounting, measuring, standards, ratings, and reporting for sustainable finance is emerging, including the following examples from equities, fixed income, and natural and human resources:

- The Global Reporting Initiative (GRI) and the Sustainability Accounting Standards Board (SASB) are developing standardized approaches to ESG reporting for public companies. The Global Impact Investing Network (GIIN) is doing the same for privately held companies. The Carbon Disclosure Project (CDP), Sustainalytics, Trucost, HIP Investor, CSR Hub, CERES, and many others provide ratings of companies' ESG practices to investors. Bloomberg and others provide platforms for obtaining ESG-based data and ratings on companies and funds much like, say, Morningstar provides for traditional investors. MSCI, Dow Jones, and Standard and Poors have developed numerous sustainability-related indexes.
- CERES, the World Bank, and the Climate Bond Initiative have developed voluntary standards for green bonds. KPMG provides third-party assurance for climate bonds (Murphy, 2014), while Barclays and MSCI have developed a green bond index to go with several existing indices for ESG-related fixed income products. HIP Investor rates over 9,000 government and non-government entities issuing municipal bonds on ESG criteria.
- The Natural Capital Project and others are developing methods for valuing natural capital for financial statement accounting based on a blend of previous and newer research on valuing ecosystem services. Puma recently began publishing its much celebrated environmental

profit and loss statement. Numerous companies, particularly in India (such as Infosys, NTPC, and BHEL, as discussed in Kashive, 2012), report human capital resources in their financial statements. These reports are based largely on previous theoretical research (such as Lev & Schwartz, 1971).

Sustainable finance infrastructure also is necessary for liquidity, which is itself required for scaling via primary market placements, secondary markets, and exits, and in aiding price discovery. Mehrling (2011) explains in detail how traditional financial theory has largely ignored liquidity in asset pricing theory by *assuming* liquidity is forthcoming when violation of no arbitrage conditions occurs. His description of the role of the hierarchy of creating, backstopping, and restricting liquidity in the financial system, and its role in financial fragility and instability (based on the work of Hyman Minsky), is beyond the scope of this chapter, but the relevant point is that liquidity is *created* in markets deliberately. Liquidity does not magically appear because there is a mispricing; rather, liquidity is an integral part of a price in the first place. The difficult work, for instance, of (a) building liquid carbon markets; (b) building primary markets for green bonds and social impacts bonds (much less secondary markets); (c) clearing and settling alternative investments like Calvert Foundation's Community Investment Note via payments systems used by advisors, trusts, and brokers; and (d) developing methods for exiting social ventures without compromising their missions all speak to the necessary role of infrastructure for creating liquidity in order to scale sustainable finance.

A public infrastructure of sustainable finance exists alongside the private infrastructure. Voluntary reporting requirements are useful—and in many ways have been successful—but there is a reason why investors concerned with ESG factors continuously write letters to the Securities Exchange Commission (SEC). From the perspective of traditional finance and economics, public sector regulation, subsidies, taxes, and restrictions are "interventions" in "pure" markets. But "pure" markets do not exist. Any real-world market is necessarily the product of the existing infrastructure of legal liabilities and rights of business, legal forms of incorporation, subsidies, taxes, regulations, and so forth. There is no such thing as a government *not* choosing among competing interests in society or the natural environment in regard to these. For instance, traditional fossil fuel industries have been characterized by expanded drilling and mining rights, subsidies (multiple times greater than those for renewable energy; see, for instance, Cody, Parry, Sears, & Shang, 2015; Koplow, 2012; Makhijani, 2014; Pfund & Healey, 2011; and Vorrath, 2014), and the historical absence of laws or regulations requiring that carbon emissions be priced. Note further that a similar combination of laws, regulations, subsidies, and so forth provides some preference for fossil fuels use in related industries like agriculture, automobiles, and electric utilities.

Rather than seeing these as "interventions" into "free" markets, a more general theory of finance recognizes that public financial infrastructure heavily influences the ability of investors to trust the stability of a market, build an asset class, and develop financial innovations. Chen (2011) refers to such infrastructure as enabling "consistency" in markets, which is a requirement, in his view, for creating and scaling sustainable finance. Note further how alterations to legal and regulatory infrastructure such as the JOBS Act can (hopefully) lessen the challenges of creating and scaling financial tools for community-based investing (e.g., direct public offerings or community mutual funds), particularly for non-accredited investors. A similar analogy exists with respect to benefit corporation legislation.

Such an understanding of the role of infrastructure is not new—the research of Ronald Coase in the 1960s was significant in recognizing that trading allowances could be assigned in order to develop cap and trade markets for carbon, water rights, and land development rights to protect biodiversity. Still earlier, in the first decades of the 20th century, John R. Commons explained how markets were necessarily socially embedded given the particular—and unavoidable—allocation of rights, duties, liabilities, and requirements inherent in markets and prices in capitalist systems. The uneven development of carbon markets to date is an illustrative example of the importance of "consistency" provided by infrastructure in building and scaling sustainable finance and of potential difficulties that not having such "consistency" can bring.

Overall, the development and scaling of sustainable finance requires its own deliberately constructed public and private infrastructure of rights, rules, regulations, accounting/measurement/reporting standards, primary markets, secondary markets, and payments systems. Markets, prices, and financial returns are not "natural"—they emerge from an interaction of businesses, consumers, and investors within this infrastructure. A more general theory of finance recognizes that the context of public and private infrastructure is a necessary complement to finance in general, sustainable or otherwise.

What's next for sustainable finance?

All progress and success to date notwithstanding, there is more to be done for a more general theory of finance to be possible. This section discusses three cornerstones of traditional financial theory—risk, diversification, and time—with respect to their implications for sustainable finance.

Risk and diversification

Emerson (2012) presents hypothesized relationships between financial return, financial risk, and impact in three dimensions. Figure 2.1 shows the traditional "efficient frontier" from finance textbooks with a positive relationship between financial return and financial risk. Figure 2.2 shows the three-dimensional "efficient frontier" relationship between financial return, financial risk, and impact in Emerson (2012, p. 11) as a three-axis graph. Emerson's point was to

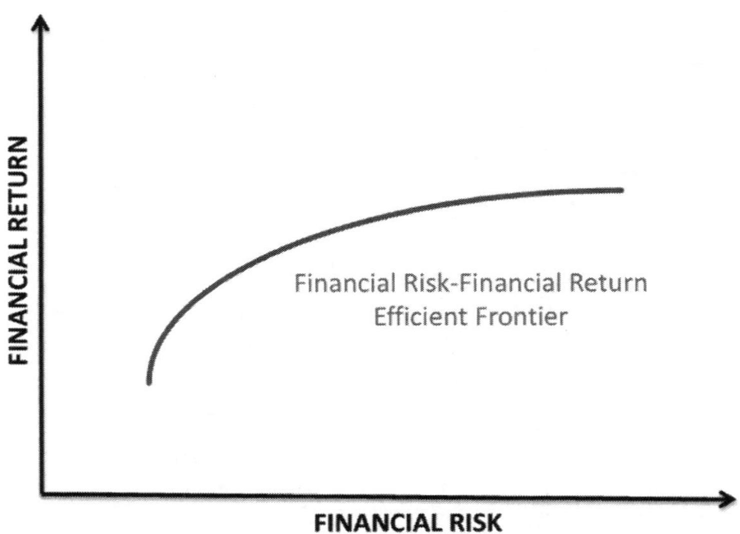

Figure 2.1 Traditional efficient frontier relationship between financial return and financial risk

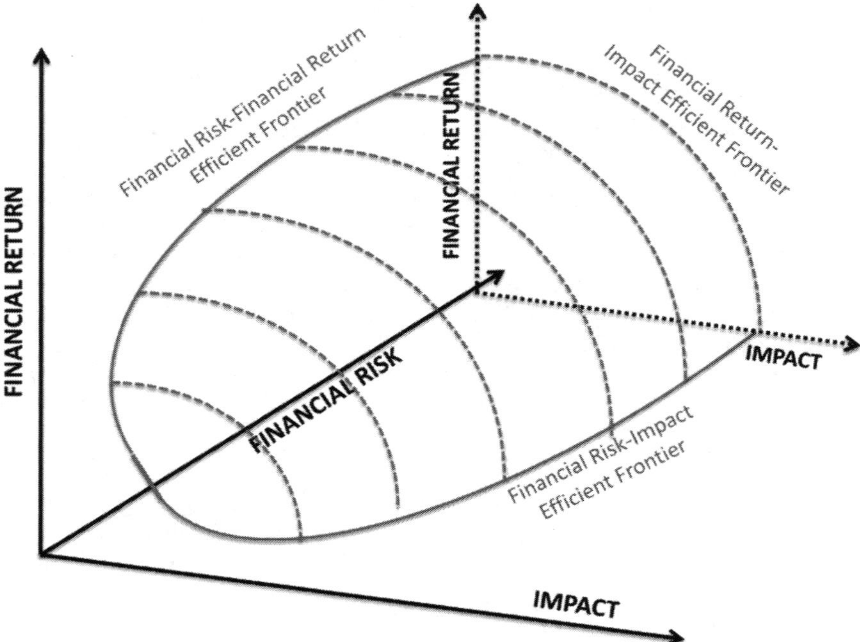

Figure 2.2 Three-dimensional efficient frontier of financial return, financial risk, and impact

demonstrate how impact investing could be viewed holistically, and it is probably a helpful representation in that sense. However, there are a few important problems with the figure. The financial return and impact axes drawn as dotted lines farther down the financial risk axis are added from Emerson's original. These clearly show that the assumed relationship in Emerson's figure between financial return and impact is negative—that is, more impact reduces financial return. Also clear from Figure 2.2 is the relationship between impact and financial risk as positive—that is, more impact raises financial risk. Both of these are counter to some of the evidence presented earlier suggesting that ESG factors appear to be able to contribute positively to return and might also possess alpha-like qualities, particularly if they are sources of systematic risk. Indeed, it is inconsistent with several of Emerson's own writings on ESG investing. To be clear, though, there is no suggestion in Emerson's paper that the graph is intended to be the result of careful theoretical analysis. As such, the reproduction and discussion here is not intended as criticism but rather a demonstration of the need for investigating the relationships he presents more rigorously both empirically and theoretically.

Additionally, while various approaches to measuring non-financial impacts and returns are available, most do not consider the risks of these impacts or how these risks might be valued or otherwise evaluated. Consider the following hypothetical scenarios:

- Two electric utilities with carbon emission reduction records that are better than their industry average, but with one company consistently reducing at a stable, regular pace and the other reducing at a highly variable pace, even increasing carbon emissions for several years at a time.
- Two large retailers score above average with respect to community impact, employee satisfaction, or some other index or ranking of social responsibility. Both consistently score

in the top 30 percent, but one's score remains quite stable regardless of the state of the economy while another "swings" with the ups and downs of the broader economy.

- Two non-profit organizations, one with a tested business model producing consistent impact in community job creation and poverty reduction, and a second with an innovative business model that could have a truly paradigm changing effect on poverty if successfully scaled, or no effect at all if the model fails.

It seems that blended value investors would in each case view the two companies differently, with the second being a riskier bet on impact. From an asset pricing perspective, if ESG factors are material and/or sources of systematic risk, the second company in each case should face a higher cost of capital and/or have a lower valuation, all else being equal. This suggests that risk to impact or to ESG factors is a fourth factor to integrate. A four-dimensional graph is obviously not possible, but Figure 2.3 presents the pairs of relationships not yet integrated into a more general theory of finance—financial return/impact, financial risk/impact, financial return/impact risk, financial risk/impact risk, and impact/impact risk. Again, the point is not to criticize Emerson's figure (i.e., Figure 2.2) per se but rather to illustrate and reiterate the importance of more fully theoretically and empirically understanding the relationships in question.

For a more general approach to finance, there are closely related theoretical and empirical questions to answer with regard to diversification. It is well known that where there are benefits to diversification, financial risk of an individual asset is less important than the financial risk to the portfolio; the benefits of diversification arise from imperfect correlations among assets in the portfolio, which if low enough can significantly reduce portfolio risk and push out the efficient frontier. While many point to the potential benefits of the financial return/financial risk tradeoff of building stock portfolios that account positively for ESG factors, is there any reason to desire imperfect correlation among these factors in order to reduce the risk to the portfolio's financial return? Or, alternatively, is the highest ESG score across all assets more desirable, as most reports published by the impact investing community implicitly assume?

Additionally, what about the relationship of impact to the risk of impact? Are there benefits to diversification of impacts across assets or of diversification across investments with less correlation for a specific impact? In other words, is there any ability to take advantage of imperfect impact correlations among assets within a portfolio and significantly reduce the risk that desired impact(s) occur(s)?

Finally, what are the potential correlative patterns for impact in the first place? For instance, it may be easier for companies to sustain greater impact or ESG ratings when the broader economy is also doing well, which would suggest a macroeconomic-based systematic component to ESG factors; if so, how valuable is it in terms of a portfolio's financial risk and its impact risk to diversify the portfolio by including investments that have less or even negative correlation with the systematic component? Perhaps there are some ESG factors for which high correlation across individual assets is desired (for instance, reduced carbon exposure or more broad diversity), while for others lower correlation might be desirable.

Developing an understanding of multiple sources and forms of risk for a new, blended-value financial system will clearly not be easy—compared to financial risks, there are few if any standards for measuring and evaluating impact risks, while investors' preferences in the face of risks to a blend of returns or impacts are obviously not as simple as the standard financial risk and financial return tradeoff of modern financial theory. But standard approaches to portfolio building and valuation rely on an analysis of financial risk and diversification. Without an understanding of the relationships in Figure 2.3 and of diversification of both financial returns and impacts, a generally agreed-upon approach to portfolio building and valuation will remain incomplete for a world of blended returns and values.

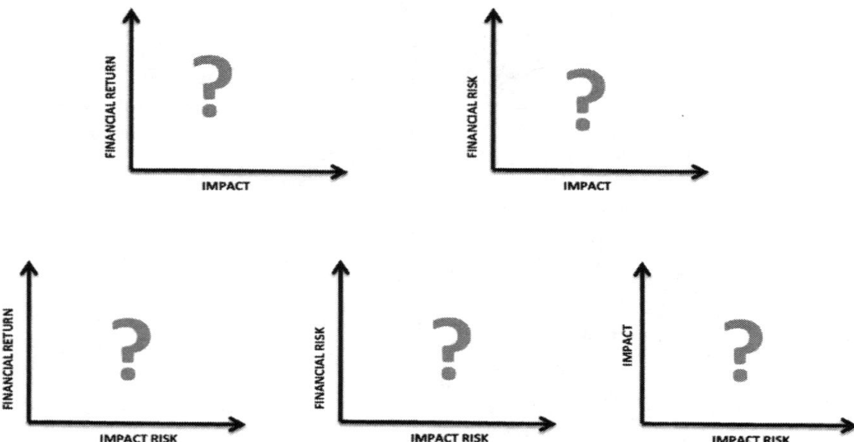

Figure 2.3 Five relationships to understand theoretically and empirically

Time

Time is fundamental to ecology *and* finance. Ecological systems have their own patterns of time sequences for interactions among parts, abilities to absorb inputs, or produce more resources (Hayden, 1993). Socio-economic systems also have *their* own time sequences. Meanwhile, traditional financial analysis assumes time is the enemy; the discount rate used for valuation of sustainability-related investments or projects is a measure of just how much an "enemy" time is assumed to be: a higher discount rate means future reductions in the effects of climate change or improvements in biological diversity are worth exponentially less today. Assuming time is the enemy may be inconsistent with integrating ecological, social, and financial time sequences. Overcoming this potential lack of integration is an important part of building a more general theory of finance.

Interestingly, within finance and economics, there is no consensus on the appropriate discount rate to use.

> Economic opinion is divided on a number of fundamental aspects, including what is the appropriate value of an uncertain future "marginal product of capital," what are the relevant efficiency distortions and how are they possibly magnified by public sector projects, how should large, long-term public investments be placed within the framework of the capital asset pricing model, how are we to view intergenerational transfers when future generations are not presently represented, how do we account for equity and other distributional effects in aggregating costs, benefits, and discount rates over individuals or across countries over time—and so forth, and so on.
>
> *(Weitzman, 2001, p. 260)*

There are essentially two competing views on the discount rate for ecological costs and benefits. The positivist position, also called the descriptive or opportunity cost view (P/D/O), is that the appropriate rate is the corresponding market rate that matches the maturity and the risk of the project, regulation, or ecosystem services under consideration. As Nordhaus (2013) puts it, "the discount rate should depend primarily on the actual returns that societies can get on alternative investments" (p. 187); to use any other rate would be to misallocate scarce financial capital among all potential investments that will affect future generations. In terms of a number, Nordhaus suggests that the risk-free real rate of interest has averaged 3 percent in the US, while the private sector rate has been 7 percent (2013, pp. 188–189). Gollier (2013) provides estimates of risk-free rates that are markedly lower than Nordhaus'—a 10-year Treasury real return of 1.9 percent—though he does have a similar private sector real return of 6.6 percent (p. 553).

The second position—known as the "ethicist" position, also called the prescriptive or philosophical view (E/P/P)—argues that the choice of discount rate for valuation or cost-benefit analysis should derive from the transfer of wealth inherent in the investment from current to future generations. Rather than existing market rates, E/P/P supporters often use the Ramsey equation of the rate of "social welfare discounting," $r = \eta g + \rho$, where r is the social rate of discount, η is a measure of diminishing marginal social benefits (i.e., larger values imply greater undesirability of wealth transfers to future generations), g is the growth rate of consumption per capital (i.e., how much wealthier future generations will be), and ρ is the pure rate of time preference (i.e., how much more the current generation's welfare should be weighted relative to the future generation's). Stern (2007) famously argued that the context of future environmental challenges required $r = 1.4$ percent via his assumptions of $\eta = 1$, $g = 1.3$ percent, and $\rho = 0.1$ percent, or $1(1.3) + .01 = 1.4$. In other words, Stern assumed that economic growth (g) would slow from that of the 20th century (i.e., the growth rate of a world with climate change is lower than a world without it), while the welfare of future generations was worth nearly the same as that of current generations ($\rho = 0.1$ percent, or nearly 0).

In a sustainability context, setting $\rho = 0$ (or nearly 0, as Stern did) is common among E/P/P supporters (e.g., Gollier, 2013; Gowdy, Howarth, & Tisdell, 2010; Posner & Weisbach, 2010). Setting g at less than historical levels is less widespread, though not necessarily uncommon, and derives from the inclusion of natural capital as another form of capital required for sustaining per capita consumption; some even set $g < 0$ for this reason (Gowdy et al., 2010, pp. 266–267). Gollier (2013) further argues that g should be reduced if future economic growth becomes more uncertain (i.e., if it becomes less certain that future generations will be wealthier). Some also claim that the discount rate should decline as the discounting horizon increases (e.g., Gollier 2013; Goulder & Williams, 2012; Gowdy et al., 2010)—in fact, the British Treasury has applied declining discount rates to ecological project evaluations (HM Treasury, 1997). This is largely at odds with the P/D/O view since an increasing term structure of interest rates is what is most commonly seen in financial markets.

Some believe that the two positions can be reconciled. Goulder and Williams (2012) argue that "neither [approach] dominates the other: the choice between them is between an approach that is more comprehensive [i.e., E/P/P] and one that might involve less subjectivity [i.e., P/D/O]" (p. 16).

> Analysts who implicitly concentrate on [the E/P/P approach], focusing on ethical considerations, tend to call for a relatively low discount rate. This leads them to argue for more aggressive abatement efforts. Analysts who implicitly focus on [the P/D/O approach], drawing attention to the (relatively high) opportunity cost of capital, tend to call for a higher rate. This leads them to support less aggressive action. The two views are not incompatible. Whether a given level of policy stringency is justified will depend on which of the two important evaluation criteria is being employed.
>
> *(2012, p. 17)*

Additionally, Gollier (2013) argues that even the P/D/O position cannot avoid being influenced by the E/P/P perspective:

> Notice that we don't observe the return of assets whose risk free cash flows mature in time horizons exceeding 30 years. The [P/D/O] approach fails to provide any clear answer to the determination of the arbitrage free discount rate for those horizons. The arbitrage argument entails a reinvestment risk in that case. If we consider a project yielding risk free cash flows in 60 years, the natural arbitrage strategy would be to invest in a bond yielding a risk free return in 30 years, and then to reinvest in another 30-year bond at that time. The problem is that we don't know today what will be the risk free rate in 30 years . . . The bottom line is that even the [P/D/O supporter] needs to rely on ethical principles when prices are not observable or when markets are incomplete.
>
> *(p. 553)*

From the view of a more general theory of finance, Goulder and Kennedy's reference to criteria and context is key. Private companies have market-based costs of capital that set the opportunity cost of their activities. Governments below the national level likewise borrow at market rates of interest. But risk-free rates are better understood as policy variables for currency-issuing national governments operating under flexible exchange rates issuing debt in their own currencies (e.g., De Grauwe, 2011; Fullwiler, 2007; Krugman, 2013). Rather than being set by "market forces," monetary authorities in these countries manipulate risk-free short-term and long-term rates (the latter more indirectly since shortly after the World War II era, though recent quantitative easing efforts moved a bit closer to more direct targeting) based upon the state of the macroeconomy relative to macroeconomic policy goals. The "market" risk-free rates that Nordhaus prefers do, in fact, ultimately rest on both policy and values.

Discount rates for private businesses or non-currency-issuing governments are not value-free even as they *are* set in private markets. Even traditional financial theory agrees that these rates are markups over the risk-free rates set by policymakers. Further, discount rates for private or public projects with negative ESG impacts should not have the same discount rates as similar projects with significantly better expected ESG impacts if markets are priced based on blended returns and blended values. If, as suggested earlier, ESG risks are systematic, then a lower rated ESG project (or company) *should* have a higher cost of capital in the efficient capital markets of traditional financial theory, all else being equal. Additionally, at all levels of public spending on the environment, the opportunity cost for an economy below full-capacity utilization could be *greater* unemployment of human resources and *less* private capital investment. Using a market rate of discount as a "hurdle" rate for a project (perhaps even one set as a policy variable) may be inconsistent with this macroeconomic context. Finally, Mazzucato (2013) provides evidence that early-stage government projects have been among the most important catalysts for future innovation and growth, while Porter (1991) famously argues similarly for environmental regulations, providing several examples of how national competitive advantage can emerge as a result (see also Ambec, Cohen, Elgie, & Lanoie, 2011; Porter & van der Linde, 1995).

Both the P/D/O and E/P/P perspectives have significant hurdles to overcome. While there is evidence that markets are beginning to incorporate ESG factors into private costs of capital and ESG-rated municipal bonds, there is no agreed-upon theory or generally accepted practice (as with, say, ratings agencies for traditional fixed-income investments) in the P/D/O literature addressing how ESG factors do or should affect the adherents' preferred market discount rates. For the E/P/P perspective, the Ramsey equation is based on the neoclassical economic theory of physical capital returns that has been criticized as being inapplicable to a modern monetary economy by Keynes (1937), then later by numerous others during the "capital controversies" of the 1960s (e.g., Cohen & Harcourt, 2003), and by contemporary economists from the Post-Keynesian school (e.g., Felipe & McCombie, 2010).

Thinking still more generally about financial theory and the natural environment, the "value" or significance of flows of ecosystem services to sustaining resilient socio-ecological systems depends on the timing, magnitude, and growth of these flows relative to the existing sufficiency of the relevant stocks of natural capital. That is, the "natural time value" of these flows is high, low, decreasing, or increasing not because of a particular discount rate but rather because of its contribution to or subtraction from the resilience of a socio-ecological system. How consistent a discount rate for financial flows of financial capital is or is not relative to the resilience of time sequences of ecosystem services flows is directly addressed by neither the P/D/O nor the E/P/P approach. Discount rates are obviously used in countless settings for determining the time value of flows of ecosystem services from natural capital, and the inclusion of ecosystem services in these valuations provides greater opportunities to protect natural capital and ecosystem resilience than would occur without their inclusion. Nevertheless, as Gowdy et al. (2010) put it,

> The bottom line is that characterizing responsibilities to future generations by a "discount rate" does not do justice to the nuances of human cultures, the heterogeneous nature of the many contributors to well being, or the pure uncertainty as to the future of *Homo Sapiens* [sic] on planet Earth.
>
> *(p. 277)*

Macroeconomists call "natural" the rate of interest that is consistent with full employment and price stability. The rate itself is not as important as the policy goals; no macroeconomist uses the interest rate as the criteria for how much unemployment must be accepted in order to reduce inflation by some percentage. Likewise, investors and policymakers at least implicitly decide how much climate change, biodiversity loss, and altered states of ecological resilience they are willing to live with, which in fact (again, at least implicitly) drives their choice of discount rates, not vice versa. To suggest otherwise is to confuse policy *goals* and related evaluative *criteria* for making policy decisions with the *levers* or *tools* policymakers use to implement policy. Stated differently, a choice to assess socio-ecological outcomes through the lens of weak (vs. strong) sustainability and monetized, time-discounted weights of costs and benefits will create the context for a particular weight selected for time discounting, and therefore it is the former choices that should be at issue more than the latter (e.g., Hiedanpää & Bromley, 2002). sustainable finance needs a more general theory of a "natural" rate of interest that recognizes this and thereby reconciles the traditional practice of discounting timed sequences of financial flows with appropriate evaluative criteria and methods for evaluating blended returns related to the "natural time value" of the resilience of ecosystem services, natural capital preservation, and socio-economic well-being.

Concluding remarks

In the end, what is *more general* about sustainable finance? In short, it recognizes (a) more values; (b) more types of returns; (c) ESG as a risk class; (d) financial innovations that encourage greater sustainability; (e) the accompanying financial and non-financial accounting to these first four; (f) that finance, economics, and markets are socially and environmentally embedded creations for social provisioning; (g) risks to impact or non-financial returns, non-financial correlations, and potential for diversification on non-financial grounds; and (h) time's effect on financial analysis needs to be socially and environmentally embedded. By comparison, in every instance above, traditional finance is a *special case*, accounting for only a narrow subset of values, returns, risks, correlations, market constructions, and time preferences.

Keynes wrote that "in the long-run we are all dead" in 1923, 13 years before *The General Theory*. Less well known is the sentence that followed, where he wrote that "economists set themselves too easy, too useless a task if in tempestuous seasons they can only tell us that when the storm is past the ocean is flat again" (Keynes, 1923, p. 80), warning of the dangers of a theory covering only special cases. More recently, Mazzucato (2013) argues that a more sustainable economy "can't develop on its own in part because of the failure of markets to value sustainability or punish pollution" (p. 119). The core premise of this chapter is that sustainable finance can aid the development of a more general theory of finance, providing the starting point for analysis of projects, portfolio management, company valuation, management/shareholder interactions, and public sector policy analysis that incorporates the socio-ecologically embedded nature of finance. When a more general theory of finance "values sustainability and punishes pollution," markets will have the analytical tools to do so, too.

References

Ambec, S., Cohen, M. A., Elgie, S., & Lanoie, P. (2011). *The Porter hypothesis at 20: Can environmental regulation enhance innovation and competitiveness?* (Discussion Paper 11-01). Washington, DC: Resources for the Future.

Bank, D. (2014, December 7). Sustainable in Seattle: A deal to meter and finance energy efficiency. *Huffington Post*. Retrieved December 8, 2014, from http://www.huffingtonpost.com/david-bank/sustainable-in-seattle-a_b_5947910.html

Barby, C., & Pedersen, M. (2014, September). *Allocating for impact*. London, UK: Social Impact Investment Taskforce Established Under the United Kingdom's Presidency of the G8.

Bonner, J., Grigg, A., Hime, S., Hewitt, G., Jackson, R., & Kelly, M. (2012). *Is natural capital a material issue?* London, UK: Association of Chartered Certified Accountants, Flora & Fauna International, & KPMG.

Bridges Ventures. (2010). *Investing for impact: Case studies across asset classes*. Boston, MA: Bridges Ventures.

Chen, D. (2011, April). *A model to build social impact and environmental based finance*. Portland, OR: Equilibrium Capital.

Cody, D., Parry, I., Sears, L., & Shang, B. (2015). How large are global energy subsidies? (Working Paper WP/15/105). Washington, DC: International Monetary Fund.

Cohen, A. J., & Harcourt, G. C. (2003). Whatever happened to the Cambridge capital theory controversies? *Journal of Economic Perspectives, 17*(1), 199–214.

De Boer, Y., & van Bergen, B. (2012, February). *Expect the unexpected: Building business value in a changing world*. Washington, DC: KPMG International.

De Grauwe, P. (2011, May). *The governance of a fragile Eurozone* (Working Document No. 346). Brussels, Belgium: Centre for Economic Policy Studies.

Digitale, R. (2014, June 15). Dale vs. Goliath. *Santa Rosa Press Democrat*. Retrieved December 1, 2014, from http://www0.pressdemocrat.com/article/20140615/business/140619730

Edmans, A., Li, L., & Zhang, C. (2014, July). Satisfaction, labor market flexibility, and stock returns around the world (Working Paper No. 20300). Cambridge, MA: National Bureau of Economics.

Emerson, J. (2003). The blended value proposition: Integrating social and financial returns. *California Management Review, 45*(4), 35–51.

Emerson, J. (2012). Risk, return, and impact: Understanding diversification and performance within an impact investing portfolio (Issue Brief #2). San Francisco, CA: Impact Assets.

Emerson, J., & Freundlich, T. (2012). *Investing with meaning: An introduction to a unified investment strategy for impact* (Issue Brief #1). San Francisco, CA: Impact Assets.

Emerson, J., & Spitzer, J. (2006, March). *Blended value investing: Capital opportunities for social and environmental impact*. Geneva, Switzerland: World Economic Forum.

Equilibrium Capital. (2010, April). *Energy efficiency: Turning negawatts into marketable securities* (Sustainability Investment Report 10-4). Portland, OR: Equilibrium Capital.

Felipe, J., & McCombie, J. (2010, January). On accounting identities, simulation experiments, and aggregate production functions: A cautionary tale for (neoclassical) growth theorists (Working Paper 01-10). Cambridge, UK: Cambridge Centre for Economic and Public Policy.

Forbes. (2013). Warren Buffet: Beware of impact investing. *Comments on Forbes 400 Panel*. Retrieved 1 December, 2014, from http://www.forbes.com/video/2886856992001/

Fullwiler, S. T. (2007). Interest rates and fiscal sustainability. *Journal of Economic Issues, 41*(4), 1003–1042.

Fulton, M., Kahn, B. M., & Sharpies, C. (2012, June). *Sustainable investing: Establishing long-term value and performance*. New York, NY: DB Climate Change Advisors, Deutsche Bank Group.

Gerlach, R., Herman, P., Hecker, S., & Bernhardt, E. (2013). How can your fixed-income portfolio spur higher impact and seek lower risk? *GreenMoney* (4). Retrieved February 26, 2016, from http://www.greenmoneyjournal.com/july-august-2013/fixed-income-portfolio

Ghoul, S. E., Guedhami, O., Kwok, C. C. Y., & Mishra, D. R. (2012). Does corporate responsibility affect the cost of capital? *Journal of Banking and Finance, 35*(9), 2388–2406.

Ghoul, S. E., Guedhami, O., Kwok, C. C. Y., & Mishra, D. R. (2014, July). Corporate environmental responsibility and the cost of capital: International evidence (Working Paper Series No. 2014-008). Daejon, South Korea: Advanced Institute of Science and Technology.

Gollier, C. (2013). The debate on discounting: Reconciling positivists and ethicists. *Chicago Journal of International Law, 13*(2), 549–562.

Goulder, L. H., & Williams, R.C., III. (2012). The choice of discount rate for climate change policy evaluation. *Climate Change Economics, 3*(4), 1–18.

Gowdy, J., Howarth, R. B., & Tisdell, C. (2010). Discounting, ethics, and options for maintaining biodiversity and ecosystem integrity. In P. Kumar (Ed.), *The economics of ecosystems and biodiversity: Ecological and economic foundations* (pp. 257–284). New York, NY: Routledge.

Harold, J., Spitzer, J., & Emerson, J. (2007, October). *Blended value investing: Integrating environmental risks and opportunities into security valuation*. Oxford, UK: Skoll Centre for social entrepreneurship.

Hayden, F. G. (1993). Order matters, and thus so does timing: Graphical clocks and process synchronicity. *Journal of Economic Issues, 27*(1), 95–115.

Herman, R. P. (2010). *The HIP investor: Making bigger profits by building a better world*. Hoboken, NJ: John Wiley & Sons, Inc.

Hespenheide, E. J., & Koehler, D. A. (2013). *Disclosure of long-term business value: What matters?* Westlake, TX: Deloitte University Press.

Hiedanpää, J., & Bromley, D. W. (2002). Environmental policy as the process of reasonable valuing. In D. W. Bromley & J. Paavola (Eds.), *Economics, ethics, and environmental policy: Contested choices* (pp. 69–84). Malden, MA: Blackwell Publishers.

Humphreys, J., Solomon, A., & Electris, C. (2012, August). *Total portfolio activation: A framework for creating social and environmental impact across asset classes*. Boston, MA: Trillum Asset Management.

Jayadev, M., & Rao, R. N. (2012). Financial resources of the microfinance sector: Securitisation deals—Issues and challenges. *IIMB Management Review, 24*(1), 28–39.

Jones, K. (2009, August). Mission insurance: How to structure a social enterprise so its social and environmental goals survive into the future. *Community Development Investment Review*, Federal Reserve Bank of San Francisco, *5*(2), 1–6.

Jussa, J., Cahan, R., Alvarez, M. A., Wang, S., Luo, Y., & Chen, Z. (2013, April 24). *The socially responsible quant*. New York, NY: Deutsche Bank Markets Research.

Kashive, N. (2012). Creating employer brands by valuing human capital in organizations and measuring intangible assets. *International Journal of Enterprise Computing and Business Systems, 2*(1). Retrieved November 15, 2014, from http://www.ijecbs.com/January2012/37.pdf

Keynes, J. M. (1923). *A tract on monetary reform*. London, UK: Macmillan.

Keynes, J. M. (1937). Alternative theories of the rate of interest. *Economic Journal, 47*(186), 241–252.

Khan, M., Serafeim, G., & Yoon, A. (2015). Corporate sustainability: First evidence on materiality (Working Paper No. 15-073). Cambridge, MA: Harvard Business School.

Kiernan, M. (2009). *Investing in a sustainable world: Why green is the new color of money on Wall Street*. New York, NY: AMACOM.

Koplow, D. (2012). *Phasing out fossil fuel subsidies in the G20: A progress update*. Washington, DC: Oil Change International.

Krosinsky, C. (Ed.). (2012). *Evolutions in sustainable investing: Strategies, funds, and thought leadership*. Hoboken, NJ: John Wiley & Sons.

Krosinsky, C. (2014). *ESG is not always material*. Retrieved October 31, 2014, from http://socialinvesting.about.com/od/Sustainable-Investing/fl/Why-ESG-isnt-Material.htm

Krugman, P. (2013, November). *Currency regimes, capital flows, and crises*. Paper presented at the 14th Jacques Polak Annual Research Conference, Washington, DC.

Leaton, J. (2014, September). *Unburnable carbon: Are the world's financial markets carrying a carbon bubble?* London, UK: Carbon Tracker Initiative.

Lev, B., & Schwartz, A. (1971). On the use of the economic concept of human capital in financial statements. *The Accounting Review, 49*(1), 103–112.

Lubber, M. S. (2010). Risks and their impact on institutional investors. In A. O. Calvello (Ed.), *Environmental alpha* (pp. 79–100). Hoboken, NJ: John Wiley & Sons.

Makhijani, S. (2014). *Cashing in on all of the above: U.S. fossil fuel production subsidies under Obama.* Washington, DC: Oil Change International.

Mazzucato, M. (2013). *The entrepreneurial state: Debunking public vs. private sector myths.* New York, NY: Anthem Press.

McGrath, M., & Lai, J. (2014, September). *Real assets primer: Research and thought leadership on impact investing.* San Francisco, CA: Sonen Capital.

Mehrling, P. (2011). *The new Lombard Street: How the Fed became the dealer of last resort.* Princeton, NJ: Princeton University Press.

Mercer. (2011a). *Climate change scenarios: Implications for strategic asset allocation.* San Francisco, CA: Mercer.

Mercer. (2011b, August 15). *Responsible investment's next decade: Developing CalPERS total fund process for ESG integration.* Discussion Document Prepared for CalPERS ESG Board Workshop, Sacramento, CA.

Milder, S. (2010). Thinking globally, acting (trans-) locally: Petra Kelly and the transnational roots of West German Green politics. *Central European History, 43*(2), 301–326.

Most, J. J., & Enzensberger, H. M. (1972). *Kapital und Arbeit: "Das Kapital" in einer handlichen Zusammenfassung.* Berlin: Suhrkamp.

Murphy, B. (2014, May 26). *KPMG's third-party assurance of green bonds.* Paper presented at the Green Bond Panel Discussion, Toronto, Canada.

Murtha, T. O., & Hamilton, A. (2012). Sustainable asset management. In C. Krosinsky (Ed.), *Evolutions in sustainable investing: Strategies, funds, and thought leadership* (pp. 53–80). Hoboken, NJ: John Wiley & Sons.

Nicola, D. (2013). *Environmental impact bonds* (Case i3 Working Paper #1). Durham, NC: Center for the Advancement of Social Entrepreneurship, Duke University.

Nordhaus, W. D. (2013). *The climate casino: Risk, uncertainty, and economics for a warming world.* New Haven, CT: Yale University Press.

Pfund, N., & Healey, B. (2011, September). *What would Jefferson do? The historical role of fossil fuel subsidies in shaping America's energy future.* San Francisco, CA: Double Bottom Line Venture Capital Investors.

Porter, M. E. (1991). America's green strategy. *Scientific American, 264*(4), 168.

Porter, M. E., & van der Linde, C. (1995). Toward a new conception of the environment-competitiveness relationship. *Journal of Economic Perspectives, 9*(4), 97–118.

Posner, E. A., & Weisbach, D. (2010). *Climate change justice.* Princeton: Princeton University Press.

Previts, G. J., & Merino, B. D. (1998). *History of accountancy in the United States: The cultural significance of accounting.* Columbus: Ohio State University Press.

Principles for Responsible Investment. (2013). *Corporate bonds: Spotlight on ESG risks.* Geneva, Switzerland: United Nations Environment Programme Finance Initiative.

Sombart, W. (1924). *Der proletarische Sozialismus. 10. neubearb. Auflage der Schrift "Sozialismus und soziale Bewegung."* Jena: Fischer.

Stern, N. (2007). *The economics of climate change: The Stern review.* New York, NY: Cambridge University Press.

Vorrath, S. (2014, December). Australian fossil fuel subsidies put at $47Bn, as RET wrestle continues. *Renew Economy.* Retrieved December 18, 2014, from http://reneweconomy.com.au/2014/australian-fossil-fuel-subsidies-put-at-47bn-as-ret-wrestle-continues-58572

Waggoner, B. (2010, March). *Put your money to work for good: RSF social finance CEO Don Shaffer.* Retrieved September 1, 2014, from http://socialenterprises.wordpress.com/2010/03/03/put-your-money-to-work-for-good-rsf-social-finance-ceo-don-shaffer/

Weitzman, M. L. (2001). Gamma discounting. *American Economic Review, 91*(1), 260–271.

Yunus, M. (2008). *Creating a world without poverty: Social business and the future of capitalism.* New York, NY: PublicAffairs.

3

THE ARCHITECTURE OF SOCIAL FINANCE

Gadaf Rexhepi

Research shows that while donations are increasing, donors are actually on the decline (Strandberg, 2006). Charity organizations are financed mainly by governments (about 80 percent) and by other sources like grants, sponsorships, donations, etc. This is the case of many important charity organizations, the oldest of which is the Benevolent Society, with an income of more than $80 million per annum, 82 percent of which coming from government sources (Tamás & Sato, 2012, p. 13). But what if governments, for some reason, fail to deliver grants to charity organizations? Will these charities continue to exist? What will happen to those who are in need then? social finance as a concept proposes a different way of dealing with poverty.

Bill and Melinda Gates are among the best known philanthropists in the world. In 2012, they gave away $3.4 billion. They also declared they will continue to give away a big portion of their wealth in the next years. Considering that their current fortune is about $77 billion and still growing, this will be a huge amount of money. Warren Buffet has also given away huge amounts of money and has pledged to donate 99 percent of his wealth. There are also a lot of other wealthy people and government organizations that are helping others and this is great, but will this solve the problem of poverty all around the world? Let me raise a hypothetical question: if all billionaires decided to give away 80 percent of their money to charities, will this eradicate world poverty? This money will be given mainly to charity organizations which will then deliver to those in need, solving the problem for some people for some years. But would it help solve the problem forever? Unfortunately, this will not be enough, mainly because of the way the money is spent.

A great way to deal with this problem is with "social finance," which is designed to help economies by providing situations where everybody will benefit. Social finance today has gained a huge interest, becoming an often discussed topic in conferences, seminars, research journals, universities, governments, municipalities, publishing, etc. Studies show that after the recent financial and economic crises, many financial organizations are pressuring corporate executives to provide reports for their non-financial performance (Cho, Lee, & Park, 2012, p. 54). This means that organizations should step up in motivating their employees, which is one of the main goals of social finance—to strike a balance between organizational profit (moderate) and employee motivation. According to a survey done by JP Morgan and the Global Impact Investing Network (GIIN) in November 2010, the US market comprises an estimated $183 billion to $667 billion, with invested capital in the range of $400 billion to nearly

$1 trillion (O'Donohoe, Leijonhufvud, Saltuk, Bugg-Levine, & Brandenburg, 2010). In May 2009, US President Barack Obama created a $50 million Social Innovation Fund and a new White House office that will coordinate the fund's efforts (Mair & Ganly, 2010, p. 103). The amount invested by the 125 leading Impact Investors in social finance is expected to grow by nearly 20 percent this year, according to the latest study by the GIIN and JP Morgan (Wilson, 2014). Recently, several G8 countries, most notably the United Kingdom and the United States, have been active in creating new social investment models as interest and activity emerge in other countries as well. These initiatives, led by governments, foundations, investors, and other stakeholders, have helped accelerate the market in the past few years (Wilson, 2014, p. 4).

An article published by renowned Harvard Business School professors Michael Porter and Mark Kramer, "The big idea: Creating shared value" (2011), argued that corporate strategies must be adopted to address social needs. Traditional thinking was that pursuing social or environmental objectives could require some financial trade-off, although not necessarily a financial loss. As market experience developed, a growing number of examples demonstrated that, in certain areas, social investments can generate both a solid financial and social return. It is in these areas that Social Investors can play a role in providing private capital to address social challenges in innovative ways (Wilson, 2014, p. 4).

But social finance is still a new concept, and not everybody is familiar with it. Research shows that social finance as an idea tends to be more familiar to people working in the niche financial sectors, such as Socially Responsible Investing and credit unions (Harji, Kjorven, Geobey, & Weisz, 2012, p. 11). This chapter is an attempt to clarify the concept of social finance and its architecture by defining it, explaining how it works, enumerating its types, and examining the benefits of social finance for society and for the future.

What is social finance?

Social finance, despite being a very modern concept, has roots that can be found much earlier. Many elements of what we know as social finance were actually proposed or used by the Islamic financial system or the holy order created by the Poor Fellow Soldiers of Christ and of the Temple of Solomon, founded in the crucible of the Crusades in 1119 (*Policy Review*, 2012, p. 92). Elements of social finance can also be found in some European countries; for example, France, during the 1950s and the early 1970s, invested a lot in social housing. During this time, some of the European economies were influenced mainly by the Keynesian approach, and they used the welfare state model. But after the global economic crisis in 1973, the welfare state model started to shrink and European countries started following neoliberal ideology (*Policy Review*, 2012, p. 92).

Social finance incorporates a number of socially orientated financial activities (Howard, 2012, p. 3):

- Impact Investment—investing for both a financial return and a social return;
- social banking—investing deposits in social enterprises;
- charitable banking—banking with a specific focus on the needs of charities;
- providing banking services and advice to financially excluded individuals;
- crowdfunding platforms for funding social ventures.

There are many definitions of social finance; unfortunately, there is no broadly acceptable definition about "what social finance is and what it incorporates." Such lack of clarity around its

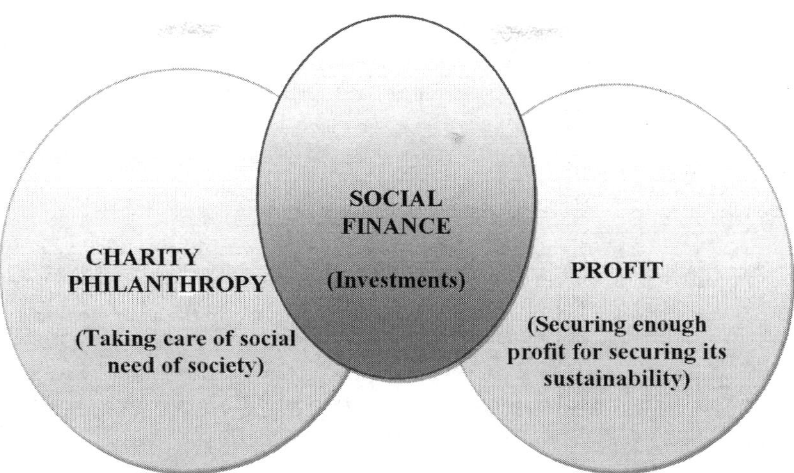

Figure 3.1 The role of social finance

definition and scope influenced the perception of investments in this area as being high risk. The perception is that non-profit organizations rely heavily on grants, which means that these organizations are not interested in managing them toward their growth and profitability (Harji et al., 2012, p. 14).

Social finance is oriented toward investments through which an organization tries to generate financial returns for sustainability by solving social or environmental challenges. Investments are generated from private investors and governments which, through social finance, create profit and bring public good for all. If we analyze the many definitions, we will see that social finance sits between charity/philanthropy and profit. Social finance tries to ensure that an organization is gaining profit so that it can secure its own existence in the future, and while doing so, it is also taking care of social and environmental needs (Figure 3.1). Organizations that are social should not depend on charities. Charities can be an initial resource and they can help in business development, but they should not be an organization's only source of financing (Cetina & Preda, 2013, p. 10).

Social finance is the deliberate, intentional application of tools, instruments, and strategies to enable capital to achieve a social, environmental, and financial return (Harji & Hebb, 2009). Organizations that engage in such investment can be found in the non-profit and for-profit sectors or in the hybrid space between them. Some suggest that social finance pursues a triple bottom-line, to deliver "social, environmental, and economic benefits" (people, planet, profit) (Harji et al., 2012, p. 6). David Hutchison, chief executive of social investment intermediary social finance Ltd., says he defines social finance as "investing capital to create social change" (Howard, 2012, p. 12). Even though there are differences among studies about what social finance represents, we can still find one thing in common: "the innovative use and combination of resources to pursue opportunities to catalyze social change" (Mair & Ganly, 2010, p. 103), which means that the use of social finance will lead to social change, which will in turn lead to a change in social behavior and the social relationship of institutions and people. Social change programs have also been made through social policy and taxation and many other ways in countries like Holland, Norway, Canada, etc. This leads to higher citizen standards and a reduction in inequality in these countries. Howard (2012, p. 3) stated that on a spectrum of investment types, social finance deals with "philanthropy and Socially Responsible Investing" because these organizations do not seek profit maximization, and they distribute their main profit to their employees and investors (usually citizens), and because "Socially Responsible Investing" organizations tend to not maximize their profits, which means when selling cheap but quality products, they usually hire people in need like the homeless, the disabled, and others. Usually they deal with a problem that is for the good of society, and they always take care of the environment.

To deserve the title "social," surely being a little bit social or social at the margins cannot be enough to warrant a totally new asset class. This probably requires a distinction to be made between investors who put capital entirely at risk in a quest to find new solutions to address social needs and those providing low-risk capital at only just below market rates while also achieving some degree of social impact. Social Investors differ from grant funders. "social investment is the provision and use of capital to generate social as well as financial returns." The following are some new and emerging sources of social finance (Strandberg, 2006, p. 5):

1 **Existing pools** of capital, including pension funds, union groups, credit unions, banks, foundations, high-net-worth individuals, investors, Venture Philanthropists, etc.
2 **New pools** of capital, such as foundations or financial intermediaries, develop donation or deposit programs for Social Investors to invest in double bottom-line projects.
3 **Leverage existing capital**, such as using assets within non-profits as loan collateral (e.g., computers, buildings, land, etc.).
4 The Federal **New Deal for Cities** program, which will be transferring tax points to municipalities for use in municipal infrastructure. Can some of this funding be harnessed to support a social economy initiative?
5 **Communities**, which can be a source of capital through credit unions or the community investment model.

In Figure 3.2, we can see an overview of social finance and the way this market operates. There are three sides to this market: the demand side, comprising actors who need social finance; the supply side, where we have the actors who provide social finance; and intermediators, that connect social actors who need additional capital with private actors who can supply capital. Note

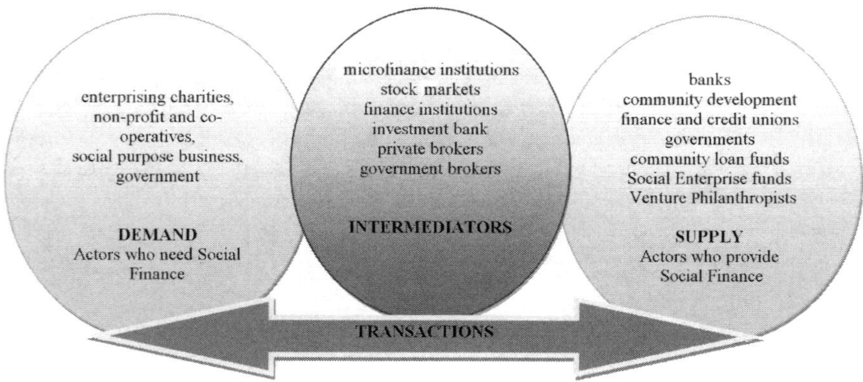

Figure 3.2 Overview of social finance marketplace

Source: Adapted according to Myers and Conte (2013).

that governments can be actors on both the supply and demand sides of the social finance marketplace (Myers & Conte, 2013, p. 9). This model also explains the way social finance works. Intermediators here appear as institutions that help investors invest their money in the demand side for social purposes.

According to the analysis made by Myers and Conte (2013, p. 4), social finance raises a new risk, and they suggest three important caveats that need to be considered:

1 Social finance approaches should not be seen as a substitute for government funding but rather as a complement.
2 Social finance approaches should not be seen as synonymous with privatization of social services. Even though there are differences in defining social finance, it is still generally accepted that social enterprises must have a social mission at the core of their operations.
3 From a more tactical standpoint, social finance approaches are not easy to support. The process of building a social enterprise is similar to starting any kind of enterprise, and having a social mission is no guarantee of success.

One of the questions raised by many actors like governments, organizations, researchers, and other relevant parties is: are there differences between social finance and Corporate Social Responsibility and not-for-profit charity work (Kerlinger & Lee, 1999)? The answer is definitely yes; social finance is conceptually a very different approach to social welfare enhancement. It uses some ideas of neoliberal markets, and it is increasing the need for social and environmental improvements, with a huge potential to make a tremendously positive impact on the economy (Massetti, 2011, p. 61). Another difference of social finance and charities and non-profit organizations is that social finance secures its own sustainability by being profitable. This means that social finance is not necessarily created by government or through donations but also by using personal funds, borrowing, taking microloans, etc.

Another dilemma is the relationship of microfinance and social finance. Is there a difference? Microfinance is a form of financing that also tries to deal with poverty. The pioneer of microfinance is Muhammad Yunus, who established the Grameen Bank, which from October 2011 gave out microcredit loans (Harji et al., 2012, p. 6). Microfinance got more attention after Yunus was awarded the Nobel Prize in 2006 and also because it was the only asset class that generated a positive financial return during the last financial and economic crisis. According to Yunus (1999), microfinance is the best way to fight world poverty in developing countries. But banks and organizations that practice microfinance, as originally proposed by its creator, are very hard to find, as Yunus stated in a 2015 interview:

> The idea of microcredit has spread across many countries. But there have been certain pain points. People are missing the concept of microcredit. They are using it to make money for themselves, rather than using it as an opportunity to help people to come out of poverty. That is not microcredit.

This is mainly because of existing laws that allow the creation of banks for the rich. You need a banking law to create a bank for the poor, according to Yunus (*Business Today*, 2015). By May 2011, one of the most influential organizations in microfinancing, Kiva, had distributed $213,942,425 to 554,116 entrepreneurs through 285,142 loans. Surprisingly, the repayment rate has been 98.8 percent (Galak, Small, & Stephen, 2011, p. 130). Even though both methods try to help those who are less fortunate, the difference is that microfinance is a form of crediting and social finance is a form of investment.

Forms of social finance

In literature and practice, there are a few forms of social finance:

1 **Social Impact Bonds (SIBs).** It is important to state upfront that an impact bond is not a "bond" in the sense of a traditional, fixed-rate-and-term security such as a municipal bond but is better understood as a rigorous, outcome-based contract between multiple parties (Shah & Costa, 2013, p. 5). An SIB is an instrument for funding projects where a prearranged amount of money is paid if performance results are achieved. SIBs combine a pay-for-performance element with an investment-based approach: private investors provide upfront capital to fund interventions and can expect to get back their principal investments and a financial return if the results are achieved (*Harnessing the PSF*, 2013). Aligning the interests of non-profit service providers, private investors, and governments, SIBs raise private investment capital to fund prevention and early intervention programs that reduce the need for expensive crisis responses and safety net services. Unlike standard bonds, they are not a form of debt security in which interest is paid by the issuer of the bond to the holder at maturity. In this form, the capital owner is actually sharing the risk with the borrower (the company that gets the capital). The impact bond concept originated in the UK, where the first SIB was launched in 2010. In 2012, it had about £600 million in available capital raised largely from unclaimed assets in British financial institutions (Shah & Costa, 2013, p. 6). New York City established the first SIB in the US. The initiative provides services to 16- to 18-year-olds who are jailed at Rikers Island and aims to reduce recidivism and its related budgetary and social costs. Services have been delivered to approximately 3,000 adolescent men per year from September 2012 to August 2015. Recently, the Harvard Kennedy School SIB Lab requested applications for additional US jurisdictions to assist. Twenty-eight state and local governments applied. Why are so many governments interested in SIBs? SIBs offer an answer to a question all policy makers face in these difficult fiscal times: how do we keep innovating and investing in new solutions when we cannot even afford to pay for everything we are currently

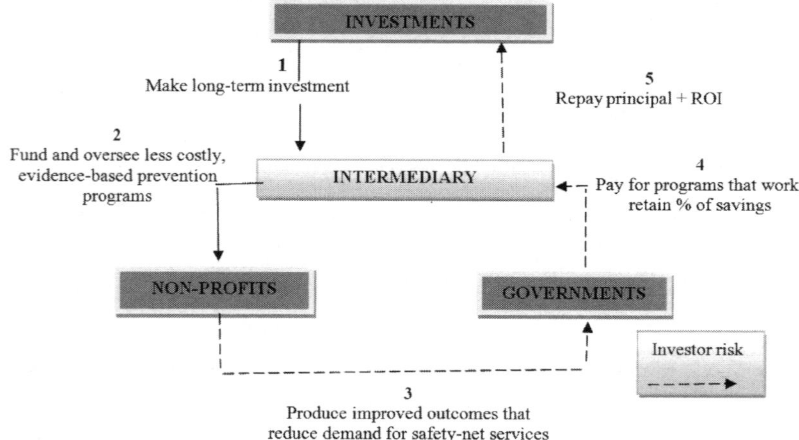

Figure 3.3 The SIB mechanism

Source: Adapted from Liebman, J. B. (2011, February). Social impact bonds. *Center for American Progress*; social finance (2012).

doing? SIBs also align well with the spread of data-driven leadership practices focused on improving government performance and with government efforts too (Azemati et al., 2014). Also, many countries such as Australia, Canada, Colombia, India, Ireland, and Israel have started exploring SIBs. Proposed projects target social problems ranging from recidivism to homelessness, unemployment, youth outcomes, and early childhood education (Azemati et al., 2014). SIBs should not be used in instances where cessation of services would harm a population or to finance critical public services such as primary and secondary education (Shah & Costa, 2013, p. 9).

- An intermediary issues the SIB and raises capital from private investors.
- The intermediary transfers the SIB proceeds to non-profit service providers, who use the funds as working capital to scale evidence-based prevention programs. Throughout the life of the instrument, the intermediary would coordinate all SIB parties, provide operating oversight, direct cash flows, and monitor the investment.
- By providing effective prevention programs, the non-profits improve social outcomes and reduce demand for more expensive safety net services.
- An independent evaluator determines whether the target outcomes have been achieved according to the terms of the government contract. If they have, the government pays the intermediary a percentage of its savings and retains the rest. If outcomes have not been achieved, the government owes nothing.
- If the outcomes have been achieved, investors would be repaid their principal and a rate of return. Returns may be structured on a sliding scale: the better the outcomes, the higher the return (up to an agreed cap).

In Figure 3.3, we can see how SIBs operate in practice. But despite the evolution of the market and the benefits previously mentioned, several challenges remain. These include a lack of products and capital across the full risk/return spectrum, a shortage of intermediaries, and a scarcity of high-quality investment opportunities into which larger amounts of capital can be deployed. Transaction costs in social investment remain high due to fragmented demand and supply and the complexity of deal structuring. As in the mainstream financial markets, there are information asymmetries between investors and investees. These asymmetries are further compounded by the lack of commonly accepted standards for measuring social investment, confusion of terminology, and lack of information about both existing investment provisions as well as related government policy. There is also imperfect competition in the market due to high transaction costs as well as the lack of brokers, advisors, exchanges, and other market mechanisms (Wilson, 2014).

2 **Social Investment Funds (SIFs).** SIFs pool capital from investors to provide loans, mortgages, and venture capital to not-for-profit social enterprises and social purpose businesses with longer payments, allowing organizations to access "patient working capital" (funding with a longer-term repayment schedule) as well as bridge loans. The Social Innovation Fund invites applications from external organizations, sometimes called intermediaries, with strong track records of finding effective social service organizations. Through a competitive process, the Social Innovation Fund grants $1 to $10 million per year for up to five years to these intermediary organizations (Shah & Costa, 2013, p. 2). These federal grants then leverage private and philanthropic dollars twice: first, the intermediaries must match the federal grant they receive dollar for dollar with non-federal sources; then, the grantees must likewise match that award one to one with other donations. This funding arrangement means that the $137.7 million awarded by the Social Innovation Fund since 2010 has leveraged $350 million in commitments from non-federal sources (Shah & Costa, 2013, p. 3).

3 **Development Impact Bonds (DIBs).** This type of bond takes the SIB model and applies it to another area that has seen a growing emphasis on measurement, evidence, and improved outcomes: international development (Shah & Costa, 2013, p. 10). DIBs are financial instruments that can bridge the gap between investors and opportunities and between financial returns and social benefits. For both SIBs and DIBs, issues around risk and risk-sharing promise to be problematic. DIBs are a new approach, and projects cannot be put together easily using the existing procurement systems of most public sector agencies. Essentially, DIBs are about forming partnerships, and to adopt this new approach, donor agencies should work closely with recipient country governments, potential investors, intermediaries, and service providers. This collaboration will help ensure that DIB contracts are attractive to investors, create the right incentives for service providers, and offer good value to outcome funders, as well as establish a good starting point for future deals. To reduce transaction costs and help build an evidence base for DIBs, pilots should be developed, implemented, and evaluated in a transparent and "open source" way. Donor agencies can drive transparency in DIB transactions by requiring that outcomes data be made public and contracts published. As a results-based approach, DIBs are meant to improve information about the impact of donor funding. This is only possible if information about how funding is being used and the results of the program are publicly known (social finance, 2012). Notably, one of the attractions of the impact bond model for governments is that it transfers away the risk that public dollars will be spent on ineffective programs; however, until the true risks of the model are better known and more predictable, many private investors are likely to balk at the all-or-nothing nature of financial returns inherent to the model (Shah & Costa, 2013, p. 12).

4 **Sector capacity-building organization.** Many submitters suggested creating tools and organizations to help actors within the sector (i.e., Social Entrepreneurs, individual and institutional investors, governments) better understand and engage in social finance. They concentrate on helping Social Entrepreneurs on how to use social finance. They help Social Investors find and evaluate social enterprises in which to invest, etc. (*Harnessing the PSF*, 2013, p. 24). These "capacity builders" seek to lower the transaction costs of social finance by preparing social enterprises for investment, helping Social Investors find appropriate social enterprises in which to invest, simplifying social impact measurement, packaging social investment opportunities for larger investors, and assisting governments with SIB negotiations (*Harnessing the PSF*, 2013).

5 **Pay-for-performance contract.** According to this contract, which is usually an agreement between a government and an external organization where the government sets an acceptable result, if this is achieved, then the government will pay the money. A pay-for-performance contract is one element of an SIB (*Harnessing the PSF*, 2013, p. 23).

6 **Program delivery scaling/leveraging.** A number of submitters to the Call for Concepts recognized the potential of social finance to augment existing programs by providing funds to increase the delivery area, widen the service offering, or add a needed new element to the program (*Harnessing the PSF*, 2013, p. 25). Although these concepts did not all delve deeply into how the financing partnerships might be structured, each provided evidence of the effectiveness of the foundational idea—as in YMCA Canada's concept to create a national, single-window solution to support youth employment through an internship framework. This concept suggests that the multitude of youth employment attachment programs offered across Canada results in a complex and redundant web of resources for youths seeking work, service providers, and employers.

> Accordingly, the YMCA suggests extending its successful national internship program, in partnership with others, to create a one-window network of governments, NFPs, and sector councils to better address the needs of the youth and employers while reducing service duplication. The submission explains: "A national, community based youth internship platform will reduce skills shortages, provide a better matching of youth skills with employer needs, address service gaps for youth, reduce government payroll and overhead costs, and streamline services." A social finance mechanism would leverage investments from multiple sectors and provide matched funding for employer contributions, with success measured through incidence of finding/retaining employment and salary levels. As evidence, the concept notes that more than 75 percent of the 11,000 participants who completed YMCA-delivered, federal government-funded internship programs either found gainful employment, returned to school, or both (*Harnessing the PSF*, 2013).

If we analyze all forms of social finance, we can conclude that the SIB has been the most used and most developed. The main benefit of this form is risk sharing, meaning the organization taking the money will repay it (principal + interest) only if it is a successful project. This is definitely great for the organization receiving the money, but is this the best way to give the money, bearing in mind that the point of social finance is to secure the sustainability of a project? We need to think about whether this money would be spent wisely if the owners knew that if they are not successful they will not have to pay anything. Maybe postponing the payment for some years could be a solution. This problem is also solved by pay-for-performance when organizations will take the money only if they achieved the result set by the government previously. The positive side of social investment funds is that the organization does not need to pay interest and they return the same amount of money, but they need to do this in five years, which sometimes might be very hard for the organization, bearing in mind that they are not for profit maximization, and expecting an ROI in five years is quite a challenge. The main advantage of DIBs is that it uses the money in more effective ways than the government, but the problem here is very similar with SIBs because it enters as a partner in risk sharing. Sector capacity-building organizations help other organizations by teaching them how to use social finance, but there are many issues like how qualified these organizations are, who is going to select them, etc. Program delivery scaling/leveraging opens a window of opportunity for young people by giving them experience.

The importance of social finance in creating social change

Social finance has different organizational intents oriented toward using the power of the marketplace to solve social and environmental problems (Massetti, 2011, p. 50). Prahalad and Hart in 2002 published a paper, "The fortune at the bottom of the pyramid," which discussed the largest but poorest socioeconomic group. According to the research, of the six billion people in the world in 2002, four billion are in the low income group living on less than $2 a day, many of which live on 60–70 cents a day. The percentage of poor people is still very similar. Can this group of people enjoy life like the middle and upper class? In the past three decades, the prices of almost every product have increased a lot. For the fourth tier of people, it will be impossible to ever have the chance to have the same kind of life as the first-tier group. The main problem is that these groups of people are not getting rich at the same speed as the price of almost everything increases, and this means that inequality will be even higher in the future.

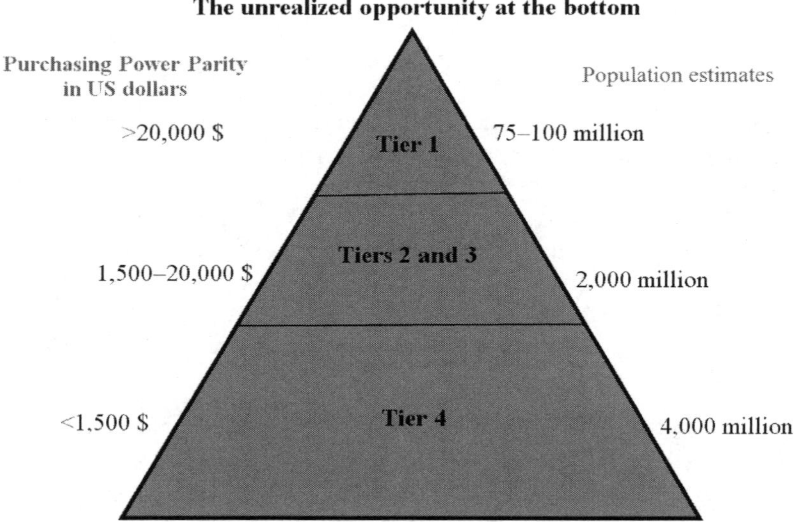

Figure 3.4 Base of the pyramid
Source: Adapted from Prahalad and Hart (2002, p. 4).

Even though every year more than $2 trillion is spent by governments of developed countries, they are still failing to increase the living standards of these people. Go to the website of almost any corporation and you can read about their commitment to the environment, to fighting poverty, to education, to health, or to the arts. None of this is true (Rippey & Subhash, 2013, p. 7). This is mainly because, as Milton Friedman noted in his famous 1962 book *Capitalism and Freedom*,

> [t]here is one and only one social responsibility of business—to use its resources and engage in activities designed to increase its profits so long as it stays within the rules of the game, which is to say, engages in open and free competition, without deception or fraud. *(Friedman, 2009, p. 133)*

Social trends are only getting worse; the number of charities is getting smaller every day, and the number of people in need is increasing especially with an aging population, unfunded pension liabilities, and pressures on the tax system (Strandberg, 2006). The world population has grown rapidly in the last century, moving from 1.6 billion in 1900 to more than 7 billion in 2015 and, according to estimates, will rise to more than 10 billion by 2050. Rapid world population growth results in rapid population aging, which will make it difficult for young people to secure retirement income. In 2011, about 17.66 percent of the Finnish population was aged 65 years or above; because the life expectancy of the Finnish population is around 79.41, it is very hard for the economy to handle figures like this (*Social Landscape*, 2012, p. 51). These and other problems like unemployment, inequality, and the like will require devoting a higher share of society's output to social protection, which needs to be shared in varying degrees between the public and private sector (Asher & Bali, 2014, p. 68).

As Joseph Schumpeter explains, during a period of crises, there will be a rising innovation. This was the case in almost all economic and financial crises (Policy Review, 2012, p. 92). This innovation is social finance and its influence on social innovation and social entrepreneurship; it proposes a better model in solving the problem, especially with the fourth tier, by creating enterprises which will not be motivated to create extra profit but reasonable profit. This means that these corporations will sell cheaper but quality products. Also, social finance will hire employees that belong to different social groups, which will influence their quality of life. The main benefit here will be that it will create an organization that will be sustainable and the government will not need to give such groups charity every year, as these people are employed. Then this money can be spent on other social problems or on creating other social finance institutions to help others. With charity, governments need to sponsor these groups of people every year and do not use their potential. social finance will not be a substitute to the actual system, but it is just offering a solution to some real problems by inspiring social change.

Thus, Ashoka, one of the leading organizations in social finance, is promoting the concept of "full economic citizenship" for civil society organizations and is engaging the corporate sector, particularly financial institutions and policy makers, in developing tools and programs to help civil society organizations meet the challenges of the century (Strandberg, 2006, p. 4). Rather than striving only to externally regulate the institutions of profit maximization, we must move to redesign them at their core (Kelly, 2012). Making the shift, over time, from the dominant extractive designs of today to generative designs, will take a combination of private innovation and government guidance (Kelly, 2012, p. 6). In trying to imagine a large-scale shift in the social architecture of the economy, it may help to recall a prediction made a half century ago by Robert Heilbroner: "Capitalism will inevitably change and in the longer run will gradually give way to a very different kind of social order" (Kelly, 2012, p. 7). social finance approaches help governments improve outcomes by aligning interests so that capital is channeled toward the most effective interventions. The potential of social finance to create incentives for increased alignment may be the most significant benefit that it can bring (Myers & Conte, 2013, p. 6). Kelly (2012) argues that multiplication of these models represents a largely unseen ownership sea change rising across the globe. At its heart is a genuinely different ownership archetype. Instead of being about maximizing financial gains, these ownership designs are about serving the community, often being financially self-sustaining, and many of these institutions are making profits. But they are not profit maximizing. They represent a new category of private ownership for the common good. Taken as a whole, these ownership designs could create the foundation of a new kind of economy, a generative economy, where economic activity again serves its original purpose of meeting human needs. social finance influences the middle class because it creates cheap products and, if the enterprise becomes successful, it will benefit more people.

The relationship of social entrepreneurship, social entrepreneurs, social innovation, and social finance

Social finance actually represents the emergence of new models. These include social enterprises, which serve a primary social mission while functioning as businesses, and these new enterprises concentrate on serving many stakeholders, not just stockholders (Kelly, 2012, p. 3). Social finance then stimulates social innovation, which in turn influences the existence of social entrepreneurship and Social Entrepreneurs. "Social entrepreneurship" emerged in the late 1990s in the United States and the UK, and it has become a global phenomenon, seen as an innovative approach to solve social problems and at the same time create economic value. Social entrepreneurship uses creative talent to develop solutions to social problems ranging from cleaning up the environment to improving conditions for workers around the world; its aim is to use businesses to make money *and* to make the world a better place to live. Social entrepreneurship in practice embraces a wide array of activities, from creative individuals devoted to making a difference to social purpose business ventures dedicated to adding for-profit motivations to the non-profit sector, to new types of philanthropists supporting venture capital-like "investment" portfolios, and to non-profit organizations that are reinventing themselves by drawing on lessons from the business world (Mair, Robinson, & Hockerts, 2006). Jeffrey Robinson defines social entrepreneurship "as a process that includes: the identification of a specific social problem and a specific solution" (Mair et al., 2006). Social entrepreneurship is related to Social Entrepreneurs. According to Francesco Perrini and Clodia Vurro,

> Social Entrepreneurs are change promoters in society; they pioneer innovation within the social sector through the entrepreneurial quality of a breaking idea, their capacity building aptitude, and their ability to concretely demonstrate the quality of the idea and to measure social impacts.
>
> *(Social Entrepreneurship, 2006)*

The origin of the phrase "Social Entrepreneur" can be traced to Bill Drayton, a former business management consultant who in 1980 set up Ashoka, the first foundation to support and fund such individuals. Today, Ashoka has over 2,000 "fellows" in more than 60 countries and continues to expand (Mair & Ganly, 2010, p. 104).

Social Entrepreneurs, then, need to create social innovation which will lead to social enterprise. Social finance is dependent on social innovation and vice versa. Recently, the European Commission published a paper titled "Guide to Social Innovation," which discussed the

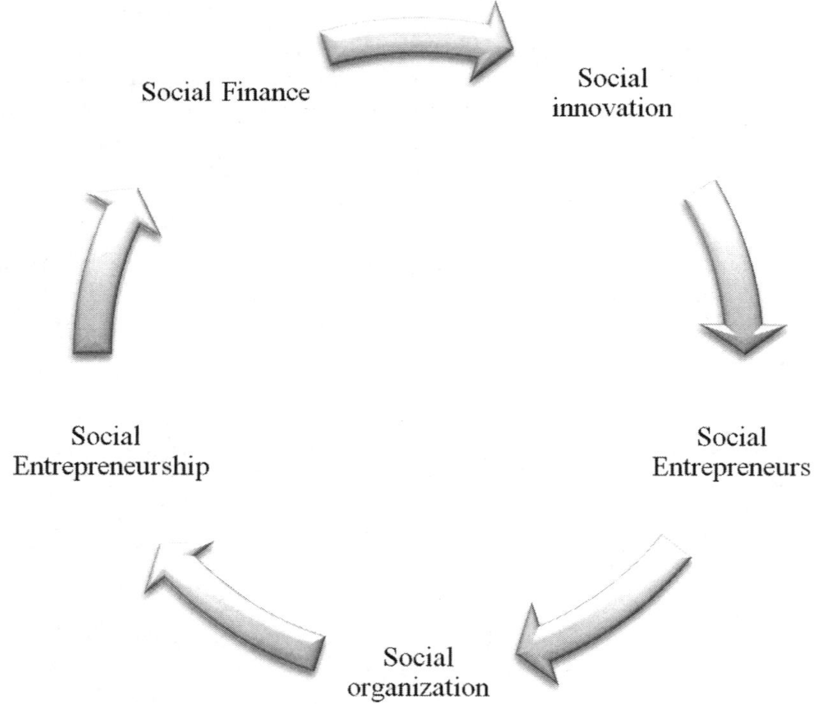

Figure 3.5 The influence of social finance

benefits of innovation and how they can offer social solutions (Myers & Conte, 2013, p. 6). The results of social innovation are all around us: self-help health groups and self-build housing; telephone helplines and telephone fundraising; neighborhood nurseries and neighborhood wardens; Wikipedia and the Open University; complementary medicine, holistic health, and hospices; microcredit and consumer cooperatives; charity shops and the fair trade movement; zero-carbon housing schemes and community wind farms; and restorative justice and community courts. All are new ideas that work to meet pressing unmet needs and improve people's lives (Mulgan, 2010, p. 7). Social innovation refers to new ideas that work in meeting social goals (2010, p. 8).

As we can see in Figure 3.5, social finance is a cycle that influences social innovation, which influences Social Entrepreneurs, which influence the creation of social organizations and, in the end, result in social entrepreneurship. If we analyze Figure 3.5 from the opposite side, we will also understand that social entrepreneurship, social organization, social entrepreneurs, and social innovation influence their existence. This means that social finance influences social innovation but it is also influenced by it.

Role of government in social finance

The role of government in social finance has been critical. One positive example of government engagement we can find is in the UK, where we can find a set of markers around ways in which the government can engage directly or indirectly in social finance (Harji et al., 2012, p. 33). The social finance sector currently struggles to produce desirable returns for investors. High start-up and regulatory costs could prevent mainstream banks from entering the sector (Howard, 2012, p. 6). For social finance to operate, the following public policy changes were identified and proposed (Strandberg, 2006, pp. 7–8):

1 Recast legislation from a for-profit/not-for-profit framework to a sustainable and effective framework.
2 Offer tax incentives to encourage investments in social finance.
3 Create a framework that permits organizations to build capacity through capital retention, for example 25 percent of earned revenues to be allocated to growth and management infrastructure.
4 Create an enabling environment for trustees to consider community investments consistent with their fiduciary duty. Clarify that it is acceptable to maximize returns as opposed to optimizing returns.
5 Create a permissive framework for foundations to support social finance. For example, clarify that foundations can provide loan guarantees and other creative financial instruments to advance the social capital marketplace.
6 Negotiate an allocation from the New Deal for Cities for the articulation of environmental, social, cultural, and economic goals into municipal sustainability plans and checklists.

These are the necessary changes that governments need to make. This is not an easy step, since not all governments have the same potential and current law framework. For some, it would be very challenging; for others, it would be very easy, and some already have this framework. The biggest challenge for underdeveloped and developing countries will be finding the necessary budget and know-how. Considering the whole discussed logic of social finance, it would be better for governments to help their countries concentrate their money on establishing and developing social finance.

Conclusion

Many governments try to deal with poverty by different means, such as social policy, taxation, social work, social welfare, or charity. This way of fighting poverty persists because we just solve problems for the short term. This is not the solution. One of the best solutions to this problem comes from "social finance," which is designed to help economies create situations where everybody will benefit. social finance will help decrease unemployment, it will reduce disparities in the long run, it will better manage poverty, it will encourage taking care of the environment, it will orient our energy toward social innovation, and so on. Social finance has three main postulates: it tries to achieve a social, environmental, and financial return. Social finance is conceptually a very different approach to social welfare enhancement. It uses some concepts of neoliberal markets on the one hand, and it increases the need for social and environmental improvements on the other. It struggles to find a way for people to stand on their own feet, because it helps organizations work profitably. Social finance takes care of enterprise sustainability as these enterprises are self-financed. Social finance is not necessarily created by governments or through donations but by private investors and different organizations using personal funds, borrowing, taking microloans, etc.

Social finance has been a solution to actual economic problems, showing positive effects that were evident in the last financial and economic crises. Should a great economic system show these problems and this very high level of inequality? Social finance does not require a new economic system but uses the actual economic neoliberal system. It tries to solve some of the problems and especially change the logic of Milton Friedman about what social responsibility is. It makes the shift of wealth from the hands of a very small number of rich owners to a huge group of people, who will earn a reasonable profit. Social enterprises are not owned by one person but by many investors giving very small amounts of money or other assets, and usually they are also employed; sometimes these enterprises can be even 100 percent employee-owned. With social finance, many people will be earning a good amount of money instead of just a small group of people getting very rich. Social finance will also lower the prices of products and services, since organizations will not charge huge prices because all of them require reasonable profits. Social finance will address inequality because there will not be extremely rich people who with their great purchasing power can increase the price of goods (e.g., prices of apartments in Manhattan), but these prices will grow very slowly as the living standard of people grows. Many people will be employed, and instances where employees are fired will drop significantly. Social finance also influences social innovation and social entrepreneurship, which can solve many problems of today's economic system. Social finance approaches enable governments to "share the risks" with the private sector. It also helps governments improve outcomes by aligning interests so that capital is channeled toward the most effective interventions. Social finance creates fundamentally different kinds of organizations, helps them stay true to their mission, and encourages different kinds of ownership. This organization will influence the existing architecture and create a different kind of economy in many ways. Social finance actually represents the emergence of new models, and these include social enterprises, which are oriented mainly toward not only solving some social problems but also gaining a reasonable profit. These enterprises are starting to be established all around the globe by many people who really care about social benefits and at the same time want to earn a reasonable profit.

References

Asher, M. G., & Bali, A. S. (2014). Financing social protection in developing Asia: Issues and options. *Journal of Southeast Asian Economies, 31*(1), 68–86.

Azemati, H., Belinsky, M., Gillette, R., Liebman, J., Sellman, A., & Wyse, A. (2014). Social impact bonds: Lessons learned so far. *Community Development Investment Review*, 23–33.

Business Today. (2015, April 12). You need a banking law to create a bank for the poor. *Business Today*, p. 1.

Cetina, K. K., & Preda, A. (Eds.). (2013). *The Oxford handbook of the sociology of finance*. New York: Oxford University Press.

Cho, S., Lee, C., & Park, C. K. (2012, June). Measuring corporate social responsibility: A survey of recent research. *The CPA Journal*, 54–60.

Friedman, M. (2009). *Capitalism and freedom: Fortieth anniversary edition*. Chicago, IL: University of Chicago Press.

Galak, J., Small, D., & Stephen, A. T. (2011). Microfinance decision making: A field study of prosocial lending. *Journal of Marketing Research, 48*, S130–S137.

Harji, K., & Hebb, T. (2009). *The quest for blended value returns: Investor perspectives on social finance in Canada*. Ottawa, ON: Carleton Centre for Community Innovation, Draft Report.

Harji, K., Kjorven, A., Geobey, S., & Weisz, A. (2012). *Redefining returns: social finance awareness and opportunities in the Canadian financial sector*. Toronto, ON: Centre for Social Innovation.

Harnessing the PSF. (2013). *Harnessing the power of social finance: Canadians respond to the national call for concepts for social finance* (Cat. No.: SP-1050-05-13E). Government of Canada.

Howard, E. (2012). *Challenges and opportunities in social finance in the UK*. London, UK: Social Finance.

Kelly, M. (2012, December). The architecture of enterprise: Redesigning ownership for a great transition. *GTI Perspectives on Critical Issues*, pp. 1–7.

Kerlinger, F., & Lee, H. (1999). *Foundations of behavioral research*. Belmont, CA: Wadsworth.

Mair, J., & Ganly, K. (2010). Social entrepreneurs: Innovating towards sustainability. In E. Assadourian (Ed.), *State of the World 2010. Transforming cultures: From consumerism to sustainability* (pp. 103–109). Washington, DC: Worldwatch Institute.

Mair, J., Robinson, J., & Hockerts, K. (Eds.). (2006). *Social entrepreneurship*. New York: Palgrave Macmillan.

Massetti, B. (2011). The duality of social enterprise: A framework for social action. *Review of Business, 33*(1), 50–64.

Mulgan, G. (2010). Measuring social value. *Stanford Social Innovation Review, 8*(3), 38–43.

Myers, K., & Conte, N. (2013). *Can social finance improve the outcomes of employment and training programs?* Ottawa, ON: Social Research and Demonstration Corporation.

O'Donohoe, N., Leijonhufvud, C., Saltuk, Y., Bugg-Levine, A., & Brandenburg, M. (2010). *Impact investments: An emerging asset class*. New York: J.P. Morgan.

Porter, M. E., & Kramer, M. R. (2011). The big idea: Creating shared value. *Harvard Business Review, 89*(1), 2–14.

Policy Review. (2012). The ongoing transformation of social housing finance in France: Towards a self-financing system? *International Journal of Housing Policy, 12*(1), 91–103.

Prahalad, C., & Hart, S. (2002, January 10). The fortune at the bottom of the pyramid. *strategy+business, 26*(1).

Rippey, P., & Subhash, H. (2013). Crossfire: We need to be cautious about accepting CSR funding for economic development initiatives since benefit to disadvantaged producers may not be the ultimate goal. *Enterprise Development and Microfinance, 24*(1). doi:10.3362/1755-1986.2013.002

Shah, S., & Costa, K. (2013, November). *Social finance: A primer. Understanding innovation funds, impact bonds, and impact investing*. Washington, DC: Center for American Progress.

Social Finance. (2012). *A new tool for scaling impact: How social impact bonds can mobilize private capital to advance social good*. New York: Social Finance Inc/Rockefeller Foundation.

Social Landscape. (2012). *PESTLE Country Analysis Report: Finland* (pp. 51–55). London, UK: Market Line.

Strandberg, C. (2006). *Exploring new sources of investment for social transformation* (Social Capital Market Roundtable #2). Vancouver, BC: PLAN Institute for Caring Citizenship.

Tamás, P. A., & Sato, C. (2012). Is the non-unitary subject a plausible and productive way to understand development bureaucrats? *Third World Quarterly, 33*(8), 1511–1525.

Yunus, M. (1999). *Banker to the poor*. New York: PublicAffairs.

Wilson, K. E. (2014, July 1). *New investment approaches for addressing social and economic challenges*. OECD Science, Technology and Industry Policy Papers, France, 15, p. 41.

4

THE EMERGENCE AND INSTITUTIONALIZATION OF THE FIELD OF SOCIAL INVESTMENT IN THE UNITED KINGDOM

Belinda Bell and Helen Haugh

Understanding the process by which new institutional fields are created is of central importance to institutional scholars. A field is a "recognized area of institutional life" (DiMaggio & Powell, 1983, p. 148) in which there is "a community of organizations that partakes of a common meaning system and whose participants interact more frequently and fatefully with one another than with actors outside the field" (Scott, 2001, p. 84). Field members therefore engage in common pursuits and face similar pressures (Powell, White, Koput, & Owen-Smith, 2005). Institutional fields develop through interactions between actors which tend to produce, and reproduce, the values and practices that constitute the field (DiMaggio & Powell, 1991; Lawrence, Hardy, & Phillips, 2002; Scott, 2001). Each institutional field is distinct from other fields on several dimensions, for example membership (Maguire, Hardy, & Lawrence, 2004), rules (Greenwood & Suddaby, 2006; Maguire & Hardy, 2009; Scott, 2001), and practices and values (Scott, 1994; Zilber, 2008). In addition to the common meaning system shared by field members then, an institutional field must in some way be distinguishable from other fields (Zietsma & Lawrence, 2010); boundaries between fields perform this function. Previous research has explored how new fields emerge around industries and technologies, and relatively little research has examined how issues influence field development (Hardy & Maguire, 2010; Hoffman, 1999).

The focus of this chapter is the creation of the field of social investment. social investment emerged in response to a combination of societal interest in, and entrepreneurial motivations to establish, businesses that seek to purposefully generate positive economic, social, and environmental impacts (Fisher & Satter, 2001). Public policy has also expressed interest in the development of new forms of capitalism that are motivated less by maximizing profits and more by striving to achieve social and environmental sustainability. To serve this collection of interests, new forms of finance have been created to direct capital toward supporting organizations that actively seek to create positive social impact. The aim of the research presented in this chapter is to analyze how social investment was established as a discrete field of activity in the UK.

The aim of social investment is to direct capital toward investments that generate social value as well as financial returns to investors (Brown & Norman, 2011). In England, social investment funds were estimated to be £165 million in 2010/11 (Brown & Norman, 2011) and predicted to exceed £1 billion by 2016 (Brown & Swersky, 2012). Although social investment is not a new phenomenon, rapid development of the field has occurred in the last 20 years (Nicholls, 2014). We set out to explore how the field of social investment was institutionalized between 2000 and 2014. To do this we employed a qualitative methodology and analyzed texts in which social investment was first described and then promoted in the UK. The first text set the agenda for the new field and influenced directly the coalescence of providers, investors, and supporters as the field developed. Subsequent texts continued to both track progress toward fulfilling the agenda and advance further recommendations to shape the field. Our analysis finds that in this process the texts were used to designate the boundaries of the new field as well as establish members and practice guidelines. This was achieved by four processes: differentiation, integration, appropriation, and innovation.

The field of social investment was intentionally created by actors from the public, private, and non-profit sectors in response to a perceived need for finance from organizations oriented toward addressing social and environmental problems. The field's development was thus guided by an explicit ethical mission to foster social change. Fields with similar ethical missions include Fairtrade (Doherty, Davies, & Tranchell, 2013; Goodman, 2004; Renard, 2003) and community-owned wind farms (Devine-Wright, 2005; Walker & Devine-Wright, 2008). Collectively we label the process of creating a new field that is guided by social mission as ethical institutional entrepreneurship.

The research makes three contributions. First, our data support prior research that field emergence involves differentiation and integration. Differentiation distinguishes the new field from existing fields, and integration builds the common bond between members of the new field. In the case of social investment the boundaries lie on the differentiation of social investment from sources of finance provided by commercial, public, and charitable organizations; and integration draws on the shared social mission and practices of members of the new field. Second, prior studies of field emergence have noted the conflicting pressures whereby isomorphism and mimesis foster conformity (DiMaggio & Powell, 1983; Lawrence & Phillips, 2004), and divergence leads to institutional entrepreneurship (Maguire et al., 2004). Our data find that the dynamics of field emergence blend mimesis with innovation. Mimesis occurred when actors and practices that are aligned with the aims of the new field were appropriated from other (source) fields. This was achieved by communicating to audiences how the appropriation of actors and the adoption of practices that are established in a source field would benefit the development of the new field. Innovation occurred in the creation of new organizations and practices that were designed to achieve the aims of the new field. Third, previous research has explored how fields form around industries and technologies and relatively little research has examined how fields form around issues (Hardy & Maguire, 2010; Hoffman, 1999; Wooten & Hoffman, 2008). In our study, the creation of the social investment field is a response to exogenous events including the demand from Social Entrepreneurs for investment finance and public sector commitment to disrupting the status quo and encouraging the growth of both social enterprises and social investment. Taken together, the contributions advance our understanding of field emergence and ethical institutional entrepreneurship.

Conceptual framework

Institutions and fields

To frame our research, we draw on theories of institutions and fields. Institutions are collective structures that set out the way that things are done in a recognized area of life. Colloquially summarized as "the rules of the game" (North, 1990, p. 3), institutions provide the guidelines that shape which behavior is deemed acceptable and that which is not acceptable. The self-reproducing recurrent patterns of behavior (DiMaggio & Powell, 1991) are socially ordered and gradually become accepted as the way to behave. In practice, institutions are enacted by actors who, through frequent interactions, collectively begin to perceive themselves to be a group that shares interests and practices. Fields refer to such structures and interactions (Emirbayer & Johnson, 2008) and are composed of norms, values, and practices that are in some way distinct from other structures and associated patterns of behavior (Scott, 2001). Fields are sustained by social interactions that maintain, by reproducing, the values and practices that guide members as to how to act and interact (Lawrence, 1999). In addition to the influence of social norms, field-level values and practices may also be formally regulated by laws, regulations, and rules. In this way governments also influence field emergence (McDermott, Corredoira, & Kruse, 2009).

Fields form around central issues and bring together actors with different perspectives (Hoffman, 1999). In a new field, institutional processes are particularly interesting to investigate as the new field is not encumbered by pre-existing structures and practices and hence the isomorphic pressures to adopt existing values and practices are not in play (Oliver, 1991). Institutional agents, or actors with the capacity to invest resources, time, and effort in promoting values and practices (Kim, Shin, Oh, & Young-Chul, 2007), have some freedom to employ their resources and skills to influence which actors and practices are aligned with the new field's goals and are therefore welcome in the new field. Actors will no doubt carry with them values and practices from other fields (Markowitz, Cobb, & Hedley, 2011; Scott, 1991) which influence how they perceive, evaluate, and respond to their environment (Ocasio, 1997); however, the relative power of actors will determine their influence on shaping the structures and interactions in a new field. Yet, just as institutional entrepreneurs are said to dis-embed themselves from existing institutional arrangements (Beckert, 1999), the intentional creation of a new field offers an opportunity to start afresh and establish new structures and practices oriented to achieving the purpose of the new field.

Boundaries and practices

The interplay of boundaries and practices is central to field emergence (Zietsma & Lawrence, 2010); they are mutually constitutive in that, by institutionalizing practices, field boundaries are also delineated. Boundaries vary in terms of their strength and permeability (Kent & Dacin, 2013). Strong boundaries may lead fields to become isolated from or unresponsive to events in the external environment (Seo & Creed, 2002); however, they may also serve to protect the distinctiveness of a field and focus resources on field expansion and growth. Permeable boundaries may be advantageous in the early stage of a field in which support is required to build the capacity of the new field and strengthen the potential to achieve the field's mission.

Practices are the shared routines that conform to social expectations and guide behavior (Whittington, 2006) and in so doing specify behaviors that are acceptable by field members as well as others seeking to join the new field. Studies of field emergence have claimed that there is a rapid tendency to isomorphism so that the connections between practices in different fields are influenced by practices in the wider institutional environment (DiMaggio & Powell, 1983; Lawrence & Phillips, 2004). Such isomorphic pressures originate from three sources: coercion, in which external forces inflict pain for non-compliance; normalization, in which societal forces impinge on the field; and mimesis, in which existing practices are imitated by others (Oliver, 1991). The transposition of existing practices to fields (Boxenbaum & Battilana, 2005) may also be explained by the efforts of boundary-spanning actors with the capacity to move between different fields and carry with them values and practices from other fields. Field-level associations are also important actors for legitimizing and ensuring member compliance with field practices (Lounsbury, 2001). For example, trade associations provide a forum for professional debates, advocating the interests of members, and play an important role in the maintenance of values and practices in mature fields through activities such as training, monitoring, and celebration (Greenwood, Suddaby, & Hinings, 2002). Formal and informal networks between field members also serve to help develop shared values, beliefs, and frames of references (DiMaggio & Powell, 1983; Podolny, 2001; Scott, 2001). Yet isomorphic pressures are likely to encounter the forcefulness of institutional entrepreneurship when new fields are under construction (Lawrence et al., 2002).

Thus we seek to investigate how the boundaries surrounding a new field are instantiated and how values and practices that become characteristic of the new field are established. This is achieved in the qualitative analysis of the social investment field in the UK.

Methodology

The research is an in-depth single case study (Yin, 2009) which is ideally suited to understanding the processual dynamics of new field creation. Case studies have proven to be a valuable method for investigating the institutional processes in the financial services industry including analyzing the competing logics in community banking (Marquis & Lounsbury, 2007), practice variation in mutual funds (Lounsbury, 2007), the origins of developmental venture capital (Rubin, 2009), and to explain how teams carry institutional logics (Almandoz, 2014). In our research, the case study method sheds light on the multiple actors involved in new field creation and the simultaneous processes of differentiation, integration, appropriation, and innovation.

Data sources

Between 2000 and 2014, five reports were published in which the agenda for and growth of the social investment market in the UK was recorded. These five reports constitute the empirical data for the study. In addition, the principal texts are complemented by two other sources of published data: first, reports produced by the Social Enterprise Unit at the Department of Trade and Industry (2002); and second, the annual reviews published by the Community Development Finance Association (CDFA) between 2004 and 2010 (see Table 4.1).

The data are historically contingent and provide a formal and legitimized record of the development of the social investment field in the UK. The texts describe the emergence of a dynamic field and in doing so capture the important actors and activities involved in establishing social investment in the UK; however, not all actors and practices that were subsequently adopted by the field are captured. It is noticeable therefore that although crowdfunding for social enterprises has become an important source of finance (Lehner, 2013; Lehner & Nicholls, 2014), it is absent from all reports except Report 5.

Context

Social investment is defined as "financial transactions intended to both achieve social objectives and to deliver financial returns to investors" (SITF, 2000, p. 3). Investing funds to generate social value is not a new phenomenon, and there are many examples of the practice of allocating funds to further social value (Nicholls, 2014); however, there has been an increase in this type of activity in recent years. Three trends in the late 20th century stimulated interest in the social investment field. First, a political climate favorable to policies to address social

Table 4.1 Data sources

Data	*Title*	*Source*
Report 1: 2000	Enterprising communities: Wealth beyond welfare. A report to the Chancellor of the Exchequer from the Social Investment Task Force	Social Investment Task Force
2002	Social Enterprise Strategy for Success (2002)	Social Enterprise Unit
Report 2: 2003	Enterprising communities: Wealth beyond welfare. A 2003 update on the Social Investment Task Force	Social Investment Task Force
2003	Social Enterprise Strategy Progress Report	Social Enterprise Unit
2004	Annual Review	CDFA
Report 3: 2005	Enterprising communities: Wealth beyond welfare. A 2005 update on the Social Investment Task Force	Social Investment Task Force
2005	Annual Review	CDFA
2006	Supporting a thriving community development finance sector. Annual Review	CDFA
2007	Annual Review	CDFA
2008	Annual Review	CDFA
2009	Speaking up for community finance. Annual Review	CDFA
Report 4: 2010	Social investment ten years on. Final report of the Social Investment Task Force	Social Investment Task Force
2010	Making an impact. Annual Review	CDFA
Report 5: 2014	Building a social impact investment market: The UK experience	UK National Advisory Board to the Social Impact Investment Taskforce

exclusion, neighborhood renewal, and community regeneration. In 1997 the newly elected Labour administration conducted a large-scale review of key aspects of civil society. Between 1998 and 2000, 18 policy action team (PAT) reports were published and their findings developed into the National Strategy for Neighbourhood Renewal (Social Exclusion Unit, 1998). The business report (Bank of England, 2000; PAT3, 1999) concluded that one of the reasons that enterprises in deprived areas failed to thrive was because entrepreneurs in such areas had limited access to finance and were therefore reliant on external sources of funds. The proposed solution was to design new sources of finance that would link deprived communities to the mainstream economy (Dayson, 2004). Second, an increase in the number of social and community organizations seeking investment finance raised demand for social investment (Nicholls, 2014). Finally, rising government and investor interest in funds that promise social as well as financial returns stimulated institutions to create new social investment vehicles (Nicholls, 2014). The effect of the 2008 economic crisis has been to further stimulate interest in social investment and impact on the flow of resources to specific categories of beneficiary, for example youth-related services (Kvist, 2013).

In 2000 senior leaders from the finance and voluntary sector were invited by Gordon Brown, then Chancellor of the Exchequer, to convene a Social Investment Task Force (SITF). The SITF was a partnership between the UK social investment Forum, the New Economics Foundation, and the Development Trusts Association, with HM Treasury acting as an observer. Its Chair was Ronald Cohen, "founding father of venture capitalism" (Casasnovas & Ventresca, 2015), who went on to hold a number of key roles in the social investment field. A core concern of the SITF was to address the barriers between enterprise and wealth creation in under-invested communities. The aim of the SITF was:

> To set out how entrepreneurial practices can be applied to obtain higher social and financial return from social investment, to harness new talents and skills to address economic regeneration and to unleash new sources of private and institutional investment.
>
> *(Report 1: 3)*

Report 1 listed five recommendations from the SITF:

1 To establish a Community Investment Tax Credit (CITC) (subsequently renamed Community Investment Tax Relief) to encourage private investment in under-invested communities via Community Development Finance Institutions (CDFIs);
2 To establish Community Development Venture Funds which would match funding from government with funding from the venture capital industry, entrepreneurs, institutional investors, and banks;
3 To advocate for increased disclosure of the lending patterns of banks;
4 To advocate for greater latitude and encouragement for charitable trusts and foundations to invest in community development initiatives;
5 To provide support to CDFIs, including through the formation of a trade association to represent their interests.

The central role played by the SITF in the creation of the social investment market is manifest in two ways. First, progress was made on four of the recommendations above such that within 3 years all but recommendation 3 had been largely accomplished. Reports 2, 3, and 4 subsequently track the impact of these recommendations, continue to seek better implementation of recommendation 3, and extend calls for additional interventions to support the development of the social investment field. Second, Report 5 acknowledges the centrality of the SITF to the development of the sector by, first, referring to it in the opening Foreword (Report 5: 3) and, second, using the establishment of the SITF as the first item on a timeline of principal developments in the UK social investment market. The texts provide a legitimized account of an intentional endeavor to create a new domain of investment activity with an explicit social mission. By analyzing the texts, our case study offers a unique insight into how the boundaries and practices of social investment came into being.

Data analysis

The analytical process was guided by the principles of grounded theory (Glaser & Strauss, 1978; Strauss & Corbin, 1998). To begin, each report was analyzed independently by the authors to gain an overview of the key actors and events relating to social investment between 2000 and 2014. This was followed by focused reading of each text, during which each phrase and sentence was analyzed in relation to the question "What does this comment tell me about the field of social investment?" Analytical memos (Glaser & Strauss, 1978) were written to label when actors and actions to create the new field were referred to; and theoretical memos (Glaser & Strauss, 1978) were written to link the texts and analytical memos to extant theory concerning institutions, fields, boundaries, and practices. Both authors created an analytical template of key words, phrases, and preliminary first-order codes. To stay close to the data in the process of theory generation, the analysis was conducted manually.

Following the independent analysis of the texts, the authors met to share their respective analytical templates. In a collaborative process, we created a chronology of events and then

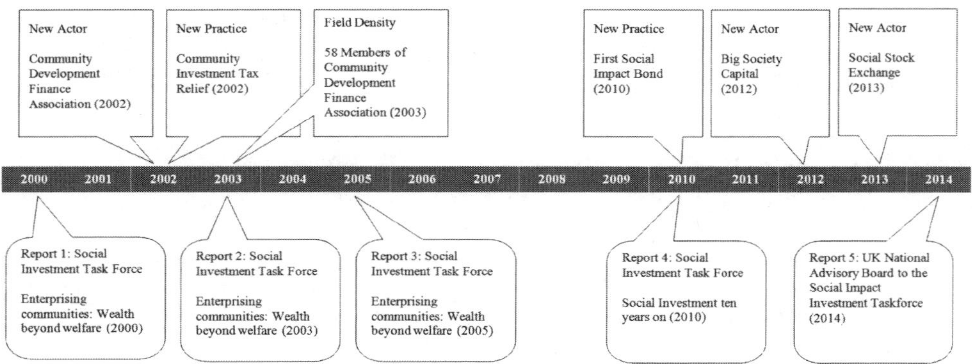

Figure 4.1 Timeline of social investment field emergence

analyzed the data. Each phrase and preliminary first-order code was subjected to critical discussion and thoughtful reflection. First-order codes were then collated and agreed for each extract. The first-order codes were then compared and contrasted, and by moving backwards and forwards between the data and the literature the first-order codes were grouped into connected themes. During this process we noted that the boundary activity consisted of emphasizing differences between social investment and commercial investment and other sources of finance; that the field was populated by actors from other fields as well as new actors that were created specifically to advance social investment; and that some practices were borrowed from other fields, whereas others were designed anew. This led to the creation of six second-order codes to group the first-order codes. The analytical process was then repeated and the second-order codes collated into three aggregate dimensions: field boundaries, field membership, and field practices.

Results

Field boundaries

Field boundaries delineate where the limit of one field metaphorically touches the limits of another. Analysis identified two themes for delineating boundaries: first, divergent discourse to highlight and specify the differences between social investment and finance available from the private, public, and charitable sectors; and second, convergent discourse to communicate the similarities between different members of the new field, that is, providers of social investment.

Field differentiation

The emergence of the new and distinct field was communicated in the use of language that specified that the nascent field is separate from other extant fields.

1 Differences between commercial and social investment.

The texts communicate that social investment is distinct from commercial investment and that the two practices, although separate, will work alongside each other:

> These CDFIs see their primary purpose as the provision of finance to self-employed individuals and businesses just outside the margins of conventional finance.
>
> *(Report 1: 11)*

> Links between the social investment and mainstream financial markets.
>
> *(Report 5: 21)*

2 Differences between social investment and finance from the public sector and charities.

The data also show that social investment is positioned as different from finance provided by the public sector, charities, and foundations. The differentiating characteristic is that social investment is repayable finance and thus borrowers are required to generate a surplus in order to repay investors. For organizations previously reliant on donated funds from public and charitable sources, the risk of failure or lack of surplus is a new concept to be factored into income portfolios. However, the SITF is clear that social investment is designed to work with, and not replace, other sources of funds available to social ventures.

> CDFIs look for higher returns than traditional public expenditure and grants.
>
> *(Report 1: 15)*

> Social challenges … cannot be addressed by government or the private sector alone.
>
> *(Report 4: 9)*

In demarcating the boundaries of the field from other sources of finance, the ethical mission of social investment to support organizations that provide services to the disadvantaged and the socially excluded is explicit:

> Access to good advice, banking services and affordable credit for those at the margins of the marketplace: CDFIs, community banks and credit unions are clearly key elements of a sustainable solution.
>
> *(Report 3: 11)*

> Actors worked collaboratively seeking solutions that started by focusing on social needs and worked backwards to provide ways in which financial or social capital could be used to help address those needs.
>
> *(Report 5: 27)*

Field density

To build field strength, the texts identify the types of social investment vehicle that would be aligned with the ethical mission of the nascent field. In doing so the aim is to foster an identity rooted in the shared ethical purpose and values of field members.

3 Field membership.

The reports specify types of organizations whose aims will align with those of social investment and community development.

> A thriving community development finance sector comprising Community Development Banks, Community Loan Funds, Micro-loan Funds and Community Development Venture Funds.
>
> *(Report 1: 6)*

Over time the range of field members is widened to include credit unions (Report 3: 11), the Social Stock Exchange (Report 4: 6), and Big Society Capital (Report 5: 21).

4 Field networks.

To foster connections between field members and assist in the promotion of a collective identity, various activities are referred to in the reports, for example networking events and training courses. To reinforce the distinctiveness of social investment, the SITF recommended that CDFIs also network with other organizations outside the new field, for example Regional Development Agencies and Local Strategic Partnerships.

> CDFIs work in such a specific environment that tailor-made training is essential if it is going to be worthwhile. As all our recruits are inevitably new to the sector it is also a good opportunity for them to meet and network with other CDFA members.
>
> *(Report 3: 13)*

> The CDFA and the Charity Commission are making efforts to define terms and disseminate their meaning.
>
> *(Report 3: 10)*

After a decade, although some concerns relating to field structure and organizational diversity persisted (Report 4: 9), the new field is reported to have been established: "Over the last ten years the SITF has succeeded in fostering the creation of a UK social investment market" (Report 4: 16).

Table 4.2 Data categories and illustrative quotes

Field boundaries
Field differentiation
1 *Differences between commercial and social investment* "These CDFIs see their primary purpose as the provision of finance to self-employed individuals and businesses just outside the margins of conventional finance" (Report 1: 11). "More than simple financing vehicles which do things banks can't, won't or don't understand" (Report 3: 13). "Links between the social investment and mainstream financial markets" (Report 5: 21). 2 *Differences between social investment and finance from the public sector and charities* "To make significant investments in entrepreneurial talent rather than put money into projects with a limited life" (Report 1: 11). "CDFIs look for higher returns than traditional public expenditure and grants" (Report 1: 15). "Social challenges … cannot be addressed by government or the private sector alone" (Report 4: 9).
Field density
3 *Field membership* "A thriving community development finance sector comprising Community Development Banks, Community Loan Funds, Micro-loan Funds and Community Development Venture Funds" (Report 1: 6). "They focused on developing an ecosystem that supported supply, demand and intermediation. They recognized that these three elements needed to be mutually supportive and interdependent" (Report 5: 27). 4 *Field networks* "CDFIs work in such a specific environment that tailor-made training is essential if it is going to be worthwhile. As all our recruits are inevitably new to the sector it is also a good opportunity for them to meet and network with other CDFI members" (Report 3: 13). "The CDFA and the Charity Commission are making efforts to define terms and disseminate their meaning" (Report 3: 10).

Field membership

Actor appropriation

5 *Appropriation of actors from the commercial finance sector*
"It is expected that the managers of the CDV Fund will be experienced business people and venture capitalists" (Report 1: 19).
"Those whose collaboration is needed: banks, large companies, venture capitalists, entrepreneurs, institutional investors, the voluntary and community sector and Government agencies" (Report 1: 7).

6 *Appropriation of actors from the public and charitable sectors*
"A key decision will be which organization will evaluate CDFI applications and allocate the tax credit. One option would be the Small Business Service, to parallel its responsibilities for the Phoenix Fund" (Report 1: 5).

Actor innovation

7 *Creation of a new trade association for social investment vehicles*
"In order to build on the pioneering work done so far, the aim should be to engage business leaders and CDFIs in the development of ... an effective trade association capable of assembling reliable information and representing the needs of CDFIs" (Report 1: 7).

8 *Appointment of a new social investment champion in government*
"The Task Force suggests the appointment within a Government department of a high ranking 'champion' for community development finance with strong links to both the Treasury and ... the Small Business Service" (Report 1: 7).

Field practices

Practice mimesis

9 *Appropriation of practices from the commercial finance sector*
"The Task Force recommends that the successful practices of venture capital, namely long term investment, business support to the entrepreneur and rapid growth of company backed, should be applied to community investment" (Report 1: 5).
"The successful disciplines of venture capital, equity investment combined with management support, could be used to speed the development of businesses in low-income neighbourhoods" (Report 3: 6).

10 *Appropriation of practices from other countries*
"Our recommendations are based on innovative approaches that have proved successful in stimulating community enterprise in under-invested communities in a number of other countries" (Report 1: 4).
"Figures from the USA support the view that the determined involvement of the banking industry is crucial to the process of turning around the UK's under-invested communities" (Report 1: 20).
"The final form of any UK Community Reinvestment Act will benefit from thirty years of experience in the US as well as from research covering the past several years" (Report 3: 12).

Practice innovation

11 *New techniques to increase the flow of funds into social investment vehicles*
"The Task Force proposes a tax credit which would provide lenders to, and equity investors in, CDFIs with a guaranteed minimum rate of return" (Report 1: 4).
"New mechanisms to collect funds at the wholesale level which can be channelled to CDFIs" (Report 1: 7).

12 *New techniques for measuring and monitoring performance in the social investment sector*
"As a new and emerging sector, CDFIs have yet to identify performance measures and benchmarks. Doing so is challenging as the sector is diverse in its activities and target markets. This work has begun and is fundamental to the next stage of the sector's growth" (Report 3: 12).

Field membership

Fields are composed of actors, and analysis of the texts identified the legitimization of actors as members of the field and the recommendation of and subsequent establishment of new actors. In Report 2, short biographies of seven key individual actors are presented. These include individuals from other sectors as well as from new actors created specifically for social investment.

Actor appropriation

5 Appropriation of actors from the commercial finance sector.

The advantages for social investment of learning from the commercial investment market are endorsed through appropriating actors from mainstream finance in the nascent field. The value of learning from the commercial venture capital market is signified in the appointment of the chair of the SITF (Sir Ronald Cohen, founder of Apax private equity group and former chair of the Venture Capital Association). In addition, SITF board members included two high-profile entrepreneurs from the private sector (Philip Hume, ComputaCenter; and Tom Singh, New Look). The inclusion of actors from the commercial sector might be achieved through direct appropriation or indirectly via networks.

> It is expected that the managers of the CDV Fund will be experienced business people and venture capitalists.
>
> *(Report 1: 19)*

> Those whose collaboration is needed: banks, large companies, venture capitalists, entrepreneurs, institutional investors, the voluntary and community sector and Government agencies.
>
> *(Report 1: 7)*

6 Appropriation of actors from the public and charitable sectors.

In addition to working with actors from the commercial finance and private sector, leading figures from government and the charitable sectors are also appropriated to join the new field. Board members of the SITF included actors from the public sector (Ian Hargreaves, University of Cardiff) and charities (David Carrington, PPP; Geraldine Peacock, Guide Dogs for the Blind; and Joan Shapiro, South Shore Bank). The texts identify actors from the public sector, for example the Small Business Service (SBS). The SBS was located in the Department of Trade and Industry to promote the interests of small business owners. The National Strategy for Neighbourhood Renewal advocated for the SBS to promote entrepreneurship among under-represented and disadvantaged groups. The SBS was also allocated responsibility for distributing £90 million (over 3 years) to support CDFIs and other initiatives to promote entrepreneurship (Fisher & Satter, 2001).

> A key decision will be which organization will evaluate CDFI applications and allocate the tax credit. One option would be the Small Business Service [part of HM Government], to parallel its responsibilities for the Phoenix Fund.
>
> *(Report 1: 5)*

Actor innovation

7 Creation of a new trade association for social investment vehicles.

One of the original recommendations in Report 1 was to create a trade association. Trade associations play an important role in field creation and maintenance. The SITF anticipated that the new trade association would play a "crucial role" (Report 1: 24), be a "critical factor" (Report 2: 12), and would aim at "achieving coherence" (Report 1: 13). To support the growth of the sector, the new trade association was established to advocate the interests of providers of social investment as well as investors.

> In order to build on the pioneering work done so far, the aim should be to engage business leaders and CDFIs in the development of ... an effective trade association capable of assembling reliable information and representing the needs of CDFIs.
>
> *(Report 1: 7)*

> A community development finance association would have a crucial role in promoting new techniques in social impact evaluation models.
>
> *(Report 1: 24)*

Also, recommendations were made to develop a community development venture fund to act as a new intermediary between government investors and commercial banks, to manage investments in social ventures. To support the new intermediary institution, the government expressed willingness to match community development venture funding.

8 Appointment of a new social investment champion in government.

To disseminate information about social investment across government and advocate for its inclusion in new policies, a new role of social investment champion was proposed:

> The Task Force suggests the appointment within a Government department of a high ranking "champion" for community development finance with strong links to both the Treasury and ... the Small Business Service.
>
> *(Report 1: 7)*

In Report 4, progress in attracting actors from commercial, public, and non-profit sectors to actively support and participate in social investment is attested:

> A wide range of new investors has been attracted to social investment since 2000. Examples include: private equity funds backing Venture Philanthropy initiatives [...] wealthy individuals and institutional investors investing directly in social enterprises and through social investment funds [...]; and foundations such as Esmée Fairbairn, which has created a social investment fund, and the Tudor Trust, which has committed to invest endowment assets in an increasingly mission related manner.
>
> *(Report 4: 6)*

The process of actor innovation is dynamic and continuous. In 2010, Report 4 presented the case for a new social investment bank. By 2014 the call has been responded to by the establishment of Big Society Capital, a new wholesale bank created to advocate for the interests of Social Investors and to provide direct support to social investment intermediaries.

Field practices

The common meaning system of a field is played out in the practices of the field. Isomorphic pressures of mimesis were identified in references to the adoption by the new field of practices from commercial finance and the venture capital industry. In addition, the texts refer to adopting practices instituted in other countries, specifically the United States. At the same time as appropriating practices established in other fields and countries, the texts refer to the creation of new practices to increase the flow of funds into social investment and ensure high standards of governance.

Practice mimesis

9 Appropriation of practices from the commercial finance sector.

Reports 1 and 3 refer to the enabling environment for venture capital in the UK and the adoption of the successful principles of venture capital by social investment vehicles.

> The Task Force recommends that the successful practices of venture capital, namely long term investment, business support to the entrepreneur and rapid growth of company backed, should be applied to community investment.
>
> *(Report 1: 5)*

> The successful disciplines of venture capital, equity investment combined with management support, could be used to speed the development of businesses in low-income neighbourhoods.
>
> *(Report 3: 6)*

10 Appropriation of practices from other countries.

To facilitate the advancement of social investment as a new field, the data outline how practices from other countries would help the establishment and growth of social investment. Specific reference is made to the positive impact of legislation to promote social investment in deprived areas in the United States. The broad approach of the US Community Reinvestment Act (1977) was to tackle the redlining of those neighborhoods where banks, building societies, and insurance companies would not invest. The Act required financial institutions to have an affirmative duty to meet the credit needs of communities where they were based (Benjamin, Rubin, & Zielenbach, 2002). The impact of the Act had been to stimulate investment in deprived areas. Further, the SITF recommended that the skills required of intermediaries in the United States be copied in the UK; for example, the leading US intermediaries, the National Community Capital Association (NCCA) and the Detroit Local Initiatives Support Corporation (LISC), advertise their accredited business expertise.

> Figures from the USA support the view that the determined involvement of the banking industry is crucial to the process of turning around the UK's under-invested communities.
>
> *(Report 1: 20)*

> The final form of any UK Community Reinvestment Act will benefit from thirty years of experience in the US as well as from research covering the past several years.
>
> *(Report 3: 12)*

Practice innovation

11 New techniques to increase the flow of funds into social investment vehicles.

Novel proposals were developed to increase the flow of finance to the field of social investment through, for example, the design of a new tax relief for investors and new social investment intermediaries. The proposed Community Investment Tax Credit was designed to encourage private investment in deprived communities through investing in CDFIs.

> The Task Force proposes a tax credit which would provide lenders to, and equity investors in, CDFIs with a guaranteed minimum rate of return.
>
> *(Report 1: 4)*

> New mechanisms to collect funds at the wholesale level which can be channelled to CDFIs.
>
> *(Report 1: 7)*

12 New techniques for measuring and monitoring performance in the social investment sector.

Impact evaluation has an important role in building trust between investors and social ventures (SEU, 2002). New practices were designed to monitor the performance of social investment funds and benchmark field members.

> Demonstrating the social returns of CDVC funds has been pioneered by BCV. Working to maintain rigorous social impact evaluation is key to the development of the sector.
>
> *(Report 3: 6)*

However, some practice innovation was intended to affect those outside field membership; specifically to promote transparency in bank lending, the SITF recommended a program of bank disclosure of lending and investment in deprived areas.

> There is a need to request much more detailed, individual disclosure by banks of their lending activities in under-invested areas.
>
> *(Report 1: 6)*

Practice innovation is a strong theme throughout the reports:

> Social investment has begun to spread more widely into investments that are diverse in terms of social mission, structure and risk-reward profile.
>
> *(Report 4: 6)*

> The result today is a rapidly growing marketplace which is providing new and innovative funding options for social entrepreneurs around the country.
>
> *(Report 5: 3)*

The continued focus on practice innovation reflects the responsiveness and the dynamism of field emergence.

Discussion and conclusion

The aim of the study was to investigate how a new field is instantiated. Previous field-level research has been dominated by studies of the role of social movements in new field creation (Fligstein & McAdam, 2012). Distinctive to social investment is the active role of government in stimulating new field creation, and the study thus joins a small group of papers that attribute to the State an important role in institutional entrepreneurship (see Vermeulen, Büch, & Greenwood, 2007). Against a context of increasing demand for finance from social entrepreneurs, State policies to promote new procurement practices, and societal interest in new forms of capitalism, the establishment of the SITF in 2000 signaled the government's commitment to supporting and promoting social change. The new field of social investment was positioned to be learning lessons from commercial finance but at the same time offering something new and innovative to investors and investees. The pressure to conform as well as innovate produced two boundary-creating responses. First, to distinguish the new field, the texts specify how social investment differs from commercial, public, and non-profit sources of funds. Second, to create a collective identity for the field, the texts specify the type of organizations whose values and practices are aligned to the new field and outline activities to further consolidate the collective identity of the field. The findings support the view that changing field-level practices involves more than legislative change (Tolbert & Zucker, 1983), and that new fields emerge from the interactions of multiple actors and actions (Powell et al., 2005).

The study finds that new field creation also involves balancing the pressures of isomorphism with innovation. The establishment of social investment combined appropriating actors and practices from fields that were already in existence in the UK and other countries. The appropriation was based on recruitment of actors that would help establish the legitimacy and profile of the new field. For example, the chair of the SITF was a successful venture capitalist, and board members included high-profile leaders from the charity sector as well as entrepreneurs. In addition to appropriating actors, the SITF promoted the appropriation of practices from commercial finance and other countries. The aim was thus to learn from practices that had been successful in other fields and implement them in the new field. As with actor appropriation, practices that promoted the interests of the new field were selected.

The isomorphic spread of existing practices was combined with innovation to invent new actors and new practices which would ensure that the new field was distinguished from existing fields. The creation of a new trade association was instrumental in building field capacity and guiding member behaviour, and membership of the new trade association grew steadily. The important role of trade and professional associations in field creation and maintenance has been noted (Greenwood et al., 2002), and in the case of social investment, the mandate for the new association is legitimized by the support of the State (McDermott et al., 2009) through the establishment of the SITF. In contrast, the intention to appoint a champion to promote awareness of social investment across government departments was proposed, but not enacted. Thus, State support of a field-creating action is not a guarantee of enactment. Some of the new practices of the field were designed to increase the awareness and attractiveness of social investment to investors. The main mechanism was the design of a tax relief that would reduce the tax to be paid on funds invested in social investment intermediaries. To ensure the integrity of the new field, new methods for measuring social performance were called for. As with the social investment champion, this practice innovation has been slow to materialize.

The aggregate dimensions of creating field boundaries, membership, and practices worked collectively to establish, and then grow, the field of social investment. The establishment of new fields is explained as a generic process of institutional entrepreneurship (Lawrence et al., 2002; Phillips, Lawrence, & Hardy, 2000). In line with previous research, the new field is constituted of boundaries, members, and practices (Fligstein & McAdam, 2012). However, the processes of boundary demarcation, defining membership criteria, and specifying acceptable practices are guided by an overt ethical mission first to provide a flow of funds to organizations with a commercial focus combined with an espoused social mission, and second to attract investors willing to accept returns on their investment that may be lower than could be earned on commercial investments and may take longer to accrue. The overt ethical mission of the field thus constitutes an institutional paradigm that shapes the creation, and subsequent growth, of the new field which we label ethical institutional entrepreneurship.

We conclude with three suggestions for future research into field-level processes. The current study investigated the policy recommendations and their implementation in the creation of a new institutional field in which the boundaries, actors, and practices are supported by legislation and formal guidelines. Scholars from across the social sciences remain interested in how formal policies are implemented in practice and the extent to which practices remain tightly coupled or become decoupled when adopted by organizations (Meyer & Rowan, 1977). A study that investigated the micro-processes of establishing and managing a social investment intermediary, such as a new organization or new fund, would provide a rich opportunity to investigate the conditions and extent of deviations between formal structures and actual processes, practices, and impacts.

A second opportunity for further research into field-level processes is to explore how and why organizations respond differently to institutional pressures to change. Responses to pressures to change by organizations range from resistance to whole-hearted adoption. In our study, we examined how practices were both borrowed and invented for the new field. The connections between the new field and extant fields provide routes for new practices to have a reciprocal influence on organizations in the source field. Thus, for example, how did commercial finance engagement with social investment influence the practices of commercial finance? How have the donor and investment practices of charities and foundations been influenced by new actors and practices engaged in social investment? Scholarly investigation into the reverse flow of influence would shed light on the permeability of boundaries and the reflexivity of institutional processes.

A third opportunity for research lies in a longitudinal investigation into field divergence over time. The narrative of the development path of social investment we presented exhibits a noticeable level of agreement between actors in which overt conflict and resistance to the new field is either not present, hidden from accounts, or takes on a new form; for example, not all of the recommendations were implemented, and new, unforeseen initiatives have been introduced. Typical of fields though is the presence of different actor positions, interests, and power structures. Institutional fields are not fixed, and over time come under pressure to change (Hoffman, 1999; Scott, 2001). As the social investment field matures, we might expect that different interests will come to the surface and impact on field topography. A study that investigated how field topography changes over time would provide valuable insights into how strategies for maintaining field values and practices respond to conflict and resistance.

References

Almandoz, J. (2014). Founding teams as carriers of competing logics. *Administrative Science Quarterly, 59*, 442–473.

Bank of England. (2000). *Finance for small businesses in deprived communities.* London: Domestic Finance Division.

Beckert, J. (1999). Agency, entrepreneurs, and institutional change: The role of strategic choice and institutionalized practices in organizations. *Organization Studies, 20*, 777–800.

Benjamin, L., Rubin, J. S., & Zielenbach, S. (2002). *Community development financial institutions: Current issues and future prospects.* Retrieved March 21, 2015, from http://www.federalreserve.gov

Boxenbaum, E., & Battilana, J. (2005). Importation as innovation: Transposing managerial practices across fields. *Strategic Organization, 3*, 355–383.

Brown, A., & Norman, W. (2011). *Lighting the touchpaper: Growing the market for social investment in England*. London: Boston Consulting Group and the Young Foundation.

Brown, A., & Swersky, A. (2012). *The first billion: A forecast of social investment demand*. London: Boston Consulting Group/Big Society Capital.

Casasnovas, G., & Ventresca, M. J. (2015). Building a robust social investment market. *Stanford Social Innovation Review*. Retrieved March 11, 2015, from http://www.researchgate.net/publication/272167718

Dayson, K. (2004). *Community finance initiatives: A policy success story*. Discussion paper, University of Salford, Salford.

Devine-Wright, P. (2005). Local aspects of UK renewable energy development: Exploring public beliefs and policy implications. *Local Environment, 10*, 57–69.

DiMaggio, P. J., & Powell, W. W. (1983). The iron cage revisited: Institutional isomorphism and collective rationality in organizational field. *American Sociological Review, 48*, 147–160.

DiMaggio, P. J., & Powell, W. W. (1991). Introduction. In W. W. Powell & P. J. DiMaggio (Eds.), *The new institutionalism and organizational analysis* (pp. 1–38). Chicago, IL: University of Chicago Press.

Doherty, B., Davies, I. A., & Tranchell, S. (2013). Where now for fair trade? *Business History, 55*, 161–189.

Emirbayer, M., & Johnson, V. (2008). Bourdieu and organizational analysis. *Theory and Society, 37*, 1–44.

Fisher, T., & Satter, D. (2001). *The state of community development finance*. London: New Economics Foundation.

Fligstein, N., & McAdam, D. (2012). *A theory of fields*. New York, NY: Oxford University Press.

Glaser, B., & Strauss, A. (1978). *The discovery of grounded theory*. New York, NY: Aldine.

Goodman, M. K. (2004). Reading fair trade: Political ecological imaginary and the moral economy of fair trade goods. *Political Geography, 23*, 891–915.

Greenwood, R., & Suddaby, R. (2006). Institutional entrepreneurship in mature fields: The big five accounting firms. *Academy of Management Journal, 49*, 27–48.

Greenwood, R., Suddaby, R., & Hinings, C. R. (2002). Theorizing change: The role of professional associations in the transformation of established fields. *Academy of Management Journal, 45*, 58–80.

Hardy, C., & Maguire, S. (2010). Discourse, field-configuring events and change in organizations and institutional fields: Narratives of DDT and the Stockholm convention. *Academy of Management Journal, 53*, 1365–1392.

Hoffman, A. (1999). Institutional evolution and change: Environmentalism and the US chemical industry. *Academy of Management Journal, 42*, 351–371.

Kent, D., & Dacin, T. (2013). Bankers at the gate: Microfinance and the high cost of borrowed logics. *Journal of Business Venturing, 28*, 759–773.

Kim, T.-Y., Shin, D., Oh, H., & Young-Chul, J. (2007). Inside the iron cage: Organizational political dynamics and institutional changes in presidential selection systems in Korean universities, 1985–2002. *Administrative Science Quarterly, 52*, 286–323.

Kvist, J. (2013). The post-crisis European social model: Developing or dismantling social investments? *Journal of International and Comparative Social Policy, 29*, 91–107.

Lawrence, T. (1999). Institutional strategy. *Journal of Management Inquiry, 25*, 161–188.

Lawrence, T., Hardy, C., & Phillips, N. (2002). Institutional effects of inter-organizational collaboration: The emergence of proto-institutions. *Academy of Management Journal, 45*, 281–290.

Lawrence, T., & Phillips, N. (2004). From Moby Dick to Free Willy: Macro-cultural discourse and institutional entrepreneurship in emerging institutional fields. *Organization, 11*, 689–711.

Lehner, O. M. (2013). Crowdfunding social ventures: A model and research agenda. *Venture Capital: An International Journal of Entrepreneurial Finance, 15*, 289–311.

Lehner, O. M., & Nicholls, A. (2014). Social finance and crowdfunding for social enterprises: A public–private case study providing legitimacy and leverage. *Venture Capital, 16*, 271–286.

Lounsbury, M. (2001). Institutional sources of practice variation: Staffing college and university recycling programs. *Administrative Science Quarterly, 46*, 29–56.

Lounsbury, M. (2007). A tale of two cities: Competing logics and practice variation in the professionalization of mutual funds. *Academy of Management Journal, 50*, 289–307.

Maguire, S., & Hardy, C. (2009). Discourse and deinstitutionalization: The decline of DDT. *Academy of Management Journal, 52*, 148–178.

Maguire, S., Hardy, C., & Lawrence, T. (2004). Institutional entrepreneurship in emerging fields: HIV/AIDS treatment advocacy in Canada. *Academy of Management Journal, 50*, 1107–1132.

Markowitz, L., Cobb, D., & Hedley, M. (2011). Framing ambiguity: Insider/outsiders and the successful legitimation project of the social responsible mutual fund industry. *Organization, 19*, 3–23.
Marquis, C., & Lounsbury, M. (2007). Vive la résistance: Competing logics and the consolidation of U.S. community banking. *Academy of Management Journal, 50*, 799–820.
McDermott, G. A., Corredoira, R. A., & Kruse, G. (2009). Public–private institutions as catalysts of upgrading in emerging market societies. *Academy of Management Journal, 52*, 1270–1296.
Meyer, J., & Rowan, B. (1977). Institutionalized organizations: Formal structure as myth and ceremony. *American Journal of Sociology, 8*, 340–363.
Nicholls, A. (2014). Filling the capital cap: Institutionalizing social finance. In S. Denny & F. Seddon (Eds.), *Social enterprise: Accountability and evaluation around the world* (pp. 161–195). London: Routledge.
North, D. C. (1990). *Institutions, institutional change and economic performance*. Cambridge: Cambridge University Press.
Ocasio, W. (1997). Toward an attention-based view of the firm. *Strategic Management Journal, 18*, 187–206.
Oliver, C. (1991). Strategic responses to institutional processes. *Academy of Management Review, 16*, 145–179.
PAT3. (1999). *Business: Policy action team*. Social Exclusion Unit. London: Cabinet Office.
Phillips, N., Lawrence, T., & Hardy, C. (2000). Inter-organizational collaboration and the dynamics of institutional fields. *Journal of Management, 37*, 23–43.
Podolny, J. M. (2001). Networks as the pipes and prisms of the market. *American Journal of Sociology, 107*, 33–60.
Powell, W. W., White, D. R., Koput, K. W., & Owen-Smith, J. (2005). Network dynamics and field evolution: The growth of inter organizational collaboration in the life sciences. *American Journal of Sociology, 110*, 1132–1205.
Renard, M.-C. (2003). Fair trade: Quality, market and conventions. *Journal of Rural Studies, 19*, 87–96.
Rubin, J. S. (2009). Developmental venture capital: Conceptualizing the field. *Venture Capital: An International Journal of Entrepreneurial Finance, 11*, 335–360.
Scott, W. R. (1991). *Institutions and organizations*. Thousand Oaks, CA: Sage.
Scott, W. R. (1994). Institutions and organizations: Towards a theoretical synthesis. In W. R. Scott & J. W. Meyer (Eds.), *Institutional environments and organizations: Structural complexity and individualism* (pp. 55–80). Thousand Oaks, CA: Sage.
Scott, W. R. (2001). *Institutions and organizations*. Thousand Oaks, CA: Sage.
Seo, M. G., & Creed, W. E. D. (2002). Institutional contradictions, praxis and institutional change: A dialectical perspective. *Academy of Management Review, 27*, 222–247.
Social Enterprise Unit (SEU). (2002). *Social enterprise: A strategy for success*. London: Department of Trade and Industry.
Social Exclusion Unit. (1998). *National strategy for neighbourhood renewal*. London: HMSO.
Social Investment Task Force (SITF). (2000). *Enterprising communities: Wealth beyond welfare*. London: Cabinet Office.
Strauss, A., & Corbin, J. (1998). *Basics of qualitative research: Grounded theory procedures and techniques*. Thousand Oaks, CA: Sage.
Tolbert, P. S., & Zucker, L. G. (1983). Institutional sources of change in the formal structure of organizations: The diffusion of civil service reform, 1880–1935. *Administrative Science Quarterly, 28*(1), 22–39.
US Community Reinvestment Act. (1977). Retrieved February 26, 2016, from https://www.usbank.com/community/reinvestment-act.html. Retrieved March 18 2016.
Vermeulen, P., Büch, R., & Greenwood, R. (2007). The impact of governmental policies in institutional fields: The case of innovation in the Dutch concrete industry. *Organization Studies, 28*, 515–540.
Walker, G., & Devine-Wright, P. (2008). Community renewable energy: What should it mean? *Energy Policy, 36*, 497–500.
Whittington, R. (2006). Completing the practice turn in strategy research. *Organization Studies, 27*(5), 613–634.
Wooten, M., & Hoffman, A. J. (2008). Organizational fields: Past, present and future. In R. Greenwood, C. Oliver, K. Sahlin-Andersson, & R. Suddaby (Eds.), *Handbook of organizational institutionalism*. London: Sage.
Yin, R. K. (2009). *Case study research methods*. London: Sage.
Zietsma, C., & Lawrence, T. (2010). Institutional work in the transformation of an organizational field: The interplay of boundary work and practice work. *Administrative Science Quarterly, 55*, 189–201.
Zilber, T. B. (2008). The work of meanings in institutional processes and thinking. In R. Greenwood, C. Oliver, K. Sahlin-Andersson, & R. Suddaby (Eds.), *Handbook of organizational institutionalism* (pp. 151–169). London: Sage.

5

ACADEMIC RESEARCH INTO SOCIAL INVESTMENT AND IMPACT INVESTING

The status quo and future research

Jess Daggers and Alex Nicholls

Academic research has a distinctive contribution to make to the development of Social Investment and Impact Investing, but it is currently lagging considerably behind practice. While practitioners develop new initiatives and tools, secure new investment deals, and convene conferences, academics are very much in the first stages of establishing this field of enquiry. By making the current status of academic research into Social Investment and Impact Investing more visible, this chapter aims to make the field more accessible and, ultimately, encourage greater volumes of academic work in this area. To this end, this chapter provides a meta-analysis of the current research landscape, followed by a proposed agenda for future academic research.

Since 2009/10 in particular, large volumes of research into Social Investment and Impact Investing have been published, but only a minority of the papers come from academic sources: 73 academic papers were found for this review, compared to 261 papers from other sources. Unlike previous reviews of literature in the field,[1] this chapter makes a careful distinction between academic and other kinds of research and focuses on the former.

The chapter is split into two sections. The first section looks to the current state of research in the field, commenting on its fragmented and diverse nature. It organizes the literature according to academic discipline and emphasizes the importance of recognizing that research in this field is very closely related to research in neighboring fields such as microfinance and socially responsible investment.

The second section of the chapter looks to the future of academic research. It draws on interviews with more than 80 practitioners, researchers, and policymakers from 13 different countries to present a framework of future possible research topics. This chapter is a condensed version of a white paper published out of the Saïd Business School at Oxford University: *The Landscape of social impact investment research: Trends and Opportunities* (2016).[2]

Definitional boundaries and terminology

Establishing common usage of terminology is a persistent problem in research into Impact Investing and Social Investment. These two areas of practice are overlapping, but are quite different in their general approach:

- *Impact Investing* concerns the *allocation of repayable capital* to organizations that have the intention to create specified social or environmental impact. The focus is, therefore, mainly on the investor.[3]
- *Social Investment* concerns providing *access to repayable capital* for social sector organizations (SSOs), where the providers of capital are motivated to create social or environmental impact. There is, therefore, more of a focus on the *investee* than in Impact Investing.[4]

The origins of these two terms are quite different. "Impact Investing" was a term coined by the Rockefeller Foundation in 2007, in a strategic attempt to create momentum behind socially and environmentally positive investing practice in the United States. The term "Social Investment," in contrast, predates its current usage and has developed in a far more organic—and less strategic—manner, mainly in Europe. Indeed, to add to this confusion, the original usage of the term "Social Investment" was in public and social policy analysis—not finance—referring to the long-term effectiveness of early-stage public welfare interventions in such sectors as health and education.[5]

The Social Investment market is concerned with building the capacity of the social sector to take on repayable finance. To do this it has proved important to engage with existing networks of charities and social enterprises. The status of the recipient organization (e.g., whether it is profit-seeking or has adopted an asset lock) is seen by many to be relevant in deciding whether a given investment counts as a "social" investment. The focus tends to be domestic activity, rather than on investors deploying capital overseas in emerging markets.[6]

The Impact Investing market, by contrast, focuses on how capital can be used to create social or environmental impact. Here the prominent concern is how investors—whether they are individuals or institutions, and whether they are driven more by a desire for impact or for financial return—should be integrating concern for impact into their investment decisions. As a consequence, the legal or "social" status of the recipient organization/investee is much less significant, and less emphasis is placed on making capital available to existing SSOs on terms suitable to them.[7]

While there are clear differences in the histories and approaches suggested by these two terms, these differences are not always clear in practice, and there is little recognition of the distinction in research to date. "Social Investment" and "Impact Investing," along with the hybrid term "Social Impact Investing" (SII), are often used interchangeably, or without making clear distinctions.

There is no simple resolution to this confusion; at this stage it is important to recognize that Social Investment and Impact Investing carry with them very different histories and sets of ideas, and that a large number of researchers interested in this space are actually focused on one or other of these domains, but not both. This is certainly the case in the UK and other European countries where there is traditionally a robust third sector, lending the idea of Social Investment more resonance.

For the sake of convenience, the remainder of this chapter will use the term "Social Impact Investing" as an umbrella term to refer to both "Social Investment" and "Impact Investing." A general definition of SII is: "investments in organisations that deliberately aim to create social or environmental value (and measure it), where the principal is repaid, possibly with a return."[8]

Methodology

In addition to the literature search—detailed in the next section—several activities were undertaken to collect primary data for this chapter. One-on-one interviews were conducted with 83 practitioners, policymakers, and academics based in 13 different countries, asking questions about the current state of research into SII and future research priorities. The majority of the interviews (67 percent) were with academics and with people based in the UK (36 percent) and the United States (31 percent). Three informant seminar meetings were also run with a total of 50 attendees.

It is important to acknowledge potential research biases. First, the research was conducted only in English, so research in other languages has not been represented. Second, there is a potential bias in the search toward research produced in the United States and the UK, as the authors are UK-based and were given access to the (US-based) MacArthur Foundation's network of contacts. These two countries were pathfinders in the creation of SII, so there is good reason to expect an existing bias in this direction, but if anything this bias would be further confirmed by the search methodology used here.

Literature review

A thorough search was conducted between April and September 2015 for academic research focused on SII.[9] Two sets of criteria for inclusion had to be established:

- By topic: is the topic of the research relevant enough for inclusion in the review?
- By type: can the research be classed as "academic"?

In deciding "topic," it was necessary to filter out research that focused closely on related fields such as microfinance or socially responsible investment. While this research is undoubtedly relevant, its inclusion would undermine the project of establishing the current state of SII research. An initial keyword search[10] identified potentially relevant papers, and then each paper was assessed in turn to ensure its relevance.

For an item to be classed as "academic" in this research requires it meeting one (or more) of the following criteria:

- *Publication in an academic peer-reviewed journal.* Journals that approximate more closely to an industry publication, such as the *Stanford Social Innovation Review*, or *MIT's Innovations*, are not treated as academic publications.
- *Publication by a researcher in an academic post*, as long as the paper is not a consultancy-style piece of descriptive analysis and is explicitly framed as a working paper or academic conference paper. Such research would typically be situated in an existing body of academic literature and theory and would set out to address a clear research question/argument with a robust methodology for data analysis (where data is used).

It is important to stress that the distinction carries no value judgment. Academic research is not considered to be necessarily of a higher standard than practitioner/policy research. Equally, not all research published by academics is of a high standard. Rather than rooting the distinction in quality, academic research should be seen as distinct from practitioner research in terms of its approach and target audiences, though a high priority does tend to be given to rigor and robustness.

Overall, this review identified 73 papers and chapters that make up a disparate and scattered body of work, without a robust core set of ideas or reference points. The review confirmed the interdisciplinary nature of the emerging SII field in terms of there being multiple points of entry—SII can equally be approached by an economic theorist as a third-sector researcher.

Almost half of the total number of papers reviewed here were published in academic journals. A further substantial proportion of the work considered here originates in two edited collections of (mostly) academic papers, *New Frontiers of Philanthropy* (2014), edited by Lester Salamon, and *Social Finance* (2015), edited by Alex Nicholls, Rob Paton, and Jed Emerson. Using only the chapters that meet the inclusion criteria here, 22 relevant items are contained in these volumes—most approaching SII from the perspective of third-sector research. The remainder of the academic research in this review is a mixture of working papers,[11] other book chapters, and reports.

For the purposes of this review, *topics* for research and academic *disciplines* are treated as distinct. Here a *topic* is a set of activities "out there" in the world that acts as the focus of enquiry. As the introduction explained, SII is itself a topic in a crowded landscape of other very similar topics, such as microfinance, responsible investment, and CSR: see Table 5.1 for a list of related topics that have been highlighted during this research.

Of course, SII as a topic for research can also be broken down into a large number of subtopics, such as the valuation of social return, social risk and return, or the influence of investee legal structure on the availability of Social Investment capital.

An academic *discipline*, in contrast, is a set of ideas, concepts, and theories that can be used to approach or better understand a topic. Disciplines such as economics and finance, or public policy research, each share its own sets of assumptions about how the world works. SII as a topic for research can be approached from a wide range of different academic disciplines, yielding different kinds of questions and interpretations.

The 73 academic papers considered here have been organized according to the academic discipline in which they are located. Set out in Tables 5.2–5.5, third-sector research was the most common discipline (22 papers), followed by finance and economics (12 papers), public policy and social policy research (11 papers), and business and management (10 papers).

The tables divide the literature into three broad types: *conceptual or theoretical work* (which is not located in any empirical setting), *landscaping or overview studies* (which attempt to provide a meta-analysis of a particular geography or set of practices), and *focused empirical studies* (which take a defined data set and analyze it according to a specified methodology).

In addition to these four main areas, a smaller number of contributions have come from other disciplines.

Table 5.1 Topics related to SII research

Community finance
Alternative finance
Crowd-funding
Cooperative and mutual finance
Ethical banking
Microfinance
SRI, ESG, responsible investment, and green investment
Payment by results
Development finance
Public–private partnerships
The social and solidarity economy
Social innovation
Social enterprise
Social impact measurement

Table 5.2 Third-sector research

Conceptual work	Steinberg (2015) asks in what situations there is a need for social investment, in light of the work of the third sector. What roles can SII play in relation to the provision of public goods? Young (2015) builds a cross-sectoral theory of social investment based on a benefits theory of not-for-profit finance.
Landscaping/ scoping	Hebb (2013) provides the editorial introduction to a special edition of the *Journal of Sustainable Finance and Investment*, giving an overview of the concept of impact investing. Lyons and Kickul (2013) scan the state of research into social enterprise financing in relation to impact investing and discusses research questions that need addressing. Salamon (2014) introduces his book on the "new frontiers of philanthropy," approaching the phenomenon of impact investing from the perspective of philanthropy. The following papers take particular aspects of SII and give an overview of their operation to date: Richter (2014) provides an overview of capital aggregators, where funds of social impact capital are pooled and used to support low-income communities. Erickson (2014) analyzes secondary markets for social impact investments in relation to both investment instruments and different actors. Shahnaz, Kraybill, and Salamon (2014) take on the issue of exchange platforms in SII, considering their scope and scale, the rationale for them, and the mechanics of how they work. Hagerman and Wood (2014) propose a range of services and actions that new intermediaries could offer to help build the market. Tuan (2014) explores the need for capacity building and investment readiness support organizations. Balboni and Berenbach (2014) set out when and how bonds and debt instruments are used in social impact investment. Nicholls and Schwartz (2014) explore the various sources of demand for social impact investment by sector and financial instrument. *Social Impact Bonds (SIBs):* Jackson (2013a) introduces the idea of SIBs for community finance professionals. Stoesz (2013) similarly looks at SIBs in the context of discussion on evidence-based policy. McHugh, Sinclair, Roy, Huckfield, and Donaldson (2013) argue that SIBs are part of a wider ideological shift taking place in the third sector in the UK. Joy and Shields (2013) similarly look at the emergence of SIBs in Canada and connect them to a broader trend of third-sector marketization. Brand and Kohler (2014) give an account of the conditions in which SIBs can operate, providing analysis of rationales and operational issues.
Empirical studies	Achleitner, Mayer, Lutz, and Spiess-Knafl (2012) report the results of a study completed with investors, where they were tested according to the criteria they used to assess the suitability of a social entrepreneur for investment. Seddon, Hazenberg, and Denny (2013) draw on interviews with Social Entrepreneurs in a discussion of the barriers to investing in social enterprises in the UK. Lyon and Baldock (2014) use SEUK survey data to analyze what kinds of finance SSOs are interested in and how this matches up to the provision of social investment. Hazenberg, Seddon, and Denny (2014) ask how social investment finance intermediaries in the UK understand investment readiness.

Table 5.3 Finance and economics

Conceptual work	Grabenwarter and Liechtenstein (2011) ground their analysis in interviews with impact investors and argue that impact investing is defined by the *lack* of a trade-off between financial return and social impact, contradicting the common "misconception" that impact investing tends to entail a trade-off. Chowdhry, Davies, and Waters (2015) seek to build a model whereby the interests of socially motivated and financially motivated investors can be aligned within the same investment deal. Evans (2013) draws on contract theory to define a theoretical framework for discussing strategy, taking account of the need for impact investors to enable financial performance without sacrificing impact. The paper aims to expand the theoretical underpinning of impact investing. Brandstetter and Lehner (2015) look at how financial and social risk and return is currently being addressed in impact investing and put forward a model for integrating the parameters of a social investment into the traditional logic of portfolio optimization, based on risk and return. Levine (2015) presents a hypothetical analysis of the transition from grant financing to repayable finance, in order to establish where greatest social benefit is created. Nicholls and Tomkinson (2015a) take theoretical principles underpinning the concept of financial risk and translate them for the social investment context, to generate a concept of "social risk and return." Nicholls and Patton (2015) extend the projection-valuation-pricing model in order to explore how social investments can be priced in the market. Schwartz, Jones, and Nicholls (2015) consider how market intermediation has developed to increase the flow of supply and demand in the SI market and builds a typology of categories of market infrastructure.
Landscaping/ scoping	Mendell and Barbosa (2013) do an initial overview of primary and secondary exchange platforms and examine whether they are helping to direct capital to SSOs. Thillai Rajan, Koserwal, and Keerthana (2014) scope the landscape of impact investing in India.
Empirical studies	Wharton Social Impact Initiative, Gray, Ashburn, Douglas, and Jeffers (2015) report their analysis of data collected from impact investing funds, considering the interplay between exiting an investment and the mission of the investee organization. Spiess-Knafl and Aschari-Lincoln (2015) compiled a data set from publicly available information about investment deals and conducted statistical analysis to investigate how beneficiary characteristics affect the kind of investment tool they use.

Table 5.4 Business and management

Conceptual work	Lazzarini et al. (2014) aim to understand how investors approach financial and social goals and then contribute a novel theoretical framework taking account of when financial and social goals are aligned and when profitability and social performance are in tension. Ormiston and Seymour (2014) use the "systems of exchange" typology as a lens through which to view social investment in Australia, arguing that SI can be understood as a moral system of exchange.

(Continued)

Table 5.4 Business and management *(Continued)*

	Bell and Haugh (2015) use institutional theory to analyze social investment in light of institutional field emergence. Morley (2015b) finds that social purpose organizations are using the language of impact reporting in order to manage their reputations with external financial stakeholders. Johnson (2015) argues that charitable donors should learn from impact investing by creating an "efficient charitable market" by creating mechanisms for directing funding to the most efficient and effective charities.
Landscaping/ scoping	Viviers, Ratcliffe, and Hand (2011) look at a range of funds in South Africa, connecting impact investing activity to RI activity. Diouf (2015) considers the barriers to impact investing in sustainable energy in West Africa. Clarkin and Cangioni (2015) present a literature review, giving an introduction to the topic of impact investing.
Empirical studies	Scheuerle and Glänzel (2013) use a series of interviews to examine how investors and investees cope with different institutional logics. Glänzel and Scheuerle (2015) also use interview data to map the impediments to impact investing in Germany.

Table 5.5 Public policy and social policy research

Conceptual work	Jackson (2013b) draws on evaluation theory to argue that theory of change should be a central component to evaluating impact investing. Mulgan (2015) asks what social investment adds, if anything, to the provision of public and social goods, with particular attention to SIBs. Addis (2015) looks at different possible relationships between government and the market, then goes on to look more specifically at the policy levers available for government to translate policy into practice.
Landscaping/ scoping	Wells (2012) uses data from the evaluation of Futurebuilders, a government-led social investment initiative in the UK, to give insight into social investment policy. Wood, Thornley, and Grace (2013) look at how US policy intersects with the specific legal requirements and investment culture characteristic of institutional investors. Anheier and Archambault (2014) survey examples of social investments in France and Germany and argue that policymakers should consider social investment options. Spear, Paton, and Nicholls (2015) look at the policy initiatives that have developed over the past 15 years, with a particular focus on the UK, US, and Canada. *SIBs* Fox and Albertson (2011) set out the challenges likely to arise from developing PbR mechanisms and question whether it is suitable in the criminal justice sector. Baliga (2011) also looks at SIBs in the United States and draws on comparisons with the privatization of prisons. Fitzgerald (2013) considers the implications of bringing SIBs to preventative health policy. Warner (2013) gives an introduction to SIBs and suggests theoretical approaches to critiquing them.
Empirical studies	n/a

From *sociology*, three conceptual pieces were identified:

- Minard and Emerson (2015) make an argument for seeing Impact Investing as intimately bound up with issues of justice.
- Morley (2015a) puts forward the theory that the aspirational norm of impact measurement was brought about in part by an elite network of professionals with ideological commitments to this practice.
- Nicholls (2010) uses a Weberian analytic lens to examine investor rationalities and suggests possible future directions for the social investment field.

One paper came from *development economics*: McWade (2012) surveys the Social Investment literature and brings it into contact with the development literature, arguing that Social Investors could have a significant role to play in bringing new capital to developing countries. Similarly, one landscaping paper takes a perspective from law: Donald, Ormiston, and Charlton (2014) explore the issue of whether superannuation fund trustees in Australia are able to engage in Social Investment, given their duties to members.

There is also a set of papers that are centered on SII as a topic, but without drawing explicitly on an established discipline. A handful of these are studies that attempt to gain an overall perspective on SII. Three papers present a survey of the range of associated activities:

- Nicholls and Pharoah's (2008) paper is a relatively early landscaping study for social investment.
- Nicholls and Emerson (2015a) explore Impact Investing, which is presented as a subset of the broader phenomenon of social finance.
- Nicholls and Emerson (2015b) introduce the book *Social Finance*, giving an overview of the development of the field to date.

Two other papers make a concerted effort to identify literature and rationalize the issues of terminology: Höchstädter and Scheck (2014) survey literature on Social Investment and offer a method for consolidating the range of terminology used in the sector, while Rizzello, Migliazza, Care, and Trotta (2015) provide a bibliometric analysis of extant literature on Impact Investing.

Nicholls and Tomkinson (2015b) give a critical account of the world's first SIB at Peterborough Prison in the UK, including an account of its early termination. Ormiston, Charlton, Donald, and Seymour (2015) analyze interview data to give an account of how existing impact investors are dealing with the difficulties of data collection.

Finally, four papers pick up on the issue of social impact measurement, which does not appear to reside within any particular discipline:

- Reeder and Colantonio (2013) create an analytical approach to understanding impact measurement among investors.
- Reeder, Jones, Loder, and Colantonio (2014) report the results of interviews with impact investors about impact measurement.
- Reeder, Colantonio, Loder, and Rocyn (2015) give an overview of the first principles of SIM and set out a framework for comparing differences in approach.
- Nicholls, Nicholls, and Emerson (2015) look at the issue of impact measurement within the context of social finance and present a "contingency model" allowing classification of the situations in which impact measurement will and will not be relevant.

Related literature

The criteria for inclusion in the list of 73 academic papers referred to above were deliberately strict. As a result there are numerous papers that have been identified throughout the review that were not sufficiently focused on SII to be included in the main list, but that are nevertheless relevant and of interest to researchers in the space. Details of this literature can be found in the accompanying white paper.

The future for research into SII

The first part of this chapter has given detailed insight into the relatively small volume of academic research that currently exists. The field has also been situated in relation to various closely related areas of enquiry and the multiple academic disciplines from which SII research topics might be approached.

Looking to the future of academic research, Table 5.6 presents a framework of research topics organized around three main research themes: *segmenting the field*; *data and transparency*; and *policy and regulation*. These themes were arrived at by compiling interviewee responses concerning where research should focus next; the themes emerged as a logical way of grouping the various types of research project. They are then broken down into a number of topics, with a (non-exhaustive) list of example subtopics and research questions.

Table 5.6 Framework of research topics within SII

Theme	*Topic*	*Example subtopics and research questions*
Segmenting the field	Distinctiveness of SII	**Defining the boundaries of SII
		Comparing SII to other approaches to solving social problems
		****Social risk and return
		**Clarification of terminology
	The investee perspective (demand)	What forms of finance are needed by Third-Sector Organizations (TSOs)? How well does SII meet these needs? What does investment-readiness mean for TSOs? What effect does it have on their ability to deliver social impact? What motivations do they have to pursue it?
		**Is the discipline of investment beneficial to TSOs?
		Take-up of the Community Interest Company's legal form in the UK How is investee demand affected by policy initiatives? Comparing multi-stakeholder collaborative outcome models, where investment is made into multiple delivery organizations for the same outcomes
	The investor perspective (supply)	What returns can be expected? How do returns vary across different sectors? Responsible exit and liquidity Integrating non-monetary return into investment decisions Cost of capital and the effect of integrating impact on cost of equity or debt Syndication of investors—incentives and implications The relevance and efficacy of different types of mission locks
		**New financial tools to suit the needs of SII
		What are the barriers preventing investors from taking part in SII?

	The market perspective	Analysis at the regional or local level, not just national. What is demand like outside urban centers such as London?
		**How SII connects to questions of social justice
		Differences in SII in the Global North and Global South Locating SII in the changing non-profit landscape Does SI displace bank finance? What happens when investees grow and are bought out?
		**The role and success/failure of SIBs
	Segmenting investees and investors	How does investment behavior differ across different kinds of investor? (high-net-worth individuals, institutional investors, family offices, pension funds, etc.) How does investment behavior differ across different kinds of investee? (social enterprises, trading charities, Benefit Corporations, etc.) How does the suitability of different kinds of capital vary across social sectors? (e.g., health compared to education)
	*The role of foundations	What role does VP or grant finance play in broader SII activity? The "Total Impact" approach for foundations Appetite for risk and motivation to build the market
	The role of intermediaries	The legal structure of intermediaries—should there be a control on profit? How much subsidy do/should intermediaries receive?
Data and transparency	****** Measurement of outcomes and impact	The different uses and drivers of impact measurement Methods and approaches to impact measurement The cost of measurement and evidencing How impact is embedded in investment deals, for example through term sheets What difference does measurement make to investment deals? Combining impact measurement with government initiatives for evidence-based policy How do the incentives of different kinds of organizations (university vs government department vs private consultancy) affect the availability/openness of data?
	(Optional) structures of accountability	**What mechanisms exist for holding investees/investors to account for the social impact they create?
		Standardization of measurement and reporting How can companies reconcile commercial sensitivity with the drive to be transparent and accountable?
Policy and regulation	Available policy options	Different legal forms available to investee organizations Tax relief—pros and cons, effectiveness What subsidy[1] options are there? How have these worked in different country contexts? Establishing a social investment bank—what effect does this have? Should countries other than the UK pursue this option? What is the justification for it?
	Role of government	What role should the government play vis-à-vis the social sector/private sector? What are the arguments for and against government intervention into investment markets? Is SII subsidy a good use of public money?

Note:

1 "Subsidy" is here meant broadly to include grant finance in support of developing the market for SII.

The example subtopics are some of the more specific subtopics suggested by interviewees. The asterisks and shading give a rough indication of topics that were mentioned more frequently.

Overall, this framework helps to lend some structure to an otherwise very diverse and potentially overwhelming area for research. Researchers might, for example, use this categorization to orient themselves against others in the field or to structure their own reading.

Conclusion

This chapter serves to make the landscape of research into SII more visible and accessible to current and future researchers in the field. It confronts some of the issues of terminology that have proven problematic in research, highlighting some key distinctions, particularly between the different origins of "Social Investment" and "Impact Investing." It provides the most comprehensive picture to date of the literature that exists, broken down according to academic discipline. And it collates the results of more than 80 conversations with stakeholders in the field and three key informant seminar meetings, presenting a wide variety of possible future research topics.

A key question for SII researchers in coming years will be whether there will be a process of consolidation where a core set of ideas evolve and gather popular support around the topic, or whether the state of fragmentation continues and different theoretical approaches persist, each with their own interpretation of what SII represents. By making the current fragmented state of SII research more visible and suggesting possibilities for future projects, this analysis represents one step toward greater consolidation of the field.

Notes

1 See Clarkin and Cangioni (2015), Höchstädter and Scheck (2014), Lyons and Kickul (2013), Nicholls and Pharoah (2008), Rizzello et al. (2015), and Smalling and Emerson (2015).

2 The white paper was made possible with support from the MacArthur Foundation.

3 See, for example, the reports from the GIIN. JP Morgan and GIIN (2011) are typical in explicitly taking "an in-depth analysis of investor perspectives."

4 Access to finance is an explicit concern of much of the material produced by the UK Cabinet Office and Big Society Capital, both of which are concerned with building the capacity of the third sector in the UK to take on repayable finance. The Alternative Commission on Social Investment (2015), for example, focuses on the question of how far social investment in the UK meets the needs of the social sector.

5 The following webpage gives a summary of this alternative "social investment" agenda: http://www.policy-network.net/event/3052/What-future-for-social-investment

6 This is a question that has been debated extensively in the UK context.

7 A similar distinction is articulated in a blog post in a UK-based online third-sector magazine: https://www.pioneerspost.com/news-views/20150907/defining-moment-what-social-investment

8 The definition used by the Global Impact Investing Network is: "Impact investments are investments made into companies, organizations and funds with the intention to generate social and environmental impact alongside a financial return." The Social Impact Investment Taskforce uses a slightly different definition: "Social impact investments are those that intentionally target specific social objectives along with a financial return and measure the achievement of both."

9 The results pertaining to the practitioner literature are not reported here—for details see the white paper *The Landscape of Social Impact Investment Research: Trends and Opportunities.*

10 The search looked for the terms "social invest," "impact invest," "Social Impact Bond," and "social impact invest" (where "invest" denotes both "investing" and "investment") in the title, abstract, executive summary, or opening paragraphs of any given document.

11 Conference papers have been classed as working papers in this analysis.

References

Achleitner, A.-K., Mayer, J., Lutz, E., & Spiess-Knafl, W. (2012). Disentangling gut feeling: Assessing the integrity of social entrepreneurs. *VOLUNTAS: International Journal of Voluntary and Nonprofit Organizations, 24*, 93–124. doi:10.1007/s11266-012-9264-2

Addis, R. (2015). The roles of government and policy in social finance. In A. Nicholls, R. Paton, & J. Emerson (Eds.), *Social finance* (pp. 383–459). Oxford, UK: Oxford University Press.

Alternative Commission on social investment. (2015). *After the rush: The report of the alternative commission on social investment.* Retrieved February 26, 2016, from https://www.clearlyso.com/wp-content/uploads/2015/04/Alternative-Commission-Report-Social-Investment.pdf

Anheier, H., & Archambault, E. (2014). Social investment: Franco-German experiences. In M. Freise & T. Hallmann (Eds.), *Modernizing democracy: Associations and associating in the 21st century* (pp. 291–300). New York: Springer.

Balboni, E., & Berenbach, S. (2014). Fixed income securities. In L. M. Salamon (Ed.), *New frontiers of philanthropy: A guide to the new tools and new actors that are reshaping global philanthropy and social investing* (pp. 341–365). New York: Oxford University Press.

Baliga, S. (2011). Shaping the success of social impact bonds in the United States: Lessons learned from the privatization of U.S. prisons. *Duke Law Journal, 63*, 437–479.

Bell, B., & Haugh, H. (2015). *Exploring institutional field emergence: Insights from social investment* (Working Paper No. 1032). Oxford, UK: Academic Research Network Oxford Centre.

Brand, M., & Kohler, J. (2014). Private equity investments. In L. M. Salamon (Ed.), *New frontiers of philanthropy: A guide to the new tools and new actors that are reshaping global philanthropy and social investing* (pp. 395–423). New York: Oxford University Press.

Brandstetter, L., & Lehner, O. M. (2015). Opening the market for impact investments: The need for adapted portfolio tools. *Entrepreneurship Research Journal, 5*(2), 87–107.

Chowdhry, B., Davies, S. W., & Waters, B. (2015, August). *Incentivizing impact investing.* Rochester, NY: Social Science Research Network.

Clarkin, J. E., & Cangioni, C. L. (2015). Impact investing: A primer and review of the literature. *Entrepreneurship Research Journal.* doi:10.1515/erj-2014-0011

Diouf, D. (2015). Exploring the barriers to impact investing in the sustainable energy area in West Africa. In S. Groh, J. van der Straeten, B. Edlefsen Lasch, D. Gershenson, W. Leal Filho, & D. Kammen (Eds.), *Decentralized solutions for developing economies: Addressing energy poverty through innovation* (pp. 177–183). New York: Springer.

Donald, M. S., Ormiston, J., & Charlton, K. (2014). The potential for superannuation funds to make investments with a social impact. *Company and Securities Law Journal, 32*(8), 540–551.

Erickson, D. J. (2014). Secondary markets. In L. M. Salamon (Ed.), *New frontiers of philanthropy: A guide to the new tools and new actors that are reshaping global philanthropy and social investing* (pp. 121–143). New York: Oxford University Press.

Evans, M. (2013). Meeting the challenge of impact investing: How can contracting practices secure social impact without sacrificing performance? *Journal of Sustainable Finance & Investment, 3*(2), 138–154. doi:10.1080/20430795.2013.776260

Fitzgerald, J. L. (2013). Social impact bonds and their application to preventive health. *Australian Health Review, 37*(2), 199–204.

Fox, C., & Albertson, K. (2011). Payment by results and social impact bonds in the criminal justice sector: New challenges for the concept of evidence-based policy? *Criminology and Criminal Justice.* doi:10.1177/1748895811415580

Glänzel, G., & Scheuerle, T. (2015). Social impact investing in Germany: Current impediments from investors' and social entrepreneurs' perspectives. *VOLUNTAS: International Journal of Voluntary and Nonprofit Organizations.* doi:10.1007/s11266-015-9621-z

Grabenwarter, U., & Liechtenstein, H. (2011, November). *In search of gamma: An unconventional perspective on impact investing* (IESE Business School Working Paper). Rochester, NY: Social Science Research Network.

Hagerman, L., & Wood, D. (2014). Enterprise brokers. In L. M. Salamon (Ed.), *New frontiers of philanthropy: A guide to the new tools and new actors that are reshaping global philanthropy and social investing* (pp. 209–220). New York: Oxford University Press.

Hazenberg, R., Seddon, F., & Denny, S. (2014). Intermediary perceptions of investment readiness in the UK social investment market. *VOLUNTAS: International Journal of Voluntary and Nonprofit Organizations, 26*(3), 846–871. doi:10.1007/s11266-014-9473-y

Hebb, T. (2013). Impact investing and responsible investing: What does it mean? *Journal of Sustainable Finance & Investment, 3*(2), 71–74.

Höchstädter, A. K., & Scheck, B. (2014). What's in a name: An analysis of impact investing understandings by academics and practitioners. *Journal of Business Ethics, 132*(2), 449–475. doi:10.1007/s10551-014-2327-0

Jackson, E. T. (2013a). Evaluating social impact bonds: Questions, challenges, innovations, and possibilities in measuring outcomes in impact investing. *Community Development, 44*(5), 608–616. doi:10.1080/15575330.2013.854258

Jackson, E. T. (2013b). Interrogating the theory of change: Evaluating impact investing where it matters most. *Journal of Sustainable Finance & Investment, 3*(2), 95–110.

Johnson, K. (2015). The charitable deduction games: Mimicking impact investing. *University of Pennsylvania Journal of Business Law, 17*(4), 1257–1294.

Joy, M., & Shields, J. (2013). Social impact bonds: The next phase of third sector marketization? *Canadian Journal of Nonprofit & Social Economy Research, 4*(2), 39–55.

Lazzarini, S. G., Cabral, S., De, L. C., Ferreira, M., Pongeluppe, L. S., & Rotondaro, A. (2014). *The best of both worlds? Impact investors and their role in the financial versus social performance debate* (U. of St. Gallen Law & Economics Working Paper No. 2015-06). Rochester, NY: Social Science Research Network.

Levine, R. (2015). *Who pays for scale? A theoretical economic analysis of impact investing* (Working Paper No. 1102). Oxford, UK: Academic Research Network Oxford Centre.

Lyon, F., & Baldock, R. (2014, June). *Financing social ventures and the demand for social investment* (Working Paper No. 124). Birmingham, UK: Third Sector Research Centre.

Lyons, T. S., & Kickul, J. R. (2013). The social enterprise financing landscape: The lay of the land and new research on the horizon. *Entrepreneurship Research Journal, 3*(2), 147–159. doi:10.1515/erj-2013-0045

McHugh, N., Sinclair, S., Roy, M., Huckfield, L., & Donaldson, C. (2013). Social impact bonds: A wolf in sheep's clothing? *Journal of Poverty and Social Justice, 21*(3), 247–257.

McWade, W. (2012). The role for social enterprises and social investors in the development struggle. *Journal of Social Entrepreneurship, 3*(1), 96–112. doi:10.1080/19420676.2012.663783

Mendell, M., & Barbosa, E. (2013). Impact investing: A preliminary analysis of emergent primary and secondary exchange platforms. *Journal of Sustainable Finance & Investment, 3*(2), 111–123.

Minard, S., & Emerson, J. (2015). *Doing justice to impact: Exploring the interplay between wealth creation, impact investing and social justice*. Boston, MA: Northeastern University.

Morley, J. (2015a). *Networks of elites and the emergence of social impact reporting*. Rochester, NY: Social Science Research Network.

Morley, J. (2015b). *Social impact reporting as reputation management: Internalisation, symbolism or business-washing?* Rochester, NY: Social Science Research Network.

Mulgan, G. (2015). Social finance: Does "investment" add value? In A. Nicholls, R. Paton, & J. Emerson (Eds.), *Social finance* (pp. 45–63). Oxford, UK: Oxford University Press.

Nicholls, A. (2010). The institutionalization of social investment: The interplay of investment logics and investor rationalities. *Journal of Social Entrepreneurship, 1*(1), 70–100. doi:10.1080/19420671003701257

Nicholls, A., & Emerson, J. (2015a). Impact investing: A market in evolution. In A. Nicholls, R. Paton, & J. Emerson (Eds.), *Social finance* (pp. 207–251). Oxford, UK: Oxford University Press.

Nicholls, A., & Emerson, J. (2015b). Social finance: Capitalizing social impact. In A. Nicholls, R. Paton, & J. Emerson (Eds.), *Social finance* (pp. 1–43). Oxford, UK: Oxford University Press.

Nicholls, A., Nicholls, J., & Emerson, J. (2015). Measuring social impact. In A. Nicholls, R. Paton, & J. Emerson (Eds.), *Social finance* (pp. 253–281). Oxford, UK: Oxford University Press.

Nicholls, A., & Patton, A. (2015). Projection, valuation and pricing in social finance. In A. Nicholls, R. Paton, & J. Emerson (Eds.), *Social finance* (pp. 311–334). Oxford, UK: Oxford University Press.

Nicholls, A., & Pharoah, C. (2008). *The landscape of social investment: A holistic topology of opportunities and challenges*. Oxford, UK: Said Business School.

Nicholls, A., & Schwartz, R. (2014). The demand side of the social investment marketplace. In L. M. Salamon (Ed.), *New frontiers of philanthropy: A guide to the new tools and new actors that are reshaping global philanthropy and social investing* (pp. 562–582). New York: Oxford University Press.

Nicholls, A., & Tomkinson, E. (2015a). Risk and return in social finance: "I am the market." In A. Nicholls, R. Paton, & J. Emerson (Eds.), *Social finance* (pp. 282–310). Oxford, UK: Oxford University Press.

Nicholls, A., & Tomkinson, E. (2015b). The Peterborough Pilot Social Impact Bond. In A. Nicholls, R. Paton, & J. Emerson (Eds.), *Social finance* (pp. 335–381). Oxford, UK: Oxford University Press.

Ormiston, J., Charlton, K., Donald, M. S., & Seymour, R. G. (2015, June). Overcoming the challenges of impact investing: Insights from leading investors. *Journal of Social Entrepreneurship*, 1–27. doi:10.1080/19420676.2015.1049285

Ormiston, J., & Seymour, R. (2014). The emergence of social investment as a moral system of exchange: The Australian experience. In H. Douglas & S. Grant (Eds.), *Social entrepreneurship and enterprise: Concepts in context*. Australia: Tilde University Press.

Reeder, N., & Colantonio, A. (2013, October). *Measuring impact and non-financial returns in impact investing: A critical overview of concepts and practice* (EIBURS Working Paper 2013/01). London: LSE Cities, London School of Economics and Political Science.

Reeder, N., Colantonio, A., Loder, J., & Rocyn, G. (2015). Measuring impact in impact investing: An analysis of the predominant strength that is also its greatest weakness. *Journal of Sustainable Finance & Investment, 5*(3), 136–154. doi:10.1080/20430795.2015.1063977

Reeder, N., Jones, G. R., Loder, J., & Colantonio, A. (2014, April). *Measuring impact: Preliminary insights from interviews with impact investors*. London: LSE Cities, London School of Economics and Political Science.

Richter, L. (2014). Capital aggregators. In L. M. Salamon (Ed.), *New frontiers of philanthropy: A guide to the new tools and new actors that are reshaping global philanthropy and social investing* (pp. 91–120). New York: Oxford University Press.

Rizzello, A., Migliazza, M. C., Care, R., & Trotta, A. (2015, April). *Social impact investing: A model and research agenda*. Abstract Proceedings for the 2015 Social and Sustainable Finance and Impact Investing (SSFII) Conference, Oxford, UK.

Salamon, L. (2014). The revolution on the frontiers of philanthropy: An introduction. In L. M. Salamon (Ed.), *New frontiers of philanthropy: A guide to the new tools and new actors that are reshaping global philanthropy and social investing* (pp. 3–88). New York: Oxford University Press.

Saltuk, Y., Bouri, A., & Leung, G. (2011). *Insight into the impact investment market: An in-depth analysis of investor perspectives and over 2,200 transactions*. Retrieved February 26, 2016, from https://thegiin.org/assets/documents/Insight%20into%20Impact%20Investment%20Market2.pdf

Scheuerle, T., & Glänzel, G. (2013). *"New ethos" with obstacles?—Empirical results on the barriers and potentials of impact investing from the perspective of investors and social entrepreneurs*. Heidelberg: Centre for social investment.

Schwartz, R., Jones, C., & Nicholls, A. (2015). Building the social finance infrastructure. In A. Nicholls, R. Paton, & J. Emerson (Eds.), *Social finance* (pp. 488–519). Oxford, UK: Oxford University Press.

Seddon, F., Hazenberg, R., & Denny, S. (2013, July). *What are the barriers to investing in social enterprises? An investigation into the attitudes and experiences of social entrepreneurs in the United Kingdom*. Paper presented at the 4th EMES European Research Network International Research Conference on Social Enterprise, University of Liege, Belgium.

Shahnaz, D., Kraybill, R., & Salamon, L. (2014). Social and environmental exchanges. In L. M. Salamon (Ed.), *New frontiers of philanthropy: A guide to the new tools and new actors that are reshaping global philanthropy and social investing* (pp. 144–164). New York: Oxford University Press.

Smalling, L., & Emerson, J. (2015). *Construction of an impact portfolio: Total portfolio management for multiple returns* (Impact Assets Issue Brief #15). Retrieved February 26, 2016, from http://impactassets.org/files/Issuebrief_No.15.pdf

Spear, R., Paton, R., & Nicholls, A. (2015). Public policy for social finance in context. In A. Nicholls, R. Paton, & J. Emerson (Eds.), *Social finance* (pp. 460–487). Oxford, UK: Oxford University Press.

Spiess-Knafl, W., & Aschari-Lincoln, J. (2015). Understanding mechanisms in the social investment market: What are venture philanthropy funds financing and how? *Journal of Sustainable Finance & Investment, 5*(3), 103–120. doi:10.1080/20430795.2015.1060187

Steinberg, R. (2015). What should social finance invest in and with whom? In A. Nicholls, R. Paton, & J. Emerson (Eds.), *Social finance* (pp. 64–95). Oxford, UK: Oxford University Press.

Stoesz, D. (2013). Evidence-based policy: Reorganizing social services through accountable care organizations and social impact bonds. *Research on Social Work Practice, 24*(2), 181–185. doi:10.1177/1049731513500827

Thillai Rajan, A., Koserwal, P., & Keerthana, S. (2014). The global epicenter of impact investing: An analysis of social venture investments in India. *The Journal of Private Equity, 17*(2), 37–50.

Tuan, M. T. (2014). Capacity builders. In L. M. Salamon (Ed.), *New frontiers of philanthropy: A guide to the new tools and new actors that are reshaping global philanthropy and social investing* (pp. 221–239). New York: Oxford University Press.

Viviers, S., Ratcliffe, T., & Hand, D. (2011). From philanthropy to impact investing: Shifting mindsets in South Africa. *Corporate Ownership and Control, 8*(4A), 25–43.

Warner, M. E. (2013). Private finance for public goods: Social impact bonds. *Journal of Economic Policy Reform, 16*(4), 303–319.

Wells, P. (2012). Understanding social investment policy: Evidence from the evaluation of Futurebuilders in England. *Voluntary Sector Review, 3*(2), 157–177. doi:10.1332/204080512X649342

Wharton Social Impact Initiative, Gray, J., Ashburn, N., Douglas, H., & Jeffers, J. (2015). *Great expectations: Mission preservation and financial performance in impact investing*. Philadelphia, PA: Wharton Social Impact Initiative.

Wood, D., Thornley, B., & Grace, K. (2013). Institutional impact investing: Practice and policy. *Journal of Sustainable Finance & Investment, 3*(2), 75–94.

Young, D. R. (2015). Financing social innovation. In A. Nicholls, R. Paton, & J. Emerson (Eds.), *Social finance* (pp. 96–112). Oxford, UK: Oxford University Press.

I.2
Introducing Impact Investing

6
IMPACT INVESTING

Olaf Weber

According to de Clerck (2009, p. 214), "money [and] capital, intelligently and wisely invested as an instrument for improving quality of life, can have a major impact on human development." However, though the number of financial institutions and investors focusing on the creation of positive societal and environmental impacts has been increasing, at least since the last financial crisis, mainly the negative impact of the financial sector on society is discussed.

In order to add some clarity to the relatively new concept of Impact Investing, the following will introduce some common definitions. In 2010, the Canadian Task Force on Social Finance provided an early definition, describing Impact Investing as "the active investment of capital in businesses and funds that generate positive social and/or environmental impacts, as well as financial returns to the investor" (Canadian Task Force on Social Finance, 2010, p. 5).

Another common definition of Impact Investment that also emphasizes the creation of both social and financial returns comes from the Monitor Institute, defining it as "making investments that generate social and environmental value as well as financial return" (Monitor Institute, 2009, p. 3). Jones (2010, p. 148) describes Impact Investment in a more general way as "the use of for-profit investment to address social and environmental problems." The Global Impact Investing Network (GIIN), the biggest global network of asset owners and managers dedicated to Impact Investing, aims "to solve social or environmental challenges while generating financial profit" (Global Impact Investing Network, 2011).

These definitions have in common the achievement of a positive societal, environmental, or sustainability impact through capital investments that create some kind of financial returns. Consequently, Impact Investing is a form of social finance, an umbrella term encompassing Impact Investing, social banking, and microfinance (Geobey & Weber, 2013) that is defined as "the application of tools, instruments and strategies where capital deliberately and intentionally seeks a blended value (economic, social and/or environmental) return" (Harji & Hebb, 2009, p. 2).

Though many definitions of Impact Investment exist, they are based on two common principles:

1 The blended value principle, claiming that social finance products and services can and should achieve *both* financial and social returns (positive social impacts).
2 The principle of sustainable financial return, guaranteeing the long-term financial viability of social finance institutions (Geobey & Weber, 2013).

On the one hand, these two principles distinguish Impact Investment from conventional investment because the latter is not striving for positive social impact but exclusively for financial returns. On the other hand, the principles distinguish Impact Investing from pure philanthropy because Impact Investing strives for financial returns in addition to social returns.

In contrast to social banking, Impact Investing tends to involve private and institutional investors instead of focusing on banking products and services such as lending and saving (Weber, 2014b), which "aims to have a positive impact on people, the environment, and culture by means of banking, i.e. savings accounts, loans, investments and other banking products and services, including 'gift money'" (Weber & Remer, 2011, p. 2). Mostly, and in contrast to social banking, Impact Investment is conducted by asset managers or foundations, while social banking is conducted by banks, credit unions, and financial cooperatives.

Impact Investing differs from Socially Responsible Investing (SRI) as well. SRI "screens" investments based on environmental, social, and governance factors. SRI avoids investments that "do bad" and focuses on social and environmental leaders in all industrial sectors, while Impact Investing seeks to make positive and measurable environmental and/or social impacts in addition to financial returns (Geobey & Weber, 2013). In other words, Impact Investing tries to "do good while doing well," while SRI tries to "do while doing less harm." Furthermore, SRI is rather an investment strategy that tries to manage environmental and societal risks that may have an impact on financial returns. It focuses on managing financial risks through the integration of environmental and social criteria into risk management processes.

As mentioned above, Impact Investing is based on the concepts of blended return (Emerson, 2003) and the shared value proposition (Porter & Kramer, 2011). Both state that social and financial returns are not a trade-off but may be concurrently maximized based on the assumption that businesses serving societal needs are able to create financial returns. Therefore, Impact Investing can be placed on a scale of blended returns between pure financial return and pure social return.

Prerequisites of successful Impact Investing

After having introduced the definitions of Impact Investing, this section will discuss the prerequisites of successful Impact Investing. Bugg-Levine and Emerson (2011) list the following conditions for being successful. First, Impact Investing works if solving social problems needs significant investments that cannot be granted by donors and governments alone. In other words, Impact Investing has to be complementary to other means of creating impacts such as government grants. Second, there must be an opportunity to connect social problem solving with a business model that is able to create financial returns for investors and lenders. This important condition does not apply for all social and environmental problems. Though it is possible to monetize social and environmental problems and their solutions, there is not always a willingness to pay for the problem solution or there is sometimes no practical way to create financial returns. In these cases, Impact Investment cannot provide support. Third, business models providing a solution for social problems are in an early stage that does not attract conventional investors yet and therefore offer opportunities for Impact Investors. Fourth, the engagement of the private sector in solving social problems has to be supported by the government and society. In some societies, for instance, creating financial returns through supporting basic societal needs is not seen positively.

Since Impact Investing provides an opportunity to invest capital to create positive impacts as well as financial returns, it broadens the group of supporters who contribute to social initiatives and problem solving. The blended approach allows one to go beyond a small group of philanthropists and to engage investors who would otherwise focus their funds in areas that prioritize financial returns. Consequently, Impact Investment may be able to use capital more efficiently than philanthropy through generating financial returns in addition to the social return. It uses the leveraging effect of loans, investments, and other financial products to enhance its impact. For institutional investors, Impact Investing offers the opportunity to connect their mission with their asset management. An environmental organization, for instance, will be able to invest their endowments in fields with positive environmental impacts instead of conventional portfolios that may be invested in sectors detrimental to the environmental organization's goals. However, in order to enable institutional investors to become active in Impact Investing, particularly risk and return measurement in Impact Investing should be compatible with those applied in conventional investing (Brandstetter & Lehner, 2015).

Finally, Impact Investing considers both the ability and willingness of a borrower or an investee to take responsibility for the achievement of the project or social enterprise's goals. It integrates the creation of positive social impacts into business decision making and consequently fosters sustainable social and environmental innovations. Consequently, Impact Investing may become a new asset class that is independent from conventional assets and one that is therefore a valuable alternative for investors' portfolios.

Impact Investors

This section will present the current players in the field of Impact Investing. The main groups of Impact Investors are asset owners including foundations, high-net-worth individuals, and banks, as well as institutional investors and asset managers such as pension funds, asset management firms, and other financial institutions (Geobey & Harji, 2014). Different types of investors, however, have different motives to engage in Impact Investing. While bigger banks and financial institutions may see Impact Investment as a new business opportunity and a value driver (Weber, 2005), others such as foundations see Impact Investing as a way to leverage their investments compared with only granting donations to create a positive societal or environmental impact. A third group are innovators that try to explore new ways of social innovations and social entrepreneurship.

The Royal Bank of Canada (RBC), for instance, provides an example of a conventional bank that is engaging in impact finance. In 2012, RBC announced $20 million in commitments to both a new social and environmental initiative and Impact Investment. The initiative is comprised of a $10-million capital fund dedicated to finance projects by organizations and entrepreneurs working on social and environmental issues. The fund invests in projects that promote environmental sustainability including water resource management and provide employment opportunities for youth and newcomers to Canada. Another $10 million is planned to be invested by the RBC Foundation into SRI funds.

RBC's CEO explains this engagement in the following way:

> We've been waiting for the right moment to launch a program of this nature, and the moment is now. We are confident that our initial investment of $10 million in the RBC Impact Fund will not only spark entrepreneurship and innovation in Canada, but also catalyze similar investments from others in the business community. We are also proud to put our money where our values are by investing an additional $10 million of our own funds through the RBC Foundation in socially and environmentally screened funds.
>
> *(Royal Bank of Canada, 2012)*

This example suggests that Impact Investment is gaining momentum in the financial industry. Of the 154 organizations that have been members of the GIIN in 2013, 12 have been conventional banks such as Citi Group, Goldman Sachs, Morgan Stanley, Robecco, RBC, and UBS that conduct some Impact Investment. In these cases the ratio of Impact Investment compared to conventional investment is rather small and Impact Investment is not included in the core business.

The spectrum of Impact Investing

As presented above, there is a broad spectrum of Impact Investing with respect to the emphasis on financial or social returns. Conventional finance is located on one end of a spectrum, and conventional non-profit investment such as donations or grants (Meehan, Kilmer, & O'Flanagan, 2004) are located on the other end. social banking, Impact Investing, and microfinance take into account both social and financial returns and consequently are located in the middle of the scale (see Figure 6.1). Thus, the main distinction of Impact Investing compared to conventional investing is the use of financial products and services as a way to achieve a positive impact on society, the environment, and sustainable development.

Compared to donations, charity, or philanthropy, Impact Investing has some benefits. Obviously, Impact Investing provides financial returns in addition to social impacts. It provides the opportunity to invest capital in order to create societal impacts combined with financial returns and opens the field to investors that rely on financial returns or that strive to leverage their investments. Additionally, Impact Investment is able to use capital more efficiently than philanthropy because invested funds will be paid back or even create an additional financial return. Therefore, Impact Investment is able to leverage the effect of capital investments, loans, and other financial services dedicated to social impacts. Furthermore, Impact Investing supports the financial feasibility of social or environmental projects or enterprises. Finally, Impact Investing acknowledges both the ability and willingness of a borrower or a project to take responsibility for the achievement of the project's or social enterprise's goals. It integrates social enterprises and projects into the economic system and hence creates sustainable social and environmental innovations.

With regard to the financial aspect it seems that Impact Investing may become a new asset class that may be independent or negatively correlated to conventional assets and therefore may become a valuable alternative for investors' portfolios. Let us demonstrate the innovative power of Impact Investing by having a look at the example of Social Impact Bonds (SIBs), an Impact Investment product that fosters public–private partnerships.

SIBs are government bonds that raise private capital that can be deployed to create improvements in the social system that, in turn, brings about cost savings. They link financial returns to the achievement of a social outcome. SIBs are applicable, for instance, to

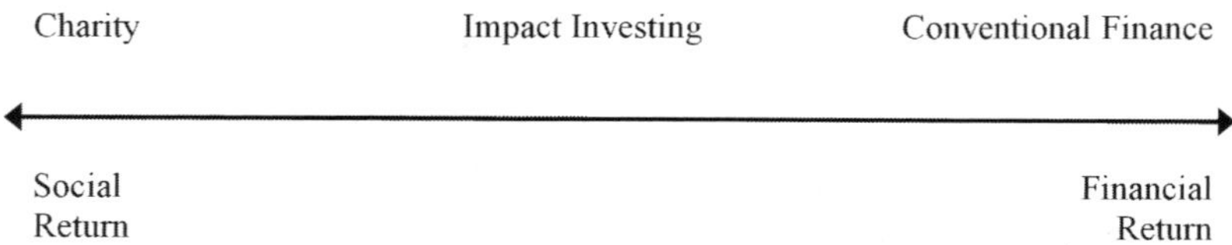

Figure 6.1 The spectrum of charity, social finance, Impact Investment and microfinance, and conventional finance

finance a social enterprise that supports the re-integration of long-term non-employed into the labor market. The government selects an institution, ensuring a high success rate. The project is then financed by private investors, whose return depends on the success of the re-integration program and the government's cost savings from lower unemployment rates. Such a project is particularly attractive during economic downturns because it provides financial returns for addressing the negative impacts of economic recession. Therefore, SIBs are innovative and offer financial returns in times of low returns of conventional investments. SIBs have been tested successfully in the UK (Mulgan, Reeder, Aylott, & Bo'sher, 2011) to prevent adult reoffending.

With regard to the future development of Impact Investing, the Monitor Institute estimated that Impact Investing in the United States in 2007 alone totaled $26 billion. Because of both innovative approaches and becoming a new asset class, the report suggests that Impact Investment will account for 1 percent of total global investments in 2018. This equals $500 billion globally and is higher than the total amount of philanthropic giving in the United States to date.

Impact Investing is a rather heterogeneous field. Therefore, the question remains as to what categories can be deployed to describe Impact Investing and Impact Investors. One characteristic that can be applied to classify Impact Investors is for-profit vs. not-for-profit. One group of Impact Investors entails for-profit organizations. They invest in order to achieve a financial return in addition to the social return, and consequently focus on the business case of Impact Investing. In contrast to conventional investors, however, for-profit Impact Investors mainly focus on achieving a social impact. An example for a for-profit Impact Investor focusing on frontier markets is Sarona Asset Management (Exhibit 6.1).

Exhibit 6.1 Sarona Asset Management: Investing in frontier markets

Sarona is a private equity firm that invests growth capital in companies and private equity funds in frontier and emerging markets around the world. Their focus is on small- to mid-market companies meeting the growing needs of the rising middle class in emerging markets. Sarona's goal is to achieve superior returns by creating world-class companies employing highly progressive business strategies, and operating to the highest standards of business, ethical, social, and environmental excellence.

> Sarona's vision is to be a leader in an industry where private capital is deployed to encourage entrepreneurship and growth while having a significant positive impact on social communities and the environment.
>
> (http://www.saronafund.com/vision.php)

The firm wants to foster investments of private investors in profitable business opportunities of local entrepreneurs and service providers in developing economies. The social venture capital firm offers private limited partnership types of investments in private companies and manages private equity funds-of-funds with a focus on the small- to mid-market sector.

As Exhibit 6.1 demonstrates, Sarona combines social impact with a focus on poverty alleviation with attractive financial returns. It demonstrates that investing in funds in developing countries helps to create successful businesses, offering both sustainable development and financial return. The case demonstrates that a commercial approach to investments in developing countries is able to create both financial and social returns. Since an involvement of institutional investors into Impact Investment can increase its power significantly, products and services that offer financial returns similar to conventional investments are a way to involve institutional investors in Impact Investing.

The other big group of Impact Investors consists of non-profit organizations. Often they originally focused on philanthropic contribution. In order to leverage their grants, however, they have been using Impact Investing. The main impact fields these organizations invest in are the environment, microfinance, health, job creation, and community development in industrialized, emerging, and developing countries (Monitor Institute, 2009). Currently, well-known foundations such as the Rockefeller Foundation or the Bill and Melinda Gates Foundation engage in Impact Investing.

The Global Impact Investing Network

The GIIN (see https://www.thegiin.org) is the main association for Impact Investors. It is a not-for-profit organization dedicated to increasing the scale and effectiveness of Impact Investing and to attract capital to alleviate poverty and find solutions for environmental problems. It has been sponsored by Rockefeller Philanthropy Advisors and other contributors. The formation of the network was officially announced in 2009. Its members are asset owners, asset managers, and service providers active in Impact Investment.

In 2014, 83 members were asset owners, 74 were asset managers, and 53 of GIIN's members were service providers. Among their members are foundations such as the Bill and Melinda Gates Foundation, banks such as J.P. Morgan, commercial Impact Investors such as SARONA Asset Management, and service providers such as Mercer. Investments are made in different types of investees such as microfinance institutions, social enterprises, and educational and health care projects, or in funds providing capital for these types of projects and enterprises.

GIIN members conduct Impact Investing from different perspectives and follow different goals. As mentioned above, a significant group conducts Impact Investing for profit and thus creates both social and financial return. Another type of Impact Investment organizations focuses on poverty reduction, development, or microfinance in developing countries. Some institutions strive to provide access to financial services for non-served or underserved people at the bottom of the socio-economic pyramid. These different approaches demonstrate the variety of Impact Investing and they show that, for instance, providing access to banking services can be an Impact Investing focus in certain regions or countries when it seems rather conventional in others.

Consequently, the missions of Impact Investors are manifold. Some of them center on industrialized countries by focusing on improving the life situation or education for children in the United States, such as the Annie E. Casey Foundation, W. K. Kellogg Foundation, and Packard Foundation. Others focus on community development, such as Deutsche Bank and Gray Ghost Ventures. A few of the Impact Investors try to change the way financial services are offered. For example, Armonia uses the triple bottom-line concept (Schaltegger & Burritt, 2010) as an investment criterion, and the Capricorn Investment Group conducts ethical, fair, and long-term investments. Shorebank International strives for an inclusive global financial system, and another investment topic is the environment. Wolfensohn & Company, for instance, focuses on low-carbon energy solutions, and the Rockefeller Foundation aims to contribute to strengthening resilience to environmental challenges.

Impact Investors offer products and services to meet their missions and targets. As expected, most of them offer investments, either in the form of funds, such as Capricorn Investment and Triodos Investments Management, or direct investments, such as Gray Ghost Ventures and IGNIA. Some of these investments focus on developing countries (e.g., Acumen Fund) and microfinance (e.g., ACCION), and others focus on domestic issues in industrialized countries (e.g., W. K. Kellogg Foundation). In addition to equity, Impact Investors use loans as their financing means. Loans are granted for both domestic and international projects and enterprises. Examples of loan-providing GIIN member organizations are the Dutch DOEN Foundation and the Packard Foundation. Various Impact Investors provide grants or guarantees as well, mostly in addition to other products and services, but also as a stand-alone service.

Opportunities and challenges of Impact Investing

Impact Investing is a relatively new phenomenon. It is still in its development phase. Therefore, it is connected with a number of opportunities and challenges. The future will show how Impact Investors will be able to manage them. The opportunities and challenges of Impact Investing are presented in Table 6.1.

Let us have a look at the opportunities first. The financial return of Impact Investing depends mainly on the success of the enterprises and projects—in other words, the success of the investees. While Impact Investing in industrialized countries often focuses on social enterprises and projects with a particular social or environmental mission, in developing countries injecting financial capital in various types of "conventional" businesses may have a positive impact. This is grounded in the inefficiency of the market in many developing countries. Often the main missing constituent for businesses becoming successful is financial capital. Consequently, investments in somewhat conventional businesses in developing countries can have a positive social impact with respect to creating jobs or helping to fulfill basic needs such as communication or transport. Connected with a significant increase of GDP in many developing countries, Impact Investments in these countries are able to achieve attractive social and financial returns.

With respect to environmental issues, Green Bonds are seen as a new way to attract investors to invest in bonds with a positive environmental impact. In addition to investing in green or climate-friendly projects, they offer financial returns similar to conventional bonds. Exhibit 6.2 describes the concept of Green Bonds.

Table 6.1 Opportunities and challenges of Impact Investing

Opportunities	*Challenges*
Financial returns	Efficiency with respect to impact assessment processes
Effective solution for environmental and societal challenges	Infrastructure
	Number of investable projects
Track record that demonstrates success	Challenges that cannot be solved by Impact Investing
	Defining impact assessment

Exhibit 6.2 Green Bonds

Broadly defined, Green Bonds are fixed-income securities that raise capital for a project or for a number of projects with particular environmental benefits. Often these environmental benefits are connected with climate change mitigation or adaptation. Green Bonds do play a role not only in project finance but also in corporate finance. They mainly address the needs of institutional investors who need investment-grade bonds.

A study of the issuance of Green Bonds found that the value of outstanding bonds in 2013 was USD 346 billion, a significant increase compared to 2012. In 2014 alone Green Bonds with a total value of $37 billion were issued. The market is dominated by bonds related to transport, followed by energy and finance. Other, significantly smaller sectors include buildings and industry, agriculture and forestry, and waste and pollution control. Nearly 80 percent of Green Bonds are government backed. A major issuer of Green Bonds is the World Bank. Recently, however, private issuers such as Toronto Dominion, HSBC, SEB, Unilever, EDF, and GDF Suez have issued Green Bonds, as well as the public institutions Export Development Canada and Korea Exim Bank.

In order to improve the transparency of Green Bonds, the Green Bonds Principles were issued in 2013 and have since been signed by a number of investment banks and other bond issuers. The Principles offer a guideline for the use of proceeds, the project evaluation and selection process, the management of the proceeds, and reporting. They do not define what types of investments are eligible for Green Bonds. However, they provide an incomplete list of the kinds of projects that would meet their criteria. These are:

- Renewable energy
- Energy efficiency (including efficient buildings)
- Sustainable waste management
- Sustainable land use (including sustainable forestry and agriculture)
- Biodiversity conservation
- Clean transportation
- Clean water and/or drinking water. (See http://www.ceres.org/greenbondprinciples)

Given that many Green Bonds issuances to date tend to be oversubscribed and that the Green Bond market is growing significantly, though their total ratio compared to the global bond market is still small, Green Bonds seem to be an appropriate tool for financing sustainable projects and could be a means to help mitigate climate change and create a sustainable future (Mathews, Kidney, Mallon, & Hughes, 2010). Furthermore, they offer investment opportunities for institutional Impact Investors that rely on standard financial return rates and try to mitigate the carbon exposure of their investment portfolios.

In addition to providing efficient and innovative solutions for societal and environmental problems, Impact Investing offers a convincing track record. Because of the effort of the Impact Reporting and Investment Standards (IRIS), a number of Impact Investors report about their businesses and investments in a transparent and reliable way. Consequently, not only financial returns but environmental and social returns can be tracked. Asset managers have the opportunity to use IRIS to report about their impacts in a way that stakeholders including investors have the information they need to make their decisions.

Nevertheless, as the second column of Table 6.1 indicates, there are also challenges for Impact Investing. First, social and environmental rating procedures that are needed to assess the financial and the societal impact of investments are still relatively inefficient and costly. Concepts such as the theory of change (Jackson, 2013), Social Return on Investment (Millar & Hall, 2012; Rotheroe & Richards, 2007), or the Impact Reporting and Investment Standards (https://iris.thegiin.org) provide ways to measure impacts but are still relatively complex and expensive. Furthermore, approaches that are able to compare Impact Investments across different types of impacts, such as assessing social value creation (Kroeger & Weber, 2014), are still in their infancy and are rather discussed academically than being implemented on the practitioners' level. Consequently, different authors express demands for compatibility in assessing risks and returns of Impacts Investments with conventional assessment procedures (Brandstetter & Lehner, 2015). Second, the infrastructure that is needed to invest efficiently in businesses is often missing. In developing countries, for instance, infrastructure that is required to conduct businesses successfully is often not developed. Consequently, financed projects are not conducted efficiently and sometimes are not able to create the expected societal and financial returns. Third, there is a lack of projects to invest in because many impact projects are exposed to high financial risks or do not deliver financial returns that are attractive for Impact Investors. An example for financial risks connected with Impact Investing delivers the case of Shore Bank that invested in social housing but was hit by financial risks arising from the last financial crisis (Post & Wilson, 2011). Fourth, some societal and environmental challenges may only be solved by activities that do not offer any kind of financial return and thus will never be targeted by Impact Investors. Fifth, as the market grows, the task of clearly defining Impact Investment and distinguishing between Impact Investment and conventional investment becomes more difficult. There is a risk that Impact Investing dilutes their mission in case of financial success similar to the mission drift in microfinance (Mersland & Strøm, 2010). It seems that, in some cases, microfinance has left the poverty alleviation approach in favor of higher financial returns and in order to attract investors. Finally, additional indicators are needed to measure the social return of Impact Investing in a way that enables comparisons between alternatives on the one hand and the calculation of the social cost-benefit ratio (Jalan & Ravallion, 2003; Sadik, 1978) on the other hand. Otherwise, Impact Investing bears the risk of feel-good rather than do-good investing (Monitor Institute, 2009), similar to the phenomenon of green washing (Laufer, 2003).

The impact of Impact Investing

The GIIN (https://www.thegiin.org) mentions food and agriculture, healthcare, education, housing, energy, water and sanitation, and IT and communication technologies as main impact sectors. Broader societal categories to create impacts are:

- economic linkages, financial inclusion, and empowerment;
- consumer protection and pricing transparency;
- crime, safety, justice, and human rights;
- poverty and income;
- nutrition and fitness;
- resource conservation and environmental protection;
- climate change;
- arts and culture.

It seems that the impact sectors are quite well aligned with main sustainability goals such as valuing the environment, mitigating and adapting to climate change, ensuring more equitable wealth distribution, improving food and water supply and distribution systems, and enhancing healthcare (Barbier, 2011; Rogers, Kazi, & Boyd, 2008). However, the question of how to assess the impact of investments in the different fields and how to compare impacts between fields still remains open.

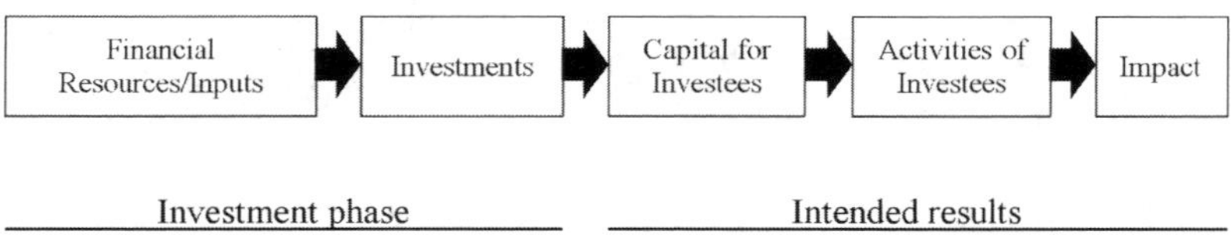

Figure 6.2 Theory of change for Impact Investment

Assessing impacts

To be able to assess impacts in the listed sectors and societal issues, impact measurement methods are needed. These methods include theory of change (Jackson, 2013), the development of output, outcome, and impact indicators (Antadze & Westley, 2012; Nicholls, 2009; Weber, 2013), quantitative and qualitative indicators (O'Dwyer, Owen, & Unerman, 2011), social cost-benefit analysis (Bebbington, Brown, & Frame, 2007; Harberger, 1984), social value creation (Kroeger & Weber, 2014), and the Social Return on Investment methodology (Millar & Hall, 2012; Nicholls, Lawlor, Neitzert, & Goodspeed, 2012; SIMPACT Strategy Group, 2009).

Generally, the measurement of impacts needs a deep understanding of causes and effects as well as a clear definition of goals. Therefore, authors such as Jackson (2013) propose to deploy the theory of change to understand and measure the effects of Impact Investing. The theory explains the creation of impacts by connecting them with the inputs, activities, outputs, and outcomes of Impact Investing. Figure 6.2 presents a modified version of the theory of change presented by Jackson (2013) that was adapted to Impact Investing.

Let us apply the theory to an Impact Investor who invests in a social enterprise that offers apprenticeships for young adults who have problems finding jobs because of a drug addiction history. The example is presented in Exhibit 6.3.

Exhibit 6.3 Social Capital Partners: Investing in accessible employment for those at a disadvantage (see http://www.socialcapitalpartners.ca/about-us.html)

SCP started their activities in 2001 with facilitating access to financing and providing advisory services for building social enterprises. The next step was the creation of a Community Employment Loan program in 2006. Instead of helping to build social enterprises, SCP engaged conventional private sector players to achieve greater social impacts and scale than could be achieved through social enterprises. SCP has been offering access to subordinate debt financing for franchisees and small business owners. Loan rates are tied directly to employment outcomes; for every person hired through an employment service provider, the interest rate on the loan is reduced. Consequently, higher social impacts are connected with more attractive financial conditions for the commercial borrower.

In 2010 SCP realized that many potential employers did not need a financial incentive to employ people with a disadvantage. Instead they were looking for an institution taking the role of an employment and training provider. Consequently, since 2012 SCP collaborates with both job seekers and employers for designing, delivering, and evaluating training and development programs.

The theory of change defines resources (inputs) and investments as parts of the financial activities during the investment phase and connects them with outputs (financial capital for investees), outcomes (activities of investees), and impacts. We will describe these components and their connections in detail in this section.

In Impact Investing, resources and inputs are financial. In contrast to many social enterprises, Impact Investors are not directly involved in creating impacts. Usually, investees such as social enterprises or projects create the impacts. The indirectness of impacts applies for the whole financial sector and for both positive and negative impacts (Weber, 2014a). Activities in the Impact Investment sector are focused on finding and assessing investees and to set up financial products and services that meet the needs of social enterprises, projects, or other investees that create positive impact. Usually, these types of activities are relatively complex tasks for Impact Investors. In addition to analyzing the financial viability of the investee, the investor has to analyze the social and environmental impact. Therefore, Impact Investing usually has relatively high administrative costs (Weber, 2012), which makes it similar to microfinance in this regard (Cull, Demirgueç-Kunt, & Morduch, 2007).

With regard to the main output of Impact Investment, we can state that these are investments in the form of venture capital, loans, fund-of-funds, and other types of investments. Outcomes of these investments are the activities the investees perform. Investees are the first in the chain from resources to outcomes that are able to create a direct impact. Finally, the impact represents the change that has been created by the investment compared to what would have changed anyway.

Based on the theory of change, Best and Harji (2013) propose the following steps to assess the effect of Impact Investing that were amended by the author:

- Value definition: Social impact goals and financial investment parameters and objectives are identified.
- Due diligence: Selecting investees that fit with the Impact Investing goals.
- Investment: Selecting the type of investment products that fits best to the investment goal and to the investee (e.g., non-profits will be financed by loans, social enterprises may need equity).
- Monitoring: Continuous evaluation to analyze whether the social impact goals are being achieved and whether the investment is financially sustainable.
- Reporting: Communicating the impact and financial returns to stakeholders using financial indicators from systems such as IRIS (https://iris.thegiin.org), Social Return on Investment (Nicholls et al., 2012), or by applying the concept of social value creation (Kroeger & Weber, 2014).
- Ongoing measurement: Measuring impact after the investment is closed to evaluate the net present value of the investment and to explore the future drop-off of the project representing the reduction of impact over time.

While trying to develop impact measurement indicators as fast as possible, it is critical to understand the *validity* of impact measurements—that is, whether or not the measurements are a true reflection of the impact and whether they are indicators of short-term or long-term success. Impact Investments often strive for a significant positive change that is long term. But what does "significant" mean in this regard? For example, if a program that has the goal to decrease youth unemployment changes the unemployment rate in a certain region from 55 percent to 50 percent, the impact may be significant but the general situation is still poor. The same is valid for long-term effects. If, for instance, the unemployment rate increases immediately after the

Impact Investment is spent, a long-term effect could not be created and the Impact Investment does not have a long-term Social Return on Investment.

Consequently, Impact Investment measures should be transparent and standardized. Only if different investments are comparable with respect to their positive and negative short- and long-term effects will it be possible to make a rational decision that does not rely on nicely told case studies and narratives but on rational indicators.

Results from ImpactAssets50

In order to give some insights into the characteristics of Impact Investors and their focus, we present data gathered from ImpactAssets50 (http://www.impactassets.org). The annually updated database illustrates what types of Impact Investments exist. The 50 firms have been selected to demonstrate the wide range of, and the state of the art in, Impact Investing. Among the fulfillment of other criteria, members of, the database have more than 3 years of experience in Impact Investment, have at least $10 million in assets under management, and measure their social and environmental impact. Though not being representative, the database gives a good overview about the different types of Impact Investments and their goals. The members of ImpactAssets50 and their managed assets are presented in Table 6.2.

As Figure 6.3 demonstrates, 14 of the 50 Impact Investors manage assets higher than $250 million. Assets between $100 and $249 million are managed by 10 Impact Investors, assets between $51 and $99 million are managed by 11 Impact Investors, and 10 manage between $26 and $50 million. The five smaller firms manage assets between $10 and $25 million. The figures

Table 6.2 ImpactAssets50 members and their managed assets

Name	*Assets in million dollars*
Accion	100–249
Acumen	51–99
Alterfin	51–99
Bamboo Finance	>250
BAML Capital Access Funds Management	>250
Blue Orchard Finance	>250
Calvert Foundation	>250
Community Reinvestment Fund	>250
Core Innovation Capital	26–50
Craft3	100–249
DBL Investors	100–249
EcoEnterprises Fund	26–50
Ecosystem Integrity Fund	51–99
Ecotrust Forest Management	51–99
Elevar Equity	100–249
Farmland LP	51–99
Global Partnerships	51–99
Grameen Foundation	10–25
Grassroots Business Fund	51–99
Habitat for Humanity International	26–50
Huntington Capital	100–249
Incofin Investment Management	>250
Insitor Management	26–50

Investisseurs & Partenaires	51–99
Iroquois Valley Farms	10–25
LeapFrog Investments	>250
Living Cities	26–50
MCE Social Capital	26–50
Media Development Investment Fund	26–50
Medical Credit Fund	10–25
MicroVest Capital	>250
Oikocredit US	26–50
Pacific Community Ventures	51–99
Renewal Funds	51–99
Responsibility Investments AG	>250
Root Capital	51–99
RSF Social Finance	100–249
Sarona Asset Management	100–249
Shared Interest	10–25
SJF Ventures	100–249
Small Enterprise Assistance Funds	>250
Symbiotics SA	>250
The Lyme Timber Company	100–249
The Reinvestment Fund	>250
Treetops Capital	100–249
Triodos Investment Management	>250
UNICEF Bridge Fund	26–50
Unitus Impact Partners	10–25
Vital Capital Fund	>250
Vox Capital	26–50

Source: Based on http://impactassets.org.

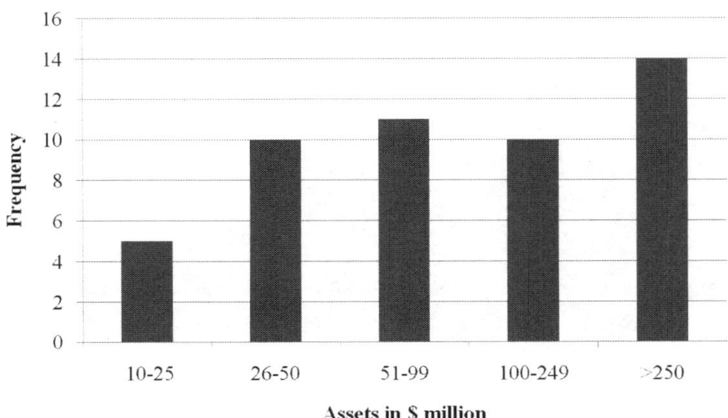

Figure 6.3 Assets under management in million dollars

demonstrate that the majority of Impact Investors manage relatively small assets compared to conventional asset management.

Figure 6.4 demonstrates that private debt (N = 32) and private equity (N = 34) are the main asset classes in Impact Investing. In the figure, frequencies can be higher than 50 because the 50

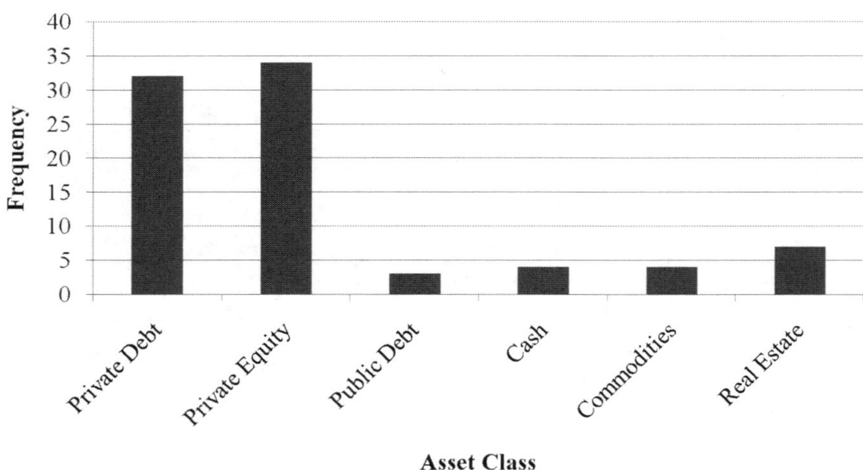

Figure 6.4 Impact Investment asset classes

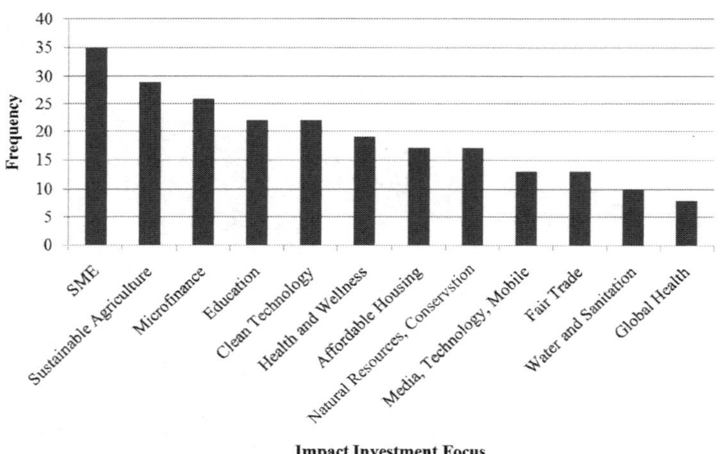

Figure 6.5 Impact Investment focus

Impact Investors may invest in more than one asset class or have more than one impact focus. Additional asset classes are public debt, cash, commodities, and real estate. The latter two are asset classes particularly deployed by investors focusing on affordable housing and sustainable agriculture.

The Impact Investment focus is presented in Figure 6.5. Similar to social banks, Impact Investors do not focus exclusively on the financial returns of the sector they are investing in but on the impact they can achieve. Consequently, 35 Impact Investors mention SMEs as investment objects. Sustainable agriculture (N = 29), microfinance (N = 26), education (N = 22), and clean technologies (N = 22) are sectors that were mentioned more than 20 times. The next group of impact sectors are those mentioned between 10 and 20 times. They are health and wellness (N = 19), affordable housing (N = 17), natural resources and conservation (N = 17), media and mobile technology (N = 13), fair trade (N = 13), and water and sanitation (N = 10). Investments in global health are conducted by eight Impact Investors.

The data suggest that Impact Investors focus on the main global sustainability issues such as natural capital, environmental issues, ensuring equitable wealth distribution, improving food and water supply and distribution systems, and enhancing healthcare (Barbier, 2011; Rogers et al., 2008).

Bugg-Levine and Emerson (2011) see future fields of Impact Investing in healthcare, affordable housing in emerging markets, education, agriculture, distributed utilities—particularly based on renewable energy—and restructured social spending. Since public budgets for social and environmental issues are shrinking, Impact Investing may step into this gap and finance some of these issues. There is a risk, however, that governments rely on Impact Investors instead of solving social and environmental problems with public monies. This could lead to situations in which only those problems will be solved that provide attractive financial returns for Impact Investors. On the other side, healthcare, affordable housing, agriculture, and distributed utilities may be sectors that are financially attractive as well and consequently will attract Impact Investors offering innovative solutions.

Conclusion

Impact Investing focuses on investments that create both financial and social returns. Consequently, it can achieve goals that neither pure philanthropic grants nor conventional investors can attain. This goal is creating a positive social impact and financial returns at the same time. Thus, Impact Investment complements SRI as a form of asset management that does not only take financial indicators into consideration but also social and environmental indicators. Theoretically, it is based on the concepts of blended returns and shared value promoted by Emerson (2003) and Porter and Kramer (2011).

Currently, Impact Investors come from many different origins. Originally, most of them descended from foundations that tried to leverage their impact through financial products and services such as loans, investments, and guarantees. At present, in addition to foundations and specialized "boutique" Impact Investors, also conventional banks and financial service providers have been integrating Impact Investment into their product portfolio.

As studies show, Impact Investors focus on poverty alleviation, job creation and mitigation of unemployment, healthcare, environmental issues, education, and affordable housing. Products and services they deploy are private and public debt, private equity, cash, commodities, and real estate. Many Impact Investors manage assets higher than $250 million, but there are also smaller players with assets under $50 million. These figures demonstrate that Impact Investing is still taking place on a relatively small scale. Newer developments such as Green Bonds and Social Impact Bonds, however, seem to increase the total value of Impact Investments dramatically because they are often based on public–private partnerships that are attractive for both investors and public authorities. Future challenges in Impact Investing are the standardization of impact assessment (Brandstetter & Lehner, 2015; Kroeger & Weber, 2014), the definition of Impact Investment relative to conventional finance and investment, and determining the future role of Impact Investing in society.

References

Antadze, N., & Westley, F. R. (2012). Impact metrics for social innovation: Barriers or bridges to radical change? *Journal of Social Entrepreneurship, 3*(2), 133–150. doi:10.1080/19420676.2012.726005

Barbier, E. B. (2011). The policy challenges for green economy and sustainable economic development. *Natural Resources Forum, 35*(3), 233–245. doi:10.1111/j.1477-8947.2011.01397.x

Bebbington, J., Brown, J., & Frame, B. (2007). Accounting technologies and sustainability assessment models. *Ecological Economics, 61*(2–3), 224–236. doi:10.1016/j.ecolecon.2006.10.021

Best, H., & Harji, K. (2013). *Social impact measurement use among Canadian impact investors* (p. 52). Toronto: Purpose Capital.

Brandstetter, L., & Lehner, O. M. (2015). Opening the market for impact investments: The need for adapted portfolio tools. *Entrepreneurship Research Journal, 5*, 87–107.

Bugg-Levine, A., & Emerson, J. (2011). *Impact investing—Transforming how we make money while making a difference*. San Francisco: Jossey-Bass.

Canadian Task Force on Social Finance. (2010). *Mobilizing private capital for public good* (p. 40). Toronto: Canadian Task Force on Social Finance.

Cull, R., Demirgueç-Kunt, A., & Morduch, J. (2007). Financial performance and outreach: A global analysis of leading microbanks. *The Economic Journal, 117*(517), F107–F133. doi:10.1111/j.1468-0297.2007.02017.x

de Clerck, F. (2009). Ethical banking. In L. Zsolnai, Z. Boda, & L. Fekete (Eds.), *Ethical prospects—Economy, society, and environment* (pp. 209–227). Dordrecht: Springer.

Emerson, J. (2003). The blended value proposition: Integrating social and financial returns. *California Management Review, 45*(4), 35–51.

Geobey, S., & Harji, K. (2014). Social finance in North America. *Global Social Policy, 14*(2), 274–277. doi:10.1177/1468018114539864d

Geobey, S., & Weber, O. (2013). Lessons in operationalizing social finance: The case of Vancouver City Savings Credit Union. *Journal of Sustainable Finance & Investment, 3*(2), 124–137. doi:10.1080/20430795.2013.776259

Global Impact Investing Network. (2011). *Global Impact Investing Network*. Retrieved June 29, 2011, from https://www.thegiin.org

Harberger, A. C. (1984). Basic needs versus distributional weights in social cost-benefit analysis. *Economic Development and Cultural Change, 32*(3), 455–474.

Harji, K., & Hebb, T. (2009). *The quest for blended value returns: Investor perspectives on social finance in Canada* (p. 25). Ottawa: Carleton Centre for Community Innovation.

Jackson, E. T. (2013). Interrogating the theory of change: Evaluating impact investing where it matters most. *Journal of Sustainable Finance & Investment*, 1–16. doi:10.1080/20430795.2013.776257

Jalan, J., & Ravallion, M. (2003). Estimating the benefit incidence of an antipoverty program by propensity-score matching. *Journal of Business & Economic Statistics, 21*(1), 19–30. doi:10.1198/073500102288618720

Jones, J. F. (2010). Social finance: Commerce and community in developing countries. *International Journal of Social Economics, 37*(6), 415–428. doi:10.1108/03068291011042300

Kroeger, A., & Weber, C. (2014). Developing a conceptual framework for comparing social value creation. *Academy of Management Review, 39*(4), 513–540. doi:10.5465/amr.2012.0344

Laufer, W. S. (2003). Social accountability and corporate greenwashing. *Journal of Business Ethics, 43*(3), 253–261.

Mathews, J. A., Kidney, S., Mallon, K., & Hughes, M. (2010). Mobilizing private finance to drive an energy industrial revolution. *Energy Policy, 38*(7), 3263–3265. doi:10.1016/j.enpol.2010.02.030

Meehan, W. F. I., Kilmer, D., & O'Flanagan, M. (2004). Investing in society. *Stanford Social Innovation Review, 1*(4), 34–43.

Mersland, R., & Strøm, R. Ø. (2010). Microfinance mission drift? *World Development, 38*(1), 28–36. doi:10.1016/j.worlddev.2009.05.006

Millar, R., & Hall, K. (2012). Social return on investment (SROI) and performance measurement. *Public Management Review*, 1–19. doi:10.1080/14719037.2012.698857

Monitor Institute. (2009). *Investing for social and environmental impact* (p. 86). Cambridge, MA: Monitor Institute.

Mulgan, G., Reeder, N., Aylott, M., & Bo'sher, L. (2011). *Social impact investment: The challenge and opportunity of Social Impact Bonds* (p. 38). London: The Young Foundation.

Nicholls, A. (2009). We do good things, don't we? "Blended Value Accounting" in social entrepreneurship. *Accounting, Organizations and Society, 34*(6–7), 755–769. doi:10.1016/j.aos.2009.04.008

Nicholls, J., Lawlor, E., Neitzert, E., & Goodspeed, T. (2012). A guide to social return on investment (p. 108). SROI Network.

O'Dwyer, B., Owen, D., & Unerman, J. (2011). Seeking legitimacy for new assurance forms: The case of assurance on sustainability reporting. *Accounting, Organizations and Society, 36*(1), 31–52. doi:10.1016/j.aos.2011.01.002

Porter, M. E., & Kramer, M. R. (2011). Creating shared value. *Harvard Business Review, 89*(1/2), 62–77.

Post, J. E., & Wilson, F. S. (2011, Fall). Too good to fail? *Stanford Social Innovation Review*, 65–71.

Rogers, P. P., Kazi, F. J., & Boyd, J. A. (2008). *An introduction to sustainable development*. London: Earthscan.

Rotheroe, N., & Richards, A. (2007). Social return on investment and social enterprise: Transparent accountability for sustainable development. *Social Enterprise Journal, 3*(1), 31–48.

Royal Bank of Canada. (2012). *RBC Announces $20 Million in Commitments to New Social and Environmental Initiative*. Retrieved February 13, 2012, from http://www.rbc.com/newsroom/2012/0124-social-finance.html

Sadik, A.-K. T. (1978). A note on some practical limitations of social cost-benefit analysis measures. *World Development, 6*(2), 221–225. doi:10.1016/0305-750x(78)90009-8

Schaltegger, S., & Burritt, R. L. (2010). Sustainability accounting for companies: Catchphrase or decision support for business leaders? *Journal of World Business, 45*(4), 375–384. doi:10.1016/j.jwb.2009.08.002

SIMPACT Strategy Group. (2009). *Social return on investment (SROI) case studies—Investing to strengthen society* (p. 44). Calgary: SIMPACT Strategy Group.

Weber, O. (2005). Sustainability benchmarking of European banks and financial service organizations. *Corporate Social Responsibility and Environmental Management, 12*, 73–87.

Weber, O. (2012, May 29–June 1). *Financing nonprofits and social enterprises: Risks and opportunities*. Paper presented at the Fifth Annual ANSER Conference, Waterloo, ON.

Weber, O. (2013). Impact measurement in microfinance: Is the measurement of the social return on investment an innovation in microfinance? *Journal of Innovation Economics (Cairn), 11*, 149–171.

Weber, O. (2014a). The financial sector's impact on sustainable development. *Journal of Sustainable Finance & Investment, 4*(1), 1–8. doi:10.1080/20430795.2014.887345

Weber, O. (2014b). Social banking: Concept, definitions and practice. *Global Social Policy, 14*(2), 265–267. doi:10.1177/1468018114539864

Weber, O., & Remer, S. (2011). Social banking—Introduction. In O. Weber & S. Remer (Eds.), *Social banks and the future of sustainable finance* (pp. 1–14). London, UK: Routledge.

7

SOCIAL IMPACT INVESTING

A model and research agenda

Alessandro Rizzello, Maria Cristina Migliazza, Rosella Carè, and Annarita Trotta

Introduction

The growth in the Impact Investing market represents one of the most exciting financial trends of the last five years in which business strategies are directly linked to a social impact goal. The idea behind Impact Investing is that investors can pursue financial returns while also intentionally addressing social and environmental challenges (Bugg-Levine & Emerson, 2011).

Social impact finance is a promising concept for addressing pressing social issues by applying a holistic approach to value creation that combines financial return and social impact (Freireich & Fulton, 2009; Jackson, 2013b). The recipients of social investments "span multiple asset classes that include real estate, private equity, infrastructure, public equities and fixed income" (Hebb, 2013, p. 71). There is a common understanding that social impact investments could be an enormous market opportunity (Martin, 2013).

However, the amount of capital currently present in the global Social Impact Investing (SII) market is difficult to calculate (Nicholls, 2010b). This is because of several factors and barriers such as the variety of types of capital and investment mechanisms present in this space or the absence of a unified market or exchange platform for social investment (Mendell & Barbosa, 2013).

Currently, the market for Impact Investing is estimated to be from $1 trillion to $14 trillion when global infrastructure investments are included (Hebb, 2013; O'Donohoe, Leijonhufvud, Saltuk, Bugg-Levine, & Brandenburg, 2010).

Recently, there has been growing policy attention focused on financing social innovation. This growth is due to the ability of social entrepreneurs to solve societal problems (Bornstein, 2007; Nicholls, 2006) with their scalable approaches and to act as intermediaries between the public and private sectors in the provision of social welfare support (Lehner, 2011; Nicholls, 2010c).

There is increasing attention to this research field in academia. However, many questions lack adequate discussion as, for example, standard impact metrics, lack in investment track record, or the industry capacity to really deliver sustainable impacts (Evans, 2013; Jackson, 2013b; Warner, 2013). Höchstädter and Scheck (2014) note that "despite all this interest and activity, a uniform definition of Impact Investing is reportedly lacking (Eurosif, 2012) as is a clear understanding of what the term stands for (Mendell & Barbosa, 2013)" (p. 2). Finally, most of the literature comes from industry-based reports and only a few academic works related to this research field (Hebb, 2013).

Addressing this void in Impact Investing research, this chapter aims to explore the stance of existing studies on Impact Investing in order to clarify the concept and to identify focal points and trends, as well as inconsistencies and research gaps.

We perform a bibliometric analysis of the literature on the topic published in peer-reviewed scientific journals and recorded by the SSCI and a content analysis by using a map of keywords that permits classification of articles according to the covered issues (Noyons, Moed, & Luwel, 1999; Verbeek, Debackere, Luwel, & Zimmermann, 2002). A literature review would be appropriate if the topic was widely researched and recent review efforts resulted in findings not completely covering the field (Short, 2009). However, our work proposes an exploratory analysis aimed at covering the complete domain by using a bibliometric analysis.

This chapter contributes to the ongoing debate on social and sustainable finance by proposing a model that is suitable for understanding the dynamics of the SII industry and serving as a guide for scholars and practitioners.

Research design and methodological approach

The main aim of analyzing the intellectual structure of a specific research field is to provide researchers with: (i) a way to "locate" their research within the field and to identify potential new directions (Locke & Perera, 2001, p. 223), and (ii) a way to suggest possible future developments of a specific theme (Petticrew & Roberts, 2008).

In the past, literature reviews (especially systematic reviews) have been used in different ways in the social science fields and they are increasingly being used to support practice and policy and to direct new research efforts (Petticrew & Roberts, 2008, p. 23).

This methodological approach is considered appropriate if a topic has been previously explored and results in findings that are not completely covering the field (Petticrew & Roberts, 2008; Short, 2009).

The bibliometric approach is particularly useful.

Locke and Perera (2001, p. 224) explain why an overall view of the intellectual structure of a disciplinary area using a bibliometric approach provides additional perspectives to traditional reviews:

> (i) it allows a great number of researchers active in the area to "unselfconsciously" provide the data for the analysis, (ii) it does not depend on the reviewers' knowledge of the literature, and (iii) it allows a more extensive overview of the literature than that possible by other ways.

Cobo, López-Herrera, Herrera-Viedma, and Herrera (2011, p. 147) highlight some advantages related to bibliometric mapping:

> Science mapping or bibliometric mapping is a spatial representation of how disciplines, fields, specialties, and individual documents or authors are related to one another (Small, 1999). It is focused on monitoring a scientific field and delimiting research areas to determine its cognitive structure and its evolution.

Despite these advantages of bibliometric analysis, this methodological approach seems to be underutilized and an exception in finance studies. This implies that academia does not provide well-established and shared procedures, but it can be considered an incentive to realize studies that use these tools to verify if and how this method contributes to the comprehension of phenomena regarding the traditional literature reviews.

In the specific field of SII, Höchstädter and Scheck (2014) are the first scholars to investigate a large number of practitioners' works, highlighting areas of similarity, overlaps, and inconsistency. In contrast, our work starts from the academic point of view with the aim to explore the structure of the SII landscape provided by scholars.

Our contribution is to draw an instructional map for scholars with research interests in this field.

The work follows the methodology proposed by Furrer, Thomas, and Goussevskaia (2008) in order to perform a bibliometric analysis and to obtain a Multiple Correspondence Analysis (MCA). MCA is an exploratory data analysis without any restrictive assumptions and it fits well with our descriptive research purpose.

More specifically this work aims: (i) to graphically map the intellectual structure and the evolution of Impact Investing research and related fields, subfields, and relationships; (ii) to debate current findings and identify the links between causes, effects, stakeholders, and key qualitative-quantitative variables involved in the Impact Investing cycle; and (iii) to design a set of themes meriting further investigation from researchers in future studies and to provide some conclusions and implications about further developments in the research agenda.

This study contains a bibliometric analysis of the literature published in peer-reviewed scientific journals and a content analysis using a map of keywords that permits classification of articles according to the covered issues (Noyons et al., 1999; Verbeek et al., 2002). To achieve these objectives, the research design is structured in four steps.

First, the work uses a process of "literature identification" by selecting articles to analyze. As discussed by Cobo et al. (2011), "there are several online bibliographic (and also bibliometric) databases where scientific works are stored" (p. 1383), and, undoubtedly, the most important are ISI WoS, Scopus, and Google Scholar.

In particular, we consider that the use of an open dataset (e.g., Google Scholar) enables an increased scale and scope and a greater collection of materials.

Considering the explorative nature of our study of this emergent research area, we have not considered only the most important journals of the field, in contrast with the study of Furrer et al. (2008), but we decided to use the following databases for the investigation: ISI WoS, Scopus, and Google Scholar, considering all journals.

The same search criteria were used for all databases. With respect to time period, we selected the algorithm "every year." Database analyses were performed on August 31, 2014 and included all works published as of that date. Search strings have been built by analyzing the keywords provided by authors and journal databases. Therefore, we decided to develop an initial list of major keywords by iteratively sorting the individual keywords and regrouping them into coherent categories and strings. The advanced search terms were grouped into 60 different search strings. The search covers only papers published in international scientific journals, as they are considered "certified knowledge." Fernandez-Alles and Ramos-Rodríguez (2009) explain: "This is the term commonly used to describe knowledge that has been submitted to the critical review of fellow researchers and has succeeded in gaining their approval" (p. 163).

An analysis of the results allowed us to detect, as expected, a large overlap among the three databases. The greater number of results is attributable to Google Scholar, which also returned results that were not a perfect match with the search expression because of its search for algorithmic structure (Mikki, 2009). All articles obtained were analyzed to verify relevance by analysis of the abstracts. This procedure reduced the number of results related to our research topic to more than 3,000. After removing the overlaps resulting from the use of the same keywords in multiple databases, 50 significant academic results were identified and serve as the basis for the present work.

By following the conceptual and methodological approach proposed by Furrer et al. (2008), in the second step a "recoding process" was carried out in order to match new macro keywords to the selected papers. The process of coding and the creation of a list of new keywords were necessary for two reasons (Furrer et al., 2008): (i) "the large number of idiosyncratic keywords provided by the authors and journal databases" (p. 5), and (ii) the presence, in our sample, of some papers without keywords.

We drafted a list of major keywords and then we grouped them into macro keywords.

To improve the reliability of our study, we decided to involve in our research some independent experts (academics or professionals) to obtain, through several rounds of discussion with these experts, a final list of major keywords (Box 7.1). Later we associated one or more of the 21 final new macro keywords with each paper (Table 7.1).

We decided to allocate each paper to one or more keywords to capture the interdisciplinary field (Furrer et al., 2008; Inkpen & Beamish, 1994). The matching was carried out considering at the same time the content of the abstract, the keywords, and the body of the article.

As suggested by the methodological approach provided by Furrer et al. (2008), three members of the research team independently coded all the papers with the main aim of ensuring better allocation of all articles.

In the third step, we computed an MCA in order to summarize the intellectual structure of the field. To do this, we defined a "units × variables" data matrix where units are represented by papers and variables by keywords codified through a complete disjunctive coding. With the aim of providing a better picture of the field, we performed the same procedure (with the same data matrix), not only by variables, but also by observations. Figures 7.1 and 7.2 summarize the positions on the map of macro keywords and authors.

The analyses were performed using XLSTAT, a statistical software suite for Microsoft Excel.

Then, using content analysis, the academic contributions were analyzed with the purpose of understanding the contextual use of the words or content. After a preliminary analysis of all works, we underlined some important aspects of various definitions of SII.

Finally, in the fourth step, we debated the main findings, proposed a model for better understanding the SII landscape, and pointed out a set of themes meriting investigation in future studies.

Table 7.1 Macro keywords and related academic works

Macro keywords	*Related terms*	*No. of related works*
Impact Invest⋆ sectors	Impact Invest⋆ sectors (e.g., health, pediatrics, preventive health, criminal justice, criminology, probation service, criminal justice incentives, crime control, prisons, recidivism, crime-control efforts, poverty, poverty reduction, education, job growth)	22
Responsible Invest⋆	Responsible Invest⋆, Responsible Invest⋆ Strategies	5
Financial Markets and Instruments	Financial Markets, Primary Markets, Secondary Markets, Crowdfunding, Exchange Platform, Financial Innovations (e.g., innovative financial investment models), Financial Instruments (e.g., asset classes)	10
Microfinance	Microfinance, Microcredit, Microfinance Institutions, Financial Inclusions	4
New Public Management	New Public Management, New Public Governance, Managerialism, Public–Private Partnership	6
Pay for Success	Pay for Success, Pay for Success Models	5
Impact Evaluation	Evaluation, Measurement, Impact Evaluation, Impact Measurement	8

(Continued)

Table 7.1 Macro keywords and related academic works *(Continued)*

Macro keywords	*Related terms*	*No. of related works*
SRI	SRI, Social Responsible Invest,* Socially Responsible Invest*	4
Investment Screening and Targeted Investment	Investment Screening, Positive Screening, Negative Screening, Ethical Policy Screenings, Economically Targeted Investment (ETI), Targeted Investment Markets, Targeted Invest,* Cause-Based Invest*	8
Social Finance	Social Finance, Social Finance Market, Social Finance Practices, Social Finance Providers, Social Finance Portfolio, Developmental Social Finance, Social Finance Industry, Social Finance Intermediaries, Social Finance Funds, Social Finance Community, Social Finance Projects, Social Finance Program, Social Return	13
Impact Entrepreneurship	Third Sector, Mission-Based Businesses, Not-for-Profit Organizations, Co-operatives, Not-for-Profit Initiatives, Not-for-Profit Business, Not-for-Profit Sector, Not-for-Profit Social Enterprises, No Profit Sector, No Profit Organizations, Fourth Sector, Benefit Corporations (e.g., B Corps, Certified B Corporations, Benefit-Corp, Benefit-Corp status, B (Benefit) Corporation), Social Enterprises (e.g., Social Enterprises, SEs, Social Enterprise, SE, Social Entrepreneurship, Social Entrepreneurs, Social Entrepreneurship, Social Enterprise Invest*)	11
Philanthropy	Philanthropic Capital, Philanthropic Toolbox, Philanthropic Activities, Philanthropic Community, Philanthropists, Philanthropic Organizations, Philanthrocapitalism (e.g., Creative Capitalism, Philanthrocapitalism, New Economy, Philanthro-capitalism)	6
*Sustainable Invest**	Sustainable Invest*, Sustainable Investment Assets, Sustainable Financial Return	5
Social Outcome	Social Outcome, Social Outcome Measurement, Outcome-Based Financial Tool, Outcome-Based Funding Models, Outcome-Based Contract	5
Payment by Results	Payment by Results, Payment by Results Models	9
Social Policy	Social Services, Social Work, Social Policy, Social Inclusion Policy, Public Policy	5
Politics of Austerity	Austerity, Politics of Austerity, Government Austerity, Austerity Measures, Economic Austerity	3
*Social Invest**	Social Invest*, Socially Conscious Invest*	4
Investment Decision	Portfolio Theory, Investor Return, Investor Behavior, Investment Decision Making, Investment Strategy	6
*Impact Invest**	Impact Investment, Impact Investing, Impact Investor	29

Invest* = Investment, Investing, Investor.

Development of the research field: Analysis and results

Development of the research field: An overview

To understand the future of Impact Investing research, it is important to provide a historical perspective on the origins of the observed changes and evolutions in the development of the field.

Our sample collection includes 50 academic papers. We identified authors whose articles appeared most frequently in our collection. The articles of our sample have been written by 77 authors. According to Furrer et al. (2008) we identified two measures to rank authors: total number of appearances (totN) and the adjusted number of appearances (adjN). The latter considers the co-authorship phenomena and it represents the amount of published articles weighted by a score assigned to each paper (1 in case of only one author, 0.5 with two authors, etc.). Authors' productions are extrémely skewed (Table 7.2). This may be due to: (i) the characteristic of a nascent field, and (ii) the multi-disciplinarity of the field. The most prolific authors ranked on adjusted appearances are Weber (totN 4, adjN 2.33) and Jackson (totN 2, adjN 2).

Our sample was comprised of authors coming from 13 countries with a clear prevalence of the US and UK. These articles represent 60 percent of our collection, followed by Canada (14 percent) and South Africa (8 percent) (Table 7.3).

Our sample was comprised of 50 papers, distributed as summarized in Table 7.4.

Table 7.2 Most contributing authors

Rank	*Author*	*Total appearances*	*Adjusted appearances*
1	Weber	4	2.33
2	Jackson	2	2
3	Hedderman	2	1.5
4	Ashta	2	1.33
5	Albertson	2	1
6	Fox	2	1
7	Geobey	2	0.83
8	Viviers	2	0.83
9	Wood	2	0.83
10	Bozesan	1	1

Table 7.3 Authors per country

Country	*No.*	*%*
US	27	35%
UK	19	25%
Canada	11	14%
South Africa	6	8%
Germany	3	4%
India	3	4%
Spain	2	3%
Other countries	6	8%

Table 7.4 Papers per year

Year	*No. of papers*	*Percentage*
2010	1	2
2011	10	20
2012	9	18
2013	18	36
2014	12	24
Total	**50**	**100**

Table 7.4 shows a significant increase in scientific production in 2013 and 2014 (60 percent) that is likely due to the recent attention on this research field. A further demonstration of the importance of this field in recent years is found in the number and in the multi-disciplinarity of journals that have published the largest number of relevant contributions. The journals come from several disciplines (e.g., criminal justice, criminology, health, business, economics and finance, community development, Entrepreneurial Finance, etc.). Furthermore, the most important journal in our sample is the *Journal of Sustainable Finance and Investment*, which provides a special issue on this topic.

Multiple correspondence analysis

To perform our MCA, we defined a "units × variables" data matrix where units are represented by papers and variables by keywords codified through a complete disjunctive coding. This means that variables are dichotomous, assuming value "1" if the keyword should be associated with the paper, and "0" if not. Data matrix was performed using the data, information, and macro keywords shown in Table 7.1. Furthermore, macro keywords were obtained by combining authors' and professionals' keywords, depicted in Box 7.1.

The analyses were performed using XLSTAT, a statistical software suite for Microsoft Excel. We used maps because they represent structural and dynamic aspects of the research

Box 7.1 Survey on the professionals' perspective

To validate the exact codification of the articles in our MCA, we proceeded with a survey. Furrer et al. (2008) suggest we consider experts' viewpoints to proceed with the identification of the "major keywords" that recognize a particular field. Following this approach, we have conducted a survey on a sample group of specialists for identifying a list of keywords that better explain the characteristics and the connections of SII research fields.

The sample group of interviewees was formed by academics and professionals that were chosen in consideration of their professional activities and studies in this particular research field all around the world (Australia, Belgium, Italy, Sweden, the UK, and the US). For our study we decided to use only keywords provided by two or more authors and to not consider those provided by only one, for two reasons:

i the interviewees' distorted perspective—too focused on a local market and without a global perspective;
ii as synonymous of non-agreement between interviewees.

The survey was conducted from August to October 2014 by email or telephone interviews. In some cases, two or more experts used the same keywords for identifying SII. The keywords that appear two or more times are as follows: Impact Investing (3), Social Impact (3), SRI (3), Social Enterprise/Entrepreneurship (3), Blended Value (2), Program-Related Investment/Investing (2), Social Impact Measurement (2), and Sustainable Investing (2). This result means that these keywords are commonly shared both by academics and by professionals and depict this particular research field.

field in an intuitive way (Noyons et al., 1999). It analyses the interdependence among a set of categorical variables and it aims to identify new latent variables. These are a combination of the original variables and explain information not directly observable (Greenacre & Blasius, 2006). The MCA implies a crucial selection of factorial axes (dimensions).

Given the different approaches, we agreed on the choice of the first factorial plan (Axis 1 and Axis 2). To select the optimal number of dimensions, we use the eigenvalues curve criteria as recommended by Furrer et al. (2008). The result of the analysis shows that a two-dimensional space is the most suitable for the graphical presentation of the data (the first four eigenvalues are 0.192; 0.113; 0.084; and 0.074). The resulting map, according to Benzecrì correction formula, summarizes 68.12 percent of overall inertia. Within the MCA literature, this value can be considered very satisfactory, given the binary nature of the data (Greenacre & Blasius, 2006). We consider different indicators as absolute and the relative contribution of each variable category to interpret the factor. While the former measures the extent to which the variable modalities contribute in the identification of a specific factor, the latter is a quality indicator measuring how much each factor contributes to the reproduction of the variable dispersion (Abdi & Valentin, 2007). Each factor has to be named according to its predominant variables. Figure 7.1 shows the results of the MCA. The output is a bi-dimensional map, where each axis represents one factor. The points correspond to the keywords, and the closeness among them means that they tend to be similar in terms of topics discussed and deepened. On this map, the proximity between keywords corresponds to shared substance: keywords are close to each other because a large proportion of articles treat them together; they are distant from each other when only a small fraction of articles discusses these keywords together (Furrer et al., 2008).

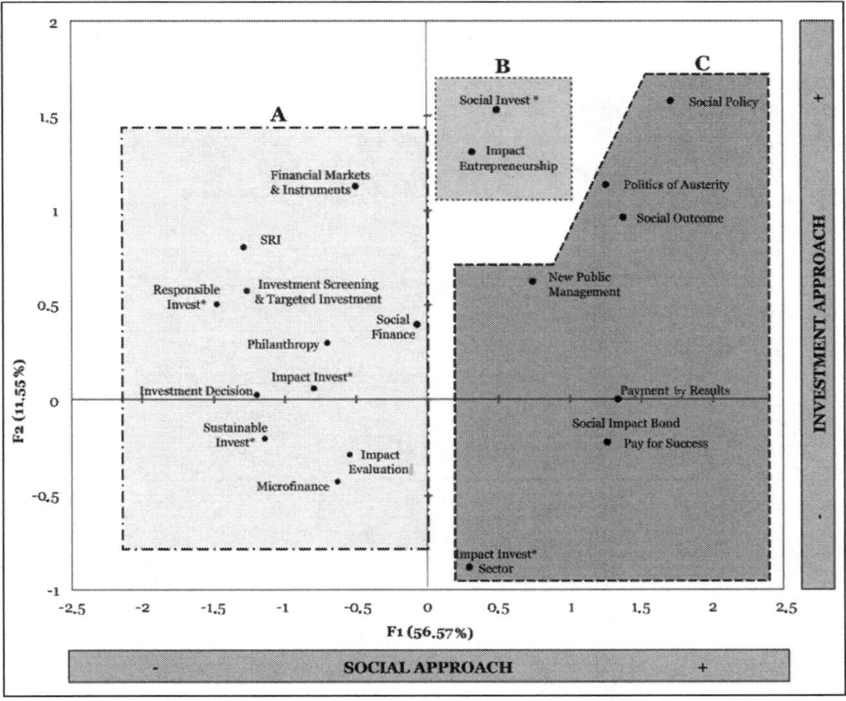

Figure 7.1 The SII academic landscape

The two dimensions of the map in Figure 7.1 that emerged from the MCA can be interpreted as follows. The first, the horizontal dimension (that summarizes 56.57 percent of overall inertia), separates keywords emphasizing a "private or market perspective" (on the left) from those related with the concept of "public or social interventions/instruments" (on the right). The second, the vertical dimension, separates keywords focusing on the concept of the Impact Investing ecosystem (e.g., the keywords financial markets and SRI) (at the top) from those focusing on the specific Impact Investment sectors (e.g., health, pediatrics, preventive health, criminal justice) (at the bottom). More specifically, the horizontal axis indicates the "social approach" (on the left, negative values show a lower social perspective but a higher market/return perspective). The vertical axis indicates the "investment approach." Our analysis shows that the macro keywords "Social Policy" and "Politics of Austerity" are relevant for both the axes (respectively F1 3.987, F2 3.689 and F1 2.215, F2 2.008). The dimensions of the map reflect the characteristic "most important themes" of topical orientation within the Impact Investment topic and depict the "Social Impact Investing academic landscape." With the aim to provide a better picture of the field, we performed the same procedure (with the same data matrix) not only by variables but also by observations. Figure 7.2 summarizes the positions on the map of authors (observations). To better explain the connections between authors and macro keywords, Figures 7.3–7.6 show a summary of each quadrant.

Positions represent articles' content and can be interpreted as such. Academic contributions from 2010 to 2014 are located in the upper left side of the map (Figure 7.3).

The purpose of these articles is to present a synthesis of the Impact Investment market (Mendell & Barbosa, 2013), of the role of an efficient social finance market (Lehner & Nicholls, 2014), and, more specifically, of the Impact Investment conceptual framework (Höchstädter & Scheck, 2014). Furthermore, authors such as Ashta, Couchoro, and Musa (2014), McGoey (2014), Pretorius and Giamporcaro (2012), Shulman and George (2012), Viviers and Firer (2013), and Viviers, Ratcliffe, and Hand (2011) are relatively concentrated in the lower part of the same quadrant. This closeness shows the similarity in the conceptual approach. More specifically, for example, Pretorius and Giamporcaro (2012), Viviers and

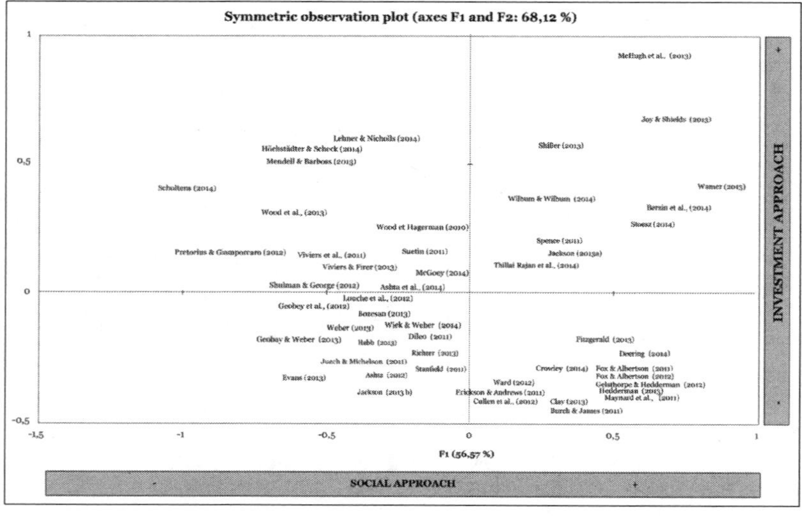

Figure 7.2 Author perspective

Figure 7.3 A focus on the academic landscape: The upper left side

Figure 7.4 A focus on the academic landscape: The upper right side

Firer (2013), and Viviers et al. (2011) show the same approach to Impact Investing as "responsible investing." Academic productions from 2011 to 2014 are positioned in the upper right side of the map (Figure 7.4).

Authors show a higher interest in the new "for-benefit" business models and to the new concept of the fourth sector (Wilburn & Wilburn, 2014) than in the role of the politics of austerity as a driver to change the government's role as a provider of services (Joy & Shields, 2013; McHugh, Sinclair, Roy, Huckfield, & Donaldson, 2013; Stoesz, 2014).

In the lower right quadrant of the map, the works from 2011 to 2014 suggest the multidisciplinarity of this field (Figure 7.5).

The purpose of these articles is to present Social Impact Bonds (SIBs). Contributions in this area relate primarily to the community development, criminal justice, and health sectors. More specifically, Jackson (2013a) shows the role of SIB as a way of supplementing the public financing of social programs; Fitzgerald (2013) as a new financing tool for the area of preventive health; and Crowley (2014) as an innovative financing strategy for pediatric health care.

In the lower left quadrant, we find authors who explore the need of evaluation in Impact Investment practices, such as Evans (2013) and Jackson (2013b) (Figure 7.6).

Figure 7.5 A focus on the academic landscape: The lower right side

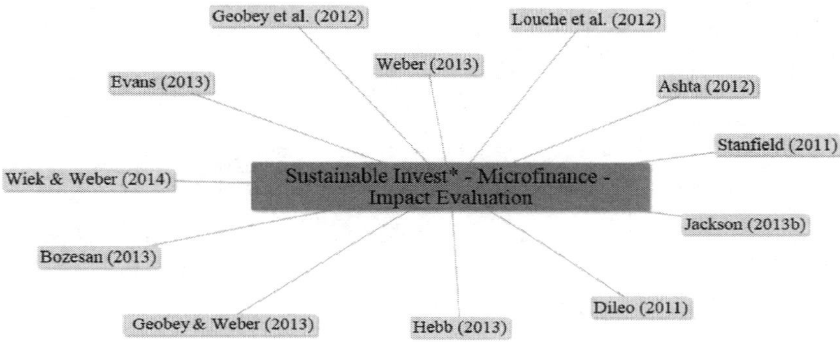

Figure 7.6 A focus on the academic landscape: The lower left side

Content analysis

Using content analysis, the academic contributions were analyzed to understand the contextual use of the words or content. Qualitative content analysis is one of numerous research methods used to analyze text data.

Content analysis is a research technique for making replicable and valid inferences from data to their context (Krippendorff, 2012).

However, there are many different approaches to perform a content analysis depending on the theoretical and substantive interests of the researcher and the problem studied (Hsieh & Shannon, 2005; Weber, 1990). As suggested by Hsieh and Shannon (2005), "research using qualitative content analysis focuses on the characteristics of language as communication with attention to the content or contextual meaning of the text" (p. 1278).

Our analysis is based only on peer review works with the aim of exploring academics' perception of Impact Investing.

After a preliminary analysis of all works, we decided to underline some important aspects of each author, but this review does not cover all authors, for two reasons: (i) authors do not always provide a direct definition; and (ii) some authors provide definitions based on practitioners' reports, and our work is based only on the academic point of view. Furthermore, our analysis shows definitions as given by authors and without interpretations.

Despite the lack of a common understanding of what Impact Investment entails (Hebb, 2013; Höchstädter & Scheck, 2014; Mendell & Barbosa, 2013; Viviers et al., 2011), the concept has been increasingly used by several authors in the period covered by our sample but not in the same way. Höchstädter and Scheck (2014) investigate a large number of practitioner works, highlighting areas of similarity and inconsistency on three levels: definitional, terminological, and strategic. According to authors, there is a clear predominant approach that defines Impact Investing around two core elements: financial return and some sort of non-financial impact.

Some scholars provide a definition of SII by pointing out several aspects as, for example, the intentionality of benefits. Others, for example Evans (2013) and Stanfield (2011), provide a definition focused on "Impact Investor" (Table 7.5).

However, as depicted by our analysis, alternative terms are used by authors interchangeably.

It is interesting to observe that a significant number of works depict intersections between SII and Responsible Investment (Table 7.6). More specifically, Viviers and Firer (2013), speaking

Table 7.5 Definitions of Social Impact Investment and Impact Investor

Definitions of Social Impact Investment	
Viviers et al. (2011, p. 214)	"However, since the turn of the millennium, a new sector has emerged at the intersection of private enterprise and non-profit service delivery, namely the so called impact investing sector. Impact investors actively invest capital in businesses and funds that generate social and/or environmental good and a range of returns (Investing for Social and Environmental Impact, 2009). Impact investments are only authentic when the social and/or environmental benefits are intentional."
Pretorius and Giamporcaro (2012, p. 9)	"According to Eurosif (2010:7), impact investing can be described as a growing area where investors look to both adopt SRI strategies and evaluate their outcomes."
Jackson (2013a, p. 609)	"Impact investing involves the placement of capital in enterprises or projects intended to produce social or environmental as well as financial returns."
Wood et al. (2013, p. 75)	"Impact investment is investment with the intent to create measurable social or environmental benefits in addition to financial return."
McGoey (2014, p. 116)	"Impact investing is the idea that individuals can earn 'market-rate' financial returns for investing in projects geared at providing environmental and social benefit."
Definitions of Impact Investor	
Stanfield (2011, p. 62)	"Impact investors invest in businesses that can provide scalable solutions that governments or purely philanthropic interventions cannot reach."
Evans (2013, p. 138)	"Impact investors seek financial return and positive economic, social or environmental impact."

Table 7.6 Impact Investment as a Responsible Investment

Louche et al. (2012, p. 302)	"Responsible investment manifests itself in many ways and, not surprisingly, goes by many names—it is variously referred to as socially responsible investing, ethical investing, sustainable investing, triple-bottom-line investing, green investing, best-of-class investing, ESG (environmental, social and governance) investing, impact investing and most simply and more recently responsible investing."
Hebb (2013, p. 71)	"Impact investing is a sub-set of responsible investing. Here the investor intentionally invests to achieve positive social and/or environmental impact in addition to financial return."

about the desire of responsible investors to improve the standard of living in local communities, for example by investing directly in social infrastructure development, included these investments, often called community, targeted, or Impact Investments, in the Responsible Investment's area. Scholtens (2014), by proposing the Eurosif definitional framework, highlights that Impact Investments are investments made into companies, organizations, and funds with the intention to generate social and environmental impact alongside a financial return. The intention to achieve positive social and/or environmental impact in addition to financial return is similarly depicted by Hebb (2013).

Furthermore, Shulman and George (2012) consider Impact Investing as a form of Socially Responsible Investing (SRI). With regard to the SII and SRI relationship, as remarked by Geobey and Weber (2013, p. 126), "SRI can screen out investments for social, environmental or governance reasons whereas impact investing is based on the assumption that investments can create financial returns and address social and environmental challenges (Bugg-Levine and Emerson, 2011)."

By confirming a different definitional approach to SII, Thillai Rajan, Koserwal, and Keerthana (2014) consider it as a form of Social Venture Capital (SVC) funding, and Ashta et al. (2014) suggest slow money, Socially Responsible Investment and Impact Investment, and crowdfunding as instruments for financing microfinance institutions. More specifically, Thillai Rajan et al. (2014, p. 39) write:

> SVC funding is also known as Impact Investing, Socially Responsible Investing, blended value, mission driven investing, mission related investing, triple bottom-line, Social Investing, values based investing, program related investing, sustainable and responsible investing, responsible investing, ethical investing, and environmental, social, and governance screening.

Some authors (Geobey & Weber, 2013; Geobey, Westley, & Weber, 2012; Suetin, 2011; Weber, 2013) consider Impact Investing and impact bond as terms included in the social finance umbrella (Table 7.7). More specifically, Geobey and Weber (2013) and Weber (2013) note that there are three forms of social finance: microfinance, Impact Investing, and social banking, and Suetin (2011) underlines that the "Social Impact Bond" can be considered the brainchild of social finance.

The social finance umbrella term can be related to the sustainable finance domain, defined as "the practice of creating economic and social value through financial models, products and markets that are sustainable over time" (Center for Responsible Investment, University of Berkeley).

In our analysis, this concept and the related terms are summarized in Section A in Figure 7.1.

Furthermore, Mendell and Barbosa (2013) highlight that "through Impact Investing, many social enterprises—for-profit and non-profit—are able to access much needed capital that is otherwise inaccessible through mainstream capital markets and/or financial institutions" (p. 111).

The topic of SII appears related by many contact points with the concept of "Impact Entrepreneurship." As depicted in Figure 7.1, this term is used both as macro keywords and as "domain." We consider these macro keywords as very broad, including many related terms (e.g., Third Sector, not-for-profit organizations, co-operatives, social enterprises) (Table 7.1).

The role and importance of these macro keywords is not only depicted by the MCA but is confirmed by the analysis of articles and of authors' points of views. The "Impact Entrepreneurship" domain is well depicted by Section B in Figure 7.1.

Table 7.7 SII as a term enclosed in the social finance umbrella

Impact Investment as a form of mission investing	
Wood and Hagerman (2010, p. 259)	"The language of mission investing includes overlapping practices such as socially responsible investing, community investing, shareholder advocacy, responsible investment, sustainable investment, impact investing, economically targeted investing, double- or triple-bottom line investing, and others. No matter what the language, the core practice is the integration of environmental and social considerations into the investment process, within the context of a disciplined financial strategy. Mission investors may differ from each other, and within their own portfolios, as to how they view the creation of environmental and social benefits in relation to achieving targeted financial returns."
Impact Investment as a form of microfinance	
Scholtens (2014, p. 383)	"Impact investments can be made in emerging and developed markets, especially microfinance can be viewed as an example of impact investment."
Social Impact Investment as a synonym of SVC	
Thillai Rajan et al. (2014, p. 39)	"SVC funding is also known as impact investing, socially responsible investing, blended value, mission driven investing, mission-related investing, triple-bottom line, social investing, values-based investing, program related investing, sustainable and responsible investing, responsible investing, ethical investing, and environmental, social, and governance screening."

In our analysis, we consider this concept as the natural intersection between "social entrepreneurship" and "Impact Investment."

The analysis shows that only a few authors explore the area of Impact Investing evaluation, especially with regard to the SIB topic. As noted by Jackson (2013a, 2013b), as more SIBs move into execution, there is a need for independent evaluations of their outcomes and impacts that promote both accountability and learning, analyze theories of change, and engage beneficiaries. This aspect seems to be, undoubtedly, related to the growing attention to the SIB market and shows the concrete need to further explore this aspect.

As a further confirmation of the increasing interest in this market opportunity, a consistent number of authors focus their attention, rather than on Impact Investing, on SIBs, providing definitions of it as a variant of payment by result (PbR) or pay for success (Table 7.8).

On the contrary, McHugh et al. (2013) show that "SIBs differ in several important ways from previous PbR models" (p. 248). At the same time, Fitzgerald (2013) and Stoesz (2014) focus on its application in the area of social work and social services; Deering (2014), Fox and Albertson (2011, 2012), and Hedderman (2013) on its application in the criminal justice service; Erickson and Andrews (2011) and Jackson (2013a) in the community development area; and Crowley (2014) and Ward (2012) in the health care sector.

The topic of SIBs is strictly related to the new approach to "public policy." As remarked by Warner (2013), "SIBs are the intellectual descendants of new public management's emphasis on markets and performance management" (p. 309). Joy and Shields (2013) underline that SIBs are said to be responsive to both taxpayer and service user interests, and McHugh et al. (2013) suggest that "SIBs could further erode the boundaries between the private, public and third sectors and expose public policy provision even more widely to the vagaries of the market" (p. 252). This aspect is well summarized by Section C in Figure 7.1.

Table 7.8 Definitions of SIB

SIB: Definitions	
Joy and Shields (2013, p. 40)	"SIBs are a financial product used to encourage private, philanthropic and/or public investors to provide upfront capital to support project-oriented service delivery by public, private, or non profit actors, or a combination of these actors."
Fox and Albertson (2011, p. 397)	"The social impact bond presents a new method of financing social outcomes via private investment. It is envisaged that the SIB will be used to raise capital for social projects in the way bonds are used for investment projects; a branch of national or local government will agree to pay for a measurable, social outcome and this prospective income is used to attract new funds to meet the up-front costs of the activity."
Warner (2013, p. 303)	"Social impact bonds (SIBs) attract private investment to social programs by paying a market rate of return if predefined outcome targets are met. SIBs monetize benefits of social interventions and tie pay to performance, limiting governmental control once the contract is designed."
Berzin et al. (2014, p. 138)	"Acting as a contract between the social sector and government, SIBs are a type of officially recognized promise, in which payment is made upon the completion of a predetermined socially beneficial outcome. SIBs create a collaboration of interested parties, attracting investments through non-traditional channels. Socially motivated investors raise capital to put toward a proven method of intervention."
SIB as PbR or pay for success	
Fox and Albertson (2011, p. 395)	"Social impact bonds (SIBs) are a form of payment by results which allow the financing of social outcomes via private investment."
Jackson (2013a, p. 611)	"Also known as pay-for-success financings, SIBs are actually not bonds in the traditional, commercial sense; rather, they are contractual obligations held (usually) by governments."
SIB as a form of outcomes-based contract	
Warner (2013, p. 303)	"SIBs are, in essence, a form of outcomes-based contract between public or nonprofit service providers and private investors, in which private financiers provide upfront funding for interventions to improve specific targeted social outcomes. SIBs operate over a fixed period of time but do not guarantee a fixed rate of return. Rather, investors can expect to receive a return on their investment, based on the savings government makes once service providers meet predetermined outcome targets."
Social Impact Investment and SIB as financial innovations	
Shiller (2013, p. 23)	"A social impact bond is not a bond in the conventional sense. It operates over a fixed period of time but does not offer a fixed rate of return. Repayment to investors is contingent on the achievement of specified social outcomes. The idea is to let the free enterprise system solve a social or even an environmental problem. The bond proceeds are used to create a financial market that will encourage and incentivize private vendors to find practical solutions for social concerns."
Warner (2013, p. 304)	"SIBs represent a new innovation in social program finance. Although not a bond in any real sense, the idea behind a SIB is that private investors can be attracted to invest in social service interventions that have a positive payoff."

Main findings

Articles defining the SII landscape were reviewed. Literature was identified and coded through the methodology described in the previous sections. Following this approach, 50 significant academic results examining the topic of SII were identified. The emerging sample was then (i) statistically evaluated as presented in Figures 7.1 and 7.2 with the MCA method and (ii) analyzed using the method of Content Analysis, with the main aim to provide a better representation of the existing literature.

The combined use of these two methodologies highlights important findings. Several preliminary interpretations can be drawn from these findings.

First, the SII landscape shows a wide range of related key terms, as summarized in Figure 7.7.

A thorough identification and a multi-disciplinary characterization of the morphology of the SII landscape are provided.

Our analysis shows that "related terms" are located in the map following a specific and not random trend. In particular, the various "related terms" revolve around two fundamental concepts: "private or market perspective" and "public or social interventions/instruments" on the left and on the right, respectively, of Figure 7.7.

Furthermore, it is not surprising to find the terms SRI and Responsible Investment on the left or Social Policy and Politics of Austerity on the right. This significant positioning suggests the usefulness of different but fundamental approaches to the SII landscape.

Linkages, similarities, and differences between SII and related terms are clarified by our analysis.

Moreover, the results of our analysis confirm that SII is a new and growing research field.

There was a growing number of works published between 2010 and 2014 (Table 7.4), with authors representing 13 countries (Table 7.3). This geographical heterogeneity of the studies helps to explain both the multi-disciplinarity and the different approaches to the SII landscape. At the same time, this aspect seems to be related to the growing interest for this topic in international academia.

Additionally, improved to better capture all the related terms of SII, our survey (Box 7.1) provided more information about the use of the various definitions of SII. Our sample group of interviewees was formed by academics and professionals from all around the world (Australia, Belgium, Italy, Sweden, the UK, the US) chosen in consideration of their professional activities and studies in this particular research field. They were pleased to provide skills and suggestions.

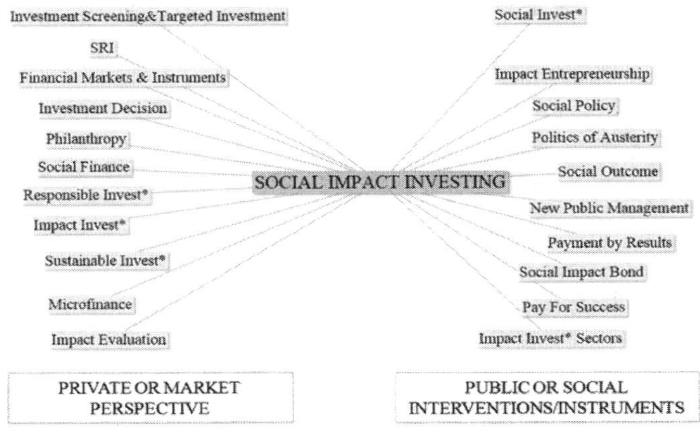

Figure 7.7 The SII landscape: An overview

Furthermore, the attention of the private sector and especially of "professionals" is better captured by the increasing number of reports and "non-peer reviewed works" found in our database analysis (for example, the GIIN website provides more than 140 publications).

This aspect seems to be related to an urgent need to clarify what really can be considered Social Impact Investment and the intersections between other terms. Academia and professionals need to reach agreement about the broad definitions.

Furthermore, our analysis pointed out three "domains" of research in SII studies: sustainable finance, impact entrepreneurship, and public policy in the social sector, directly related to social and investment approaches.

In addition, a consistent number of authors focus their attention on SIBs (Table 7.8). SIBs create a collaboration of public and private sectors in delivering a project-oriented service (Jackson, 2013a; Joy & Shields, 2013) in which payment is made upon the completion of predetermined social outcomes (Berzin, Pitt-Catsouphes, & Peterson, 2014). Since the launch by the UK government of the first SIBs in 2010, 25 other SIBs have been commissioned around the world (Social Finance, 2014). The adaption of the SIB approach for developing countries is the most recent financial innovation derived from the Impact Investing industry.

These financial instruments are a bridge between the social and the investment approach (see Figure 7.8, Section 7), and their implementation is one of the major challenges for the future of SII.

A model and research agenda

Our analysis indicates that in recent years a great number of publications have focused on Impact Investing through a variety of conceptual lenses, ranging from sustainable finance, impact entrepreneurship, and public policy in the social sector (see Sections 1–3 of Figure 7.8). The contamination between these three domains of research in SII studies could be identified in Sections A, B, and C and are indicated in Figure 7.1. In Figure 7.8, we identify emerging lines for further researches in the overlapping areas (see Sections 4–7) between the three domains mentioned above.

In Figure 7.8, Section 1 relates to the contributions of finance researches focused on investment approaches that provide not just a financial benefit but also social and environmental returns. The variety of types of Sustainable Investments, such as double or triple bottom-line investing, mission-related investing, microfinance, Socially Responsible Investing, ESG, and CSR investing, have been captured in academic propositions through different lenses derived from managerial or financial studies (Emerson, 2003; Porter & Kramer, 2011; Weber & Remer, 2011). Contributions in sustainable finance have been concentrated in the global and mature sub-field of finance research and especially in microfinance (Fischer & Ghatak, 2011) and SRI (Sandberg, Juravle, Hedesström, & Hamilton, 2009) as well as in "regional" and mature research sub-domains such as Community Development Finance (Affleck & Mellor, 2006). This aspect is better captured by Section A in Figure 7.1.

Section 2 identifies the entrepreneurship research focused on organizations that seek opportunities by bringing new value creation to meet unfulfilled social needs (Clark, Emerson, & Thornley, 2014). Based on business-driven and business-supported discourses characterized as "philanthro-capitalism" (Edwards, 2010; McGoey, 2012; Sabeti, 2011; Shiller, 2013; Yunus, 2007), this research space encompasses the continuum between for-profit and non-profit enterprises. In our analysis, Section B in Figure 7.1 is related to this approach.

Section 3 covers studies focused on public policies in the social sector. Research in this multi-disciplinary conceptual space examines new management approaches and models derived from recent periods of reforms in this sector. Contributions in this domain are based

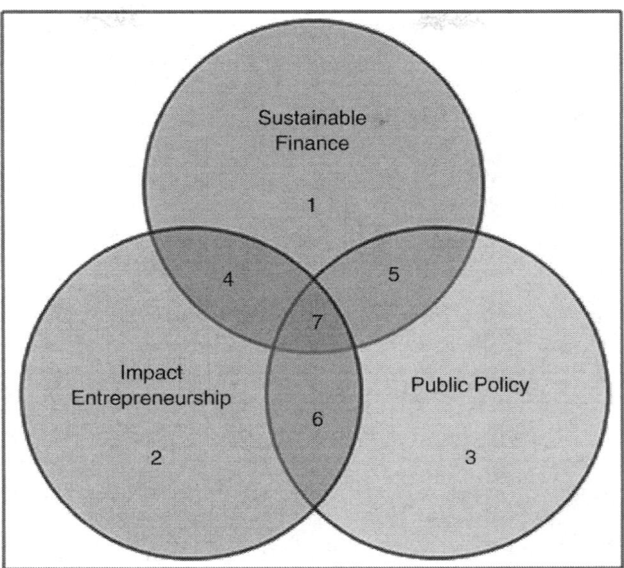

Figure 7.8 A model for Impact Investing and future research areas

on studies on social improvements in the delivery of public services born from the discourses of New Public Management (Osbourne & Gaebler, 1992; Walsh, 1995) and quasi-markets (LeGrand & Bartlett, 1993), as well as international development research (Bebbington, 2001). Section C in Figure 7.1 summarizes this information.

The overlap between sustainable finance and impact entrepreneurship (Section 4) permeates SII by including activities that contribute to new social venture creation or existing impact business organizations that are growing. Research in this domain focuses on practices, processes, and financial instruments able to achieve investor and entrepreneur alignment. Existing studies derived from the fields mentioned above and converging in this area have explored investment logic and type of Impact Investors (Hebb, 2013; Nicholls, 2010a), stage of social venture creation (Haugh, 2007; Miller, Wesley, & Curtis, 2010), and mission alignment (Evans, 2013; Ormiston & Seymour, 2011). Future contributions in this conceptual space should therefore look in an operational and evaluation perspective that aims to capture evidence for the availability of best practice impact measurement models and to investigate the barriers and the levers able to disseminate a more effective impact assessment more suitable for both investors and investees.

Section 5 highlights the commonality between the domain of the public sector and sustainable finance issues. Studies in this domain focus primarily on the public policies enabling the financial impact ecosystem and on creating social value through community development finance and innovative financial mechanisms bridging the gap between social finance and social innovation (Geobay & Weber, 2013; Lehner, 2013; Moore, Westley, & Nicholls, 2012). Research efforts in this domain should be directed at case studies that explore the role of the state in Impact Investing market building policies (Berzin et al., 2014). Future research questions should also explore the area of institutional Impact Investing, especially in case studies directed at mapping co-investment practices in which public investments leverage private market participation (Wood, Thornley, & Grace, 2013). Finally, further exploration should consider adapting vehicles and techniques from mainstream finance to the Impact Investing market, starting, for example, with examining existing initiatives with the mission to improve financial efficiency and effectiveness on the demand side of the Impact Investing market (Mendell & Barbosa, 2013).

Overlap in Section 6 is based on the contributions of discourses related to the broad research area of social innovation that embraces the perspective of execution of social policies and development programs by existing impact enterprises and public sector organizations. Through this lens, social value is co-created and delivered using practices and processes that are unique to entrepreneurship (Austin, Stevenson, & Wei-Skillern, 2006; Bovaird, 2006). The interplay of the politics of austerity with incumbent social development goals and social business opportunities may be the foremost questions to be asked in the "hybrid context" of opportunity recognition for impact enterprises in impact business.

Finally, Section 7 includes contamination from all three domains: sustainable finance, impact entrepreneurship, and public policy in the social sector. Research in this context focuses on financial models and instruments creating and balancing social and economic value for the collective benefit of addressing the social issue. The foremost research questions in this context should cover the topic of financial innovation derived from the lack of financing instruments in public efforts to address social issues (Phillips & Hebb, 2010). Further studies on new financial instruments in this area, such as crowdfunding for social ventures, SIBs, and the connected research topic of evaluation, should be conducted, as suggested by Jackson (2013a), Lehner and Nicholls (2014), and Warner (2013). However, further investigation should explore the emerging trend of public–private community partnerships between civil society, government, and financial institutions (Mendell & Nogales, 2009) from the perspective of risk mitigation, thanks to dedicated social finance intermediaries.

Conclusion and limitations

The literature relating to Impact Investing is wide and multi-faceted. As remarked by Hebb (2013), the conceptual framework that underpins Impact Investing is best captured by the "Blended Value Proposition" articulated by Emerson in the early 2000s. This approach could be enriched by the concept of "Shared Value" proposed by Porter and Kramer (2011), which can be defined as policies and operating practices that enhance the competitiveness of a company while simultaneously advancing the economic and social conditions in the communities in which it operates. Despite the widespread use of the term "Impact Investment," our study showed significant variations in its conceptualization and, at the same time, the need to clarify differences and to provide a broader and more comprehensive conceptual framework. The multiplicity of studies found in the literature and more generally the different disciplinary domains involved in the debate about Impact Investment seem to focus alternatively on different and single aspects of the phenomenon while missing the whole picture of the elements that may hinder or facilitate its development.

To the authors' knowledge, this study represents the first academic effort that provides an exploratory analysis of the existing stance of SII academic literature in order to draw an instructional map for scholars with research interests in this field.

The bibliometric and content analyses used in this work allow us to obtain a landscape of the SII field while monitoring the evolution of academic studies about this topic in order to identify its shared areas. This method takes into consideration only scientific papers published in peer-reviewed journals in order to consider only "certified knowledge" and to understand the further developments of academic studies concerning this topic. Our bibliometric analysis does not consider works such as reports, books, or working papers different from academic papers, and for this reason, these types of publications are excluded from the analysis. This aspect is relevant for SII because this field could be considered nascent, and many contributions are derived from works written by professionals or academics using these particular forms of publication. Specifically, our bibliometric and content analysis do not intercept important authors such as Martin, Bugg-Levine, or Emerson. Nevertheless, this lack is filled by the inclusion of academic works such as Höchstädter and Scheck (2014), which depict the important contribution provided by reports or professional publications.

Authors' note

This chapter is the result of a collaboration between the authors. In particular, Rizzello contributed to the introductory text and the section "A model and research agenda"; Migliazza contributed to Box 7.1 ("Survey on the professionals' perspective") and the section "Conclusion and limitations"; Carè contributed to the sections "Development of the research field: an overview," "Multiple correspondence analysis," and "Content analysis"; and Trotta contributed to the sections "Research design and methodological approach" and "Main findings."

Acknowledgments

The authors thank the Editor—Professor Othmar M. Lehner—for the opportunity to contribute to this book, the anonymous reviewers, and participants of the ACRN SSFII—Social and sustainable finance and Impact Investing Conference—for their useful comments. They also wish to recognize the important contribution of the leaders interviewed for this project: Rosemary Addis (Impact Investing Australia), Lisa Hehenberger and Priscilla Boiardi (European Venture Philanthropy Association), Meg Voorhes (The Forum for Sustainable and Responsible Investment), Luciano Balbo (Oltre Venture Capital), Simon Howard (UK Sustainable Investment and Finance Association), Roberto Randazzo (Impact Investing Lab), and Shawn Westcott (Impact Invest Scandinavia).

References

The academic contributions analyzed in bibliometric and content analysis are indicated by an asterisk (*):

Abdi, H., & Valentin, D. (2007). Multiple correspondence analysis. In N. Salkind (Ed.), *Encyclopedia of measurement and statistics* (pp. 651–657). Thousand Oaks, CA: Sage.

Affleck, A., & Mellor, M. (2006). Community development finance: A neo-market solution to social exclusion? *Journal of Social Policy, 35*(2), 303–319.

*Ashta, A. (2012). Co-creation for impact investment in microfinance. *Strategic Change, 21*(1–2), 71–81.

*Ashta, A., Couchoro, M., & Musa, A. S. M. (2014). Dialectic evolution through the social innovation process: From microcredit to microfinance. *Journal of Innovation and Entrepreneurship, 3*(1), 4.

Austin, J., Stevenson, H., & Wei-Skillern, J. (2006). Social and commercial entrepreneurship: Same, different, or both? *Entrepreneurship Theory and Practice, 30*(1), 1–22.

Bebbington, J. (2001). Sustainable development: A review of the international development, business and accounting literature. *Accounting Forum, 25*(2), 128–157.

*Berzin, S. C., Pitt-Catsouphes, M., & Peterson, C. (2014). Role of state-level governments in fostering social innovation. *Journal of Policy Practice, 13*(3), 135–155.

Bornstein, D. (2007). *How to change the world: Social entrepreneurs and the power of new ideas*. New York, NY: Oxford University Press.

Bovaird, T. (2006). Developing new forms of partnership with the "market" in the procurement of public services. *Public Administration, 84*(1), 81–102.

*Bozesan, M. (2013). Demystifying the future of investing. *Journal of Integral Theory and Practice, 8*(1–2), 19–56.

Bugg-Levine, A., & Emerson, J. (2011). Impact investing: Transforming how we make money while making a difference. *Innovations, 6*(3), 9–18.

*Burch, I. I., & James, H. (2011). Encouraging innovation on the foundation of evidence. *Criminology & Public Policy, 10*(3), 609–616.

*Clay, R. F. (2013). Health impact bonds: will investors pay for intervention?. *Environmental Health Perspectives, 121*(2), a45.

Clark, C., Emerson, J., & Thornley, B. (2014). *The impact investor: Lessons in leadership and strategy for collaborative capitalism.* San Francisco, CA: John Wiley & Sons.

Cobo, M. J., López-Herrera, A. G., Herrera-Viedma, E., & Herrera, F. (2011). Science mapping software tools: Review, analysis, and cooperative study among tools. *Journal of the American Society for Information Science and Technology, 62*(7), 1382–1402.

*Crowley, D. M. (2014). The role of social impact bonds in pediatric health care. *Pediatrics, 134*(2), e331–e333.

*Cullen, F. T., Jonson, C. L., & Eck, J. E. (2012). The accountable prison. *Journal of Contemporary Criminal Justice, 28*(1), 77–95.

*Deering, J. (2014). A future for probation? *The Howard Journal of Criminal Justice, 53*(1), 1–15.

*Dileo, P. (2011). Repositioning microfinance with impact investors: Codes of conduct and 'social first'MFIs. *Enterprise Development and Microfinance, 22*(4), 276–290.

Edwards, M. (2010). *Small change: Why business won't save the world.* San Francisco, CA: Berrett-Koehler.

Emerson, J. (2003). The blended value proposition: Integrating social and financial returns. *California Management Review, 45*(4), 35–51.

*Erickson, D., & Andrews, N. (2011). Partnerships among community development, public health, and health care could improve the well-being of low-income people. *Health Affairs, 30*(11), 2056–2063.

Eurosif (2012). *European SRI Study 2012.* Brussels, BE: Author.

*Evans, M. (2013). Meeting the challenge of impact investing: How can contracting practices secure social impact without sacrificing performance? *Journal of Sustainable Finance & Investment, 3*(2), 138–154.

Fernandez-Alles, M., & Ramos-Rodríguez, A. (2009). Intellectual structure of human resources management research: A bibliometric analysis of the journal *Human Resource Management*, 1985–2005. *Journal of the American Society for Information Science and Technology, 60*(1), 161–175.

Fischer, G., & Ghatak, M. (2011). *Spanning the chasm: Uniting theory and empirics in microfinance research.* Singapore, SGP: World Scientific Publishing.

*Fitzgerald, J. L. (2013). Social impact bonds and their application to preventive health. *Australian Health Review, 37*(2), 199–204.

*Fox, C., & Albertson, K. (2011). Payment by results and social impact bonds in the criminal justice sector: New challenges for the concept of evidence-based policy? *Criminology and Criminal Justice, 11*(5), 395–413.

*Fox, C., & Albertson, K. (2012). Is payment by results the most efficient way to address the challenges faced by the criminal justice sector? *Probation Journal, 59*(4), 355–373.

Freireich, J., & Fulton, K. (2009). *Investing for social and environmental impact.* New York, NY: Monitor Institute.

Furrer, O., Thomas, H., & Goussevskaia, A. (2008). The structure and evolution of the strategic management field: A content analysis of 26 years of strategic management research. *International Journal of Management Reviews, 10*(1), 1–23.

*Gelsthorpe, L., & Hedderman, C. (2012). Providing for women offenders the risks of adopting a payment by results approach. *Probation Journal, 59*(4), 374–390.

*Geobey, S., & Weber, O. (2013). Lessons in operationalizing social finance: The case of Vancouver City Savings Credit Union. *Journal of Sustainable Finance & Investment, 3*(2), 124–137.

*Geobey, S., Westley, F. R., & Weber, O. (2012). Enabling social innovation through developmental social finance. *Journal of Social Entrepreneurship, 3*(2), 151–165.

Greenacre, M., & Blasius, J. (Eds.). (2006). *Multiple correspondence analysis and related methods.* Boca Raton, FL: Taylor & Francis Group.

Haugh, H. (2007). Community-led social venture creation. *Entrepreneurship Theory and Practice, 31*(2), 161–182.

*Hebb, T. (2013). Impact investing and responsible investing: What does it mean? *Journal of Sustainable Finance & Investment, 3*(2), 71–74.

*Hedderman, C. (2013). Payment by results: Hopes, fears and evidence. *British Journal of Community Justice, 11*(2–3), 43–58.

*Höchstädter, A. K., & Scheck, B. (2015). What's in a name: An analysis of impact investing understandings by academics and practitioners. *Journal of Business Ethics, 132*(2), 449–475.

Hsieh, H. F., & Shannon, S. E. (2005). Three approaches to qualitative content analysis. *Qualitative Health Research, 15*(9), 1277–1288.

Inkpen, A. C., & Beamish, P. W. (1994). An analysis of twenty-five years of research in the *Journal of International Business Studies*. *Journal of International Business Studies, 25*(4), 703–713.

*Jackson, E. T. (2013a). Evaluating social impact bonds: Questions, challenges, innovations, and possibilities in measuring outcomes in impact investing. *Community Development, 44*(5), 608–616.
*Jackson, E. T. (2013b). Interrogating the theory of change: Evaluating impact investing where it matters most. *Journal of Sustainable Finance & Investment, 3*(2), 95–110.
*Joy, M., & Shields, J. (2013). Social impact bonds: The next phase of third sector marketization? *Canadian Journal of Nonprofit and Social Economy Research, 4*(2), 39–55.
*Juech, C., & Michelson, E. S. (2011). Rethinking The Future of Sustainability: From silos to systemic resilience. *Development, 54*(2), 199–201.
Krippendorff, K. (2012). *Content analysis: An introduction to its methodology* (3rd ed.). Thousand Oaks, CA: Sage.
LeGrand, J., & Bartlett, W. (1993). *Quasi-markets and social policy*. London, UK: Palgrave Macmillan.
Lehner, O. M. (2011). *Social entrepreneurship perspectives: Triangulated approaches to hybridity* (Vol. 111). Jyväskylä, FI: Jyväskylä Studies in Business and Economics.
Lehner, O. M. (2013). Crowdfunding social ventures: A model and research agenda. *Venture Capital, 15*(4), 289–311.
*Lehner, O. M., & Nicholls, A. (2014). Social finance and crowdfunding for social enterprises: A public–private case study providing legitimacy and leverage. *Venture Capital, 16*(3), 271–286.
Locke, J., & Perera, H. (2001). The intellectual structure of international accounting in the early 1990s. *The International Journal of Accounting, 36*(2), 223–249.
*Louche, C., Arenas, D., & van Cranenburgh, K. C. (2012). From preaching to investing: Attitudes of religious organisations towards responsible investment. *Journal of Business Ethics, 110*(3), 301–320.
Martin, M. (2013). *Making impact investible* (Impact Economy Working Papers, 4). Lausanne, CH: Impact Economy.
*Maynard, A., Street, A., & Hunter, R. (2011). Using 'payment by results' to fund the treatment of dependent drug users-proceed with care!. *Addiction, 106*(10), 1725–1729.
McGoey, L. (2012). Philanthrocapitalism and its critics. *Poetics, 40*(2), 185–199.
*McGoey, L. (2014). The philanthropic state: Market-state hybrids in the philanthrocapitalist turn. *Third World Quarterly, 35*(1), 109–125.
*McHugh, N., Sinclair, S., Roy, M., Huckfield, L., & Donaldson, C. (2013). Social Impact Bonds: A wolf in sheep's clothing? *Journal of Poverty and Social Justice, 21*(3), 247–257.
*Mendell, M., & Barbosa, E. (2013). Impact investing: A preliminary analysis of emergent primary and secondary exchange platforms. *Journal of Sustainable Finance & Investment, 3*(2), 111–123.
Mendell, M., & Nogales, R. (2009). Social enterprises in OECD member countries: What are the financial streams? In A. Noya (Ed.), *The changing boundaries of social enterprises* (pp. 89–138). Paris, FR: OECD Publishing.
Mikki, S. (2009). Google Scholar compared to Web of Science: A literature review. *Nordic Journal of Information Literacy in Higher Education, 1*(1), 41–51.
Miller, T. L., Wesley, I. I., & Curtis, L. (2010). Assessing mission and resources for social change: An organizational identity perspective on social venture capitalists' decision criteria. *Entrepreneurship Theory and Practice, 34*(4), 705–733.
Moore, M. L., Westley, F. R., & Nicholls, A. (2012). The social finance and social innovation nexus. *Journal of Social Entrepreneurship, 3*(2), 115–132.
Nicholls, A. (2006). *Social entrepreneurship: New models of sustainable social change*. New York, NY: Oxford University Press.
Nicholls, A. (2010a). The institutionalization of social investment: The interplay of investment logics and investor rationalities. *Journal of Social Entrepreneurship, 1*(1), 70–100.
Nicholls, A. (2010b). *The landscape of social investment in the UK*. Birmingham, UK: Third Sector Research Centre & Health Services Management Centre.
Nicholls, A. (2010c). The legitimacy of social entrepreneurship: Reflexive isomorphism in a pre-paradigmatic field. *Entrepreneurship Theory and Practice, 34*(4), 611–633.
Noyons, E. C. M., Moed, H. F., & Luwel, M. (1999). Combining mapping and citation analysis for evaluative bibliometric purposes: A bibliometric study. *Journal of the American Society for Information Science, 50*(2), 115–131.
O'Donohoe, N., Leijonhufvud, C., Saltuk, Y., Bugg-Levine, A., & Brandenburg, M. (2010). *Impact investments: An emerging asset class*. London, UK: J.P. Morgan Global Research.
Ormiston, J., & Seymour, R. (2011). Understanding value creation in social entrepreneurship: The importance of aligning mission, strategy and impact measurement. *Journal of Social Entrepreneurship, 2*(2), 125–150.

Osbourne, D., & Gaebler, T. (1992). *Reinventing government*. Reading, MA: Addison-Wesley.

Petticrew, M., & Roberts, H. (2008). *Systematic reviews in the social sciences: A practical guide*. Oxford, UK: Blackwell Publishing.

Phillips, S., & Hebb, T. (2010). Financing the third sector: Introduction. *Policy and Society, 29*(3), 181–187.

Porter, M. E., & Kramer, M. R. (2011). Creating shared value. *Harvard Business Review, 89*(1–2), 62–77.

*Pretorius, L., & Giamporcaro, S. (2012). Sustainable and responsible investment (SRI) in South Africa: A limited adoption of environmental criteria. *Investment Analysts Journal, 75*, 1–19.

*Richter, L. (2013). Social Impact Investing at the Intersection of Health and Community Development. *National Civic Review, 102*(4), 67–71.

Sabeti, H. (2011). The for-benefit enterprise. *Harvard Business Review, 89*(11), 98–104.

Sandberg, J., Juravle, C., Hedesström, T. M., & Hamilton, I. (2009). The heterogeneity of socially responsible investment. *Journal of Business Ethics, 87*(4), 519–533.

*Scholtens, B. (2014). Indicators of responsible investing. *Ecological Indicators, 36*, 382–385.

*Shiller, R. J. (2013). Capitalism and financial innovation. *Financial Analysts Journal, 69*(1), 21–25.

Short, J. (2009). The art of writing a review article. *Journal of Management, 35*(6), 1312–1317.

*Shulman, J. M., & George, B. (2012). Growing jobs and getting returns: Impact investing through entrepreneurs. *Journal of Global Business Management, 8*(1), 123–132.

Small, H. (1999). Visualizing science by citation mapping. *Journal of the American Society for Information Science, 50*(9), 799–813.

Social Finance. (2014). *The global social impact bond market*. London, UK: Author.

*Stanfield, J. (2011). Impact investment in education. *Economic Affairs, 31*(3), 62.

*Stoesz, D. (2014). Evidence-based policy reorganizing social services through accountable care organizations and social impact bonds. *Research on Social Work Practice, 24*(2), 181–185.

*Spence, A. (2011). Achieving Financial Sustainability in Today's Changed World. *The Philanthropist, 24*(2), 97–102.

*Suetin, A. (2011). Post-crisis developments in international financial markets. *International Journal of Law and Management, 53*(1), 51–61.

*Thillai Rajan, A., Koserwal, P., & Keerthana, S. (2014). The global epicenter of impact investing: An analysis of social venture investments in India. *The Journal of Private Equity, 17*(2), 37–50.

Verbeek, A., Debackere, K., Luwel, M., & Zimmermann, E. (2002). Measuring progress and evolution in science and technology I: The multiple uses of bibliometric indicators. *International Journal of Management Reviews, 4*(2), 179–211.

*Viviers, S., & Firer, C. (2013). Responsible investing in South Africa—A retail perspective. *Journal of Economic and Financial Sciences, 6*(1), 217–242.

*Viviers, S., Ratcliffe, T., & Hand, D. (2011). From philanthropy to impact investing: Shifting mindsets in South Africa. *Corporate Ownership and Control, 8*, 25–43.

Walsh, K. (1995). *Public services and market mechanisms: Competition, contracting, and the new public management*. London, UK: Palgrave Macmillan.

*Ward, J. E. (2012). New money for chronic diseases: Can clinicians and entrepreneurs deliver outcomes eluding governments? *The Medical Journal of Australia, 197*(5), 268–270.

*Warner, M. E. (2013). Private finance for public goods: Social impact bonds. *Journal of Economic Policy Reform, 16*(4), 303–319.

*Weber, O. (2013). Impact measurement in microfinance: Is the measurement of the social return on investment an innovation in microfinance? *Journal of Innovation Economics & Management, 11*, 149–171.

Weber, O., & Remer, S. (2011). *Social banks and the future of sustainable finance*. New York, NY: Routledge.

Weber, R. P. (1990). *Basic content analysis*. Beverly Hills, CA: Sage.

*Wiek, A., & Weber, O. (2014). Sustainability challenges and the ambivalent role of the financial sector. *Journal of Sustainable Finance & Investment, 4*(1), 9–20.

*Wilburn, K., & Wilburn, R. (2014). The double bottom line: Profit and social benefit. *Business Horizons, 57*(1), 11–20.

*Wood, D., & Hagerman, L. (2010). Mission investing and the philanthropic toolbox. *Policy and Society, 29*(3), 257–268.

*Wood, D., Thornley, B., & Grace, K. (2013). Institutional impact investing: Practice and policy. *Journal of Sustainable Finance & Investment, 3*(2), 75–94.

Yunus, M. (2007). *Creating a world without poverty: Social business and the future of capitalism*. Philadelphia, PA: PublicAffairs.

8
IMPACT INVESTING
Funding social innovation

Rebecca Tekula and Archana Shah

This chapter outlines the current state of funding for social impact and in particular the growing field of Impact Investing, its background and definition, and the challenges and potential of this emerging asset class. In addition, this chapter examines the various actors in the field, the measurement metrics utilized, and presents a model of the interactions within the Impact Investing ecosystem.

The emphasis of this chapter is on three questions: What is the current state of funding for social impact and, in particular, Impact Investing? How is impact identified and measured? What intermediaries and other actors are at play in this field?

Funding social innovation: The emergence of Impact Investing

The origins of social finance can be traced back at least to the mid-1700s when the Quakers prohibited their members from participating financially in the slave trade (Royal Bank of Canada, 2010). More recently, we have seen concerns about the environment and sustainability influence many socially conscious investors. Ethical investors have also driven the growth of Corporate Social Responsibility through the 1980s and 1990s, yet during this time, Socially Responsible Investing was concentrated on screening investments for businesses that did not meet an investor's standards and encouraging responsibility through shareholder activism. Evolving from this, we have also seen mission-related investing (MRI) and program-related investing (PRI), most often in relation to charitable foundation investments.

Funders of social innovation include governments, charitable foundations, philanthropists, and high-net-worth individuals that have the capacity to be first movers as well as provide grant and first loss capital during the early stages of a social enterprise, allowing an enterprise to become financially viable and scale its operations.

There is developing interest and discussion among investors, governments, philanthropists, and nonprofits around the topic of Impact Investment, along with a growing number of early adopters of this asset class. Estimates of the market potential range from $400 billion to $1 trillion in invested capital (O'Donohoe, Leijonhufvud, & Saltuk, 2010, p. 11). There is an emerging government policy focus on social finance and specifically Impact Investing. The United Kingdom has developed a Social Investment Task Force; Canada has created a Ministerial Advisory Council on Social Innovation; and the United States now has a Social Innovation Fund (SIF). Building upon the United Kingdom's reputation as a global leader in social innovation development and domestic innovations including Big Society Capital, during the United Kingdom's presidency of the G8 in 2013, Prime Minister David Cameron announced the Social Impact Investment Task Force with the aim to "catalyze the development of the social Impact Investment market" (2014). Bringing together government officials and leaders from industries including finance, business, and philanthropy from G8 nations, the taskforce held its first meeting at the White House in Washington, DC in Fall 2013 and developed working groups focused on (1) impact measurement, (2) asset allocation, (3) international development and Impact Investing, and (4) mission alignment (2014).

Related to this effort, also in 2013, the US Small Business Administration (SBA) announced that it would nearly double its Impact Investment funds, from $80 million to $150 million. In the United States in 2014, the White House hosted roundtables on Impact Investing, and the Obama administration has committed to catalyzing additional private sector Impact Investments and supporting the involved companies and entrepreneurs (Office of Science and Technology Policy [OSTP], 2014a, p. 2). These commitments include an increase of the reach and flexibility of the SBA Small Business Investment Company (SBIC) Impact Fund, a US Agency for International Development (USAID) managed $60 million loan guarantee facility for green base-of-the-pyramid serving businesses; and pay-for-success (PFS) field-building support through the SIF (OSTP, 2014b).

As the field grows in size, it is increasingly important to clarify the definition of Impact Investing. Essentially, Impact Investing is dual-purpose financing: the pursuit of social benefit together with financial profit. While Impact Investing is generally considered to include many of the investment activities previously included in definitions of Socially Responsible Investing, Impact Investing goes beyond traditionally passive investments whereby investors apply a set of negative or positive filters to a group of publicly listed securities, for example avoiding investments in tobacco, alcohol, and firearms, while favoring businesses that provide socially beneficial goods or services. In contrast to this more passive, "do no harm" approach, Impact Investing has come to mean an active, intentional selection of investments in companies, organizations, projects, or funds that have the potential to create measurable positive economic, social, or environmental change, while also earning a relatively attractive financial return. Entrepreneurs, investors, and philanthropists are moving away from the duality of maximizing profits in their business activities while unconnectedly giving away donations to charity.

The notion of a financially attractive solution to solving societal problems is intriguing for a growing number of institutional and private investors around the world, and in particular those who already have an inclination toward social and environmental responsibility. Recent discussions around the precise definition of Impact Investing have focused on intentionality, or intention of positive impact when making an investment, as an essential factor distinctive from other Socially Responsible Investments. Microfinance, which gained momentum in the latter half of the last century, is an established and specific sector ripe for Impact Investments along with others including clean technology, sustainable agriculture, and affordable energy.

The rise of Impact Investing corresponds with a desire among charitable donors, both individual and institutional, for greater accountability and performance measurement from the organizations they fund philanthropically. These donors are requesting and requiring metrics: evidence and measurement of social impact. Furthermore, going beyond the risk-taking flair of Venture Philanthropy, Impact Investments aim to deliver community-based solutions on a scale

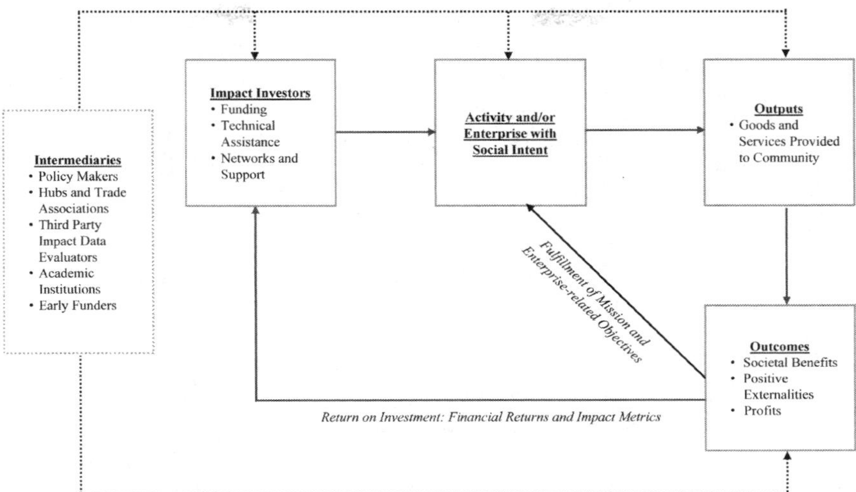

Figure 8.1 A model of the Impact Investing ecosystem

that most donations cannot. Figure 8.1 provides a model of the Impact Investment ecosystem, including relationships among various actors and the flow of outcomes and impact metrics.

In addition to the private equity investments we may typically think of as Impact Investments, there are a number of vehicles and instruments that fall into the category of Impact Investing. Impact Investments come in the form of traditional asset classes including private debt, deposits, guarantees, and real assets. Additionally, new instruments have been created in this arena including community investment notes, PFS bonds, and Social Impact Bonds (SIBs), which are discussed later in the chapter in more detail. Public–private partnerships and infrastructure projects in particular have also grown to be ripe ground for Impact Investments in often unique and creative deals that can be interesting to myriad investors and supporters, including nonprofits and government entities.

Identifying and measuring social impact

As the social finance sector develops, there are an increasing number of questions on how to assess impact. Achieving some form of social impact or outcome is a *raison d'être* for social enterprises, and Impact Investments typically require the measurement of this impact. These social enterprises, sometimes referred to as Impact Enterprises, are firms, organizations, and entities that pursue both profit and social impact by creating jobs, essential goods and services, or environmental benefit (Rodin & Brandenburg, 2014, p. 35) and are thus the typical recipient of Impact Investment funds. While these entities may be unified in creating impact, they differ greatly and in their individual purpose or theory of change.

Common areas of impact for these firms are at the point of output: producing products and services that create societal good or have a positive impact on the environment, as illustrated in Figure 8.1. Many firms also endeavor to create jobs in underemployed communities, with a growing emphasis on quality jobs, which is explored later in this chapter. Creating positive social impact across the supply chain is also seen in the field: ranging from fair trade to reforestation and sustainable agriculture. To address the need for impact metrics, these enterprises must, at a minimum, engage in a systematic outcome assessment in which they develop and implement a methodology with which to monitor their performance relative to the desired outcome.

Much can be learned from the efforts of the nonprofit and charity sectors which have employed program evaluation, and increasingly outcomes assessment, to both define the specific role their organizations played in producing any observed beneficial changes and to satisfy funder requirements. Typically, these organizations employ an impact or logic model to visualize and illustrate the ways that their various goals are projected to produce desired outcomes (Thomas, 2010). Outcomes are then measured using a series of indicators. Additionally, a growing number of government and nonprofit agencies are utilizing scorecards or dashboards to systematically analyze and report upon data collected on program effectiveness (Carman, 2007, p. 65).

While the use of such assessments in measuring the social outcomes of programs has increased in recent years, the interpretation of data can prove difficult. In particular, outcome metrics must be carefully analyzed when implying causality. In other words, impact metrics cannot always be read as resulting from an enterprise activity itself and not from other independent factors such as shifts in the economy. Furthermore, it is important to assess and address side effects or unintended consequences of the activities invested in. For example, an infrastructure investment outcome of reducing crime in one neighborhood may have in fact shifted crime to elsewhere in community. A number of organizations in the social enterprise space have endeavored to measure the impact value of social investments in monetary terms. Return on investment (ROI) is a common measure of financial value creation, and those who invest in organizations that create social (or environmental) impact similarly are looking to measure this value. Sometimes this is referred to as social return on investment (SROI), a term coined and defined by the Roberts Enterprise Development Fund (REDF). This concept, which has been refined by various actors in the field, is an effort to measure and achieve maximum value from social investments. However, assigning a value to social impact is a notoriously difficult endeavor. The addition of externalities, benefits, and costs that are not limited to the producer of a good causes the traditional market mechanisms to break down. Because of the difficulty associated with valuing intangible benefits like a lowered crime rate or a drop in the homeless population, there are many hurdles to overcome when endeavoring to measure social change.

While a great deal of focus has been placed on the measurement and communication of impacts resulting from program or enterprise outputs, there is emerging interest and focus on product impact and operational impact. Product impact can be defined as the effect of goods and services produced by an enterprise (e.g., clean water or anti-malaria mosquito nets), while operational impact is the impact of the enterprise function on the community, employees, and effects of its supply chain and operations (Brest & Born, 2013).

Social impact metrics

There is clear demand for metrics among the various actors in the Impact Investing sector including philanthropists, venture capitalists, foundations, and government agencies. And dozens of toolkits and analytics platforms have been developed in response to the growing interest and investment in this sector. However, to attract meaningful investment capital, to the extent possible, there are growing calls in the sector for standardized, measurable, and reportable outputs and outcomes. For some impact sectors such as microfinance, randomized control trials (RCTs) and/or longitudinal studies are the standard; however, these are expensive and time-consuming and not relevant to many other social innovations.

Impact reporting and investment standards

The growth in emphasis on measuring impact has resulted in a noteworthy response from the Global Impact Investment Network (GIIN), a nonprofit Impact Investing trade association with the mission to "increase the scale and effectiveness of Impact Investing" (GIIN, 2014a). The GIIN has been an early actor in developing Impact Investment-specific metrics with the establishment of the Impact Reporting and Investment Standards (IRIS), a directory of standardized metrics for articulating social, environmental, and financial performance. There appears to be general agreement that IRIS has been increasingly adopted as the industry standard tool.

IRIS is built on existing industry best practices and is designed to provide users with a foundation from which to build their social and environmental performance assessments. The IRIS library defines and provides indicators to measure financial performance; operational performance such as governance policies and employment practices; and product performance to help communicate the social or environmental benefits of the products or services offered. There are also measurements to evaluate overall sector performance that could be used as benchmarks (GIIN, 2014b). This catalog, which can be used across geographies and sectors, is freely accessible on the web and easily downloadable for use.

While IRIS can be adopted as part of an organization's impact evaluation process, the onus is on IRIS users to define their impact measurement program. Organizations can use the IRIS catalog to identify relevant metrics that best define their own impact intentions, in line with their stakeholder and shareholder commitments. Using IRIS standardizes the way impact indicators are described. As more organizations adopt standardized IRIS metrics, social impact reporting becomes more uniform, which in turn helps when evaluating different Impact Investment opportunities.

For example, an investor focused on quality jobs may look for impact metrics such as wages compared to average minimum wage, the percentage of healthcare paid by the company, and quality or availability of retirement benefits, and training for employees, to name a few. The latest IRIS 3.0 catalog, updated March 2014 (GIIN, 2014b), offers several detailed indicators including full-time wages (i.e., total value of wages including bonuses, excluding benefits, paid to all full-time employees of the organization during the reporting period); employment benefits (i.e., health insurance, dental insurance, disability coverage, life insurance, maternity/paternity leave, retirement provisions, stock ownership, etc.); and fair compensation practices (i.e., whether the organization has a written policy to compensate employees fairly and equally) (B-Lab, 2014b).

The field of social innovation continues to evolve and grow. For more recent innovations where IRIS metrics do not exist yet, organizations can collect, verify, and report on data using a combination of their own identified set of metrics and the available standardized IRIS metrics (GIIN, 2014b). An effectively designed impact measurement program is an iterative process, and many early actors in the sector caution against implementation paralysis with the aphorism: "Don't let perfection be the enemy of good."

Global Impact Investment Rating System

The Global Impact Investment Rating System (GIIRS) is a complementary tool to IRIS. "[It] is a comprehensive and transparent system for assessing the social and environmental impact [...] with a ratings and analytics approach analogous to Morningstar investment rankings and Capital IQ financial analytics" (B-Lab, 2014b). GIIRS is being developed by B-Lab, a nonprofit organization that focuses on advocating for change in legislation in favor of social enterprises and supporting the growth of the Impact Investment (B-Lab, 2014a). Organizations that have adopted IRIS metrics to self-assess and self-report on their impact can now choose to be GIIRS-rated and assessed. Adopting GIIRS is not a reinvention of an impact management strategy; GIIRS integrates IRIS metrics. A GIIRS Impact Assessment includes the analysis of data, largely drawn from IRIS, to assess an organization's impact. An independent third-party evaluator validates the data shared by the organization. GIIRS reports on the analyzed data with relevant stakeholders and shareholders on behalf of the company or fund. One of GIIRS' primary objectives is to allow Impact Investors to have a uniform system to compare and contrast the impact characteristics of different investment opportunities: "As of July 2013, 52 investment funds representing $2.7 billion in assets under management had GIIRS ratings" (Johnson & Lee, 2013). In order for the sector to scale, anecdotes are no longer a sufficient means of demonstrating effectiveness: robust, user-friendly, standardized assessment tools are the key to unlocking capital toward impact.

Intermediaries

At this nascent stage, a spectrum of intermediaries including government, private sector, innovative foundations, and independent institutions such as hubs and academic institutions all play a part in the growth of this sector (see Table 8.1).

While social innovation and well-articulated impact metrics are important, the scalability and financial viability of these innovations makes them investable enterprises. However, currently there are limited relevant and appropriate finance products for social enterprises. Rutherford and von Glahn (2014) articulate a critical issue in this sector with regard to matching appropriate investors and investees: "much of the available supply of Impact Investment capital is seeking [...] attractive financial returns combine[d] with positive social, economic or environmental

Table 8.1 Intermediaries involved in Impact Investing

Type of intermediary	*Immediate role*	*Long-term role*	*Support needed*
Early funders Philanthropists, such as high-net-worth individuals, innovative foundations	Provide initial capital, patient capital, technical expertise, reputational assets, and access to networks	Develop and participate in innovative and appropriate financial solutions, provide first loss protection to help catalyze other investors	Investable, scalable, and financially viable solutions to social and environmental problems
Policy makers Government organizations and agencies	Develop supportive legislation, convene intermediaries, bring mainstream capital and impact-oriented capital together, provide specific incentives, and leverage public funds	Rally financial and other resources to support and scale innovative social and environmental interventions	Public–private partnerships and cross-national collaboration
Trade associations and hubs	Develop rigorous and accessible metrics frameworks, help identify and address ongoing inefficiencies, communicate with Impact Investors, and provide technical assistance	Educate the market on impact metrics, establish best practices, connect investors and investees	Feedback from early adopters of metrics, market growth, and sector development
Academic institutions and university centers	Provide frameworks and analysis, faculty expertise, education and awareness building	Incubate and support the development of impact funds and social enterprises	Access to the sector

impact [...] meanwhile, there is an unmet demand from social enterprises [...] ready to absorb financial support." Intermediaries are stepping in to help close the capital void by developing creative non-traditional types of capital and financial structures with pay-offs appropriate for social enterprises (e.g., SIBs, first loss capital, etc.) (Rutherford & von Glahn, 2014). These institutions are also providing the varied technical assistance so critical in the early stages of any enterprise. Some key problem areas include: weak operational capacity, poorly defined business models, a general lack of awareness of how to raise capital, and poor supportive capacity.

In addition to traditional and non-traditional capital, social enterprises need ideas, talent, influence, and deep social networks: intermediaries are critical to accessing these resources. As detailed in Table 8.1, intermediaries in Impact Investing can be categorized into four distinct groups: early funders, policy makers, trade associations and hubs, and academic institutions and university centers.

Early funders

Funders serving as intermediaries include the innovative foundations, philanthropists, and high-net-worth individuals that have the capacity to be first movers as well as provide grant and first loss capital during the early stages of a social enterprise. This group not only brings funding to the sector but can also help investees with technical assistance in the form of operational and organizational capacity and access to their networks. Through their actions they can help the enterprise to become financially viable and scale its operations. These funders can also harness and influence non-traditional sources of capital, such as venture capital and private equity for investment in the sector.

US-based foundations hold over $550 billion in assets invested in the financial markets (Roeger, Blackwood, & Pettijohn, 2012), and evolving foundation strategies have the potential to unlock these assets toward mission. A growing number of foundations in the United States are making their first MRI, which will in effect test this process in each individual operating structure. Support among intermediaries is also crucial as more actors start getting involved in the sector. Changing the ecosystem of philanthropy is challenging—it requires a complete overhaul in the skill set of the personnel from traditional grant makers to investment analysts. It also requires a robust risk management system; with assets invested toward impact, both pre-investment rigorous due diligence and ongoing risk management become crucial. MRIs are the foundation and precursor for much of the Impact Investing market. It is worth noting that US private markets hold an estimated $210 trillion in assets, with $80 trillion in pension and institutional funds alone (Rodin, 2014). Needless to say, unlocking private capital for social change has the potential to be transformative.

Example

The F.B. Heron Foundation is an innovative foundation in the United States that is playing a significant role in the development of the Impact Investing sector. In their 2011 strategy, the foundation declared a move to deploy all their assets toward mission (F.B. Heron, 2014). Over the past three years, F.B. Heron's approach has evolved from solely grant-making, to making a combination of grants and investments in the form of patient capital—patient capital, as the name suggests, is longer term capital, critical for early-stage enterprise development. In this case, the investor is not looking for a quick return on capital, but rather is willing to wait for their investment to pay off. F.B. Heron is making PRI and MRI, depending on the need and capacity of the intended organization or investment. Through this progression, their goal is to have 100 percent of their assets deployed for mission by 2017; as of 2015 they had already reached 75 percent. To quote the organization: "We no longer believe that the legal requirement of using just five percent of endowment assets to make grants, while leaving the rest traditionally invested, is adequate to achieve the scale of social change we would like to see" (F.B. Heron, 2014).

Policy makers

The public sector in the form of government agencies and task forces is critical to the development of the impact investing sector. From the US Office of Social Innovation and Civic Participation to the G8 Social Investment Taskforce, the support and backing of the public sector is necessary to grow the capacity of this area. From developing legislation and providing incentives to creating supportive frameworks and leveraging agency funding, there are a growing number of success stories of policy makers effectively calling attention to the field and setting standards, and thus motivating investors to join the sector.

Example

In the United States, we have seen policy maker involvement in support of Benefit Corporations, or B Corps; "B Corp registration (the 'B' stands for 'benefit') allows a company to subordinate profits to social and environmental goals" (Alperovitz, 2011). This legislation, for example, protects a CEO from being sued by stockholders, if they make a decision that compromises maximizing profits in favor of a social and/or environmental objective. The state of Maryland became the first state to pass Benefit Corporation legislation in April 2010. Four-and-a-half years later, 20 states have signed B Corp legislation into law, with a growing number of states following suit. This law creates a new class of investable entities that embeds social mission into corporate purpose.

Trade associations and hubs

Trade associations and hubs such as the Global Impact Investing Network (GIIN) are also important actors for the development of the sector. By providing outreach, network connections, and research resources, these intermediaries can help to address the need for resources and services in the field including supportive capacity, matching of investors and investees, educating new entrants on best practices, and connecting new talent to opportunities.

Example

ImpactBase is an initiative of the GIIN that aims to provide a centralized database of information on investment opportunities. Developed out of conversations on the type of market infrastructure needed to address inefficiencies in this emerging sector, ImpactBase is a resource which responds to the type of concerns and challenges regarding a lack of quality investment opportunities with a demonstrated track record (Saltuk & Idrissi, 2014). This tool is searchable across categories including asset class, impact objectives, geographic area, fund status, etc. (GIIN, n.d.). Within six months of launch, ImpactBase included the profiles of 85 management firms and 106 funds (GIIN, n.d.).

Academic institutions and university centers

Academic institutions can play an integral role in attracting new entrants to the sector. University centers typically focus on a particular industry or field and generally have a goal related to thought leadership and knowledge creation in that area. Ideally, such centers also reflect a partnership of academia, government, and industry. Impact Investing as an emerging field is ripe ground for the academe to play an active role, offering resources and support during nascent development stages, while consequently developing opportunities for engagement, experiential learning, and access for students, faculty, and community. By positioning the university as incubator, whether formal or informal, centers can become a direct provider and intermediary of resources in an emerging field. Furthermore, as the field develops, there is an immediate need for data, research, and analysis, which faculty and researchers are able to provide. Conversely, Impact Investing is great fodder for case study development. Students at both the undergraduate and graduate levels are also a key resource to new ventures as interns and part-time staff.

Example

The Helene and Grant Wilson Center for Social Entrepreneurship at Pace University has an established Social Enterprise in Residence program which during the 2013–2014 academic year hosted the Impact America fund (Tekula, Shah, & Jhamb, 2015). Impact America is an early-stage GIIRS-rated equity firm that invests $250,000 to $2,000,000 in high-growth companies generating real financial returns while improving the well-being of underserved communities and creating quality jobs in the US (Impact America, n.d.). As part of the in-residence program, the Center provided Impact America with a full-time summer student intern to help with due diligence on potential fund investments. Wilson Center staff helped co-manage the intern and guide his work. In addition, a series of on-campus events have been held to develop awareness and share insights among both practitioners and students. Acting as a catalyst and supportive partner in this emerging field has allowed learning opportunities and real-time access and cases for research and teaching.

It is worth noting that none of these intermediaries acting alone is sufficient; collaborations enable innovative social sector solutions to further scale.

Social Impact Bonds (SIBs): Intermediaries in action

SIBs or PFS bonds are an example of what effective collaborations in the social impact space can achieve: a first-generation vehicle for Impact Investment. The impact bond concept originated in the United Kingdom. These bonds were developed through a unique public–private partnership and designed as a vehicle to catalyze private capital toward advancing social good. This innovative financial product leverages investment capital to support and expand effective social or environmental interventions (Social Finance, n.d.).

These bonds can be developed in a process whereby a public sector agency identifies a discrete social or environmental issue to be addressed and defines a specific, measurable outcome over a period of time. With defined outcomes and timeline in mind, the public sector agency contracts with an external organization which is responsible for (1) hiring a reputable nonprofit service organization to provide services to achieve the identified outcomes and (2) convening funders to provide the working capital needed to fund the service providers' programs (Shah & Costa, 2013). An independent evaluator then measures and verifies the outcomes, as defined by the contract. If achieved, the public sector entity makes a payout to repay the investors' principal, plus an agreed-upon return for taking the financial risk. If the contracted outcome is not achieved, the government agency does not pay out and investors typically lose their entire principal.

These types of contracts, if successful, save taxpayer money and expand the reach of effective social or environmental interventions. Rigor and accountability are vital to ongoing growth in this market. The estimated future savings are used to pay a return to investors.

Example

In January 2014, the state of Massachusetts announced a PFS program targeted at reducing youth crime. This intervention raised $18 million from private funders such as the Goldman Sachs Social Impact Fund and the Kresge Foundation, among others. Third Sector Capital Partners, the external organization, is managing the project, and a nonprofit youth intervention group, Roca, is the service provider. Roca's youth intervention program has a proven track record, including mechanisms to measure and report on outputs and outcomes. With the working capital injection, Roca will work with almost a thousand young men recently released or about to be released from jail, with the goal of reducing repeat criminal violations and prison terms.

The contracted outcome is a reduction in number of incarceration days by 40 percent over the 7-year contract period, as measured by an independent third-party evaluator. If this is achieved, the state of Massachusetts will pay principal plus some interest to the private investors; this amount is roughly equal to the estimated money the state would save through the decrease in incarceration days (Johnson, McGilpin, Hanscom, & Kelly, 2014).

Conclusion

What is the future of social innovation funding? Will Impact Investing grow to reach predicted market size? Can this industry ever function without heavily involved intermediaries? Can and should the industry create its own metrics of social impact?

As the landscape for social innovation funding evolves, it is evident that the growth of the Impact Investing sector will be an important driver of social innovation in the near future. A large number of actors are now active in the field, which includes a multinational group of nonprofit organizations and foundations, for-profit corporations, national governments and local government agencies, private bankers, asset managers, and institutional investors, among others.

Current forecasts of the market size of the Impact Investing sector alone range from $400 billion to $1 trillion. These forecasts are dependent upon the successful implementation of standardized and meaningful metrics for measuring social impact. However, there are a multitude of challenges to creating uniform metrics, and much can be learned from the work of innovative nonprofits and charities that have responded to the increasing demand for performance analytics from both individual and institutional philanthropic funders. While the measurement of SROI and rates of return are most commonplace among the Impact Investment community, there is a long history in the social change sector of the use of logic models, outcome measurement, impact evaluation, and specific approaches including RCTs.

Trade associations and conveners have emerged in an effort to support and sustain the Impact Investing industry. Supporting the implementation and use of metrics is just one way that the role of intermediaries has important implications for the evolution of the sector. Other supportive mechanisms include policy implementation, awareness building, and developing the investor-investee matching processes. There is the potential for these associations to foster and develop ratings agencies, as seen in the microfinance industry. Finally, much work can be done to present success stories where both market rate financial returns and meaningful social impact result from an investment—this could go a long way toward building the credibility of the field.

Early adopters in the US foundation sector are beginning to move the needle on expectations of how their peers invest assets. Impact Investments by these sources, which are by law only required to donate five percent of their assets to charity each year, have the potential to unlock much more of the aggregate $550 billion in foundation assets than what is currently at work for societal benefit.

Understanding the challenges of scale and the key factors limiting growth remain important areas for future exploration of the Impact Investing sector. While much work is underway in supporting these activities, and movements are being made toward an industry standard of measuring impact, it is only meaningful and visible examples of successful investments that will stimulate and reveal the potential of this emerging sector.

Acknowledgments

We are grateful for the support of the Helene T. and Grant M. Wilson Center for Social Entrepreneurship at Pace University. We benefited from discussions with Kesha Cash, Clarissa Middleton, and Nikita Singhal, the support of Adrian Rivero, and the research assistance of Jordan Jhamb. All figures and tables are our own.

References

Alperovitz, G. (2011, May 25). The new-economy movement. *The Nation*. Retrieved November 20, 2014, from http://www.thenation.com/article/new-economy-movement/

B-Lab. (2014a). *Powered by B-Lab*. Retrieved November 25, 2014, from http://www.benefitcorp.net/about-b-lab

B-Lab. (2014b). *About Global Impact Investing Rating System (GIIRS)*. Retrieved October 24, 2014, from http://b-analytics.net/giirs-ratings

Bouri, A. (2011). How standards emerge: The role of investor leadership in realizing the potential of IRIS. *Innovations: Technology, Governance, Globalization, 6*(3), 117–131.

Brest, P., & Born, K. (2013). When can impact investing create real impact? *Stanford Social Innovation Review, 11*(4), 22–27.

Carman, J. G. (2007). Evaluation practice among community-based organizations: Research into the reality. *Journal of Evaluation, 26*(1), 60–75.

F.B. Heron Foundation. (2014). Frequently Asked Questions. Retrieved October 24, 2014, from http://heron.org/engage/resources

Global Impact Investing Network (GIIN). (2014a). *About us*. Retrieved October 24, 2014, from http://www.thegiin.org/cgi-bin/iowa/investing/index.html

GIIN. (2014b). *Getting started with IRIS*. Retrieved October 24, 2014, from https://iris.thegiin.org/guides/getting-started-guide

GIIN. (n.d.). *ImpactBase, a database of impact investing funds, continues to attract subscribers*. Retrieved November 25, 2014, from https://thegiin.org/assetsbinary-data/MEDIA/pdf/000/000/20-1.pdf

Impact America. (n.d.). *About us*. Retrieved November 25, 2014, from http://www.impactamericafund.com

Johnson, H., McGilpin, B., Hanscom, J., & Kelly, M. (2014). *Massachusetts launches landmark initiative to reduce recidivism among at-risk youth*. Retrieved February 24, 2016, from http://rocainc.org/wp-content/uploads/2014/02/Pay-For-Success-Announcement-from-Govs-office.pdf

Johnson, K., & Lee, H. (2013). *Impact investing: A framework for decision making*. Boston, MA: Cambridge Associates LLC.

O'Donohoe, N., Leijonhufvud, C., & Saltuk, Y. (2010). *Impact investments, an emerging asset class* (pp. 7–23, 60–63, 66–72). New York: J.P. Morgan Global Research.

Office of Science and Technology Policy. (2014a). *Background on the White House Roundtable on Impact Investing: Executive actions to accelerate impact investing to tackle national and global challenges* [Electronic Version]. Retrieved November 24, 2014, from http://www.whitehouse.gov/sites/default/files/microsites/ostp/background_on_wh_rountable_on_impact_investing.pdf

Office of Science and Technology Policy. (2014b). *Executive actions to accelerate impact investing to create jobs and strengthen communities* [Electronic Version]. Retrieved November 24, 2014, from http://www.

whitehouse.gov/blog/2014/06/25/executive-actions-accelerate-impact-investing-create-jobs-and-strengthen-communities

Rodin, J. (2014, September). Innovations in finance for social impact. Rockefeller Foundation. *News&Media*. Retrieved February 24, 2016, from https://www.rockefellerfoundation.org/about-us/news-media/remarks-by-dr-judith-rodin-socap-2014/

Rodin, J., & Brandenburg, M. (2014). *The power of impact investing: Putting markets to work for profit and global good*. Philadelphia, PA: University of Pennsylvania, Wharton Digital Press.

Roeger, K. L., Blackwood, A., & Pettijohn, S. L. (2012). *The Nonprofit Almanac 2012*. Washington, DC: The Urban Institute Press.

Royal Bank of Canada. (2010, November). *An overview of impact investing*. Vancouver, BC: Phillips, Hager, & North Investment Management.

Rutherford, R., & von Glahn, D. (2014). *A fault in funding* [Electronic Version]. Retrieved November 17, 2014, from http://www.ssireview.org/articles/entry/a_fault_in_funding

Saltuk, Y., & Idrissi, A. E. (2014). *Spotlight on the market: The Impact Investor Survey*. New York: J.P. Morgan Social Finance.

Shah, S., & Costa, K. (2013). *Social finance: A primer. Understanding innovation funds, impact bonds, and impact investing*. Washington, DC: Center for American Progress.

Social Finance. (n.d.). *What is a social impact bond?* Retrieved November 25, 2014, from http://socialfinanceus.org/social-impact-financing/social-impact-bonds/what-social-impact-bond

Social Impact Investment Taskforce. (2014). *Social Impact Investment Taskforce report* [Electronic Version]. Retrieved November 24, 2014, from https://www.gov.uk/government/groups/social-impact-investment-taskforce

Tekula, R., Shah, S., & Jhamb, J. (2015) Universities as intermediaries: Impact investing and social entrepreneurship. *Metropolitan Universities Journal, 26*(1), 35–51.

Thomas, J. C. (2010). Outcome assessment and program evaluation. In D. O. Renz (Ed.), *Jossey-Bass handbook of nonprofit leadership and management* (pp. 401–430). San Francisco, CA: Jossey-Bass.

I.3
Special Instruments

9

CROWDFUNDING SOCIAL VENTURES

A model and research agenda

Othmar M. Lehner

Introduction

Media and public alike recognize the promise of crowdfunding (CF) for social entrepreneurs in the news; however, few to none scholarly articles exist that address the inner workings and implications of CF in such a context. The author therefore set out to thematically analyse existing nascent enquiries by reviewing extant literature, draws up a schema as a model and derives an agenda of eight-related research themes from it.

On the very basis, CF means tapping a large dispersed audience, dubbed as 'the crowd', for small sums of money to fund a project or a venture. CF is typically empowered by the social media communication over the Internet, through for example embracing user-generated content as guides for investors. CF has been addressed in the literature so far mostly in the context of creative industries, such as producing Indie music records or retro software games (Belleflamme et al. 2010a; Ward and Ramachandran 2010). The context of social ventures has remained largely unexplored so far.

Improving our knowledge of CF seems especially important for social entrepreneurship (SE) as traditional means of finance have proven as subpar or sometimes even inadequate in starting and sustaining growth of the many forms of SE (Agrawal et al. 2010; Brown and Murphy 2003; Fedele and Miniaci 2010; Ridley-Duff 2008).

Differences of SEs to traditional for-profits are shown in the literature to stem from

- ambiguous and sometimes dichotomous aims of SEs (Dacin et al. 2010), torn between the social and commercial (Lehner 2011b; Moss et al. 2011),
- alien corporate governance and legal and organizational structures in SEs that are difficult to accept for traditional investors and lenders (Agrawal et al. 2011; Gundry et al. 2011),
- cultural and cognitive distance-related barriers between for-profit investors and SEs that hinder communication (Bauer-Leeb and Lundqvist 2012),
- social entrepreneurs' narrations that are being hooked in the 'social' sphere (Brown and Murphy 2003) and are lacking the managerial terminology, which leads to severe scepticism in their managerial capabilities.

Such peculiarities of social ventures additionally aggravate the already difficult financing situation that many start-ups find themselves in (Cosh et al. 2009). Recent developments such as the financial crisis also contribute to the situation and increase pressure to find alternative access to funding and financing new social ventures, as the public sector has to reduce spending to cope with the high-accumulated governmental debts (Bielefeld 2009; Ferrera et al. 2004; Lehner 2011b).

Finding alternative, tailored methods of funding and financing by innovatively combining existing factors, such as everyday people's values and opinions, social media platforms and alternative reward systems, seems a consistent step for social entrepreneurs and fits well to the new emancipation of the crowd (Drury and Stott 2011; Reyes and Finken 2012; Valenzuela et al. 2012).

CF may offer one especially suited answer to the financing needs of social ventures, as crowd investors typically do not look much at collaterals or business plans, but at the ideas and core values of the firm (Ekedahl and Wengström 2010) and thus at its legitimacy. Aspects that are typically regarded as very positive in social entrepreneurial initiatives, and thus in theory CF and SE should match well (Dart 2004).

Such crowd-based processes may bring the additional benefit of being perceived by the public as per se democratic (Drury and Stott 2011), thus addressing critics of SEs' capitalist steering (Meyer 2009). In addition, the recent passing of the Jumpstart Our Business Start-ups (JOBS) act in the USA (Martin 2012; Parrino and Romeo 2012), which legalizes certain forms of equity CF for small businesses and start-ups based on volume criteria, shows that governments are becoming aware of the untapped potential and are trying to reduce legal barriers for entrepreneurs (Parrino and Romeo 2012).

Despite this potential for social entrepreneurs, few academic articles exist so far that address CF in this context – apart for a small stream focusing solely on donations (Firth 2012; Muller and Kräussl 2011). Even in the business-venturing domain as a whole, research on CF is only starting to emerge and is often based on anecdotal evidence with a focus on finite projects and the creative industry (Agrawal et al. 2010).

As for a definition of SE, the author addresses all kinds of ventures that have a social or environmental mission as their primal goal, which aim to be financially and legally independent and strive to become self-sustainable by means of the market. Such a broad characterization acknowledges the ongoing discussion on definitions, for example from the EMES or the social enterprise London (SEL; Defourny and Nyssens 2009a; Lehner 2011b; SEL 2001; Zahra et al. 2009), while it is open and wide-ranging enough not to exclude needlessly and perhaps even too early in this pre-paradigmatical field (Nicholls 2010c).

Addressing this void in literature, this paper thus set out to propose future research themes of CF in a social entrepreneurial context. It first debates current findings on financing and funding of social ventures. Subsequently, the small existing research canon on CF is explored in the literature and the author draws up a schema of CF.

Examining the perspectives of this schema in an SE context, eight themes are derived and proposed as a future research agenda.

Funding SE

As stated earlier, funding and financing in the SE domain have to deal with idiosyncrasies of social ventures (Shaw and Carter 2007). Some of these may arise from the entrepreneurs or founders themselves, as they often originate from traditional non-profit organizations and have a non-business-related educational background. The terminology thus used and the values implied in their narrations make it difficult to communicate with traditional investors and financial intermediaries (Bauer-Leeb and Lundqvist 2012). Social entrepreneurs' presentations often primarily deal with the social vision, impact and outcome and at the same time neglect aspects of cash-flow liquidity, long-term financial returns and planning and forecasting (Brown and Murphy 2003; Ridley-Duff 2009). A 2003 study of the Bank of England consequently finds that social entrepreneurs indeed have a hard time accessing traditional debt finance.

In addition to these idiosyncratic hurdles for social entrepreneurs, many of the known problems for start-ups also hold true in SE (Berger and Udell 2006; Dushnitsky and Shapira 2010; Irwin and Scott 2010; Lam 2010) – for example the effectuation principles used by entrepreneurs are barely compatible with the traditional rationales of banks, basing their financing decisions in project finance upon the long-term planning of stable cash flows (Chandler et al. 2011; Perry et al. 2012).

Centred upon these specifics, a specialized financial market has started to emerge for social entrepreneurs (Bull and Crompton 2006; Fedele and Miniaci 2010; Ridley-Duff 2009; SEC 2004). It includes very different forms of rewards, narrations and discourses as a whole, compared to traditional financial markets. Instead of focusing on financial returns on investments, for example, entrepreneurs have to participate with their social ideas in competitions organized by foundations such as Skoll or Ashoka, or increasingly by traditional for-profit companies as part of their CSR activities (Baron 2007; Cornelius et al. 2008; Gallego-Álvarez et al. 2011; Janney and Gove 2011). Specialized investment and performance metrics such as the social return on investment (SROI) have been proposed as instruments in decision-making and legitimization of investments (Flockhart 2005).

Many social ventures, however, still rely at least partially on donations and public grants (Bull and Crompton 2006; Fedele and Miniaci 2010; Ridley-Duff 2009) despite their aim of financial independence. This is especially true for developed countries with a corporate-statist welfare regime (Esping-Andersen 2006), where social enterprises often act as intermediaries between the public and private sectors in the provision of social welfare support (Lehner 2011a). However, recent cut-downs on welfare spending make it increasingly difficult for SEs to access public money, and on the other hand, donations are already highly competed for.

On the progressive side, several special banks, such as Kiva (Larralde and Schwienbacher 2012; Pope 2011; Rubinton 2011) or the Grameen Bank (Yunus and Weber 2007), have emerged, dealing with micro-financing of socially desirable and sustainable investments, especially in the realm of local micro-loans. In addition, several philanthropic venture capital funds and related investors/donors have surfaced, delivering funds, and also other resources such as networks and advice to social ventures (Scarlata and Alemany 2012). Investors' rewards often lie in a certain social impact, and amongst the tailored management performance measurement instruments, the SROI plays an important role, in which cascading social effects of the (social) venture are computed as monetary impact on public spending and income (Flockhart 2005).

Reporting practices of social entrepreneurs have been examined by Nicholls (2009, 2010b) in the context of the community interest company (CIC) in the UK. He found that the reporting practices not only account for financial performance but also include discussions on the social and environmental impacts, a logic that seems necessary when dealing with a multitude of stakeholders with differing aims, some driven by the social mission, others by financial sustainability.

One important aspect for financing social ventures has been almost neglected so far in literature; the trustworthiness of social entrepreneurs is regarded to be much higher due to the primacy of the social aim, and thus the costs of fraudulent risk should be reduced in theory (Lambert et al. 2012). We see early empirical claims for this based on the traditional non-profit literature (Frumkin and Kim 2001; Hansmann 1987; Haugh 2006; Herman and Renz 2008;

Kerlin 2006; Laratta 2010), but so far it has not improved social entrepreneurs' situation when seeking money from traditional sources.

Nicholls (2010a) examines types of social investors and their respective investment logics based upon a Weberian analytic lens between value and purpose. He creates a matrix of nine distinct models and captures early evidence of the actual flow of capital within the social investment landscape in the UK. His conclusion, based upon the dominance of a singular investor reality, will provide an interesting counterproposition to the rationale of the crowd, consisting of equal investors with various logics.

In Tables 9.1 and 9.2, the author presents a list of investor types, clustered by debt and equity claims, based on the literature as examined earlier and adapting and enhancing previous work by Larralde and Schwienbacher (2012). These tables specifically address the stage in which the various means are most applicable. Although previous literature hints that CF may be especially suitable in the start-up phase (Firth 2012; Lambert and Schwienbacher 2010; Ward and Ramachandran 2010), its potential for funding growth and expansion (Hynes 2009) has yet to be empirically examined.

CF literature in an SE context

Widespread Internet access and functioning social networking platforms together with the emancipation of the crowd (Drury and Stott 2011) propose interesting opportunities (Reyes and Finken 2012). Leveraging these phenomena in a process called CF can help entrepreneurs gain necessary start-up capital. Such a quest for alternative start-up capital is relevant as new ventures do not easily gain access to the necessary external finance at their early stages (Cosh et al. 2009). In later periods, business angels and venture capital funds may fill gaps for larger amounts; however, costs for proof-of-concepts and the first entrepreneurial steps are often only financed by the entrepreneur, family and friends (Cumming 2012; Dushnitsky and Shapira 2010; Irwin and Scott 2010). Early debt finance in such ventures is often brought up through a process identified in the literature as Bootstrapping (Lam 2010).

So, instead of relying on decisions made by a small group of relatively high-sophisticated investors and bank managers, the idea of CF is to tap and motivate a large audience, with each individual member of the crowd contributing only little (Belleflamme et al. 2010b) but with a high combined impact.

CF may thus provide a much-needed alternative for raising start-up capital for ventures seeking donations, debt or equity finance. CF as a constructed term is often considered in the literature as project-based funding only and so the term in its current usage does not fully comprise its full potential, which would also include more long-term commitments such as debt or equity shares (Crowdsourcing 2012). Also a distinct focus on donation-based CF for social entrepreneurs leaves out important market alternatives, where crowd members actually become shareholders. Especially equity-based CF will thus inevitably cross the border of simple project financing (Larralde and Schwienbacher 2012).

Scholars see the roots of CF in a movement that has been labelled as crowdsourcing, which comprises using the crowd to obtain ideas, feedback and solutions in order to develop corporate activities (Brabham 2008; Howe 2006; Kleemann et al. 2008). A distinct feature of the 'crowd' is seen in the literature as consisting of a large number of people, each contributing little, but with a possible high combined impact (Belleflamme et al. 2010b). However, such a crowd is supposed to behave in unforeseen, chaotic and complex manners (Drury and Reicher 1999; Drury and Stott 2011; Ivancevic et al. 2010; Massink et al. 2010), and therefore, a careful examination of the influential factors and functions is necessary.

Table 9.1 Equity investor types, SE accessibility and stages

Equity claims			
Type	*Description*	*Accessible for SE*	*Stage*
Entrepreneur and Family	Investing his/her own money into the social venture, or money borrowed privately from friends and family.	+++	Early start-up.
Social Target Group	A form of crowd sourcing by tapping the beneficiaries. Successful when the entrepreneurial innovation is understood and the leverage is perceived high enough. Suitable when many people are involved with small contributions from each individual. Complex forms of governance.	+++	Innovating, perhaps after some initial proof. Great impact on Corporate Governance.
Business Angels	Wealthy individuals, willing to invest in small social projects that fit to their intrinsic values and agenda.	++	Early stages, difficult to tap and scarce.
Venture Capitalists	Specialized investors, placing their fund-investors' money into larger projects for a longer period of time, but with a clear exit strategy. Fiduciary duties, lots of reporting necessary.	+	Growth. More specialized VC firms for SE emerge, not suitable for early start-ups.
Other Companies	Decide to invest in projects that have a strategic value for them. Perhaps from a Real-options logic to secure certain environmental patents, or as part of their CSR activities. Strategic Entrepreneurship.	–	All stages, but only as addition. Often highly selective, and with a negative impact on ventures' reputation.
Stock Markets	Public offering to invest in the company. Often problematic in social ventures due to the expected risk-adjusted return on investment. Some specialized funds targeting 'ethical' investments exist however. Possible negative consequences due to loss of control and high regulative efforts.	–	Globalization and tremendous scaling up of established and recognized social solutions.

Source: Adapted from Larralde and Schweinbacher (2012).

CF in an SE perspective can provide additional legitimacy to the venture, as the selection process by the crowd is perceived as per se democratic, and the crowd will thus select the social ideas it deems worthy and needed (Belleflamme et al. 2010b; Drury and Stott 2011; Rubinton 2011).

The concept of CF has been demonstrated in cases to work miraculously well. The amounts of money obtained even reach GBP 1 million, as in the case of Trampoline Systems UK, a high-tech start-up (Belleflamme et al. 2010b). The involved processes, from communication, utility functions to legal aspects, however, are far from being clear. Much need for experimentation, last minute changes and unforeseen legal hurdles have put the effort of Trampoline almost in jeopardy.

Belleflamme et al. (2010a) examine CF from an industrial organization perspective and associate CF with pre-ordering and the resulting price discrimination. Such a model may not hold well in an SE context as the investors' motives for investment may differ in that they are less concerned about costs but the outcome (Delanoë 2011; Fayolle et al. 2005; Shaw and Carter 2007). Belleflamme et al. also provide some theoretical underpinnings why non-profit organizations tend to be more successful in using CF by examining the literature on contract failure theory. This theory is based on the view that limiting monetary motivations of owners, such

Table 9.2 Debt investor types, SE accessibility and stages

Debt claims			
Type	*Description*	*Accessible for SE*	*Stage*
Banks	Loans. Special banks for social ventures exist. Often Project finance with little mutual understanding between (social aim) seeker and provider. Problems in terminology and cultural distance.	++	All stages, depending on the entrepreneurs' preferences for control and risk-taking. Increasing importance due to specialized banks.
Leasing Companies	Providing machinery and equipment to entrepreneurs against lease payments. Suitable for all types of ventures, when cash flows are stable and investment is relatively standardized.	+	Start-up and Expansion, for certain types of investment only. Often investment as collateral.
Government, Agencies	Subsidies, grants and credit to improve rating. Perhaps forms of PPP (public–private partnerships). Also service-based public funding. Highly competed for, problematic in times of government austerity.	++	High importance for socially desirable projects that can be run sustainably with a managerial attitude, but would not be attractive for traditional investors and entrepreneurs.
Customers/ Suppliers	Trade credit and upfront payments for future goods and services. Sometimes used in crowdfunding for special niche products.	++	Operational Expenses, depending on industry.
Bootstrapping	Clever use of working capital management (WCM) and Bricolage to start a business, together with a strict eye on expenses. Often used by small social entrepreneurial initiatives.	+++	Early stages, when motivations of stakeholders and entrepreneurs are high. Perhaps based upon personal traits.
Donations	While given for free, donors expect a certain type of reward, for example through achieving a certain social impact. This reward can also be personal, for example through creating a noble feeling or a better standing in society.	++	Still many social ventures rely partly on donations. Will become scarce with more competitors. Often used in crowdfunding initiatives with a honorary element.

Source: Adapted from Larralde and Schweinbacher (2012).

as prohibiting or limiting dividend payouts in some forms of SE (Lehner 2011b), attracts donations more easily and invites other forms of participation, such as voluntary work. Such a limit on monetary motivation for owners can also be seen as a strong signal that the owners put a significant weight on the quality of the outcome and less on monetary gains (Chillemi and Gui 1991; Van Slyke 2006). This invites perspectives from information economics and signalling on CF (Akerlof 1970; Balakrishnan and Koza 1993; Lambert et al. 2012).

Pope (2011) identifies legal hurdles for equity-based CF in the USA, asserted by the Security Exchange Commission, which can be transferred to some extent also to Europe and many other countries with a regulated capital market. He scrutinizes difficulties for micro-start-ups in gaining necessary equity capital and their willingness to bootstrap, using their own available resources. As the public offering of equity is highly regulated, it brings tremendous costs for auditing, creating prospectuses and consulting law firms and financial intermediaries. Pope thus observes equity-based CF in start-up ventures as being severely limited in the current legal situation. It is therefore logical that many forms of CF so far do not offer equity shares but other forms of rewards, for example early access to products, honorary recognition or some interest payments. However, to reflect on CF origins in crowdsourcing, equity stakes may on the one hand provide a pronounced democratic corporate governance (CG) model for social ventures, and on the other hand be the one missing opportunity for small investors in the crowd, seeking for ethical investments and rewards on alternative financial markets (Fox 2012). As reported earlier, legal and regulatory hurdles for equity CF are addressed in a perhaps ground-breaking manner by the recently passed JOBS act by the US President Obama. It lowers restrictions on Rule 506 offerings and frees seekers for small CF volumes, 100k USD, and to a lesser extent, 500k USD, from several costly regulations (Heminway and Hoffman 2011; Pope 2011; Rubinton 2011).

Larralde and Schwienbacher (2012) identify business models for CF, namely donations, passive and active investments by the crowd. Donation-based CF has been a long-established means of finance for NPOs and NGOs (Hansmann 1987; Nyssens et al. 2006). However, as the number of CF initiatives and platforms rises, the resource 'crowd' for donations becomes highly competed for and thus scarce. Larralde and Schwienbacher distinguish between active and passive CF. Passive CF sees some reward for its investors, for example tailored products, honorary recognition or other forms of revenue sharing. However, the interaction between the company and its crowd investors is limited to the rewarding function. Active CF differs in that aspect, as its investors are not only supplying money but are also in the best manner of crowdsourcing included in a constant dialogue with the company, helping for example in designing new features, testing products, suggesting paths for the company and supplying their network scope and individual expertise. This active form of CF is also very fruitful in providing a means for corporate communication and public relations, and through the dispersed positive discourse, dubbed 'buzz', it ultimately improves a company's legitimacy.

Such a quest for legitimacy is of high value especially for social ventures because of their dealing between the market, civil society and public sphere (Kerlin 2006). Social entrepreneurs on one hand address social voids by market activities but on the other hand also work as social change makers by influencing systems and policies (Cho 2006; Drayton 2006; Gunn et al. 2008). Such attempted policy change, however, may inevitably see resistance from incumbent powers and institutions (Ahlstrom and Bruton 2010; Bonoli and Palier 2009; Levander 2010; Lim et al. 2010; Mair and Marti 2009; Meyer et al. 2009), and therefore, needs to be backed by the power of the people in what they perceive as a legitimate case.

CF activities are also demonstrated to have a true global outreach through the means of the Internet and specialized social media platforms. Agrawal et al. (2011) examine this on the case of the record industry, and find that CF indeed shows a broad geographic dispersion of investors and that the negative impact of distance-sensitive costs is mitigated; a finding standing in contrast to traditional finance theory, which would hold a perspective of a rising distrust with distance. This broad geographic dispersion, however, also reflects well on SE, which is also designated as a truly global phenomenon (Zahra et al. 2009, 2008), and in which many initiatives work on a very international level even from the beginning (Korsgaard 2011; Meyskens et al. 2010; Zahra et al. 2008).

A proposed schema of CF

Based on the previously examined literature and some early empirical evidence as discussed in the previous sections, the author presents an early schema of the inner workings of CF, which is then applied and discussed in an SE context (Figure 9.1).

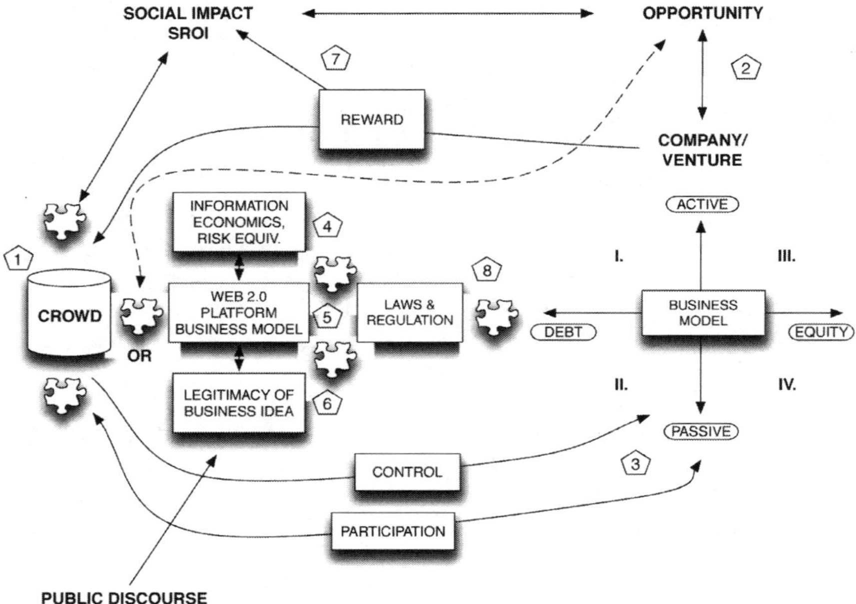

Figure 9.1 Schema of crowdfunding

Overview of the schema

This schema displays the matchmaking process between the venture, offering debt or equity investments, and the crowd. Opportunity recognition (OR) in this schema is essential, as not only the entrepreneur but also the crowd has to recognize it, informed through communication channels and the user-generated content on the Web platforms. Matchmaking takes place when members of the crowd decide to participate in the exploitation of this opportunity based upon its perceived legitimacy. This participation in the venture can take place within one of the four quadrants, spanning business models (active–passive) as well as type of capital (debt–equity). Communication and business strategies of the Web-based CF platforms as intermediaries; networks of crowd members pointing to these and aspects of information economics (reducing the asymmetry) together with the crowd members' individual risk equivalents will form the so-called motivational block (based upon utility functions). The outcome will be moderated by reward, levels of control and participation offered, but more so by the intermediary platform's business model. Laws and regulations (including related costs) finally will form a strong mediator block between the crowd, the CF platform and the desired participation in the venture.

The four quadrants describe the actual nature of the investment offering, between debt and equity, and active or passive participation. Debt or equity financing, however, is not a purely deliberate choice of investors and entrepreneurs likewise. Rather the stage and phase of the venture, aspects of risk dispersion, legal regulations, as well as nonmonetary goals such as CG and reputation, have a big influence on capital formation (Berger and Udell 1998; Kreiser et al. 2010).

The enthusiasm of the investing group regarding the desired outcome (Duckett and Swerissen 1996; Qiongzhi 2007; Ruebottom 2011) of the crowd-funded venture seems to be a much higher motivation for an active participation than to ensure monetary, interest-like incentives and influence risk taking. As has been seen in the cases of Kittur (2010), Kleemann et al. (2008)

and Whitla (2009), such active participation can take many forms of crowdsourcing (Brabham 2008), from testing early prototypes to advertising and viral marketing and from volunteering work such as translating texts to serving at events. It seems beneficial even to the funding process itself to offer and invite some form of investors' partaking. Participation of the crowd will typically create 'buzz' in the social media that may draw even more future potential investors to the CF platform site (Belleflamme et al. 2010b). However, previous literature by Larralde and Schwienbacher suggests there will be a recurring shift between active and passive involvements, depending on the individuals' circumstances as well as on the stage of the venture.

Capital formation is essential to economic developments, as it enables entrepreneurs to create new solutions to opportunities (Cumming 2012; Seghers et al. 2012). This also holds true for social entrepreneurs in their opportunity seeking and exploitation strategies (Cha and Bae 2010; Korsgaard 2011; Lehner and Kaniskas 2012).

Due to legal restrictions, so far few long-term maturing, crowd-funded bonds have been issued outside of the traditional regulated market, so we can only guess on required interest rates or the level of control and reporting expected from long-term lenders in CF (Larralde and Schwienbacher 2012; Pope 2011; Rubinton 2011). Most cases of debt financing so far have been of the type of advance payments (Agrawal et al. 2010; Firth 2012; Larralde and Schwienbacher 2012; Ward and Ramachandran 2010) for future goods or services; however, another interesting aspect of debt may be crowd-funded donations and grants.

Equity financing may provide the greatest challenges but also the greatest opportunities for crowd-funded social ventures (Artiach and Clarkson 2011). Typically, equity investments are legally linked with several rights, among the rights of information and control, and the right to participate in the earnings or added value of the company (Berger and Udell 1998). Selling shares of equity is ultimately a means of distributing risk onto the shoulders of many investors, compared to debt finance, in which the entrepreneur shoulders all risk himself/herself (Amit et al. 1990; Sharfman and Fernando 2008). Equity-based CF does therefore come at a much higher cost for the ventures, but perhaps contrary to the traditional theories less in a monetary sense but more so in terms of control, governance and stewardship (Meuleman et al. 2009; Williamson 1988).

Dispersing control is counted as a detrimental aspect in traditional for-profit financing; however, this impact on CG may hold positive merits in social ventures, as increased shareholder participation will improve legitimacy in the eyes of the public and may also refine the actual approach to the social needs towards higher effectiveness (Beckmann 2011; Bull et al. 2010; Ridley-Duff 2009, 2010). However, besides the positive, an increased dispersion of control may well hinder thoughtful experimentation and necessary changes of strategy by the founders, lessening the chances of entrepreneurial innovation (Huarng and Yu 2011; Ruvinsky 2012; Vaccaro et al. 2012).

The challenges for equity-based CF are thus multi-faceted; they comprise legal and regulatory hurdles (Heminway and Hoffman 2011; Larralde and Schwienbacher 2012; Pope 2011; Rubinton 2011; Schwienbacher and Larralde 2010), as well as considerations about governance and control. Public offering (exceeding to a certain amount of people) of a company's equity is highly regulated in most developed countries – the main reasons given to prevent fraud (Altman and Sabato 2007; Hmieleski and Baron 2008) and to enable an efficient market through reducing information asymmetry (Deakins and Hussain 1994; Lambert et al. 2012; Schnatterly et al. 2008). Even the sharing of net revenues to investors is seen as a security offering and thus highly regulated. Therefore, CF platforms in various countries such as the UK or the Netherlands, which allow CF for equity, need to use complex schemes of partaking and control in the entity to avoid legal pitfalls.

Concerning the traditional reward systems of shareholder value and dividends, possible utility functions of equity investors in crowd-funded social ventures may differ from those of traditional for-profit investors, such as business angels or venture capital funds. Several legal forms, tailored for social enterprises, such as the CIC in the UK or L3C in the USA, have some kind of dividend pay-out prohibition (Nicholls 2009, 2010b; Ridley-Duff 2008, 2009) and any accumulated wealth cannot be paid out to shareholders, even after closure of such a firm. These rules may thus prevent interest from many investors and the ongoing discussion on the usefulness of distinct SE legal forms has a new facet (Galera and Borzaga 2009).

There are also the more strategic and for-profit considerations based upon real-options logic (Levitas and Chi 2010; Scherpereel 2008; Tong and Reuer 2007) that may bring crowd-investors to fund social ventures with equity finance. Some relatively small financing early at the beginning may provide access and control over the investment if it turns out to be successful later (Husted 2005; Levitas and Chi 2010; Scherpereel 2008; Tong and Reuer 2007; Wang and Lim 2008). In an SE context, this option may well be embedded in the CSR strategy of larger companies and can also provide a very tangible competitive advantage later for example through access to patents that may come in handy in ever changing energy and other environmental regulations (Block 2012; Brettel et al. 2012; Cuervo Cazurra and Annique Un 2010; Husted 2005; Mcwilliams and Siegel 2010).

Proposing a research agenda

Derived from the proposed schema, eight themes are identified (see related numbers in Figure 1) to further the field by using a stepwise refinement research methodology based upon the maturity of the theory (Edmondson and Mcmanus 2007). The first steps need to be descriptive in nature, to assess the relevance of the individual blocks, find variables and come up with theories of quantification, subsequent correlation and ultimately explanation (Bluhm et al. 2011; Connelly et al. 2010). It is these explanations that can later be put into recommendations for policy-makers and businesses alike.

Types and utility functions of crowd investors

Using the 'crowd' to obtain ideas, feedback and solutions in order to develop corporate activities (Brabham 2008; Howe 2006; Kleemann et al. 2008) is nothing new. The widely available access to social media and networks makes it easy to tap a large number of people instantly. A distinct feature of the crowd was carved out in the previous paragraphs as consisting of a large number of people, each contributing little, but with a possible high combined impact (Belleflamme et al. 2010b; Whitla 2009). It has been examined that such a crowd is behaving in unforeseen, chaotic and complex manners (Drury and Reicher 1999; Drury and Stott 2011; Ivancevic et al. 2010; Massink et al. 2010) and that small activities by the company (including the omission of certain actions) can lead to a hyperbolic response by the crowd. However, what we do not know is what motivates the individuals being part of the crowd. Do these motivations differ for certain types of offered crowd investments? Previous research seems to hint at that, as there is a distinctiveness in the handling of investors between CF for donations, projects or equity (Larralde and Schwienbacher 2012).

Kozinets et al. (2008) distinguish between four types of online consumer communities, Crowds, Hives, Mobs and Swarms, and find that collective innovation is produced both as an aggregated byproduct of everyday information consumption and as a result of the efforts of talented and motivated groups of innovative e-tribes. Their proposed typology may provide a starting point to address types of collective investors from a macro-marketing perspective, as the difference between crowd consumers and investors in CF is often only marginal.

Motivational factors, such as financial reward systems or personal involvement, may well be positively correlated to one type, but deter others. Nicholls (2010a) identifies types of social investors and their respective investment logics and creates a matrix of nine distinct models. His scenarios, each based upon the dominance of a singular investor reality, will provide an interesting counterproposition to the rationale of the crowd, consisting of equal investors with various logics.

Research in this area should therefore look into the perspective of the crowd as an emancipated entity, as well as on the individual members and their motivations stemming from the psychological to the economical. Answers will allow SEs to serve a broader spectrum of approaches to attract and retain crowd investors and to increase efficiency through tailored approaches for target audiences.

Opportunity recognition and matchmaking

OR is at the very heart of venture creation; some scholars regard OR even as the basis of entrepreneurship (Short et al. 2010). As Lehner and Kaniskas (2012) and Corner and Ho (2010) examine, existing SE literature on OR draws upon a multitude of theoretical frameworks for their research. Among others, theories from Austrian School economists such as Schumpeter, Kirzner and Hayek (Murphy and Coombes 2009; Zahra et al. 2009) are employed and the behavioural theory of the firm (Zahra et al. 2008) is applied. In addition, closely related concepts to OR, such as Bricolage or innovation, are used to integrate OR and exploitation into a broader perspective of SE (Archer et al. 2009; Corner and Ho 2010; Di Domenico et al. 2010; Fuglsang 2010; Nicholls 2010c; Shaw and Carter 2007). Some scholars maintain that SE opportunities are different from those found in for-profit ventures (Corner and Ho 2010; Mair and Noboa 2006; Robinson 2006). Different views on OR exist, depending on the activeness of the entrepreneur and the dispersion of available information. In CF, another perspective is added. Not only the entrepreneurs have to identify an opportunity, but also the crowd has to recognize and evaluate it. This brings an additional hurdle to the actual exploitation. In traditional financing, entrepreneurs have to deal with few, relatively sophisticated investors and need to convince them, often using business plans and forecasts. In CF, opportunities need to be communicated to a great mass of heterogeneous people, using different instruments and strategies. The individual crowd members in this model can be either (a) passive listeners acting on the available information or (b) active seekers looking for opportunities. Future research in this area will need to address this dual OR of the entrepreneur and the crowd alike, and take an eye on the SE context of OR. Findings will deliver insights on how an OR transfer can take place, from the entrepreneurs' alertness or informedness, to the crowd.

Business models and corporate governance

A distinct CG with a broad stakeholder inclusion is seen as one central and defining element in the SE literature (Beckmann 2011; Nicholls 2010b). Stakeholder participation, the division of control power not based on the number of shares, and community-based decision-making processes are part of everyday life for many social ventures (Borzaga et al. 2008; Defourny and Nyssens 2009a, 2009b; Mason et al. 2007; Travaglini 2009).

With the inclusion of the crowd, consisting of a multitude of (partly anonymous) individuals as stakeholders or even shareholders, new approaches to CG models in SE need to be addressed.

It may be difficult to include the crowd in traditional decision-making processes; therefore, communication means and forms need to be created and adapted, often powered by Web-based services over the Internet. The impact of such a large number of involved people can nevertheless have several beneficial aspects. Among them are an increased legitimacy, bringing with it a higher acceptance and attractiveness to invest and work for such a company (Lumpkin 2011; Patriotta et al. 2011), or a refined outlook of what is really needed through the feedback of the many. The interplay of organizational forms, types of involvement, stakeholder tailored reporting (Nicholls 2009) and means of participation in CF may be the foremost questions to be asked in this context.

CG structures differ between countries, based upon legal requirements as well as different cultures and mindsets. Therefore, careful longitudinal enquiries in the CG structures of crowd-funded social ventures, scrutinizing the hurdles and opportunities for CF within existing CG structures, as well as respective public acceptance in a comparative fashion, will provide further insights into this theme. Carmel and Harlock (2008) examine governance in the 'third sector' and bring new perspectives on the governance of what they call the 'dispersed state', which may provide an interesting starting point in such discussions.

Information economics, reporting and risk

A growing body of research literature on communication strategies in the field of investor relations (IR) is available (Bassen et al. 2010; Kirchhoff and Piwinger 2009). Different approaches to potential and existing investors are laid out, united by the commonly accepted ambitions to attract new and keep current investors, fulfil legal requirements concerning reporting and disclosure and reduce the perceived idiosyncratic risk (differing from systemic risk stemming from industry). Ultimately, the intent of these measures is to reduce the cost of capital (Millo and Mackenzie 2009) and provide a true and fair view on the risk/return ratio.

Specialized platforms on the Internet, such as Kickstarter, have been brought to life as distinct business models, addressing the perceived communication needs of ventures seeking for CF and slowly taking over the role of financial intermediaries. IR literature holds much about communication in the web-age (Singer and Cacia 2009) including the importance of network domino effects for the dispersion of information. The primacy of the simply understood socially desirable mission of a venture, however, is unique in CF IR, compared to the more ample capital market stories typically drawn up in traditional companies (Bassen et al. 2010).

Reporting practices of social entrepreneurs have been examined by Nicholls (2009, 2010b), which he describes as 'blended value accounting'. Not only financial performance is disclosed, but the reports also include discussions on the social and environmental impacts. Exactly how reporting will take place in the area of highly dispersed investors remains unclear so far. Research in this theme therefore needs to look at the role of risk and information dispersion, enquire about legal proceedings, examine the risk equivalents of crowd-investors and perhaps challenge agency theory as a whole (Heracleous and Lan 2012).

Networking and the role of platforms

Crowd-funded ventures rely heavily upon networks, mainly brought together by the Internet. Networking theory has already proven to be highly predictive in modelling the flow of various resources, such as materials and workforce, but also more generally capabilities, information, business partners and opportunities in various situations (Dobrow et al. 2011; Hoang and Antoncic 2003; Mahmood et al. 2011; Martinez and Aldrich 2011; Soh 2010; Sullivan and

Marvel 2011). Early research in CF for example sees a distinct approach to geographical closeness, compared to other forms of venture financing (Agrawal et al. 2011). Geographical distance does not come with the expected risk premium in CF. Also the importance of structural holes in linking cycles of crowd investors (Batjargal 2010) in order to globally disperse information about the investment opportunity may provide a fascinating lens for enquiry.

Nodes in these networks will be the individual crowd members but more so the platforms and their respective followers. The examination of the role of these platforms as amplifiers and mediators, creating quasi super-nodes, as well as of the ties, ruled and regulated by payment providers, will be crucial in getting the whole picture. Research thus would take existing networking theory and adapt it where possible in order to model the flow of communication and resources.

Discourse and legitimacy of CF

Higher legitimacy of a venture (or better of its respective opportunity) increases acceptance of its activities and helps accessing resources such as materials or workforce. In the case of CF, the legitimacy of a venture will ultimately moderate the crowd's willingness to invest in it. Legitimacy, however, is built up in a complex, recursive process, involving the individuals' values, self-pictures, needs and wants and the perceptions of the venture created by public discourse (Cornelissen and Clarke 2010; Dart 2004; Nicholls 2010c; Patriotta et al. 2011), which is difficult to predict when targeting a large heterogeneous audience.

The success of social entrepreneurs dealing in between the market, civil and public sector already depends on positive communication and thus ultimately on perceived legitimacy of their doings (Di Domenico 2009; Di Domenico et al. 2010; Lehner 2011b).

Are crowds then per se democratic, and is the dispersion of control in such ventures therefore always a positive thing (Drury and Reicher 1999)? Does CF for example help overcome the criticism of leaving social welfare provision in the hands and decisions of a few, as has been raised in the literature (Meyer 2009; Palier 2010)?

Research in this theme needs to be downright interdisciplinary, borrowing from the interplay between the domains of sociology and psychology, looking at the diverse fields of politics, law, international relations, communication and business, applying and modifying a diverse range of theories such as new institutionalism or contract failure theory.

There is also a methodological challenge included, as Büscher and Urry (2009) see the need for new strategies of enquiry in the age of mobile devices, which allow access to 'information at your fingertips'. This information is however condensed and often reduced of the richness of context specifics. They examine and propose the 'mobilities' paradigm in how to conduct empirical studies that better grasp the nature of movements of people, objects, information and ideas.

Challenging finance metrics and instruments in a CF environment

The capital asset pricing model (CAPM) in its various forms is still seen as a basis to many of the finance-related metrics and instruments (Andersen et al. 2007; Berger and Udell 2006; Hovakimian et al. 2001; Millo and Mackenzie 2009). The assumptions in the calculation of the weighted average cost of capital, influenced by the costs of equity based on CAPM, are still widespread accepted (Artiach and Clarkson 2011; Brown 2011; Kunc and Bhandari 2011) and serve as a guiding principle in making traditional investment decisions.

Theory claims that investors will make use of derived models to compute the necessary return on investment based on risk comparisons. However, early empirical evidence shows that in CF, most members of the crowd are more motivated by the either explicitly or implicitly proposed non-monetary value and return (Belleflamme et al. 2010b; Drury and Stott 2011). Literature suggests the further development and inclusion of the SROI as a metrics in social ventures (Flockhart 2005) to help investors choose the highest leverage of their (social) investment.

However, so far, it has remained unclear whether such complex investment metrics really provide a decision-making tool, or are rather used to maintain some form of rationalization after the investment – which was in fact originally based upon more intrinsic choices. Especially the public sector, however, needs such tools to have a rational answer to questions about their investments and grants to social initiatives (Hennala et al. 2011; Hood 2011; Patriotta et al. 2011).

In the CF field, especially when investing in equity shares, real-options logic (Husted 2005; Levitas and Chi 2010; Scherpereel 2008; Tong and Reuer 2007), which is derived from financial markets, can provide another frame of thinking to explain investors' choices. Such thinking leads to limiting potential losses to the price of the option (the small initial investment), allows holding a bundle of strategic investment options as an answer to uncertainty and ultimately enables investors to claim their stakes when some of the ventures later gain movement and the proof of concept has been made.

Research in this theme needs to address the adaption of traditional metrics and explore new ways to measure and predict investment decisions. Perspectives from Behavioural Finance, such as 'herding', may also provide insights into the inner rationale of crowd investors (Fairchild 2011; Lehner 2004; Shleifer 2000).

Legal and regulatory perspectives in CF

Platforms addressing equity-based CF often come up with a complex scheme of control and partaking in order to avoid costly rules and regulations. Due to high public pressure in a reclining economy, the recently passed JOBS act is celebrated in the media as a giant step for entrepreneurship in the USA, as it exempts some equity CF from excessive regulatory schemes (Heminway and Hoffman 2011; Parrino and Romeo 2012; Pope 2011). Such a scheme, as suggested in this act, allows smaller ventures to offer equity or securities via crowd activities, while the necessary regulations are held at a minimum. It is thus seen as a big alleviation for entrepreneurs and newly founded ventures to travel further down the growing path after the initial steps – before venture capitalists of all sorts would find the investment attractive.

Research in this theme needs to address the implications of such rules and regulations, costs being one side, but the diminished value of reporting and auditing may well be a backlash for the efforts to attract crowd-based equity investors due to rising information asymmetry, and the fear of moral hazards.

Besides international legal and comparative studies, it might also be fruitful to apply agency theory and identify for example lobbying groups and their motives (Heracleous and Lan 2012). Also the long-term impact of these new rules and regulations for crowd-funded initiatives on traditional finance market rulings for small ventures may provide further perspectives.

In addition, the role of intermediaries in CF, for example the platforms themselves, with their perceived fiduciary duties, needs to be addressed in order to provide guidance to both investors and ventures (Rubinton 2011). It will be interesting to see case studies on how courts decide on the role of these intermediaries when the first moral hazards and cases of fraud appear.

Is the legal system prepared for the complex scheme of CF with so many and often globally dispersed participants? A special focus might also be necessary on the payment providers. Besides taxation and currency exchange issues, their activities are under strict oversight and control by individual governments and thus politics may exert influence.

The choice and interplay of legal business forms with their inherent organizational forms has been seen to matter in capital formation (Belleflamme et al. 2010a; Dushnitsky and Shapira 2010; Edwards and Edwards 2008; Lambert et al. 2012). The SE sector shows tailored and often highly complex legal forms such as community interest companies (e.g. the CIC or L3C) with unusual organizational structures (Hill et al. 2010), providing interesting perspectives for future research in how the crowd perceives these as investment opportunities.

Conclusion

This paper has reviewed extant literature on CF and its financial underpinnings in an SE context, and has outlined eight CF-related research themes that would provide valuable information for academics, policy-makers and practitioners.

Once more we see that the complex and ambiguous nature of SE provides a fascinating playground for researchers from various disciplines (Mair and Marti 2006). The almost undefined and disputed field of CF for donations, equity or debt, even increases this convolution of terms, concepts and actions. The proposed schema of the inner workings of CF shall thus reduce ambiguity and provide a framework for researchers to find a common ground.

We need to see rigorous and robust conceptual and empirical research, drawing and developing from existing proven theories from a multitude of disciplines. Such solid research endeavours ultimately need to address and inform policy-makers and practitioners likewise in order to increase the success of CF of new (social) ventures – a worthwhile scholarly pursuit.

Acknowledgement

With permission to reprint, this chapter was originally published as: Lehner, O. M. 2013. Crowdfunding social ventures: A model and research agenda. *Routledge Venture Capital*, 15 (4): 289–311.

References

Agrawal, A. K., C. Catalini, and A. Goldfarb. 2010. "Entrepreneurial Finance and the Flat-World Hypothesis: Evidence from Crowd-Funding Entrepreneurs in the Arts." Working Papers.

Agrawal, A. K., C. Catalini, and A. Goldfarb. 2011. "The Geography of Crowdfunding." NBER Working Paper No. w16820. http://ssrn.com/abstract=1770375

Ahlstrom, D., and G. D. Bruton. 2010. "Rapid Institutional Shifts and the Co Evolution of Entrepreneurial Firms in Transition Economies." *Entrepreneurship Theory and Practice* 34 (3): 531–554.

Akerlof, G. A. 1970. "The Market for 'Lemons': Quality Uncertainty and the Market Mechanism." The *Quarterly Journal of Economics* 84: 488–500.

Altman, E. I., and G. Sabato. 2007. "Modelling Credit Risk for SMES: Evidence From the US Market." *Abacus* 43 (3): 332–357.

Amit, R., L. Glosten, and E. Muller. 1990. "Entrepreneurial Ability, Venture Investments, and Risk Sharing." *Management Science* 36 (10): 1232–1245.

Andersen, T. G., T. Bollerslev, P. Christoffersen, and F. X. Diebold. 2007. *Practical Volatility and Correlation Modeling for Financial Market Risk Management*. Chicago: University of Chicago Press.

Archer, G., T. Baker, and R. Mauer. 2009. "Towards an Alternative Theory of Entrepreneurial Success: Integrating Bricolage, Effectuation and Improvisation." *Frontiers of Entrepreneurship Research* 29 (6): 4–26.

Artiach, T. C., and P. M. Clarkson. 2011. "Disclosure, Conservatism and the Cost of Equity Capital: A Review of the Foundation Literature." *Accounting & Finance* 51 (1): 2–49.

Balakrishnan, S., and M. P. Koza. 1993. "Information Asymmetry, Adverse Selection and Joint-Ventures 1: Theory and Evidence." *Journal of Economic Behavior & Organization* 20 (1): 99–117.

Baron, D. P. 2007. "Corporate Social Responsibility and Social Entrepreneurship." *Journal of Economics & Management Strategy* 16 (3): 683–717.

Bassen, A., H. Basse Mama, and H. Ramaj. 2010. "Investor Relations: A Comprehensive Overview." *Journal für Betriebswirtschaft* 60 (1): 49–79.

Batjargal, B. 2010. "The Effects of Network's Structural Holes: Polycentric Institutions, Product Portfolio, and New Venture Growth in China and Russia." *Strategic Entrepreneurship Journal* 4 (2): 146–163.

Bauer-Leeb, M., and E. Lundqvist. 2012. "Social Entrepreneurs and Business Angels – A Quest for Factors Facilitating Business Relationships." PhD thesis, Danube University Krems.

Beckmann, M. 2011. "The Social Case as a Business Case: Making Sense of Social Entrepreneurship from an Ordonomic Perspective." In *Corporate Citizenship and New Governance*, edited by I. Pies and P. Koslowski, 91–115. Heidelberg: Springer-Verlag.

Belleflamme, P., T. Lambert, and A. Schwienbacher. 2010a. "Crowdfunding: An Industrial Organization Perspective." Paper presented at *Digital Business Models Conference: Understanding Strategies*, Paris, France, June 25–26.

Belleflamme, P., T. Lambert, and A. Schwienbacher. 2010b. "Crowdfunding: Tapping the Right Crowd." CORE Discussion Paper No. 2011/32. http://ssrn.com/abstract=1578175

Berger, A. N., and G. F. Udell. 1998. "The Economics of Small Business Finance: The Roles of Private Equity and Debt Markets in the Financial Growth Cycle." *Journal of Banking and Finance* 22 (6–8): 613–673.

Berger, A. N., and G. F. Udell. 2006. "A More Complete Conceptual Framework for SME Finance." *Journal of Banking & Finance* 30 (11): 2945–2966.

Bielefeld, W. 2009. "Issues in Social Enterprise and Social Entrepreneurship." *Journal of Public Affairs Education* 15 (1): 69–86.

Block, J. H. 2012. "R&D Investments in Family and Founder Firms: An Agency Perspective." *Journal of Business Venturing* 27 (2): 248–265.

Bluhm, D. J., W. Harman, T. W. Lee, and T. R. Mitchell. 2011. "Qualitative Research in Management: A Decade of Progress." *Journal of Management Studies* 48 (8): 1866–1891.

Bonoli, G., and B. Palier. 2009. "How Do Welfare States Change? Institutions and Their Impact on the Politics of Welfare State Reform in Western Europe." *European Review* 8 (3): 333–352.

Borzaga, C., G. Galera, and R. Nogales. 2008. *Social Enterprise: A New Model for Poverty Reduction and Employment Generation. An Examination of the Concept and Practice in Europe and the Commonwealth of Independent States*. Bratislava: UNDP, EMES.

Brabham, D. C. 2008. "Crowdsourcing as a Model for Problem Solving: An Introduction and Cases." *Convergence: The International Journal of Research into New Media Technologies* 14 (1): 75–90.

Brettel, M., R. Mauer, A. Engelen, and D. Küpper. 2012. "Corporate Effectuation: Entrepreneurial Action and Its Impact on R&D Project Performance." *Journal of Business Venturing* 27 (2): 167–184.

Brown, H., and E. Murphy. 2003. *The Financing of Social Enterprises: A Special Report by the Bank of England*. Domestic Finance Division, Bank of England, London. London: Bank of England.

Brown, S. J. 2011. "The Efficient Markets Hypothesis: The Demise of the Demon of Chance?" *Accounting & Finance* 51 (1): 79–95.

Bull, M., and H. Crompton. 2006. "Business Practices in Social Enterprises." *Social Enterprise Journal* 2 (1): 42–60.

Bull, M., R. Ridley-Duff, D. Foster, and P. Seanor. 2010. "Conceptualising Ethical Capital in Social Enterprise." *Social Enterprise Journal* 6 (3): 250–264.

Büscher, M., and J. Urry. 2009. "Mobile Methods and the Empirical." *European Journal of Social Theory* 12 (1): 99–116.

Carmel, E., and J. Harlock. 2008. "Instituting the 'Third Sector' as a Governable Terrain: Partnership, Procurement and Performance in the UK." *Policy & Politics* 36 (2): 155–171.

Cha, M.-S., and Z.-T. Bae. 2010. "The Entrepreneurial Journey: From Entrepreneurial Intent to Opportunity Realization." *Journal of High Technology Management Research* 21 (1): 31–42.

Chandler, G. N., D. R. Detienne, A. Mckelvie, and T. V. Mumford. 2011. "Causation and Effectuation Processes: A Validation Study." *Journal of Business Venturing* 26 (3): 375–390.

Chillemi, O., and B. Gui. 1991. "Uninformed Customers and Nonprofit Organization: Modelling Contract Failure Theory." *Economics Letters* 35 (1): 5–8.

Cho, A. H. 2006. "Politics, Values and Social Entrepreneurship: A Critical Appraisal." In *Social Entrepreneurship*, edited by J. Mair, J. Robinson, and K. Hockerts, 34–56. Hampshire: Palgrave.

Connelly, B. L., R. D. Ireland, C. R. Reutzel, and J. E. Coombs. 2010. "The Power and Effects of Entrepreneurship Research." *Entrepreneurship Theory and Practice* 34 (1): 131–149.

Cornelissen, J. P., and J. S. Clarke. 2010. "Imagining and Rationalizing Opportunities: Inductive Reasoning and the Creation and Justification of New Ventures." *Academy of Management Review* 35 (4): 539–557.

Cornelius, N., M. Todres, S. Janjuha-Jivraj, A. Woods, and J. Wallace. 2008. "Corporate Social Responsibility and the Social Enterprise." *Journal of Business Ethics* 81 (2): 355–370.

Corner, P. D., and M. Ho. 2010. "How Opportunities Develop in Social Entrepreneurship." *Entrepreneurship Theory and Practice* 34 (4): 635–659.

Cosh, A., D. Cumming, and A. Hughes. 2009. "Outside Entrepreneurial Capital." *The Economic Journal* 119 (540): 1494–1533.

Crowdsourcing, O. 2012. *Crowdfunding Industry Report.* New York: Ellenoff Grossman & Schole LLP.

Cuervo Cazurra, A., and C. Annique Un. 2010. "Why Some Firms Never Invest in Formal R&D." *Strategic Management Journal* 31 (7): 759–779.

Cumming, D. 2012. *The Oxford Handbook of Entrepreneurial Finance.* Oxford: Oxford University Press.

Dacin, P. A., M. T. Dacin, and M. Matear. 2010. "Social Entrepreneurship: Why We Don't Need a New Theory and How We Move Forward From Here." *The Academy of Management Perspectives* 24 (3): 37–57.

Dart, R. 2004. "The Legitimacy of Social Enterprise." *Nonprofit Management and Leadership* 14 (4): 411–424.

Deakins, D., and G. Hussain. 1994. "Risk Assessment with Asymmetric Information." *International Journal of Bank Marketing* 12 (1): 24–31.

Defourny, J., and M. Nyssens. 2009a. "Conceptions of Social Enterprise and Social Entrepreneurship in Europe and the United States." Paper presented at the *International Conference on Social Enterprise*, Trento, July 16.

Defourny, J., and M. Nyssens. 2009b. "Conceptions of Social Enterprise and Social Entrepreneurship in Europe and the United States: Convergences and Divergences." Paper presented at the second *EMES International Conference on Social Enterprise*, in Trento, Italy.

Delanoë, S. 2011. "An Individual-Level Perspective for Assessing Nascent Venturing Outcomes." *Journal of Small Business and Enterprise Development* 18 (2): 232–250.

Di Domenico, M. 2009. "The Dialectic of Social Exchange: Theorising Corporate-Social Enterprise Collaboration." *Organization Studies* 30 (8): 887–907.

Di Domenico, M., H. Haugh, and P. Tracey. 2010. "Social Bricolage: Theorizing Social Value Creation in Social Enterprises." *Entrepreneurship Theory and Practice* 34 (4): 681–703.

Dobrow, S. R., D. E. Chandler, W. M. Murphy, and K. E. Kram. 2011. "A Review of Developmental Networks: Incorporating a Mutuality Perspective." *Journal of Management* 38 (1): 210–242.

Drayton, B. 2006. "Everyone a Changemaker: Social Entrepreneurship's Ultimate Goal." *Innovations* 1 (1): 80–96.

Drury, J., and S. Reicher. 1999. "The Intergroup Dynamics of Collective Empowerment: Substantiating the Social Identity Model of Crowd Behavior." *Group Processes & Intergroup Relations* 2 (4): 381–402.

Drury, J., and C. Stott. 2011. "Contextualising the Crowd in Contemporary Social Science." *Contemporary Social Science* 6 (3): 275–288.

Duckett, S., and H. Swerissen. 1996. "Specific Purpose Programs in Human Services and Health: Moving from an Input to an Output and Outcome Focus." *Australian Journal of Public Administration* 55 (3): 7–17.

Dushnitsky, G., and Z. Shapira. 2010. "Entrepreneurial Finance Meets Organizational Reality: Comparing Investment Practices and Performance of Corporate and Independent Venture Capitalists." *Strategic Management Journal* 31 (9): 990–1017.

Edmondson, A., and S. Mcmanus. 2007. "Methodological Fit in Management Field Research." *Academy of Management Review* 32 (4): 1155–1179.

Edwards, J. M., and M. E. J. M. Edwards. 2008. *Hybrid Organizations: Social Enterprise and Social Entrepreneurship.* Honolulu: Lulu.Com.

Ekedahl, M., and Y. Wengström. 2010. "Caritas, Spirituality and Religiosity in Nurses' Coping." *European Journal of Cancer Care* 19 (4): 530–537.

Esping-Andersen, G. 2006. "The Three Worlds of Welfare Capitalism." In *The Welfare State Reader*. 2nd ed. Cambridge: Polity Press.

Fairchild, R. 2011. "An Entrepreneur's Choice of Venture Capitalist or Angel-Financing: A Behavioral Game-Theoretic Approach." *Journal of Business Venturing* 26 (3): 359–374.

Fayolle, A., P. Kyro, and J. Ulijn. 2005. "The Entrepreneurship Debate in Europe: A Matter of History and Culture?" In *Entrepreneurship Research in Europe: Outcomes and Perspectives*, edited by A. Fayolle, P. Kyrö, and J. Ulijn, 1–34. Cheltenham: Edward Elgar Publishing Limited.

Fedele, A., and R. Miniaci. 2010. "Do Social Enterprises Finance Their Investments Differently from For-Profit Firms? The Case of Social Residential Services in Italy." *Journal of Social Entrepreneurship* 1 (2): 174–189.

Ferrera, M., A. Hemerijck, and M. Rhodes. 2004. *The Future of European Welfare States: Recasting Welfare for a New Century*. Oxford: Oxford University Press.

Firth, N. 2012. "Crowdfunding Successes Show Value of Small Donations." *The New Scientist* 213 (2858): 1–22.

Flockhart, A. 2005. "Raising the Profile of Social Enterprises: The Use of Social Return on Investment (SROI) and Investment Ready Tools (IRT) to Bridge the Financial Credibility Gap." *Social Enterprise Journal* 1 (1): 29–42.

Fox, S. 2012. "The New Do-It-Yourself Paradigm: Financial and Ethical Rewards for Businesses." *Journal of Business Strategy* 33 (1): 21–26.

Frumkin, P., and M. T. Kim. 2001. "Strategic Positioning and the Financing of Nonprofit Organizations: Is Efficiency Rewarded in the Contributions Marketplace?" *Public Administration Review* 61 (3): 266–275.

Fuglsang, L. 2010. "Bricolage and Invisible Innovation in Public Service Innovation." *Journal of Innovation Economics* 1 (5): 67–87.

Galera, G., and C. Borzaga. 2009. "Social Enterprise: An International Overview of Its Conceptual Evolution and Legal Implementation." *Social Enterprise Journal* 5 (3): 210–228.

Gallego-Álvarez, I., J. M. Prado-Lorenzo, and I.-M. García-Sánchez. 2011. "Corporate Social Responsibility and Innovation: A Resource-Based Theory." *Management Decision* 49 (10): 1709–1727.

Gundry, L. K., J. R. Kickul, M. D. Griffiths, and S. C. Bacq. 2011. "Creating Social Change Out of Nothing: The Role of Entrepreneurial Bricolage in Social Entrepreneurs' Catalytic Innovations." *Social and Sustainable Entrepreneurship* 13: 1–24.

Gunn, R., C. Durkin, G. Singh, and J. Brown. 2008. "Social Entrepreneurship in the Social Policy Curriculum." *Social Enterprise Journal* 4 (1): 74–80.

Hansmann, H. 1987. "Economic Theories of Nonprofit Organization." In *The Nonprofit Sector: A Research Handbook*, edited by W.W. Powell, 27–42. New Haven: Yale University Press.

Haugh, H. 2006. "Nonprofit Social Entrepreneurship." In *The Life Cycle of Entrepreneurial Ventures*, edited by S. Parker, 401–436. Cambridge: University of Cambridge.

Heminway, J., and S. Hoffman. 2010–2011. "Proceed at Your Peril: Crowdfunding and the Securities Act of 1933." *Tennessee Law Review* 78: 879–922.

Hennala, L., S. Parjanen, and T. Uotila. 2011. "Challenges of Multi-Actor Involvement in the Public Sector Front-End Innovation Processes: Constructing an Open Innovation Model for Developing Well-Being Services." *European Journal of Innovation Management* 14 (3): 364–387.

Heracleous, L., and L. L. Lan. 2012. "Agency Theory, Institutional Sensitivity, and Inductive Reasoning: Towards a Legal Perspective." *Journal of Management Studies* 49 (1): 223–239.

Herman, R., and D. Renz. 2008. "Advancing Nonprofit Organizational Effectiveness Research and Theory: Nine Theses." *Nonprofit Management and Leadership* 18 (4): 399–415.

Hill, T., T. Kothari, and M. Shea. 2010. "Patterns of Meaning in the Social Entrepreneurship Literature: A Research Platform." *Journal of Social Entrepreneurship* 1 (1): 5–31.

Hmieleski, K. M., and R. A. Baron. 2008. "Regulatory Focus and New Venture Performance: A Study of Entrepreneurial Opportunity Exploitation Under Conditions of Risk Versus Uncertainty." *Strategic Entrepreneurship Journal* 2 (4): 285–299.

Hoang, H., and B. Antoncic. 2003. "Network-Based Research in Entrepreneurship: A Critical Review." *Journal of Business Venturing* 18 (2): 165–187.

Hood, C. 2011. "Public Management Research on the Road from Consilience to Experimentation?" *Public Management Review* 13 (2): 321–326.

Hovakimian, A., T. Opler, and S. Titman. 2001. "The Debt-Equity Choice." *Journal of Financial and Quantitative Analysis* 36 (1): 1–24.
Howe, J. 2006. "The Rise of Crowdsourcing." *Wired Magazine* 14 (6): 1–4.
Huarng, K.-H., and T. H.-K. Yu. 2011. "Entrepreneurship, Process Innovation and Value Creation by a Non-Profit SME." *Management Decision* 49 (2): 284–296.
Husted, B. W. 2005. "Risk Management, Real Options, Corporate Social Responsibility." *Journal of Business Ethics* 60 (2): 175–183.
Hynes, B. 2009. "Growing the Social Enterprise – Issues and Challenges." *Social Enterprise Journal* 5 (2): 114–125.
Irwin, D., and J. M. Scott. 2010. "Barriers Faced by SMEs in Raising Bank Finance." *International Journal of Entrepreneurial Behaviour & Research* 16 (3): 245–259.
Ivancevic, V. G., D. J. Reid, and E. V. Aidman. 2010. "Crowd Behavior Dynamics: Entropic Path-Integral Model." *Nonlinear Dynamics* 59 (1): 351–373.
Janney, J. J., and S. Gove. 2011. "Reputation and Corporate Social Responsibility Aberrations, Trends, and Hypocrisy: Reactions to Firm Choices in the Stock Option Backdating Scandal." *Journal of Management Studies* 48 (7): 1562–1585.
Kerlin, J. 2006. "Social Enterprise in the United States and Europe: Understanding and Learning from the Differences." *Voluntas: International Journal of Voluntary and Nonprofit Organizations* 17 (3): 246–262.
Kirchhoff, K. R., and M. Piwinger. 2009. *Praxishandbuch Investor Relations: Das Standardwerk der Finanzkommunikation*. Wiesbaden: Gabler.
Kittur, A. 2010. "Crowdsourcing, Collaboration and Creativity." *XRDS* 17 (2): 22–26.
Kleemann, F., G. G. Voß, and K. Rieder. 2008. "Un(der) Paid Innovators: The Commercial Utilization of Consumer Work Through Crowdsourcing." *Science, Technology & Innovation Studies* 4 (1): 5–26.
Korsgaard, S. 2011. "Opportunity Formation in Social Entrepreneurship." *Journal of Enterprising Communities: People and Places in the Global Economy* 5 (4): 265–285.
Kozinets, R. V., A. Hemetsberger, and H. J. Schau. 2008. "The Wisdom of Consumer Crowds: Collective Innovation in the Age of Networked Marketing." *Journal of Macromarketing* 28 (4): 339–354.
Kreiser, P. M., L. D. Marino, P. Dickson, and K. M. Weaver. 2010. "Cultural Influences on Entrepreneurial Orientation: The Impact of National Culture on Risk Taking and Proactiveness in SMES." *Entrepreneurship Theory and Practice* 34 (5): 959–983.
Kunc, M., and M. R. Bhandari. 2011. "Strategic Development Processes During Economic and Financial Crisis." *Management Decision* 49 (8): 1343–1353.
Lam, W. 2010. "Funding Gap, What Funding Gap? Financial Bootstrapping: Supply, Demand and Creation of Entrepreneurial Finance." *International Journal of Entrepreneurial Behaviour & Research* 16 (4): 268–295.
Lambert, R. A., C. Leuz, and R. E. Verrecchia. 2012. "Information Asymmetry, Information Precision, and the Cost of Capital." *Review of Finance* 16 (1): 1–29.
Lambert, T., and A. Schwienbacher. 2010. "An Empirical Analysis of Crowdfunding." Working Paper, University de Louvain, France.
Laratta, R. 2010. "Ethical Climate in Nonprofit and Government Sectors: The Case of Japan." *Social Enterprise Journal* 6 (3): 225–249.
Larralde, B., and A. Schwienbacher. 2012. "Crowdfunding of Small Entrepreneurial Ventures." In *The Oxford Handbook of Entrepreneurial Finance*, edited by D. Cumming. Vol. 369. New York: Oxford University Press.
Lehner, O. M. 2004. "A Survey of Behavioral Finance." *Journal of Banking and Finance in Austria* 1 (2): 1–22.
Lehner, O. M. 2011a. "The Phenomenon of Social Enterprise in Austria: A Triangulated Descriptive Study." *Journal of Social Entrepreneurship* 2 (1): 53–78.
Lehner, O. M. 2011b. *Social Entrepreneurship Perspectives: Triangulated Approaches to Hybridity. Studies in Business and Economics*, edited by T. Tuomo. Vol. 111. Jyväskylä: JSBE.
Lehner, O. M., and J. Kaniskas. 2012. "Opportunity Recognition in Social Entrepreneurship: A Thematic Meta Analysis." *Journal of Entrepreneurship* 21 (1): 25–58.
Levander, U. 2010. "Social Enterprise: Implications of Emerging Institutionalized Constructions." *Journal of Social Entrepreneurship* 1 (2): 213–230.
Levitas, E., and T. Chi. 2010. "A Look at the Value Creation Effects of Patenting and Capital Investment Through a Real Options Lens: The Moderating Role of Uncertainty." *Strategic Entrepreneurship Journal* 4 (3): 212–233.

Lim, D. S. K., E. A. Morse, R. K. Mitchell, and K. K. Seawright. 2010. "Institutional Environment and Entrepreneurial Cognitions: A Comparative Business Systems Perspective." *Entrepreneurship Theory and Practice* 34 (3): 491–516.

Lumpkin, G. T. 2011. "From Legitimacy to Impact: Moving the Field Forward by Asking How Entrepreneurship Informs Life." *Strategic Entrepreneurship Journal* 5 (1): 3–9.

Mahmood, I. P., H. Zhu, and E. J. Zajac. 2011. "Where Can Capabilities Come From? Network Ties and Capability Acquisition in Business Groups." *Strategic Management Journal* 32 (8): 820–848.

Mair, J., and I. Marti. 2006. "Social Entrepreneurship Research: A Source of Explanation, Prediction, and Delight." *Journal of World Business* 41 (1): 36–44.

Mair, J., and I. Marti. 2009. "Entrepreneurship in and around Institutional Voids: A Case Study from Bangladesh." *Journal of Business Venturing* 24 (5): 419–435.

Mair, J., and E. Noboa. 2006. "Social Entrepreneurship: How Intentions to Create a Social Venture Are Formed." In *Social Entrepreneurship*, edited by J. Mair, J. Robinson, and K. Hockerts, 121–135. New York: Palgrave Macmillan.

Martin, T. 2012. "The Jobs Act of 2012: Balancing Fundamental Securities Law Principles with the Demands of the Crowd." Available at SSRN 2040953.

Martinez, M. A., and H. E. Aldrich. 2011. "Networking Strategies for Entrepreneurs: Balancing Cohesion and Diversity." *International Journal of Entrepreneurial Behaviour & Research* 17 (1): 7–38.

Mason, C., J. Kirkbride, and D. Bryde. 2007. "From Stakeholders to Institutions: The Changing Face of Social Enterprise Governance Theory." *Management Decision* 45 (2): 284–301.

Massink, M., D. Latella, A. Bracciali, and J. Hillston. 2010. "Combined Process Algebraic, Agent and Fluid Flow Approach to Emergent Crowd Behaviour." CNR-ISTI Technical Report.

Mcwilliams, A., and D. S. Siegel. 2010. "Creating and Capturing Value: Strategic Corporate Social Responsibility, Resource-Based Theory, and Sustainable Competitive Advantage." *Journal of Management* 37 (5): 1480–1495.

Meuleman, M., K. Amess, M. Wright, and L. Scholes. 2009. "Agency, Strategic Entrepreneurship, and the Performance of Private Equity Backed Buyouts." *Entrepreneurship Theory and Practice* 33 (1): 213–239.

Meyer, K. E., S. Estrin, S. K. Bhaumik, and M. W. Peng. 2009. "Institutions, Resources, and Entry Strategies in Emerging Economies." *Strategic Management Journal* 30 (1): 61–80.

Meyer, M. 2009. "Wie viel wirtschaft verträgt die zivilgesellschaft? Über möglichkeiten und grenzen wirtschaftlicher rationalität in npos." In *Bürgergesellschaft als projekt*, edited by I. Bode, A. Evers, and A. Klein, 127–144. Wiesbaden: VS Verlag für Sozialwissenschaften.

Meyskens, M., C. Robb-Post, J. A. Stamp, A. L. Carsrud, and P. D. Reynolds. 2010. "Social Ventures from a Resource-Based Perspective: An Exploratory Study Assessing Global Ashoka Fellows." *Entrepreneurship Theory and Practice* 34 (4): 661–680.

Millo, Y., and D. Mackenzie. 2009. "The Usefulness of Inaccurate Models: Towards an Understanding of the Emergence of Financial Risk Management." *Accounting, Organizations and Society* 34 (5): 638–653.

Moss, T. W., J. C. Short, G. T. Payne, and G. Lumpkin. 2011. "Dual Identities in Social Ventures: An Exploratory Study." *Entrepreneurship Theory and Practice* 35 (4): 805–830.

Muller, A., and R. Kräussl. 2011. "Doing Good Deeds in Times of Need: A Strategic Perspective on Corporate Disaster Donations." *Strategic Management Journal* 32 (9): 911–929.

Murphy, P., and S. Coombes. 2009. "A Model of Social Entrepreneurial Discovery." *Journal of Business Ethics* 87 (3): 325–336.

Nicholls, A. 2009. "'We Do Good Things, Don't We?': 'Blended Value Accounting' in Social Entrepreneurship." *Accounting, Organizations and Society* 34 (6–7): 755–769.

Nicholls, A. 2010a. "The Institutionalization of Social Investment: The Interplay of Investment Logics and Investor Rationalities." *Journal of Social Entrepreneurship* 1 (1): 70–100.

Nicholls, A. 2010b. "Institutionalizing Social Entrepreneurship in Regulatory Space: Reporting and Disclosure by Community Interest Companies." *Accounting, Organizations and Society* 35 (4): 394–415.

Nicholls, A. 2010c. "The Legitimacy of Social Entrepreneurship: Reflexive Isomorphism in a Pre-Paradigmatic Field." *Entrepreneurship Theory and Practice* 34 (4): 611–633.

Nyssens, M., S. Adam, and T. Johnson. 2006. *Social Enterprise: At the Crossroads of Market, Public Policies and Civil Society*. Routledge Studies in the Management of Voluntary and Non-Profit Organizations. London and New York: Routledge.

Palier, B. 2010. *A Long Goodbye to Bismarck?: The Politics of Welfare Reform in Continental Europe*. Amsterdam: Amsterdam University Press.

Parrino, R. J., and P. J. Romeo. 2012. "Jobs Act Eases Securities-Law Regulation of Smaller Companies." *Journal of Investment Compliance* 13 (3): 27–35.

Patriotta, G., J.-P. Gond, and F. Schultz. 2011. "Maintaining Legitimacy: Controversies, Orders of Worth, and Public Justifications." *Journal of Management Studies* 48 (8): 1804–1836.

Perry, J. T., G. N. Chandler, and G. Markova. 2012. "Entrepreneurial Effectuation: A Review and Suggestions for Future Research." *Entrepreneurship Theory and Practice* 36 (4): 837–861.

Pope, N. 2011. "Crowdfunding Microstartups: It's Time for the Securities and Exchange Commission to Approve a Small Offering Exemption." *Journal of Business Law* 13 (4): 973–1002.

Qiongzhi, L. 2007. "Efficiency Measurement and Quantity Optimization of Public Outcome: Based on Objective of Social Justice Output." http://en.cnki.com.cn/Article_en/CJFDTOTAL NDSP200702007.htm

Reyes, L. F. M., and S. Finken. 2012. "Social Media as a Platform for Participatory Design." In *Proceedings of the 12th Participatory Design Conference: Exploratory Papers, Workshop Descriptions, Industry Cases – Volume 2, 89–92.* ACM, Roskilde, Denmark, August 12–16.

Ridley-Duff, R. 2008. "Social Enterprise as a Socially Rational Business." *International Journal of Entrepreneurial Behaviour and Research* 14 (5): 291–312.

Ridley-Duff, R. 2009. "Co-Operative Social Enterprises: Company Rules, Access to Finance and Management Practice." *Social Enterprise Journal* 5 (1): 50–68.

Ridley-Duff, R. 2010. "Communitarian Governance in Social Enterprises: Case Evidence from the Mondragon Cooperative Corporation and School Trends Ltd." *Social Enterprise Journal* 6 (2): 125–145.

Robinson, J., ed. 2006. *Navigating Social and Institutional Barriers to Markets: How Social Entrepreneurs Identify and Evaluate Opportunities.* New York: Palgrave Macmillan.

Rubinton, B. J. 2011. "Crowdfunding: Disintermediated Investment Banking." http://ssrn.com/abstract=1807204

Ruebottom, T. 2011. "Counting Social Change: Outcome Measures for Social Enterprise." *Social Enterprise Journal* 7 (2): 173–182.

Ruvinsky, J. 2012. "Making Businesses More Responsible." *Stanford Social Innovation Review*, Winter 2012: 7–10.

Scarlata, M., and L. Alemany, eds. 2012. *Philanthropic Venture Capital from a Global Perspective.* Oxford: Oxford University Press.

Scherpereel, C. M. 2008. "The Option Creating Institution: A Real Options Perspective on Economic Organization." *Strategic Management Journal* 29 (5): 455–470.

Schnatterly, K., K. W. Shaw, and W. W. Jennings. 2008. "Information Advantages of Large Institutional Owners." *Strategic Management Journal* 29 (2): 219.

Schwienbacher, A., and B. Larralde. 2010. "Crowdfunding of Small Entrepreneurial Ventures." In *The Oxford Handbook of Entrepreneurial Finance*, edited by Douglas Cumming, 369–392. Oxford: Oxford University Press.

SEC (Social Enterprise Coalition). 2004. *Unlocking the Potential: A Guide to Finance for Social Enterprises.* London: Social Enterprise Coalition.

Seghers, A., S. Manigart, and T. Vanacker. 2012. "The Impact of Human and Social Capital on Entrepreneurs' Knowledge of Finance Alternatives." *Journal of Small Business Management* 50 (1): 63–86.

SEL (Social Enterprise London). 2001. Introducing Social Enterprise. London: Social Enterprise London.

Sharfman, M. P., and C. S. Fernando. 2008. "Environmental Risk Management and the Cost of Capital." *Strategic Management Journal* 29 (6): 569–592.

Shaw, E., and S. Carter. 2007. "Social Entrepreneurship: Theoretical Antecedents and Empirical Analysis of Entrepreneurial Processes and Outcomes." *Journal of Small Business and Enterprise Development* 14 (3): 418–434.

Shleifer, A. 2000. *Inefficient Markets: An Introduction to Behavioral Finance.* Oxford: Oxford University Press.

Short, J., D. Ketchen, C. Shook, and R. Ireland. 2010. "The Concept of 'Opportunity' in Entrepreneurship Research: Past Accomplishments and Future Challenges." *Journal of Management* 36 (1): 40–65.

Singer, P., and C. Cacia. 2009. "The Role of Web Investor Relations for Mitigating and Manage Stock Exchange Liquidity and Enterprise Risks." Paper presented at 9th *Global Conference on Business & Economics*, Cambridge University, UK, October 16–17.

Soh, P. H. 2010. "Network Patterns and Competitive Advantage Before the Emergence of a Dominant Design." *Strategic Management Journal* 31 (4): 438–461.

Sullivan, D. M., and M. R. Marvel. 2011. "Knowledge Acquisition, Network Reliance, and Early-Stage Technology Venture Outcomes." *Journal of Management Studies* 48 (6): 1169–1193.

Tong, T. W., and J. J. Reuer. 2007. "Real Options in Strategic Management." *Advances in Strategic Management* 24: 3–28.

Travaglini, C. 2009. "Social Enterprise in Europe: Governance Models." In Second *EMES International Conference on Social Enterprise*. Trento: EMES.

Vaccaro, I. G., J. J. P. Jansen, F. A. J. Van Den Bosch, and H. W. Volberda. 2012. "Management Innovation and Leadership: The Moderating Role of Organizational Size." *Journal of Management Studies* 49 (1): 28–51.

Valenzuela, S., A. Arriagada, and A. Scherman. 2012. "The Social Media Basis of Youth Protest Behavior: The Case of Chile." *Journal of Communication* 62 (2): 299–314.

Van Slyke, D. M. 2006. "Agents or Stewards: Using Theory to Understand the Government-Nonprofit Social Service Contracting Relationship." *Journal of Public Administration Research and Theory* 17 (2): 157–187.

Wang, H., and S. S. Lim. 2008. "Real Options and Real Value: The Role of Employee Incentives to Make Specific Knowledge Investments." *Strategic Management Journal* 29 (7): 701–721.

Ward, C., and V. Ramachandran. 2010. "Crowdfunding the Next Hit: Microfunding Online Experience Goods." Paper presented at *Computational Social Science and the Wisdom of Crowds*, Whistler, Canada, December 10.

Whitla, P. 2009. "Crowdsourcing and Its Application in Marketing Activities." *Contemporary Management Research* 5 (1): 15–28.

Williamson, O. E. 1988. "Corporate Finance and Corporate Governance." *Journal of Finance* 43 (3): 567–591.

Yunus, M., and K. Weber. 2007. *Creating a World Without Poverty: Social Business and the Future of Capitalism*. New York: Public Affairs.

Zahra, S., E. Gedajlovic, D. Neubaum, and J. Shulman. 2009. "A Typology of Social Entrepreneurs: Motives, Search Processes and Ethical Challenges." *Journal of Business Venturing* 24 (5): 519–532.

Zahra, S., H. Rawhouser, N. Bhawe, D. Neubaum, and J. Hayton. 2008. "Globalization of Social Entrepreneurship Opportunities." *Strategic Entrepreneurship Journal* 2 (2): 117–131.

10

SOCIAL IMPACT BONDS

Exploring and understanding an emerging funding approach

Jim Clifford and Tobias Jung

The last decade has seen an increasing focus on developing new and alternative funding approaches for leveraging social impact. As part of this, Social Impact Bonds (SIBs) have emerged as a widely hailed innovation, as an "audacious idea for solving the world's problems" (Schmid, 2012, p. 64). Aimed at raising investments for preventative services that improve social outcomes for a defined population and cause (Social Finance, 2011, 2013b), SIBs combine governmental "payment by results" approaches with private sector investments and risk sharing. Thereby, SIBs are perceived to offer three major benefits: improved performance and lower costs of public and social services; greater innovation and uptake of new solutions; and accelerated knowledge exchange and sharing of "best practice" (Liebman, 2011). Unsurprisingly, this has led to widespread interest in, and support of, SIBs across policy, funders, investors, and practice (e.g., Bensoussan, Ruparell, & Taliento, 2013; Fletcher, 2013; McKinsey & Company, 2012; Social Finance, 2012, 2014). Whether vision for, and rhetoric on, SIBs reflects developments on the ground is, however, often unclear; critical voices question whether SIBs are indeed the most appropriate tools for achieving their envisaged results (Demel, 2013) and raise concerns about SIBs' structure, regulation, and underlying agenda (Baliga, 2013; Humphries, 2014; Leventhal, 2013).

Given the emergent nature of, and diverse activities within, the SIB field, there is a strong need for both stronger conceptualization and better practical understanding. To this end, our chapter proposes a multi-dimensional conceptual typology of SIBs. Grounded in our ongoing work on mapping global SIB developments and trajectories, this typology combines three overarching analytical dimensions of SIBs—social, financial, and governance and structure aspects—and identifies and describes eight categories within these.

While across the social sciences there have been long-standing debates about the nature and appropriate role of typologies and their relationship with taxonomies and classifications (e.g., Delbridge & Fiss, 2013; Doty & Glick, 1994), there is no doubt that typologies provide a basis for developing learning and understanding. By combining complexity with parsimony, typologies provide a comparative basis without discounting the richness and diversity existing within each type; through breaking up, subdividing, and arranging phenomena into discrete and collective categories, typologies provide the foundations for strong research; and by providing constructs, relationships, and a basis for falsification, typologies are steps toward theory development: in short, typologies assist in developing more systematic knowledge and practice

(Collier, LaPorte, & Seawright, 2012; Doty & Glick, 1994; Filion, 2000; Fiss, 2011; Hay & Kinchin, 2006; Rich, 1992). With limited academic analysis and comparison of SIBs to date, a SIB typology can thus lay an important stepping stone in taking the area forward.

In the next section, our chapter provides a short historical overview of SIBs. This is followed by an examination of the nature of SIBs, an outline of the growing diversity in the field, and a discussion of some of the key challenges with SIBs. Drawing on the wider social investment literature, the chapter proceeds by describing our analytical framework for examining SIBs. Discussing our findings from a detailed analysis of 10 SIBs, we then propose a SIB typology and conclude with reflections on next steps and further research needs.

The emergence and growth of SIBs

In the late 1980s, New Zealand economist Ronnie Horesh proposed the idea of a social policy bond, a bond that would only be redeemable when a specific social objective had been achieved (Horesh, 1988). While it took another two decades before the first SIB was actually launched, important developments occurred during that interim period. Central to these were the establishment of two initiatives within the UK: the Social Investment Task Force (SITF) and Social Finance Ltd.

SITF was set up by the UK government in April 2000. Led by Sir Ronald Cohen, founder of venture capitalist and private equity firm Apax Partners, SITF's overarching remit was to facilitate social innovation and outcomes through the use of capital from outside the public sector. To this end, it was asked to:

> set out how entrepreneurial practices could be applied to obtain higher social and financial returns from social investment, to harness new talents and skills, to address economic regeneration and to unleash new sources of private and institutional investment.
>
> *(SITF, 2010, p. 2)*

While the remit of SITF emphasized and focused strongly on communities (SITF, 2000, 2003, 2005), its work and support prompted the foundation of Social Finance Ltd in 2007. This brought together a team of experts involved in the social sector, finance, and government. Its aim was the exploration of opportunities and obstacles for voluntary and community organizations in the provision of services for disadvantaged and vulnerable groups (Social Finance, 2015). Realizing that making finance available was only one concern, social finance sought to change the way in which public service commissioners engaged with potential providers and their funders. To this end, a new contracting structure was developed. This became the first SIB.

Initiated in the aftermath of the financial crash of 2008 and a signaled reduction in government spending across the globe, the first SIB, the Peterborough Prison Social Impact Bond, was launched in the UK in September 2010. It focused on addressing male offender recidivism numbers and was considered to be an opportunity to trial payments-by-results that drew on funds from, and shifted risk to, non-government investors (see Disley, Rubin, Scraggs, Burrowes, & Culley, 2011; Nicholls & Tomkinson, 2013). The idea was quickly picked up, both internationally and across different sectors. The New York Rikers Island SIB in the United States, the UK Department for Work and Pensions (DWP) Innovation Fund, and bonds in New South Wales rapidly followed, building up a variety of commissioner-led models. After the Scope Bond in 2010, a broader social investment issue which was listed on the Luxembourg Stock Exchange, other SIBs started to emerge with a general fundraising profile and which latterly are approaching the retail investment market (Palmer, 2013). While at that time all SIBs were public-sector driven, in 2013 the UK's Consortium of Voluntary Adoption Agencies (CVAA) set up the first non-public sector-arranged SIB, the Adoption Bond, It's All About Me (IAAM). Providing a sector response to a perennial failing in UK adoption placements, IAAM also featured a number of other unique characteristics. Unlike other SIBs, which offered lower commercial yields in view of the social impact being delivered, IAAM was both a debt instrument and carried a return designed to match its risk profile (Clifford, Markey, & Malpani, 2013; Patton, 2013).

With an ongoing growth trajectory and increasing global spread, a total of 28 SIBs were active in early 2015. Their emergence and geographic spread within the UK and internationally are illustrated in Figures 10.1–10.3.

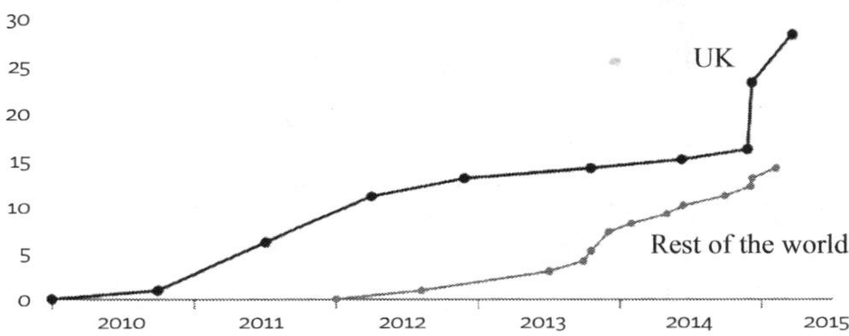

Figure 10.1 SIBs launched—UK and worldwide

Source: Based on and recreated from Tomkinson (2015).

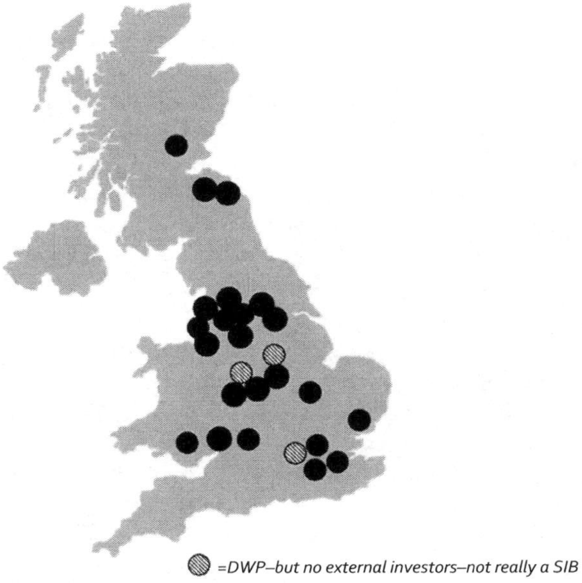

Figure 10.2 SIBs—UK spread

Source: Based on and recreated from Tomkinson (2015).

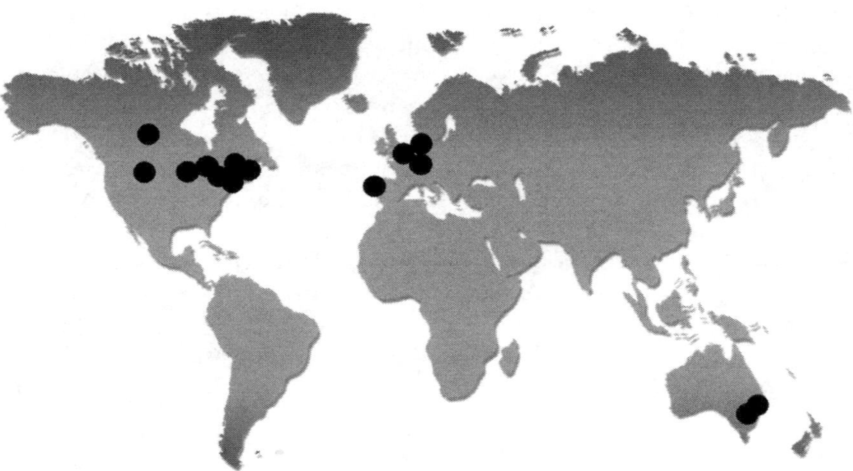

Figure 10.3 SIBs (agreed)—international spread

Source: Based on and recreated from Tomkinson (2015).

The nature of, and challenges with, SIBs

The global growth in SIBs has been accompanied by a proliferation of terminologies, features, and ideas. Reflecting the various policy and practice contexts within which SIBs have emerged—including education, healthcare, social welfare, criminal justice, and international aid—reference is being made to Pay for Success Bonds (US Government, 2014), Social Policy Bonds (Horesh, 1988), Social Benefit Bonds (NSW Treasury, 2014), Health Impact Bonds (Clay, 2013), Climate Stability Bonds (Horesh, 2002), and Development Impact Bonds (Social Finance, 2013a). As such, it is important to clarify what actually constitutes a SIB.

While some commentators have focused on SIBs' investment aspects, a SIB is essentially a contract for the delivery of social services (Callanan & Law, 2012; Cameron, 2013; Costa, Shah, & Ungar, 2012; Social Finance, 2013b). It can be defined by four characteristics: it is a contract between a commissioner, that is, a public sector or other buyer of services, and an external delivery agent; it focuses on the delivery of a specific social outcome or outcomes, which will result in a payment by the commissioner; at least one investor exists who is neither commissioner nor delivery agent; and some, or all, of the delivery risk sits with the investor (Rotheroe, 2014). In relation to these characteristics, three aspects warrant further reflection: the financial and structural aspects of SIBs and the provider's role.

The financial aspect of SIBs can mirror the five types of capital finance requirements expected in the wider social investment markets: fixed assets; short-term working capital; long-term (permanent) working capital; growth capital (what tends to be referred to as scaling in this arena); and various project-specific needs. These may be fulfilled from the investment of financial capital or may be partly applied in kind, through Venture Philanthropy models or through the contribution of intellectual property or other assets (Cabinet Office, 2011, 2012; Clifford, Hehenberger, & Ors, 2014). Structurally, SIBs bring together a diversity of parties and stakeholders. These can extend beyond those who pay and those who deliver, including the government contracting authority (commissioner); the social service provider; the private investor; the intermediary; and the independent evaluator (Burand, 2013). Further adding to the perceived and actual structural diversity within the field, some SIBs also entail the use of an evaluation advisor. The increasing complexity resulting from these factors might not only act as a deterrent for potential participants in the SIB field, but it may risk increasing the costs of a tool that is intended to cut them. Finally, while within SIBs the provider's role is central, and providers may frequently bring much of the delivery expertise, in traditional SIBs they take no risk and have little direct control over the delivery plans and mechanisms. This presents the danger that providers take on a responsive rather than an active, innovative, and leading role, thereby falling short of contributing the full potential value they could offer (Clifford et al., 2013; Rotheroe, 2014; Sheil, 2014).

Rotheroe's (2014) definition is cast slightly wider than some of the original assumptions. For example, there was an initial perception that the delivery agent would always be an entity formed for that purpose, which then would contract out to one or more social providers as deliverers of the service(s) (e.g., Costa et al., 2012; Mulgan, Reeder, Aylott, & Bo'scher, 2011). Furthermore, this definition avoids various random and unnecessary, stated or implied, boundaries that can be identified within the literature, as illustrated by Goodall's (2014) idea that funders should be directly financially interested in the outcomes delivered. Although this might be reflected in the desirability of funders taking some of the risk, if this was used to impose a direct contractual link between outcomes and yield to investors, it would potentially disqualify several of those SIBs that are now generally accepted as mainstream examples, such as IAAM.

Accompanying the growth of SIBs, various concerns have been raised in the media, by public commentators, and across academic and gray literatures (e.g., Cohen, 2014; Demel, 2013; Godoy, 2013; McKay, 2013). These can be roughly clustered into three overarching themes: measurement, financialization, and governance. First of all, in focusing on outcomes, and basing the financial models around the delivery thereof, SIBs face the challenge of measuring these outcomes. In light of wider debates about the challenges of social impact measurement (NAO, 2009; NCVO, 2011; SITF, 2014), this is especially pertinent for SIBs: SIBs face the requirement to satisfy multiple stakeholders as well as their different needs and perspectives. Furthermore, they touch upon highly nuanced and complex social changes in perhaps hard-to-reach or hard-to-track groups of beneficiaries. Second, with wider concerns about the marketization and financialization of the "social" (e.g., Moran, 2008; Nickel & Eikenberry, 2009; Thümler, 2015), there is the perception that the existence of SIBs, and the skewing of the market for finance and for services that may follow from them, could bring negative consequences to the structure, independence, and operation of the social sector. Third, SIBs demand careful and independent governance (McHugh, Sinclair, Roy, Huckfield, & Donaldson, 2013). In general, the challenges SIBs are trying to address are potentially the same six areas as those for social investment in general: they must create investible business models, and they demand the development of financial skill and experience among those operating them; they require an understanding of risk and how to price it, and they demand improvement in commissioning capabilities; they must embrace operating with multi-party reporting of metrics and the validation or audit that that demands; and they need to address, or better still use as a capital market management tool, the distortive effects of grants and other soft finance (Brown & Norman, 2011; Clifford et al., 2014; Corry, 2012). Whether, and to what extent, these concerns are warranted and how they play out in practice is an area for further research and beyond the scope of this chapter. However, a clearer understanding of SIB types and developments should help in that process.

Laying the foundations for a SIB typology

Despite some attempts at standardization, there is no "one size fits all" formula for SIBs. While, with the growing number of SIBs, certain commonalities have started to emerge (Rotheroe, 2014; Tomkinson, 2015), overall frameworks on SIBs are highly abstract and do not reach into underlying structures and applications required of a more detailed typology (e.g., Palandjian & Hughes, 2014). To this end, it appears useful to look toward the wider academic and gray literature on social entrepreneurship and social investment, of which SIBs form a part (Cabinet Office, 2011; Patton, 2013). Within this context, the development of appropriate classifications and frameworks has featured more prominently, and some can offer useful insights for building a basis on which to develop a stronger SIB typology.

Nicholls (2010), for example, provides a broad analytical framework for social investment. This maps three types of investor rationality against three types of investment logic. It takes two aspects, the financial (means-end driven) and the social/environmental (values driven), across each of the two axes and places a blended (systematic) one that combines aspects of the other two in between them. While this gives a possible mapping approach and adds much to the examination of the comparative motivations of parties, SIBs probably only fit within the blended systematic space as few use the other areas of Nicholls' (2010) matrix. Similarly, the mapping of social investment in *The First Billion* (Brown & Swersky, 2012), a combined report by the Boston Consulting Group and Big Society Capital geared toward forecasting social investment demand, contextualizes social investment within a wider capital market. Although this is an important facet on which to reflect, it too is not detailed enough for SIBs. SITF (2010) maps the social purpose of the investment against the capital market return and explains its relevance to the emerging market from both investor and social provider perspectives. The capital market return includes both investor income yield and the capital performance itself. McHugh et al. (2013) highlight a range of challenges in SIBs, a central one being the aforementioned governance issue, while Goodall (2014) categorizes bonds as direct (delivered by the provider contracting directly with the commissioner or payor, such as IAAM), intermediated (using a Special Purpose Vehicle [SPV], such as Peterborough Prison, Essex MST, or Newpin in New South Wales), and managed (where a service provider provides the performance management, such as Rykers Island).

Taking these factors, and combining them with insights from the literature on corporate and contractual structures (e.g., Kohli, Besharov, & Costa, 2012a, 2012b), an analytical framework that spans three broad dimensions of SIBs seems to be appropriate, covering: the financial facets—focusing on the capital market performance of the investment; the social purpose;

Table 10.1 Exploratory framework

Dimensions	*Categories*
Financial	• Finance use and quantum • Financial return • Economic/financial risk • Financial risk management • Capital sources
Social	• Area of focus/need being addressed • Outcomes addressed • Social risk • Social risk management • Payment by results (payment for success) approach
Governance and structure	• Corporate vehicle and structure • Contractual arrangements • Governance and control • Accountabilities • Systems and implementation

Table 10.2 SIBs analyzed

SIB	*Area/need*	*Outcomes addressed*
1 Peterborough Prison (UK—England—local area, single site)	Looking at a cohort of 3,000 prisoners: 3 × 2 year cohorts of 1,000 each 18-year-old+; incarceration at least 365 days 60 percent re-offend within 1 year	Reduction in reoffending vs control group from Police National Computer of 10 comparators per 1 cohort participant Reasonable expectation of longer term improvement
2 It's All About Me (UK-wide, networked "Adoption Bond")	Finding, training, and supporting therapeutic adopters for harder-to-place children who do not usually find homes Targeting steady state of 300 children p.a.—initial target of 100 children	Finding families to turn around children's lives Supporting to deliver that; effects in attachment; development; education; well-being of child and family Case selection to a free (spot purchase) model to match social work decision-making Systemic change in adoption support and parent training to assess child's needs
3 BSSBB (NSW—supporting vulnerable families keeping their children out of state care)	Targeting 300 families. Highlighted by FACs (state agency) as having child at risk of going into care. Across three RFS regions	Service innovation and further development Direct outcomes of keeping child in the family and sustaining them in supporting them. Covered during crisis period plus 9 months and post-program checking
4 Newpin (NSW—supporting vulnerable families taking their children back out of state care)	Restoration of children in state care to their families with appropriate support 700 families supported; 55 percent with a child under 5 Targeting to restore 400 children of this group	Poorer outcomes for children who stay in care than those who return to sound, supportive, and supported family structures. Focus on education; health; social engagement; development; attachment
5 Essex Multi-Systemic Therapy (UK—England—regional—supporting families/children at risk of needing state care)	Children in care have poor outcomes, but families may be unable to sustain them Work with child and family in multi-systemic therapy (blend of CBT, Systemic Family Therapy, Social Learning Therapy)	Educational attainment Future employment Keep out of criminal justice system Improve parenting/relationships Focus on 11–17-year-olds
6 Massachusetts Roca (young offenders/gang members re-engaging with society/work)	Youth offending in Boston, Chelsea, Springfield areas 55 percent return to crime <3 years of release Get into employment Inc. 380 housing units for homeless young people	Only felons; in gang/supervision; no GEDs 1 Engage—work to change attitude and start hope 2 Transitional employment with Roca/tried employers @ $8/hr 3 Full-time employment (with partner employer) 2 years on scheme plus 2 years follow-up

(Continued)

Table 10.2 SIBs analyzed *(Continued)*

SIB	*Area/need*	*Outcomes addressed*
7 Rykers Island (NYC—reducing re-offending rates)	50 percent young people leaving RI back within a year Targeting 2,500–3,000 YPs each of 4 years. Pre-defined cohort CBT-based intervention improving social decision-making: Adolescent Behavioral Leaving Experience	Reduce re-offending Reduce effects of crime on self and third parties Re-engage with employment
8 Innovation Fund/ DWP (Adviza) (1 of 10 DWP SIBs getting people into work)	Disadvantaged YPs 14–24 Re-engagement with employment Get into employment Basic skills development NEET avoided	Re-engagement with employment Get into employment. Basic skills development 3 paths: 1 3 year prog. 12 weeks intensive, 2 residential 2 1 resi; 6–10 weeks intensive 3 No resi All with follow-ups extended
9 Innovation Fund/ DWP (Coui) (1 of 10 DWP SIBs getting people into work)	Disadvantaged YPs 14–24 29 schools and Youth Offending Teams as referrers 18 afternoons across 18 weeks mentoring for struggling students and gain level 1 interpersonal skills. Working in groups of 8–10 with foundation	Outcomes and indicators present in bid documents (see PbR outcomes) SROI at 1:6 Experience was 93 percent in education and employment training @ 16–18 y.o., vs teachers' predictions of 50 percent
10 GLA Homeless People (UK—London area)	Persistent rough sleepers not caught by "No Second Night" or by intensive program for "top 205" 63 percent rough sleepers around for 4 years+ 831 persistent rough sleepers 1/6th of these have 47 percent nights out Stats worsening at 10.4 percent	Avoid early death (age 40–44) Reduce rough sleeping Health outcomes Employment outcomes Eval. £37k NPV Public Saving over 5 years

and the governance and structural features. A number of sub-themes in relation to these dimensions can also be extracted from these literatures, leading to our exploratory framework provided in Table 10.1.

This exploratory framework forms the basis for our detailed analysis of 10 SIBs currently in existence. The SIBs selected came from a combination of those listed in February 2014 on the UK Cabinet Office Knowledge Hub website, the PayforSuccess Learning Hub in the US, and information from the New South Wales government and from commentators from within that context. At the time, a total of 24 SIBs were identified globally. Of these, we selected two of the group of 10 DWP bonds (UK), and eight others—two in the US, two in Australia, and four others in the UK—the full list being provided in Table 10.2. Bearing in mind that DWP can be counted as a single type example, this effectively covered 18 of the 24, or 9 of the 15, SIBs then in existence.

The data obtained on these SIBs covered three categories: documentation by those who designed the SIB; material by the operators or providers under each scheme; and, where available, public records. There were some limitations, where individual parties were unwilling or unable to disclose some of the relevant documentation, so that some SIBs could be more fully analyzed than others. Using our exploratory framework and an "insider-outsider" perspective approach (see Brannick & Coghlan, 2007; Evered & Louis, 1981), the similarities and differences for the SIBs were analyzed against our framework using a mixture of quantitative and qualitative approaches: financial and statistical information was analyzed to find means and deviations therefrom; structural maps were analyzed from a network analysis perspective to look at common purposes and relationships; and the measurement, social intervention, and other aspects were reviewed using qualitative thematic analysis.

Toward a SIB typology

Financial dimension

Looking at SIBs' financial aspects, particularly of earlier bonds, such as Peterborough Prison, the returns on capital are below those expected in the general capital markets. While there are indications of this being around 4 percent to 7 percent below, further information would be required to provide a more robust and reliable answer. However, there is evidence of a progression, with later bonds showing debt funding elements, for which the market yields, between 5 percent and 15 percent, are not unreasonable for senior and junior debt. This is being achieved by passing risk away from the investors in these elements and into the hands of equity or quasi-equity investors (creating multi-tiered, or geared, capital structures such as in BSSBB), the providers (e.g., Massachusetts Roca or IAAM), the commissioners (with minimum committed funding in several), and the introduction of grants (e.g., Guarantee in Rykers Is., or Massachusetts Roca).

The capital repayment profile is generally away from regular repayment and toward the final third of a 5- to 9-year bond period. However, several pay regular income yields on the finance. Only one appears to release all capital right at the end, paying income as a premium on redemption, with the majority using a mixture of draw down as needed and release when funds are no longer needed to keep down overall funding costs.

Further financial risk management is evident in the operating finances. This includes what is described as "risk arbitrage" in IAAM, that is, analyzing risk in detail and allocating elements of it to those parties most able to manage and sustain it. In IAAM's case this includes the risk of not achieving milestones for some of the children's placements. This factor, after averaging across both the 10-year bond period and across all placements under the scheme UK-wide, is then passed for the first 10 percent of the cohort to the funder pool and, above that, to providers. The former can budget for the potential shortfalls; the latter can control the selection of individual children at the take-on stage and the service delivery in order to manage their risk.

As regards the use to which funding is put, all of these schemes appear to use it for working capital, both short and long term, and for growth (scaling). That should not, however, suggest a boundary since none of the interventions being described and funded appear to have a significant fixed capital requirement.

Social dimension

Turning to the social frame, the interventions chosen are primarily in the fields of young people and children, families, and offender management (recidivism). There are none for older people, for medical conditions, and for general health and fitness. There are no indications that the SIB approach cannot work in these fields, provided there is a payor for the services. It might thus simply be a matter of time before such SIBs emerge. With regard to that payor, it appears that all SIBs exhibit one or more points in the commissioning or commitment-to-pay cycle at which a potential payor for the service(s) makes a decision to commission, or to refer someone to the scheme, when they know that they stand to gain (largely financially but also in delivery of policy imperatives) from the successful delivery of the targeted outcomes, and that they believe these are reasonably achievable. These gateways to service are perhaps a key feature of the SIB model.

The interventions being used seem to fall into two types: simpler services, focused on a basic "one outcome" achievement for a single beneficiary (e.g., Peterborough Prison's recidivism, or Rykers Island with similar targets), and the more complex multi-streamed services, requiring several delivery streams to converge, and then to affect multiple parties and their relationships (e.g., family provisions in Newpin and BSSBB, and adoptive families in IAAM).

In contracting form, three approaches to defining the beneficiary group seem to have emerged. Firstly there is the predefined cohort, such as the "all prisoners serving at least twelve months" at Peterborough Prison. This requires a definition for that cohort that can be locked in at the outset, notwithstanding any changes in the operating environment or the nature of that cohort over future years. While simple and encouraging for the commissioner for a pilot of a new model, it is perhaps a less flexible arrangement than the other two models. This may be a reason as to why it appears less after Peterborough and Rykers Island. It may be, though, that it is simply better suited to more easily self-defining cohorts in homogenous situations such as offenders. The second approach is of a pre-boundaried group with a referral or contract call-off system. This is apparent in Newpin and Massachusetts Roca. Both these have a minimum cohort, or under-referral provisions, to cover the consequent risk of the commissioner losing interest to the cost of the scheme. This is more flexible. It enables the beneficiaries to be matched to the intervention; it focuses provision on where it is most needed and where it is most likely to be effective. The third approach is the free-market purchase system of IAAM, the only bond exhibiting this model to date. It firstly defines a service, a market, and a means for buyers to buy it. Thereafter, it markets its services to them in a conventional market-making approach. It is consequently exposed to the risk of non-take-up of those services and must ensure that it manages this risk. The approach seems to suit markets where, as with IAAM, there is a highly nuanced selection process against highly individualized criteria that are hard, if not impossible, to pre-define.

All of these SIBs—given that they are remunerated on results (success), defined as a change in the lives of beneficiaries—require a counterfactual to give a benchmark against which to test the achievement of outcomes according to a pre-researched theory of change. With regard to the theory of change, this is clear in all cases. However, it may arise from, or build on, multiple sources, including sample cohort studies (e.g., IAAM), one or more pilot studies (e.g., Massachusetts Roca), or from randomized control trials (where it is possible to use these to isolate the effects of often complex and highly nuanced provision to a cohort which may vary demographically from the subjects of the intervention).

Three broad approaches to the counterfactual seem to be emerging. First, there is the comparison to a continuing general population. This is the traditional approach. It is exemplified by Peterborough Prison, where there is reliable national data about reoffending and the subject cohort is sufficiently small that the effectiveness of the intervention for that group does not cause a shift in the benchmark. The second approach is the matched cohort, which allows the benchmark to emerge and to vary over time (e.g., Essex MST and BSSBB). It relies on the quality of the matching, which, it appears, is often a matter of professional judgment by the payor (commissioner) and entails fail-safe provisions to cover the situation of unusual shifts in the comparator group. The third approach is to match the life track of individual subject beneficiaries against individual targets as indicators of success (e.g., IAAM, Newpin, BSSBB, DWP). This seems to work where there are measurable points which are widely accepted as indicators of success. These may not be the ultimate outcomes, but are likely to be milestones on the route to them that are commonly accepted by stakeholders as giving a high probability of success. In this, they can be what in social impact measurement terms is known as an output, being a point of interface with the beneficiary (Clifford et al., 2014), and may best be distinguished from the selection of output measures in the abstract by the term "informed output." Perhaps the ideal informed outputs are ones which may also be direct measures of outcomes for the payor. This is also illustrated in IAAM, where the ultimate outcomes are a change in expected life course for the child and family, with effects felt for many years into the future, if not a whole lifetime. The payment is against two years of milestones in therapeutic placement after which period it is apparently widely accepted by stakeholders that the placement is likely to succeed. Those two years also mark cashable savings to the commissioner of twice what they are paying for the scheme, so are also outcomes in their own right for the payor.

Structure and governance

The final part of our exploratory framework is that of structure and governance. Contrary to early definitions of SIBs, it emerges that there is an appreciable number of SIBs that do not use a SPV as a contracting entity. They do, however, all use contracts as the primary link between the parties instead of ownership structures. Three types of corporate and contracting structure can be identified. Firstly there is the traditional model, in which a SPV is established as a core contracting vehicle. This receives funds from the investors, enters into a contract to deliver public services with the commissioner, and contracts out that delivery to one or more service providers, such as NGOs or private sector entities. The second approach is that the SPV is formed but acts as a contract manager, with the commissioner contracting directly with the provider. In this case, the funding generally comes through the SPV, often from a trust fund holder, with the SPV also acting as a gatherer of scheme surpluses to be distributed to investors and providers as appropriate. The third approach is the managed network. Only one example of this, IAAM, exists to date. Similar to the trust fund holder in the second approach, here the fund still stands separately. However, the SPV is dispensed with in favor of a project manager that acts as the hub of the network. The contracting is between commissioners and individual providers on what in IAAM is a free-market purchase arrangement, although it is hard to see why it should not work with a pre-boundaried and call-off approach instead.

As part of the payment-by-results (for success) regime, control systems are central to SIBs. Diverse in their focus, they underpin internal control arrangements for funding and operational management and support the gathering of evidence for research. They may also be necessary for other forms of compliance, such as dealing with sensitive data (e.g., in IAAM or Essex MST, where regulated personal data about children is handled), or compliance with external licensing of methodologies or other intellectual property (e.g., Essex for the MST system and approach). The approaches in respect of the payment systems again seem to fall into three types. Firstly, some use complex measurement systems tracking a mixture of service delivery (volume, timing, and quality) and meeting financial triggers. Secondly, there are those approaches that use natural systemic gateways or milestones that appear within a normal flow of events for the payor (such as the milestones in IAAM that follow statutory review or decision events for a looked-after child). Thirdly, there are multiple indicator approaches that offer a series of targets, each with its own value. These latter are applied where there are several potential routes to different positive outcomes (e.g., DWP).

Taken together, these insights result in the conceptual typology of the SIB arena proposed in Figure 10.4. In line with Collier et al.'s (2012) conceptualization of typologies, our typology starts to explore and reflect the meaning of SIBs by mapping out their dimensions with the aim to develop better identification, description, and understanding of the field. Unlike the expectation that developments might follow one set of types for each of the three dimensions in the framework (financial, social, and governance and structure), or be based around a financial market typology as suggested in SITF (2010) and by Brown and Swersky (2012), Figure 10.4 highlights that there seem to be subsets of two or three types within each dimension. In financial, it is suggested that there are financial value criteria (income and capital yields mapped against risk, and market benchmarking) and application of the funding. In social we have intervention type (simple, single; or complex, multiple), cohort selection, or market approach (pre-defined; pre-boundaried and referral or call-off; open market or spot purchase), and approach to counter factual (general population; matched cohort; or self-, market-, or expert-defined). All three areas herein have a risk and risk management perspective layered across them. Finally, in governance and structure there is corporate structure (traditional SPV as contractor; SPV as manager; managed network) and the control and measurement approach (complex, multi-aspect; systemic milestones; multi-indicator flexible).

While so far insufficient evidence has been gathered, it may also be that accountability and approach thereto is a third range of alternatives within this area. Given each area has risks associated

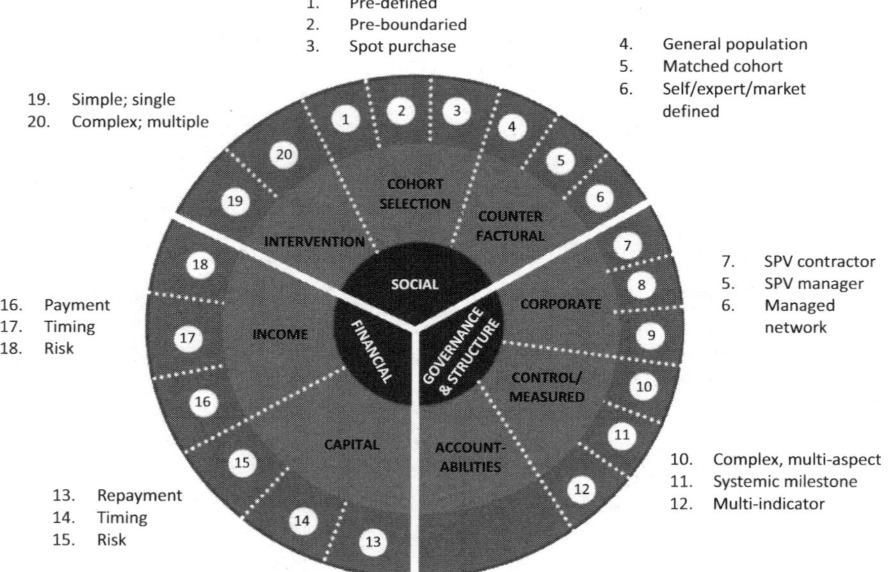

Figure 10.4 Conceptual typology of SIBs

with it, further work might look at how different types of risk match what is seen here. Bearing in mind that risk relates to both the social and financial aspects of SIBs—intended outcomes might not be delivered, or unintended and potentially detrimental outcomes might occur—it might be useful to consider six risk categories within this context: interventional model—does the work proposed to be done achieve the outcomes targeted at a theoretical level?; execution risk—does it achieve them in practice?; intermediary risk—can the parties concerned deliver and sustain?; political risk—will the climate of need or policy-driven payment change?; financial risk—does the model work with financial sensitivities?; and reputational risk—will reputation and brand drive social engagement effectively, and will failure cause reputational damage that spills over into other programs? (Social Finance, 2012). Against this complexity of risk and risk management, it is notable that although later SIBs, such as IAAM, have introduced risk sharing and management by the provider(s), the traditional SIB approach exhibits little sophistication in risk management and risk sharing (Cabinet Office, 2013).

Concluding remarks

There are strong indications that SIBs can perform an important role in the changing social finance and Impact Investing landscape. Although envisioned by some as a way to replace normal, government-provided and -funded public services, SIBs' real potential is their promise of additionality. By bringing together a variety of non-governmental stakeholders and alternative forms of resources, SIBs allow for the development of social interventions in areas where a government agency does not have the funding for, or is not prepared to take the risk of, doing so. Furthermore, SIBs enable multi-area or larger-scale development of interventions where local government is not focused on promulgating interventions outside its area, or where a substantial capital investment in asset base and scaling infrastructure cannot be afforded out of constrained government budgets, even if such interventions would bring future savings. To those involved in the development and delivery of social interventions, SIBs allow for the more efficient averaging, sharing, and managing of risk. Taken together, SIBs thereby offer the potential for social interventions that may otherwise not occur at all, that may not happen right now, or that may not happen at an envisioned scale.

While the purpose and future use of SIBs may vary in different areas of the world, so far there appear to be three dominant applications of SIBs. Based on their location, and the political and social context in which they are set, these can be described as US, UK, and Australian perspectives. In the US, the emphasis seems to be on scaling evidence-based, fully tried-and-tested interventions. This differs from the Australian approach, where the focus is on innovation, developing interventions which are expected to be taken into government and directly funded once they have run their first, bond-funded cycle. While the idea of innovation also runs through the UK perspective, despite some national schemes, such as IAAM, there is no apparent intention of taking the services into direct government provision after the initial investment cycle. As the fit of each type is driven by factors within the economies and societies in which the bond is operating, further research around the interaction between these innovations, their stated aims of systemic change, and whether these demographic and cultural focuses change over time seems warranted. This rings especially true in light of future visions for SIBs, such as Development Impact Bonds as a funding tool for international development (see Social Finance, 2013a).

To this end, however, SIBs need to be well understood. Our chapter has provided an overview of the emergence of SIBs, their global growth, and diverse development trajectories. Based on an inductive approach that utilized three overarching dimensions derived from the literature on social finance—the social, the financial, and governance and structure—10 SIBs were analyzed, and eight sub-categories across the three dimensions, each with its own set of types, were identified and a conceptual typology was developed. Breaking up the diversity of SIBs' characteristics, this typology offers a structured basis for further research with the aim to understand the subtleties, differences, flexibilities, and appropriateness of SIBs, both to enable them to deliver on their promise and to strengthen our knowledge base on the area.

References

Baliga, S. (2013). Shaping the success of social impact bonds in the United States: Lessons learned from the privatisation of U.S. prisons. *Duke Law Journal, 63*(2), 437–479.

Bensoussan, E., Ruparell, R., & Taliento, L. (2013). *Innovative development financing*. Retrieved February 24, 2016, from http://www.mckinsey.com/industries/social-sector/our-insights/innovative-development-financing

Brannick, T., & Coghlan, D. (2007). In defence of being "native": The case for insider academic research. *Organisational Research Methods, 10*(1), 59–74.

Brown, A., & Norman, W. (2011). *Lighting the touchpaper: Growing the market for social investment in England*. London, UK: The Boston Consulting Group/The Young Foundation.

Brown, A., & Swersky, A. (2012). *The first billion—A forecast of social investment demand*. London, UK: The Boston Consulting Group/Big Society Capital.

Burand, D. (2013). *Globalizing social finance: How social impact bonds and social impact performance guarantees can scale development*. Retrieved June 30, 2015, from http://repository.law.umich.edu/cgi/viewcontent.cgi?article=2086&context=articles

Cabinet Office. (2011). *Growing the social investment market: A vision and strategy*. London, UK: HM Government.

Cabinet Office. (2012). *Growing the social investment market: Progress update*. London, UK: HM Government.

Cabinet Office. (2013). *The knowledge box: Centre for social impact bonds*. Retrieved June 30, 2015, from http://data.gov.uk/sib_knowledge_box

Callanan, L., & Law, J. (2012). *Will social impact bonds work in the United States?* Retrieved June 30, 2015, from http://payforsuccess.org/sites/default/files/will_social-impact-bonds_work_in_the_us.pdf

Cameron, D. (2013). *Social investment can be a great force for social change*. London, UK: Social Impact Investment Forum.

Clay, R. F. (2013). Health impact bonds: Will investors pay for intervention? *Environmental Health Perspectives, 121*(2), A45.

Clifford, J., Hehenberger, L., & Ors, F. M. (2014). *Proposed approaches to social impact measurement in European Commission legislation and in practice relating to: EuSEFs and the EaSI*. Retrieved June 30, 2015, from http://ec.europa.eu/internal_market/social_business/docs/expert-group/social_impact/140605-sub-group-report_en.pdf

Clifford, J., Markey, K., & Malpani, N. (2013). *Measuring social impact in social enterprise: The state of thought and practice in the UK*. London, UK: Social Business International and Baker Tilly.

Cohen, R. (2014, June 12). Eight sobering thoughts for social impact bond supporters. *Nonprofit Quarterly*. Retrieved June 30, 2015, from https://nonprofitquarterly.org/policysocial-context/24346-eight-sobering-thoughts-for-social-impact-bond-supporters.html

Collier, D., LaPorte, J., & Seawright, J. (2012). Putting typologies to work: Concept formation, measurement, and analytic rigor. *Political Research Quarterly, 65*(1), 217–232.

Corry, D. (2012, January 26). Social investment: A revolution or a bubble? *The Guardian*. Retrieved June 30, 2015, from http://www.theguardian.com/voluntary-sector-network/2012/jan/26/social-investment-revolution-bubble

Costa, K., Shah, S., & Ungar, S. (2012). *Frequently asked questions: Social impact bond*. Retrieved June 30, 2015, from https://cdn.americanprogress.org/wp-content/uploads/2012/12/FAQSocialImpactBonds-1.pdf

Delbridge, R., & Fiss, P. C. (2013). Styles of theorizing and the social organization of knowledge. *Academy of Management Review, 38*(3), 325–331.

Demel, A. (2013). Second thoughts on social impact bonds. *NYU Journal of Law & Business, 9*(2), 503–509.

Disley, E., Rubin, J., Scraggs, E., Burrowes, N., & Culley, D. M. (2011). *Lessons learned from the planning and early implementation of the social impact bond at HMP Peterborough*. Cambridge, UK: RAND Europe.

Doty, D. H., & Glick, W. H. (1994). Typologies as a unique form of theory building: Towards improved understanding and modelling. *Academy of Management Review, 19*(2), 230–251.

Evered, R., & Louis, M. R. (1981). Alternative perspectives in the organisational sciences: "Inquiry from the Inside" and "Inquiry from the Outside." *Academy of Management Review, 6*(3), 385–395.

Filion, L. J. (2000). Entrepreneurial typologies: Are they really useful? In E. Brauchlin & J. H. Pichler (Eds.), *Unternehmer und Unternehmensperspektiven fuer Klein- und Mittelunternehmen* (pp. 163–172). Berlin: Duncker & Humboldt.

Fiss, P. (2011). Building better causal theories: A fuzzy set approach to typologies in organisational research. *Academy of Management Journal, 54*(2), 393–420.

Fletcher, M. (2013). *Can investors make money in social services?* Retrieved June 30, 2015, from http://www.washingtonpost.com/business/economy/can-investors-make-money-in-social-services/2013/06/07/a010e7f6-ced6-11e2-8845-d970ccb04497_story.html

Godoy, E. (2013). *Critics question impact of "pay for success" bonds.* Retrieved June 30, 2015, from http://www.ipsnews.net/2013/10/critics-question-impact-of-pay-for-success-bonds

Goodall, E. (2014). *Choosing social impact bonds: A practitioner's guide.* London, UK: Bridges Impact+, Bridges Ventures.

Hay, D. B., & Kinchin, I. M. (2006). Using concept maps to reveal conceptual typologies. *Education and Training, 48*(2/3), 127–142.

Horesh, R. (1988, July). *Social policy bonds.* Paper presented at the New Zealand Branch Australian Agricultural Economics Society Conference, Blenheim.

Horesh, R. (2002, September). Better than Kyoto: Climate stability bonds. *IEA Economic Affairs*, 48–52.

Humphries, K. W. (2014). Not your older brother's bond: The use and regulation of social impact bonds in the United States. *Law and Contemporary Problems, 76*(3), 433–452.

Kohli, J., Besharov, D., & Costa, K. (2012a). *Inside a social impact bond agreement: Exploring the contract challenges of a new social finance mechanism.* Washington, DC: Center for American Progress.

Kohli, J., Besharov, D., & Costa, K. (2012b). *Defining terms in a social impact bond agreement: Explaining essential clauses in a SIB contract.* Washington, DC: Centre for American Progress.

Leventhal, R. (2013). Effecting progress: Using social impact bonds to finance social services. *NYU Journal of Law & Business, 9*(2), 511–534.

Liebman, J. B. (2011). *Social impact bonds: A promising new financing model to accelerate social innovation and improve government performance.* Washington, DC: Center for American Progress.

McHugh, N., Sinclair, S., Roy, M., Huckfield, L., & Donaldson, C. (2013). Social impact bonds: A wolf in sheep's clothing? *Journal of Poverty and Social Justice, 21*(3), 247–257.

McKay, K. (2013, April 8). Debunking the myths behind social impact bond speculation. *Stanford Social Innovation Review.* Retrieved June 30, 2015, from http://www.ssireview.org/blog/entry/debunking_the_myths_behind_social_impact_bond_speculation

McKinsey&Company. (2012, May). *From potential to action: Bringing social impact bonds to the US.* New York: Callanan, L., Law, J., & Mendonca, L.

Moran, M. (2008, March 26–29). *The 800 pound gorilla: The Bill & Melinda Gates Foundation, the GAVI Alliance and philanthropy in international public policy.* Paper presented at the International Studies Association 49th Annual Convention, San Francisco.

Mulgan, G., Reeder, N., Aylott, M., & Bo'sher, L. (2011). *Social impact investment: The challenge and opportunity of social impact bonds.* London, UK: The Young Foundation.

National Audit Office (NAO). (2009). *Building the capacity of the Third Sector. Report by the Comptroller and Auditor General.* HC 132 Session 2008–2009. London, UK: NAO.

National Council for Voluntary Organisations (NCVO). (2011). *Efficiency and value for money.* Retrieved June 30, 2015, from http://ncvoforesight.org/drivers/efficiency-and-value-for-money

Nicholls, A. (2010). The institutionalization of social investment: The interplay of investment logics and investor rationalities. *Journal of Social Entrepreneurship, 1*(1), 70–100.

Nicholls, A., & Tomkinson, E. (2013). *The Peterborough Pilot Social Impact Bond.* Oxford, UK: Said Business School, University of Oxford.

Nickel, P. M., & Eikenberry, A. M. (2009). A critique of the discourse of marketised philanthropy. *American Behavioral Scientist, 52*(7), 974–989.

NSW Treasury. (2014). *Social benefit bonds.* Retrieved June 30, 2015, from http://www.treasury.nsw.gov.au/site_plan/social_benefit_bonds

Palandjian, T., & Hughes, J. (2014). A strong field framework for SIBs'. *Stanford Social Innovation Review.* Retrieved June 30, 2015, from http://www.ssireview.org/blog/entry/a_strong_field_framework_for_sibs

Palmer, A. (2013, February 23). Social impact bonds: Commerce and conscience. *The Economist*. Retrieved June 30, 2015, from http://www.economist.com/news/finance-and-economics/21572231-new-way-financing-public-services-gains-momentum-commerce-and-conscience/print

Patton, A. (2013). *The social investment market: The role of public policy in innovation and execution*. London and Oxford, UK: Cabinet Office/Said Business School.

Rich, P. (1992). The organisational taxonomy: Definition and design. *Academy of Management Review, 17*(4), 758–781.

Rotheroe, A. (2014). *Lessons and opportunities: Perspectives from providers of social impact bonds*. London, UK: New Philanthropy Capital.

Schmid, E. (2012, January–February). Pay businesses to keep people out of prison. *Harvard Business Review*, 64.

Sheil, F. (2014). *Failing the public? A provocation paper*. London, UK: New Philanthropy Capital.

Social Investment Task Force (SITF). (2000). *Enterprising communities: Wealth beyond welfare*. A Report to the Chancellor of the Exchequer, London. Retrieved June 30, 2015, from http://www.socialinvestment taskforce.org/downloads/SITF_Oct_2000.pdf

SITF. (2003, July 2–3). *Enterprising communities: Wealth beyond welfare. A 2003 update on the Social Investment Task Force*. Paper presented at CDFA Conference, Cardiff. Retrieved June 30, 2015, from http://www.socialinvestmenttaskforce.org/downloads/SITF_July_2003.pdf

SITF. (2005, July 6–8). *Enterprising communities: Wealth beyond welfare. A 2005 update on the Social Investment Task Force*. Paper presented at CDFA Conference, Melton Mowbray.

SITF. (2010). *Social investment ten years on: Final report of the Social Investment Task Force*. London, UK: Social Investment Task Force.

SITF. (2014). *Measuring impact: Subject paper of the impact measurement working group*. Retrieved June 30, 2015, from http://www.thegiin.org/binary-data/IMWG_Whitepaper.pdf

Social Finance. (2011). *Peterborough Social Impact Bond*. London, UK: Social Finance.

Social Finance. (2012). *A new tool for scaling impact: How social impact bonds can mobilise private capital to advance social good*. Retrieved June 30, 2015, from http://www.socialfinance.org.uk/wp-content/uploads/2014/05/small.SocialFinanceWPSingleFINAL.pdf

Social Finance. (2013a). *Investing in social outcomes: Development impact bonds*. Retrieved June 30, 2015, from http://www.socialfinance.org.uk/resources/publications/investing-social-outcomes-development-impact-bonds

Social Finance. (2013b). *Social impact bonds*. Retrieved June 30, 2015, from http://www.socialfinance.org.uk/work/sibs

Social Finance. (2014). *Vision*. Retrieved June 30, 2015, from http://www.socialfinance.org.uk/about/vision

Social Finance. (2015). *History*. Retrieved June 30, 2015, from http://www.socialfinance.org.uk/about-us/history

Thümler, E. (2015). The financialisation of philanthropy. In T. Jung, S. D. Phillips, & J. Harrow (Eds.), *The Routledge companion to philanthropy*. London, UK: Routledge.

Tomkinson, E. (2015). *Social impact bonds*. Retrieved June 30, 2015, from http://emmatomkinson.com/category/social-impact-bonds

US Government. (2014). *Paying for success* (Office of Management and Budget). Retrieved June 30, 2015, from http://www.whitehouse.gov/omb/factsheet/paying-for-success

11

LENDING TO SOCIAL VENTURES

Existing demand for finance and the potential roles of social investment

Fergus Lyon

There is a growing interest in the provision of Social and Sustainable Investment and loan finance for social enterprises and other social purpose organizations. These organizations, operating at the intersections of the commercial world and civil society, face particular challenges with tensions between their social or environmental objective and the financial imperative of running a business. These tensions become particularly apparent when examining the use of repayable loan finance (Doherty, Haugh, & Lyon, 2014). social investment is financed by investors that seek opportunities to lend to organizations that create social value at the same time as generating a financial return (Nicholls, 2010). It has become a focus for policy around the world, but particularly in the UK where it was selected as a key theme to be promoted by the UK's presidency of the G8 in 2013. In this chapter we specifically focus on the use of repayable loan finance that might come from specialist Social Investors or from conventional sources such as banks. This is distinguished from other forms of finance such as retained profit/surplus, investment from owners/staff, or grants.

While the supply of investment for social enterprise may be expanding in the UK, there remain questions over the nature of the demand for loan finance for social organizations. There is evidence that some funds find it hard to distribute resources and find investees (Alcock, Millar, & Hall, 2012; Gregory, Hill, Joy, & Keen, 2012; Hall, Alcock, & Millar, 2012). Gregory et al. (2012, pp. 8–9) state:

> After a number of years bemoaning the lack of access to capital and suggesting that "if you build it they will come" (Sir Ronald Cohen), the emphasis has shifted amongst the experts to regret the absence of investment ready propositions. In the midst of a global credit crisis and with access to finance at the top of social ventures' concerns, we perversely see significant pools of unapplied capital with slow dispersal rates.

A further review of the UK experience by the Social Impact Investment Taskforce (2014, 29) found that "The social Impact Investing market has more capital available than demand side organizations can reasonably absorb. This has been attributed to a lack of 'investment-readiness' among social organizations particularly due to skills gaps in financial and strategic management."

With an ever-growing community of Social Investors and policy interest around the world, there is a need for greater understanding of the demand for social investment from different types of business and social organizations. While much literature produced by the social investment community is focused on aspirations, there is also a need for sensitive reflective research that explores the challenges and unpicks existing assumptions. In particular, there is a need to examine the role of commercial banks in lending to social organizations and the relationships of the social investment providers to commercial lenders. Questions remain concerning the role of social investment with regard to filling gaps in the market left by banks. For example, Social Investors are not explicit in their aims: are they operating to lend where banks will not lend, or are they aiming to take a market share from commercial lenders?

Finally there are questions over which business and social organizations are eligible for social investment. As investors struggle to lend to charities, Community Interest Companies, and other socially regulated organizations, there is a strong impetus to redefine who can access social investment. The language and labels of social investment have been kept loose with broad definitions adopted that can allow flexibility and multiple interpretations. As shown with explorations of the definition of social enterprise (Lyon & Sepulveda, 2009; Teasdale, Lyon, & Baldock, 2013), definitions of these hybrid concepts can shift. The combination of multiple logics (social, environmental, financial) within hybrids creates tensions but also offers room for maneuver. social investment is, therefore, at a cross-roads with challenges related to demonstrating that there is a market failure and a lack of clarity regarding who is eligible.

To explore these issues, this chapter will address the following questions: What is the current use of repayable finance? What is the evidence of a gap in the provision of repayable finance for social organizations? What is the role of social investment? Which organizations can be eligible for social investment and what is the size of this market?

The current use of repayable finance by social organizations

There is now a growing body of evidence about the use of social investment and repayable finance by social organizations. This analysis separates the use of grants from repayable finance and explores which organizations are seeking, the amount sought, and the sources. Earlier work found repayable finance is only of interest to a minority of social enterprises, with most being cautious of debt finance (Bank of England, 2003; Sunley & Pinch, 2012). More recently, a survey of 1,811 charities with incomes of more than £60,000 found that 61 percent were unlikely to take out repayable finance in the future and 12 percent currently had repayable finance (Charities Aid Foundation, 2014). A study of 2,200 third-sector organizations in the north of England (including a large proportion of smaller organizations) found that 4.2 percent had borrowed in the past two years and 14 percent stated that "borrowing money is of importance" (Chapman, 2015). A study of 878 organizations defining themselves as social enterprises found that 47 percent sought external finance (including grants) but only 15 percent were seeking repayable finance[1] (Lyon & Baldock, 2014). This is slightly lower than the borrowing by all Small and Medium Enterprises (BIS, 2013).

Commercial banks are found to provide a very large proportion of the lending. NCVO (2014) reports that bank lending to charities was £4 billion, although Big Society Capital (2014b) reports a figure of £2.9 billion. Charities Aid Foundation (2014) found that 56 percent of borrowing charities (larger than £60,000 turnover) were going to banks. The survey of social enterprises also found that banks were used by 64 percent of borrowers (Lyon & Baldock, 2014).

Table 11.1 Amount of debt finance sought from different providers of debt finance

	N	Min (£)	Max (£)	Median (£)	Mean (£)	Trimmed mean
Bank	74	2,000	30,000,000	80,000	1,352,064	505,164
All Social Investors	29	15,000	7,000,000	250,000	705,414	437,174
Other (not Social Investors)	38	6,000	5,500,000	100,000	620,547	386,140

Source: Lyon and Baldock (2014). Includes examples of multiple finance seeking from different sources. The trimmed mean excludes the lowest and highest 5% (outliers) of responses.

The amount of social investment from social banks and other social lenders has been estimated as £595 million (Big Society Capital, 2014b), although GHK (2013) report a lower figure of £202 million. These figures exclude community shares, charitable bonds, and investment by social enterprises in other social enterprises. This remains a small fraction of all repayable finance to social organizations. The survey of social enterprises found that 3.6 percent of social enterprises were using social lenders, or a quarter of all borrowers. As Table 11.1 shows, these social lenders were found to be lending larger amounts, with a median loan of £250,000 compared to the median loan from banks of £80,000 (Lyon & Baldock, 2014).

The study of social enterprises found that larger organizations (with turnovers of more than £1 million) were twice as likely to be borrowing (Lyon & Baldock, 2014), with similar results found by Chapman (2015). As would be expected, the more established are more likely to borrow, but there is only a weak association between the percentage of trading income and borrowing in both these studies. This raises questions over the importance of commercial income opportunities as a driver for social investment. Social enterprise borrowing was found to have a higher success rate of 69 percent receiving some and 63 percent receiving all that they requested (Lyon & Baldock, 2014). This is similar or marginally better than other SMEs (BIS, 2013; Fraser, 2009).

There is limited data on how social organizations currently use social investment. Chapman (2015) found that 4.3 percent of third-sector organizational borrowing was made up of 1.6 percent borrowing to invest in the development of new services, 1 percent taking out a mortgage to buy a property, and 0.8 percent seeking working capital to bridge a cash flow gap. While investment is evident for those organizations that are growing, there can also be investment as a stepping stone, ensuring survival when an organization loses a major contract or grant (IVAR, 2013). Repayable finance can therefore be sought from organizations that are not growing. The study of social enterprises found that of the 18 percent of organizations with a declining income, 11 percent were seeking loans (Lyon & Baldock, 2014).

Finance gaps and the need for social investment

The actual unmet demand for repayable finance by social organizations is also an ongoing debate in the UK. Interest in social investment has arisen as a large proportion of organizations report that "access to finance" is a major constraint. Survey data using this term has been used to justify the need for public sector involvement in the market. While the term "access to finance" refers to repayable finance for private sector organizations, for charities and other social organizations, "access to finance" refers predominantly to the desire for more grants or donations. However, access to finance can also refer to the need for any financial resource, including repayable finance and even income for delivering services. There is therefore a need for more detailed examination of the evidence on the unmet demand for repayable finance by social organizations.

The literature on social investment has not focused on this lack of demand, although it is now recognized as a central issue for the development of the social investment market. The UK National Advisory Board to the Social Impact Investment Taskforce reported that "Developing a robust pool of social organizations that want, need and can service Social Impact Investment remains critical to building the social investment market" (Social Impact Investment Taskforce, 2014, p. 28).

Much of the literature from the Social Investors themselves has made assumptions that a gap in the supply of repayable finance will arise when there is an increase in business opportunities. The most notable report is the modestly titled *The First Billion: A forecast of social investment demand* prepared for Big Society Capital by Boston Consulting Group (2012b). They forecast a rise in the demand for social investment from £165 million in 2011 to £1 billion by 2016. The report states that this is dependent on a number of assumptions. First, an increase in public procurement by 37 percent in sectors where social organizations operate; second, an increase in the market share captured by social organizations from 22 percent to 32 percent; third, an increase in the use of social investment within social organizations with repayable finance as a percentage of total investment needs rising from 5 percent to 7.4 percent; and finally, a change in policy from Social Investors resulting in unsecured lending increasing from 11 percent of their portfolio to 58 percent (Big Society Capital, 2012b). Data available from 2011 to 2012 shows that many of these trends have been moving in the opposite direction with dramatic cuts in public expenditure, the income from public procurement declining for charities (NCVO, 2014), large areas of procurement such as criminal justice reforms, focusing contracts on large corporate businesses, and a decline in the number of social enterprises spinning out from the public sector. Furthermore, the proportion of unsecured lending from the Big Society Capital-supported social investment finance intermediaries was reducing and secured lending increasing lending from 84 percent in 2010/11 to 90 percent in 2011/12 (GHK, 2013).

However, if the finance gap is partly due to the capabilities and competences of social organizations and their desire for using repayable finance, there is a need to understand where this gap is and to segment the social investment market. A segmentation model shown in Figure 11.1 distinguishes between those not interested in repayable finance, those receiving investment, and

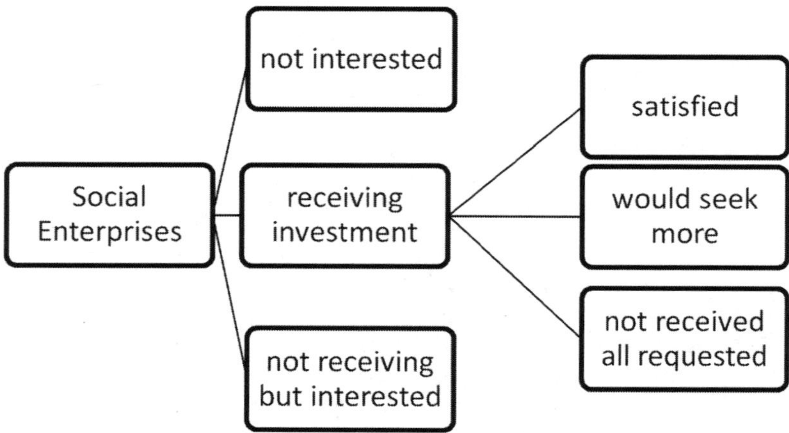

Figure 11.1 Segmentation model for social enterprises seeking finance

Source: Adapted from Lyon and Baldock (2014).

finally those not receiving social investment but are interested. Of those that are already receiving repayable finance, there may be a demand for more investment or more favorable terms being offered by Social Investors. The additional impact of social investment taking a market share from commercial banks is discussed in the next section.

Lyon and Baldock (2014) found that 21 percent of social enterprises had not sought social investment in the last year but might have done so if circumstances were different. Many will be limited by the lack of opportunities in their sector and this may be shaped by the economic downturn and the period of public spending austerity. Within this 21 percent, there is evidence of 9 percent that felt that the cost of finance was too high, terms too stringent, or the process too onerous.

These "discouraged borrowers" (Fraser, 2009) also included those that did not know where to apply to, who did not have confidence, or were discouraged by a previous application. The social enterprise survey found that these discouraged borrowers are significantly more likely to be smaller and younger organizations (Lyon & Baldock, 2014). The National Survey of Charities and social enterprises (2010) found that 8 percent were dissatisfied with access to loan finance, and the survey of all third-sector organizations in the north of England (35 percent of those who had turnovers under £10,000) found that 10 percent said they may need social investment but needed information and support (Chapman, 2015, p. 36).

Figure 11.2 segments the market for social investment further, by exploring the different elements of those that are not receiving social investment but are interested. First, there are those that have to try to access repayable finance but have not succeeded. This was 24 percent of the social enterprises seeking repayable finance (or 3.5 percent of all social enterprises) (Lyon & Baldock, 2014).

Existing research suggests that these applications could have failed for three reasons. First, it could be due to the approach of the application and capabilities of the organization. IVAR

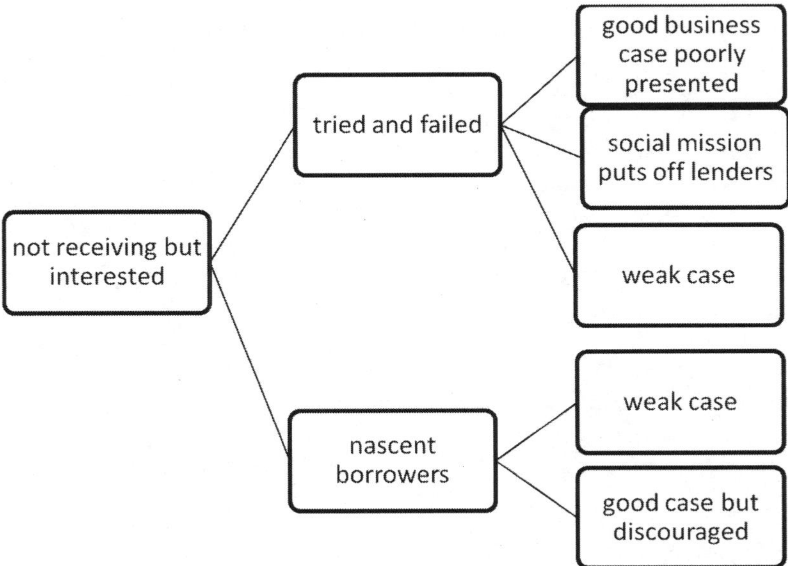

Figure 11.2 Segmentation model for social enterprises seeking but not receiving repayable finance
Source: Adapted from Lyon and Baldock (2014).

(2013) identifies key factors for success as willingness of trustees to engage with investment, leadership, ability to present a business plan, and understanding of investment requirements. Second, good applications may be rejected as the social mission of the organization may put off conventional lenders. More research is needed on the perception of conventional lenders, but the large amount of lending to social organizations from commercial banks suggests that social organizations can be perceived as good borrowers. Indeed, commercial lenders may be actively seeking borrowers who are less risky, conducting careful diligence, and not likely to go bankrupt. Third, there may be rejections for those social organizations that do not have a strong business case with safe streams of income or security. Promoting repayable finance to such organizations would be unwise and an example of "sub-prime" lending. These organizations require support in developing their basic business rather than specific investment readiness support.

The final category can be classified as the "nascent borrowers" and would be the organizations where more attention should be given by Social Investors. Again this category can be divided into those with a good business case but discouraged and those needing support to develop income streams that can repay any borrowing. They may be requiring support in the form of advice, mentoring, and coaching.

The role of social investment

With the development of the supply of social investment and the growing evidence of a lack of immediate demand, there is a need for reflection on the role of social investment. This requires examination of how social investment can fill a gap left by commercial lenders and support innovation that might be risky.

Social investment is promoted as it is

> able to take risks on innovations with primarily social, rather than financial, returns ... This is especially true in the case of innovative social enterprise start-ups with untested business models ... Social Investors may, therefore, be willing to invest in these organizations to support greater experimentation, and therefore, innovation in the social sector.
>
> *(Brown & Swersky, 2012, p. 6)*

This aim is laudable and very important for the development of new ways of having greater social outcomes. Such riskiness of investment is likely to lead to dramatic winners, but also many unsuccessful experiments. The extent of unsuccessful lending to innovative organizations is not evident from the existing literature on social investment.

Some social investment funds have aimed to encourage innovation, with the social enterprise Investment Fund promoted by the Department of Health being designed with a specific innovation fund and a target of 15 percent of all deals to have a degree of innovation, as determined by an external committee (TSRC, 2010). The design of this fund accepted that innovation entails a degree of risk and therefore potential failure, with the policy makers expecting annual losses on loans up to 15 percent. An early evaluation (3 years after the fund started) found that 13 percent of social enterprises were not trading (Alcock et al., 2012). Similarly, BCG (2015) reviewed data on the Future Builders Fund 10 years after that started and found that 14 percent of loans had been written off. However, such data is not provided from other Social Investors. This may be due to the conservative nature of Social Investors not wanting the negative publicity that comes when loans have to be called in or social organizations are forced to close. The lack of data may also be due to competitive pressures facing different intermediaries and their lack of ability to share such commercially sensitive data.

Social investment is promoted as a way of addressing market failure and the gap in finance provision. There are a range of social investment providers in the UK, and their scale has increased through additional funds from Big Society Capital and other sources. Big Society Capital was set up under the Dormant Bank and Building Society Accounts Act passed in November 2008. Using unclaimed assets, it is a wholesale provider of finance to social investment financial intermediaries investing £150 million to intermediaries up to December 2013, with £600 million committed to building the social investment market (Big Society Capital, 2014c).

The Dormant Bank and Building Society Accounts Act states in Section 16:

> Subject to the provisions of this Part, the Big Lottery Fund shall distribute dormant account money for meeting expenditure that has a social or environmental purpose.
>
> The Fund may make grants or loans, or make or enter into other arrangements, for the purpose of complying with subsection … For the purposes of this Part, distributing money for meeting expenditure of a particular description includes distributing money for the purpose of establishing, or contributing to, endowments (including permanent endowments) in connection with expenditure of that description.

Section 18 of the Act on "Distribution of money for meeting English expenditure" states:

> A distribution of dormant account money for meeting English expenditure must be—
>
> (a) made for meeting expenditure on or connected with the provision of services, facilities or opportunities to meet the needs of young people,
> (b) made for meeting expenditure on or connected with—(i) the development of individuals' ability to manage their finances, or (ii) the improvement of access to personal financial services, or
> (c) made to a social investment wholesaler … In this section—"social investment wholesaler" means a body that exists to assist or enable other bodies to give financial or other support to third sector organizations; "third sector organization" means an organization that exists wholly or mainly to provide benefits for society or the environment.

Interestingly, this legislation does not specify the type of finance being provided and so creates an opportunity for social investment providers to distribute grant finance as well as repayable finance.

In order to use "public funds" in a competitive market, Big Society Capital had to ensure that it complied with the European Commissioners' State Aid rules. The interpretation of the State Aid rules draws on a submission from the UK government, and states:

> According to the UK authorities, there are market failures which prevent the social sector from accessing private money. Among those market failures are capital shortage and misperception of the risk/return couple. As regards capital shortage, for example nearly half of all social enterprises see access to finance as a key obstacle to their success (compared to only one third of SMEs). Although 16% of frontline social sector organizations access finance from public sources, the remaining 84% do not and thus are denied sufficient access to finance, limiting the efficiency of the frontline social market.
>
> *(European Commission, 2011, p. 4)*

This data on "access to finance" needs closer examination as it conflates access to grants with access to repayable finance. The gap therefore relates to the demand for grants or blended capital that mixes grants with loans. "Blended capital funding" is particularly important for younger organizations and those wanting to build their revenue models (Davison & Heap, 2013). However, combining loans with grants presents further challenges for the social investment market as all social organizations will prefer a provider who can provide support in grant form rather than repayable finance. This therefore can act as a subsidy and can be challenged by commercial lenders who are being displaced. Furthermore, this chapter has shown that the market failure with respect to purely repayable finance is not so evident and that commercial banks are the major players in lending to social organizations. The challenge for social investment is to maximize social benefit in addition to existing forms of investment. Big Society Capital does have a Displacement policy which states:

> To ensure Dormant Accounts money is used in the most effective and efficient way, and to avoid unduly distorting functioning markets, all of BSC investments must be additional and must not displace existing capital. In practice this means that, for every investment it makes, BSC will need to ensure that the SIFI (or fund) BSC is investing in as well as the frontline social sector organizations that the SIFIs/funds are on-lending to are unable to access funding elsewhere. BSC will require potential investee SIFIs to show clearly that they cannot obtain the investment from elsewhere and that the frontline social sector organizations they invest in (or will be investing in) cannot obtain investment from elsewhere. This might be evidenced in a straightforward manner. In most cases, however, this will not be possible because no market exists for most asset classes. The onus will be placed on the SIFI to justify to BSC why they cannot raise finance elsewhere and demonstrate that they will not be investing in frontline social sector organizations that are able to raise finance elsewhere.
>
> *(Big Society Capital, 2012a, p. 51)*

In the past, displacement by public sector-supported social investment in the early stages of the Future Builders Fund was minimized by having independent Social Investors on the investment committee with the ability to take on deals if these were perceived to be "bankable" with non-public sector funds (BCG, 2015; TSRC, 2010). However, there is much evidence that social investment is being offered to those who can have bank finance. Big Society Capital (2012b, p. 6) reports that

> Social investment can be an attractive form of finance even for social organizations that are able to secure commercial lending. This is because Social Investors share with their investees an overall desire to create social impact. By taking on social capital, organizations can align their mission with that of their financiers. Where trade-offs emerge between financial and social returns, commercial investors are likely to force a resolution in favour of profit, whereas Social Investors would have a more balanced view.

Measuring additionally is highly complex. Evaluations of social investment are limited and very few assess the additionality and consider what might have happened without the social investment (what can be termed the deadweight). social investment can have additional benefits compared to commercial finance when social organizations are attracted to Social Investors because of the strong relationships, mutual trust, and shared vision (IVAR, 2013). Similarly, Chapman (2015) explored the different aspects of loan arrangements that are considered very important.

They found that 44 percent of the borrowers found relationships with lenders very important, and 47 percent considered the ethics of the lender very important. These can be classified as the non-financial reasons for preferring social investment over commercial lending. However, the same survey found 68 percent of borrowers felt that the length of the loan was important, 70 percent felt the fees and conditions were important, and 78 percent considered that the rate of interest was important.

There are further challenges in measuring additionally, as Social Investors may see their role as developing a social investment market and attracting further investment into social investment intermediaries. They report that they need to invest in "bankable" social ventures so they can demonstrate the profitability of social investment to other investors. Social Investors may also be trying to "crowd in" social investment by leveraging further investment for social organizations from commercial sources. The long-term impact of these strategies will therefore require further exploration.

The changing eligibility of social investment

There are ongoing debates regarding the organizational forms that can receive social investment. Much social investment has been targeted at those organizations that have a regulated social form, with an asset lock. This is also the basis for the finance provided by Big Society Capital which emphasizes the role of lending to third-sector organizations and organizations with a social purpose. In order to lend to this specific group, BSC had to ensure it was not breaking any State Aid rules. As it aims to grow the number of potential investees, there is attention being paid to widening the types of organizations eligible beyond those with asset locks and regulated by the Charity Commission and the Community Interest Company regulator. The Social Impact Investment Taskforce (2014, p. 28) suggests that "Redefining the social business frontier to ensure that businesses delivering social value can be recognized will enable them to be supported by Social Impact Investors."

The redrawing of the social investment eligibility and the social enterprise definitions will be a fast way of increasing the demand for social investment. The loose definitions of social investment, social enterprise, and third sector allow for reinterpretation, although it is also fraught with definitional issues and the risk of diluting the social and philanthropic aims of social investment. There has been a long-standing debate over the interpretation of definitions of social enterprise in the UK and the number of organizations that can be called social enterprises or social organizations. There is good information on those organizations that are registered as charities and Community Interest Companies, which requires them to have an asset lock whereby the capital and assets held by the organization cannot be sold for individual benefit. There are 161,000 organizations registered as charities (excluding those controlled by government, religious organizations, or independent fee-paying schools) (NCVO, 2014), as well as 10,000 Community Interest Companies and 10,000 Industrial and Provident Societies/Cooperatives (Big Society Capital, 2014a).

Greater challenges arise when estimating the number of social enterprises. There have been a range of different approaches over the past 12 years, with early attempts focusing on those organizations with asset locks but having trading elements. A figure of 15,000 was identified in 2005 based on this approach. This increased to 55,000 in 2005 and then to 62,000 in 2007, as the methodology was adjusted to include private businesses reporting that they operated as social enterprises (Lyon, Teasdale, & Baldock, 2010). This increase therefore reflects changing political debates concerning the types of organizations that can be called social enterprises (Teasdale et al., 2013). In 2013, the methodology was adjusted further, with a looser definition of social enterprise and a renewed estimate of 180,000 social enterprises or 688,000 if sole traders are included (BMG, 2013). These figures were reported widely as the UK selected the topic of social investment as a key area of work while president of the G8. The G8 Factsheet defines social enterprises as

> businesses that tackle social or environmental problems and work in communities to improve people's lives. Social enterprises can include charitable non-profits or businesses that make money. The majority of social enterprises reinvest their profits in the communities they work in.
>
> *(Cabinet Office, 2013)*

However, like much literature on social enterprise populations in the UK, these reports fail to report that an overwhelming proportion of these enterprises have private sector business legal forms such as Companies Limited by Share. They have no required asset lock (or other forms of locking in the social mission or performance) and so would not be entitled to much of the social investment available, such as investments originating from Big Society Capital. Closer analysis of the figure of 180,000 social enterprises shows that only 7 percent of these social enterprises have legal forms that ensure an asset lock (BMG, 2013; Teasdale et al., 2013).

With a lack of demand for social investment from social organizations with asset locks, parts of the social investment community are seeking other ways to demonstrate the social objectives of social enterprises that have private sector legal forms and thereby increase the number of organizations eligible for social investment. Big Society Capital is now exploring other forms of mission and performance "locks" as "there are many other ways to align financial and social goals with different levels of effectiveness that need not involve a regulator or an asset lock" (Big Society Capital, 2014a, p. 3). There is also recognition of the need to move beyond self-identification as this "presents a real risk of 'social washing' by companies wanting to appear more socially conscious than they really are" (Big Society Capital, 2014a, p. 3). The UK National Advisory Board to the Social Impact Investment Taskforce has supported the need to improve the recognition of those organizations delivering social outcomes but without a regulated social form, what they term profit-with-purpose businesses (Social Impact Investment Taskforce, 2014).

Conclusion

This chapter has set out to explore the demand from social enterprise and other social organizations for repayable finance. While much of the social investment industry is based on the premise that there is a market failure, there is evidence of a shortage of demand from existing eligible social organizations to meet the supply being provided. There is also evidence that commercial lenders provide a large majority of repayable finance for social organizations at present. If social investment is to be focused on the socially regulated sectors such as charities and Community Interest Companies, then these organizations require other forms of grant finance rather than conventional repayable finance (Davison & Heap, 2013). If social investment has to be focused on repayable finance, then its role has to be redefined and its eligibility criteria changed to include social purpose (or profit with a purpose) businesses. These are predominantly private businesses without asset locks and may not fit the criteria of philanthropic public funding.

As the social investment industry matures, there is a need to reflect and understand where it is working and where it can be improved. At present the evidence base of "what works" is particularly weak. The pressure from Social Investors on social organizations to measure their social impact is not being replicated with respect to the investors themselves or the providers of funds to the social investment finance intermediaries. Evaluation of the impact of social investment is required, taking into consideration the displacement of commercial bank lending by Social Investors and the additionality of the social investment funds when this happens.

The issue of displacement and the lack of demand by charities and social enterprises also raises questions of the evidence of market failure. In a period of global financial crisis, social investment was established as an alternative form of finance that aimed to fill gaps left by conventional finance. The need for alternative forms of resourcing social organizations becomes more pressing as public sector austerity results in cuts in funding to delivery organizations and puts pressure on social organizations through increasing demand from service users who are not being provided for by the public sector. Repayable finance may not be the radical alternative for these organizations. An alternative future may involve using philanthropic social investment funds for those areas of civil society where there is demand for external finance in the forms of grants or blend of loan and grant. If social investment has to retain its focus on repayable finance, then it has to reframe its target market and eligibility criteria beyond the conventional socially regulated organizations. Both of these scenarios would be expected to have social benefits, and evaluations of the UK experience can explore how such social value can be maximized. social investment is therefore at a crossroads.

Note

1 This survey found that loans were used by 10 percent of social enterprises and overdrafts used by 6 percent of social enterprises. The mix of repayable and grant finance was found to be important, with 87 percent of repayable finance seekers also seeking grants (Lyon & Baldock, 2014).

References

Alcock, P., Millar, R., & Hall, K. (2012). *Start-up and growth: National evaluation of the Social Enterprise Investment Fund (SEIF)*. Report submitted to the Department of Health Policy Research Programme, Third Sector Research Centre, Birmingham.

Bank of England. (2003). *The financing of social enterprises: A special report by the Bank of England*. London: Bank of England.

BCG. (2015). *A tale of two funds: The management and performance of Futurebuilders England*. London: Boston Consulting Group.

Big Society Capital. (2012a). *Big Society Capital: Vision, mission and activities*. Retrieved March 3, 2015, from http://www.bigsocietycapital.com

Big Society Capital. (2012b, September). *The first billion: A foreceast of social investment demand*. Retrieved February 24, 2016, from http://www.bigsocietycapital.com/sites/default/files/attachments/The%20First%20Billion.pdf

Big Society Capital. (2014a). *The social business frontier*. Prepared for the UK National Advisory Board to the Social Impact Investment Taskforce. Retrieved March 3, 2015, from http://www.bigsocietycapital.com/sites/default/files/pdf/Binder1.pdf

Big Society Capital. (2014b). *Social Investment Compendium 2014: Portfolio of research and intelligence on the social investment market*. Retrieved March 2, 2015, from http://www.bigsocietycapital.com/sites/default/files/pdf/20140912_Market%20Intelligence%20Compendium_2014_FINAL%20%282%29.pdf

Big Society Capital. (2014c). *Social investment: From ambition to action. Annual review 2013*. Retrieved March 3, 2015, from http://www.bigsocietycapital.com/sites/default/files/BSC_AR_2013.pdf

BIS. (2013, April). *Small Business Survey 2012: SME employers*. Report by BMG to the Department for Business Innovation and Skills.

BMG Research. (2013). *Social enterprise: Market trends*. Report for Cabinet Office, London.

Brown, A., & Swersky, A. (2012). *The first billion: A forecast of social investment demand*. London: Boston Consulting Group. Retrieved November 7, 2015, from https://www.bcg.com/documents/file115598.pdf

Cabinet Office. (2010). *National survey of charities and social enterprises*. Cabinet Office. Office of the Third Sector.

Cabinet Office. (2013). *G8 factsheet: Social investment and social enterprise*. Retrieved February 2, 2015, from https://www.gov.uk/government/publications/g8-factsheet-social-investment-and-social-enterprise/g8-factsheet-social-investment-and-social-enterprise

Chapman, T. (2015). *An assessment of the willingness of organisations to borrow money in the Third Sector: Findings from studies in Yorkshire, North East England and Cumbria*. Report for Northern Rock Foundation, Newcastle.

Charities Aid Foundation. (2014, March). *In demand: The changing need for repayable finance in the charity sector*. Retrieved March 3, 2015, from https://www.cafonline.org/docs/default-source/about-us-publications/in_demand_0314.pdf

Davison, R., & Heap, H. (2013). *Can social finance meet social need?* Retrieved February 2, 2015, from http://www.tomorrows-people.org.uk/files/blog/can-social-finance-meet-social-need-heap-and-davison-june-20131.pdf

Doherty, R., Haugh, H., & Lyon, F. (2014). Social enterprises as hybrid organizations: A review and research agenda. *International Journal of Management Reviews, 16*(4), 417–436.

European Commission. (2011). *State Aid No. SA.33683 (2011/N)—United Kingdom: Big Society Capital*. Letter to William Hague from European Commission. Retrieved February 2, 2015, from http://www.bigsocietycapital.com/sites/default/files/EU%20State%20Aid%20Decision_BSC_website.pdf

Fraser, S. (2009). *Small firms in the credit crisis: Evidence from the UK survey of SME finances*. Warwick Business School, University of Warwick.

GHK. (2013). *Growing the social investment market: The landscape and economic impact report to City of London*. London: Guildhall.

Gregory, D., Hill, K., Joy, I., & Keen, S. (2012). *Investment readiness in the UK*. London: Big Lottery Fund.

Hall, K., Alcock, P., & Millar, R. (2012). Start up and sustainability: Marketisation and the Social Enterprise Investment Fund in England. *Journal of Social Policy, 41*(4), 733–749.

IVAR. (2013). *Charities and social investment: A research report for the Charity Commission*. London: Institute for Voluntary Action Research. Retrieved June 11, 2015, from http://www.ivar.org.uk/publications/reports-and-publications/charities-and-social-investment-research-report-charity-commis

Lyon, F., & Baldock, R. (2014, June). *Financing social ventures and the demand for social investment* (TSRC Working Paper 124). Birmingham: Third Sector Research Centre. Retrieved February 24, 2016, from http://www.birmingham.ac.uk/generic/tsrc/documents/tsrc/working-papers/working-paper-124.pdf

Lyon, F., & Sepulveda, L. (2009). Mapping social enterprises: Past approaches, challenges and future directions. *Social Enterprise Journal, 5*(1), 83–94.

Lyon, F., Teasdale, S., & Baldock, R. (2010). *Approaches to measuring the scale of the social enterprise sector in the UK* (TSRC Working Paper 43). Birmingham: Third Sector Research Centre.

NCVO. (2014). *NCVO UK civil society almanac*. London: National Council for Voluntary Organisations.

Nicholls, A. (2010). The institutionalization of social investment: The interplay of investment logics and investor rationalities. *Journal of Social Entrepreneurship, 1*(1), 70–100.

Social Impact Investment Taskforce. (2014). *Building a social impact investment market: The UK experience*. UK National Advisory Board to the Social Impact Investment Taskforce. Retrieved February 2, 2015, from http://www.socialimpactinvestment.org/reports/UK%20Advisory%20Board%20to%20the%20Social%20Investment%20Taskforce%20Report%20September%202014.pdf

Sunley, P., & Pinch, S. (2012). Financing social enterprise: Social bricolage or evolutionary entrepreneurialism? *Social Enterprise Journal, 8*(2), 108–122.

Teasdale, S., Lyon, F., & Baldock, R. (2013). A methodological critique of the social enterprise growth myth. *Journal of Social Entrepreneurship, 4*(2), 113–131.

TSRC. (2010). *Social Enterprise Investment Fund (SEIF) evaluation. Phase one: Scoping, review and methodology development*. Third Sector Research Centre. Retrieved February 2, 2015, from http://www.birmingham.ac.uk/generic/tsrc/documents/tsrc/reports/SEIF/SEIFPhaseOneReport.pdf

PART II

Challenges, Suggestions, Critiques, and Debates

II.1
Social Responsibility in Finance: ideology, risk, and new models

12
SOCIAL RESPONSIBILITY IN ISLAMIC FINANCE

Ainulashikin Marzuki and Andrew C. Worthington

Over the past few decades, the provision and use of Islamic Financial products and services has grown dramatically around the world. However, while there is now a wider understanding of many of the objectives for these products and services from the perspective of *Shariah* (Islamic law), less is known about the inherent social objectives of Islamic Finance, many of which it shares with the Social Responsibility movement more broadly.

The principles of Islamic Finance, as defined by *Shariah*, prescribe that, among other things, finance must serve society. These revolve around the axioms of Islamic ethical philosophy, which comprises the concepts of unity (*tawhid*), justice or equilibrium (*al-'adl*), freewill or freedom (*ikhtiyar*), responsibility (*fard*), and benevolence (*ihsan*). Further, because *Shariah* prohibits usury (the receiving and paying of interest), Islamic Finance is equity-based and therefore shares a common thread with community and ethical banking and with Socially Responsible Investing. Islamic Finance, therefore, requires a balance between financial and social objectives that necessitates a disciplined approach toward long-term sustainability.

In this chapter, we begin by considering the social dimension of Islamic Finance, as it presently exists in the various products and services. We outline the religious background for these beliefs and the expectation of how the characteristics of each product and service benefit society. Apart from the societal benefits of debt alternative finance, we particularly focus on social responsibility as demonstrated in Islamic managed funds (IMFs).

We then discuss the various risks faced by Islamic Financial institutions, firms, and individual and institutional investors and how these incorporate issues of social responsibility in their behavior. Finally, we discuss the increasing societal pressure for banks, non-financial firms, and investors to act responsibly toward the community and how the environment has translated into businesses engaging in socially responsible activities. Lastly, we examine how well Islamic financial and non-financial institutions are incorporated into existing national and international socially responsible frameworks.

The social dimension of Islamic Finance

Islamic Finance is part of a broader Islamic economic system regulated by *Shariah*, with the main sources being the Holy Quran and Sunnah. *Shariah* guides all Muslim activities, which reflect Islamic moral and ethical values. The overall objective of *Shariah* is to promote the well-being of humankind, which lies in safeguarding its faith (*din*), life (*nafs*), intellect (*'aql*), progeny (*nasl*), and wealth (*mal*). This responsibility falls on the shoulders of the Islamic economic system, specifically Islamic Financial institutions.

The social dimension of Islamic Finance exists in the various products and services offered by Islamic Financial institutions. Primarily, finance must serve society. The social dimension of Islamic Finance is embedded in Islamic ethical philosophy and the foundation of the Islamic economic system, which comprises the concepts of unity (*tawhid*), justice or equilibrium (*al-'adl*), freewill or freedom (*ikhtiyar*), responsibility (*fard*), and benevolence (*ihsan*) (Beekun & Badawi, 2005; Naqvi, 1981). This foundation provides guidance to all aspects of human life, including economic activities and financial practices, for individuals, organizations, governments, and society as a whole.

The concept of unity (*tawhid*) refers to the recognition of the oneness of Allah (the God) and the role of man as a vicegerent on earth, also referred to as the vertical dimension of Islam, wherein it deals with the relationship between human beings and Allah (Naqvi, 1981). Allah is the creator and the owner of the universe, and human beings as trustees are entrusted to use and manage the resources wisely in accordance with Allah's will as prescribed in *Shariah*. In the sight of Allah, all individuals are equal, save their piety and righteousness (Dusuki, 2008).

In addition to a responsibility toward Allah, human beings are also responsible to society (people) and the environment (planet), the so-called horizontal dimension of Islam (Naqvi, 1981). This is the concept of justice or equilibrium (*al-'adl*), which emphasizes that all individuals have a responsibility to contribute to social justice. This responsibility to society includes both a balance between those who have and those who have not, and individuals are entitled to equal treatment in their dealings, regardless of their status, race, religion, or gender (Zinkin, 2007). The responsibility to the environment is to preserve the environment for future generations.

Despite the fact that *Shariah* regulates human beings, there is the freedom (*ikhtiyar*) to choose the way they desire to lead their own life, to decide the best behavior they would like to follow, to use their own capabilities, and to utilize any economic resources in this world. That is, they have the ability to think and make judgments. For those who adhere with the prescribed rules and guidelines, they will behave ethically, acknowledging that they have a responsibility toward Allah, themselves, society, and the environment.

Following the concept of free will, the concept of responsibility (*fard*) aims to make human beings ultimately accountable for their actions. The implication is that the achievement of social justice is not for individuals alone but mandatory for all human beings. Thus, all individuals need to be conscious of their actions, as they will be held responsible for the consequences of their actions on the Day of Judgment (Farook, Hassan, & Lanis, 2011; Graafland, Mazereeuw, & Yahia, 2006).

Benevolence (*ihsan*) is an act that benefits persons other than those from whom the act proceeds without any obligation (Beekun & Badawi, 2005). In other words, the doer does the actions without any expectation of rewards and this action benefits others. Unlike justice, which is mandatory, benevolence lies beyond the mandatory (Qurtubi, 1966 as cited in Beekun & Badawi, 2005). In order to achieve socioeconomic justice, human beings are obliged to bring about justice and at the same time observe the principle of benevolence.

Further, *Shariah* prohibits *riba* (usury/interest), *gharar* (uncertainty), *maysir* (gambling), and other impermissible activities, such as those related to pork, tobacco, and pornography, as clearly stated in the Quran and Sunnah. The implication is that many interest-based products and services provided by conventional financial institutions are not permissible. Interest means making money from money. In Islam, money is not to serve as an asset or a commodity to generate profits, as it is purely a medium of exchange to create social value rather than wealth. Islam also encourages equity participation in business activities, implying the sharing of both business risks and profits.

Islamic Finance also prohibits any element of *gharar* (uncertainty) in any business dealings. Examples of *gharar* are uncertainty in relation to the quantity, quality, deliverability, and existence of assets. In order to avoid risk, Islam requires transparency, such as full information disclosure in the contract, to remove any asymmetric information, and rejects excessive risk-taking or suggestion of speculation. Concomitantly, any financial transactions should link to some physical economic transaction.

Other social dimensions of Islamic Finance include the obligations of Muslims and Islamic institutions to pay *zakat*. The recipients of *zakat* contributions, as specified in verse 9:60 of the Quran, include the poor, the deprived, those unable to pay their debts, destitute travelers, and those on the path of Allah. This injunction obliges Muslims to provide social safety to the needy. In addition, Islam also encourages Muslims to participate in voluntary donations or *sadaqah* to help these vulnerable groups.

Societal benefits of debt alternative finance

The main implication of the prohibition of interest under *Shariah* is debt alternative finance in the form of risk- and profit-sharing. In practice, risk is the volatility (or standard deviation) of the net cash flows of a firm. In Arabic, a similar word to risk is *mutakharah*, which means "the situation that involves the probability of deviation from the path that leads to the expected or usual result" (Elgari, 2003). The definition implies that risk is uncertainty about the future and, therefore, is a possibility a business will bear losses as well as profits. One of the differences between Islamic and conventional finance is this concept of risk. While the former advocates risk-sharing, the latter promotes risk-shifting or transfer.

The foundation for profits in Islamic Finance is *al-ghumn bil-ghurm*, which means "one is entitled to a gain (profit) if one agrees to bear the responsibility for the loss (risk)" (Rosly & Zaini, 2008). Thus, compensation without bearing any kind of risk is impermissible. On this basis, Islamic law prohibits *riba*, but still encourages trade, as it is the predetermined repayment in addition to the principal, which increases contractually over the length of time outstanding to the creditor.

Thus, as capital providers, Islamic Financial institutions become partners and investors in the businesses owned by entrepreneurs. As business partners, Islamic Financial institutions share any profits or losses. This arrangement benefits the entrepreneur as it provides the flexibility needed to repay capital from the project cash flows. This also benefits the project as it reduces project risk and enhances the prospects of a successful outcome. Besides, it also promotes cooperation between Islamic Financial institutions and entrepreneurs, contributes to economic and societal well-being, and avoids the exploitation of any party to the transaction.

This contrasts with conventional banking, which employs a creditor–debtor relationship. In this relationship, there is a guarantee for financial institutions as creditors of income from any capital lent to others without risk. That is, entrepreneurs, as debtors, still have to pay interest even if the project is unsuccessful and loses money. Thus, by providing money today for more money in the future, the financial institutions effectively transfer risk to the entrepreneurs.

In addition, it is a widespread feature that a conventional financial institution will require collateral for a loan or credit contract. The basic argument is that the purpose of this is "to create a strong relationship to the lender" and that it benefits the borrower in the case of financial distress (Elsas & Krahnen, 2002). However, if fully secured, the loan contract is free from default risk. In this case, "the interest income which is acquired by the lender is without potential losses since there is no uncertainty about loan recovery when the borrower fails to pay up" (Rosly & Zaini, 2008). The lender then creates wealth by assuming no risk but instead transferring all risk to the borrower, a feature totally prohibited in Islam. In Islamic Finance, the only type of borrowing permitted is interest-free borrowing, known as *qard hassan*, a form of benevolent loan given to those in financial hardship in an attempt to alleviate severe poverty.

Socially responsible IMFs

The ethical and social responsibility demonstrated by IMFs make them potentially attractive to not only Muslim investors, but also other socially and ethically conscious investors desiring a socially just financial and capital market. The objective of IMFs is to generate a *Shariah*-compliant portfolio with social, ethical, and environmental impact alongside some financial return.

Shariah governs every aspect of IMF investment management, including fund selection (portfolio formation, asset allocation, portfolio screening), operation of the business (investment and trading practices), income distribution, and those concerning income purification (*zakah* and cleansing any impure elements through charitable giving) (Elfakhani & Hassan, 2005). The unique features of IMFs lie in three main elements. These are the presence of *Shariah* advisory boards (SABs), the process of security selection through *Shariah* screening to form a *Shariah*-compliant portfolio, and the income purification activities.

The SABs oversee the structure of financial products and services as well as their operation to ensure compliance with *Shariah*. The board is responsible for closely monitoring every aspect of business activity, such as stock selection, trading, record keeping, and reporting. At the end of the financial year, the board produces a *Shariah* compliance report as part of the IMF's annual report verifying that the invested funds comply with *Shariah*. This is one of the important elements in a *Shariah* governance framework, representing an additional layer of corporate governance.

Screening is the process of portfolio construction that excludes companies from the potential pool of investments for *Shariah* mutual funds. Typically, an IMF will apply negative screening in portfolio formation whereby it excludes the stocks of companies involved in interest, uncertainty, and other prohibited activities (including short selling, derivatives, and speculation) as also prescribed by *Shariah*. The expectation is that *Shariah* screening will generate long-term positive externalities for society as it acts as a risk management tool for negative externalities.

Income purification is an ex post tool used to fulfill the social obligations of mutual fund companies and investors following investment, being the process of "deducting from the returns on one's investment those earnings, the source of which is not acceptable from a *Shariah* point of view" (Elgari, 2002, p. 156). In other words, it refers to the process of taking out that portion of income derived or generated from any prohibited activities. The need to purify income arises from the nature of economic transactions in the modern world whereby the strict avoidance of prohibited activities is almost impossible. For example, if the portfolio inadvertently earns interest-contaminated income, fund managers will need to undertake income purification by donating that portion of income to charity. IMFs are also obliged to cleanse income through paying *zakat*. This also acts as a mechanism for wealth distribution and thus social welfare.

Risks facing Islamic Financial and non-financial institutions and investors

Islamic Financial institutions, firms, individuals, and institutional investors face various risks in conducting their daily business affairs. In order to protect themselves from these risks, they are instructed by *Shariah* to behave ethically and to be concerned about the impact of their investments, financing, and operations on society, the community, and the environment. Importantly, not only businesses have to be responsible for their own unethical actions—the financial institutions that provide financing or investment to these businesses are also required to be responsible for those actions.

The recent global financial crisis, corporate scandals, and accounting failures have awoken all parties to the importance of incorporating socially responsible frameworks in business policy and strategic decision making as an important risk management strategy. The benefits of incorporating social responsibility may also enhance the value of the business, avoid negative perceptions about the company, reduce incidents of reputational damage, and lower the risk of economic and financial crisis. Better human resources, customer loyalty, reduced reputational and legal risk, improved corporate reputation, and enhanced public image may result (Davis, 1973). Coles, McWilliams, and Sen (2001) also found that companies with better corporate governance enjoy higher valuations.

One of the risks that businesses and financial institutions face are reputational risks that result from brand damage from bad press and consumer boycotts, as well as dealing with the threat of legal action. A corporate reputation that took decades to establish could be lost overnight or even in a few hours if there are incidents involving corruption or environmental scandals. Thus, social responsibility enables the avoidance of reputational risk.

A company that ignores the importance of being socially responsible may also face commercial risk involving the loss of customers to competing firms. In a situation where people are concerned about society and the environment, firms are better off acting socially responsibly. Social risks have also become a major concern for corporations. In order to mitigate social risks, many financial and non-financial institutions are attempting to construct a positive Islamic image (i.e., being socially responsible), as a negative corporate image can have serious economic implications for the organization (Buhr & Freedman, 2001, p. 294).

Islamic Financial institutions face two types of risk. These are risks concerning their financing activities similar to conventional finance, and risks related to their *Shariah*-compliant operations. The former generic risks comprise credit risk, liquidity risk, market risk, operational risk, reputational risk, and macroeconomic risk. The latter specific risks are unique to Islamic Financial institutions because of their risk-sharing principles. These risks are rate of return risk, *Shariah* non-compliance risk, displaced commercial risk, and equity investment risk. This suggests that Islamic Financial institutions face additional challenges in fulfilling the requirement for balance between the maximization of shareholder wealth and concern for socially responsible behavior.

Unlike conventional finance systems where financial institutions largely transfer fund provider risk to entrepreneurs, Islamic Financial institutions share these risks. Because of this, Islamic Financial institutions require a modified risk management framework. For instance, the risk of moral hazard and information asymmetry are more critical in Islamic Finance than in conventional finance. The problem of moral hazard arises when Islamic Financial institutions are "unable to monitor the actual efforts performed by the customers or debtors" (Dar & Presley, 2000), while information of asymmetry is critical when customers manipulate operating cost to minimize any profits shared with Islamic Financial institutions (Hassan & Kayed, 2009).

In order to mitigate these risks, Islamic Financial institutions are required to increase their participation in the entrepreneur's business and implement proper monitoring. Proper monitoring helps to reduce information asymmetry and improve the social and financial performance of the business, and ensures that the business operations accord with *Shariah*, legal, environment, and social values.

Shariah non-compliance risk is the most significant risk for Islamic Financial institutions. These risks arise when Islamic banks fail to comply with *Shariah* principles. Non-compliance with *Shariah* has a negative impact on the image of Islamic Financial institutions and increases reputational and legal risks. Examples of *Shariah* non-compliance risks include when Sheikh Taqi Usmani declared in 2007 that the majority of *Sukuk* (Islamic bonds) were not *Shariah*-compliant, and when the International Council of Fiqh Academy declared in 2009 that some *tawarruq* contracts contained interest elements (Dinar Standard and Dar Al-Istithmar, 2010).

Displaced commercial risks arise when Islamic banks face commercial pressure to pay returns that exceed the rate that has been earned on its assets financed by *mudharabah* deposits. The Islamic bank may have to forgo part or its entire share of profit in order to retain the fund providers and dissuade them from withdrawing their funds. For example, Islamic bank depositors may transfer their funds to conventional banks when the rate of return provided by the Islamic banks is significantly lower. Unlike conventional banks, which operate on a predetermined return-sharing agreement with deposit holders that guarantees them principal and a fixed rate of return, Islamic banks operate a profit-sharing agreement with their depositors. The profit-sharing agreement exposes the deposit holders to the loss of principal, which Islamic banks are not legally obligated to indemnify. Because of this profit-sharing nature, the expectation is that Islamic banks will follow a higher standard of morality and ethics and hence forgo profit opportunities that involve any compromise on these core values.

In relation to IMFs, investors face diversification risk where the portfolio of managed funds contains more idiosyncratic risks than conventional funds due to *Shariah* screening. However, ethical screening can also be part of a fund management company's risk management strategy. For example, avoiding unethical stocks may minimize the risk of future litigation from unethical activities such as pollution. IMFs may also indirectly benefit from avoiding high-risk speculative activities, short selling, and investment in derivatives.

Individual and institutional investors are also becoming more concerned about business activities, and the operations of firms are as much a concern as the financial performance their portfolios provide. They are especially concerned about how their investment affects the community and environment. In addition, ethical or Muslim investors seek their funds to be utilized in ethical or *halal* activities, respectively, in that they may potentially suffer from the risk of losing their investment if the company is involved in litigation. Therefore, investors are better off not supporting unethical behavior, avoiding speculation, and focusing on the social impact of their investment.

Thus, investors choose *Shariah* or ethical investment as the screenings serve as risk management tools that limit the exposure the investor could face to activities that are suspicious and contain elements of uncertainty (*gharar* and *maysir*). While not all investment activities that link to real economic activities are included in the investment portfolio, *Shariah* screenings are still able to play a central role in regulating the market (Hassan & Kayed, 2009).

Societal pressure for businesses to act responsibly

Nowadays, there is increasing social pressure that obliges financial and non-financial institutions to act socially responsible or to be more responsible for their behavior. These social pressures come from internal (employees, managers, *Shariah* board, shareholders) and external stakeholders (customers, consumers, regulators, NGOs, investors). As examples, these pressures could be in the form of regulation and government enforcement, consumer boycotts, media and internet campaigns, brand damage, and harm to a firm's reputation or brand equity from NGOs and social activists (Baron, Harjoto, & Jo, 2009, p. 2).

Firms are attentive to these kinds of pressure as these could directly affect the firm's market value and profits, by driving some investors away from the firm and by damaging brand equity or reputation, respectively (Baron et al., 2009, p. 2). Studies have shown that societal pressures are able to influence the behavior of firms to act responsibly toward the community. The greater the social pressure they receive, the higher would be their social performance results (Baron et al., 2009; Orlitzky, Schmidt, & Rynes, 2003; Refiner, 2001).

Recent financial crisis and corporate scandals (such as Enron) have made society more aware of the impact financial institutions and the corporate sector can have through their financing and investment policies. These have raised important concerns about the roles and responsibilities of financial institutions and companies, and they have begun to feel pressure from the public, government, and NGOs demanding them to act socially and environmentally responsibly. For employees, it has now become common for younger generations to look for employers that integrate social and ethical values into their business policy and operations. Socially conscious consumers, entrepreneurs, and leaders are now expecting businesses to play their role in generating social goods.

In addition, both individual and institutional investors are becoming more aware of the benefits of *Shariah*-compliant and Socially Responsible Investment. They are expecting that the companies in which they invest perform well both in terms of financial and social performance and act responsibly beyond mere legal and *Shariah* compliance. Ethical investors are keen to know the full activities of these companies, including the impact on the environment, local communities, and the workforce. NGOs and investors are also putting pressure on customers and institutional investors, such as fund management companies, to invest in ethical companies. For example, consumer-based corporate sectors such as Nike, Walmart, and BP have recently begun to adhere to the needs of society for social responsibility.

Islamic socially responsible frameworks

Despite a strong social dimension in *Shariah* principles, there has been significant criticism of the practices of Islamic Finance and non-financial institutions, mainly involving the divergence from theory, the overdependence on prohibition, and the lack of social disclosure.

First, one argument is that Islamic institutions continue to pursue profit maximization and maximization of shareholder value over their fundamental *Shariah*-based objectives. In evidence, despite *Shariah* promoting socioeconomic justice by offering profit- and loss-sharing financial contracts, the practice of Islamic banking institutions is more toward sales-based instead of equity-based contracts. Alarmingly, Chong and Liu (2009) found that the practice of Islamic banking differs little from conventional banking. For example, despite the fact that *Shariah* prohibits *riba* and promotes equity participation, they found that only 0.5 percent of financing involved equity participation. The divergence in the practice of Islamic Financial and non-financial institutions from its initial philosophy to serve society has then become critical.

Elsewhere, Haron and Hisham (2005) conducted a study involving two Islamic banks in Malaysia and found that they lacked any aspect of socioeconomic development. Socioeconomic performance was measured in terms of the proportion of *qard hassan* (benevolent loans) dispensed, the distribution of financing by economic sector, *zakah* contribution, and overdrafts and activities to support the preservation of Islamic culture (Haron & Hisham, 2005). The expectation is that Islamic banks should, but frequently do not, promote charitable *takaful* savings plans, social impact-based investment programs, and *Shariah*-compliant microfinance initiatives (Dinar Standard and Dar Al-Istithmar, 2010).

Second, the practices of Islamic Finance often excessively focus on avoidance or negative prescriptions, and this diverts them from the socioeconomic dimension (see Lewis, 2010; Sairally, 2007; Wilson, 1997). For Islamic banks, this is amply evidenced by the prohibitive nature of *Shariah* and the minimal attention to positive practice (Barom, 2013; Derigs & Marzban,

2008; Marzuki, 2012; Nainggolan, 2011). There is also minimal social disclosure save *zakah* payments. Overall, Islamic Financial institutions should offer more socioeconomic welfare products, including those relating to microfinance, social banking, ethical banking, community reinvestment, and *qard hassan* to help the poor. Islamic Financial institutions may also be able to demonstrate their social responsibility by giving priority in their financing to health and social (affordable housing projects) projects, providing scholarships for the poor, and financially supporting community events.

Finally, few Islamic institutions disclose corporate social responsibility (CSR) initiatives in their annual reports. Maali, Casson, and Napier (2006) investigated the social reporting of 29 Islamic banks from 19 countries and found that social reporting by Islamic banks was significantly below expectations. Their results suggest that Islamic banks that are subject to pay *zakah* or Islamic religious tax provide more social disclosure than those that are not, further supported by a more recent study by Hassan and Harahap (2010), which concluded that CSR strangely did appear a major concern for Islamic banks.

However, Maali et al. (2006) suggest that financial institutions in developing countries behave differently than financial institutions in developed countries in their commitment to social welfare. They found that issues such as the environment are of less concern in developing countries where most Islamic Financial institutions reside. This influences the results whereby Islamic Financial institutions report lesser concern for social issues. They also suggest that less disclosure on social issues by Islamic Financial institutions may be because of Islamic teachings that preach that it is better not to publicize one's own good conduct.

A study by Al-Sabir and Ahmad (2013) found that Tadhamon International Bank in Yemen partly financed its social responsibility from tainted sources of revenue/income. However, the bank still managed to fulfill its *Shariah* obligations by participating in socioeconomic activity such as providing scholarships to poor families and financing health and social projects. In addition, it also assisted government with natural disaster and other social problems (Al-Sabir & Ahmad, 2013). This well recognizes the complexity of Islamic Financial institution decision making and strategy.

According to a recent survey on social responsibility practices among 29 Islamic Financial institutions worldwide, the practices of social responsibility in these institutions were not limited to *Shariah* and legal compliance but also expanded to other areas of responsibility such as community contribution and environmental concerns (Dinar Standard and Dar Al-Istithmar, 2010). The survey also found that there is a significant improvement in their CSR initiatives.

In relation to socially responsible frameworks, Islamic Financial institutions and the regulators have come out with their own frameworks which follow the rules and regulations or values prescribed by *Shariah*. Even though many aspects of the frameworks used in Western countries such as the OECD principles and the UN Global Compact are not against *Shariah* values (Abu-Tapanjeh, 2009; Williams & Zinkin, 2010; Zinkin, 2007), some may not be suitable for the structure of Islamic Financial institutions.

For example, Bursa Malaysia, the Malaysian stock exchange, introduced a CSR framework applicable to listed companies in 2006. Malaysia has also come out with an Islamic Corporate Social Responsibility framework (i-CSR) ready for adoption by Malaysian Islamic banks and financial institutions after 2015 (Hamzah, 2014). This draws on Islamic ethical values and philosophy divided into two categories: obligatory and recommended dimensions.

In relation to international socially responsible frameworks, the Accounting and Auditing Organization for Islamic Financial Institutions (AAOIFI)[1] has released its own standards for CSR. This is Governance Standard No. 7: Corporate Social Responsibility, Conduct, and Disclosure for Islamic Financial Institutions, which covers 13 areas of social responsibility.

Among the recommended areas are responsibilities toward clients, employees, charity, responsible investments, and *zakah* or *waqaf* management. CSR as defined by AAOIFI comprises "all activities carried out by Islamic Financial institutions to fulfil its religious, economic, legal, ethical and discretionary responsibilities as financial intermediaries as individuals and institutions" (AAOIFI, 2010). This definition requires IFIs to practice CSR as part of their religious obligation and ethical commitments to *Shariah* and socioeconomic development.

The Islamic Financial Services Board in Malaysia also issued its guiding principles on social responsibility, the "Guiding Principles on Shariah Governance Systems for Institutions Offering Islamic Financial Services," in 2009 (amended version). However, even though these Islamic Finance institutions have developed guiding standards and principles for social responsibility, including corporate governance principles, they are not fully accepted or applied and none is enforceable. They also do not have the authority to enforce implementation. For example, the AAOIFI standards have been adopted in only a few Islamic Finance jurisdictions, including Bahrain, the Dubai International Financial Center, Jordan, Qatar, Sudan, Syria, and the Islamic Development Bank Group (Dinar Standard and Dar Al-Istithmar, 2010).

At the regional level, the launch of the Hawkamah Index for the Middle East and North Africa (MENA) region offers investors investment products that address a broader range of social responsibilities within Muslim countries (Barom, 2013). Hawkamah is a joint collaboration between a Dubai-based institution and Standard & Poor's, supported by the International Finance Corporation, which launched the first MENA-wide Environmental, Social and Corporate Governance Index, the S&P-Hawkamah Pan Arab ESG Index. This ranks and tracks the performance, transparency, and disclosure of regional companies on ESG issues. The constituents of the index include the largest companies listed on the stock exchanges of the United Arab Emirates, Saudi Arabia, Qatar, Bahrain, Oman, Kuwait, Jordan, Egypt, Lebanon, Morocco, and Tunisia (Saidi, 2011).

Other positive developments include the launch of the Dow Jones Islamic Sustainability Index in 2006. This index ranks companies based on their practices in Islamic investment principles and sustainability criteria (Lewis, 2010) and acts as a mechanism or pressure tool to influence corporations to behave ethically and responsibly. Companies that are listed in the index provide an indication of their commitment to incorporate social responsibility into their investments (Barom, 2013), and they enjoy a good reputation, which is able to attract investors, individuals, and institutions concerned with religious and ethical obligations.

Conclusion

This chapter examined social responsibility in Islamic Finance, with a particular focus being how Islamic Financial products and services may not only meet their religious requirements, but may also benefit society more broadly. The chapter also discussed the risks faced by Islamic Financial and non-financial institutions and individual and institutional investors, and how these incorporate issues of social responsibility through Islamic principles in their behavior. Likewise, the chapter considered the increasing societal pressure for banks, non-financial firms, and investors to act responsibly toward their communities by engaging in socially responsible activities. Lastly, the chapter surveyed the interplay between general national and international socially responsible frameworks and specific Islamic socially responsible frameworks. The chapter concluded that even though the principles of Islamic Finance theory advocate that finance must serve society, the practices of Islamic Financial and non-financial institutions often depart from their fundamental basis.

We suggested that the Islamic Finance industry should be more proactive in promoting its social objectives by actively communicating their social activities in their financial statements and other mediums such as the media and social media. Islamic Finance players should also be more innovative in developing new products and services based on equity participation rather than relying excessively on debt-based finance, particularly as these can enhance the social responsibility credentials of Islamic Finance. In terms of future studies, it would be interesting to compare the social responsibility performance of conventional and Islamic Financial institutions. It would also be interesting to explore in detail the impact of Islamic and conventional social responsibility frameworks upon each other.

Note

1 The international organization responsible for development and issuance of standards on accounting, auditing, ethics, governance, and *Shariah* standards for the Islamic finance industry.

References

AAOIFI. (2010). *Governance Standard No. 7: Corporate social responsibility, conduct, and disclosure for Islamic Financial institutions*. Bahrain: AAOIFI.

Abu-Tapanjeh, A. M. (2009). Corporate governance from the Islamic perspective: A comparative analysis with OECD principles. *Critical Perspectives on Accounting, 20*(5), 556–567.

Al-Sabir, W. M., & Ahmad, I. (2013). Assessing the social responsibility (SR) of Tadhamon International Islamic Bank of Yemen. *Journal of Emerging Economies and Islamic Research, 1*(1), 1–13.

Barom, M. N. (2013). Conceptualising a strategic framework of social responsibility in Islamic economics. *International Journal of Economics, Management and Accounting, 21*(1), 65–95.

Baron, D. P., Harjoto, M. A., & Jo, H. (2009). *The economics and politics of corporate social performance* (Rock Center for Corporate Governance Working Paper 45). Rochester, NY: Social Science Research Network.

Beekun, R. I., & Badawi, J. A. (2005). Balancing ethical responsibility among multiple organizational stakeholders: The Islamic perspective. *Journal of Business Ethics, 60*(2), 131–145.

Buhr, N., & Freedman, M. (2001). Culture, institutional factors and differences in environmental disclosure between Canada and the United States. *Critical Perspectives on Accounting, 12*(3), 293–322.

Chong, B. S., & Liu, M.-H. (2009). Islamic banking: Interest-free or interest-based? *Pacific-Basin Finance Journal, 17*(1), 125–144.

Coles, J. W., McWilliams, V. B., & Sen, N. (2001). An examination of the relationship of governance mechanisms to performance. *Journal of Management, 27*(1), 23–50.

Dar, H., & Presley, R. (2000). Lack of profit and loss sharing in Islamic banking: Management and control imbalances. *International Journal of Islamic Finance, 2*(2), 3–18.

Davis, K. (1973). The case for and against business assumption of social responsibilities. *The Academy of Management Journal, 16*(2), 312–322.

Derigs, U., & Marzban, S. (2008). Review and analysis of current *Shariah*-compliant equity screening practices. *International Journal of Islamic and Middle Eastern Finance and Management, 1*(4), 285–303.

Dinar Standard and Dar Al-Istithmar. (2010). *Social responsibility trends at Islamic financial institutions: Based on 2009 social responsibility survey*. Dinar Standard and Dar Al-Istithmar.

Dusuki, A. W. (2008). Understanding the objectives of Islamic banking: A survey of stakeholders' perspectives. *International Journal of Islamic and Middle Eastern Finance and Management, 1*(2), 132.

Elfakhani, S. M., & Hassan, M. K. (2005, December). *Performance of Islamic mutual funds*. Paper presented at the 12th Economic Research Forum Conference, Economic Research Forum, Egypt.

Elgari, M. A. (2002). Islamic equity investment. In S. Archer & R. A. Abdel Karim (Eds.), *Islamic finance: Innovation and growth*. London: Euromoney Books and AAOIFI.

Elgari, M. A. (2003). Credit risk in Islamic banking and finance. *Islamic Economic Studies, 10*(2), 25.

Elsas, R., & Krahnen, J. P. (2002). *Collateral, relationship lending, and financial distress: An empirical study on financial contracting* (Unpublished manuscript). Center for Financial Studies, Frankfurt.

Farook, S., Hassan, M. K., & Lanis, R. (2011). Determinants of corporate social responsibility disclosure: The case of Islamic banks. *Journal of Islamic Accounting and Business Research, 2*(2), 114–141.

Graafland, J. J., Mazereeuw, C., & Yahia, A. (2006). Islam and socially responsible business conduct: An empirical research among Dutch entrepreneurs. *Business Ethics: A European Review, 15*(4), 390–406.

Hamzah, S. R. (2014). *Islamic CSR framework ready for adoption next year*. Retrieved November 1, 2014, from Malaysian National News Agency: http://www.bernama.com

Haron, S., & Hisham, B. K. (2005). Wealth mobilisation by Islamic banks: The Malaysian case. In M. Iqbal & R. Wilson (Eds.), *Islamic perspectives on wealth creation* (pp. 49–68). Edinburgh: Edinburgh Scholarship Online.

Hassan, A., & Harahap, S. S. (2010). Exploring corporate social responsibility disclosure: The case of Islamic banks. *International Journal of Islamic and Middle Eastern Finance and Management, 3*(3), 203–227.

Hassan, K. M., & Kayed, R. N. (2009). The global financial crisis, risk management and social justice finance. *ISRA International Journal of Islamic Finance, 1*(1), 33–58.

Lewis, M. K. (2010). Accentuating the positive: Governance of Islamic investment funds. *Journal of Islamic Accounting and Business Research, 1*(1), 42–59.

Maali, B., Casson, P., & Napier, C. (2006). Social reporting by Islamic banks. *ABACUS, 42*(2), 266–289.

Marzuki, A. (2012). *Performance, screening and fund flows in Malaysian Islamic mutual funds* (PhD thesis). Griffith University, Nathan, Australia.

Nainggolan, Y. (2011). *Taking a leap of faith: Are investors left short changed?* (PhD thesis). Queensland University of Technology, Brisbane, Australia.

Naqvi, S. N. H. (1981). *Ethics and Islamic economics: An Islamic synthesis*. Leicester: The Islamic Foundation.

Orlitzky, M., Schmidt, F. L., & Rynes, S. L. (2003). Corporate social and financial performance: A meta-analysis. *Organization Studies, 24*(3), 403–441.

Refiner, U. (2001). Social banking: Products for community development. In C. Guene & E. Mayo Charlbury (Eds.), *Banking and social cohesion: Alternative response to a global market*. Oxfordshire: Jon Carpenter.

Rosly, S. A., & Zaini, M. M. A. (2008). Risk-return analysis of Islamic banks' investment deposits and shareholders' fund. *Managerial Finance, 34*(10), 695–707.

Saidi, N. (2011). *Innovating for sustainable investment in MENA: The Hawkamah/S&P ESG Index*. Retrieved October 1, 2014, from http://www.hawkamah.org

Sairally, S. (2007). *Evaluating the social responsibility of Islamic finance: Learning from the experience of socially responsible investment funds*. Paper presented at the 6th International Conference on Islamic Economics and Finance, Islamic Research and Training Institute, Jeddah, Saudi Arabia.

Williams, G., & Zinkin, J. (2010). Islam and CSR: A study of the compatibility between the tenets of Islam and the UN Global Compact. *Journal of Business Ethics, 91*(2010), 519–533.

Wilson, R. (1997). Islamic investment and ethical investment. *International Journal of Social Economics, 24*(11), 1325–1342.

Zinkin, J. (2007). Islam and CSR: A study of the compatibility between the tenets of Islam, the UN Global Compact and the development of social, human and natural capital. *Corporate Social Responsibility & Environmental Management, 14*(4), 206–218.

13

SEEING OURSELVES AS OTHERS SEE US

Incorporating reflexivity in Corporate Social Responsibility

Christopher Mason and John Simmons

This chapter presents a rationale for and a method of achieving a more inclusive and value-based approach to Corporate Social Responsibility (CSR) that incorporates due recognition of an organization's obligations to its stakeholders, the environment, and wider society. Its theoretical underpinning draws from the constructs of stakeholder theory and reflexivity and gains from their synergistic application. Synergism enables us to address the fundamental question "what does CSR do for stakeholders and how do stakeholders react to CSR?" (Hildebrand, Sen, & Bhattacharya, 2011). Reflexive analysis requires understanding of the complex business context that confronts organizations engaging in CSR and awareness of an organization's position in its environment, together with an understanding of the expectations and values of salient stakeholders (Barratt & Korac-Kakabadse, 2002). Commentators have identified the instrumental version of CSR that dominates mainstream research as an intellectual blockage that prevents the field from achieving critical reflexivity and thereby a justifiable *raison d'être* (Jones, 2009). Utilizing stakeholder theory in a reflexive analysis of CSR also responds to a recently proposed research agenda urging focus on conflicts of interest between stakeholders and the challenge that management faces in coping with these diverse objectives (Mainardes, Alves, & Raposo, 2011). Viewing stakeholder theory through a reflexive lens enables its application in a normative way so that organizations "can see their CSR activities as their stakeholders see them." It also aligns with a view of CSR as "context-specific organizational actions and policies that take into account stakeholders' expectations and the triple bottom line of economic, social and environmental performance" (Aguinis, 2011, p. 855). We therefore construe CSR-related relationships between the focal organization and its stakeholder constituencies as a form of psychological contract that enables evaluation of the level of justice that these represent (Mainardes et al., 2011).

The chapter is structured as follows. First, we critically appraise current theoretical and practical approaches to corporate governance to demonstrate how these hegemonic standpoints prevent the field from achieving critical reflexivity. Second, we examine the use of reflexivity in critical management studies (CMS) to identify implications of the concept to the new approach to CSR that we advocate. The third section introduces the notion of syncretism and assesses the claim that it can balance two potentially opposing expectations of CSR—namely prioritizing profitability or emphasizing the significance of stakeholder beliefs and values. Fourth, the challenge of adapting the reflexive perspective to organizational change contexts is addressed via the concept of strategic reflexivity. Strategically reflexive companies create knowledge-based mechanisms which enable them to react reflexively to environmental changes that have implications for organizational strategy. Fifth, we propose a stakeholder responsive philosophy of CSR together with a method of operationalizing this and show how this approach aligns with new perspectives on measuring sustainable development performance. Finally, we examine how corporate governance should change in response to these issues. Proposals include the development of a strategic audit tool that provides a broad-based and more stakeholder-aware evaluation of CSR. Our analysis provides a rationale for putting CSR at the heart of this new mode of corporate governance and for the stakeholder systems model to be the means by which this can be achieved.

Criticisms of mainstream CSR

The specter of irrelevance that haunts CSR (Marens, 2010) relates both to the lack of a valid philosophical basis for the precepts that are proposed to guide ethical business practice, as well as to the negligible impact that these precepts have had on how contemporary organizations conduct their affairs. Taking these in turn, a trenchant critique of the logic used to generate the principles that should underpin socially responsible business is advanced by Donaldson (2012), who exposes the epistemic fault line in corporate governance by those who claim to derive normative principles from positivist theories. A similar stark assessment is made of the negligible influence that CSR has had on contemporary business operations (Marens, 2010), as "the dismal reality speaks for itself" (Fleming, Roberts, & Garsten, 2013, p. 338). The scale of corporate malfeasance in the financial crisis of the 1990s and its recurrence in the early years of the twenty-first century—together with the prevalence of erosion of labor rights, rampant consumerism, and environmental despoliation—attest to the conclusion that CSR research has had no significant impact on management decision making, nor on the quality of CSR reporting. Rather, what has transpired is merely an exercise in superficial compliance (Fleming et al., 2013; Knox, Maklan, & French, 2005) or a subtle method of ideological capture that denies any antagonistic relationship between capitalism and the social good (Cederstrom & Marinetto, 2013). Neither should the recurrent nature of business sidelining CSR come as a surprise, as evidence shows that a significant number of company directors failed to exercise due diligence even after the financial crisis (Fram & Zoffer, 2005), while others substituted the stringent codes of conduct sought by regulators with more malleable internal ones (Okhmatovskiy & David, 2011). The extent of this disconnect between CSR rhetoric and the reality experienced by many stakeholders implies improved evaluation systems (Fassin & Buelens, 2011), better risk management to protect stakeholder interests (Chong, 2004), and the need for a two-way perspective on CSR (Bartlett, Tywoniak, & Hatcher, 2007). Nevertheless, as we discuss in a subsequent section, the disparity between CSR communication and CSR action can represent a leverage point for social and organizational change (Christensen, Morsing, & Thyssen, 2013).

We challenge not only the dominant philosophy of CSR but also organizational practice in managing it. Research shows that most organizations adopt an institutional approach to CSR (one that replicates the organization's product market strategy) rather than a strategic stance (one that views CSR as a response to salient stakeholders) (Husted & Allen, 2006). The chapter therefore proposes a new mode of corporate governance that includes a periodic stakeholder audit to identify stakeholders' CSR-related expectations and the extent to which stakeholders believe that their expectations have been met. This more outwardly focused perspective on corporate governance acknowledges the evolving nature of stakeholder relations in a highly complex business environment (Raghavendran & Rajagopalan, 2011) in contrast to more inwardly focused analyses based on agency theory (Ruhanen, Scott, Richie, & Tkacynski, 2010). This also aligns with the wider accountancy context in which non-financial reporting is widely accepted as a means of corporate sustainability reporting and represents a significant means of communication between a company and its stakeholders (Caliskan, 2014). Studies also show that less stakeholder-responsive organizations which pursue policies aimed at maximizing shareholder value sub-optimize the social and economic benefits to society as a whole (McSweeney, 2008). The changes to the corporate governance process—the system of rights, processes, and controls established internally and externally over the management of a business entity with the objective of protecting the interests of all stakeholders (Ruhanen et al., 2010)—that we propose also address the incompatibility between traditional, top-down administrative structures and organization responsiveness to the expectations of salient stakeholders (Donaldson & Fafaliou, 2007). Research suggests the way forward is to identify practical methods of identifying and meeting stakeholder expectations (Donaldson & Fafaliou, 2007), and the recent GRI (2013) G4 Guidelines emphasize the need to identify salient stakeholders and their concerns to assess the organization's social and environmental impact. The stakeholder systems model of corporate governance we advocate therefore identifies the CSR-related expectations that stakeholders have of the focal organization; how these constituencies evaluate organizational CSR policy, outcomes, and reporting; and how organizational awareness of stakeholder evaluations can lead to more responsive and responsible corporate governance.

Reflexivity and CMS

In this section we explore the concept of reflexivity within CMS prior to demonstrating commonalities and applications of the concept to the new CSR philosophy and practice that we advocate. We confirm the relevance of reflexivity to our critique of mainstream CSR, show how reflexivity can be applied to organizational change contexts by utilizing the concept of strategic reflexivity, and relate its philosophy and application to the stakeholder systems model of CSR that we propose.

In positivist enquiry the subjectivity of the researcher is of little importance (Renganathan, 2009) as objectivity requires separation between the investigator and the phenomenon under investigation (Orr & Bennett, 2009). In contrast, reflexivity questions the researcher's stance toward the subject of enquiry (Wang, 2012), as well as researcher influence on the outcomes of this investigation. The essence of qualitative research is the investigator's attempt to reconstruct the reality of how those being studied view the world (Khalid, 2009), with reflexivity regarded by many in the field as essential to confirm the integrity of those endeavors (Wang, 2012). However, reflexivity is a contested term (Cunliffe & Jun, 2005), and researchers use varying terminology to identify different facets of it and the level of critical thinking that these represent. One school of thought views reflexivity as a method of questioning and legitimizing research practice (Wang, 2012) through reflection and recursion (Mahadevan, 2011). Reflection is conceptualized as a form of mirror image that enables researchers to reflect on the nature of the research enquiry, while recursion is the process of validating whether the description of a phenomenon is true to participants' experience of it (Hibbert, Coupland, & Macintosh, 2010).

However, reflection does not question the assumptions on which practice is based, and a more fundamental examination requires critical reflexivity. Researchers draw on Heidegger's (1969) distinction between calculative and meditative thinking to show how reflection represents only a limited form of reflexivity (Cunliffe & Jun, 2005). Calculative thinking aligns with reflection by representing something as those observing it believe it to be—but without questioning the assumptions that underpin this belief. In contrast, meditative or reflexive thinking generates new insights by a more fundamental appraisal of practices and relationships. Reflexive practitioners are therefore more aware of their limitations and those of their institutions, as well as how these limitations can marginalize particular stakeholders in policy formulation and implementation (Cunliffe & Jun, 2005).

Recursion can take two forms (Hibbert et al., 2010). One is a researcher-directed process with the aim of correcting for bias by an enhanced understanding of the subject's point of view or by revising the researcher's conceptual framework. The other is where change is instituted by involving the subject in the research activity. Here researchers abrogate autonomous direction of the research enquiry and deliberately open themselves up to the insights and challenges of others (Mahadevan, 2011). This mode of recursion aligns with the process that Hibbert et al. (2010) describe as participative reflexivity. They claim participative reflexivity is the only fully conceived view as researchers engage with a particular community and are willing for this involvement to alter their world view. Others' accounts of their experiences are regarded as authoritative and are used to reconcile differences. Involvement of research subjects in a genuinely participative way also incorporates a moral dimension into the process of enquiry. Respect for the expectations and evaluations of others and the use of these to reconcile differences between researchers and participants underpin reflexivity's claim for greater investigative legitimacy (Hibbert et al., 2010). Similarly, reflexive practitioners respect stakeholder voice, are willing to engage in ethical discourse, and have a sense of justice that goes beyond institutional interests (Cunliffe & Jun, 2005).

CSR as "aspirational talk"

With this in mind, it is also evident that CSR is caught in the paradox of aspirational pragmatism. Recognition of the difference between CSR rhetoric and reality is fundamental to the stakeholder systems approach that we advocate. However, a recent analysis challenges the view that this disparity is necessarily viewed as superficial, a diversionary tactic, or corporate spin (Christensen et al., 2013). While acknowledging that legislation to regulate CSR is imperative, these researchers argue that CSR rhetoric represents "aspirational talk," so a reflexive process that makes organizations aware of this discrepancy offers a parallel strategy to move CSR practice to higher goals and standards (Kostera, 1997). Drawing on social identity theory, they recognize that organizations are likely to orientate their CSR aspirations toward issues perceived as important by their stakeholders as this has the potential to enhance corporate reputation. However, encouraging organizations to articulate their CSR aspirations to external media, and stimulating stakeholder and societal evaluation of these, represents a form of leverage that can stimulate the organizational effort to bridge the gap between current practice and the aspirations they articulate. Moreover, their analysis identifies that progression from aspirational reality to CSR practice can become a continuous process if organizations have new aspirations to hand when old aspirations are fulfilled. We contend that a periodic audit of stakeholder CSR expectations and experience can provide additional leverage that stimulates organizations to bridge the rhetoric reality gap—as well as providing revised stakeholder expectations that enable incremental improvement.

Strategic reflexivity and organizational change

A particular challenge for those who adopt a reflexive perspective is to adapt its principles and techniques to organizational change contexts. Recent research has developed the concept of "strategic reflexivity" as a response to the ineffectiveness of conventional business strategy in a turbulent and hypercompetitive environment (Vrontis, Thrassou, Chebbi, & Yahiaoui, 2012). Three factors are seen as necessary for long-term corporate competitiveness: rethinking the concept of strategy; building flexible organizations that are responsive to change; and developing value propositions that align with stakeholder preferences. A value-defining approach utilizes strategic reflexivity to identify what stakeholders expect, evaluates the extent to which stakeholders believe the organization provides this, uses a common currency to measure stakeholder perceptions of value, and responds by developing organizational capabilities that enhance stakeholder evaluation. Strategic reflexivity is premised on the belief that companies can no longer rely on top-down linear planning to achieve their aims, but rather should create knowledge-based mechanisms that enable them to react reflexively to environmental changes (Vrontis et al., 2012).

The chapter utilizes the concept of reflexivity as a rationale for its philosophy and for the feedback mechanisms in the stakeholder systems model that we propose. Taking these in turn, researchers have identified reflexivity as part of a broader shift in attitudes to organizations. Changes in the "expectations of publics" have resulted in a central shift from one-way perspectives (where organizations seek to influence stakeholders) to two-way relationships (where organizations engage, consult, and negotiate with them) (Bartlett et al., 2007). Reflexivity aligns with this in seeking alternatives to prevailing organization "imperatives" in its unorthodox, constructivist take on the organization realm (Brewis & Wray-Bliss, 2008). In corporate governance, reflexivity is identified as a core feature of critical approaches to CSR (Rhodes, 2009) through its counter-hegemonic discourse (Duarte, 2006). Reflexive approaches also address the crisis in organizational analysis in relation to representing the views of others—both in terms of accuracy and by acknowledging the possibility of variation over time (Tsoukas & Chia, 2002). In relation to the latter, reflexivity holds that knowledge obtained by organizational enquiry can no longer be regarded as "intellectual finitude" but should be open to difference and change (Rhodes, 2009). This has parallels with the concept of organization enactments of CSR "traveling" over time and being the subject of interpretation and evaluation by those receiving them (Aguinis & Glavas, 2012; Jensen, Sandstrom, & Helin, 2009). Our model relates this to the "travel" of espoused CSR and the need to obtain stakeholder evaluation of it at various stages of its journey.

However, alongside the organizational benefits of strategic reflexivity, this approach enhances and advances the process of enquiry. Specifically, the idea is of a "virtuous circle" whereby reflexive sensitivity leads to better research that in turn produces greater reflexive sensitivity (Tomkins & Eatough, 2010). In this situation, each reflexive research enquiry into CSR produces something new—both about the research topic and the ways in which researchers access and interpret it (Tomkins & Eatough, 2010).

Reflexive CSR and stakeholder engagement

A reflexive analysis of CSR responds to calls to re-orientate management science so that it engages with organizational change more consistently and openly (Tsoukas & Chia, 2002) and focuses on the processes and power relations between an organization and its stakeholders (Mahadevan, 2011). The approach adopted by the chapter captures the dynamism of organizational life by treating CSR not as an accomplished event but as an unfolding business process that encompasses endogenous and exogenous change (Tsoukas & Chia, 2002).

Stakeholder engagement is defined as "a process of relationship management that seeks to enhance understanding and alignment between a company and its stakeholders" (Gable & Shireman, 2005) and is fundamental to any debate about the nature of this relationship (Connor,

2006). Many organizations engage with stakeholders, but commentators have expressed reservations as to whether stakeholder engagement necessarily represents responsible management practice or a means of achieving sustainability (Greenwood & De Ceiri, 2007). Stakeholder engagement spans many areas of organization activity—public relations, customer liaison, supplier links, and human resource management—but it can be a mechanism for achieving consensus or for stakeholder manipulation. Moreover, even if organizational intentions regarding stakeholder engagement are genuine, assumptions that stakeholders are socially and ecologically orientated, have the time and resources to become engaged in this way, and will adopt a common stance on CSR issues are contested (Greenwood & De Ceiri, 2007). More significantly, radical commentators attest that morally grounded CSR and sustainable business practice go beyond stakeholder engagement and require a fundamental revision of the traditional business model (Collins, Kearins, & Roper, 2005).

The stakeholder systems model that we propose responds to the limitations of current organizational stakeholder dialogue and to concerns regarding the transparency and authenticity of stakeholder engagement. In an employment relations context, demands for the ethical treatment of a particular stakeholder constituency (employees) include both the moral treatment of the workforce and employee involvement in decision making (Greenwood & De Ceiri, 2007). We argue that the same principles apply to organizational relationships with all stakeholder groups and that the stakeholder systems model offers both a reflexive philosophy and a syncretistic method of achieving this.

Reflective and recursive enquiry within strategically reflexive CSR

Brown and Starkey (2000) apply a psychodynamic perspective to analyze the processes of organization identity and learning. They contend that organizational learning is often hampered by a reluctance to question self-concepts in order to preserve an existing identity. Ego defenses maintain organizational self-esteem by failing to challenge the assumptions that underpin current identity or by a reluctance to promote dialogue that may identify possible future identities. However, these maladaptive defense mechanisms can be challenged by processes of organizational learning in the form of critical reflexivity.

Figures 13.1–13.3 illustrate the differences between reflective and recursive forms of reflexivity and how the latter can be applied within a strategically reflexive approach to CSR.

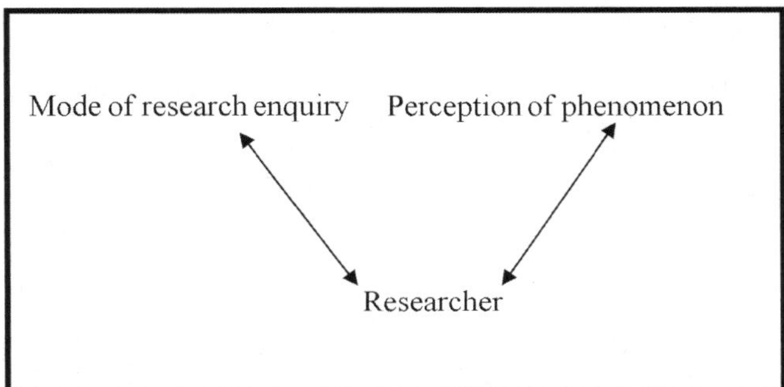

Figure 13.1 A reflective form of reflexivity

Source: Hibbert et al. (2010).

Mode of research enquiry
Perception of phenomenon
Researcher
Insights and challenges of research subjects

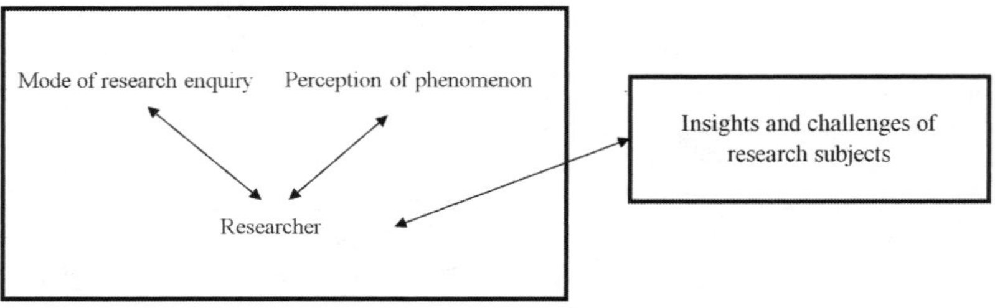

Figure 13.2 A recursive form of reflexivity
Sources: Hibbert et al. (2010) and Mahadevan (2011).

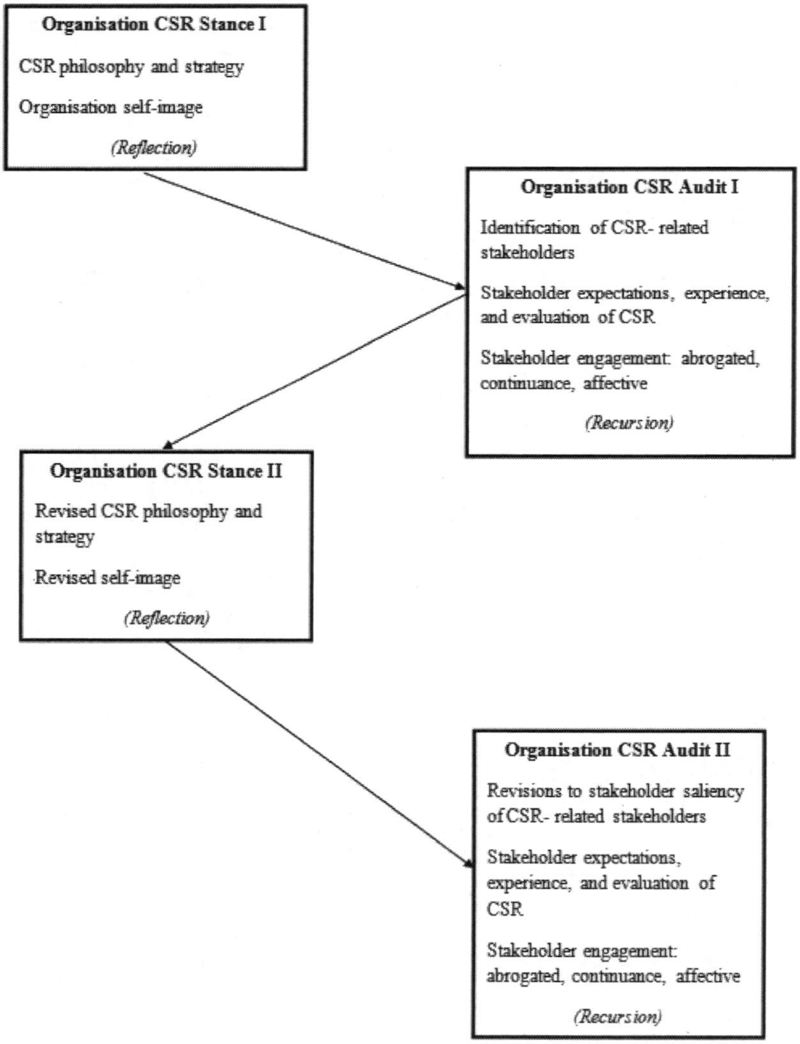

Organisation CSR Stance I
CSR philosophy and strategy
Organisation self-image
(Reflection)
Organisation CSR Audit I
Identification of CSR- related stakeholders
Stakeholder expectations, experience, and evaluation of CSR
Stakeholder engagement: abrogated, continuance, affective
(Recursion)
Organisation CSR Stance II
Revised CSR philosophy and strategy
Revised self-image
(Reflection)
Organisation CSR Audit II
Revisions to stakeholder saliency of CSR- related stakeholders
Stakeholder expectations, experience, and evaluation of CSR
Stakeholder engagement: abrogated, continuance, affective
(Recursion)

Figure 13.3 How reflection and recursion shape CSR philosophy and strategy

Figure 13.1 represents a reflective mode of reflexivity in which the researcher reflects on their method of research enquiry and perception of the phenomenon being studied so as to minimize bias from gendered, status-driven, organizational, or ideological standpoints. However, this internal and self-regulatory process is entirely reliant on the soul-searching and confessional capability of the researcher. In contrast, in the recursive mode shown in Figure 13.2, the researcher combines internal reflection with deliberately opening themselves up to the insights and challenges of research subjects. This represents a more democratic mode of enquiry and may result in a fundamental revision of the initial research stance.

Incorporation of the recursive mode of enquiry within a strategically reflexive approach to CSR enables the views of salient stakeholders to inform the development and refinement of an organization's CSR stance. A reflexive approach to current practice in evaluating sustainability and CSR is essential if their transformation is to be achieved (Frame & Cavanagh, 2009). Figure 13.3 illustrates how recursion can shape and refine CSR philosophy and strategy. At the start of the process, the organization is either formulating a CSR stance or is conscious of the need to refine an existing one. Strategic reflexivity involves both inward reflection on the organization's current approach to CSR together with outward recursion to identify stakeholder perspectives on this. A CSR-focused stakeholder audit includes the identification of salient stakeholder constituencies together with their expectations, experience, and evaluation of the organization's CSR initiatives. Figure 13.3 shows the initial position of Organization CSR Stance I where organization self-image in the form of current CSR philosophy and strategy—whether embryonic or developed—is reflected on internally by relevant organization decision makers. The organization then seeks stakeholder perspectives and evaluation of these. Organization CSR Audit I confirms the salience of stakeholder constituencies, identifies their CSR-related expectations, and evaluates their experience of enacted CSR. Results from this organizational audit of stakeholder views then inform Organization CSR Stance II and contribute to a revised CSR philosophy, strategy, and self-image. The process becomes a continuous one and is incorporated into wider performance management and auditing processes. In this way a strategically reflexive perspective on CSR makes a distinct and significant contribution to organizational learning and development.

Organizational assessment of how stakeholders view CSR policy and practice is paralleled by stakeholders' own informal evaluation. Specifically, stakeholders evaluate how closely organizational CSR aligns with their expectations and experience. These evaluations then impact on the level of subsequent stakeholder engagement that can be categorized as abrogated (alienated and hostile), continuance (willing to continue the association), or affective (enhanced loyalty from recognition of shared values).

We suggest that stakeholder evaluation of organizational CSR is best conceptualized by developing the notion of organizational justice from employment relations research (Erdogan, Kraimer, & Liden, 2001). Organizational justice represents an employee's view—or, as we propose in the corporate governance context, stakeholder perception—of how fairly they are treated by an organization. Organizational justice has been delineated into the dimensions of procedural justice (perceptions of the equity of the process used to determine the outcome), interactional justice (perceptions of the level of trust and openness between the two parties), and distributive justice (perceptions of the fairness of process outcomes). These dimensions can be related to stakeholder perceptions of CSR in the following ways. The extent to which an organization's CSR stance (espoused CSR) matches stakeholder expectations is a measure of its procedural justice; the degree to which stakeholders experience CSR practice (enacted CSR) as equitable and open is a measure of its interactional justice; while the extent to which CSR outcomes (evaluated CSR) deliver what stakeholders believe has been promised is a measure of its distributive justice.

CSR—A syncretistic perspective

Increasing recognition of the detrimental impact of business activities on society and the environment is used by Martinez (2012) to advocate syncretism as a means of integrating CSR into business operations. However, application is challenging due to terminological confusion (Droogers, 1989). The concept of syncretism originates from theology and describes the merger of different schools of religious thought to achieve a federation of ideas. The outcome can be viewed positively or negatively according to the perspective adopted. Positive assessment views it as unifying previous standpoints that emerge stronger as a result, whereas negative evaluation sees a betrayal of principles where unity is pursued at the expense of truth (Droogers, 1989). In business contexts, syncretistic incorporation of CSR into corporate strategy seeks to combine two potentially opposing influences: a systemic one that prioritizes the organization's profitability obligations together with a constructivist one that emphasizes the significance of stakeholder beliefs and values. Syncretism can achieve equilibrium between the two whereby both economic and CSR performances are optimized within a more holistic and longer-term business strategy. Here, the organizational performance dimensions of CSR (economic and legal) are balanced with societal ones (ethical and philanthropic) (Martinez, 2012). This challenge to the "zero sum game" view of CSR whereby acceptance of a business contribution expectation of CSR obviates its societal obligations is supported by some recent studies (Halal, 2000). Ethical principles are compatible with long-term profitability as sustainable business necessitates consideration of organizational impact on wider society and the environment (e.g., Fleming & Jones, 2012). Further support for the syncretistic stance is found in a recent review of opposing perspectives on sustainability accounting in which the critical theory view is contrasted with that emanating from a management orientation (Burritt & Schaltegger, 2010). It concludes that, while the critical view rightly highlights the limitations of the management perspective, it fails to address sustainability in a realistic way. Therefore, a managerial perspective that also addresses particular concerns of the critical stance can contribute to real progress in sustainability accounting. However, others question whether reconciliation is fully achievable and claim that firms' approach to CSR is primarily driven by economic motives (Fleming & Jones, 2012).

Nevertheless, strong justification for linking syncretism to the stakeholder systems approach is found by viewing it as a management philosophy that reflects a corporate effort to respond to the potentially disparate views of a diverse set of stakeholders (Berger, Cunningham, & Drumwright, 2007). This research study utilized survey evidence from a wide range of organizations in different countries to identify the rationales companies use for mainstreaming CSR as a core component of business strategy. Three distinct profiles emerged: firms that emphasized the business case for CSR; those that were motivated by social values; and those that recognized the interdependence of economic and non-economic objectives and achieved a syncretistic combination of the two. "Syncretic stewardship" organizations acknowledge the significance of stakeholder perceptions of the organization as representing the reality of how constituencies perceive it and recognize the importance of negotiating mutually acceptable trade-offs between diverse stakeholder groups. These organizations also rigorously evaluate their CSR initiatives by using surveys to gauge stakeholder reaction (Berger et al., 2007).

Support for the stakeholder systems approach

In summary, the studies we have reviewed support the philosophy and method of our approach. Taking philosophy first, we concur with du Plessis (2008) that the issues of ethics and economics are indivisible and that stakeholder theory can bridge the conceptual divide that has hampered corporate governance research to date. Viewing these disciplines through a stakeholder lens results in a more pragmatic "ethical strategist" stance that is essential for the long-term sustainability of the firm and of wider society (Noland & Phillips, 2010). A key challenge for corporate decision makers is therefore to design a CSR strategy that addresses social issues and generates business benefits for the organization (Bhattacharyya, Sahay, Arora, & Chaturvadi, 2008). Organizations that adopt a "syncretic stewardship" philosophy of corporate governance recognize the importance of stakeholder perceptions of the organization as well as the necessity of negotiating acceptable compromises between diverse stakeholder constituencies (Berger et al., 2007). Research analyses also support our method of implementation. Advocates of a "post-positivist" approach to corporate governance attest that ethical CSR can only be achieved through a process of "deliberative democracy" with salient stakeholders (Brown & Starkey, 2000). The probability of organizational defense mechanisms that seek to maintain didactic information flows to stakeholders is acknowledged, but evidence suggests that these mechanisms can be challenged by the incorporation of strategic reflexivity into processes of stakeholder engagement (Vrontis et al., 2012). Moreover, contrary to conventional assumptions, divergence between CSR rhetoric and practice is not necessarily devoid of possibilities for incremental enhancement of firm performance (Christensen et al., 2013).

Further support for the stakeholder systems model is found in a recent investigation into the extent of stakeholder inclusivity in social and environmental report assurance (SERA). Researchers examined the benefits, degree of stakeholder inclusivity, and extent of managerial capture of SERA processes (Edgley, Jones, & Solomon, 2010). Although the SERA framework is endorsed by the EC, it is currently a voluntary involvement for UK companies. It constitutes a quality assurance frame of reference developed from the reporting standards of sustainability and accountancy bodies. Assurors with either environmental or accountancy backgrounds are retained by companies to assess and report back to them on social and environmental issues with the aim of enhancing the credibility of organization sustainability claims. A typical assurance and reporting service claims that assurance from a trusted adviser enables client companies to assess stakeholder expectations, provide independent verification that their sustainability report meets regulatory requirements and benchmark standards, review current reporting against best practice, and align sustainability objectives with corporate strategy (PWC, 2013). Prior studies have questioned the value of the SERA process in relation to the extent of its managerial capture, as well as limitations in its stakeholder inclusivity and dialogic nature. However, Edgley et al. (2010, p. 536) attest that SERA has the potential to break down "hegemonic discourse by ensuring dialogic communication between companies and their stakeholders." They claim that reporting and assurance processes can become truly dialogic if they identify social and environmental issues, engender change, involve action and reflection that results in organization transformation, and are informed by an inclusive stakeholder dialogue.

The study contrasts indirect and direct methods of stakeholder inclusivity. In the former, assurors facilitate company awareness of stakeholder views of its CSR practice by observation of company stakeholder interaction or data analysis. Direct methods involve assurors engaging directly with stakeholders by conducting interviews, issuing questionnaires, or undertaking stakeholder mapping. While indirect methods of stakeholder inclusivity currently represent good practice, direct involvement of a wider range of stakeholders who have greater influence in determining SERA issues is identified as an emerging trend. Managerial capture is acknowledged as a continuing limitation, but evolving stakeholder inclusivity indicates that SERA is becoming an important link in the reporting chain. We contend that the stakeholder systems model we advocate aligns with and builds on the SERA framework by formalizing stakeholder inclusivity within a more reflexive and dialogic process.

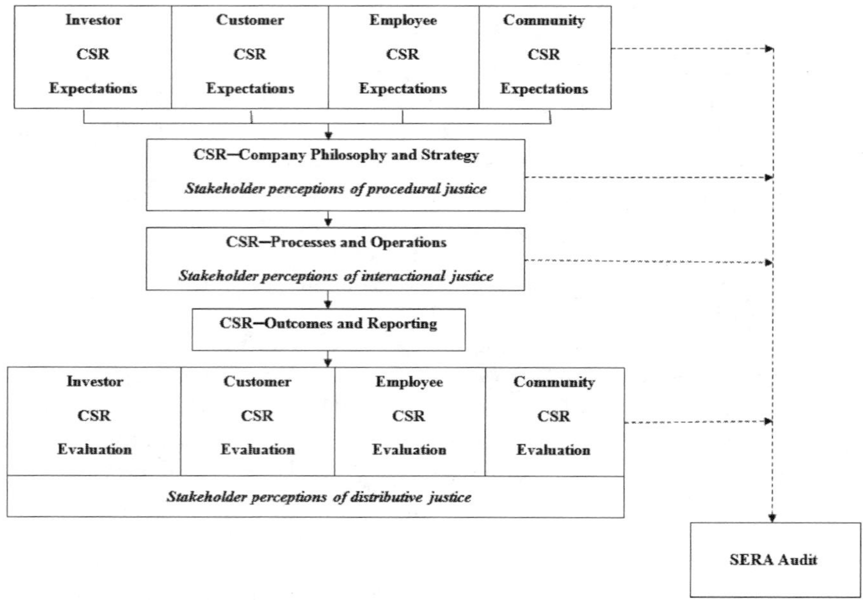

Figure 13.4 Stakeholder expectations of company CSR and the SERA audit process

In Figure 13.4 we show how the SERA audit process would operate by using a framework based on the stakeholder systems model. The starting point is the CSR-related expectations that major stakeholder constituencies have of a focal organization—namely the expectations of investors, customers, employees, and social and environmental groups. The focal organization identifies the CSR-related expectations that relevant constituencies have of the company and evaluates these in relation to the constituency's perceived saliency. CSR-related expectations that are acknowledged by the organization will inform its CSR philosophy and strategy. CSR philosophy and strategy are then enacted through CSR operations and processes that in turn produce specific CSR outcomes. Stakeholder groups evaluate the equity and effectiveness of each stage of the CSR process with varying levels of formality and cohesion: CSR philosophy and strategy are assessed by stakeholder perceptions of their procedural justice; CSR processes and operations by their perceived interactional justice; and CSR outcomes by their perceived distributive justice.

A SERA audit could therefore obtain stakeholder views on the effectiveness and equity of a company's CSR strategy, processes, and outcomes; or could focus on CSR outcomes alone. The audit would utilize quantitative data on company CSR alongside qualitative insights from questionnaires, interviews, and focus groups to assess how well each stakeholder group's expectations have been met, and whether the company should be required to take action to address any shortfalls. SERA audits would include stakeholders' CSR expectations that the company failed to acknowledge but which SERA regards as valid. Action points arising from such audits would be classified as mandatory or advisory—with SERA being able to impose financial penalties on companies if mandatory requirements are not complied with. We also suggest that our SERA proposals respond to calls for innovations in accounting that address challenges that cannot be resolved by existing protocols and contribute to the development of new national standards (Caliskan, 2014).

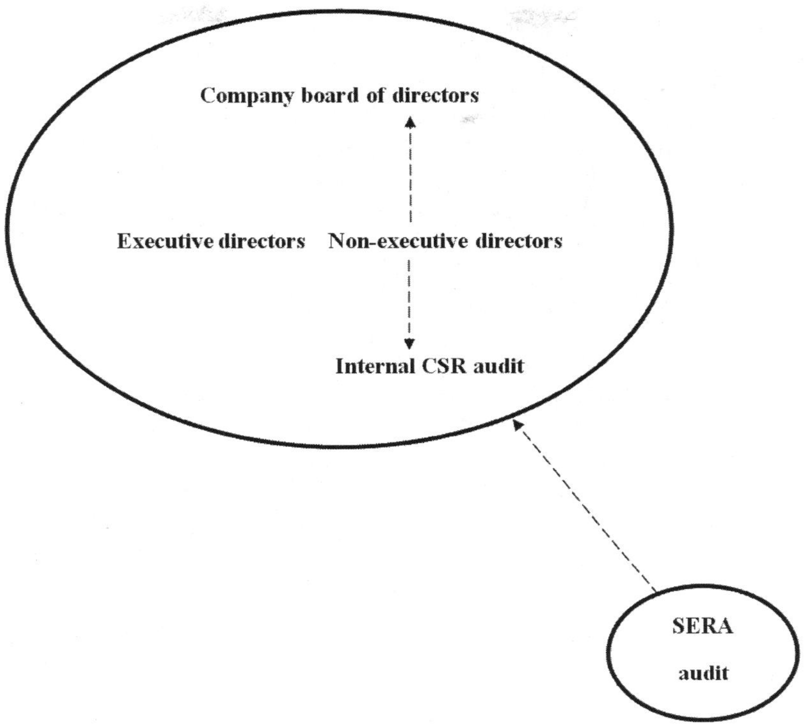

Figure 13.5 Internal and external audit of company CSR

Figure 13.5 shows the complementary nature of internal and external CSR audits of a focal organization. In the internal audit component, non-executive directors (NEDs) would have a responsibility under a revised Companies Act to monitor company CSR by conducting an appropriate internal audit. This would be paralleled by legislation that establishes a new governmental agency empowered to conduct external SERA audits on UK-based companies of a certain size. The SERA agency would authorize suitable consultancies to undertake SERA audits in specified geographical or industrial sectors using the precepts of the stakeholder systems model—with appropriate penalties for companies that fail to comply with the new audit regime. Companies that met SERA standards would be entitled to display an "Investor in CSR"-type kite mark similar to the "Investors in People" logo. (Investors in People accreditation is awarded to organizations that meet rigorous standards of people management practice and is recognized as a mark of excellence; see http://www.investorsinpeople.co.uk.) NEDs would not be required to adhere to a stakeholder systems-type audit, but would be aware that this is the framework that SERA consultancies use when assessing how well stakeholders' legitimate expectations of company CSR have been met.

We recognize that reflexivity "purists" will view our development of the strategic reflexivity concept as a form of organization capture of CSR which emasculates its social responsibility initiatives so that CSR remains primarily driven by profit maximization (Fleming & Jones, 2012). In response, we utilize Noland and Phillips' (2010) identification of two modes of stakeholder engagement that they term "Habermasian" and "Ethical Strategist." They attest that, while the Habermasian approach is purer in a moral sense, its requirement that CSR decision makers prioritize ethical purity over alignment with strategy renders this mode of stakeholder engagement impractical in a business context. Moreover, Ethical Strategists argue that the Habermasian distinction between morality and strategy is misguided. Good strategy necessarily incorporates moral concerns as the sustainability of the firm requires the creation of value for all stakeholders. The question is, how can an organization demonstrate that it creates a valued form of CSR for its stakeholder constituencies? We contend that the stakeholder perceptions of the ethicality of the CSR strategy, process, and outcomes which the stakeholder systems model provides are measures of corporate social performance (Secchi, 2007, 2009). Moreover, if an organization modifies its CSR philosophy and practice as a result of stakeholder feedback, this evidences the leverage that ethical stakeholder engagement can exert. We therefore contend that those who hold to a purist Habermasian stance on CSR are indulging in a form of organization train spotting as they observe, classify, and critique research approaches to CSR—but without any real hope of "boarding the CSR train" and influencing its destination!

Purists who adopt this position are akin to the situation described in the old joke when a person who is lost asks a passerby for directions and is given the advice "If I were you, I wouldn't start from here." However, those seeking to address CSR issues should recognize their starting position in that they are "boarding a train that is already moving" (Landry & Malouin, 1983); and that particular structures, cultures, power relationships, and stakeholder attitudes have evolved during CSR's "journey" so far. Pursuing the analogy, "on board" CSR are various stakeholder groups that differ in their definitions of the problem and what action should be taken in response to it. Failure to recognize the significance of identifying and interpreting the stakeholder viewpoints renders the process of enquiry sterile and irrelevant. Therefore, the chapter offers a structured methodology for identifying train "passengers" (stakeholders with a vested interest in CSR) and their "luggage" (perspectives on CSR that accompany them on their journey) via a new mode of analysis based on strategic reflexivity. The reflexive mode of stakeholder analysis facilitates a synthesis of stakeholder views that enables CSR "passengers" to travel to a new destination (a point where there is agreement as to how CSR problems should be responded to).

Comparing CSR practice with stakeholders' CSR-related expectations can create new insights that can accommodate disparate stakeholder interests. The type of strategic reflexivity advocated by Ethical Strategists aligns with the reflexive mode of stakeholder analysis we advocate. It combines robust methods of enquiry with an interpretivist approach that recognizes the contested nature of CSR within the contemporary organizational context.

Conclusion

There is a developing view that current modes of corporate governance and sustainability accounting are inadequate in philosophy and practice. The limitations of current stakeholder dialogue have led to calls to "mainstream" CSR so that responsible and sustainable corporations develop new frameworks for stakeholder engagement (Banerjee, 2008). The chapter presents a rationale for the reformation of the philosophy and practice of corporate governance through the synergistic application of reflexivity and stakeholder theory. Adoption of a pragmatic and syncretistic stance enables it to draw from reflexive awareness of stakeholder perceptions alongside company concerns for effectiveness and profitability. A strategically reflexive audit of stakeholder perceptions of CSR also enables stakeholder theory to be used in an empowering way rather than as "a sophisticated ideology of control" (Antonacopoulou & Meric, 2005, p. 22). Its more radical perspective on corporate governance/CSR is given greater significance by the evidence that many corporations have failed to learn the lessons of history. Recent financial crises and corporate malfeasance demonstrate limited due diligence concerns by directors, the failure of NEDs to confront management on contentious governance issues, and the inadequacy of existing governance rules. In particular, commentators suggest that NEDs and company managers require a powerful strategic management tool capable of conducting a comprehensive and robust stakeholder audit of CSR (Murray, 2003). Calls for reform regarding what is required are paralleled by outwardly disparate, but in reality complementary, views on how this type of audit mechanism could be developed. For example, while conventional and critical management views of the relevance of sustainability accounting to CSR appear diametrically opposed, recent research attests that they can be deployed synergistically (Burritt & Schaltegger, 2010). Similarly, the one-dimensional and retrospective focus of traditional audit approaches is challenged by those who advocate a multidisciplinary and comprehensive assessment of organization performance (Kaplan & Norton, 1992). The stakeholder systems model that we offer presents a novel and reflexive way to audit stakeholder perspectives on CSR. It responds to calls for researchers to focus on stakeholder expectations and achieve greater sophistication in managing stakeholder responses. The approach aligns with a new philosophy of corporate governance that advocates incorporation of the four Ps (planet, people, profit, and posterity) in organizational performance management (Kakabadse & Kakabadse, 2003). It is grounded in a more relational view of the corporation, as research has identified the departure point of responsible and sustainable corporations as the company's relationships with its stakeholders (Aguilera, Rupp, Williams, & Ganapathi, 2007; Jamali, 2008).

Transformative organizational learning requires decision makers and groups to develop a vision of the future that challenges current philosophy and practice. The outcome of this process of critical reflexivity is to question the validity of existing organizational philosophy and practice in a radically different business environment. Organizational development therefore depends on a firm's ability to understand and manage discord (Brown & Starkey, 2000). In the CSR context depicted by the stakeholder systems model, this type of transformative change is achieved when an organization's reflexive awareness of the dissonance between its espoused CSR stance and stakeholder expectation and experience results in initiatives to achieve greater congruence between them.

CSR standards constitute an institutional infrastructure for CSR (Bjartmarz & Pedersen, 2015). The mandatory element of the quality assurance system that we advocate aligns with developments in social reporting and accounting, and specifically the inclusion of third-party verification within this (Bjartmarz & Pedersen, 2015). The assessment of sustainable development is a current concern of academics and practitioners. This is evidenced by the burgeoning literature on the topic (Frame & Cavanagh, 2009) and the significance of the measurement issue to those in the accountancy profession (Gasparatos, El-Haram, & Horner, 2009). Currently, most sustainability assessments are derived from a diverse range of metrics that are then aggregated into one composite measure. However, this stance has come under significant challenge, as collapsing a multiplicity of measures from diverse areas of expertise into a single metric is seen as reductionism (Gasparatos et al., 2009). Such approaches are regarded as unjustifiable because of the limitations of the metrics used and the impossibility of encapsulating the outcomes of a dynamic and complex system in a single measure. These limitations make a strong case for methodological pluralism alongside stakeholder contribution to improve both the outcome and the acceptability of the evaluation process. Pluralist approaches that combine different ways of knowing with increased stakeholder involvement are identified as a route to more informed policy making (Gasparatos et al., 2009). In summary, the significance of decision making in sustainable development for present and future generations and the high level of epistemological and ethical uncertainty involved implies the inclusion of an increasing number of salient stakeholders in system evaluation (Bebbington, 2009).

What then are our model's implications? First, while it can play a vital role in aligning CSR philosophy and practice with the reality of the 21st-century corporation, it requires complementary changes in legislation, regulatory practice, and company culture. Detailed plans for implementing strategic reflexivity in CSR are outside the scope of this chapter. However, we contend that two related proposals should represent key components of this. First, we suggest the introduction of a new due diligence role for NEDs that requires them to conduct a periodic stakeholder audit to ascertain stakeholder expectations and experience of their company's CSR. The results would then form part of the organization's annual report. Second, we advocate the establishment of a robust, uniform, and mandatory SERA system for the external audit of CSR that would operate in a similar way to the current auditing of financial accounts. The proposals—which would only apply to companies of a certain size—would require new legislation, and critics will identify issues of cost and stakeholder identification as barriers to implementation. However, we contend that the same arguments could have been made against company responsibility for health and safety standards in their supply chains; but these objections are now recognized as untenable from moral, reputational, and financial perspectives. Our recommendations constitute a multi-prong approach to CSR that incorporates legislation, directors' duties, and managerial responsibility (Waring, 2008). Our proposals also align with ideas from the emerging field of integrated reporting, and specifically the second component of this. The approach combines two strands of corporate reporting: one that provides information to investors so that they can appraise the company's economic prospects; the other that demonstrates the company's willingness to be accountable to a range of stakeholder expectations regarding social and environmental impacts (de Villiers, Rinaldi, & Unerman, 2014).

Societal requirement for responsible and sustainable corporations grows more urgent by the day. To complete Santayana's dictum referred to above, if companies, their stakeholders, and society fail to learn the lessons of history and accord CSR the importance it deserves, they will be compelled to relive them and contend with greater penalties for their failure.

References

Aguilera, R. V., Rupp, D. E., Williams, C. A., & Ganapathi, I. (2007). Putting the S back into corporate social responsibility: A multilevel theory of social change. *Academy of Management Review, 32*(3), 836–863.

Aguinis, H. (2011). Organizational responsibility: Doing good and doing well. In S. Zedeck (Ed.), *APA handbook of industrial and occupational psychology* (Vol. 3, pp. 855–879). Washington, DC: American Psychological Association.

Aguinis, H., & Glavas, A. (2012). What we know and don't know about corporate social responsibility: A review and research agenda. *Journal of Management, 38*(4), 932–968.

Antonacopoulou, E. P., & Meric, J. (2005). A critique of stakeholder theory: Management science or a sophisticated ideology of control? *Corporate Governance, 5*(2), 22–33.

Banerjee, S. B. (2008). Corporate social responsibility: The good, the bad and the ugly. *Critical Sociology, 34*(1), 51–79.

Barratt, R., & Korac-Kakabadse, N. (2002). Developing reflexive corporate leadership. *Corporate Governance, 2*(3), 32–35.

Bartlett, J., Tywoniak, S., & Hatcher, C. (2007). Public relations professional practice and the institutionalisation of CSR. *Journal of Communication Management, 11*(4), 281–299.

Bebbington, J. (2009). Measuring sustainable development performance: Possibilities and issues. *Accounting Forum, 33*(3), 189–193.

Berger, I. E., Cunningham, P. H., & Drumwright, M. E. (2007). Mainstreaming corporate social responsibility: Developing markets for virtue. *California Management Review, 49*(4), 132–157.

Bhattacharyya, S. S., Sahay, A., Arora, A. P., & Chaturvadi, A. (2008). A toolkit for designing firm level strategic corporate social responsibility. *Corporate Governance, 4*(3), 265–282.

Bjartmarz, T., & Pedersen, E. R. G. (2015). CSR standards and social accounting. In E. R. G. Pedersen (Ed.), *Corporate social responsibility* (pp. 103–123). London: Sage.
Brewis, J., & Wray-Bliss, E. (2008). Re-searching ethics: Towards a more reflexive critical management studies. *Organization Studies, 20*(12), 1521–1540.
Brown, A. D., & Starkey, K. (2000). Organizational identity and learning: A psychodynamic perspective. *Academy of Management Review, 25*(1), 102–120.
Burritt, R. L., & Schaltegger, S. (2010). Sustainability accounting and reporting: Fad or trend? *Accounting, Auditing and Accountability Journal, 23*(7), 829–846.
Caliskan, A. O. (2014). How accounting and accountants may contribute to sustainability. *Social Responsibility Journal, 10*(2), 248–267.
Cederstrom, C., & Marinetto, M. (2013). Corporate social responsibility a la the liberal communist. *Organization, 20*(3), 416–432.
Christensen, L. T., Morsing, M., & Thyssen, O. (2013). CSR as aspirational talk. *Organization, 20*(3), 372–393.
Chong, Y. Y. (2004). Corporate governance: Risk management starts at the top. *Balance Sheet, 12*(5), 42–47.
Collins, E., Kearins, K., & Roper, J. (2005). The risks in relying on stakeholder engagement for the achievement of sustainability. *Electronic Journal of Radical Organisation Theory, 9*(1). Retrieved February 29, 2016, from http://www.management.ac.nz/ejrot/Vol9_1/CollinsKearinsRoper.pdf
Connor, K. T. (2006). Assessing organization ethics: Measuring the gaps. *Industrial and Commercial Training, 38*(3), 145–155.
Cunliffe, A. L., & Jun, J. S. (2005). The need for reflexivity in public administration. *Administration and Society, 37*(2), 225–242.
de Villiers, C., Rinaldi, L., & Unerman, J. (2014). Integrated reporting: Insights, gaps and an agenda for future research. *Accounting, Auditing and Accountability Journal, 27*(7), 1042–1067.
Donaldson, T. (2012). The epistemic fault line in corporate governance. *Academy of Management Review, 37*(2), 256–271.
Donaldson, T., & Fafaliou, I. (2007). Principles of administration revisited. *International Journal of Social Economics, 34*(5), 297–309.
Droogers, A. (1989). Syncretism: The problem of definition, the definition of the problem. In J. D. Gort, H. M. Vroom, R. Fernhout, & A. Wessels (Eds.), *Dialogue and syncretism: An interdisciplinary approach* (pp. 7–25). Grand Rapids, MI: Wm B. Eerdmans Publishing.
Duarte, F. (2006). Spivs, shonks and sharks: The HIH collapse as a moral tale of corporate capitalism. *Social Responsibility Journal, 2*(3/4), 282–290.
du Plessis, C. J. A. (2008). Ethical failure under the agency logic: Grounding governance reform in a logic of value. *Groups and Organization Management, 33*(6), 781–804.
Edgley, C. R., Jones, M. J., & Solomon, J. F. (2010). Stakeholder inclusivity in social and environmental report assurance. *Accounting, Auditing and Accountability Journal, 23*(4), 532–567.
Erdogan, B., Kraimer, M. L., & Liden, R. C. (2001). Procedural justice as a two-dimensional construct. *Journal of Applied Behavioral Science, 37*(2), 205–222.
Fassin, Y., & Buelens, M. (2011). The hypocrisy-sincerity continuum in corporate communication and decision making: A model of corporate social responsibility and business ethics practices. *Management Decision, 49*(4), 586–600.
Fleming, P., & Jones, M. T. (2012). *The end of corporate responsibility*. London: Sage.
Fleming, P., Roberts, J., & Garsten, C. (2013). In search of corporate social responsibility: Introduction to special issue. *Organization, 20*(3), 337–348.
Fram, E. H., & Zoffer, H. J. (2005). Are American corporate directors still ignoring the signals? *Corporate Governance, 5*(1), 31–38.
Frame, B., & Cavanagh, J. (2009). Experiences of sustainability assessment: An awkward adolescence. *Accounting Forum, 33*(3), 195–208.
Gable, C., & Shireman, B. (2005). Stakeholder engagement: A three-phase methodology. *Environmental Quality Management, 4*(3), 9–24.
Gasparatos, A., El-Haram, M., & Horner, M. (2009). The argument against a reductionist approach to measuring sustainable development performance and the need for methodological pluralism. *Accounting Forum, 33*(3), 245–256.
Greenwood, M., & De Ceiri, H. (2007). Stakeholder theory and the ethics of HRM. In A. H. Pinnington, R. Macklin, & T. Campbell (Eds.), *Human resource management: Ethics and employment* (pp. 119–136). Oxford, UK: Oxford University Press.

GRI. (2013). *G4 sustainability reporting guidelines*. Amsterdam: GRI. Retrieved May 21, 2015, from http://www.globalreporting.org/reporting/g4/Pages/default.aspx

Halal, W. E. (2000). Corporate community: A theory of the firm uniting profitability and responsibility. *Strategy and Leadership, 28*(2), 10–16.

Heidegger, M. (1969). *Identity and difference*. New York: Harper and Row.

Hibbert, P., Coupland, C., & Macintosh, R. (2010). Reflexivity: Recursion and relationality in organizational research processes. *Qualitative Research in Organizations and Management—An International Journal, 5*(1), 47–62.

Hildebrand, D., Sen, S., & Bhattacharya, C. (2011). Corporate social responsibility: A corporate marketing perspective. *European Journal of Marketing, 45*(9/10), 1353–1364.

Husted, B. W., & Allen, D. B. (2006). Corporate social responsibility in the multi-national corporation: Strategic and institutional approaches. *Journal of International Business Studies,* 7(3), 538–549.

Jamali, D. (2008). A stakeholder approach to corporate social responsibility: A fresh perspective into theory and practice. *Journal of Business Ethics, 82*(1), 213–231.

Jensen, T., Sandstrom, J., & Helin, S. (2009). Corporate codes of ethics and the bending of moral space. *Organization, 16*(4), 529–545.

Jones, M. T. (2009). Disrobing the emperor: Mainstream CSR research and corporate hegemony. *Management of Environmental Quality—An International Journal, 20*(3), 335–346.

Kakabadse, N. K., & Kakabadse, A. (2003). Polylogue as a platform for governance: Integrating people, planet, profit and posterity. *Corporate Governance, 3*(1), 5–28.

Kaplan, R. S., & Norton, D. P. (1992). The balanced scorecard: Measure that drive performance. *Harvard Business Review, 70*(1), 71–79.

Khalid, S. N. A. (2009). Reflexivity in qualitative accounting research. *Journal of Financial Reporting and Accounting,* 7(2), 81–95.

Knox, S., Maklan, S., & French, P. (2005). Corporate social responsibility: Exploring stakeholder relationships and programme reporting across leading FTSE companies. *Journal of Business Ethics, 61*(1), 7–28.

Kostera, M. (1997). Personal performatives: Collecting poetical definitions of management. *Organization, 4*(3), 345–353.

Landry, M., & Malouin, J.-L. (1983). Pour une meilleure utilization des experts-conseils en administration. *Gestion, 8*(2), 4–11.

Mahadevan, J. (2011). Reflexive guidelines for writing organizational culture. *Qualitative Research in Organizations and Management, 6*(2), 150–170.

Mainardes, E. W., Alves, H., & Raposo, M. (2011). Stakeholder theory: Issues to resolve. *Management Decision, 49*(2), 225–252.

Marens, R. (2010). Destroying the village to save it: Corporate social responsibility, labour relations and the rise and fall of American hegemony. *Organization, 17*(6), 743–766.

Martinez, F. (2012). The syncretism of environmental and social responsibility with business economic performance. *Management of Environmental Quality—An International Journal, 23*(6), 597–614.

McSweeney, B. (2008). Maximising shareholder value: A panacea for economic growth or a recipe for economic and social disintegration? *Critical Perspectives on International Business, 4*(1), 56–74.

Murray, K. (2003). Reputation: Managing the single greatest risk facing business today. *Journal of Communication Management, 8*(2), 142–149.

Noland, J., & Phillips, R. (2010). Stakeholder engagement, discourse ethics and strategic management. *International Journal of Management Reviews, 12*(1), 39–49.

Okhmatovskiy, I., & David, R. J. (2011). Setting your own standards: Internal corporate governance codes as a response to institutional pressure. *Organization Science, 23*(1), 155–176.

Orr, K., & Bennett, M. (2009). Reflexivity in the co-production of academic-practitioner research. *Qualitative Research in Organizations and Management: An International Journal, 4*(1), 85–102.

Porter, B. A. (2009). The audit trinity: The key to securing corporate accountability. *Management Auditing Journal, 24*(2), 156–182.

PWC. (2013). *Assurance and reporting*. Retrieved April 1, 2015, from http://www.pwc.com/gx/en/services/sustainability/assurance-verification-reporting.html

Raghavendran, S., & Rajagopalan, P. S. (2011). Sense making of complexity: Leadership in financial services. *Journal of Business Ethics, 32*(3), 19–25.

Renganathan, S. (2009). Exploring the researcher-participant relationship in a multiethnic, multicultural and multilingual context through reflexivity. *Qualitative Research Journal, 9*(2), 3–17.

Rhodes, C. (2009). After reflexivity: Ethics, freedom and the writing of organization studies. *Organization Studies, 30*(6), 653–672.

Ruhanen, L., Scott, N., Richie, B., & Tkacynski, A. (2010). Governance: A review and synthesis of the literature. *Tourism Review, 65*(4), 4–16.

Secchi, D. (2007). Utilitarian, managerial and relational theories of corporate social responsibility. *International Journal of Management Reviews, 9*(4), 347–373.

Secchi, D. (2009). The cognitive side of social responsibility. *Journal of Business Ethics, 88*, 565–581.

Tomkins, L., & Eatough, V. (2010). Towards an integrative reflexivity in organisational research. *Qualitative Research in Organizations and Management, 5*(2), 162–181.

Tsoukas, H., & Chia, R. (2002). On organizational becoming: Rethinking organization change. *Organization Science, 13*(5), 567–582.

Vrontis, D., Thrassou, A. S., Chebbi, H., & Yahiaoui, D. (2012). Transcending innovativeness towards strategic reflexivity. *Qualitative Market Research—An International Journal, 15*(4), 420–437.

Wang, G. G. (2012). Indigenous Chinese HRM research: Phenomena, methods and challenges. *Journal of Chinese Human Resource Management, 3*(2), 88–99.

Waring, P. (2008). Rethinking directors' duties in changing global markets. *Corporate Governance, 8*(2), 159–164.

14

SOCIALLY RESPONSIBLE INVESTMENT AS EMERGENT RISK PREVENTION AND MEANS TO IMBUE TRUST IN THE POST-2008/2009 WORLD FINANCIAL CRISIS ECONOMY

Julia M. Puaschunder

Globalization, political changes, and societal trends, but in particular the current world economy, have leveraged the societal demand for social responsibility in market systems to regain trust in the global economy (*The Economist*, July 7, 2012). Our time has been referred to as the "Age of Responsibility" in US President Barack Obama's 2009 inauguration speech (*Washington Post*, January 21, 2009). In the wake of the 2008 financial crisis, President Obama called for a new spirit of responsibility that serves the greater goals of society. Former World Bank President Robert Zoellick describes the "new era of responsibility" as featuring "changed attitudes and co-operative policies" that promote responsible corporate conduct (Zoellick, 2009).

The 2008/09 World Financial Crisis climaxed the call for responsibility in financial markets. The announcement of the recapitalization of the banking system in October 2008 created a demand for social responsibility in a newly defined economic order. Financial market regulations and consumer protection agencies set out to re-establish trust in the corporate and finance world. In July 2010, the US Congress approved a sweeping expansion of federal financial regulations in response to the 2008 financial excesses that caused the worst recession since the Great Depression (*The New York Times*, July 15, 2010). The 2,300-page legislative catalog of repairs and additions to the financial regulatory system in the wake of the most important Wall Street reform legislation in 75 years implements social responsibility in financial markets and protects from human ethical decision-making failures imposing systemic risks (Summers, *CNBC news*, July 21, 2010).

For academia, the 2008/09 World Financial Crisis clearly underlines how classical finance and economic theories do not truly capture human cognition in economic markets. An accurate understanding of socio-economic market behavior in the interaction of financial markets and real-world economic outcomes is needed (Duchac, 2008). Mainstream economics must be complemented by heterodox insights on socio-psychological notions of fallible market actors and pay attention to the harmful contagion effects of their limited decisions (*The Economist*,

July 7, 2012). Ways must be found to lower emergent risks stemming from financial social irresponsibility and solutions to regain trust in economic markets. With the LIBOR/EURIBOR scandal revealing additional risks in the finance world, attention on how to manage systemic financial market risks and restore trust in the finance world has reached unprecedented momentum (*The Economist*, July 7, 2012). In the aftermath of the 2008/09 World Financial Crisis, debt may reach a level at which capital markets lose confidence, requiring a large increase in interest rates for the continued attraction of capital in North America in order to avert lower economic growth rates (Milberg, 2013). Unsustainable debt in the sense that the government will not be able to meet its debt payments or will have to raise interest rates significantly in order to continue to borrow because of a decline in market confidence will affect economic growth in a negative downward spiral. The economic system's market actors will need more confidence in declining market options to maintain the functioning of economic markets.

In the eye of the many negative consequences of the 2008/09 world financial downturn, the crisis appears to hold less acknowledged potentials to raise social responsibility in economic markets. As a window of opportunity to focus on human values in economic market interaction, we can also see the crisis as a driver of Financial Social Responsibility and Socially Responsible Investment (SRI) and these market options as a means to regain trust in the global economy.

To strategically foster a successful rise of SRI in the aftermath of the 2008/09 world economic downturn, a better understanding of the essential stakeholders' view on SRI is needed. A thorough investigation of SRI, however, is a formidable task. As a novel concept, SRI is construed by diverse stakeholders who lack concerted oversight of this complex phenomenon. Given the negative consequences of the 2008/09 World Financial Crisis, the Western world also appears to be challenged by the growing complexity of interactive relationships between individuals and organizations in the age of globalization.

As a first step toward resolving societal losses imbued in the complex interconnectedness of global institutional systems and innovatively exploring new opportunities to foster social responsibility within globalized market economies as an emergent risk panacea in times of mistrust in financial markets, the following sections capture how Financial Social Responsibility can stabilize financial and economic markets in the post-2008/09 World Financial Crisis era. With special attention to the 2008/09 World Financial Crisis and the United States, investigating SRI as a means to imbue trust in financial markets will help portray crises as opportunities to heighten ethicality in economic markets, and Financial Social Responsibility as a way to stabilize markets through trust (Puaschunder, 2011a).

Socially Responsible Investment

Today social responsibility has emerged into an en vogue topic for the corporate world and the finance sector. Contrary to classic finance theory that attributes investments to be primarily based on expected utility and volatility, the consideration of social responsibility in financial investment decisions has gained unprecedented momentum (*The Economist*, January 17, 2008; *The Wall Street Journal*, August 21, 2008).

Financial Social Responsibility is an ethical imperative that includes social concerns in financial investments (Puaschunder, 2011c; Schueth, 2003; Soana, 2011). Foremost, SRI, which accounts for the implementation of Financial Social Responsibility, imbues personal values and social concerns into financial investments (Schueth, 2003). The 2006 Social Investment Forum Report on Socially Responsible Investing outlines CSR as the basis for SRI—an asset allocation style, by which securities are selected not only on the basis of profit return and risk probabilities but in regard to the social and environmental contributions of the issuing entities (Beltratti, 2003;

Williams, 2005). Pursuing economic and social value maximization alike, Socially Responsible Investors incorporate CSR into financial decision making (Renneboog, Horst, & Zhang, 2007; Schueth, 2003; Steurer, Margula, & Martinuzzi, 2008). Socially conscientious investors fund socially responsible corporations based on evaluations of the CSR performance as well as the social and environmental risks of corporate conduct. SRI assets combine social, environmental, and financial aspects in investment options. Socially Responsible Investors are attributed explicit and implicit socio-psychological motives to pursue financial goals while catalyzing positive change (Beltratti, 2003; Matten & Crane, 2005; Mohr, Webb, & Harris, 2001; Puaschunder, 2011c). Profit maximization goals are thereby supplemented by incorporating social, environmental, and global governance factors into investment options. Socially Responsible Investors allocate financial resources based on profit maximization goals as well as societal implications. Thereby SRI becomes an investment philosophy that combines profit maximization with intrinsic and social components (Ahmad, 2008; Matten & Crane, 2005; Wolff, 2002). SRI allows the pursuit of financial goals while catalyzing positive change in the corporate and financial sectors as well as the international political arena (Mohr et al., 2001; Schueth, 2003). In the case of political divestiture, Socially Responsible Investors use their market power to attribute global governance goals. By foreign direct investment flows, SRI relocates capital with the greater goal of advancing international political development (Schueth, 2003; Starr, 2008).

As of today, SRI has been adopted by a growing proportion of investors around the world in screenings, shareholder advocacy, community investing, and social venture capital funding. SRI has leveraged into a multi-stakeholder phenomenon that comprises economic, organizational, and societal constituents. In recent years, SRI has increasingly become an element of fiduciary duty, particularly for Western world investors with long-term horizons that oversee international portfolios. As of today, SRI accounts for an emerging multi-stakeholder phenomenon with multifaceted expressions in the Western world. Today's unprecedented SRI diversity can be traced back to Financial Social Responsibility rising during times of crisis (Nilsson, 2008).

International emergence

In recent decades, SRI grew qualitatively and quantitatively in the Western world due to historical incidents, legislative compulsion, and stakeholder pressure (Carroll, 1979; Wolff, 2002). Originally stemming from a small number of specialist ethical investment funds, SRI emerged into an investment philosophy adopted by a growing proportion of Western investment houses and governmental agencies reporting on social, ethical, and environmental corporate aspects (Knoll, 2008; Mohr et al., 2001). Financial social conscientiousness increasingly became an element of fiduciary duty, particularly for long-term investors overseeing international portfolios (Social Investment Forum Report, 2006).

Today the United States features the broadest variety of SRI options and socially responsible performance measurement indices in a landscape of highly dispersed share ownership. Starting with the 1981-enacted American Social Investment Forum as a professional body for individual and institutional SRI constituents, SRI prospered in the wake of corporate social externalities' disclosure and shareholder activism on socio-political concerns (Broadhurst, Watson, & Marshall, 2003). From 1995 to 2005 the combined assets held in socially screened portfolios have increased more than tenfold in the United States (Williams, 2005). Three hundred and forty-eight resolutions on social and environmental issues were proposed, of which 177—over 50 percent—reached a proxy vote in 2005 (Social Investment Forum Report, 2006). The same year, assets worth

US$ 2.5 trillion were attributed as socially responsible funds, accounting for 20.7 percent of all US investments (Williams, 2005).

Europe has the longest tradition of incorporating social facets into institutional investments (Stavins, Reinhardt, & Vietor, 2008; Sutton, 2004). European legal systems emphasize stakeholder participation in corporate governance. Civil laws codify profit-sacrificing corporate behavior for the sake of societal good. European corporate boards often include employee representatives. The European Union institutionalizes SRI in sustainability, social, environmental, and ethical screenings. While the liberal UK permits corporate managers to engage in socially beneficial activities as long as they are in the shareholders' interests, social democracies—like the German-speaking world—legally back stakeholder interests (Lynch-Fannon, 2007; Stavins et al., 2008). According to Eurosif, SRI funds accounted for up to 18 percent of the market share in 2011.

In the UK, the European SRI leader, Victorian concerns about employment conditions sparked corporate social conduct (Sparkes, 2002). Ethical finance was established by Mercury Provident in 1974 and introduced to retail banking in 1992. In 1997, academics launched a campaign for ethical and environmental pension funds. Since 2000, Sustainable and Responsible Investment policies required all occupational pension funds to formally consider adopting social, ethical, and environmental policies (Sparkes & Cowton, 2004; Williams, 2005). UK government regulations similarly regulate pension funds to declare the extent to which environmental, social, or ethical concerns are taken into consideration in the selection, retention, and realization of investments (Sparkes, 2002). Similar regulations have been passed in Germany and are currently being considered by the European Parliament (Steurer et al., 2008). In the wake of peace and environmental protection movements, SRI was propelled in German-speaking Roman Law countries, with the "Gemeinschaftsbank" and "Ökobank" becoming the first SRI traders. Major influences are attributed to Green Parties, the 1991 Renewable Energy Act, information campaigns, and tax exemptions (Williams, 2005).

As of today, a variety of commercial SRI retail, mutual, and pension funds are offered to the public around the world. The establishment of retail funds and the adoption of SRI by major institutional investors matured SRI from a niche segment solution into a more mainstream option (Mathieu, 2000; Rosen, Sandler, & Shani, 1991; Sparkes & Cowton, 2004). The rise in SRI goes hand in hand with an upcoming of social and environmental stock exchange rating agencies, SRI impact measurement, social reporting, and environmental certifications in the Western world (Steurer, 2010). With the SRI market having reached unprecedented momentum, SRI nowadays accounts for a global phenomenon encompassing a wide range of different forms and diverse constituents.

Forms

SRI features various forms and foci to align financial considerations with ethical, moral, and social endeavors. The most common are "socially responsible screenings, shareholder advocacy, community investing and social venture capital funding" (Steurer et al., 2008). "Socially responsible screenings" are "double bottom-line analyses" of corporate economic performance and social responsibility. In screenings, financial market options are evaluated based on economic fundamentals as well as social features and corporate conduct externalities (Schueth, 2003). In addition to the traditional scanning of expected utility and volatility, screenings include qualitative examinations of intra- (e.g., corporate policies and practices, employee relations) and extra-organizational (e.g., externalities on current and future constituents) features of corporate conduct (Schueth, 2003). In general, screenings are based on the corporate track records of societal impacts, environmental performance, human rights attribution, and fair workplace policies, as well as health and safety standards outlined in CSR reports. Consequentially, screening leads to the inclusion or exclusion of corporations from portfolios based on social, environmental, and political criteria.

"Positive screenings" feature the selection of corporations with sound social and environmental records and socially responsible corporate governance (Renneboog et al., 2007). Areas of positive corporate conduct are human rights, the environment, health and safety, and labor standards, as well as customer and stakeholder relations. Corporations that pass positive screenings meet value requirements expressed in their social standards, environmental policies, labor relations, and community-related corporate governance. "Negative screenings" exclude corporations that engage in morally, ethically, and socially irresponsible activities. Proactive negative screenings refrain from entities with corporate conduct departing from international legal standards and/or implying negative social externalities (Renneboog et al., 2007). Negative screenings may address addictive products (e.g., liquor, tobacco, gambling), defense (e.g., weapons, firearms), and environmentally hazardous production (e.g., pollution, nuclear power production), but also social, political, and humanitarian deficiencies (e.g., minority discrimination, human rights violations). Specialty screens feature extraordinary executive compensations, abortion, birth control, animal testing, and international labor standard infringements. In 2005 the most common screenings in the United States were targeted at tobacco (US$ 159 billion in total net assets; approximately 28 percent); liquor (US$ 134 billion; 25 percent); gambling (US$ 41 billion; 7 percent); defense/weapons (US$ 34 billion; 6 percent); community impact (US$ 32 billion; 5 percent); labor concerns (US$ 31 billion; 5 percent); environmental issues (US$ 31 billion; 5 percent); consumer safety (US$ 28 billion; 5 percent); workplace diversity and equal employment opportunity (US$ 27 billion; 5 percent); faith-based objections (US$ 12 billion; 2 percent); adult entertainment (US$ 12 billion; 2 percent); human rights (US$ 11 billion; 2 percent); animal testing (US$10 billion; 2 percent); and abortion, healthcare, biotechnology, medical ethics, youth concerns, anti-family entertainment, and excessive executive compensation (US$ 5 billion; 1 percent).

Post-hoc negative screening implies divestiture as the removal of investment capital from corporations and/or markets. Divestiture is common to steer change in politically incorrect regimes, but also used to promote environmental protection, human rights, working conditions, animal protection, and health and safety standards (Broadhurst et al., 2003; McWilliams & Siegel, 2000). "Political divestiture" describes foreign investment flight from politically incorrect markets based on CSR information (Steurer, 2010). Political divestiture aims at forcing political change by imposing financial constraints onto politically incorrect regimes that depart from international law resulting in war, social conflict, terrorism, and human rights violations. Prominent cases are South Africa during the Apartheid regime and governmental human rights violations in Burma, as well as the current humanitarian crisis in Sudan's Darfur region.

Up to now the effects of negative screenings on corporations and whether divestment is associated with an increase or decrease of shareholder value are unclear. Unanswered remains the question if political divestiture grants first-mover advantages for early withdrawing entities, as politically fractionate markets lead to long-term economic decline (Posnikoff, 1997; Puaschunder, 2015a). Empirical investigations of political divestiture are primarily based on event studies. This methodology is limited as for refraining to take externalities on the wider constituent group into consideration, relatively short time frames under scrutiny, small sample sizes, and the irreplicability of unique political events (McWilliams, Siegel, & Teoh, 1999; Puaschunder, 2015b; Teoh, Welch, & Wazzan, 1999).

The majority of socially screened funds use multiple screens and sometimes complement screening with shareholder advocacy, community investing, and political interests. Based on transparent and accountable corporate policies and procedures, "shareholder advocacy" is the active engagement of shareholders in corporate policy making, managerial practices, and corporate social conduct (Little, 2008). Shareholder advocacy comprises "shareholder activism" and "dialogues" as well as "active endowments."

In their role as corporate owners, socially conscientious investors aim at positively influencing corporate conduct in "shareholder activism" (Schueth, 2003). Shareholder activism refers to shareholder groups engaging in "coordinated action to utilize their unique rights to facilitate corporate change" (Sparkes & Cowton, 2004, p. 51). Positive shareholder activism implies advocating for socially responsible corporate conduct in shareholder meetings in the United States. Shareholder resolutions provide formal communication channels on corporate governance among shareholders, management, and the board of directors. Resolutions can request information from the management and ask for changes in corporate policies and practices. In resolutions shareholders use their voting rights as a means to influence corporate behavior and steer corporate conduct in a more socially responsible direction (Little, 2008). In the United States, shareholder resolutions are managed by the US Securities and Exchange Commission. Shareholders who wish to file a resolution must own at least US$ 2,000 in shares in a given corporation or 1 percent of the corporate shares 1 year prior to filing proposals. Resolutions appear on the corporate proxy ballot, where they can be voted on by all shareholders or their representatives electronically, by mail, or in person at the annual meeting. The vast majority of shareholders exercise their voting rights by proxy. Proxy resolutions grant third parties rights to vote for shareholders on matters before the corporation (Little, 2008). Proxy resolutions on social issues and corporate governance generally aim at improving corporate policies and practices as well as encourage management to exercise good corporate citizenship with the goal of an increase in long-term shareholder value. Current trends comprise transparent and accountable proxy voting policies to support social and environmental responsibility. For example, mutual fund proxy disclosure regulations aim at making corporate records publicly available. Negative shareholder activism exerts activist influence and ranges from political lobbying, consumer boycotts, and confrontations geared by negative publicity to pressure corporations into socially responsible corporate conduct (Sparkes & Cowton, 2004).

Parties engaging in "shareholder dialogues" seek to influence corporate policies and practices without introducing a formal resolution for their concerns. Corporate management is attentive to shareholder dialogues about avoiding formal proxy resolutions and investment withdrawal. "Active endowments" emerged from academics establishing procedures for integrating social responsibility in university endowments. SRI campus advisory committees issue proxy voting guidelines as recommendations on proxy ballot votings. "Community investing" started in the 1970s with direct investment for unserved communities. Community investing involves investor set-asides and earmarks of investment funds for community development, but also features access to traditional financial products and services such as credits, equity, and banking products to low-income and at-risk communities (Schueth, 2003). Community development banks focus on lending and rebuilding lower-income segments. Community development credit unions grant access to credits to unserved communities. Community development loans provide credit for small businesses with a focus on sustainable development and resource conservation, but also sponsor community services. For individuals, community loans open avenues to affordable housing, education, and child and health care (Little, 2008; Schueth, 2003). Financial empowerment of micro-enterprises helps disadvantaged minorities by providing financial education, mentoring, and technical assistance. "Social venture capital funding" finances socially responsible start-ups and Social Entrepreneurs to foster the positive social impact of capital markets. Community development venture capital funds provide capital for small start-ups with growth potential in traditionally un(der)developed regions. The very many forms of Financial Social Responsibility embrace a wide range of SRI stakeholders and entities.

Stakeholders

Bridging the financial world with society, SRI comprises public and private economic (e.g., institutional and private investors), organizational (e.g., labor union representatives, banking executives, fiduciaries), and societal (e.g., representatives of international organizations, NGOs, public policy specialists, media representatives, academics) stakeholders. As information agents, banking executives inform clients about SRI and the benefit of Financial Social Responsibility. The largest segment of screened accounts includes private and institutional portfolios managed by fiduciaries (e.g., private equity executives, fund managers, investment managers) who are opinion leaders with a strong potential to advocate for SRI (Nilsson, 2008). Institutional investors range from public pension funds to small non-profit organizations featuring corporations, state and municipal governments, religious organizations, hospital and healthcare facilities, college and university endowments, and foundations and trade unions driving social and environmental endeavors. Private investors choose SRI for efficiency and long-term competitive advantages coupled with altruistic and personal social responsibility values and the need for innovation and self-expression (Cheah, Jamali, Johnson, & Sung, 2011; Puaschunder, 2011b).

In globalized financial markets, international organizations harmonize differing SRI practices by defining SRI standards and guiding Financial Social Responsibility implementation from a global governance perspective (Puaschunder, 2010). The UN Global Compact division leads the international administration of Financial Social Responsibility with the Principles for Responsible Investment (PRI) and the Responsible Investment in Emerging Markets Initiative. Throughout the Western world, public policy specialists regulate finance accountability and aid the adoption of socially responsible market evaluation criteria. NGOs monitor corporate conduct and shareholder activism as SRI prerequisites (Mohr et al., 2001). Labor union representatives implement social responsibility in financial markets—foremost in the areas of human rights, labor conditions, and minority empowerment. SRI was spearheaded by the academic community, especially finance experts, behavioral economists, sociologists, and social psychologists. Media representatives select and process information about socially responsible corporate conduct and Financial Social Responsibility.

While preliminary research connects leadership to responsibility (Druyen, 2012), our knowledge of stakeholder-specific SRI notions remains an open, cutting-edge research gap waiting to be investigated, not only due to the economic power and socio-political impetus of Financial Social Responsibility stakeholders, but foremost in the eye of the economic crises caused by social irresponsibility and ethical downfalls (Druyen, 2010).

SRI emergence in times of crisis

Social and ethical considerations have a long tradition in the wake of humanitarian, social, and environmental deficiencies (Williams, 2005). The first interest in corporate social conduct led ethical investors to fund socially responsible corporations at the beginning of the 20th century in the Western world (Ahmad, 2008; Sparkes, 2002; *The Wall Street Journal*, August 21, 2008). With the gradual post-World War II lifting of financial market restrictions in the United States, an individualization of financial asset allocations propelled ethical investing (Soros, 2008). Stakeholder pressure in connection with legislative information disclosure reforms and policy compulsion to develop social responsibility drove SRI throughout the Western world (Puaschunder, 2011c; Solomon, Solomon, & Norton, 2002).

SRI prospered in the wake of shareholder activism, civil rights campaigns, and social justice movements. Anti-Vietnam War institutional investors sold napalm-producing corporations' shares in the United States (Biller, 2007). Minority empowerment, consumer rights activism, and environmentalism leveraged sensitivity for Financial Social Responsibility in the industrialized world (Renneboog et al., 2007). Since 1969, the Council on Economic Priorities has rated corporate social and environmental performances. Starting in the 1970s, financial markets increasingly became attentive to socio-political circumstances in the Western world. SRI was introduced in the United States at a Yale University conference. Subsequently, universities established committees advocating for international oversight of social, environmental, and institutional aspects. The Investor Responsibility Research Center and Interfaith Center on Corporate Responsibility promoted shareholder advocacy and proxy resolutions in the United States. In 1971, the first modern SRI mutual fund was created by US Methodist clergy that aimed at divestiture from Vietnam War-involved corporations (Broadhurst et al., 2003). The Dreyfus Third Century Fund started avoiding "sin stocks" and improved labor standards in the following year in the United States. In 1972, activists criticized Harvard University for owning shares in petroleum corporations. Around the same time, political divestiture was first discussed in the case of the repressive Angolan government in the international context (Alperson, Tepper-Marlin, Schorsch, & Wil, 1991). By the mid-1970s, a significant number of governments enacted shareholder rights to address corporate activities that caused "social injury," and many universities established committees to advise trustees on SRI and shareholder rights in the United States. The Sullivan Principles fostered equal remuneration and workplace opportunities to empower minorities (Voorhes, 1999). Environmental catastrophes in Chernobyl and Bhopal, as well as the Exxon Valdez oil spill, triggered anti-nuclear and environmental concerns in stakeholders around the globe. Socially conscientious investors started positive screenings to identify and support corporations that paid attention to human rights, equal opportunities, labor relations, environmental protection, consumer safety, and community concerns. In 1981, the American Social Investment Forum was formed as a professional body for individual and institutional SRI constituents (Broadhurst et al., 2003). Political divestiture became prominent in the fight against the South African Apartheid regime, triggering a widespread divestiture trend of socially concerned investors, churches, cities, and states (Merriam Webster Dictionary, 2008; Puaschunder, 2015b).

In the 1990s, Financial Social Responsibility increasingly leveraged into global governance means and was perpetuated by the micro-finance and co-operative banking revolution in North America (Brenner, 2001). Corporate social conduct information and benchmarking of corporate social codes in combination with governmental regulation developed SRI in the United States. Institutional investors concurrently influenced corporate conduct and actively demanded corporate governance reforms to act on societal concerns. SRI reached unprecedented diversity, featuring a wide range of stakeholder social engagement and monitoring the possibilities of social, ethical, and environmental corporate performances (McCann, Solomon, & Solomon, 2003; Nilsson, 2008; Rosen et al., 1991; Steurer et al., 2008).

Around the turn of the millennium, the diminishing power of nation states in a globalizing world coupled with political libertarianism placed a greater share of social responsibility onto the private sector in the global context (Ahmad, 2008). An unprecedented interconnectivity of globalized financial markets strengthened the societal role of financial institutions, and global governance increasingly became a financial market feature (Soros, 2008). Financial Social Responsibility leveraged into an implicit fiduciary responsibility norm (Solomon et al., 2002; Sparkes & Cowton, 2004). In the given literature on contemporary Corporate Social

Responsibility (CSR) models, SRI has primarily been integrated in CSR models in the wake of legislative compulsion, global governance advocacy, and stakeholder pressure (Steurer, Martinuzzi, & Margula, 2012). Attentive to this trend, the UN Global Compact division launched the PRI to standardize SRI (Puaschunder, 2010). The 2008/09 World Financial Crisis perpetuated the demand for SRI (Puaschunder, 2011c).

Since the outbreak of the crisis, the societal call for social responsibility in corporate and financial markets has reached unprecedented momentum in the Western world. The revelation of corporate social misconduct and financial fraud steered consumers and investors to increasingly pay attention to social responsibility within market systems (Roberts, 2010). Media coverage of corporate scandals, fiduciary breaches, and astronomic CEO remuneration drove financial social conscientiousness. Stakeholder pressure advocated for information disclosure of corporate activities and governmental assistance of corporate social conduct. Governmental bail-outs fueled public claims for financial market regulation to lower the future negative consequences of agency default risks. Regained regulatory power was meant to implement social responsibility as a standard of sustainable markets. Public and private leaders as well as academics searched for financial social conscientiousness to enhance market structures and restore public trust in financial markets in the eye of corporate capital hoarding, liquidity traps, and the latest London Inter-bank Offered Rate scandal (*The Economist*, July 7, 2012; Tumpel-Gugerell, 2009).

The current widespread acknowledgment of financial social conscientiousness as a vital economic market ingredient, and regulatory renaissance in the finance world, are predicted to advance SRI (Duchac, 2008). SRI is an idea whose time has come. Financial Social Responsibility is fueled by socio-political deficiencies and economic turmoil. Socially responsible funds offer crisis-stable market options that are less volatile and not influenced by cyclical changes and whimsical market movements. Especially negative screenings are extremely robust in times of uncertainty—as socially conscientious investors remain loyal to values (McLachlan & Gardner, 2004; Puaschunder, 2011d). Given this track record of stability during times of societal and economic downturns, SRI nowadays appears as a favorable market strategy for lowering emergent risks.

Emergent risk theory

Globalization led to an intricate set of interactive relationships between individuals, organizations, and states (Centeno & Tham, 2012). To an increasing degree, the business of the world nowadays depends on other parts of the world doing their business well. Deepening nets of interactions challenge human foresight as fastened transactions transmit positive and negative externalities. Perturbations arising from novel interdependencies impose dangers for mankind. Over time and in crowds, one individual decision has no longer limited local effects but global consequences (Centeno & Tham, 2012; Centeno et al., 2013; Summers & Pritchett, 2012).

Globalization presents specific risks and challenges over and above those associated with other forms of market or system failure. The very logic of increasing globalization carries within it the seeds of its own destruction. Global systemic risk has increased exponentially in recent years and now affects the health, safety, quality of life, and standard of living of almost every citizen of the world. We now live in a world with the potential for natural and manmade disasters that we have never seen before, where our imaginations are often limited by narrow academic knowledge and the problem of induction regarding past experience. With the interdependence of massive global systems having caused systemic risk to increase exponentially, tangible risks in the finance sector now threaten global political, economic, and financial systems that affect citizens of every nation.

In webs of unconscious and fallible decision making, responsibility blurring over time can turn hard-to-foresee risks for collectives (Bazerman & Moore, 2008; Centeno & Tham, 2012; Leonhardt, Keller, & Pechmann, 2011). With growing globalization and a rising population, as well as a quickening of transfer speed, emergent risks developed into overlooked large-scale systemic problems (Centeno & Tham, 2012; Okamoto, 2009; Summers & Pritchett, 2012). Due to the global interconnectedness of the world, system failures can have potentially disastrous global consequences that can impact energy supplies, cause food shortages, threaten manufacturing processes, and jeopardize asset values ranging from housing prices to retirement savings to university endowments (Centeno et al., 2013).

Nowadays, the global web of trade, finance, travel, and communication can be best understood as a complex adaptive system. Featuring a large number of actors and a multitude of relations between them in a dense network of transactions, these webs are further complicated by their interactions and the causal loop of feedback. Also, adaptation occurs over time. The structure, nature, and challenges of this complex interactive system imbues undescribed emergent risks that no single authority or set of authorities can direct solely (Centeno et al., 2013). Emergent risks describe these threats of system failures, which emerge through individual parts' participation in and interaction with the system itself being prone to failures and collective action problems. The emergence of these risks may reflect both systemic causality and limitations of available information and human analytical ability—they are inevitably caused by the nature of the system, and yet we do not have the capacity to foresee these black swan risks with a small probability to occur but that have extreme impacts if they do so (Centeno et al., 2013).

The systemic risks associated with such emergent properties are significant and growing. Not only are we increasingly dependent on the continuous flow of complex global transactions for our daily lives, but increased connectivity and the exponential rise of associated interactions make the system more fragile even as its apparent robustness increases (Centeno et al., 2013). While some strategic attention has been paid to the susceptibility of the global system to intentional attack on critical nodes, much less has been attributed to the fact that interactions and apparently insignificant failures in distant and seemingly inconsequential nodes could produce a catastrophic outcome. The probability of such causal reactions may be small, yet the subsequent severity of such outcomes and even the increases in unexpected variance are high enough as to merit significant attention (Centeno et al., 2013).

Currently evolving emergent risk theory captures these insufficiently described shadows of the invisible hand in the era of globalization (Centeno & Tham, 2012; Miller & Rosenfeld, 2010). Building on behavioral economics research insights about fallible decision making, emergent risk theory sets out to capture the economic contagion of mutually dependent market actors. Emergent risk theory thereby depicts how individual decision-making fallibility can echo in economic systems and impose systemic risks within markets over time and in crowds. In seeking to understand the leap from the individual decision maker failing to recognize unethical consequences down the road and the mass of individuals being unaware of the cumulative and potentially disastrous outcomes of their actions, emergent risk theory innovatively sheds light on unexpected dangers in the age of globalization.

The Global Financial Crisis of 2007–08 is a stark example of global systemic risk. Emergent interdependencies among participants in capital markets thereby made it almost impossible for actors in the system to estimate the real risk of many transactions and their shared, and therefore blurred, social responsibility levels. Consequent failures produced a ramifying crisis through contagion and excess leverage. In the aftermath of the financial meltdown, the heightened demand for the understanding of emergent risks heralds a call for novel economic thinking. As prevailing behavioral economics have shed less attention on the collective outcomes of economic choices over time in the pre-2008 Financial Crisis era, new economic thinking must widen the interdisciplinary lens to study emergent risks in economic markets.

As globalization has led to an unprecedented interdependency of massive global systems causing systemic risk to increase exponentially (Centeno et al., 2013), emerging societal long-term downfalls have created a quest for global governance on systemic risks imbued in fallible market systems (Puaschunder, 2015a). Global systemic risks of over-indebtedness in the aftermath of the 2008/09 World Financial Crisis currently focus attention on implementing social responsibility and future orientation in financial markets (Puaschunder, 2015a). Systemic transnational risks and pressing social dilemmas beyond the control of singular nation states call for corporate social activities to back governmental regulation in crisis mitigation (Puaschunder, 2015a).

Future directions for SRI research

Globalization raises challenges of systemic market failure. Global systemic risks have increased exponentially in recent years and now affect all economic systems. We currently live in a world with the potential for economic market downfalls that we have never seen before, where our imaginations are often limited by incomplete information and missing knowledge that may, if gained, be biased by drawing from an obsolete past experience (Centeno et al., 2013). The systemic risks associated with financial systems are growing due to the increasing dependence on the continuous flow of complex global financial transactions. The exponential rise of financial market connections and associated interactions make the finance world more fragile. While some strategic attention has been paid to the susceptibility of the global financial system to critical nodes and times (e.g., the Millennium bug), much less focus has been given to the fact that interactions and apparently insignificant failures in distant and seemingly inconsequential nodes could produce catastrophic outcomes. The probability of such causal reactions may be small, yet the subsequent severity of such outcomes and even the increases in unexpected variance are high enough as to merit significant attention (Centeno et al., 2013). Understanding these novel, yet hardly described, risks arising because of the novel interconnectedness of global financial markets will help to design favorable governance structures and institutional arrangements that reduce the probability of system downfall dangers.

At first, the risks that unexpectedly lead to unpredicted dangers to system survival could become subject to scrutiny. With a special focus on the intangible dimensions of risk, attitudes toward risk may thereby become reflected. As the number and complexity of transactions and interactions makes any kind of conventional description or analysis arguably impossible to compute or comprehend, future research may seek to better understand the structure, nature, and challenges of this novel and complex interactive system (Centeno et al., 2013). A variety of systemic financial market risks can be explored, including catastrophic threats arising from individual failures, accidents, or disruptions present in financial markets through the process of contagion. Emerging risk as the problem that arises from new technologies or interdependencies may be contrasted to emergent risk as the threat to the individual parts produced by their participation in and interaction with the system itself (Centeno et al., 2013). The emergence of these risks may reflect both systemic causality and limitations of available information and also human analytical ability limitations to foresee the outcomes of cumulative actions. In an increasingly interconnected and fragile global network, small risks can become tipping points for catastrophic systemic failure. The development of new interpretations, understandings, and concepts of these risks will help estimate and weight the tradeoffs between the benefits of more risk and the concomitant threats. Capturing the negative consequences of international financial markets featuring a global web that has created a meta-structure with the potential for negative or catastrophic impacts on the real economy would thereby allow one to estimate the social and economic costs of emergent risks arising in the finance sector and the extent to which different countries are exposed to these dangers.

Research on emergent risk and concerted actions will lead to financial and economic systems gaining from long-term robustness. While the private sector and the finance world can benefit from more nuanced and realistic understandings of the nature of emergent risks, NGOs can focus their efforts on developing and strengthening economic infrastructures to avert emergent risks. A clearer definition of systemic risks in the finance world from different academic perspectives will not only prepare for policy-making studies to estimate the likelihood and costs of crises occurring, but also help understand the systemic characteristics of global networks and the inherent uncertainties within them. The information retrieved will help decide whether policies might best focus on remediating failures—in post-hoc clean-up after approaches, such as facilitating and speeding up responses to crises—or on constructing governance and preemptive regulatory regimes that make dangerous intra-system interactions less likely to occur (Centeno et al., 2013).

By paying attention to previous lessons in risk education and the cases in which such lessons have been effective in preventing risks, future research could include a meta-analysis of risk and its various meanings, beginning with the distinction between risk and uncertainty. An analysis of specific global networks and flows could comprise the fragility of the global financial system as exposed by the Global Financial Crisis of 2007–08 and systemic risk within global networks in a multidisciplinary fashion in order to derive regulatory and policy solutions to reduce the global dangers of systemic risk and create more robust systems. Adjusted risk-limiting regulations could be proposed alongside monitoring, inspection, and surveillance of economic and financial market systems. A precautionary principle approach to avert emergent risk could be introduced in the form of SRI.

Not only helping to understand emergent risks as a social construction and the politics thereof, SRI's potential to imbue trust in the 2008/09 World Financial Crisis economy can also be explored. After outlining the importance of emergent risk, the insights gained could be used to emphasize how education and the communication of risk can encourage SRI to limit the potential for future system failures and public policy conclusions to craft legislation and regulation to imbue financial social responsibility in economic markets. As a remedy, Financial Social Responsibility appears as an emergent risk prevention and viable means to avert future socially irresponsible financial conduct. Future research may comprise how SRI may be able to affect the nature of global systemic risk in economic theory and the prescriptive government regulation of financial networks. Studies related to the causes and consequences of global systemic risk could lead to recommendations on how SRI can be used to structure increasingly fragile systems and mitigate emergent risks. Understanding SRI as a means to lower systemic risks will allow one to strengthen the robustness of the global human-made organizational system and avert the negative externalities of globalized financial markets. Focusing on endogenous threats to the system but also endogenous remedy potentials will help to predict the threats to systems by individual actors or agents by the possible downfalls of financial markets.

In particular, SRI trend analyses with attention on the socio-economic success factors of Financial Social Responsibility and stakeholder-specific views in the aftermath of the 2008/09 World Financial Crisis could innovatively capture the crisis as a window of opportunity for acknowledging SRI. Through the prism of the interplay of financial markets and the real economy, an overall investigation of the social perception of SRI in the aftermath of the 2008/09 financial downturn could determine in what ways the financial crisis has changed the financial community's view of economic markets' social responsibility. Currently once-in-a-lifetime information on the social representations of financial social conscientiousness in post-crisis markets not only offers a unique historic snapshot of the prevailing economic Zeitgeist but also helps portray the potential of economic downturns to fortify ethicality in economic markets. Retrieving information on SRI success factors would allow recommendations on the optimum balance of deregulated market systems and governmental control. Concurrently investigating SRI supply and demand changes implied by the 2008/09 World Financial Crisis could foster our knowledge on the impact of organizational, institutional, and political factors on SRI development in times of crisis and allow one to derive recommendations on how SRI can serve in emergent risk prevention. Introducing financial social conscientiousness in emergent risk mitigation within globalized economic markets and a means to avert future financial crises could help imbue public trust in financial markets as a countercyclical means to overcome our current Age of Angst featuring corporate capital hoarding and liquidity traps perpetuated by the additional LIBOR/EURIBOR scandal (Coen & Roberts, 2012). Future research may thus advocate for understanding Financial Social Responsibility as a means to overcome emergent risks in order to improve financial market stability but also to restore trust in the global economy in the aftermath of the 2008/09 World Financial Crisis.

A preliminary literature review revealed a limited scientific investigation of SRI. Most studies focus on describing Financial Social Responsibility forms (De La Cuesta González & Valor Martinez, 2007; Little, 2008; Rosen et al., 1991; Williams, 2005). Holistic, empirical SRI studies are rare (Menz, 2010). The current qualitative and quantitative emergence of Financial Social Responsibility options coupled with the engagement of various stakeholders result in differing, novel SRI practices. Recently weakened market economies due to a missing understanding of real-world financial market responsibility underline the importance of a whole, rounded SRI picture to overcome socio-economic losses implied by the various Financial Social Responsibility notions of stakeholders. Building on state-of-the-art research on the social representations of the economy in times of crisis, a further in-depth scrutiny of stakeholder-specific perceptions of Financial Social Responsibility would help gain a holistic yet nuanced description of SRI.

A more stakeholder-specific investigation of Financial Social Responsibility with special attention to SRI success factors to imbue trust in financial markets in the aftermath of the 2008/09 World Financial Crisis could be gained by interviewing stakeholders about their opinion on Financial Social Responsibility during economic turmoil. Capturing social representations of SRI as a trust-bestowing means in times of crisis would allow the harmonizing of SRI standards and avert multi-stakeholder conflicts in understanding Financial Social Responsibility as a market-stabilizing means.

Financial Social Responsibility emerged out of social, environmental, and political deficiencies during times of crisis. In the past, financial social conscientiousness was propelled by a combination of humanitarian and environmental downfalls, stakeholder pressure, and constituents' social demands in combination with legislative coercion and policy compulsion. But what the current aftermath of the 2008/09 World Financial Crisis implies on SRI's supply and demand given an unprecedentedly globalized economic financial market may be explored in future research. As the number and complexity of transactions and interactions makes any kind of conventional analysis of the leap between fallible decision making and institutional ethicality downfalls impossible, SRI's potential to become a means to overcome emergent risks in the aftermath of the 2008/09 World Financial Crisis and a way to imbue trust in financial markets during times of economic upheaval could also be investigated with the help of large-scale mapping of globalization methods and quantitative databases.

Future theoretical and empirical research may feature qualitative and quantitative methodology in order to rationalize Financial Social Responsibility while imbuing ethicality in economic markets. After a stakeholder-specific literature review of Financial Social Responsibility, qualitative research may aim at gaining an in-depth understanding of stakeholder views on Financial Social Responsibility in order to determine SRI success factors in relation to the 2008/09 World Financial Crisis. Quantitative market analyses would thereby aim at capturing SRI supply-demand changes as well as Financial Social Responsibility potentials to avert emergent risks and bestow market actors with trust in post-crisis markets.

Shedding light on stakeholder-specific SRI facets will advance our knowledge on the vital ingredients for the functioning of market economies and drivers of trust in the global market economy (*The Economist*, July 7, 2012). The insights gained from qualitative expert interviews could be coupled with quantitative market analyses of the SRI supply and demand changes in the aftermath of the 2008/09 World Financial Crisis. Temporal comparisons of financial social conduct could retrieve information about the ongoing adaptation and adoption of SRI with attention on the interplay of public and private contributions in the aftermath of the 2008/09 World Financial Crisis.

Promoting socially conscientious investment as a financial market-stabilizing means has manifold implications. Knowledge of the stakeholder-specific success factors of Financial Social Responsibility will allow a harmoniously concerted SRI administration and reduce socio-economic losses due to the complexity of the novel phenomenon. Social representations of the economy during times of crisis will capture historically valuable insights on the societal echo of economic crisis and at the same time stimulate a vital dialogue among Financial Social Responsibility stakeholders to help social responsibility become more integrated in everyday financial decision making. Building on the preliminary findings of the current financial crisis as a driver of attention to ethicality (Puaschunder, 2015a), outlining the role of SRI in market risk mitigation will help stabilize financial markets. Aiding a rise of financial social conscientiousness will lower emergent risks while lifting entire market industries onto a more socially conscientious level (Glac, 2009). Overall, averting the emergent risks of irresponsible financial market conduct will help to foster a positive societal climate of trust in the post-2008/09 World Financial Crisis era. Unraveling financial social conscientiousness may thereby serve the overarching goal of financial market stability and improved economic conditions for this generation and the one following.

Conclusion

The 2008/09 World Financial Crisis underlined the importance of social responsibility for economic markets. Financial Social Responsibility is implemented in SRI, which bridges the finance world with society. In a plethora of emerging SRI options, a structured multi-stakeholder analysis of SRI in the aftermath of the 2008/09 World Financial Crisis is missing. Future research may capture SRI as a real-world relevant means to avert emergent risks within a globalized economy. A nested approach featuring qualitative and quantitative global measurements may aim at gaining information about the interaction of financial markets with the real-world economy. A qualitative analysis of Financial Social Responsibility could retrieve SRI as a means to lower emergent risks within institutionalized market systems in order to avert future economic failures. Capturing stakeholder-specific Financial Social Responsibility practices may aim at determining SRI success factors and aid in promoting SRI to diverse groups. Mapping globalization market tools and financial market databases could concurrently depict qualitative and quantitative SRI changes in the aftermath of the 2008/09 World Financial Crisis in order to delineate the potential of SRI to avert emergent risks in the aftermath of the 2008/09 financial market downturn. Outlining SRI during this unprecedented time of economic change and regulatory reform holds invaluable historic opportunities to outline the potential of a crisis to ingrain social responsibility and bestow market actors with trust in the global market economy. At the same time, spearheading financial social conscientiousness aids a successful SRI implementation in averting future economic market downfalls and follows the greater goal of economic stability and a sustainable global market economy.

Acknowledgments

The financial support of the Austrian Academy of Sciences, Fritz Thyssen Foundation, Inter-University Consortium of New York, Max Kade Foundation (New York), the New School for Social Research, the University of Vienna, and the Vienna University of Economics and Business is gratefully acknowledged. The author declares no conflict of interest. The author thanks the audiences of her presentations at the 2015 Academic Research Network Oxford Social and Sustainable Finance and Impact Investment Conference as well as at the Department of Global Business and Trade Vienna University of Economics and Business in March 2014 for valuable feedback. All omissions, errors, and misunderstandings in this piece are solely the author's.

References

Ahmad, M. (2008, January 24). Global CEOs at the World Economic Forum Annual Meeting cite sovereign wealth funds as the new power broker. *BI-ME.*

Alperson, M., Tepper-Marlin, A. T., Schorsch, J., & Wil, R. (1991). *The better world investment guide: One hundred companies whose policies you should know about before you invest your money. From the Council on Economic Priorities.* New York, NY: Prentice Hall.

Bazerman, M. H., & Moore, D. (2008). *Judgment in managerial decision making.* Hoboken, NJ: Wiley.

Beltratti, A. (2003). *Socially responsible investment in general equilibrium.* Retrieved August 12, 2015, from http://papers.ssrn.com/sol3/papers.cfm?abstract_id=467240

Biller, A. (2007). Socially responsible investing now part of the landscape. *Benefits Compensation Digest, 44,* 12.

Brenner, R. (2001). *The force of finance: Triumph of the capital markets.* New York, NY: Texere.

Broadhurst, D., Watson, J., & Marshall, J. (2003). *Ethical and socially responsible investment: A reference guide for researchers.* München, Germany: Saur.

Carroll, A. B. (1979). A three-dimensional model of corporate social performance. *Academy of Management Review, 4,* 497–505.

Centeno, M. A., Cinlar, E., Cloud, D., Creager, A. N., DiMaggio, P. J., Dixit, A. K., . . . Shapiro, J. N. (2013, April). *Global systemic risk* (Unpublished manuscript for research community). Princeton Institute for International and Regional Studies, Princeton University, Princeton, NJ.

Centeno, M. A., & Tham, A. (2012). *The emergence of risk in the global system* (Unpublished working paper). Princeton University, Princeton, NJ.

Cheah, E., Jamali, D., Johnson, J. E. V., & Sung, M. (2011). Drivers of corporate social responsibility attitudes: The demography of socially responsible investors. *British Journal of Management, 22*(2), 305–323.

Coen, D., & Roberts, A. (2012). The new age of uncertainty. *Governance, 25,* 5–9.

De La Cuesta González, M., & Valor Martinez, C. (2007). Fostering corporate social responsibility through public initiative: From the EU to the Spanish case. *Journal of Business Ethics, 55*(3), 275–293.

Druyen, Th. (2010, October). Reich ist nicht vermögend. Über die Verwirklichung des Guten. *Soziologie heute.*

Druyen, Th. (2012, May 22). Geld allein macht nicht glücklich. *Südwestdeutsche Zeitung.*

Duchac, J. (2008, December 15). *The perfect storm: A look inside the 2008 financial crisis.* Vienna University of Economics and Business talks special notes.

Glac, K. (2009). Understanding socially responsible investing: The effect of decision frames and trade-off options. *Journal of Business Ethics, 87,* 41–55.

Knoll, M. S. (2008). *Socially responsible investment and modern financial markets* (Unpublished working paper). University of Pennsylvania Law School, Philadelphia, PA.

Leonhardt, J. M., Keller, L. R., & Pechmann, C. (2011). Avoiding the risk of responsibility by seeking uncertainty: Responsibility aversion and preference for indirect agency when choosing for others. *Journal of Consumer Psychology, 21*(4), 405–413.

Little, K. (2008). *Socially responsible investing: Put your money where your values are*. New York, NY: Penguin.

Lynch-Fannon, I. (2007). The corporate social responsibility movement and law's empire: Is there a conflict? *Northern Ireland Legal Quarterly, 58*(1), 1–22.

Mathieu, E. (2000). *Response of UK pension funds to the SRI disclosure regulation*. London, UK: UK Social Investment Forum.

Matten, D., & Crane, A. (2005). Corporate citizenship: Toward an extended theoretical conceptualization. *Academy of Management Review, 30*, 166–179.

McCann, L., Solomon, A., & Solomon, J. F. (2003). Explaining the growth in UK socially responsible investment. *Journal of General Management, 28*(4), 15–36.

McLachlan, J., & Gardner, J. (2004). A comparison of socially responsible and conventional investors. *Journal of Business Ethics, 52*(1), 11–25.

McWilliams, A., & Siegel, D. (2000). Corporate social responsibility and financial performance: Correlation or mis-specification? *Strategic Management Journal, 21*, 603–609.

McWilliams, A., Siegel, D., & Teoh, S. W. (1999). Issues in the use of the event study methodology: A critical analysis of corporate social responsibility studies. *Organizational Research Methods, 2*, 340–365.

Menz, K. (2010). Corporate social responsibility: Is it rewarded by the corporate bond market? A critical note. *Journal of Business Ethics, 96*(1), 117–134.

Merriam Webster Dictionary. (2008). Retrieved August 12, 2015, from http://www.merriam-webster.com/

Milberg, W. (2013). A note on economic austerity in science, morality, and political economy. *Social Research: An International Quarterly, 80*(3), 697–714.

Miller, G., & Rosenfeld, G. (2010). Intellectual hazard: How conceptual biases in complex organizations contributed to the crisis of 2008. *Harvard Journal of Law and Public Policy, 33*(2), 807–840.

Mohr, L. A., Webb, D. J., & Harris, K. E. (2001). Do consumers expect companies to be socially responsible? The impact of corporate social responsibility on buying behavior. *Journal of Consumer Affairs, 35*(1), 45–72.

Nilsson, J. (2008). Investment with a conscience: Examining the impact of pro-social attitudes and perceived financial performance on socially responsible investment behavior. *Journal of Business Ethics, 83*(2), 307–325.

Okamoto, K. S. (2009). After the bailout: Regulating systemic moral hazard. *UCLA Law Review, 57*(1), 183–236.

Posnikoff, J. F. (1997). Disinvestment from South Africa: They did well by doing good. *Contemporary Economic Policy, 15*(1), 76–86.

Puaschunder, J. M. (2010). *On corporate and financial social responsibility* (Unpublished doctoral thesis). University of Vienna, Vienna, Austria.

Puaschunder, J. M. (2011a). *Ethical decision making under social uncertainty: An introduction of Überethicality*. Library of Congress United States of America Copyright Office, Copyright Catalogue TXu00178 2130/2011-11-04.

Puaschunder, J. M. (2011b). *Intergenerational equity as a natural behavioral law*. Library of Congress United States of America Copyright Office, Copyright Catalogue TXu001743422/2011-03-08.

Puaschunder, J. M. (2011c). *On the emergence, current state and future perspectives of socially responsible investment*. Harvard University Weatherhead Center for International Affairs Working Paper. Retrieved August 12, 2015, from http://wcfia.harvard.edu/publications/emergence-Current-State-And-Future-Perspectives-Socially-Responsible-Investment

Puaschunder, J. M. (2011d). *Socio-psychological motives of socially responsible investors*. Harvard University Weatherhead Center for International Affairs Working Paper. Retrieved August 12, 2015, from http://wcfia.harvard.edu/publications/socio-Psychological-Motives-Socially-Responsible-Investors

Puaschunder, J. M. (2015a). *On eternal equity in the fin-de-millénaire* (Unpublished manuscript). The New School, New York, NY.

Puaschunder, J. M. (2015b). When investors care about politics: A meta-synthesis of political divestiture studies on the capital flight from South Africa during Apartheid. *Business, Peace and Sustainable Development, 5*(24), 29–52.

Renneboog, L. D. R., Horst, J. R. T., & Zhang, C. (2007). *Socially responsible investments: Methodology, risk and performance* (Discussion Paper 2007-2031). Tilburg University Center for Economic Research, Tilburg, The Netherlands.

Roberts, A. S. (2010). *Disciplined democracies: Global capitalism and the new architecture of government*. Oxford, UK: Oxford University Press.

Rosen, B. N., Sandler, D. M., & Shani, D. (1991). Social issues and socially responsible investment behavior: Preliminary empirical investigation. *Journal of Consumer Affairs, 25*(2), 221–234.

Schueth, S. (2003). Socially responsible investing in the United States. *Journal of Business Ethics, 43*(3), 189–194.

Soana, M. (2011). The relationship between corporate social performance and corporate financial performance in the banking sector. *Journal of Business Ethics, 104*(1), 133–148.

Social Investment Forum Report. (2006, January 24). *Report on socially responsible investing trends in the United States*. Social Investment Forum Industry Research Program 10-year review.

Solomon, J. F., Solomon, A., & Norton, S. D. (2002). Socially responsible investment in the UK: Drivers and current issues. *Journal of General Management, 27*(3), 1–13.

Soros, G. (2008). *The new paradigm for financial markets: The credit crisis of 2008 and what it means*. New York, NY: Public Affairs.

Sparkes, R. (2002). *Socially responsible investment: A global revolution*. Cornwall, UK: Wiley.

Sparkes, R., & Cowton, Ch. J. (2004). The maturing of socially responsible investment: A review of the developing link with corporate social responsibility. *Journal of Business Ethics, 52*, 45–57.

Starr, M. (2008). Socially responsible investment and pro-social change. *Journal of Economic Issues, 42*(1), 51–73.

Stavins, R. N., Reinhardt, F. L., & Vietor, R. H. (2008). Corporate social responsibility through an economic lens. *Review of Environmental Economics and Policy, 2*, 219–239.

Steurer, R. (2010). The role of governments in corporate social responsibility: Characterizing public policies on CSR in Europe. *Policy Science, 43*, 49–72.

Steurer, R., Margula, S., & Martinuzzi, A. (2008). *Socially responsible investment in EU member states: Overview of government initiatives and SRI experts' expectations towards governments. Analysis of national policies on CSR, in support of a structured exchange of information on national CSR policies and initiatives*. Final report to the EU High-Level Group on CSR provided by the Research Institute for Managing Sustainability. Vienna University of Economics and Business.

Steurer, R., Martinuzzi, R.-A., & Margula, S. (2012). Public policies on CSR in Europe: Themes, instruments and regional differences. *Corporate Social Responsibility and Environmental Management, 19*, 206–227.

Summers, L. H., & Pritchett, L. (2012). *Societies of the world: The future of globalization: Issues, actors, and decisions*. Cambridge, MA: Harvard University Faculty of Arts and Sciences.

Sutton, M. (2004). Between a rock and a judicial hard place: Corporate social responsibility reporting and potential legal liability under Kasky v. Nike. *University of Missouri-Kansas City School of Law Review, 72*, 1159.

Teoh, S. H., Welch, I., & Wazzan, C. P. (1999). The effect of socially activist investment politics on the financial markets: Evidence from the South African boycott. *Journal of Business, 72*(1), 35–89.

Tumpel-Gugerell, G. (2009, June 15). *Monetary policy challenges in the light of the current financial market development* (Unpublished lecture notes). Vienna Alpbach Talks, Vienna, Austria.

Voorhes, M. (1999). *The US divestment movement: How sanctions work. Lessons from South Africa*. New York, NY: St. Martin's.

Williams, G. (2005). *Are socially responsible investors different from conventional investors? A comparison across six countries* (Unpublished working paper). University of Bath, UK.

Wolff, M. (2002). Response to "Confronting the critics." *New Academy Review, 1*, 230–237.

Zoellick, R. (2009, January 17). Time to herald the age of responsibility. *The Economist*.

15

SOCIALLY RESPONSIBLE INVESTMENTS AND ISLAMIC INVESTMENTS

Is there a difference?

Saeed Binmahfouz

The concept of Socially Responsible Investment (SRI) started with religious groups hundreds of years ago, when they made conscious efforts to avoid investing in sin industries such as those involved with alcohol, tobacco, gambling, and arms (Kinder & Domini, 1997; Sauer, 1997). In particular, in the early 1900s, the Methodist Church of the UK began to exclude sin stocks, and subsequently churches in the United States and Europe played an important role in spreading the concept of SRI to such markets (Louche & Lydenberg, 2006; White, 2005).

Despite the fact that SRI originated with religious groups, modern SRI activities started during the activist political climate in the 1960s and 1970s (Bauer, Koedijk, & Otten, 2005; Statman, 2005). These decades are considered a significant turning point for the contemporary practice of SRI. This is because this period witnessed the rise of "human rights," anti-war activism against the Vietnam War, opposition to apartheid in South Africa, increasing awareness of environmental protection, and employees' unions also becoming more involved and active (Hamilton, Jo, & Statman, 1993; Sauer, 1997; Statman, 2005; White, 2005).

During the late 1980s and early 1990s, the concept of SRI evolved and continued to grow. Instead of applying only negative screening criteria to exclude sin industries, positive screening criteria were also employed (Hamilton et al., 1993; Sauer, 1997; Statman, 2005). This approach would involve investing in companies that use alternative energy sources, support the community, have a good record in equal employment opportunities, adopt corporate governance practice, etc. More recently, the concept of SRI has been further developed and broadened by the entrance of mainstream institutional investors using the best-in-class and engagement approaches rather than just applying traditional exclusion and inclusion criteria.

The UN introduced the Principles for Responsible Investment (PRI) mandate in 2006 to promote awareness of environmental, social, and/or governance (ESG) issues and to thus ensure that they are considered in the investment process. This SRI mandate provides the framework for global SRI practice and is gaining acceptance among institutional investors around the world. In 2010, the principles were used by over 808 leading global institutional investors with over $22 trillion in total assets under management (AuM; EUROSIF, 2010). This shows that SRI is no longer considered a niche market for religious groups only. In fact, the current practice of SRI is indeed largely dominated by mainstream institutional investors (EUROSIF, 2014; USSIF, 2014).

As a result, the SRI market has witnessed tremendous growth in recent years, controlling around 40 percent and 18 percent of the total European and US assets, respectively, under professional management (EUROSIF, 2014; USSIF, 2014). Consequently, internationally recognized mainstream indices providers, such as FTSE, Dow Jones, Morgan Stanley, and Standard & Poor's, have introduced SRI indices to their indices family. This was done to meet the growing demand for such types of investments and in recognition of the acceptability of the SRI industry by mainstream investors.

The Islamic economic and finance system is perceived as a socio-economic and finance system which requires that ethicality and morality be considered in economic activities, because of the religion's embedded ethical values such as fairness, justice, and equity (Chapra, 1985; Obaidullah, 2005; Siddiqi, 2004). The underlying features of an Islamic economic system derive from the objectives of *Sharia* (Islamic Law), which Al Ghazali identifies as promoting human beings' welfare through the protection of their five basic interests (*masalih*): religion, life, reason, progeny, and property (Siddiqi, 2004). These five objectives are, however, not exhaustive. For example, Ibn Taymiya argued that securing benefits for people and protecting them from harm was the general umbrella under which the *Sharia* objectives could be covered, whereas Ibn Aashur stated that the objectives of *Sharia* are to reform this world and to eliminate corruption (Siddiqi, 2004).

The Ethical Investment Research Services defines a green or ethical SRI fund as a fund where the choice of investments is influenced by one or more social, environmental, or other ethical criteria. Thus, by definition, Islamic investment can be considered under the broad umbrella of SRI, since, similar to SRI, it applies ethical screening criteria that exclude certain industries for non-financial reasons.

The modern Islamic Finance and Investment practice started in the 1970s with the establishment of the first Islamic banks. Subsequently, such Islamic banks spread around Muslim countries, as well as being accommodated by global commercial and investment banks, such as HSBC, Deutsche, Citigroup, UBS, Barclays Capital, Merrill Lynch, and Morgan Stanley (Ghoul & Karam, 2007; Hussein & Omran, 2005). As at 2014, it was estimated that the global total of Islamic Finance assets is $1.87 trillion, and this figure is expected to grow further in the coming years (IFSB, 2015). These figures cover 1,161 Islamic funds around the world, with a total estimated AuM of $75.8 billion as of 2014 (IFSB, 2015).

Similar to SRI indices, the introduction of Islamic indices by globally reliable index providers, such as Dow Jones and FTSE, in the late 1990s, and subsequently by Morgan Stanley and Standard & Poor's, was also a significant turning point for the development of the Islamic investment industry. It supports the Islamic mutual fund industry by promoting transparency, as well as by showing the acceptance of Islamic investment by mainstream players in the industry.

This chapter aims to provide an overview and comparison of two growing types of investments: socially responsible and Islamic.

The chapter is structured as follows:

- Fundamentals and screening process
- Growth and market share
- Sector exposure and investment style of SRI and Islamic investments
- Convergences and divergences between SRI and Islamic investments
- Social responsibility of Islamic investments
- Classification of Islamic investments
- Conclusion.

Fundamentals and screening process

This section discusses the fundamentals and the screening process of both SRI and Islamic investments.

Socially Responsible Investments

Although the concept of SRI started with religious groups avoiding investing in sin industries, as indicated earlier, there is no clear definition of the current practice of SRI. In fact, the definition of SRI is too broad and can vary greatly, as SRI criteria tend to be subjective and controversial, since they rely on individuals' values and beliefs, rather than agreed-upon criteria. While one criterion is acceptable according to one Socially Responsible Investor, it might not be acceptable or may even be totally ignored by another. For example, some Socially Responsible Investors may consider the ethical aspects of the investment, whereas others focus more on the environmental issues. Therefore, Socially Responsible Investors should consider all the available SRI products or approaches to find which fits best with their philosophy, as well as their risk and return requirements.

Nevertheless, it is generally accepted that SRI combines investors' financial objectives with their concerns about ESG issues (EUROSIF, 2014; USSIF, 2014). Clearly, the concept of SRI has significantly evolved and broadened from only excluding certain stocks to now covering one or more of the elements indicated above. There are various approaches/strategies that are used for SRI, such as screening (negative and positive criteria), best in class, engagement, and community investing (USSIF, 2012). These approaches can be used in combination or individually. A brief description of the major SRI approaches/strategies follows.

Screening approach

There are two main branches of SRI screening criteria: negative and positive. Negative screening criteria describe a traditional SRI approach that excludes certain sectors/companies which do not meet social, environmental, or ethical standards from the SRI portfolios (UKSIF, 2007). Such a screening method was used solely by the earlier "religious" Socially Responsible Investors to avoid sin stocks, such as tobacco, alcohol, gambling, etc. In contrast, positive screening has also been adopted by Socially Responsible Investors to invest in companies with a commitment to socially responsible business practices (UKSIF, 2007). This is to invest in profitable companies which also make positive contributions to society, such as companies that use alternative energy sources, contribute to the control of pollution, have equal employment opportunities, have good employee relations, etc. (USSIF, 2010).

In fact, Socially Responsible Investors tend to use a combination of both negative and positive screening criteria rather than just one or the other (Hamilton et al., 1993; Sauer, 1997). Thus, it is a common mistake to assume that SRI screening is simply exclusionary and only involves negative screening (USSIF, 2010). The screening approach also known as "ESG" incorporation is sometimes used to select companies that support ESG practices. Currently, there are specialized "thematic" SRI mutual funds that apply positive screening to invest in a particular positive industry, for example a fund that focuses on environmental technology (EUROSIF, 2010).

It should be noted that SRI screening criteria, both negative and positive, vary from one Socially Responsible Investor to another, since there is no consensus on a fixed set of negative/positive screening criteria (UKSIF, 2007). In fact, Socially Responsible Investors can set their own negative and positive criteria in order to fulfill their beliefs and concerns. For example, some Socially Responsible Investors may screen out a tobacco company from their investment portfolios, since it is against their religion or belief. In contrast, other Socially Responsible Investors might invest in a tobacco company because it has equal employment opportunities or supports the local community.

The best-in-class approach

While a screening approach might screen out certain sectors/companies, the best-in-class approach is used to select the companies that are best in their sectors, in terms of financial performance, the environment, and social and corporate governance. This is the case regardless of the sector that the companies are involved in. In particular, the best-in-class approach, adopted by the Dow Jones Sustainability Index (DJSI), tends to concentrate equally on three elements (economic, environmental, and social criteria) without excluding certain sectors (Dow Jones, 2013). For example, an oil company can be screened if it has a distinguished record in terms of financial, environmental, and social performance when compared to its peers (UKSIF, 2007). The concept of the best-in-class approach has been adopted by mainstream indices providers such as Dow Jones, which launched the DJSI in 1999. Subsequently, other sustainability indices have also adopted the best-in-class approach to meet the growing demand for such types of market benchmarks (White, 2005).

The best-in-class approach aims to achieve an industry weighting, which approximates the weighting of the relevant conventional benchmark index, since it does not totally exclude certain industries. For example, the DJSI and the Dow Jones Sustainability Index Europe (DJSISTOXX) both select the top 10 percent and 20 percent in each sector, from their broader conventional indices Dow Jones Industrial Average (DJIA) and Dow Jones STOXX (DJSTOXX), respectively (Dow Jones, 2013). This ensures that each sector will be represented in the SRI index. As a result, unlike other SRI approaches, the best-in-class approach does not seem biased toward certain sectors or small companies. This is because each sector will be represented in the index; also, the best-in-class companies tend to be large in nature (Vermeir, Velde, & Corten, 2005). Thus, it is argued that the best-in-class approach is about creating long-term value and managing the investment risk, rather than being about a set of ethical beliefs.

Engagement approach (or shareholder resolutions/voting)

Unlike the screening and the best-in-class approaches, the engagement approach does not require certain criteria for inclusion or exclusion of companies from SRI portfolios. Rather, it influences the companies to adopt environmental, social, ethical, and/or corporate governance practice by opening dialogue with senior management or using shareholder advocacy through a voting proxy (UKSIF, 2007). In particular, shareholder advocacy involves Socially Responsible Investors who take an active role as the owners of stock in a corporation by filing and co-filing shareholder resolutions on SRI business practice topics. Then, shareholder resolutions are presented, as a vote, to all owners of a corporation. Such action in turn puts pressure on company management, often gets media attention, and educates the public on SRI issues (USSIF, 2010). Also, different fund managers may engage in different SRI issues, operating either unilaterally or in collaboration with other managers (UKSIF, 2007).

The engagement approach can be either combined with the exclusion/inclusion screening approach or used on its own. Socially Responsible Investors who only adopt the engagement approach do not choose companies based on predetermined criteria other than financial performance. Therefore, applying the engagement approach on its own as an SRI approach does not tend to affect the investment universe, the investment strategy, or the investment practice and decisions (such as asset allocation, stock selection, level of diversification, or any other strategic or tactical investment decision). Such an approach has been adopted by large mutual funds and mainstream institutional investors—especially pension funds—and many of the socially responsible pension funds tend to concentrate solely on this approach (EUROSIF, 2010; UKSIF, 2007; USSIF, 2010). This might be because this SRI approach allows mainstream institutional investors to adopt socially responsible practice, while in the meantime their investment universe and choice are not affected.

According to USSIF (2014), from 2012 through to 2014, 27 management firms and 175 institutional investors, including public funds, labor funds, religious investors, foundations, and endowments, filed or co-filed proposals that supported SRI practices. These institutions and money managers in the United States collectively controlled $1.72 trillion in assets at the end of 2014. In contrast, in Europe, the engagement approach represented €3.27 trillion of the total managed assets in 2013; the UK is the leader among EU countries with half of European assets, followed by the Netherlands (EUROSIF, 2014).

Community investing approach (Impact Investing)

Unlike other SRI approaches which involve investing in stock markets (or companies), community investing pools capital from investors and lenders to provide access to basic banking products to local communities underserved by traditional financial services (UKSIF, 2007; USSIF, 2010). This can be done either directly or through channels such as local community development banks, credit unions, loan funds, and community development venture capital funds (EUROSIF, 2012). Thus, community investing aims to support local communities by financing housing, healthcare, small business creation, the development of facilities, and the empowerment of women and minorities, creating local jobs, and also providing the required training and expertise for such groups to enable them to succeed and return the loan (USSIF, 2010).

It is worth emphasizing that community investing is not a charity, but is rather an investment strategy used by Socially Responsible Investors to get competitive returns on their investment and in the meantime helping the underserved communities (USSIF, 2010). According to EUROSIF (2012), the biggest motivation for social investing is to contribute to sustainable development and local communities, but interestingly, financial considerations such as return and risk management feature higher than philanthropic or fiduciary concerns. However, the main investor concerns for such an investment are on product access and design, as well as the relative lack of expertise.

It should be noted that the European Social Investment Forum (EUROSIF) further classifies the screening approach to exclusions and norm-based screening. Norm-based screening involves the screening of investments according to their compliance with international standards and norms such as those developed by the UN and UN agencies. Moreover, EUROSIF considers the integration approach, whereby investors consider ESG risk within traditional financial analysis as an approach toward SRI. Such an SRI approach is gaining more and more popularity and became the second largest SRI approach in Europe, controlling €5,232,120 billion in 2013 (EUROSIF, 2014).

Table 15.1 illustrates SRI screening criteria applied by the major global indices providers. As can be seen from Table 15.1, while Dow Jones applies the best-in-class SRI approach, FTSE employs various sets of positive and negative screening criteria. On the other hand, to meet the demand of different Socially Responsible Investors, Morgan Stanley Capital International

Table 15.1 SRI screening criteria of the major global indices providers

Dow Jones		To meet the sustainability requirements, companies must be in the top 10 percent of their industries based on a sustainable business practice model established by SAM (Sustainability Asset Management Group) that covers long-term economic, environmental, and social criteria. Thus, the sustainability index follows the positive best-in-class social responsibility screening approach where no sector is excluded.
FTSE		*Inclusion Criteria*: eligible companies must meet criteria requirements in five areas (working toward environmental sustainability, upholding and supporting universal human rights, ensuring good supply chain labor standards, countering bribery, and mitigating and adopting to climate change). *Exclusion Criteria*: companies which have involvement in the following industries are excluded: producing tobacco, manufacturing either whole, strategic parts, or platforms for nuclear weapon systems, or manufacturing whole weapon systems.
MSCI	Socially Responsible	*Inclusion Criteria*: these indices target companies with high ESG ratings relative to their sector peers, to ensure the inclusion of the best-in-class companies from an ESG perspective. *Exclusion Criteria*: companies that are involved in the following activities are excluded: alcohol, gambling, tobacco, military weapons, civilian firearms, nuclear power, adult entertainment, and genetically modified organisms. Additionally, in order to ensure a high minimum level of ESG performance, any company that has an ESG rating of "BBB" or lower, or an Impact Monitor controversy assessment of severe or very severe, is not eligible for inclusion.
MSCI*	Sustainability	The indices are designed to provide exposure to companies that have high ESG performance. Any company which has an ESG rating of "B" or lower or an Impact Monitor controversy assessment of severe or very severe is not eligible for inclusion in the index. This rating criterion ensures a high minimum level of ESG performance, consistent with the aim of including only the best-in-class companies in the index.

Source: Based on official indices websites (2013).

* MSCI provides a range of different SRI indices such as Socially Responsible, Sustainability, Catholic Values, Broad ESG, and ESG Select. The table presents only two types of MSCI SRI indices.

(MSCI) provides a range of different SRI indices such as Socially Responsible, Sustainability, Catholic Values, Broad ESG, and ESG Select, which all adopt various SRI approaches. Thus, Table 15.1 confirms that there is no set of agreed SRI criteria adopted by all Socially Responsible Investors, as such investors choose to adopt the SRI criteria that comply with their value systems and beliefs.

Islamic investments

According to Obaidullah (2005), the most distinctive feature of the Islamic economic and finance system is the prohibition of *ribā* (refers to interest-based activities in this chapter), *gharar* (ambiguity or deception in commercial contracts), *maysir* (pure game of chance "gambling"), and *Sharia* (impermissible businesses such as those involving alcohol, tobacco, and pork-related products). There are two categories of *Sharia* investment screening criteria: sector screening criteria and financial screening criteria (Binmahfouz & Habib, 2014). These two

Sharia screening criteria ensure the compliance of the company with *Sharia* principles. *Sharia* sector screening and financial screening criteria are discussed next.

Sector screening criteria

There are certain businesses that violate *Sharia* rules and hence must be excluded from any Islamic investments, such as tobacco, alcohol, pornography, the casino, pork-related products, conventional finance and insurance, etc. (Obaidullah, 2005). Once a company passes the sector screening criteria and its core business is *Sharia*-permissible, it must pass the financial screening criteria in order to be a *Sharia*-compliant company. However, if the company fails to pass the sector screening criteria, it will be excluded from any further *Sharia*-compliant investment consideration. Derigs and Marzban (2008) indicate that *Sharia* sector screening alone excludes around 23 percent of the conventional Standard & Poor's 500 investment universe for their *Sharia* non-compliance.

According to Derigs and Marzban (2008), there are different industry classification codes used across the industry for *Sharia* screening. Standard & Poor's and MSCI perform screening based on the Global Industry Classification Standard (GICS), a standard which was jointly developed by both. Dow Jones and FTSE also use a self-developed coding system called the Industry Classification Benchmark (ICB) that is very similar to the GICS coding system.

Financial screening criteria

Unlike conventional SRI, Islamic investments have to comply with certain financial screening criteria, in order to be *Sharia*-compliant (Ghoul & Karam, 2007). The purpose of the financial screening criteria is to exclude companies with unacceptable levels of conventional debt, liquidity, interest-based investment, and/or impure income (Binmahfouz & Habib, 2014).

Table 15.2 shows both qualitative sector screening criteria and quantitative financial screening criteria employed by the major global Islamic indices providers and Accounting and Auditing Organization for Islamic Financial Institutions (AAOIFI) standards (AAOIFI, 2004).

Table 15.2 Sector and financial screening criteria based on the major global Islamic indices providers and AAOIFI standards

Dow Jones	*Industry Type*—excludes companies that represent the following lines of business: alcohol, tobacco, pork-related products, conventional financial services, defense/weapons, and entertainment.
	Financial Ratios—excludes companies that exceed 33 percent of the following: total debt divided by trailing 24-month average market capitalization, the sum of a company's cash and interest-bearing securities divided by trailing 24-month average market capitalization, and accounts receivables divided by trailing 24-month average market capitalization.
	Industry Type—excludes companies that represent the following lines of business: alcohol, tobacco, pork-related products and non-*halal* food, conventional financial services, defense/weapons, and entertainment.
FTSE	*Financial Ratios*—excludes companies where the following is true: total debt divided by total assets less than 33 percent, the sum of a company's cash and interest-bearing securities divided by total assets less than 33 percent, accounts receivables and cash divided by total assets less than 50 percent, and total interest and non-compliant activities income should not exceed 5 percent of total revenue.

(Continued)

Table 15.2 Sector and financial screening criteria based on the major global Islamic indices providers and AAOIFI standards *(Continued)*

MSCI	*Industry Type*—excludes companies that represent the following: alcohol, tobacco, pork-related products, conventional financial services, defense/weapons, and gambling/casino, music, hotel, cinema, and adult entertainment. *Financial Ratios*—excludes companies that exceed 33 percent of the following: total debt over total assets, sum of a company's cash and interest-bearing securities over total assets, and sum of a company's accounts receivables and cash over total assets.
Standard & Poor's	*Industry Type*—excludes business activities related to the following: advertising and media, alcohol, conventional financial services, gambling, pork, pornography, tobacco, cloning, and the trading of gold and silver on a cash-deferred basis. *Financial Ratios*—excludes companies that exceed 33 percent of the following: total debt divided by trailing 36-month average market capitalization, the sum of a company's cash and interest-bearing securities divided by trailing 36-month average market capitalization, and accounts receivables divided by trailing 36-month average market capitalization.
AAOIFI	*Industry Type*—excludes companies whose nature of business is not *Sharia*-permissible. *Financial Ratios*—excludes companies whose interest-based debt or interest-based deposit exceeds 30 percent of market capitalization. The total market value of assets, benefits, and rights should not be less than 30 percent of the total asset value of the corporation. The amount of income generated from the prohibited component does not exceed 5 percent of the total income of the corporation.

Source: Based on official indices websites (2013).

As can be seen from Table 15.2, there is agreement among the *Sharia* supervisory boards of the major Islamic indices providers to exclude sectors/companies which have involvement in industries involving alcohol, tobacco, pork-related products, conventional financial services, and entertainment, as these areas of business are deemed *Sharia*-impermissible. However, there tends to be disagreement between *Sharia* supervisory boards as to whether to consider weapons/defense and advertising and media sectors as *Sharia*-impermissible or not, as Standard & Poor's Islamic index does not exclude the weapons/defense sector but excludes the advertising and media sector.

In contrast, it can also be noticed that there seems to be no general consensus among *Sharia* supervisory boards on financial screening criteria in terms of financial ratios, thresholds, and the divisor used, and the disagreement among scholars in such screening is much more pronounced than in sector screening.

Growth and market share

The growth and market share of SRI and Islamic investment are discussed next in this section.

Socially Responsible Investment

As pointed out previously, SRI has enjoyed a massive growth in market share over the last decade, with total global SRI controlling around 40 percent and 18 percent of the total European and US AuM, respectively (EUROSIF, 2014; USSIF, 2014). Also, recently, SRI has gained popularity in other countries such as Canada, Australia, and Japan (EUROSIF, 2010). This section illustrates the growth and market shares of SRI in the United States and Europe, since they are the major markets for SRI.

US SRI market

US SRI accounted for $6.57 trillion in 2014, which reflects the fact that around 18 percent of the total $36.8 trillion AuM in the United States applies at least one SRI approach (USSIF, 2014). This implies that nearly one out of every six dollars invested in the United States is involved in SRI.

Table 15.3 shows several important things regarding the US SRI market. First, it can be seen that there was a tremendous rate of growth in the US SRI market between 1995 and 2014, increasing from only $639 billion to $6.57 trillion. This implies that, from 1995 to 2014, the US SRI universe has increased 929 percent, with a compound annual growth rate (CAGR) of 13.1 percent (USSIF, 2014). Second, in terms of SRI approaches, the total of $6.57 trillion in the United States—as of 2014—is made up of ESG incorporation, accounting for $6.20 trillion, whereas shareholder resolutions control around $1.72 trillion. It should be noted that the overlapping strategies ($1.4 trillion) must be subtracted to avoid double counting. Third, while the ESG incorporation approach dominates the US SRI market with tremendous growth between 2012 and 2014, shareholder resolution and community investing recently has gained acceptance.

It can be seen from Table 15.4 that the US SRI funds industry has also increased dramatically between 1995 and 2014, in terms of both total NAV and number of funds. The total NAV of US SRI funds rose from only $12 billion with 55 funds to $4.306 trillion with 925 funds, over the period of 1995 to 2014. This figure consists of all different types of investment funds, including mutual funds, annuity funds, closed end funds, exchange traded

Table 15.3 US SRI market between 1995 and 2014 (figures in trillions)

SRI approach	*1995*	*1997*	*1999*	*2001*	*2003*	*2005*	*2007*	*2010*	*2012*	*2014*
ESG Incorporation	$0.16	$0.53	$1.49	$2.01	$2.14	$1.68	$2.09	$2.51	$3.25	$6.20
Shareholder Resolutions	$0.47	$0.73	$0.92	$0.89	$0.45	$0.70	$0.74	$1.49	$1.53	$1.72
Community Investing	$0.00	$0.00	$0.01	$0.01	$0.01	$0.02	$0.03	$0.04	$0.06	N/A
Overlapping Strategies*	N/A	($0.08)	($0.26)	($0.59)	($0.44)	($0.11)	($0.15)	($0.98)	($1.12)	($1.40)
Total	$0.63	$1.18	$2.16	$2.32	$2.16	$2.29	$2.71	$3.06	$3.72	$6.52

Source: Adapted from USSIF (2010, 2012, 2014).

* Overlapping strategies involved in some combination of ESG incorporation, filing shareholder resolutions, or community investing are subtracted to avoid the potential effects of double counting.

Table 15.4 Figures of US Socially Responsible funds incorporating ESG screening from 1995 to 2014 (NAV figures in billions)

	1995	*1997*	*1999*	*2001*	*2003*	*2005*	*2007*	*2010*	*2012*	*2014*
Number	55	144	168	181	200	201	260	493	720	925
NAV	$12	$96	$154	$136	$151	$179	$202	$569	$1,013	$4,306

Source: USSIF (2014).

funds, alternative investment funds, and other types of pooled products, but excludes separate account vehicles and community investment institutions (USSIF, 2014). It can also be seen that the US SRI fund industry has continued to enjoy sharp growth since 2007, and remarkably between 2012 and 2014. It rose from 720 funds with $1.013 trillion NAV in 2012 to 925 funds with $4.306 trillion NAV in 2014.

European Socially Responsible Investment market

Similar to the US market, the European market enjoyed a rapid increase in SRI with a significant growth in market share. According to EUROSIF (2014), around 40 percent of the total €16.8 trillion European AuM have policies in place to exclude certain companies believed to be socially irresponsible.

According to Table 15.5, there was a rapid growth in most of the European SRI strategies between 2005 and 2013. Furthermore, Table 15.5 illustrates the main European SRI strategies applied and their market share. As can be seen, among the European SRI strategies, exclusion is the dominant strategy; second is integration, followed then by norms-based screening and engagement strategies respectively, whereas best-in-class, sustainability themed, and Impact Investing strategies account only for a small portion of overall European SRI. It should be noted that the market share and the growth rate of each SRI strategy varies greatly from one European country to another.

Furthermore, according to EUROSIF (2014), institutional investors account for 96.6 percent of total European SRI, whereas retail investors account only for 3.4 percent (as of 2013). This is despite the fact that 31 percent of European AuM are in retail (EUROSIF, 2012). Figure 15.1 shows the main types of European institutional investors and their SRI market share, by volume of SRI assets. It can be seen that the largest player is the public pension fund which accounts for 63.4 percent of total SRI of European institutional investors, followed by universities and other academics with 20.3 percent, and then insurance companies and mutual funds with 12 percent. Also, the figure indicates that corporate/occupational pension funds, religious institutions and charities, and public authorities control only 1.9 percent, 1.3 percent, and 0.4 percent of total SRI of European institutional investors, respectively. This shows that religious institutions account for only a negligible portion of the total European SRI market, which implies a shift of the SRI market toward mainstream institutional investors.

Table 15.5 European SRI market growth by strategy between 2005 and 2013 (figures in € millions)*

EUROPE (13 countries)	*2005*	*2007*	*2009*	*2011*	*2013*
Sustainability Themed	6,941	26,468	25,361	48,090	58,961
Best in Class	57,816	130,315	132,956	283,206	353,555
Norms-Based Screening	N/A	N/A	988,756	2,132,394	3,633,794
Exclusions	335,544	1,532,865	1,749,432	3,584,498	6,853,954
Engagement/Voting	728,837	1,351,303	1,668,473	1,762,687	3,275,930
ESG Integration	639,149	1,024,925	2,810,506	3,164,066	5,232,120
Impact Investing	N/A	N/A	N/A	8,750	20,269

Source: Adapted from EUROSIF (2014).

* Overlapping strategies should be considered to avoid double counting.

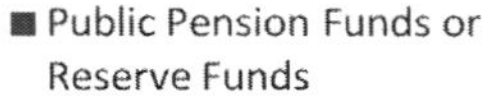

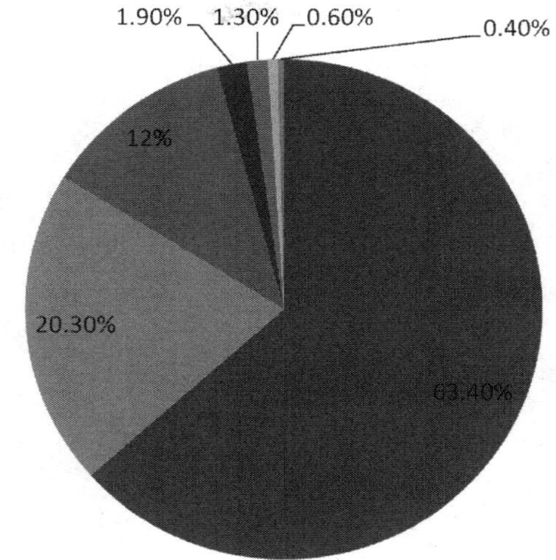

Figure 15.1 Types of European institutional investors and their SRI market share
Source: Based on EUROSIF (2010).

Drivers for growth and market share of SRI

There seem to be several main causes of the high growth in the market share of SRI. These are illustrated below.

PUBLIC AWARENESS AND CONCERNS

There has been a demand increase for SRI, as a result of increased public awareness of the negative impact of ignoring SRI on the environment, such as global warming and climate change (EUROSIF, 2010). Equally important are corporate scandals, such as Enron, Tyco, and WorldCom, which have also increased awareness in both regulators and the general public of the importance of corporate governance practice; this also strongly supports SRI. In addition, the recent financial crisis has made investors more aware of the need to integrate ESG risk in the investment selection process (EUROSIF, 2010).

LEGISLATION AND DISCLOSURE REQUIREMENTS

SRI legislation in the United States and Europe is one of the key drivers of SRI practice. It influences pension funds to disclose their attitudes and actions toward SRI practice, and how they manage ESG risk, despite not necessarily requiring them to adopt SRI policies (EUROSIF, 2010; USSIF, 2010). For example, under the 1995 UK Pensions Act, occupational and stakeholder pensions are required to have a "Statement of Investment Principles," which must in turn be made available to members on request and must set out the scheme's approach to disclose ethical and SRI issues (UKSIF, 2007). Also, pension funds in other European countries are required by regulation to disclose the socially responsible attitudes and actions of their investment to their clients (EUROSIF, 2010).

At a European parliamentary level, there is discussion about forcing institutional investors into further SRI disclosure (EUROSIF, 2010). In Australia, regulation goes beyond forcing the financial product providers to disclose the social responsibility position of their investment. It also requires financial advisors to ask if their clients regard environmental, social, or ethical considerations as being important in their investment choice, which in turn increases public awareness about the availability of such investment products (Bauer, Otten, & Rad, 2006). According to USSIF (2010), more than 52 percent of institutional investors said they incorporate SRI due to regulation or legislation above any other reason. EUROSIF (2014) finds that legislation is the second most important driver for SRI in Europe.

EXTERNAL PRESSURE

External pressure—such as media and international organizations—has put a greater burden on companies and institutional investors to adopt SRI practices (EUROSIF, 2010). For example, at the UN level, the introduction in 2006 of the PRI mandate—which has been signed up to by leading global institutional investors—provides a framework for global SRI practice to ensure that ESG issues are considered in the investment process. Such a mandate is gaining global acceptance for institutional investors around the world, and the principles in 2010 were signed up to by over 808 leading global institutional investors, with over $22 trillion total AuM (EUROSIF, 2010).

ACADEMIC RESEARCH AND FINDINGS

Academic research also supports SRI by providing empirical evidence that the performance of SRI does, on average, not differ significantly from that of conventional investment. This implies that Socially Responsible Investors can combine their beliefs or environmental and social concerns in the investment process without sacrificing returns. See, for example, Bauer et al. (2005, 2006), Binmahfouz and Hassan (2013a), Cortez, Silva, & Areal (2009), Gregory and Whittaker (2007), Guerard (1997), Hamilton et al. (1993), Sauer (1997), Scholtens (2005), Statman (2000, 2006), and Vermeir et al. (2005).

IMPROVEMENT OF SRI APPROACHES AND PRODUCTS

The improvement of SRI practice and its current broad coverage (ESG and/or ethical) has led to the development of new SRI approaches and products, which have also been adopted by mainstream investors. In other words, while the initial practice of SRI was driven by religious groups and its main purpose was to avoid investing in sin industries, the concept has evolved over time to consider broader ESG issues. This attracts investors with different beliefs and value systems.

THE ENTRANCE OF MAINSTREAM INSTITUTIONAL INVESTORS

As a result of the above-mentioned reasons, SRI has shifted from being a niche market targeting only religious and minority groups to being adopted by institutional investors and hence being prominent in the mainstream market (EUROSIF, 2014; USSIF, 2014). This is considered one of the main forces behind such tremendous growth in the market share of SRI. For example, institutional investors account for 96.6 percent of the total SRI market in Europe (EUROSIF, 2014). This shows that the SRI market is significantly dominated and driven by institutional investors. EUROSIF (2014) argues that the main driver for European SRI demand comes from institutional investors, and this trend will continue in the coming years. Similarly, USSIF (2014) indicates that institutional investors hold a substantial portion of assets in the US SRI universe.

Islamic finance and investment

The Islamic Finance industry has been developed with different segments such as banking, insurance/*takaful* (*Sharia*-compliant alternative to conventional insurance), risk management instruments, and the capital market, including stocks, *sukuks* (*Sharia*-compliant alternative instruments to conventional fixed-income bonds), and mutual funds, all of which should operate in an Islamic manner. This is to enable Muslims to engage with the modern finance system without violating their religion. According to the Islamic Financial Services Board's report (IFSB, 2015), the estimated global Islamic Finance assets accounted for $1.87 trillion as of 2014, representing a 17 percent CAGR between 2009 and 2013.

To meet such a growing demand, conventional banks are also offering Islamic products and services, including international banks such as HSBC, Lloyds TSB, Barclays, Citibank, and Deutsche Bank, as well as investment banks such as Merrill Lynch and Morgan Stanley (Ghoul & Karam, 2007; Hussein & Omran, 2005). Also, several Islamic market indices benchmarks were introduced by globally reliable mainstream indices providers, including FTSE, Dow Jones, MSCI, and Standard & Poor's, to track the performance of Islamic investment.

Table 15.6 shows the breakdown of Islamic Financial assets in 2014, in terms of both geographical focus and sectors of Islamic Finance (banking, *sukuk*, investment funds, and *takaful*). It can be seen that the total estimated size of Islamic Financial assets as of 2014 is $1.87 trillion. This shows that, despite the rapid growth of Islamic Finance, it is still much below that of SRI. Furthermore, it can be seen that the banking sector dominates the Islamic Finance market by controlling around 79 percent of total Islamic Finance assets, *sukuk* outstanding accounts for 15.7 percent, and finally Islamic funds and *takaful* contributions controlling only 4 percent and 1.2 percent, respectively. The market trend of each sector of Islamic Finance is highlighted briefly below.

Islamic banking

There has been a sustainable growth rate of Islamic banking assets over the last decade. According to the IFSB (2015), assets with Islamic banks and Islamic banking windows have grown at a CAGR of 16.9 percent between 2008 and 2013 to reach $1.48 trillion in 2014, with GCC and MENA representing over 80 percent of total Islamic banking assets. The Islamic banking sector has been the major driver of Islamic Finance industry growth over the past decade, taking the largest share of financial assets.

Islamic mutual funds

According to the IFSB (2015), the total AuM of Islamic funds reached $75.8 billion with 1,161 funds in 2014. However, this is in sharp contrast with SRI funds, which represent over $4 trillion (NAV) in the United States alone over the same period (USSIF, 2014). Thus, the figure implies that, similar to Islamic banking, the Islamic funds industry represents a small

Table 15.6 Breakdown of Islamic financial assets (figures in USD billions, 2014)

Geographical focus	*Takaful contributions*	*Islamic funds' assets*	*Sukuk outstanding*	*Banking assets*
Asia	3.9	23.2	188.4	203.8
GCC	9	33.5	95.5	564.2
MENA (exc. GCC)	7.7	0.3	0.1	633.7

Source: IFSB (2015).

niche market compared to the total global conventional and SRI funds' AuM. Furthermore, Islamic funds' AuM are concentrated in three jurisdictions—namely, Saudi Arabia, Malaysia, and Jersey, holding about 74 percent of total AuM domiciled (IFSB, 2015).

Sukuk

The *sukuk* market has been the most rapidly expanding Islamic Finance sector in the last few years, based on growth rate. According to the IFSB (2015), there was a continued growth trend in the amount of *sukuk* outstanding in the secondary market between 2008 and 2013 at a CAGR of 20.8 percent, reaching $294.7 billion in 2014, with an average annual *sukuk* issuance of $95.3 billion from 2010 to 2013. Moreover, there has been a shift in the trend of the type of *sukuk* issuers from corporate to government, as sovereign and quasi sovereign *sukuk* issuances have accounted for an average of 80 percent of the total annual volume of *sukuk* issued since 2009 (IFSB, 2015). In terms of market share, Malaysia is the dominant *sukuk* market for both number of deals and amount raised through *sukuk* instruments (IFSB, 2015).

Takaful

There has been a continued growth rate of the global *takaful* contributions as it grew at a CAGR of 15.8 percent between 2008 and 2013, reaching $21.4 billion with 206 *takaful* operators globally (IFSB, 2015). The *takaful* industry is concentrated in the GCC and Malaysian markets, as these two domiciles collectively controlled around 43.7 percent of total global gross *takaful* contributions in 2013 (IFSB, 2015).

Sector exposure and investment style of SRI and Islamic investments

Sector exposure

Tables 15.7 and 15.8 show the sector exposure and the component number of different types of investment portfolios—conventional, conventional socially responsible, Islamic, and Islamic socially responsible—based on the global Dow Jones and FTSE indices. It can be seen that Islamic and Islamic SRI portfolios tend to be more exposed to the technology, health care, basic materials/resources, oil and gas, and industrial sectors, but have almost no exposure to the financial sector. In contrast, the conventional SRI portfolio seems to be more exposed to the financial, consumer goods, industrial, health care, and technology sectors. Excluding financial sectors from the composition of Islamic indices is due to the prohibition of "*riba*"—interest-based activities—by Islamic teaching.

In addition, the composition of the indices shows that around 60 percent and 50 percent of the unrestricted conventional index (Dow Jones and FTSE, respectively) did not pass the *Sharia* screening process. Also, it can be seen that applying SRI criteria to the investment selection process results in a very restricted investment portfolio, when compared to the broad unrestricted portfolios. Incorporating sustainability criteria into the *Sharia* screening process leads to even greater restriction. This is because Dow Jones' sustainability criteria screen considers only the top 10 percent of companies in each industry.

This raises the question (though it is beyond the scope of the present study): would SRI and *Sharia* screening processes have a significant adverse impact on the investment characteristics due to restriction of the investment universe? Binmahfouz (2012) and Binmahfouz and

Table 15.7 Sector exposure and component number of four Dow Jones indices groups (as per June 30, 2011)

Sector	*Dow Jones Global Index*	*Dow Jones Sustainability World Index*	*Dow Jones Islamic Market World Index*	*Dow Jones Islamic Market Sustainability Index*
Health Care	7.89%	11.62%	15.68%	24.83%
Technology	9.33%	9.82%	17.86%	21.54%
Basic Materials	8.96%	11.22%	14.64%	19.55%
Oil and Gas	10.96%	7.81%	19.28%	12.54%
Industrials	13.38%	12.24%	14.25%	9.70%
Consumer Goods	11.83%	13.43%	8.31%	7.90%
Consumer Services	9.17%	5.43%	6.05%	2.20%
Telecommunication	4.12%	4.68%	2.49%	1.56%
Utilities	3.86%	3.63%	1.05%	.18%
Financials	20.51%	20.13%	.38%	–
Component Number	6,805	324	2,599	100

Source: Adapted from Dow Jones official documents (June 30, 2011).

Table 15.8 Sector exposure and component number of the FTSE indices groups (as per August 29, 2014)*

Sector	*FTSE All-World Index*		*FTSE Sharia All-World Index*		*FTSE4GOOD Global Index*	
	*No. of cons***	*Wgt%****	*No. of cons*	*Wgt%*	*No. of cons*	*Wgt%*
Oil and Gas	173	9.45	133	18.35	18	4.13
Chemicals	119	2.97	96	5.66	34	2.85
Basic Resources	161	2.72	122	5.03	22	2.08
Construction and Materials	117	1.32	90	2.32	18	.92
Industrials	406	10.84	224	12.40	85	6.27
Automobiles and Parts	94	2.90	70	2.78	17	2.27
Food and Beverage	148	4.81	66	4.81	27	3.91
Personal and Household	155	5.09	111	6.39	57	5.46
Health Care	150	10	107	15.14	58	13.33
Retail	168	4.95	65	5.22	33	3.38
Media	89	2.98	20	.93	39	4.26
Travel and Leisure	112	2.24	18	.4	32	1.63
Telecommunications	95	3.68	41	3.51	36	5.43
Utilities	164	3.41	84	3.35	29	2.04
Banks	238	11.31	1	.01	73	16.73
Insurance	113	4.62	———	———	50	4.95
Real Estate	157	2.71	51	.88	44	2.48
Financial Services	134	3.55	13	.28	37	3.35
Technology	172	10.46	103	12.54	71	14.54
Component Number	2,965	100.00	1,415	100.00	780	100.00

Source: Adapted from FTSE official documents, September (2014).

* The sector exposure and the component number of the FTSE4GOOD Global Index (as per September 30, 2014).

** Number of constituents.

*** Weight of the sector.

Table 15.9 Sector exposure screening result based on Standard & Poor's 500 (as per 2007)

Sector	*Halal**	*Haram***	*Standard & Poor's 500 constituents*
Consumer Discretionary	71	17	88
Consumer Staples	32	7	39
Energy	32		32
Financials	14	78	92
Health Care	53		53
Industrials	42	11	53
Information Technology	75		75
Materials	28		28
Telecommunication Services	9		9
Utilities	31		31
Standard & Poor's 500 Constituents	387	113	500

Source: Derigs and Marzban (2008).

* "Sharia-permissible."
** "Sharia-impermissible."

Hassan (2013a) provide empirical evidence that, despite the investment restrictions associated with Islamic and SRI portfolios, both types of investment groups do not underperform their unrestricted conventional counterpart investments. Also, they find that there is no statistically significant performance difference between Islamic investment and SRI, based on both absolute return and risk-adjusted return.

Furthermore, it can be seen from Table 15.9 that 387 companies of Standard & Poor's 500 constituents passed the *Sharia* sector screening criteria, whereas 113 companies (about 23 percent) were removed because of their non-compliance with the *Sharia* sector screening criteria. Furthermore, 78 companies out of the 113 excluded companies (70 percent) were filtered out as they operate in the conventional financial sector. In addition, sectors such as consumer discretionary, industrials, and consumer staples were also affected by the *Sharia* sector screening criteria. However, all companies in the energy, health care, information technology, materials, telecommunication services, and utilities sectors passed the *Sharia* sector screening process.

Investment style

Binmahfouz (2012) and Binmahfouz and Hassan (2013a) investigate the investment style of different types of investment portfolios—conventional, conventional socially responsible, Islamic, and Islamic socially responsible—based on the global Dow Jones and FTSE indices. They provide evidence that there is no significant difference between Islamic and SRI portfolios in terms of size factor (large or small) in most subgroups examined. However, there is a significant difference between the two groups of the investment portfolios in terms of the book-to-market factor. While Islamic investment portfolios tend to be relatively more growth stocks-oriented, SRI portfolios seem to lean more toward value stocks. This implies that the returns drivers of each type of investment seem to be different. While Islamic investment portfolios seem to be driven by growth stocks, the returns of SRI portfolios tend to be relatively driven by value stocks.

Finding a growth cap tilt associated with Islamic indices is in line with Abderrezak (2008), Forte and Miglietta (2007), Girard and Hassan (2005, 2008), and Kraussl and Hayat (2008). The aforementioned studies show that Islamic investment portfolios tend to have a significant exposure to growth companies. This implies that, in general, growth companies are more likely to pass *Sharia* screening criteria compared to value companies. In other words, *Sharia* screening criteria seem to influence Islamic investment portfolios having a higher exposure to growth companies.

The source of the growth investment style bias associated with Islamic investment portfolios might be due to excluding conventional financial sectors, which tend to be value companies by nature (Forte & Miglietta, 2007). In addition, the *Sharia* restriction on the level of liquidity might be another reason behind targeting growth companies which are relatively associated with lower liquidity, due to them reinvesting available cash in potential growth projects. Furthermore, Islamic investment portfolios tend to have a high exposure to technology companies due to their lower leverage (Ghoul & Karam, 2007). This might be another source of the growth cap tilt, since technology is a typical growth cap sector.

Moreover, finding that SRI indices are relatively skewed toward value stocks is consistent with Bauer et al. (2006) and Scholtens (2005), who document a value stock tilt associated with SRI portfolios. However, it is not in line with Bauer et al. (2005), Cortez et al. (2009), Gregory and Whittaker (2007), Guerard (1997), and Statman (2006), who find a growth cap bias associated with SRI portfolios. Such deviation in terms of investment style might be because different SRI portfolios implement different criteria. Statman and Glushkov (2009) show that applying different SRI criteria influences investment style differently.

In addition, Binmahfouz (2012) and Binmahfouz and Hassan (2013a) find evidence that neither the *Sharia* nor the SRI screening process tends to influence the investment portfolio to target a small cap. This rejects the argument that *Sharia* and SRI screening criteria are likely to lead to a small cap bias. In fact, they find evidence that conventional and Islamic sustainability indices tend to be relatively more exposed to a large cap compared to the broader conventional index. This is consistent with Vermeir et al. (2005), who find that sustainability indices (including the Dow Jones Sustainability Index) tend to be more exposed to a large cap. This seems to be because Dow Jones sustainability criteria screen in the top 10 percent of companies in their sectors in terms of financial, environmental, and social responsibility criteria. Furthermore, large companies have more resources to adopt sustainability criteria, and they are more able to communicate with SRI agencies, in addition to the coverage effect where SRI agencies initially concentrate their analysis on large caps (Vermeir et al., 2005).

Convergences and divergences between SRI and Islamic investments

Convergences

There are some similarities between SRI and Islamic investment in terms of excluding certain industries/companies that are believed to be unethical. This results in having a relatively restricted investment universe compared to broad conventional unrestricted investments. These issues are further discussed in the following section.

Excluding "sinful" industry

Similar to SRI, Islamic investments started with religious groups' avoidance of investing in industries that operate in a manner that violates their value systems and beliefs. Those involved in alcohol, tobacco, arms defense, pornography, etc., are excluded from their investment universe (Ghoul & Karam, 2007). It should be noted that not all Socially Responsible Investors employ exclusion criteria to exclude certain industries, as the exclusion approach is just one of various SRI approaches employed by Socially Responsible Investors.

Restricted investment universe

Both types of investment portfolio, SRI and Islamic, impose non-financial screening criteria for their investment selection to screen out companies that violate their beliefs and value systems. This implies that, unlike unrestricted conventional investment portfolios, SRI and Islamic investment portfolios tend to be more restricted and have a relatively smaller investment universe. For example, 50 percent of the conventional Standard & Poor's 500 index constituents were removed from the Domini Social Index for their SRI criteria violation (Statman, 2006). Hakim and Rashidian (2002) state that 75 percent of the companies which are included in the Wilshire 5000 index failed to pass the US Dow Jones Islamic Market Index (DJIM) *Sharia* screening criteria. Also, around 60 percent of the MSCI and Dow Jones conventional indices' constituents had to be removed from their Islamic subset indices due to their *Sharia* non-compliance (Binmahfouz, 2012).

Similarly, Tables 15.7 and 15.8 show that applying SRI or *Sharia* screening leads to a restricted investment portfolio. This indicates that applying either an SRI or a *Sharia* screening process significantly reduces the investment universe for socially responsible and Muslim investors, as compared to conventional investors.

Divergences

There are dissimilarities between SRI and Islamic investment in several aspects, which are discussed next.

Financial screening and excluding the conventional financial sector

Unlike SRI, Islamic investments exclude the conventional financial sector and have to comply with certain financial screening criteria (Ghoul & Karam, 2007). The purpose of the financial screening criteria is to exclude companies with unacceptable levels of conventional debt, liquidity, interest-based investment, and impure income. In addition, inconsistent with SRI, Islamic investment portfolios are not allowed to invest in fixed income instruments, in order to avoid having exposure to interest-bearing securities (Elfakhani, Hasan, & Sidani, 2005). Furthermore, Islamic mutual funds are not permitted to use derivatives contracts, such as futures, forwards, options, and swaps, since they are not *Sharia*-compliant (Obaidullah, 2005; Usmani, 2009).

In contrast, SRI does not have an issue with the conventional financial sector or with conventional interest-based activities, since such businesses/activities are not perceived as unethical or socially irresponsible by conventional Socially Responsible Investors. In fact, as shown in Tables 15.7 and 15.8, SRI usually tends to overweight the conventional financial sector in their portfolio. In addition, SRI has no objection to investing in interest-bearing securities, using any kind of derivative contracts. These are in sharp contrast with Islamic investment principles.

Excluding pork-related products

Unlike SRI, for religious purposes, Islamic investments also exclude any pork-related products.

ESG concerns

Unlike Islamic investments, SRI places much importance on issues such as environmental risk, social aspects, corporate governance, and the ethical practice of the corporation with its stakeholders, such as employees, investors, customers, etc. SRI has also been shifted from only traditional exclusionary screening criteria to promoting a proactive shareholders' approach.

In contrast, criteria such as human rights, employee rights, environmentally friendly production, etc., are not captured in the contemporary Islamic investment screening process (Forte & Miglietta, 2007; Wilson, 2004). This is despite the embedded social and ethical concerns in Islamic principles. This implies that, unlike SRI, *Sharia* screening criteria adopt only exclusion criteria to avoid investing in *Sharia*-impermissible companies while they lack ESG concerns. In other words, unlike SRI screening, the Islamic screening process focuses on whether the output of the business is *Sharia*-permissible or not, as well as the level of exposure to interest-based activities. However, non-income-generating aspects such as social and environmental issues are not incorporated into the traditional *Sharia* screening process (Dar Al Istithmar, 2009; Wilson, 2004).

Nevertheless, there has been a recent development in the *Sharia* screening process, when the Dow Jones introduced the first Islamic Sustainability index in 2006, which combines both *Sharia* and sustainability screening criteria (Dow Jones, 2013). This is to create *Sharia*-compliant investments to target Muslim investors who are also socially and environmentally concerned. However, unlike conventional sustainability investment, incorporating the sustainability criteria into the traditional *Sharia* screening criteria is still in its infancy.

Regulation influence and institutional investors' dominance

Unlike Islamic investment, SRI is influenced by regulations (legislation) and pressure groups, not only at the domestic level but also at the global level—such as the UN. This has influenced mainstream institutional investments to enter the SRI market and become a key player in such markets. In fact, institutional investors are the most important driver for SRI demand, and this trend will continue in the coming years (EUROSIF, 2014; USSIF, 2014). According to USSIF (2010), more than 52 percent of institutional investors said that they incorporate SRI, due to regulation or legislation rather than any other reason. EUROSIF (2010) also attributes the high growth in European SRI to the adopting of integration strategies and screening of specific criteria—such as climate change—by large asset owners.

On the other hand, Islamic investment seems to be still rather largely supported and sustained by the demand of retailers/individuals who want to comply with religious guidelines. This is, of course, besides the demand from institutions in the industry, such as Islamic banks and Islamic insurance/*takaful* companies.

Income purification

The purification process, whereby *Sharia*-compliant investors are required to donate the *Sharia*-impermissible portion of their income, seems to be unique to Islamic investment, since conventional SRI does not require such purification.

Figure 15.2 summarizes the major similarities and dissimilarities between SRI criteria and Islamic investment criteria. As can be seen, Islamic investment screens out the conventional financial sector and highly leveraged and highly liquid companies (to reduce the exposure of the

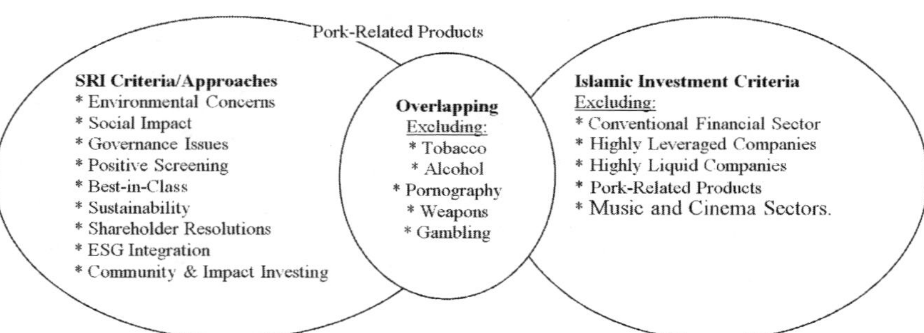

Figure 15.2 SRI criteria/approaches vs. Islamic investment criteria

investment to *riba*), as well as excluding pork-related products and music and cinema sectors. In contrast, SRI criteria emphasize much broader aspects of the investment such as ESG concerns, sustainability issues and positive screening, best-in-class, and being proactive shareholders to influence companies to adopt SRI practices. Furthermore, there are some similarities between the two types of investments in terms of excluding some sectors, such as tobacco, alcohol, pornography, military weapons, and gambling/casinos.

Social responsibility of Islamic investments

One of the main criticisms associated with Islamic investment screening is that aspects such as ESG are not incorporated into the contemporary Islamic investment screening process. Ahmed (2009) indicates that, in 2007, Vedanta Resources (a diversified metals and mining company listed on the London Stock Exchange and a constituent of the FTSE 100 index and the FTSE *Sharia* index, UK) was divested from the Norway Government's Pension Fund. This is because the Council on Ethics of the fund found a violation of human rights and environmental damage associated with its subsidiary in India. However, such an action was not taken by the *Sharia* board of the FTSE *Sharia* index, since this was not a violation of their *Sharia* screening criteria. This raises the question of whether Islamic investment portfolios are socially responsible. In order to address such a question properly, SRI needs to be defined first.

By applying the broad definition of SRI proposed by global and highly credible independent SRI authorities, indicated earlier, Islamic investment portfolios can be classified under the broad umbrella of SRI. This is because they apply negative screening criteria to exclude certain sectors/companies that are deemed to be unethical, such as alcohol, tobacco, pornography, and weaponry. This is despite not adopting other SRI approaches such as positive screening, sustainability criteria, or proactive SRI approaches, as well as ignoring broad ESG issues in the screening process. This is similar to some other SRI "religious" funds which only apply negative screening to exclude "sin" industries from their investments. In spite of this, these "religious" funds are classified as ethical investments. This is because, by definition, adopting only one of the SRI criteria/approaches—including negative screening—still classifies the fund as SRI.

It should be noted that not all conventional SRI funds place equal concerns regarding the impact of their investments on the social and environmental surroundings, since Socially Responsible Investors can set their own criteria that fulfill their specific beliefs and concerns. For example, a Socially Responsible Investor might exclude oil and gas sectors from the investment portfolio due to their environmental risk, whereas another Socially Responsible Investor might invest in such sectors as long as they have equal employment opportunities and support from the community. While the former investor is more concerned about the environmental issues, the latter emphasizes the social aspects of the investments, yet both investors by definition are considered socially responsible.

Another example, the Dow Jones SRI index, applies sustainability criteria whereby the best companies in each sector in terms of financial performance and environmental and social impact are selected regardless of the sector that the companies are involved in. In contrast, the FTSE SRI index applies a combination of positive and negative screening that excludes certain sectors such as tobacco and nuclear weaponry. This is clearly unlike the Dow Jones SRI index, which does not totally exclude any sector.

However, Islamic investment might not be deemed as SRI for those investors who emphasize ESG of their investments since the contemporary *Sharia* screening process does not capture such issues. The plausible question that needs to be addressed is whether *Sharia* really has no objection to socially or environmentally irresponsible investments. In other words, is it *Sharia*-compliant to invest in companies which are involved in serious environmental damage or human rights violations? This question is raised because the traditional *Sharia* investment screening process does not exclude these companies.

As indicated earlier, ethicality and morality are promoted by *Sharia*, and religious values forbid any income from exploitation, deceit, and other unethical sources. The rights of others, including laborers, owners, neighbors, etc., are also important throughout the religion. In fact, not only humans have such privileges in Islam—animals, plants, and society as a whole do too. Thus, it is argued that any Islamic investment screening process should focus on both negative and positive screening criteria to invest in companies that make positive contributions to society and to avoid investing in companies that cause any harm (Dar Al Istithmar, 2009; Wilson, 2004).

In other words, positive social and environmental screening criteria should not be separated from the Islamic investment screening process to reward criteria such as human rights, community investing, and environmental protection. This is because such separation does not seem to be in line with the fundamental beliefs of Islam in general, and with the fundamentals of the Islamic economic and finance system in particular, since morality and ethics is essential in all aspects of Islam. Surprisingly, the contemporary *Sharia* investment screening process does not capture these social and ethical issues, though they are usually incorporated into the conventional SRI screening. This seems to be rather paradoxical, since it contradicts the *Sharia*-embedded ethical values of fairness, justice, and equity.

Classification of Islamic investments

Examining the sector exposure of Islamic investments compared with their conventional SRI counterparts shows that the conventional SRI indices tend to have a high exposure to the financial sector (as shown in Table 15.7, around 20 percent of the overall weight of their investment portfolio, and by far the highest sector they have exposure to). Islamic investments, on the other hand, have almost no exposure to such sectors because the operation of the conventional financial sector violates *Sharia* principles (see Tables 15.7 and 15.8).

Unlike excluding the financial sector, excluding companies that involve alcohol- and tobacco-related activities (food and beverage and retail sectors) does not seem to have a significant influence on the exposure of Islamic investment portfolios to such sectors, compared to conventional portfolios (see Table 15.8). In addition, employing financial screening criteria to exclude highly leveraged and highly liquid companies for their *Sharia* non-compliance also plays a crucial role in identifying the Islamic investment universe (Derigs & Marzban, 2008).

Derigs and Marzban (2008) indicate that, as of 2007, the total number of companies of the conventional Standard & Poor's 500 that passed the *Sharia* screening criteria was 271 out of 500 (229 companies were excluded for their *Sharia* non-compliance). They further break down the total 229 screened-out companies from the conventional Standard & Poor's 500 as follows: 113 companies were excluded due to sector screening (78 of which were due to operating in the financial sector), whereas 116 companies were removed as a result of financial screening, to exclude highly leveraged and highly liquid companies. This implies that around 34 percent of the excluded companies from the conventional Standard & Poor's 500 were due to removing the conventional financial sector, whereas financial screening alone excludes about 51 percent of the screened-out companies. Thus, the total excluded companies for *riba* purposes (from the conventional financial sector and from financial screening) accounts for around 85 percent of the total excluded companies from the conventional Standard & Poor's 500. This phenomenon is unique to Islamic investment portfolios, as compared to any other SRI.

Thus, unlike conventional SRI, the main driving force for identifying a *Sharia*-compliant investment universe is avoiding or reducing the exposure of the investment to *riba* through removing the conventional financial sector and highly leveraged and highly liquid companies. The question that arises here is whether excluding the conventional financial sector as well as highly leveraged and highly liquid companies—all of which play a significant role in the *Sharia* screening process—is for a socially responsible purpose.

From a conventional SRI point of view, the financial sector and highly leveraged and highly liquid companies are not perceived as socially irresponsible businesses by nature. In fact, as shown in Table 15.7, conventional SRI tends to have high exposure to the financial sector, which might be because the financial sector is considered as a green sector. Besides, companies in the financial sector tend to be large by nature and hence are likely to have the financial capacity to adopt SRI practices such as corporate governance, community investing, etc.

There is a clear contradiction between the Islamic and conventional SRI screening criteria. While the driving force for the *Sharia* screening process is to avoid or reduce the exposure to *riba* (for religious purposes), such activities are not perceived by conventional SRI as socially irresponsible or unethical. On the other hand, issues such as ESG are significant components in contemporary SRI, yet such issues seem to be totally ignored in the Islamic investment screening process.

Hence, it seems to be more appropriate to classify Islamic funds as religious funds, rather than SRI funds. This finding is consistent with Forte and Miglietta (2007), who also advocate for defining norm-based funds (such as Catholic, Islamic, Lutheran, or Methodist) as "religious funds" or "faith-based funds" in order to underline their religious basis and to give investors a clear understanding of the values that characterize each fund and its potential risk-and-return profile. Forte and Miglietta also find that Islamic and SRI investments are two different portfolios, not only in terms of country and sector exposure but also in terms of the econometric trends that characterize each portfolio. Similarly, Binmahfouz and Hassan (2013a) show that, despite performance similarity between both types of investment (Islamic and conventional SRI), the return drivers tend to be different.

Conclusion

There is no consensus on a unified definition of SRI. Rather, SRI depends on individuals' values and beliefs, which can vary greatly from one person to another. However, it is generally accepted that SRI is where the choice of investments is influenced by one or more environmental, social, or other ethical criteria. The main approaches/strategies that are used for SRI include negative and positive screening, best-in-class, engagement, and community investing. These approaches can be used individually or in combination.

There are some similarities between SRI and Islamic investment in terms of excluding certain industries/companies that are considered unethical. However, SRI in general emphasizes the importance of issues such as environmental risk, social impact, corporate governance, and the ethical practice of the corporation with its stakeholders. In contrast, the contemporary Islamic screening process focuses on whether the output of the business is *Sharia*-permissible or not, as well as its exposure to interest-based activities. However, non-income-generating aspects such as social, corporate governance, and environmental concerns are not incorporated into the traditional *Sharia* screening process.

In addition, unlike SRI, Islamic investments also exclude the conventional financial sector and impose additional financial screening ratios. This ensures that the level of conventional debt and interest-bearing securities does not exceed the threshold tolerated by *Sharia*, as interest-based activities are not *Sharia*-compliant. Also, Islamic investment portfolios are not allowed to invest in interest-bearing securities, or use conventional derivative contracts. *Sharia*-compliant investors are also required to purify their *Sharia* non-compliant income; such issues are not considered in SRI.

The chapter concludes that Islamic and conventional SRI are two different investment groups, despite having similarities and "overlapping" in terms of excluding certain sectors/companies that are deemed to be unethical. This is because, unlike all conventional SRI, the major driving forces of Islamic investment are avoiding *riba* (for religious concerns) by excluding the conventional financial sector and excluding highly leveraged and highly liquid companies. However, SRI emphasizes issues such as environmental, social, and corporate governance and has no objection to investing in the conventional financial sector or in interest-bearing activities. Furthermore, sector exposure and investment-style studies also confirm that the returns drivers of Islamic investments and SRI tend to be different. Clearly, there is a contradiction between Islamic investments and conventional SRI in terms of the screening criteria, the purposes of the screening used, the sector exposure and investment style, as well as the underlying investment universe.

Thus, although by definition Islamic investment portfolios can be viewed under the broad umbrella of SRI portfolios since they apply negative screening criteria, the practices of the two groups of investments differ significantly. Therefore, it seems to be more appropriate to classify Islamic investments as religious investments, rather than SRI. This is in order to underline their religious basis and to give investors a clear understanding of the values that characterize each type of investment and its potential risk-and-return profile.

Finally, *Sharia* scholars should review the contemporary *Sharia* investment screening process to be more socially responsible. Islamic screening should at least expand its exclusion criteria by adding norm-based criteria, to exclude companies that violate human rights, cause damage to the environment, etc. By doing so, Islamic investment screening will not only be focusing on financial screening and sector screening (at the product level) but will also consider the ethical practices of the companies that are deemed to be *Sharia*-compliant. This is in order to be more in line with the *Sharia*-embedded ethical values of fairness, justice, and equity, since morality and ethics are essential in all aspects of Islam.

References

AAOIFI. (2004). *Shari'a standards, accounting and auditing organization for Islamic financial institutions*. Manama, Bahrain: AAOIFI.

Abderrezak, F. (2008). *The performance of Islamic equity funds: A comparison to conventional, Islamic and ethical benchmarks* (Thesis submitted to the Department of Finance). University of Maastricht, the

Netherlands. Retrieved March 10, 2012, from http://www.failaka.com/downloads/AbderrezakF_Perf_IslamicEquityFunds.pdf

Ahmed, I. (2009). *Incorporating socially responsible investing in Islamic equity investments*. London: Cass Business School.

Bauer, R., Koedijk, K., & Otten, R. (2005). International evidence on ethical mutual fund performance and investment style. *Journal of Banking & Finance, 29*(7), 1751–1767.

Bauer, R., Otten, R., & Rad, A. (2006). Ethical investing in Australia: Is there a financial penalty? *Pacific-Basin Finance Journal, 14*(1), 33–48.

Binmahfouz, S. (2012). *Investment characteristics of Islamic investment portfolios: Evidence from Saudi mutual funds and global indices* (PhD thesis). Durham Business School, UK.

Binmahfouz, S., & Habib, A. (2014). Sharia investment screening criteria: A critical review. *Journal, King Abdul Aziz University: Islamic Economics, 27*(1), 111–145.

Binmahfouz, S., & Kabir Hassan, M. (2013a). Sustainable and socially responsible investing: Does Islamic investing make a difference? *Humanomics Journal, 29*(3), 164–186.

Binmahfouz, S., & Kabir Hassan, M. (2013b). A comparative study between the investment characteristics of Islamic and socially responsible investment portfolios: Evidence from FTSE indices family. *Islamic Capital Markets Resilience and Competitiveness*, 177–204.

Chapra, M. (1985). *Towards a just monetary system*. Leicester: Islamic Foundation.

Cortez, M., Silva, F., & Areal, N. (2009). The performance of European socially responsible funds. *Journal of Business Ethics, 87*(4), 573–588.

Dar Al Istithmar. (2009). *A universal platform for Shari'a compliant equity screening*. Oxford Islamic Finance—Dar Al Istithmar.

Derigs, U., & Marzban, S. (2008). Review and analysis of current Sharia-compliant equity screening practices. *International Journal of Islamic and Middle Eastern Finance and Management, 1*(4), 285–303.

Dow Jones Official Website. Retrieved April 2, 2013, from http://www.djindexes.com/

Elfakhani, S., Hasan, K., & Sidani, Y. (2005). *Comparative performance of Islamic versus secular mutual funds*. Proceedings of the 12th Economic Research Forum, University of New Orleans, Louisiana, US.

Europe Social Investment Forum Report (EUROSIF). (2010). Retrieved February 20, 2013, from http://www.eurosif.org/

EUROSIF. (2012). Retrieved February 20, 2013, from http://www.eurosif.org/

EUROSIF. (2014). Retrieved July 5, 2015, from http://www.eurosif.org/

Forte, G., & Miglietta, F. (2007). Islamic mutual funds as faith-based funds in a socially responsible context. *Social Science Research Network (SSRN)*. Retrieved March 9, 2012, from http://ssrn.com/abstract=1012813

FTSE. Retrieved April 12, 2013, from http://www.ftse.com/

Ghoul, W., & Karam, P. (2007). MRI and SRI mutual funds: A comparison of Christian, Islamic (morally responsible investing), and socially responsible investing (SRI) mutual funds. *Journal of Investing, 16*(2), 96–102.

Girard, E., & Hassan, K. (2005, May 9–10). *Faith-based ethical investing: The case of Dow Jones Islamic indexes*. Proceedings of the Malaysian Finance Association (MFA) Conference, Kuala Terengganu (Malaysia).

Girard, E., & Hassan, K. (2008). Is there a cost to faith-based investing? Evidence from FTSE Islamic indices. *The Journal of Investing, 17*, 112–121.

Gregory, A., & Whittaker, J. (2007). Performance and performance persistence of "ethical" unit trusts in the UK. *Journal of Business Finance & Accounting, 34*(7), 1327–1344.

Guerard, J. (1997). Is there a cost to being socially responsible in investing? *Journal of Investing, 6*(2), 11–18.

Hakim, S., & Rashidian, M. (2002, October 26–28). *Risk and return of Islamic stock market indexes*. Proceedings of the 9th Economic Research Forum Annual Conference, Sharjah, UAE.

Hamilton, S., Jo, H., & Statman, M. (1993). Doing well while doing good? The investment performance of socially responsible mutual funds. *Financial Analysts Journal, 49*(6), 62–66.

Hussein, K., & Omran, M. (2005, Fall). Ethical investment revisited: Evidence from Dow Jones Islamic indexes. *The Journal of Investing*, 105–124.

IFSB. (2015). *Islamic financial services industry stability report*. Retrieved August 18, 2015, from http://www.ifsb.org

Kinder, P., & Domini, A. (1997, Winter). Social screening: Paradigms old and new. *The Journal of Investing*, 12–19.

Kraussl, R., & Hayat, R. (2008). Risk and return characteristics of Islamic equity funds. *Emerging Markets Review, 12*(2). Retrieved February 7, 2012, from http://ssrn.com/abstract=1320712

Louche, C., & Lydenberg, S. (2006). *Socially responsible investment differences between Europe and United States*. Vlerick Leuven Gent Management School, Working Paper.

Morgan Stanley Capital International (MSCI). Retrieved April 12, 2013, from http://www.msci.com/

Obaidullah, M. (2005). *Islamic financial services*. Islamic Economics Research Centre, King Abdul Aziz University, Jeddah, Saudi Arabia.

Sauer, D. (1997). The impact of social-responsibility screens on investment performance: Evidence from the Domini 400 social index and Domini equity fund. *Review of Financial Economics, 6*, 23–35.

Scholtens, B. (2005). Style and performance of Dutch social responsible investment funds. *Journal of Investing, 14*(1), 63–72.

Siddiqi, M. (2004). *Riba, bank interest and the rationale of its prohibition* (Visiting Scholars' Research Series No. 2). Islamic Research and Training Institute, Islamic Development Bank.

Standard & Poor's (S&P). Retrieved April 12, 2013, from http://www.standardandpoors.com/

Statman, M. (2000). Socially responsible mutual funds. *Financial Analysts Journal, 56*(3), 30–39.

Statman, M. (2005, Fall). The religions of social responsibility. *The Journal of Investing*, 14–22.

Statman, M. (2006). Socially responsible indexes: Composition, performance and tracking error. *Journal of Portfolio Management, 32*(3), 100–109.

Statman, M., & Glushkov, D. (2009). *The wages of social responsibility*. Retrieved March 9, 2012, from http://www.cfapubs.org/doi/pdf/10.2469/faj.v65.n4.5

UK Social Investment Forum Report (UKSIF). (2007). Retrieved December 17, 2011, from http://uksif.org/

USSIF. (2010). Retrieved February 25, 2013, from http://uksif.org/

USSIF. (2012). Retrieved February 25, 2013, from http://uksif.org/

USSIF. (2014). Retrieved July 11, 2015, from http://uksif.org/

Usmani, M. (2009). *Examining the prudence of Islamic banks: A risk management perspective* (Islamic Finance Review). Euromoney Yearbooks, 5–8.

Vermeir, W., Velde, E., & Corten, F. (2005, Fall). Sustainable and responsible performance. *The Journal of Investing*, 94–100.

White, C. (2005, Fall). SRI best practices learning from the Europeans. *Journal of Investing, 14*(3), 88–94.

Wilson, R. (2004). Screening criteria for Islamic equity funds. In S. Jaffer (Ed.), *Islamic asset management: Forming the future for Shari'a-compliant investment strategies* (pp. 35–45). London: Euromoney Institutional Investor PLC.

16

SOCIAL INVESTMENT AND FIDUCIARY RESPONSIBILITIES

Tommi Lehtonen

In this chapter the concepts of social investment and fiduciary duty are explored with a focus on the following factual, definitional, and ethical questions:

- What is social investment, and what forms does it take? How is the concept of social investment related to the concept of Sustainable Investment? How can social investment be useful?
- What means are available for promoting social investment? Which of them are ethically the best and why? How can social investment be economically sustainable?
- What are fiduciary responsibilities? To whom are they related? On what are they based?
- How unconditional are fiduciary responsibilities and what is the relationship between them and other social and ethical responsibilities related to investment?

The discussion of these questions is divided into three parts. In the first part, I focus on the principles of Socially Responsible Investment (SRI). In the second part, I discuss fiduciary and other investment responsibilities. In the last part, I introduce a procedure called "corporate responsibility indexing," which facilitates social investment through an ethical rating of different investment types. The main thesis of this chapter is that investors are, and should consider themselves to be, moral agents and not "doormats" for impersonal market forces. Since this ethical self-conception of investors has received relatively less attention in the literature than the related topic of corporate social responsibility, this gap is sought to be filled in this chapter. The contribution is thus to provide insights into the ethical implications of social investment in terms of the role and responsibility of investors. These implications concern both investment portfolio recommendations and the expected benefits of investment.

Principles for Socially Responsible Investment

Social investment is briefly defined here as the provision of finance to achieve social outcomes and gain a financial return. Another way to say it is that social investment is about harnessing the power of financial markets to help effect positive social impact.

Moreover, a non-profit and for-profit orientation of social investment can be distinguished. A non-profit social investment is any investment a company makes to contribute to society that is not primarily motivated by generating a direct financial return (Howard, 2012, p. 12). Such investments include philanthropy and charitable giving through which social change is sought without expectation of repayment. To give an example, companies around the world and their charitable foundations invest billions each year in social programs that aim to address poverty, lack of access to healthcare or education, natural disasters, climate change, and much more. A for-profit social investment, in turn, takes the social, ethical, and environmental impacts of investment as well as a financial return into account. These investments can be conventional, while simultaneously they are expected to deliver beneficial social outcomes, such as higher employment rates, a general increase in welfare, or environmental protection. This type of investing is often referred to as SRI.

The different orientations of social investment form a continuum in which one end is about promoting the desired social transformation without necessarily seeking financial return, while at the other end more attention is paid to economic outcomes. One could say that the former end represents humanitarian values and public sector objectives, whereas the latter is more private sector-oriented, with a stronger focus on the owners' economic benefit (Figure 16.1).

Further, three types of criteria for social investment can be distinguished: investment-based, investor-based, and beneficiary-based. Thus, an investment can be considered as social not only because of the type of the investment but also because the investor is a state, municipality, or a public or a non-profit organization. Other criteria for social investment include the weak social or economic position of the beneficiaries and the case that the beneficiaries are ordinary citizens such as health and pension insurance holders. Most commonly, however, the investment-based criteria, including expectations for good social and environmental impacts, are decisive for considering an investment as social.

In what follows, the focus is on the for-profit orientation of social investment, because it involves many issues important from the perspective of fiduciary responsibilities, a major topic of this chapter. Such issues are, for example, the difference between legal and ethical responsibilities, the relationship between owners' rights and general moral obligations, as well as the relationship between social and financial investment goals.

The economic goals of investment are often condensed into financial profitability, but they can also include benefits such as risk management and liquidity boost. We have already seen that the social goals of investment are diverse, including the promotion of education, gender equality, and environmental sustainability, to mention only a few. Accordingly, the following three-part goal can be set for profit-oriented social investment: (i) to secure a good return on investment, (ii) to advance the common good and social justice, and (iii) to manage the investment risks related to potential economic, social, and environmental losses and negative impacts upon the reputation of the investor (Bardy & Massaro, 2013). These goals are illustrated in Figure 16.2.

The primary risk management objectives of social investment are social stability and environmental protection. These also include more specific objectives such as equalizing the economic differences related to beneficiaries' personal risks (e.g., illness and unemployment). Such beneficiaries are, for example, employees of policyholders and other insured persons.

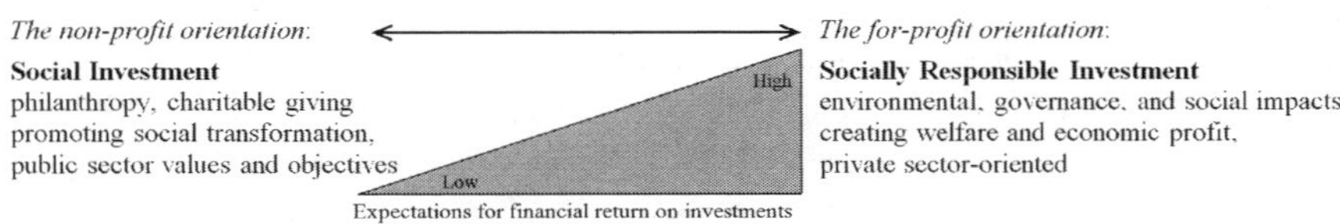

Figure 16.1 The continuum of the non-profit- and profit-oriented concepts of social investment

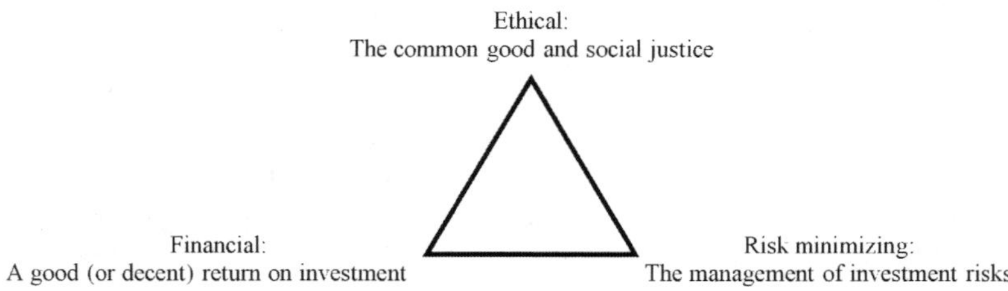

Figure 16.2 The triangle of social investment objectives

The interrelated goals of social investment are thus financial, ethical, and risk-minimizing. The distinction between these different objectives of social investment is part of a more general "division of moral labor." The division refers to the ways in which the responsibility for the political, social, and economic dimensions of society is divided among social institutions and individuals (Porter, 2009; Scheffler & Munoz-Dardé, 2005). Based on the division, the agents responsible for social welfare are institutions including markets and governments, actors such as corporations and public sector organizations, and individuals whose responsibility and identity are defined in relation to institutions and other actors. Accordingly, responsible investors (be they institutional or individuals) are those who recognize their share of moral labor and manage their role in—and liability for—social, economic, and environmental development, an issue to which I will return later in this chapter.

The "moral division of labor," a related concept, refers to the particular roles and agreements that endow people with specific moral rights and duties toward each other—rights and duties that exceed the universal moral precepts that apply to all individuals irrespective of their social roles and occupations (Koller, 2009, p. 313). An example of a role-related moral duty, which was argued for by Milton Friedman (1970), is the manager's obligation to maximize the profit of a company, an obligation that is based on the agreement between the business owners and the manager. In view of this, a major risk related to both managing a company and investing in a business is to underperform in terms of economic profit.

Financial risks related to social investment (with for-profit orientation) are managed in similar ways as in investments in general: through dispersion and allocation among different asset classes such as stocks, bonds, interest rates, real estate, and capital investments. Dispersion can also be made among investee regions, fields of business, property managers, and styles such as direct, indirect, active, and passive investment.

We have already stated that in SRI special attention is paid to environmental, social, and corporate governance issues (e.g., board procedures, accounting frameworks and rules, anti-corruption measures, and tax planning). Thus, SRI aims toward sustainability both in terms of social stewardship and economic results. These aims seem conventional and conservative in comparison to more radical views that completely question the legitimacy of investment. Such questioning can be based, for example, on social, political, and environmental critiques of the market economy, capitalism, and financial structures that support the goal of economic growth and which are blamed for causing serious social and environmental problems, such as increasing income differences, pollution, and climate change. Because this radical criticism suggests the complete elimination of investment under the assumption that no possible type of financial investment is ultimately sustainable and acceptable, I will limit this discussion to these few words, as it is beyond the scope of our topic and could easily comprise another chapter. It suffices to add that the "degrowth movement" represents a more or less moderate form of investment criticism and anti-capitalism (Jackson, 2009) that is not without historical precedent. For example,

Aristotle quite straightforwardly considered it unnatural to acquire riches with the aims of gaining profit and increasing one's property (*Politics* I, 9, 1257a–1258b—Aristotle, 1998).

Let us get back to the issue of how investors can accomplish their part in the division of moral labor. The following approaches to SRI provide different examples of how ethical considerations can be incorporated into investment decisions. The most typical approaches are responsibility analyses of investee companies and property management services, active ownership and influencing, as well as impact investing. When the issue is examined more closely, the following partially overlapping and non-exclusive approaches to responsible investment can be identified:

- In a responsibility analysis, the responsibility of investments is estimated in terms of environmental, social, and governance-related criteria. Based on the information thus acquired, certain companies can be favored or avoided in an investment portfolio.
- In a norm-based consideration, the investor estimates the responsibility of companies based on the level of their compliance with international norms, such as those of the United Nations and the Organisation for Economic Co-operation and Development (OECD).
- In integrated investing, the investor includes environmental, social, and governance issues in an investment analysis in conjunction with economic considerations.
- The investor can also categorize the companies in an investment universe according to their measured or otherwise identified and indexed corporate responsibility. The best rated companies from each field of business are then included in the investment portfolio. The internationally best known stock indices of sustainable development are the Dow Jones Sustainability Indices and FTSE4Good.
- In thematic investing, the investor favors companies in a certain field, products that support sustainable development, or companies that give services that support sustainable development.
- The investor can also exclude companies that manufacture products or offer services considered to be controversial or unethical. Typical means for such exclusion include various national and international ban lists, which name companies and fields of business to be avoided.
- In active ownership and influencing, investee companies must act perseveringly and control risks to the benefit of the owner. An active owner meets and engages with companies and their management to change their course of action if necessary. The divestment or abandonment of stocks would not necessarily lead to changes in the operations of companies. Instead, the abandonment would entail the renouncement of the rights of ownership. Withdrawing from the investment can therefore be considered only after the failure of other means, such as an impact discussion.
- Impact investment means investing in companies, organizations, and funds that aim to make measurable social and environmental changes that coincide with obtaining a return on investment. The forms of impact investment include microloans and "green" obligations. Capital investment is a noteworthy subtype of impact investment because a capital investor has the possibility to influence early entrepreneurship and thereby the construction of a sustainable enterprise culture.

As these various approaches indicate, the notions of sustainable and Socially Responsible Investment have quickly developed and expanded internationally. Regular updating of the guidelines for these new investment policies is therefore required, especially since the tools of analysis, types of property, and the themes of sustainable development and economy are continually changing.

Basically, the present investment objectives are twofold: social and economic. Economic objectives are well established, but social goals represent a partly new frontier in investment—a frontier that has been created because of the global concern over various social and environmental problems, including the widening gap between the rich and the poor, the use of child labor, waning natural resources, prolific pollution, and climate change. For these reasons, among others, many investors' organizations have recently introduced various national and international guidelines, principles, and recommendations (Blowfield & Murray, 2008, pp. 281–282; Ransome & Sampford, 2011, pp. 52–54). UN initiatives such as the Global Compact (2000) and the Principles for Responsible Investment (UNPRI) (2006) are the most famous of these.

The negative recommendations included in various guidelines suggest avoiding investment in companies that

- use child labor, damage the health of workers, exploit local populations, pollute the environment, or use vivisection to test their products;
- produce or sell weapons (especially nuclear weapons, landmines, cluster bombs) or ammunition, furs, addictive substances (e.g., alcohol and tobacco), or addictive and morally questionable entertainment (e.g., gambling and pornography);
- operate in countries where, for instance, corruption, sexual harassment, racial discrimination, and lack of concern for the environment are common social evils;
- try to reduce their tax bill by using tax havens or other questionable tax avoidance schemes.

In view of the above list (cf. Lehtonen, 2013, p. 591), the basis for social and responsible investment is demarcative, and responsible investments are assumed to be distinguishable from irresponsible ones. A common way to implement this demarcation is to compile lists of prohibited investments ("sin stocks") or areas of business. In this "negative screening," companies that operate in certain areas are excluded from being investment options.

Compiling adequate ban lists is, however, complicated, because it first requires determining the criteria that set certain investments as morally or socially reprehensible. Second, compiling such lists also requires determining criteria that classify certain investments as more reprehensible than others. Thus, both the basis for and the degree of reprehensibility must be determined. The making of ban lists may therefore involve expert discussions, public deliberation (e.g., citizens' juries, workshops, and other forms of deliberative democracy), and voting. Independent experts and citizens can help to broaden the perspective of investment evaluation and can help to take into account different interests related to investment. Moreover, the involvement of experts and citizens can dispel suspicions about the neutrality of the ban lists.

The exclusion of investments can be categorical, but often it focuses only on such corporations that have at least 10 percent of their business concentrated in the alcohol, tobacco, or weapons industries, fossil fuels, gambling, or pornography. This exclusion can also concern countries and companies that do not respect human rights or basic workers' rights as stated by the International Labour Organization, or that otherwise show economic, environmental, or social irresponsibility (Blowfield & Murray, 2008, pp. 283–284).

Ban lists and the exclusion of investments are often criticized for naivety and insufficient or controversial justification. However, a larger problem may be that ban lists oversimplify and freeze ethical deliberation as well as prevent a full consideration of the different aspects of ethical choices (Ransome & Sampford, 2011, p. 54). Additionally, a prohibition to invest in companies that operate in certain countries regarded as "problematic" can be criticized as being neo-colonial because the prohibition allegedly distinguishes between countries based on Western standards.

Many investors consider the exclusion of whole business sectors to be incompatible with the necessity for a return on investment. Therefore, private investors, in particular, criticize ethical investment for being too demanding (Ransome & Sampford, 2011, p. 12).

Because of these and other problems, the guidelines for SRI may also include positive recommendations, which many investors prefer instead of ban lists. In short, these recommendations suggest types of investments other than those mentioned in bans. An investment is considered sustainable or socially responsible usually because of the type of business that the investee company conducts. Companies that operate according to internal social responsibility (or social responsibility in their primary entrepreneurship) are typically expected to be in the areas of renewable energy, low emissions, communication, education, and healthcare sectors, among others. Although charity is rarely a company's main task, social responsibility can also refer to charity work, corporate donations, humanitarian programs, or other forms of external social responsibility adhered to by a company (Table 16.1).

Internal social responsibility is always recommendable, whereas external social responsibility can in some cases be seen as a marketing ploy or an attempt to compensate for the harmful effects of a company's activities (i.e., to appease angry citizens or ease a bad corporate conscience, or to avoid legal action).

In an important positive sense, social investment refers to taking a "dialogic approach" to environmental, social, and corporate governance issues as a condition and criterion for investment and ownership (Ransome & Sampford, 2011, pp. 12, 28). This "positive screening" involves the constructive but critical review and evaluation of different investment options. An investor may expect that investing helps to redirect the activity of the investee company and influence the way the company acts as a responsible member of society and of the global economy. This view of responsible investment is ambitious and optimistic. Some may even consider it wishful thinking, because the proper implementation of such a "participative investment strategy" would require that the investor has a seat on the board of directors of the invested company. However, only the major owners sit on the boards of directors, which significantly decreases the chances of small investors being able to influence companies' activities.

The basis of positive screening in investment, and of socially responsible business in general, is the conviction that companies have social tasks and obligations other than merely to profit their owners. As an expression of that conviction, people throughout the world are united in their concern over environmental, social, and corporate governance issues (Garriga & Melé, 2004). Concern over pollution and the depletion of natural resources, among other issues, has prompted many citizens to re-evaluate the scope and limits of economic growth and examine more closely the notion of sustainable business (Jackson, 2009, chs. 9–10). The promotion of social justice and the safeguarding of human rights have also been portrayed as demands directed toward companies and industry (Smith, Voß, & Grin, 2010). Such demands are justified because large companies and corporations in the global economy have significant political power and resources that must be used prudently and responsibly.

Table 16.1 Examples of different forms of social responsibility

Internal social responsibility	*External social responsibility*
• renewable energy	• charity work
• low-emissions industry	• corporate donations
• media and communication sector	• sponsorship
• education	• humanitarian programs
• healthcare	

Citizens are thus increasingly interested in business ethics and issues related to corporate social responsibility. The point of view of other interest groups of the company, besides that of owners, is taken into account in interest group-based management, which is believed to be profitable in the long run for shareholders as well. However, the status and importance of other interest groups in investment, besides those of owners and shareholders, is a controversial topic (see Bakan, 2005; Ransome & Sampford, 2011, p. 13). At the same time, a central economic aspect of responsible investment is the ability of an investment to increase in financial value (cf. Friedman, 1970). Particularly from the point of view of investors who invest others' money, such as pension or health insurance contributions or donated resources, it is both a legal and ethical imperative that investments be, at least in the long run, economically profitable insofar as the investors can affect the situation.

Ethical guidelines for investment therefore recommend that investments be chosen from among ethically acceptable alternatives based on an evaluation of profitability because it would be careless to invest in a long-term losing proposition. Thus, investment ethics incorporates considerations of both economic profitability and ethical acceptability, two different aspects that are not easily reconcilable for two main reasons. First, the regulation and evaluation of human activities are the main functions of ethics, whereas in the market economy, at least in its neo-liberal form, regulation is sometimes considered to be an enemy of free trade. Second, ethics as an imperative is autonomous, meaning that ethical norms and principles are not based on any other norms or principles, as useful as those other principles (such as business norms) may be from a non-ethical (such as economic, political, or legal) standpoint. This fact entails a possible conflict between ethics and business norms, because ethical norms are, from an ethical standpoint, more fundamental and binding than any financial goals. This means, for example, that nothing can justify violating human rights or destroying other things that are regarded as intrinsically valuable, such as cultures and ecosystems, in the name of economic growth and progress.

Another increasingly important requirement for Socially Responsible Investing is that the investee company is known for being a reliable taxpayer everywhere it operates. Accordingly, the taxes paid should reflect the economic activity of the company, and taxes should be paid in the different countries of operation according to the actual activity taking place in them (Fuest & Riedel, 2009, pp. 43–44; Pasternak & Rico, 2008, pp. 58, 75). One could expect that the weight of this criterion increases on a global scale because many countries are suffering from deep budget deficits and are therefore struggling to maximize their tax revenue. The prohibition of tax havens is thus related to a social responsibility to all citizens and taxpayers. Some other norms and recommendations for SRI are more closely related to special groups such as owners, shareholders, or employees. These norms are often discussed under the title of fiduciary responsibilities.

The concept and problems of fiduciary responsibilities

The term *fiduciary* refers to a relationship in which one person (such as managing director, president of the board of directors, property manager, or fund manager) has the responsibility of caring for the assets or rights of another. *Fiduciary responsibility* means accordingly an obligation to act in the best interest of the beneficiary or ultimate owners of the shares (Mallin, 2012, p. 181). Such responsibility involves diligence and loyalty obligations to shareholders, bondholders, employees, customers, and suppliers. Accordingly, for example, the fiduciary duty of retirement fund trustees is to invest the assets of the fund in a prudent manner to ensure the best returns for members.

Moreover, fiduciary responsibility means adherence to one's promises and a constant and earnest effort to accomplish what has been undertaken. This is required from investee companies, corporations, and organizations as well as from property management services. Of course, the duty to keep one's promises is also more generally a basic ethical obligation. Making promises and signing contracts activate the moral obligation to keep one's word, the breaking of which is (prima facie) morally reprehensible and can be a basis for legal and economic sanctions. Fiduciary responsibilities thus have both legal (covenanted, promise, or agreement-based) and ethical (categorical) aspects.

Accordingly, fiduciary responsibility refers to the legal and ethical accountability of an organization to its stakeholders. On the one hand, stakeholders are the entities and individuals that can reasonably be expected to be significantly affected by the organization's activities, products, and services. On the other hand, stakeholders are those whose actions can reasonably be expected to affect the ability of the organization to successfully implement its strategies and achieve its objectives. From a very wide perspective, stakeholders may include the whole human race and the planet itself. However, stakeholders are often limited to the most obvious actors including investors, employees, suppliers, and customers (Mallin, 2013, pp. 69–73).

The above individual and organization-related aspects of fiduciary responsibility are summarized in Table 16.2.

In investment, fiduciary responsibilities are related to the pursuit of economic gain, which is of course essential for any business. On the other hand, the pursuit of economic gain may cause social problems because the "invisible hand" of the economy (e.g., the general increase in the standard of living, income redistribution through taxation and transfers) does not always work as well as it should, meaning that wealth tends to accumulate in the hands of only a few people (Piketty, 2014). An increasingly unequal income distribution is a global problem and a major threat to social and international peace. Therefore, one argument is that institutional investors, such as banks, insurance companies, and pension, mutual, and private equity funds, should conduct the majority of investing, because broad social responsibility in addition to more narrow fiduciary responsibility can be demanded of them (Langley, 2008; Mallin, 2012; Monks, 2001; Useem, 1996). Social responsibility can be demanded from them because of their large economic influence and importance for the public good in terms of taxation and social welfare. Thus, individual investors would be distinguished from institutional investors with good reason, and investing could be left primarily as a matter of institutions acting for the public good. This is not merely wishful thinking, for individual share ownership has been declining and institutional share ownership increasing across many countries (Mallin, 2012, p. 179).

Two additional reasons can be given for placing a focus on institutional investors. First, they are usually committed to long-term investment strategies, even if investments can in the short term be exposed to significant changes in value. Thus, institutional investors are not (supposedly) speculators who wish to profit from the rises and falls they expect in share prices, interest rates, or exchange rates. Second, many institutional investors have special informational and

Table 16.2 Different aspects of fiduciary responsibility

Fiduciary responsibility
• a relationship in which one person has the responsibility of caring for the assets or rights of another
• the accountability of an organization to its stakeholders
• an obligation to act in the best interest of the beneficiary
• diligence and loyalty obligations to shareholders
• adherence to one's promises and an earnest effort to accomplish what has been undertaken

human resources, such as experts in responsible investment, who prepare the guidelines for responsible investment, produce annual responsibility reports, and make recommendations to the board of directors concerning Sustainable Investment. Thus, institutional investors are far better equipped for social investment than most private investors, which makes institutional investors the most recommendable actors in the investment world (Mallin, 2013, pp. 140–144).

Fiduciary responsibilities are based on legislation, written agreements, and implicit expectations. Investment funds and property management services explicitly promise to take proper and professional care of beneficiaries' investments, with utmost honesty and good faith, so that the value of the investments increases insofar as a fund has any influence over the matter. Keeping this promise concerning the value retention and appreciation of investments is a major legal and moral responsibility of fund managers and the management of exchange listed companies (Ransome & Sampford, 2011, pp. 125–126). On the other hand, if the activities of an investee company cause significant harm to the environment or threaten human life and well-being, fiduciary responsibilities to investors in no way excuse such harm or justify such risk taking. Thus, the fiduciary responsibilities to investors and the ethical norms that concern all people potentially conflict (Simon, 1994, pp. 163–164). In such cases, universal moral obligations should be put before fiduciary responsibilities, because none but moral obligations are unconditionally binding and therefore the most important ones.

Moreover, we would be committing a serious intellectual and perhaps even a moral error if we were to think that some human practices are beyond moral criticism. It would be equally problematic to assume that some financial activities cannot or should not be evaluated from a moral point of view. Thus, the point of view of morality encompasses all human acts and practices, financial as well as non-financial.

The questions of the extent to which fiduciary responsibilities are absolute, and based on these, what other responsibilities could be neglected, exemplify a more general issue of the hierarchy of duties. In ethical theory, this is known as the issue of prima facie (or *pro tanto*) duties or duties that are more incumbent than others in various situations. Thus, prima facie duties are actual duties only if no stronger conflicting prima facie duty exists. Examples of prima facie duties are keeping promises, making reparation for injuries, paying for services rendered, distributing rewards in accord with merit, and not injuring others. These and many other duties are conditional in the sense that they require an appropriate basis to be obligatory such as moral grounds. For example, even if your prima facie duty is to be on time for a work meeting, a more urgent duty is to stop to help the victims of a traffic accident. This is so because helping people in an extraordinary emergency in which a life is endangered is morally more important than fulfilling your (non-vital) work duties. Correspondingly, even if a prima facie duty for property managers is to do everything possible to secure the growth in value of their clients' capital, more urgent duties (that are independent of occupational or other roles of any human being) for them include preventing child labor and unchecked pollution, insofar as it is in the property managers' power to do so.

However, this general view is made more complex by the duties related to professionalism that allow limiting a professional's viewpoint in favor of her or his clients. We have already referred to this issue when discussing the "moral division of labor." Based on the division, a professional can rightly safeguard the client's interest against other legitimate interests. For example, an advocate may limit her or his viewpoint and may focus on and advantage her or his client's interests against other persons' equally justified interests, even if the client is accused of a crime. This right is, however, limited, because professionals such as advocates must also not lie or break promises, including the promise to act professionally, ethically, and with integrity. This limitation also concerns property managers and their accountability in investment. General moral obligations set limits within which investors and businesses that aim at maximizing profit can act in a way that is morally acceptable. In summary, for different professions there are different bases for deciding which prima facie or conditional duties are, in the case of the profession concerned, the actual duties. Such decisions are not, however, bound to be arbitrary or unlimited—they are limited by general moral duties and are based on the right of professionals to limit their viewpoint in favor of their clients.

But then, how can general moral duties override, in practice, the fiduciary responsibilities? "Ought implies can" is an ethical formula, ascribed to Kant, that is highly relevant here. According to that rule, a person has a duty to do (or not to do) something only if the person is capable of performing (or omitting) the action (Kant, 2004, p. 70; 2007, p. 472). For example, what a property manager ought to and supposedly can do in a case in which an investee company operates in a morally questionable way is to recommend her or his clients to seriously consider the morality of continuing to own the stocks of that company. The client, however, has the ultimate authority and responsibility to decide. Of course, focusing on the morally problematic aspects of an investment does not necessarily imply the decision to withdraw the investment from the company in question. Instead, having an impact on operations and taking active steps to influence the company's policy may be, in many cases, more productive. Thus, the right course of action depends on the specific circumstances of the case in question.

We have already seen that the direct influence of investment activity includes discussions with company representatives in business meetings and seminars, participation in shareholders' meetings, as well as participation in voting (Mallin, 2012). Discussions can concern strategic issues, the appointment of directors, incentive schemes, and executive directors' remuneration packages, to name only a few examples. Indirect influencing includes a property manager's or a consultant's discussions with companies and participation in shareholders' meetings on behalf of an investor. Participating in shareholders' meetings is, however, very labor-intensive, and funds may accept that not all property managers are able to commit themselves to these kinds of practices.

Direct and indirect forms of influencing are defined by the OECD Principles of Corporate Governance (2004). In view of these, the owner's guidance can emphasize the following, among others: modesty in rewarding management and administration, the selection of responsible members for business administration, a predictable staff policy, a public and foreseeable dividend policy, and the transparent and comprehensive reporting of issues of economy and responsibility.

Having an impact on operations demands consistency and patience, because all cases are different and obtaining positive results may take years. Sometimes impact efforts cannot change a company's course of action, and then it may be best to renounce such an investment. However, many funds invest in international markets through investment or mutual funds, and in such cases renouncing individual stocks is not always possible.

Fiduciary responsibilities also include the responsibility not to negatively taint beneficiaries through morally questionable investments—an important concern in social investment. For this reason, among others, investors must have accurate information about investee companies. It must be emphasized that the moral responsibility for investment cannot, however, be outsourced to external consultancies, property management services, or to other sources of information. Instead, investors themselves should periodically review their investments from a social-ethical point of view. All stock and interest investments should be screened twice a year in order to obtain an up-to-date general view of the content of the investment portfolio and to identify possible breaches of contract, for example related to UN conventions on human rights, labor laws, operations against corruption and bribery, or environmental protection. Thus, active supervision and follow-up of the courses of action of the companies invested in is a necessary requirement for responsible investment. This oversight should be internal and external and thus be conducted both by companies themselves and by investors and their organizations.

Another way to express the importance of screening investments from an ethical point of view is to emphasize that investors are, and should consider themselves to be, moral agents and not non-moral ones or "doormats" for impersonal market forces. Thus, morally passive behavior is unacceptable for investors (and for all human beings, for that matter), who should act more as shareowners rather than just shareholders. The self-conception of investors is therefore of crucial importance for the ethics of investment: they should consider themselves first and foremost as human persons with moral obligations. Investors are thus obliged to submit to social-ethical regulation and self-control, which is again assumed to bring about stability and predictability in investment. This is the dominant view of the normative requirements of investment today, and very few people, except for perhaps a number of neo-liberals, would like to free stock investment of all regulations. This is an even more crucially important issue because an increasingly large number of stock market transactions are robotized or automated today. However, the rules and principles of robotized transactions, too, are planned and programmed by human beings, at least for the time being. Robotized transactions by no means free investors from moral and legal responsibility.

In order to enhance fiduciary responsibility, property managers' know-how about responsibility analysis should be evaluated and augmented by presenting the investors' goals and expectations in calling for offers of investment products. Investors should favor property management services that are committed to the principles of responsible investment, and investors should dialogue with companies about responsible entrepreneurship. As we have seen, such dialogue can take place, for example, through participating in general meetings of investee companies and through direct discussions with management (Mallin, 2012). The dialogic approach also includes investors' initiatives in which a group of investors pool their resources to highlight their joint position to companies. Many investors' initiatives aim to promote companies' responsibility reporting. Such initiatives include the Carbon Disclosure Project, the Water Disclosure Project, the Global Reporting Initiative, and the Global Compact.

Open communication is also more generally an important part of companies' corporate responsibility policies. In line with this conviction, a company is credible in claiming responsibility if it can show that the demands of responsibility have led to real strategic changes in its activities. Proper accounting and financial reporting play a major role in this. Open communication also includes the company's reporting on their tax policy and tax footprint. All these belong to the communicative aspects of fiduciary responsibility.

Property managers commonly make individual investment analyses and choices, especially for institutional investors such as health and pension insurance funds. Therefore, successful and responsible property managers should not only be sought out but also collaborated with in complying with the principles of responsibility and in developing investment operations. Other external experts are used in the examination of the responsibility of the portfolio and in impact operations, which include obligating investee companies to operate according to laws and regulations. Choosing a property manager is therefore one of the most critical stages in responsible investment. Institutional investors, in particular, are recommended to add their guidelines on responsible investment to all calls for bids so that property managers participating in the call understand the expectations of the fund in relation to the investment strategy offered. A good start is that the property manager is committed to the UN's Principles of Responsible Investment. The property manager should also follow a responsible environmental and personnel policy as well as a good method of administration. Institutional investors should also

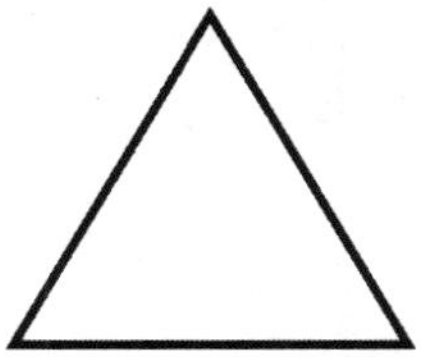

Social issues and investor responsibilities

Economic profitability

Business reputation and other risks

Figure 16.3 The triangle of social investment challenges

examine the way in which the property manager combines impact operations with investment decision making.

Institutional investors are themselves committed to operating according to tax laws and regulations, and they do not (supposedly) use dirty tricks to achieve tax advantages. At the same time, institutional investors also try to advance the accumulation of assets by avoiding the multiple taxation of investment returns and by achieving an optimal asset allocation that is taxed as little as possible. For these and other reasons, the transparency and justness of investment activities are especially important for institutional investors. This is demonstrated by the fact that institutional investors have formulated various national and international guidelines and principles for responsible investment. Their efforts also include respecting and considering central interest groups and those influenced by investment. Although these fiduciary responsibilities are also recognized in the UN's Principles of Responsible Investment, the general audience often expects more concrete recommendations and measures, including investment prohibitions and ban lists, which the signatories to the UN Principles leave open. It suffices to say that the UN's Global Compact principles provide a few more detailed standards in the areas of human rights, labor, the environment, and anti-corruption. With more than 12,000 corporate participants and other stakeholders from over 145 countries, the Global Compact is the largest voluntary corporate responsibility initiative in the world.

In what follows, I will introduce another general scheme for SRI decisions. The scheme is based on indexing the companies in an investment universe according to their measured or otherwise identified corporate responsibility. This indexing system can give useful information to investors when they attempt to find a balance between (i) the social issues and investor responsibilities related to the selection and monitoring of investment options, (ii) reputation and other risks related to investments, and (iii) the economic profitability of investments, which together form the triangle of social investment challenges (Figure 16.3).

A suggestion for Socially Responsible Investment

As we have seen, the implementation of social investment policies is made complicated by several factors, including the fact that compliance with both universal (or context independent) moral precepts and local (or context dependent) laws and statutes must be reviewed and taken into consideration when monitoring investee companies. Investors may therefore need an ethics "tool kit" to support decision making on investment priorities. Kantian ethicists state that ethics concerns our rational duty and that universally binding norms, or "categorical imperatives," should be followed in all circumstances. Utilitarian ethicists, for their part, may think that the most useful or beneficial course of action may vary from case to case and context to context. Because of the dual goal of the ethicality and profitability of social investment, one might be inclined to think that a utilitarian moral theory is the most suitable for investment considerations. On the other hand, a Kantian deontological model seems to fit well with investment ban lists.

In what follows, a social and environmental eligibility evaluation model is introduced, with the intention of assisting investors in making ethically justified decisions to invest or not to invest. The model is a mixed one, with both utilitarian and deontological inclinations. It is utilitarian in its emphasis on the social and financial return of investment. The model is deontological in considering some actions to be absolutely wrong and unethical. One may consider this duality to be a weakness, but rather there is reason to consider it to be a benefit that adds to the plausibility of the model. Mixed grounds are often used in ethical argumentation both in everyday life and when engaged in theorizing.

The initiatives of SRI include as an essential element a distinction between advisable (i.e., beneficial, ethically good, or neutral) and inadvisable (i.e., harmful, ethically wrong, or problematic) investments. The following model is based on the idea that exchange-listed and other companies can be rated according to the following categories, for example on the basis of a careful expert judgment or on the verdict of citizens' juries or other democratic bodies:

- Prohibited investments—morally or socially questionable fields of business;
- Non-prohibited investments—morally neutral businesses;
- Morally neutral businesses that are expected to develop in a morally sound way and in a morally good direction through the help and guidance of investors—companies that are ethically "best in their class"; and
- Investments that are presumed to promote favorable social and environmental development.

I distinguish between and justify these categories based on the positive and negative principles for SRI discussed at the outset of this chapter.

Investments can be classified, for example, according to Table 16.3, or on the basis of an equivalent eligibility evaluation that assists in making justified investment decisions (Lehtonen, 2013, pp. 598, 601–602). The coefficients at the bottom of the table show the relative ethical value of different types of investments (on different indices of responsible investment, see Blowfield & Murray, 2008, pp. 284–285).

Table 16.3 A suggestion for the evaluation of the relative moral value of different investments

Ethical value	*Negative (forbidden)*	*Neutral (acceptable, decent)*	*Positive (recommendable, praiseworthy)*
A. Prohibited investments—morally questionable fields of business	B. Non-prohibited investments—morally neutral businesses	C. Morally neutral businesses that are expected to develop in a morally sound way and in a morally good direction through the help and guidance of investors—companies that are ethically "best in their class"	D. Investments that promote favorable social and environmental development
An undefined negative value (×¬∞)	×*1*	×*2*	×*3*

Source: Based on Lehtonen (2013, p. 598).

The coefficients mentioned in Table 16.3 are to be used to multiply decimals that express the percentage portion of each type of investment in a portfolio (or in a mutual or exchange-traded fund). Stricter or looser criteria for responsible investment can be created by changing these coefficients.

In addition, many investors might be ready to temporarily tolerate investing in a morally problematic business if it can be expected to develop in a morally sound way and in a morally good direction through help and guidance from investors. A stronger requirement is that the development should continue up to the elimination of moral faults; a weaker requirement is that a minor positive development may also be good enough. The sum of the weighted portions of each type of investment should be, for example, at least 1.1 in order for the investment portfolio in question to be considered ethically good and responsible. If an investment is categorically prohibited, its coefficient is $\neg\infty$. Two examples of the use of the coefficients are shown in Table 16.4.

Management that is based on this kind of numeric evaluation could be applied to the investment decisions of major investors, including institutional ones, but minor-scale investors and their interest groups could also begin to demand from investment funds, among others, this kind of rating.

However, for this investment evaluation to be reasonable and serve its proper purpose, the following questions must be answered:

1. On what basis (including both factual and normative information) is the ethical classification of investments to be made? And how should the classification body (i.e., an advisory committee or a citizens' jury) be formed?
2. How are the financial risks to be dispersed and allocated among different types of investments in a portfolio (or investment product)? For example, can greater financial risks be endured from investments that promote favorable social and environmental development than from morally neutral businesses? Should the weighted coefficients for financial risks be added to the rating scheme?
3. To what extent should the expected profit from individual investments be evaluated ethically and be taken into account in the rating procedure?
4. What would be a reasonable coefficient for each type of investment?
5. What should be chosen as the minimum value (i.e., the sum of the weighted portions of each type of investment) for an ethically good and responsible portfolio?

Table 16.4 Examples of rating stock portfolios

Example portfolio I
1% prohibited investments: $0.01 \times \neg\infty = \neg\infty$
60% morally neutral businesses: $0.6 \times 1 = 0.6$
10% businesses that are expected to develop in a morally good direction: $0.1 \times 2 = 0.2$
29% investments that promote favorable social and environmental development: $0.29 \times 3 = 0.87$
Total: $\neg\infty + 0.6 + 0.2 + 0.87 = \neg\infty$ (This investment is ethically irresponsible based on the assumption of a categorical ban, which many people may criticize because the main part of the portfolio's content is still ethically acceptable.)

Example portfolio II
60% morally neutral businesses: $0.6 \times 1 = 0.6$
20% businesses that are expected to develop in a morally good direction: $0.2 \times 2 = 0.4$
20% investments that promote favorable social and environmental development: $0.2 \times 3 = 0.6$
Total: $0.6 + 0.4 + 0.6 = 1.6$ (This investment can be considered ethically responsible because the total sum surpasses 1.1.)

Source: Based on Lehtonen (2013, pp. 601–602).

If these and other related issues can be negotiated and resolved adequately—as I believe they can—there is a strong case to say that an ethical justification of investment can be systematically combined with the goal of economic profit, which is a combination that SRI aims to achieve in the first place. Different countries can support social investment by giving tax relief to those who invest in companies that are considered responsible based on commonly accepted extra financial criteria. This encouragement would most likely promote responsible investment more effectively than prohibitions that completely prevent individual investment.

Conclusion

In this chapter, we have explored and detailed the relationship between general moral duties and fiduciary responsibilities related to investments—an issue that often remains vague and ill-defined despite its importance. Improving our understanding of the issue is important because the fiduciary responsibilities to investors and the ethical norms that concern all people potentially conflict, causing doubt about the right action to take in investing. This uncertainty can, at its worst, paralyze investment decision making and thereby cause serious social and economic harm. Despite these utilitarian concerns, a major result of this chapter emerges as the deontological principle that moral obligations are primary of all commitments, fiduciary responsibilities included, because only moral obligations are unconditionally binding. Thus, universal moral duties set limits within which investors and businesses that aim at maximizing profit can act in a way that is morally acceptable. It follows that ethical reasons may demand, for example, that property managers recommend their clients to divest instead of invest. Accordingly, investors and money managers are, and should consider themselves to be, moral agents and not non-moral ones. The self-conception of investors is therefore of crucial importance for the ethics of investment. Other major results and recommendations of this chapter include the following:

- social investment was defined as the provision of finance to achieve a combination of economic and social goals, such as educational development, gender equality, and environmental sustainability.
- social investment takes a "dialogic approach" to environmental, social, and corporate governance issues. This involves the constructive but critical review and evaluation of different investment options. The basis of this "positive screening" is the conviction that companies have social tasks and obligations other than merely to profit their owners.
- Fiduciary responsibility refers to an obligation to act in the best interest of the beneficiary or the ultimate owners of the shares.
- Investing should be dominated by institutional investors, such as pension funds, insurance companies, and mutual funds, of whom broad social responsibility can be demanded in addition to more narrow fiduciary responsibility.
- Ethical decisions are integral in making investment decisions. This conviction is incorporated into the following maxim: Businesses that are ethically responsible and companies that are expected to benefit from socially and environmentally sustainable development should be preferred investment targets.

References

Aristotle. (1998). *Politics*. Transl. by Ernest Barker, revised with an introduction by R. F. Stalley. Oxford: Oxford University Press.

Bakan, J. (2005). *The corporation: The pathological pursuit of profit and power*. New York: Free Press.

Bardy, R., & Massaro, M. (2013). Shifting the paradigm of return on investment: A composite index to measure overall corporate performance. *Corporate Governance, 13*(5), 498–510.
Blowfield, M., & Murray, A. (2008). *Corporate responsibility: A critical introduction*. Oxford: Oxford University Press.
Dow Jones Sustainability Indices. Retrieved March 12, 2015, from http://www.sustainability-indices.com
Friedman, M. (1970, September 13). The social responsibility of business is to increase its profits. *The New York Times Magazine*. Retrieved March 12, 2015, from http://www.colorado.edu/studentgroups/libertarians/issues/friedman-soc-resp-business.html
FTSE4Good Index Series. Retrieved March 12, 2015, from http://www.ftse.com/products/indices
Fuest, C., & Riedel, N. (2009). *Tax evasion, tax avoidance and tax expenditures in developing countries: A review of the literature*. Retrieved March 12, 2015, from https://www.sbs.ox.ac.uk/sites/default/files/Business_Taxation/Docs/Publications/Reports/TaxEvasionReportDFIDFINAL1906.pdf
Garriga, E., & Melé, D. (2004). Corporate social responsibility theories: Mapping the territory. *Journal of Business Ethics, 53*(1–2), 51–71.
Howard, E. (2012). *Challenges and opportunities in social finance in the UK*. London: Cicero.
Jackson, T. (2009). *Prosperity without growth? The transition to a sustainable economy*. London: Sustainable Development Commission.
Kant, I. (2004). *Religion within the boundaries of mere reason and other writings*. Ed. by Allen Wood & George di Giovanni, introduction by R. M. Adams. Cambridge: Cambridge University Press.
Kant, I. (2007). *Critique of pure reason*. Transl. and ed. by M. Weigelt. London: Penguin Books.
Koller, P. (2009). On the legitimacy of political communities: A general approach and its application to the European Union. *Rationality, Markets, and Morals: Studies at the Intersection of Philosophy and Economics*, Part 3: Perspectives on Justice and Rights, 309–325.
Langley, P. (2008). Pension fund capitalism, pension fund socialism, and the politics of dissent. In M. Taylor (Ed.), *Global economy contested: Power and conflict across the international division of labor* (pp. 141–157). London: Routledge.
Lehtonen, T. (2013). Philosophical issues in responsible investment: A care-ethical approach. *Social Responsibility Journal, 9*(4), 589–603.
Mallin, C. (2012). Institutional investors: The vote as a tool of governance. *The Journal of Management and Governance, 16*(2), 177–196.
Mallin, C. (2013). *Corporate governance* (4th ed.). Oxford: Oxford University Press.
Monks, R. A. G. (2001). *The new global investors: How shareowners can unlock sustainable prosperity worldwide*. Oxford: Capstone.
OECD. (2004). *OECD principles of corporate governance*. France: OECD. Retrieved March 12, 2015, from http://www.oecd.org/corporate/ca/corporategovernanceprinciples/31557724.pdf
Pasternak, M., & Rico, C. (2008). Tax interpretation, planning, and avoidance: Some linguistic analysis. *Akron Tax Journal, 23*, 33–79.
Piketty, T. (2014). *Capital in the twenty-first century*. Cambridge, MA: Belknap Press.
Porter, T. (2009). The division of moral labor and the basic structure restriction. *Politics, Philosophy & Economics, 8*(2), 173–199.
Ransome, W., & Sampford, C. (2011). *Ethics and socially responsible investment: A philosophical approach*. Surrey: Ashgate.
Scheffler, S., & Munoz-Dardé, V. (2005). The division of moral labor. *Proceedings of the Aristotelian Society, Supplementary Volumes, 79*, 229–253, 255–284.
Simon, R. L. (1994). *Neutrality and the academic ethic*. Lanham, MD: Rowman & Littlefield.
Smith, A., Voß, J.-P., & Grin, J. (2010). Innovation studies and sustainability transitions: The allure of the multi-level perspective and its challenges. *Research Policy, 39*(4), 435–448.
The Principles for Responsible Investment (2006). Retrieved March 12, 2015, from http://www.unpri.org
The United Nations Global Compact (2000). Retrieved March 12, 2015, from http://www.unglobalcompact.org
Useem, M. (1996). *Investor capitalism: How money managers are changing the face of corporate America*. New York: Basic Books.

17

CORPORATE SOCIAL RESPONSIBILITY AND FINANCIAL PERFORMANCE IN ITALIAN CO-OPERATIVE BANKS

Eleonora Broccardo, Ericka Costa, and Maria Mazzuca

In recent years, banking systems have undergone profound transformation, moving away from a relationship banking model toward a more standardized and impersonal model (Ayadi, Llewellyn, Schmidt, Arbak, & De Groen, 2010). Co-operative banks (hereafter CBs) have been relatively less involved, showing sustainability and resilience to financial shocks compared to commercial and investment banks (Draghi, 2009; European Association of Co-operative Banks [EACB], 2010a). Today, CBs continue to constitute an important segment of the European and Italian banking sectors. In Europe, CBs represent almost 4,000 banks and hold an average market share of around 20% (EACB, 2013). Out of 684 banks in Italy, 422 were popular banks and co-operative credit banks; of those, 385 (over 90%) were CBs (Bank of Italy, 2013).

For a long time, CBs characteristics and performance remained unexplored or underdeveloped (Kalmi, 2007); however, the unexpected response of CBs to the recent economic crisis has initiated considerable debate from both academia and practitioners (EACB, 2010a). CBs differ from commercial and investment banks because they are based on member ownership; thus, they reflect an approach that is not anchored solely to the maximization of value for shareholders like shareholder value banks, that is, commercial banks. Instead, CBs aim to maximize value for a larger and more diversified group of subjects representing varied interests, such as stakeholder value banks (Coco & Ferri, 2010). CBs thus pursue a twofold objective: they provide the community with both economic and social benefits. From a managerial point of view, CBs constitute a dual challenge: as a financial institution, they have to consider their economic performance and financial performance (FP) in terms of profitability, solvency, and efficiency (Relano & Paulet, 2012); as an association of persons, they have to pursue the well-being of their stakeholders and the development of the local economy in a socially responsible way. Therefore, they must encapsulate their activities within strong Corporate Social Responsibility (CSR) practices (EACB, 2010a).

Due to their stakeholder orientation and values-based approach, CBs are expected to fulfill their CSR, including accountability. However, although co-operative principles and values (International Co-operative Alliance, 1995) are based on concepts of responsibility and solidarity, it is not possible to define CBs as socially responsible *a priori* since they have to deliver value to their stakeholders (Harvey, 1995). To understand how CBs interpret these principles today, CBs require a clear strategy to communicate and account for their values and to translate these into relevant products and services (Davis & Worthington, 1993):

> The challenge for co-operative banks is to combine their co-operative specificities [...] with external guidelines for CSR (i.e. Global Reporting Initiative, UN Global Compact, OECD, etc.) in order to enshrine the co-operative banks' contribution to a more sustainable economic and social development.
>
> *(EACB, 2010b, p. 4)*

The existing body of literature on CSR in the banking sector can be grouped into two main strands. The first strand adopts content analysis to examine the themes, locations, extent, and trends of CSR in the annual and/or stand-alone social and environmental reporting of banking institutions (Bravo, Matute, & Pina, 2012; Maali, Casson, & Napier, 2006; Roca & Searcy, 2012). The second strand of literature investigates the relationship between corporate social performance (CSP) and FP (Mallin, Faraga, & Ow-Yong, 2014; Wu & Shen, 2013). This second strand remains in an early stage and—to the best of our knowledge—there are no studies that address the CSP-FP link in the CBs context.

Due to the economic and social role that banks and CBs play in the European context, the aim of this chapter is to answer two urgent questions: does the CBs model discharge accountability in social responsibility, and does CSP positively affect long-term FP?

This chapter makes two incremental contributions to the literature on CSR and co-operative banks. First, the chapter completely considers CSR disclosure by investigating both the quantity and quality of disclosure in the stand-alone social and environmental reports, thus going beyond limitations associated with CSR disclosure analysis (Mallin et al., 2014). Second, although there have been a few empirical studies investigating the link between CSR and FP in the banking sector, as far as we are aware, this is the first study that empirically investigates this relationship in a non-profit context, specifically with reference to the co-operative bank system.

The remainder of this chapter follows a succinct structure. The next two sections introduce the theoretical debate regarding the link between CSP and corporate FP, clarifying these concepts in further detail. The section after provides the chapter's research design before moving to a section that presents the results and discussion of the findings. This chapter concludes with some final remarks regarding this research.

The link between corporate social performance and corporate financial performance

The relationship between companies' and organizations' social performance and FP has been a topic of research for some time (e.g., Griffin & Mahon, 1997; Preston & O'Bannon, 1997; Waddock & Graves, 1997); however, the connection between an organization's economic and financial dimension and its social behavior remains underexplored. More specifically, even if banks play a central role as financial resource providers to broad economic sectors, a limited number of studies focus on the banking sector and the relationship between social performance and FP (Carnevale & Mazzuca, 2014; Mallin et al., 2014; Simpson & Kohers, 2002; Wu & Shen, 2013); there is no previous study that empirically investigates this relationship in the co-operative banking context.

Researchers have employed different theories and methodologies in order to assess the above-mentioned relationship, obtaining various results. On one hand, supporters of stakeholder theory argue that social performance and FP tend to be positively associated in the long run (Freeman, 1984): if the organization is able to meet the stakeholders' claims, it will have positive financial effects in the long term. On the other hand, critics of this theory—dating back to the neoclassical thinking of Friedman (1970)—argue that a firm is an instrument for economic efficiency, disregarding any specific role for social activities or ethical consequences and values.

The controversy about the relationship between social performance and FP is not only limited to the existence (or not) of this relationship, but it also considers the *direction* and the *sign* of this relationship (Preston & O'Bannon, 1997; Waddock & Graves, 1997). Preston and O'Bannon (1997) propose a typology of possible social performance and FP relationships in which they summarize six different approaches and theories on the basis of this relationship. By running a longitudinal analysis on a database of 67 large US firms covering a 11-year time period, the authors highlight that there is no support for a *negative* association between social performance and FP; on the contrary, the majority of the analysis reveals a positive link between CSP and FP, thus reducing their typology scheme to three main theories: social impact (social performance affects FP), available funding (FP affects social performance), and positive synergy (social performance and FP are synergetic). Similarly, Griffin and Mahon (1997) developed a review of empirical studies on the social finance performance relationship from 1972 to 1997, shedding light on the need to better investigate this relationship because of the controversy of the results. The majority of studies show a *positive* link between social performance and FP even if some empirical evidence has been inconclusive, revealing both positive and negative links in the same sample of analysis.

Social impact theory

Preston and O'Bannon (1997) support the so-called social impact theory (or good management theory according to Waddock & Graves, 1997). This theory holds that there is a high correlation between the capacity of companies to meet various corporate stakeholders' needs and FP. Similarly, Waddock and Graves (1997) argue that companies that foster satisfaction by maintaining positive relationships with all stakeholders (employees, community members, and customers) enjoy better FP; improvements in reputation deliver increasing revenues while reducing costs.

Wu and Shen (2013) consider the beneficial adoption of CSR practices both at the micro and macro level. At the macro level, they note environmental improvements and reductions in social injustices and inequalities; at the micro level, they emphasize the company's reputation enhancement as a consequence of CSR behavior. CSR initiatives and practices therefore lead to financial benefits that are greater than the resulting costs, thereby improving the company's long-term FP: "Accordingly, adopting CSR can be beneficial to both corporate shareholders and stakeholders, which creates a potential win–win situation" (Wu & Shen, 2013, p. 3529). Social impact theory therefore suggests that CSR practices enhance the reputation of the company, which later leads to a better FP.

In the banking sector, Simpson and Kohers (2002) studied 385 US commercial banks, solidly supporting the hypothesis that the link between social performance and FP is positive. The results of this analysis are consistent with both social impact theory and good management theory and show that the financial resources required to put socially responsible actions into practice are not so relevant as to make the bank unprofitable. Furthermore, the results clearly show that the creation of favorable stakeholder relationships could be a competitive driver in terms of FP (Waddock & Graves, 1997).

Available funding theory

From another perspective, Preston and O'Bannon (1997) again suggest that social performance and FP could be positively associated, but the causal relationship goes from financial to social performance. Motivation thus should be found in the level of available funds or slack resources (Waddock & Graves, 1997); when (and if) slack resources are available, the company could, at its own discretion, allocate these resources to social performance outcomes, such as improving employee and community relations or fostering environmental programs. In the banking industry, Mallin et al. (2014) analyzed a sample of 90 Islamic banks from 2010 to 2011 and found that the surpluses generated by Islamic banks from high FP encouraged them to invest in socially responsible activities. Islamic banks with high FP have slack resources to devote to undertaking socially responsible activities, benefiting all stakeholders, including the community.

Finally, Preston and O'Bannon (1997) recognize the possibility that social performance and FP are positively synergetic, interacting over time in a simultaneous relationship, a "virtuous circle" (Waddock & Graves, 1997) that is difficult to detect through statistical analysis.

In the case of the CBs, we have to consider the impact of their mutualistic nature in analyzing the CSP-FP link. Since CBs have to be loyal to their co-operative values and answer to the economic and social needs of their members, they cannot adopt risky financial instruments that are potentially profitable but not anchored to their mutualistic purposes. Slack resources, therefore, are not automatically available in the CBs context.

Referring to the analysis of Waddock and Graves (1997), this chapter applies "social impact theory" (Preston & O'Bannon, 1997) because of the need to consider mission-based performance for the CBs. Indeed, the mission of CBs is strongly driven by a commitment to ethical/social values so that their banking model is embedded in values and beliefs connected to social/ethical issues. This attitude impacts the creation of relational capital with all the stakeholders and affects the development of lending activities oriented toward local economic growth. The aim of a CB is not reducible merely to profit margin achievement because of its role as a local player in the development of the economic and social community.

As a consequence, the creation, development, and maintenance of the social capital relationship is the fundamental prerequisite for FP. Social performance is therefore a predictor of FP for Italian CBs. Accordingly, we propose the following hypothesis:

Hypothesis: Improved CB social performance leads to higher FP.

How to measure social and financial performance in co-operative banks

Wu and Shen (2013) point out that the conflicting results presented in several studies (Griffin & Mahon, 1997; Margolis & Walsh, 2003; Simpson & Kohers, 2002) may be attributable to two main factors: motivation and measurement problems. Companies indeed have different motives for promoting CSR initiatives, and these differences exhibit different CSR-FP relationships. Furthermore, the analyses employed different samples, methods, and periods, causing the results to be plausibly divergent. This section will briefly review different measures for evaluating CSP and FP, thus introducing the methodological choices that form the basis of this chapter.

The social performance measurement challenge

CSP is a complex and multifaceted concept (Carroll, 2000; Griffin & Mahon, 1997; Wood, 1991) that includes inputs for CSR strategies, managers' behaviors, outputs for programs, or reporting initiatives; it ranges differently across countries and activity sectors. As Margolis and Walsh (2003) clearly show, CSP measures have mainly included the *Fortune* reputation rating or other kinds of *rating systems* (e.g., KLD Index, the Domini 400 Social Index), *content analysis* of reports, *surveys* on stakeholders' perceptions, social and environmental *awards*, and observation of *CSR practices*.

These measurements offer some benefits, but simultaneously have limitations due to the fact that they focus only on one dimension of CSR while ignoring its complexity and broader context. As suggested by Carroll (2000), research must continue to find a way to assess CSP, because it is such an important topic to businesses and to society. The author suggests that, in looking for consistent CSP measures, scholars have to take care not to isolate social performance into one social issue or stakeholder: "At a minimum, I believe the firm's social performance with respect to at least four to five key stakeholder groups—employees, consumers, owners, community, and, perhaps, the environment [...] are needed if we are to talk about CSP" (Carroll, 2000, p. 473).

Moving from these measurement problems, we become aware that "good social disclosure does not automatically mean good CSR practices"; however, the accounting literature has provided a substantial number of studies that focus on organizations' social disclosures in their annual reports as a proxy for social and environmental responsibility activity (Milne & Adler, 1999).

The accounting literature has traditionally engaged in measuring a firm's financial transactions/performance. Nonetheless, a body of literature within this broad discipline (social accounting) has begun to study how to evaluate, measure, and account for social impact in the firm's accounting system (Abbott & Monsen, 1979).

Therefore, this chapter will assess CSP in Italian CBs by addressing a comprehensive content analysis that considers all of the social and environmental issues reported by Italian CBs in their stand-alone social and environmental reports. Content analysis of corporate publications is indeed one of the most developed and popular methods of research used in the social accounting discipline (Parker, 2014), and it is later described in the chapter's methodological section.

The financial performance

In the banking literature, the concept of FP reflects different perspectives and takes into account different profiles of profitability. More recently, given the importance of the risk system in banks, FP has been viewed as a complex concept strictly connected to both profitability and risk. By focusing on CBs, FP has been investigated within four main literature streams: (i) profitability and efficiency; (ii) capitalization's role and resilience during the crisis (Cannata, D'Acunto, Allegri, Bevilacqua, & Chionsin, 2013; Hesse & Cihák, 2007); (iii) the relationship between performance and corporate governance (Fonteyne, 2007); and (iv) competition (Fonteyne, 2007). For the purpose of this study, the chapter focuses on the first strand of the literature, which considers efficiency and profitability as a measure of FP.

Some studies address the efficiency dimension in the CBs context and highlight that CBs are more cost-efficient compared to commercial banks (Altunbas, Evans, & Molyneux, 2001; Girardone, Nankervis, & Ekaterini-Fotini, 2009). Fiordelisi and Mare (2013) point out that higher efficiency levels have a positive link with the probability of CB survival. Moreover, Manetti and Bagnoli (2013) studied Italian CBs efficiency compared to non-co-operative banks, finding that CBs appear efficient and mission-oriented.

Other researchers focus on the profitability dimension of CBs and consider its relationship with different variables, such as the governance ownership structure and concentration. For example, Iannotta, Nocera, and Sironi (2007) studied the relationship between the performance and risk of a sample of 181 banks from 15 European countries from 1999 to 2004 while also evaluating the impact of alternative ownership models (privately owned stock banks, mutual banks, and government-owned banks). Their study measured profitability as the ratio of operating profit to total earning assets. The research showed that mutual banks have better loan quality and lower asset risk than both private and public sector banks; meanwhile, ownership concentration does not significantly affect a bank's profitability.

By focusing on Italian CBs and commercial banks from 2006 to 2009, Stefancic and Kathitziotis (2011) study the determinants of performance, as measured by return on equity (RoE). They show that, in contrast to commercial banks, Italian CBs do not perceive profit making as a principle in and of itself. These banks have been able to accumulate capital and provide credit to customers despite the ongoing crisis. On average, they manage their loan portfolio better than commercial banks.

Ayadi, Schmidt, and Carbò Valverde (2009) investigate profitability, efficiency, competition, earning stability, and role on regional growth of savings banks in Europe from 1996 to 2006. They measure bank performance using accounting ratios (RoE, RoA, cost-to-income ratio, and total operating costs/total operating income). Additionally, they use z-scores (considered as measures of banks' capacity to absorb deviations in income) to test the earnings stability of savings and commercial banks. Their results show that Italy is the only country where a notable difference exists between savings banks and commercial banks in terms of performance indicators. Furthermore, they highlight two distinguishing aspects of savings banks: (i) savings banks fulfill an important role in assisting regional economic growth; and (ii) in some countries, savings banks cope with income volatility better than other banks. By also considering CBs in their analysis, Ayadi et al. (2010) confirm the previous research of Ayadi et al. (2009).

Following the analyses of Stefancic and Kathitziotis (2011) and Ayadi et al. (2009, 2010), this chapter measures FP, as resulting from RoE, RoA, and z-scores. Although these ratios have been widely discussed and criticized (Karr, 2005), in this chapter they are used as the most reliable indicators of profitability because of their standardization. However, the mutualistic nature of CBs imposes judgment and caution in interpreting the results.

Research design

Sample

The empirical evidence presented in this chapter is based on a study of both the annual report and the stand-alone social and environmental report from 88 CBs in Northern Italy from 2007 to 2011 (5 years). The research builds a complete database of CBs by retrieving information from the official website of the Co-operative Movement and from the Bank of Italy, mapping out all CBs in Northern Italy. A list of 228 CBs in Northern Italy was compiled. Out of these 228 CBs, 98 published at least one stand-alone social report from 2007 to 2011. This sample was reduced to 88 based on the availability of the annual report, thus enabling an analysis of 440 bank year observations (see Table 17.1).

A large number of studies on CSR consider the annual report as *the* document to analyze (Gray, Kouhy, & Lavers, 1995). As argued by Mallin et al. (2014), one of the main limitations of the CSP-FP literature is that these studies assume that CSR disclosure can be inferred from the annual report. In order to methodologically contribute to this literature and extend beyond these limitations, this research considers stand-alone social and environmental reports.

Table 17.1 Research sample

Year	*Number of banks without social report*	*Number of banks with social report*	*Number of banks with social report on their website*	*Total*
2007	34	54	45	88
2008	16	72	49	88
2009	15	73	70	88
2010	20	68	54	88
2011	22	66	57	88
Total	107	333	275	440

Additionally, in Italy, there are no binding requirements to integrate social and environmental issues into annual reports. In order to promote the diffusion of CSR disclosure practices, in 2001 and later in 2006, the Italian Banking Association (ABI) built up a specific standard for the banking sector's social and environmental reporting (Zappi, 2007), which has been taken as a reference for this study.

Content analysis

Content analysis enables the researcher to collect large amounts of textual information and systematically identify its properties (Krippendorff, 2004). Beck, Campbell, and Shrives (2010) suggest that accounting research has used content analysis in two broad ways, either interpretative or mechanistic. Within the mechanistic approach, content analysis can usually be classified into two main groups.

The first group consists of counting every word, sentence, page, or page proportion (for a review, see Pesci & Costa, 2014; Unerman, 2000). This research is based on the assumption that the volume of disclosure signifies the importance of the disclosure (Unerman, 2000). The second group uses a scoring system to assess the quality of the information. Different kinds of scoring systems have been employed (for a review, see Al-Tuwaijri, Christensen, & Hughes, 2004), including binary code (presence/absence) and completeness ratings (information only mentioned, detailed information, and information supported by numerical data).

Following Al-Tuwaijri et al. (2004), this study employs a quantitative manual content analysis in order to fully capture both the volume and the quality score of the disclosed information employed in stand-alone social and environmental reporting in northern Italian CBs. Manual content analysis, although labor-intensive and time-consuming, allows the researchers to conduct a more detailed and sophisticated analysis (Brennan, Guillamon-Saorin, & Pierce, 2009).

In order to guarantee reliability (Gray et al., 1995; Unerman, 2000), we conducted a pilot test on a few corporate social reports. The extent and the quality of the disclosure was independently carried out three times by two researchers. Discrepancies between them were re-analyzed and differences resolved (Milne & Adler, 1999).

The volume of CSR disclosure

Following previous studies (Unerman, 2000), the volume was measured by selecting sentences as the unit of analysis. By starting from the list of indicators/information suggested by the ABI standard, the analysis considers all the narrative information presented in the stand-alone social report. The researchers read the 88 reports more than once to count all of the sentences belonging to the following five areas: economics, customers, human resources, community, and environment (Guthrie & Parker, 1990). In constructing our final volume measure for every CB, we calculated a ratio between the total number of sentences per area and the total number of indicators presented within the same area. This procedure was carried out within each of the five areas of the disclosure.

The quality score of CSR disclosure

The second measure investigates the quality score of the disclosure. According to previous studies, the level of informational detail can vary from a vague and descriptive statement to quantified and numerical data. Non-quantified information is generally considered less significant when compared with numerical information because it is more susceptible to the "green washing" technique. After considering existing scales, we employed a four-point score (0–3) like Al-Tuwaijri et al. (2004). Following this scoring scale, the quantitative numerical disclosure receives the greatest weight (+3). The next highest weight (+2) is assigned to non-quantitative narrative information, which provides a rich and comprehensive description of the topic. Finally, vague qualitative disclosures receive the lowest weight (+1). When certain information is not presented in the report, it is attributed a zero score.

This approach is an attempt to provide a more complete and comprehensive measure of disclosure than simply a binary code (present or absent) of the extent of information. However, we are aware that this kind of scoring may increase the subjectivity of the content analysis and that some scholars criticize the quality evaluation scoring system (Botosan, 2004).

Regression analysis: The effects of CSR on financial performance

The analysis has been developed in two steps. First, the chapter presents a panel data analysis (with fixed effects) over the period of 2007–2011 to test the relationship between CSP and FP. Over this period, CSP has been evaluated with a binary approach considering the presence or absence of a social report. Second, a cross-sectional analysis assesses the relationship, in 2009, between FP and CSP, as captured by the volume and quality score variables. The year 2009 was selected because of the available data on 2008 CSP quality and volume. The data were coherent with previous empirical studies highlighting that, in 2008, the stand-alone report was still considered predominant within Italian companies (KMPG, 2011).

Following previous literature, in both types of analyses, the CSP measures were collected in 2008 and the FP measures in 2009, thus considering a lead-lag effect. This effect is explained by Preston and O'Bannon (1997) and Simpson and Kohers (2002) as implying that social performance, and therefore social reputation, develops first; then, FP follows.

To assess whether the presence or absence of the social report produces effects on banks' FP, the following panel regression model is estimated [1]:

$$perf_{it} = \beta_0 + \beta_1 CSR_{it-1} + \beta_2 TA_{it} + \beta_3 EQTA_{it} + \beta_4 DF_{it} + \beta_5 LOANTA_{it} + \beta_6 INTMARG_{it} + \beta_7 COST_{it} + \beta_8 TIER1_{it} + \beta_9 BLR_{it} + \mu_{it} \quad [1]$$

where:

$perf_{it}$ = FP measures RoA, RoE, and z-score for bank i at year t,
CSR_{it-1} = dummy variable for bank i at year $(t-1)$, equal to 1 if social report is present and 0 if not,
TA_{it} = total assets value of bank i at year t,

$EQTA_{it}$ = book value of equity/total assets of bank i at year t,
DF_{it} = retail deposits/total funding of bank i at year t,
$LOANTA_{it}$ = loans/total assets of bank i at year t,
$INTMARG_{it}$ = interest margins of bank i at year t,
$COST_{it}$ = cost/income ratio of bank i at year t,
$TIER1_{it}$ = Tier1 ratio of bank i at year t,
BLR_{it} = bad loans ratio of bank i at year t,
μ_{it} = error.

For the panel regression, the analysis includes 308 bank year observations because of the exclusion of bank year observation where the data were not available.

The dependent variables are measures of bank performance aiming at capturing profitability and risk. We employed RoE and RoA (Ayadi et al., 2009; Stefancic & Kathitziotis, 2011) to capture the banks' profitability. To capture the bank (insolvency) risk we employ the z-score (Ayadi et al., 2009; Boyd & Runkle, 1993; Hesse & Cihák, 2007).

The z-score measures the number of standard deviations a return realization has to fall in order to deplete equity (under the assumption of the normality of banks' returns) (Hesse & Cihák, 2007). Combining profitability, leverage, and return volatility in a single measure, the z-score increases with higher profitability and capitalization levels, and decreases with unstable earnings (Berger, Klapper, & Turk-Ariss, 2008). It has become a popular measure of bank soundness because it directly relates to the probability of a bank's insolvency—the probability that the value of its assets will become lower than the value of its debt. Compared to other risk measures, the z-score seems better able to capture the overall riskiness of the bank—for instance, if the non-performing loans are considered, the risk captured is only the loan risk (Berger et al., 2008). In addition, given the new rules of Basel III—that includes a leverage ratio—the z-score appears a relevant measure of risk, also from the perspective of the regulators. It has been used in studies focusing on CBs (Ayadi et al., 2009; Beck, Hesse, Kick, & von Westernhagen, 2009; Garcia-Marco & Robles-Fernandez, 2008; Hesse & Cihák, 2007), also in the Italian setting (Cioli & Giannozzi, 2014), and given its ability to capture a bank's overall insolvency risk, the z-score has been employed, even recently, to make comparisons between different types of banks and to conduct cross-country analyses (e.g., Barry, Lepetit, & Tarazi, 2011; Demirgüç-Kun & Huizinga, 2009; Hesse & Cihák, 2007; Köhler, 2012). Finally, since the z-score can be considered a forward-looking measure of performance, it seems capable of grasping the dynamics of change taking place in the system of the co-operative banks while remaining less susceptible to market manipulation.

The regressors include the key independent variable on CSP plus a vector of bank-specific variables. The first control variable, total assets, captures the size of the bank. Since larger banks have better risk diversification opportunities, and thus lower costs of funding than smaller ones, they should exhibit relatively higher levels of performance (McAllister & McManus, 1993); a positive sign of the coefficient is expected. Better capitalized banks should be associated with higher management quality, lower expected bankruptcy costs (Berger, 1995), and riskier assets portfolios (also due to Basel Accord pressure). As a result, the sign of the coefficient should be positive. The same considerations can be applied to the Tier1 variable. The direction of the relationship between the incidence of retail deposits and performance is an open empirical question. Retail deposits carry a lower interest cost with respect to other types of liabilities. On the other hand, retail deposits are costly in terms of the required branching network. As a result, the sign of the coefficient could be either positive or negative (Iannotta et al., 2007). Since loans might be more profitable than other assets, we expect a positive coefficient sign of the ratio of loans to total assets. The relationship between net interest margin and profitability is expected to be positive, as interest forms the main positive component of banks' income statements. The bad loans ratio captures the banks' asset quality (Iannotta et al., 2007; Stefancic & Kathitziotis, 2011). Since the profitability of riskier loans is expected to be higher, the relationship with performance could be positive. On the other hand, since a poorer asset quality should increase the bank's cost of funding, this typically implies more resources on credit underwriting and loan monitoring, thus increasing costs (Mester, 1996); therefore, the relationship could be negative.

To assess whether the volume and quality score of CSP is linked to FP we perform a cross-section regression, by adding the one-year lagged volume and quality CSR measures. Due to the exclusion of cases where data were unavailable, the cross-section regression analysis includes 59 bank year observations.

Findings and discussion

Volume and quality score of CSR

This section provides the results for CSR disclosure volume and quality score for 88 Italian co-operative banks in 2008. Table 17.2 presents the descriptive statistics for CSR volume with a focus on different areas of the disclosure.

The data show that the average sentence length for each indicator provided in the stand-alone social and environmental report in the Italian CBs is 3.7, ranging from a minimum of 1.0 to a maximum of 8.3. When considering single areas of the disclosures, significant differences appear. We find that the economic and community areas generally disclose highly, whilst the environment has an average number of sentences equal to 2.0, which is almost half of the average for the sample. In particular, the *economic area* has a 5.3 average sentence length for CBs, with a maximum value of 32.0 sentences by indicator; it also shows the highest deviation standard (6.7). This result aligns with that of Roca and Searcy (2012) who make clear that the banking sector mostly emphasizes the economic dimension of sustainability. The attention paid to the economic area calls into question the role of the stand-alone social report as a voluntary mechanism, which theoretically should go beyond traditional financial disclosure (Gray et al., 1995). In the case of Italian CBs, the role of social reporting seems to be affected by the prominence of financial and economic performance.

However, these results are partially mitigated by the relevant role of the *community area*, which accounts for 5.1 average sentences by indicator. This finding is consistent with that of Mallin et al. (2014), a study that shows that the vision and mission statement dimensions are highly represented across all countries. Bravo et al. (2012) also point out the significance of the community area by providing evidence that savings banks publish more information regarding their contribution to the achievement of the community's general interests. Similarly, Khan et al. (2011) discovered an extension of indicators about banks' social and community involvement in Bangladesh. This

Table 17.2 Volume of CSP (2008)

Area	*Average*	*Min*	*Max*	*Median*	*DS*
Economic	5.3	0.0	32.0	3.0	6.7
Customer	2.5	0.0	14.5	2.2	2.2
HR	2.3	0.0	6.3	2.3	1.5
Community	5.1	1.0	17.2	4.0	3.9
Environmental	2.0	0.0	13.3	1.0	2.8
Total	3.7	1.0	8.3	3.3	1.7

Table 17.3 Quality score of CSP (2008)

Area	*Average*	*Min*	*Max*	*Median*	*DS*
Economic	2.58	0.0	3.0	3.0	1.04
Customer	2.19	0.0	3.0	2.5	1.0
HR	2.34	0.0	3.0	2.71	0.93
Community	2.4	1.0	3.0	2.5	0.6
Environmental	0.5	0.0	2.0	0.5	0.48
Total	2.4	1.3	3.0	2.4	0.4

finding reflects the mutualistic aim of CBs, which are devoted to creating value for the local community in which they operate.

Table 17.3 shows the data regarding the CSR disclosure quality scores, highlighting the fact that social and environmental reports are still used in a descriptive way; indeed, the average score is 2.4. Therefore, CBs still employ social and environmental reports to provide detailed information to stakeholders regarding their economic, social, and environmental performance rather than quantitatively providing a measure. The economic area remains the most prominent for CBs, with a quality score of 2.58. It has to be noted that economic impact lends itself to measurement mainly by numerical information; therefore CBs are favorable to adapting quantitative data to measure this dimension.

The lowest quality score appears in the *environmental area* (0.5). This result is consistent with previous studies (Branco & Rodrigues, 2008; Herzig, Giese, Hetze, & Godemann, 2012; Mallin et al., 2014). It confirms that, even if banks and banking institutions are starting to pay attention to the impact of their activities on the environment (both directly and indirectly), this attention is not widespread enough. Some studies have provided evidence of the scant or complete absence of environmentally related issues in corporate social reports in banking institutions (Maali et al., 2006; Zeghal & Ahmed, 1990).

The CSP-FP link

Table 17.4 shows the results obtained by estimating the panel regression model [1], in which the dependent variables are, in turn, represented by RoA (column 1), RoE (column 2), and z-score (column 3). Overall, the results are mixed. When RoA is considered, the results provide evidence that the presence or absence of the stand-alone social and environmental report produce negative effects on the performance of the sample banks from 2008 to 2011. The CSR variable is slightly statistically significant at 10%. The CSR is not statistically significant when RoA and z-score are investigated; however, the sign of the coefficients seems to confirm the negative influence of CSR on bank performance.

Contrary to our expectations, focusing on RoA showed a strongly negative influence. However, this evidence is not confirmed by other performance measures. The cost-to-income ratio (COST) is strongly significant, and the sign of the coefficient is coherent with our expectations. In the case of the z-score, the variable on bank's capitalization (EQTA) is strongly significant with the expected positive sign.

To examine whether the volume and the quality score of CSR affect banks' FP, we conducted a cross-sectional analysis by running a modified model [1], in which the CSR dummy variable is substituted by the quality (Q_CSP) and the volume (V_CSP) score variable.

We first conducted two regressions in which the quality score and volume of CSR were considered separately. The results of these estimates did not prove the existence of a statistically

Table 17.4 CSR-report on FP (2008–2011)

	(1) *RoA*	(2) *RoE*	(3) *z-score*
CSR	−0.102* (−2.16)	−15.30 (−0.56)	−0.288 (−1.05)
TA	−0.0000** (−2.51)	−0.000000872 (−1.20)	6.23e−10 (0.26)
EQTA	2.096 (0.58)	−265898.8 (−1.15)	300.0*** (9.77)
DF	−0.0959 (−0.14)	2927.5 (1.20)	4.211 (0.88)
LOANTA	−0.645 (−1.07)	1132.0 (0.98)	0.555 (0.16)
INTMARG	1.56e−08 (0.86)	0.0000190 (1.09)	−3.41e−08 (−0.54)
COST	−1.346** (−2.14)	−311.6 (−0.96)	0.630 (0.34)
TIER1	−5.532** (−2.07)	9855.0 (1.21)	7.161 (0.48)
BLR	5.772 (1.14)	−3872.5 (−0.90)	9.334 (0.59)
CONST	3.435** (2.59)	−156.3 (−0.25)	4.931 (0.87)
N	308	308	308
R-sq	0.3541	0.2408	0.8530
adj. R-sq	0.3345	0.2178	0.8485
F (9.79)	.	0.18	53.86

* Significant at level <0.10, ** significant at level <0.05, *** significant at level <0.01.

Table 17.5 CSP (measured in terms of both quality and quantity) on FP (year 2009)

	(1) *RoA*	(2) *RoE*	(3) *z-score*
Q_CSP	0.0767 (−0.97)	−0.579 (−1.01)	−21.20 (−1.67)
V_CSP	0.0345 (1.71)	0.229 (1.84)	0.757 (0.27)
TA	−0.00000 (−0.62)	−0.00000 (−0.46)	0.00000 (0.41)
EQTA	−1.271 (−0.40)	−21.19 (−1.00)	678.6 (1.06)
DF	0.696* (2.06)	5.973* (2.47)	−13.70 (−0.24)
LOANTA	0.00147 (0.30)	−0.00000310 (−0.00)	−0.136 (−0.19)
INTMARG	−6.55e−09 (−1.26)	−5.41e−08 (−1.74)	−0.00000156 (−0.99)
COST	−2.870*** (−4.51)	−19.40*** (−7.17)	−92.84 (−1.68)
TIER1	0.338 (0.15)	−7.670 (−0.43)	−316.6 (−0.83)
BLR	−5.238 (−1.52)	−58.74 (−1.88)	867.3 (0.95)
CONST	2.330*** (4.21)	20.24*** (7.02)	145.2 (1.64)
N	59	59	59
R-sq	0.7155	0.6753	0.1332
adj. R-sq	0.6563	0.6077	−0.0474
F (10, 48)	.	.	0.45

* Significant at level <0.10, ** significant at level <0.05, *** significant at level <0.01.

significant relationship between the FP of Italian co-operative banks and CSR quality score or volume, respectively. We successively estimated a regression in which the CSR quality score and volume variables were both included as independent variables. Table 17.5 shows the results of these estimates. Ultimately, these findings do not provide evidence that CSR dimensions produce effects on the banks' FP. The negative sign of the CSR quality variable seems to confirm the results of previous estimates, while the positive coefficient of the CSR volume variable seems to indicate that the volume of CSR information disclosed positively influences the banks' performance. The significance of the other variables' coefficients substantially confirms the results of the previous panel regressions.

In conclusion, the results of the regression analysis fail to provide evidence that CSR affects banks' performance. However, especially in the case of the cross-sectional analysis, these findings have to be interpreted with caution because the sample was limited and because the variability of the CSR quality score was not very high. Similar to Griffin and Mahon (1997), our analysis is inconclusive, depending on the volume-based or quality-based variable considered. Two main interpretations can be made for these findings.

First, differences have emerged when adopting the volume and the quality of the disclosure. Indeed, on one side, the volume of the disclosure signifies the importance of the disclosure (Unerman, 2000); therefore, it is significant that the more CBs disclose on social and environmental issues, the more it is associated with the bank's economic performance and FP. However, the relevance of the economic dimension within the overall volume variable is very high, questioning the role of the social report as a company document oriented to disclose non-financial information (Parker, 2014). Within the volume variable, this effect is partially mitigated by the relevance of community issues; within the quality variable, however, this effect is not mitigated and therefore negatively affects the model.

Second, as the previous point is strictly related to the second consideration, we would like to move on with this chapter and discuss our initial hypothesis. Consistent with social impact theory (Preston & O'Bannon, 1997), we expected CBs to deliver social and environmental reporting in order to meet the needs of various non-owner corporate stakeholders, which will positively impact FP. Our results also call into question the role of social reporting for Italian co-operative banks, which seem disconnected from the need to disclose their social impact to customers, members, and the community. Rather, social reports are composed primarily of economic and financial information, thus diminishing the values and beliefs on which CBs are grounded (EACB, 2010b). Therefore, this study offers a sectorial perspective regarding the banking sector and contributes to the study of Simpson and Kohers (2002) by pointing out that when focusing on one particular type of bank—the co-operative bank—the positive relationship between CSP and FP may be questioned.

Summary and conclusion

This chapter investigates CSR and its disclosure within the co-operative bank context. A sample of 88 northern Italian CBs from 2007 to 2011 has been used in the analysis in order to better understand if CBs discharge accountability on their social responsibility and to assess if CSP may positively affect long-term FP.

In order to make a contribution to the theoretical debate regarding CSR disclosure, this chapter considers both the annual report and the stand-alone social and environmental reports while holistically assessing the volume and quality of the disclosures in five different areas: economics, customers, employees, community, and environment. The chapter also empirically investigates the CSP-FP link in order to support social impact theory (Preston & O'Bannon, 1997; Waddock & Graves, 1997).

The empirical results of the volume and quality score of the CSR disclosures show that Italian co-operative banks seem to show more commitment to the following: economic and FP information, the vision and mission statement, the community, and the local development, thus confirming previous studies (Bravo et al., 2012; Khan et al., 2011; Mallin et al., 2014; Roca & Searcy, 2012). Furthermore, the analysis reveals that, consistent with previous research (Branco & Rodrigues, 2008; Herzig et al., 2012; Mallin et al., 2014), little attention is paid to the environmental dimension. These results confirm the importance of approaching CSR disclosure in a complete manner, considering both the volume of the information reported as well as its quality.

The regression analysis represented a first attempt to analyze the relationship between banks' FP and CSP. It provided evidence that CSR fails to produce effects on the banks' performance. These results open new avenues of research to understand why a higher FP would remain unaffected by higher social performance in the co-operative bank context. Due to the mutualistic nature of the co-operative banks analyzed, many possibilities could explain our results, and each of them requires further research and explanation. First, by referring to Wu and Shen's (2013) arguments, any future investigation should consider alternative CSP and FP measures in order to avoid miscalculating the economic dimension within the volume and quality score of CSR disclosure. Moreover, CB FP could be better interpreted in terms of economic added value or other measures of risk related to the Basel II requirements (such as measures aimed at specifically capturing the credit risk and the banks' capitalization). Future research could also extend the analysis by adopting a larger sample of CBs and using a longer time span, in order to better test different lead-lag effects.

References

Abbott, W. F., & Monsen, R. J. (1979). On the measurement of corporate social responsibility: Self-reported disclosures as a method of measuring corporate social involvement. *Academy of Management Journal, 22*(3), 501–515.

Al-Tuwaijri, S., Christensen, T. E., & Hughes, K. E. (2004). The relations among environmental disclosure, environmental performance, and economic performance: A simultaneous equations approach. *Accounting, Organizations and Society, 29*(5–6), 447–471.

Altunbas, Y., Evans, L., & Molyneux, P. (2001). Bank ownership and efficiency. *Journal of Money, Credit and Banking, 33*(4), 926–954.

Ayadi, R., Llewellyn, D. T., Schmidt, R. H., Arbak, E., & De Groen, W. P. (2010). *Investigating diversity in the banking sector in Europe*. Brussels: Centre for European Policy Studies.

Ayadi, R., Schmidt, R. H., & Carbò Valverde, S. (2009). *Investigating diversity in the banking sector in Europe: The performance and role of savings banks*. Brussels: Centre for European Policy Studies.

Bank of Italy. (2013). *Relazione Annuale*. Banca d'Italia, Roma.

Barry, T. A., Lepetit, L., & Tarazi, A. (2011). Ownership structure and risk in publicly held and privately owned banks. *Journal of Banking & Finance, 35*, 1327–1340.

Beck, A. C., Campbell, D., & Shrives, P. J. (2010). Content analysis in environmental reporting research: Enrichment and rehearsal of the method in a British-German context. *British Accounting Review, 42*(3), 207–222.

Beck, T., Hesse, H., Kick, T., & von Westernhagen, N. (2009). *Bank ownership and stability: Evidence from Germany*. Tilburg University mimeo.

Berger, A. N. (1995). The relationship between capital and earnings in banking. *Journal of Money, Credit and Banking, 27*(2), 432–456.

Berger, A. N., Klapper, L. F., & Turk-Ariss, R. (2008). Bank competition and financial stability. The World Bank. *Policy Research Working Paper*, No. 4696, 1–24.

Botosan, C. A. (2004). Discussion of a framework for the analysis of firm risk communication. *The International Journal of Accounting, 39*(3), 289–295.

Boyd, J. H., & Runkle, D. E. (1993). Size and performance of banking firms. *Journal of Monetary Economics, 31*(1), 47–67.

Branco, M. C., & Rodrigues, L. L. (2008). Social responsibility disclosure: A study of proxies for the public visibility of Portuguese banks. *The British Accounting Review, 40*(2), 161–181.

Bravo, R., Matute, J., & Pina, J. M. (2012). Corporate social responsibility as a vehicle to reveal the corporate identity: A study focused on the websites of Spanish financial entities. *Journal of Business Ethics, 107*, 129–146.

Brennan, N. M., Guillamon-Saorin, E., & Pierce, A. (2009). Impression management: Developing and illustrating a scheme of analysis for narrative disclosures—A methodological note. *Accounting, Auditing and Accountability Journal, 22*(5), 789–832.

Cannata, F., D'Acunto, G., Allegri, A., Bevilacqua, M., & Chionsin, G. (2013). Il credito cooperativo alla sfida di Basilea 3: tendenze, impatti, prospettive. *Questioni di Economia e Finanza*, Banca d'Italia, No. 158.

Carnevale, C., & Mazzuca, M. (2014). Sustainability report and bank valuation: Evidence from European stock markets. *Business Ethics: A European Review, 23*(1), 69–90.
Carroll, A. B. (2000). A commentary and an overview of key questions on corporate social performance measurement. *Business & Society, 39*(4), 466–478.
Cioli, V., & Giannozzi, A. (2014). Banche di credito cooperativo come leva di stabilità finanziaria. Un'analisi comparata con le banche commerciali. *Economia e diritto del terziario, 2,* 239–268.
Coco, G., & Ferri, G. (2010). From shareholder to stakeholder finance: A more sustainable lending model. *International Journal of Sustainable Economy, 2*(3), 352–364.
Davis, P., & Worthington, S. (1993). Cooperative values: Change and continuity in capital accumulation. The case of the British Cooperative Bank. *Journal of Business Ethics, 12*(11), 849–859.
Demirgüç-Kun, A., & Huizinga, H. (2009). Bank activity and funding strategies: The impact on risk and returns. The World Bank. *Policy Research Working Paper,* No. 4837, 1–64.
Draghi, M. (2009, December 10). *Solidarietà nella crisi. Il credito cooperativo nelle economie locali.* Speech of the Governor of the Bank of Italy, Città della Pieve, Italy.
European Association of Co-operative Banks (EACB). (2010a). *European co-operative banks in the financial and economic turmoil: First assessments. Research paper.* Brussels, Belgium.
EACB. (2010b). *Corporate social responsibility in cooperative banks: CSR report.* Brussels, Belgium.
EACB. (2013). *Annual report: More than a bank, a cooperative bank.* Brussels, Belgium.
Fiordelisi, F., & Mare, D. S. (2013). Probability of default and efficiency in cooperative banking. *Journal of International Financial Markets, Institutions & Money, 26,* 30–45.
Fonteyne, W. (2007). *Cooperative banks in Europe—Policy issues* (IMF Working Papers No. 07/159). Washington, DC: International Monetary Fund.
Freeman, R. E. (1984). *Strategic management: A stakeholder approach.* Boston: Pitman.
Friedman, M. (1970, September 13). The social responsibility of business is to increase its profits. *New York Times Magazine,* pp. 32–33, 122, 126.
Garcia-Marco, T., & Robles-Fernandez, M. D. (2008). Risk-taking behaviour and ownership in the banking industry: The Spanish evidence. *Journal of Economics and Business, 60*(4), 332–354.
Girardone, C., Nankervis, J. C., & Ekaterini-Fotini, V. (2009). Efficiency, ownership and financial structure in European banking: A cross-country comparison. *Managerial Finance, 35*(3), 227–245.
Gray, R. H., Kouhy, R., & Lavers, S. (1995). Methodological themes: Constructing a research database of social and environmental reporting by UK companies. *Accounting, Auditing & Accountability Journal, 8*(2), 78–101.
Griffin, J. J., & Mahon, J. F. (1997). The corporate social performance and corporate financial performance debate. *Business & Society, 36*(1), 5–31.
Guthrie, J., & Parker, L. D. (1990). Corporate social disclosure practice: A comparative international analysis. *Advances in Public Interest Accounting, 3,* 159–175.
Harvey, B. (1995). Ethical banking: The case of the cooperative bank. *Journal of Business Ethics, 14*(12), 1005–1013.
Herzig, C., Giese, N., Hetze, K., & Godemann, J. (2012). Sustainability reporting in the German banking sector during the financial crisis. *International Journal of Innovation and Sustainable Development, 6*(2), 184–218.
Hesse, H., & Cihák, M. (2007, January). Cooperative banks and financial stability. *IMF Working Paper,* No. 07/02.
Iannotta, G., Nocera, G., & Sironi, A. (2007). Ownership structure, risk and performance in the European banking industry. *Journal of Banking & Finance, 31*(7), 2127–2149.
International Co-operative Alliance (ICA). (1995). Statutes, revised by the General Assembly, November 20, 2009.
Kalmi, P. (2007). The disappearance of cooperatives from economics textbooks. *Cambridge Journal of Economics, 31*(4), 625–647.
Karr, J. (2005). Performance measure in banking: Beyond RoE. *Journal of Performance Management, 18*(3), 56–70.
Khan, H., Islam, M. A., & Fatima, J. K. (2011). Corporate sustainability reporting of major commercial banks in line with GRI: Bangladesh evidence. *Social Responsibility Journal, 7*(3), 347–362.
KMPG. (2011). *KMPG international survey of corporate responsibility reporting 2011.* Amsterdam: Holland.
Köhler, M. (2012). Which banks are more risky? The impact of loan growth and business model on bank risk-taking. Deutsche Bundesbank. *Discussion Paper,* No. 33, 1–53.
Krippendorff, K. (2004). *Content analysis: An introduction to its methodology* (2nd ed.). Thousand Oaks, CA: Sage.

Maali, B., Casson, P., & Napier, C. (2006). Social reporting by Islamic banks. *Abacus, 42*(2), 266–289.

Mallin, C., Faraga, H., & Ow-Yong, K. (2014). Corporate social responsibility and financial performance in Islamic banks. *Journal of Economic Behavior & Organization, 103*, S21–S38.

Manetti, G., & Bagnoli, L. (2013). Mutual and social efficiency of Italian cooperative banks: An empirical analysis. *Annals of Public and Cooperative Economics, 84*(3), 289–308.

Margolis, J. D., & Walsh, J. P. (2003). Misery loves companies: Rethinking social initiatives by business. *Administrative Science Quarterly, 48*(2), 263–305.

McAllister, P. H., & McManus, D. A. (1993). Resolving the scale efficiency puzzle in banking. *Journal of Banking and Finance, 17*(2–3), 389–405.

Mester, L. (1996). A study of bank efficiency taking into account risk preferences. *Journal of Banking and Finance, 20*(6), 1025–1045.

Milne, M. J., & Adler, R. W. (1999). Exploring the reliability of social and environmental disclosures content analysis. *Accounting, Auditing & Accountability Journal, 12*(2), 237–252.

Parker, L. (2014). Constructing a research field: A reflection on the history of social and environmental accounting. *Social and Environmental Accountability Journal, 34*(2), 87–92.

Pesci, C., & Costa, E. (2014). Content analysis of social and environmental reports of Italian cooperative banks: Methodological issues. *Social and Environmental Accountability Journal, 34*(3), 157–171.

Preston, L. E., & O'Bannon, D. P. (1997). The corporate social–financial performance relationship. *Business & Society, 36*(4), 419–429.

Relano, F., & Paulet, E. (2012). Corporate responsibility in the banking sector: A proposed typology for the German case. *International Journal of Law and Management, 54*(5), 379–393.

Roca, L. C., & Searcy, C. (2012). An analysis of indicators disclosed in corporate sustainability reports. *Journal of Cleaner Production, 20*(1), 103–118.

Simpson, G. W., & Kohers, T. (2002). The link between corporate social and financial performance: Evidence from the banking industry. *Journal of Business Ethics, 35*(2), 97–109.

Stefancic, M., & Kathitziotis, N. (2011). An evaluation of Italian banks in the period of financial distress. *International Business & Economics Research Journal, 10*(10), 103–113.

Unerman, J. (2000). Methodological issues: Reflections on quantification in corporate social reporting content analysis. *Accounting, Auditing & Accountability Journal, 13*(5), 667–681.

Waddock, S. A., & Graves, S. B. (1997). The corporate social performance–financial performance link. *Strategic Management Journal, 18*(4), 303–319.

Wood, D. J. (1991). Corporate social performance revisited. *Academy of Management Review, 16*(4), 691–718.

Wu, M. W., & Shen, C. H. (2013). Corporate social responsibility in the banking industry: Motives and financial performance. *Journal of Banking & Finance, 37*, 3529–3547.

Zappi, G. (2007). Corporate responsibility in the Italian banking industry: Creating value through listening to stakeholders. *Corporate Governance, 7*(4), 471–475.

Zeghal, D., & Ahmed, S. A. (1990). Comparison of social responsibility information disclosure media used by Canadian firms. *Accounting, Auditing & Accountability Journal, 3*(1), 38–53.

18

INTEGRAL SUSTAINABILITY OR HOW EVOLUTIONARY FORCES ARE DRIVING INVESTORS' TRUST AND THE INTEGRATION OF PEOPLE, PLANET, AND PROFIT

Mariana Bozesan

Researchers argue that most reforms implemented thus far at national and European Union level have failed to impact economic development in a positive manner (Fichtner, Fratzscher, & Gorning, 2014). Moreover, without massive private investments, Europe is in danger of falling into an economic stagnation similar to that of Japan in the 1990s. According to Fichtner et al. (2014) the "persisting climate of distrust in the stability of economic development" (p. 635) could be addressed by closing the existing investment gap. Further research shows that "current investment in the Eurozone remains markedly below the level corresponding to macroeconomic conditions. When measured against this baseline, there was an underinvestment of around two percent on average in relation to gross domestic product between 2010 and 2012" (Baldi, Fichtner, Michelsen, & Rieth, 2014, p. 651). To address the investment gap, Fichtner et al. (2014) recommended (1) an efficient competitive landscape that should become more attractive for private investment capital; (2) an investment-friendly tax policy; and (3) a three-digits Billion Euros EU Investment Fund that would complement the current European Investment Fund (EIF), which is dedicated to Venture Capital and is rather moderate (pp. 633–634). Although the authors refer to the overall decreasing investment landscape including infrastructure, the same is true for seed and early-stage investing.

In the United States,

> the activity level of the US venture capital industry [in 2013] is roughly half of what it was at the 2000-era peak. For example, in 2000, 1050 firms each invested $5 million or more during the year. In 2013, the count was roughly half that at 548. (Thomson Reuters, 2014, p. 9)

Within the European Union, we can witness a similar downward trend. The aggregate data on Venture Capital investments shows "relative weakening of the UK at 0.013% of GDP (down from 0.028% in 2011), Denmark (0.01% against 0.029% in 2011), and Sweden (0.029%, down from 0.031% in 2011)" (European Commission, n.d.). This tendency can be seen also in more stable economies like Germany, France, and Italy but also in Spain, and "it is increasingly clear that the market is not providing the scale of investment that firms need" (European Commission, n.d.). The smaller investment market, namely that of business angels, also represents a cause of concern for policymakers, which address it through government-backed venture schemes and tax breaks for angel investors in various countries. Moreover, the 2012 European Private Equity and Venture Capital Association (EVCA) data (European Commission, n.d.) suggests that the later stage Venture Capital market also suffered from the systemic weaknesses and the 2013 EVCA report (2014) shows only modest increases in most areas compared with 2012. However, despite the economic downturn of the past decade, European Small and Medium Enterprises (SMEs)

> have retained their position as the backbone of the European economy, with some 20.7 million firms accounting for more than 98 per cent of all enterprises, of which the lion's share (92.2 percent) are firms with fewer than ten employees.
>
> *(Wymenga, Spanikova, Barker, Konings, & Canton, 2012, p. 9)*

At the same time, the funding for this type of essential innovation and creativity, upon which our future depends, either has diminished or is growing too slowly to have a significant impact.

Hence, in the light of current financial, economic, and environmental crises (Randers, 2012), the growing inequality (Stieglitz, 2011), and the resulting geo-political radicalization (Becerra et al., 2010; Boeckler, 2009; Hughes & Church, 2010; Maloney & Schumer, 2010; Tachibanaki, 2009), the obvious question remains: How can the trust of private investors be increased and the gap between the demand side and the availability of capital be closed? The answer is multifaceted and just as complex as the problem, of course. One potential answer and a solution could provide the €315 billion investment plan presented by the European Commission president Jean-Claude Juncker on November 26, 2014 (Juncker, 2014). In his initiation speech, president Juncker confirmed that, "despite the huge liquidity in the world's money markets and corporate bank accounts, investment in Europe is not rebounding" and argued that "confidence, credibility and trust" could be built through this investment plan. The future will show whether it will work or not, and we can only hope that it does, for our future depends on it. This chapter attempts to contribute to these efforts by corroborating that trust is a feeling that, when positive, could lead to the much-needed transformation. The chapter shows two pathways on how investors' trust could be increased. The first pathway shares research results on investors who have presumably reached higher levels of intrinsic trust through vertical personal development. The second pathway introduces a few de-risking tools based on integral theory (Wilber, 2000) that (a) expand and go beyond traditional financial and legal due diligence; (b) include Environmental, Social, and Governance (ESG) measurements; (c) add cultural, behavioral, and consciousness metrics; and (d) are embedded in Ken Wilber's Integral Theory (1998, 2000, 2000a, 2000b, 2006) as the underlying theoretical foundation.

Part I: Building trust through vertical growth

Part I of this chapter focuses on the hidden determinants that led the researched investors to an investment behavior based on more trust through personal growth and vertical development. It elucidates the profound motivations behind the inner transformation and change of mind, attitude, and behavior of the researched high-net-worth and ultra-high-net-worth investors. It proposes, furthermore, that the current crises in economy, finance, ecology, climate, water, health care, education, food, security, energy, natural resources, poverty, and biodiversity could also be in part condensed to and addressed by one common denominator, namely a consciousness crisis (Bozesan, 2010; Mackey & Sisodia, 2013; Scharmer, 2013). This consciousness crisis appears to be tackled by different investors—private or institutional—from their own cultural, social, and environmental perspectives as well as their own level of interior human development. Preliminary research (Bozesan, 2010, 2013a, 2013b; Kelly, 2011) supports this view and shows that a few but growing number of leading wealth owners seem to have awakened to later stages of consciousness called integral (Wilber, 2000, 2000a, 2000b), a second tier, yellow meme (Beck & Cowan, 1996), or strategist (Cook-Greuter, 2005, 2008).

The motivation for the current transformation of these leading-edge money owners is indisputably diverse. Triggered by personal crises but also driven by the major emergencies of our time, a certain percentage of high- and ultra-high-net-worth individuals have, however, begun to act more boldly (Balandina, 2011; Bozesan, 2010; Giving Pledge, 2010; Godeke et al., 2009; Soros, 2008; Strong, 2009). They ask and try to answer fundamental questions (Gardner, 2004) that have preoccupied humanity all along. Such questions are: Why am I here? What is the meaning of my life? How am I fulfilling my life's purpose in the face of global crises? The investors' individual response to these questions appears to influence their investment behavior, culture, environment, and portfolios in a significant way. As a result, a new paradigm in investing, philanthropy, business, and leadership is emerging in (1) organizations such as the Social Venture Network (2012), Investors' Circle (2012), and the TBLI Group (2012); and (2) when ultra-high-net-worth individuals such as Warren Buffett (Kelly, 2011), Bill Gates (Giving Pledge, 2010), Al Gore (Gore, 1992, 2006, 2011), or George Soros (Soros, 2008) use investing apparently as a self-actualizing and a legacy-building vehicle.

Literature review, hypothesis, and research questions

There is a rather significant amount of information and research that focuses on transformation in investing (Bugg-Levine & Emerson, 2011; Faust & Scholz, 2014; Freireich & Fulton, 2009; Robeco, Booz & Co., 2009), finance (Panwar & Blinch, 2012; Spinkart & Gottwald, 2013), economics (Arnsperger, 2010; Lietaer, Arnsperger, Goerner, & Brunnhuber, 2012), leadership (Randers, 2012; Scharmer, 2013), and business (Mackey & Sisodia, 2013). From the perspective of integral theory (Wilber, 2000), which is the foundation of the presented research, however, it could be argued that many studies address some aspects and neglect others. For instance, the exterior transformations in investing that led to new investment forms and paradigms such as Impact Investing, mission-related investing, and sustainable and responsible investing (Bugg-Levine & Emerson, 2011; Freireich & Fulton, 2009; Robeco, Booz & Co., 2009) seem more attractive and easier to replicate than the interior transformation of the participating agents who initiated these transformations (Bozesan, 2010; Bryce, Drexler, & Noble, 2013; Kelly, 2011; Porras, Emery, & Thompson, 2007). Moreover, the developmental lines (Wilber, 2006, pp. 23–25) along with the inner transformation of the participating agents took place, and questions on how, when, and why they reached their new understanding still need to be researched in more depth. Such a line of development is cognition, but morals, psychology, and emotional intelligence (Goleman, Boyatzis, & McKee, 2002) are also important or may be even more important. Although increased vertical development appears to have become a megatrend (Aburdene, 2005), the phenomenological investigation on the interior transformation of the participating agents is relatively rare but is increasing (Adams, 2005; Boyatzis & McKee, 2005; Cook-Greuter, 2004; Goleman et al., 2002; Hendricks & Ludeman, 1996; Jaworski, 1996; Kelly, 2011; Lietaer, 2001; Marques, Dhiman, & King, 2007; Mitroff & Denton, 1999; Pauchant, 2002; Paulson, 2002; Ray & Anderson, 2000; Ray & Myers, 1989; Ray & Rinzler, 1993; Renesch, 2002; Rooke & Torbert, 1998, 2005; Senge et al., 2005; Taylor, 2005). Thus, the hypothesis of this research is that vertical growth could lead to an increased sense of inherent trust.

Therefore, the main question for this phenomenological research was: What were the most significant cognitive, emotional, physical, spiritual, or other experiences that characterized the interior transformation of an investor leading toward building more intrinsic trust? Secondary questions included: (1) How do people become the integral change agents required to change current investment practices from for-profit-only investment metrics toward the integration of people, planet, and profit measurements? (2) What facilitated their change of mind? (3) How do they keep high levels of awareness and consciousness in a hostile environment dominated by less conscious investors and shareholders in a litigation-friendly environment? (4) How do they close the gap between the soul of wealth and the wealth of their souls? (5) What triggered their personal growth that led to more trust, causing more peak experiences (Grof, 2006; Maslow, Stephens, & Heil, 1998; White, 1998); flow feelings (Csikszentmihalyi, 1990; Kjaer et al., 2002); and states and stage development (Wilber, 2003)?

Research method and data collection

This research has been performed over a period of more than seven years and still continues. The research method used is called heuristic structuralism and is a qualitative, pluralistic mode of inquiry in which each point of view is respected as a potential source of insight. It is a combination of Moustakas' (1990) in-depth heuristic method and Wilber's (2006) Integral Methodological Pluralism, which contains "at least eight fundamental and apparently irreducible methodologies, injunctions, or paradigms for gaining reproducible knowledge or verifiable repeatable experiences" (p. 33). A quantitative evaluation of data will not be performed in this chapter.

The data collection was taken from 136 interviews performed with global early-stage investors between the ages of 30 and 70 who were personally known to the researcher. They are located all over the world including the United States of America, Western Europe, India, China, Bali/Indonesia, Singapore, and Thailand. They are independently wealthy individuals who are active as Venture Capitalists or angel investors, presidents of Fortune 100 or Fortune 500 companies, serial entrepreneurs, Wall Street financiers, lawyers, musicians, artists, and medical doctors, or who pertain to the entertainment business. All research participants are active investors and Venture Philanthropists who have earned top academic degrees including doctorate degrees, MBAs, or other Master's degrees from some of the most reputable global universities. To these universities belong MIT, KIT (Karlsruhe Institute of Technology, Germany), LMU (Ludwig Maximilian University, Munich), IIT (Indian Institute of Technology), Sorbonne/Paris, London School of Economics, INSEAD/France, Stanford, Yale, or Harvard. The current research focused on identifying, researching, and analyzing the transformational experiences of individual high-net-worth individuals prior, during, and after the 2008 financial crisis. The following descriptions are based on real quotes given by research participants during the interviews performed over several years. In order to allow for an easy understanding and reading flow, the dates, interview numbers, and other data pertaining to these quotes are not included each time. For more details, the reader is invited to refer to Bozesan (2010), where the largest amount of data has been described, analyzed, and synthesized.

Data analysis and composite synthesis

This phenomenological study indicated that the interior evolution toward later stages of consciousness occurs along multiple intelligences (Gardner, 1993), also called lines of human development, which include the cognitive, moral, value, physical, emotional, and psycho-spiritual lines of evolution (Wilber, 2000b). Bozesan (2010) illustrated the evolutionary journey (Figure 18.1) of the research participants toward later stages of consciousness in detail using Joseph Campbell's Hero's Journey (Campbell, 1949/1968).

The reason for choosing Campbell's Hero's Journey (Campbell, 1949/1968) as a demonstration vehicle over more advanced evolutionary models such as Graves' (Beck & Cowan, 1998), Gilligan's (1982/1993), Cook-Greuter's (2005), Kegan's (1982), Kohlberg's (Kohlberg & Ryncarz, 1990), or Wilber's (2000a) has to do with Campbell's (1949/1968) familiarity to a much larger audience other than academia. Campbell's Hero's Journey (Campbell, 1949/1968) is rather well known due to its application in various legends, tales, myths, and cultures, and in Hollywood movies such as the Star Wars films, the Matrix Trilogy, or *The Lion King*. This chapter, however, will only summarize the results within the context of their implications with respect to early-stage investing and leadership development.

Physical and emotional pain as transformation triggers

All research participants are high achievers and can be characterized through exceptional levels of intelligence, postgraduate education, massive drive, determination, hard work, outcome orientation, and competitiveness. The yearning to reach their maximum human potential was fueled by their innate inquisitiveness, creativity, and impulse to work hard. Their unique ability to manifest extraordinary material and financial wealth confirmed their self-reinforcing "outside in mentality" (Bozesan, 2010, p. 63). This individualistic, egocentric, mentality seemed to confirm that their actions were the unique source of happiness and success in the world. It helped them achieve remarkable social status, accumulate extraordinary wealth, build strong egos, and attain the conviction that one is in control of life. The rising spiral of success seemed secure until it was not. As a result, the research participants decided to leave their old world, along with their egocentric model of the world occurring, when they were afflicted by terrible pain that apparently took control away from them as individuals. The source of pain was initially physical in nature. It showed up at the beginning as relatively simple "back problems," "heart hurting," "migraines," "colds and sore throats," weight gain, or food allergies (Bozesan, 2010). Some other times, the pain was of an emotional nature and was caused by a "horrible divorce," death of "mother," being "fired" from a prestigious position, or by not getting the desired job. The emotional pain was perceived as "high degree of anxiety," "worry and fear," "heartbreak," tension between "fear and desire," "grief," the "need" to be accepted by the outside world, and frustration. It was powered by "unhappiness," "lack of fulfillment," "deep sadness and almost shame," "lack

Figure 18.1 The interior journey toward more trust and unity consciousness

of love," "unrest," "lack of trust," and "lack of joy." At the beginning, most participants tried to address their agony by using their cognitive abilities and the same skills that made them outstanding achievers. One of these skills was their ability to control people and outcomes. Initially, they became "a control freak" and "closed down" their hearts to "never" be emotionally available again or they were "wearing a coat of armor" and dealt "with the symptoms" of their physical and emotional pain by studying books or consulting with experts (Bozesan, 2010). They took better care of their bodies through exercises, massages, and better nutrition. As soon as the pain subsided, they went back to the old behavior until the next painful challenge showed up.

Facing the worst nightmares—Shadow work

However, over time the pain increased significantly and more resources were needed to hold it under control. Thus, the research participants decided to spend more money, to hire better "teachers," to attend more "seminars," to get better "counseling," and even to receive psychotherapy. In the end, the pain became unbearable and they were all forced to face their "worst nightmares," namely their own shadows (Bozesan, 2010). The tipping point that eventually led to interior transformation was triggered by their courage and conscious decision to face straight on their shadows and the challenges at hand. This process took several years and was different for each individual research participant. It included (a) the decision to experience the "dark night of the soul" (Bozesan, 2010, p. 120) through holotropic breathwork (Grof, 2006); (b) the willingness to face the "worst [emotional] pain" after "chopping wood" for several hours (Bozesan, 2010, p. 67); and (c) various types of "meditation" or "vision quests." They all began asking essential questions regarding the true meaning of life. The results of the shadow work led in all cases to significant human experiences and are known as Maslow's transcendent or peak experiences (Maslow, 1968/1999), meditative experiences (Alexander et al., 1990), contemplative experiences (Beauregard & O'Leary, 2007), near death or out of body experiences (Alvarado, 2000), exceptional human experiences (White, 1998), and other states of unity consciousness and awe (Vaughan, 2000, 2005). Research indicated that such exceptional human experiences could move humans beyond duality—the good and the bad, the beautiful and the ugly—and toward later stages of consciousness (Alexander et al., 1990; Beauregard & O'Leary, 2007; Commons, Armon, Kohlberg, Richards, & Grotzer, 1990; Commons, Richards, & Armon, 1984; Cook-Greuter, 2005, 2008; Loevinger, 1977; Pauchant, 2002; Torbert et al., 2004; Torbert, Livne-Tarandach, Herdman-Barker, Nicolaides, & McCallum, 2008).

The research participants described these experiences as a "lightning bolt [that] moved through" the body and caused a feeling "so powerfully strong that it was almost to the point where you couldn't walk" (Bozesan, 2010). Or as a "mystical experience," "divine light," or "divine intelligence" (Bozesan, 2010). In some cases, it was a feeling in which the "heart was exploding with love" and in which the "body turned into an intense beam of light" that opened the heart. They "could feel every bird and insect" as being part of them. These "grand openings" enabled the perception of "an energy that's greater than we are" (Bozesan, 2010).

Not religion, but spirituality

When relating to these extraordinary human experiences within the context of investing or business, it is important to note that, without exception, the researched asset owners are non-religious people who enjoyed high academic, scientific, and/or business educations and possessed extremely successful careers. At that time, many of them did not have any framework or the proper language to explain or make sense of the extraordinary experiences they were having. The old worldview was shattered as soon as the research participant gave up control and surrendered to their shadows, the unknown, and to the "unbearable fear" and pain. Their "spiritual" experiences caused a "major shift" and a "quantum leap in consciousness" (Bozesan, 2010) and their lives would never be the same again. Neuroscientific research indicates that such extraordinary human experiences can contribute to achieving higher levels of personal integration and/or move the participant to later stages of ego development (Beauregard & O'Leary, 2007; McCraty, 2001; Newberg & Lee, 2005) and developmental investigations (Alexander et al., 1990; Commons et al., 1990; Cook-Greuter, 2005, 2008; Damasio, 2006; Goleman, 2000, 2003; Goleman, Boyatzis, & McKee, 2003; Kegan, Lahey, & Souvaine, 1990; Koplowitz, 1984, 1990; Wilber, 2000b).

The closet mystic existence

Driven by these extraordinary human experiences that gave them a taste of the hidden and much more comprehensive dimensions of a greater reality, the research participants pursued their shadow work and inner growth with the same dedication with which they had developed their careers. However, for a while, they lived the life of a "closet mystic" (Bozesan, 2010, p. 224) and practiced certain meditative rituals for longer periods of time, sometimes for several decades. A notable fact shared by all research participants was their inner yearning for a common-sense spirituality that elucidated their mystical experiences and transcended traditional religious norms, which all of them rejected. Originally, their extraordinary experiences conflicted also with their scientific education, which had neither room nor the proper language to explain them. Yet, their ability to experience these peak states on an ongoing basis paired with the enormous amount of research data available in this field permitted them to come to terms with their new insights. One investor described this phase of his life like

> going through a college program, which is a rapid introduction to something and exposure to something—Like turning on a fire hose. This was like drinking out of a fire hose. In this area, MIT and Stanford Business School were like drinking out of a fire hose for academic and business issues. This was like drinking out of a fire hose for emotional, spiritual, and consciousness issues. We need both.
>
> *(Bozesan, 2010, p. 168)*

Gaining a deeper understanding of reality

Their "unitive experiences" transformed the research participants in significant ways. They (a) learned how to "reconnect to that authentic self"; (b) realized that we are all "part of oneness, a greater whole"; (c) developed the ability to understand their "own consciousness," the "collective consciousness," and how we "are part of that greater human consciousness and then beyond"; (d) understood the "dimensions and interconnectedness of body, mind, and spirit"; (e) became more "rounded [and] balanced"; and (f) received "structure and specific knowledge" on how to continue to grow on the path to self-actualization. In short, the research participants moved from a previous orientation of the exterior dimensions of life toward a deep interior transformation, only to integrate these later on.

More trust through fear transcendence

One of the most significant outcomes of this transformation was related to fear transcendence, which then led to intrinsic trust. For example, after having a deep spiritual experience, one research participant, who has a Ph.D. in distributed computer systems and was a co-founder of a major Silicon Valley company, realized that he has "absolutely no fear of death." Thus, he sees death as a "great opportunity to move forward" on his path through life. To various degrees, all research participants have transcended their fear of failure because they realized that (a) "nobody can take" from them who they are, (b) "fear of failure is not sustainable," and (c) they are no longer "afraid to" face fear. Facing their "worst nightmares" trained them how to "listen to [the] inner voice" and how to connect with their "divine nature" to access their "unlimited potentials" (Bozesan, 2010). Fear turned into deep trust.

Asking essential questions—Who am I?

Furthermore, their transformative experiences led the investors to ask essential questions such as "Who am I?," "Why am I here?," "Is this it?," and "Why do I let the mob psychology [of Wall Street] tell me whether I was having a good day or not?" Their transformation induced significant doubt regarding their old worldviews. This more integrated lifestyle encouraged them to question more deeply the status quo of their own lives and that of the world as a whole. Eventually, they noticed the "collective insanity" of the "money game" and decided that the "standard operating procedure" for a "successful" person was no longer the game they wanted to play (Bozesan, 2010). Furthermore, they realized that (a) they were not "manifesting" their true mission in life, (b) the values they had "adopted" were not "self-selected" but imposed by society, and (c) they were "following a script that was not authored" by them. As they "looked into the future" and saw the "endless stream of closing quarters" that are the essential driving force in the financial and business worlds, they detected the "almost mind numbingly impossible monotony around the trajectory" on which they were operating (Bozesan, 2010). They understood that the rewards "were running out," the next "gold ring" was no longer tempting, that there were "fewer [attractive] jobs left" in the world, and that "maximizing shareholder value" was no longer the only goal in life (Bozesan, 2010). As a result, their value system shifted from the need to control the future to being present now (Senge, Scharmer, Jaworsky, & Flowers, 2005).

Transitioning from an ego-centric view to a world-centric view of the world

Without exception, all research participants moved over time from an ego-centric view of the world to a world-centric view of the world in which they decided to be of service to a greater good (Bozesan, 2010). One investor, for example, described his transformational shift from the ego-centric to the world-centric level of consciousness, from "me" to "we," in the following way:

> [Initially], it was me, me, me and my fabulous career and how do I help create more money for the company, so I can create more money for me and more success for me and more power for me? But suddenly when I was rewired, it felt like the smallest game in the universe. When you really make that shift and you start playing for an idea bigger than yourself and you start sensing into what is that divine creative impulse that's seated within me that is my gift to the planet? Within that surrendering was recognizing that there's something unique within me that I was born to become and that by surrendering to that, by paying attention to that, by allowing that to emerge within myself, that I could play a much bigger game, a much more fulfilling game, a much more meaningful game in terms of being able to create from that space in service to a much deeper and broader concept.
>
> *(Bozesan, 2010, p. 200)*

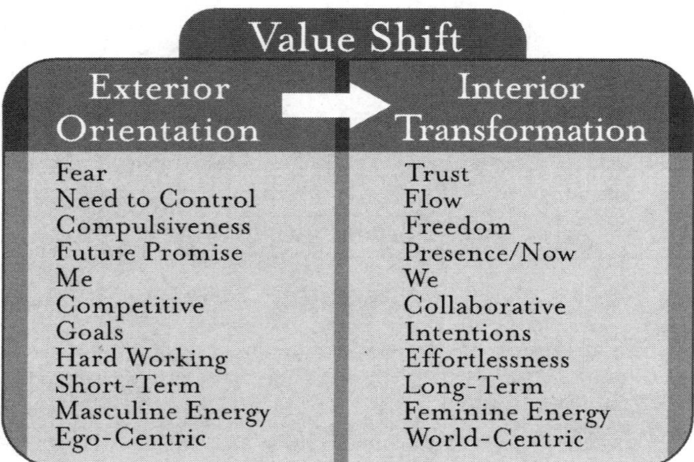

Figure 18.2 Interior transformation resulted in an exterior values shift

Values shift

The tremendous transformation resulted also in new and "self-selected" values (Figure 18.2), which, as a consequence, had to be tightly connected with their current *raison d'être* in the world (Bozesan, 2010).

These new values are integrity, authenticity, truth, truthfulness, honesty, humility, and unity consciousness. With the support of these high moral standards they can today (a) "stick" their "neck" out to fight for what they believe in without fear, (b) perform "social justice," and (c) "do the right thing whether it's popular or not." Along with this new sense of identity, their self-confidence also increased. They grew beyond being "ego-driven" to being more self-confident and feeling "more comfortable" in their own skin. This includes (a) trusting their intuition and (b) an increased sense of awareness, as well as (c) being willing to "take the risk," and (d) declaring "more fully" what they want (Bozesan, 2010).

Letting go of control

After many years of trials and tribulations, the research participants arrived at the realization that they can achieve much more when they let go of "efforting" and by having intentions rather than outcomes (Bozesan, 2010). As a result, they have learned to "get rid of" their "outcomes," "life plan," or even "personal career." As they set intentions instead of outcomes, they became more open and were able to "see [more] opportunities" than before. If they "simply get out of the way," "the universe constantly positively surprises" them "with its potential." The more they were willing to let go of control, the more success they had, and the more accepting they became of themselves and life in general. As they began meeting "people where they are" at instead of where they wanted them to be, the greater was their sense of "relief."

Meaning versus money

Without exception, all researched participants are now "less concerned with material things" as they were before (Bozesan, 2010). They do not seem to "need as many things as" they "used to need." In fact, "things sometimes get in the way" of what they are "trying to do." Furthermore, they seem to not "care about showing off" or "accumulating things" anymore. Through their transformation, they also "saw the hollowness" of a money-only and material-only orientation. They realized that there are "a lot of problems that money doesn't solve," and that "it's not all about the money" but also about "freedom of expression and creativity" (Bozesan, 2010).

Cultivating presence

Another significant structural change of which the participants in the current study were cognizant is their ability to have intrinsic trust through their newly gained ability to stay present within the stressful environment in which they live (Scharmer, 2013; Senge, Scharmer, Jaworski, & Flowers, 2005). Cultivating presence and "being the observer" has become a key transformative practice in the lives because it helps them "stay sane" (Bozesan, 2010). By being present they can now get "down into the basic elements of life," connect with the people in their lives at a much deeper level, and be more efficient and effective. Presence helps them "quiet" their minds, and in doing that they "feel absolutely grateful and joyful to be alive in this moment." Cultivating presence has become part of their daily integral life practice, which some even declared publicly through an action or event that "felt" like a "coming out party."

Leaving the old world

In all cases, the research participants quit their old and unsupportive environment to pursue a more integrated life. While preserving their old façades, they followed their transformative paths using their "creative side that was always crying to emerge" (Bozesan, 2010) to make movies, write books, or start new and more socially and environmentally oriented organizations and businesses. There was "no going back" to their old ways, and "change became unavoidable." Being outstanding leaders in their field of investing, finance, and economics, the research participants felt the responsibility to follow their higher calling and have a greater impact in the world. Their calling was in all cases driven by "the realization of what a purposeful life actually means," and they needed to leverage their "talents to make a meaningful and impactful contribution to the sustainability of the planet" (Bozesan, 2010).

Changing the old paradigm

Following their major transformation, the research participants began viewing their new life purpose in bringing "consciousness" into the domain of investing, economics, philanthropy, and business "in a way that creates sustainable change relative to the human beings on the planet and ultimately bringing spirit into manifestation" (Bozesan, 2010). One of them expressed the new purpose as being

> not so blatantly devoid of my personal own interests. But I think I've become much more decentralized in my thinking to where it's much easier for me to have other people have certain things and not worry about myself. I'm about mission and I'm about helping.
>
> *(Bozesan, 2010, p. 229)*

Through their changed behaviors and actions, the researched investors were determined to have an even "bigger impact" in the finance and business world than before and in a much more integrated way. They saw investing, economics, and business as an "incredible laboratory of consciousness" (Bozesan, 2010) in which the integration of the interior and exterior dimensions of life is of utmost significance. The research participants realized that "everything is either moving towards that state of expanded consciousness or is retarding it" (Bozesan, 2010). Their newly gained capabilities enabled them also to impact both their own culture and social environments. They became better at relationships because they are able to build a bridge between the mind and the heart, between the inner and the outer, between having an "enjoyable business as well as mak[ing] money." They became Venture Philanthropists parallel to or alternative to investing. They now view "business as a service" to humanity. Over time, they became involved with the creation of Sustainable Investing, economic, and business models (a) by promoting long-term thinking through the realization that it "was not necessarily the shorter term end state you are working toward but the greater good, the greater end state"; (b) by "creating social enterprises and different financing mechanisms that are behind that"; (c) by ceasing to support the "ideology" of "rampant consumerism"; and (d) by creating social justice and seeking a more integral "political leadership." Through their evolutionary process, they have developed more trust, self-esteem, and a deeper understanding of "interconnectedness" between people, planet, and profit as well as their own life's purpose and their passion (Bozesan, 2010). In an unassuming way, their mission in life has become more important to them than personal achievement and outer success.

Part II: Discussion and implications in early-stage investing

Through their major shift in consciousness, the research participants, called here integrally acting investors, realized that their new investing approach must be based on the integration or parity of people, planet, and profit rather than preferring one aspect at the expense of the other two. They saw that, without a full understanding of the problem, no sustainable solution is possible. Through their transformation, these investors noted how crucial the interior aspects of the individual and the collective are in determining a full-spectrum investing philosophy and portfolios. They saw that, collectively, we do not only have ecological, financial, inequality, water, or poverty crises, we also have interior human crises that must be taken into consideration equally. They realized that their action in the world must be grounded in the quintessence of life as a whole with its interior as well as exterior reality.

Part II of this chapter shows how (1) vertical growth is at work in the above transformations of consciousness; (2) these developmental dimensions are co-arising whether we are aware of them or not; and (3) Wilber's (2006) Integral Theory could provide a workable framework for the future of investing. The Theta Model is then briefly introduced as an investing process in early-stage investing that includes, transcends, and reflects such a transformation. It shows how the integration of people, planet, and profit measurements could increase trust in the investment process through more comprehensive de-risking tools.

Vertical growth as the driving force behind the scene

The desired changes toward integral sustainability occur within a very complex context. That includes what is obvious to the eye from the outside, namely the environmental, financial, economic, and social structures, as well as individual behavior. However, it includes also what cannot be seen from the outside, namely the interiors—emotions, psychology, cognition—of participating agents, both the individual as well as collective players. What Krugman (2009) called "obsolete doctrines that clutter the minds of men" (p. 191) are actually socio-political and inter-objective contexts, rules, systems, and regulations. But they also contain cultural inter-subjective and deeply ingrained norms, such as ethics and morals that influence our individual and collective behaviors (Baier, 1994/1996; Gilligan, 1993; Kohlberg & Ryncarz, 1990).

These collective behaviors have evolved over thousands of years of human evolution (Wilber, 2000a, 2000b) and have been represented by Maslow (Maslow, Stephens, & Heil, 1998) in his pyramid of needs. According to Maslow (Maslow et al., 1998), humans apparently evolve during their lifetime along his pyramid. The model contains consecutive stages of development, starting with (a) survival/physiological needs for air, food, water, sex, and sleep; and then moving to (b) safety/security needs for health and property needs; (c) social needs for love; (d) ego/self-esteem needs for confidence and achievement; (e) self-actualization needs for high morals and creativity with lack of prejudice and acceptance of facts; and finally (f) self-transcendence needs (Maslow, 1999; Maslow et al., 1998). As individuals are able to fulfill their basic needs, they are able to grow into the next stages. On the moral line of development, Gilligan (1923) names these stages: (1) selfish/pre-conventional stages; (2) care/conventional stages; and (3) universal care/post-conventional stages. As humans grow to these later stages, they apparently begin to take a more global view on life and adapt higher moral standards (Commons, Armon, Kohlberg, Richards, & Grotzer, 1990; Commons, Richards, & Armon, 1984; Cook-Greuter, 2004, 2005, 2008; Gardner, 1993, 2004; Gebser, 1984; Gilligan, 1993; Kohlberg & Ryncarz, 1990; Wilber, 2000a, 2000b). In other words, only at the later stages of personal development do people appear to be in a position to fulfill higher ethical requests. That could mean that commandments and regulations can only be fulfilled if people are at the later stages of interior development and their basic needs are satisfied and they have higher ethical standards. This could explain why a LIBOR and a subprime crisis had to occur despite SEC and other regulations (Lewis, 2014). Ensuring that the participating agents in such key positions are at the later stages of human and moral development could provide additional certainty and avoid similar disasters in the future. In other words, individuals at the later stages of development and of higher ethical standards (Baier, 1994/1996; Dalai Lama, 1999) might be in a much better position to apply Kant's categorical imperative (Kant, 1949/1993).

However, what also resulted from this research is that vertical, interior transformation occurs over many years; it is rather painful, elaborate, and not guaranteed. This may also explain in part why mandating through legislation that people behave in an ethical manner does not guarantee that they will. Most world religions have tried to cultivate higher ethics for millennia with modest success (Armstrong, 1993).

Current transformations in investing

From an investing perspective, there is a lot of reason for hope. The current transformative developments in the investing industry today appear to be occurring through investors such as the ones researched. Such investors seem to be changing the current investment paradigm through various initiatives and activities that attempt to re-establish trust in our economy, financial systems, the environment, and geo-political systems by showing various paths toward "integral sustainability" (Brown, 2007, p. 1; Esbjörn-Hargens & Zimmermann, 2009, p. 245).

One such initiative is the Natural Capital Declaration (The Natural Capital Declaration, n.d.) made by 37 banks, investment funds, and insurance companies, which aims at integrating natural capital criteria such as soil, air, water, flora, and fauna in their products and services.

Another is the Sustainable Stock Exchanges Initiative (Panwar & Blinch, 2012), a commitment made by five major stock exchanges that collectively list more than 4,600 companies, with the intention to promote Sustainable Investments through a global call for sustainability disclosure and performance by the companies listed on their trade floors. The Giving Pledge, launched on August 4, 2010, is another initiative through which some "of the wealthiest families and individuals in the United States [and the rest of the world] have committed to returning the majority of their wealth to charitable causes" (Giving Pledge, 2010).

The AVIVA (2011) coalition, an alliance of more than 40 like-minded private and institutional investors managing collectively approximately US $2 trillion, is yet another alliance of investors who have agreed to promote the long-term sustainability of their investees through more reliable information and more robust measurement criteria that could drive more sustainable performance and demonstrate reliably the value of non-financial information including Environmental, Social, and Governance (ESG) criteria (Tomorrow's Capital Markets, 2012).

Moreover, the Global Alliance for Banking on Values provides hope through an independent network of more than 24 of the world's leading Sustainable Banks. Their report (GABV, 2012) assessed the performance of banks over 10 years from 2002 to 2011 and demonstrated how they are (a) eliminating the myth about lower returns through sustainability, (b) showing that Sustainable Banks have higher returns on assets than regular banks, (c) indicating significantly higher levels of growth in loans and deposits than traditional banks, (d) exhibiting higher and better quality capital inflows, and (e) revealing that Sustainable Banks are both investing more successfully in a greener and fairer society while having more robust and resilient business models than traditional banks. Furthermore, the International Integrated Reporting Council (IIRC) is a "global coalition of regulators, investors, companies, standard setters, the accounting profession and NGOs that share the view that communication about businesses' value creation should be the next step in the evolution of corporate reporting" (The IIRC, 2013).

And last but not least, the Global Sustainable Investments study (GSIA, 2015) showed that investments using some kind of ESG criteria reached an invested amount of US$ 21.4 trillion, equivalent to 30.2 percent of total AuM worldwide in 2014.

Moving beyond both traditional investing and Impact Investing

On one hand, there is traditional investing that is profit-oriented and thus challenges investors to earn superior financial returns consistently. On the other hand, it has become obvious over the past decades that an increasing number of investors have begun integrating their values within their investment decisions by looking for more responsible investment opportunities that make a profit in addition to having a social and/or an environmental impact (GSIA, 2015). The transformation of the participating agents' mindset paved the way toward the development of Impact Investing in 1985, which is considered to be its birth year (Robeco, Booz & Co., 2009). As a result, Impact Investing appears to have become a separate asset class according to the same source. Similar forms of investing with comparable criteria are also known as Socially Responsible Investing (SRI), Program-Related Investing (PRI), Mission-Related Investing (MRI), or Triple Bottom Line Investing (TBLI).

Impact Investing appears to be rather promising because it is driven by the investors' intention to make a difference (Bugg-Levine & Emerson, 2011) and is measured through financial criteria alongside ESG criteria (Freireich & Fulton, 2009; Robeco, Booz & Co., 2009). Unfortunately, according to Randall Kempner, Executive Director of the Aspen Network of Development Entrepreneurs, Aspen Institute, "Impact Investing is currently growing linearly. In order for it to grow exponentially, we need to find a way to incorporate mainstream investors into the mix" (Bryce, Drexler, & Noble, 2013). In order for this industry to grow exponentially,

Impact Investing must become mainstream through better integrated and more easily measurable criteria for mainstream investors (Bryce et al., 2013). However, what appears to impede Impact Investing from becoming mainstream is not only the missing critical mass of world-centric-oriented investors discussed above, but also the outdated current incentive structures. These incentive structures are the result of the old for-profit-only investment paradigm that is predominantly influenced by short-term financial performance, market indices, benchmarks, market share, personal security, success, and reputation, as well as regulatory compliance, few of which contain long-term sustainability aspects, which are currently tagged as externalities (Tomorrow's Capital Markets, 2012). New compensation structures should aim at discouraging unsustainable behaviors in the participating agents that in the past led to goal misalignment, cultures of fear, growing self-interest, communication gaps, and high levels of remuneration that were linked to short-term profits.

Building trust through Integral Investing

Investors are the custodians of financial capital and natural capital, but also human capital—including interior values such as purpose, joy, and happiness. In order to ensure the accurate integration of these significant factors in investing, that is, the financial sustainability metrics of traditional investing with the ESG criteria of Impact Investing, as well as the cultural and individual metrics, the application of Wilber's (2000) Integral Theory represented in Figure 18.3 is herewith proposed.

Wilber's (2000) theory informs the investment thesis of Integral Investing, with the Theta Model at its center providing a post-post-modern framework that is based on theory of evolution while integrating humanity's indivisible value spheres described by Plato as the True/science, the Good/morals, and the Beautiful/art (Plato, 1938/1961). Wilber's (2000a) Integral Theory is based not only on Plato's (1938/1961) irreducible value spheres, but it also includes Kant's (1949/1993) Big Three critiques: the Critique of Pure Reason (the True, "IT," or objective rationality), the Critique of Practical Reason (the Good, "WE," or morals), and the Critique of Judgment (Beauty, "I," or subjective reality). It is, furthermore, rooted in Habermas' (1992) indivisible three Worlds: the objective, the subjective, and the cultural. Integral Investing

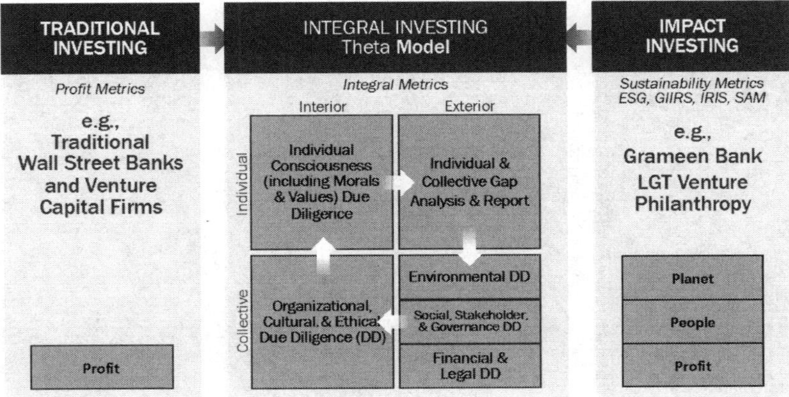

Figure 18.3 Integral Investing provides the integration between traditional investing and Impact Investing
Source: Based on Bozesan (2014).

contributes to (a) honoring the truth in all there is, including people, planet, and profit; (b) appreciating diversity in culture and society; and (c) seeing reality as an indivisible whole. In this reality, every exterior, such as the social, political, and geographical context, has an interior, such as cultural and ethical norms that influence it.

For example, an average entrepreneur who lives in a postmodern society such as Western Europe will, most likely, have a different view of the world and therefore other behavior and leadership skills than an entrepreneur from an emerging economy such as the BRIC states (Brazil, Russia, India, and China). Thus, the application of Wilber's (2000) Integral Theory enables the development of a rather powerful de-risking tool. Within the context of early-stage investing, it provides one with a differentiated view of investees and a reality that is made up of a complex web of interrelated and intra-connected ecological structures, social systems, and cultural determinants, all of which are subject to evolution. From a collective perspective, the evolution of social systems and/or cultural structures can be categorized either (a) according to the infrastructural and techno-economic base of society, which includes evolutionary periods such as the foraging, horticultural, agrarian, industrial, and informational stages of development (Beck & Cowan, 1996); or (b) according to the predominant worldview of the culture such as archaic, magic, mythic, scientific, rational, pluralistic, and integral (Gebser, 1949/1984) or simply pre-modern, modern, and postmodern. The cultural worldviews are intimately correlated with the social techno-economic structures because they occurred together and are influencing each other. They are different facets of the same coin. Therefore, understanding and acknowledging the fact that the multitude of societies and cultures on earth are at different levels of evolution, and apparently at different levels of consciousness, is key for building investors' trust. This understanding, helps one to invest much more sustainably and compassionately by meeting people at their own levels of consciousness and not our own. It helps acknowledge, honor, and celebrate the fact that humanity, as a whole, is completely heterogeneous. This is true at large and within the context of a start-up company.

From the investing perspective in early-stage companies, it is important that the integration of people, planet, and profit occurs along the entire value creation process. This investment thesis must be included in execution of deal screening and the due diligence process, but also be part of the execution of the investment, as well as during start-up monitoring and development and up to the investment exit. The stages of value creation from deal screening to due diligence, investment execution, monitoring, and wealth actualization through the investment exit are shown in Figure 18.4.

DEAL SCREENING	DUE DILIGENCE	INVESTMENT EXECUTION	MANAGEMENT/ MONITORING	WEALTH ACTUALIZATION
Deal Sourcing	*Theta Model Toolbox & Process*	*Integral Alignment*	*Grow for Success*	*Exit*
Integrally Informed Business Model Screening According to Theta Model Criteria **Integral Founders Screening**	**Financial & Legal DD** **ESG/B-Corp Assessment** **Cultural & Organizational Assessment** **Team Alignment Test** **Individual Assessment**	**Secure Mission Aligned Co-investors** **Closing** **Setting Up Integrally Informed Company** **Consciousness Leadership Alignment**	**Board Representation** **Org. Development** **Integrally Informed Human Resources** **Integrally Informed Strategy** **Corporate & Stakeholder Alignment**	**Secure Top Rating** **IPO/Trade Sale** **Liquidat ion** **Ongoing Dividends**
Integrally Screened Deal Flow Theta Model Alignment Potential Term Sheet	AQAL Scoring/Certificate Go/No go Recommendation	Integrally Informed Investment Executed Investment Aligned with Investee's Strategy	Ongoing Theta Model Alignment Ongoing Management & Monitoring	Delivered Outstanding ROI and Integral Impact Integral Wealth Creation Self-actualization

Figure 18.4 The value creation process in early stage investing using integral theory

Source: Bozesan, 2014.

The due diligence procedure, Step 2 in Figure 18.4, is discussed in more detail in the following paragraphs in order to provide a better understanding of the role of trust in investing and how it could be increased through a more thorough de-risking process.

Trust is an emotion: Why better de-risking tools could deliver more investors' trust

Trust is an emotion, and emotional intelligence (Goleman, 1995) plays an important role not only in our everyday, mundane, life but more so in the context of any type of investing as well as with the "global casino" (Henderson, 2013) on Wall Street, for example. At 1:08 PM on April 23, 2013 a fake tweet from a hacked Associated Press account asserted that explosions at the White House had injured Barack Obama. Stock prices immediately dropped, wiping more than $130 billion off the value of the S&P 500. This number actually understates the severity of the episode because in several cases liquidity simply disappeared altogether (*The Economist*, April 23, 2013). Therefore, the inclusion of emotional intelligence (Goleman, 1995) along with other human intelligences (Gardner, 1993) such as cognition and intrapersonal and interpersonal intelligences in the due diligence process has been shown to provide better informed investment decisions, leading to greater success (Bozesan, 2013a; Kelly, 2011; Rooke & Torbert, 1998, 2005; Torbert, Livne-Tarandach, Herdman-Barker, Nicolaides, & McCallum, 2008).

Moreover, the scientific community, from economics, finance, and behavioral finance to neuroscience and psychology (Camerer & Loewenstein, 2004; Yazdipour, 2011) appears to be united in the fact that behavior is influenced by our psyche "in here" rather than "out there." These various dimensions of consciousness are permanently co-arising and are deeply influencing our decisions about whether we consider them or not (Beauregard & O'Leary, 2007; Kahneman & Tversky, 1982; McCraty, 2001; Newberg & Lee, 2005; Wilber, 2000b).

The decision to include most significant de-risking dimensions including those for people, the planet, and profit using Integral Theory (Wilber, 2000) led 15 years ago to the development of the Theta Model in my own investment practice. With respect to measurement criteria discussed in more detail below, the Theta Model implements (a) the integration between traditional, profit-oriented, investing criteria (financial and legal due diligence tools); (b) Impact Investing measurements with their ESG (UN PRI, 2013) metrics; and (c) behavioral, cultural, and consciousness criteria as defined in Wilber's (2000) integral framework. Moreover, the Theta Model is an accelerator for screening and decision making as well as a vehicle for the speedy creation of successful and sustainable companies from the very beginning.

The Theta Model

The Theta Model provides a de-risking framework, which integrates traditional due diligence, that is shown in Step 2 in Figure 18.4, with integral Impact Investment performance measurements. The five steps of the Theta Model are represented in Figure 18.5 and will be briefly discussed below.

Step 1: Financial and Legal Due Diligence

In Step 1 of Figure 18.5, the Theta Model addresses traditional financial and legal due diligence components that try to identify the unknown by validating the business plan, uncovering

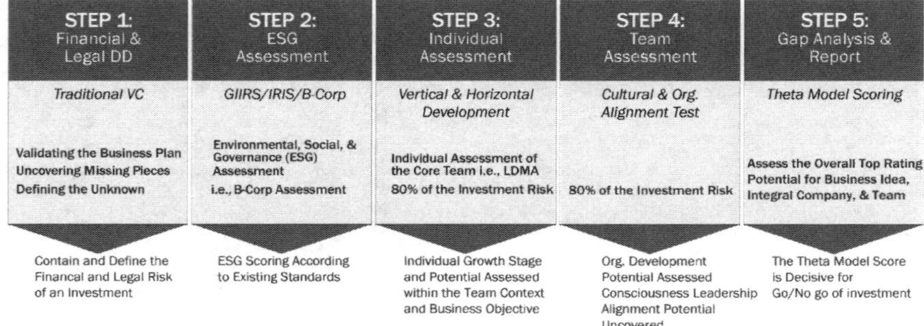

Figure 18.5 The Theta Model: De-risking steps of the due diligence process

Source: Bozesan, 2014.

missing pieces, and defining the financial and legal risks, as well as other risks associated with the market, competition, and intellectual property (IP).

Step 2: Environmental, Social, and Governance Assessment

In Step 2, the Theta Model implements Environmental, Social, and Governance (ESG) criteria and thus helps fulfill Brundtland's (World Commission on Environment and Development, 1987/2009) request for integral sustainability by meeting "the need of the present without compromising the ability of future generations to meet their own needs" (p. 43). The adoption of the ESG metrics of the United Nations (UN PRI, 2013) helps (1) reduce risk; (2) create sustainable and responsible companies from the very beginning; (3) produce more transparency (IIRC, 2013); and (4) generate compliance with the International Stock Exchange Initiative to receive a good rating in case an initial public offering (IPO) occurs (Panwar & Blinch, 2012). There are several tools that can be applied to accomplish the goals in Step 2. The GIIRS-based (Global Impact Investing Rating System) self-assessment offered by B Corp (2015) is highly recommended.

Step 3: Individual Assessment

Any good real estate agent would agree that "location, location, location" are the three most important attributes of a successful real estate investment. In a similar way, any experienced high-risk/VC investor would agree that investing in high-quality management is arguably the litmus test not only for the success of the start-up, but more importantly for the success of the partnership between investors, entrepreneurs, the community, suppliers, and other stakeholders. In my experience, more than 80 percent of the investment risk can be addressed by performing an integral due diligence on the team.

Most due diligence tools used by investors to assess individuals and the team of a start-up are frequently limited to assessing exterior factors such as the ones described by social scientists as (a) mental characteristics such as "the need for achievement, need for power, belief that one is in control of one's own destiny, and risk preferences"; (b) behavioral characteristics that include "determination, resourcefulness, a sense of urgency to get things done, and a realistic approach to facts"; (c) physical characteristics such as "energy level, a better than average ability to speak and communicate, and mental stamina"; and (d) moral characteristics such as "honesty, partnership orientation, and a desire for fair play" (Gladstone & Gladstone, 2004). The traditional

VC assessment process includes individual and team interviews, background checks, personal history assessments, and the observing of body language during personal interactions. Some venture capital firms "resort to personality or psychology tests, but this is not frequently done" (Wong, 2005). This is unfortunate for both the start-up and the investor side.

Given the fact that both parties are actually looking for a mutually fruitful relationship, the results of these tests would help cement the potential relationship and lead it to success. According to research by renowned Harvard scholar Susanne Cook-Greuter (2004), only 10–20 percent of adults demonstrate high ethics and high levels of ego development. Identifying those in a start-up setting would help ensure that what is being promised on the outside is authentically true on the inside. According to CEO-oriented research (Rooke & Torbert, 1998, 2005; Torbert, Livne-Tarandach, Herdman-Barker, Nicolaides, & McCallum, 2008) performed on 10 organizations over four years by Action Inquiry experts Rooke and Torbert (2005), there appears to be a direct correlation between levels of consciousness of the CEO and the survival of the business. In this research, all five organizations led by CEOs rated at high ethics levels were transformed into successful businesses—financially and otherwise. Only two of the organizations that were led by CEOs assessed at conventional levels of consciousness were still around, while the others went out of business. Additional research involving financial service advisors at American Express by leading Stanford researcher and forgiveness expert Fred Luskin (Luskin et al., 2009) "demonstrated a 50–400 percent improvement in productivity over their peers, which led to an average increase in sales of 25 percent. This was coupled with a marked decrease in stress and a large improvement in life satisfaction."

Beginning with Step 3, the Theta Model goes, therefore, well beyond traditional investing, sustainable and responsible investing, or Impact Investing criteria. It includes additional aspects of reality—such as interior, evolutionary, behavioral, inter-objective, and inter-subjective—that are constantly co-arising and which affect us whether we are aware of them or not (Wilber, 2000). The detailed explanation of Wilber's Integral Theory and its application in early-stage investing is not within the scope of this chapter. For more details, please refer to Bozesan (2010, 2011a, 2011b, 2012, 2013a, 2013b, 2014). The underlying premise of this application is that leaders can be developed through vertical learning (Brown, 2014). Vertical learning is considered the number one future trend in leader development (Petrie, 2011) and is thus very important, especially in the success of early-stage companies. Vertical learning occurs naturally, yet can be accelerated by three to five times under the right conditions (Brown, 2014). Applied correctly, it appears to broaden our worldview and to heighten our awareness. Leaders with greater vertical development are perceived as more effective and more capable of addressing complex challenges (Brown, 2014). Research indicates that vertical learning can have the following impact: (1) Vertical learning helps transform how people think and behave, not just what they know. It literally alters brain functioning and recreates a leader's worldview. (2) Studies of the CEOs of industry-leading public companies, mid-market executives, military cadets, and consultants all show that vertical learning creates a new operating system—a more complex mindset—that makes leaders considerably more effective than their counterparts. (3) Leaders with mature vertical development not only appear to see and feel situations and people differently, but they seem to see and feel more than other leaders.

With vertical development, leaders seem to perform better across a host of mission critical domains: (a) inspiring vision and leading transformational change; (b) strategic, systemic, and contextual thinking; (c) building relationships, collaborating, and resolving conflicts; (d) decision-making, reframing challenges, and creating innovative solutions; (e) developing themselves and others; and (f) tolerating ambiguity and navigating complexity (Nicolaides, 2008). There are various tools that can be applied within Step 3 of the Theta Model. Within the context of this chapter, LDMA (Leadership/Lectical Decision-Making Assessment) will be mentioned (Stein, Dawson, & Fischer, 2009). LDMA "is a learning tool that supports the development of leaders' decision-making skills" that "focuses on three aspects of decision-making: (1) collaborative capacity: the ability to bring together diverse perspectives to develop inclusive, innovative, and effective solutions; (2) contextual thinking: the ability to consider problems in terms of the broader systems and contexts in which they are embedded; and (3) cognitive complexity: the ability to think well about complex issues" (Lectica, 2014). The tool is based on work performed at Harvard University's Graduate School of Education. It was initiated by Prof. Kurt W. Fischer and later enhanced by Stein et al. (2009).

Step 4: Team Assessment

In support of team assessment and development, Brown (2014) stated that high-performing teams exhibit a ratio of positive interactions (support, encouragement, appreciation) to negative interactions (disapproval, sarcasm, cynicism) of between 3:1 and 11:1. Such teams also balance advocacy with inquiry and balance a focus on self with a focus on others. In layman's terms, they care about one another and work well together. These behaviors enable the teams to operate in a dynamic flow-like state—a bit like a championship basketball team. Medium and low-performing teams exhibit lower ratios of positive to negative interactions, favor advocacy over inquiry, and participants focus more on themselves than on each other.

Possessing this type of data on the entrepreneurs in whom one invested could significantly increase trust and the likelihood of success, and reduce the investment risk related to the team. Here too, there are a myriad of tools that can be applied to team assessment. The Five Dysfunctions of a Team is such a tool and process that is based on the book with the same title by Patrick Lencioni (2002). The Five Dysfunctions of a Team are (1) Absence of Trust, (2) Fear of Conflict, (3) Lack of Commitment, (4) Avoidance of Accountability, and (5) Inattention to Results.

Step 5: Gap Analysis and Report

Step 5 contains the summary of the integral due diligence process contained in the Theta Model. It offers a gap analysis and report and makes the final recommendation for the investment based on the Theta Factor, which will not be discussed further in this chapter. In short, the Theta Factor is a number that results from the summary of each due diligence step. A positive investment decision will be made only if more than 80 percent of all requirements have been fulfilled in order of importance.

Conclusion

Through the application of the Theta Model in early-stage investing, an investor has the opportunity to not only decrease the investment risk but also increase his/her own trust in the success of his/her investment because of the utilization of a much more elaborated and more thorough de-risking process and tools. The premise is that his/her portfolio companies must (1) solve real customer problems; (2) implement innovative business ideas; (3) have a specific-sector focus such as transformative technology, climate change, lifestyle, cultural innovation, and/or megatrends; and (4) have the ability to massively scale into a worldwide marketplace. The Theta Model ensures that the portfolio companies (1) are led by dedicated, resilient, and integrally acting management teams; (2) are committed to integral sustainability criteria including, financial, environmental, social, and governance measurements; (3) display ethical behavior; (4) create a corporate culture based on higher values and levels of consciousness; and (5) support transparent reporting.

At the same time, the following can be carried out so that mistakes can be avoided: (1) failure to identify early enough the lack of team alignment and missing common values; (2) the companies must be easily accessible and geographically and culturally close to the immediate circle of influence through the investor and other stakeholders; (3) the technology must not be introduced too early that it takes too much capital and time to materialize; (4) do not neglect the importance of a regulated market; (5) the main founder(s) must want to provide some kind of exit in order for the cost of the investment to be retrieved within a reasonable period of time; (6) do not be too hands off; (7) allocate enough capital so you can continue investing in the company's growth to avoid unnecessary dilution; (8) do not invest against your intuition and gut feeling; (9) do not trust the entrepreneurs at face value; (10) always use proper scientific tools to assess the levels of morals and ethics; (11) do not underestimate the importance of proper legal advice; (12) being fast is key to success in order to avoid being eliminated by faster and hungrier competition; and (13) be well prepared for crises. Early-stage investing is a risky business, but if homework is comprehensively done there should be no regrets.

When the Theta Model is applied in full, it could be argued that the main key to success is the team, including all stakeholders such as investors, suppliers, the start-up team, and other contributors. The intention of the Theta Model is the cultivation of a stakeholder culture based on trust, interdependency, integrity, transparency, caring, passion, and fun, in addition to the desire to be financially and otherwise sustainable. The result could be not only happier employees and higher customer stickiness, but also significantly higher returns of integral Impact Investments.

More research would have to be performed to achieve higher data granularity, but it appears that, by adding multiple worldviews and perspectives within the Wilber (2000) quadrants, the investment risk could be significantly reduced and a better integral impact can be achieved (Bozesan, 2013b, 2014; Rooke & Torbert, 1998, 2005; Torbert, Livne-Tarandach, Herdman-Barker, Nicolaides, & McCallum, 2008).

Summary

This chapter argued that lack of investors' trust in the stability of economic development could be one of the main reasons for current global stagnation. It contended that investing is driven by emotional intelligence that depends upon the levels of consciousness of the participating agents. The research performed on 136 global investors was presented, and the hypothesis that intrinsic trust in the future could be achieved through personal growth and vertical development was tested. The chapter asserted, furthermore, that more trust in investing could be cultivated through the external integration of appropriate measurements for people, planet, and profit. The Theta Model was subsequently introduced as an evolution-based, de-risking tool grounded in Ken Wilber's Integral Theory. Much more research will have to be performed to make the Theta Model applicable at large scale in early-stage investing. As technological innovation will continue to grow at historical rates, this model could provide an enhanced de-risking tool toward integral sustainability. It could make sure that the available capital is integrally de-risked to address further resource degradation, increasing pollution, massive climate change, growing inequity, substantial social unrest, and geo-political conflict. The Theta Model could provide the necessary de-risking tools and due diligence processes required during the transition from a fossil-fueled economy toward an integrally sustainable economy rooted in well-being for all human kind and our blue planet. From the research shared on vertical development in adults, one could gain additional hope in the intelligence and resilience of the human species and in our collective ability to turn crises into opportunities.

Acknowledgments

With permission to reprint by the publisher: Bozesan, M. (2014). De-risking VC investing for outstanding ROI: An interdisciplinary approach toward the integration of people, planet and profit. *ACRN Journal of Finance and Risk Perspectives, 4*(1), 49–71.

In no particular order, I would like to express my gratitude to the following extraordinary people for their inspiration and support. Without you this chapter would not exist. Thank you Prof. Dr Ernst-Ulrich von Weizsaecker, Prof. Dr Othmar Lehner, MBA, Prof. Dr Bernhard R. Katzy, Prof. Dr Marcel Fratzscher, Prof. Dr Otto Scharmer, Dr h.c. mult. Hazel Henderson, NASA Scientist Dennis M. Bushnell, Prof. Dr Mark McCaslin, Prof. Dr Rosemarie Anderson, Dr Ruth Judy, Prof. Dr Marius Koga, Prof. Dr Ana Perez Chisti, Prof. Dr Kartik Patel, Prof. Dr Henry Poon, Prof. D. Judy Schavrien, and last but not least Ken Wilber.

References

Aburdene, P. (2005). *Megatrends 2010.* Charlottesville, VA: Hamptonroads.

Adams, J. D. (Ed.). (2005). *Transforming leadership.* New York, NY: Cosimo on Demand.

Alexander, C. N., Davies, J. L., Dixon, C. A., Dillbeck, M. C., Drucker, S. M., Oetzel, R. M., . . . Orme-Johnson, D. W. (1990). Growth of higher stages of consciousness: Maharishi's Vedic psychology of human development. In C. L. Alexander & E. J. Langer (Eds.), *Higher stages of human development: Perspectives on adult growth* (pp. 286–341). New York, NY: Oxford University Press.

Alvarado, C. S. (2000). Out of body experiences. In E. Cardena, S. J. Lynn, & S. Krippner (Eds.), *Varieties of anomalous experience: Examining the scientific evidence* (pp. 183–218). Washington, DC: American Psychological Association.

Armstrong, K. (1993). *A history of God: The 4000-year-old quest of Judaism, Christianity, and Islam.* New York, NY: Ballantine Books.

Arnsperger, C. (2010). *Full-spectrum economics: Toward an inclusive and emancipatory social science.* New York, NY: Routledge.

AVIVA. (2011, September 20). *Aviva convenes Corporate Sustainability Reporting Coalition.* Retrieved August 7, 2012, from http://www.aviva.com/research-and-discussion/articles-and-research/13023

Baier, A. C. (1994/1996). *Moral prejudices.* Cambridge, MA: Harvard University Press.

Balandina, J. J. (2011). *Guide to impact investing: Managing wealth for impact and profit for family offices and high net worth individuals.* Self-published by the author. Own copy received from the author in August 2011.

Baldi, G., Fichtner, F., Michelsen, C., & Rieth, M. (2014, July 2). Schwache Investitionen dämpfen Wachstum in Europa. *DIW Wochenbericht: Wirtschaftliche Impulse für Europa.* Nr. 27, 2014, pp. 636–651. Retrieved August 6, 2014, from http://www.diw.de/documents/publikationen/73/diw_01.c.469130.de/14-27.pdf

B Corp. (2015). *Benefit Corporation official website.* Retrieved May 1, 2015, from http://www.bcorporation.net

Beauregard, M., & O'Leary, D. (2007). *The spiritual brain: A neuroscientist's case for the existence of the soul.* New York, NY: HarperCollins.

Becerra, J., Damisch, P., Holley, B., Kumar, M., Naumann, M., Tang, T., & Zakrazewki, A. (2010). *Regaining lost ground: Resurgent markets and new opportunities.* Retrieved September 10, 2010, from http://www.bcg.com.cn/en/files/publications/reports_pdf/BCG_Regaining_Lost_Ground_Global_Wealth_Jun_10_ENG.pdf

Beck, D. E., & Cowan, C. C. (1996). *Spiral dynamics: Mastering values, leadership, and change.* Malden, MA: Blackwell.

Boeckler, H., & Stiftung. (2009). *Neue Studie warnt vor Altersarmut: Vermoegen in Deutschland zunehmend ungleich verteilt.* Pressedienst Hans_Boeckler-Stiftung. Retrieved October 10, 2010, from http://www.boeckler.de/pdf/pm_fofoe_2009_01_21.pdf

Boyatzis, R., & McKee, A. (2005). *Resonant leadership.* Boston, MA: Harvard Business School.

Bozesan, M. (2010). *The making of a consciousness leader in business: An integral approach* (Published PhD dissertation). ITP Palo Alto, SageEra, Redwood City, CA.

Bozesan, M. (2011a, April 28–30). *The future of investing and business: An integral view from an investor's perspective.* Paper presented at the 14th International Business Research Conference, Dubai, UAE.

Bozesan, M. (2011b, June 16–18). *The future of Wall Street: An investor's perspective from the intersection of capital, philanthropy, business, and human evolution.* Paper held at the 2011 SIBR Conference on Interdisciplinary Business and Economics Research, Bangkok, Thailand.

Bozesan, M. (2012). *Why some investors care about the parity of people, planet, and profit, and others do not* (Wirtschaftspsychologie, 3/2012, pp. 100–111). Lengerich, Germany: Wolfgang Pabst Science.

Bozesan, M. (2013a, June). Demystifying the future of investing. Parts 1 & 2: An investor's perspective. *Journal of Integral Theory and Practice, 8*(1 & 2), 19–56.

Bozesan, M. (2013b, July 18–21). *Integral venture investing: An inclusive and sustainable model for investing in our future.* Award-winning paper presented at ITC 2013 conference, San Francisco. Retrieved November 7, 2015, from https://foundation.metaintegral.org/sites/default/files/Bozesan_ITC2013.pdf

Bozesan, M. (2014). De-risking VC investing for outstanding ROI: An interdisciplinary approach toward the integration of people, planet and profit. *ACRN Journal of Finance and Risk Perspectives, 4*(1), 49–71.

Brown, B. (2007, February 20). *The four worlds of sustainability: Drawing upon four worlds of perspectives to support sustainable initiatives.* Retrieved November 7, 2015, from http://nextstepintegral.org/wp-content/uploads/2011/04/Four-Worlds-of-Sustainability-Barrett-C-Brown.pdf

Brown, B. (2014). Dr. Brown quoted this research by Losada—*American Behavioral Scientist, 47*(6), February 2004, 740–765—in a personal conversation on March 10–11, 2014.

Bryce, J., Drexler, M., & Noble, A. (2013, September). *From the margins to the mainstream assessment of the impact investment sector and opportunities to engage mainstream investors.* A report by the World Economic Forum investors industries prepared in collaboration with deloitte touche tohmatsu. Retrieved November 7, 2015, from http://www3.weforum.org/docs/WEF_II_FromMarginsMainstream_Report_2013.pdf

Bugg-Levine, A., & Emerson, J. (2011). *Impact investing: Transforming how we make money while making a difference.* San Francisco, CA: Jossey-Bass.

Camerer, C. F., & Loewenstein, G. (2004). Behavioral economics: Past, present, future. In C. F. Camerer, G. Loewenstein, & M. Rabin (Eds.), *Advances in behavioral economics* (pp. 3–51). Princeton, NJ: Princeton University Press.

Campbell, J. (1968). *The hero with a thousand faces.* Princeton, NJ: Princeton University Press (Original work published 1949).

Club of Rome. (2013). *On the edge.* Retrieved November 7, 2015, from http://www.clubofrome.org

Commons, M. L., Armon, C., Kohlberg, L., Richards, F. A., & Grotzer, T. A. (Eds.). (1990). *Adult development: Models and methods in the study of adolescent and adult thought.* New York, NY: Praeger.

Commons, M. L., Richards, F. A., & Armon, C. (Eds.). (1984). *Beyond formal operations: Late adolescent and adult cognitive development.* New York, NY: Praeger.

Cook-Greuter, S. R. (2004). Making the case for a developmental perspective [Electronic version]. *Journal of Industrial and Commercial Training, 36*(7), 275–281.

Cook-Greuter, S. R. (2005). *Ego development: Nine levels of increasing embrace.* Retrieved October 4, 2008, from http://newpossibilitiesassociates.com/uploads/9_levels_of_increasing_embrace_update_1_07.pdf

Cook-Greuter, S. R. (2008). Mature ego development: A gateway to ego transcendence? [Electronic version]. *Journal of Adult Development, 7*(4), 227–240.

Csikszentmihalyi, M. (1990). *Flow: The psychology of optimal experience.* New York, NY: HarperPerennial.

Dalai Lama. (1999). *Ethics for the new millennium.* New York, NY: Riverhead Books.

Damasio, A. (2006). *Descartes' error: Emotion, reason and the human brain.* London: Vintage Press.

Esbjörn-Hargens, S., & Zimmermann, M. E. (2009). *Integral ecology: Uniting multiple perspectives on the natural world.* Boston, MA and London, England: Integral Books.

European Commission. (n.d.). *Enterprise and industry: Venture capital.* Retrieved December 24, 2014, from http://ec.europa.eu/growth/tools-databases/smaf/venture-capital/index_en.htm

European Private Equity and Venture Capital Association (EVCA). (2014). *2013 European private equity activity: Statistics on fundraising, investments & divestments.* Retrieved August 22, 2014, from http://www.evca.eu/media/142790/2013-European-Private-Equity-Activity.pdf

Faust, M., & Scholz, S. (Eds.). (2014). *Nachhaltige Geldanlagen: Produkte, Strategien und Beratungskonzepte.* Frankfurt, Germany: Frankfurt School.

Fichtner, F., Fratzscher, M., & Gorning, M. (2014, July 2). Eine Investitionsagenda für Europa. *DIW Wochenbericht: Wirtschaftliche Impulse für Europa*. Nr. 27, 2014, pp. 631–636. Retrieved August 6, 2014, from http://www.diw.de/documents/publikationen/73/diw_01.c.469130.de/14-27.pdf

Freireich, J., & Fulton, K. (2009). *Investing for social and environmental impact: A design for catalyzing an emerging industry* (Monitor Institute Report). Retrieved March 22, 2010, from http://www.monitorinstitute.com/impactinvesting/documents/InvestingforSocialandEnvImpact_FullReport_004.pdf

GABV. (2012, March). *Global Alliance for Banking on Values: Strong, straight forward, and sustainable banking* (Financial capital and impact metrics of value based banking. Full report). Retrieved May 15, 2013, from http://www.gabv.org/wp-content/uploads/Full-Report-GABV-v9d.pdf

Gardner, H. (1993). *Multiple intelligences*. New York, NY: Basic Books.

Gardner, H. (2004). *Changing minds: The art and science of changing our own and other people's minds*. Boston, MA: Harvard Business School Press.

Gebser, J. (1984). *The ever-present origin*. Athens, OH: Ohio University Press (Original work published 1949).

GIIRS. (n.d.). *Global Impact Investing Rating System*. Retrieved November 7, 2015, from http://www.giirs.org

Gilligan, C. (1993). *In a different voice: Psychological theory and women's development*. Cambridge, MA: Harvard University Press (Original work published 1982).

Giving Pledge. (2010). *Forty U.S. families take Giving Pledge: Billionaires pledge majority of wealth to philanthropy*. Retrieved September 10, 2010, from http://givingpledge.org/Content/media/PressRelease_8_4.pdf

Gladstone, D., & Gladstone, L. (2004). *Venture capital investing: The complete handbook for investing in private businesses for outstanding profits* (p. 30). New Jersey: Prentice Hall.

Global Sustainable Investment Alliance (GSIA). (2015). *Global Sustainable Investment Review 2014*. Retrieved May 15, 2015, from http://www.gsi-alliance.org/members-resources/global-sustainable-investment-review-2014/

Godeke, S., Pomares, R., Bruno, A. V., Guerra, P., Kleissner, C., & Shefrin, H. (2009). *Solutions for impact investors: From strategy to implementation*. New York, NY: Rockefeller Philanthropy Advisors.

Goleman, D. (1995). *Emotional intelligence: Why it can matter more than IQ*. New York, NY: Bantam Books.

Goleman, D. (2000, March–April). Leadership that gets results [Electronic version]. *Harvard Business Review*, 78–91. Reprint No. R00204. Retrieved November 8, 2008, from https://hbr.org/2000/03/leadership-that-gets-results

Goleman, D. (Ed.). (2003). *Healing emotions: Conversations with the Dalai Lama on mindfulness, emotions, and health*. Boston, MA: Shambhala.

Goleman, D., Boyatzis, R., & McKee, A. (2002). *Primal leadership: Realizing the power of emotional intelligence*. Boston, MA: Harvard Business School Press.

Gore, A. (1992). *Earth in the balance: Ecology and the human spirit*. Santa Monica, CA: Dove Audio Cassettes.

Gore, A. (2006). *An inconvenient truth: The planetary emergency of global warming and what we can do about it*. New York, NY: Rodale.

Gore, A. (2011). Climate of denial [Electronic version]. *Rolling Stones*, June 22, 2011. Retrieved November 7, 2015, from http://www.rollingstone.com/politics/news/climate-of-denial-20110622

Grof, S. (2006). *When the impossible happens: Adventures in non-ordinary realities*. Boulder, CO: Sounds True.

Habermas, J. (1992). *Postmetaphysical thinking: Philosophical essays*. Cambridge, MA: MIT Press.

Henderson, H. (2014). *Mapping the transition to the solar age: From "economism" to earth systems science*. London: ICAEW and The Centre for Tomorrow's Company.

Hendricks, G., & Ludeman, K. (1996). *The corporate mystic: A guidebook for visionaries with their feet on the ground*. New York, NY: Bantam Books.

Hughes, M., & Church, J. (2010, July 6). *Social trends: Correction notice*. 40. Office for National Statistics. Government of the United Kingdom. Retrieved October 18, 2010, from http://www.statistics.gov.uk/downloads/theme_social/Social-Trends40/ST40_2010_FINAL.pdf

Jaworski, J. (1996). *Synchronicity: The inner path of leadership*. San Francisco, CA: Berrett-Koehler Publishers.

Juncker, J. C. (2014, November 26). *Investing in Europe: Speech by President Juncker in the European Parliament plenary session on the €315 billion Investment Plan*. Retrieved November 31, 2014, from http://europa.eu/rapid/press-release_SPEECH-14-2160_en.htm

Kahneman, D., & Tversky, A. (1982). On the study of statistical intuitions. In D. Kahneman, P. Slovic, & A. Tversky (Eds.), *Judgment under uncertainty: Heuristics and biases*. Cambridge, UK: Cambridge University Press.

Kant, I. (1949/1993). *The philosophy of Kant: Immanuel Kant's moral and political writings*. New York, NY: The Modern Library.

Kegan, R. (1982). *The evolving self: Problem and process in human development*. Cambridge, MA: Harvard University Press.

Kegan, R., Lahey, L. L., & Souvaine, E. (1990). Life after formal operations: Implications for a psychology of the self. In C. N. Alexander & E. J. Langer (Eds.), *Higher stages of human development* (pp. 229–257). New York: Oxford University Press.

Kelly, E. J. (2011). Exercising leadership power: Warren Buffett and the integration of integrity, mutuality and sustainability. In D. Weir & N. Sultan (Eds.), *From critique to action: The practical ethics of the organizational world* (pp. 315–337). Newcastle, UK: Cambridge Scholars.

Kjaer, T. W., Bertelsen, C., Piccini, P., Brooks, D., Alving, J., & Lou, H. C. (2002, April). Increased dopamine tone during meditation-induced change of consciousness. *Cognitive Brain Research, 13*(2), 255–259.

Kohlberg, L., & Ryncarz, R. A. (1990). Beyond justice reasoning: Moral development and consideration of a seventh stage. In C. N. Alexander & E. J. Langer (Eds.), *Higher stages of human development: Perspectives on adult growth* (pp. 191–207). New York, NY: Oxford University Press.

Koplowitz, H. (1984). A projection beyond Piaget's formal operations stage: A general system stage and a unitary stage. In M. L. Commons, F. A. Richards, & C. Armon (Eds.), *Beyond formal operations: Late adolescent and adult cognitive development* (pp. 272–296). New York, NY: Praeger.

Koplowitz, H. (1990). Unitary consciousness and the highest development of mind: The relationship between spiritual development and cognitive development. In M. L. Commons, C. Armon, L. Kohlberg, F. A. Richards, T. A. Grotzer, & J. D. Sinnott (Eds.), *Adult development. Volume 2: Models and methods in the study of adolescent and adult thought* (Chap. 6, pp. 105–111). New York, NY: Praeger.

Krugman, P. (2009). *The return of depression economics and the crisis of 2008*. New York, NY and London, England: W.W. Norton Company.

Lectica. (2014). *Lectica official website*. Retrieved May 1, 2015, from https://dts.lectica.org/_about/showcase.php?instrument_id=LDMA

Lencioni, P. (2002). *The five dysfunctions of a team*. San Francisco, CA: Jossey-Bass.

Lewis, M. (2014). *Flash boys: A Wall Street revolt*. New York, NY and London, England: Norton & Company.

Lietaer, B. (2001). *The future of money: Creating new wealth, work, and a wiser world*. London, England: Random House.

Lietaer, B., Arnsperger, C., Goerner, S., & Brunnhuber, S. (2012). *Money and sustainability: The missing link*. Devon, UK: Triarchy Press.

Loevinger, J. (1977). *Ego development: Conceptions and theories*. San Francisco, CA: Jossey-Bass.

Luskin, F., Aberman, R., & DeLorenzo, Sr, A. E. (2009). Effects of training of emotional competence in financial services advisors. *Losada, American Behavioral Scientist, 47*(6), February 2004, 740–765. Retrieved August 28, 2014, from http://learningtoforgive.com/research/effect-of-training-of-emotional-competence-in-financial-services-advisors/

Mackey, J., & Sisodia, R. (2013). *Conscious capitalism: Liberating the heroic spirit of business*. Boston, MA: Harvard Business Press.

Maloney, C. B., & Schumer, C. E. (2010, September). *Income inequality and the great recession*. Report by the U.S. Congress Joint Economic Committee. Retrieved October 10, 2010, from http://jec.senate.gov/public/?a=Files.Serve&File_id=91975589-257c-403b-8093-8f3b584a088c

Marques, J., Dhiman, S., & King, R. (2007). *Spirituality in the workplace*. Fawnskin, CA: Personhood Press.

Maslow, A. H. (1999). *Toward a psychology of being*. New York, NY: John Wiley & Sons (Original work published 1968).

Maslow, A. H., Stephens, D. S., & Heil, G. (1998). *Maslow on management*. New York, NY: John Wiley & Sons.

McCraty, R. (2001). *Science of the heart: Exploring the role of the heart in human performance*. Boulder Creek, CA: Institute of HeartMath.

Mitroff, I. I., & Denton, E. A. (1999). *A spiritual audit of corporate America: A hard look at spirituality, religion, and values in the workplace*. San Francisco, CA: Jossey-Bass.

Moustakas, C. (1990). *Heuristic research: Design, methodology, and applications*. London, England: Sage.

Newberg, A. B., & Lee, B. Y. (2005, June). The neuroscientific study of religious and spiritual phenomena: Or why God doesn't use biostatistics. *Zygon, 40*(2), 469–489.

Nicolaides, A. (2008). *Learning their way through ambiguity: Explorations of how nine developmentally mature adults make sense of ambiguity* (Unpublished doctoral dissertation). Teachers College, Columbia University, NY.

Panwar, J. S., & Blinch, J. (2012, June 18). *The sustainable stock exchanges: A progress report on progress*. Retrieved August 7, 2012, from http://www.unglobalcompact.org/docs/issues_doc/Financial_markets/Sustainable_Stock_Exchanges.pdf

Pauchant, T. C. (Ed.). (2002). *Ethics and spirituality at work: Hopes and pitfalls of the search for meaning in organizations*. Westport, CT: Quorum Books.

Paulson, D. (2002). *Competitive business, caring business*. New York, NY: ParaView Press.

Petrie, N. (2011). *Future trends in leadership development*. Greensboro, NC: Center for Creative Leadership.

Plato. (1961). *The collected dialogues of Plato: Including the letters*. Princeton, NJ: Princeton University Press (Original work published 1938).

Porras, J., Emery, S., & Thompson, M. (2007). *Success built to last: Creating a life that matters*. Upper Saddle River, NJ: Wharton School.

Randers, J. (2012). *2052: A global forecast for the next forty years*. A report to the Club of Rome commemorating the 40th anniversary of The Limits to Growth. White River Junction, VT: Chelsea Green.

Ray, M., & Myers, R. (1989). *Creativity in business*. New York, NY: Doubleday.

Ray, M., & Rinzler, A. (Eds.). (1993). *The new paradigm in business: Emerging strategies for leadership and organizational change*. New York, NY: Jeremy P. Tarcher/Pedigree.

Ray, P., & Anderson, S. R. (2000). *The cultural creatives: How 50 million people are changing the world*. New York, NY: Three Rivers Press.

Renesch, J. (Ed.). (2002). *Leadership in a new era: Visionary approaches to the biggest crises of our time*. New York, NY: ParaView Press.

Robeco, Booz & Co. (2009). *Responsible investing: A paradigm shift*. Rotterdam and London: From Niche to Mainstream.

Rooke, D., & Torbert, W. (1998). Organizational transformation as a function of CEOs' developmental stage. *Organizational Development Journal, 16*(1), 11–28.

Rooke, D., & Torbert, W. (2005, April). *Seven transformations of leadership*. Harvard Business Review OnPoint Article, 1–11. Reprint No. R0504D.

Scharmer, O. (2013). *Leading from the emerging future: From ego-systems to eco-systems economies*. San Francisco, CA: Berrett-Koehler Publishers.

Senge, P., Scharmer, C. O., Jaworski, J., & Flowers, B. S. (2005). *Presence: An exploration of profound change in people, organizations, and society*. New York, NY: Currency Doubleday.

Soros, G. (2008). *The new paradigm for financial markets: The credit crisis of 2008 and what it means*. New York, NY: PublicAffairs.

Spinkart, K. P., & Gottwald, F.-T. (2013). *FairFinance: Das Kapital der Zukunft; Auswege aus dem Raubtierkapitalismus* (p. 162). München: Herbig.

Stein, Z., Dawson, T., & Fischer, K. W. (2009). Redesigning testing: Operationalizing the new science of learning. In M. S. Khine & I. M. Saleh (Eds.), *The new science of learning: Computers, cognition, and collaboration in education* (pp. 207–224). New York, NY: Springer Press.

Stiglitz, J. (2011, May). *Of the 1%, by the 1%, for the 1%*. VanityFair. Retrieved April 12, 2011, from http://www.vanityfair.com/society/features/2011/05/top-one-percent-201105

Strong, M. (2009). *Be the solution: How entrepreneurs and conscious capitalists can solve all the world's problems*. Hoboken, NJ: Wiley & Sons.

Tachibanaki, T. (2009). *Confronting income inequality in Japan: A comparative analysis of causes, consequences, and reform*. Cambridge, MA: MIT Press.

Taylor, J. B. (2009). The Financial Crisis and the Policy Responses: An Empirical Analysis of What Went Wrong, NBER Working Paper 14631. Cambridge, MA: National Bureau of Economic Research.

The Economist. (2013, April 23). The Twitter crash. *The Economist*. Retrieved May 14, 2013, from http://www.economist.com/news/finance-and-economics/21576671-hacked-tweet-briefly-unnerves-stock market-newscrashrecover

The IIRC. (2013). *The Integrated Reporting Committee*. Retrieved from http://www.theiirc.org

The Natural Capital Declaration. (n.d.). Retrieved August 7, 2012, from http://www.naturalcapitaldeclaration.org/wp-content/uploads/2012/04/NaturalCapitalDeclaration.pdf

Thomson Reuters. (2014). *2014 National Venture Capital Association Yearbook*. Retrieved August 22, 2014, from http://www.nvca.org/index.php?option=com_content&view=article&id=257&Itemid=103

Tomorrow's Capital Markets. (2012). *Tomorrow's Capital Markets: A private invitation to work with tomorrow's company to set new incentive structures for a sustainable world*. Retrieved May 9, 2013, from http://www.unepfi.org/fileadmin/documents/Tomorrow_s_Capital_Markets_web.pdf

Torbert, W. R., Cook-Greuter, S., Fisher, D., Foldy, E., Gauthier, A., Keeley, J., . . . Tran, M. (2004). *Action inquiry: The secret of timely and transforming leadership*. San Francisco, CA: Berrett-Koehler Publishers.

Torbert, W. R., Livne-Tarandach, R., Herdman-Barker, E., Nicolaides, A., & McCallum, D. (2008, August 9). Developmental action inquiry: A distinct integral theory that actually integrates developmental theory, practice, and research. In S. Esbjörn-Hargens (Ed.), *Integral theory in action* (pp. 413–429). Albany, NY: State University of New York Press.

UN PRI. (2013). Overcoming strategic barriers to a sustainable financial system: A consultation with signatories on a new PRI work programme. Authors were requested to participate via email on January 21, 2013, by the United Nations Principle for Responsible Investing (UN PRI). Retrieved May 15, 2013, from http://www.unpri.org/viewer/?file=wp-content/uploads/2013Strategicbarriersconsultation.pdf

Vaughan, F. (2000). *The inward arc: Healing in psychotherapy and spirituality*. Lincoln, NE: IUniverse.

Vaughan, F. (2005). *Shadows of the sacred: Seeing through spiritual illusions*. Lincoln, NE: IUniverse.

White, R. A. (1998). Becoming more human as we work: The reflexive role of exceptional human experience. In W. Braud & R. Anderson (Eds.), *Transpersonal research methods for the social sciences* (pp. 128–145). Thousand Oaks, CA: Sage.

Wilber, K. (1998). *Marriage of sense and soul*. New York, NY: Random House.

Wilber, K. (2000). *Sex, ecology, spirituality: The spirit of evolution*. Boston, MA: Shambhala.

Wilber, K. (2000a). *Integral psychology: Consciousness, spirit, psychology, therapy*. Boston, MA: Shambhala.

Wilber, K. (2000b). *A theory of everything: An integral vision for business, politics, science, and spirituality*. Boston, MA: Shambhala.

Wilber, K. (2003). *Kosmic consciousness* [6 CDs]. Boulder, CO: Sounds True.

Wilber, K. (2006). *Integral spirituality: A startling new role for religion in the modern and postmodern world*. Boston, MA: Integral Books.

Wong, L. W. (2005). *Venture capital fund management: A comprehensive approach to investment practices & the entire operations of a VC firm* (p. 160). Boston, MA: Aspatore Books.

World Commission on Environment and Development. (2009). *Our common future*. Oxford, England: Oxford University Press (Original work published 1987).

Wymenga, P., Spanikova, V., Barker, A., Konings, J., & Canton, E. (2012). *EU SMEs in 2012 at the crossroads: Annual report on small and medium-sized enterprises in the EU, 2011/12*. Retrieved May 15, 2015, from http://ec.europa.eu/growth/smes/business-friendly-environment/performance-review/files/supporting-documents/2012/annual-report_en.pdf

Yazdipour, R. (Ed.). (2011). *Advances in entrepreneurial finance: With applications from behavioral finance and economics*. New York, NY: Springer.

II.2
Critical Perspectives on Markets, Institutions, and Ideology

19

STUDYING CROWDFUNDING THROUGH EXTREME CASES

Cursory reflections on the social value creation process of a potato salad project

Pascal Dey and Laurent Marti

> A very popular error: having the courage of one's convictions; rather it is a matter of having the courage for an attack on one's convictions!!!
>
> —*Friedrich Nietzsche (Beyond Good and Evil)*

Crowdfunding is a fairly novel phenomenon, both in taxonomic as well as in technological terms. Whilst at first mainly used to finance projects in the arts and the broader field of the creative industries (Bradford, 2012), political campaigns (Belleflamme, Lambert, & Schwienbacher, 2010) as well as entrepreneurial start-ups and SMEs (de Buysere, Gajda, Kleverlaan, & Marom, 2012), crowdfunding has been increasingly employed as a vehicle for financing social and sustainable ventures or projects (Lehner, 2013; Thorpe, 2012)—which forms the focal attention of this chapter.

In general, so-called social purpose crowdfunding forms an alternative means of financing the overall operation of social ventures, or isolated projects or programs (Lehner, 2013, 2014; Lehner & Nicholls, 2014; Lehner, Grabmann, & Ennsgraber, 2014). The main assumption is that social purpose crowdfunding offers project initiators or Social Entrepreneurs a financial remedy under conditions of increasing restrictions on traditional means of funding (Meyskens & Bird, 2015). Simultaneously, social purpose crowdfunding offers attractive investment opportunities to those investors who are more interested in producing social value than in earning a profit (Meyskens & Bird, 2015).

The basic contention the present chapter makes is that, despite the almost univocally accepted promise of crowdfunding as an innovative tool for social value creation, relatively little is known about how this emergent technology works, and what kind of contingent effects it produces. This chapter argues that substantially new insights about crowdfunding in general and its relationship to social value creation more specifically can be derived from the investigation of *queer cases*—particular types of investigation which does not simply deviate from, but largely upsets and potentially changes the very essence of the phenomena under consideration. To attain this goal, we follow a potato salad crowdfunding campaign, which started as a fairly modest initiative before turning into one of the most prominent crowdfunding projects in the US. The project in question, which was perceived by many as a blatant hoax, challenges the linear "cause and effect" model underlying many conceptualizations of crowdfunding. It also makes us aware that social value creation is not necessarily attributable to the ingenuity of the project initiator or located in the proclaimed goal of a campaign; instead, social value in the case of the analyzed project forms a contingent effect emerging from the specific relations between an initial idea, the distinct agency of the crowdfunding platform, and the backers' staging of an event.

The chapter proceeds as follows. First, we offer a tentative overview of crowdfunding research, placing particular heed on how the crowdfunding process is framed in normative terms. Second, we introduce the concept of "*queer cases*" and draw on speech act theory to develop a provisional framework to analyze the infelicitous usages of crowdfunding. This is followed, third, by the introduction of our empirical vignette, a Kickstarter project by Zack Brown aimed at producing a potato salad. Fourth, Brown's potato salad project is analyzed in terms of how it breaches existing conditions of felicity. Fifth, we reflect on a more general level of how attentiveness to ostensible misfires and abuses of crowdfunding through such queer cases puts an opportunity in front of us to experiment with new perspectives on the matter. The chapter concludes by calling for prospective research that invokes queer crowdfunding projects and ventures to uproot our dearly held convictions about how and where social value gets created.

The crowdfunding process: A very brief introduction

The core concept of crowdfunding as a mobilization of financial resources via a large amount of small-scale investors is anything but new. Crowdfunding found its antecedents several centuries ago—yet its proliferation and prominence coincides with the invention of new social media technologies in the most recent years (Frydrych, Bock, Kinder, & Koeck, 2014). The first studies have largely been conducted from disciplinary angles such as entrepreneurship and new venture research (Belleflamme, Lambert, & Schwienbacher, 2013) or legal studies (Bradford, 2012). Different theoretical approaches, such as signaling theory (Ahlers, Cumming, Günther, & Schweizer, 2015), institutionalism (Kshetri, 2015), or Bourdieu's (social) capital theory (Lehner, 2014), have been used to explain the subject. Apart from definitional work, a significant part of this nascent body of research has focused on the motivation and behavior of the funders, or the geographic proximity and the quality of social networks (Agrawal, Catalini, & Goldfarb, 2015). Other studies exhibit an interest in the transformative effect crowdfunding has on traditional financing practices in particular (Hollas, 2013) or established capital demanding industries (Sorensen, 2012).

While many scholars describe crowdfunding as a process (e.g., Mollick, 2014), only few have made the processual dimension of the phenomenon the focal object of their study. Notable exceptions do exist, such as Macht and Weatherston (2015), who, from the point of view of the project initiator, suggest that the funding process can be differentiated into two main phases: a pre-investment phase and a post-investment phase. One of the most comprehensive crowdfunding (investment) process models, however, has been put forward by Tomczak and Brem (2013). Based on a literature review, the crowdfunding-based investment process is delineated as a linear decision tree path proceeding along a series of decisions, which the project initiator must take. These decisions are typologized into five broad phases, among others comprising the type of crowdfunding choice, the funding model, and reward modes. However, such models advance a very particular type of normative framework, which prescribes how the crowdfunding process should ideally unfold (if looked at from the perspective of the project initiator).

Even though Tomczak and Brem's process model was not related to crowdfunding campaigns with a social focus, its root premises are clearly compatible with the extant literature on social purpose crowdfunding. Social purpose crowdfunding ostensibly starts with an idea, which

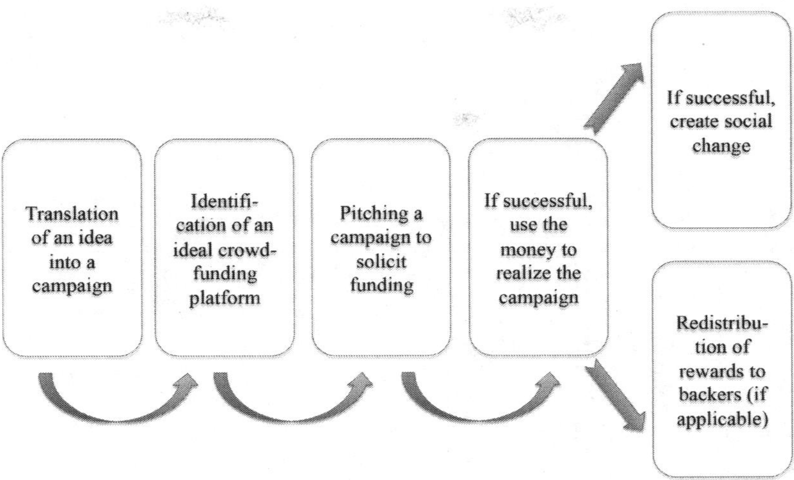

Figure 19.1 The process of crowdfunding social projects and ventures

Source: Based on Meyskens & Bird, 2015, p. 157.

is then molded by the project initiator or social entrepreneur into a crowdfunding campaign (cf. Figure 19.1). Unlike traditional crowdfunding projects, the project goal in social purpose crowdfunding is less directly related to the potential reward for investors (e.g., receiving pre-funded and thus a pre-purchased music album, or taking part in an aesthetic experience such as a concert), but more to tackling a particular social problem such as education, malnutrition, or inequality. During the translation of the idea into a proper campaign, the project initiator or social entrepreneur selects the crowdfunding platform most conducive to the social purpose he/she seeks to pursue. Once the campaign has been approved by the respective crowdfunding platform, the project initiator or social entrepreneur pitches his/her idea by communicating the purpose of the campaign, the duration of the fundraising, and the incentives to the backers. If successful, the project initiator or social entrepreneur puts the money towards realizing his/her campaign. The ideal outcome of the crowdfunding process is social value, which essentially consists of effectively solving the identified social problem. Depending on the campaign, the project initiator or social entrepreneur completes the process by giving rewards to the backers. Unlike commercial campaigns whose rewards often include direct and indirect monetary contributions, social purpose campaigns often deliver rewards that hold value for the backers but are still relatively "low cost," such as the recognition of all backers supporting a given project (Larralde & Schwienbacher, 2012).

We are reluctant to embrace the normative model in Figure 19.1 uncritically, for it tends to misconceive crowdfunding as a linear process moving effortlessly through a set of stages towards a predefined end. Feeling ill at ease with the model, not least due to the kind of omnipotence it attributes to the project initiator, we now aim at provoking its normative assumption through a "queer case."

Going against the norm with "*queer cases*"

Studying a new phenomenon such as crowdfunding usually entails defining and circumscribing its apparent essence with an eye towards demarcating it from related phenomena. It is not uncommon in academic work to use illustrative cases or anecdotal evidence to shed light on the defining features of a phenomenon such as crowdfunding. Such typical cases are used primarily to sketch out the very essence of crowdfunding by making distinctions between what crowdfunding is and what it is not, with the effect of rendering the subject matter into an object of knowledge. Typical cases, thus, help make crowdfunding intelligible and discussable.

The pertinence of typical cases notwithstanding, we must not forget that the attribute "typical" is a semi-fiction, which effectively masks how these cases exclude other ways of knowing. In other words, typical cases—by establishing an authoritative account of what crowdfunding "really is"—exclude alternative ways of knowing crowdfunding by labeling them as unintelligible and vulgar. Hence, although typical cases permit us to get a grip on our phenomenon, the "matter-of-factness" such cases engender comes at the cost of prematurely stifling the potential of crowdfunding to take on very different meanings. This is where extreme cases gain relevance.

Extreme cases are—per the etymological meaning of "extreme" as the "opposite end of anything"—cases that largely deviate from prevailing rules and traditions. As Eisenhardt and Graebner (2007) convincingly argue, scholars tend to "make the faulty assumption that the cases should be representative of some population" (p. 27). Case selection in this logic, as they clarify, simply means to identify cases that are "particularly suitable for illuminating and extending relationships and logic among constructs" (2007, p. 27). Where Eisenhardt and Graebner commend, among other things, "single-case research" as a means "to explore a significant phenomenon under rare or extreme circumstances" (2007, p. 27), what ultimately makes a case "extreme" remains fairly elusive, leaving considerable scope for different, and potentially incompatible, interpretations. For the sake of clarity and precision, we suggest "*queer cases*" as our sensitizing concept to properly heed the experimental and inventive dimension of extreme cases. The prefix "queer" designates cases that deviate from what is deemed normal. More specifically, apart from alluding to phenomena that are odd, eccentric, or unconventional, the attribute queer has for quite some time formed a derogatory term for describing lesbians and gays (Turner, 2000). However, starting in the 1980s, "queer" was less and less seen merely as a homophobic slur and has been increasingly used as a reference point for lesbians and gays (as well as bisexuals and transgender people). The term has also become popular in academia through what is commonly referred to as "queer theory." The lynchpin of queer theory is the attempt to counteract heteronormative belief systems (i.e., dominant representations conditioned by heterosexual ideologies), with an eye toward revealing that gender and sex are not essential features of the self, but socially constructed realities and identities.

"Queer" is used here to denote extreme cases, which are at odds with and thereby tend to problematize that which is deemed normal or dominant (Green, 2007). Thus, in line with Halperin (1995), we define queer cases not through their positive content but through their "positionality vis-à-vis the normative" (p. 62). This essentially means that queer cases, which might be quite heterogeneous in terms of their stated objectives, focus, or reason for being, are united by how they upset and potentially suspend the field of normalization in which they are located. Consider, as an example, a recent article by Farnel (2014) that looked at the crowdfunding of gender and sexual reassignment surgeries. A key insight from Farnel's sagacious investigation is that queer cases spark controversy around normative beliefs informing both the perception and practice of crowdfunding. For instance, one of the three campaigns that were analyzed by Farnel was critiqued directly by the CEO of the crowdfunding platform who issued a statement saying that he disapproved of how his platform was (mis)used to finance gender and sexual reassignment surgeries. Framed in terms of speech act theory, the CEO flagged the reassignment campaign in question as an act of "infelicity" (Austin, 1975), that is, as a failure or abuse of crowdfunding, something which, in his eyes, should not have happened.

However, although queer cases such as gender and sexual reassignment surgery campaigns might appear as a failure if viewed from the standpoint of dominant perception, it should be borne in mind that the infelicity such cases epitomize always bears the potential of transforming the conventions it violates. More poignantly, Judith Butler, whose work builds on John Austin's, suggested that the ostensible failure of infelicitous cases essentially exposes the "bounds of the felicitous and the normal" (Medina, 2007), thus "disrupting and subverting the effects produced by such [felicitous] speech, a fault line exposed that leads to the undoing of this process of discursive constitution" (Butler, 1997, p. 19).

While we are largely supportive of queer theory's theoretical premises and political ambitions, we in this chapter, we do not focus on issues explicitly related to gender and sexuality. Instead, we use the term "queer" to denote cases which disrupt the boundaries between felicitous and infelicitous uses of crowdfunding, thus kindling profound questions over how crowdfunding works. Queer cases bear the unique potential of discovering something new and truly unexpected about crowdfunding, even if these discoveries might stir feelings of unease and estrangement. Revealing normative structures of meaning making, queer cases open the field of signification so that inventive propositions can be uttered, propositions which challenge orthodoxies by dint of surprise and evocation.

At this decisive point in our argument, we would like to demonstrate how queer cases can be used to fundamentally rethink what else crowdfunding is and how it participates in the creation of social value by introducing our empirical vignette, a Kickstarter campaign geared towards producing a potato salad.

Zack Brown's potato salad project

The crowdfunding campaign in question was started by Zack "Danger" Brown on July 3, 2014. Brown pitched his campaign on the crowdfunding platform Kickstarter by saying: "I'm making a potato salad, and for a few bucks, I'll give you a bite." Described by a journalist as a pitch written in a "hilarious, deadpan style" (Forbes Magazine, 2014), Brown's plan to make a potato salad was ostensibly triggered by a discussion with friends about his favorite side dish being served on the impending 4th of July barbecue. Although he had eaten a lot of potato salad in the course of time, he had never made one. Brown's Kickstarter campaign was anything but pompous, comprising a picture of him as well as of a potato salad (which was not his own creation). His financial requirements were modest, to say the least, as he only requested $10 to realize his campaign. Already on day one of his pitch, the accumulated funds exceeded Brown's aim by a factor of twenty. Thirty days after placing his pledge, he ended up receiving an astounding $55,000 from approximately 7,000 backers. Brown repeatedly admitted that he was dumbstruck by the success of his project. For instance, three days after his campaign was initiated, Brown expressed on a local TV news channel his amazement at how successful his idea was in attracting money (at the time he had fewer than 200 backers). Only a few days later, the potato salad project hit the big stage as Brown's campaign was simultaneously picked up by Yahoo! News, Slate, and the Huffington Post. On July 7, Brown was invited to talk about his campaign on ABC's nationally televised "Good Morning America" (ABC News, 2014). At the time, the idea had gathered $35,000, and Brown kept no secret that the project was "crazy" and might have been blown out of proportion.

Nevertheless, Brown obviously enjoyed his overnight stardom. At one point, he called television channels to ask whether they would offer him a job as a comedian. Although his wish did not come true, Brown mentioned on several occasions that the experiences gathered during his campaign were worthwhile, and that he was having fun throughout. Indeed, fun was a key element of his project. For instance, in an interview, Brown jokingly said that the "thing that drew me to crowdfunding is what draws a lot of people: I am risk-averse [...]. I needed to be supported in my venture and know that I was not going alone" (The Columbus Dispatch, 2014). The irony is obvious here, as the risk involved in Brown's campaign was literally inexistent, for neither did the making of the potato salad form a particularly risky task, nor were the negative ramifications of potential failure particularly eerie. Further, Brown used, if unintentionally, irony to suggest that the success of his potato salad campaign was largely beyond his own control. He did so by stating that the critical lesson he had learned from his campaign is that project initiators must communicate their ideas clearly (read "I'm making a potato salad"; YouTube, 2014a).

Despite his apparent sense of humor, Brown did not treat his financial success lightly. On the contrary, he immediately embraced the responsibility that came with the amount of money his project had raised. On "Good Morning America" Brown was quick to suggest that he planned to do as much good as possible with the money. "Doing good," according to Brown, involved continuously adding further incentives for backers. While the campaign was initially predicated on the idea that every backer contributing $3 would get a portion of potato salad, Brown kept adding further stretch goals as the funds exceeded his original financial goals. In a first step, Brown started producing hats (for backers contributing at least $25) and T-shirts (for backers contributing at least $35), stating that the project was backed. Later on, he promised to recognize backers by reading their names on camera while doing his first potato salad. His honorary recognition (Larralde & Schwienbacher, 2012) of almost 7,000 backers, from over 74 countries, took Brown nearly 4 hours (YouTube, 2014b).

Brown's financial success was not without its obstacles. Most notably, Kickstarter's regulations prevented Brown from donating the money earned during his campaign to a good cause in Columbus, Ohio, where he lived. As the "Rules" section of Kickstarter stipulates: "We're all in favor of charity [...], but they're not permitted on Kickstarter. Projects can't promise to donate funds raised to a charity or cause" (Kickstarter, 2015a). This stipulation obviously put Brown's promise of using the money for a good cause in jeopardy. But Brown eventually found a way to simultaneously spend the money in accordance with Kickstarter's rules, while serving a good cause. This consisted of setting up a music festival called PotatoStock 2014 (cf. thepotatostock.com) comprising cooking demonstrations for kids, radio DJs, and different local bands. According to Brown, approximately 1,500 people attended the festival, where he and his team distributed 450lbs of potato salad. Admitting that he had hoped for a bigger turn-out, Brown noted that he nevertheless "felt like everyone in attendance was really happy to be there celebrating something so silly" (Interviewly, 2014). While the organization of the festival cost $28,492, Brown spent roughly $20,000 on the incentives backer, $2,000 on taxes, and $5,000 to set up a for-profit limited liability company which he and some friends planned to use for producing further content such as funny movies (Columbus Monthly, 2014). Brown's vision was to match the costs of the festival through corporate sponsorships, and to give the money to the Columbus Foundation, a local charity fighting hunger and homelessness in Central Ohio. It only took Brown and his team an hour to sell out their 300 festival T-shirts, $10 from each going to the Columbus Foundation. Together with $18,000 from sponsorship, Brown was able to donate over $20,000 to the Columbus Foundation to support the fight against hunger and homelessness in Central Ohio. As Lisa Jolley, the Columbus Foundation's director of donors and development, mentioned, the funds "will have potential way after this potato salad is forgotten" (CBS News, 2014).

How a potato salad upsets normative assumptions about crowdfunding

Meeting opposition: The critique of Brown's campaign

As we write this chapter, Brown's project is listed as the fourth most visited site on Kickstarter, outweighed only by a well-known games console (backed with more than $8.5 million), a watch (backed with more than $10 million), and a major feature film (backed with more than $5.5 million). However, regardless of the fact that Brown's campaign was touted as an economic exemplar which conveys serious lessons about the factors success—defining crowdfunding, such as the right timing (the project was launched right before the 4th of July) or the brevity and simplicity of the campaign description (Forbes Magazine, 2014), other commentators earmarked the campaign as "spoof," "nonsense," or "hoax." Hence, unlike those who regarded the potato salad campaign as original or simply a "good laugh," Brown's project was attacked, at times fiercely, for mocking the cause of crowdfunding by misusing it for largely illegitimate ends. For instance, on July 8, the New York Magazine (2014) described Brown's campaign as an "incredibly stupid" project whose only opportunity consisted of having "a stranger flush your money down the toilet so you don't have to." It was also mentioned that the campaign might be dangerous since Brown had never made a potato salad before (Forbes Magazine, 2014). Considerably harsher critiques were posted in the comments section of the Kickstarter homepage, such as "Jason Kreiger" who complained that Brown's campaign was "a slap in the face for any serious creators out there and muddles up the credibility of having a Kickstarter." "Andy Jennings" feared that Brown's project would inspire "hundreds, if not thousands, of stupid copycat projects" with the effect of sapping Kickstarter's reputation as a serious platform "where you can get your great idea funded by the people who want to see it brought to life." "Dale Taylor," in turn, insisted that Kickstarter had destroyed its brand by becoming the "Monty Python of crowdfunding." And "Terrance Grace" added that Kickstarter was well on its way to becoming a "trash sourcing platform."

Some commentators pointed out that Brown's campaign might have simply slipped the attention of Kickstarter, as the platform had recently changed from evaluating each project individually to using an algorithm to check whether a given project was in line with its general rules. At the time, a Kickstarter spokesperson insisted that quality would not suffer as a result of the procedural change. However, the critique triggered by the potato salad campaign compelled Kickstarter to account for its laissez-faire approach. Kickstarter maintained on its "Trust and Safety" page that "Kickstarter doesn't evaluate a project's claims [...]—*backers* decide what's worth funding and what's not" (Kickstarter, 2015b; emphasis in original). On its company blog, Kickstarter tried to divert attention from Brown's campaign by pointing at what it deemed a more representative Kickstarter project that tried to raise money to produce virtual reality headsets: "It's funny to think that more people have seen the potato salad project than Oculus Rift, but hey, the internet is a crazy place."

What these tentative comments are bound to show is that Brown's campaign upset the felicity conditions delineating the proper usage of crowdfunding. While crowdfunding campaigns, to become recognizable as pertinent or sound, need to meet certain "felicity conditions" (Austin, 1975), these conditions are not necessarily obvious. Given the elusiveness of felicity conditions, we would like to throw some light on the precise ways in which Brown's potato salad campaign violates prevailing understandings of crowdfunding. Out of all the breaches Brown's campaign precipitates, we selectively focus on three violations we deem most illuminative.

Felicity condition 1: Capital is in short supply

The significance of crowdfunding largely derives from its ability to raise capital to finance ventures and projects otherwise barely financed (Harrison, 2016). In the particular case of social projects and ventures, crowdfunding offers an alternative means of financing under conditions of declining public funds, private donations, or the mere non-existence of traditional means of capital investment more generally. The attentive reader will understand that crowdfunding campaigns are predicated on the idea that capital is a scarce resource. If we now turn toward the potato salad campaign, which asked for only $10, it becomes difficult to believe that Brown was not able to finance the project through his own resources (or those of his friends and family). Hence, if it gets accepted that Brown, a co-owner of a successful tech company focusing on building web and mobile applications, was not using Kickstarter out of economic necessity, as he would have been able to finance the potato salad without any difficulties, this suggests that the potato salad project formed an infelicitous use of Kickstarter, since its success did in no way depend on the monetary contributions of the crowd.

Felicity condition 2: Crowdfunding campaigns get financed if they convey a compelling idea

What is crucially at stake in social purpose crowdfunding is that the project initiator or social entrepreneur offers a compelling account of why backers should finance their idea or venture. A crowdfunding project will only receive financial support if backers are able to recognize its value, potential, and, importantly, legitimacy (Lehner, 2013). Given the competitive nature of crowdfunding, this implies that the idea of a project or campaign must be communicated in a persuasive manner so that backers eventually deem it "worthy and needed" (Lehner, 2013, p. 6). While it is said that backers who are passionate about a project or idea will "easily invest small amounts of capital" (Meyksens & Bird, 2015, p. 155), we wonder what triggered the passion of those who invested in Brown's campaign. It is thereby fairly uncontroversial to suggest that the potato salad project did not rest upon a particularly good idea or opportunity (Görling & Rehn, 2008). Even Brown admitted the profanity of his campaign by ironically claiming that the aim of his campaign was to revolutionize the making of potato salad: "We set out to redefine what a side dish could be and together we are building a movement" (YouTube, 2014c). Brown's campaign can be regarded as infelicitous insofar as it contradicts the idea that backers will only support an idea if they perceive it as innovative and legitimate (Lehner, 2013).

Felicity condition 3: Crowdfunding campaigns need to offer backers attractive rewards

Crowdfunding campaigns offer different forms of incentives (i.e., donations and passive and active investments) (Rubinton, 2011) to garner the interest of potential backers. The traditional literature on commercial crowdfunding purports that backers are mostly driven by financial rewards as well as the prospect of active participation (Rubinton, 2011). There is the belief that if a given project bears utility from the backer's point of view (e.g., expected returns in the form of, for instance, delivery of a copy of the physical good, access to services, or free admission to special events), then he/she will invest money to support the project. While Brown in the early stages of his campaign promised to deliver a portion of the potato salad to each backer, it is hard to believe that this prospect was a significant driver of backers' monetary support. At any rate, even if one accepts that backers might invest their money for irrational reasons, their investment behavior nevertheless appears infelicitous, as it is not brought into equipoise by a corresponding material or symbolic reward.

While these three brief reflections convey the realization that the potato salad project breaches existing conditions of felicity on different levels, we will now turn our attention towards how Brown's seeming abuse of crowdfunding allows us to experiment with fresh ways of thinking about our subject matter, notably as concerns the process of social value creation.

Experimenting with novel understandings of crowdfunding

As tangentially mentioned at the outset, crowdfunding is increasingly discussed in the academic literature as a vehicle for social value creation. The idea of social value, which remains a notoriously ill-defined term (a point already stressed by Schumpeter (1908) more than a century ago), is based on the assumption that project initiators or social entrepreneurs use crowdfunding to access capital as a missing factor of production, which then allows them to solve their identified social problem. In this schema, social value gets conceived as teleology (the targeted end goal of social purpose crowdfunding), against which the actual outcome of a given project can eventually be assessed. The project initiator thereby defines what kind of social value the respective project should produce (e.g., decreasing rates of illiteracy or juvenile delinquency), and by which means social value is being realized. Backers, in turn, operate as facilitators who enable social value by financing the respective project goals defined by the project initiator.

As revealed in the previous section dealing with how Brown's campaign violates crowdfunding's conditions of felicity, the normative understanding of crowdfunding as a linear process that proceeds along a series of predefined steps geared toward unleashing social value is utopic. This fantasy, however, is productive in the sense that it invites us to reconsider the ways in which we understand how crowdfunding and social value intersect. In the remainder of this chapter, we aim at reinterpreting Brown's project as indicative of how social value results from a contingent and co-emergent (and not from a linear) process. The main objective is to demonstrate, if only tangentially, how the social value produced by the potato salad project was less the "logical" outcome of a compelling idea than of the unique interplay between a rather peculiar idea, the technology of the crowdfunding platform, the backers, and an entrepreneur in-the-making.

The project initiator and the contingency of social value creation

Let us begin our reflection with the project initiator, Zack Brown, and his potato salad campaign. Judging from publicly available information, Brown's project never pursued a social purpose to begin with.[1] Indeed, Brown, at the outset of this journey, was not in the least trying to act on vulnerable people by solving a specific social problem, and he was overtly surprised by the role he came to play in helping eradicate hunger and homelessness in his home town. The transformation of the potato salad campaign into a project with a social purpose became visible when Brown proclaimed that he would use the attracted funding to do "as much good as possible" (ABC News, 2014). To properly understand how Brown's mockery project was transformed into a social purpose campaign, we move away from the idea of the project initiator as the originator of social value.

To say it without hesitation, even if the potato salad project eventually helped create social value, this was definitively not the result of Brown's visionary foresight and entrepreneurial imagination. Truly, the way in which Brown eventually created social value was, from his point of view, purely random, a success by accident (Görling & Rehn, 2008). This interpretation is inter alia supported by a Twitter comment of a follower of Brown's campaign, saying: "Nice to see that what initially seemed like the dumbest idea turned into a great thing. Congrats!" However, once we have agreed that social value, if looked at from the perspective of the project initiator, is a product of arbitrariness, this immediately suggests a need to make palpable the complex processes from which social value emerged.

Soon after the pitch of his campaign, Zack Brown rather quickly acted as a comedian entrepreneur by respectively making fun of or acting surprised about the epic funds his project had attracted. His celebrity status helped him, wittingly or unwittingly, to make his project palatable for a broader audience, which in turn led to even more excess capital. An important turning point occurred when Brown promised to use the funds to do good. By organizing a festival whose proceeds were donated to the Columbus Foundation, Brown found a way to transform his capital from being mere excess to being an input for creating social value. At the same time as Brown transformed the meaning of his funds and of his project at large (from mockery project to social purpose campaign), he too went through a metamorphosis of becoming a social entrepreneur.

Obviously enough, the unfolding of Brown's campaign explodes any pretensions of a linear "cause and effect" sequence between the project's initial idea and the creation of social value (see Figure 19.1 above). Social value rather emerged from how the project initiator was able to adapt his role (from comedian to social entrepreneur) to his polymorphous project, which changed as a result of the funders' excessive investing (cf. below). On this read, social value in the case of Brown's campaign can be regarded as contingent in the best sense of the term, as it was not intended but nevertheless occurred as an emergent possibility (Harmeling & Sarasvathy, 2013). Contending that social value is a contingent effect, we are thereby not suggesting, as Castoriadis (1997) reminds us elsewhere, that social value merely emerges "out of blue sky" (or cum nihilo, with nothing; 1997, p. 404). Instead, what is crucially at stake in Brown's campaign is that social value did not already exist as a possibility of the initial idea of the campaign, but rather emerged from the distributed agency (Korsgaard, 2011) of an emerging set of specific relations between an apparently nonsensical idea, the project initiator, the technology, that is, the Kickstarter platform, and the crowd. The idea of contingency further suggests that the notion of agency needs to be understood in a broader sense. As Latour once proposed: "An actor is what is made to act by many others [...] not the source of action but the moving target of a vast array of entities swarming toward it" (Latour, 2005, p. 46). Hence, Brown's agency in creating social value is an effect of both the resources already put to work with his campaign as much as his clever use of the contingent possibilities that emerged from it, such as the surplus of funding, the prohibition of donations by Kickstarter, and the publicity of "his" project. We thus seem well advised to replace the linear causation logic which informs normative understandings of crowdfunding with an effectuation logic (Sarasvathy, 2001), which acknowledges that the outcome of crowdfunding campaigns, although not predictable at the outset, can nevertheless be shaped by taking advantage of the contingent effects emerging throughout the venture process (Harmeling & Sarasvathy, 2013).

Technology and co-emergence

Crowdfunding platforms are suggestive of how web 2.0 technologies open up new possibilities of social value creation. Common wisdom tells us that technology is the medium which enables communication between project initiator and members of the crowd, as well as exchange of resources. The question that lingers here is how technology, the initiator, and the project are actually related. To address this question, it is important to first have a look at the two dominant ways in which technology is interpreted, which can then be used to make sense of Brown's campaign. Following Orlikowski (1992), the first portrayal can be paraphrased as the "technological imperative position." For our context, this view would imply that the crowdfunding technology shapes human behavior in a more or less deterministic manner by defining, for instance, what the project initiator must do so that his or her project becomes eligible for funding, or how the initiator can communicate his or her project. Conjuring up an imagery in which technology barely offers the individual any room for maneuver, the "technological imperative position" essentially implies that the agency of project initiators ends when they decide to pitch their project on a particular platform. Perhaps surprisingly, this position holds true in our case to the extent that Brown's behavior was indeed shaped by the pre-given options of Kickstarter, from the early project presentation to the definition of his stretch goals, Brown's behavior was always a reflection of Kickstarter's formal rules.

The second portrayal of technology derived from Orlikowski can be labeled as a "strategic choice position." Diametrically opposed to the first position, technology is no longer conceived of as a given object. Rather, how technologies are used, and what they eventually signify, remains largely open to its users, from defining the interpretive schemes to designing their functionalities for the predefined ends.[2] This position too seems to have explanatory value for our case, as Brown was at no point in time "forced" by technology to operate his campaign in a predetermined way. Indeed, Brown would not only have been able to stop the project, opt for another funding channel, or ask the crowd to stop backing his project with further capital. Rather, the "strategic choice position" advances an image of the individual who *possesses* the agency to deliberately and continuously redefine the appropriate interpretive schemes through which other actors would re-read his campaign in a favorable way.

Concurring with Orlikowski, both approaches are inapt for acknowledging the duality of technology. While the deterministic perspective denies project initiators any agency (beyond the submission of their project to a pre-given structure), the strategic choice perspective tends to overestimate the autonomy of individuals. Judging from our queer case, we believe that a more nuanced position is needed to strike a balance between these two views so as to recognize the relation of the crowdfunding technology and the projects in terms of co-emergence. Since not only did the crowdfunding technology shape the form and content of Brown's campaign; the campaign too had an effect on the politics of the technology in terms of its project valuation and admission. Specifically, the respective platform started to foreground the more "conventional" or desired projects to attenuate the publicity the potato salad project had garnered. In other words, the newness (or strangeness) of Brown's campaign turned into a liability of newness for the platform. This corresponds with the sexual reassignment project mentioned earlier (Farnel, 2014); while positioning itself as a neutral "enabler" of projects, the platform in question eventually tried to bar sexual surgeries from being financed through its technology. Together this shows that the fate of a crowdfunding project is not solely determined by the acts of its initiator or the causal effect of technology; instead, the initiator and the technology are related in such a way as to establish the project as a co-emergent effect.

Backers and the appropriating of the potato salad campaign as event

Having argued that technology shapes the reality of crowdfunding projects (and vice versa), we would like to expand on this argument by taking a closer look at the agency of backers. To put it bluntly, available research conjures an image of backers of social purpose campaigns as opportunistic individuals who invest their money in anticipation that the campaign will create social value somewhere in the future. The general thinking is that backers systematically trade off the expected charitable outcomes of a social purpose campaign against potential risks. As research shows, enthusiasm about the anticipated outcome of a social venture or project is a better predictor of backers' willingness to invest than particular monetary rewards (Lehner, 2013). However, Brown's campaign casts a different light on how social purpose crowdfunding works by raising intriguing questions around why almost 7,000 backers came to commit themselves to a nonsensical project in ways that only the "higher potential" projects seem capable of doing.

Now, a first point to be raised here is that the erratic behavior of the backers of Brown's campaign is perhaps less surprising than initially assumed. As Lehner (2013) insightfully comments, crowds might act in a largely unforeseen way since individuals are not entirely rational when assessing their investment opportunities. Evidence has it that backers often spend their money on what they expect will give them most satisfaction. This hedonistic imagery of backers receives anecdotal support from a Kickstarter project which offered backers fancy pens as a reward. One of the backers offered revealing insights while reflecting on the value of this reward:

> It's five inches of machined metal with a pen in it. It's nice, I guess, but I'm still using a $2 roller ball to sketch notes in my Moleskine. Yet the Pen Type A is more than a $100 metal pen that never gets used, *it's a memento of the excitement I felt after first seeing the product.*
>
> *(Bogost, 2012; emphasis added)*

The message conveyed here is that backers engage in crowdfunding not so much because they expect the project to engender a particular outcome but because of the novel experiences their participation in crowdfunding enable. As Bogost (2012) remarks in this context: "We're paying for the sensation of a hypothetical idea, not the experience of a realized product. [...] For the experience of watching it succeed beyond expectations or to fail dramatically."

Bogost's remark has an intuitive ring to it, as backers of Brown's campaign were arguably less interested in the prospect of a bite of potato salad but in how the project could be transformed into something entirely different, that is, an experience which offers satisfaction by eliciting desires. What we are suggesting here is that backers endowed Brown's campaign with a particular type of value which is not so much related to utility or "use value" than to the release of new experiences. Thus, in contrast to Marx (1990) who famously said that nothing can have value which does not have utility, the potato salad project reveals how backers, by dint of their ongoing and excessive investments, created a spectacle whose social value resides precisely in the satisfaction they received from participating in it.

That the crowd kept investing in Brown's campaign even after it had reached its official funding goal is not a sign of backers' approval, but an attempt to enact the social value of the project after their own image. In light of what we know about the campaign, one can surmise that backers reenacted the potato salad project as what in philosophical parlance is called an event. This event into which the potato salad project was transformed forms a creative and active movement, which affected everyone who participated in it (Lundborg, 2012). Obviously enough, there is a ruptural element to the event (Robinson, 2015), as the excessive financing of the potato salad project indicated that another *use* of Brown's campaign was possible. Whereas backers reshaped the locus and meaning of "social value" by refusing to interpret Brown's campaign literally (read "I'm making a potato salad, and for a few bucks, I'll give you a bite"), the event subverts many of the root assumptions of social purpose crowdfunding, such as that only the best ideas will receive funding, that backers will finance a project or venture only if its (social) value proposition appears compelling, or that the likelihood of receiving funding is correlated with the backers' rewards (cf. above).

On the other hand, even though Brown's campaign brings into focus how backers used crowdfunding to enact social value in largely novel ways, experience shows that the event remained unrepeatable and inimitable. For instance, although copy cats were quick in emulating the example put forward by the backers of Brown's campaign, they were not in the least able to mobilize similar experiences. That the event enacted by backers necessarily remained an ephemeral moment is also evident from Brown's attempt to repeat it through his music festival PotatoStock 2014. The relatively low attendance at the festival is indicative of how the event enacted by the backers of the potato salad project was already over when Brown tried to actualize it into a "real" encounter between "real" people.

In conclusion, it should be borne in mind that the event enacted by backers was by no means the result of backers' strategic choice. Backers never met in person, and it is highly unlikely that the event they enacted formed an orchestrated endeavor. Instead, the event "happened" as dispersed individuals simultaneously watched how their accumulated micro contributions collapsed existing expectations around how crowdfunding ideally works. Even more, backers' infelicitous use of crowdfunding redefined what *else* crowdfunding can be. It is this iconoclastic experience that constituted the crowd of backers as a "common people" of disparate but connected individuals.

Concluding thoughts

The basic contention advanced in this chapter is that research on (social purpose) crowdfunding has much to learn from the investigation of queer cases. During a time where empirical research on crowdfunding is rapidly growing, we have tried to intervene in this still nascent endeavor by introducing a crowdfunding campaign that occupies a position outside the realm of normative thinking. Unsurprisingly, challenging notions pertaining to linearity, the atomistic agency of the project initiator, or the predictability (and hence mere functionality) of technology, which typify normative renditions of crowdfunding, the potato salad project is notable by the level of critique it has evoked, all sharing a common message: that Brown's campaign represents an infelicitous abuse of crowdfunding. We have put this sweeping pretension into perspective by arguing that what gives Zack Brown's campaign its acute significance is how it permits us to ask important questions about how crowdfunding operates, and especially how it engenders social value.

Hence, while Brown's campaign at first sight makes it difficult to say with any sense of certainty if this is still crowdfunding or not, it is precisely this sense of uncertainty and estrangement which eventually prompts intriguing debates around what else crowdfunding could be(come). As such, we have used the potato salad campaign to suggest that any attempt at understanding necessarily demands a holistic view of the intermingling of the various actors involved in it. A key contribution of our chapter was to cultivate sensitivity for the contingency of crowdfunding by pinpointing the unforeseeable effects it precipitates. On the most general level, we have established the heterodox contention that the social value produced by the potato salad project in the form of a charitable donation to the Columbus Foundation does not emanate "naturally" from a good idea developed by an ingenious (already existing) social entrepreneur. Rather, the potato salad project's contribution to fighting hunger and homelessness in Central Ohio forms a contingent and therefore largely unpredictable effect resulting from the co-emergent relationship between a ridiculous idea, the technology of the Kickstarter platform, the community of backers, and an entrepreneur in-the-making. More specifically, our musing has thrown into sharp relief that the agency of crowdfunding is best thought of in collective rather than in individual terms. For instance, Brown's campaign helped us bring into focus that the outcome of crowdfunding projects is strongly conditioned by the backers that participate in it. In the end, backers do not simply provide the requisite money to support a specific cause or idea; instead, Brown's campaign has offered a paradigmatic example of the formative power of backers who actively shape rather than only finance the reality of the project with which they interact. Lastly, we have argued that technology plays a constitutive role in the crowdfunding process. Rather than only supporting the exchange of information between project initiators or social entrepreneurs and the crowd, technology, via its rules, regulations, project categories, etc.—helps to enact—while recursively being shaped by—reality in particular ways.

It hardly goes without saying that our conceptual exercise formed a tentative thought experiment rather than a self-contained treatise. Notwithstanding this caveat, the key lesson to be gleaned from this chapter is that queer cases such as Brown's potato salad project revitalize thinking by throwing our convictions of crowdfunding into crisis. Such crises are productive in making palpable the felicity conditions that determine our self-evidences and convictions about crowdfunding in general and social value creation more specifically. Shedding light on the separation of felicitous and infelicitous uses of crowdfunding, queer cases cultivate sensitivity that the empirical cases we invoke in our research on crowdfunding largely condition what can be known about our subject matter. Queer cases intervene in this situation by revealing the other against which the norm gets defined, and, on the other hand, by creating opportunities for new and different (potentially horrifying) understandings. Succinctly put, queer cases offer possibilities, but they also threaten what is known. Evidently then, queer cases have critical purchase; not so much to question the legitimacy of crowdfunding *in toto* or by asking whether crowdfunding merits its current hype, but by suggesting an injunction to take a look at the sort of knowledge our empirical cases eventually enact. If it is accepted that the empirical cases we use in our research beget our understanding of what crowdfunding is, then this implies the need to forego, at least occasionally, our beloved assumptions and to engage with cases that are counter-intuitive (if viewed from a canonical perspective).

Indeed, queer cases are still mostly excluded from academic and public debate precisely because they endanger existing convictions (Farnel, 2014). But if it is true, as Nietzsche (1986) tells us, that prevailing "convictions are more dangerous enemies of truth than lies" (p. 483), then it becomes exigent to keep a vigilant eye on how our choice of empirical cases determine what can eventually be known about our subject. To fulfill the promise heralded by queer cases, we need to work up the courage to swim against the canon of common wisdom by refusing to compromise our curiosity and will to know. This is no small postulation, for sure; but the potential danger involved in this endeavor does not absolve us from the responsibility to ask questions which might be uncomfortable yet necessary to prevent trite conventions to congeal into scholarly certainties. To keep knowledge about crowdfunding moving, we must not shy away from using empirical cases which repel normative assumptions about crowdfunding to their core. Despite forming a dangerous endeavor which potentially yields stigma or expulsion from the scholarly community, in our estimate it remains important to embrace what Michel Foucault (2001) elsewhere called the ethos of *parrhesia* or "fearless speech," that is, the unrelenting will to tell potentially disturbing truths (about crowdfunding) regardless of any negative consequences that might ensue. Metaphorically speaking, let us "risk death to tell the truth instead of reposing in the security of a life where the [Other] truth goes unspoken" (Foucault, 2001, p. 17).

Notes

1 To be fair, one could argue that Brown's campaign always had a social purpose, as it aimed at producing a potato salad in the context of an official holiday, the 4th of July. Also, the making of the potato salad was a social happening from the outset, as it was made public through an online campaign. But although these observations are relevant in their own right, they do not form the focus of this chapter.

2 It has to be noted that the reading of the strategic choice position in Orlikowski's paper potentially exaggerates the agency of *managers* (not the users) in shaping a technology to achieve a particular goal or behavior of *users* or how shared meaning emerges from the use of a technology annulling the material-structural conditions.

References

ABC News. (2014). *Potato salad Kickstarter goes global.* Retrieved September 23, 2015, from http://abcnews.go.com/GMA/video/zach-danger-browns-potato-salad-kickstarter-global-24464503

Agrawal, A., Catalini, C., & Goldfarb, A. (2015). Crowdfunding: Geography, social networks and the timing of investment decisions. *Journal of Economics & Management Strategy, 24*(2), 253–274.

Ahlers, G. K. C., Cumming, D., Günther, C., & Schweizer, D. (2015). Signaling in equity crowdfunding. *Entrepreneurship Theory and Practice, 39*(4), 955–980.

Austin, J. L. (1975). *How to do things with words.* Cambridge, MA: Harvard University Press.

Belleflamme, P., Lambert, T., & Schwienbacher, A. (2010). *Crowdfunding: Tapping the right crowd* (CORE Paper No. 32). Retrieved June 3, 2015, from http://ssrn.com/abstract=1578175

Belleflamme, P., Lambert, T., & Schwienbacher, A. (2013). Individual crowdfunding practices. *Venture Capital, 15*(4), 313–333.

Bogost, I. (2012). *Kickstarter: Crowdfunding platform or reality show?* Retrieved September 23, 2015, from http://www.fastcompany.com/1843007/kickstarter-crowdfunding-platform-or-reality-show

Bradford, C. S. (2012). The new federal crowdfunding exemption: Promise unfulfilled. *Securities Regulation Law Journal, 40*(3), 195–249.

Butler, J. (1997). *Excitable speech: A politics of the performative.* New York: Routledge.

Castoriadis, C. (1997). *The Castoriadis reader.* New York: Blackwell.

CBS News. (2014). *Man who raised $55,000 for potato salad throws huge public party.* Retrieved September 30, 2015, from http://www.cbsnews.com/news/man-who-raised-55000-for-potato-salad-throws-huge-public-party/

Columbus Monthly. (2014). *Potato salad guy and the prank that raised £55,000.* Retrieved September 23, 2015, from http://www.columbusmonthly.com/content/stories/2014/09/potato-salad-guy-and-the-prank-that-raised-55000.html

de Buysere, K., Gajda, O., Kleverlaan, R., & Marom, D. (2012). *A framework for European crowdfunding.* Retrieved August 18, 2015, from http://www.crowdfundingframework.eu

Eisenhardt, K. M., & Graebner, M. E. (2007). Theory building from cases: Opportunities and challenges. *Academy of Management Journal, 50*(1), 25–32.

Farnel, M. (2014). Kickstarting trans*: The crowdfunding of gender/sexual reassignment surgeries. *New Media & Society, 17*(2), 215–230.

Forbes Magazine. (2014). *Potato salad Kickstarter campaign raises over $46,000.* Retrieved September 23, 2015, from http://www.forbes.com/sites/johngreathouse/2014/07/08/potato-salad-kickstarter-campaign-raises-over-41000/

Foucault, M. (2001). *Fearless speech.* Los Angeles: Semiotext(e).

Frydrych, D., Bock, A. J., Kinder, T., & Koeck, B. (2014). Exploring entrepreneurial legitimacy in reward-based crowdfunding. *Venture Capital, 16*(3), 247–269.

Görling, S., & Rehn, A. (2008). Accidental ventures—A materialist reading of opportunity and entrepreneurial potential. *Scandinavian Journal of Management, 24*(2), 94–102.

Green, A. I. (2007). Queer theory and sociology: Locating the subject and the self in sexuality studies. *Sociological Theory, 25*(1), 26–45.

Halperin, D. (1995). *Saint Foucault: Towards a gay hagiography*. Oxford: Oxford University Press.
Harmeling, S. S., & Sarasvathy, S. D. (2013). When contingency is a resource: Educating entrepreneurs in the Balkans, the Bronx, and beyond. *Entrepreneurship Theory & Practice, 37*(4), 713–744.
Harrison, R. T. (2016). *Crowdfunding and entrepreneurial finance*. New York: Routledge.
Hollas, J. (2013). Is crowdfunding now a threat to traditional finance? *Corporate Finance Review, 18*(1), 27–31.
Interviewly. (2014). *Zack Danger Brown*. Retrieved October 2, 2015, from http://interviewly.com/i/zack-danger-brown-oct-2014-reddit
Kickstarter. (2015a). *Our rules*. Retrieved November 20, 2015, from https://www.kickstarter.com/rules
Kickstarter. (2015b). *Trust and safety*. Retrieved November 20, 2015, from https://www.kickstarter.com/trust
Korsgaard, S. (2011). Entrepreneurship as translation: Understanding entrepreneurial opportunities through actor-network theory. *Entrepreneurship & Regional Development, 23*(7), 661–680.
Kshetri, N. (2015). Success of crowd-based online technology in fundraising: An institutional perspective. *Journal of International Management, 21*, 100–116.
Larralde, B., & Schwienbacher, A. (2012). Crowdfunding and small entrepreneurial ventures. In D. Cumming (Ed.), *The Oxford handbook of entrepreneurial finance*. New York: Oxford University Press.
Latour, B. (2005). *Reassembling the social: An introduction to actor-network theory*. Oxford: Oxford University Press.
Lehner, O. M. (2013). Crowdfunding social ventures: A model and research agenda. *Venture Capital, 15*(4), 289–311.
Lehner, O. M. (2014). The formation and interplay of social capital in crowd funded social ventures. *Entrepreneurship & Regional Development, 26*(5–6), 478–499.
Lehner, O. M., Grabmann, E., & Ennsgraber, C. (2014). Entrepreneurial implications of crowdfunding as alternative finance source for innovations. *Venture Capital, 17*(1–2), in-print.
Lehner, O. M., & Nicholls, A. (2014). Social finance and crowdfunding for social enterprises: A public–private scheme providing legitimacy and leverage. *Venture Capital, 16*(3), 271–286.
Lundborg, T. (2012). *Encountering the "event" in international politics: Gilles Deleuze, "9/11", and the politics of the virtual*. London: Routledge.
Macht, S. A., & Weatherston, J. (2015). Academic research on crowdfunders: What's been done and what's to come? *Strategic Change, 24*(2), 191–205.
Marx, K. (1990). *Capital, Volume 1*. London: Penguin Books.
Medina, J. (2007). How to undo things with words: Infelicitous practices and infelicitous agents. *Essays in Philosophy, 8*. Retrieved July 17, 2015, from https://commons.pacificu.edu/eip/
Meyskens, M., & Bird, L. (2015). Crowdfunding and value creation. *Entrepreneurship Research Journal, 5*(2), 155–166.
Mollick, E. (2014). The dynamics of crowdfunding: An exploratory study. *Journal of Business Venturing, 29*(1), 1–16.
New York Magazine. (2014). *12 other incredibly stupid Kickstarter projects that could be the next potato salad*. Retrieved October 2, 2015, from http://nymag.com/daily/intelligencer/2014/07/12-other-incredibly-stupid-kickstarter-projects.html
Nietzsche, F. (1986). *Human, all too human*. Cambridge: Cambridge University Press.
Orlikowski, W. J. (1992). The duality of technology: Rethinking the concept of technology in organizations. *Organization Science, 3*(3), 398–427.
Robinson, A. (2015). *Alain Badiou: After the event*. Retrieved November 20, 2015, from https://ceasefiremagazine.co.uk/alain-badiou-event-2/
Rubinton, B. (2011). *Crowdfunding: Disintermediated investment banking* (MPRA Working Paper). Retrieved May 30, 2015, from https://mpra.ub.uni-muenchen.de/31649/
Sarasvathy, S. D. (2001). Causation and effectuation: Toward a theoretical shift from economic inevitability to entrepreneurial contingency. *The Academy of Management Review, 26*(2), 243–263.
Schumpeter, J. (1908). On the concept of social value. *Quarterly Journal of Economics, 23*(2), 213–232.
Sorensen, I. E. (2012). Crowdsourcing and outsourcing: The impact of online funding and distribution on the documentary film industry in the UK. *Media, Culture & Society, 34*(6), 726–743.
The Columbus Dispatch. (2014). *$10 potato salad Kickstarter idea nets $35,000 in pledges for Columbus man*. Retrieved September 23, 2015, from http://www.dispatch.com/content/stories/life_and_entertainment/2014/07/07/potato-kickstarter.html

Thorpe, D. (2012). *Eight crowdfunding sites for social entrepreneurs*. Retrieved July 21, 2015, from http://www.forbes.com/sites/devinthorpe/2012/09/10/eight-crowdfunding-sites-for-social-entrepreneurs/

Tomczak, A., & Brem, A. (2013). A conceptualized investment model of crowdfunding. *Venture Capital, 15*(4), 335–359.

Turner, W. B. (2000). *A genealogy of queer theory*. Philadelphia: Temple University Press.

YouTube. (2014a). *Three Kickstarter tips from the $55,000 potato salad guy*. Retrieved September 23, 2015, from https://www.youtube.com/watch?v=_ymfzPJpwz0

YouTube. (2014b). *Potato salad Kickstarter: The reading of the names*. Retrieved September 23, 2015, from https://www.youtube.com/watch?v=gacUgnNHh7Y&feature=youtube

YouTube. (2014c). *Potato salad: Behind the scenes*. Retrieved September 23, 2015, from https://www.youtube.com/watch?v=SCPbIW7JCTE

20

INSTITUTIONAL ANALYSIS OF VENTURE PHILANTHROPY

Tamaki Onishi

Venture Philanthropy, sometimes called Philanthrocapitalism (Bishop & Green, 2010), generally refers to applying the venture capital investment model to philanthropy (Frumkin, 2008; Moody, 2008). A notion of Venture Philanthropy emerged in the US from the mid-1980s to early 1990s, later expanding into the UK, continental Europe, and other nations (John, 2006; Mair & Hehenberger, 2014; Moody, 2008). This ostensibly "perfect marriage" between social mission and business has attracted a "new breed" of philanthropists (Greenfeld, 2000), including high-tech entrepreneurs and venture capitalists (Brainerd, 1999), as well as management scholars (Porter & Kramer, 1999). Proponents argued that Venture Philanthropy would be one of the most prominent innovations in philanthropic practice (Frumkin, 2003). Wide coverage in popular media outlets, such as *Time* (Greenfeld, 2000), *Forbes* (Gupte, 1999), and *Fortune* (Colvin, 2001; Whitford, 2000), helped popularize this unconventional form of philanthropy beyond the traditional philanthropic circle. The proponents' rationale has been that by adopting the venture capital model used so successfully to identify and grow start-up business ventures, Venture Philanthropy would be more effective than traditional funding approaches in growing social ventures as well (Letts, Ryan, & Grossman, 1997).

Despite much buzz about its potential, Venture Philanthropy has been a highly controversial idea within the non-profit and philanthropic communities (Edwards, 2009; Frumkin, 2003; Sievers, 2001). By incorporating the venture capital model into philanthropy, the hybrid model has become embedded in competing institutional logics: social and philanthropic logics guide organizations to pursue a mission, whereas business and venture capital logics seek profit (Dacin, Dacin, & Matear, 2010; Nicholls, 2010a; Pache & Santos, 2010). In essence, Venture Philanthropy was a concept deviating from the institutional norms of traditional philanthropy. Even as Venture Philanthropy was becoming institutionalized, these competing logics created tension and sparked intense debate over the benefits and risks of utilizing a business model for philanthropy.

Institutional theory suggests that organizations must conform to demands from their institutions, which are "composed of regulative, normative and cultural cognitive elements that, together with associated activities and resources, provide stability and meaning to social life" (Scott, 2008a, p. 48). Conformity to external constraints presses organizations toward "institutional isomorphism" (DiMaggio & Powell, 1983)—processes that lead organizations in a specific organizational field to become homogeneous over time in search of legitimacy. Isomorphism among organizations then often results in the creation of a new organizational field (DiMaggio, 1991). Prior literature confirms that a new field was being created for Venture Philanthropy (Mair & Hehenberger, 2014; Moody, 2008). The literature of institutional theory tends to examine established fields rather than early stage processes of institutionalization (DiMaggio, 1991). To explore such early processes, we ask: how has the new organizational field of Venture Philanthropy emerged and evolved while facing multiple and competing institutional demands from both social and business logics?

To address this question, I apply institutional perspectives to analyze a new hybrid field of Venture Philanthropy in the US. I argue that exploring the first two decades of Venture Philanthropy's history offers insights into the dynamics—promotions, conflicts, and constraints arising from competing logics—in the initial evolution of this emerging field. Because institutional theory (DiMaggio & Powell, 1983; Scott, 2008a) explores how institutional elements become established as dominant forces and how these elements are diffused and adapted towards institutionalization, it is a highly useful theoretical lens for analyzing social entrepreneurship (Nicholls, 2010a) and Venture Philanthropy (Mair & Hehenberger, 2014; Moody, 2008). Institutions are "historical accretions of past practices and understandings that set conditions on action" (Barley & Tolbert, 1997, p. 99). As institutional theory attends to deeper, historical, and more resilient aspects of social structure, it is appropriate to apply institutional theory to analyze the development of Venture Philanthropy.

In light of the theoretical implications discussed here, this study addresses four broad aspects: (1) naturalistic approaches and agent-based approaches to understanding the rise of a new organizational field; (2) the social carriers that diffuse and institutionalize innovative ideas; (3) the effects of business influence on isomorphism; and (4) institutional constraints of traditional philanthropy on the new field of Venture Philanthropy. I ask: (1) How do institutions of Venture Philanthropy emerge? Who are the actors and what are the forces by which new institutions emerge?; (2) How are institutions constructed? What effects are created by isomorphism?; and (3) How do elements from prior institutions constrain Venture Philanthropy's efforts to mimic venture capital culture and practices? The subsequent sections begin with a brief overview of Venture Philanthropy and institutional theory as a framework for the analysis, based on prior literature. Then, I discuss the mechanism of field construction, and institutional effects and constraints on Venture Philanthropy practices.

Venture Philanthropy

As a philanthropic form of social finance (Lehner & Nicholls, 2014; Nicholls, 2010b), Venture Philanthropy pursues social mission and business entrepreneurship simultaneously (Miller & Wesley, 2010)..In this regard, Venture Philanthropy is often situated in the movement toward social entrepreneurship and enterprises adapting business concepts and practices for use in the non-profit sector (Dart, 2004; Dees, 1998; Eikenberry & Kluver, 2004; Jegen, 1998). Similar to social entrepreneurship, the field of Venture Philanthropy suffers from definitional challenges. To clarify the term Venture Philanthropy, this section provides an overview of various definitions and core practices put forth by prior studies. This overview also underscores the diversity within the field of Venture Philanthropy.

Definitions

Prior literature points to the difficulty of proposing a succinct and encompassing definition of Venture Philanthropy, because of the diversity of specific activities taking place under its umbrella (Moody, 2008). Some scholars use the term "Venture Philanthropy" as part of "social

Table 20.1 Definitions of Venture Philanthropy by selected prior literature

Authors	*Term used*	*Definition*	*Organization types included in the study*
Community Wealth Ventures, Inc. (2000)	Social venture funds	"[W]e defined a social venture fund as follows: a multi-donor fund specifically created to address social issues that utilizes venture capital practices to maximize investor value and impact" (p. 8).	Non-profit organizations including giving circles and foundations
Eikenberry (2006)	Venture Philanthropy	"[I]s structured to follow a Venture Philanthropy model—applying venture capitalist principles to philanthropy" (p. 522).	Non-profit organizations including giving circles and foundations
Fleishman (2009)	Venture Philanthropy	"In this approach, the foundation provides financing in exchange for significant involvement in and some degree of control of the program being supported. For instance, a foundation that is basically playing a Partner role might ask for the right to specify particular strategic implementation tasks to be performed by the grantees according to an agreed upon timeline, with specified benchmarks and required performance reports" (p. 7).	Foundations
Frumkin (2003)	Venture Philanthropy	"Rather than simply being a purveyor of charitable funds for deserving organizations of all sorts, Venture Philanthropy promised to turn donors into hard-nosed Social Investors by bringing the discipline of the investment world to a field that had for over a century relied on good faith and trust" (p. 8).	Non-profit organizations including giving circles and foundations
James and Marshall (2006)	Venture Philanthropy	"[W]hat *is* arguably new is that [Venture Philanthropy] folds these practices into a systematic framework that mimics the vaunted for-profit venture capital model. In short, venture philanthropists aspire to build the capacity of nonprofit organizations" (p. 108).	Foundations
John (2006)	Venture Philanthropy	"There is no single accepted definition of Venture Philanthropy. Several terms are used interchangeably, including strategic philanthropy, high engagement philanthropy, effective philanthropy or philanthropic investment. For the purpose of this paper, Venture Philanthropy is defined primarily by the relatively high level of engagement of the funder in the organisation being supported, over an extended time period, injecting skills or services in addition to finance" (p. 7).	Non-profit and for-profit organizations that provide a wide range of funding including grants and equity (UK focused)
Mair and Hehenberger (2014)	Venture Philanthropy	"The Venture Philanthropy model of giving prescribes investing in and strengthening the organizational capacity of social purpose organizations as defining practices" (p. 10).	Organizations that use organized philanthropy in Europe

Miller and Wesley (2010)	Social venture capitalists (SVCs)	"Social venture capital (also called patient capital or Venture Philanthropy) uses a new model for funding social ventures. Like commercial venture capital, this model allows the entrepreneur to exchange involvement in the operations for continued funding as SVCs often invest through equity in the early stages of social ventures using limited liability corporations or partnerships" (p. 707).	Non-profit and for-profit organizations that make equity investments
Moody (2008)	Venture Philanthropy	"[A] core set of principles and practices that are espoused by the majority of Venture Philanthropy organizations… 1) Investments in a long-term (3–6 year) plan for social change; 2) A managing partner relationship; 3) An accountability-for-results process; 4) Provision of cash and expertise; and 5) An exit strategy." "Venture Philanthropy involves close monitoring of predetermined performance goals and measurements as well as joint problem solving with nonprofit investees throughout the long-term duration of the funding" (p. 9).	Non-profit organizations including giving circles and foundations
Scarlata and Alemany (2008)	Philanthropic venture capitalists (PhVCs)	"Philanthropic venture capitalists are social subjects whose aim consists of investing those funds raised from various donors—who may be wealthy individuals, enterprises, and/or foundations—in organizations with high social impact. In order to maximize the social return from the investment, PhVCs engage in a value added partnership with the target organization and mete out financing based on the reaching of milestones. As such, PhVCs monitor the progress of the firms they back, not only providing capital but also expertise and strategic guidance. Besides, in case PhVCs take a seat on the board of directors of the organizations they back, they retain important rights which allow them to intervene in the company's operations when necessary" (p. 3).	Non-profit organizations including foundations (European for-profit funds included)
Scarlata and Alemany (2010)	Philanthropic venture capitalists	"[A]n intermediated investment in small and medium SEs with a potential for a high social impact. Financial return considerations may, however, also be taken into account but must be of secondary importance to the attainment of social impact."	Non-profit and for-profit organizations that provide a wide range of funding including grants and equity (European funds included)
Van Slyke and Newman (2006)	Venture Philanthropy	"[P]rivate, or corporate foundation, venture philanthropists and their philosophy of high engagement regard funding as a long-term investment. Whereas many foundations have traditionally provided grants for a single year or perhaps as long as three years, venture philanthropists and their organizations, funders, and staff, such as Venture Philanthropy Partners and the Roberts Enterprise Development Fund, generally enter into a relationship with a social enterprise nonprofit organization for a longer period of time because they believe the nonprofit can benefit from long-term engagement and substantial financial investments and levels of strategic assistance in the organization" (p. 347).	Community foundations primarily

venture capital investment funds" (Miller & Wesley, 2010), or "Impact Investing" in more recent years (Bugg-Levine & Emerson, 2011). Others discuss Venture Philanthropy as a new strategic-giving approach of philanthropic foundations (Fleishman, 2009; Standlea, 2006).

To highlight this definitional challenge, I explicate how prior studies have defined Venture Philanthropy (see Table 20.1). Many studies, including those by Community Wealth Ventures, Inc. (2000, 2002), examine non-profits structured as Internal Revenue Code (IRC) 501(c)(3) public charities (they are "organized and operated exclusively for religious, charitable, scientific, testing for public safety, literary, or educational purposes" under the US Tax Law [Internal Revenue Service, n.d.]), but focus on those applying the Venture Philanthropy model to their funding activities. Some (Fleishman, 2009; Standlea, 2006) probe the Venture Philanthropy activities of long-standing private independent foundations (e.g., the William and Flora Hewlett Foundation, the Rockefeller Foundation, and the W.K. Kellogg Foundation), as well as private independent foundations more recently established by dotcom millionaires (e.g., the Bill & Melinda Gates Foundation and the Skoll Foundation). Others (Miller & Wesley, 2010) use for-profit venture capital funds investing in social and green businesses as their samples. Further, hybrid funds often are explicated as cases of Venture Philanthropy (Moody, 2008). A notable example of hybrid funds is the Omidyar Network, which is structured as two legal entities, a limited liability company (Omidyar Network LLC) and a private foundation (Omidyar Network Fund, Inc.) (Omidyar Network, n.d.).

This study aims to explore dynamics arising from diverse and competing institutional logics between the philanthropic field and the venture capital field. And, relative to for-profit organizations, non-profit organizations typically experience greater resistance and difficulty in adapting to the social business hybridity (Kistruck & Beamish, 2010). Hence, my analysis focuses on Venture Philanthropy activities by non-profit funds and foundations, but it does not exclude for-profit venture capital funds, as they are part of this Venture Philanthropy field.

Core practices

Table 20.1 displays a wide range of legal structures in Venture Philanthropy, as examined by prior studies. Certain activities taking place under the Venture Philanthropy banner vary greatly. For instance, leaning toward for-profit social investment approaches, Miller and Wesley (2010) limit their sample to organizations that: (1) directly fund ventures on a competitive basis (excluding foundations and angel investors); (2) dedicate at least 10 percent of the assets to social ventures through equity investment; (3) invest in early stage ventures; and (4) employ executives with experience and some decision-making authority in funding decisions. Criteria used by Scarlata and Alemany (2010) to select their US sample are broader and more general. That is, Venture Philanthropy organizations (1) provide financial and non-financial resources; (2) fund social enterprises; (3) have exit strategies; and (4) seek social impact. Further, Frumkin (2008) refers to three core principles guiding a variety of Venture Philanthropy practices, namely (1) a close relationship between a funder and a fundee; (2) unconventional funding tools; and (3) rigorous performance measurement.

Despite these discrepancies in definitions of Venture Philanthropy, my review of prior studies sheds light on a core set of principles and practices that define Venture Philanthropy organizations. In line with Frumkin's (2008) three core principles, Table 20.2 summarizes main Venture Philanthropy practices discussed in prior publications, comparing Venture Philanthropy to traditional philanthropy. To compile this table, the reviewed publications were selected by the following criteria: (1) seminal publications (e.g., Community Wealth Ventures, Inc., 2002; Letts et al., 1997); (2) publications, including websites, generated by leading Venture Philanthropy

Table 20.2 Core practices discussed as Venture Philanthropy versus traditional philanthropy

Principle	*Traditional philanthropy*	*Venture philanthropy*
Characteristics of funding tools	• Shorter funding term • Smaller amounts • Philanthropic funding tools (grants) • Specific program support • Limited provision of technical assistance	• Longer funding term • Larger amounts • Market-based funding tools (e.g., equity, loans) • General operational support • Greater provision of technical assistance
Performance measurement	• Less rigorous measurement • Measurement system developed primarily by a funded social venture • Less rigorous due diligence • No clear exit strategy	• Rigorous measurement • New metrics developed by funders via adaptation of for-profit systems • Rigorous due diligence • A clear exit strategy
Funder–fundee relationship	• Low involvement in a funded social venture • Not serve on the board	• High involvement in a funded social venture • Serve on the board

organizations (e.g., Acumen Fund, REDF, Venture Philanthropy Partners); (3) industry reports; and (4) scholarly publications on Venture Philanthropy and case studies developed by academic institutions (Acumen Fund, 2013; Bill & Melinda Gates Foundation, n.d.; Community Wealth Ventures, Inc., 2000, 2001, 2002; Emerson, 2000, 2003; Fleishman, 2009; Frumkin, 2003, 2008; Letts et al., 1997; Miller & Wesley, 2010; Omidyar Network, n.d.; REDF, 2013; Standlea, 2006; Venture Philanthropy Partners, 2013).

While the debate over Venture Philanthropy being a wholly new funding approach is not conclusive, it appears reasonable to say a Venture Philanthropy approach is distinguished from a traditional grantmaking approach in the elements reviewed by Frumkin (2008) (i.e., a larger amount of their financial support over a longer period of time and provision of different kinds of capital; high involvement in fundees' operations and programs; and new metrics of organizational performance). It should, however, also be noted that the way Venture Philanthropy organizations reflects these characteristics is not uniform. For instance, Acumen Fund, a non-profit whose funding approach is almost identical to that of a for-profit venture capital fund, shows a heightened focus on using market-based funding tools and complex metrics to measure performance of its funded organizations (Acumen Fund, 2013; Trelstad, 2009). Another non-profit Venture Philanthropy organization, Venture Philanthropy Partners, takes a close relationship with funded organizations, even shifting the terminology from "Venture Philanthropy" to "high engagement grantmaking" (Community Wealth Ventures, Inc., 2002). Standlea's (2006) case studies provide evidence that Venture Philanthropy has influenced the practices of private foundations, but to a varying degree.

Institutional analysis of the Venture Philanthropy field

Traditional philanthropy and venture capital investment as distinct institutional fields

A core hypothesis of institutional theory is that legitimacy and social acceptability are critical for organizations to survive and thrive in their institutional environment (Scott, Ruef, Mendel, & Caronna, 2000). To determine a source and a form of institutional demand, Scott (2008a) has argued that institutions comprise three nominal "pillars"—incorporating regulative (legal), normative (social), and cultural cognitive elements. Regulative pillars commonly take the form of regulations, laws, and rules (North, 1990): the state and powerful actors both encourage and constrain organizational action through coercion (DiMaggio & Powell, 1983) or threat of legal sanctions (Hoffman, 1999). Normative pillars generally symbolize professional practices, occupational standards, and appropriate ways to pursue goals (Scott, 2008a): organizational action and beliefs are guided largely by social obligation, norms, or professionalization (Honig & Karlsson, 2004; Kirkpatrick & Ackroyd, 2003; Ruef & Scott, 1998; Scott, 2008b). Lastly, cognitive cultural pillars embody shared conceptions, symbols, language, and frameworks that constitute the nature of social reality (Meyer & Rowan, 1977).

Such regulations, rules, norms, and shared conceptions established in a particular field both promote and constrain organizational behaviors. Organizations in a mature field face more severe institutional resistance to any attempt to engage in activities differing from accepted institutional rules, norms, and culture than do those in an emerging field. Venture Philanthropy organizations are embedded in two mature fields, that is, traditional philanthropy and venture capital investment. Many prior studies (Zacharakis, McMullen, & Shepherd, 2007) point to the highly institutionalized practices of the venture capital industry, but traditional philanthropy has also become highly developed as a distinct field. After the beginning of the 20th century (Cutlip, 1965), American philanthropy became quickly institutionalized as a professional field that today contributes charitable giving totaling $335 billion (Giving USA, 2014). Approximately 15 percent of this US giving comes from foundations, in which Venture Philanthropy organizations are often included (Moody, 2008).

A challenge for Venture Philanthropy organizations lies in the fact that the venture capital field and the traditional philanthropic field comprise diverging institutional logics (business versus mission), and their demands often conflict. This study argues that the significant variations in structure and behavior among Venture Philanthropy organizations result from the dynamics of these competing institutional demands.

Structuration

While macro-environmental conditions—most notably, the political climate of the 1980s and the high-tech economy's boom in the 1990s—underpinned the emergence of Venture Philanthropy, careful and deliberate efforts by institutional actors were major forces driving and expanding this new organizational field. For instance, Letts et al.'s (1997) seminal article advocating for a notion of Venture Philanthropy reports that "some foundations have been studying venture capital firms and their techniques" (p. 35) to look for ways to improve upon traditional grantmaking. Moody's (2008) exploratory study also testifies how philanthropic-minded entrepreneurs deliberately drew on venture capital practices and adjusted their unconventional approaches in a way that Venture Philanthropy would be accepted in philanthropic circles. Thus, when we explore how the field of Venture Philanthropy emerged, we should probe not only the environmental stimuli, but also actors' deliberate efforts. In the subsequent section, I explore two different accounts illuminating the early evolution of the Venture Philanthropy field.

From the institutional perspective, the early evolution of the new Venture Philanthropy field was promoted by the duality of agency and structure and the integration of the two (Giddens, 1979, 1984). To understand the dynamics of constructing the new field of Venture Philanthropy, I apply the concept of structuration (Giddens, 1979, 1984) to my analysis. Structuration theory is a process-oriented theory that treats structure as both a product of and a constraint upon human action. Its fundamental premise is that social structures involve the patterning of actors' activities and communications that persist over time and space (Jarzabkowski, 2008). While the context (structure) enabled early Venture Philanthropists and proponents (agents) to act, their actions altered the sociopolitical context (structure), which set a foundation of institutional creation for Venture Philanthropy. During the process of institutionalization, organizations embody "institutionalized features in the forms of symbolic systems, relational systems, routines and artifacts within their own boundaries" (Scott, 2008a, p. 85). Such institutional rules, norms, and cultural meanings are generated, preserved, and modified collectively by interactions between institutions' members.

Two approaches to new field construction: Naturalistic and agent-based

Institutionalists have debated how institutions are constructed. Strang and Sine (2002) classify the approaches of institutional construction into two distinct methods: naturalistic accounts and agent-based accounts. The gaps between naturalistic accounts and agent-based accounts may lie at the heart of the "structure versus agency debate" over whether organizational behavior is the product of macro social forces or of organizational agency (Hirsch & Lounsbury, 1997). Whereas traditional structure-based naturalistic views emphasize institutional forces that reinforce conformity, agent-based views call attention to creative forces that bring about institutional creation and change (Garud, Hardy, & Maguire, 2007).

Naturalistic accounts of institutions recognize institutionalization as a natural and undirected process (Strang & Sine, 2002), whereby collective sense-making and problem-solving behavior are habitualized through social interaction among organizations (Berger & Luckmann, 1966; Scott, 2008b). On the other hand, agent-based accounts stress the agentic actions and roles in institutional construction, assuming the extent to which intentionality and self-interest are at work (Scott, 2008a). The latter is linked to the notion of "institutional entrepreneurs" (Battilana, Leca, & Boxenbaum, 2009; Garud, Jain, & Kumaraswamy, 2002; Greenwood & Suddaby, 2006; Maguire, Hardy, & Lawrence, 2004). The term is most closely associated with DiMaggio (1988), who argued that "new institutions arise when organized actors with sufficient resources see in them an opportunity to realize interests that they value highly" (DiMaggio, 1988, p. 14).

Using both naturalistic accounts and agent-based accounts allows us to understand the complex process of constructing a new organizational field. Applying both accounts helps us illuminate the very origin of the Venture Philanthropy field before the notion of Venture Philanthropy became popularized (using the naturalistic approach), as well as the primary surge of growth in Venture Philanthropy during the dotcom era (using the agent-based approach).

Phase one: Naturalistic construction

The 1980s and 1990s were marked by the growing influence of anti-welfare state ideologies and the neoconservative faith in market-based approaches for non-profits (Dart, 2004), which prepared the base for a naturalistic construction of a new field of Venture Philanthropy. For instance, the Task Force on Private Sector Initiatives, appointed by President Reagan, promoted an idea that the private business sector could help solve community needs (Berger, 1986). The Task Force urged practitioners, scholars, and policy-makers to reexamine the roles of non-profit and philanthropic organizations in society.

Further, sociopolitical forces and budget cuts during the Reagan administration coerced non-profit and philanthropic organizations to coexist with, and compete against, for-profit businesses in certain industries. There was heightened public concern that federal spending cuts would cripple philanthropic organizations (Salamon & Abramson, 1982). On the contrary, the ostensibly devastating situation urged non-profit organizations to hone their managerial skills and adopt market-based entrepreneurship approaches for their survival. The resilience of these organizations was evidenced by an increase in the number of charitable tax exempt entities by more than 30 percent during this time (Hall, 2001).

These years of non-profits' adjustment to a drastic change in the sociopolitical climate shaped a new public perception of the "preferred" type of non-profit organization, a perception that began altering norms in the field of non-profit organizations. One new norm emerging during the 1980s and 1990s advocated that seeking a market-based strategy is a legitimate approach for non-profit and philanthropic organizations (Dart, 2004). Entrepreneurship was no longer restricted to for-profit firms; scholars began exploring a notion of "non-profit entrepreneurship" (Young, 1986). As a result, the sociopolitical climate during the 1980s and 1990s facilitated the emergence of a field of Venture Philanthropy in a naturalistic way, while forces from the state—a distinctive type of actor exercising legitimate coercion (Streeck & Schmitter, 1985)—triggered the field's creation.

Phase two: Agent-based construction

The primary wave of institutional creation for Venture Philanthropy came during the dotcom era when high-tech entrepreneurs accumulated wealth and began entering the philanthropic field. Here, institutional creation was driven by the deliberative actions of a variety of "institutional actors" (Lawrence, Suddaby, & Leca, 2009). In institutional theory, those who change an extant institutional arrangement or create a new institutional field are institutional actors, such as the nation state, professional associations or managers, and corporate or social elites (DiMaggio & Powell, 1983; Dorado, 2005; Garud et al., 2002; Greenwood & Suddaby, 2006; Maguire et al., 2004). The actors who played a central role in structuring the Venture Philanthropy field came from both the venture capital field and the philanthropic field. As detailed in the subsequent section, notable examples of corporate elites and professions advancing a new field of Venture Philanthropy include high-tech millionaires and venture capitalists, such as George R. Roberts (founding partner of hedge fund KKR & Co, who developed REDF) and Paul Tudor Jones (hedge fund manager, who created the Robin Hood Foundation). Actors from the philanthropic field include Jed Emerson at REDF and, later, those from long-standing influential foundations, such as the W.K. Kellogg Foundation and the Rockefeller Foundation. Involvement of these two distinct groups of actors, who have diverging goals and professional backgrounds, further complicated the field of Venture Philanthropy.

To become truly established, a new institutional field must achieve some degree of sociopolitical legitimation, which is facilitated by "opinion leaders" (Aldrich & Fiol, 1994). The public prestige of these opinion leaders is vital to the success of institutional legitimation. Those leaders infuse the organization with values beyond mere technical requirements, help select the social base and central personnel, and determine the nature and timing of the formalization of structure and procedures (Selznick, 1957). From its early history, the field of Venture Philanthropy has included influential opinion leaders from the business community, such as Michael Porter at Harvard Business School (Moody, 2008).

Diffusion research (Abrahamson, 1991; Galaskiewicz & Burt, 1991; Haunschild, 1993; Rogers, 1995) has established that the diffusion of practices (practices spread from one organization to another through resource dependence or network ties) promotes the process of institutionalization. In this process, opinion leaders work deliberately and diligently to construct the culture and promote the field, developing a cohesive and legitimate repertoire of principles and practices, and strategically communicating those principles across networks (DiMaggio, 1991). Influential business people played a vital role as opinion leaders in creating the field of Venture Philanthropy. For instance, Bill Gates has often actively cultivated new donors to enter the field (Moody, 2008); at the World Economic Forum in Davos, he encouraged other corporate and political leaders to financially support philanthropic organizations. Other Venture Philanthropists (e.g., Jed Emerson and Jeffrey Skoll) have diffused the ideas and practices of Venture Philanthropy internationally to Oxford University's Saïd Business School in the UK, where the research and practices of Venture Philanthropy have been advanced to study social finance under the direction of Alex Nicholls (2010b).

Carriers of new field institutionalization

Institutionalization, or structuration, of a new organizational field is carried by social structures, routines, and cultures. Structuration is characterized by increases in the number of interactions among organizations in a field. These increased interactions, in turn, accelerate the exchange of information and the development of a consensus on organizational forms and the processes by which work should be accomplished—a process that contributes to isomorphism (DiMaggio & Powell, 1983; Giddens, 1979). The initial stage of structuration entails the encoding of institutional principles in the scripts used in specific settings (Barley & Tolbert, 1997). Encoding frequently takes place during socialization and involves an individual internalizing the rules and interpretations of behavior appropriate for particular settings (Berger & Luckmann, 1966). Thus, understanding what "carriers" (Jepperson, 1991) facilitate the encoding of institutional norms is vital for examining how a new organizational field becomes institutionalized.

Building on prior literature, Scott (2008a, 2008b) identifies a variety of carriers that promote such institutionalization. Those carriers include (1) professions (e.g., educators at all levels, lawyers, librarians, missionaries, and consultants), (2) symbolic systems (e.g., the emergence of language and developments in communication technology), (3) relational systems (e.g., networks and role systems), (4) routines (e.g., habitualized and patterned behaviors, and standard operating procedures), and (5) artifacts (discrete material objects consciously produced or transformed by human activity, such as tools and technology). Building on Moody's (2008) exploratory study about Venture Philanthropy, the following subsections examine professions (opinion leaders), networks, media, and new language as the primary carriers that promoted the diffusion of business ideas and practices to institutionalize Venture Philanthropy.

Professions

The literature of institutional theory examines professions as powerful institutional actors who induce the construction of a new field. These professional actors are usually resource-rich professional people, such as accountants (Greenwood & Suddaby, 2006), lawyers (Scott, 2008b), and human resource professionals. Likewise, the creation of the new field of Venture Philanthropy was also prompted by business people.

Although the philanthropic field traditionally has not emphasized the importance of business management acumen, prior literature (Dart, 2004; Moody, 2008) documents the appearance of new professions—management, high technology, and financial professionals—as a dominant factor accelerating the structuration of Venture Philanthropy. Moody (2008) finds a disproportionately greater number of business people—MBA graduates, former investors, and management consultants—involved in Venture Philanthropy organizations as board or staff members. Notably, Venture Philanthropy organizations deliberately seek to hire MBA graduates from top business schools, whereas philanthropic foundations traditionally do not require business degrees or expertise (Letts et al., 1997). Job descriptions of Venture Philanthropy organizations, such as Acumen Fund and Omidyar Networks, explicitly state that qualified candidates should possess work experience in business management, finance, or consulting. Hiring business people not only shaped new practices for "investing in" social ventures but also accelerated the diffusion of business ideas and practices over the Venture Philanthropy field, because professions tend to share the same terminology, culture, and ways of thinking and of doing business. As discussed below, new language and business norms arose among these professionals, who had similar educational and work training, and increased interactions within their closed networks, which promoted the structuration of the Venture Philanthropy field.

Networks

Institutional theorists (DiMaggio & Powell, 1983; Galaskiewicz, 1985; Meyer & Rowan, 1977; Scott, 2008a) stress the importance of communication across networks as part of the relational systems of institutionalization. Communications are further enhanced if they are facilitated among those who share common meanings, values, and goals. By using a notion of the diffusion of innovation, Rogers (1995) finds that innovations spread through communication across networks particularly well when they are promoted by opinion leaders. We witness the same phenomena in the Venture Philanthropy field. Moody's (2008) study reveals that early Venture Philanthropists became part of various networks in order to diffuse and exchange their unconventional ideas and practices. Since the early stages, proponents for Venture Philanthropy have established a network-based community primarily concentrated in Silicon Valley. While the institutional literature tends to probe formal networks, such as professional associations (DiMaggio & Powell, 1983; Galaskiewicz, 1985), the networks promoting communication among early Venture Philanthropists were rather informal. In fact, Moody (2008) found informal networks, such as connections between former classmates at business school and gatherings at which corporate leaders and Venture Philanthropists interact, to be highly effective for diffusing novel ideas during the experimental stages of Venture Philanthropy.

Networks not only connect prominent actors in Venture Philanthropy, they are also structurally designed to be important recruitment and training devices (Moody, 2008). For instance, Paul Shoemaker, a former manager at Microsoft Corporation, utilized a network-based "giving circle" model (Eikenberry, 2006) to recruit new partners for the local chapters of his organization, Social Venture Partners (Brainerd, 1999). The networks of Social Venture Partners further helped spread a model of Venture Philanthropy nationally and internationally, educating their partners about how to create philanthropic investment (i.e., donations) for their local communities. Shoemaker and his colleagues first structured original training seminars at their headquarters in Seattle and then offered the training programs to local chapters on a regular basis.

Media

Institutional theorists discuss media as the main carriers to transmit symbolic systems of norms and values that facilitate the institutional process (Scott, 2008a). As such, popular business media have been important vehicles to diffuse the novel ideas of Venture Philanthropy since the early days. Letts and her co-authors' seminal article pioneering a Venture Philanthropy approach (1997) was published in *Harvard Business Review*, instead of in periodicals for nonprofit managers. Prominent actors promoting Venture Philanthropy, such as Michael Porter at Harvard Business School (Porter & Kramer, 1999), used popular management magazines skillfully as central domains in which the structuration of Venture Philanthropy was manifested. During the mid- to late 1990s, the notion of Venture Philanthropy was promoted by business magazines, such as *Forbes* (Gupte, 1999), *Time* (Greenfeld, 2000), *Fortune* (Colvin, 2001; Whitford, 2000), the *Financial Times* (Bibby, 2004), and *The Economist* ("The birth of philanthrocapitalism," 2006). Whereas the articles in non-profit-focused publications, such as the *Chronicle of Philanthropy*, were generally critical about Venture Philanthropy, the business media outlets encouraged dialog among different actors who developed a consensus on what Venture Philanthropy should be.

Language

Institutionalization is a multifaceted, durable social structure composed of a variety of symbolic elements, such as language (Scott, 2008a). Collective beliefs emerge from processes of repeated interactions among actors, and categorizations of their exchanges achieve the status of objectification and finally constitute social reality (Berger & Luckmann, 1966; Zucker, 1977). Artifacts, such as distinctive terminology and a model of practices, are critical carriers during this process. In particular, language enables actors to frame the issue (Hirsch, 1986) and make sense of new concepts to facilitate institutional construction (Fiss & Hirsch, 2005; Maguire & Hardy, 2009; Phillips, Lawrence, & Hardy, 2004).

The amount of communication and information transfer has increased during the evolution of the Venture Philanthropy field. Venture philanthropists mimicked not only an investment model of venture capitalists, but also their business and investment terminology. For instance, "philanthropic grant" became an "investment," and "donors" became "investors" (Frumkin, 2003). Although this new terminology did not receive as much acclaim as hoped from the traditional philanthropic circle, it was an important step for Venture Philanthropists to invent new business language mimicking that of mainstream venture capitalists. The new terminology facilitated the construction of a new social reality for Venture Philanthropy, gaining legitimacy from business people, and helping institutionalize its new field.

Outcomes of isomorphism

Organizations' quests for legitimacy and the process of structuration result in the isomorphism of organizations with respect to their most visible attributes (Lynall, Golden, & Hillman, 2003). Incorporating various institutional elements, such as rules and norms, from different fields, organizations become more homogeneous over time. Because of the widely accepted validity of business in American culture, Venture Philanthropy organizations have attempted to gain legitimacy by integrating market-based models and concepts with non-market-based, philanthropic grantmaking practices (Dart, 2004; Moody, 2008). Their attempts result in isomorphism characterized in particular by (1) the closeness of funder–recipient relationships, (2) the distinct characteristics of investment tools, and (3) metrics to assess performance (Emerson, Wachowicz, & Chun, 2000; Fleishman, 2009; Frumkin, 2008; Letts et al., 1997; Miller & Wesley, 2010).

Funder–recipient relationships

The funder–fundee relationship was an important element for Venture Philanthropy from its beginning. Letts and her co-authors (1997) propose a closer and longer-term relationship between funders and fundees to achieve more effective funding practices. They note that of the grants made in 1995 in the five states with the highest number of foundations, only 5.2 percent were for more than one year, and the multi-year grants were 2.5 years in length on average (Letts et al., 1997). The 2000 and 2001 reports (Community Wealth Ventures, Inc., 2000, 2001) indicate Venture Philanthropy organizations make grants with a longer timeframe (over three years) than traditional foundations do.

However, a more revealing outcome from isomorphism is a change in the nature of the funder–fundee relationship. Business venture capitalists are known for their close relationship with their invested ventures, often through seats on boards, to monitor organizational performance and provide financial resources and strategic assistance to nascent entrepreneurs (Busenitz, Fiet, & Moesel, 2004; De Clercq & Sapienza, 2006; Macmillan, Kulow, & Khoylian, 1989). Mimicking the practices of venture capitalists, Venture Philanthropists began taking an approach called "high engagement philanthropy" (Community Wealth Ventures, Inc., 2002). High engagement philanthropy refers to an approach in which funders (called "investors" by Venture Philanthropists) are directly involved with the various operations of their funded organizations in order to help build their organizational capacity. While traditional grantmaking practices sometimes entail the provision of technical assistance, the extent to which Venture Philanthropists intervene in their fundees' operations is significantly greater. As a result, the relationship between Venture Philanthropists and their funded organizations has departed from a traditional philanthropic relationship. Ostrander (2007) calls this new type of funder–fundee relationship of Venture Philanthropy "donor controlled philanthropy"—donors oversee operations of the recipient organizations as authorial partners—as opposed to traditional "donor centered philanthropy"—a two-way, mutual, and interactive relationship between funders and recipients. A report surveying the Venture Philanthropy field reveals that some Venture Philanthropy organizational funds, such as New Profit Inc., indeed plan to take seats on the boards of their funded organizations (Community Wealth Ventures, Inc., 2000). Likewise, one of the case organizations featured in Moody's (2008) study about Venture Philanthropy, Omidyar Network, specifies that they often serve on the boards of funded organizations, as well as consulting as a strategic partner (Omidyar Network, 2015a).

Characteristics of investment tools

Proponents for Venture Philanthropy (Letts et al., 1997) argue that a traditional philanthropic strategy (providing a grant to a specific program) does not address a fundamental need for organizational capacity building—a vital condition that enables non-profits to provide high-quality services and programs. They dictate that supporting the organizational development of non-profit fundees requires a more holistic approach. Turning to the venture capital approach that focuses on organizational development, early venture philanthropists mimicked practices and tools used by venture capitalists. In addition to a longer duration and a larger amount of funding, venture philanthropists experimented with using market-based tools, provided added value strategic assistance, and shifted funding focus from a specific program to operations. For instance, Venture Philanthropy Partners provides grants of \$3–\$50 million combined with technical and strategic assistance (Venture Philanthropy Partners, 2015). Acumen Fund's typical investment size ranges from \$0.25 million to \$3 million, structured primarily as market-based tools, that is, either debt or equity (Acumen Fund, 2013). As a hybrid Venture Philanthropy organization, Omidyar Network makes grants and program-related investments in non-profits through its non-profit entity and equity investment in for-profit businesses through its for-profit entity (Omidyar Network, 2015b). Despite this wide variety, Venture Philanthropists claim that these funding tools are the best for improving the organizational health and capacity building of funded organizations.

Metrics to assess performance

The success of venture capital investment relies on accurate assessment (Franke, Gruber, Harhoff, & Henkel, 2008; Shepherd & Zacharakis, 2002). Traditional capital markets evaluate the performance of venture capital investment based on quantifiable and standardized criteria, such as Return on Investment (ROI). Often bringing a background in venture capital investment and entrepreneurship, many early Venture Philanthropists were familiar with such performance measurement (Anheier & Leat, 2006; Frumkin, 2008).

Program assessment was not new in the philanthropic field. Even before the notion of Venture Philanthropy became popularized by the *Harvard Business Review* article (Letts et al., 1997), philanthropic funders, such as United Way, had developed and implemented tools to evaluate the programs that they funded (Kanter & Summers, 1987). Nonetheless, there are still considerable disparities between Venture Philanthropists' measurement methods and those of traditional philanthropic funders. Prior literature points to the degree of specificity of measurable goals, rigor of measuring organizational health (rather than programs), and application of venture capitalists' measurement methods to measure outcomes of funding (Fleishman, 2009; Frumkin, 2008; Letts et al., 1997). Notable examples include Social Return on Investment (SROI) developed by REDF (Emerson, 2003). Mimicking the standardized performance measurement and accounting methods of commercial ventures, such as ROI, SROI "monetizes" the social as well as financial results of funded organizations. Further, these metrics were posted on the Internet for other organizations to share and utilize (Emerson et al., 2000; Trelstad, 2009), which furthered their diffusion.

Constraints from the prior institutions

Up to this point, we have delineated a variety of factors promoting the creation of a new field of Venture Philanthropy. However, "institutions do not emerge in a vacuum; they always challenge, borrow from, and, to varying degrees, displace prior institutions" (Scott, 2008a, p. 94). Beliefs, norms, and practices inherited from the past continue to be part of the initial conditions in the processes of new field construction (Greif, 2006). Organizations that engage in unconventional practices, such as Venture Philanthropy, must deal with path dependency and constraints created by their embeddedness in their own institutional fields. The ideas and practices of Venture Philanthropy departed from philanthropic norms, and as a result, these actors needed to refine their approach to receive acceptance from the non-profit philanthropic field. In this section, I discuss three areas to illustrate the main constraints from traditional philanthropy, namely (1) access to funding tools, (2) primary funding goals, and (3) performance assessment.

Constraints on access to funding tools

State influence through government mandates and regulations represents regulative pressures from institutional environments (Baum & Oliver, 1991; DiMaggio & Powell, 1983). The main legal structure of Venture Philanthropy organizations and their funded organizations is non-profit, and US charitable tax law regularizes certain practices of non-profit organizations. Under US tax law, non-profits, especially IRC 501(c)(3) public charities, receive various tax benefits, that is, exemption from property, sales, and corporation income taxes, to a greater degree than do for-profit firms (Brown & Slivinski, 2006). In return for such benefits, IRS regulations restrict the types of funding and financing tools available for non-profits. While for-profit businesses regularly seek funding resources in the form of equity, non-profits are not allowed to finance by equity capital from the mainstream capital markets (Hansmann, 1980; Tuckman, 1993). Thus, major funding resources in the philanthropic field have traditionally been philanthropic donations and grants.

In recent years, new market-based funding tools have been developed for philanthropic funders. A notable example is program-related investments (PRIs), which are defined as investments by the regulations under US Code Section 4944(c) (Federal Register, n.d.). While PRIs are funding tools based on market-based mechanisms (e.g., equity and debt), the primary purpose of PRIs is to accomplish one or more of the charitable purposes described in US Code Section 170(c)(2)(B). That is, private foundations are required to substantially further the accomplishment of their exempt activities when using PRIs (Internal Revenue Service, n.d.).

Some Venture Philanthropy organizations, in particular those created during the dotcom era, such as Acumen Fund and Omidyar Network, explored debts and equity investment to invest in their funded organizations. However, to use equity, these Venture Philanthropy organizations have chosen for-profit ventures as their portfolio. Investment in business ventures requires human capital with tacit knowledge about and experience in entrepreneurship and investment—vastly different from human capital in traditional grantmaking and non-profit management, which usually entails deep understanding about programs and the social mission of organizations. Compliance with legal and practical requirements necessitates additional resources on the part of Venture Philanthropy organizations. Consequently, as the institutional field of non-profits and philanthropy is resource-constrained, many Venture Philanthropy organizations, as non-profits, have chosen not to use market-based funding tools due to possible costs. They instead have refined their approach in accordance with the norms and practices of the philanthropic community (Moody, 2008; Venture Philanthropy Partners, 2013).

Constraints on primary funding goals

Norms specify how things should be done and designate appropriate ways to pursue goals (Scott, 2008a, pp. 54–55). Given this, norms within a particular institution direct a funder's attempts to evaluate information for the decision process and set the primary goal of investment (Zacharakis et al., 2007). Normative systems impose considerable constraints on the behavior of philanthropic organizations as tax exempt entities. The charitable exemption for philanthropic organizations has been defended by Congress because of what charities offer the larger community: public benefit or reduction of government burden (Simon, Dale, & Chisolm, 2006).

Hence, by playing a primary role in the provision of public goods or facilitating it as funders, philanthropic organizations are under enormous pressure to behave in accordance with social norms. To monitor their behavior, many professional and trade associations exist, for example the Council on Foundations for philanthropic foundations. These professional associations collectively promote professional codes of conduct in order to enhance the field's legitimacy, accountability, and transparency, and protect the public, especially donors. As a result, the primary funding goal in the philanthropic field is normalized as maximization of the social good for the public. Due to such a normative goal being set by the philanthropic institution, although Venture Philanthropy funds began creating a new field for themselves, their investment goal remains similar to that of other philanthropic organizations.

Constraints on performance assessment

As discussed above, Venture Philanthropy organizations have attempted to mimic venture capitalists' measurement methods. Application of such metrics to investment performance is one of their signature practices, yet this practice has been sharply criticized within philanthropic circles (Edwards, 2009; Sievers, 2001). The central concern of venture capital investment is to maximize ROI and the value of the portfolio ventures (Zacharakis et al., 2007). However, the nature of philanthropic funding, such as charitable donations, hinders capital markets from an accurate valuation for social benefit (Zietlow, 2001). Quantitative performance measurement does not fit a philanthropic culture that gives the greatest weight to the quality of the social good. Cultural perceptions about the primary goal of philanthropic funding suggest that organizations are expected to pursue a mission for the public good. The complexity and multiplicity of their goals require holistic, qualitative comprehension of the unique nature of social phenomena (Kanter & Summers, 1987). Multicausality of underlying factors (Haugh, 2005), lengthy temporal manifestation of outcomes (Austin, Stevenson, & Wei-Skillern, 2006), non-monetary benefits and costs (Zietlow, 2001), and different bottom lines (Chell, 2007) all complicate, or even make impossible, the quantification and precise measurement of social impact. Since the core principle of philanthropy is to serve the public, understanding the needs and interests of diverse stakeholders is vital for assessing organizational and funding performance (Kanter & Summers, 1987).

From an institutional perspective, organizations' conformity to institutional demands may initially be to improve efficiency and productivity, but later, it primarily serves a legitimacy purpose (DiMaggio & Powell, 1983). After confronting the complex nature and goals of philanthropic work, early Venture Philanthropists admitted the limitations of their measurement tools (Moody, 2008). Measurement metrics developed by early Venture Philanthropists (e.g., SROI) have been significantly adjusted or eliminated. Further, cultural cognitive constraints of traditional philanthropy have affected the types of business language used for measurement metrics. Instead of using the exact terms used by venture capitalists, Venture Philanthropy organizations have refined their terminology to receive acceptance within traditional philanthropic circles. As a result, more indirect business terms have been used to describe market-based criteria, such as "measurable goals" or "specific outcomes," rather than "profit goals."

Conclusion

This study explores the emerging field of Venture Philanthropy in the US through the theoretical lens of institutionalism and structuration. The emergence and evolution of this field originated not only from external (political and economic) factors, but also other factors, such as the deliberative actions of business professions and opinion leaders.

One of the main contributions of this study is to analyze the institutional construction of Venture Philanthropy based on two different approaches, that is, a naturalistic approach focusing on the exogenous stimuli of institutional creation and an agent-based approach highlighting the endogenous drive of agents in institutional creation. Using both approaches, this study is in line with a recent development in the institutional theory literature. Whereas institutional theory stresses dominance of institutional environments and organizations' passivity to them (DiMaggio & Powell, 1983; Meyer & Rowan, 1977), more recent studies of institutional entrepreneurship recognize an agentic role that actors play in institutional creation or change (Greenwood & Hinings, 1996; Hirsch & Lounsbury, 1997; Powell & DiMaggio, 1991). Prior studies about institutional change tended to focus on agent-based accounts exploring the roles of institutional entrepreneurs, rather than looking into both naturalistic accounts and agent-based accounts. Through analysis based on both approaches, this study allows us to understand a more complex process involving endogenous and exogenous processes in the creation of the new field of Venture Philanthropy.

Giddens (1979, 1984) proposes structuration theory as a process-oriented theory that treats structure as both a product of and a constraint upon human action. Building on his argument over the "duality of agency and structure," this study investigates structural carriers that have helped to institutionalize Venture Philanthropy, along with the resulting isomorphism that mimicked business practices and constraints from traditional philanthropy.

This study further shows that competing institutional logics from traditional philanthropy and venture capitalism created interactions between actors and structure in the institutionalization of Venture Philanthropy. The case of Venture Philanthropy underscores that the evolution of a new innovative field results from "push" and "back," or as Mair and Hehenberger (2014) suggest, "front stage" and "backstage," interactions. That is, the front stage interactions in public spaces made Venture Philanthropy models accessible to a broad audience, whereas the backstage interactions deconstructed these models. The process is multifaceted; while investors and entrepreneurs promote the innovative ideas and practices of Venture Philanthropy (explicated as outcomes of isomorphism), traditional philanthropists and non-profit managers resist these ideas and practices (explicated as institutional constraints). As a result, the institutional elements of the Venture Philanthropy field have been constantly refined and revised. The evolution of a new innovative field requires the process of negotiation (Mair & Hehenberger, 2014), seeking the most agreeable conditions among different actors in the new institutional field.

Among the main challenges in studies of Venture Philanthropy has been a lack of systematic data (Van Slyke & Newman, 2006). As a result, theory-grounded, scholarly research to understand Venture Philanthropy has lagged behind. Nonetheless, more recent years have seen important advancement concerning Venture Philanthropy and social investment. Moody's (2008) study explored processes legitimizing the controversial model of Venture Philanthropy as a response to criticisms in traditional philanthropic circles. By scrutinizing a case of European Venture Philanthropy, Mair and Hehenberger (2014) refined the institutional argument illuminating how conflicts resulting from competing institutional logics could be negotiated and resolved. Nicholls (2010b) expanded theoretical and empirical analysis to the entire field of social investment, including Venture Philanthropy for the first time. These groundbreaking studies demonstrate that Venture Philanthropy is a worthy topic for future scholarly endeavors. Recently, scholars have undertaken research examining the legitimacy aspect of Venture Philanthropy as part of a crowd funding case (Lehner & Nicholls, 2014). Another empirical study (Onishi, 2014) probes how the interaction between institutional constraints and organizational attributes, in particular entrepreneurial orientation (Covin & Slevin, 1989; Lumpkin & Dess, 1996), shapes the behavior of Venture Philanthropy organizations. One contribution of this study (Onishi, 2014) is to show that a stronger entrepreneurial nature enables organizations to respond to and resist institutional constraints. An approach linking institutional literature and entrepreneurship literature may be among the most important avenues for future research about Venture Philanthropy, given that the effects of more traditional entrepreneurial activity on institutional entrepreneurship or vice versa have remained largely unexplored (Battilana et al., 2009; Pacheco et al., 2010; Phillips & Tracey, 2007).

References

Abrahamson, E. (1991). Managerial fads and fashions: The diffusion and rejection of innovations. *Academy of Management Review, 16*(3), 586–612.

Acumen Fund. (2013). Acumen is a bold new way of tackling poverty. *Acumen*. Retrieved May 14, 2013, from http://acumen.org/

Aldrich, H. E., & Fiol, C. M. (1994). Fools rush in? The institutional content of industry creation. *Academy of Management Review, 19*(4), 645–670.

Anheier, H. K., & Leat, D. (2006). *Creative philanthropy: Toward a new philanthropy for the twenty-first century*. New York, NY: Routledge.
Austin, J., Stevenson, H., & Wei-Skillern, J. (2006). Social and commercial entrepreneurship: Same, different, or both? *Entrepreneurship Theory and Practice, 30*(1), 1–22.
Barley, S. R., & Tolbert, P. S. (1997). Institutionalization and structuration: Studying the links between action and institution. *Organization Studies, 18*(1), 93–117.
Battilana, J., Leca, B., & Boxenbaum, E. (2009). How actors change institutions: Towards a theory of institutional entrepreneurship. *Academy of Management Annals, 3*(1), 65–107.
Baum, J. A. C., & Oliver, C. (1991). Institutional linkages and organizational mortality. *Administrative Science Quarterly, 36*(2), 187–218.
Berger, P. L., & Luckmann, T. (1966). *The social construction of reality: A treatise in the sociology of knowledge*. Garden City, NY: Anchor Books.
Berger, R. A. (1986). Private-sector initiatives in the Reagan Administration. *Proceedings of the Academy of Political Science, 36*(2), 14–30.
Bibby, A. (2004, December 30). Charity begins with rigorous due diligence. *Financial Times*, p. 7.
Bill & Melinda Gates Foundation. (n.d.). *How we make grants—Bill & Melinda Gates Foundation*. Retrieved May 14, 2013, from http://www.gatesfoundation.org/How-We-Work/General-Information/How-We-Make-Grants#OurApproachtoShapingFundingandManagingGrants
Bishop, M., & Green, M. (2010). *Philanthrocapitalism: How giving can save the world*. New York, NY: Bloomsbury Press.
Brainerd, P. (1999). Social Venture Partners: Engaging a new generation of givers. *Nonprofit and Voluntary Sector Quarterly, 28*(4), 502–507.
Brown, E., & Slivinski, A. (2006). Nonprofit organizations and the market. In W. P. Powell & R. Steinberg (Eds.), *The nonprofit sector: A research handbook* (2nd ed., pp. 140–158). New Haven, CT: Yale University Press.
Bugg-Levine, A., & Emerson, J. (2011). *Impact investing: Transforming how we make money while making a difference*. San Francisco: Jossey-Bass. Retrieved April 30, 2013, from http://site.ebrary.com/id/10494625
Busenitz, L. W., Fiet, J. O., & Moesel, D. D. (2004). Reconsidering the venture capitalists' "value added" proposition: An interorganizational learning perspective. *Journal of Business Venturing, 19*(6), 787–807.
Chell, E. (2007). Social enterprise and entrepreneurship: Towards a convergent theory of the entrepreneurial process. *International Small Business Journal, 25*(1), 5–26.
Colvin, G. (2001, December 24). The gift of arrogance: It's blessed to give—But it's a lot harder than Nethead philanthropists thought. *Fortune*.
Community Wealth Ventures, Inc. (2000). *Venture Philanthropy 2000: Landscape and expectations*. Washington, DC: Venture Philanthropy Partners.
Community Wealth Ventures, Inc. (2001). *Venture Philanthropy 2001: The changing landscape*. Washington, DC: Morino Institute.
Community Wealth Ventures, Inc. (2002). *Venture Philanthropy 2002: Advancing nonprofit performance through high-engagement grantmaking*. Washington, DC: Venture Philanthropy Partners.
Covin, J. G., & Slevin, D. P. (1989). Strategic management of small firms in hostile and benign environments. *Strategic Management Journal, 10*(1), 75–87.
Cutlip, S. M. (1965). *Fund raising in the United States: Its role in America's philanthropy*. Piscataway, NJ: Transaction Publishers.
Dacin, P. A., Dacin, M. T., & Matear, M. (2010). Social entrepreneurship: Why we don't need a new theory and how we move forward from here. *Academy of Management Perspectives, 24*(3), 37–57.
Dart, R. (2004). The legitimacy of social enterprise. *Nonprofit Management and Leadership, 14*(4), 411–424.
De Clercq, D., & Sapienza, H. J. (2006). Effects of relational capital and commitment on venture capitalists' perception of portfolio company performance. *Journal of Business Venturing, 21*(3), 326–347.
Dees, J. G. (1998). The meaning of social entrepreneurship. *Comments and suggestions contributed from the Social Entrepreneurship Funders Working Group*, p. 6.
DiMaggio, P. J. (1988). Interest and agency in institutional theory. In L. G. Zucker (Ed.), *Institutional patterns and organizations: Culture and environment* (Vol. 1, pp. 3–22). Cambridge, MA: Ballinger.
DiMaggio, P. J. (1991). Constructing an organizational field as a professional project: US art museums, 1920–1940. In W. W. Powell & P. J. DiMaggio (Eds.), *The new institutionalism in organizational analysis* (pp. 267–292). Chicago, IL: University of Chicago Press.
DiMaggio, P. J., & Powell, W. W. (1983). The iron cage revisited: Institutional isomorphism and collective rationality in organizational fields. *American Sociological Review, 48*(2), 147–160.

Dorado, S. (2005). Institutional entrepreneurship, partaking, and convening. *Organization Studies, 26*(3), 385–414.

Edwards, M. (2009). Why "philanthrocapitalism" is not the answer: Private initiatives and international development. In M. Kremer, P. V. Lieshout, & R. Went (Eds.), *Doing good or doing better: Development policies in a globalizing world* (pp. 237–254). Amsterdam, the Netherlands: Amsterdam University Press.

Eikenberry, A. M. (2006). Giving circles: Growing grassroots philanthropy. *Nonprofit and Voluntary Sector Quarterly, 35*(3), 517–532.

Eikenberry, A. M., & Kluver, J. D. (2004). The marketization of the nonprofit sector: Civil society at risk? *Public Administration Review, 64*(2), 132–140.

Emerson, J. (2000). *The nature of returns: A social capital markets inquiry into elements of investment and the blended value proposition*. Boston, MA: Harvard Business School.

Emerson, J. (2003). The blended value proposition: Integrating social and financial returns. *California Management Review, 45*(4), 35–51.

Emerson, J., Wachowicz, J., & Chun, S. (2000). Social return on investment: Exploring aspects of value creation in the nonprofit sector. In *The box set: Social purpose enterprises and venture philanthropy in the new millennium* (Vol. 2, pp. 130–173). San Francisco, CA: The Roberts Foundation.

Federal Register. (n.d.). *Examples of program-related investments*. Retrieved June 22, 2013, from https://www.federalregister.gov/articles/2012/04/19/2012-9468/examples-of-program-related-investments

Fiss, P. C., & Hirsch, P. M. (2005). The discourse of globalization: Framing and sensemaking of an emerging concept. *American Sociological Review, 70*(1), 29–52.

Fleishman, J. L. (2009). *The foundation: A great American secret; how private wealth is changing the world*. New York, NY: PublicAffairs.

Franke, N., Gruber, M., Harhoff, D., & Henkel, J. (2008). Venture capitalists' evaluations of start-up teams: Trade-offs, knock-out criteria, and the impact of VC experience. *Entrepreneurship Theory and Practice, 32*(3), 459–483.

Frumkin, P. (2003). Inside venture philanthropy. *Society, 40*(4), 7–15.

Frumkin, P. (2008). *Strategic giving: The art and science of philanthropy*. Chicago, IL: University of Chicago Press.

Galaskiewicz, J. (1985). Professional networks and the institutionalization of a single mind set. *American Sociological Review, 50*(5), 639–658.

Galaskiewicz, J., & Burt, R. S. (1991). Interorganization contagion in corporate philanthropy. *Administrative Science Quarterly, 36*(1), 88–105.

Garud, R., Hardy, C., & Maguire, S. (2007). Institutional entrepreneurship as embedded agency: An introduction to the special issue. *Organization Studies, 28*(7), 957–969.

Garud, R., Jain, S., & Kumaraswamy, A. (2002). Institutional entrepreneurship in the sponsorship of common technological standards: The case of Sun Microsystems and Java. *Academy of Management Journal, 45*(1), 196–214.

Giddens, A. (1979). *Central problems in social theory: Action, structure, and contradiction in social analysis* (Vol. 241). Berkeley: University of California Press.

Giddens, A. (1984). *The constitution of society: Outline of the theory of structuration*. Berkeley: University of California Press.

Greenfeld, K. T. (2000). The new philanthropy: A new way of giving. *Time, 156*(4), 48–51.

Greenwood, R., & Hinings, C. R. (1996). Understanding radical organizational change: Bringing together the old and the new institutionalism. *Academy of Management Review, 21*(4), 1022–1054.

Greenwood, R., & Suddaby, R. (2006). Institutional entrepreneurship in mature fields: The big five accounting firms. *Academy of Management Journal, 49*(1), 27–48.

Greif, A. (2006). *Institutions and the path to the modern economy: Lessons from medieval trade*. Cambridge, UK: Cambridge University Press.

Gupte, P. (1999, May 31). Venture capitalist to the poor. *Forbes*. Retrieved November 26, 2014, from http://www.forbes.com/forbes/1999/0531/6311058a.html

Hall, P. D. (2001). *"Inventing the nonprofit sector" and other essays on philanthropy, voluntarism, and nonprofit organizations*. Baltimore, MD: Johns Hopkins University Press.

Hansmann, H. B. (1980). The role of nonprofit enterprise. *The Yale Law Journal, 89*(5), 835–901.

Haugh, H. (2005). A research agenda for social entrepreneurship. *Social Enterprise Journal, 1*(1), 1–12.

Haunschild, P. R. (1993). Interorganizational imitation: The impact of interlocks on corporate acquisition activity. *Administrative Science Quarterly, 38*(4), 564–592.

Hirsch, P. M. (1986). From ambushes to golden parachutes: Corporate takeovers as an instance of cultural framing and institutional integration. *American Journal of Sociology, 91*(4), 800–837.

Hirsch, P. M., & Lounsbury, M. (1997). Ending the family quarrel toward a reconciliation of "old" and "new" institutionalisms. *American Behavioral Scientist, 40*(4), 406–418.

Hoffman, A. J. (1999). Institutional evolution and change: Environmentalism and the U.S. chemical industry. *Academy of Management Journal, 42*(4), 351–371.

Honig, B., & Karlsson, T. (2004). Institutional forces and the written business plan. *Journal of Management, 30*(1), 29–48.

Internal Revenue Service. (n.d.). *Instructions for form 990-PF (2012).* Retrieved June 23, 2013, from http://www.irs.gov/instructions/i990pf/ch02.html

James, C., & Marshall, P. (2006). Journeys in venture philanthropy and institution building. In W. V. B. Damon & S. Verducci (Eds.), *Taking philanthropy seriously: Beyond noble intentions to responsible giving* (pp. 108–124). Bloomington, IN: Indiana University Press.

Jarzabkowski, P. (2008). Shaping strategy as a structuration process. *Academy of Management Journal, 51*(4), 621–650.

Jegen, D. L. (1998). Community development venture capital: Creating a viable business model for the future. *Nonprofit Management and Leadership, 9*(2), 187–200.

Jepperson, R. L. (1991). Institutions, institutional effects, and institutionalism. In P. DiMaggio & W. P. Powell (Eds.), *The new institutionalism in organizational analysis* (Vol. 6, pp. 143–163). Chicago, IL: University of Chicago Press.

John, R. (2006). *Venture philanthropy: The evolution of high engagement philanthropy in Europe.* Oxford, UK: Skoll Centre for Social Entrepreneurship Oxford Said Business School.

Kanter, R., & Summers, D. V. (1987). Doing well while doing good: Dilemmas of performance measurement in nonprofit organizations and the need for a multiple-constituent approach. In W. P. Powell (Ed.), *The nonprofit sector: A research handbook* (1st ed., pp. 154–165). New Haven, CT: Yale University Press.

Kirkpatrick, I., & Ackroyd, S. (2003). Archetype theory and the changing professional organization: A critique and alternative. *Organization, 10*(4), 731–750.

Kistruck, G. M., & Beamish, P. W. (2010). The interplay of form, structure, and embeddedness in social intrapreneurship. *Entrepreneurship Theory and Practice, 34*(4), 735–761.

Lawrence, T. B., Suddaby, R., & Leca, B. (2009). *Institutional work: Actors and agency in institutional studies of organizations.* Cambridge, UK: Cambridge University Press.

Lehner, O. M., & Nicholls, A. (2014). Social finance and crowdfunding for social enterprises: A public–private case study providing legitimacy and leverage. *Venture Capital, 16*(3), 271–286.

Letts, C. W., Ryan, W., & Grossman, A. (1997). Virtuous capital: What foundations can learn from venture capitalists. *Harvard Business Review, 75*(2), 36–50.

Lumpkin, G. T., & Dess, G. G. (1996). Clarifying the entrepreneurial orientation construct and linking it to performance. *Academy of Management Review, 21*(1), 135–172.

Lynall, M. D., Golden, B. R., & Hillman, A. J. (2003). Board composition from adolescence to maturity: A multitheoretic view. *Academy of Management Review, 28*(3), 416–431.

Macmillan, I. C., Kulow, D. M., & Khoylian, R. (1989). Venture capitalists' involvement in their investments: Extent and performance. *Journal of Business Venturing, 4*(1), 27–47.

Maguire, S., & Hardy, C. (2009). Discourse and deinstitutionalization: The decline of DDT. *Academy of Management Journal, 52*(1), 148–178.

Maguire, S., Hardy, C., & Lawrence, T. B. (2004). Institutional entrepreneurship in emerging fields: HIV/AIDS treatment advocacy in Canada. *Academy of Management Journal, 47*(5), 657–679.

Mair, J., & Hehenberger, L. (2014). Front-stage and backstage convening: The transition from opposition to mutualistic coexistence in organizational philanthropy. *Academy of Management Journal, 57*(4), 1174–1200.

Meyer, J. W., & Rowan, B. (1977). Institutionalized organizations: Formal structure as myth and ceremony. *American Journal of Sociology, 83*(2), 340–363.

Miller, T. L., & Wesley, C. L. (2010). Assessing mission and resources for social change: An organizational identity perspective on social venture capitalists' decision criteria. *Entrepreneurship Theory and Practice, 34*(4), 705–733.

Moody, M. (2008). "Building a culture": The construction and evolution of venture philanthropy as a new organizational field. *Nonprofit and Voluntary Sector Quarterly, 37*(2), 324–352.

Nicholls, A. (2010a). The legitimacy of social entrepreneurship: Reflexive isomorphism in a pre-paradigmatic field. *Entrepreneurship Theory and Practice, 34*(4), 611–633.

Nicholls, A. (2010b). The institutionalization of social investment: The interplay of investment logics and investor rationalities. *Journal of Social Entrepreneurship, 1*(1), 70–100.

North, D. C. (1990). *Institutions, institutional change and economic performance.* New York, NY: Cambridge University Press.

Omidyar Network. (2015a). *Who we are.* Retrieved May 6, 2015, from https://www.omidyar.com/who-we-are

Omidyar Network. (2015b). *Financials.* Retrieved May 6, 2015, from https://www.omidyar.com/financials

Omidyar Network. (n.d.). *Why we use both investments and grants in service of our mission.* Retrieved November 27, 2014, from http://www.omidyar.com/blog/why-we-use-both-investments-and-grants-service-our-mission

Onishi, T. (2014). Moderating effect of entrepreneurial orientation on institutional forces and venture philanthropy. *Academy of Management Annual Meeting Proceedings*, 1595–1600.

Ostrander, S. A. (2007). The growth of donor control: Revisiting the social relations of philanthropy. *Nonprofit and Voluntary Sector Quarterly, 36*(2), 356–372.

Pache, A.-C., & Santos, F. (2010). When worlds collide: The internal dynamics of organizational responses to conflicting institutional demands. *Academy of Management Review, 35*(3), 455–476.

Pacheco, D. F., York, J. G., Dean, T. J., & Sarasvathy, S. D. (2010). The coevolution of institutional entrepreneurship: A tale of two theories. *Journal of Management, 36*(4), 974–1010.

Phillips, N., Lawrence, T. B., & Hardy, C. (2004). Discourse and institutions. *Academy of Management Review, 29*(4), 635–652.

Phillips, N., & Tracey, P. (2007). Opportunity recognition, entrepreneurial capabilities and bricolage: Connecting institutional theory and entrepreneurship in strategic organization. *Strategic Organization, 5*(3), 313–320.

Porter, M. E., & Kramer, M. R. (1999). Philanthropy's new agenda: Creating value. *Harvard Business Review, 77*, 121–131.

Powell, W. W., & DiMaggio, P. (Eds.). (1991). *The new institutionalism in organizational analysis.* Chicago, IL: University of Chicago Press.

REDF. (2016). *The REDF portfolio: Investing in what works.* Retrieved March 1, 2016, from http://redf.org/what-we-do/invest/

Rogers, E. M. (1995). *Diffusion of innovation* (4th ed.). New York, NY: Free Press.

Ruef, M., & Scott, W. R. (1998). A multidimensional model of organizational legitimacy: Hospital survival in changing institutional environments. *Administrative Science Quarterly, 43*(4), 877–904.

Salamon, L. M., & Abramson, A. J. (1982). *The federal budget and the nonprofit sector.* Washington, DC: Urban Institute Press.

Scarlata, M., & Alemany, L. (2008). *Philanthropic venture capital: Can the key elements of venture capital be applied successfully to social enterprises?* (SSRN Scholarly Paper No. ID 1099277). Rochester, NY: Social Science Research Network. Retrieved May 5, 2013, from http://papers.ssrn.com/abstract=1099277

Scarlata, M., & Alemany, L. (2010). *Deal structuring in philanthropic venture capital investments: Financing instrument, valuation and covenants* (SSRN Scholarly Paper No. ID 1635307). Rochester, NY: Social Science Research Network. Retrieved May 5, 2013, from http://papers.ssrn.com/abstract=1635307

Scott, W. R. (2008a). *Institutions and organizations: Ideas and interests* (3rd ed.). Thousand Oaks, CA: Sage.

Scott, W. R. (2008b). Lords of the dance: Professionals as institutional agents. *Organization Studies, 29*(2), 219–238.

Scott, W. R., Ruef, M., Mendel, P., & Caronna, C. A. (2000). *Institutional change and organizations: Transformation of a healthcare field.* Chicago, IL: University of Chicago Press.

Selznick, P. (1957). *Leadership in administration: A sociological interpretation.* Los Angeles, CA: University of California Press.

Shepherd, D. A., & Zacharakis, A. (2002). Venture capitalists' expertise: A call for research into decision aids and cognitive feedback. *Journal of Business Venturing, 17*(1), 1–20.

Sievers, B. (2001). If pigs had wings: The appeals and limits of venture philanthropy. In A. Waldemar (Ed.), *Nielsen Issues in Philanthropy Seminar*, Georgetown University.

Simon, J., Dale, H., & Chisolm, L. (2006). The federal tax treatment of nonprofit organizations. In W. P. Powell & R. Steinberg (Eds.), *The nonprofit sector: A research handbook* (2nd ed., pp. 267–306). New Haven, CT: Yale University Press.

Standlea, N. (2006). Old problems, new solutions: The creative impact of venture philanthropy. In W. V. B. Damon & S. Verducci (Eds.), *Taking philanthropy seriously: Beyond noble intentions to responsible giving* (pp. 205–221). Bloomington, IN: Indiana University Press.

Strang, D., & Sine, W. D. (2002). Interorganizational institutions. In J. A. C. Baum (Ed.), *The Blackwell companion to organizations* (pp. 497–519). Oxford, UK: Blackwell.

Streeck, W., & Schmitter, P. C. (1985). Community, market, state—and associations? The prospective contribution of interest governance to social order. *European Sociological Review, 1*(2), 119–138.

The birth of philanthrocapitalism. (2006, February 23). *The Economist*. Retrieved November 26, 2014, from http://www.economist.com/node/5517656

Trelstad, B. (2009). *The nature and type of "social investors."* New York, NY: Acumen Fund.

Tuckman, H. P. (1993). How and why nonprofit organizations obtain capital. In D. C. Hammack & D. R. Young (Eds.), *Nonprofit organizations in a market economy* (pp. 203–252). San Francisco, CA: Jossey-Bass.

Van Slyke, D. M., & Newman, H. K. (2006). Venture philanthropy and social entrepreneurship in community redevelopment. *Nonprofit Management and Leadership, 16*(3), 345–368.

Venture Philanthropy Partners. (2013). *Approach*. Retrieved May 14, 2013, from http://www.vppartners.org/about-us/approach

Venture Philanthropy Partners. (2015). *How we select: Investment criteria*. Retrieved May 6, 2015, from http://www.vppartners.org/about-us/approach/select/investment-criteria

Whitford, D. (2000, June 12). The Internet generation is bringing the principles of venture capital to philanthropy. It's innovative—but is it effective? *Fortune*.

Young, D. R. (1986). Entrepreneurship and the behavior of nonprofit organizations: Elements of a theory. In S. Rose-Ackerman (Ed.), *The economics of non profit institutions: Studies in structure and policy* (pp. 161–184). New York, NY: Oxford University Press.

Zacharakis, A. L., McMullen, J. S., & Shepherd, D. A. (2007). Venture capitalists' decision policies across three countries: An institutional theory perspective. *Journal of International Business Studies, 38*(5), 691–708.

Zietlow, J. T. (2001). Social entrepreneurship: Managerial, finance and marketing aspects. *Journal of Nonprofit & Public Sector Marketing, 9*(1–2), 19–43.

Zucker, L. G. (1977). The role of institutionalization in cultural persistence. *American Sociological Review, 42*(5), 726–743.

21

THE CONVERGENCE PARADOX OF ISLAMIC FINANCE

A sociological reinterpretation, with insights for proponents of social finance

Aaron Z. Pitluck

How is "social" finance distinctive from conventional finance? We can analytically distinguish available answers to this question by whether the "social" applies to distinctively social ends or to distinctively social means. Said differently, social finance can be understood as distinctive from conventional finance by applying morality and ethics to how finance is applied to the non-financial sector (a focus on ends) or by focusing on the morality and ethics of the finance industry itself (a focus on means).

I suggest that the orthodox understanding of social finance is that it is structured equivalently to "conventional finance" except insofar as it has distinctively "social" ends. *Conventional finance* is typically conceived of as a morally neutral technology that can be applied to financial problems (Davis, 2009). This perspective of finance as technology is well represented in *Finance and the Good Society*, where the Nobel prize-winning financial economist Robert J. Shiller (2012, p. 6) defines finance as

> the science of goal architecture—of the structuring of the economic arrangements necessary to achieve a set of goals and of the stewardship of the assets needed for that achievement… Finance does not embody a goal. Finance is not about "making money" per se. It is a "functional" science in that it exists to support other goals—those of the society.

In contrast to conventional finance, which like cash itself can be used for any purpose, *orthodox social finance* is finance earmarked to ameliorate social problems and promote social justice. This spectrum between conventional finance and orthodox social finance shares a conception of financiers and finance as analogous to engineers and engineering; the same experts and their technologies can be used to either build bridges or destroy them.

In the social finance literature, we can illustrate this orthodox understanding with Lehner and Nicholls (2014, pp. 271–272), who implicitly define "social finance" as any financial intermediary that channels capital to "social enterprises." Therefore, while "social enterprises" may be narrowly defined,[1] "social finance" itself is structurally equivalent to

Table 21.1 Distinguishing social from conventional finance

		Emphasize social ends?	
		No	**Yes**
Emphasize social means?	**No**	Conventional finance	Orthodox social finance
	Yes	Radical social finance	Visionary finance

conventional finance—a black box of "market participants" with a diverse "array of different concerns, needs and motivations" that invest in distinctively social enterprises (e.g., Lehner & Nicholls, 2014, p. 272).

Rather than viewing finance as a neutral technology potentially applicable to pro-social ends, the *radical* conception of social finance emphasizes distinctively social means. In this perspective, finance is conceived of not as a morally neutral technology but as social relationships (de Goede, 2005; Graeber, 2011; Ingham, 2004). In this understanding of social finance, attention shifts from *what* is financed to *how* financing is accomplished. This understanding of social finance is a radical critique of the conventional finance industry insofar as it explicitly outlines the ethical or moral failings of conventional finance and seeks to rectify them. This is the inverse of Lehner and Nicholls (2014) insofar as "social finance" can potentially finance anything—but attention shifts to the morality and ethics of the financial instruments themselves and how financiers and their firms behave.

Although social finance may empirically tend to bifurcate into an emphasis on ends or means, certainly there is no analytic reason why a critic, firm, or industry could not seek social change in both. As illustrated in Table 21.1, the remaining quadrant—*visionary finance*—represents the furthest departure from conventional finance, in that it seeks to change both what is financed and the social relationships embedded in financial instruments and services.

This typology is fundamental for understanding what benchmarks for success are appropriate in appraising a financial service or instrument. A vibrant orthodox social finance industry would be an ethical market niche within the larger industry. So long as social enterprises are successfully financed (or social outcomes achieved) either by the social or conventional finance markets, one could consider orthodox social finance as successful. In contrast, radical social finance is critical of how conventional finance is practiced, and so normative success would be superior distinctive financial practices. Arguably, the ultimate goal of radical social finance is to change the conventional finance industry or replace it. Success in visionary finance is even more daunting, as it requires not merely the transformation or replacement of the conventional finance industry, but seeks to alter society as well.

For example, consider "green bonds," debt instruments designed to finance new and existing projects that are identified as promoting environmental sustainability. As discussed by Sean Kidney, the chief executive of The Climate Bonds Initiative, a London-based non-profit seeking to promote the green bond market, "[t]he labelling of green is really just a marketing question for the underwriter" (Cherney, 2015). From the perspective of orthodox social finance, the bond is "successful" insofar as the underwriters and the third party credentials it enlists can credibly attest that the proceeds are designed to promote environmental sustainability. From the perspective of radical social finance, a "green bond" is a failure insofar as it is structurally identical to a conventional bond—the social relationship between issuer and investor is identical, as is the distribution of risk and reward.

In contrast, consider the example of social investment bonds (also known as social benefit bonds, or pay for success bonds). Broadly defined, these are private sector securities designed to finance government (or private non-profit) social interventions, in which the rate of return for investors is guaranteed by government, contingent on the social project achieving successful (non-financial) social outcomes, typically at a below-market rate of return (Fitzgerald, 2013; Pauly & Swanson, 2014). In this second illustration, the social investment bonds would be perceived by orthodox social finance as successful as green bonds insofar as it has distinctive social ends—namely, social outcome contingent returns on investment designed to yield below-market rates of return. However, in contrast to green bonds, social investment bonds may be viewed as successful from the perspective of radical social finance as well, insofar as the relationship between issuer and investor has been changed (from an arms' length relationship to a collaborative relationship involving shared expertise, as observed in Silicon Valley venture capital firms) and the distribution of risk and reward has shifted so that investors absorb some of the financial risks formerly borne by non-profit agencies (Pauly & Swanson, 2014).

With these three contested types of social finance in mind, coupled with an understanding of how these analytic categories shape whether a financial instrument or service could be appraised as successful, we are now in a position to examine the contested success of Islamic finance as radical social finance.

The radical critique of Islamic finance

Although Islam dates from the seventh century, until recently modern banking institutions in Muslim-majority countries were organizationally and institutionally similar to European conventional banking systems. The development of modern banking in Islamic countries originated with colonial administrations, and was modeled on the colonizers' experiences in metropole and colonial banking. Following independence, many of these banks were nationalized, or ownership was slowly acquired by Muslim nationals; however, such shifts in ownership did not alter the banks' essential banking practices based on such concepts as interest-bearing savings accounts and interest-based debt financing (Imam & Kpodar, 2013; Pollard & Samers, 2007; Warde, 2010).

Contemporary Islamic banking and finance originated approximately four decades ago as an Islamic alternative. Therefore, with few exceptions, Islamic banks and financial institutions compete in a market dominated by conventional finance. In our typology, Islamic finance would generally be understood as either radical social finance or visionary finance.[2]

Relative to orthodox social finance markets, Islamic finance is unusual in the depth and sophistication of its radical critique of the conventional market with which it competes. Islamic finance prohibits *riba*—roughly understood as making money from money without entrepreneurial risk. Ideally, Islamic banks must tether all financial investment to real economic activity and forgo speculation in financial markets. In contrast, conventional financial theory celebrates financial capitalists seeking speculative arbitrage, and argues that such profit seeking improves the accuracy of prices (El-Gamal, 2003, 2006; Maurer, 2005; Vogel & Hayes, 1998, pp. 72–87; Warde, 2010).

Islamic finance also prohibits *gharar*—transactions that are gambling-like in character or that involve the exploitation of ambiguous or superior information. In contrast, conventional bankers argue that risk is a product that can be traded like any other, and that speculation directs capital to its most productive uses (El-Gamal, 2001; Vogel & Hayes, 1998, pp. 87–93, especially 90).

Islamic finance also necessitates *fairness* between transacting parties. In contrast, conventional finance practitioners celebrate the principle of *caveat emptor* (literally, "buyer beware") to be exercised by sophisticated financiers, arguing for the social benefit of allowing self-interested parties to pursue hard negotiations with one another.

Finally, like some other forms of social finance, Islamic finance insists on integrating *religious and ethical imperatives* in daily economic life. Businesses must be "Sharia compliant," a phrase typical of Islamic finance in that it bridges the language of religion and accounting. The Sharia (or Shari'ah or Shariah) is divine law, and therefore "Sharia-compliant" activities are those interpreted as permitted by the Sharia. For example, non-Sharia-compliant activities typically include profiting from pork or alcohol, as these are widely interpreted as dietary restrictions on pious Muslims. Often, Islamic banking is also a form of religious and cultural expression. More rarely, firms and projects are expected to conform to an Islamic-inflected form of corporate social responsibility.

As a consequence of this radical critique of the finance industry, numerous banking practices that pervade the conventional industry are usually prohibited in Islamic finance, including profiting from interest, the trading of speculative derivatives, the exploitation of information asymmetries, and financing projects perceived as harmful to the Islamic community (Islamic Development Bank, Islamic Research and Training Institute, & Islamic Financial Services Board, 2007).

Just as there is no single ethical or moral manifesto as to what constitutes social finance (Nicholls, 2010) or social entrepreneurship (Lehner & Kansikas, 2013), there are active technical debates regarding what constitutes Islamic banking and finance that stretches back four decades (Siddiqi, 2007). As a consequence, there is no single theory of how to interpret *riba*, *gharar*, and fairness in contemporary economic transactions, and thus no singular definition as to what constitutes Islamic finance and what does not (Maurer, 2005; Pollard & Samers, 2007; Warde, 2010).

This lack of consensus has a number of causes. Intellectually, religious scholars and practitioners continue to engage in a global conversation regarding hermeneutic understandings of *riba*, *gharar*, and other moral concepts in the Sharia, as well as how to interpret complex contemporary products and services in light of these moral concepts. Institutionally, Islam is not a hierarchical or static religion; the Sharia is interpreted through four major schools of interpretation, with distinctive regional interpretations and diverse traditions (e.g., Indonesian/Malay, Indo-Pakistani, Persian, and Turkic) that differ significantly from the diverse practices of the Arabian Peninsula and that change over time (Warde, 2010). Moreover, few countries have national Sharia bodies to interpret economic life, and therefore there is a great deal of diversity within countries. As a consequence, worldwide, each Islamic financial institution must assemble its own Sharia supervisory body to issue *fatwa* (authoritative legal opinions). Whenever a fatwa is issued by an Islamic scholar or a Sharia supervisory board that permits transaction X,

> one should not conclude that transaction X is "Islamic" for all parties and for all time. The itjihads [interpretations] of different scholars may legitimately vary. Moreover, if the fatwa is based on utilitarian choice, assessments of utility can change with place and time. And lastly, a fatwa might rest on nothing more than temporary, and changeable, necessity.
>
> *(Vogel & Hayes, 1998, p. 41)*

In the terms of the framework outlined in Table 21.1, relative to both conventional finance and orthodox social finance, Islamic finance is noteworthy for its intellectually coherent and yet internally debated radical critique of the conventional finance industry as well as its visionary aspirations to also constrain finance to Sharia-compliant activities.

Islamic finance is vanishingly similar to conventional finance

Interpreting *riba*, *gharar*, and fairness in contemporary banking products and services is not straightforward. Therefore, what distinguishes Islamic from conventional finance remains passionately contested, both within countries and internationally.

Viewed through the lens of orthodox or radical social finance, as well as the visionary social and solidarity economy paradigm (Arnsperger, 2013; United Nations Inter-Agency Task Force on Social and Solidarity Economy, 2014), I suspect that many readers would perceive Islamic finance as decidedly less radical. Islamic banks are not paragons of workplace democracy—they are typically hierarchical, profit-oriented public corporations accountable to shareholders rather than other stakeholders. Moreover, Islamic finance rarely incorporates unique social safety nets into its products, or concerns itself with the environmental sustainability of the projects it finances. Islamic banks also have a mixed record with regard to women's empowerment. Yet there are certainly many voices advocating that Islamic finance should pursue a social and solidarity economy paradigm, such as Mahmoud El-Gamal (2006, 2007) and Mehmet Asutay (2012).

More controversially, many experts of Islamic finance are skeptical whether it is a kind of social finance, or merely a religious analogue to "greenwashing" conventional financial products so that they appear moral, good, and compliant with submission to Islam. These immanent critiques are built on three key arguments.

First, the paradigmatic form of Islamic finance is rarely practiced. This paradigmatic form is profit and loss risk-sharing arrangements, in contrast to debtor–lender relationships in which lenders are entitled to interest payments regardless of the outcome of the debtor's financial project (Chapra, 2007, p. 57; Chong & Liu, 2009; ElGindi, Said, & Salevurakis, 2009; Kamla, 2009; Khan, 2010; Kuran, 2004; Mirakhor & Zaikdi, 2007; Nienhaus, 2007; Zaher & Hassan, 2001). As the influential Islamic finance practitioner Muhammad Taqi Usmani (2002, p. 1; also see 41) observes, "It is an ideal alternative for the interest-based financing with far reaching effects on both production and distribution." In a UK survey, nearly two-thirds of Islamic banking customers associate Islamic banking with profit- and loss-sharing (Akbar, Zulfiqar Ali Shah, & Kalmadi, 2012, p. 362), and in interviews with Muslim Americans, Maurer (2006, p. 75) finds that they have a "fondness" for such contracts.

Yet in spite of the theological and ideological importance of profit- and loss-sharing financial contracts between financial institutions and their clients, it is widely acknowledged and well documented that very little capital is invested in such relationships. An examination of assets in the 10 largest Islamic banks in 1994–1996 documents that on average they held only 14 percent of assets in profit- and loss-sharing arrangements (Khan, 2010, p. 809). In an analysis of 81 private Islamic banks between 1994 and 1995, the percentage of financing made up of profit- and loss-sharing contracts averaged 14 percent in the Middle East and North Africa, 30 percent in East Asia, 8 percent in South Asia, and 44 percent in Sub-Saharan Africa (Yousef, 2005, p. 65). In a more recent study, Jan (2011, as cited in Asutay, 2012, pp. 102–103) finds that 10 international Islamic banks based in West Asia and Southeast Asia had negligible to no financing by profit- and loss-sharing arrangements between 2006 and 2010. As a consequence, a number of social scientists have evaluated the radical promise of Islamic finance fulfilling its paradigmatic form of profit- and loss-sharing between banker and client and have documented that Islamic finance rarely enters into such transactions (Chong & Liu, 2009; Kamla, 2009; Khan, 2010; Kuran, 2004). By the criteria of radical social finance, Islamic finance is failing to live up to the high standards it has set for itself.

A second immanent critique by scholars of Islamic finance is that financial engineering is used to mask debt-based financing (with interest payments that constitute *riba*) as commodity financing (with scheduled payments that include profit). This is perceived as an "ancient ruse" (Kuran, 2004, p. 15) when the commodity itself is not desired by the client. For example, consider a client who requires $10,000. Rather than lending $10,000 at 5 percent interest for 24 months, the bank purchases $10,000 of a liquid commodity such as oil on behalf of their client and finances the commodity over 24 months with a 5 percent markup for the bank's financing services. Since the client desires cash rather than the commodity, the commodity is immediately sold on the open market in exchange for $10,000 minus transaction costs. Numerous critics have called such "*murabahah*" financing to avoid *riba* as merely a "semantic difference" (Kuran, 2004, p. 10) in which the word "interest" is replaced with terms such as "fee," "service charge," "profit," or "markup." For some financial products, the distinction between interest and profit grows even fainter because many Islamic banks benchmark their administrative fees to an international benchmark interest rate (LIBOR) or to the interest rates charged by their conventional competitors (El-Gamal, 2006, pp. 74–80). By the criteria of radical social finance or visionary finance, some scholars of Islamic finance evoke theology to question whether Islamic finance is in fact distinctive from conventional finance.

A third immanent criticism is that Islamic finance pursues "form over substance" (El-Gamal, 2006) and "Shari'ah compliant finance" rather than "Islamic based finance" (Asutay, 2012, p. 100). As forcefully argued by Mehmet Asutay (2012, pp. 94–96), contemporary Islamic Financial institutions fall short of the human-centered goal of socio-economic development advocated in the 1970s by proponents of an Islamic moral economy (also see Siddiqi, 2007). Drawing on our earlier typology of social finance, essentially this is an argument that Islamic finance is sacrificing social ends by emphasizing social means. That is, judged by Asutay's standards of visionary finance, or by the secular standards of orthodox social finance, Islamic finance falls short of both promoting social justice and humanizing economic outcomes.

Taken together, these three immanent critiques have led numerous social scientists, critics, Islamic finance practitioners, and prospective clients to argue that Islamic finance is on the surface identical to conventional finance (Chong & Liu, 2009; Kamla, 2009; Khan, 2010). An alternative variation of this argument is that Islamic finance is identical to conventional finance, except that it is more economically inefficient, has higher transaction costs, and bears additional economic and legal risks (El-Gamal, 2006; Kuran, 2004).

The convergence paradox

Regardless of whether one adopts the lens of visionary finance or the less challenging vision of radical social finance, we confront the puzzling empirical observation that contemporary Islamic finance bears a remarkable surface similarity to conventional finance in spite of its radical intent to morally distinguish itself from conventional financial products. Elsewhere, I have argued that although Islamic finance is superficially similar to conventional finance, it is not identical (Pitluck, 2013). Moreover, in ongoing ethnographic research in a number of Islamic investment banks in Malaysia, a robust early finding is that Islamic finance is not a cynical façade to peddle conventional products with Arabic terms to the pious. Investment bankers and Sharia scholars within investment banks go to great lengths to apply Islamic finance's radical critique to conventional finance.

The convergence paradox is that in spite of the sincere and substantial efforts of practitioners to apply a radical critique to conventional finance, the resulting products and services are remarkably similar to those in conventional financial markets.

While I do not intend to position myself as an apologist for the Islamic finance industry, and I do have considerable sympathy for the immanent criticisms advanced by my colleagues, the empirical existence of the convergence paradox is both a puzzle and a useful puzzle to explain. I suggest that the convergence paradox of Islamic finance has much to teach the proponents of social finance about the potential benefits and dangers of upscaling visionary finance projects.

Four social mechanisms promote the convergence paradox

Drawing on ongoing research in Islamic banks in Malaysia and the existing academic literature on Islamic finance, here I draw on the scholarship of two influential organizational sociologists, Paul DiMaggio and Woody Powell (1983), to identify four social mechanisms that I use to explain the convergence paradox. On the one hand, these four social forces have helped finance entrepreneurs to harness capital and rapidly expand Islamic finance into a global, trillion dollar market. However, these same social forces simultaneously mold Islamic finance to increasingly resemble the very industry that it scorns. By viewing Islamic finance as subject to these four social forces, we may be able to better understand how an industry with such radical intent could nevertheless grow to strongly resemble the conventional finance industry. More importantly, the case of Islamic finance provides a lens through which we can understand the promise and dangers for social and sustainable financial institutions seeking to use the engine of capitalist innovation to rapidly upscale.

Competitive convergence

The most readily acknowledged of the four convergence mechanisms is efficiency-based rationality (DiMaggio & Powell, 1983). The winnowing effects of market competition, combined with firms' emulation of existing best practices, combine to push Islamic banks to offer a similar portfolio of products as their conventional competitors. This is an evolutionary argument in which social financial institutions survive by efficiently adapting to fit an environmental niche.

Islamic finance competes with conventional finance by creating such a market niche. It distinguishes itself as having superior morality, by identifying with Islam, and by harnessing referrals from charismatic religious and community leaders.

In financial markets, we can imagine a "moral premium" in which clients are willing to forgo a degree of quality and pay higher prices for the opportunity to participate in Islamic finance. In markets where this premium is high and stable, Islamic banks can afford to offer distinctive products even when they are not as cost effective as conventional financial products. In all social finance markets, competition from prospective competitors drives the "moral premium" to decrease over time, just as it does other costs. If the niche is profitable, we observe increasing competition among banks to enter this moralizing market niche, thereby reducing the moral premium that clients are willing to pay. If the niche is unprofitable, existing Islamic banks will desperately seek to appeal to clients to increase the moral premium—however, such appeals have limitations and grow tiring over time. Ultimately, Islamic banks facing the existential requirement of survival will attempt to mimic their more successful competitors, including their conventional competitors.

In social and sustainable enterprises, we often observe firms seeking to appeal to clients to pay a moral premium—either by forgoing quality or paying higher prices—so as to support the survival of the firm or to promote the market niche. Such moral premiums are invaluable in insulating social enterprises from market competition. However, such appeals may be insufficient for economic survival, or the premiums may be too volatile. Under such circumstances, the case of Islamic finance suggests that we should expect social financial institutions to grow increasingly similar to the conventional sector as they rationalize their operations and attempt to cut costs. Market competition forces social enterprises to rationalize and thereby converge with the very industry from which they seek to distinguish themselves.

The remaining three social forces that jointly explain the convergence paradox are not premised on a highly competitive market and do not require a "moral premium." Most distinctive of all, the remaining three social forces are efficiency neutral—that is, they may enhance or erode the social financial institution's bureaucratic capacity to efficiently provide social services, maximize profits, or lower costs.

Mimetic convergence

The second social force that produces the convergence paradox is the strategy of imitation. Because of uncertainty and risk aversion, all organizations imitate—with minor variations—pre-existing products and organizations (DiMaggio & Powell, 1983). Two common sources of uncertainty are the social financial institution's clients, and contradictions between internal and external gatekeepers (particularly regulators).

Consider the uncertainty generated by clients in Islamic finance. As a rapidly forming industry, there is a great deal of uncertainty regarding what clients want an Islamic Financial product to look like. After all, clients' knowledge of financial markets is shaped by their experience with the conventional banking sector, and this in turn shapes their expectations for niche markets, including the Islamic finance sector. One could make a similar argument with organic food. Prospective customers' expectations of what organic food should look and taste like is shaped, in large part, by the pre-existing food market with which organic produce competes. So uncertainty of clients' demand is a mimetic force pushing Islamic finance to resemble conventional financial products.

A second source of uncertainty is the tension between the demands of internal and external gatekeepers. In Islamic finance, new Islamic financial products must meet the requirements of two kinds of gatekeepers with very different criteria: the firm's internal Sharia scholars, and the external market regulators. Each financial product must be crafted so that it satisfies the internal Sharia scholars who evaluate whether bank products and practices are compliant with Islam. Each innovation must also meet the requirements of external gatekeepers. Regardless of their sympathy or antipathy to the social financial institution or social finance, market regulators must use conventional market regulations as their standard for appraising the legality and safety of new products and services. These regulations were developed in a historic response to the interests and functional needs of the conventional financial market, and may conflict with the values and processes of the social financial institution.

Conflicting demands by clients, internal gatekeepers, and external gatekeepers generate uncertainty for social financial institutions. To satisfy external gatekeepers—as well as customers who use the conventional market as their reference point—organizations strategically mimic conventional products and only deviate insofar as it is necessary to satisfy their internal gatekeepers. While such a strategy may allow for the rapid expansion of social financial institutions, it also produces a rapid convergence with the conventional market so that their products bear a strong superficial resemblance to their conventional competitors.

Coercive convergence

Social financial institutions, like all organizations, are dependent on other organizations and institutions for economic resources, political legitimacy, and for status. It is not uncommon for these parties to require, persuade, or invite social financial institutions to increasingly resemble their conventional competitors (DiMaggio & Powell, 1983).

Probably the strongest such structure pushing Islamic financial institutions and products to resemble those in the conventional sector is a secular legal system that has coevolved with an interest-based financial services industry. Although each country's existing regulatory structure and legal precedent poses unique challenges for Islamic finance (both to exist and to maintain its distinctiveness), there are also cross-national similarities. For example, Islamic finance practitioners routinely highlight how national tax regimes that had evolved within the conventional financial system systematically disadvantage contemporary Islamic finance. In Islamic finance, many financial products replace debt relationships with joint ownership relationships; an asset is jointly purchased by the financial institution and the client, and over time the client gains a greater share of ownership, until the client ultimately has financed the purchase of the asset. In many tax jurisdictions, relative to taxes associated with debtors making interest payments to lenders, implementing the incremental transfer of ownership from bank to client can be prohibitively costly because of capital gains tax and stamp duties associated with each commercial transaction. To provide another common discrepancy, in many tax jurisdictions interest charged by a conventional financier is deductible, while the Islamic bank's "profit charge" embedded in an Islamic finance product—although equivalent in function—is either not deductible or this is a costly area of legal ambiguity (Freudenberg & Nathie, 2012, pp. 60–61). To summarize, in earlier decades, states, self-regulatory authorities, and civil watchdog groups have made numerous legal and technical requirements of financial institutions that may be ill-suited for radical or visionary social financial institutions offering products that are contractually dissimilar to conventional financial products.

Equally problematic, all social financial institutions share the common problem that regulatory and accounting authorities can independently verify that the social financial institution is conforming to conventional criteria, but the authorities are unable to verify or audit that it adheres to its own radical or visionary social criteria. For example, Islamic financial institutions must demonstrate to clients, potential clients, and religious authorities that all relevant products and processes are Sharia compliant without the aid of conventional regulatory authorities, accountancy firms, or national religious regulations, thus producing extreme challenges for corporate governance (Alkhamees, 2013; Bassens, Derudder, & Witlox, 2012; Ghoul, 2008; Nienhaus, 2007; Safieddine, 2009). Thus through both omission as well as commission, existing conventional financial regulations and taxation policies are two of many social mechanisms of coercive convergence pushing Islamic finance to very closely resemble conventional financial products.

Professional convergence

When social financial institutions hire professionals—as they often must—the new employees are Trojan horses promoting convergence from within the organization. Professionals are distinguished from other employees by their collective struggle to control their work practices and their occupational knowledge and skills base (Freidson, 1984). Social financial institutions benefit when they hire professionals because it allows them to tap into established industry-wide education and training systems, professional industry associations, as well as pre-existing cross-organization career ladders. However, hired professionals also exert potentially conflicting normative pressure, as their body of expertise may conflict with the knowledge, beliefs, and practices that make the social financial institution distinctive from the larger conventional market. By practicing their profession, professionals within social financial institutions promote isomorphism and thus the convergence paradox (DiMaggio & Powell, 1983).

In the early decades of the Islamic finance industry, in university and professional training, all investment bankers were inculcated with expertise in conventional finance, and this was reinforced inside investment banks by on-the-job socialization and career ladders. The social force of professionalization is alleviated in some countries as Islamic finance has developed its own on-the-job training in Islamic investment banks, and as post-secondary education institutions have promoted Islamic finance certificates, coursework, and some degree programs (Bassens et al., 2012; Rudnyckyj, 2014; but see Yaacob, Shafeek, & Nahar, 2013). Nevertheless, even in Malaysia and countries where such training in the public and private sector is rather mature, the bulk of investment bankers' training is in conventional finance, and this approach to solving problems, with its related ontological view of the world, is deeply embedded in the professionalization of investment bankers.

When social financial institutions hire professionals (no matter how dedicated the hired individuals may be to the organization's distinctive values), the organization is in effect staffing itself with individuals with conflicting values—those of the organization and those of their profession. A potential consequence of these conflicting interests is a persistent pressure from within the organization to resemble the profession's perceived best practices, typically of their conventional competitors.

Discussion

This chapter has argued that Islamic banking and finance (IBF) can be interpreted as "radical social finance" or "visionary finance" insofar as it provides a radical critique of existing financial practices, and seeks to replace these practices with visionary alternatives associated with being a good Muslim, while simultaneously financing projects that could be perceived as beneficial (or at least not harmful) from a religious perspective. However, in spite of such radical intentions, and as numerous critics have already noted, Islamic finance is vanishingly similar to conventional finance. I refer to this empirical observation as the convergence paradox. The convergence paradox is that in spite of the sincere and substantial efforts of practitioners to apply a radical critique to conventional finance, the resulting products and services are remarkably similar on the surface to those in conventional financial markets. Drawing on DiMaggio and Powell's (1983) four mechanisms of isomorphic change, the existing literature on IBF, and my own ongoing research observing the production of Islamic finance in Malaysian investment banks, I have identified four social forces that mold Islamic finance to increasingly resemble the very industry that it critiques. I have also argued that these same social forces have contributed to the rapid growth of Islamic finance into a 1.3 trillion dollar global industry. Specifically, these four social forces have contributed to a successful upscaling by: (1) helping Islamic finance compete with conventional finance, (2) solving problems of uncertainty in a market in formation, (3) solving problems of religious legitimacy for the Muslim community while simultaneously meeting the political requirements of secular regulatory authorities, and (4) benefiting from professionalization. In short, the convergence paradox reveals that the same social forces contributing to the successful upscaling of Islamic finance are also contributing to the convergence paradox, thereby threatening that very success.

What lessons can we draw from IBF for secular financial reform projects and for Social and Sustainable Finance?

First, IBF demonstrates that a social movement seeking to restructure global financial markets can be successful without imposing a uniform reform program. IBF is a market in formation, with factious voices claiming certain economic activity as "Sharia compliant" or "Islamic," while other voices claim the same economic activity to be outside of, if not contrary to, Islam. Yet the industry has grown in a relatively short period to a trillion dollar industry, and continues to grow significantly faster than many conventional financial markets. Intellectual disagreement among scholars regarding how to define "social finance" or how to enact sustainable finance need not prevent the launch of successful markets.

Second, in spite of IBF's radical vision of an alternative financial system grounded in the needs of a moral economy, and IBF's longstanding and persistent efforts to absolutely prohibit *riba* and *gharar* (two characteristics of conventional markets that many financial economists consider natural if not essential characteristics of contemporary financial markets), nevertheless IBF is surprisingly similar to conventional financial markets. A number of scholars have interpreted this to mean that IBF is merely a marketing ploy to dress conventional financial products in Islamic garments (Chong & Liu, 2009; El-Gamal, 2006; Kamla, 2009; Khan, 2010; Kuran, 2004). Although I have disagreed with this line of argument elsewhere (Pitluck, 2013), nevertheless the critics are empirically correct that Islamic financial instruments and products have a strong surface similarity to those in the conventional sector. The convergence paradox is an established and puzzling empirical finding; an explanation for it is desirable, as it has important implications for the proponents of social finance.

Third, the case of Islamic finance demonstrates that it is not sufficient to build a parallel social finance in competition with the conventional market (Lai, 2014; Rethel, 2011). To prevent the convergence paradox requires an *additional* regulatory project to ameliorate convergence. Otherwise social finance, like Islamic finance, may experience such grave self-criticism that its very legitimacy is threatened from within. Therefore, this regulatory project is not a tangential nicety, but rather a requirement to ensure that, over time, radical social finance and visionary finance remains a distinctive alternative to conventional finance. This additional regulatory project must be designed to counteract the four social processes that DiMaggio and Powell (1983) identified—competition, mimesis, coercion, and professionalization.

Fourth, scholars of social finance are well positioned to formulate the important elements of this additional regulatory project by researching ongoing experiments in Social and Sustainable Finance (Davis, 2013, pp. 304–305). We need historical and qualitative researchers to document and compare cases of social finance that have succeeded or failed to ameliorate the convergence paradox. Such cases are also invaluable for generating "stylized facts" for scholars to create deductive financial models to better understand the social forces promoting or inhibiting the convergence paradox.

Islamic banking and finance is an ideal case for such scholarship because it is currently one of the largest radical social finance or visionary finance projects, and also one in which industry practitioners and academics are well aware of the existence and dangers of the convergence paradox. As a consequence, worldwide there is ongoing experimentation in every Islamic financial institution seeking to clarify to clients and regulators what Islamic finance is, what it should be, and how to maintain its distinctiveness from conventional finance.

Policy implications

It is beyond the scope of this chapter to summarize the regulatory lessons learned from the IBF case that could potentially be applied to promote secular Social and Sustainable Finance. I conclude with a few such potential regulatory lessons, in part to inspire such scholarship, and also to demonstrate the utility of understanding the convergence paradox as a product of competition, coercion, mimesis, and professionalization.[3]

Competitive isomorphism

An explicit argument in this chapter is that IBF's competition with the conventional financial market has yielded both benefits and costs. The benefits include rapid growth and rapid firm-level financial innovation which has diffused throughout national jurisdictions. But the principal cost is competitive isomorphism—where IBF products and instruments closely resemble those existing in the conventional sector.

One solution is to apply the well-known tools of industrial policy (Chang, 1994; Lai, 2014) to insulate the young social finance market from competition with the conventional sector. Over time, as the social finance market matures, this creates a grave political economic problem of how to withdraw the market protection and subsidies (Amsden, 1989; Wade, 1990).

A politically simpler solution is to promote mutualization of social financial institutions so that they become cooperatively owned by their key stake holders (e.g., by becoming a credit union or building society). In the IBF sector, Mahmoud El-Gamal (2007) has advocated that firms pursue mutualization, both to insulate them from competition, but also to resolve numerous corporate governance problems plaguing the IBF sector (cf., Alkhamees, 2013).

Coercive isomorphism

This social force is the most amenable to correction by regulation and legislation. However, regulatory advocacy by Islamic financial institutions tend to be centered on creating a "level playing field" where IBF can compete on an equal footing with the conventional financial sector. The paradigmatic example of this is tax policy, which in most jurisdictions is inadvertently punitive for IBF due to double taxation or subsidy programs to encourage interest-based debt markets. However, such tricky political economic issues are merely the tip of the iceberg for coercive isomorphism.

To reduce coercive isomorphism, regulators in coordination with legislators must rethink the financial system in social finance terms (Rethel, 2011). For example, in the UK, the Islamic Bank of Britain (now Al Rayan Bank) desired to offer a profit- and loss-sharing deposit account in which the depositor accepts the potential risk of loss of the original capital, in conformance with local interpretations of Sharia. However, "[t]his was not consistent with the [Financial Services Authority's] interpretation of the legal definition of a 'deposit' which requires capital certainty" (Financial Services Authority et al., 2007, p. 14). "After extensive discussions," the Islamic Bank of Britain acquiesced that its depositors were legally entitled to a full repayment; however, "customers had the right to turn down deposit protection after the event on religious grounds, and choose instead to be repaid under the Sharia compliant risk-sharing and loss bearing formula" (p. 14). To prevent such coercive isomorphism, UK regulators and legislators would have needed to dialogue with ideas unique to IBF (such as *riba* and *gharar*) in order to create new regulatory categories such as profit- and loss-sharing deposit accounts. One potential example of such legislation is Malaysia's Islamic Financial Services Act 2013, which clearly distinguishes between capital-guaranteed deposits and risk-bearing investment accounts.

For secular social reform projects such as social finance, the case of IBF demonstrates that it is necessary not merely to build a parallel, alternative social finance market, but to also create new legal and regulatory categories applicable to that market.

Mimetic processes

If coercive isomorphism is the social force most amenable to change by legislators and regulators, mimetic processes are likely to be the least amenable. Mimetic isomorphism (i.e., imitation of other firms and trivially incremental financial innovation) is a product of social financial institutions' strategic response to uncertainty. Therefore, policy-makers have essentially two strategies to reduce uncertainty. First, regulators can use all of the tools in their arsenal to reduce regulatory uncertainty for social finance institutions. In Malaysia, this is attempted by creating high-level social financial institutions (i.e., Shariah Advisory Councils) within the Central Bank and the Securities Commission, both of which engage in extensive public deliberations. Regulatory uncertainty is also reduced by the publication of indicative planning documents (e.g., Malaysia's two consecutive 10-year *Capital Market Masterplans*). Second, policy-makers can reduce mimetic processes by expending government resources to educate consumers on what makes social financial products and services distinctive from those in the conventional sector. Such education is a public good undersupplied by the private social finance sector. Social financial institutions certainly have an incentive to educate potential customers regarding what makes social finance a distinctive alternative from their conventional counterparts; however, government can both amplify this message, and also provide information that may be perceived by the public as more accurate and neutral, given the self-evident conflict of interest involved in firms marketing their own distinctiveness. By reducing regulatory uncertainty and increasing the sophistication of market demand (Porter, 1990), government can potentially inhibit mimetic processes so that social finance need not converge in form with the conventional sector. Malaysia has numerous organizations and institutions dedicated to promoting Islamic finance and educating potential clients of how this form of social finance is distinctive from conventional finance. Several such organizations are mentioned in endnote 4, but it is noteworthy that Malaysia organized the Malaysia International Islamic Financial Centre (housed in the Central Bank) to coordinate these efforts.

Professionalization processes

To capitalize on professional knowledge, or as a coercive requirement of regulations, social financial institutions hire numerous professionals, including lawyers, accountants, and a diverse range of licensed banking professionals. Each of these professionals is a Trojan horse brought into the social financial institution with distinctive worldviews and perceived best practices shaped by professional organizations oriented to the conventional financial market. To help mitigate such professionalization contributing to the convergence paradox is relatively straight forward: promote educational institutions and research institutes that create professionals in social finance. Malaysia has an exceptionally rich organizational and institutional infrastructure to create professionals in Islamic finance (Lai, 2014; Rudnyckyj, 2014; Wan Abdul Rahim, 2014).[4] We might expect social finance professionals' voices to be overlooked or overridden unless there are corporate governance reforms implemented to staff social financial institutions with credentialed social finance professionals with institutionally derived authority. In Malaysia, the aforementioned Islamic Financial Services Act 2013 (and earlier, the Shariah Governance Framework issued by the Central Bank) required that Islamic financial institutions have a Sharia Committee staffed by credentialed and experienced Sharia scholars. Through a number of institutional devices, this committee is partially insulated from the CEO or management and reports directly to the Board of Directors. Moreover, the Sharia Committee is invested with substantial institutional power vis à vis other professionals staffed in the organization. For example, publicly listed corporations must publish quarterly reports, and in one section the Sharia Committee must verify that the bank's products, services, and operations are Sharia compliant (Hassan & Hussain, 2013). By wielding this gatekeeping authority, the Sharia Committee can potentially require the corporation to alter any aspect of its operation (although in practice, there are also significant lapses of control by Sharia Committees (see Alkhamees, 2013; Pitluck, 2014)). Such legislation and regulations substantially strengthen the influence of social finance professionals vis à vis other professionals staffed in the social finance firm.

Conclusion

The case of Islamic finance provides a vivid illustration of the promise and dangers that many social enterprises and social movements face in developing Social and Sustainable Finance. How can we tap into the growth and dynamism of conventional capitalist markets and preserve the radical intent of social finance? While we are unlikely to find a simple answer to such a question, the four social forces and corresponding policy implications that I have outlined may provide readers with a theoretical lens through which to understand the strategic challenge of upscaling social financial institutions while resisting the convergence paradox.

Acknowledgments

This research has benefited from a lengthy gestation originating in the seed of Pitluck (2013). I've received invaluable feedback from colleagues at the European Association for Banking and Financial History conference at the University of Sarajevo (2012), the online World Economic Association Conference 3 (2012), and the International Workshop "Emulation or Contestation? Comparing the Development and Effectiveness of Islamic finance" held in Melbourne (2014). I am particularly indebted to fine comments and suggestions from Ercument Aksak, Ahmad Alkhamees, Mehmet Asutay, Alberto Brugnoni, Valentino Cattelan, Almir Colan, Nick Foster, Haider Ala Hamoudi, Kabir Hassan, Ahmad Kaleem, Jikon Lai, Imran Lum, Lena Rethel, and Kerstin Steiner, and the encouragement of David A. Westbrook. All views and errors are my own. This research was partially sponsored by Budapesti Közép-Európai Egyetem Alapítvány (CEU BPF). The views expressed in this chapter are those of the author and do not necessarily reflect the views of Central European University Budapest Foundation.

Notes

1 In contrast to the black-boxed definition of "social finance," Lehner and Nicholls (2014, pp. 271–272) define "social enterprises" more narrowly, as "institutions and actors...that combine social, economic and environmental components of value, together with personal values and the disciplined pursuit of financial returns" (also see Jones, 2010; Yunus & Weber, 2007).

2 In recent years, an orthodox social finance niche market has developed *within* Islamic finance, appropriately referred to as "Islamic social finance." "The Islamic social finance sector broadly comprises the traditional Islamic institutions based on philanthropy—*zakah*, *sadaqah* and *awqaf*; those based on mutual cooperation, e.g. *qard* and *kafala*; and also the contemporary Islamic not-for-profit microfinance institutions that use for-profit modes primarily to cover costs and sustain their operations" (Zawya Thomson Reuters & Islamic Research and Training Institute, 2013, p. 14).

3 The remainder of this chapter is not intended to portray Malaysia as a template or best practice model. Nor is it intended to suggest that these institutions have succeeded in ameliorating the convergence paradox in Malaysia—they certainly have not. Nor is this section intended to suggest that the institutional innovations are unqualified successes; their country-specific limitations are simply beyond the scope of this chapter. My pedagogic purpose is simply to illustrate how organizations and institutions can be designed to counteract the social forces of competition, coercion, mimesis, and professionalization that contribute to the convergence paradox.

4 There are numerous such organizations and institutions in Malaysia created by the government, private sector, and public–private partnerships. A partial list includes: the Securities Industry Development

Corporation (the training and development arm of the Securities Commission Malaysia); the Islamic Banking and Finance Institute Malaysia; INCEIF—The Global University of Islamic finance, and its research arm, The International Shari'ah Research Academy for Islamic finance (ISRA); the Institute of Islamic Banking and Finance housed at the International Islamic University Malaysia (IIUM); and the Research Center for Islamic Economics and Finance (EKONIS) at National University Malaysia (UKM).

References

Akbar, S., Zulfiqar Ali Shah, S., & Kalmadi, S. (2012). An investigation of user perceptions of Islamic banking practices in the United Kingdom. *International Journal of Islamic and Middle Eastern Finance and Management, 5*(4), 353–370.

Alkhamees, A. (2013, April). The impact of Shari'ah governance practices on Shari'ah compliance in contemporary Islamic finance. *Journal of Banking Regulation, 14*, 134–163.

Amsden, A. H. (1989). *Asia's next giant: South Korea and late industrialization*. New York: Oxford University Press.

Arnsperger, C. (2013). Want to really help expand Social and Solidarity Economy? Then start rethinking money! *Social and Solidarity Economy Think Piece*. Retrieved July 8, 2015, from http://www.unrisd.org/unrisd/website/newsview.nsf/%28httpNews%29/F479064990225049C1257B5D005A14ED?OpenDocument

Asutay, M. (2012). Conceptualising and locating the social failure of Islamic finance: Aspirations of Islamic moral economy vs. the realities of Islamic finance. *Asian and African Area Studies, 11*(2), 93–113.

Bassens, D., Derudder, B., & Witlox, F. (2012). "Gatekeepers" of Islamic financial circuits: Analysing urban geographies of the global Shari'a elite. *Entrepreneurship and Regional Development, 24*(5–6), 337–355.

Chang, H.-J. (1994). *The political economy of industrial policy*. New York: St. Martin's Press.

Chapra, M. U. (2007). Challenges facing the Islamic finance industry. In M. K. Hassan & M. K. Lewis (Eds.), *Handbook of Islamic banking* (pp. 325–357). Cheltenham, UK and Northampton, MA: Edward Elgar.

Cherney, M. (2015). Making a green bond. *Wall Street Journal MoneyBeat*. Retrieved July 8, 2015, from http://blogs.wsj.com/moneybeat/2015/03/12/making-a-green-bond/

Chong, B. S., & Liu, M.-H. (2009). Islamic banking: Interest-free or interest-based? *Pacific-Basin Finance Journal, 17*, 125–144.

Davis, G. F. (2009). *Managed by the markets: How finance reshaped America*. Oxford, UK and New York: Oxford University Press.

Davis, G. F. (2013). After the corporation. *Politics & Society, 41*(2), 283–308.

de Goede, M. (2005). *Virtue, fortune and faith: A genealogy of finance*. Minneapolis, MN: University of Minnesota Press.

DiMaggio, P., & Powell, W. W. (1983). The iron cage revisited: Institutional isomorphism and collective rationality in organizational fields. *American Sociological Review, 48*(2), 147–160.

El-Gamal, M. A. (2001). An economic explication of the prohibition of *gharar* in classical Islamic jurisprudence. *Islamic Economic Studies, 8*(2), 29–58.

El-Gamal, M. A. (2003). "Interest" and the paradox of contemporary Islamic law and finance. *Fordham International Law Journal, 27*(1), 108–149.

El-Gamal, M. A. (2006). *Islamic finance: Law, economics, and practice*. Cambridge, UK and New York: Cambridge University Press.

El-Gamal, M. A. (2007). Mutualization of Islamic banks. In M. K. Hassan & M. K. Lewis (Eds.), *Handbook of Islamic banking* (pp. 310–324). Cheltenham, UK and Northampton, MA: Edward Elgar.

ElGindi, T., Said, M., & Salevurakis, J. W. (2009). Islamic alternatives to purely capitalist modes of finance: A study of Malaysian banks from 1999 to 2006. *Review of Radical Political Economics, 41*(4), 516–538.

Financial Services Authority, Ainley, M., Mashayekhi, A., Hicks, R., Rahman, A., & Ravalia, A. (2007). *Islamic finance in the UK: Regulation and challenges*. London: Financial Services Authority. Retrieved July 30, 2015, from http://www.fsa.gov.uk/pubs/other/islamic_finance.pdf

Fitzgerald, J. L. (2013). Social impact bonds and their application to preventive health. *Australian Health Review, 37*(2), 1–204.

Freidson, E. (1984). The changing nature of professional control. *Annual Review of Sociology, 10*(1), 1–20.

Freudenberg, B., & Nathie, M. (2012). Chasing Islamic finance: A framework to assess the potential benefits of Australian tax reforms to facilitate Islamic finance. *Review of Business, 32*(2), 58–70.

Ghoul, W. A. (2008). Shari'ah scholars and Islamic finance: Towards a more objective and independent Shari'ah-compliance certification of Islamic financial products. *Review of Islamic Economics, 12*(2), 87–104.
Graeber, D. (2011). *Debt: The first 5,000 years*. Brooklyn, NY: Melville House Publishing.
Hassan, R., & Hussain, M. A. (2013). Scrutinizing the Malaysian regulatory framework on Shari'ah advisors for Islamic financial institutions. *Journal of Islamic Finance, 2*(1), 38–47.
Imam, P., & Kpodar, K. (2013). Islamic banking: How has it expanded? *Emerging Markets, Finance & Trade, 49*(6), 112–137.
Ingham, G. (2004). *The nature of money*. Malden, MA: Polity Press.
Islamic Development Bank, Islamic Research and Training Institute, & Islamic Financial Services Board. (2007). Islamic Financial Services industry development: Ten year framework and strategies. *Policy Dialogue Paper, 1*. Retrieved July 8, 2015, from http://www.ifsb.org/docs/10_yr_framework.pdf
Jones, J. F. (2010). Social finance: Commerce and community in developing countries. *International Journal of Social Economics, 37*(6), 415–428.
Kamla, R. (2009). Critical insights into contemporary Islamic accounting. *Critical Perspectives on Accounting, 20*(8), 921–932.
Khan, F. (2010). How "Islamic" is Islamic banking? *Journal of Economic Behavior & Organization, 76*(3), 805–820.
Kuran, T. (2004). *Islam and mammon: The economic predicaments of Islamism*. Princeton, NJ and Oxford, UK: Princeton University Press.
Lai, J. (2014). Industrial policy and Islamic finance. *New Political Economy, 20*(2), 178–198.
Lehner, O. M., & Kansikas, J. (2013). Pre-paradigmatic status of social entrepreneurship research: A systematic literature review. *Journal of Social Entrepreneurship, 4*(2), 198–219.
Lehner, O. M., & Nicholls, A. (2014). Social finance and crowdfunding for social enterprises: A public–private case study providing legitimacy and leverage. *Venture Capital, 16*(3), 271–286.
Maurer, B. (2005). *Mutual life, limited: Islamic banking, alternative currencies, lateral reason*. Princeton, NJ: Princeton University Press.
Maurer, B. (2006). *Pious property: Islamic mortgages in the United States*. New York: Russell Sage Press.
Mirakhor, A., & Zaikdi, I. (2007). Profit-and-loss sharing contracts in Islamic finance. In M. K. Hassan & M. K. Lewis (Eds.), *Handbook of Islamic banking* (pp. 49–63). Cheltenham, UK and Northampton, MA: Edward Elgar.
Nicholls, A. (2010). The institutionalization of social investment: The interplay of investment logics and investor rationalities. *Journal of Social Entrepreneurship, 1*(1), 70–100.
Nienhaus, V. (2007). Governance of Islamic banks. In M. K. Hassan & M. K. Lewis (Eds.), *Handbook of Islamic banking* (pp. 128–143). Cheltenham, UK and Northampton, MA: Edward Elgar.
Pauly, M., & Swanson, A. (2014). *Social impact bonds: New product or new package?* (Unpublished work). University of Pennsylvania, Wharton School, and NBER.
Pitluck, A. Z. (2013). Islamic banking and finance: Alternative or façade? In K. Knorr Cetina & A. Preda (Eds.), *The Oxford handbook of the sociology of finance* (pp. 431–449). Oxford, UK: Oxford University Press.
Pitluck, A. Z. (2014, August 16–19). *How to control an investment banker: Theorizing counter-financialization from the case of Islamic finance*. Paper presented at the American Sociological Association Annual Meeting, San Francisco, CA.
Pollard, J., & Samers, M. (2007). Islamic banking and finance: Postcolonial political economy and the decentring of economic geography. *Transactions of the Institute of British Geographers, 32*(3), 313–330.
Porter, M. E. (1990). *The competitive advantage of nations*. New York: Free Press.
Rethel, L. (2011). Whose legitimacy? Islamic finance and the global financial order. *Review of International Political Economy, 18*(1), 75–98.
Rudnyckyj, D. (2014). Islamic finance and the afterlives of development in Malaysia. *Political and Legal Anthropology Review, 37*(1), 69–88.
Safieddine, A. (2009). Islamic financial institutions and corporate governance: New insights for agency theory. *Corporate Governance: An International Review, 17*(2), 142–158.
Shiller, R. J. (2012). *Finance and the good society*. Princeton, NJ: Princeton University Press.
Siddiqi, M. N. (2007). Shari'ah, economics and the progress of Islamic finance: The role of Shari'ah experts. *IIUM Journal of Economics and Management, 15*(1), 93–113.
United Nations Inter-Agency Task Force on Social and Solidarity Economy. (2014). *Social and solidarity economy and the challenge of sustainable development: A position paper by the United Nations Inter-Agency Task Force on Social and Solidarity Economy (TFSSE)*. Retrieved July 30, 2015, from http://unsse.org/?page_id=499

Usmani, M. T. (2002). *An introduction to Islamic finance*. The Hague: Kluwer Law International.
Vogel, F. E., & Hayes, S. L. (1998). *Islamic law and finance: Religion, risk, and return*. Boston: Kluwer Law International.
Wade, R. (1990). *Governing the market: Economic theory and the role of government in East Asian industrialization*. Princeton, NJ: Princeton University Press.
Wan Abdul Rahim, K. (2014). Malaysia: World's Islamic finance marketplace. In S. Thiagaraja, A. Morgan, A. Tebbutt, & G. Chan (Eds.), *The Islamic finance handbook: A practitioner's guide to the global markets* (pp. 303–336). Singapore: John Wiley & Sons Singapore Pte. Ltd.
Warde, I. (2010). *Islamic finance in the global economy* (2nd ed.). Edinburgh, UK: Edinburgh University Press.
Yaacob, H., Shafeek, F., & Nahar, H. S. (2013). Exploring undergraduate students' understanding of Shari'ah based audit: Implications for the future of Shari'ah auditing labor market in Brunei. *Asian Journal of Finance & Accounting, 5*(2), 84–100.
Yousef, T. M. (2005). The *murabaha* syndrome in Islamic finance: Laws, institutions and politics. In C. M. Henry & R. Wilson (Eds.), *The politics of Islamic finance* (pp. 63–80). Edinburgh, UK: Edinburgh University Press.
Yunus, M., & Weber, K. (2007). *Creating a world without poverty: Social business and the future of capitalism*. New York: PublicAffairs.
Zaher, T. S., & Hassan, M. K. (2001). A comparative literature of Islamic finance and banking. *Financial Markets, Institutions & Instruments, 10*(4), 155–199.
Zawya Thomson Reuters & Islamic Research and Training Institute. (2013). *Islamic Social Finance Report 2014*. Thomson Reuters.

II.3
Hybridity, Business Models, and Measurement

22

JOINT SOCIAL-FINANCIAL VALUE CREATION IN SOCIAL ENTERPRISE AND SOCIAL FINANCE AND ITS IMPLICATIONS FOR MEASUREMENT CREATION AND MEASUREMENT OF PROFIT AND IMPACT IN SOCIAL FINANCING

Sean Geobey

Social entrepreneurship and the social financing that supports such entrepreneurial activity can be considered as two related strategies for intervening in complex socio-ecological systems while also generating financial returns. These strategies straddle the public, private, and social sectors, yet using any of those three lenses alone would not provide the analytical tools needed to evaluate and compare social entrepreneurial approaches. This chapter argues that there are three categories of value creation here: production synergies, strategic resilience, and increases to adaptive capacity. For social enterprises and social financiers to operationalize their activities, creating these sources of value measurement is critical. However, each category of value creation requires different measurement approaches. Metric, valuation, and learning systems are the three broad measurement approaches needed to operationalize joint social and financial value creation, though the balance between the three approaches will depend on the situational context of the strategy undertaken.

Overview of argument

The generation of both social and economic returns is the central objective of social financing, making the clear identification of how joint social-financial gains could arise an important aspect. As the social financing market develops, it is critical that both academics and practitioners clarify where gains from combining social and financial objectives arise. Without this clarity we risk wasting resources on faddish investments that will have little lasting impact, often at the expense of relatively well-functioning public sector and charitable investment. The risk here is high, as the premise underpinning social financing and social entrepreneurship—that combining separate goals into a single economic strategy—is fundamentally at odds with Adam Smith's classical argument in favor of economic specialization. The argument inherent in the strategies of social entrepreneurship and social financing is that moving away from an economy in which some organizations specialize in socially oriented economic activity and other organizations specialize in for-profit economic activity can produce superior outcomes than those we are currently seeing. However, the burden lies with social financiers and Social Entrepreneurs to prove that their models can produce greater social returns, financial returns, or both than standard for-profit companies and mission-driven organizations. This chapter will clarify where these additional sources of social and financial value can be developed; how impact measurement can support value creation; and what this means for the operationalization of impact measurement. A graphical approach will be taken to draw out the key trade-offs and opportunities inherent in following a joint social-financial value-generating strategy. A fictitious social enterprise is used to illustrate how these strategies would look in practice.

Specifying the sources of value creation allows for the further clarification of the role of impact measurement in operationalizing joint social-financial impact creation. Exploiting these value creation sources requires different measurement operations that can be viewed as tools for the reduction of transaction costs. Coase argued that there are three types of transaction costs: policing enforcement, bargaining, and information search costs (1973). The use of measurement systems can be seen as providing accountability to social financiers, which is analogous to reducing policing enforcement costs; aiding the prioritization of social investment opportunities, which is analogous to reducing bargaining costs; and the identification of opportunities for innovation, reducing information search costs. Best and Harji (2013) identified three broad types of measurement approaches that are used in social financing: impact methods, monetization methods, and process methods. This chapter will build on that work to argue that there are three more generalizable categories of measurement systems that focus on reducing each of these three transaction costs: impact metrics that focus on policing enforcement costs; valuation methods that focus on bargaining costs; and learning processes that focus on information search costs.

Value creation overview

There are three ways that undertaking a strategy of social enterprise or Social Financing can produce additional social or financial value. First, value can be created through production synergies between social and financial output. Second, value can be created over time by opportunistically shifting focus between financial and social objectives in response to external shocks, building greater resilience. Third, value can be created through an improved understanding of the social ecological systems being impacted and subsequent adaptation in response to changes in these systems. This is not to say that any or all of these value creation opportunities will occur in a social enterprise, only that these are the three broad categories of additional value creation in a social enterprise.

To further illustrate these sources of value creation, a hypothetical social enterprise, Exemplar Retrofits, will be used. Exemplar Retrofits provides services such as new window installation, roofing, and insulation for homes and commercial properties with the end result of providing more comfortable spaces for people to live and work that consume less electricity. As a result, Exemplar Retrofits' customers have lower electricity bills, some gains from which can be used by customers to pay for or finance these retrofits. Reduced electricity consumption also reduces a property's greenhouse gas emissions, reducing the consumer's contribution to global climate change. Exemplar Retrofits also has the option of purchasing credible carbon offsets. These offsets are sold by organizations elsewhere whose work unrelated to Exemplar Retrofits', such as a company in Thailand that may grow bamboo and bury it to remove atmospheric carbon, and purchasing these offsets can further reduce greenhouse gas emissions. This social enterprise is used as an example because the relative simplicity of its business model allows for greater clarity in distinguishing between types of value creation. However, these general lessons hold true for other social enterprises and for social financing strategies, albeit with greater complexity.

Value creation—Synergies

The first source of value creation comes from immediate synergies between social and financial value creation. A social enterprise can be viewed as a multiproduct firm with a choice to make between producing some combination of financial and social returns. We will call this the Strategic Choice Frontier (SCF; see Figure 22.1). Without synergies between the two types of returns, the SCF is simply a straight-line budget constraint. What this implies is that when the social enterprise wishes to produce greater social returns it comes at the expense of financial returns on a direct one-to-one basis. In effect, the social enterprise is purchasing social returns using their profits. This would make sense if increasing a unit of the targeted social return through an external donation or purchase could be done at a lower marginal cost than doing so by changing internal operations. For example, Exemplar Retrofits could employ a synergistic value creation strategy by taking a portion of their profits and using them to purchase carbon offsets. This linear trade-off does not imply that the profit-maximizing strategy produces no positive social impact; just that social impact is an externality that does not directly change operational decision-making and thus change an enterprise's SCF. It may be the case that Exemplar Retrofits could maximize profits when they make revenue of $10,000,000 per year and reduce greenhouse gas emissions for their clients by 100,000 tons, or 1 ton per $100 in revenue. If Exemplar Retrofits has an increasing marginal cost function, then increasing output further would reduce their profits because they would be producing where marginal cost exceeds marginal revenue, even though it would reduce greenhouse gas emissions further.

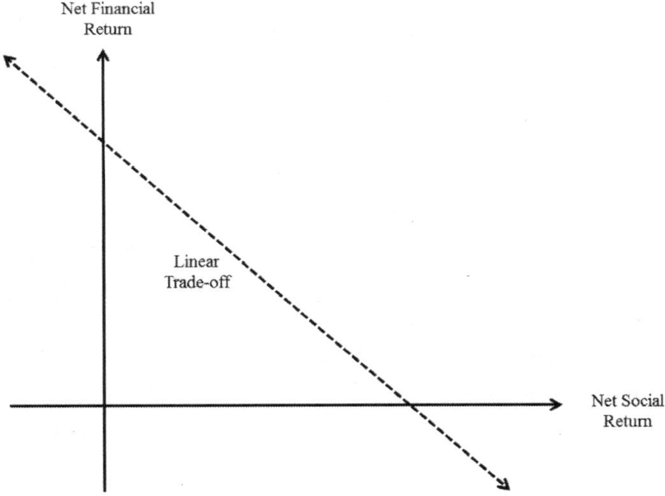

Figure 22.1 Strategic Choice Frontier—Linear trade-off

However, if carbon offsets were available for purchase at a cost of $20 per ton, then the most cost-effective way of reducing carbon emissions for Exemplar Retrofits would be to purchase offsets, not increase output. If they are using a profit-maximization strategy then their baseline greenhouse gas emission impact is 100,000 tons, a positive externality but not one that changes operational decision-making in the firm. This positive externality is effectively a social analogue to a "market rate of return" for a financial investment.

Selecting a strategy along the SCF is not a straightforward exercise in practice. All organizations convert inputs into some combination of social and economic outputs, though it is impossible to fully identify all of the inputs and outputs of production (Simon, 1982). Within the organization, much of the technology used to create outputs is embedded within social systems, individual people, and the physical structure of capital (Nelson & Winter, 1982).

Beyond the linear trade-off are combinations of social and environmental returns that demonstrate true production synergies. Combining social and economic returns in a non-separable way can take advantage of synergies in combining inputs, outputs, and a range of new production technologies. The existence of synergistic opportunities in the short term can come about when there are diminishing returns in social returns, economic returns, or both. Diminishing returns occur when there are "low hanging fruit" to be taken advantage of, meaning that the highest return projects per resource investment are undertaken first, followed by falling returns per resource investment as more resources are invested. If either social returns or economic returns are diminishing with respect to resource investment, the shape of the curve moves away from linear trade-off to a curved trade-off line (see Figure 22.2). It is not necessarily the case that returns will be constant or diminishing in either economic or social output. However, it is necessary for the social returns to be internalized to the extent that it expands the SCF to allow a range of financial and social return strategies beyond the simple linear trade-off. In effect, a synergistic strategy offers a range of operational choices that would be unavailable if there had not been synergies between the two types of returns. Unlike the linear trade-off without synergies,

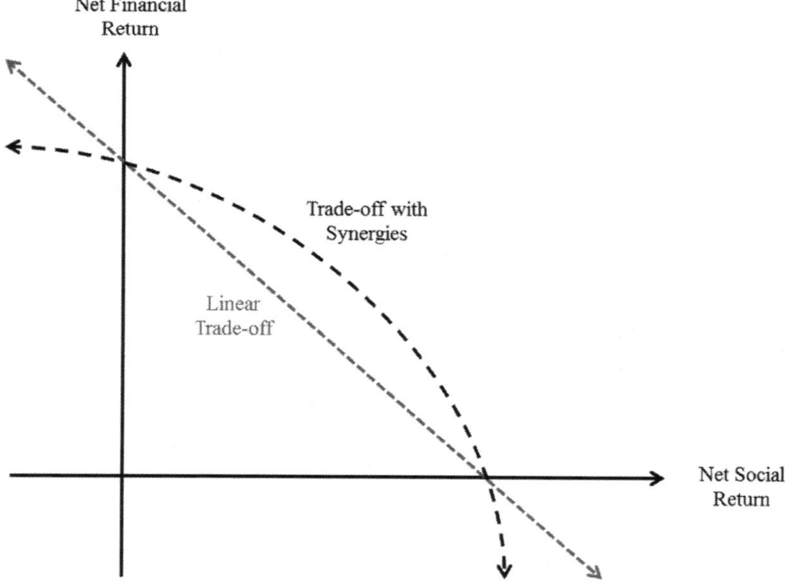

Figure 22.2 Strategic Choice Frontier—Synergies

for synergistic strategies it is not more cost-effective to create an additional unit of social impact by reducing some financial return or vice versa. For example, if Exemplar Retrofits can reduce carbon emissions by a ton when they generate revenues of less than $20, it means that even if the marginal cost is greater than $20—a case where any additional output would be at a loss—this per ton loss could be smaller than the cost of purchasing an emissions permit. If this is the case then Exemplar Retrofits could decide to take a lower profit by producing some output at a loss but have a greater social impact than could be achieved by focusing operations on profit maximization and using some of those gains to purchase carbon offsets. Indeed, the trade-off with synergies model clarifies that the SCF could include areas where some net financial return is negative to achieve slightly higher social returns, or net social returns are negative to achieve slightly higher financial returns.

When there are opportunities for synergies in the production of joint profitability and social gains, a strategy that creates both will produce different outcomes than a strategy of using financial returns to provide resources for social gains. When there are production synergies between social and financial returns, following an investment strategy that seeks a purely short-term financial return exposes the system and investor to negative social impacts that exceed the potential profitability. Similarly, following a purely philanthropic strategy exposes the social ecological system to investor losses far in excess of the potential social benefits. If financial and social returns are linked in the long run, committing to either pure strategy in the short run can be to the long-term detriment of the targeted goal. In addition to these two pure strategies, social financiers and social entrepreneurs may use mixed strategies and synergistic strategies to create social impact. Mixed strategies are those that place some resources into a pure profit-seeking strategy and some into a purely philanthropic strategy without operationally integrating these approaches, approaches that all lay along the simple linear trade-off line. For example, an approach in which a for-profit company takes some of their financial returns and donates them to an arm's length charity is an example of a mixed strategy. In contrast, a synergistic strategy integrates the seeking of financial and social returns operationally, making the two inseparable. This makes it more difficult to change strategies quickly, as removing investments in producing social returns will necessarily reduce financial returns as well, and vice versa. While a synergistic strategy may be more difficult to change when compared to a mixed strategy, it exposes the organization to fewer risks. Because a mixed strategy is simply the combination of two pure strategies, it leaves the organization exposed to the same downside risks as either pure strategy without the potential returns of a synergistic strategy (Emerson, 2003; Porter & Kramer, 2011).

The operationalization of the range of synergistic options does not come without its costs. There will likely be switching costs involved in changing business operations to move between different points on the SCF, and these may be much higher than those involved in changing the intended strategy with the linear SCF. For example, if Exemplar Retrofits changes output to achieve greater or lesser social return, this may involve fixed costs tied to changing the internal operations, which could range from trivial changes in pricing to larger changes in marketing and distribution strategy, staff training, or switching facilities. However, the alternative to purchasing greater or fewer carbon offsets effectively has a negligible cost associated with it. Not all social enterprises will have high internal switching costs, and not all donation or purchasing alternatives to making a social return will be as low cost as those available to Exemplar Retrofits.

Effective measurement systems are critical to being able to identify and operationalize synergistic value creation opportunities. Without clear metrics it is difficult to tell how costly it is to generate social impact, which is critical in determining whether the internalization of an externality will be viable as a value-creating option. For Exemplar Retrofits this means identifying how costly it is to produce a reduction of 1 ton of CO_2 emissions and how that cost structure compares to purchasing carbon offsets. If the cost of producing a CO_2 emission reduction through their retrofit services is greater than the cost of a carbon offset then it would not make sense for Exemplar Retrofits to internalize CO_2 emission reductions into their strategy and they should instead focus on profit maximization. What is critical for identifying opportunities to exploit synergies is that social enterprises have clear, comparable metrics that can be used to clarify their own cost structures and to compare their own operations to external alternatives. Here, specific impact metrics are important, and sets of standardized metrics such as the Impact Reporting Investment Standards (IRIS) or the International Standards Organization (ISO) standards provide the infrastructure needed to develop and implement impact metrics at a lower cost than trying to develop them internally.

Value creation—Resilience

The second source of value creation comes from nimbly taking advantage of external shocks to build organizational resilience and increase financial or social impact over time. The overall effect is to change the synergistic long-term trade-off from a curved short-term line to a bowed-out long-term trade-off line, which in turn creates a wider range of strategic opportunities for social and economic growth (outlined in Figure 22.5). These can increase the range of potential social returns beyond what a social value creation-alone strategy could achieve. There are two broad real-world ways in which this can manifest. First, the existence of positive economic returns allows for investment in productivity-enhancing capital. Second, by reducing the possibility that the organization will suffer losses and go out of operation, the negative risk borne by those dependent upon these services is reduced. Similarly, an organization following a Corporate Social Responsibility strategy geared toward economic return would be better placed over the long term to produce some positive net social returns. This area of improved financial return comes in part from the reduction of negative risk caused by creating negative social returns within the niche on which the organization relies. Unlike synergistic value creation, resilient value creation from blended value, shared value, or both can directly contribute to organizational longevity.

The gains from resilience occur when Social Entrepreneurs and social financiers can respond to external changes. It may be that in a resilient value creation model a SCF is relatively predictable, but in the short term there are fluctuations in its shape, sometimes skewed in the direction of higher financial returns and sometimes skewed in the direction of higher social returns. If the cost of shifting the balance between a relatively high financial return strategy and a relatively high social return strategy is not prohibitive, then over time greater financial and social returns can be achieved than would occur if a single strategy on the synergistic SCF were rigidly adhered to. Figure 22.3 shows how this could work when there is a financial return-skewed shock. For Exemplar Retrofits such a scenario could easily arise if there were an exogenous increase in electricity prices. Net financial returns would increase because higher electricity prices would make retrofits that would reduce consumer electricity usage far more attractive, increasing demand and the prices that Exemplar Retrofits could charge. At the same time, anticipated net social returns could fall. This might seem counterintuitive given that output may rise, but higher electricity prices could lead consumers to reduce their electricity usage regardless of whether or not they use Exemplar Retrofits' services. Consequently, the actual greenhouse gas emission reductions that could be directly attributed to Exemplar Retrofits per unit of output would fall. What is interesting is how Exemplar Retrofits could react to this change in pricing. Figure 22.3 shows different intended strategies and the possible outcomes of following these strategies when there are short-term changes to financial and social returns.

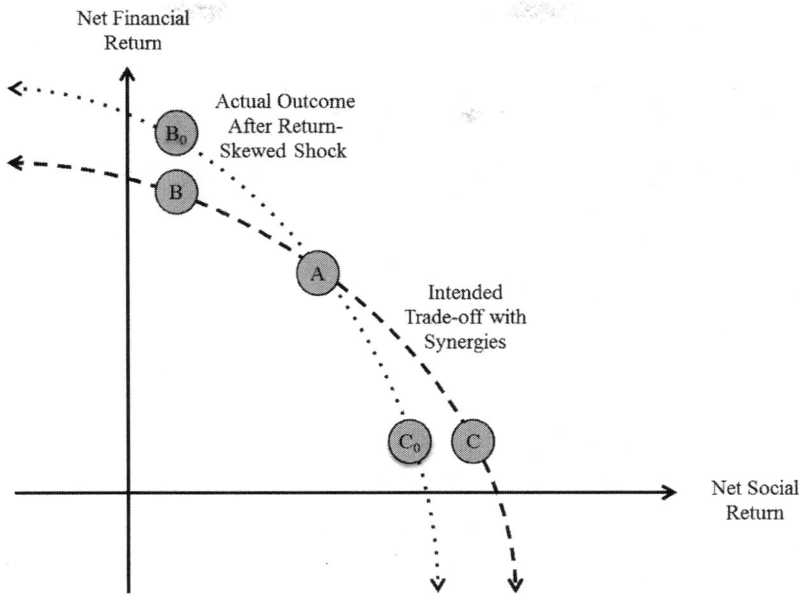

Figure 22.3 Strategic Choice Frontier—Financial return-skewed shock

At point A they could maintain their current strategy without any change. However, a shift toward the B strategy, which is more financial return-oriented, could lead to financial returns beyond what the longer term SCF would otherwise produce at B_0. Conversely, adhering to the more socially oriented strategy, C, would lead to some disappointment, as either financial returns or social returns, or both, would have to be sacrificed, as in the case C_0.

Similarly, a social return-skewed shock could provide an opportunity to generate abnormally high social returns. Here the converse example of low electricity prices would have the opposite effect of what we just saw with a financial return-skewed shock for Exemplar Retrofits. Lower electricity prices would reduce consumer demand for retrofit services and therefore reduce financial returns, but the increased electricity usage and greenhouse gas emissions resulting from higher usage would likely increase social returns for those retrofits that do occur. As a general case a socially skewed shock presents an opportunity to shift short-term strategies to take advantage of a temporary opportunity to create a higher social return (see Figure 22.4). Trying to maintain a relatively high financial return at level E would likely fail, forcing a choice between losing social or financial returns, as at level E_0. In effect the maintenance of higher financial returns can come from reducing social returns, possibly even to the level of drawing down accumulated social capital. For example, Exemplar Retrofits could aggressively push retrofits on customers for whom the economic and environmental effects would be limited, such as promoting new efficient windows on customers who have already recently replaced their windows. However, using the opportunity to increase social returns could move beyond the standard SCF into a point such as F_0. Such a level of social output may not be generally sustainable, but if an opportunistic strategy is coupled with one that also takes advantage of higher financial returns when they are available, the financial cushion provided could subsidize an otherwise unsustainable level of social return.

Taken together, if the costs of shifting between these strategies are relatively low, then a flexible strategy can actually produce returns beyond the bounds of the expected SCF. Critical

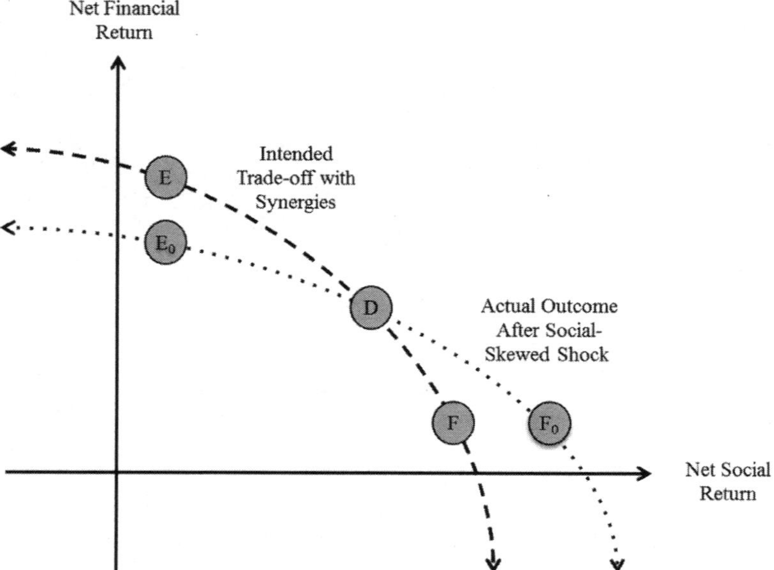

Figure 22.4 Strategic Choice Frontier—Social return-skewed shock

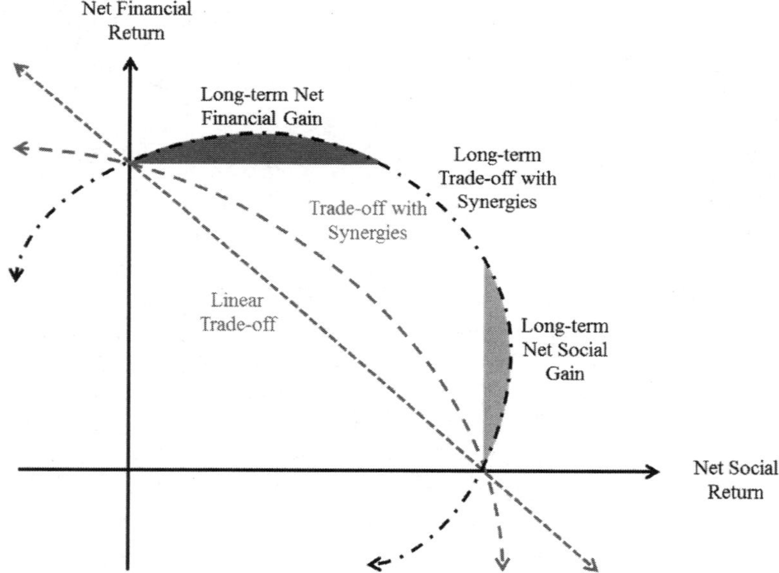

Figure 22.5 Strategic Choice Frontier—Long-term resilience

to making the strategic flexibility that makes these additional returns possible is the capacity to identify and choose between strategies as circumstances change, which necessitates adequate social performance metrics. However, the measurement systems that are even more critical here are valuation methods such as cost–benefit analysis (CBA) and social return on investment analysis (SROI). These tools allow decision-makers to more easily guide their decisions to make the necessary trade-offs needed to exploit these opportunities as they arise. Ultimately this improves the resilience not only of the social enterprise but also of the systems they seek to positively impact by increasing net social returns over time. Additionally, to the extent that the social ecological systems the enterprises operate in become increasingly tied to and dependent upon a social enterprise, the sustainability of the social enterprise becomes increasingly important for the resilience of these systems.

Value creation—Adaptation

The final source of value creation comes from adaptive strategies. When seeking joint social and financial returns there is an inherent imbalance between the two. While financial returns are relatively straightforward to measure, there are a wide variety of possible social returns. Land preservation, food security, poverty alleviation, international economic development, and a likely endless variety of other social goods can all be targeted for social returns. Furthermore, even within a particular type of social return the metrics that are used to capture impact are always imperfect proxies for actual social impact. Learning about the complex social and ecological systems Social Entrepreneurs and social financiers seek to impact can lead to the development of better proxy metrics for social impact. Interventions in a complex system are all conducted in somewhat mysterious landscapes where the interventions themselves reveal elements and relationships in the complex systems that were previously unknown. Navigating such systems is an inductive process where models are held onto as long as they work well, and once better models are found they are adopted instead (Arthur, 1994), making theory evaluation a comparative process. While a capacity for learning, adaptation, and innovation is central to generating social innovation over time, identifying the depth of this capacity would require broadening the scope of what is measured and a blurring of the boundaries between measurement and action.

As explored earlier, the application of complex systems theory and bounded rationality to the problem of measurement implies that system super observation is impossible. A super observer would be an observer whose view of the system ultimately dominates all other views of the system, consequently knowing the observer-independent "truth" about the system. As Weinberg (1975) notes, "the concept of observer independent truth is the ultimate egocentrism" (p. 53). What we include or exclude from our view of the system through the selection of measurement systems consequently changes how the system is acted upon and the resource flows that will follow from that (Westley, Zimmerman, & Patton, 2007). If there is no observer-independent truth, the observation is necessarily impacted by the observer who is, therefore, an element of the system, making measurement itself a system intervention. Moreover, because of this a change in the perspective of the observer actor will necessarily change their role in the system, since it will drive their activity actors in the system.

Adaptation can range from small improvements to radical innovations. The small improvements can amount to having proxies better hone in on the core type of impact being sought. For example, Exemplar Retrofits may have initially used CO_2 emission reductions as their social impact metric and shifted toward the use of CO_2-equivalent emission reductions to account for other greenhouse gases such as methane. Such improvements increase the efficacy of the activities they undertake. However, the strategic adaptations that scale up social impact require a fundamental reframing of how the social or ecological system being impacted works (Westley, Antadze, Robinson, Riddell, & Geobey, 2014). In Exemplar Retrofits' case it may be that they have noticed that some of their retrofits have made high-density urban facilities much more attractive, so much so that they are converting some consumers away from suburban living to higher density urban living. Recognizing that higher density-built environments produce not only lower per person greenhouse gas emissions in each facility but also reduce transportation emissions and production of other effluents, Exemplar Retrofits decides to reframe its impact metrics and valuations to promote intensification directly rather than greenhouse gas emissions. This reframing may induce additional strategic changes such as releasing intellectual property for free or licensing retrofit designs to bring their impact to scale in a way that had previously been completely outside their strategic scope of action. As measurement systems, learning processes grounded in complexity such as developmental evaluation can aid in converting learning into adaptive strategy change (Patton, 2011).

Visually this is not really a movement along a current Strategic Choice Frontier, but a move from a Strategic Choice Frontier aligned to one model of social value to one aligned to a different model of social value. For the social enterprise or social financier this new conception of social value will be seen as one that provides a more accurate picture of the social ecological system, initiating a strategic pivot. From this a modified set of synergistic and resilience value creation opportunities can be developed that will have greater impact than the pre-adaptation opportunities offered (see Figure 22.6). This new net social return axis will provide a "better" understanding of the complex social ecological system from a Social Entrepreneur or Social Investor's perspective. However, the new Strategic Choice Frontier will not have the same shape as the initial one, either short-term or long-term, and this will impact the most effective strategies that come from this. In particular, if the new Strategic Choice Frontier does not provide financial-social synergies it may suggest a move away from a social entrepreneurship or social finance strategy toward a simpler one of financial return maximization coupled with contributions to an organization seeking social-only returns. Less extreme shifts may simply change the balance between financial and social returns that will achieve the preferred return combination, though this will still necessitate an operational change, as the strategies that will best exploit synergistic and resilience returns will change.

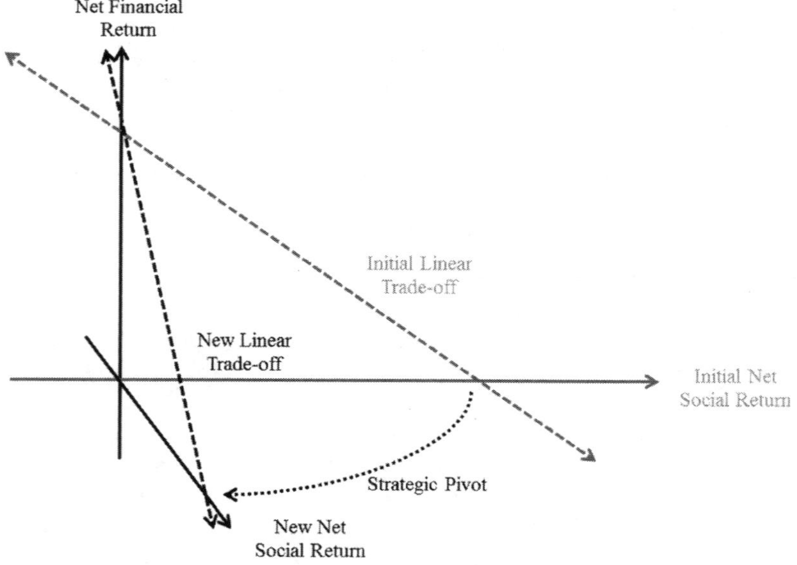

Figure 22.6 Shifting perception of new social return and new Strategic Choice Frontier

Bounded rationality implies that identifying these opportunities for change is costly (Simon, 1982). Moreover, there is a trade-off between learning what is needed to maximize social impact and identifying the variety of social impacts available. An expenditure on identifying the shape of the landscape reduces short-term economic returns but may be able to help in adapting to system shifts. However, that expenditure will be limited in the scope of how much of the landscape it can uncover. A narrow search will not provide many alternatives to the current construct of social returns a decision-maker uses but may help identify the social return strategy that will maximize social returns. On the other hand, a wide search will provide a number of alternatives and may uncover a greater variety of system shifts without providing the means to maximize impact. Wide search strategies are particularly important when there have been radical system shifts and little is known about the new landscape, and can include Arthur's (1994) inductive search model.

There is room for broader social innovation when co-evolutionary forces connect social impact or financial return at one level in a complex system with social impact or financial return at a higher level in a complex system. Although neither "blended value", or "shared value" concepts are explicitly grounded in a framework that connects activities at different scales, both models of value creation can be applied to cross-scale impact in their conception of moving beyond a "financial or social return" mindset to a mutually reinforcing "financial and social return" way of thinking (Emerson, 2003; Porter & Kramer, 2011). Shifting perceptions to create new opportunities for radically transformative change that positively impacts both financial and social returns combines the shared or blended value concepts with social innovation theory. However, these changing perceptions are most likely to arise from those who have experience within a complex social ecological system reframing their understanding of it. This, in turn, builds on the corridor principle underlying much innovation, which is the idea that entrepreneurs are best positioned to create new ventures in areas similar to those in which they already operate (Holt, 1992).

Measurement system interactions

Impact measurement is not valuable in and of itself; it is valuable because of how it is integrated into strategic and operational decision-making. This includes decisions made by social financiers, as well as the recipients of social financing, the intended beneficiaries, policymakers, other social financiers, and those engaged in other market-making enterprises. Consequently, different strategies for creating both social and economic value must be considered in the assessment of impact while remembering that the ability of people to consciously design any strategy, even an investment strategy, is limited and the resulting strategies are emergent in practice (Cyert & March, 1963; Mintzberg, 2009; Mintzberg & Waters, 1985). By modeling the perceived trade-off between economic and social returns in different social financing strategies, this chapter argues that we can identify sources of real social and financial value generation that can be used to guide not only the conscious strategies of social financiers and social entrepreneurs, but also the often unconscious collective learning needed to enable large-scale social innovation.

Impact metrics monitor the ecological impact of a social financing strategy. Valuation methods weight the relative value of profitability and the set of social impacts that social financiers intend on advancing. Learning processes seek to identify new impact metrics and to better understand the workings of the complex social, ecological, and economic systems a social financier seeks to influence. The language differs from that used by Best and Harji to account for the more general nature of strategies and measurement approaches analyzed here. Impact metrics are used rather than impact methods to sharpen the role of individual items being measured. Valuation methods are used rather than monetization to account for the possibility of systems that value impacts relative to each other without directly converting them into monetary units, thus including a larger possible set than monetization methods. Finally, learning processes are used rather than process methods to clarify that the primary importance of these types of measurement systems is in systemic learning, which then feeds into strategy development. This separates the strategic component from the measurement and evaluation component, though in practice they are usually co-evolutionary approaches.

Measuring impact is vital to many system interventions, but system complexity presents a number of challenges. Within the context of social entrepreneurship, measurement contributes to the internal controls needed to generate consistent impact, planning for innovation, and accountability to stakeholders (Nicholls, 2010). However, for measurement and management, the challenge of complexity is threefold. First, the underlying properties of complex systems mean that there is no single observer-independent way of optimally measuring impact. Second, the underlying phenomena that social impact measurement attempts to capture change over time. Finally, there will always be system elements and relationships that are real but beyond measurement.

The framework for value creation developed here speaks to strategic objectives, not the means to achieve them. Operationalization of these strategies requires a careful and humble understanding of the role of measurement. The full social impact of any intervention will always be impossible to grasp because of the complexity of the social phenomena at play. This is an ontological challenge, as even if the phenomena were fully observable—which they are not—the different values each social entrepreneur and social financier place on different elements of the phenomena will make it impossible to have a single "correct" understanding of the impact on the system. Complicating this further, there is an epistemological challenge in the inadequacy of metrics. All metrics are a proxy measurement of some social phenomena. In some cases these proxy metrics are relatively good, while in other cases proxy metrics or sets of proxy metrics are only loosely correlated with the underlying phenomena. While an organization that is only seeking profits will not have to worry about these nuances, the distinction between what is knowable, what is known, and what can be used is pivotal for the operationalization of a joint social-financial generating strategy. In all, there are three broad objectives that underpin measurement systems for social financiers and social entrepreneurs:

- accountability to social financiers;
- prioritization of social investment opportunities; and
- identification of opportunities for innovation.

These three objectives are analogous to the three types of transaction costs, policing enforcement, bargaining, and information search, that are drawn from Coase (1937). Operationally, impact measurement also differs based on the measurement systems used. In Best and Harji's (2013) overview of the types of measurement systems used by social financiers in Canada, three broad types of measurement approaches were found: impact methods, monetization methods, and process methods. In this chapter slightly different language is used, but measurement systems still fall into three broad categories:

- impact metrics;
- valuation methods; and
- learning processes.

In the relationship between value generated through resilience and value generated through adaptation, it is important to highlight the distinction between social enterprise and social financing. First, social entrepreneurs and social financiers have access to different metrics. A social enterprise primarily has its own social and financial indicators to work with, whereas a social financier will have access to a portfolio of social investments with different social impact metrics. Although the appropriate balance between focusing on developing resilience and adaptation will primarily be context-dependent, given their different access to metrics it may be relatively easier for social enterprises to focus on resilience and relatively easier for social financiers to focus on adaptation. For social enterprises the smaller set of outcome indicators and hands-on access to and knowledge of internal cost structures may make it easier to develop strategies to take advantage of short-term environmental changes. On the other hand, the access social financiers have to a wide variety of impact metrics can make it relatively easy for them to analyze these findings and convert them into actionable knowledge (Geobey, Westley, & Weber, 2012). Furthermore, while there can be substantial fixed costs to initially develop this systemic learning, in principle the dissemination of this knowledge should be close to costless. A social financier's portfolio of investments provides both a source for new knowledge and a channel for knowledge mobilization. Even if there are additional costs for enterprises to operationalize this learning, its broad availability can provide the platform for innovation.

Both at the level of the social enterprise and the level of the social financier, the three different value creation approaches interact with each other in a complex manner. Impact metrics are necessary to identify synergies. Valuation methods rely on impact metrics to operationalize, but systems such as SROI can be adapted to ongoing changes in the complex systems social enterprises and social financiers operate within. Learning processes are vital for strategic adaptation, but without some sense of organizational valuation or prioritization it becomes harder to focus on identifying learning opportunities and, ultimately, the creation of better proxy impact metrics. Each of these measurement processes is costly, and it will depend on the context where the balance of costs will fall. In the case of Exemplar Retrofits, CO_2 emission reductions are using established impact metrics that would be relatively low cost to administer, whereas generating value through resilience and adaptation in a relatively competitive industry would likely be more expensive. With another social enterprise the balance may be quite different. For example, for an international development project in a region in which no social enterprise has operated before, the costs may weigh quite heavily on learning and metric development.

Conclusion

There are real opportunities for value creation by combining social and financial returns. However, it is incumbent on Social Entrepreneurs and social financiers to clarify where they are generating value if they are going to be able to build sustainable organizational models. Production synergies, organizational resilience, and adaptive capacity are the three sources of value creation for joint social and financial returns. To operationalize these a combination of impact metrics, valuation systems, and learning processes are required, though the balance between the three will depend on the economic, social, and ecological context within which they work.

References

Arthur, W. (1994). Inductive reasoning and bounded rationality. *The American Economic Review, 84*(2), 406–411.

Best, H., & Harji, K. (2013). *Social impact measurement use among Canadian impact investors*. Toronto, ON: Purpose Capital.

Coase, R. H. (1937). The nature of the firm. *Economica, 4*(16), 386–405.

Cyert, R., & March, J. (1963). *Behavioral theory of the firm*. Englewood Cliffs, NJ: Prentice Hall.

Emerson, J. (2003). The blended value proposition: Integrating social and financial returns. *California Management Review, 45*(4), 35–51.

Geobey, S., Westley, F. R., & Weber, O. (2012). Enabling social innovation through developmental social finance. *Journal of Social Entrepreneurship, 3*(2), 151–165.

Holt, D. (1992). Entrepreneurship and innovation. In D. H. Holt (Ed.), *Entrepreneurship: New venture creation*. Englewood Cliffs, NJ: Prentice Hall.

Mintzberg, H. (2009). *Managing*. San Francisco, CA: Berrett-Koehler Publishers, Inc.

Mintzberg, H., & Waters, J. A. (1985). Of strategies, deliberate and emergent. *Strategic Management Journal, 6*(3), 257–272.

Nelson, R., & Winter, S. (1982). *An evolutionary theory of economic change*. Cambridge, MA: Belknap Press of Harvard University Press.

Nicholls, A. (2010). The functions of performance measurement in social entrepreneurship: Control, planning and accountability. In K. Hockerts, J. Mair, & J. Robinson (Eds.), *Values and opportunities in social entrepreneurship* (pp. 241–272). New York: Palgrave Macmillan.

Patton, M. Q. (2011). *Developmental evaluation: Applying complexity concepts to enhance innovation and use*. New York: The Guilford Press.

Porter, M., & Kramer, M. (2011). Creating shared value: How to reinvent capitalism—and unleash a wave of innovation and growth. *Harvard Business Review, 89*(1–2), 62–77.

Simon, H. A. (1982). *Models of bounded rationality: Behavioral economics and business organization, 2*. Cambridge, MA: MIT Press.

Weinberg, G. (1975). *An introduction to general systems thinking*. New York, NY: Wiley.

Westley, F., Antadze, N., Riddell, D. J., Robinson, K., & Geobey, S. (2014). Five configurations for scaling up social innovation: Case examples of nonprofit organizations from Canada. *The Journal of Applied Behavioral Science, 50*(3), 234–260.

Westley, F., Zimmerman, B., & Patton, M. Q. (2007). *Getting to maybe: How to change the world*. Toronto, ON: Vintage Canada.

23

ORGANIZATIONAL HYBRIDITY IN SOCIAL FINANCE

A comparative analysis

Gunnar Glänzel and Björn Schmitz

The "hybrid movement" (Battilana, Lee, Walker, & Dorsey, 2012) is a description of the recent trend in organizational forms that are combining highly heterogeneous sectoral elements in general and commercial and non-profit practices in particular in new ways and more intensively. The body of academic literature on hybrid organizations has increased vastly in the last decade (e.g., Billis, 2010; Boyd, Henning, Reyna, Wang, & Welch, 2009; Bromberger, 2011; Doherty, Haugh, & Lyon, 2014; Evers, 2008; Glänzel & Schmitz, 2012; Jäger & Schröer, 2013; Jay, 2013; Schmitz, 2013; Skelcher, 2012; Smith, 2010). Best-known hybrid organizations are active in fair trade (e.g., Huybrechts & Defourny, 2008; Nicholls & Opal, 2005) or work integration (e.g., Garrow & Hasenfeld, 2010; Pache & Santos, 2010). But also organizations in the field of social finance are interesting and of increasing importance, as these organizations might serve as part of the ecosystem for hybrid organizational forms like social enterprises (e.g., Battilana & Dorado, 2010; Harvey, 1995; Moore, Westley, & Brodhead, 2012).

The debate on hybrid organizations active in finance is prevalent in the literature on social investment and social finance (e.g., Moore, Westley, & Nicholls, 2012; Nicholls, 2010). As social mission organizations find it hard to attract resources for their operations and most of the common investment options do not come without restrictions (Glänzel, Krlev, Schmitz, & Mildenberger, 2013; Schmitz & Glänzel, 2013), financial organizations that are hybrid as well are interesting solutions for at least two central reasons: (1) due to their own hybridity, they might be able to establish a better fit with social enterprise investees; and (2) also based on hybridity, they should be in a better position to attract and raise capital for investment in hybrid ventures. That is, because they are hybrids themselves, they should have the capacities required for bringing together supply and demand for social finance, or in other words for "hybrid capital." What do these capacities consist of? We use three case studies to illuminate that question and argue for the hypothesis that central capacities lie in the ability to communicate way more extensively (in terms of quantity) and intensively (in terms of quality) with different types of stakeholders. That is, we will analyze financial hybrid organizations' communication channels and their approaches in systematically creating legitimacy for hybrid investment through these media.

Hybrid organizations in finance

Dees and Anderson (2003, p. 18) define hybrid organizations as "formal organizations, networks or umbrella groups that have both for-profit and non-profit components." Hybrid organizations span and bridge institutional boundaries (Brandsen & Karré, 2011; Jay, 2013; Pache & Santos, 2013; Smith, 2010; Tracey, Phillips, & Jarvis, 2011) and "allow the co-existence of values and artefacts from two or more categories" (Doherty et al., 2014, p. 418). They are "intermediate forms" (Wamsley & Zald, 1973) that blur sector boundaries (e.g., Anheier & Then, 2004; Billis, 2010; Dees, Emerson, & Economy, 2004; Nederveen, 2001; Wilson & Post, 2013). In general terms hybrid organizations are "heterogeneous arrangements, characterized by mixtures of pure and incongruous origins, (ideal) types, 'cultures,' 'coordination mechanisms', 'rationalities,' or 'action logics' (Brandsen, van de Donk, & Putters, 2005, p. 750; Brandsen & Karré, 2011; Jay, 2013; Pache & Santos, 2010; Skelcher, 2012; Smith, 2010; Brandsen & Karré, 2011; Jay, 2013; Pache & Santos, 2010). From an empirical point of view every organization is in fact hybrid, because one hardly finds organizations not embracing both commercial and social elements (Skelcher, 2012); however, they differ in their degree and patterns of hybridity (see Glänzel & Schmitz, 2012; Schmitz & Glänzel, 2016).

Recently scholars have tried to describe hybrid organizational forms with the help of neo-institutional theory (Mason, Kirkbride, & Bryde, 2007; Pache & Santos, 2010; Skelcher & Smith, 2015) and use tensions between institutional logics as a point of departure (Purdy & Gray, 2009). An institutional logic is generally defined as "taken for granted social perceptions that guide actors' behavior (e.g., Friedland & Alford, 1991; Suddaby & Greenwood, 2005; Thornton, 2004; Thornton & Ocasio, 2008) in fields of activity" (Battilana & Dorado, 2010, p. 1419). From this perspective, financial hybrid organizations combine a banking or profit logic, targeting turnover and high margins on the one hand, and a solidarity logic that aims at helping marginalized groups, for example, with below-market-rate loans or even just access to the banking system. From a distinct social perspective, the greatest threat to such organizations is mission drift (e.g., Battilana & Dorado, 2010; Weisbrod, 1998), that is, giving up part of the social mission to generate more turnover and profits, or simply reducing complexity. In those cases the commercial logic becomes dominant over the other/s (see Selznick, 1949).

Scholars expect tensions and conflicts arising predominantly when organizational arrangements combine sector logics and therefore face conflicting institutional demands (Battilana & Dorado, 2010; Battilana et al., 2012; D'Aunno, Sutton, & Price, 1991; Pache & Santos, 2013; Zahra, Gedajlovic, Newbaum, & Shulman, 2009). In these cases demands from multiple stakeholder groups are hard to balance (Bridgstock et al., 2010). On the one hand, market or commercial logics hold hybrid organizations responsible for financial and overall economic success. On the other hand, hybrids have to fulfill demands according to social welfare or solidarity logics, that is, create social value at the same time (Doherty et al., 2014; Mullins, Czischke, & van Bortel, 2012; Pache & Santos, 2010; Schmitz & Glänzel, 2016; Thompson & Doherty, 2006; Tracey et al., 2011). Due to these conflicting demands, there are tensions arising calling for trade-offs within the organization (Doherty et al., 2014), but the nature of the tensions has rarely been explored in detail (Austin, Stevenson, & Wei-Skillern, 2006).

Besides conflicting institutional logics, financial hybrid organizations also face the "liability of newness" (Stinchcombe, 1965) in established institutional fields. In this respect, the main barrier they face to ensure organizational survival is to establish legitimacy (Suchman, 1995). Forms of isomorphism (DiMaggio & Powell, 1983) might not be appropriate to generate such legitimacy, as these would likely cause hybrid organizations to become purely commercial. Interventions that shape logics actively or that manipulate mechanisms have been underexposed in institutional theory (see Hirsch & Lounsbury, 1997; Walgenbach, 2006, p. 390). Most important exceptions to this are approaches that focus on "institutional entrepreneurs" (DiMaggio, 1988), such as academics, consultants, or social movements, who are the drivers for organizational change (see Czarniawska & Sevón, 1996; Sahlin-Andersson & Engwall, 2002; Scott, 2003).

Institutional entrepreneurs have been defined as "actors who are interested in particular institutional arrangements and who leverage resources to create new institutions or to transform existing ones" (Maguire, Hardy, & Lawrence, 2004, p. 657). They use multiple frames at hand, combine them and apply discursive strategies to alter the existing frames, justify projects and organizations, and maximize their resonance (Creed, Scully, & Austin, 2002; Suddaby & Greenwood, 2005). In this sense institutional entrepreneurs "create a whole new system of meaning that ties the functioning of disparate sets of institutions together" (Garud, Hardy, & Maguire, 2007). Institutional entrepreneurs break with existing norms, rules, and practices that are connected to the dominant institutional logic/s in the field and at the same time implement new rules, new norms, and new practices while rearranging the old ones, and therefore institutionalize these (Battilana, 2006; Garud & Karnøe, 2001; Leca, Battilana, & Boxenbaum, 2008). New institutions can arise "when organized actors with sufficient resources see in them an opportunity to realize interests that they value highly" (DiMaggio, 1988, p. 14).

From an institutional entrepreneurship perspective the discursive dimension is of crucial importance (e.g., Creed et al., 2002; De Holan & Phillips, 2002; Dorado, 2005; Fligstein, 1997, 2001; Hensmans, 2003; Lounsbury, Ventresca, & Hirsch, 2003; Maguire & Hardy, 2006; Rao, 1998; Rao, Morill, & Zald, 2000; Seo & Creed, 2002; Suddaby & Greenwood, 2005), because discourse is the most effective way to change institutions (Munir & Phillips, 2005, p. 1669; Phillips, Lawrence, & Hardy, 2004). Discourse can challenge and change taken-for-granted perceptions and reframe situations (Habermas, 1981). Maguire et al. (2004) distinguish three discursive strategies being used for institutional transformation: (1) occupation of positions with wide legitimacy and bridging diverse stakeholders; (2) theorization of new practices; and (3) connecting these practices to stakeholders' routines and values. Most importantly, institutional entrepreneurs intentionally and actively import and translate discourses and communicative signals from other arenas (Boxenbaum, 2006; Creed et al., 2002; Lawrence & Phillips, 2004). In this sense, Doherty et al. (2014, p. 431) recently stated:

> In practice, this means that the strategy development process will involve time and resources devoted to networking, communicating, lobbying and negotiating with stakeholders to achieve a consensus on key issues to avoid mission drift, build and retain legitimacy contemporaneously with developing new approaches to mobilize financial resources and manage people.

Particularly in the financial sector, this latter aspect has become of utmost importance, as this sector has been facing a severe legitimacy crisis (Benedikter, 2011).

In the following subsections, we analyze the communication channels and strategies of three cases of hybrid organizations active in finance and banking. We argue that hybrids send and receive signals as other types of organizations do too; concerning stakeholder management, this is what hybrids have in common with conventional organizations as laid out by stakeholder theory (Freeman, 1984; etc.), that is, hybrids have the same communication channels. However, what we assume is that for hybrid organizations both quality and quantity of what is transmitted through these channels differ significantly. Trust and integrity are created due to communication and transparency. And both are important for organizations in the field of social finance (Achleitner, Lutz, Mayer, & Spiess-Knafl, 2013; Harrison, Dibben, & Mason, 1997).

Charity Bank

In 2002, Charity Bank (CB) was registered in Tonbridge, Kent, UK, with the central objective to collect funds from investors and act as a bank for community development projects and organizations that are underfinanced due to commercial banks' reluctance to serve them. As its name indicates, CB at that time was registered and regulated both as a bank and charity, the rationale being governance aspects and the goal to go to scale as a bank while continually and dependably serve its social mission in close co-operation with its major stakeholders: customers/borrowers and investors/depositors.

As a result, the organization has enjoyed dual legitimacy and trust: As a bank it has been trusted to manage funds professionally and efficiently, and as a charity it has been believed to effectively contribute to the common welfare. Five years after its foundation, CB had grown the original capital of GBP 500,000 into GBP 6.4 million; the organization had lent to about 200 organizations and had not lost any money by that time.

In detail, hybridity consists in combining two interrelated processes: First, ensure a level of trust and accountability necessary for receiving donations or equivalent for a social cause (fundraising principle of charities); and second, leverage that disposition by raising the initial level of trust through both effective investment and repayment of the funds (banking principle).

> [I]t seemed to us from the market research we did that if somebody was willing to give away a pound they would be probably willing to lend us ten pounds.
>
> *(Interviewee 1)*

CB is capable of initiating this leverage mechanism, because it is trusted as an effective and accountable banking institution in which people actually deposit more than they would donate: They can expect to get their money back, and the money is committed to an effective financial recycling circle, that is, it can make an impact several times. This process thus increases two critical dimensions: First, the amount of total funds people are willing to make available for investment, because these funds are withdrawable and therefore remain assets of the depositor; and second, the funds' total impact increases in relation to donations, because they are recycled and thus impact the charitable sector repeatedly; proof of that impact in turn increases potential depositors' willingness to invest and so forth.

CB invites charitable sector organizations to apply for a loan if they meet certain criteria. CB has these applications assessed by two groups of professionals each representing one of the spheres outlined above: There are banking professionals evaluating the economic viability of the project to be financed and the so-called assessors, that is, people providing the necessary experience in and knowledge of the charitable sector. It is the joint responsibility of these two groups to balance credit risk with the social benefit of making loans and the source and/or generate information on which investment decisions can be taken and communicated to investors:

> There is a problem in the third sector that organizations are very poor in general about providing financial information. But it's also about a level of relationship with the borrower. For them to understand why we need this information. We start from the point of view that when they come to approach us in the first place we need to understand what they need the money for. (…) [I]f we don't get this information we won't have money to lend because then people won't invest in us.
>
> *(Interviewee 1)*

So CB co-operates and interacts closely with borrowers in order to get to know about the applicants' business and social case, and what performance indicators can be provided to evidence effectiveness. This part is crucial to build a close and lasting relationship based in the flows of information necessary to manage hybridity:

> I mean if an organization has a great mission but it does not have a robust financial model we would try and suggest ways that it could become more robust. (...) That tension between, if you like, the mission and the money is very often the root of [problems] and we really do have to walk trustees through this and get them to understand why it's helping to strengthen the organization even if it's not attractive to them.
>
> *(Interviewee 1)*

So besides the economic risk, the "social risk," that is, the risk of failing to make a social impact, has to be assessed and communicated accurately; that adds vastly to the total complexity of assessing risk. Concerning risk, CB differs significantly from mainstream banks: While of course complying with the same rules of the FSA, CB takes risks that these institutions avoid (ceteris paribus)—if these risks are compensated for through potential social impact. That potential is not accounted for by mainstream banks' credit calculations, yet constitutes a central factor in CB's assessment. That translates into a rather unfavorable risk-and-return ratio from a banking perspective which CB strives to compensate for by the intensely close co-operation with borrowers. And that "handholding" also builds another constituent of investor relations:

> [I]n this market place if you don't do that your risk just rises. So, you have two choices: you are to provide for much larger loss rate or you do the handholding. And I worry if we provide for much higher loss rates although depositors won't lose out, psychologically if they see us making larger losses every year they would begin to question the safety of their deposits.
>
> *(Interviewee 1)*

Such short-term economic trade-offs for long-term socio-economic win-win results based on communication make up CB's hybrid business model. It is to assure (a) economic success of borrowers and (b) legitimacy and the trust required for attracting new capital for growth.

So CB investors are also integrative constituents of this communicative strategy.

> We want to select investors who we can work together with, so that there is engaged investment; it's not just a passive investment. So we are looking at organizations who have similar objectives to us; who may become co-investors in deals that we do; who may have skills or introduction sources that can help us and we can help them. So it's around a growing relationship rather than a passive relationship.
>
> *(Interviewee 1)*

From the credit committee's individual members and their discussions and decisions, hybridity is spread throughout various spheres around that origin; it is forwarded to external actors in the course of negotiations about terms, conditions, and objectives of the loan agreement as well as by means of "handholding" through which the borrower learns about the hybrid rationale behind the loan. The loan is tied or leads to hybridization of the borrower organization (if not present already). The same holds true for (potential) investors: They have to understand the hybrid rationale either in advance or through learning about them. And new capital is attracted by communicating the success of the business model as well as overall transparency and accountability.

Oikocredit

Oikocredit was founded in 1975 as a co-operative in the Netherlands with the initial idea to supply the poor in developing countries with affordable credit finance instead of non-returnable development aid. Today it is one of the world's largest sources of private funding to the microfinance sector, also providing credit to trade co-operatives, fair trade organizations, and SMEs:

> Our main goal is to provide resources for poor people, but not to give away the money, but to use the money for these people now for a certain period of time, and they pay back, and then we use it for the next group of people. So, it's a sort of recycling process.
>
> *(Interviewee 2)*

Founding members were Europe's Catholic and Protestant churches, while today other important member groups are supporter associations in various European countries. Despite its share ownership structure, Oikocredit is governed through a one-member-one-vote principle; this extent of hybridity is unusual for a financial institution:

> But first of all, we are a corporative society, so in that sense, [the organization] already has some [hybrid] aspects in its structure. [Being] a corporative society with members, one member, one vote (...) is a special feature (...) for an organization involved in the sector where we are, in the financial world.
>
> *(Interviewee 2)*

Most of Oikocredit's capital (more than 80 percent) comes from the 34 support associations and their 30,000 individual members worldwide. Support associations are located in Europe (Austria, Belgium, Denmark, France, Germany, Italy, the Netherlands, Spain, Sweden, and Switzerland), in the Americas (Canada, the United States, Mexico, and Uruguay), and in Asia (Japan, Korea, and the Philippines). The largest investor groups are those from Germany (~17,000), followed by the Netherlands (~9,000), Switzerland, Austria, and the US (~2,000 each). They are permanently provided with information about Oikocredit's operations and important developments. Through this channel, Oikocredit can generate and increase awareness well beyond its organizational boundaries and immediate scope. Thus, individual investors provide not only financial but also social capital, that is, important ties with Oikocredit's wider societal environment. To maintain, cultivate, and enhance these relations that go well beyond investor relations common in the financial sector, Oikocredit proactively seeks to "nourish" them with information as regards questions such as: Is Oikocredit reaching the poor? Are interest rates fair? How can we be sure loans alleviate poverty rather than creating over-indebtedness? What broader impact is made? But also, how stable are financial performance and sound risk management? Yet to Oikocredit, it is important to facilitate and enhance the smooth flow of information in both directions; that is, Oikocredit also values and actively seeks feedback from investors by arranging open dialogue with them regularly.

Oikocredit considers its *raison d'être* in its role as a unique kind of risk-taker:

> And when I talk about risk-taker, it's mainly a financial risk-taker. The banks take risks maybe here, and then there are maybe some sorts of development banks that go here, but we go still a bit further than those in financial risks. That's why we exist; otherwise, we wouldn't have any role, the banks can do it. So, we are really taking a lot of risk, financial risk, but of course there is a limit. (…) [W]e have to also make a little bit of return for our investors and also for our balance sheet.
>
> *(Interviewee 2)*

To determine an economically and socially reasonable and justifiable relation of risk and return is the organization's most critical internal task. Depending on the volume of the potential investment, the identified project risk needs to be balanced with Oikocredit's total risks, particularly liquidity risk and country risk; one decisive change of strategy in Oikocredit's history consisted in acknowledging and coping with these requirements more professionally: "We have emphasized more professionalism and more financial expertise in analyzing projects (…)" (Interviewee 2).

These social and financial risk professionals engage with investees to assess their particular needs. Thus, both due diligence and also later the investment process requires an extensive degree of transparency (to create a common language and a common pool of knowledge) and flexible co-operation. In this sense, Oikocredit distinguishes itself from competitors as to the following communication strategies with its primary stakeholder groups:

- By favoring small and young MFIs in its investment decisions Oikocredit takes a high-risk strategy. Yet they themselves are closer to beneficiaries actually needing microfinance, and these close communicative ties yield more potential for social impact, because they understand the actual needs.
- Providing technical/business assistance to its microfinance partners is another distinguishing communicative strategy of Oikocredit and a structural ingredient in connecting social and economic practices and goals.
- Systematically assessing and communicating risks of over-indebtedness of MFIs' clients is an attempt to fight this problem, which is one of the major threats to the entire MF sector and to the very concept.
- The organization has many regional and country offices run by locals; that is, rather costly, yet strengthens communicative strategies, and thus tightens the relationships with the local community and the beneficiaries.

All these efforts for increased transparency and proactive communication with numerous stakeholders generate costs, reduce the profitability, or increase the risk of finance business transactions while at the same time increasing the economic sustainability of the lenders. Oikocredit selects these lenders according to their need and their potential for social impact, while its competitors often select rigidly according to favorable risk-and-return ratios ("cherry picking").

Nevertheless, the economic viability must be ensured; but Oikocredit rather works on enhancing creditors' viability by co-operating with them to promote their economic progress.

As to the investors' side, although most of them seek an economically secure investment, people and institutions invest in Oikocredit primarily for it to achieve social impact: "They do it because we make them believe in what we are doing. They believe that their money can do something good somewhere, and that's why they want to put their money here (…)" (Interviewee 2).

To communicate and evidence that impact, the organization has implemented a social performance management (SPM) system which is permanently improved and complemented through the development of new SPM tools. The recent establishment of what is called the social performance and financial analysis department documents both the importance of the issue and how closely intertwined social and economic impact are for Oikocredit's relations with investors.

Oikocredit puts much effort into building up trust and loyalty through transparency. It is the first MF investor to undergo a full audit by CERISE, a French knowledge exchange network NGO auditing MF institutions, and Oikocredit in turn applies CERISE's social audit tools to some of its MF partner institutions in order to evaluate their performance and to jointly identify ways to improve it. Oikocredit's social performance and financial analysis department has developed a comprehensive social performance and capacity-building strategy to illustrate the relations between its closest stakeholder groups at five levels:

- Beneficiaries: Promote transparency about interest rates and risk of indebtedness.
- Project partners: Increasing awareness for SPM within the investee MF institutions offers capacity-building support.
- Oikocredit's own operations: Make social impact internally and ensure staff everywhere, are well informed about related issues.
- The MF industry: Commitment to co-operate with other organizations in the field to develop and promote SPM, to address industry issues, and to initiate joint industry efforts.
- Investors: Most of the output of its SPM assessments is made available to investors and used to attract new ones.

This last point illustrates how closely Oikocredit's organizational output and input interfaces are connected: Delivering a social return means for Oikocredit to make its operations and impact transparent in a comprehensive and assuring way. To extend transparency as far along forward in the value chain as possible is an integral part of Oikocredit's operating model. That is, hybridity must be made transparent along the entire value chain. So to a large extent SPM is a governance tool to make hybridity visible within its investment cycle; therefore, it is a governance tool for communicating and extending hybridity to actors beyond its own organizational boundaries, yet within its immediate reach. Therefore, its hybridity is "forwarded" to and also shaped by them. Oikocredit has put much effort into increasing this interaction also on a governance level, that is, through having an effective and representative board elected by its shareholders:

> [W]e also emphasized more that the board has to have certain expertise. And we have listed a number of areas that they have to be experts in, like finance, development, communication, strategic communication, ecumenical things, and things like that we have to be represented in the board. So and secondly comes the geographic distribution.
>
> *(Interviewee 2)*

So Oikocredit's strategies and practices are determined in co-operation with these stakeholders with which Oikocredit maintains direct and regular relations. The co-operative legal form ensures and fosters this sort of interaction:

> [T]he members' voice is so strong, and the members are members because of a certain commitment or a certain similarity in a co-operative, that's why they are in

> this co-operative. (...) So, we have to have a dialogue, regular dialogue with the supporters, with the members on certain issues.
>
> *(Interviewee 2)*

Beyond this realm, however, Oikocredit aims at making an impact as well: "We are interested in that it has a broader impact on the society" (Interviewee 2).

Yet the organization does not target society as a whole; it concentrates on its own fields, that is, finance and development, and the actors in these fields. In particular, within the MF industry and its various networks and associations, Oikocredit follows a strategy of co-operation instead of competition: "For example in this country, we have a platform of micro-finance funders. We meet regularly and discuss issues, discuss developments, discuss co-operation. So, it's not the fierce competition at all" (Interviewee 2).

By "radiating" hybridity through these channels, Oikocredit leverages its resources to achieve a higher social impact in relatively distant societal spaces. Most of these policies are communicative efforts that generate effects through the joint efforts of many different actors. While the attraction of profit-oriented investors by the MF industry has been discussed quite controversially, Oikocredit networks with like-minded actors to influence the development of the industry.

Regionalwert AG

Regionalwert AG[1] (RWAG) was founded as an incorporated company in 2006 in order to collect funds from investors and to provide finance to agricultural operations in the region of Freiburg, Germany. It combines two parallel and interrelated goals: First, economic return generation; and second, a socio-ecological return based on a sophisticated set of agricultural, social, and environmental indicators. By establishing and stimulating stakeholder dialogues along and around the entire agricultural value chain, RWAG pursues broad and long-term objectives such as building regional networks, enhancing community development, and increasing awareness for socio-economic value creation in a regional environment.

In the early 1990s, RWAG's founder Christian Hiß and some like-minded individuals held regular meetings for 1–2 days, bringing together participants from various fields besides agriculture, for example academia, retailers, community politics, etc. The goal was to have as many potential stakeholders as possible to identify deficits in agricultural production and distribution. Based on these discussions an actionable idea was derived: Both intended and unintended consequences of agriculture have to be measured continuously and integrated into a new approach to do agriculture.

Further discussions and systematic research indicated that an innovative type of organization had to be set up, an organization to connect input and output interfaces on the basis of an altered, more holistic concept of agriculture. The most suitable type of organization was found in the corporation with its unique "power of capital" (Hiß), that is, its capability to promote action based on serious and binding forms of communication between investors and investees. The obligation to continuously generate and deliver necessary information establishes the basis for communication and empowers shareholders to get involved in decision-making:

> That was the trick, not to find some but the organizational form most powerful and dynamic, determining conditions worldwide: corporations. This I wanted to get hold of. The corporation bears [this power] in its form, and I employ it for socio-ecologically sustainable developments.
>
> *(Interviewee 3)*

The foundation of RWAG in 2006, therefore, followed 15 years of focused meetings and discussions, and 3 years of research to finalize the organizational concept. So the initial idea for the organization was developed in a discursive way actively involving multiple perspectives from the public:

> That is very essential to me, and this entire story has this character. So, [an issue] is exposed to the public space or to the semi-public I would say, and then the contents are worked on. And that was special about our discussion meetings: To open that space for people to speak.
>
> *(Interviewee 3)*

Ever since, the corporation has sought to gain and exert influence on companies along the entire agricultural value chain to promote and secure an ecologically and socially sustainable agriculture and food production in the Freiburg region. By connecting various nodes of the chain, RWAG seeks to build a regional network of producers, processors, and distributors of agricultural products. RWAG's targeted investors are actors in the region and that makes the overall goal of the organization clear: Building a co-operative type of network connection between all involved in the value chain; and opening space to jointly discuss the production and distribution of values along the chain:

> We want to get access to retail and wholesale, actually we have already. (…) [Our] business forum is another instrument for us to get all entrepreneurs involved together every two months, retailers, wholesalers, farmers. And they all have to report. That is an obligation. (…) And then [value distribution] should get more explicit, who gets what?
>
> *(Interviewee 3)*

So the businesses involved in the network discuss the distribution of values (economic and socio-ecological) generated in the network which they produce and receive as businesses. All investors in RWAG shares accept a typically below-market financial return in exchange for a "double return" with socio-ecological value parameters besides financial ones; the relationship between the two value sets is also to be negotiated by shareholders and laid down in operating criteria which serve as targets for the tenants and other businesses RWAG holds shares in. So by means of intermediation by RWAG, the community and its agricultural environment and value chain are linked to communicate about their relationship as investors and investees:

> So to stick to the [operating] criteria is part of the partnership or tenancy agreement. And what's special about this is that [RWAG] does not prescribe criteria, instead we rather provide the [underlying] indicators. And what's mandatory is the reporting duty. That is very important to me. And if a business has problems concerning socio-ecological indicators, then the entrepreneur has to report, enter discourse, discussion, debate with our shareholders. (…) I rather want people to have discussions about actual situations than RWAG to prescribe the way how to do things. (…) Then you simply have to enter the discussion and also so to speak help your partner do the first step.
>
> *(Interviewee 3)*

The form of investment RWAG heads for depends on the financial, organizational, and/or legal situation of the investment assets as well as the needs and competencies of their designated tenant. RWAG may supply equity capital and dormant equity capital, invest in partners' interest shares, or buy entire agricultural, food production, and/or distribution companies.

> So we have applications of entrepreneurs whose approaches and ideas we value. Yet the entrepreneur has little capital and thus cannot bear much of the risk, and his management skills are limited. This is a case I would say for us to go in with partnership shares, with a vote, in order to have a formal senior management role [in the business]. (...) In some cases shares with voting power are appropriate.
>
> *(Interviewee 3)*

It is one of RWAG's precepts to provide the tenant with as much entrepreneurial freedom as possible. However, tenants are mostly farmers or gardeners lacking business skills. To compensate for these deficits, RWAG may provide experience and consulting services. The composition of the competencies, resources, and requirements of an object and its tenant forms the basis on which risk and an appropriate investment instrument are assessed. That is also done jointly and discursively: "We have to develop common business plans. (...) [Co-operation on business issues] is a laborious, also joyful, process, important and constructive, but it is long (...)" (Interviewee 3).

With the goal of connecting all individual and organizational actors involved in regional agriculture utilizing the "power" of capital, RWAG continuously develops its set of indicators. With the aim of vastly increasing both the amount and the quality of information about value chains and their externalities, RWAG and its partners aim to use this information for improving production processes, for education and showcasing, and most importantly for attracting and satisfying investors interested in active involvement.

> So, a very important instrument [of investor relations] is our business reporting. (...) The main instrument for dialogue is to make sure that the reporting is differentiated and sophisticated. That is very important. Then the second major instrument is the general assembly and to open the room for discussion there. (...) We are planning a symposium for shareholders to take place annually, to deal with issues in depth, value chain and the like.
>
> *(Interviewee 3)*

So this reporting innovation is an integral part of RWAG's major organizational innovation. RWAG has re-functionalized (Padgett & McLean, 2006, p. 1468) the "glue" of financial capital and put it to a new use, not confined to the field of agriculture but rather applicable to meet several community needs (Christian Hiß imagines, for instance, that a community's water supply could be handled in a similar way). The corporate organizational form based on financial capital has been combined with co-operative-type organizational characteristics and goals. The result of this recombination is a highly innovative type of organization utilizing the best attributes of both organizational types: It has the strong interest power of financial capital combined with the integrative and communicative features of a co-operative.

Discussion

Our data supports our hypothesis that hybrid organizations in general and social finance hybrids in particular communicate in distinct qualities and quantities with different types of stakeholders. They do inject social elements in investment and legitimize this hybridization through proactive and targeted communication. Therefore, a central element of organizational hybridity consists of communication, and an important ingredient to the success of hybrid organizations is communicating about hybridity and what it takes to implement it—that is, establishing legitimacy through communication. Legitimacy in turn may take different forms, in our case mainly "market legitimacy" and "social legitimacy": By providing business development support, financial hybrids help to develop sustainable business models, that is, to establish market legitimacy; and by constantly ensuring social impact, they establish social legitimacy. By doing "handholding" and maintaining close stakeholder relationships, hybrid organizations under investigation are all able to influence stakeholders to implement hybridity. And by communicating systematically they are successfully managing key stakeholder relations. Yet even more important are integrative activities: Through the communicative processes and stakeholder involvement, various expectations can be balanced and streamlined. A conception of hybrid capital and investment is communicated throughout the various interaction spheres to gain broad legitimacy for this conception and also the practices and actions required for making it real. That is, legitimacy is established to activate stakeholders to contribute their part to the success of the hybrid investment process.

Table 23.1 depicts the various types of stakeholders with whom social finance hybrids may communicate in fulfilling their hybrid missions. Table 23.1 also shows the influence the organizations exert on other actors regarding hybridity in different interaction spheres: internal communication, interaction with stakeholders of different degrees of closeness, and communication with parts of society at large. It also illustrates what this influence consists of, how it is executed, and how in turn external signals and influences are taken up and processed.

So the hybrids under investigation here are concentrating on the interaction sphere, while concentration and influence here do not leave the other spheres unaffected. On the contrary, as we have seen, hybrid organizations in finance first need to be clear internally about their own conception of hybridity in investment. So from the internal sphere and the intra-organizational communication we may derive a first proposition to guide further research and financial hybrid organizations' practices:

> Proposition 1: Financial hybrid organizations need to be clear internally what their own conception of hybridity is. That is, they must know and communicate internally about their social and their financial objectives and how to bring the two together sustainably.

But then also this concept of hybridity must be communicated to key stakeholders in the various interaction spheres. This process must be supported systematically and strategically, as we see that our sample organizations differ significantly concerning their target audiences, the stakeholder groups, and thus as to the composition of the institutional fields they seek to shape: We see the field of local food production and retail chains in one example (RWAG), nonprofit social services mostly in the urban UK community field (CB), and also a field in which actors from Christian faith-based communities engage to improve the lives of people in poorer countries (Oikocredit). So the composition of actors on investor and investee sides is marked by some apparent similarities concerning hybridity, but they also differ significantly as to their socio-economic contexts, rationales, motives, etc., that is, their institutional logics. Based on this, we formulate our second proposition:

> Proposition 2: Financial hybrid organizations need to have and implement a communication strategy targeted towards and tailored specifically for different types of stakeholders. Thus in total, they will have to communicate more (in terms of quantity) and also in more diverse ways (in terms of quality), emphasizing different aspects of their concept of hybridity when addressing different stakeholders.

Table 23.1 Overview of the interaction spheres relevant for the cases presented

	Internal; intra-organizational	*Interactive; spheres of direct influence on/from and interaction with individual and organizational actors*			*Societal*
		Interactive I	*Interactive II*	*Interactive III*	
Modes/ objectives of interaction	Day-to-day business; regular and irregular internal meetings	Regular direct interaction with chartered influence; strong and direct (financial) interest	Regular direct interaction w/out strong/direct, but with considerable/indirect influence/interest	Irregular direct contact; relatively weak and/or diffuse interest, yet (at least partly) observable/ expected indirect influence	Generally no direct observable influence or interaction of the organization on the societal level; yet significant influence in the opposite direction, and (at least partly) the organizational intention to shape this level over the long-run
RWAG	Development/ improvement of indicator model; balance economic with social risks and opportunities in investment decisions; prepare discussion and determination of operating criteria to be implemented for abstract shareholder goals in day-to-day agricultural business	Input (shareholder-directed) and output (tenant-directed) hybridity, connected through the "power of capital" as the sustainable and long-term binding force between investors and investees, based on which to discuss, and jointly determine desirable relation between economic and socio-ecological objectives; output hybridity: collaboratively implement operating criteria in day-to-day agricultural business	Value chain actors; tenure applicants	Community; local agriculture; local food industry	Communities, agriculture, and food industry on regional, national, and EU levels; parts of academia

(Continued)

Table 23.1 Overview of the interaction spheres relevant for the cases presented *(Continued)*

	Internal; intra-organizational	*Interactive; spheres of direct influence on/from and interaction with individual and organizational actors*			*Societal*
		Interactive I	*Interactive II*	*Interactive III*	
Oikocredit	Risk-taker: balance economic and social risks with opportunities based on sound and sophisticated discussion and collaborative due diligence by personnel with widely differing professional backgrounds	Input (member-/investor-directed) and output (lender-directed) hybridity: transparency (social performance measurement) and "handholding" (consulting/professionalization) to "radiate" hybridity; co-operations with other hybrids and hybrid change agents	MF markets; beneficiary affiliates. "Radiate" downward (investor-related) hybridity by communicating investment goals, impacts, and best practices; "radiate" upward hybridity (lender-related: MFIs, etc.); by providing support in capacity building and business development	Inner church communities; wider beneficiary community (17.5 m); investment market; MF/SRI scene	Christian community, financial markets (particularly SRI-/MF-affiliated market sectors); parts of academia
Charity Bank	Assess and discuss economic risk and social opportunities taking account of the organization's growth objective; collaborate on (financial and social) due diligence; prepare credit committee decisions	Input (saver-/investor-directed) hybridity: social impact measurement and communication of results; output (borrower-directed) hybridity: "handholding" (consulting/professionalization)	Charity and social finance/banking sectors. Attract large sums of capital from savers and institutional investors for financial recycling/leverage	Local charities; SRI scene; some sectors of regular banking	Regional/national charities; financial markets (particularly SRI-/MF-affiliated market sectors); parts of academia

Also we see that legal forms are an interesting factor, both concerning the flows of communication (how regular does information have to be provided, how obligatory are which types of information, what are decision-making and governance based on, etc.?) and for protection against mission drift. As we have seen, the danger of a mission drift is bigger when competitive pressure from purely commercial actors threatens the economic bottom-line of hybrids. It might then be tempting to also go for more lucrative deals, sometimes laying less emphasis on social impact. Oikocredit's one-member-one-vote governance ensures some balance between the members and avoids single members becoming too powerful and pushing the organization towards singular interests or a too commercial orientation. Not being registered as a bank decouples it from strict reporting regulations. In contrast, as a stock corporation RWAG does face tight reporting requirements, but it does so willingly in order to exploit the bonding capacity of investment capital. Instead of a one-member-one-vote decision-making process, RWAG is set up to exploit the strong interests people connect to their money—they should get involved and engage, and the more money they invest, the more they should actually be eager to do so.

So overall among our sample, RWAG appears to seek the closest ties between investors and investees, and it employs investment capital as a tool to let both parties co-determine the hybrid character of their business. In comparison, Oikocredit ties less voting power to the amount of capital an individual investor has brought in, but together the total of shareholders remains key in decision-making, and voting power remains with them. In the case of CB, the situation is a bit different: Here decision-making and voting power are with a credit committee, that is, shareholder investors do have a direct say, yet the other major investor group (depositors) does not. Therefore, we see three quite different forms and also the communicative directions of stakeholder involvement in shaping hybrid strategies. This leads to different types of options for hybrids to involve actors who help them in remaining sustainable (banking and business experts) while at the same time reducing risks of mission drift (non-profit actors).

Our third proposition is based on this observation:

> Proposition 3: Different legal forms and related governance structures are important elements in building and implementing hybridity, as they can be used to involve necessary stakeholders to various degrees.

Further research will have to shed light onto how these differing legal forms and related governance structures affect the long-term development of hybridity in finance and banking as to its chances of success and resilience against crises, such as strong commercial competitors.

Conclusion

Hybrid organizations active in (social) finance communicate more and also in more heterogeneous ways. To make hybrid investment processes successful, they have seen the need to establish legitimacy in order to activate stakeholders and make them contribute actively to the success of social investment processes. Our three cases of hybrids in finance have revealed some important hints to understand how.

Through a theoretic lens we may conclude that combining a commercial and solidarity logic creates a field in which actors face at least two very distinct kinds of institutional demands. They must be commercially successful under conditions of strong competition (very much often from purely commercial competitors), while at the same time they need to evidence that they do not fall victim to the threat of mission drift. This causes severe tensions that hybrid organizations have to cope with both internally and externally. They do so by making the nature of these tensions explicit through systematic communication about them, addressing stakeholders' specific institutional demands in very much targeted ways, and thus shaping institutional logics proactively as "institutional entrepreneurs."

Communicative strategies are therefore central aspects of organizational hybridity, because it requires addressing hybrid organizations' "liability of newness" and establishing legitimacy when taken-for-granted practices and cognitive frames are challenged. The framework we suggest may help to distinguish these strategies as to the institutional closeness and distance of various kinds of stakeholders to any organization under observation. It may also provide hints about how these organizations use transparency as a strategic tool, importing and translating discourses and communicative signals from multiple fields. Further research may be worthwhile to shed more light on what are the exact constituents of the arising institutional field of social finance as compared to more established ones (Thornton, 2004; Thornton & Ocasio, 2008).

Note

1 The German legal form AG represents a stock corporation.

References

Achleitner, A.-K., Lutz, E., Mayer, J., & Spiess-Knafl, W. (2013). Disentangling gut feeling: Assessing the integrity of social entrepreneurs. *Voluntas, 24*, 93–124.

Anheier, H. K., & Then, V. (2004). *Zwischen Eigennutz und Gemeinwohl: Neue Formen und Wege der Gemeinnützigkeit*. Güthersloh: Verlag Bertelsmann Stiftung.

Austin, J., Stevenson, H., & Wei-Skillern, J. (2006). Social and commercial entrepreneurship: Same, different or both? *Entrepreneurship Theory and Practice, 30*, 1–22.

Battilana, J. (2006). Agency and institutions: The enabling role of individuals' social position. *Organization, 13*(5), 653–676.

Battilana, J., & Dorado, S. (2010). Building sustainable hybrid organizations: The case of commercial microfinance organizations. *Academy of Management Journal, 53*, 1419–1440.

Battilana, J., Lee, M., Walker, J., & Dorsey, C. (2012). In search of the hybrid ideal. *Stanford Social Innovation Review, 10*(3), 51–55.

Benedikter, R. (2011). *Social banking and social finance: Answers to the economic crisis*. New York: Springer.

Billis, D. (Ed.). (2010). *Hybrid organizations and the third sector: Challenges for practice, theory and policy*. New York: Palgrave Macmillan.

Boxenbaum, E. (2006). Lost in translation: The making of Danish diversity management. *American Behavioral Scientist, 49*(7), 939–948.

Boyd, B., Henning, N., Reyna, E., Wang, D. E., & Welch, M. D. (2009). *Hybrid organizations: New business model for environmental leadership*. Sheffield: Greenleaf.

Brandsen, T., & Karré, P. M. (2011). Hybrid organizations: No cause for concern. *International Journal of Public Administration, 34*, 827–836.

Brandsen, T., van de Donk, W., & Putters, K. (2005). Griffins or chameleons? Hybridity as a permanent and inevitable characteristic of the third sector. *International Journal of Public Administration, 28*(9–10), 749–765.

Bridgstock, R., Lettice, F. M., Özbilgin, M. F., & Tatli, A. (2010). Diversity management for innovation in social enterprises in the UK. *Entrepreneurship & Regional Development, 22*, 557–574.

Bromberger, A. R. (2011, Spring). A new type of hybrid. *Stanford Social Innovation Review*, 49–53.

Creed, W. E. D., Scully, M., & Austin, J. (2002). Clothes make the person? The tailoring of legitimating accounts and the social construction of identity. *Organization Science, 13*(5), 475–496.

Czarniawska, B., & Sevón, G. (1996). *Translating organizational change*. Berlin and New York: De Gruyter.

D'Aunno, T., Sutton, R. I., & Price, R. (1991). Isomorphism and external support in conflicting institutional environments: A study of drug abuse treatment centers. *Academy of Management Journal, 34*, 636–661.

Dees, J. G., & Anderson, B. B. (2003). Sector-bending: Blurring lines between nonprofit and for-profit. *Society, 40*(4), 16–27.

Dees, J. G., Emerson, J., & Economy, P. (2004). *Strategic tools for social entrepreneurs: Enhancing the performance of your enterprising nonprofit* (Vol. 207). New York: John Wiley & Sons.

De Holan, P. M., & Phillips, N. (2002). Managing in transition: A case study of institutional management and organizational change. *Journal of Managing Inquiry, 11*(1), 68–83.

DiMaggio, P. J. (1988). Interest and agency in institutional theory. In L. G. Zucker (Ed.), *Institutional patterns and organizations* (pp. 3–21). Cambridge, MA: Ballinger.

DiMaggio, P. J., & Powell, W. W. (1983). The iron cage revisited: Institutional isomorphism and collective rationality in organizational fields. *American Sociological Review, 48*(2), 147–160.

Doherty, B., Haugh, H., & Lyon, F. (2014). Social enterprises as hybrid organizations: A review and research agenda. *International Journal of Management Reviews, 16*(4), 417–436.

Dorado, S. (2005). Institutional entrepreneurship, partaking, and convening. *Organization Studies, 26*(3), 383–413.

Evers, A. (2008). Hybrid organizations: Background, concept, challenges. In S. P. Osborne (Ed.), *The third sector in Europe: Prospects and challenges* (pp. 279–292). Abingdon: Routledge.

Fligstein, N. (1997). Social skill and institutional theory. *American Behavioral Scientist, 40*(4), 397–405.

Fligstein, N. (2001). Social skills and the theory of fields. *Sociological Theory, 19*(2), 105–125.

Freeman, E. R. (1984). *Strategic management: A stakeholder approach.* Boston, MA: Pitman.

Friedland, R., & Alford, R. R. (1991). Bringing society back in: Symbols, practices, and institutional contradictions. In W. W. Powell & P. J. DiMaggio (Eds.), *The new institutionalism in organizational analysis* (pp. 2320–2363). Chicago, IL: University of Chicago Press.

Glänzel, G., Krlev, G., Schmitz, B., & Mildenberger, G. (2013). *Report on the feasibility and opportunities of using various instruments for capitalizing social innovators.* A deliverable of the project: "The theoretical, empirical and policy foundations for building social innovation in Europe" (TEPSIE). European Commission: 7th Framework Programme, DG Research, Brussels.

Habermas, J. (1981). *Theorie des kommunikativen Handelns* [2 Bände]. Frankfurt/Main: Suhrkamp.

Harrison, R. T., Dibben, M. R., & Mason, C. M. (1997). The role of trust in the informal investor's investment decision: An exploratory analysis. *Entrepreneurship Theory & Practice, 21*(4), 63–81.

Harvey, B. (1995). Ethical banking: The case of the Co-operative Bank. *Journal of Business Ethics, 14*(12), 1005–1013.

Hensmans, M. (2003). Social movement organizations: A metaphor for strategic actors in institutional fields. *Organization Studies, 24*(3), 355–382.

Hirsch, P. M., & Lounsbury, M. (1997). Ending the family quarrel: Toward a reconciliation of "old" and "new" institutionalism. *American Behavioral Scientist, 40*, 406–418.

Jäger, U., & Schröer, A. (2013). Integrated organizational identity: A definition of hybrid organizations and a research agenda. *Voluntas, 25*, 1281–1306.

Jay, J. (2013). Navigating paradox as a mechanism of change and innovation in hybrid organizations. *Academy of Management Journal, 56*(1), 137–159.

Garrow, E., & Hasenfeld, Y. (2010). Theoretical approaches to human service organizations. *Human Services as Complex Organizations, 2*, 33–58.

Garud, R., Hardy, C., & Maguire, S. (2007). Institutional entrepreneurship as embedded agency: An introduction to the special issue. *Organization Studies, 28*(7), 957–969.

Garud, R., & Karnøe, P. (2001). Path creation as a process of mindful deviation. In R. Garud & P. Karnøe (Eds.), *Path and dependence and creation* (pp. 1–38). Mahwah, NJ: Lawrence Earlbaum Associates.

Glänzel, G., & Schmitz, B. (2012). Hybride organisationen: Spezial- oder Regelfall? In H. Anheier, A. Schröer, & V. Then (Eds.), *Soziale investitionen* (pp. 181–203). Wiesbaden: VS Verlag.

Huybrechts, B., & Defourny, J. (2008). Are fair trade organisations necessarily social enterprises? *Social Enterprise Journal, 4*(3), 186–201.

Lawrence, T. B., & Phillips, N. (2004). From Moby Dick to Free Willy: Macro-cultural discourse and institutional entrepreneurship in emerging institutional fields. *Organization Studies, 11*(5), 689–711.

Leca, B., Battilana, J., & Boxenbaum, E. (2008). *Agency and institutions: A review of institutional entrepreneurship* (HBS Working Paper 08-096). Boston, MA: Harvard Business School, Harvard.

Lounsbury, M., Ventresca, M. J., & Hirsch, P. M. (2003). Social movements, field frames and industry emergence: A cultural perspective on US recycling. *Socio-Economic Review, 1*, 71–104.

Maguire, S., & Hardy, C. (2006). The emergence of new global institutions: A discursive perspective. *Organization Studies, 27*(1), 7–29.

Maguire, S., Hardy, C., & Lawrence, T. B. (2004). Institutional entrepreneurship in emerging fields: HIV/AIDS treatment advocacy in Canada. *Academy of Management Journal, 47*, 657–679.

Mason, C., Kirkbride, J., & Bryde, D. (2007). From stakeholders to institutions: The changing face of social enterprise theory. *Management Decision, 15*(2), 284–301.

Moore, M.-L., Westley, F. R., & Brodhead, T. (2012). Social finance intermediaries and social innovation. *Journal of Social Entrepreneurship, 3*(2), 184–205.

Moore, M.-L., Westley, F. R., & Nicholls, A. (2012). The social finance and social innovation nexus. *Journal of Social Entrepreneurship, 3*(2), 115–132.

Mullins, D., Czischke, D., & van Bortel, G. (2012). Exploring the meaning of hybridity and social enterprise in housing organizations. *Housing Studies, 27*, 405–417.

Munir, K. A., & Phillips, N. (2005). The birth of "Kodak Moment": Institutional entrepreneurship and the adoption of new technologies. *Organization Studies, 26*(11), 1665–1687.

Nederveen, P. (2001). Hybridity, so what? The anti-hybridity backlash and the riddles of recognition. *Theory, Culture and Society, 18*(2/3), 219–245.

Nicholls, A. (2010). The institutionalization of social investment: The interplay of investment logics and investor rationalities. *Journal of Social Entrepreneurship, 1*, 70–100.

Nicholls, A., & Opal, C. (2005). *Fair trade: Market-driven ethical consumption*. London: Sage.

Pache, A. C., & Santos, F. (2010). When worlds collide: The internal dynamics of organizational responses to conflicting institutional demands. *Academy of Management Review, 35*, 455–476.

Pache, A. C., & Santos, F. (2013). Inside the hybrid organization: Selective coupling as a response to competing institutional logic. *Academy of Management Journal, 56*, 972–1001.

Padgett, J. F., & McLean, P. D. (2006). Organizational invention and elite transformation: The birth of partnership systems in Renaissance Florence. *American Journal of Sociology, 111*(5), 1463–1568.

Phillips, N., Lawrence, T. B., & Hardy, C. (2004). Discourse and institutions. *Academy of Management Review, 29*(4), 635–652.

Purdy, J. M., & Gray, B. (2009). Conflicting logics, mechanisms of diffusion and multilevel dynamics in emerging institutional fields. *Academy of Management Journal, 52*(2), 355–380.

Rao, H. (1998). Caveat emptor: The construction of nonprofit consumer watchdog organizations. *American Journal of Sociology, 103*(4), 912–961.

Rao, H., Morill, C., & Zald, M. N. (2000). Power plays: How social movements and collective action create new organizational forms. *Research in Organizational Behaviour, 22*, 239–282.

Sahlin-Andersson, K., & Engwall, L. (Eds.). (2002). *The expansion of management knowledge: Carriers, flows, and sources*. Stanford: Stanford University Press.

Schmitz, B. (2013). Muster organisationaler Hybridität: Ein Indikatorenmodell zur Messung von Hybridität in Organisationen. In J. Gebauer & H. Schirmer (Eds.), *Unternehmerisch und verantwortlich wirken? Forschung an der Schnittstelle von Corporate Social Responsibility und Social Entrepreneurship* (pp. 69–104). Schriftenreihe des IÖW 204/13, Berlin.

Schmitz, B., & Glänzel, G. (2013). *Resourcing social innovation in Germany: An empirically based concept of matching social innovators with social investors*. Retrieved December 16, 2014, from http://de.scribd.com/doc/193264913/Resourcing-social-innovation-in-Germany-an-empirically-based-concept-of-matching-social-innovators-with-social-investors

Schmitz, B., & Glänzel, G. (2016). Hybrid organizations: Concept and measurement. *International Journal of Organizational Analysis, 24*(1).

Scott, W. R. (2003). Institutional carriers: Reviewing modes of transporting ideas over time and space and considering their consequences. *Industrial and Corporate Change, 12*, 879–894.

Selznick, P. (1949). *TVA and the grass roots: A study in the sociology of formal organization*. Los Angeles, CA: University of California Press.

Seo, M., & Creed, D. W. E. (2002). Institutional contradictions, praxis and institutional change: A dialectical perspective. *Academy of Management Review, 27*(2), 222–247.

Skelcher, C. (2012). *What do we mean when we talk about "hybrids" and "hybridity" in public management and governance?* Working Paper, Institute of Local Government Studies, University of Birmingham, Birmingham.

Skelcher, C., & Smith, S. R. (2015). Theorizing hybridity: Institutional logics, complex organizations, and actor identities: The case of nonprofits. *Public Administration, 93*(2), 433–448.

Smith, S. R. (2010). Hybridization and nonprofit organizations: The governance challenge. *Policy and Society, 29*(3), 219–229.

Stinchcombe, A. L. (1965). Organizations and social structure. In J. March (Ed.), *Handbook of organizations* (pp. 153–193). Chicago, IL: Rand McNally.

Suchman, M. (1995). Managing legitimacy: Strategic and institutional approaches. *Academy of Management Review, 20*(3), 571–610.

Suddaby, R., & Greenwood, R. (2005). Rhetorical strategies of legitimacy. *Administrative Science Quarterly, 50*(1), 35–67.

Thompson, J., & Doherty, B. (2006). The diverse world of social enterprise: A collection of social enterprise stories. *International Journal of Social Economics, 33*(5–6), 361–375.

Thornton, P. (2004). *Markets from culture: Institutional logics and organizational decisions in higher education publishing*. Stanford: Stanford Business Books.

Thornton, P. H., & Ocasio, W. (2008). Institutional logics. In R. Greenwood, C. Oliver, R. Suddaby, & K. Sahlin-Andersson (Eds.), *The Sage handbook of organizational institutionalism*. London: Sage.

Tracey, P., Phillips, N., & Jarvis, O. (2011). Bridging institutional entrepreneurship and the creation of new organizational forms: A multilevel model. *Organization Science, 22*(1), 60–80.

Walgenbach, P. (2006). Neoinstitutionalistische Ansätze in der Organisationstheorie. In A. Kieser & M. Ebers (Eds.), *Organisationstheorien* (6th ed.). Stuttgart: Kohlhammer.

Wamsley, G. L., & Zald, M. N. (1973). *The political economy of public organizations: A critique and approach to the study of public administration*. Lexington, MA: Indiana University Press.

Weisbrod, B. A. (Ed.). (1998). *To profit or not to profit: The commercial transformation of the nonprofit sector*. Cambridge: Cambridge University Press.

Wilson, F., & Post, J. E. (2013). Business models for people, planet (& profits): Exploring the phenomena of social business, a market-based approach to social value creation. *Small Business Economics, 40*, 715–737.

Zahra, S. A., Gedajlovic, E., Newbaum, D. O., & Shulman, J. M. (2009). A typology of social enterprise: Motives, search processes and ethical challenges. *Journal of Business Venturing, 24*, 519–532.

24

MEASURING AND COMPARING SOCIAL VALUE CREATION

Advantages and disadvantages of a new comparability method, IRIS, GIIRS, and SROI

Arne Kroeger and Christiana Weber

Measuring and comparing social value creation is a topic of continuing interest in society, politics, science, business, and economics. Assessing social value creation helps decision-makers improve the allocation of resources when interventions in the not-for-profit sector become necessary. Additionally, it facilitates the comparison of interventions in light of best practice. It also aids the reporting of an intervention's social effectiveness to governmental institutions, foundations, and impact investors for fund-raising purposes and helps prove their social status to society. In turn, funders use evaluations to choose between different funding options and to monitor the development of the interventions they finance. Scholars, social analysts, and managers of foundations and social enterprises have therefore repeatedly tried to develop appropriate frameworks for measuring and comparing social value creation (Brandstetter & Lehner, 2015; McLoughlin et al., 2009). By 2012 the Trasi Database contained as many as 178 approaches and tools for measuring and comparing social value (Foundation Center, 2012). However, the wide range of instruments for such measurement and comparison is overwhelming. Literature on not-for-profit management, social entrepreneurship, and program evaluation lacks analyses and comparative discussions of instruments, particularly approaches that have been developed through and applied in practice.

To close this gap, we aim to investigate the question of which method of measuring and comparing social value creation makes the most sense in a given context. As a starting point, we focus on the most frequently adopted approaches—the Impact Reporting and Investment Standards (IRIS), the Global Impact Investment Rating System (GIIRS), and the Social Return on Investment (SROI). We compare these approaches to a recently published method well received in research and academic education: the Comparability Method (Kroeger & Weber, 2014). This chapter provides scholars, not-for-profit managers, social analysts, and impact investors with an overview of the strengths and limitations of each approach. Because assessments of social value creation serve various purposes, this chapter is intended to provide initial help in selecting the most appropriate approach for the given purpose. We start with a brief review of the logics, strengths, and limitations of the IRIS, the GIIRS, the SROI, and the Comparability Method. We then discuss the advantages and disadvantages of the four approaches on the basis of six key criteria and conclude by summarizing the primary findings of the discussion.

Frequently used approaches for measuring and comparing social value creation: The IRIS, the GIIRS, and the SROI

Scholars and practitioners have suggested a vast number of instruments for measuring and comparing social value creation. Some of these tools are often applied in the not-for-profit sector. According to Saltuk, El Idrissi, Bouri, Mudaliar, and Schiff (2014), the most frequently used approach for measuring social value creation is the IRIS. Building on the IRIS, the Global Impact Investing Network (GIIN) and a private company called "B Lab" developed the GIIRS, which, according to these two actors, makes it possible to compare GIIRS-rated interventions. Another much discussed method for assessing social value creation in the context of social entrepreneurship is the SROI (Davis & Pett, 2002; Emerson, 2003; Hehenberger, Harling, & Scholten, 2013; Lingane & Olsen, 2004; Nicholls, 2009; Polonsky & Grau, 2011; Yates, 2009). When it comes to program evaluation, experimental and quasi-experimental research designs (Baker, 2000; Caspari & Barbu, 2008; Reichardt, 2011)—such as randomized control trials, difference-in-difference technique, and propensity score matching—are also found to be crucial (Angrist, 2004; Kromrey, 2001; Shadish, Cook, & Campbell, 2002). However, because these approaches are taken into account by the suggestions made in the Comparability Method, the overlap of strengths and limitations makes a comparison obsolete. Our chapter is therefore focused on the comparison of advantages and disadvantages of the IRIS, the GIIRS, and the SROI with those of the Comparability Method developed by Kroeger and Weber (2014).

The IRIS

Description of the IRIS approach

The IRIS was developed by the GIIN (Busenhart, 2012; Hehenberger et al., 2013). The 4.0 version of the IRIS comprises a catalogue of 559 metrics related to social value creation and a glossary with 149 standardized definitions of key terms that analysts often use during their impact assessments (https://iris.thegiin.org/metrics; see also Gelfand, 2012; Jackson, 2013). Some metrics are appropriate for assessing qualitative data such as the social impact objectives or the mission statement of an organization, but most metrics allow for quantitative assessment of an intervention's outputs such as job placement rate or the number of beneficiaries treated. Up to 358 metrics can be applied across sectors, and 201 indicators are specified for one of nine sectors, including education, health, or environment. For each metric, the IRIS provides its name, its definition, usage guidance, reporting format, and instructions on how to calculate the indicator. Social analysts who work with the IRIS can choose from the catalogue those metrics appropriate for the intervention to be assessed (Gelfand, 2012). Additionally, the standardized definitions of the terms in the IRIS glossary help analysts align their assessment with what, according to the IRIS, should be the common understanding in the not-for-profit sector. For instance, a charitable donation is defined as "financial contributions and in kind donations of goods and services to charities, private foundations, non-profits, or non-governmental organizations" (IRIS 4.0 Taxonomy, 2016). This definition avoids the case in which one analyst refers only to financial contributions while another refers to financial contributions as well as in-kind donations.

Strengths and limitations of the IRIS approach

The most obvious strength of the IRIS is its character as a "pragmatic and easy-to-use metrics tool" (Gelfand, 2012). It is highly flexible, for analysts simply choose the metrics that fit the respective social value created by an evaluated intervention selected from a list of 599 metrics. It is thus easy and quick to learn and use the IRIS. Because of this simple and flexible applicability, the approach has been widely adopted (Saltuk et al., 2014). It has strong credibility (Busenhart, 2012) in the field, and hence has great legitimacy too.

We consider the major drawback of the IRIS to be its limited number of indicators—599 metrics. That number seems insufficient to capture all the facets of social value creation, which can satisfy the myriad needs of different treatment groups. The second prominent limitation of the IRIS we see is that it does not offer a comprehensive guideline for interpreting the results yielded by its application. For instance, an organization's decision-makers who assess the IRIS metric known as the "number of unique individuals who were active clients of the organization as of the end of the reporting period" (IRIS 4.0 Taxonomy, 2016) may find it difficult to judge whether their calculated number of these clients is "good" or "bad."

The GIIRS

Description of the GIIRS approach

The GIIRS is a rating methodology (Brandenburg, 2012; Jackson, 2013; Richardson, 2012), "an analogue of the Standard and Poor's or Morningstar Rating systems" (Jackson, 2013, p. 98), that grants up to five social impact stars to rated companies and funds, with five stars being the best score. The number of stars awarded is based on the number of points a company scores, the highest possible score being two hundred. Before an intervention is rated, it must be categorized in terms of its market of operation (emerging market, frontier market, or developed market), its sector affiliation (manufacturing, wholesale, service, or agriculture), its number of full-time equivalents (FTEs) according to the World Bank's scale of employment in small- to medium-sized enterprises (0, 1–9, 10–49, 50–249, and 250+ FTEs), and its impact business model. More than 13 different impact business models offered by the GIIRS categorize different ways in which an intervention can combine its social activity and the financial business model. Taking into account the specified market, sector, size, and impact business model, the GIIRS generates one of 40 alternative company assessment questionnaires. All questionnaires contain 50–120 weighted questions based on IRIS metrics (Brandenburg, 2012) and take 60–90 minutes to answer. The number and weighting of the questions depend on the details specified in the first step. The questions are grouped into subcategories, which, in turn, are clustered into four different "impact areas" (governance, worker, community, and environment). The total score is the weighted sum of points that are assigned to responses to items in the questionnaire about a given intervention. The number of points granted for an answer depends on assumptions, or rationales, such as "flexible work environments create better places to work and improve work/ life balance" (http://giirs.nonprofitsoapbox.com/about-giirs/how-giirs-works). Interventions can only score points. No points are deducted in the GIIRS. The responses given by not-for-profit managers are verified in a one-hour telephone call with a GIIRS staff member and in a desk review of selected documents uploaded by the respective managers. Additionally, annual site visits are conducted by the GIIRS staff for 10 percent of all GIIRS-rated companies (http://giirs.nonprofitsoapbox.com/about-giirs/how-giirs-works).

Strengths and limitations of the GIIRS approach

A major strength of the GIIRS is that it draws on the well-known and easily understood metrics of the IRIS (Gelfand, 2012). The GIIRS takes the IRIS a step further by aggregating several IRIS metrics into one number and thereby affords external stakeholders an overall indication of the intervention's performance. A second main strength that advocates of the GIIRS often cite is that an intervention's GIIRS rating value can be compared across sectors and treatment groups (Brandenburg, 2012; Richardson, 2012). The third major strength is that the GIIRS rating can even be calculated for social investment funds (Brandenburg, 2012; Busenhart, 2012).

The principal limitation of the GIIRS is that the final overall rating it yields may convey little information apart from whether an intervention performs rather good or bad. The reasoning behind the integrated weightings of the discrete variables is not apparent. For instance, it is unclear why the maximum number of points for a manufacturing company employing 50 or more people and operating in a developed market is weighted with 10 points for Worker Benefits and with 5 points for Training and Education as the highest possible scores in these categories. Furthermore, the rationales that determine the final rating may not apply to all cultures. For instance, the aforementioned rationale of "flexible work environments create better places to work and improve work/life balance" (http://giirs.nonprofitsoapbox.com/about-giirs/how-giirs-works/174) may not hold for cultures in which people "accept and expect power [that is] distributed unequally" (Hofstede, 1991, p. 28), as is the case in Malaysia, the Philippines, and Mexico (p. 26). Another serious limitation a critical auditor may detect is that the data review process is highly liable to lead an intervention's not-for-profit managers to report incorrect information—intentionally or unintentionally.

The SROI

Description of the SROI approach

The SROI is a sophisticated technique that allows for the extrapolation of results. It captures the value of accrued benefits, which, when compared to the level of investment, produces the SROI ratio (Rotheroe & Richards, 2007). The SROI is basically a cost-benefit analysis (Jackson, 2013; Krlev, Münscher, & Mülbert, 2013). To calculate the SROI, analysts first assess how much social value an intervention creates and/or reduces for its most important stakeholders (Lingane & Olsen, 2004). Based on proxies and assumptions, this social value that is created or reduced is then monetized (converted into monetary values) (Krlev et al., 2013; Nicholls, 2009). For instance, the financial proxy for 5 fewer days of police presence in Vineburgh per month is £8,640 (http://www.globalvaluexchange.org/valuations/). Hence, one can use this indicator to monetize the social value created by an intervention that reduces the crime rate. The monetized social value created or reduced for the different stakeholder groups is summarized and compared to the resources invested to generate this social value (Polonsky & Grau, 2011). One calculates the SROI by dividing the net present value of benefits projections by the net present value of investment for a specific period (Somers, Nicholls, Mackenzie, & Sanfilippo, 2005). Moore, Boardman, Vining, Weimer, and Greenberg (2004) suggest a social discount rate of between 1.1 percent and 3.5 percent.

Strengths and limitations of the SROI approach

The SROI's key strength as an approach to measuring and comparing social value creation lies in providing a structured understanding of an intervention's customized theory of change (Rotheroe & Richards, 2007). The SROI framework "offers valuable insights into an intervention's specific internal processes and [main] drivers of social value" (Kroeger & Weber, 2014,

p. 517; see also Lingane & Olsen, 2004). The SROI therefore facilitates resource allocation. The second convincing argument in favor of the SROI is that its sole measurement unit is money. The SROI ratio, which monetizes social value created per dollar invested, is not only well understood by financial players in the market, it also allows for interventions in which the SROI is used to balance costs and impact (Yates, 2009).

The SROI's most problematic limitations are threefold. First,

> different socioeconomic and institutional contexts and different treatment groups result in different theories of change for each evaluated intervention. Comparing two interventions on the basis of SROI requires similar interventions and becomes problematic with increasing heterogeneity in the socioeconomic and institutional contexts of the target groups whose social needs are served.
>
> *(Kroeger & Weber, 2014, p. 517)*

Second, the SROI is replete with various assumptions to be made when one calculates it, so two analysts might end up with two significantly different SROI ratings even when evaluating the same intervention (Krlev et al., 2013; Lingane & Olsen, 2004). A third pitfall of the SROI approach to measuring and comparing social value creation is, as social entrepreneurs perpetually point out, that users perceive it to be time-consuming and unsuitable for the contractual impact investment relationship.

Although scholars and practitioners continue to suggest and discuss new tools and instruments for measuring and comparing social value creation in the not-for-profit sector, they predominantly state that comparing social value creation across sectors and countries is not possible (Dacin, Dacin, & Matear, 2010; Emerson, 2003; Mair & Marti, 2006; Nicholls, 2009; Polonsky & Grau, 2011; Ryan & Lyne, 2008; Zahra, Gedajlovic, Neubaum, & Schulman, 2009). In answer to these convictions, however, Kroeger and Weber (2014) developed a method that makes such comparisons possible. It is summarized in the following section.

The Comparability Method: comparing social value creation across sectors, target groups, and countries

Description of the Comparability Method

Kroeger and Weber (2014) began by identifying three constantly reported problems that seem to complicate efforts to compare social value creation. First, scholars and practitioners lack a unified measure for comparing interventions that serve different target groups in different sectors (e.g., Mair & Marti, 2006; Polonsky & Grau, 2011). For instance, while the social intervention "Cotton Made in Africa" improves the economic, educational, and health situations of small impoverished cotton farmers in Africa, another social intervention in Germany called "Dialogue in the Dark" aims to (re-)integrate blind people into both society and the first employment market that allows them to live independently.

Second, it is not clear what the construct "social" in the not-for-profit context means (Austin, Stevenson, & Wei-Skillern, 2006; Choi & Majumdar, 2014; Dacin et al., 2010; Herman & Renz, 2008; Hervieux, Gedajlovic, & Turcotte, 2010; Mair & Marti, 2006; Nicholls & Cho, 2008; Phills, Deiglmeier, & Miller, 2008; Polonsky & Grau, 2011; Tan, Williams, & Tan, 2005). There is presumably an implicit understanding of what is considered "social." However, scholars and practitioners have remained vague about an explicit differentiation between a social program and a non-social program.

Third, social interventions may take place in different countries with different living standards (Donaldson, 2001; United Nations, 2013).

> As a result, two interventions might increase their social value creation by the same amount, but the growth rate in the richer country will, by definition, be lower than the growth rate in the poorer country. Rates of improvement tend to be relatively high in low-number ranges, a fact that might exaggerate the effectiveness of a social intervention.
>
> *(Kroeger & Weber, 2014, p. 519)*

For instance, the social intervention of Cotton Made in Africa takes place in Zimbabwe, which has a much lower living standard than Germany, where Dialogue in the Dark operates.

The model proposed by Kroeger and Weber (2014) enables social analysts and managers of not-for-profit organizations, foundations, and investment funds to solve these three central problems. First, the authors suggest using life satisfaction indicators as a unified unit of measurement for all interventions that benefit people in the not-for-profit sector. For instance, Cotton Made in Africa improves the life satisfaction of poor farmers, and Dialogue in the Dark raises the life satisfaction of blind people. For the evaluation of regions and nations, data on life satisfaction is already assessed by national and supranational institutions such as the Organisation for Economic Co-operation and Development (OECD), the World Values Survey, the Corporación Latinobarómetro, the Buthan government, and the Gallup Company. Indicators of life satisfaction have proven to be statistically reliable, and surveys gathering data on which to base such indicators achieve very high response rates (Diener, Inglehart, & Tay, 2013). In addition, previous research has shown that gross domestic product (GDP) and similar benchmarks heretofore used to calculate national well-being are inadequate for that task. For example, factors such as the social support by the family go unaccounted for in GDP. To assess life satisfaction, persons of a region or country are asked how high they rate their life satisfaction on a Likert scale ranging from 1 (dissatisfied) to 10 (satisfied) when they consider their life situation as a whole (Anand et al., 2009; Beja & Yap, 2013; Finsterbusch, 1985; Georgopoulos & Mann, 1962; Lawless & Lucas, 2011; Layard, 2010; Price, 1972; Veenhoven, 2000). Overall life satisfaction can also be subdivided into domains such as education, security, or health, which then permit the various social programs, interventions, and their impacts to be linked by domain, or even better to the different needs of the beneficiaries (Cox, 2012; Cummins, 1996; Gonzalez, Coenders, Saez, & Casas, 2010; Hsieh, 2003; Rojas, 2006; Schimmack, 2008). In this case a domain satisfaction index is compiled from the interviewee's perceived satisfaction in various areas of life, such as his or her own training or health (Gonzalez et al., 2010; Kroeger & Weber, 2014; Rojas, 2006). This kind of index can thus adequately approximate life satisfaction.

To solve the second problem that seems to complicate attempts to compare social value creation, the authors draw on secondary data. With national and supranational institutions already evaluating regional and national data on life satisfaction, Kroeger and Weber (2014) suggest taking the mean level of life satisfaction in a region or country as the threshold that differentiates social from non-social interventions. Accordingly, social interventions are those interventions that treat people whose reported level of regional or national life satisfaction is below the mean. These people are disadvantaged relative to respondents exceeding that level. Hence, the purpose of a social intervention is to reduce the relative disadvantage of its target groups. If the mean level of life satisfaction of a group of poor women is below that in the region or country in which they live, one can use the difference between the two means to calculate the social need of this group (Kroeger & Weber, 2014).

To solve the third problem with comparing social value creation, the Comparability Method is based on the theory of organizational effectiveness (Cameron, 1986; Connolly, Colon, & Deutsch, 1980; Cunningham, 1977; Lecy, Schmitz, & Swedlund, 2012; Lewin & Minton, 1986; Rojas, 2000; Sowa, Selden, & Sandfort, 2004; Yuchtman & Seashore, 1967; Zammuto, 1982). In this theory effectiveness is understood as a relative construct (Lewin & Minton, 1986). Accordingly, one can calculate the efficacy of a social program by taking the improvement that a program initiates in the life situation of a socially disadvantaged treatment group and dividing it by that group's social need (Kroeger & Weber, 2014):

$$\text{Degree of SVC}_{i,t+1} = \left(\left(\frac{\text{LS improved}_{i,j,t+1}}{\text{Social Need}_{i,j,t+1}}\right) - \left(\frac{\text{LS improved}_{i,j,t}}{\text{Social Need}_{i,j,t}}\right)\right),$$

with i = intervention, $\varepsilon = \{i = 1, 2,. . ., I\}$; t = point in time, $\varepsilon = \{t = 1, 2, 3,. . ., T\}$; j = treatment group, $\varepsilon = \{j = 1, 2,. . ., J\}$, LS = life satisfaction.

The improvement in the life situation of a socially disadvantaged treatment group can be calculated with established scientific procedures, including randomized control trials or the difference-in-difference technique (Duflo & Kremer, 2008; Epstein & Klerman, 2012; Meyer, 1995; White, 2013). By establishing a control group, they take into account the fact that "extraneous" influences such as economic cycles or a bountiful harvest can affect a social program (Caspari & Barbu, 2008; Rubin, 1974). A control group is observed to tell how satisfied the members of the treatment group would be if they were to go without the program (e.g., if the group targeted by Cotton Made in Africa in Zimbabwe were to receive no training or fair contracts). On average, the persons in the control group would have the same characteristics (e.g., age, origin, and level of life satisfaction) as the persons in the treatment group but would not be beneficiaries of the social program. Both groups would be subject to extraneous influences, but only one of the groups would benefit from the program. In other words, improvement in the socially disadvantaged group's life situation when it is measured would amount to the difference between the average level of life satisfaction in the group of beneficiaries and that in the control group.

Social interventions that are to be compared usually involve different numbers of disadvantaged people. Therefore, comparing these interventions requires one to take each social intervention's calculated degree of social value created and multiply it again by the corresponding numbers of treated beneficiaries. As shown in Kroeger and Weber (2014), the weighted degree of social value created is thus calculated as

$$\text{Weighted Degree of SVC}_{i,t} = w_{i,j,t+1} \star \left(\left(\frac{\text{LS improved}_{i,j,t+1}}{\text{Social Need}_{i,j,t+1}}\right) - \left(\frac{\text{LS improved}_{i,j,t}}{\text{Social Need}_{i,j,t}}\right)\right),$$

with i = intervention, $\varepsilon = \{i = 1, 2,. . ., I\}$; t = point in time, $\varepsilon = \{t = 1, 2, 3,. . ., T\}$; j = treatment group, $\varepsilon = \{j = 1, 2,. . ., J\}$; w = weighting = number of beneficiaries, $\varepsilon = \{w = 1, 2,. . ., W\}$.

Strengths and limitations of the Comparability Method

The Comparability Method has four notable strengths. First, it enables the user to compare social value creation across sectors and treatment groups by adopting life satisfaction as a unified measurement unit for assessing the performance of social interventions. Second, it helps clearly define the fuzzy construct "social" by using the mean level of life satisfaction in a region or a country as a threshold between social and non-social value creation. Third, the user can take a social intervention's social value created and compare it across regions and countries by contextualizing it within the corresponding social need of the treatment group in the relevant region or country. Fourth, the Comparability Method is readily understood and grounded in theory, namely organizational effectiveness theory.

Scholars and practitioners desiring to work with this new method should also keep two limitations in mind. First, it places the emphasis on comparing the effectiveness rather than the efficiency of different social interventions and thereby leads users to disregard the means and resources necessary to achieve the intended social value. However, scholars and analysts interested in having their analyses include these inputs could, for instance, compare the weighted social efficiency, which one calculates by taking the weighted degree of social value creation and dividing it by all the resources used in the investigated period of time to achieve this degree of social value created:

$$\text{Weighted Efficiency}_{i,j,t+1} = \frac{\left(w_{i,j,t+1} \star \left(\left(\frac{\text{LS improved}_{i,j,t+1}}{\text{Social Need}_{i,j,t+1}} \right) - \left(\frac{\text{LS improved}_{i,j,t}}{\text{Social Need}_{i,j,t}} \right) \right) \right)}{\text{Inputs}_{i,j,t \to t+1}},$$

with i = intervention, $\varepsilon = \{i = 1, 2, \ldots, I\}$; t = point in time, $\varepsilon = \{t = 1, 2, 3, \ldots, T\}$; j = treatment group, $\varepsilon = \{j = 1, 2, \ldots, J\}$; w = weighting = number of beneficiaries, $\varepsilon = \{w = 1, 2, \ldots, W\}$.

The second limitation of the new framework that may be solved is the application of subjective indicators. Because the Comparability Method draws on ratings of life satisfaction, analysts who use this method interview people of target groups and collect their subjective responses to their current life situation. However, the evaluations of individuals' subjective life satisfaction risk being manipulated by social project managers who are interested in a highly weighted degree of social value created. For instance, disadvantaged individuals may be told that a low life satisfaction rating will result in termination of the social intervention. Additionally, Diener and Lucas (2000) found that chronically disadvantaged individuals will adapt to their misfortune. That is, these people may rate their life satisfaction higher than it actually is. For example, the longer a woman has been blind, the higher the life satisfaction she might report, but this increase in satisfaction may be due only to the ever longer time she has spent in learning to cope with her condition, and not to any objective improvement in it.

A way to factor out the effect of coping with manipulation and adaptation to misfortune could be the complementary assessment of additional control variables such as "non-self-report measures" (Sandvik, Diener, & Seidlitz, 1993, p. 317; Kroeger & Weber, 2014). Moreover, creating a domain satisfaction index makes it possible to link the various social interventions and their effect even better with the different needs of the beneficiaries than by using overall life satisfaction (Gonzalez et al., 2010; Rojas, 2006). Any distortions can thereby be offset by socially desired answering behavior.

Comparing the IRIS, the GIIRS, and the SROI with the Comparability Method

In this section, we compare the Comparability Method with the IRIS, GIIRS, and SROI approaches and highlight their respective advantages and disadvantages on the basis of six criteria.

Output, outcome, and impact

Social value creation can be assessed at three levels: output, outcome, and impact. In the social context, the term output not only comprises products and services provided by a social enterprise (e.g., speech-to-text-transcription for people with impaired hearing) but also to accomplished activities (e.g., creating jobs for individuals with autism). Outcome means a change (e.g., increased education) in the well-being of a social intervention's target group. Of course, this change of well-being may also be the result of causes (e.g., socioeconomic trends) other than that of the social intervention (White, 2010). If analysts exclude these effects originating from outside a social intervention's area of influence, they can gauge the change that an assessed social intervention has brought about in the treatment group's well-being. This change is called *impact* (Kroeger & Weber, 2014; McLoughlin et al., 2009; Nicholls, 2009). The Comparability Method and the SROI both control for external effects and therefore make it possible to assess the impact of social interventions. Most IRIS metrics address outputs. Few IRIS metrics, such as the Student Tests Pass Rate, address outcome. Drawing on the IRIS, the GIIRS partially includes specific outcomes:

> ...for example, in workforce development, we ask if a company tracks the workers it has trained after they "graduate"—beyond existing employment—and whether those workers have attained gainful employment in the medium and long-term ... In other areas, particularly around outcomes associated with a specific product or service, we ask more general questions whether a company has defined desired outcomes, created targets for meeting those outcomes, measured against those targets and have *[sic]* had success in meeting the targets.
>
> *(http://www.bcorporation.net/blog/an-evolution-in-impact-measurement)*

Neither the IRIS nor the GIIRS enables one to evaluate the impact of interventions.

Comparability across sectors and target groups

By drawing on the life satisfaction indicator as a unified unit of measurement, the Comparability Method allows analysts to compare social interventions across sectors and target groups (Kroeger & Weber, 2014). The IRIS, the GIIRS, and the SROI are also able to do so, albeit in a limited way. The IRIS, for instance, is able to compare different social interventions across sectors and target groups only as long as the IRIS metric list contains cross-sector indicators that are suitable for the interventions to be compared. The overall GIIRS rating can also be compared across sectors and target groups because sector differences are adjusted by different questions and weightings for each sector (see the section "Description of the GIIRS approach"). However, users and other stakeholders such as investors may find this customization of the GIIRS questionnaire implausible, for the weightings are not well reasoned (see the section "Strengths and limitations of the GIIRS approach"). To deal with the problem of comparing across sectors and target groups, the SROI sets a unified measurement unit (monetary proxies) for social value created. (The Comparability Method uses the life satisfaction indicator for this purpose.) However, necessary assumptions for defining the monetary equivalent of social value created may be problematic, for the conversion of social value to financial value is not standardized, some benefits cannot be monetized, and other benefits may be under- or overvalued (Jackson, 2013; Krlev et al., 2013; Lingane & Olsen, 2004; Nicholls, 2009; Polonsky & Grau, 2011).

Type of data

Unlike the analyses based on the IRIS, the GIIRS, and the SROI, those of the Comparability Method are built on subjective data that its users collect by asking the members of an intervention's target group how they perceive their current life satisfaction. As noted above, this approach harbors at least two potential risks. The first is manipulation. People who must fear exclusion from a social intervention if they honestly report what they perceive might rate their life satisfaction higher than they would otherwise. The second risk arises when respondents who have adapted to their misfortune rate their life satisfaction higher than can be expected given their objective life situation. However, as Kroeger and Weber (2014) discuss, this accommodation of misfortune (a) might not characterize all life situations; (b) might not necessarily complicate comparisons of life satisfaction or domain satisfaction indices among countries; and (c) might not occur if a domain satisfaction index is assessed "because not all D[omain] S[atisfaction]s may be affected when disadvantaged individuals adapt somewhat to miserable life situations" (p. 529). Consequently, such a potential adaptation effect would not be fully reflected at the aggregated level of the domain satisfaction index. The most important argument against this potential criticism comes from the findings reported by Layard (2010), Oswald and Wu (2010), and Lawless and Lucas (2011), who all assert that perceptual ratings correlate highly with "non-self-report measures" (Sandvik et al., 1993, p. 317).

The IRIS, the GIIRS, and the SROI use only non-subjective data, which, however, entail other risks. The greatest of them is that of working with indicators that do not correspond to what the treatment group really cares about or needs. In this case, the social analysis would not capture the actually generated impact. Moreover, the 599 indicators offered by the IRIS might not include the indicator that best corresponds to the type of social intervention that is underway.

Defined difference between advantaged and disadvantaged

The second main problem of comparing social value creation is the question of whether an approach distinguishes between social and non-social value creation. In the Comparability Method the mean level of life satisfaction in the social intervention's target region or country is defined as the threshold between social and non-social value creation (Kroeger & Weber, 2014). The IRIS approach does not explicitly differentiate between social and non-social value creation. Instead, it encompasses metrics such as "Number of unique individuals who belong to minority or previously excluded groups and were clients of the organization during the reporting period" and "Number of unique poor households that were clients of the organization during the reporting period" (IRIS 4.0, Taxonomy, 2016). These metrics address target groups that may be disadvantaged as classified by the Comparability Method. The same is true for GIIRS ratings and the SROI, which assess the social value creation for all stakeholders regardless of whether these stakeholders are disadvantaged or not. However, the GIIRS at least discloses how many clients in need have been benefited and "whether chronically underemployed individuals have been hired" (http://www.bcorporation.net/blog/an-evolution-in-impact-measurement).

Comparability across countries

The Comparability Method offers the possibility of comparing social value creation across countries. This kind of analysis cuts across differing socioeconomic and institutional contexts because different living standards and cultures are reflected by the different mean levels of life satisfaction in the region or country in which social interventions take place. They are also reflected in the different social needs of a social intervention's benefited target group through which the Comparability Method contextualizes the social value created. To capture these relationships, users of the Comparability Method assume cultural coherence within the regions and countries studied. Although this assumption may not reflect reality entirely, it is common practice with prominent economic indicators such as the Human Development Index or Gross National Product (Kroeger & Weber, 2014). Unlike the Comparability Method, the IRIS does not allow cross-regional or cross-national comparisons. However, some IRIS metrics are specified for target groups located in urban, suburban, or rural areas. By contrast, the GIIRS approach takes account of socioeconomic and institutional differences by providing different questionnaires for social interventions that operate in emerging, frontier, and developed markets. This segregation may raise the same problem as that experienced with the comparability of GIIRS ratings across sectors and target groups, for the corresponding weightings of the customized GIIRS questionnaire may also be perceived as implausible by users and their stakeholders. The SROI does not allow one to compare social interventions that operate in different regions or countries (see the section "Strengths and limitations of the SROI approach").

Negative social value

Although scholars and practitioners usually emphasize social value creation, some social interventions reduce the living standard of their beneficiaries (Antonie, 2010; Finsterbusch, 1995). For example, microloans are sometimes tied to extremely poor conditions for the receiver or are granted without proper training. The consequence has been that some beneficiaries use up such microfinance without being able to meet the loan and interest repayments and are thus worse off after the program than loan recipients who had not received microfinance (Kroeger & Weber, 2014). The Comparability Method and the SROI approach include the possibility that negative social value is initiated (Kroeger & Weber, 2014; Lingane & Olsen, 2004). By contrast, none of the 599 IRIS metrics captures negative social value. The GIIRS also provides limited information on negative social value initiated by a social intervention. On the GIIRS website B Lab explicitly emphasizes that "no points are deducted for negative performance" (http://b-analytics.net/articles/company-ratings-methodology). Instead, the GIIRS report contains a section called "Disclosure Questionnaire", in which the rated interventions indicate whether or not the intervention has been subject to unethical behavior such as "bribery, fraud or corruption" (http://b-analytics.net/sites/default/files/documents/Education_Tools_R_Us_Company_Report.pdf).

Conclusion

We set out in this chapter to provide scholars, not-for-profit managers, social analysts, and impact investors with initial guidance for selecting the best method for measuring and comparing social value creation in a given situation. To do so, we introduced the Comparability

Method developed by Kroeger and Weber (2014) and compared it to the most frequently used approaches for measuring and comparing social value creation—the IRIS, the GIIRS, and the SROI—highlighting their respective strengths and limitations. Whereas the IRIS is used best in contexts characterized by scarce resources and a low level of complexity, the SROI lends itself particularly to situations in which users and investors wish to gain a deep understanding of an intervention's impact value chain, its theory of change, and its most important drivers for social value creation. The Comparability Method should be used in contexts where social interventions are highly heterogeneous and complex and where the overriding objective is to compare these heterogeneous social interventions for the social value they create across different sectors, target groups, and countries. We hope our work inspires other scholars to advance the Comparability Method or to develop alternative approaches that promote cross-sector and cross-national comparisons of social value creation and encourage practitioners to begin drawing on the Comparability Method in their daily work.

References

Anand, P., Hunter, G., Carter, I., Dowding, K., Guala, F., & Van Hees, M. (2009). The development of capability indicators. *Journal of Human Development and Capabilities, 10*(1), 125–152.

Angrist, J. (2004). American education research changes tack. *Oxford Review of Economic Policy, 20*(2), 198–212.

Antonie, R. (2010). Social impact assessment models. *Transylvanian Review of Administrative Sciences, 29*, 22–29.

Austin, J., Stevenson, H., & Wei-Skillern, J. (2006). Social and commercial entrepreneurship: Same, different, or both? *Entrepreneurship Theory and Practice, 30*(1), 1–23.

Baker, J. (2000). *Evaluating the impact of development projects on poverty: A handbook for practitioners*. Washington, DC: World Bank.

Beja, E. L., & Yap, D. B. (2013). Counting happiness from the individual level to the group level. *Social Indicators Research, 114*(2), 621–637.

Brandenburg, M. (2012). Impact investing's three measurement tools. *Stanford Social Innovation Review*. Retrieved July 24, 2015, from http://ssir.org/articles/entry/impact_investings_three_measurement_tools

Brandstetter, L., & Lehner, O. M. (2015). Opening the market for impact investments: The need for adapted portfolio tools. *Enterprise Research Journal, 5*(2), 87–107.

Busenhart, B. (2012). Using the right tools. *Stanford Social Innovation Review*. Retrieved July 24, 2015, from http://ssir.org/articles/entry/using_the_right_tools

Cameron, K. S. (1986). Effectiveness as paradox: Consensus and conflict in conceptions of organizational effectiveness. *Management Science, 32*(5), 539–553.

Caspari, A., & Barbu, R. (2008). *Wirkungsevaluierungen: Zum Stand der internationalen Diskussion und dessen Relevanz für Evaluierungen der deutschen Entwicklungszusammenarbeit* [Evaluating effect: The state of the international discussion and its relevance for evaluations of German development cooperation]. Evaluation Working Papers, 1–44. Bonn: Bundesministerium für wirtschaftliche Zusammenarbeit und Entwicklung.

Choi, N., & Majumdar, S. (2014). Social entrepreneurship as an essentially contested concept: Opening a new avenue for systematic future research. *Journal of Business Venturing, 29*(3), 363–376.

Connolly, T., Colon, E. J., & Deutsch, S. J. (1980). Organizational effectiveness: A multiple-constituency approach. *Academy of Management Review, 5*(2), 211–218.

Cox, K. (2012). Happiness and unhappiness in the developing world: Life satisfaction among sex workers, dump dwellers, urban poor, and rural peasants in Nicaragua. *Journal of Happiness Studies, 13*(1), 103–128.

Cummins, R. A. (1996). The domains of life satisfaction: An attempt to order chaos. *Social Indicators Research, 38*(3), 303–328.

Cunningham, J. B. (1977). Approaches to the evaluation of organizational effectiveness. *Academy of Management Review, 2*(3), 463–474.

Dacin, P. A., Dacin, M. T., & Matear, M. (2010). Social entrepreneurship: Why we don't need a new theory and how we move forward from here. *Academy of Management Perspectives, 24*(3), 37–57.

Davis, P. S., & Pett, T. L. (2002). Measuring organizational efficiency and effectiveness. *Journal of Management Research, 2*(2), 87–97.

Diener, E., Inglehart, R., & Tay, L. (2013). Theory and validity of life satisfaction scales. *Social Indicators Research, 112*, 497–527.

Diener, E., & Lucas, R. E. (2000). Subjective emotional well-being. *Handbook of Emotions, 2*, 325–337.

Donaldson, T. (2001). The ethical wealth of nations. *Journal of Business Ethics, 31*(1), 25–36.

Duflo, E., & Kremer, M. (2008). Use of randomization in the evaluation of development effectiveness. *Boston: MIT Economics*. Retrieved March 21, 2015, from http://economics.mit.edu/files/2785

Emerson, J. (2003). The blended value proposition: Integrating social and financial returns. *California Management Review, 45*(4), 35–51.

Epstein, D., & Klerman, J. A. (2012). When is a program ready for rigorous impact evaluation? The role of falsifiable logic model. *Evaluation Review, 36*(5), 375–401.

Finsterbusch, K. (1985). State of the art in social impact assessment. *Environment and Behavior, 17*(2), 193–221.

Finsterbusch, K. (1995). In praise of SIA—A personal review of the field of social impact assessment: Feasibility, justification, history, methods, issues. *Impact Assessment, 13*(3), 229–252.

Foundation Center. (2016). *About Trasi*. Retrieved March 3, 2016, from http://trasi.foundationcenter.org/about.php

Gelfand, S. (2012). Why IRIS? *Stanford Social Innovation Review*. Retrieved July 24, 2015, from http://ssir.org/articles/entry/why_iris

Georgopoulos, B. S., & Mann, F. C. (1962). *The community general hospital*. New York, NY: Macmillan.

Gonzalez, M., Coenders, G., Saez, M., & Casas, F. (2010). Nonlinearity, complexity and limited measurement in the relationship between satisfaction with specific life domains and satisfaction with life as a whole. *Journal of Happiness Studies, 11*(3), 335–352.

Hehenberger, L., Harling, A.-M., & Scholten, P. (2013). *A practical guide to measuring and managing impact*. Brussels, Belgium: European Venture Philanthropy Association.

Herman, R. D., & Renz, D. O. (2008). Advancing nonprofit organizational effectiveness research and theory: Nine theses. *Nonprofit Management and Leadership, 18*(4), 399–415.

Hervieux, C., Gedajlovic, E., & Turcotte, M. F. B. (2010). The legitimization of social entrepreneurship. *Journal of Enterprising Communities: People and Places in the Global Economy, 4*(1), 37–67.

Hofstede, G. (1991). *Cultures and organizations: Software of the mind*. New York, NY: McGraw-Hill.

Hsieh, C.-M. (2003). Counting importance: The case of life satisfaction and relative domain importance. *Social Indicators Research, 61*(2), 227–240.

IRIS 4.0 Taxonomy (2016). The complete version of the IRIS 4.0 Standards, released in March 2016. Retrieved April 4, 2016, from https://iris.thegiin.org/metrics/downloads.

Jackson, E. T. (2013). Interrogating the theory of change: Evaluating impact investing where it matters most. *Journal of Sustainable Finance & Investment, 3*(2), 95–110.

Krlev, G., Münscher, R., & Mülbert, K. (2013). *Social Return on Investment (SROI): State-of-the-art and perspectives*. A Meta-Analysis of Practice in Social Return on Investment (SROI) studies published 2002–2012. Retrieved September 3, 2015, from http://www.ub.uni-heidelberg.de/archiv/18758

Kroeger, A., & Weber, C. (2014). Developing a conceptual framework for comparing social value creation. *Academy of Management Review, 39*(4), 513–540.

Kromrey, H. (2001). Evaluation—ein vielschichtiges Konzept: Begriff und Methodik von Evaluierung und Evaluationsforschung [Evaluation—A multilayered concept: Terminology and methodology of evaluation and evaluation research]. *Sozialwissenschaften und Berufspraxis, 24*(2), 1–23.

Lawless, N. M., & Lucas, R. E. (2011). Predictors of regional well-being: A country level analysis. *Social Indicators Research, 101*(3), 341–357.

Layard, R. (2010). Measuring subjective well-being. *Science, 327*, 534–535.

Lecy, J. D., Schmitz, H. P., & Swedlund, H. (2012). Nongovernmental and not-for-profit organizational effectiveness: A modern synthesis. *Voluntas: International Journal of Voluntary and Nonprofit Organizations, 23*(2), 434–457.

Lewin, A. Y., & Minton, J. W. (1986). Determining organizational effectiveness: Another look, and an agenda for research. *Management Science, 32*(5), 514–538.

Lingane, A., & Olsen, S. (2004). Guidelines for social return on investment. *California Management Review, 46*(3), 116–135.

Mair, J., & Marti, I. (2006). Social entrepreneurship research: A source of explanation, prediction, and delight. *Journal of World Business, 41*(1), 36–44.

McLoughlin, J., Kaminski, J., Sodagar, B., Khan, S., Harris, R., Arnaudo, G., & McBrearty, S. (2009). A strategic approach to social impact measurement of social enterprises: The SIMPLE methodology. *Social Enterprise Journal, 5*(2), 154–178.

Meyer, B. D. (1995). Natural and quasi-experiments in economics. *Journal of Business and Economic Statistics, 13*(2), 151–161.

Moore, M. A., Boardman, A. E., Vining, A. R., Weimer, D. L., & Greenberg, D. H. (2004). "Just give me a number!" Practical values for the social discount rate. *Journal of Policy Analysis and Management, 23*(4), 789–812.

Nicholls, A. (2009). We do good things, don't we? "Blended value accounting" in social entrepreneurship. *Accounting, Organizations and Society, 34*(6–7), 755–769.

Nicholls, A., & Cho, A. (2008). Social entrepreneurship: The structuration of a field. In A. Nicholls (Ed.), *Social entrepreneurship: New models of sustainable social change* (pp. 99–118). Oxford: Oxford University Press.

Oswald, A. J., & Wu, S. (2010). Objective confirmation of subjective measures of human well-being: Evidence from the USA. *Science, 327*(5965), 576–579.

Phills, J. A., Deiglmeier, K., & Miller, D. T. (2008). Rediscovering social innovation. *Stanford Social Innovation Review, 6*(4), 34–43.

Polonsky, M., & Grau, S. L. (2011). Assessing the social impact of charitable organizations—Four alternative approaches. *International Journal of Nonprofit and Voluntary Sector Marketing, 16*(2), 195–211.

Price, J. L. (1972). The study of organizational effectiveness. *Sociological Quarterly, 13*(1), 3–15.

Reichardt, C. (2011). Evaluating methods for estimating program effects. *American Journal of Evaluation, 32*, 246–270.

Richardson, B. (2012). Sparking impact investing through GIIRS. *Stanford Social Innovation Review*. Retrieved July 24, 2015, from http://ssir.org/articles/entry/sparking_impact_investing_through_giirs

Rojas, M. (2006). Life satisfaction and satisfaction in domains of life: Is it a simple relationship? *Journal of Happiness Studies,* 7(4), 467–497.

Rojas, R. R. (2000). A review of models for measuring organizational effectiveness among for-profit and nonprofit organizations. *Nonprofit Management and Leadership, 11*(1), 97–104.

Rotheroe, N., & Richards, A. (2007). Social return on investment and social enterprise: Transparent accountability for sustainable development. *Social Enterprise Journal, 3*(1), 31–48.

Rubin, D. (1974). Estimating causal effects of treatments in randomized and nonrandomized studies. *Journal of Educational Psychology, 66*(5), 688–701.

Ryan, P. W., & Lyne, I. (2008). Social enterprise and the measurement of social value: Methodological issues with the calculation and application of the social return on investment. *Education, Knowledge and Economy, 2*(3), 223–237.

Saltuk, Y., El Idrissi, A., Bouri, A., Mudaliar, A., & Schiff, H. (2014). Spotlight on the market—The impact investor survey. *JP Morgan*. Retrieved February 23, 2015, from http://www.jpmorganchase.com/corporate/socialfinance/document/140502_Spotlight_on_the_Market.pdf

Sandvik, E., Diener, E., & Seidlitz, L. (1993). Subjective wellbeing: The convergence and stability of self-report and non-self-report measures. *Journal of Personality, 61*(3), 317–342.

Schimmack, U. (2008). *The structure of subjective wellbeing* (Working Paper 1). Toronto, ON: Department of Psychology.

Scholten, P. (2005). *Social return on investment, performance measurement for social entrepreneurs*. Paper presented at the IESE Social Enterprise Conference, Barcelona.

Shadish, W., Cook, T., & Campbell, D. (2002). *Experimental and quasi-experimental designs for generalized causal inference*. Boston, MA: Houghton.

Somers, A., Nicholls, J., Mackenzie, S., & Sanfilippo, L. (2005). *Measuring value creation in social firms: A do-it-yourself training manual for SROI*. Social Firms UK and New Economics Foundation. Retrieved August 15, 2011, from http://www.socialfirmsengland.co.uk/product/measuring-value-creation-in-social-firms-a-do-it-yourself-training-manual-for-sroi

Sowa, J. E., Selden, S. C., & Sandfort, J. R. (2004). No longer unmeasurable? A multidimensional integrated model of nonprofit organizational effectiveness. *Nonprofit and Voluntary Sector Quarterly, 33*(4), 711–728.

Tan, W.-L., Williams, J., & Tan, T.-M. (2005). Defining the "social" in "social entrepreneurship": Altruism and entrepreneurship. *The International Entrepreneurship and Management Journal, 1*(3), 353–365.

United Nations. (2013). *Millennium Development Goals Report 2013*. Retrieved July 24, 2015, from http://www.un.org/millenniumgoals/pdf/report-2013/mdg-report-2013-english.pdf

Veenhoven, R. (2000). Wellbeing in the welfare state: Level not higher, distribution not more equitable. *Journal of Comparative Policy Analysis, 2*(1), 91–125.

White, H. (2010). A contribution to current debates in impact evaluation. *Evaluation, 16*(2), 153–164.

White, H. (2013). An introduction to the use of randomized control trials to evaluate development interventions. *Journal of Development Effectiveness, 5*(1), 30–49.

Yates, B. T. (2009). Cost-inclusive evaluation: A banquet of approaches for including costs, benefits, and cost-effectiveness and cost-benefit analysis in your next evaluation. *Evaluation and Program Planning, 32*(1), 52–54.

Yuchtman, E., & Seashore, S. E. (1967). A system resource approach to organizational effectiveness. *American Sociological Review, 32*(6), 891–903.

Zahra, S., Gedajlovic, E., Neubaum, D., & Schulman, J. (2009). A typology of social entrepreneurs: Motives, search processes and ethical challenges. *Journal of Business Venturing, 24*(5), 519–532.

Zammuto, R. F. (1982). *Assessing organizational effectiveness: Systems change, adaption, and strategy*. Albany, NY: State University of New York.

25

SUSTAINABLE INSTITUTIONAL INVESTMENT MODELS AND THE HUMAN CAPITAL ANALYTICS APPROACH

A great gap to be filled

Carol Royal and G. Sampath S. Windsor

The power base of institutional investors is changing with tighter financial market regulation, fear of large-scale sovereign default, and increased consumer apprehension within an investment climate. Furthermore, corporate sustainability and Corporate Social Responsibility (CSR) have become mainstream and non-negotiable. A common theme within these fundamental market changes is the concept of human capital and human capital risk.

At a macro level, human capital is a measure of the economic value of an employee for employers and for the economy as a whole. Human capital is the stock of knowledge, habits, social and personality attributes, and creativity, embodied in people's ability to perform labor, to produce economic value. The concept also recognizes that not all labor is equal. The chapter explores human capital, how to analyze it, and how to see human capital as an opportunity for institutional investors, regulators, and investing public and corporate leaders to make more Sustainable Investment and leadership decisions as well as to mitigate against corporate and investment risk.

After recent corporate collapses, institutional investors have focused more on the human element as a key indicator of risk and of potential future value in firms (Akerlof & Shiller, 2010). This requires institutional investors to interpret the ambiguity inherent in the early warning signs of risk and uncertainty, implying a move away from "lag" to "lead" indicators of a firm's financial performance. Some human capital analytical models used in this regard have been adapted from the discipline of accounting. However, these models do not interpret the more complex process of managing the uncertainty and ambiguity of human capital in ways that can be readily understood by investors or corporate leaders. As such, investors and indeed corporate stakeholders today lack a coherent way to assess whether the configuration of human capital within a firm is internally consistent and provides a context for a firm to deliver its stated strategy.

Initiatives such as the United Nations Principles for Responsible Investment (UNPRI) provide a context for investment markets to broaden equities research to incorporate themes such as human capital that are more ambiguous. However, while attempting to capitalize on this emerging mandate, most institutional investors and corporate leaders fall into the trap of measuring what they can measure. Such data include those on health and occupational safety incidents, staff turnover, and headcount, and simplify what they should truly measure (Creelman, 2006). The environmental, social, and governance (ESG) principles of UNPRI also incorporate the role of boards and directors' duties, corporate accountability and disclosure, risk management, corporate responsibility, major trends in financial accounting, as well as "doing the right thing" (Williams, 2007). Yet, there is insufficient detail in these themes to sufficiently interpret the key elements of ambiguity and uncertainty in relation to human capital and related risks within organizations. Traditionally, risk management within organizations has evolved around risk identification, quantification, management, monitoring, and review. This process has then led to a situation where corporate leaders are identifying and quantifying risks themselves. However, this process fails to readily identify the dynamism of human capital risks, most of which can exist simultaneously in the "known," "unknown," and "unknowable" states. A more robust process is to identify the drivers of risk in an institution, and then to develop an appreciation of how these drivers influence the various risks that may arise.

A recent report from a coalition of institutional investors made the observation, "Today, while investors know a lot about a firm's profits and cash flow, they don't know much about a firm's sustainability" (Aviva, 2012). For institutional investors, firms' sustainability translates to CSR record and Socially Responsible Investment (SRI) concepts. However, the knowledge gaps surrounding CSR and SRI can be minimized if institutional investors move beyond first- and second-generation interpretations of CSR and SRI models. First-generation interpretations advocate that investors screen investments based on socially harmful aspects or negative filters, such as tobacco, arms dealings, and related industries. The second generation of CSR and SRI was typically based on positive filters, that is, finding and encouraging appropriate CSR role models, such as above-average environmental and social engagement practices. Third-generation CSR and SRI were based on integrated filters, which combined both negative

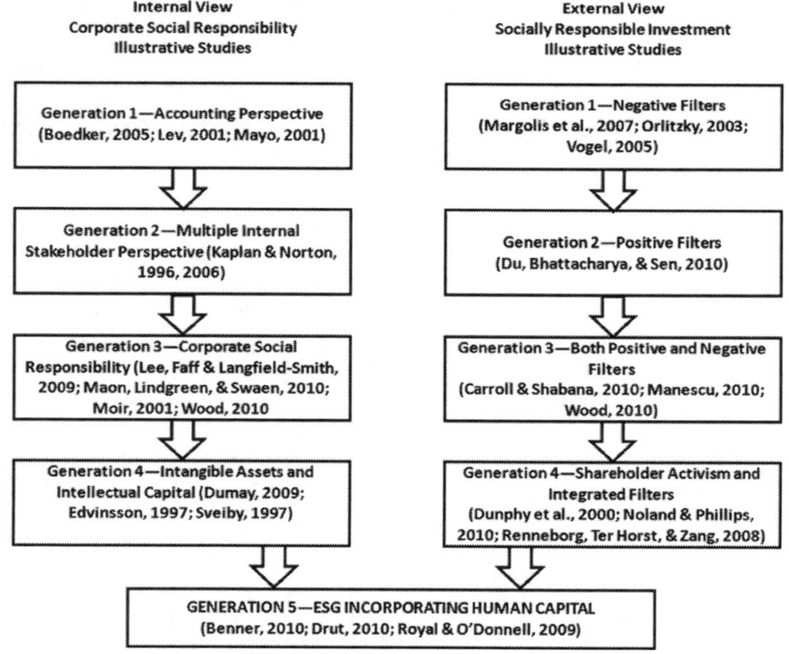

Figure 25.1 ESG as the fifth generation of Corporate Social Responsibility analysis and reporting

and positive filters. Fourth-generation CSR and SRI incorporated integrated filters and social interrelations such as stakeholder activism, which was seen as the ability to blend social, environmental, and corporate practices with substantial cost savings. While the later models were more sophisticated than the previous generation of investment filters, they are still limited in their scope and benefit.

In the current investment climate, institutional investors' power will increasingly rely on their ability to invest with the aid of fifth-generation CSR and SRI models that incorporate key elements of intangible value creation such as human capital and identification of human capital risk in corporate entities. Fifth-generation CSR and SRI models rely on a sophisticated approach to define and analyze human capital as a critical component in the ESG base of corporations which CSR depends on (see Figure 25.1 for a summary of the evolvement of these approaches).

Traditionally, institutional investors have been seen to hold significant power, some of which is embedded in the various regulatory regimes, via the power to vote on substantial corporate governance issues, such as executive remuneration and appointments to governance structures such as risk committees and boards. The power of institutional investors is only as strong as the quality of the information they use to make governance and investment decisions on behalf of clients. However, the power of institutional investors is currently based on incomplete information from listed companies on how they create value. This implies a suboptimal context for investing, as noted by a research report from a coalition of institutional investors, which notes:

> Markets are driven by information. If the information they receive is short-term and thin, then these characteristics will define the markets. If the information the board and management produce is long-term and strategic, then the market can move toward a sustainable future...capital markets currently allocate capital to corporate activity in a way that undermines sustainable development...capital markets should be the primary facilitator of a globally sustainable and just economy...development that provides short-term benefits but creates significant costs over the long-term will reduce the absolute value of long-term investment portfolios.
>
> *(Aviva, 2012)*

This chapter supports the argument that the role of institutional investors as advocates for social change in the sustainability debate is hampered by incomplete information on ESG investing, which is based on UNPRI. Traditional models of investment analysis, even when ESG considerations are included, are not sufficient as a means of articulating and communicating value in listed firms (Cohan, 2009; Creelman, 2006). Yet, fifth-generation SRI incorporating human capital capacity and human capital risk analysis has not been exploited to its full potential. For institutional investors to recognize the future performance of firms, they require knowledge of the "S" in the ESG base of corporations and their CSR actions in order to systematically analyze human capital capacity, along with the human capital risks of the firm. Finally, we conclude that the strong desire of institutional investors to make positive change will only be possible when ESG investment utilizes fifth-generation models comprehensively, which systematically incorporates all aspects of the "S" dimension, including human capital analysis.

Internal and external perspectives of a firm's value creation

As the 2012 Australian Stock Exchange declaration on sustainability implies, incorporating a corporate ESG perspective requires both an inside and an outside perspective on firm value. The internal view incorporates all three aspects of ESG beyond an analysis of financial data and includes environmental and governance data. The concept amalgamates the disciplinary areas of human resource management, strategy, organizational behavior, and management. The external view draws on corporate finance, accounting, and governance. Furthermore, both the internal and external perspectives of future firm value need to be understood by corporate leaders and then communicated to markets in a coherent manner to show how their organization is performing in these arenas for institutional investors to make investment decisions.

UNPRI, incorporating ESG base approaches to investment, has the potential to provide a fundamental shift in the power of institutional investors to interpret the creation and the destruction of value in listed companies, which has enhanced the case for SRI. SRI emerged in the United States in the 1960s, and later in the United Kingdom, Canada, and Australia. Values-based SRI (Kinder, 2005) or "value-seeking SRI" identifies social and environmental criteria that might affect future financial performance (Kinder, 2005), including perceptions of non-financial risk and risk management. Because of lack of clarity around these topics, it is still unclear which ESG concerns institutional investors need to prioritize in their SRI decisions (Mănescu, 2011). Moreover, the additional cost that is discussed in terms of SRI by detractors is dependent on investors' risk understanding and aversion perspectives (Drut, 2010).

Wood (2010) and Crifo and Forget (2013), in their studies of the private equity industry in Europe, found that SRI concepts were now mainstream and had moved beyond basic screening for specific investments when building a portfolio. Such screens can be based on ethical, social, or environmental norms, or best practices in terms of being proactive within an ESG aspect. An additional approach noted in research is shareholder activism, where voting rights are used to directly foster CSR in portfolio companies by integrating ESG issues into investment practices. In this context, each of the three ESG components is important in analysis and for the debate on the future direction of SRI. However, out of the ESG aspects, the least understood aspect is the "S" or social dimension.

Current investment indexes, such as the KLD Index (Wood, 2010), are not sufficiently measuring all "S" aspects of the firm to be interpreted by financial analysts, because they do not clearly articulate the strategic role of human capital or the minimization of human capital risk in the ESG value creation process linked to SRI. Yet, the current ESG and CSR literature and debates explore the social aspects in the investment process by incorporating some, but not all, of the role of human capital, including the role of boards and directors' duties; corporate accountability and disclosure; risk management; corporate responsibility and "doing the right thing"; as well as major trends in financial accounting (Williams, 2007). However, in this debate there is a tendency to focus on superficial human capital or social metrics, which do not provide the depth and richness required for a theoretical or practical interpretation of future value creation. It is asserted that the first-, second-, and third-generation models of SRI, although necessary for furthering the debate, did not have sufficient conditions for the successful enhancement of SRI. Furthermore, the fourth-generation model of SRI, while helpful and usable, remains incomplete. As such, it is noted that the next generation of models should incorporate hard-to-measure, yet essential, themes such as human capital capacity and risk mitigation analysis, for the true potential of SRI investing to be achieved. Furthermore, academics and institutional investors need to systematically work toward the enrichment of the fifth generation of SRI models, which incorporate value creation, which in turn will demand a clear understanding of both the internal and external views of human capital in order for institutional investors to analyze human capital.

Human capital and SRI nexus

Conception of value is immensely different in a knowledge economy in comparison to traditional economies. In the knowledge economy, employees are no longer regarded as labor but as capital (Drucker, 2002). Knowledge-based companies originate profits from the commercialization of the knowledge created by their employees. Bassi, Lev, Low, McMurrer, and Siesfeld (2000) define knowledge as "the accumulated insights and understanding, both explicit and implicit, that the employees of a firm use to accomplish their assignments every day." They see knowledge as the thoughtfulness and attention people bring to doing their job in pursuit of the firm's goals. Often these new workers are labeled "knowledge workers," and they are highly skilled, qualified, trained, and experienced. In essence, they are workers who deal with a high degree of complexity and uncertainty that requires a high degree of judgment (Dunphy, Benveniste, Griffiths, & Sutton, 2000).

The stock of competencies, knowledge, and social and personality attributes, including creativity, embodied in the ability to perform work to produce economic value is generally termed human capital. The human capital systems of corporations are mechanisms by which employees are managed, and therefore become observable in an organization and comparable, across industry sectors and across time. Royal and O'Donnell (2008) assume that human capital is manifested in a firm's unique configuration as observable aspects such as training and development, performance management, knowledge management, career planning, and succession planning. In this context, human capital is broader than employee engagement, and incorporates management systems as well as human capital risk mitigations (Royal & O'Donnell, 2008). This definition is consistent with that of Werbach (2009) and Raisch, Birkinshaw, Probst, and Tushman (2009). Human capital analysis links human resource management systems with the future performance of the firm (Royal & O'Donnell, 2003). However, for sustainable competitive advantage, all HR functions need to be in synchronization with each other as well as with the firm's broader strategic infrastructure. HR management systems are difficult to replicate, to implement, and to change. It is argued that firms that have superior HR management systems also have a potential long-term source of competitive advantage (Bassi & McMurrer, 2007; Becker, Becker, Ulrich, Huselid, & Huselid, 2001). The term "human capital" is distinguishable from the more commonly used term "social capital," which is defined by Dunphy et al. (2000) as human sustainability, which implies building human capability and skills for sustainable high-level organizational performance for community and societal well-being while reducing human capital risk, as well as other aspects of risk related to social aspects.

The "first wave" of ESG incorporating investment, prior to UNPRI, was launched by selected large European institutional investors in November 2004. The aim of the Enhanced Analytical Initiative (EAI) was to encourage sell-side analysts to systematically examine intangibles by allocating 5 percent of their broker commissions for superior intangibles research (Bauer, Koedijk, & Ottenc, 2005). This initiative, now a component of UNPRI, was an implicit acknowledgment of a knowledge gap in securities analysts to distinguish material non-financial data. It also implies that human resources professionals, as well as senior executives, will increasingly be required to be aware of the dialogue between the board and institutional investors working within regulatory regimes, which requires the board to clarify the company's business model and to explain the nature and extent of the significant risks it is willing to take. Such explanations are required to include human capital capacity to assist companies' business models as well as mechanisms to minimize human capital risk.

The impact of poor corporate governance practices on shareholder value, accentuated by the global financial crisis, has also lifted issues such as transparency, corruption, board structure, shareholder rights, business ethics, risk management, and executive compensation to the top of the investor agenda. In response, UNPRI offers a menu of possible actions for incorporating ESG issues into investment practices. The UN Principles are voluntary and aspirational. UNPRI is seen as a process that must be tailored to fit each organization's investment strategy, approach, and resources. The Principles are designed to be compatible with the investment styles of large, diversified, institutional investors that operate within a traditional fiduciary framework. A UNPRI and ESG focus ensures that listed companies are increasingly judged on their quality of management. For human capital accountability, it is expected that boards have to be composed carefully, based on merit and diversity, and be reviewed at least every 3 years. All directors of FTSE350 companies should be put forward for re-election every year. Also, "proper boardroom debate" is demanded, and that the chairman and the non-executive directors are required to provide the same constructive challenges and time commitment expected of all directors. As such, human capital analysis is becoming strategic to CEOs, boards, and institutional investors. However, institutional investors need to move through the four preceding generations of SRI investing to optimize the insights from the fifth and more powerful approach to SRI investing, which incorporates human capital analysis (see Figure 25.1). It is asserted that using the fifth-generation models, institutional investors are more likely to and would be able to analyze and interpret elements of human capital risk, which is a significant issue, as highlighted by the Lehman Brothers collapse.

Early generations of CSR and SRI, while well intentioned, did not incorporate all three aspects of ESG at the appropriate level of detail. The incomplete knowledge base of the ESG base of corporations used by institutional investors means incomplete power over investment advice. While superficial aspects of human capital, as a key component of the "S" in ESG investing, were measured using traditional accounting and quantitative data, measuring the efficient and effective management of "human capital" and analysis has progressed to an increasingly imperative and complex process. Both qualitative and systems thinking are required to analyze the open, generative systems that drive human capital value. Such qualitative data can be benchmarked using appropriate fifth-generation models.

Known, unknown, and unknowable human capital risk and epistemic uncertainty

Investment recommendations are made on a relative basis, comparing a company's performance within a sector or industry. Such analyses cover all relevant publicly available information about the company and its business and the sector in which it operates. "It is not limited to financial statements, [and includes] research on the company, industry, product or sector, and public statements by and interviews with executives of the company, its customers and suppliers" (Fernandez, 2001). These underpinning disciplines of econometrics and finance are effective in training graduates to model risk and even uncertainty, but they typically do not teach analysts to model ambiguity.

Human capital risk exists in "known," "unknown," and "unknowable" states within corporations. Yet, corporations neither focused on specifically, nor espoused to analyze, human capital data or risk. To make matters worse, inconsistency exists between the rhetoric espoused at the top levels of the organization as opposed to the reality of what is practiced within organizations, in regards to human capital risk and risks in general. Although some blame the corporate regulators and internal governance committees for lacking definitive guidance and creating confusion, others acknowledge that corporations are unprepared to tackle human capital risk despite corporate leaders' genuine efforts to reduce risk exposures. However, corporate leaders still believe that intangible human capital aspects or risk is the main cause of scandals or corporate collapses, and that human capital is a lead indicator or predictor of these kinds of situations.

Understanding the performance of a firm requires an analysis of the ambiguities inherent in employee behavior. Although specific financial results cannot be predicted precisely via human capital, the human capital patterns shaping superior performance can be understood (Senge, 2000) and can provide insight into future value creation and destruction within listed firms. As such, corporate regulators can provide a context for market participants to analyze and interpret human capital and associated risk at the level of patterns and systems. Quantitative techniques are valuable to appreciate outcomes within multiple uncertain inputs, but users need to understand the imperfections of their assumptions. There are also non-readily quantifiable issues to take into account. Quantitative valuation methods, such as the BSM and Gaussian Cupola models, are necessary but not sufficient for predicting future value in complex, knowledge-based markets. They need to be supplemented by rigorous qualitative research that incorporates interpreting the ambiguity inherent in human capital as experienced by firms in changing economic conditions. Human capital professionals are trained in the disciplines of organizational psychology, strategic human resource management, and interpreting ambiguity. This is distinctly different to the overly simplistic use of accounting principles in human capital metrics, especially when those metrics were designed for internal corporate use, not market use. They do not allow institutional investors to assess whether a listed company has reduced ambiguity through appropriate configurations of human capital and human capital systems.

It appears that institutional investors do not systematically acquire the skills which underpin human capital analysis, including strategic human resource management and organizational change management systems. Most finance professionals are trained in a very different set of underlying disciplinary fields, and these do not typically account for high levels of environmental ambiguity and episodic uncertainty. The nominal function of financial markets analysis is to conduct thorough research investigations into all aspects of the current and prospective financial condition of publicly listed companies and to provide an analysis of the findings in the form of a research report, which serves as a basis for making an investment recommendation (Royal & Althauser, 2003). However, in spite of significant regulation on all aspects of the recruitment, training, development, remuneration, and promotion of financial analysts, regulators do not currently focus on the acquisition of skills to analyze inherently ambiguous human capital within listed firms. However, institutional investors indicate they benefit from the timeliness of human capital information, which they see as essential for providing a better balance of "real time" and "right time" financial and non-financial information. It is noted that such human capital information provides opportunities for sensing and responding to corporate events before their implications are widely known and understood.

The uncertainty can be minimized if institutional investors move beyond analysis and interpretation of traditional data sets, as urged by the UNPRI initiatives. However, even these principles are not adequate to ensure the widespread adoption of appropriate levels of modeling episodic uncertainty. While the first- and second-generation interpretations of CSR and SRI serve to challenge traditional quantitative risk models, they can be misinterpreted, and have been used as an over-simplistic proxy for human capital analysis and risk management (Royal & O'Donnell, 2011). For investment analysis, these approaches attempt to minimize ambiguity for investors by providing relatively simple industry-based screens, such as tobacco, arms dealing, and related industries. More comprehensive third and fourth generations of CSR and SRI are based on negative–positive filters and integrated filters associated with sustainable business practices, and the ability to blend social, environmental, and corporate practices with substantial cost-savings efficiency improvements. While these filters are more sophisticated than the previous generation of investment filters, they are still limited in their scope and benefit. Investors will need to increasingly rely on their ability to invest in the context of fifth-generation CSR and SRI involving a sophisticated approach to modeling to avoid (or minimize) risk and uncertainty in investment decision-making.

Why it is difficult to quantify human capital and associated risk

During uncertain economic times, institutional investors overemphasize the short-term gains, concentrating more on quarterly results than on the foundation for long-term success (Bassi et al., 2000). Such an obsession with short-term profits is contrary to the spirit of sustainability, which requires the firm to meet the needs of its stakeholders in the future as well as today. However, due to the difficulties of measuring human capital, corporate leaders find it difficult to reliably report the information. Therefore, Bassi et al. (2000) argue that capital market impressions are driving the valuation of company stocks. According to Shiller (2000), variations in assessing also occur due to various external influences like the media. In some cases, analysts provide estimates for selected elements of SRI without attempting to provide comprehensive reasoning (Royal & O'Donnell, 2003).

Although there are policies regarding continuous disclosure in the Australian Stock Market, it was found that efforts in HR were not readily disclosed publicly. The corporate sector does not yet recognize the benefits of disclosing such information and view government efforts to get comprehensive disclosure as intrusive (Bassi et al., 2000). Possible reasons for not disclosing human capital information included shareholder backlash due to conflicting ideologies on investment in areas such as training. Gallery, Gallery, and Hsu (2002), in their research which investigated the link between analysts' earnings forecasts and ASX's continuous disclosure, state that corporate leaders strategically issue less informative confirmatory forecasts because confirmatory forecasts minimize disclosure costs and help foster good relations with analysts, investors, and corporate regulators. They further argue that the current system is somewhat defective, as the research indicated a selective disclosure environment and lack of actions by corporate regulators. They concluded that 63.3 percent of earning forecasts made to ASX did not provide any new information to investors apart from what was already available through analysts' forecasts, and 75 percent of forecasts were qualitative and lacked precision.

The second major problem was found to be the lack of standardized tools that the institutional investors could easily utilize. This lack of standardization also meant that questions were raised about the ability of institutional investors to properly use the tools, and the tools' ability to measure sustainability among all industries. Furthermore, regardless of the tool used, institutional investors and brokerage firms still lack the necessary competencies and skills to analyze sustainability (Royal & O'Donnell, 2002). It is suggested that one either needs to come up with more practical models, which includes human capital analysis for institutional investors, or institutional investors should purchase such analysis reports from relevant human capital analysis experts.

Attributes of effective human capital measurement and analysis

Bassi and McMurrer (2007) and Creelman (2006) describe the ideal attributes of human capital measurement systems. Such a system should be credible, descriptive, predictive, detailed, actionable, and cost-effective. Jhunjhunwala (2009) observes that indicators should be easy to measure. This is consistent with the Statement of Financial Accounting Concepts (CON) 2:

Qualitative Characteristics of Accounting Information of Financial Accounting Standards Board (FASB). FASB note that indicators should be understandable and beneficial, consistent, comparable, relevant, and reliable. While some may argue that traditional financial metrics achieve these goals, recent behavior leading to the global financial crisis would suggest that even the more mathematically elegant equations used by dominant analysts in equity research and derivatives can be wrong and misleading (Salmon, 2009).

From an accounting perspective, Mayo (2001) suggests that human capital measures should be "roughly right" rather than "precisely wrong," simple to understand, clearly defined, and able to be interpreted in the same way. They should have integrity, be consistent and reliable, have no inherent biases, nor be influenced by a person's judgment, and make sense in the context of other measures. Further, they should focus on what is important and comprise key outputs linked to them, and have the right level of detail for action to be taken, for tracking change, and for showing clear ownership by an individual or team. It is also noted that such measures should have the right frequency for measurements and to provide useful trending and comparisons. While ambitious, these measures are not wildly impossible conditions to meet. However, it would be difficult to reach all such standards (Pike & Roos, 2004). From a mathematical perspective, there are five conditions for measurement: completeness (the attributes must completely describe the company); distinctness (which eliminates double counting); independence (this concerns the relationship between entities so that aggregation to overarching measures can be undertaken safely); agreeability (mapping from an empirical to numeric system); and commensurability (measurements must be observed using a ratio scale and be normalized onto a common scale). Qualitative human capital data can meet equally high standards of rigor (Denzin & Lincoln, 2005).

Initiatives like UNPRI provide scope to broaden the analysis process. However, such initiatives do not specify specific tools for the analysis of non-financial elements. Though helpful, traditional approaches to human capital metrics tend not to be able to be readily used by institutional investors and securities analysts (see Table 25.1).

Table 25.1 Summary of 10 traditional approaches to human capital metrics

Model	*Author(s)*	*Date*	*Attributes*
Human Capital Index	Watson Wyatt Worldwide	2002	Indicates human capital systems are a lead indicator of future financial performance.
European Business Excellence Model	European Foundation for Quality Management (EFQM)	2009 updated	Compares real human capital situation with ideal benchmarks.
Malcolm Baldrige Criteria for Performance Excellence	Baldrige National Quality Program, National Institute of Standards and Technology, MD	2009 updated	Is used for both corporates and not-for-profit organizations to compare standards of quality of management.
William Mercer's Human Capital Wheel	William Mercer	1997	Is tailored to individual organizations.
Return on Investment in Human Capital	Jac Fitz-Enz	2000	Focuses on total remuneration rather than headcount as key unit of analysis.
Balanced Scorecard	R. S. Kaplan and D. P. Norton	1996	Is double-loop feedback process to focus attention of management on a small number of critical issues. Widely used across a variety of industry sectors.

(Continued)

Table 25.1 Summary of 10 traditional approaches to human capital metrics *(Continued)*

Model	*Author(s)*	*Date*	*Attributes*
Skandia Navigator	Leif Edvinsson and M. S. Malone	1997	Is influential model, developed for one firm, drawing on Kaplan and Norton's ideas. This model is applied globally.
HR Scorecard	Brian Becker, Mark Huselid, and Dave Ulrich	2001	Forms a bridge between strategic HRM practices and Balanced Scorecard practices.
Human Capital Monitor	Andrew Mayo	2001	Works on the fundamental assumption that human capital is a key strategic asset in organizations. Applies accounting principles to human capital systems.
Intellectual Capital Index	R. D. Stacey	2001	Acknowledges that measures of human capital, such as patents, are useful only if they indicate dynamic processes between people in organizations.

Source: Based on O'Donnell and Royal (2010).

Table 25.2 Five stages of organizational decline

Stage 1: Hubris born of success

- Arrogance, success as entitlement, and loss of understanding of why they were successful

Stage 2: Undisciplined pursuit of more

- More scale, more growth, more acclaim, and more "success" (however defined)
- Can't fill seats with the right people—danger of overreaching

Stage 3: Denial of risk and peril

- Internal warning signs are ignored or explained away
- Positive news is accentuated—blame external factors

Stage 4: Grasping for salvation

- Choice to lurch for salvation or go back to the discipline that created the initial greatness
- For example, bold but untested strategy; charismatic visionary leader; radical transformation; dramatic cultural revolution; blockbuster product; and game-changing acquisition. Initial positive results are not sustainable.

Stage 5: Capitulation to irrelevance or death

- Accumulated setbacks erode financial strength and individual spirit—some abandon all hope
- Some leaders sell out and other institutions atrophy into insignificance or die

Source: Based on Collins (2009).

The research of Collins (2009) on the stages of organizational decline is a significant contribution to the debate on investing in the human capital and social aspects of sustainability. Collins found five stages, which represent the decline of an organization. Typically, not always, the sequence is maintained, but with varying times in different stages (see Table 25.2).

Collins (2009) also found that stages can overlap, and that there can be different periods between stages. It can take months to move from one stage to the other (as in the Lehman Brothers example discussed below), or decades. His analysis found that firms like IBM and Disney fell into Stage 4 and reversed their declines, and so too have 3M, Johnson and Johnson, and

Procter and Gamble. They suggest that Stage 1 does not inevitably lead to Stage 5. The main finding that investors need to consider is that Stage 5 can be prevented when leadership instills disciplined management practices, which also requires rigor around organizational human capital capacity and minimization of human capital risk through robust human capital systems.

A lack of human capital measurement and analysis lead to five stages of organizational decline; examples in brief—Enron and Lehman Brothers collapses

To illustrate the five stages of organizational decline, incomplete ESG reporting, as well as the lack of power of institutional investors to formally and systematically predict future financial failure, it is worth noting a few examples of recent corporate collapses in brief.

The Enron scandal revealed in October 2001 eventually led to the bankruptcy of Enron. Enron is a large American energy company based in Houston, Texas. The scandal also caused the de facto dissolution of Arthur Andersen, one of the world's five largest audit and accountancy firms.

At the time of the Enron collapse, human capital was not seen as an essential theme in ESG reports and/or other investment reports by the corporations as well as institutional investors. However, Enron won a spot for 3 years in a row on the list of the best companies to work for in America (Waddock, Bodwell, & Graves, 2002). In 2000, it received six environmental awards. Enron issued a triple bottom-line report and had policies on climate change, human rights, and anti-corruption. The Enron CEO was a guest speaker at ethics conferences. Enron featured in many SRI funds' recommendation to invest before it collapsed. However, a closer look at Enron from a human capital perspective could have revealed a different picture. A culture of dysfunctional human capital, including performance management, remuneration, and career planning, was shown to be inconsistent internally and with the strategy of the organization, leading to a contradictory picture from the quantitative accounting-based one.

Evidence uncovered later showed that Jeffrey Skilling, the CEO of Enron, promoted executives that used accounting loopholes, special entities, and substandard financial reporting to hide billions of dollars in debt. Chief Financial Officer Andrew Fastow and other executives misled Enron's board of directors and audit committee on high-risk accounting practices. The majority of the causes that led to bankruptcy were perpetuated by the indirect knowledge or direct actions of Ken Lay, Jeffrey Skilling, Andrew Fastow, and other executives. Ken Lay served as the chairman of the company and approved of the actions of Skilling and Fastow without inquiring about the details. On paper, Enron had a model board of directors comprising mainly outsiders with significant ownership stakes. It also had a talented audit committee. In its 2000 review of best corporate boards, *Chief Executive Magazine* included Enron among its five best boards. Even with its complex corporate governance, Enron executives were still able to hide a questionable business model and conceal its true performance while encouraging hype around its stock to unsustainable levels.

Enron's compensation and performance management system was dysfunctional and created a corporate culture that focused on short-term earnings to maximize executive and employee bonuses. In 1998, Enron's top 200 highest paid employees received $193 million from salaries, bonuses, and stock. Two years later, the figure was at $1.4 billion. Employees constantly focused on getting good performance reviews at the cost of risk mitigation and following regulations to maximize their bonuses. Company executives were also compensated extensively using stock options. Using Enron's January 2001 stock price of $83.13, the value of direct stock ownership of Lay was $659 million and $174 million for Skilling (Gillan & Martin, 2002). The compensation policy using stock options caused management to create expectations of rapid growth in stock to keep up with expectations from Wall Street and to maximize their own wealth. The stock publishing monitors were located in lobbies, elevators, and on company computers to promote the culture of stock price maximization within all ranks of the company. Executives also went to extreme lengths to lift the stock price. In 1998, when analysts were given a tour of the Enron Energy Services office, analysts were impressed to see employees working energetically on the office floor. In reality, Skilling had moved other employees from other departments to the office and instructed them to pretend to work hard to create the appearance of a tightknit high-performing division that was larger than it was (Sorkin, 2008). This ruse was used several times to fool analysts about the progress of different areas of Enron to help improve the stock price.

Skilling constantly focused on meeting Wall Street expectations and advocated the use of mark to market accounting (accounting based on market value). However, market value could inflate. This led Skilling to pressure Enron executives to find new ways to hide its debt. Enron's complex financial statements were confusing to shareholders and analysts. Its unethical practices required the company to use deliberately complex financial statements aided by accounting limitations to misrepresent earnings to show a favorable balance sheet and performance at each year-end. Before the scandal, Enron was lauded for its sophisticated financial risk management tools. Enron's aggressive accounting practices were not hidden from the board of directors, as later learned by a Senate subcommittee. Although not all of Enron's widespread improper accounting practices were revealed to the board, the practices were dependent on board decisions. Enron extensively relied on derivatives for its business. The company's finance committee and board did not have enough experience with derivatives to understand what they were being told. However, Enron's audit committee had more expertise than many other contemporary corporations' audit committees. But Enron's audit committee did not have the technical knowledge to question the auditors properly on accounting issues related to the company's special purpose entities. The committee was also unable to question the company's management due to pressures applied on the committee.

Enron's auditor, Arthur Andersen, was accused of applying reckless standards in its audits due to the significant consulting fees it generated through Enron. In 2000, Arthur Andersen earned $25 million in audit fees and $27 million in consulting fees. Enron hired numerous Certified Public Accountants (CPAs) who had worked on developing accounting rules with the FASB. The accountants searched for new ways to save the company money, including capitalizing on loopholes found in the accounting industry's standards. Finding loopholes was seen as opportunities to be exploited as weaknesses in the system. Andersen's auditors were pressured by Enron's management to defer recognizing the charges arising from the special purpose entities, as such information would have exposed its credit risks. To pressure Andersen into meeting Enron's earnings expectations, Enron occasionally allowed accounting companies Ernst & Young and PricewaterhouseCoopers to complete accounting tasks to create the illusion of hiring a new company to replace Andersen. Although Andersen was equipped with internal controls to protect against the opposed incentives of clients, it also failed to prevent a conflict of interest. After the collapse Enron's auditor Arthur Andersen was found guilty of illegally destroying documents relevant to the investigation and ultimately had to cease operations.

Many executives at Enron were indicted on a variety of charges and sentenced to prison. Employees and shareholders received limited returns in lawsuits, despite losing billions in pensions and stock prices. As a consequence of the Enron scandal, new regulations such as the Sarbanes-Oxley Act were introduced with increased penalties for destroying, altering, or fabricating records in federal investigations or for attempting to defraud shareholders.

Lehman Brothers' subsequent bankruptcy was many times the size of the Enron collapse. This indicates that institutional investors, analysts, corporate executives, and regulators may not have learned enough about the strategic role of human capital analysis as a lead indicator of future sustainability and performance after Enron declared bankruptcy a decade earlier.

Financial services firm Lehman Brothers was the fourth largest investment bank in the US. Citing a bank debt of $613 billion, it filed for chapter 11 bankruptcy protection in the US on September 15, 2008. It remains the largest bankruptcy filing in US history (Mamudi, 2008). On the day the Lehman Brothers investment bank filed for bankruptcy, the three top credit ratings agencies had rated the firm as above average in its ability to meet its financial commitments. S&P rated the investment bank's debt as A, a "strong" capacity to meet financial commitments (Swedberg, 2010). Moody's had rated Lehman A2, "low credit risk." Fitch rated Lehman A+ or "high credit quality" (Evans & Salas, 2009). Furthermore, Lehman Brothers won numerous awards that year while cultivating a reputation for being an industry leader and an innovative company to be emulated by its peers. For example, in 2008, which was the year of the collapse, at ALB China Law Awards, Lehman Brothers was crowned Debt Market Dealer of the Year and the Equity Market Dealer of the Year. Similarly, superficial analysis of selected "S" indicators from an ESG perspective indicated that the bank was also doing well in its social, human capital, and human capital risk mitigation aspects. On the surface, it seemed that Lehman performed quite well under long-term Chairman and CEO Richard S. Fuld, Jr. The incompleteness of human capital analysis and the company's "S" information became evident later that year after the collapse.

In 2006, Fuld, the CEO, was named No. 1 CEO in the Brokers & Asset Managers category, by *Institutional Investor* magazine. In June 2008, rival CEOs, including Lazard's Bruce Wasserstein, stated their confidence in Fuld as a top CEO in the US and a worthy corporate opponent. However, Fuld's personal experience was as a bond trader who thrived on risk-taking in unilateral behaviors for profit-making. He had little experience of financial instruments such as collateralized debt obligations and credit default swaps (McDonald & Robinson, 2009). Lehman's last CFO was a lawyer, without qualifications in Finance or Accounting. As the subprime mortgage crisis took hold, the CEOs of rivals like Bear Stearns, Merrill Lynch, and Citigroup were forced to resign (Plumb & Wilchins, 2008). However, Lehman's board of directors, which included retired CEOs like Vodafone's Christopher Gent and IBM's John Akers, were reluctant to challenge Fuld even as the firm's share price descended (Plumb & Wilchins, 2008).

In 2007, Dick Fuld received a $22 million bonus while Lehman achieved a net profit increase of 5 percent. However, the collapse and subsequent crisis exposed a controversy around executive pay in Lehman Brothers. During the investigation by the US House of Representatives' Committee, it was noted that Fuld had received about $300 million in pay and bonuses over the past 8 years (Swaine, 2008). Despite Fuld's defense of his high remuneration, Lehman Brothers' executive pay, which was reported to have increased significantly before the bankruptcy, was criticized as unjustifiable by investigation committees.

Investment banks such as Lehman Brothers were not subject to the same regulations applied to depository banks to restrict their risk-taking (Labaton, 2008). Lehman Brothers borrowed significant amounts to fund its investing in a process known as leveraging (gearing). A significant portion of this investing was vulnerable to a downturn in markets. During the US subprime mortgage crisis and the Asian Financial Crisis, such investments led to unprecedented loss, contributing to the collapse. Fuld was accused of underestimating the downturn in the US housing market and its effect on Lehman Brothers' mortgage bond underwriting business and the subsequent attempt to hide the losses.

In March 2010, the report of *Bankruptcy Examiner* drew attention to the use of cosmetic accounting gimmicks such as "Repo 105" transactions to boost the bank's financial position in the year-end balance sheet. "Repo 105" was a Lehman Brothers term for an accounting maneuver that classified a short-term repurchase agreement as a sale to temporarily remove securities from the company's balance sheet. It was reported that Lehman accountants used the accounting maneuver to reduce $50 billion in liabilities on their balance sheet before year-end earnings were announced. This created "a materially misleading picture of the firm's financial condition in late 2007 and 2008" (Trumbull, 2010). New York attorney general Andrew Cuomo also filed charges against Lehman Brothers' auditors Ernst & Young in December 2010. It was alleged that the firm "substantially assisted ... a massive accounting fraud" by approving such accounting treatments (Reed, 2010). Furthermore, it was revealed that Lehman Brothers had used a small company, Hudson Castle, to move a number of transactions and assets off Lehman's books as a means of manipulating Lehman's finances and risks. One-quarter of Hudson Castle was owned by Lehman Brothers; Hudson Castle's board was controlled by Lehman Brothers; and most Hudson Castle staff members were former Lehman employees (Story & Dash, 2010).

Fuld ran Lehman in an authoritarian manner, creating the competitive corporate culture characteristic of investment banks. Anyone who was perceived as a threat by Fuld was eliminated, and so were the critics who argued that Lehman was "heading for trouble" (McDonald & Robinson, 2009). Whistle blower Matthew Lee, a former senior vice president of the Finance Division in charge of global balance sheet and legal entity accounting, was sacked in late June 2008. In May 2008, Lee wrote a letter to senior management warning that the firm may have been masking the true risks on its balance sheet (Corkery, 2010). Analysts who had tried to highlight the negative aspects of Lehman Brothers' corporate culture, including the executive performance management and remuneration systems, were criticized (Swedberg, 2010). Hedge Fund Greenlight Capital's president, Timothy Einhorn, highlighted some of these human capital themes in October 2007, March 2008, and May 2008, but was criticized by other journalists in the business press and by Lehman Brothers for being inexperienced, arguing his analysis was "underdone." However, after the collapse the Street website stated that Dick Fuld "ruled with an iron fist, and ultimately his poor leadership and management led to one of the largest bankruptcy filings in history," noting that "A single man's leadership style resulted in the financial ruin of tens of thousands of employees and shareholders." During hearings on the bankruptcy filing, Fuld argued that a host of factors including a crisis of confidence and short-selling attacks followed by false rumors contributed to the collapse of Lehman Brothers. With the benefit of hindsight and documents that became publicly available after the Lehman bankruptcy, US House Committee Chairman Henry Waxman said evidence portrayed a company in which there was "no accountability for failure" (Moore, 2008; Smith, 2008).

Analysis of human capital and human capital risk through a fifth-generation model would have uncovered these systemic inconsistencies, which could have posed the questions around the sustainability of these corporations. By examining any inconsistencies between human capital systems, such as remuneration and performance management systems, a human capital analysis can raise questions about the sustainability and internal–external consistency of such practices. In the case of Enron and Lehman Brothers, the inconsistencies between rewards, remuneration, and performance management systems have been implicated in the downfall of the firms. In its broadest sense, the question Enron and Lehman Brothers pose is, "Can this organization survive?" Furthermore, it could be argued that every stage of Collins' (2009) Five Stages of Organizational Decline model played itself out in these examples from hubris born of success to undisciplined pursuit of more, to denial of risk and peril, to grasping for salvation, and ending in capitulation to irrelevance or death. The assertion is a systematic analysis of "S" and human capital system insights, and human capital risk analysis needs to be embedded in the investment analysis and recommendations of institutional investors as an early warning or lead indicator of trouble brewing within a corporation.

Conclusion

Without a full analysis of the "S" in ESG investing, human capital and human capital risk can lead to devastating consequences, as can be seen by the Enron and Lehman cases and others.

Although human capital analytical tools are available to institutional investors, securities analysts, and the broader investment community, changing the quantitative nature of corporate analysis to a more qualitative, human capital-oriented, approach is a complex process.

Human capital is a strategic competitive advantage and a necessary aspect of qualitative risk management tools. Strategic significance motivates organizations to assess their capabilities as well as limitations in terms of measuring and managing human capital and human capital risk. Furthermore, knowledge of human capital and human capital risk management would allow institutional investors to make better decisions in terms of choosing the appropriate risk evaluation tools, understanding their limitations, and developing new strategic tools that incorporate human capital into investment decision-making and risk assessments.

In conditions of episodic uncertainty, more knowledge in human capital systems within listed firms is likely to be useful to institutional investors than less knowledge. The specific outcomes of human capital risk cannot be fully known. While markets are continually subjected to "black swan" events, it is feasible for corporate leaders and regulators to consider embedding a more systematic analysis of human capital into the regulatory system. Systemic analysis of human capital risks can also potentially prepare institutional investors for the financial market equivalent of tsunamis, through clearer analysis of previously underestimated qualitative data.

Studies indicate that there is an important knowledge and skills gap of strategic importance, with institutional investors and finance professionals, in regards to human capital analysis and risk mitigation. Human capital risk analysis can provide a complementary approach to financial models, such as the Gaussian Cupola formula. It is acknowledged that the human element can create more variables and complexities. However, regulators in the future may need to consider the significance of systematically incorporating human capital risk assessment into all aspects of the financial industry, as one approach to reduce ambiguity—especially to accommodate conditions of episodic uncertainty due to human capital drivers that act as lead indicators of the future financial performance of investments while at the same time highlighting ensuing risk.

As Isern, Meaney, and Wilson (2009) found, since the global financial crisis, companies across all sectors are already undergoing significant change. Additional turbulent change triggers are likely to create more complexity, unless policy-makers and industry leaders are able to offer a fifth-generation model that systematically incorporates critical intangibles, such as human capital, to mitigate hidden corporate risk. A fifth-generation model can also be considered as the new investment bridge to the future, which can highlight clear and achievable milestones toward specified ESG targets and clear regulatory structures to support the change.

References

Akerlof, G. A., & Shiller, R. J. (2010). *Animal spirits: How human psychology drives the economy, and why it matters for global capitalism.* Princeton, NJ: Princeton University Press.

Aviva. (2012). *Corporate sustainability reporting coalition, promoting corporate sustainability reporting.* UN Conference on Sustainable Development, Rio+20, A Briefing for Participants.

Bassi, L., & McMurrer, D. (2007). Maximizing your return on people. *Harvard Business Review, 85*(3), 115.

Bassi, L. J., Lev, B., Low, J., McMurrer, D. P., & Siesfeld, G. A. (2000). Measuring corporate investments in human capital. In M. M. Blair & T. A. Kochan (Eds.), *The new relationship: Human capital in the American corporation* (pp. 334–381). Washington, DC: Brookings Institution.

Bauer, R., Koedijk, K., & Ottenc, R. (2005). International evidence on ethical mutual fund performance and investment style. *Journal of Banking & Finance, 29*(7), 1751–1767.

Becker, B., Becker, B. E., Ulrich, D., Huselid, M. A., & Huselid, M. (2001). *The HR scorecard: Linking people, strategy, and performance.* Boston, MA: Harvard Business School Press.

Cohan, W. D. (2009). *House of cards: How Wall Street's gamblers broke capitalism.* London, UK: Penguin Books Ltd.

Collins, J. C. (2009). *How the mighty fall: And why some companies never give in.* New York, NY: HarperCollins.

Corkery, M. (2010). The Lehman whistleblower's letter. *The Wall Street Journal.* Retrieved May 16, 2015, from http://blogs.wsj.com/deals/2010/03/19/breaking-news-here-is-the-letter-at-the-center-of-the-lehman-report

Creelman, D. (2006). *Reporting on human capital: What the Fortune 100 tells Wall Street about human capital management.* School of Accounting, Edith Cowan University.

Crifo, P., & Forget, V. D. (2013). Think global, invest responsible: Why the private equity industry goes green. *Journal of Business Ethics, 116*(1), 21–48.

Denzin, N. K., & Lincoln, Y. S. (2005). *The Sage handbook of qualitative research* (3rd ed.). Thousand Oaks, CA: Sage.

Drucker, P. F. (2002). They're not employees, they're people. *Harvard Business Review, 80*(2), 70.

Drut, B. (2010). *Social responsibility and mean-variance portfolio selection* (CEB Working Paper No. 10/002). Solvay Brussels School of Economics and Management, Université Libre de Bruxelles, Belgium.

Dunphy, D., Benveniste, J., Griffiths, A., & Sutton, P. (2000). *Sustainability: The corporate challenge of the 21st century.* Sydney, Australia: Allen & Unwin.

Edvinsson, L., & Malone, M. S. (1997). *Intellectual capital: Realizing your company's true value by finding its hidden brainpower.* New York, NY: HarperCollins.

Evans, D., & Salas, C. (2009, April 29). Flawed credit ratings reap profits as regulators fail investors. *Bloomberg News.*

Fernandez, F. A. (2001). The role and responsibilities of securities analysts. *Securities Industry Association Research Reports, 2,* 3–10.

Gallery, G., Gallery, N., & Hsu, C. M. G. (2002). *The association between management and analysts' earnings forecasts in the Australian continuous disclosure environment* (Working Paper). Brisbane: Queensland University of Technology.

Gillan, S., & Martin, J. D. (2002). *Financial engineering, corporate governance, and the collapse of Enron* (U. of Delaware Coll. of Bus. and Econ. Ctr. for Corp. Governance Working Paper No. 2002-001).

Isern, J., Meaney, M. C., & Wilson, S. (2009, April). Corporate transformation under pressure. *McKinsey Quarterly,* 7–14.

Jhunjhunwala, S. (2009). Monitoring and measuring intangibles using value maps: Some examples. *Journal of Intellectual Capital, 10*(2), 211–223.

Kaplan, R., & Norton, D. (1996). *The balanced scorecard.* Boston, MA: Harvard Business School Press.

Kinder, P. D. (2005). *Socially responsible investing: An evolving concept in a changing world.* Boston, MA: KLD Research & Analytics, Inc.

Labaton, S. (2008, October 2). Agency's '04 rule let banks pile up new debt. *The New York Times.* Retrieved May 16, 2015, from http://www.nytimes.com/2008/10/03/business/03sec.html?_r=0

Mamudi, S. (2008, September 15). Lehman folds with record $613 billion debt. *MarketWatch.* Retrieved May 16, 2015, from http://www.marketwatch.com/story/lehman-folds-with-record-613-billion-debt

Mănescu, C. (2011). Stock returns in relation to environmental, social and governance performance: Mispricing or compensation for risk? *Sustainable Development, 19*(2), 95–118.

Mayo, A. (2001). *The human value of the enterprise: Valuing people as assets—Monitoring, measuring, managing.* London, UK: Nicholas Brealey Publishing.

McDonald, L. G., & Robinson, P. (2009). *A colossal failure of common sense: The inside story of the collapse of Lehman Brothers.* New York, NY: Crown Business.

Moore, H. N. (2008, October 7). Dick Fuld's Vendetta Against Short-Sellers—and Goldman Sachs. *The Wall Street Journal.* Retrieved May 16, 2015, from http://blogs.wsj.com/deals/2008/10/07/dick-fulds-vendetta-against-short-sellers-and-goldman-sachs

O'Donnell, L., and Royal, C. (2010). The business case for human capital metrics. In J. O'Connell & S. Teo (Eds.), *Strategic HRM: Contemporary issues in the Asia Pacific Region* (pp. 98–125). Melbourne, Victoria: Tilde University Press.

Pike, S., & Roos, G. (2004). Mathematics and modern business management. *Journal of Intellectual Capital, 5*(2), 243–256.

Plumb, C., & Wilchins, D. (2008, September 14). Lehman CEO Fuld's hubris contributed to meltdown. *Reuters, New York.* Retrieved May 16, 2015, from http://www.reuters.com/article/us-lehman-backstory-idUSN1341059120080914

Raisch, S., Birkinshaw, J., Probst, G., & Tushman, M. L. (2009). Organizational ambidexterity: Balancing exploitation and exploration for sustained performance. *Organization Science, 20*(4), 685–695.

Reed, K. (2010, December 21). E&Y sued over Lehmans audit. *Accountancy Age*. Retrieved May 16, 2015, from http://www.accountancyage.com/aa/news/1934026/-sued-lehmans-audit

Royal, C., & Althauser, R. P. (2003). The labor markets of knowledge workers: Investment bankers' careers in the wake of corporate restructuring. *Work and Occupations, 30*(2), 214–233.

Royal, C., & O'Donnell, L. (2002). The human factor: Taking a less subjective approach to investment decisions. *B+ FS, 116*(6), 10.

Royal, C., & O'Donnell, L. (2003). *The human capital classification process: Evaluating companies using a qualitative lens*. Sydney: School of Industrial Relations, University of New South Wales.

Royal, C., & O'Donnell, L. (2008). Emerging human capital analytics for investment processes. *Journal of Intellectual Capital, 9*(3), 367–379.

Royal, C., & O'Donnell, L. (2011). Investment and sustainability: The importance of the "S" in ESG. In G. Jones (Ed.), *Current research in sustainability* (1st ed., pp. 133–151). Victoria, Australia: Tilde University Press.

Salmon, F. (2009, February). Recipe for disaster: The formula that killed Wall Street. *Wired Magazine*, 17.03.

Senge, P. (2000). The puzzles and paradoxes of how living companies create wealth: Why single-valued objective functions are not quite enough. In M. Beer & N. Nohria (Eds.), *Breaking the code of change* (pp. 59–81). Boston, MA: Harvard Business School Press.

Shiller, R. J. (2000). *Irrational exuberance*. Princeton, NJ: Princeton University Press.

Smith, A. (2008, October 6). Fuld blames "crisis of confidence." *money.cnn.com*. Retrieved May 16, 2015, from http://money.cnn.com/2008/10/06/news/companies/lehman_hearing/index.htm?postversion=2008100616

Sorkin, A. R. (2008, September 14). Lehman files for bankruptcy; Merrill is sold. *New York Times*. Retrieved March 4, 2016, from http://www.nytimes.com/2008/09/15/business/15lehman.html?partner=rssuserland&emc=rss&pagewanted=all

Stacey, R. D. (2001). *Complex responsive processes in organizations: Learning and knowledge creation*. London, UK: Psychology Press.

Story, L., & Dash, E. (2010). Lehman channeled risks through "Alter Ego" firm. *New York Times*. Retrieved May 16, 2015, from http://www.nytimes.com/2010/04/13/business/13lehman.html?pagewanted=all

Swaine, J. (2008). Richard Fuld punched in face in Lehman Brothers gym. *The Daily Telegraph* (London). Retrieved May 16, 2015, from http://www.telegraph.co.uk/finance/financialcrisis/3150319/Richard-Fuld-punched-in-face-in-Lehman-Brothers-gym.html

Swedberg, R. (2010). The structure of confidence and the collapse of Lehman Brothers. *Research in the Sociology of Organizations, A30*, 71–114.

Trumbull, M. (2010). Lehman Bros. used accounting trick amid financial crisis—and earlier. *The Christian Science Monitor*. Retrieved May 16, 2015, from http://www.csmonitor.com/USA/2010/0312/Lehman-Bros.-used-accounting-trick-amid-financial-crisis-and-earlier

Waddock, S. A., Bodwell, C., & Graves, S. B. (2002). Responsibility: The new business imperative. *The Academy of Management Executive, 16*(2), 132–148.

Werbach, A. (2009). *Strategy for sustainability: A business manifesto*. Boston, MA: Harvard Business School Press.

Williams, T. (2007). *Measuring, managing, and reporting what matters. The state of ESG: An introduction—What language are we speaking?* (Regnan Working Paper).

Wood, D. J. (2010). Measuring corporate social performance: A review. *International Journal of Management Reviews, 12*(1), 50–84.

26

OPENING THE MARKET FOR IMPACT INVESTMENTS

The need for adapted portfolio tools

Lisa Brandstetter and Othmar M. Lehner

While tackling worldwide social and environmental challenges through providing the means and funds for innovative entrepreneurs is maintained to be the core vision of the social finance movement, the market has developed in different directions. Over the last couple of years, the field of such investments advanced in terms of market structures, involved participants, and investment vehicles. Among the diverse set of streams within the social finance sphere, progress achieved in Impact Investing currently receives exceptional attention in practice and in the media. Involved parties express their strong belief in an even more promising future of Impact Investing, with its potential to revolutionize how we think about investing itself (Salamon, 2014; social investment Research Council, 2014; Wilson, 2014).

According to investors' perceptions, the two key constraints limiting the expected growth are a "lack of appropriate capital across the risk/return spectrum" and the "shortage of high quality investment opportunities with a track record" (Saltuk, El Idrissi, Bouri, Mudaliar, & Schiff, 2014)—a somewhat vicious circle, as one implies the other.

Large institutional asset owners, such as pension funds, endowments, and insurers, are an especially important category of current and prospective Impact Investors as they play a fundamental role in domestic and world capital markets with total assets of over $20 trillion. In addition to their potential ability to grow the market, recognition by large institutional investors can help further legitimize the field for asset management intermediaries, financial institutions, consultants, and policymakers. However, the road to unlock this potential is still paved with several barriers (Wood, Thornley, & Grace, 2012, 2013).

First, institutional investors are demanding an infrastructure in terms of investable financial products (asset classes, metrics, and instruments) and intermediaries, which the Impact Investment market cannot yet provide.

Second, embedded into regulatory frameworks, institutional investors are bound by their fiduciary duties and are committed to asset class-specific benchmarks for expected financial risk and return. While some asset owners, such as family offices or certain funds, are already implicitly or explicitly acknowledging environmental and social targets as part of their investment strategies, others are still tied to conservative legal and policy-related requirements.

Third, institutional investors apply conventional portfolio allocation frameworks built on the evaluation of financial risk and returns in order to make rational investment decisions (Buckland, 2014; Clark, Emerson, & Thornley, 2013; Richardson, 2011; Wood et al., 2012, 2013) and have not yet found a way to include social risks and returns other than through negative screening (non-investments because of high social and environmental riskiness). Currently, only small and often dedicated funds apply some sort of positive screening, as the instruments and metrics used by large institutional investors are not compatible with these constructs.

Since Impact Investments differ significantly from traditional investments through their hybrid goals (Doherty, Haugh, & Lyon, 2014; Lehner, 2012), such investments do not yet match the logic of traditional finance tools. Measuring the potential social and environmental impact of these investments in a generally agreed fashion will thus be a key component of new approaches, since Impact Investing explicitly seeks to intentionally generate quantifiable social and financial returns (see Figure 26.1). Not only investors but also intermediaries, governments, and social businesses themselves are currently striving for standardized, transparent, and comprehensible industry-wide measurement metrics to create a market. Across sectors, there are already a number of measurement systems in use, endorsed by various actors. Among them are the Impact Reporting and Investment Standards (IRIS), the Global Impact Investing Rating System (GIIRS), and the B Impact Assessment powered by B Lab (Antadze & Westley, 2012; Jackson, 2013). Social Responsible Investing (SRI) presents itself as a broad category in literature, consisting of a range of different investment activities, such as negative screening. For a detailed elaboration on the issue of SRI, see, for example, Renneboog, Ter Horst, and Zhang (2008); Sandberg, Juravle, Hedesström, and Hamilton (2008); Lee, Humphrey, Benson, and Ahn (2010); Harji and Hebb (2010); and Berry and Junkus (2012).

On the other hand, investors struggle to allocate capital toward the social sector, because the above proposed performance measurement metrics do neither fully assess risks associated with the generation of impact nor consider relationships and interdependencies between parameters of risks and return. This becomes an aggravated problem when looking at a portfolio level, due to inevitable covariances that remain unaccounted for. Portfolio models can only be applied in situations where risk and return metrics are accurately measurable and comparable. Unfortunately, such consistent metrics are largely absent within the emergent field of social finance (Geobey, Westley, & Weber, 2012)

Therefore, since an optimized asset allocation is an indispensable necessity for institutional investors, the expected market growth of Impact Investing will be dampened as long as Impact Investments' characteristics do not match conventional portfolio tools.

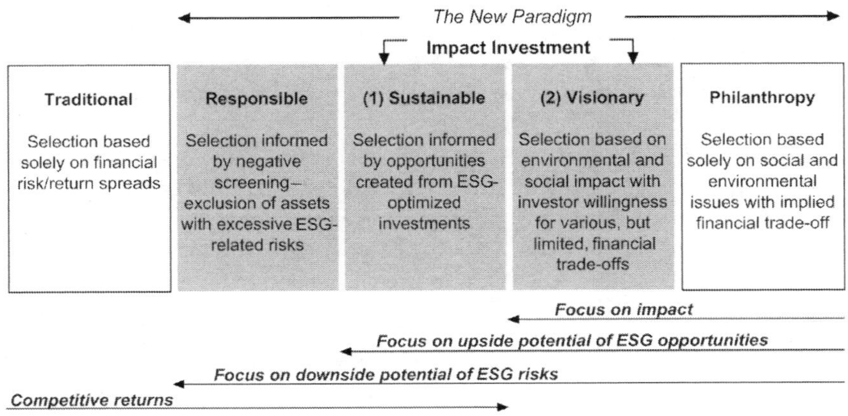

Figure 26.1 Investment philosophies

Source: Adapted from Nicklin (2012), and Clara Barby, Bridges Ventures.

Already some researchers point out the need for adapted financial tools (e.g., Geobey et al., 2012; Lyons and Kickul, 2013), yet there are few scholarly publications so far addressing the integration of Impact Investments into traditional portfolio optimization tools. There is some substantial ground work, as some authors already propose further research referring to the decision framework and investment criteria of Social Investors (Lyons & Kickul, 2013) and others see financial risks as one of the most severe barriers to social innovation and ask for mechanisms of risk reduction through the inclusion of ESG (Environmental, Social, Governance) criteria (Krlev, Glänzel, & Mildenberger, 2013). There are some fundamental paradigms implied, however, as much debate is dedicated to negative screening, meaning the exclusion of certain non-ESG-compliant investments. The active search for investments in creating a social impact as "positive screening" is still somewhat limited in literature, yet early evidence suggests even a financial ueber-return in some of these Impact Investments.

One mathematical approach that seems most suitable to bridge the gap between the social and financial logics in the context of Impact Investing is the Black-Litterman (BL) model by Black and Litterman (1992), with major contributions by Bevan and Winkelmann (1998); He and Litterman (1999); Idzorek (2005); Mankert and Seiler (2011); and Walters (2014). Other innovative mathematical approaches to the topic can be found in Dorfleitner and Utz (2012) and Dorfleitner, Leidl, and Reeder (2012).

The current ongoing research by the authors thus seeks to bridge social and financial return and risk considerations in portfolio optimization by adapting the BL model to the specific needs in Impact Investing. To overcome the sub-problem of measuring social returns and risks given various institutional policies, the authors turn to an ex ante examination of factors as capabilities, which can be individually defined to fit the specific institution's logic. These factors are currently the focus of research in the work of highly valued colleagues around the globe and can then be easily integrated into the proposed model.

Social finance and Impact Investments

As Social and Environmental Finance, and especially Impact Investing, is a nascent field of research, the number of purely academic and theory-building publications is still quite limited and major leaps in literature have been written by only a handful of highly interconnected scholars. At the moment, it is mostly practitioners' reports and documents that are driving the field forward, partly because of the fast pace of innovations in practice.

As the recent economic crisis showed, businesses and the capitalist system are in many respects capable of dealing with its financial consequences. Unfortunately, the same cannot be said of the social consequences.

Going back to the roots of the current movement, social finance partly emerged because governments, charities, and philanthropists alone are no longer capable of dealing with the 21st century's social and environmental challenges. Focusing on the act of charitable giving rather than on achieving social outcomes and a dependence on unpredictable funding hindered many charitable organizations from realizing their full potential concerning innovations, effectiveness, and scale. Realizing that governments are not best placed to find solutions to social issues and fiscal expenditures fall far short of expected needs, the third sector adapted methods and logic of the business sector to become more "businesslike" (Canadian Task Force on social finance, 2010; Cohen, 2014). To do so, however, the public has to be aware of the critical role that financiers play to help achieve social goals and mitigate social ills (Shiller, 2013). Given the nature of how resources are distributed in the world, private investors may have a special role and responsibility in addressing social challenges (World Economic Forum, 2013).

Social finance also serves as a mechanism for channeling capital toward social innovation that contributes to a public benefit. It comprises a spectrum of approaches, such as Impact Investing, governmental-backed finance, and mission-related philanthropic investments. The motivations of investors are widespread, and range from impact first investors who are willing to provide funding for organizations that are not able to generate market returns, to more financially focused investors who are interested in achieving both an adequate financial as well as a social return (Moore, Westley, & Brodhead, 2012; Wilson, 2014).

As in traditional finance, social investment instruments can include grants, loans, guarantees, quasi-equity, bonds, and equity. Additionally, Impact Investments may also fall in the category of real assets. Ranging from forest and farmland to affordable residential developments, these projects usually require a substantial sum of capital (Rodin & Brandenburg, 2014; Wilson, 2014). Given that the sector is still a small niche in traditional financial markets, existing products however do not always align with mainstream definitions of asset classes (Harji, Reynolds, Best, & Jeyaloganathan, 2014) because of the idiosyncrasies of the underlying ventures.

One significant aspect about social enterprises is that their features characterize them as hybrid organizations, which incorporate elements of different institutional logics (Pache & Santos, 2012). For hybrids, the strategic challenge is the integration and balance of public and private values so that these apparently competing goals leverage each other to maximize operational efficiency and effective delivery of social and environmental impact (Florin & Schmidt, 2011). Especially in terms of capital allocation, these two quite distinct and historically incompatible logics are by nature arenas of contradiction. The social welfare logic implies the well-established practice of gift-giving, state spending, and mutualism primarily used to create public goods appropriated by specific beneficiaries or society at large. In contrast to that, the traditional business aspect draws on the investment logics and practices of mainstream financial investment management to reframe the processes by which capital generates social or environmental returns (Nicholls, 2010). The confluence of these two traditions has generated a good deal of innovation in social enterprises so far, and the perceived boundaries that previously delineated not-for-profits from for-profits and investments from philanthropy may no longer apply. However, the different institutional logics and emerging norms have also introduced increased complexity in the markets (Antadze & Westley, 2012; Nicholls, 2010).

Apart from the early research by Nicholls (2010), who outlines an institutional matrix by conceptualizing investors' logics and rationalities through a Weberian analytic lens, there are few scholarly publications dealing with the landscape of the sector on a macro level. Tackling the void and need, practitioners have already developed frameworks to structure the market in order to facilitate the communication with investors and advisers (e.g., Lai, Will, Joshua, & Raúl, 2013; Nicklin, 2012).

The heterogeneity within the social investment movement suggests that a variety of risk and return models may be applied in practice and the spectrum of financial instruments and investment approaches is quite diverse. Since underlying investment logics typically determine the financial instruments and deal structures in a market, this variety and inherent complexity currently undermines efforts of standardization.

Drawing on previous work by Nicklin and Barby, the authors provide an overview of what can be seen as Impact Investments in Figure 26.1. While the research and the model currently developed by the authors may well serve the "Responsible" logic (negative screening of ESG risks) as well, the motivation of and following sections in this chapter deal with the positive screening, actively looking for ESG opportunities.

Voices in the social sector have long been stressing the fact that the allocation of funding needs to be optimized for social enterprises (Desjardins, 2011; Trelstad & Katz, 2011). For example,

Bishop and Green (2010) argue that the sector needs an efficiently functioning social capital curve to fill pressing funding gaps, starting at the stage of a good idea to scalable business models. Installing such a curve would ensure that available resources are directed to the most promising ventures at different critical levels. One prerequisite for this however would be an in-depth examination of underlying (social and impact) risks and hybrid returns.

Two-dimensional performance framework of risk and return

One of the particularly outstanding features of Impact Investments is the simultaneous generation of financial and social returns. Yet this interplay of objectives increases complexity when it comes to risk/return spectrums.

As outlined earlier, especially institutional investors commonly use a two-dimensional framework of risk and return to select investment opportunities and arrange portfolios. Since Impact Investors' focus is to generate an additional social impact alongside a financial return, applying the traditional lens evokes the following questions:

a How does financial risk change when adding a second return perspective?
b What kind of risks influences the social returns?

While risk is already perceived as an important factor for evaluating social innovation in general (Krlev et al., 2013), a deeper understanding of risk and how it is financially priced in terms of investing has yet to be developed (Brown & Swersky, 2012). For the measurement of social impact on the other hand, various market participants have already developed different sets of metrics and frameworks (e.g., IRIS, GIIRS, and SROI). However, these look at the investments from an ex post point of view, and thus are only helpful if the ventures are already well established in the markets, and do little for the judgment of potential investments from an ex ante point of view.

To gain a comprehensive overview of current efforts made by market participants to conceptualize the logic of measuring ex ante Impact Investments' performance, the authors reviewed existing literature and reports and talked to investors. One of the striking, yet not unexpected, outcomes is that the perception and interpretation of an investment's impact performance is directly dependent on the particular author's or institution's inherent perspective on the market (see Figure 26.2). Performance metrics are either three or four dimensional (social and financial risk separate or together), and the chosen set of factors is highly influenced by practicability rather than completeness.

Concerning the social return, Hornsby and Blumberg (2013), as well as Puttick and Ludlow (2012), define impact, in particular impact generation in Hornsby and Blumberg (2013), as the effect of outputs on outcomes and address the potential for real change presented by the organization and investment opportunity together. Compared to traditional investments, impact generation is equivalent to the prospective financial return.

Both reports are using the term impact risk to describe a measure of uncertainty that an organization will deliver on its proposed impact. By considering six key qualities that help to assess the social risk, Hornsby and Blumberg (2013) for example focus the evaluation particularly on the validity of the impact plan. The starting point for any structured and rational treatment of impact is to check whether the impact plan is explicit in all particulars. Second, attention has to be focused on how well reasoned and compelling the theory of change is presented. Third, a potential tension within the organization may arise between its impact-generating and revenue-generating activities. In order to reduce this risk, the generation of impact should be integral to the organization's business strategy, operations, and revenue model. Fourth, the feasibility of the impact plan has to be assessed concerning the necessary resources, capacity, skills, and relevant experience besides its operational and financial strengths. Fifth, some kind of evidence has to be found which supports the impact plan's approach to impact generation. Sources of evidence may include track records, precedents, research, or control groups. Finally, the impact plan has to be evidenceable to ensure that carrying out the plan will produce sufficient evidence to demonstrate the impact and prove the approach.

Puttick and Ludlow (2012), on the other hand, refer—in terms of risk—to Standards of Evidence which consist of five levels representing different stages of how impact evidence is gathered, interpreted, and assessed. At the lowest level, the organization, respectively the venture's manager, can give an account of impact by using existing data to provide a set of logical reasons why products or services could have an impact on the intended outcomes. At the highest level, the product or service could be operated up by someone else, somewhere else, and be scaled-up while continuously achieving a positive and direct impact on the outcome. In general, a higher level of evidence suggests a lower level of risk.

While the two already mentioned reports see social and financial risk as two independent parameters, three other publications describe only one aggregated measure of risk. Emerson (2012) and Saltuk (2012) use a three-dimensional framework consisting of risk, return, and impact.

Saltuk (2012) uses the three dimensions to map a profile of each investment. The impact assessment consists of a due diligence to come to a view on the intent and the impact of the proposed investment opportunity. After the analysis, they assign a ranking from one to five on questions regarding the people, products, or processes through which the impact will be delivered. Summarizing the results of each scorecard gives a weighted average ranking between one and five for each investment. The scorecards are used to quantify impact relative to the investor's mission. In a second step, the return of the portfolio is assessed on a blended basis including the aggregate financial return and social impact. In practice, this means that impact objectives can outweigh returns below the usually required threshold. The risk parameter within the framework comprises several risk factors which are analyzed from a traditional finance and a specific impact perspective. In addition to the risks of traditional investments, they consider further aspects listed in Table 26.1.

In the first report published by JP Morgan (O'Donohoe, Leijonhufvud, & Saltuk, 2010), the Rockefeller Foundation and GIIN state that the risks of Impact Investments are similar to those for venture capital or high-yield debt instruments. Besides typical risks associated with early-stage companies and small scales, the report focuses particularly on legal and reputational risks, which arise especially when operating in emerging markets and with vulnerable populations. Besides these explicitly mentioned risks, another section concentrates on social impact risk which refers to difficulties regarding standardized performance measurement and reporting (O'Donohoe et al., 2010). These further risk factors are added in Table 26.1. From a forward-thinking view, the report also takes asset class and thematic area risk into consideration because the type of investment vehicle and the particular vehicle's thematic area affect the assessment of an investment's real risk. Beyond these aspects, the report further differentiates between perceived and real risk, since new investments often seem more risky than they really are.

Similar to Saltuk (2012), the two-dimensional metrics of Laing et al. (2012) expand the traditional risk/return framework with combined risks and combined returns. The combined return accounts for both the investment's financial return and any social return that is relevant to the investor's objectives. While the combined risk incorporates the financial risk measured by an

Table 26.1 Risk factors

Risk factor	*Description*
Early stage of the market	Risks might arise from the market's small size, the short track record of performance, small portfolio and deal sizes, and fund managers little experienced with dual return objectives.
Ecosystem risk	The Impact Investment market depends on infrastructure, for example policy support and measurement systems, which adds risk.
Mission drift	Investees might drift away from the intended mission without the approval of investors.
Combination of investment capital	Impact Investments combine grant and investment capital. This combination risks not achieving the expectations and intentions of the respective funders.
Moral hazard	Similar to traditional investment, but extended by the failure of not delivering on the impact mission. Additionally, funders not only aim at helping the investee but also have to maintain rigor with respect to loss recognition.
Legal risk	In addition to legal and regulatory challenges at the beginning of a business, there may also be changes to different regimes over time or changes to transferring the business as it grows. Difficulties in scaling the business or changing ownership will introduce a challenge to the growth of Impact Investments, but with the help of local management teams it will be easier to maneuver within local regimes.
Reputational risk	An Impact Investment must constantly balance the dual imperative of generating positive social impact and profit. However, these two objectives can also create tensions. In pursuit of more profit a business may be inclined to target relatively better-off customers, raise prices to take advantage of the lack of competition, or take cash out of the business rather than invest in innovation to enable even broader customer reach.

Source: Modified from Saltuk (2012) and O'Donohoe et al. (2010).

investment's volatility, the social risk only refers to a reputational risk through which an institution's investments might alienate key stakeholders and compromise the values of the organization.

Finally, the report by Barby and Gan (2014) focuses exclusively on Impact Investments' risks. In general, the approach is based on the assumption that risk is multi-factored since poor performance can be driven by a range of factors and risk is subjective and always relative to the expectations of a particular investor. Beyond the traditional risk factors, such as market risk, operational risk, and currency risk, which are obviously equally relevant for Impact Investments, they discovered five further idiosyncratic factors, quite similar to those reported earlier (see Figure 26.2).

Although the considered risk factors seem diverse, the comparison in Figure 26.2 shows that there are several conceptual overlappings. In this figure, the authors present a snapshot of "risks in focus" at various institutions, building the comparison based on underlying assumptions rather than on the individually applied terminology. As indicated by the formatting, many definitions overlap. The legend at the bottom of the figure simultaneously represents a summary of resulting risk categories which are arranged in an order representing their frequency of occurrence.

Based on the findings in the document analysis, the overall perception of practitioners is that Impact Investments face a multifaceted set of interdependent risks, and further research is desperately needed to define risk factors and empirically analyze interdependencies between those risks and their effects on financial and social returns. These interdependencies would form the basis for the building of efficient portfolios. In accordance with the proposed definition of performance parameters, the evaluated reports propose different approaches concerning portfolio building.

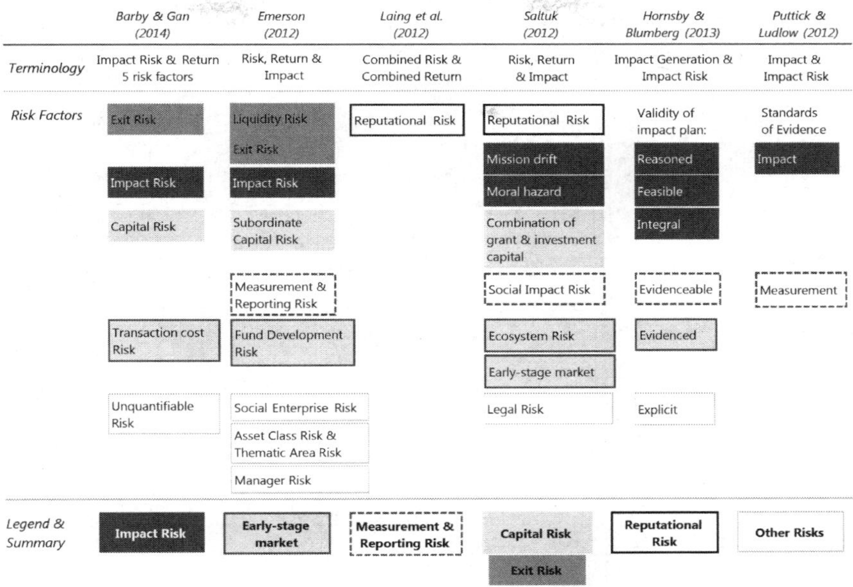

Figure 26.2 A comparison of risk factors in practice

Source: The authors based on the above-mentioned reports.

From a practical perspective, Laing et al. (2012) recommend the integration approach for investors focused on minimizing social risk and the carve-out approach for investors looking to maximize social impact.

As opposed to the previously explained portfolio frameworks following a more or less conventional approach, Bridges Ventures (2013) developed a four-dimensional Bridges IMPACT Radar, which plots impact risk and impact return of each of the four criteria: "Target outcome," "Additionality," "Alignment," and "ESG," which are evaluated from a return as well as a risk perspective based on a scoring model.

Besides their internally used methodology, Bridges Ventures also look at the entire market applying a risk lens. The interviews conducted by Barby and Gan (2014) suggest that a significant portion of asset owners simply cannot participate in the market today because of a variety of risk factors. In an attempt to broaden the market, the range of lower risk opportunities available for investors needs to grow. However, reducing risk is not a one-size-fits-all approach, as the relevance of risk factors differs considerably depending on the target investor and performance expectations. One of the proposed possibilities to reduce capital as well as transaction cost risk is to use portfolio diversification and bundling. A traditional fund structure, for example, offers investors the opportunity to buy a single product that comprises different underlying investments and consequently spreads the risk. Beyond that, sufficiently dissimilar products can be bundled to provide diversification. The financial and impact exposure can either be spread across asset classes or different sectors and geographies. Since diversification is only possible if the respective products are available, the report encourages asset owners to challenge intermediaries to bring opportunities forward that match their needs and preferences.

Although Hornsby and Blumberg (2013) describe the relationship between the four performance measures of financial risk and return as well as impact generation and risk, they do not provide a systematic framework for selecting a portfolio. Besides pointing out that a certain balance among the investments should be maintained, they highlight the importance of paying attention to the anticipated development of investments.

Combining financial and social risk into one risk figure constitutes difficulties, since social risk is not easily quantifiable. For that reason, Laing et al. (2012) recommend increasing the combined risk if a relevant social risk is identified so that it is meaningfully higher than the financial risk measure. With this approach they attempt to imply that a strategy with exposure to social risk is less attractive from a risk/return standpoint than an investment disregarding social risk.

Although the report by Emerson (2012) neither deals with the relationship between the defined parameters of risk, return, and impact in detail, he postulates the creation of a New Efficient Frontier that is not bifurcated, but rather spherical.

Concerning the expected return, however, it is mentioned that over the past 5 years Impact Investors have changed their perception of return. Consequently, they no longer ask what the market may deem as an appropriate financial return, but rather define a level of financial performance integrated with measurable social and environmental value creation. With the created slogan "I AM the market," it is expressed that the investor will determine an appropriate rate of return. Further, investors perceive blended financial and social returns not only acceptable but a significant driver for their investment decisions.

Saltuk (2012) discusses the debate in the Impact Investment market whether there needs to be trade-off in financial returns in order to gain impact or not. From their point of view, we should not aim to describe the diverse set of assets with one overall statement about the relationship between return and impact. To characterize such a broad universe of opportunities with just an average seems to have little meaning. For that reason, investors are encouraged to assess each opportunity individually and let the economics of the intervention determine the return profile.

Looking at the issue from a practical perspective, the fund described by Puttick and Ludlow (2012) aims at investing in early-stage innovations where potential impact and impact risk are both high. Through the investment, they believe to be able to reduce the impact risk and deliver public benefit by scalingup output. Besides, increasing impact performance will eventually lead to an increase in financial value.

To a certain extent, all approaches are based on the traditional model of risk and return and are predominantly adjusted by an additional subjective evaluation. However, none of the reports describe how the parameters are concretely evaluated, measured, or systematically embedded into a portfolio allocation framework. In addition, an impact portfolio can be interpreted either with or without traditional assets.

Following the lead from the practitioners' voices, the authors are currently working on a BL model to operationalize the concepts and allow for rational decision-making based upon a verifiable mathematical theory. Alongside this research, an innovative mathematical approach, albeit not based on BL, can be found in Dorfleitner and Utz (2012) and Dorfleitner et al. (2012).

A proposed model for portfolio optimization

Drawing from current hurdles which investors face when approaching the Impact Investment market, the authors are working on an approach that incorporates social investments' specific parameters alongside financial values into the traditional logic of portfolio optimization, based on risk and return. To do so, social measures are quantified and included in an adapted optimization process based on the BL model as depicted in Figure 26.3. The authors remodeled the investors' view perspective Q to allow for an operationalization of social and impact considerations based upon expert panels and subsequent Monte Carlo computations.

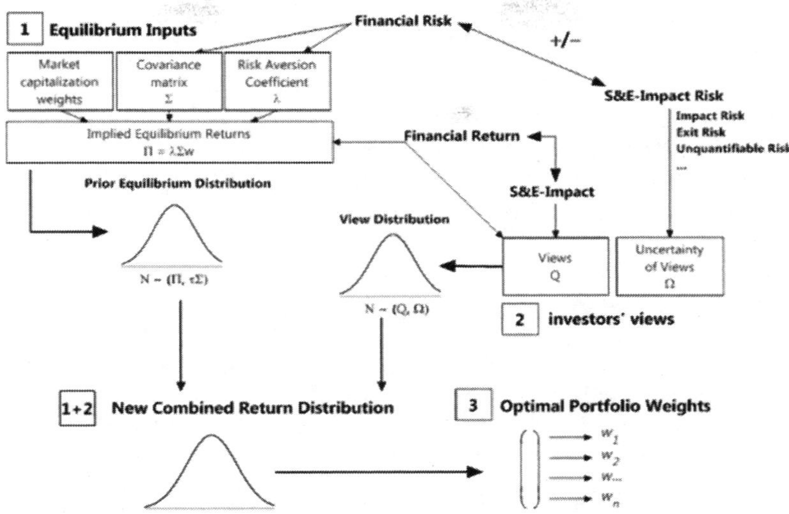

Figure 26.3 The proposed model, including social risks and returns in previously optimized portfolios

The S&E impact score (S&E IS) describes an investment's social and environmental contribution by looking at the antecedents of impact. S&E impact risk (S&E IR), on the other hand, represents the risk of successfully generating the intended positive impact as a deviation of the S&E impact score.

To include the S&E perspective in the traditional optimization logic, these two measures are derived from investor-specific expectations and standardized evaluation processes (Monte Carlo Simulations based upon expert panels and scoring models). Since each social investment generates different outcomes and investors have different objectives, a holistic approach ensuring both comparability and enabling rational decision-making is required.

Figure 26.4 shows how the concept quantifies and determines financial and S&E input parameters before applying a rebalancing based on the traditional BL model. According to the numbering in Figure 26.4, the following section breaks the entire process down into four major steps whereby the first three explain how the measures are derived and the last aligns both perspectives to arrive at optimized weights.

First, an investment's financial perspective includes financial values for risk and return, which are inferred from a mean-variance optimum. Based on historical data and individual portfolio constraints, equilibrium market weights are computed. These in turn serve as a starting point for a reverse optimization to come up with a vector of implied expected financial returns and the covariance matrix. This approach makes use of the traditional BL model, while BL's feature of formulating and incorporating an investor's individual views has been reworked to include the S&E perspectives.

Second, the next step aims at calculating an S&E impact score that ensures comparability and an objective evaluation of an investment's impact. In order to evaluate each investment's performance in accordance with the investor's unique set of mission targets, the authors propose a weighted scoring model that can be filled with different S&E criteria and corresponding weights. By asking independent experts carrying out due diligence to evaluate investments based on these predefined categories, investors have the opportunity to express motivations and preferences while still collecting objective opinions. The list of ex ante criteria may differ among investors and be either broadly or narrowly defined. It should however be compatible to a standard framework of reporting social impact (such as GIIRS) to allow for back testing and validity reviews. After collecting experts' views, the S&E scores serve as input for a Monte Carlo Simulation to generate expected average scores that are randomly distributed. To get reasonably optimized returns which are proportional to and comparable with the implied financial returns, the scores need to be normalized to arrive at the S&E impact.

Third, the S&E IR is derived by comparing individual investments' characteristics within a portfolio to detected cluster risks. As argued before, risk within Impact Investing is multifaceted and cannot be easily summarized and quantified. However, cluster risks within a portfolio can be determined by comparing different objective settings such as the group of beneficiaries, geographical area, or service provider. Classifying each investment into predefined categories and assigning each category with individual weights expresses the investor's attitude toward different risk factors and results in an S&E IR covariance matrix.

Fourth, after computing the parameters for the financial and the S&E perspective (via matrix algebraic operations), these isolated values serve as input for the BL rebalancing process (see formulas 1 and 2) at an assumed estimation error Tau to arrive at likewise financially and socially optimized returns. The underlying logic would also allow for further individual constraints to comprise investors' preferences. By assigning a risk aversion coefficient Lambda, investors are also able to operationalize their risk appetite, and the "social value ratio" describes the desired (policy determined) trade-off between the financial and the S&E perspective.

$$E[R]=\left[(\tau\Sigma)^{-1}+P'\Omega^{-1}P\right]^{-1}\left[(\tau\Sigma)^{-1}\Pi+P'\Omega^{-1}Q\right] \tag{1}$$

$$\Sigma_p=\Sigma+((\tau\Sigma)^{-1}+P^T\Omega^{-1}P)^{-1} \tag{2}$$

Finally, BL-optimized weights are computed in formula 3 (the authors chose a 100 percent investment constraint, yet individual investment policies concerning leverage can be implemented).

$$w=\frac{\Sigma^{-1}I}{I^T\Sigma^{-1}I}+\frac{1}{\lambda}\Sigma^{-1}\star\left(R-\frac{I^T\Sigma^{-1}R}{I^T\Sigma^{-1}I}\star I\right) \tag{3}$$

The streams of logic and the variable names are explained in Figure 26.4.

Applying this optimization concept, the authors suspect that such portfolios provide slightly lower financial returns while generating a positive S&E impact within the planned range. At the same time, volatility typically decreases because of the low correlation between social investments and traditional investment alternatives. In several simulations based upon available data, these assumptions were valid; however, in terms of the overall suggested concept and model, further efforts are needed to validate the model with real data, and the underlying assumptions of normality and regression will need to be carefully considered to understand the model's constraints. We therefore invite the community to contact us and work together. A very early simulation (with rather steep differences in social impact scores to exemplify) is displayed in Table 26.2. Computations for A1–A3 are based on real-world data from Bloomberg, and A4–A5 (proposed social projects) are based on business plans. Social impact potential was estimated by experts. Details on the Monte Carlo Simulations and Social Covariances are omitted because of space restrictions.

What can be seen in this early simulation is that a BL rebalancing reduces the financial return by 18.05 percent (from 13.51 percent to 11.07 percent). It also reduces volatility by 11.97

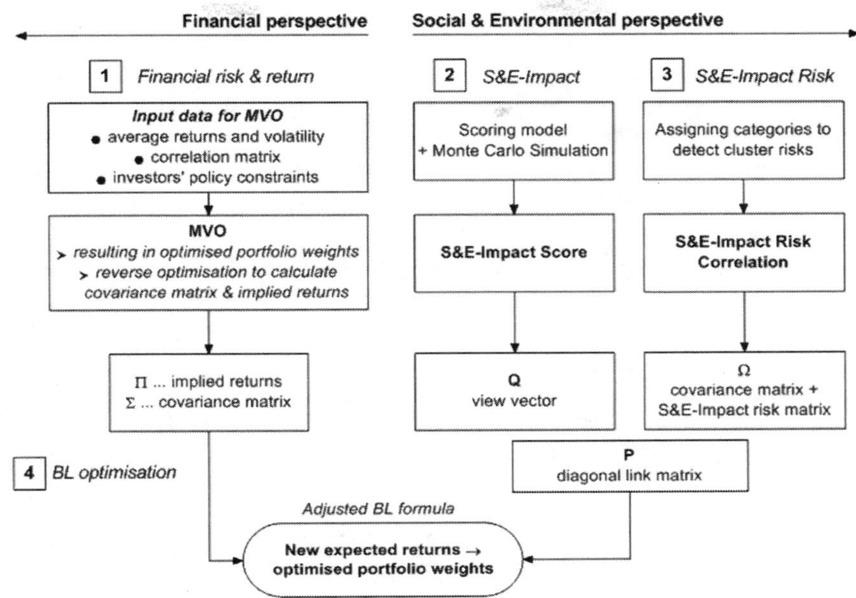

Figure 26.4 Explaining the streams of logic in the BL model leading to optimized portfolio weights based on social and financial inputs

Table 26.2 Simulation on five assets with portfolio returns, volatility, and social impact scores

Asset	*Fin.-returns mean (%)*	*Fin.-std. dev (%)*	*Markowitz-Sharpe ratio optimized portfolio weights*	*Social impact score (antecedent)*	*BL optimized portfolio weights*	*Delta*
A1	18.20%	23.16%	11.33%	0.90	*6.54%*	*−42.27%*
A2	23.00%	26.00%	18.40%	1.82	*10.05%*	*−45.38%*
A3	13.69%	14.97%	31.59%	0.60	*21.68%*	*−31.37%*
A4	7.00%	12.70%	20.21%	6.60	*33.44%*	*+65.46%*
A5	8.00%	14.29%	18.46%	7.40	*28.30%*	*+53.30%*
	Portfolio-return	Markowitz	13.51%	BL Opt.:	11.07%	*−18.05%*
	Volatility	Markowitz	9.96%	BL Opt.:	8.76%	*−11.97%*
	Social impact score	Markowitz	3.32p	BL Opt.:	4.67p	*+40.47%*

percent and strongly improves on the potential social impact of this portfolio by 40.47 percent. The assumptions were a 20 percent social impact orientation, a 5 percent estimation error, and a risk policy parameter Lambda of 1. Overall, despite a quite significant rebalancing toward the social projects, a stable financial return was achieved, while overall risk was reduced and a vastly higher social impact potential was created through the investments.

Several issues need to be addressed by the authors in the near future before the whole model can be presented to the public: among the topics are the severely restricted liquidity of social projects, leading to potential rebalancing problems, problematic differences in investment sizes in the market, and other, more mathematically relevant factors such as parametric sensitivity issues, distributional assumptions, and model constraints. Yet this conceptualization provides a universe for experimentation and a common ground to start a discussion with investors.

Future outlook and ideas

Over the last couple of years, Impact Investing has advanced from being a niche within the social investment spectrum to a promising investment philosophy blending financial and social values. What became clear in the authors' journey is that when striving to unlock the market's untapped social and financial potential, participants are still facing a number of hurdles—among them is the leap from diffuse and idiosyncratic concepts to operationalized practical instruments guiding rational decision-making. While the landscape of investors and intermediaries is continuously growing, large institutional investors such as pension funds, insurance companies, and hedge funds have limited tools and metrics at hand that would provide a solid basis for their decision-making and are therefore still reluctant when it comes to entering the market. This is a vicious circle, because without a market such tools will inevitably be severely limited in practice because of liquidity problems.

Future research may also need to look at possible correlations between financial and social returns as well as between the respective risks. Early voices argue that positive social investments are often little correlated to mainstream market investments, thus leading to the possibility of attractive diversification strategies and additional risk mitigation strategies. Much work lies ahead. Besides further validating and back-testing the proposed model in this chapter, the authors will embark on a journey to mathematically model a multivariate formula that incorporates the intercorrelation between financial and social risks for further inclusion in the portfolio-building tool. In order to unlock the potential of social innovation at large and of Impact Investments in a narrower sense, future activities will necessarily require an intense collaboration across sectors, countries, and organizations. Exchanging perspectives and experiences from various fields might not only accelerate the growth of the impact sector but also provide room for reflection on traditional finance and investments.

Acknowledgments

With permission to reprint by De Gruyter. Chapter previously published as: Brandstetter, L., & Lehner, O. M. (2015). Opening the market for Impact Investments: The need for adapted portfolio tools. *Entrepreneurship Research Journal, 5*(2), 87–107.

The authors would like to express their gratitude for great discussions and numerous inspirations to Prof. Alex Nicholls, Said Business School, University of Oxford; Dr John Hoffmire, Said Business School, University of Oxford; Dr Ashby Monk, Stanford University; Dr Clara Barby, Bridges Ventures; and Prof. Gordon Clark, Smith School of Enterprise and the Environment, University of Oxford.

References

Antadze, N., & Westley, F. R. (2012). Impact metrics for social innovation: Barriers or bridges to radical change? *Journal of Social Entrepreneurship, 3*(2), 133–150.

Barby, C., & Gan, J. (2014). *Shifting the lens: A de-risking framework for impact investments*. London: Bridges Ventures.

Berry, T. C., & Junkus, J. C. (2012). Socially responsible investing: An investor perspective. *Journal of Business Ethics, 112*(4), 707–720.

Bevan, A., & Winkelmann, K. (1998). Using the Black-Litterman global asset allocation model: Three years of practical experience. In R. A. Krieger (Ed.), *Fixed income research—Goldman Sachs* (pp. 1–15). New York, NY: Goldman Sachs.

Bishop, M., & Green, M. (2010). The capital curve for a better world. *Innovations: Technology, Governance, Globalization, 5*(1), 25–33.

Black, F., & Litterman, R. (1992). Global portfolio optimization. *Financial Analysts Journal, 48*(5), 28–43.

Bridges Ventures. (2013). *Bridges IMPACT report—A spotlight on our methodology* (pp. 1–27). London: Bridges Ventures.

Brown, A., & Swersky, A. (2012). *The first billion: A forecast of social investment demand* (pp. 1–32). London: Big Society Capital.

Buckland, L. (2014). *Social impact strategies for banks—Venture philanthropy and social investment* (pp. 1–109). London: EVPA.

Canadian Task Force on social finance. (2010). *Mobilizing private capital for public good* (pp. 1–38). Toronto: Canadian Task Force on social finance.

Clark, C., Emerson, J., & Thornley, B. (2013). *Impact Investing 2.0: The way forward—Insight from 12 outstanding firms* (pp. 1–41). Durham, NC: Duke University, Fuqua School of Business.

Cohen, R. (2014). *Revolutionising philanthropy—Impact investment* (pp. 1–11). London: Social Impact Investment Taskforce.

Desjardins, S. (2011). The need for a smarter funding ecosystem. *Innovations: Technology, Governance, Globalization, 6*(3), 85–92.

Doherty, B., Haugh, H., & Lyon, F. (2014). Social enterprises as hybrid organizations: A review and research agenda. *International Journal of Management Reviews, 16*(4), 417–436.

Dorfleitner, G., Leidl, M., & Reeder, J. (2012). Theory of social returns in portfolio choice with application to microfinance. *Journal of Asset Management, 13*(6), 384–400.

Dorfleitner, G., & Utz, S. (2012). Safety first portfolio choice based on financial and sustainability returns. *European Journal of Operational Research, 221*(1), 155–164.

Emerson, J. (2012). *Risk, return and impact: Understanding diversification and performance within an impact investing portfolio* (pp. 1–14). Bethesda, MD: Impact Assets.

Florin, J., & Schmidt, E. (2011). Creating shared value in the hybrid venture arena: A business model innovation perspective. *Journal of Social Entrepreneurship, 2*(2), 165–197.

Geobey, S., Westley, F. R., & Weber, O. (2012). Enabling social innovation through developmental social finance. *Journal of Social Entrepreneurship, 3*(2), 151–165.

Harji, K., & Hebb, T. (2010). *Impact investing for social finance* (pp. 1–20). Carleton, Canada: Carleton Centre for Community Innovation.

Harji, K., Reynolds, J., Best, H., & Jeyaloganathan, M. (2014). *State of the nation—Impact investing in Canada* (pp. 1–94). Toronto, ON: MaRS.

He, G., & Litterman, R. (1999). *The intuition behind Black-Litterman model portfolios* (pp. 1–18). New York, NY: Goldman Sachs.

Hornsby, A., & Blumberg, G. (2013). *The good investor: A book of best impact practice* (pp. 1–94). London: The Good Investor.

Idzorek, T. M. (2005). *A step-by-step guide to the Black-Litterman model* (pp. 1–32). Chicago, IL: Ibbotson Associates.

Jackson, E. T. (2013). Interrogating the theory of change: Evaluating impact investing where it matters most. *Journal of Sustainable Finance & Investment, 3*(2), 95–110.

Krlev, G., Glänzel, G., & Mildenberger, G. (2013). *Capitalising social innovation: A short guide to the research for policy makers* (pp. 1–23). Bruxelles, Belgium: TEPSIE of the European Commission.

Lai, J., Will, M., Joshua, N., & Raúl, P. (2013). *Evolution of an impact portfolio: From implementation to results* (pp. 1–68). San Francisco, CA: Sonen Capital.

Laing, N., Long, C., Marcandalli, A., Matthews, J., Grahovac, A., & Featherby, J. (2012). *The U.K. social investment market: The current landscape and a framework for investor decision making* (pp. 1–24). Cambridge: Cambridge Associates Limited.

Lee, D. D., Humphrey, J. E., Benson, K. L., & Ahn, J. Y. K. (2010). Socially responsible investment fund performance: The impact of screening intensity. *Accounting & Finance, 50*(2), 351–370.

Lehner, O. M. (2012). *Social entrepreneurship perspectives: Triangulated approaches to hybridity*. Jyväskylä, Finland: University of Jyväskylä.

Lyons, T. S., & Kickul, J. R. (2013). The social enterprise financing landscape: The lay of the land and new research on the horizon. *Entrepreneurship Research Journal, 3*(2), 147–159.

Mankert, C., & Seiler, M. J. (2011). Mathematical derivations and practical implications for the use of the Black-Litterman model. *Journal of Real Estate Portfolio Management, 17*(2), 139–159.

Moore, M. L., Westley, F. R., & Brodhead, T. (2012). Social finance intermediaries and social innovation. *Journal of Social Entrepreneurship, 3*(2), 184–205.

Nicholls, A. (2010). The institutionalization of social investment: The interplay of investment logics and investor rationalities. *Journal of Social Entrepreneurship, 1*(1), 70–100.

Nicklin, S. (2012). *The power of advice in the UK sustainable and impact investment market* (pp. 1–72). London: Bridges Ventures.

O'Donohoe, N., Leijonhufvud, C., & Saltuk, Y. (2010). *Impact investments: An emerging asset class* (pp. 1–93). London: JP Morgan.

Pache, A. C., & Santos, F. (2012). Inside the hybrid organization: Selective coupling as a response to competing institutional logics. *Academy of Management Journal, 56*(4), 972–1001.

Puttick, R., & Ludlow, J. (2012). *Standards of evidence for impact investing* (pp. 1–16). London: Nesta.

Renneboog, L., Ter Horst, J., & Zhang, C. (2008). Socially responsible investments: Institutional aspects, performance, and investor behavior. *Journal of Banking & Finance, 32*(9), 1723–1742.

Richardson, B. J. (2011). From fiduciary duties to fiduciary relationships for socially responsible investing: Responding to the will of beneficiaries. *Journal of Sustainable Finance & Investment, 1*(1), 5–19.

Rodin, J., & Brandenburg, M. (2014). *The power of impact investing: Putting markets to work for profit and global good*. Philadelphia, PA: Wharton Digital Press.

Salamon, L. M. (2014). *New frontiers of philanthropy: A guide to the new tools and new actors that are reshaping global philanthropy and social investing*. Oxford: Oxford University Press.

Saltuk, Y. (2012). *A portfolio approach to impact investment* (pp. 1–35). London: JP Morgan.

Saltuk, Y., El Idrissi, A., Bouri, A., Mudaliar, A., & Schiff, H. (2014). *Spotlight on the market—The impact investor survey* (pp. 1–50). London: JP Morgan.

Sandberg, J., Juravle, C., Hedesström, T. M., & Hamilton, I. (2008). The heterogeneity of socially responsible investment. *Journal of Business Ethics, 87*(4), 519–533.

Shiller, R. J. (2013). Capitalism and financial innovation. *Financial Analysts Journal, 69*(1), 21–25.

Social Investment Research Council. (2014). *New specialist sources of capital for the social investment market*. London: City of London.

Trelstad, B., & Katz, R. (2011). Mission, margin, mandate: Multiple paths to scale. *Innovations: Technology, Governance, Globalization, 6*(3), 41–53.

Walters, J. (2014). *The Black-Litterman model in detail* (pp. 1–65). Retrieved March 4, 2016, from http://papers.ssrn.com/sol3/papers.cfm?abstract_id=1314585

Wilson, K. (2014). New investment approaches for addressing social and economic challenges. *OECD Science, Technology and Industry Policy Papers, 15*, 1–41.

Wood, D., Thornley, B., & Grace, K. (2012). *Impact at scale—Policy innovation for institutional investment with social and environmental benefit* (pp. 1–34). San Francisco, CA: Pacific Community Ventures.

Wood, D., Thornley, B., & Grace, K. (2013). Institutional impact investing: Practice and policy. *Journal of Sustainable Finance & Investment, 3*(2), 75–94.

World Economic Forum. (2013). *From the margins to the mainstream: Assessment of the impact investment sector and opportunities to engage mainstream investors* (pp. 1–36). New York, NY: World Economic Forum.

PART III

Markets and Institutions

III.1
Social and Sustainable Banking

27

SOCIAL BANKS' MISSION AND FINANCE

Olaf Weber

Alternative Bank Switzerland announces on its website that it invests in, and finances, sustainable projects and businesses, and that it does not insist on maximizing profit. Instead, it places a rational emphasis on sustainability and ethical principles (https://www.abs.ch). The Canadian VanCity communicates that their commitment to building an accountable, sustainable, supportive financial model guides everything they do (https://www.vancity.com). Both financial institutions—a bank and a credit union—can be called social, ethical, or alternative banks that offer products and services such as loans for social enterprises, renewable energy projects, or social housing.

But what are social banks and how can social banking be defined? In contrast to conventional banks, social banks provide loans in order to create a social or environmental benefit (da Silva, 2007; Edery, 2006). All their products and services focus exclusively on creating and sustaining social value through financial products and services (Geobey, Westley, & Weber, 2012; Martin & Osberg, 2007; Weber, 2011). For social banks, financial products and services are a means to create a positive societal impact. According to the Global Alliance for Banking on Values (GABV), a global association of social banks, and of which the two mentioned institutions are members, social banking follows the following principles:

1 "Triple bottom line approach at the heart of the business model
2 Grounded in communities, serving the real economy and enabling new business models to meet the needs of both
3 Long-term relationships with clients and a direct understanding of their economic activities and the risks involved
4 Long-term, self-sustaining, and resilient to outside disruptions
5 Transparent and inclusive governance
6 All of these principles embedded in the culture of the bank." (http://www.gabv.org/about-us/our-principles)

The GABV principles as well the social banking principle mentioned above, however, are very broad and do not provide a clear picture about what social banking is. Therefore, this chapter will introduce a further definition of social banking and will analyze the missions, visions, products, and services of current social banks.

Background

Recently, and particularly during and shortly after the last financial crisis, social banks demonstrated an impressive balance sheet and market share increase (Remer, 2011). However, social banks are still a niche phenomenon. In 2013, the total amount of the balance sheet of the members of the GABV was a little more than $76 billion (see http://www.gabv.org). According to the GABV's website, the members of the organization serve about 10 million clients in 25 countries. On the one hand, this is an impressive number. On the other hand, it is still a small fraction of the total market, though not all social banks are members of the GABV.

Generally all banks have some kind of social responsibility (Schuster, 2001) because they channel financial capital into different sectors and projects. Obviously, they have a strong impact on the economy and on society (Allen & Santomero, 2001), as the last financial crisis demonstrated. Different concepts exist, however, about the connection between social and environmental impacts, and banking and financial services. On the one side of the spectrum, we find philanthropy that has one explicit target, achieving a positive social impact without considering any financial return for the investor, in this case a donor. On the other end of the scale, we find financial products and services that only strive for high financial returns without taking any social impacts into account. This is the case for the majority of financial products and services offered by conventional banks and other financial institutions.

Socially Responsible Investment (SRI) integrates some social, environmental, or governance inclusion or exclusion criteria into investment decisions and thus is located between philanthropy and conventional finance, though it is a very heterogeneous field (Sandberg, Juravle, Hedesström, & Hamilton, 2009). It integrates social or environmental criteria into the set of investment indicators (Koellner, Suh, Weber, Moser, & Scholz, 2007) and includes "social" screening, community investment, and shareholder advocacy (O'Rourke, 2003) in the investment process to guarantee higher and more sustainable financial returns. The main goals of SRI, however, differ from those of social banks. In contrast to achieving a positive social impact, SRI focuses on guaranteeing attractive financial returns through investments that take long-term sustainability concerns into account (Weber, Mansfeld, & Schirrmann, 2011), and to channel capital towards sustainable businesses (Buttle, 2007; Weber, 2006). In this case, SRI is based on the assumption that it pays to integrate environmental and social indicators into investment decision-making.

Definition of social banking

In contrast to conventional banking, philanthropy, and SRI, social banks invest in a way that generates social and environmental returns in the first place (Weber, 2014b; Weber & Remer, 2011). They strive to create a positive impact on sustainable development and thus follow the sustainability case of business (Weber, 2014a). Consequently, they analyze the financial returns only of projects or clients that demonstrate positive impacts on the environment, society, and sustainability. social banks look for a blended value return (Emerson, 2003; Harji & Hebb, 2009) with "corporate social responsibility as the core of their business model" (Kaufer, 2014, p. 76). Cornée and Szafarz (2013) define social banks as institutions that pay attention to the social and environmental consequences of their activity and as banks that act as drivers of Corporate Social Responsibility through supporting community-oriented projects and social enterprises. A similar definition of social banking that puts societal impacts into the core of the banking business comes from Relaño (2011). He defines social banks as banks that integrate ethics in the whole project of finance and use profitability to serve ethical goals.

Therefore, to summarize the definitions, social banking:

- focuses on achieving positive social, environmental, and sustainability impacts through financial products and services,
- bases all its business and its operations on ethical goals, and
- uses financial products and services to achieve a blended value return consisting of social, environmental, and financial returns.

The core business of social banks centers on loans for creating a social, environmental, or sustainability benefit. However, as for social enterprises in general, the distinction between social and commercial banking is not dichotomous. It is rather a continuum ranging from purely social to purely economic (Austin, Stevenson, & Wei-Skillern, 2006). Consequently, social banks also have to create enough income in order to be financially sustainable.

History of social banking

In a historical perspective, the first modern social banks were founded in the 1970s in order to emphasize financial ethics and with the goal to use finance as a means to influence society and business (Kaufer, 2014; Milano, 2011). These banks are based on environmental, social, or ethical principles, or focus on development issues. Another group of social banks is based on credit union principles. They are community based and emphasize the integration of communities and members into financial decision-making.

Social Banks and management theory

From a management theoretical perspective, the success of social banks can be explained through resource-based theory (Wernerfelt, 1984) and its specification "environmental resource-based theory" (Hart, 1995). The theory states that internal tangible and intangible resources such as environmental and sustainability knowledge is needed to create successful products and services in the short term that serve as models for further expansion. Empirical studies demonstrated that internal resources are an important condition for successful business and environmental performance (Russo & Fouts, 1997), especially for business activities that are outside conventional business activities. Consequently, Battilana and Dorado (2010) demonstrated that social banks build their organizational identity through hiring and socialization policies. Based on this finding, it can be stated that the main assets of social banks are their employees who follow the ethical guidelines provided by their organizations.

Social and financial return of social banking

The remainder of the chapter will present an analysis of social banks that were members of the GABV in 2014. First, the analysis will focus on exploring whether the mission, the history, and the products and services of social banks stand for business practices that correspond with the concept of social finance. Second, we will present financial data that suggest that social banks are financially successful in addition to their social impact.

Founding years and mission of the banks in the sample

The GABV is a global membership organization of sustainable banks. The member banks of this organization are presented in Table 27.1. In 2014, banks came from 19 countries from all

Table 27.1 Social banks, their country of origin, mission, and mission category

Institution	*Country of origin*	*Mission*	*Mission category*
Affinity Credit Union	Canada	Enhancing the economic and social well-being of the members	Members' and community well-being
Alternative Bank Switzerland	Switzerland	Emphasizing ethical principles instead of maximum profits	Ethical principles first
Assiniboine Credit Union	Canada	Providing accessible financial services for the well-being of members, employees, and the community	Members' and community well-being
Banca Etica	Italy	Offering transparent and responsible management of financial resources	Ethical principles first
Banco Fie	Bolivia	Microfinance	Microfinance
Banco Sol	Bolivia	Microfinance for Base of the Economic Pyramid clients	Microfinance
Bankmecu	Australia	Enhancing economic well-being of its customers in responsible ways	Members' and community well-being
Beneficial State Bank	United States	Improving economic opportunity for low-to moderate-income communities throughout California	Members' and community well-being
BRAC	Bangladesh	Microfinance	Microfinance
Centenary Bank	Uganda	Microfinance	Microfinance
Clean Energy Development Bank	Nepal	Creating a sustainable and energy-efficient future through comprehensive and innovative financial services	Renewable energy
Credit Cooperatif	France	Financing "social economy" organizations	Social economy financing
Cultura	Norway	Financing projects which benefit society and contribute to a better natural environment	Members' and community well-being
Ecology Building Society	UK	Supporting and promoting ecological building practices and sustainable communities	Ecological building practices
First Green Bank	United States	Doing the right thing for: the environment, its people, its community, and its shareholders	Members' and community well-being
GLS	Germany	Investing exclusively in companies and projects whose social, ecological, and economic performance is outstanding	Investing in high ecological, social, and economic performance
Merkur	Denmark	Including environmental, social, and ethical aspects in addition to financial considerations	Investing in high ecological, social, and economic performance
Mibanco	Peru	Providing access to the financial system	Microfinance
New Resource Bank	United States	Advancing sustainability with everything the bank does—the loans it makes, the way it operates, and its commitment to putting deposits to work for good	Members' and community well-being

SAC Appoyo Integral	El Salvador	Microfinance	Microfinance
Sunrise Bank	United States	Improving the urban community	Members' and community well-being
Triodos	The Netherlands	Financing companies, institutions, and projects that add cultural value and benefit people and the environment	Investing in high ecological, social, and economic performance
VanCity	Canada	Being a democratic, ethical, and innovative provider of financial services to its members. Serving as a catalyst for the self-reliance and economic well-being of its membership and community through strong financial performance.	Members' and community well-being
Vision Banco	Paraguay	Microfinance	Microfinance
XAC	Mongolia	Providing equitable access to transparent, reliable, and responsive banking products and services to the bank's clients, including its traditional micro-entrepreneurs as well as small and medium businesses	Microfinance

Source: Based on data provided by http://www.gabv.org.

continents, with eight European and seven North American banks. In 2015, three more banks became members of the organization. However, these banks were not integrated into the analysis because their financial data were only disclosed for the years 2010 to 2014. Five banks are located in South America; three banks are from Asia; and there is one each from Africa and Australia respectively. The banks from Asia and Latin America can be classified as microfinance institutions. The common denominator of all these banks is that they follow the guidelines of the GABV presented above. All these banks focus on social impacts as their main mission.

If we distinguish between specific social banks on the one hand and co-operative banks and credit unions on the other hand, social banking seems to be a relatively new phenomenon. The French Credit Cooperatif, however, was already founded in 1893 as an association that supported the social economy through lending to co-operatives. The specific social bank with the longest history in our sample is GLS bank, founded in 1974. GLS, as well as Triodos, founded in 1980, and Merkur, have an anthroposophist basis. Alternative Bank Switzerland was founded in 1990 by environmental, social, and development organizations. Other banks like Cultura Bank and Banca Etica followed in the 1990s. The only European social bank in the sample focused on one specific issue, fostering ecological building practices, is the Ecology Building Society founded in 1981 in the UK. Generally, this data suggest that social banking is a relatively new phenomenon in Europe.

The Asian and Latin American social banks, as well as Centenary Bank, the only GABV member from Africa, can be classified as microfinance institutions. BRAC's microfinance program was launched in 1974 and is the basis of the bank's business. XAC was founded as a merger of two non-bank financial institutions in Mongolia in 2001 in order to provide access to transparent, reliable, and responsive products and services for small, medium, and micro-enterprises.

The newest Asian bank in the sample is Clean Energy Development Bank, founded in 2006 in Nepal. In contrast to the other two Asian members, it focuses on financial services related to renewable energy and especially on hydropower.

Both Banco Sol, founded in 1992, and Mibanco, founded in 1998, focus on microfinance as well. The first was founded by international and Bolivian investors and the latter by entrepreneurs. Like some of the other banks, Mibanco is based on a social project that was already initiated in 1970. The bank, however, was founded in 1998. All the other South American members of the GABV were founded in the 1990s. These are Banco Fie (in 1998), SAC Appoyo Integral (in 1992), and Vision Banco (in 1992). They all follow the concept of microfinance and support micro-entrepreneurs. In this regard, they are similar to Centenary Bank in Uganda, founded in 1993 in order to provide microfinance especially to rural areas in Uganda.

The North American social banks in the sample are quite heterogeneous with respect to their history. They consist of three Canadian credit unions, Affinity Credit Union, founded in 1929, Assiniboine Credit Union, founded in 1943, and VanCity, founded in 1947. Affinity's mission is to enhance the economic and social well-being of its members. It has strong ties to local first nations, being the only Canadian credit union with an on-reserve branch. Assiniboine Credit Union's goal is to provide accessible financial services for the well-being of members, employees, and the community. It offers a full range of financial services. VanCity was founded as a community-based credit and savings co-operative in a neighborhood that was not considered a place to give mortgages to (Geobey & Weber, 2013).

The other North American institutions in the sample are US-based. With Sunrise Bank being the oldest of the US social banks in the sample (founded in 1986), social banks seem to be a relatively new phenomenon in the United States. Shore Bank, founded in 1973, however, was the best known and biggest social bank in the US but became insolvent and closed in 2010. New Resource Bank, founded in 2006, Beneficial State Bank, founded in 2010, and First Green Bank, founded in 2009, are much younger. New Resource Bank is the only social bank in the sample founded by technology entrepreneurs and green business pioneers. Because of that, the bank's focus is on financing green technologies. Beneficial State Bank was founded on the premise that conventional banks failed to serve businesses in low- and moderate-income markets. First Green Bank has a social and environmental mission and combines local community banking with positive environmental impacts.

The credit union Bankmecu, founded in 2001, is the only Australian institution in the sample. It is the first customer-owned bank in Australia and its mission is to enhance the economic well-being of its customers in responsible ways.

The results of the analysis of the data in Table 27.1 suggest that the banks were founded on the basis of a mission other than creating or maximizing profits. Their goal is to provide financial services that help create a positive societal and environmental effect. With the oldest banks being founded in the 1970s, the phenomenon of social banking seems to be relatively new, though some authors see their roots even in the credit and savings organizations that have operated since the 15th century (Milano, 2011).

Social impact sectors

After having discussed the institutions' missions, we will now have a look at the sectors the banks are lending to or investing in. Figure 27.1 demonstrates that social banks are involved in sectors connected with sustainable development such as microfinance. Loans and mortgages for housing are provided by 17 percent of the banks, followed by 16 percent engaged in the environment and renewable energy. These sectors are followed by education, community

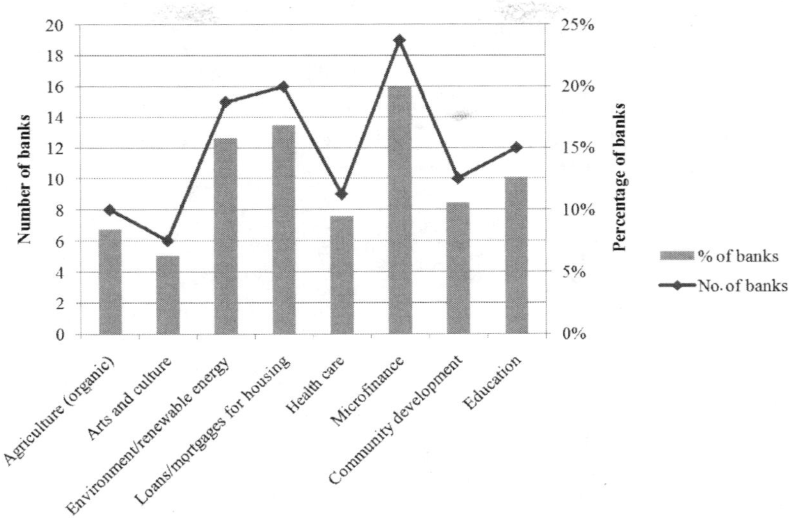

Figure 27.1 Sectors financed by social banks

Source: Based on data provided by http://www.gabv.org.

development, health care, agriculture, and arts and culture. The engagement in these sectors reflects the core goals of social banks, indicating that they are dedicated to supporting social issues and sustainable development.

The insights presented above speak of an approach that addresses important environmental and societal issues. However, can this approach be conducted in a financially successful way? In order to examine the financial success of the banks in the sample, we analyzed their key financial figures. The results are presented in the following section.

Social banks' financial figures

We present important financial figures for 2013 such as total assets, loans, deposits, and equity, as well as the indicators' equity/assets, loans/assets, and deposits/assets, in Table 27.2.

With total assets of $77.1 billion in 2013, the total balance sum of all the banks in the group is still small. As a comparison, the average total assets of all members of the World Council of Credit Unions (WOCCU) globally equals $1.7 trillion (World Council of Credit Unions, 2014). The mean for the total assets for the GABV sample was $3.1 billion. The median with $1.1 billion is even smaller, suggesting that some bigger social banks such as VanCity, Credit Cooperatif, and Triodos are rather exceptions than typical representatives of social banks with regard to their size. The median of the social banks' assets in the sample, however, is significantly higher than the average assets of WOCCU members with $30.65 million (2012 data).

In 2013, the average loan sum provided by the banks in the sample was $3.25 billion, with a median of $891 million. With $18.0 billion in loans, Credit Cooperatif had the biggest loan portfolio. The average loan sum of WOCCU members in 2013 was $57 million (World Council of Credit Unions, 2014). The loans of the GABV members seem to be secured by the deposits in the banks. With a total of $59 billion, the value of the deposits is slightly lower than the total loan portfolio with $61 billion, leading to a loans-to-deposit ratio of 96 percent. The ratio demonstrates that a large part of the savings in social banks is actually used for providing loans, mostly

Table 27.2 Banks' assets, loans, deposits, and equity in $ million, and loans/assets for the year 2013

Bank	*Total assets*	*Total loans*	*Total deposits*	*Total equity*	*Total loans/total assets*
Affinity	3,699	3,048	3,363	291	82.4%
Alternative Bank	1,546	997	1,438	88	64.5%
Assiniboine	3,323	2,939	3,118	180	88.4%
Banca Etica	1,509	868	913	84	60.5%
Banco Fie	1,165	913	807	87	78.4%
Banco Sol	1,125	934	788	94	83.0%
Bank Mecu	2,699	2,048	2,315	304	75.9%
Beneficial State Bank	437	300	354	49	68.6%
BRAC	2,373	1,434	1,668	155	60.4%
Centenary Bank	582	270	387	102	46.3%
Clean Energy Development Bank	97	66	73	13	68.0%
Credit Cooperatif	22,394	18,043	16,751	1,871	80.6%
Cultura Bank	91	59	78	9	65.3%
Ecology Building Society	206	137	192	11	66.7%
First Green Bank	248	199	212	28	80.1%
GLS Bank	4,457	3,802	3,858	272	85.3%
Merkur Cooperative Bank	446	239	375	38	53.3%
Mibanco	2,164	1,502	1,467	238	69.4%
New Resource Bank	216	157	186	29	72.6%
SAC Appoyo	82	66	18	13	79.9%
Sunrise	848	426	750	38	50.2%
Triodos	8,876	4,881	7,779	900	55.0%
VanCity	16,408	14,083	13,999	899	85.8%
Vision	1,018	707	705	95	69.5%
XAC	1,125	647	392	76	57.5%
Total	77,134	58,810	61,157	5,880	69.9%

Source: Based on data provided by http://www.gabv.org.

in the same community, given the local nature of the banks in the sample. Some banks, however, deployed less than 70 percent of their deposits for loans, such as Alternative Bank Switzerland, Merkur, Sunrise, and Triodos. This may be due to multiple reasons, such as fast-growing deposits, the lack of borrowers with acceptable financial risks, or a diverse product portfolio.

Regarding the indicator loans/assets, on average 69.8 percent of the assets were used for loans in 2013. Banca Etica, Centenary, Merkur, Triodos, Sunrise, and XAC presented ratios below 60 percent, demonstrating high liquidity and diversified sources of revenue on the one hand. On the other hand, a low ratio means that a significant part of the assets was not channeled into loans. As a benchmark, however, WOCCU members presented a loan-to-asset ratio of 65 percent in 2013. A one sample t-test suggests that the loan-to-asset ratio of the GABV members was significantly higher than the ratio of 65 percent of WOCCU members ($p_{\text{single sided}} = 0.03$).

To analyze the profitability and the financial security of the social banks, the total minimum, maximum, average, and median revenue, net profit, BIS ratio, and return on equity for 2009–2013 is presented in Table 27.3.

The average total revenue from 2009 to 2013 was $111.4 million. We found a high variance, however, between the banks with respect to this indicator. The bank with the lowest total revenue with $4.0 million was Clean Energy Development Bank, while Credit Cooperatif achieved

Table 27.3 Total revenue and net income in $ million, return on equity, cost-income ratio, and Bank of International Settlement (BIS) ratio in % between 2009 and 2013

	Total revenue	*Net income*	*Return on equity*	*Cost-income ratio*	*BIS 1 ratio*
Minimum	4.0	0.5	2.0	33.8	7.0
Maximum	568.0	76.6	29.8	86.7	27.6
Mean	111.4	14.7	10.6	69.6	13.0
Median	83.0	12.2	8.4	69.4	12.3

Source: Based on data provided by http://www.gabv.org.

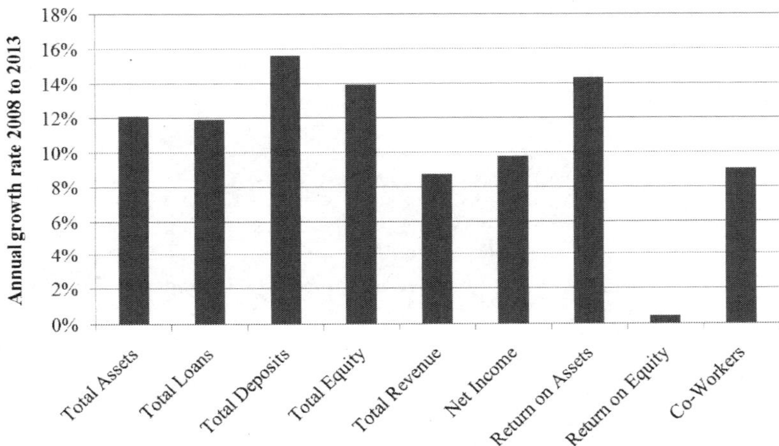

Figure 27.2 Annual growth rates for different financial indicators of the social banks in the sample between 2008 and 2013

Source: Based on data provided by http://www.gabv.org.

$568 million in 2013. The average net income was $14.7 million, with a median of $12.2 million. The most profitable social bank in the sample was VanCity with a net income of $76 million.

With 57.4 percent, Banco Sol achieved the highest return on equity (RoE) in the sample. The average RoE was 10.7 percent, and the median was 8.2 percent. As a comparison, the RoE in the banking sector globally was 7.6 percent in 2011 (Daruvala et al., 2012), while the banks in the sample achieved an average RoE of 11.3 percent in the same year.

As an indicator for measuring the efficiency of the banks, we used the cost-income ratio. The average cost-income ratio in 2013 was 69.6 percent. Consequently, social banks had a significantly higher cost-income ratio (T-test: $p < .00001$) than banks globally in 2011, presenting a cost-income ratio of 50.8 percent (Daruvala et al., 2012).

The BIS 1 or tier 1 ratio, expressing the ratio of a bank's core capital to its risk-weighted assets, is used by the Bank of International Settlements (BIS) and domestic regulators in order to guarantee that banks are able to cover unexpected risks. In our sample, the ratio varied from 7.0 percent for Banco Sol to 27.6 percent for Centenary Bank, with an average of 13.0 percent and a median of 12.3 percent. According to BIS, the tier 1 ratio should not be smaller than 3 percent (Basel Committee on Banking Supervision, 2013). Globally the BIS 1 ratio in 2011 was 12.7 percent (Daruvala et al., 2012), compared with a 2011 average of 12.9 percent in the sample, suggesting no significant difference.

Generally our data suggest that the social banks in the sample presented similar income and risk figures as conventional banks and credit unions globally. However, the question remains whether the similarity is also valid for the growth rate between 2007 and 2012, a time that was very much influenced by the financial crisis. In order to demonstrate the growth of social banks over the last few years, we present the annual growth rates between 2008 and 2013 in Figure 27.2.

Between 2008 and 2013, average annual growth rates of assets, loans, and deposits, total equity, and return on assets have been higher than 10 percent. The strongest growth has been achieved in deposits. The increase in deposits can be explained by the fact that during the financial crisis social banks gained many new clients from conventional banks who wanted to deposit their funds in a more secure and ethical way. In parallel, the banks could achieve a growth of more than 8 percent per year in total revenue, net income, and the amount of co-workers, while conventional banks suffered from a net income decrease (Korslund & Spengler, 2012) between 2008 and 2013. These figures suggest that social banks have been successful during and after the financial crisis.

Discussion and conclusion

The chapter has presented an analysis of social banking. The members of the GABV, the only global social banking association, were analyzed with respect to their social finance missions, their investments and loans, and their financial sustainability. The banks in the sample focus on achieving positive social, environmental, and sustainability impacts, and strive for a blended, sustainable income consisting of both social and financial returns. Following a social enterprise approach (Austin et al., 2006), the goal of social banks is to achieve financial returns and not to maximize profit.

Our analysis was conducted in order to explore whether the mission, products, and services of social banks indicated business practices in line with the concept of social banking. Additionally, the analysis explored whether social banks fulfill the second part of the concept of social banking, creating a sustainable financial return. In order to answer these questions, we analyzed the missions of the banks qualitatively, and financial figures, such as assets, loans, savings, equity, etc., and their respective growth rates, in a quantitative way. We also compared the financial results of social banks with other banks and credit unions. The 25 banks in the sample were all members of the GABV and originated from 19 countries in Europe, Asia, North and South America, Australia, and Africa. Eight of them were microfinance institutions and 17 were social banks.

The qualitative analysis of the missions of the banks, as well as the sectors the banks invested in, suggest that the banks in the sample follow the principles of social banking and social entrepreneurship (Austin et al., 2006; Kaeufer, 2010; Weber & Remer, 2011), as well as blended return (Bugg-Levine & Emerson, 2011; Chertok, Hamaoui, & Jamison, 2008; Emerson, 2003; Harji & Hebb, 2010). None of the banks named profit maximization or the maximization of shareholder value as their mission. Instead, the well-being of members or financing projects with environmental and societal benefits has been at the core of social banks' activities. All analyzed institutions followed the concept of creating social impact as the principal vision and strategy, in contrast to conventional banks and many other financial institutions that usually have profit maximization as their main goal. The mission of social banks is also different from conventional credit unions and co-operative banks that usually have a strong relation to their community and try to empower people (World Council of Credit Unions, 2012) through financial services but do not strive for other social and sustainability goals.

Consequently, social banks follow an inside-out approach of Corporate Social Responsibility (Porter & Kramer, 2006) that emphasizes the impacts of business activities on the environment and society instead of following an outside-in approach that focuses mainly on the management of sustainability risks and benefits for a bank. In other words, they focus on the sustainability case of business rather than on the business case of sustainability (Weber, 2014a, 2014b).

In order to analyze whether the missions of social banks could be found in their actual business activities, we analyzed the sectors and projects social banks provide loans to and invest in. Microfinance, social housing, the environment/renewable energy, and education have been the sectors with the highest portion in the portfolio of banks in the sample. This result suggests that social banks channel financial capital into different sectors than conventional banks do. Social banks focus on sectors with high sustainability impacts, while conventional banks usually lend to and invest in sectors proportional to the ratio in their respective economic environment. Furthermore, financing sectors with a positive social or environmental impact is not a niche offering in social banks, but is the main part of their core business.

The social banks in the sample have been successful with respect to financial returns as well. Their revenues, net income, cost-income ratio, and tier 1 capital ratio, also called the BIS 1 ratio, demonstrate that they are financially sustainable. Furthermore, between 2008 and 2013, they provided positive annual growth rates. For instance, they outperformed big conventional banks with respect to net income and European banks with respect to revenue growth (Korslund, 2013), demonstrating that a social enterprise approach can be successful in the financial sector. This growth, however, does not come with higher risks. With an average of 13 percent, the banks in the sample significantly exceeded the capital ratio that is suggested by the Basel Committee on Banking Supervision (Basel Committee on Banking Supervision, 2013). In addition, the banks showed a significant increase in loans, deposits, assets, and equity.

The years 2007–2013 were characterized as a time of turmoil affecting the business success of many banks and financial institutions (Weber et al., 2011). This, however, was not the case for social banks. Clients changing from conventional banks to social and ethical banking organizations, particularly in Europe and in the United States, where the financial crisis of 2008 had a significant influence on the financial sector, could be the reason for the growth, mostly in deposits. The more risk-aversive business of social and ethical banks that relies on deposits that are needed to provide loans and less on highly speculative financial products such as derivatives, options, and asset-backed securities could be another explanation for the success of social banks, though their financial figures exceeded those of credit unions with similar business models as well. Consequently, our findings suggest that the concept of social banking as a business strategy can be financially successful even in times of turmoil.

Despite the positive results, however, the social banking sector is still small and represents a small niche of the banking industry. In 2013, Credit Cooperatif as the biggest institution in the sample provided $22.4 billion in assets, and the total assets in the sample in 2013 added up to $77.1 billion. Given this small market share, the sustainability effect of these banks is less caused by their direct impact, but rather by being a model for a new successful way of banking that focuses on the sustainability case rather than on profit maximization. Similar to other sectors, social banks could play the role of sustainability innovators (Koellner, Weber, Fenchel, & Scholz, 2005) that lay the ground for social finance products and services to be integrated into conventional banking. Nevertheless, social banks will have to follow the path of sustainable growth and to widen their client base to generate more impact in the future.

The consequent transformation of the social mission to successful core products and services speaks to the availability of the respective resources. Resource-based theory defines resources as tangible and intangible assets that are available in a firm and that lead to short-term and long-term competitive advantages (Wernerfelt, 1984). In the case of social banks, resources such as knowledge about how environmental, societal, community, or sustainability issues can be positively influenced by financing clients who address these issues leads to both short-term balance effects and long-term capabilities for further expansion. In addition, the respective sustainability products and services support further expansion because they demonstrate that a bank focusing on sustainability issues can create both a positive sustainability impact and attractive financial returns. As mentioned above, Hart (1995) has already broadened resource-based theory to environmental resource-based theory. Consequently our study suggests that the theory can be broadened to become a sustainability resource-based theory that is able to explain the success of social banks.

Further research in the field is needed in analyzing the long-term success of social banks and in analyzing risks. The bankruptcy of Shore Bank, one of the most well-known social banks, demonstrates that social banks are at risk as well and are not immune against financial shocks. Furthermore, indicators have to be developed that will be able to measure the social impact of banks in a more reliable, valid, and objective way. Only through the use of valid, reliable, and comparable indicators will social banks be able to demonstrate their sustainability case in comparison to conventional banks (Brandstetter & Lehner, 2015).

References

Allen, F., & Santomero, A. M. (2001). What do financial intermediaries do? *Journal of Banking & Finance, 25*(2), 271–294. doi:10.1016/s0378-4266(99)00129-6

Austin, J., Stevenson, H., & Wei-Skillern, J. (2006). Social and commercial entrepreneurship: Same, different, or both? *Entrepreneurship Theory and Practice, 30*(1), 1–22. doi:10.1111/j.1540-6520.2006.00107.x

Basel Committee on Banking Supervision. (2013). *Revised Basel III leverage ratio framework and disclosure requirements* (p. 22). Basel, Switzerland: Bank for International Settlements.

Battilana, J., & Dorado, S. (2010). Building sustainable hybrid organizations: The case of commercial microfinance organizations. *Academy of Management Journal, 53*(6), 1419–1440. doi:10.5465/amj.2010.57318391

Brandstetter, L., & Lehner, O. M. (2015). Opening the market for impact investments: The need for adapted portfolio tools. *Entrepreneurship Research Journal, 5*, 87–107.

Bugg-Levine, A., & Emerson, J. (2011). *Impact investing—Transforming how we make money while making a difference.* San Francisco, CA: Jossey-Bass.

Buttle, M. (2007). "I'm not in it for the money": Constructing and mediating ethical reconnections in UK social banking. *Geoforum, 38*(6), 1076–1088. doi:10.1016/j.geoforum.2006.12.011

Chertok, M., Hamaoui, J., & Jamison, E. (2008). The funding gap. *Stanford Social Innovation Review, 6*(2), 44–51.

Cornée, S., & Szafarz, A. (2013). Vive la différence: Social banks and reciprocity in the credit market. *Journal of Business Ethics, 125*(3), 361–380. doi:10.1007/s10551-013-1922-9

da Silva, A. F. C. (2007). Social banking: The need of the hour. In A. F. C. da Silva (Ed.), *Social banking—Perspectives and experiences* (pp. 3–9). Hyderabad, India: The Icfai University Press.

Daruvala, T., Dietz, M., Härle, P., Sengupta, J., Voelkel, M., & Windhagen, E. (2012). *The triple transformation—Achieving a sustainable business model* (p. 52), McKinsey & Company.

Edery, Y. (2006). Ethical developments in finance: Implications for charities and social enterprise. *Social Enterprise Journal, 2*(1), 82–100.

Emerson, J. (2003). The blended value proposition: Integrating social and financial returns. *California Management Review, 45*(4), 35–51.

Geobey, S., & Weber, O. (2013). Lessons in operationalizing social finance: The case of Vancouver City Savings Credit Union. *Journal of Sustainable Finance & Investment, 3*(2), 124–137. doi:10.1080/20430795.2013.776259

Geobey, S., Westley, F. R., & Weber, O. (2012). Enabling social innovation through developmental social finance. *Journal of Social Entrepreneurship, 3*(2), 151–165. doi:10.1080/19420676.2012.726006

Harji, K., & Hebb, T. (2009). *The quest for blended value returns: Investor perspectives on social finance in Canada* (p. 25). Ottawa, ON: Carleton Centre for Community Innovation.

Harji, K., & Hebb, T. (2010). *Investing for impact: Issues and opportunities for social finance in Canada.* Ottawa, ON: Carleton Centre for Community Innovation.

Hart, S. (1995). A natural resource-based view on the firm. *Academy of Management Review, 20*, 986–1014.
Kaeufer, K. (2010). *Banking as a vehicle for socio-economic development and change: Case studies of socially responsible and green banks* (p. 6). Cambridge, MA: Presencing Institute.
Kaufer, K. (2014). Social responsibility as a core business model in banking: A case study in the financial sector. *Journal of Sustainable Finance & Investment, 4*(1), 76–89. doi:10.1080/20430795.2014.887350
Koellner, T., Suh, S., Weber, O., Moser, C., & Scholz, R. W. (2007). Environmental impacts of conventional and sustainable investment funds compared using input-output life-cycle assessment. *Journal of Industrial Ecology, 11*(3), 41–60.
Koellner, T., Weber, O., Fenchel, M., & Scholz, R. (2005). Principles for sustainability rating of investment funds. *Business Strategy and the Environment, 14*(1), 54–70.
Korslund, D. (2013). *Real banking for the real economy: Comparing sustainable bank performance with the largest banks in the world* (p. 12). Zeist, the Netherlands: Global Alliance for Banking on Values.
Korslund, D., & Spengler, L. (2012). *Strong, straightforward and sustainable banking—Financial capital and impact metrics of values based banking* (p. 195). Zeist, the Netherlands: Global Alliance for Banking on Values.
Martin, R., & Osberg, S. (2007). Social entrepreneurship: The case for definition. *Stanford Social Innovation Review, 5*, 28–39.
Milano, R. (2011). Social banking: A brief history. In O. Weber & S. Remer (Eds.), *Social banks and the future of sustainable finance* (Vol. 64, pp. 15–47). New York, NY: Routledge.
O'Rourke, A. (2003). The message and methods of ethical investment. *Journal of Cleaner Production, 11*(6), 683–693.
Porter, M. E., & Kramer, M. R. (2006). Strategy & society: The link between competitive advantage and corporate social responsibility. *Harvard Business Review, 84*(12), 78–92.
Relaño, F. (2011). Maximizing social return in the banking sector. *Corporate Governance, 11*(3), 274–284.
Remer, S. (2011). Social banking at the crossroads. In O. Weber & S. Remer (Eds.), *Social banks and the future of sustainable finance* (pp. 136–195). London, UK: Routledge.
Russo, M. V., & Fouts, P. A. (1997). A resource-based perspective on corporate environmental performance and profitability. *Academy of Management Journal, 40*(3), 534–559.
Sandberg, J., Juravle, C., Hedesström, T., & Hamilton, I. (2009). The heterogeneity of socially responsible investment. *Journal of Business Ethics, 87*(4), 519–533. doi:10.1007/s10551-008-9956-0
Schuster, L. (2001). The societal responsibility of commercial and savings banks. In C. Guene & E. Mayo (Eds.), *Banking and social cohesion* (pp. 159–163). Charlbury, UK: John Carpenter.
Weber, O. (2006). Investment and environmental management: The interaction between environmentally responsible investment and environmental management practices. *International Journal of Sustainable Development, 9*(4), 336–354.
Weber, O. (2011). Social banking: Products and services. In O. Weber & S. Remer (Eds.), *Social banks and the future of sustainable finance* (pp. 96–121). London, UK: Routledge.
Weber, O. (2014a). The financial sector's impact on sustainable development. *Journal of Sustainable Finance & Investment, 4*(1), 1–8. doi:10.1080/20430795.2014.887345
Weber, O. (2014b). Social banking: Concept, definitions and practice. *Global Social Policy, 14*(2), 265–267. doi:10.1177/1468018114539864
Weber, O., Mansfeld, M., & Schirrmann, E. (2011). The financial performance of RI funds after 2000. In W. Vandekerckhove, J. Leys, K. Alm, B. Scholtens, S. Signori, & H. Schaefer (Eds.), *Responsible investment in times of turmoil* (pp. 75–91). Berlin, Germany: Springer.
Weber, O., & Remer, S. (2011). Social banking—Introduction. In O. Weber & S. Remer (Eds.), *Social banks and the future of sustainable finance* (pp. 1–14). London, UK: Routledge.
Wernerfelt, B. (1984). A resource-based view of the firm. *Strategic Management Journal, 5*(2), 171–180.
World Council of Credit Unions. (2012). *2011 statistical report* (p. 4). Madison, WI: World Council of Credit Unions.
World Council of Credit Unions. (2014). *2013 statistical report* (p. 4). Madison, WI: World Council of Credit Unions.

28

GROWING SOCIAL BANKING THROUGH (BUSINESS) ASSOCIATIONS

Daniel Tischer and Sven Remer

Social banks—values-based financial service providers with a mission to have a positive impact on society as a whole—have a long tradition of operating in niche markets across Europe, but have they have remained largely unnoticed, not only by the wider public, but also by conventional banks and academics alike. This is despite them having a number of interesting characteristics. social banks have shown not only a great deal of resilience during the latest financial crisis of 2008, but have even experienced almost exponential growth since then. As a consequence, ever more experts consider them "shining examples" for the financial sector overall (e.g., Roland Berger, 2012; zeb, 2012).

While the exact factors contributing to social banks' apparent success are just beginning to be researched and understood in detail, there are indications that they also face a number of distinctive obstacles to organizational growth and outreach, amongst them a lack of size, public awareness, qualified staff, equity capital, and lobbying power (Käufer, 2011; Weber & Remer, 2011; zeb, 2012).

Here, joining forces to promote their cause and to deal with the above obstacles seems an obvious recommendation, not least because cooperation and the coordination of activities has a long history in European cooperative banking in, for example, Germany and the Netherlands. Collaboration between individual cooperative banks has also proven an effective means to re-establish the ailing cooperative banking sector in Finland (Yeoman & Tischer, 2015). Yet these examples are nationally negotiated, and by virtue of being an international movement, social banks' ambition to collaborate required a more nuanced approach that acknowledges international and organizational diversity.

Indeed, social banks have been shown to cooperate through associational life (Tischer, 2013a, 2013b), a feature emerging in the 1980s with the establishment of INAISE, the International Association of Investors in the Social Economy. Since then, new challenges have intensified and led to the emergence of new, specialized associations, offering different benefits to the diverse range of social banks within Europe and globally.

Given their geographical separation, resulting competition between social banks is limited and should allow them to collaborate closely. Still, international collaboration also comes with challenges. Most obvious in this context are differences in the founding impulses of social banks, along with differences in their cultural and regulatory settings. Thus, it is surprising to see that the specific characteristics of these collaborations and their importance to social banking have received little scholarly attention to date.

Therefore, in this chapter our objective is to shed some light on why and how the sector organizes its affairs collectively through membership in associations. We are particularly interested in the type and purpose of associations being established, as well as how membership responds to wider changes to their operating environment through associational life. Moreover, the analysis will show that associational life-bridging national contexts can be an effective and beneficial mechanism to organize geographically dispersed yet collectively minded niche sectors, such as social banking.

In the first part, we provide a sector overview, covering definition(s), historic origins, more recent developments, and future opportunities and threats. In the following part, we examine the associational life of social banks by first summarizing key features of the four main associations and why they have been established, before substantiating some developments in membership empirically using a network analytic approach to describe developments since 1999. In the final part, we discuss the findings, followed by our conclusion and discussion of future research prospects in the closing part.

Sector overview

Definition

When it comes to social banking, there is considerable confusion about this term and its underlying concepts. The very same term can mean very different things, and seemingly different terms can refer to similar concepts.

Reflecting the disagreement on fundamental aspects including the terminology used, some argue that the word "social" in social banking could and should be replaced by "sustainable" or "ethical," while others insist that these terms are not to be used interchangeably. De Clerck (2009), for instance, suggests that a precise and unified definition of financial activities such as "social, ethical, alternative, sustainable development and solidarity banking and finance" is not available and perhaps not possible because of the different traditions from which the ethical finance actors have emerged.

This notwithstanding, in the limited literature available on social banking, there appears to be a perception of a "common denominator" of various organizations in this field (e.g., Carboni, 2011; ISB, 2011; Tischer, 2013a; Weber & Remer, 2011): Based on a strong set of non-monetary values, their core objective lies in using money and finance to contribute to the "common good," as well as sustainable—social, environmental, and economic—development. While their activities obviously need to be economically viable, they do not strive for profit maximization. social banks often employ an explicit set of negative and positive sustainability criteria to reject funding into "unsustainable" sectors (e.g., arms production or nuclear power) or speculative activities, concentrating funding into "sustainable" sectors (e.g., organic agriculture or multigenerational housing) (De Clerck, 2009; GLS, 2015; Triodos Bank, 2015). They refrain from speculative activities and focus instead on the actual needs of clients from the social economy and civil society. They strive for long-term relations rather than short-term transactions. Many social banks also show a high degree of transparency—and even have clients participating in decision-making processes—particularly with respect to the usage of deposit funds.

This common denominator clearly differentiates social banks not only from conventional banks that mainly pursue profit-maximizing strategies, but also from many savings and cooperative banks that arguably have lost much of their "social heritage" over the past decades.

Social banking of this particular form is essentially a European phenomenon. Here, one can identify a small group of social banks—in Germany (GLS Bank), the Netherlands (Triodos Bank),

Scandinavia (Merkur Bank, Ekobanken, and Cultura-Bank), Switzerland (Alternative Bank Schweiz and Freie Gemeinschaftsbank), Italy (Banca Etica), the UK (Charity Bank), and some others.

Having said that, one also finds noteworthy similarities between (European) social banks and socially oriented banks in other parts of the world, such as community (development) banks and savings/credit unions in the Anglo Saxony area or many Microfinance Banks (GABV, 2015a). While the latter focus more on social development in a narrower sense (leaving other—environmental or cultural—aspects of relevance in social banking aside), this has begun to change.

Historic origins

Social banking has a long history, reaching back to the 18th and 19th centuries at least, but has also been shaped by ideas and movements in the 20th century too. There is no single answer to explain their historic origins; instead, it helps to think of social banking as "emergent"—a multiplex phenomenon drawing from impulses from a variety of areas and historic developments.

Of the many factors influencing the development of social banking, three are particularly noteworthy:

1 *The emergence of cooperative and savings banks in Europe in the late 18th century.* Most social banks today are cooperatives that share the basic values with their predecessors, such as a focus on the social and financial inclusion of underprivileged groups, the principle of "self-help," and a members-oriented governance structure (Milano, 2011).
2 *The anthroposophical movement originating in the early 20th century based on the ideas of Rudolf Steiner.* Many social banks have an anthroposophic founding impulse (e.g., Cultura, Ekobanken, Freie Gemeinschaftsbank, GLS, Merkur, Triodos), although only a few still adhere strictly and publicly to this world view, which puts great consciousness on how economic activity impacts on wider society and the environment (Perlas, 2002; Wachsmuth, 1920). Still, in most social banks, anthroposophic ideas are manifest in providing gift money to support cultural and educational needs (Benedikter, 2011; Steiner, 2013 [1922]) and in lending to areas that, according to anthroposophic ideas, have a positive impact but were long excluded from mainstream finance, such as biodynamic agriculture, alternative medicine, or independent ("Steiner") schooling (Dodwell, 2012).
3 *The social (justice) and environmental movements of the 1970s and 1980s.* Most social bank(er)s today are also heavily influenced by concerns on issues that first came to the public agenda in the 1970s, such as global poverty, gender inequality, financial exclusion, unfair international trade relations, environmental pollution, global warming, and, more recently, the contributions of the mainstream financial sector to those issues. Some social banks—such as Alternative Bank Schweiz, Banca Etica, and Charity Bank—have explicitly been initiated (often by charities, NGOs and/or social enterprises) to tackle these issues by providing access to finance and banking services for those un(der)-served by the mainstream or by offering financial products to and encouraging investments in green energy, social housing, etc. (Tischer, 2013b).

While, as noted above, social banking essentially is a European phenomenon that has existed for over 40 years, similar activities can be found in the financial sectors of many other regions, particularly in the Anglo Saxony area, partly driven by their very own contextual settings.

With a view to North America, Geobey and Harji (2014), for instance, note the importance of the passing of the 1977 Community Reinvestment Act in driving the development of "a plethora of community development financial institutions that deploy significant amounts of capital in affordable housing, renewable energy and local economic development across the

United States," for example Beneficial State Bank (California) and Sunrise Bank (Minnesota). In Canada, by contrast, "social finance finds its roots in credit unions and cooperatives across the country, and particularly in the province of Quebec." Thus, it is more historically and culturally embedded, with the notable examples of Vancity and the Desjardins group of credit unions taking a more considerable market share.

More recently there has been some (limited) activity in setting up new social banks outside Europe. In the US, First Green Bank and New Resource Bank opened in 2006; Xac Bank of Mongolia opened in 2001/2; and the Nepalese Clean Energy Development Bank started trading in 2006.

Recent developments and success factors

Although social banking clearly still represents a niche, it is one with significant momentum. When looking at the social banking sector, one has to acknowledge its small size, even in Europe where it has its origins. There, social banks, with balance sheets between $100 million and $10 billion, reach less than 1 percent of all possible banking customers (Carboni, 2011; Weber & Remer, 2011; zeb, Alanus Hochschule, & Puls Marktforschung, 2012). And for a long period, social banking was only known by a small number of clients and largely ignored by the wider public, conventional peers, and academics.

This changed dramatically when it became apparent that most social banks had been "astonishingly" resilient toward the initial shockwaves of the financial crisis (Benedikter, 2011). Once the word spread that conventional retail banking was not only in an economic crisis but also an ethical one, social banks suddenly began to attract previously unseen attention. On the one hand, this is visible in the increased media coverage, expert discussions, and research featuring social banks (Remer, 2011; Tischer, 2013b). On the other hand, it is visible in the actual growth of social banks. While most social banks have seen a healthy organic development since their foundation, growth figures have risen sharply since the financial crisis of 2007/8, averaging 20–30 percent per annum—quite different to the performance of most conventional banks (Carboni, 2011; Niven, 2014; zeb et al., 2012).

A regular report of the Global Alliance for Banking on Values (GABV)—which compares the performances of an international group of social/sustainability-focused banks (SFBs) with 28 of the world's largest and most influential banks, Globally Systemically Important Financial Institutions (GSIFIs)—shows that social banks are outperforming GSIFIs (GABV, 2014). Comparing pre- and post-crisis data (Table 28.1), figures have developed positively for social banks, whereas both loans and deposits to total asset ratios have declined for GSIFIs, suggesting that social banks are becoming more active players in the market as they represent an interesting alternative to conventional banks (Benedikter, 2011; Carboni, 2011; Remer, 2011; San-Jose, Retolaza, & Gutierrez-Gloria, 2011).

It is important to note that these developments are not purely in response to the financial crisis of 2007/8 and the ensuing failure of retail banking, as many social banks had grown at similar rates in the years leading up to the financial crisis, as illustrated by pre-crisis data provided by GABV (2014).

To many observers, these developments might seem surprising for a number of reasons. First, the adverse global economic developments resulted in diminished earning opportunities linked to low interest rates and spreads (Carboni, 2011). Second, social banks do not strive for growth to improve the underlying profitability of operations as they usually do not seek to compensate outside investors through dividend payments. For social banks, growth and financial sustainability are prerequisites to lend and invest incoming funds to social and economic activities that fit their missions (De Clerck, 2009; San-Jose et al., 2011). Third, social banks primarily serve clients deemed

Table 28.1 Recent developments in social banking (SFBs) and mainstream banking (GSIFIs), 2003–2013

		2003	*2008*	*2013*
Loans to Assets				
	SFBs	77.1%	76.0%	76.2%
	GSIFIs	43.4%	38.8%	40.5%
Deposits to Total Assets				
	SFBs	71.4%	71.5%	80.4%
	GSIFIs	47.3%	42.0%	48.8%
Equity/Total Assets				
	SFBs	6.2%	7.3%	7.7%
	GSIFIs	5.2%	5.0%	6.6%
		2003–2013	2009–2013	
Return on Assets				
	SFBs	0.68%	0.66%	
	GSIFIs	0.58%	0.46%	

Source: Based on GABV (2014).

too risky and unprofitable to be served by most conventional banks. Thus in theory, social banks should face significant levels of bad debt; however, ongoing profitability over the years suggests that this might not be necessarily true.

So what factors contribute to the apparent success of social banks?

In this context, a number of likely reasons come to mind, and have been suggested by the limited literature on social banking. For instance, with their strong values orientation, traditional approach to core banking activities, and reliable economic performance, social banks present a very attractive proposition to an increasing number of clients. This development is characterized not only by a general change in values systems toward sustainable lifestyles and consumption, but also by a significant distrust toward conventional banks developing in the aftermath of the latest financial crisis (zeb, 2010). social banks' ability to innovate products and services by including social and environmental criteria is likely to meet an increasing demand for sustainable financial services from society at large (Käufer, 2012). In addition, it has also been pointed out that social banks certainly benefit from a loyal and supportive base of like-minded owners, clients, and other stakeholders (Remer, 2011).

Yet to date there are only a few studies that systematically and empirically examine the characteristics and practices that are potentially linked to the success of social banks.

For instance, focusing on deposit clients, a study by zeb et al. (2012) found that 23 percent of those participating in a representative study in Germany acknowledged the potential "social return" earned when depositing their funds with a social bank. They appreciate the transparent and positive social and environmental investment criteria of social banks and the ability of customers to influence lending and investment decisions. This perceived additional benefit increases the attractiveness of savings and investment products that, by conventional measures, only pay average interest rates (zeb et al., 2012).

Focusing on the bank borrower relationships, Cornée, Masclet, and Thenet (2011) and Cornée (2012) have shown that the long-term-oriented bank customer relationships and the collection of "soft information" on creditors reduce the risk of loans not being repaid. In addition, Cornée and Szafarz (2013) found that relationship banking in this context may be mutually beneficial as it provides customers with access to reasonably priced lending that, despite an apparently lower credit rating, reduces the risk of those customers defaulting.

Pointing to a similar direction, Tischer (2013b) has shown that social banks customers' demand, in particular from charities and social enterprises, but also from private customers, for socially and environmentally responsible investments, is voiced through relatively close knit, mutually dependent relationships between the social banks and their customers.

Future developments and challenges

Developments in social banking over the past decade have been impressive, particularly in the face of various financial, economic, socio-cultural, and environmental problems which had clearly limited the possibilities to expand business activity when compared to mainstream banking. Accordingly, experts are forecasting a bright future for the sector (Becchetti, 2011; Carboni, 2011; Milano, 2011; Remer, 2011; zeb, 2010; zeb et al., 2012). Yet in spite of the overwhelmingly positive expectations for development in the future, some literature also highlights the challenges social banks face on the road ahead, as summarized in Table 28.2.

Table 28.2 Challenges to social banks' future growth and development

Challenges	*Authors*
Lack of visibility beyond niche markets, due to their small scale operations compared with mainstream finance	Remer (2011) and zeb et al. (2012)
Threat of growth and turning "mainstream" that could water down their values base and impact	De Clerck (2009), Remer (2011), and Tischer (2013b)
Comparatively limited level of professionalization and limited range of products and services that could put off new, arguably less loyal but more demanding, customers	De Clerck (2009), Remer (2011), and Weber and Remer (2011)
Limited availability of lending and investing opportunities that match Social banks' negative and positive criteria, leading to a need to "park" excess funds in ways not appreciated by depositors	Weber and Remer (2011)
Need for a more systematic assessment and reporting of their actual (positive) impact (instead of merely "story telling") in the face of a more critical (new) clientele	Remer (2011)
Necessity for an ongoing open but resource-consuming dialog with clients and other stakeholders	Becchetti (2011), Milano (2011), and San-Jose et al. (2011)
Need to continuously develop innovative financing solutions to address the ever-changing sustainability problems on a regional, national, and global level	Arnsperger (2014), Remer (2011), San-Jose et al. (2011), and Weber and Remer (2011)
Changing competitive landscape, with the emergence of disruptive forces such as crowd-funding, challenger banks using digital platforms, and classic banks competing for the customer base of social banks	Hayday (2014) and Tischer (2013a)
Need to identify, hire, and retain new staff with the suitable "double" qualifications in banking and sustainability that cannot yet be obtained from most conventional training institutions and universities	Hayday (2014), Remer (2011), and Von Passavant (2011)
Tightening regulations that put new demands on equity capital, documentation, and qualification, which are particularly hard to fulfill for small banks	Becchetti (2011), Hayday (2014), and Remer (2011)
Low interest regimes that disproportionally affect small banks focusing on core-banking activities and having to live on the interest spread	Remer (2011)

As a consequence, Remer (2011) sees the sector at a crossroads with no clear indication towards its likely growth in the future. Questions about how sustainable the current growth of social banks is are equally problematic and, indeed, the closure of South Shore Bank, United States, and the near failure of the Co-operative Bank plc, Britain's first bank to brand itself an ethical bank, are clear indications that rapid expansion may jeopardize social banks' development in the longer term (Hayday, 2014; Tischer, 2013c).

The above challenges, and especially higher regulatory demands with a view to the equity capital of banks in most countries, as well as a shortfall of good lending opportunities in some countries and a lack of investable deposits in others, undoubtedly ask for a variety of different activities and responses by the social banks. Still, one particularly promising route clearly lies in strengthening their networks and joining forces in tackling these challenges (Tischer, 2013b).

The role of networking in social banking

Social banks have indeed opted to team up to combat the various challenges they face. At a basic level, evidence for this can be found in the existence of four specialized social banking membership associations: INAISE, FEBEA, ISB, and GABV (see Table 28.3 for an overview). Usually, there are very few representatives of social banking in any domestic market and, as a result, there is limited potential to organize collectively on a national level. Thus national associations, like those found in the mainstream banking sector, are of little or no value to social banks. Instead, they require associations with a more international outlook, particularly focused on specific needs such as tailor-made training for co-workers and funding for projects too large or risky for individual banks.

The existence of these four associations suggests that social banks see value in associating and cooperating on different levels and for different purposes. This is particularly true for larger European social banks who often hold multiple associational memberships (Figure 28.1).

Yet it is likely that, even in the case of organizations that share many non-monetary values, the willingness to cooperate depends on the contextual and competitive settings, which might well change over time. For instance, the possible shortening of available lending opportunities could, in future, also have repercussions for how social banks interact and cooperate with one another.

Indeed, a series of interviews conducted by Tischer in 2013 with social banks in Germany (unpublished) suggests that, while considering the current market as big enough for ethical banks to operate alongside one another, this might change in future because good quality lending and investments into the social economy is finite in a consumerist and growth-oriented economy. Especially the expansion of Triodos in Western European markets could impact on the performance of smaller national, or regional, ethical banks that are unable to reallocate investable funds to markets abroad that exhibit a higher demand for lending and investments from social banks.

On the other hand, by developing a culture of cooperation, and making it central to the sector's identity, social banks should be able to avoid the negative impact competition can have in the longer term, as shown by Tischer's (2013a) analysis of building societies in the UK. In his analysis, Tischer points out how competitive practices between building societies came to dominate the sector, making it increasingly difficult to re-introduce the idea of "collaboration" (265ff.).

At the same time, looking at the four existing social banking associations, they appear to have a specific orientation and function which, at least to some extent, seem to get more focused when comparing the earlier associations with the later ones (see Table 28.3).

Table 28.3 Main features of social banking associations

	INAISE	*FEBEA*	*ISB*	*GABV*
	International Association of Investors in the Social Economy	European Federation of Ethical and Alternative Banks	Institute for social banking	Global Alliance for Banking on Values
	http://www.inaise.org	http://www.febea.org	http://www.social-banking.org	http://www.gabv.org
	1989, Brussels, Belgium	2001, Brussels, Belgium	2006, Witten, Germany	2009, Zeist, the Netherlands
Aim	to further the development of finance organizations involved in the social economy	to develop ethical and solidarity banking in Europe	to devise and initiate training courses and research activities for people interested in finance and banking based on ethical, social, and ecological principles	to grow the impact of sustainable banking globally
Functions	encourages and supports member cooperation	supports collaboration and the exchange of information between national networks and practitioners of the social economy and finance across Europe	offers study programs and conducts research projects in cooperation with universities and other educational institutions	seeks to drive member competitiveness through development and support
	serves as information desk for those interested in the field of social economy financing	represents its members vis-à-vis the EU institutions and other financial and political organizations	reviews publications and research projects and stimulates a public discourse	encourages joint ventures to drive sustainable social and environmental change
	plays an active role in representing the movement of social investors and disseminates information on its members, new publications, conferences, and training courses	creates instruments to support member organizations, including: 1) the guarantee fund "Solidarity Guarantee," 2) the investment fund "Solidarity Choice," and 3) the financing company "SEFEA"	offers the first ever practice-oriented Master "social banking and social finance" (with Plymouth University/UK), a regular international Summer School, and a Certificate Course "Socially Responsible Finance" (with Alanus University in Alfter/Germany)	supports the development of innovative financial products oriented towards generating positive social and environmental impact

(Continued)

Table 28.3 Main features of social banking associations *(Continued)*

	INAISE	*FEBEA*	*ISB*	*GABV*
	contributes to and coordinates research projects in the field of social economy financing, sponsored by national and international institutions	sets up several working groups "Financing the South and Fair Trade" and "Microcredit"	organizes and promotes international conferences, seminars, and similar events	provides a forum for member banks to ensure engagement at executive and senior management level
Membership	Full members: banks, cooperative financial institutions, and non-bank organizations Associate members: non-financial organizations, including businesses, organizations, public authorities, and (groups of) individuals	25 members: 11 banks, 6 savings and loan cooperatives, 5 investment companies, and 3 foundations financial institutions with balance sheet >€1 million and focused on social finance	15 members: 8 social banks, 4 non-bank social finance providers, 2 foundations, and 1 insurance company—currently all from Europe open to organizations that support ISB's aims and are approved by ISB's existing members	25 members including microfinance banks in emerging markets, credit unions, community banks, and sustainable banks 1) are independent and licensed banks focused on retail customers; 2) have a minimum balance sheet of \$50 million; and 3) are committed, at their core, to social banking and the triple bottom line

Source: Based on associations' websites.

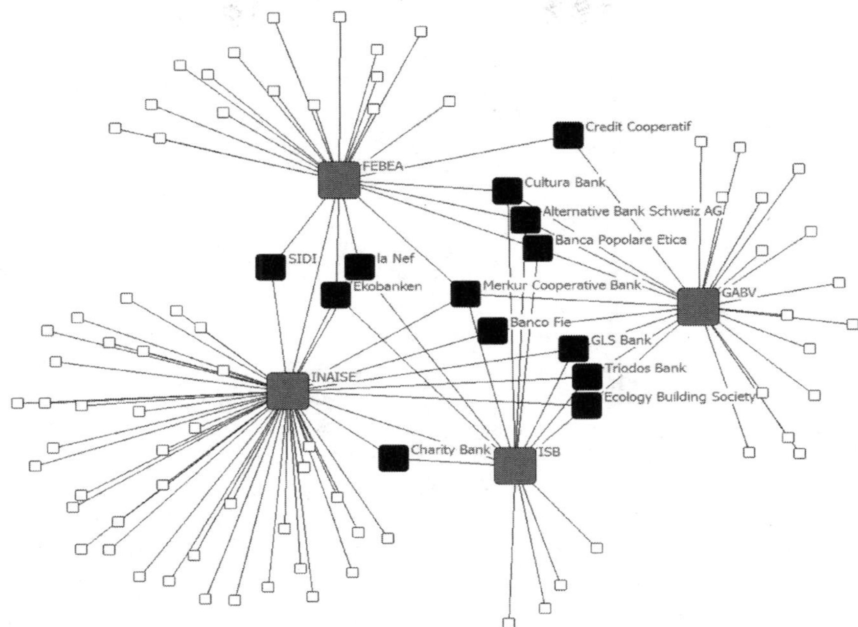

Figure 28.1 Social bank associational membership in 2014

Legend: gray squares (labeled) = social bank associations; black squares (labeled) = social banks with multiple memberships; white squares (not labeled) = social banks with only one membership.

Source: Based on INAISE, FEBEA, ISB, and GABV websites; own calculations.

INAISE, the oldest association established in 1989, has a rather heterogeneous membership, with both small and large numbers of members from around the world, some with a banking license and some without, although all are sympathetic to the cause of social development, thus effectively connecting social banks with stakeholders in the social economy and charitable sectors. Yet, its objectives and corresponding activities are rather broad.

FEBEA, the second oldest association, by contrast, is slightly more focused, in terms of its members (all European social banks and financial service providers—although its largest and arguably dominating membership is considered by some to be merely a socially oriented cooperative bank, not a fully fledged "social" bank) and in terms of a more defined set of activities. It takes on a more technocratic role within social banking: not only is it representing member banks at European level, but it also provides financial support for members through guarantee, financing, and investment funds.

The ISB's members are similarly homogeneous, covering mostly European social banks and a few "befriended" banks like financial service providers and foundations—all "social" in the narrow sense. But the ISB's activities are even more focused, providing research and tailor-made training for (future) social bankers who need a multitude of competences not only in finance but also in social, environmental, and ethical issues, as well as values-centered reflectivity. This reflects its members' perceived need to develop crucial human resources and to ensure that the core values of social banks are being retained in a period of growth alongside a growing need for additional staff. This is crucial because, in previous experiences, the Co-operative Bank in the UK, for example, has shown that growth can have a negative impact on sustaining social, ethical, and/or environmental values as operations and practices adjust to the mainstream (Tischer, 2013a).

Finally, GABV—despite having a seemingly broad membership, from various continents and with various business models and core values—is rather strict in requiring its members to be banks with assets of at least $50m (and in support of GABV's Principles of Sustainable Banking). Moreover, with its objective to serve as a platform mainly for CEOs and high-level management, as well as its five distinct working programs (Advocacy & Engagement, Human Capital, Expanding the Network, Measuring Impact, and Raising Financial Capital), it pursues a rather well-defined mission.

Having said that, it seems that GABV's activities show a significant overlap with those of older associations. For instance, one could argue that GABV's PR and lobbying activities for the social banking sector replicate those of INAISE and FEBEA, at least to some extent. This is in line with GABV's wider ambitions to facilitate cooperation between social banks and to increase their impact and visibility overall, but it could lead to some competition between the different sector associations. For instance, the recent (2015) introduction of GABV's own investment fund "SFRE" to support existing and new social banks with long-term capital (GABV, 2015b) could ultimately have repercussions for FEBEA's current offering of financial support for social banks. Similarly, GABV's newly set up "Leadership Academy" (which currently only offers a leadership course in values-based banking for "high potential" social bankers, but is also contemplating offering MOOCs to a wider audience) could be seen as competing with some of the ISB's offers—and as of now, there is no obvious indication of the two associations cooperating to make their training offers more complementary.

It therefore seems interesting to take a closer look at the development and changes within social banking associations over time. Gaining a better understanding of this aspect might not only provide theoretical insights into the cooperation of (values-based) organizations, but it might also result in more practical suggestions with view to the—possibly changing—success factors for such joint ventures in practice.

Empirical insights

To understand the importance of and changes to social banks' associational life, membership data on each association has been collected for the years 1999–2014. Instead of solely focusing on the development of overall membership data for each year and association, data has been analyzed using UCINet, a network analysis software program (Borgatti, Everett, & Freeman, 2006).

Without going into too much detail, which is beyond the scope of this chapter, it is worth briefly describing the method. A series of networks containing associational membership data for two consecutive years—for example, 1999 and 2000—has been generated from the collected data. These networks have then been analyzed using the UCINet function of Egonet Change. This function counts the change in the number of ties in each egonetwork (defined as "ego" = association and "alter" = member) of a whole network at two time periods; in other words, we were able to detect changes to associational membership from one year to another. Repeating this process for all 15 time periods gives us changes to associational membership from 1999 to 2014.

Instead of only reporting changes in overall membership numbers, the function also provides us with information about "new," "lost," and "kept" alters, enabling us to further assess membership with respect to continuity, change, and stability over time. For example, while overall membership in an association may remain the same for two consecutive years (y=20), we cannot make any statements about whether membership has changed; however, if we know that four members have each joined and left the association and 16 members have kept their membership, we know that, for that year, membership has changed by 20 percent. This

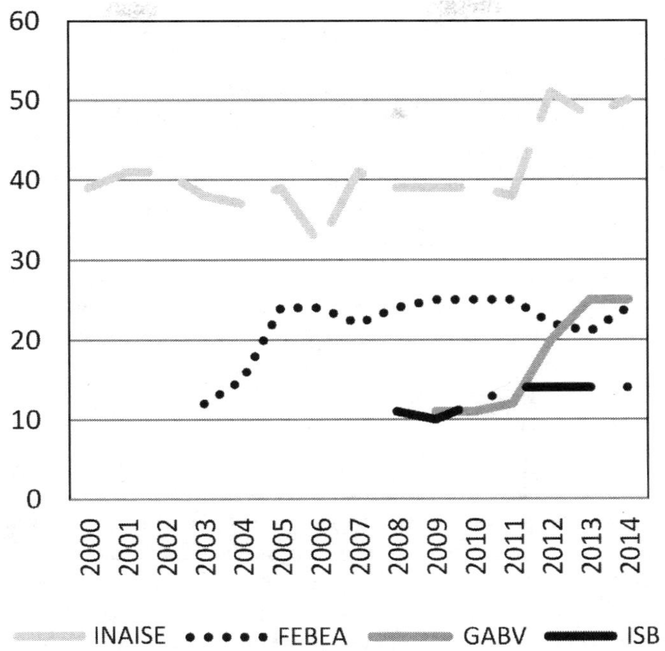

Figure 28.2a Associational membership for each year

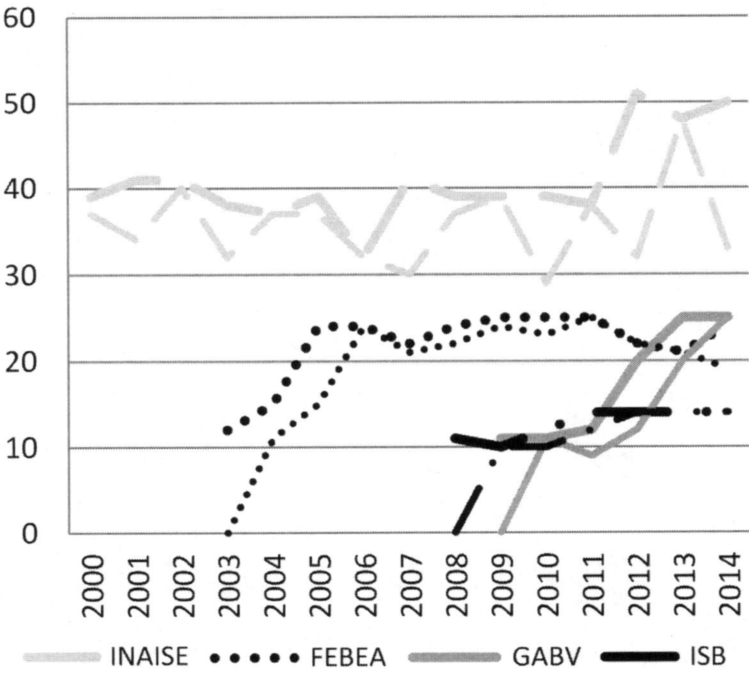

Figure 28.2b Kept (thin lines) ties in relation to overall (bold lines) ties

provides additional valuable detail on changes to associational membership in social banking, as will be discussed below.

In the period between 1999 and 2014, overall associational membership more than doubled from 47 to 113, coinciding with the increase in numbers of ethical banks. The increase in number of associations from one in 1999 (INAISE), to four a decade later, suggests that social banks find value in being members of associations. At the same time, growth in membership has varied across associations (Figure 28.2a): membership in INAISE only increased from 47 (1999) to 50 (2014), whereas GABV has increased its membership from 11 members in 2009 (its founding year) to 25, tendency rising. FEBEA, founded in 2003, saw an initial increase in members to around 25, before stabilizing between 20 and 25. However, to speak of a steady growth in membership ignores a more turbulent development of associational membership; for example, only 10 of the 47 original INAISE members continue to be a member in 2014, partially mimicking wider developments in the sector reflecting takeovers and failures, but also suggesting that maintaining its diverse membership (of banks and non-banks around the world) is difficult compared to other associations. For instance, in comparison, FEBEA, with its more homogeneous group of European bank members, has maintained membership of 10 of its 12 original members.

To allow us to understand the more complex developments depicted by the sector's associational membership, it is useful to look into the additional outputs given by the routine: the number of new, lost, and kept ties, corresponding to new, lost, and kept members. Figure 28.2b illustrates "kept" ties as part of overall ties. The difference between the thick dark line and the corresponding lighter-colored thin line highlights the amount of movement in membership for each year. This gap is clearly greatest for INAISE for most years, especially in 2007, 2010, 2012, and 2014, providing further evidence for the instability of INAISE membership. For other associations, the difference between the lines for most years is small, if not non-existent, suggesting

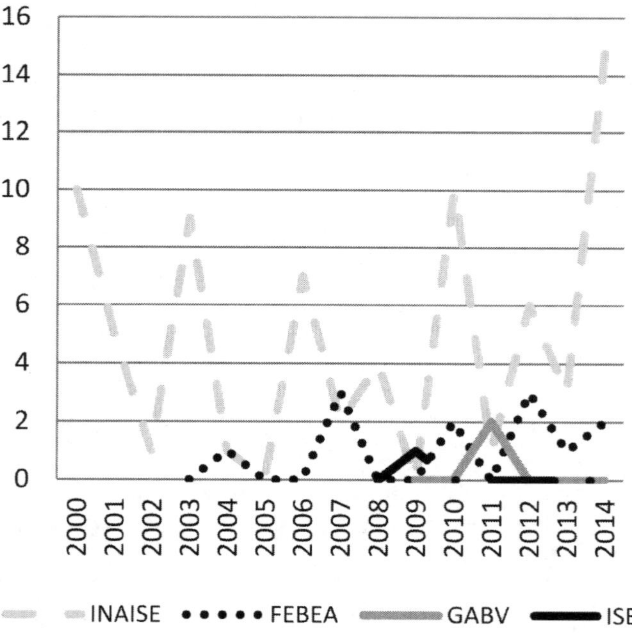

Figure 28.2c "Lost" membership in associations p.a.

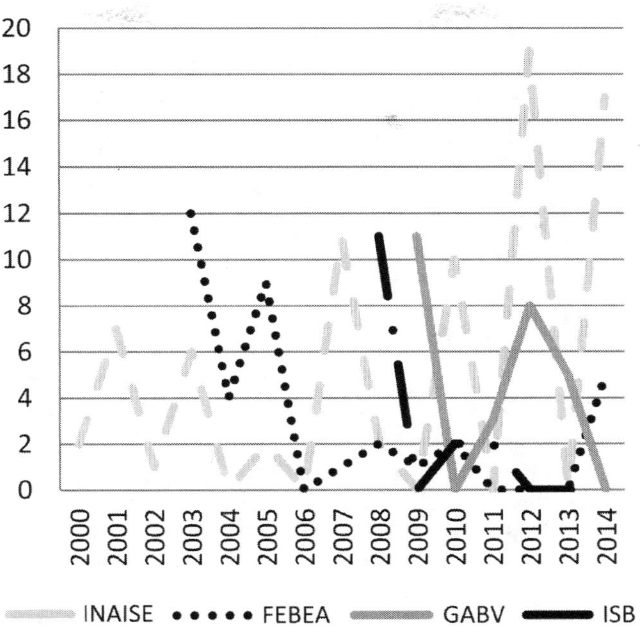

Figure 28.2d "New" membership ties p.a.

less fluctuations of membership annually. Underlying the increasing volatility of INAISE membership, Figure 28.2c highlights that the association frequently loses 10 or more members in a single year, more than twice the rate seen in other association. One possible explanation of this could be that INAISE is the largest association with the most diverse members and, subsequently, their objectives. Moreover, some of INAISE's small members—and particularly those from developing countries—can be assumed to lack resources to participate and network in INAISE annual conferences. Moreover, they may simply lack the funds in a given year and thus drop out, but then rejoin the association when funds are once again available. On the other hand, INAISE's lost members are replaced quickly with new members, suggesting that membership in INAISE is still valued by organizations linked to social banking and financing of the social economy more generally. Indeed, most larger ethical banks that have been a member of INAISE—including Triodos, La Nef, and Merkur—retain membership in INAISE, and it is only Banco Populare Etica and Credal who have recently left INAISE. Figure 28.2d further underlines the growth in associational membership, with the new ties added exceeding lost membership ties for most years. Yet at the same time, growth is uneven, with FEBEA adding fewer members in recent years compared with GABV, before seeing a marked increase in membership from 2013 to 2014. Likewise, ISB membership has shown little growth since its establishment, yet this is likely to be linked to it providing publically available research and educational services, which do not require formal membership status.

Discussion

The findings presented in this chapter add to our understanding of how social banking is organized and especially how it seeks to pre-empt potential pitfalls caused by the growth of individual organizations and the sector as a whole.

Overall, we found encouraging developments in the sector both in terms of the growth of individual organizations and the sector overall, as well as the developing associational life between organizations within the sector. social banks have started to outgrow their niche, and one of the contributing factors is arguably their willingness to join forces and associate with other social banks. Given that banks operate within national boundaries (with the exception of Triodos), competition amongst most players in the market is rather limited, which facilitates meaningful interaction between social banks globally (Vandemeulebroucke, Beck, & Käufer, 2010).

Membership in associations has developed strongly over the past years and has managed to maintain a coherent sector at the international level by offering support on technical/business issues (technocratic, human resources) and maintaining the cultural values of social banking. Different associations, overall, offer complementary services and do not appear to replace existing ones, thus accepting the diverse needs of different constituents while at the same time ensuring a collective identification with the needs and values of social banking. This helps social banks to sustain their outlook, as well as social and business interests, during times of increased public awareness and mainstream competition.

The growth in the number of sector-specific associations and membership in conjunction with the expansion of social banking can be understood as a collective *professionalization* of the sector and its members through the development and setting of standards for professional and organizational development and behavior in line with the values underpinning social banking. It also suggests that social banks consider associations useful, arguably for a number of reasons.

First, social banks are somewhat isolated in any national setting, given their particular values and business principles, and would find little value in associating with savings, cooperative, or mainstream banks in those markets. Thus, becoming a member in a more specialized association is attractive as it provides opportunities for mutual learning with similarly minded actors—social banks and other social finance providers—internationally.

Second, social banking associations offer additional benefits by giving members access to products and services that are specifically tailored toward social banks' needs and interests, and thus have practical implications for developments in the sector more generally. For example, many issues, including increased capital requirements for lending activities or the need for new products/services that are less dependent on the interest margins but more focused on the impact or outcome they generate, as well as the need for additional qualified staff, affect social banks in similar ways. Thus associations may serve as a platform for members to collaborate on developing solutions that are of benefit to its members.

Third, associations represent social banks as a collective and thus may be able to influence policy-making more effectively than individual social banks would be able to. In addition, associations promote social banks' achievements to outsiders through research and reports made available to members and stakeholders alike, thus increasing the visibility of social banking more generally.

In this context, the professionalization of the sector facilitated through these associations should also be crucial in dealing with the likely suspicions both of the public and of the regulators—many people might see a danger in banking with smaller banks that do not share the symbolic history of Barclays, Deutsche Bank, or Wells Fargo (even though the fact that social banks present an alternative to those institutions has conversely been attracting customers since the financial crisis began in 2007/8). However, by embarking on producing quality research and educating its staff through the Institute for social banking and GABV, social banks have taken a step towards becoming a clearly identifiable sub-sector within the wider financial services industry.

In the same vein, an additional benefit of associating—whether conscious or not—lies in the potential to "safeguard" the collective values of the group and to prevent individual members from adopting a more mainstream (and risk-prone) behavior. While failure in social banking is not a frequent event, it does happen, and it is the failure of higher profile social banks that could have major implications for other member banks. For example, as the failure of the British Co-operative Bank hit the headlines in 2013, regulators, politicians, and mainstream finance started voicing concerns about the sustainability of social banking even though the Co-operative Bank was not considered a social bank by the social banking sector itself. Yet, its failure tarnished social banks and raised question marks as to whether a different kind of banking can exist and perform sustainably alongside the mainstream, especially with respect to future market downturns. While associations do not have direct mechanisms in place to penalize members who are seen to turn away from the values of social banking, they can be seen as strengthening the cultural values and norms of social banking and therein bind members to follow them.

At the same time, the data also suggest that associational life has become more specialized over time, bringing together more homogeneous members and concentrating on more concrete activities. Early associational membership, as seen in INAISE, is less directed toward influencing policy-making and provides few, if any, services aimed at supporting member needs directly. GABV and the ISB, however, both founded after 2006, have much more clearly defined agendas in supporting and professionally developing member organizations, as discussed in this chapter. This specialization is also likely to have had an impact on membership: INAISE has lost and added more members than the other organizations combined; indeed, the ISB and GABV have only lost one and two members respectively.

Some of this can be linked to individual member organizations struggling with their resources to participate in all possible associations and some even exiting the market.

Yet, it also points towards some likely "competition" between the various associations. This may be particularly the case where activities are being duplicated at least to some extent across associations. Some social banks are more likely to leave one association for another, but they also might feel that their particular needs are better met by other associations (e.g., FEBA, GABV), which might focus more on certain activities of particular interest to some organizations and/or enjoy greater public visibility compared to other associations. To some extent, these "competitive pressures" have encouraged INAISE to revisit its own organization, leading to a current re-organization of its structure to more strongly represent member needs. Yet at the same time, it is important to not overstress competition; INAISE have been operating for a long time, and thus the organizational change can be argued to be reflective of changing environments and requirements, and not felt to be from competition with other associations.

Still, membership transfers from one association to another are likely to continue to occur, while possibly also increasing in the future. This is not necessarily detrimental for the sector. For instance, GABV's new fund (SFRE) seeks to collect funds for investors to give social banks access to long-term capital, making the association attractive to social banks with ambitions to expand their service and grow their business. Yet not all social banks consider these to be the right solutions for them, and while SFRE has the potential to have far larger resources than FEBEA's "social capital" financing tool "SEFEA," FEBEA's options remain attractive to members precisely because its financing options are not focused on generating the growth of individual organizations, but seeking to develop the *European* social banking sector more generally (FEBEA, 2012). Therefore, the establishment of SFRE effectively means that more social banks around the world may receive much-needed support to shore up their capital base and/or expand their businesses to meet borrowing demands across the world.

Likewise, additional training offerings tailored to the needs of future leaders in social banking, such as currently developed by GABV, could indeed be of benefit to the sector. Also, providing online-based learning may improve access to organizations geographically distanced and with limited resources, so may indeed help the sector as a whole.

While creating some competition between associations, these developments could be simply taken as indications for GABV's attempt to further develop and professionalize the sector, also driven by the pragmatic "Dutch mercantile" style of Triodos Bank, its founding chairman's organization. The ambitions of GABV speak to those social banks that seek a future in which commercial viability is an important criterion for success alongside the generation of positive impact on social and environmental matters. Here, specialist requirements for membership, for example a banking license and a focus on retail banking as demanded by GABV, would enable social banks with similar aims to be more pro-active in shaping the sector beyond otherwise restrictive national boundaries.

Conclusion

In summary, the analysis has revealed some interesting findings. The social banking sector's expansion following the financial crisis has been accompanied by the development of additional associations offering specific and relevant support to members. These more recent associations increasingly focus on the requirements of specific types of social banks—those focused on growth of the individual banks and those that consider the development of the sector more generally as the prevailing goal. Despite some overlap between the products and services offered, competition between the associations as well as members remains limited. Moreover, the network analysis has shown that developments in membership differs across associations in three main ways—they can be (relatively) static (FEBEA, ISB), expanding (GABV), or turbulent (INAISE)—suggesting that the organization of social banks within the sector is not yet settled and this may indeed be of relevance for the future development of the social banking sector—and, for that matter, of other sectors characterized by values-oriented organizations.

Yet it is evident that, given the lack of previous research and by merely taking a bird's eye (social network) perspective, the research findings only draw an initial picture of the associational life of social banks. Still, these outcomes are useful in highlighting areas for future research into this area.

As such, further research in this area could focus on a number of aspects that are not investigated in this chapter to further our understanding of the social banking sector.

Given the findings of this study, the most obvious area for further research lies in an in-depth qualitative research to expand existing knowledge of the organization of the social banking sector and associations, with a particular focus on the corresponding motives and perceived benefits of different kinds of social banks. In doing so, it might also make sense to analyze the actual differences and similarities of the respective associations—including their members and activities—in more detail.

On the other hand, it could also be interesting to expand on what has been briefly touched upon here—the currently weak competition between social banks, which might change with increasing geographic overlap of their activities, limited lending, and investment opportunities, as well as its potential impact on the likelihood of (lasting) association.

Finally, notwithstanding the likely benefits, it is also fair to speculate about the potential risks of concentration and specialization. A more narrow focus in terms of membership (of larger banks)—and a concentration of activities tailored to these (larger banks)—particularly if combined with the development of a leading association (i.e., GABV), could ultimately translate into a loss of diversity and flexibility. Arguably, diversity and flexibility are two key ingredients for the success of "niche" social banks trying to prosper in an environment that remains dominated by profit-oriented mainstream banks, many of which are still "too large to fail." As this environment has undoubtedly turned more instable and is more difficult to predict, with more and more (non-banking) competitors entering from the edges, a focus on one type and size, as well as a narrow adaptation of organizations and their associations, might be a risky evolutionary path to follow. Instead, it could be argued that the DNA of social banks—which is essentially their values base and their mission to have a positive impact—might be better served by keeping up and fostering the variety of organizations, with or without banking licenses, and their associations. While not the immediate focus of the present chapter, this certainly would be one interesting avenue to follow in future research on the sector.

References

Arnsperger, C. (2014). *Social and sustainable banking and the Green Economy project. Part I: A hypothetical diachronic scenario.* Paper for the 2014 Annual Conference of the Society for the Advancement of Socio-Economics (SASE).

Becchetti, L. (2011). Why do we need social banking? In O. Weber & S. Remer (Eds.), *Social banking and the future of sustainable finance* (pp. 48–68). New York, NY: Routledge.

Benedikter, R. (2011). *Social banking and social finance: Answers to the economic crisis.* New York, NY: Springer.

Borgatti, S., Everett, M., & Freeman, L. C. (2006). *UCINet 6.* Lexington, KY: Analytic Technologies.

Carboni, V. (2011). *Banking on ethics: Challenges and opportunities for the European ethical banking industry in the aftermath of the financial crisis.* Rome: Campagna per la Riforma della Banca Mondiale.

Cornée, S. (2012, July). *Predicting default events in social banks: On the relevance of soft information in credit rating.* Working Paper, University of Rennes, Rennes.

Cornée, S., Masclet, D., & Thenet, G. (2011, April). *Credit relationships: Evidence from experiments with real bankers.* Working Paper, University of Rennes, Rennes.

Cornée, S., & Szafarz, A. (2013). Vive la difference: Social banks and reciprocity in the credit market. *Journal of Business Ethics, 125*(3), 361–380.

De Clerck, F. (2009). Ethical banking. In L. Zsolnai (Ed.), *Ethical prospects—Economy, society, and environment* (pp. 209–227). Berlin: Springer.

Dodwell, N. (2012). *Financial crisis, threefold social order and Rudolf Steiner's organic system of money.* Berlin: Institut für Soziale Dreigliederung.

FEBEA. (2012). *SEFEA—European ethical and alternative financing company.* Retrieved October 8, 2015, from http://www.febea.org/content/sefea-european-ethical-and-alternative-financing-company

GABV. (2014). *Real economy—Real returns: The business case for sustainability focused banking.* Zeist, the Netherlands: Global Alliance for Banking on Values.

GABV. (2015a). *Our principles.* Retrieved August 1, 2015, from http://www.gabv.org/about-us/our-principles

GABV. (2015b). *New fund with ambition to provide $1 billion capital for new banking paradigm.* Retrieved July 17, 2015, from http://www.gabv.org/our-news/sustainability-finance-real-economies#.VTkAOyFVhBc

Geobey, S., & Harji, K. (2014). Social finance in North America. *Global Social Policy, 14,* 274–277.

GLS. (2015). *Anlage- und Finanzierungsgrundsätze.* Bochum: GLS Bank.

Hayday, M. (2014). Social banks: What do they need to be successful? *Global Social Policy, 14,* 272–274.

ISB. (2011). *Our definition of social banking.* Retrieved February 12, 2015, from http://www.social-banking.org/uploads/media/ISB_Social_Banking_Definition_English_110614.pdf

Käufer, K. (2011). *Banking as if society mattered—The case of Triodos Bank.* Retrieved March 4, 2016, from http://colab.mit.edu/sites/default/files/Banking_as_if_Society_Mattered.pdf

Käufer, K. (2012). *Banking as if the world mattered—The case of Triodos Bank.* Cambridge, MA: Massachusetts Institute of Technology.

Milano, R. (2011). Social banking: A brief history. In O. Weber & S. Remer (Eds.), *Social banking and the future of sustainable finance* (pp. 15–47). London, UK: Routledge.

Niven, J. (2014). Change-makers: The global alliance for banking on values. *Global Social Policy, 14,* 269–272.

Perlas, N. (2002). *Shaping globalization: Civil society, cultural power and threefolding.* Manila: Centre for Alternative Development Initiatives.

Remer, S. (2011). Social banking at the cross-roads. In O. Weber & S. Remer (Eds.), *Social banking and the future of sustainable finance* (pp. 136–195). London, UK: Routledge.

Roland Berger. (2012). *"Green Banking": Banken können mit nachhaltigen Finanzprodukten in Deutschland stark wachsen.* Retrieved March 4, 2016, from http://www.rolandberger.de/expertise/branchenexpertise/financial_services/Green_banking_bietet_hohes_Potenzial.html

San-Jose, L., Retolaza, J., & Gutierrez-Gloria, J. (2011). Are ethical banks different? A comparative analysis using the radical affinity index. *Journal of Business Ethics, 100*, 151–173.

Steiner, R. (2013 [1922]). *Price, cultural activity, and gift.* In R. Steiner (translated by A. O. Barfield & T. Gordon Jones), *Rethinking economics: Lectures and seminars on world economics.* Great Barrington, MA: SteinerBooks & Anthroposophic Press.

Tischer, D. (2013a, October). Co-op Bank: The David that wanted to be a Goliath. *Red Pepper.*

Tischer, D. (2013b). *The embeddedness of ethical banking in the UK* (PhD thesis). University of Manchester, Manchester, UK.

Tischer, D. (2013c). Swimming against the tide: Ethical banks as countermovement. *Journal of Sustainable Finance & Investment, 3*, 314–333.

Triodos Bank. (2015). *Triodos Bank minimum standards for direct lending and investments.* Retrieved August 20, 2015, from https://www.triodos.com/downloads/investment-management/research/minimum-standards.pdf

Vandemeulebroucke, V., Beck, K., & Käufer, K. (2010). *Networking social banking.* Retrieved March 4, 2016, from http://www.social-banking.org/fileadmin/isb/Artikel_und_Studien/Networking_Social_Finance_Beck_Kaeufer_Vandemeulebrouke.pdf

Von Passavant, C. (2011). Inside social banks. In O. Weber & S. Remer (Eds.), *Social banking and the future of sustainable finance* (pp. 71–95). London, UK: Routledge.

Wachsmuth, G. (1920). *From the basic ideas of Rudolf Steiner on the threefold social order.* New York, NY: Anthroposophic Press.

Weber, O., & Remer, S. (2011). *Social banks and the future of sustainable finance.* London, UK: Routledge.

Yeoman, R., & Tischer, D. (2015). *Re-envisioning mutuality.* London, UK: BSA and AFM.

zeb. (2010). Social-banking-trend ungebrochen. *zeb.* Retrieved August 20, 2015, from http://www.pressebox.de/inaktiv/zebrolfesschierenbeckassociates-gmbh/Social-Banking-Trend-ungebrochen/boxid/381325

zeb. (2012). *Social Banking Study 2012.* Retrieved March 4, 2016, from https://www.alanus.edu/fileadmin/downloads/fachbereiche_und_studienanbegote/fb_wirtschaft/fachbereich/Social_Banking_Study_2012.pdf

zeb, Alanus Hochschule, & Puls Marktforschung. (2012). *Social Banking Study 2012.* Retrieved August 20, 2015, from https://bankinghub.de/banking/privatkunden/zeb-social-banking-study-2012-management-summary

29

COMMON GOOD DISCLOSURE

A framework for analysis

Clelia Fiondella, Marco Maffei, Rosanna Spanò, and Claudia Zagaria

Disclosure in annual reports has raised growing attention in the accounting field, and previous literature has investigated the motivations behind its development, such as the need for more transparency and accountability (Uyar & Kılıç, 2012). What emerges is that disclosure improves the credibility of financial reporting (Healy & Palepu, 1993) and contributes to the understanding of the role of accounting information in firm valuation and corporate finance (Core, 2001). The issues relating to disclosure, especially in the Corporate Social Responsibility (CSR) domain (de Villiers & Alexander, 2014), are even more relevant in the context of ethical banks—such as mutual credit cooperative banks (Caldarelli, Fiondella, Maffei, Spanò, & Zagaria, 2014)—for two main reasons. First, these banks' mission is characterized by a strong commitment to ethical values, thus encompassing in their business models social and environmental variables. The latter are usually not included in mandatory reports, but they can be voluntarily disclosed through other documents, helping ethical banks to report their broadest performance to stakeholders in order to meet their accountability and transparency needs. Second, these financial intermediaries are expected to provide disclosure—especially to satisfy stakeholders' information needs—on the relationship between performance and exposure to risk factors (Frolov, 2007; Maffei, Aria, Fiondella, Spanò, & Zagaria, 2014).

In other terms, traditional banks may incorporate ethical and social aspects through CSR (De la Cuesta-González, Munõz-Torres, & Fernández-Izquierdo, 2006), which acts as a self-regulating apparatus whereby entities monitor and guarantee their adherence to law and international norms, especially in terms of the triple bottom-line. This does not necessarily imply any ethical commitment in decision-making (Kakabadse, Rozuel, & Lee-Davies, 2005; Votaw, 1972) that, nevertheless, is the main feature for ethical banks (see Caldarelli et al., 2014).

Some authors addressing the issues relating to ethics in finance (Caldarelli, Fiondella, Maffei, Spanò, & Zagaria, 2011, 2014; Caldarelli & Maffei, 2012; Ferri & Messori, 2000; Usai & Vannini, 2005) show the importance of ethical banks in creating close and long-lasting stakeholder relationships with households and firms, promoting a favorable allocation of credit for economic growth. Literature regards these aspects as common good values, which are an integral part of the mission and of the operational activities of mutual credit cooperative banks. However, there is a lack of information about how this way of doing business is translated into disclosure practices; there are no studies examining the common good disclosure provided by these types of banks from an empirical perspective.

On this ground, this research aims to more deeply explore the issues relating to the disclosure delivered by ethical banks, especially in the Italian context. A possible theoretical starting point could be the common good theory, classified by Garriga and Melé (2004) as an ethical theory that has potential in practically addressing CSR questions (Mahon & McGowan, 1991; Velasquez, 1992). However, literature has warned that the implementation of the common good is complex; it is difficult for an entity to identify what the common good consists of in practical terms (Alford & Shcherbinina, 2008). In this regard, recent research (Caldarelli et al., 2011, 2014; Costa & Ramus, 2012) has highlighted that the Italian *Economia Aziendale* theory, as a common good-driven theory, has the potential to overcome the above-cited limitation of practical applicability. Thus, on the basis of this theoretical approach, our research proposes a framework for the analysis of common good disclosure that is valuable in interpreting the information provided by Italian mutual credit cooperative banks. It is worth noting that despite the importance of common good values in conducting the activity and the necessity of being accountable to local territories in relation to this aspect (Pesci & Costa, 2014), still little is known about the categories of information that should be disclosed by banks in their annual reports. Hence, the framework developed from the theoretical perspective is used to understand whether disclosure provided by Italian mutual credit cooperative banks in annual reports provides a whole picture of their common good-oriented practices.

Our research employs the case study of the Banca di Credito Cooperativo del Garda, an Italian mutual credit cooperative bank founded in the 19th century. This is an example of success in contributing not only to the common good of the local community but also to the growth of the mutual credit cooperative banking system.

The remainder of the chapter is structured as follows:

- *Economia Aziendale* as a common good-driven theory
- The characteristics of the Italian mutual credit cooperative banking system
- Research design and dataset
- Results
- Conclusion.

Economia Aziendale as a common good-driven theory

The notion of common good employed in this chapter derives from the interpretation of the Roman Catholic Church, which states that the common good is "the total sum of social conditions which allow people, either as groups or as individuals, to reach their fulfilment more fully and more easily" (Papal Council for the Justice and the Peace, 2010). A number of authors (Abela, 2001; Alford & Naugthon, 2002; Alford & Shcherbinina, 2008; Argandoña, 1998; Caldarelli et al., 2011, 2014; Costa & Ramus, 2012; Koslowski, 2006; Melé, 2002; Sandelands, 2009; Santos & Laczniak, 2009; Sison, 2007; Vaccaro & Sison, 2011; Zamagni, 2011) have already applied this conception of common good to management studies. However, previous literature (Alford & Shcherbinina, 2008) has already highlighted that it is not easy to find out what the common good consists of in practical terms. Thus, we adopt the theoretical framework of *Economia Aziendale* because it can be regarded as a useful guide for the effective application of common good principles in business (Caldarelli et al., 2014; Costa & Ramus, 2012). On the basis of this theory, we develop a common good disclosure framework applicable to interpreting the disclosure provided by Italian mutual credit cooperative banks.

Economia Aziendale is an Italian normative entity theory, which studies the conditions of the existence and the manifestation of the life of the *azienda* (Zappa, 1927). *Azienda* is defined as an economic institution intended to last for an indefinite length of time and that, with the aim of meeting human needs, manages the production, procurement, or consumption of resources in continuous coordination (we quote here the English translation of Zappa (1956) provided by Signori and Rusconi (2009)).

According to the *Economia Aziendale* theory, *azienda* as a whole has to be analyzed from three interrelated perspectives—that is, management, organization, and accounting—taking into consideration their interdependencies and systematic relationships. A distinguishing feature of the theory is the unitary view of the *azienda*, which leads to a holistic approach (Caldarelli et al., 2014; Costa & Ramus, 2012; Signori & Rusconi, 2009) that permeates the decision-making process and is not narrowed to the internal elements.

The *azienda* is an open and dynamic system that plans its activities considering its stakeholders and, broadly, the social community's needs. Accordingly, the goal of the *azienda* is to create value, for itself—and not for individual persons within the institution—and for the various socially recognized stakeholders involved (Sidrea, 2009). Furthermore, the *azienda* not only achieves social values but also respects ecological and environmental factors (Catturi, 2003). Recently, *Economia Aziendale* has been gradually affirming its theoretical relevance in the international arena. It presents remarkable methodological and heuristic potential for international studies in business economics, management, and accounting (Dagnino & Quattrone, 2006).

To our knowledge, there are no studies discussing the content and the characteristics of the disclosure of the common good. In order to identify the main disclosure categories useful to orient disclosure practices of the common good, we rely on recent literature on the *Economia Aziendale* theory (Caldarelli et al., 2014) suggesting two dimensions—that is, the ethical dimension and the economic dimension—to apply this thinking to ethical banks.

As far as the ethical dimension is regarded, there are two disclosure categories that should be discussed: (i) the development of relationships towards the common good goals; and (ii) the constant effort toward economic and social development.

With reference to the first disclosure category (the development of the relationships towards the common good goals), it is important to highlight that the theory was developed to formulate a set of best practices to ensure the joint achievement of all the systemic goals of the *azienda*. Such best practices are conceived in a way that allows the alignment of the individual's interests to the social community's interests to avoid any attempt by the main economic actor (Zambon & Zan, 2000) to pursue his own advantages to the detriment of those of the stakeholders. The disclosure of this category implies the provision of information on both external and internal relationships. The effective transparent relationships with external clients are central for a preliminary recognition of their needs and of the propensity to achieve satisfactory results. Also, the identification of internal transparent relationships between the internal members of the *azienda* is to be regarded as an essential aspect to comprehend and disclose.

With reference to the second disclosure category (the constant effort toward economic and social development), it is important to consider that the *azienda* is a holistic system that must (and is potentially able to) create value (Zappa, 1956). Creating value implies a practical effort by the *azienda* to encompass a broader perspective in its everyday management to contribute to the growth of the social and environmental system of reference. For the *azienda*, being oriented towards the common good means that it has to pay attention to the issues of a large number of subjects, which are usually not fully considered when management issues are addressed. For this reason, the disclosure of this category should contain information on the processes conducted to engage a large number of stakeholders and their consequences on the community's growth.

As far as the economic dimension is concerned, there are two categories that should be discussed in the common good disclosure: (i) the identification of the goals; and (ii) the identification of roles and responsibilities within the organization and internal communication.

Considering the identification of the goals, it is worth remarking that the *azienda* should be able to preserve or even improve its level of functionality over time through the continuous realization of a positive difference between the benefits obtained and the resources employed (i.e., economic equilibrium) (Catturi, 2003; Cavalieri, 2010; Sciarelli, 2007). Moreover, the *azienda* should pay attention to the asset-liability and cash flow dimensions (i.e., financial equilibrium and monetary equilibrium) to avoid any imbalances that could create financial dependence on third parties or compromise the financial expectations of stakeholders. Although *Economia Aziendale* regards profit as an indicator to ensure that the *azienda* is preserving the above-mentioned equilibrium, it is not intended to be sufficient to assess the value created, as it is possible to pursue profits without encompassing the social dimension within economic activities (Giannessi, 1960). Moreover, *Economia Aziendale* suggests the conditions that the *azienda* should meet to ensure in the long term either the persistence of the institution or the accomplishment of the purposes for which it was founded (Sidrea, 2009). Long-term durability is to be intended as the achievement of economic and social goals, which ensures the durable existence of the *azienda* (Potito, 2012). Also, the *azienda* can be either profitable but unable to contribute to the creation of a diffused value, or not profitable but operating in accordance with the common good. The disclosure of this category implies providing information on the identification and the degree of achievement of the economic objectives, understood as a *viaticum* to reach the social purposes of the *azienda*. Disclosure should therefore allow the understanding of the degree of economic profitability and its drivers, the degree of social profitability and of the actions taken to achieve social aims, and the management choices that determine a real contribution to community flourishing, thus ensuring the development and the durable existence of the *azienda*.

With reference to the disclosure category related to the identification of roles and responsibilities within the organization and internal communication, the *azienda* must be capable of reconciling multiple interests—for example, those who invest their capital and those who provide a labor force (Masini, 1976; Zambon & Zan, 2000)—and of enlarging the sphere of responsibilities to include social and environmental actions (Sciarelli, 2007). This is realized when the *azienda* reaches a good level of competitiveness, achieves "winning" goals (Coda, 1988), and monitors the internal information flows, leading to the creation of interfunctional and interpersonal harmony to stimulate productivity, creativity, and innovation (Cafferata, 2005). Thus, the disclosure of this category passes through the correct and clear identification of roles and responsibilities with regard to the activities carried out. Also, a full disclosure of the processes undertaken to involve the broadly identified stakeholders, their contribution to decision-making, and of the strategies to foster communication and transparency at any level is greatly advisable.

The characteristics of the Italian mutual credit cooperative banking system

The cooperative banking sector represents a growing proportion of banking activity in Italy, and the trend is likely to continue in the years to come. It serves about 6,700,000 clients, and the total weight on the loan market is close to 8 percent. There are 382 mutual credit cooperative banks in 101 provinces and 2,711 municipalities, with about 4,458 branches. Furthermore, the system includes about 1,180,000 members and 37,000 employees.

A distinguishing feature of the Italian mutual cooperative banking system is its strong roots in local territories, its relationships with entities and families, and its activities to maximize social utility for the community. Mutual credit cooperative banks play a very important role in the Italian banking sector through widespread distribution in many cities, especially in the underdeveloped areas, sometimes representing the sole bank in a local community where there are neither local branches of a financial institution nor a traditional post office. These banks support local economies and communities, protect the wealth of many households, and allow small firms to endure the worst moments of economic recession, carrying out economic actions with social advantages for the local community via common good principles. Indeed, since the very beginning, these banks have been characterized by the firm commitment of their funding principles to the core values of Catholic social teaching (Zamagni, 2011).

These banks are regulated by a specific chapter of Italian banking law, and they are under the supervision of the National Banking Authority (Bank of Italy). Accordingly, mutual credit cooperative banks must comply with specific requirements pertaining to the governance structure and the mutuality principle. Mutual credit cooperative banks run their business primarily for their members, whose number cannot be lower than 200. The governance mechanism is characterized by one vote per shareholder in the general assembly, independently of the number of shares owned, which cannot exceed the nominal value of 50,000 euros. To become a member of a mutual credit cooperative bank, one must prove that the residence, the registered office, or the continuous activities are within the local territory of the bank. Moreover, mutual credit cooperative banks must devote 70 percent of their profits to the legal reserve, allocating another portion to the Mutual Fund for the Development of the Cooperation, and the remaining part, if not distributed to the members, is used for mutuality or charity purposes.

The Italian mutual credit cooperative banking system operates within a three-level network (local, regional, and national) characterized by an associative structure and a corporate system. More specifically, it is possible to identify mutual credit cooperative banks at the local level, federations at the regional level, and Federcasse at the national level. Each mutual credit cooperative bank is associated, according to the geographic area of reference, with a federation (encompassing one or more regions). Federations are, in turn, members of the national association Federcasse, which represents and protects the rights of its associated banks, offering them legal, fiscal, and organizational assistance while providing support in communications and training so as to provide benefits to the mutual credit cooperative system as a whole. At the corporate level, the Italian mutual credit cooperative banking system also includes several service companies working together to guarantee a complete and diversified range of financial products, which help these small banks to reach their own economic and social aims. The network combines the traditional features and the economic constraints of banking activity with the peculiar social purposes of such banks, as it is characterized by a flexible organizational structure. At the same time, it also ensures a high degree of autonomy for each mutual credit cooperative bank, thus enabling them to better meet their local members' needs.

In addition, in contrast with traditional financial institutions, mutual credit cooperative banks carry out their activities on the basis of the values and strategies formalized in two documents (the Agreement Charter of Values and the Agreement Charter of Cohesion) shared within the network and defined at the national level. Indeed, the two documents, identifying the goals of mutual credit cooperative banks, clearly state that these banks must promote the bottom-up development of society through attention to "non-bankable persons" and young people, as well as the sustainable growth of SMEs and protecting the environment and artistic heritage. The Agreement Charter of Values establishes that these banks are characterized by two complementary logics: economic profitability to ensure that the members' needs are met, and social responsibility to foster the development of local communities and territories. In this regard, article 2 of the mutual credit cooperative banking system statute states:

> The Bank aims to serve the interests of its stakeholders and the members of the local community through the provision of financial operations and services, to improve their moral, cultural and economic conditions, promoting collaboration and teaching the benefits of saving and forward planning as well as encouraging social unity and responsible, sustainable growth in the surrounding territory. The Bank distinguishes itself through its support for the community and its commitment to further the common good.

The ethical nature of the Italian network of cooperative banks goes beyond the "conventional" and "well stated" compliance with banking law and the above-mentioned agreements; it is also influenced by the evolving society's needs. In this regard, it is interesting to highlight that Federcasse has recently realized a national employment agreement for people working in the mutual credit cooperative banking system. In particular, the "Fund for New Employment" has been established, in order to reserve new recruitment for young people and disadvantaged groups.

Attention has also been paid to the role of the network. In particular, the oldest and largest mutual credit cooperative banks act as *mentors* for younger and smaller banks belonging to the federation. The network and the mentoring ensure a constant effort to reach the economic and social target of the banks as well as to manage the bad consequences of a financial crisis.

Hence, the Italian mutual credit cooperative banks act as financial intermediaries—with their fundamental activities of loans and savings accounts—and as ethical companies. They provide all the banking services normally offered by traditional financial institutions, but they differ from other large banks in that their primary objectives are the well-being of their stakeholders and the development of the local economy. Moreover, they require alternative guarantees (i.e., the reputation and the integrity of the entrepreneur, the trust relationship with the bank, as well as the evaluation of the environmental, occupational, and cultural benefits of the project for the local area), which enhance the bank's awareness of the quality of its loans.

What should be appreciated of the Italian banking system is that mutual credit cooperative banks are able to operate while satisfying the above-mentioned conditions and, at the same time, they are characterized by good patrimonialization, funds availability, and liquidity, the stability of which over time has allowed them to provide credit during the recent financial crisis, replacing other banks suffering more from the credit crunch (Tarantola, 2011).

On the basis of the above considerations, and acknowledging the great attention paid to social issues, mutual credit cooperative banks are expected to provide public information on their banking activity, explaining the goals they achieve (both economic and social) and how they pursue the common good of society.

Research design and data set

This research employs a longitudinal case study (Scapens, 1990), that allows us to examine, on the basis of the framework developed, common good disclosure practices over the years and how these practices have been shaped by such a specific organizational context.

Our analysis mainly refers to the Banca di Credito Cooperativo del Garda (BCC del Garda), which is the most ancient mutual credit cooperative bank founded in Italy. The case is of particular interest because BCC del Garda represents a clear example of what the driving values of the Italian cooperative banking sector entail in practice, which can therefore be regarded as *best practices* for the activities carried out within the network. Indeed, the bank acts as a mentor for other young mutual credit cooperative banks and devotes attention to stimulating collaboration between other banks and financial institutions belonging to the Italian Federation of Cooperative Banks. Therefore, BCC del Garda should strive to fully communicate the ethical nature of its banking activity through the practices of disclosure of the common good.

Our case study covers the period 2011–2013 because, starting from 2011, the bank has made available to the public all information pertaining to both economic and social performance through its annual reports (at the moment, available until the year 2013), which can be accepted as an appropriate source of a company's attitudes towards the voluntary reporting of social information (Gray, Owen, & Adams, 1996).

Data collection involved gathering all types of evidence from both external and internal sources of information on the common good disclosed by BCC del Garda from 2011 to 2013.

Because the purpose of the analysis is to examine the disclosure, our case study mainly relies on the annual reports to verify *whether* the Bank provides information on the common good. Specifically, we performed a rigorous analysis, coding, and understanding of data and facts disclosed in the documents, distinguishing them from the background noise (Krippendorff, 2004).

Our research also draws on interviews with people who are directly and indirectly involved in the disclosure process of BCC del Garda. In particular, we rely on formal and informal dialogs with the CEO of BCC del Garda, which allows us to understand the process of common good disclosure. We also interviewed the Chairman of BCC di Napoli—a bank that benefits from mentoring BCC del Garda—in relation to the issues pertaining to the common good information to be disclosed. In addition, we had the opportunity to attend some important corporate meetings. Attendance at such public events allowed us to collect evidence on the corporate environment and made us aware of the *iter* that BCC del Garda is following towards the achievement of a reporting package that explains the effects (both economic and social) of its activity. This evidence allows us to better understand the managerial practices and how they relate to (and shape) the reporting data made available to the public.

The data gathered from our investigation have been summarized according to the common good disclosure framework, which relies on the categories derived by the *Economia Aziendale* theory, as explained earlier. These categories were related to the *ethical dimension* (the development of a relationship with the common good goals and the constant effort for common good development) and the *economic dimension* (the identification and achievement of the goals and the identification of roles and responsibilities and internal communication) of the *azienda*. The framework was completed taking into account the peculiarities of the operational activities of the Italian mutual credit cooperative banking system—that is, the involvement in the cooperative network to be added to the ethical dimension—and the alternative system of guarantees is integrated to be added to the economic dimension.

For each disclosure category, we developed an argument taxonomy. Some categories may incorporate subcategories, to be intended as *sub*-arguments. Thus, we organized the information provided by BCC del Garda according to the taxonomy presented in Tables 29.1 and 29.2.

On the basis of the above-described framework, we attempted to evaluate *how* information is revealed by assessing the thoroughness of the common good information disclosed by BCC del Garda. To this end, we refer to a qualitative range of judgments that allow us to classify the common good disclosure as:

- *total*: information in each subcategory is fully completed and detailed, as required by the (sub)arguments;
- *partial*: information in each subcategory is lacking and not fully completed and detailed, as required by the (sub)arguments;
- *absent*: no information is disclosed in each subcategory.

Table 29.1 Arguments taxonomy—Ethical dimension

Arguments	*Description*
Development of relationship towards the common good goals	
a) External relationships	Effective transparent relationships with the external clients, for a preliminary understanding and recognition of their needs and achievement of satisfactory results
b) Internal relationships	Effective transparent relationships between the internal members of the bank about the exchange of knowledge, dialog, and cooperation towards common goals
Constant effort for common good development	
a) Of the local community	Attention towards "non-bankable persons" and young people, the sustainable growth of small to medium-sized entities, as well as environmental safeguard and protection of artistic heritage
b) Of the federation itself	Constant effort towards regional growth and development
Involvement in the cooperative network	
a) Cooperation within the network	Cooperation within the network between different mutual credit cooperative banks and other firms belonging to the federation
b) Mentoring for the network	Mentoring activities for other banks belonging to the federation

Table 29.2 Arguments taxonomy—Economic dimension

Arguments	*Description*
Identification and achievement of the goals	
a) Economic goals	Identification and degree of achievement of economic goals, to be intended as a *viaticum* to achieve the social purposes of the bank
b) Social goals	Identification and degree of achievement of social goals (i.e., closeness to small and medium entities—including start-ups—and to entrepreneurs, encouraging international openness, promotion of ideas with environmental benefits, etc.)
c) Long-term durability goals	Identification and achievement of a degree of both economic and social profit that ensures the durable existence and the fitting development of the *azienda*
Identification of roles and responsibilities and internal communication	The correct and clear identification of roles and responsibilities, to ease the monitoring process and the information flow with regard to: • the activities carried out; • eligibility criteria to become a member or director to avoid the deep-seated problems of crime and corruption Discussion between people with different backgrounds from different organizational functions contributing to the achievement of both economic and social results
Alternative systems of guarantees	Description of guarantees other than financial (i.e., the reputation and the integrity of the entrepreneur, the trust relationship with the bank, as well as the evaluation of the environmental, occupational, and cultural benefits of the project for the local area)

To prevent the individual perspective of each researcher from affecting the data, the members of the team shared the framework as developed in light of the theory so as to contribute to the analysis of the documents as well as to the definition of the key topics for the interviews. In this way, the evidence collected and analyzed on the basis of the agreed-upon parameters allowed us to reach a unitary interpretation of the phenomena.

Results

In this section, we show and discuss the results of the analysis carried out in the case of BCC del Garda from 2011 to 2013, with reference to the disclosure of the common good. The results are summarized in Tables 29.3 and 29.4. In the examined period, we did not find any significant difference in terms of thoroughness of the disclosure of the common good categories.

Overall, the results suggest that disclosure is more thorough for the aspects relating to ethical commitment and less thorough for the aspects relating to the economic dimension.

As far as the ethical dimension is regarded, the thoroughness of the disclosure of the common good in relation to the arguments selected according to the theoretical framework is total only for the argument *involvement in the cooperative network*. The thoroughness is partial for the *development of relationship towards the common good goals* and for the *constant effort towards the economic and social development of the local community*. We did not find any information about the *constant effort for the economic and social development of Federcasse itself*. With reference to the external and internal relationship of the sub-arguments, the disclosure of BCC del Garda is partial because it generically states a commitment to foster relationships with local communities and partners, including the appointment of a contact person. However, this cannot be considered a complete disclosure on effective transparent relationships. The disclosure on the constant effort for the economic and social development of the local community is partial because it simply reports a generic commitment to improving the moral, cultural, and economic needs of people belonging to the local area, without specifying which categories of persons are preferred and what action plans are to be implemented. The reports do not include information on the actions that BCC del Garda undertakes to ensure the economic and social development of the federation itself, for example through regional growth plans.

As far as the economic dimension is regarded, the thoroughness of the disclosure of the common good in relation to the arguments selected according to the theoretical framework is total only for the sub-argument *identification and achievement of economic goals*. It is partial for the

Table 29.3 Results of the analysis—Ethical dimension

Ethical dimension					
Development of relationship towards the common good goals		*Constant effort for common good development*		*Involvement in the cooperative network*	
External relationships	Internal relationships	Of the local community	Of the federation itself	Cooperation within the network	Mentoring for the network
Partial	Partial	Partial	Absent	Total	Total

Table 29.4 Results of the analysis—Economic dimension

Economic dimension				
Identification and achievement of the goals			*Identification of roles and responsibilities and internal communication*	*Alternative systems of guarantees*
Economic goals	Social goals	Long-term durability goals		
Total	Partial	Partial	Absent	Absent

identification and achievement of the social objectives and for long-term durability. We did not find any information with reference to the remaining arguments. Apart from the involvement of BCC del Garda in the cooperative network and its role of mentor, which are well documented, it is not surprising that the disclosure on economic goals, due to its mandatory nature, shows a total thoroughness in comparison to the other theoretical sub-arguments. The interpretation of the results related to the sub-arguments *social objectives* and *long-term durability* is less obvious. The disclosure shows a partial thoroughness with respect to the theoretical sub-arguments, especially concerning the identification of social goals that are vaguely declared. Moreover, there is no information on the specific objectives of long-term durability. More details are available on the achievement of the (not declared) goals, but users cannot fully appreciate the goodness of the results due to the absence of a clear disclosure on what the goals were and how they were identified. Finally, there is no information on the alternative systems of guarantees—that is, guarantees other than financial—that the bank certainly is required to provide in separate reports.

Many deficiencies are understandable, arguably because the common good disclosure is not mandatory. Although the disclosure of BCC del Garda covers various aspects addressed in the theoretical framework, the information is poorly systematic and fragmented, losing usefulness in terms of the common good. In this regard, it is worth noting that the findings of the analysis carried out on the annual reports can be better interpreted in light of the issues covered during the conversations with people directly and indirectly involved in the disclosure process. Indeed, such conversations allowed us to depict additional elements useful to comprehend the whole of the phenomenon.

First, the information provided on the economic dimension—which clearly privileges economic rather than social goals—is perceived as a crucial issue that deserves further attention. People expressed the view that the bank must pay attention to economic and financial concerns, but that more commitment is needed to divulge more systematically among stakeholders the impact of their social and network-related activities. The ambition is to enhance such information to increase the awareness of both internal and external subjects of the fact that—as the chairman stated during the celebration of the 10th anniversary of BCC Mediocrati—BCC del Garda and Federcasse intend "Finance, Credit, and Trust as synonyms" and want to realize this vision in daily business practice.

Moreover, it is worth noting that despite the not completely satisfactory results in relation to the disclosure of the ethical dimensions—which is still partially lacking in information on the development of a relationship with the common good goals—and the efforts to encourage economic and social development, there is increasing consciousness of the importance of these aspects. Indeed, also in the light of the financial crisis, these are crucial reasons to render clear to the community of reference the role of BCC del Garda as "a part of the solution rather than a part of the problem." One of the declared aims of the bank—also in the wake of the attention that this question is receiving by Federcasse, which has recently issued a coherence report—is to improve this area of information. Indeed, BCC del Garda has a strong perception of the importance of measuring and divulging its multifaceted performance. For this reason, in the foreseeable future, it is reasonable to expect further improvements in the above-mentioned areas of disclosure because the bank will have the chance to rely upon the work carried out by Federcasse to prepare the coherence report, thus providing more thorough and systematic information not only on the economic dimension but also on the social, ecological, and cooperative ones.

The central importance assigned by BCC del Garda to a multidimensional disclosure divulged among a broad range of stakeholders is also confirmed by the Chairman of BCC di Napoli, a mutual credit cooperative bank located in the South of Italy, which has been mentored since the very beginning by BCC del Garda. During the interviews, the Chairman highlighted that

> an essential part of our role for the growth of the territories passes through our communication. We constantly put effort towards disclosing our activities to engage our stakeholders, thus fostering a virtuous circle towards the common good. For example, bearing in mind the importance of new media, we developed a video [on] financial reporting for the year 2013.

The findings of the case study reveal interesting aspects that should not be underestimated. Although mutual credit cooperative banks are well known as ethical banks effectively operating for the common good, they are not fully able to communicate their positive achievements to stakeholders. This seems quite surprising; communication represents a crucial part of the common good process because it keeps the stakeholders engaged in striving to reach common good goals. However, the bank is correctly aware of the importance of disclosure and is progressively putting more effort into improving it. What emerges from the case study is that the lack of a commonly agreed-upon disclosure model that is consistent with the common good-oriented management model is likely to render inadequate the information divulged. Moreover, although there are some sub-arguments derived from the *Economia Aziendale* framework (which have been fully disclosed), as the economic goals, this information itself does not reach the common good disclosure aims.

In summary, our results suggest that additional efforts should be made to adopt a single common good report by referring to the disclosure categories addressed in our framework. In this way, it should be possible to disclose the interrelationships between different kinds of information and encourage a process of harmonization for the disclosure of the common good.

Conclusion

The purpose of this research is to develop a framework for the analysis of the disclosure of the common good provided by the Italian mutual credit cooperative banking system, which is understood to be an ethical banking system. The framework is theoretically developed and used to examine the practice of disclosure of the common good in the annual reports of Italian mutual credit cooperative banks. To this end, the disclosure of the most representative Italian ethical bank was analyzed by employing a case study method, which relied on both interviews and documentary analysis.

This chapter is valuable because it has the potential to identify a theoretical framework that would be useful in guiding mutual credit cooperative banks towards enhanced information on the common good. On this basis, we can conclude that this study contributes to the current debate in several ways. First, it fills the gap in the existing literature on disclosure provided in the annual reports by ethical banks, with particular reference to the disclosure of the common good. Although common good values are an integral component of the Italian mutual credit cooperative banking system, little is known about the categories of information disclosed. It is also worth noting the that reporting practices of Italian banks have evolved in line with changes in regulatory and legislative initiatives, and also as a consequence of financial crises and corporate collapses. In this regard, our chapter shows what kind of information is provided by a mutual credit cooperative bank. From this perspective, the research is also of interest to practitioners and regulators because it sheds light on the fact that there has never been an attempt to develop disclosure on mutual cooperative activities, despite the Italian banking law requirement that mutual credit cooperative banks be managed with reference to specific values.

An interesting further development of this research could be the analysis of the determinants of disclosure of the common good by considering how the governance of the mutual cooperative banks, regulations, and the economic and social needs of the local community may influence corporate communication.

References

Abela, A. V. (2001). Profit and more: Catholic social teaching and the purpose of the firm. *Journal of Business Ethics, 31*(2), 107–116.

Alford, H., & Naugthon, M. J. (2002). Beyond the shareholder model of the firm: Working toward the common good of a business. In S. A. Cortright & M. J. Naugthon (Eds.), *Rethinking the purpose of business: Interdisciplinary essays from the Catholic social tradition* (pp. 27–47). Notre Dame, IN: Notre Dame University Press.

Alford, H., & Shcherbinina, Y. (2008). Corporate social responsibility and common good. In E. Bettini & F. Moscarini (Eds.), *Responsabilità Sociale di Impresa e nuovo umanesimo* (pp. 14–30). Genova: Sangiorgio Editrice.

Argandoña, A. (1998). The stakeholder theory and the common good. *Journal of Business Ethics, 17*(9), 1093–1102.

Cafferata, R. (2005). *Organizzazione e direzione aziendale.* Roma: Aracne Editrice.

Caldarelli, A., Fiondella, C., Maffei, M., Spanò, R., & Zagaria, C. (2011). The common good and Economia Aziendale theory: Insights for corporate social responsibility from the Italian perspective. *Journal of the Asia-Pacific Centre for Environmental Accountability, 17*(4), 197–216.

Caldarelli, A., Fiondella, C., Maffei, M., Spanò, R., & Zagaria, C. (2014). Banking for the common good: A case study. *International Journal of Business, Governance and Ethics, 9*(4), 330–355.

Caldarelli, A., & Maffei, M. (2012). Bene Comune ed Economia Aziendale: primi spunti di riflessione. *Economia Aziendale On Line, 3*(2), 185–190.

Catturi, G. (2003). Valori Etici e Principi Economici: Equilibrio Possibile. *Studi e Note di Economia Aziendale, 3*(1), 7–37.

Cavalieri, E. (2010). *Le nuove dimensioni dell'equilibrio aziendale. Contributo alla rivisitazione della teoria.* Torino: Giappichelli.

Coda, V. (1988). *L'orientamento strategico dell'impresa.* Torino: Unione Tipografica Editrice Torinese.

Core, J. E. (2001). A review of the empirical disclosure literature. *Journal of Accounting & Economics, 31*(1–3), 441–456.

Costa, E., & Ramus, T. (2012). The Italian Economia Aziendale and Catholic social teaching: How to apply the common good principle at the managerial level. *Journal of Business Ethics, 106*(1), 103–116.

Dagnino, G. B., & Quattrone, P. (2006). Management and business research Italian style: The methodological contribution of Economia Aziendale to business economics. *Journal of Management History, 12*(1), 36–52.

De la Cuesta-González, M., Munõz-Torres, M. J., & Fernández-Izquierdo, M. A. (2006). Analysis of social performance in the Spanish financial industry through public data: A proposal. *Journal of Business Ethics, 69*(3), 289–304.

de Villiers, C., & Alexander, D. (2014). The institutionalisation of corporate social responsibility reporting. *The British Accounting Review, 46*(4), 98–212.

Ferri, G., & Messori, M. (2000). Bank–firm relationships and allocative efficiency in Northeastern and Central Italy and in the South. *Journal of Banking and Finance, 24*(6), 1067–1095.

Frolov, M. (2007). Why do we need mandated rules of public disclosure for banks? *Journal of Banking Regulation, 8*(2), 177–191.

Garriga, E., & Melé, D. (2004). Corporate social responsibility theories: Mapping the territory. *Journal of Business Ethics, 53*(1), 51–71.

Giannessi, E. (1960). *Le Aziende di Produzione Originaria.* Pisa: Colombo Corsi.

Gray, R., Owen, D., & Adams, C. (1996). *Accounting and accountability: Changes and challenges in corporate social and environmental reporting.* London, UK: Prentice Hall.

Healy, P. M., & Palepu, K. G. (1993). The effect of firms' financial disclosure strategies on stock prices. *Accounting Horizons, 7*(1), 1–11.

Kakabadse, N. K., Rozuel, C., & Lee-Davies, L. (2005). Corporate social responsibility and stakeholder approach: A conceptual review. *International Journal of Business Governance and Ethics, 1*(4), 277–302.

Koslowski, P. (2006). The common good of the firm as the fiduciary duty of the manager. In G. J. Rossuw & A. J. Sison (Eds.), *Global perspectives on the ethics of corporate governance* (pp. 67–76). New York, NY: Palgrave-Macmillan.
Krippendorff, K. (2004). *Content analysis: An introduction to its methodology*. Thousand Oaks, CA: Sage.
Maffei, M., Aria, M., Fiondella, C., Spanò, R., & Zagaria, C. (2014). (Un)useful risk disclosure: Explanation from the Italian banks. *Managerial Auditing Journal, 29*(7), 621–648.
Mahon, J. F., & McGowan, R. A. (1991). Searching for the common good: A process-oriented approach. *Business Horizons, 34*(4), 79–87.
Masini, C. (1976). *Lavoro e Risparmio*. Torino: Utet.
Melé, D. (2002). Not only stakeholder interests: The firm oriented towards the common good. In S. A. Cortright & M. Naugthon (Eds.), *Rethinking the purpose of business: Interdisciplinary essays from the Catholic social tradition* (pp. 190–214). Notre Dame, IN: Notre Dame University Press.
Papal Council for the Justice and the Peace. (2010). *Compendio della Dottrina Sociale della Chiesa*. Città del Vaticano: Libreria Editrice Vaticana.
Pesci, C., & Costa, E. (2014). Content analysis of social and environmental reports of Italian cooperative banks: Methodological issues. *Social and Environmental Accountability Journal, 34*(3), 157–171.
Potito, L. (2012). *Economia Aziendale*. Torino: Giappichelli Editore.
Sandelands, L. (2009). The business of business is the human person: Lessons from the Catholic social tradition. *Journal of Business Ethics, 85*(1), 93–101.
Santos, N., & Laczniak, G. R. (2009). "Just markets" from the perspective of Catholic social teaching. *Journal of Business Ethics, 89*(1), 29–38.
Scapens, R. W. (1990). Researching management accounting practice: The role of case study methods. *The British Accounting Review, 22*(3), 259–281.
Sciarelli, S. (2007). *Etica e responsabilità Sociale nell'Impresa*. Milano: Giuffè.
Sidrea. (2009). *La ragioneria e l'Economia Aziendale: dinamiche evolutive e prospettive di cambiamento*. Milano: Franco Angeli.
Signori, S., & Rusconi, G. (2009). Ethical thinking in traditional Italian Economia Aziendale and the stakeholder management theory: The search for possible interactions. *Journal of Business Ethics, 89*(3), 303–318.
Sison, A. J. G. (2007). Toward a common good theory of the firm: The tasubinsa case. *Journal of Business Ethics, 74*(4), 471–480.
Tarantola, A. (2011). Il Credito Cooperativo del domani: sviluppo, efficienza e solidarietà, *XIV congresso nazionale del credito cooperativo*. Banca d'Italia.
Usai, S., & Vannini, M. (2005). Banking structure and regional economic growth: Lessons from Italy. *Annals of Regional Science, 39*(4), 691–714.
Uyar, A., & Kılıç, M. (2012). Value relevance of voluntary disclosure: Evidence from Turkish firms. *Journal of Intellectual Capital, 13*(3), 363–376.
Vaccaro, A., & Sison, A. J. G. (2011). Transparency in business: The perspective of Catholic social teaching and the Caritas in veritate. *Journal of Business Ethics, 100*(1), 17–27.
Velasquez, M. (1992). International business, morality, and the common good. *Business Ethics Quarterly, 2*(1), 27–40.
Votaw, D. (1972). Genius becomes rare: A comment on the doctrine of social responsibility part 1. *California Management Review, 15*(2), 25–31.
Zamagni, S. (2011). Caritas in veritate, market and firms: The Catholic church's position on economy. An interview by Renato Mangano. *European Company & Financial Law Review, 8*(1), 65–69.
Zambon, S., & Zan, L. (2000). Accounting relativism: The unstable relationship between income measurement and theories of the firm. *Accounting, Organizations and Society, 25*(8), 799–822.
Zappa, G. (1927). *Tendenze evolutive negli studi di ragioneria*. Milano: Istituto Editoriale Scientifico.
Zappa, G. (1956). *Le produzioni nell'economia delle imprese*. Milano: Giuffrè.

30

THE QUALITY OF BANK CAPITAL IN COOPERATIVE BANKS

Lessons from history and the current financial crisis

Andrea Bonoldi, Eleonora Broccardo, Luca Erzegovesi, and Andrea Leonardi

A recent report on the value of "biodiversity" in the European Banking System, published by the Centre for European Policy Studies (Ayadi, Llewellyn, Schmidt, Arbak, & de Groe, 2010), highlights how cooperative banks (CBs), in their broadest definition, have performed better during and after the financial crisis than their shareholder-based counterparts, supplying more stable credit to the real economy, preserving competition among banks, and fostering financial inclusion. Additionally, in the aftermath of the financial crisis, the validity of the universal banking model, based upon wide diversification of the business mix and shareholder value maximization, has seriously been called into question.

This chapter aims to assess whether banks oriented to a stakeholder perspective—such as CBs—can be considered a positive example of sustainable finance and whether they are more resilient, particularly during periods of turmoil (Birchall, 2013). Taking an historical perspective, we will identify and discuss the critical success factors that have always been characteristic of sound and sustainable CBs. More specifically, we aim to answer the following questions: (1) From an historical perspective, what are the recurring and common strengths and weaknesses experienced by the CBs in the processes of local development and during different historical crises? (2) From a bank capital management perspective, how have the new regulatory and market environments affected CBs? Our analysis shows that "virtuous" CBs are those that have been strikingly loyal to their cooperative principles, namely responding to the economic or social needs of their members.

The remainder of the chapter is structured as follows. The next section introduces the concept of sustainable finance and stakeholder value maximization in banking. The section after focuses on the performance of CBs in the processes of local development and in periods of economic and financial crises. More specifically, taking an historical perspective, we will consider the development of the cooperative banking sector in the last century, with a particular focus on some European countries, especially Germany and Italy, where cooperative credit has contributed importantly to the processes of local development, by following two models: the Raiffeisen model (rural banks) and Schulze's model (urban CBs). Today, CBs are also important in other countries, such as Austria, Finland, France, and the Netherlands. We intend to verify the recurring presence of common success factors in different historical experiences. But, where are the factors that have made CBs "diverse" and successful actors in situations of economic and social distress to be found? From a bank capital management perspective, and building upon the previous historical survey, we will subsequently analyze the features of credit policies and capital management, which are typical of CBs, with a focus on the credit performance and capital adequacy of CBs in Italy. We intend to verify whether CBs' specificities may have made them weaker or stronger in the new regulatory and market environment, after the introduction of new international guidelines for bank capital regulation and prudential supervision in the Basel II and Basel III frameworks (Basel Committee on Banking Supervision, 2006, 2010). In the penultimate section, we discuss how to reconcile stakeholder value maximization and quality of bank capital in CBs. The final section concludes with a set of policy recommendations and suggestions for further research.

The concept of sustainable finance and stakeholder value maximization in banking

In the literature, the concept of Social and Sustainable Finance has not been defined clearly. Also, the meaning of social banking has gained different definitions and understanding. As highlighted by Weber and Remer (2011), the concept of social finance and social banking have been developed through many and different perspectives, such as being used: (i) to refer to banks that serve socially oriented clients; (ii) to indicate government banking; (iii) to equate to microfinance; and (iv) to mean ethical finance. Others conclude that a clear definition of sustainable/social banking is still lacking in the literature (De Clerk, 2009).

For the purpose of this chapter, we conceive a social and sustainable financial institution as an entity that aims to improve the well-being of its members as well as of that of the local community in which it is set. This purpose translates into a "philosophy" that historically has developed within the dimension of various forms of stakeholder-oriented institutions, which often takes the form of a cooperative institution. The International Co-operative Alliance (ICA) defines a cooperative as "an autonomous association of persons united voluntarily to meet their common economic, social, and cultural needs and aspirations through a jointly owned and democratically controlled enterprise" (International Co-operative Alliance, 1995, p. 3). According to this definition, any kind of cooperative institution is founded on the following principles: (i) autonomy and independence; (ii) voluntary association and withdrawal; (iii) democratic structure (each member having one vote); and (iv) fair and just distribution of economic results (European Commission, 2015). Referring to the banking sector, such institutions took the form of savings banks, CBs, and, in more recent times, ethical banks. Among these forms, cooperative institutions show a wider geographical diffusion, a longer-lasting historical presence, and a clearer and more robust governance and business model.

For the purpose of this chapter, we therefore identified the social and sustainable intermediary with CBs. Together with the aforementioned common principles, and with regard to financial institutions, what defines CBs is the purpose to maximize stakeholder surplus, which is not merely economic but is complemented by additional goals that increase their well-being. Stakeholders can be parties other than members (e.g., employees, community, and environment). On the contrary, commercial banks publicly state their pursuit of the maximization of profit. By paying attention to both the economic and social needs of their members, CBs contribute to the sustainable development of their local communities through policies approved by their members.

Within the financial context, the social and sustainable nature of CBs helps to meet the credit needs of the local communities (by avoiding overly risky investments) and promotes member loyalty.

The economic strength of CBs mainly consists in their peculiar capability to provide credit to local enterprises. Due to their legal status and geographical responsibility, CBs tend to have no exposure to global financial markets and focus mainly on servicing local borrowers (Jassaud, 2014).

Moreover, as pointed out by Fonteyne (2007), CBs have a crucial comparative advantage in overcoming opportunistic behavior by banks because, as supported by Kay (2006), their institutional features favor the establishment of trust between members. Given that CBs are owned by their members—and that they explicitly pursue the maximization of value for those members—they are perceived as trustworthy, and the members consider the risks and monitoring costs involved to be low. However, as stressed by Kay, trust is easy to lose when CBs pursue growth diversification and are not loyal to their cooperative principles, that is, when they start to act like commercial banks.

Historically, sustainable CBs are characterized by a stable respect for the accomplishment of their mutualistic aim, their greater attention to the demand for credit on the part of actors located in a limited area, and the avoidance of risky financial instruments that are potentially profitable but entirely devoid of mutualistic purpose. These features, together with the constant update of operational and organizational processes, contribute to substantially strengthening CBs, which are then able to sustain local development even in times of financial and economic difficulties (Goglio & Alexopoulos, 2013). This has not always been the case, however. Historically, there have been periods during which, in some CBs, the pursuit of profit maximization was predominant to the mutualistic aim. Nonetheless, over the long period, and especially during the financial crisis, those CBs were more oriented to the stakeholder model and more devoted to making the local economy succeed by promoting stable cooperative credit.

The performance of CBs in the processes of local development and in periods of economic and financial crises

Strengths and weaknesses of the cooperative banking model in Europe in the last century: An historical perspective

The origins of the modern conception of mutualism, which took concrete form in the complex reality of the cooperative movement, reside in the profound changes brought about by the industrial revolution. This was an extraordinary historical phenomenon that engendered unprecedented economic development but was accompanied, at least in the short term, by significant social costs. On the one hand, the emergence of a capitalist market economy generated a substantial and generalized increase in income; on the other hand, however, it resulted in the disintegration of an important part of the relational networks of traditional society, and the construction of new ones took a rather long time. In this context, the impetus behind the creation of mutual benefit organizations to support workers and small businesses in rural and urban settings had a twofold economic and social nature, and it gave rise to institutions capable of supporting long-period development (Birchall, 1994; Sapelli, 1998). The first consumer cooperative, created in Rochdale, Lancashire, in 1844, was soon followed by others. In Central European societies, the cooperative model established itself, particularly in rural areas. In Germany, it became the distinctive instrument with which to expand small- and medium-sized enterprises, which viewed cooperative credit as the means to drive the process of "Selbsthilfe" (self-help), enabling them to meet the challenges raised by the expansion of the market economy (Birnstein & Schwikart, 2014). Following careful observation of the situation in the countryside and small towns of the Rhineland and Saxony, Friedrich Wilhelm Raiffeisen (1818–1888) and Hermann Schulze-Delitzsch (1808–1883) concluded that a lack of capital prevented the weaker classes from escaping the marginalization transferred from the economic to the social level (Klein, 1997; Schulze-Delitzsch, 1987). Both Raiffeisen and Schulze-Delitzsch therefore set about creating cooperative associations based on the concept of mutual aid. The organizations thus created—"Darlehenskassen-Vereine" and "Volksbanken"—issued personal credit of even small amounts to persons hitherto largely excluded from the credit system. Moreover, credit cooperatives underpinned a complex system of societies operating in both consumption and production. However, there were significant differences between the two models of cooperative credit concerning aspects such as management methods, range of operations, the amount of shares, the duration of loans, and the distribution of profits, which also reflected their differing social bases. The Raiffeisen banks dealt almost entirely with small farmers, who possessed real estate but lacked working and liquid capital and were interested in loans that could not be short term because they had to be calculated across the crop year. Instead, the cooperative credit banks (*Volksbanken*) were used mainly by urban artisans and retailers, who had larger liquid capital and wanted investments with shorter maturities (Goglio & Leonardi, 2012). From the outset, therefore, cooperative credit was a flexible instrument able to meet the specific needs of stakeholders.

As these institutes grew in number, it became necessary to aggregate them to enhance their efficiency and coordinate their actions (Engelhardt, 1995). Consequently, bodies were created for representation, tutelage, and supervision, such as the "Anwaltschaftsverbandes ländlicher Genossenschaften" of 1877 and, subsequently, the "Generalverband der deutschen Raiffeisengenossenschaften," for rural banks (Stickdorn, 2004). Already established in 1864 was an inter-bank equalization fund: the "Zentralinstitut für die Vorschussvereine" (Guinnane, 2013). At the end of the 19th century and the beginning of the 20th century, cooperative credit banks flourished throughout Germany, and their lending activities were further strengthened by reorganization of the entire German agricultural cooperation movement, with the purpose to enable farm businesses to compete on the market (Weisser & Engelhardt, 1968; applicable to other European contexts are the considerations on Austria set out in Bruckmüller, 1977). This was achieved by using, for economic purposes, the trust and social role recognition mechanisms typical of small communities, thereby promoting a model of democratic participation (Boscia & Di Salvo, 2009). In the early 20th century, the German cooperation movement involved more than 12,000 enterprises with around 3 million members. In 1930, the difficulties of the long post-war period led to the creation of a first unitary body comprising 36,000 cooperatives with 4 million members. Not until 1972, however, were the various forms of German cooperative credit definitively merged together (Guinnane, 2013).

At the end of the 1870s, amid the "Great Depression" of the European countryside, the "Raiffeisenkassen" model crossed Germany's borders, spreading through Belgian, French, Austrian, and Italian rural areas (Bruckmüller & Werner, 1998; Leonardi, 2000). Particularly incisive was the presence of credit unions in the "Länder" of the Habsburg monarchy due to the efforts of distinguished scholars like Gustav Marchet and the advocacy of the cooperative model by provincial parliaments (Bruckmüller, 1977; Werner, 1988).

In Italy, credit cooperation was successful thanks to the action of such pioneers as Luigi Luzzatti (1841–1927)—a jurist, economist, and politician (also head of government)—and Leone Wollemborg (Cafaro, 2001; Fornasari & Zamagni, 1997; Ianes, 2013; Leonardi, 2000; Zaninelli, 1996). The banks spread rapidly; by 1878 there were already 124 of them, with around 100,000 members, mainly small entrepreneurs in manufacturing, commerce, and agriculture. Five years later, in 1883, when the first rural bank was established, their number had risen to 250 (De Rosa, 1999). In the opinion of Alessandro Rossi, a wool industrialist and passionate supporter of Leone Wollemborg's cooperative initiative, Italian "banche popolari" had lost with time the genuine mutualistic nature of Schulze Delitzsch's model. In a note dated from 1895 in favor of Raiffeisen's system, Rossi wrote that "people's banks [banche popolari], which should be more appropriately named bourgeois banks, are not co-operatives: they are shareholders' property" (Rossi, 1895).

At the end of 1887, 34 rural banks were active in the Italian countryside. In the following years, the spread of this model was supported by the creation of local reference bodies according to the Raiffeisen example (Cafaro, 2001) and by the Catholic movement's programmatic commitment to carrying the project forward (Leonardi, 2000). At the turn of the century in Italy, in addition to the Catholic variant, there also arose robust lay and socialist cooperation, although not in the banking sector.

From the years of the "belle époque" onwards, rural banks helped broad strata of the rural population escape marginalization. Both credit and consumption cooperation led to the better allocation of resources in areas traditionally considered to be on the margins of development (Goglio & Leonardi, 2012). On the eve of World War I, the volume of deposits clearly demonstrated the greater economic vitality of places where rural banks were active. Immediately after the war, the number of small CBs in Italy reached its peak, with more than 3,000 units. But in the second half of the 1920s there began, amid severe difficulties for the entire Italian banking system, a marked decline of cooperative credit. The great crisis would sweep away two-thirds of the rural banks operating in Italy. The causes of rural banks' defaults included the policy of the Fascist government in favor of public or state-controlled banks and the new Banking Law of 1936, both of which reduced the role of CBs in the banking system. Since many of the failed rural banks were unlimited liability cooperatives, their members paid for the cost of bankruptcy from their personal wealth, transforming banks' failures into a social issue.

When the crisis subsided, however, cooperative credit rapidly recovered, demonstrating the vitality of the model (Leonardi, 2012). This was also made possible thanks to support from local communities interested in the availing of banks strongly connected to local needs. Unlimited or multiple liability again constituted an important factor of stability and members' commitment. On the other hand, supervision by the Bank of Italy carefully enforced the requisite territoriality to ensure the stability of the rural bank system.

Within a few years, the growth of production and trade channeled a large amount of capital into cooperative credit institutions. The comprehensive action of the banks in favor of the small businesses then multiplying enabled rural banks to regain ground. Consequently, for Italian cooperative credit, there began a period of buoyant growth that contributed to the country's overall development. As an effect of the new Banking Law of 1993, legislation on rural CBs has been in part homologated to the rules applied to other banks; for example, limited liability of members has been made mandatory. At the same time, the new Law confirmed, albeit in an updated form, the restrictions on territoriality and on members' composition that are necessary to preserve the typical mutualistic nature of the CB model (Cafaro, 2001).

The economic events that characterize today's scenario can be related to previous experiences. Among these, a leading role is assumed by the culture of responsibility, which underpins the various forms of active mutualism. The extent of these phenomena plays an important role, for example, in information management because it allows a more efficient allocation of resources. As already pointed out by Joseph Stiglitz, when markets are spoiled by a lack of information or by strong asymmetries in its distribution, the presence of trust relationships and a knowledge network makes it possible to generate greater well-being (Stiglitz, 1999). The ability to promote sustainable development also depends on social capital, that is, the quality of institutions and the thickness of relational networks (Durlauf & Fafchamps, 2005; Granovetter, 1985).

Consequently, cooperative credit has over time acquired the role of a global provider of solutions. It is able to withstand difficult conjunctures and adapt to changing conditions (Leonardi, 2011). But achieving this outcome has required a constant effort of renewal, which has involved not only members in the strict sense but also entire communities.

The financial crisis of 2007–2008 and the effects of the new economic and regulatory environment on CBs

The great financial crisis of 2007–2008 also hit CBs, producing manifold implications in the following years. The first period after the outbreak of the crisis marked a rediscovery of the merits of stakeholder value-oriented (STV) banking. In Europe, CBs were acclaimed not only for having remained immune to the excesses leading to the crisis but also for resisting and reacting to its impact on the real economy (Ayadi et al., 2010; Leogrande, 2012). The strong capital base built before the crisis, which was unaffected by losses on subprime mortgages, allowed CBs to adhere to their mission of supporting credit for families and small businesses. Consequently, they gained a higher share in the lending markets. As noted in Groeneveld and de Vries (2009), at the outset of the post-crisis era, there was an opportunity to demonstrate several of the virtuous features of the CB model, particularly the "impact presence" of CBs in financially and economically turbulent times. Owing to their financial solidity and steady mission-oriented strategy, CBs should be able to back their customers for longer periods, which would be reflected in stable profit growth, lower credit losses, and stronger capitalization vis-à-vis commercial banks. In Groeneveld (2014), the ideal cooperative bank model is characterized by five features: (a) strong customer focus and client proximity thanks to dense branch networks, (b) austerity and efficiency in operations, (c) a stable focus on retail banking, (d) strong capitalization and a low-risk profile, and (e) impact presence. Such assertions are verified by means of a comparative analysis of the performance indicators of cooperative banking groups from 10 European countries vis-à-vis all other banks in 1997–2011. The empirical analysis supports all five of the differentiating features. For example, cooperative groups show a lower variability of both deposit and credit growth rates (Figure 30.1) thanks to a stable focus on retail banking and better indicators of financial stability, based on a distance-to-default metric (Z-score) (Figure 30.2). As a result of a more stable performance in financial turmoil, the market share of CBs increased steadily in the period covered by the analysis (Figure 30.3).

From 2012 onwards, weak economic conditions caused a long period of defaults by firms and the consequent build up of problem loans in banks with higher exposure to domestic loan markets. Stable credit support for local businesses, which was previously appreciated as a strength, had become a weakness. Credit losses eroded the capital buffers of STV banks, especially in countries that were hit by more severe and prolonged recessions. The Italian case provides impressive evidence of this phenomenon and deserves closer scrutiny because it allows for a comparison of the different ways in which the crisis impacted the two institutional categories of CBs that are considered in the previous historical survey, that is, "banche popolari" (BP) and "banche di credito cooperative" (BCC).

In Italy, as in other Eurozone countries (Cyprus, Greece, Ireland, Portugal, and Slovenia), non-performing loans (NPLs) have grown beyond 10 percent of total assets, placing a heavy burden on the banks' willingness and ability to supply credit (International Monetary Fund, 2015, p. 19). Statistical data on loans to non-financial entities by bank category in December 2014 compiled by the Bank of Italy (Table 30.1) show a higher incidence of NPLs on gross exposures among CBs (BPs and BCCs) vis-à-vis shareholder banks. Both categories of CBs also exhibit a lower coverage ratio of NPLs through loan provisions, a clue about the delayed

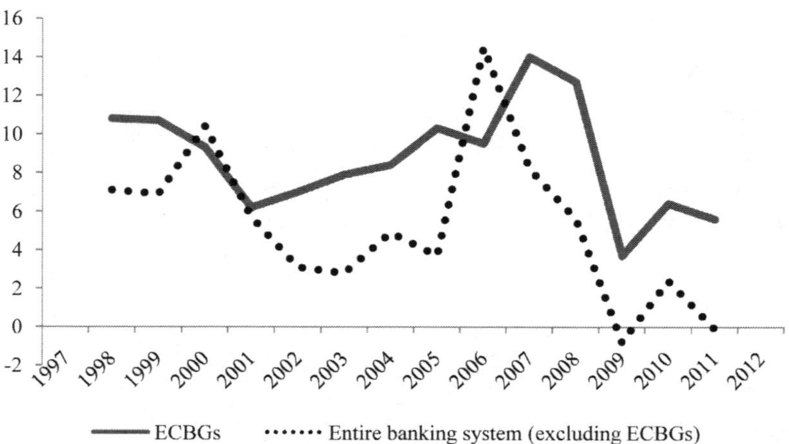

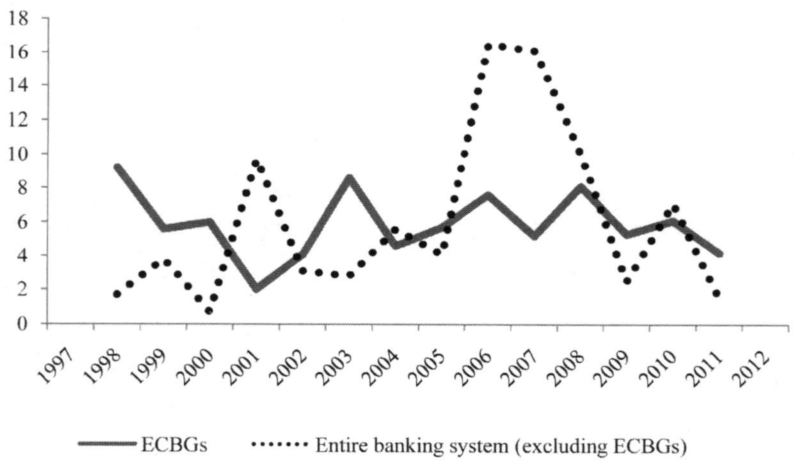

Figure 30.1 Average credit and deposit growth rates (percentages)

Source: Based on Groeneveld (2014). Data from ECBGs, TBS, and national statistics. ECBGs and TBS stand for European cooperative banking groups and total banking sectors, respectively. The credit data refer to all (inter)national credits and loans to the non-financial private sector of ECBGs and all other banks. The deposit data refer to all (inter)national credits and loans to the non-financial private sector of ECBGs and all other banks.

recognition of latent credit losses. BPs may also have inadequate capital buffers with respect to potential losses, as signaled by the "Texas ratio," that is, the ratio of non-performing loan amount (net of provisions) to total capital, named after the crisis of savings and loans institutions in Texas in the 1980s where failed intermediaries were characterized by a high level of this indicator in the years before defaulting (Jassaud & Kang, 2015). Conversely, BCCs have the lowest value of this indicator thanks to a stronger capital base composed almost exclusively of best

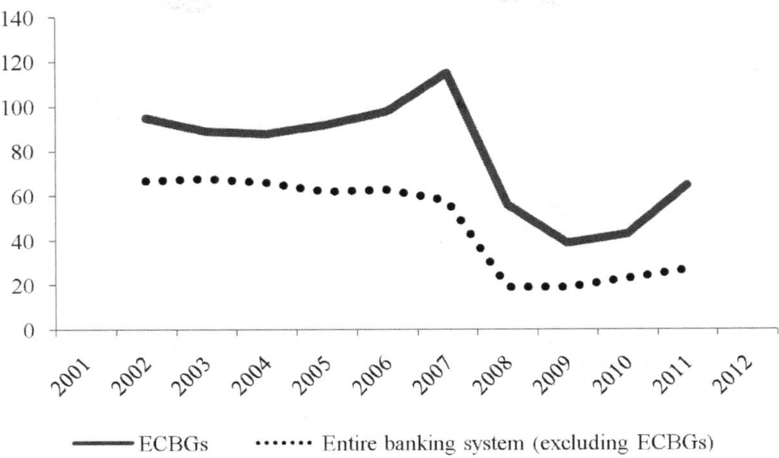

Figure 30.2 Average Z-scores

Source: Based on Groeneveld (2014). Data from ECBGs, European Central Bank, International Monetary Fund, and national supervisory authorities. The figure displays the average Z-score of 15 ECBGs in 10 countries and the Z-score of the entire banking sector in these countries. The Z-score is a widely used measure of a bank's distance to default monotonically associated with the bank's probability of failure. A higher Z-score implies a lower probability of insolvency.

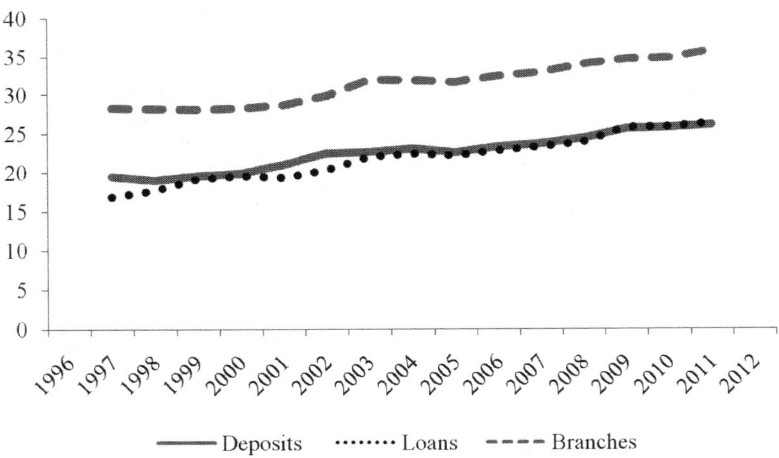

Figure 30.3 Average market share of the deposits, loans, and branches of ECBGs (percentages)

Source: Based on Groeneveld (2014). Data from individual ECBGs and the ECB. The unweighted market shares pertain to domestic loans to private households (mortgages and/or consumer loans) and the domestic retail deposits of households. The market share of branches is defined as the branches of local CBs as a percentage of total bank offices.

quality common equity tier 1 (CET1) capital (Table 30.2). BPs also show the higher frequency and severity of the weakness that occurs in banks that are missing their target capital ratios.

The financial weakness that is observable in BPs may be attributed to the challenges resulting from their ownership and governance structure. As discussed in Jassaud (2014), restrictions

Table 30.1 Bank loans to non-financial entities, by bank category and credit quality (at December 31, 2014)

Category of bank or banking group	*Classification of credit quality*	*Share of total loans (gross of provisions)*	*Coverage ratio (a)*	*Texas ratio (b)*
Shareholder banks	Total loans	100.0	8.8	
	Performing	82.9	0.6	
	Non-performing, of which	17.1	48.0	80.1
	Bad debts	10.0	62.0	34.2
	Substandard	5.5	29.7	
	Restructured	1.0	26.6	
	Past due	0.6	17.0	
Banche popolari	Total loans	100.0	7.6	
	Performing	80.3	0.7	
	Non-performing, of which	19.7	35.7	118.7
	Bad debts	10.2	49.3	48.5
	Substandard	7.2	23.2	
	Restructured	1.3	18.3	
	Past due	0.9	8.9	
Banche di credito cooperativo	Total loans	100.0	7.0	
	Performing	82.0	0.5	
	Non-performing, of which	18.0	36.6	74.0
	Bad debts	9.1	52.0	28.4
	Substandard	7.6	22.7	
	Restructured	0.5	16.4	
	Past due	0.9	7.0	
All categories	Total loans	100.0	8.4	
	Performing	82.3	0.7	
	Non-performing, of which	17.7	44.4	86.5
	Bad debts	10.0	58.7	36.2
	Substandard	6.0	27.5	
	Restructured	1.0	24.1	
	Past due	0.7	13.9	
Top five banking groups	Total loans	100.0	9.2	
	Performing	81.5	0.7	
	Non-performing, of which	18.5	46.6	95.6
	Bad debts	10.7	60.3	41.1
	Substandard	6.1	29.0	
	Restructured	1.2	26.7	
	Past due	0.6	16.9	

Source: Modified from Bank of Italy Annual Report (Relazione annuale sul 2014, Appendice, Tavola a13.14). (a) Coverage ratio: ratio of loan loss provisions to gross loan amount. (b) Texas ratio: ratio of non-performing loan amount (net of provisions) to total capital.

on ownership make it difficult for any shareholder, even with a large capital stake, to change the governance structure and replace poorly performing BP managers. Thanks to the close ties established with partners/customers (clientele) that are controlling the majority of votes, incumbent directors and top managers accumulate arbitrary power with limited accountability. In times of bad economic conditions, these relationships can distort the allocation of credit and slow down the work-out procedures with some types of creditors.

As reported by Barbagallo (2015), some of the larger BCCs in Northern Italy have reproduced on a smaller scale the same governance criticalities observed among BPs; consequently,

Table 30.2 Regulatory capital ratios by bank category (at December 31, 2014)

Category of bank or banking group	*Total capital (€ millions)*	*CET1 (a) ratio (%)*	*Tier 1 ratio (%)*	*Total capital ratio (%)*	*Risk weighted assets on total assets (%)*	*Capital shortfall (b)*	
						No. of banks	*Shortfall amount (€ millions)*
Shareholder banks	159.203	11.5	12.1	14.6	50.4	1	5
Banche popolari	43.892	11.5	11.6	13.6	56.0	2	330
Banche di credito cooperativo	20.170	16.1	16.1	16.5	54.9	6	51
Total	224.909	11.8	12.3	14.5	52.5	9	386
Top five banking groups	127.506	11.4	12.0	14.7	47.0	0	0

Source: Based on Bank of Italy Annual Report (Relazione annuale sul 2014, Appendice, Tavola a13.21). (a) CET1: core equity tier 1 capital. (b) Capital shortfall: difference, if positive, between total available CET1 capital and minimum requirements as of Basel III rules (estimated as 7% of Risk Weighted Assets).

they have suffered from the same problems of excessive risk assumption and distorted allocation of credit. In addition to small BCCs that are mainly established in the South of Italy, these larger northern BCCs are a matter of concern for national supervisors (Cannata et al., 2013).

Apart from a limited number of BCCs that are in bad financial shape, the cooperative credit system as a whole has performed better than the rest of the banking system. However, the earnings reported by BCCs in 2012–2014 have benefited from extraordinary circumstances, mainly the provision of low-cost funding by the European Central Bank through Long-Term Refinancing Operations, coupled with high returns on Italian government bonds due to the reduction of the country risk premiums embedded in the Italian bond yields. In those years, the carry margin and capital gains that BCCs earned on their treasury portfolio represent a windfall profit that might turn into a loss if the same spreads on Italian bonds widen in the future. Moreover, the earnings capacity of BCCs has some structural weaknesses that originate from a rigid cost base and a limited capacity to develop new lines of business in a changing market (Barbagallo, 2015).

The pressure to challenge the adequacy of the business models of Italian CBs has become stronger in the long-phase process of the Basel III reform of the prudential regulation and supervision of banks; this is especially the case in the Eurozone where a Single Supervisory Mechanism and a Single Resolution Mechanism for bank crises are being implemented in the context of the so-called "Banking Union" (European Commission, 2014). Consequently, the attitude of policy-makers and supervisors towards CBs in Italy has changed from encouraging to worried. Both categories of CBs are undergoing a radical process of reform and reorganization. A decree law enacted in January 2015 (Decreto-legge, "Investment Compact," 2015, art. 1) enforces the demutualization of BPs with assets greater than 8 billion euros. On the other hand, national bank supervisors have been encouraging BCCs through moral suasion to evolve towards a more centralized group model that should be similar to Crédit Agricole in France and Rabobank in the Netherlands (Barbagallo, 2015). If the Federation of BCCs fails to develop and implement a credible restructuring plan on a voluntary basis, the reorganization may be forcibly enacted by law.

Verifying whether CBs' specificities have made them weaker or stronger in the new regulatory and market environment is a complex endeavor. Among the issues relevant to CBs, we consider the following:

1 How the evolving capital regulation has affected their intermediation model, and how their typical sources of equity financing have made them more or less capable of achieving credit growth targets, covering credit losses, and handling capital adequacy constraints. In this respect, a shortage of external equity capital in times of stress may be a relevant weakness.
2 How the revision of the criteria defining core equity capital in the Basel III framework may question the eligibility of shares subscribed by clients (mainly by borrowers) of the bank and how it can be maintained as long as the client relationship persists.

Shortage of external equity capital in times of stress

As shown in Fonteyne (2007), in good times CBs benefit from a higher organic growth of their capital base (i.e., growth that does not require external capital) thanks to a higher share of retained earnings, sometimes reinforced by a lower corporate tax rate. On the contrary, in bad times they suffer from the lack of external sources of capital. External equity investors are kept away by constraints on the distribution of dividends and the absence of voting power proportional to the number of shares owned. For example, the Swedish cooperative banking sector did not survive the domestic banking crisis of the early 1990s, and the need to restore capital was a major factor in the decision to demutualize (see Brunner, Decressin, Hardy, & Kudela, 2004).

The ability to raise a substantial amount of equity on the stock market is seen as a key factor of success in the current debate on Basel III and the EU Single Supervisory Mechanism (Merler & Wolff, 2013). Banks are hard pressed to build up a large buffer of capital and loss-absorbing debt—and to do it quickly—to reassure governments that bailouts of insolvent banks at the expense of the taxpayer are no longer a possibility.

STV banks appear disadvantaged on this front. Investors may be attracted by the opportunity to participate in the demutualization of the cooperative (as attempted with a large "banca popolare" in Italy; see Jassaud, 2014), but this is clearly a destructive solution. Bigger cooperative banking groups may create affiliates in the form of joint stock companies to attract capital from equity investors. Although cooperatives may benefit from externalizing part of their activities in joint stock companies exposed to market discipline, such hybrid groups must reach compromises between their different stakeholders and are thus sometimes unable to enjoy the advantages of either governance form (see Fonteyne, 2007).

In the wake of a dramatic restructuring of the global financial system, there is undoubtedly a huge base of investors (global banks, private equity groups, hedge funds, and sovereign funds) eager to bet on the probable winners—or on the probable acquisition targets of the winners. One may question whether such endowment of capital will provide a strong and resilient foundation for financial stability or if it will make the system weaker and more fragile because of prevailing speculative motivations and cross-shareholdings among investors and banks.

Eligibility of member shares as core equity tier 1 capital

The Basel III framework has introduced higher and stricter minimum requirements for core equity tier 1 capital (CET1). CBs are generally in a position to meet the stricter requirements with ease, having a capital base composed almost entirely of common equity. However, because of criteria set in the Basel III rules, shares issued by CBs have been at risk of being excluded from CET1 in the case where a member exercises the generic right of withdrawal with reimbursement of his shares. Such a provision conflicts with the requirement set by Basel III for eligible CET1 instruments in the following terms: "Principal is perpetual and never repaid outside of liquidation (setting aside discretionary repurchases or other means of effectively reducing capital in a discretionary manner that is allowable under relevant law)" (BCBS, 2010, p. 14). The implementation of Basel III in the European Union by means of the Capital Requirement Regulation of 2013, article 29, has moderated the severity of the new criterion, allowing national supervisors the discretion to admit the issued capital of cooperative, mutual, and savings banks as core tier 1 even if redeemable in force of national law. The Basel Committee on Banking Supervision in their Regulatory Consistency Assessment Programme (BCBS, 2014) has deemed the concessions made by the EU not fully compliant with eligibility criteria for CET1 set by Basel III.

In order to comply with the new rules, Italian BCCs (see Cannata et al., 2013) were required to modify their statutes according to the new template elaborated by their national federation (Federcasse), in which the option of redeeming social shares for the generic needs of a member has been removed. In June 2015, the Bank of Italy issued an update to national bank supervisory standards (Banca d'Italia, 2015) requiring both BPs and BCCs to adopt stricter statutory clauses limiting share redemption; in the force of such clauses, banks' boards of directors will be given the power to delay or deny the reimbursement of capital whenever it may conflict with prudential requirements.

Therefore, Basel III is acting as a stimulus towards a strict application of the concept of cooperative capital as a permanent, inter-generational endowment without final owners. As pointed out earlier, this view is rooted in Raiffeisen's principles. In contrast, Schulze Delitzsch's view of cooperative capital as a fund pooled by members with a common interest in obtaining credit is rejected by the new prudential framework on the grounds that withdrawal of members—or sales of their shares on a secondary market supported by the issuing bank—impairs the loss-absorption capacity of capital.

In its quest for "more resilient bank and banking systems," Basel III apparently fosters the strengthening of ties among cooperative members, beyond self-interest. In principle, this is a desirable outcome. In practice, however, CBs will find more difficulties in raising capital since paid-in shares will be perceived as an unrecoverable expense by member customers. In the case of large CBs, this could further stimulate demutualization to make their listed shares more attractive.

How to reconcile stakeholder value maximization and quality of bank capital in CBs

Both the SHV and STV banking models have been challenged and sometimes shaken at their roots by the Great Crisis. The prevailing view among academics and policymakers seems to favor the SHV model for being more adaptable to a financial system that is increasingly dynamic and globally integrated.

In this context, CBs face strategic threats; they must bear the cost of a higher and more stable lending volume in a prolonged negative credit cycle while at the same time being menaced by competition from commercial banks in the richer segments of the same domestic markets. Competitive pressure may arise on different fronts: product innovation, the cost of distribution networks, and, obviously, access to capital and direct and indirect public subsidies. The inflexibility of the cost base, which originates from a dense branch network, coupled with negative profitability in lending, may lead to an irreversible decline (Barbagallo, 2015).

As reported by Oliver Wyman (2014), a subtle threat is coming from shareholder-owned banks, which are evolving their service models and brand positioning to mirror some of the historic strengths of cooperatives—in particular, trust, proximity to customers, and social responsibility—in an attempt to restore the tarnished reputation of the banking sector.

CBs can meet these challenges, either by diluting their distinctive characteristics or by preserving and building upon them. In order to make the latter option viable, other challenges must be faced (see Oliver Wyman, 2014):

1 CBs must continue supporting local economies despite the capital and cost pressures mentioned above. This requires cost discipline and a new kind of governance and decision-making in credit risk selection and management.
2 They must emphasize the cooperative difference, trying to increase the number of customers who are members and increase the engagement of members. They should also communicate the social value created for the local community with transparent reports, although social benefits and spillovers are even more difficult to measure and compare than financial performance.
3 They must be at the forefront of technological and process innovation in order to rejuvenate the cooperative relationship, thereby achieving greater cost efficiency and increased quality.

Returning to the main issue considered in this chapter, which is the need for a stronger capital base, simple or universal recipes cannot be devised.

To respond to the need to expand the capital buffer available during crises, one may consider solutions experimented with in the glorious tradition of cooperative credit, such as member shares with unlimited or multiple liability, which prevailed in the period before World War II and which had been gradually abandoned after the widespread bank insolvencies following the Great Depression. Provisions of that kind are still present in the statutes of some German and Swiss CBs (see Fonteyne, 2007), where members are personally liable for losses subject to a limit that exceeds the value of their member shares. It is questionable, though, whether this liability can be called upon without disconcerting the member guarantors.

Another solution might be a capital-raising campaign through extraordinary share issues motivated by a collective interest in rebuilding the permanent endowment of the cooperative for the benefit of younger generations. Similar endeavors are certainly significant from the perspective of cooperative ethics, but it is highly improbable that a substantial amount of capital can be raised on a *pro bono* basis.

Capital gaps in CBs are usually filled by institutional sponsors, typically central cooperative institutions. In Italy, the Banking Law has been recently amended in order to introduce a new class of shares (azioni di finanziamento) issuable by CBs in situations of financial distress. Those shares can be purchased by the Deposit Guarantee Fund or other funds for the promotion and development of the cooperative movement (Barbagallo, 2015).

Financial innovation should be the answer here.

As an alternative to external equity, Basel III allows for the emission of contingent convertible debt instruments eligible as tier 1 capital (the Rabobank group has issued such securities; see Groeneveld, 2011). Subordinated or hybrid debt issued by cooperative banking groups in reasonable amounts may be appreciated by professional investors, who may concede a cheaper systemic risk premium vis-à-vis commercial banking groups.

CBs in Europe, usually with support from their central banks or shared service centers, have been early adopters of credit risk transfer and funding solutions, for example, in the form of multi-bank securitizations and sales of distressed assets. Starting in 2012, Italian CBs structured multi-originator true sale securitizations that often have been used for refinancing operations with the European Central Bank. A recent transaction securitized more than two million euros of loans extended to small and medium enterprises by 28 BCCs (BCC SME Finance, 2012).

Sophisticated financial engineering is also a condition for accessing new programs by governments, development agencies (in the form of credit guarantees and sponsored private equity funds), or central banks, like the Targeted Long-Term Refinancing Operations or the asset-backed securities (ABS) purchase program, both of which are promoted by the European Central Bank. Modern credit risk transfer, although conceived by SHV-oriented global banks, can more credibly ensure the flow of additional financing into the real economy (as envisaged by the Bank of England and the European Central Bank, 2014) if it is placed into the hands of STV-oriented banks.

From a more general perspective, participation in publicly sponsored programs is a key generator of margins at a moderate risk, which is a necessary condition for rebuilding reserves from retained earnings in today's uncertain environment.

Conclusion and policy recommendations

The CB vs. SHV bank controversy heated up after the great financial crisis of 2007–2008. In the first after-crisis phase, CBs were proud of themselves for two valid reasons: they bore no responsibility for the crisis and they emerged undamaged by its first major strike. In a later stage, SHV banks counterattacked on the grounds of their superior capacity for reorganizing, raising capital, and reducing risk. The profound revision of the international framework for bank regulation and supervision takes the SHV model implemented by the so-called "Global Systemically Important Financial Institutions" as its primary target. However, complex requirements designed with SHV banks in mind are being placed on banks in general, and this spill-over effect is particularly acute in the Eurozone, as a side effect of the Banking Union.

The ongoing debate is not just academic: access to public aid and exemption from stricter prudential rules (or from costlier bail-in mechanisms) are at stake.

Ostensibly, the CB community defends a more credible thesis in the debate, that is, the soundness of its evergreen intermediation model. Our brief historical survey showed how the ideas conceived by the founding fathers of the CB movement spread around the world and crossed more than one century of economic up- and downturns. The movement laid its roots during major agricultural or credit crises. The Great Depression of the Thirties had a profound impact, but CBs were able to start again by remaining true to their original mission, although with updated statutes.

Critics of CBs point to their weaknesses, which may be idiosyncratic or systematic. Examples of possible idiosyncratic flaws include unbalanced governance leading to capture by local conflicting interests, excessive informality in credit selection, diseconomies of scale, and limited capacity for innovating and operating in global financial markets. The idiosyncratic flaws are by definition not generalizable, and they are also in many cases rebutted by empirical evidence. More worrisome are the systematic weakness that may emerge in periods like the current one, that is, vulnerability to prolonged negative cycles of the domestic economy, especially when they are triggered by the boom-bust cycles of dominant local industries (usually construction), as happened in Sweden in the 1990s and in some European economies after 2008.

The repeated shocks produced by the great financial crisis sounded a call to reality in the debate on STV vs. SHV banking. The theoretical merits of each model are irrelevant unless one is able to translate them into sound and viable implementations, which are contingent upon circumstances that may change from time to time, and dramatically so. The value of diversity in the financial system should be out of the question: the presence of CBs has proven to be a factor of resiliency that has also ultimately benefited the SHV-oriented banking sector (Chiaramonte, Polli, & Oriani, 2013). CBs that remain true to their mission may make financial systems more resilient simply by being exposed to financial shocks differently from SHV banks, without necessarily being more resilient. As verified in Blank and Dovern (2009), for the German banking system during 1994–2004 this distinction created resilience at the systemic level as banks are not equally exposed, and episodes of bank distress following macroeconomic shocks feed back into the macroeconomic environment in a mitigated way.

Arguments in favor of a definitive demutualization of the banking system are pretentious since they do not acknowledge the merits of such diversity, both direct (support to the real economy) and indirect (reduction of systemic risk). However, CBs should learn from their critics and take remedies against the dysfunctions emphasized in their analyses.

The major challenge to be addressed is the impact that the lack of access to external capital on the stock market has on the capital management of CBs. In addition to issuing capital instruments directly into the market, CBs may be asked by prudential supervisors to create additional capital buffers at the banking group level to cover potential or underestimated losses. Networks of CBs (Fonteyne, 2007) are the ideal setting for establishing mutual support mechanisms that compensate for the credit and liquidity risk concentration of an individual cooperative. Such mechanisms, established within the "institutional networks" of banks, take several forms (see Ayadi et al., 2010), typically as insurance schemes protecting depositors or other liability holders, or as guarantee funds covering the risk of member defaults on interbank deposits. Within the Eurozone, mutual support schemes are in need of a radical redesign in order to adapt to the new forms of bank crisis management introduced in the Bank Recovery and Resolution Directive of 2014. In the early stage of the crisis, forms of mutual support have been at risk of being crowded out by the extraordinary aid that governments have provided to banks (by means of rescue and restructuring programs or bank liability insurance). In the second phase of the crisis, mutual self-help may be ruled out by state aid compatibility criteria as set out in the European Commission's Banking Communication of 2013, or crowded out by official interventions by bank resolution authorities. Moreover, the support schemes established by CBs could become incentive incompatible and, therefore, unsustainable: when the risk of bank crises among the group's members is higher, the solvent members are hit by unforeseen losses and their incentive and motivation to stay in the network are seriously challenged. While the mutual resources are adequate to cover defaults due to idiosyncratic factors, they cannot cope with systematic credit crises, such as those in countries that were hit harder by the recession. This issue warrants investigation in future research.

The founders of the seminal cooperative banking movements were charismatic leaders with an urgent desire to respond to the people's needs (material as well as non-material). In today's complex financial environment, the same human attitude remains a distinctive trait and a potential strength of CBs. Serving the needs of people through proximity defines their mission. In times of compelling strategic challenges, the same principle dictates the method to follow in order to stay true to that mission. As an example, CBs should explore, side by side with firms and public bodies, the best avenues to economic growth in their territory as well as how best to retract from declining sectors in an orderly way, limiting the social and economic impact of discontinued activities. Problem loans may be seen as a mere deadweight, something to lay off with the aim of minimizing capital consumption, either by selling assets to distressed debt investors or by reclaiming state aid. Hopefully, banks rooted in the genuine cooperative tradition will go beyond such a cold, self-interested attitude, striving instead to do their best to preserve the value of the assets owned by the defaulted families or firms without denying the persons involved care and respect (presuming it is deserved). The search for equitable and low-cost solutions to a high number of small-scale bankruptcies may originate new, socially responsible forms of distressed debt management. Nothing so good is likely to happen by chance or economic calculus alone.

As documented in the brief survey presented in this chapter, the history of cooperative credit is marked by repeated, exciting episodes of "Mission: Impossible." Now, again, the time has come to surprise the unbelieving, and once again the human factor has to make a difference.

References

Ayadi, R., Llewellyn, D. T., Schmidt, R. H., Arbak, E., & de Groe, W. P. (2010). *Investigating diversity in the banking sector in Europe: Key developments, performance and role of cooperative banks*. Brussels: Centre for European Policy Studies.

Banca d'Italia. (2015). *Banche in forma cooperativa, 9° Aggiornamento delle Disposizioni di vigilanza per le banche, Circolare n. 285 del 17 dicembre 2013 (Capitolo 4)*. Rome, Italy: Author. Retrieved June 30, 2015, from http://www.bancaditalia.it/compiti/vigilanza/normativa/archivio-norme/circolari/c285/CIRC_285_9_AGGTO.pdf

Bank of England and European Central Bank. (2014, April 11). *The impaired EU securitisation market: Causes, roadblocks and how to deal with them* (paper). London and Frankfurt: Author. Retrieved June 30, 2015, from http://www.bankofengland.co.uk/publications/Documents/news/2014/paper070.pdf

Bank Recovery and Resolution Directive 2014/59/EU of the European Parliament and of the Council. EU (2014, May 15).

Banking Communication 2013/C 216/01 of the European Commission. EU (2013, July 30).

Barbagallo, C. (2015, February 12). *Le banche locali e di credito cooperativo in prospettiva: vigilanza europea ed evoluzione normativa*. Paper presented at Federazione delle Cooperative Raiffeisen, Bolzano. Rome, Italy: Banca d'Italia. Retrieved June 30, 2015, from https://www.bancaditalia.it/pubblicazioni/interventi-vari/int-var-2015/Barbagallo-12022015.pdf

Basel Committee on Banking Supervision (BCBS). (2006, June). *International convergence of capital measurement and capital standards: A revised framework. Comprehensive version*. Basel, Switzerland: Bank for International Settlements. Retrieved June 30, 2015, from http://www.bis.org/publ/bcbs128.htm

Basel Committee on Banking Supervision (BCBS). (2010, December). *Basel III: A global regulatory framework for more resilient banks and banking systems*. Basel, Switzerland: Bank for International Settlements. Retrieved June 30, 2015, from http://www.bis.org/publ/bcbs189_dec2010.htm

Basel Committee on Banking Supervision (BCBS). (2014). *Regulatory Consistency Assessment Programme (RCAP): Assessment of Basel III regulations—European Union*. Basel, Switzerland: Bank for International Settlements. Retrieved June 30, 2015, from http://www.bis.org/bcbs/publ/d300.pdf

BCC SME Finance. (2012). *BCC SME Finance 1 S.r.l. Offering Circular*. Retrieved June 30, 2015, from http://www.bccsmefinance1.cartolarizzazioni.com

Birchall, J. (1994). *Co-op: The people's business*. Manchester and New York: Manchester University Press.

Birchall, J. (2013). *Resilience in a downturn: The power of financial cooperatives*. Geneva: International Labour Office.

Birnstein, U., & Schwikart, G. (2014). *Friedrich Wilhelm Raiffeisen—Hermann Schulze-Delitzsch: genossenschaftlich gegen die not*. Berlin: Wichert.

Blank, S., & Dovern, J. (2009). *What macroeconomic shocks affect the German banking system? Analysis in an integrated micro-macro model* (Discussion Paper, Series 2: Banking and Financial Studies, No. 15/2009). Frankfurt, Germany: Deutsche Bundesbank. Retrieved June 30, 2015, from https://www.bundesbank.de/Redaktion/EN/Downloads/Publications/Discussion_Paper_2/2009/2009_11_13_dkp_15.pdf

Boscia, V., & Di Salvo, R. (2009). The theory and experience of cooperative banking. In V. Boscia, A. Carretta, & P. Schwizer (Eds.), *Cooperative banking: Innovations and developments* (pp. 9–38). London, UK: Palgrave Macmillan.

Bruckmüller, E. (1977). *Landwirtschaftliche organisation und gesellschaftliche modernisierung. Vereine, genossenschaften und politische modernisierung der landwirtschaft in Österreich im Vormärz bis 1914*. Salzburg: Neugebauer.

Bruckmüller, E., & Werner, W. (1998). *Raiffeisen in Österreich: Siegeszug einer idee*. St. Pölten: Österreichischer Raiffeisenverband.

Brunner, A., Decressin, J., Hardy, D., & Kudela, B. (2004). *Germany's three-pillar banking system—Cross-country perspectives in Europe* (IMF Occasional Paper 233). Washington, DC: International Monetary Fund.

Cafaro, P. (2001). *La solidarietà efficiente. Storia e prospettive del credito cooperativo in Italia (1883–2000)*. Roma and Bari: Laterza.

Cannata, F., D'Acunto, G., Allegri, A., Bevilacqua, M., Chionsini, G., Lentini, T., & Francesco Marino e Gianluca Trevisan. (2013, April). *Il credito cooperativo alla sfida di Basilea 3: Tendenze, impatti, prospettive* (Questioni di economia e finanza—Occasional Papers, 158). Rome, Italy: Banca d'Italia.

Capital Requirement Regulation No. 575/2013 of the European Parliament and of the Council. EU (2013, June 26).

Chiaramonte, L., Polli, F., & Oriani, M. E. (2013). On the relationship between bank business models and financial stability: Evidence from the financial crisis in OECD countries. In J. Falzon (Ed.), *Bank stability, sovereign debt and derivatives* (pp. 7–30). London, UK: Palgrave Macmillan.

De Clerk, F. (2009). *Our common future*. Oxford and New York: Oxford University Press.

De Rosa, L. (1999). Le banche popolari nell'economia dell'Italia liberale. In P. Pecorari (Ed.), *Le banche popolari nella storia d'Italia* (pp. 7–12). Venezia: Istituto veneto di scienze lettere ed arti.

Decreto-legge, "Investment Compact," n. 3. Italy (2015, January 24).

Durlauf, S. N., & Fafchamps, M. (2005). Social capital. In P. H. Aghion & S. Durlauf (Eds.), *Handbook of economic growth* (pp. 1639–1699). North Holland: Elsevier.

Engelhardt, W. W. (1995). *Hundert jahre genossenschaftliches spitzeninstitut: zum hundertjährigen jubiläum der DG-bank, Deutsche genossenschaftsbank*. Frankfurt am Main: Vandenhoeck & Ruprecht.

European Commission. (2014, April 15). *Banking union: Restoring financial stability in the Eurozone* (memo). Brussels: Author. Retrieved June 30, 2015, from http://ec.europa.eu/finance/general-policy/docs/banking-union/banking-union-memo_en.pdf

European Commission. (2015). *Defining characteristics of cooperatives*. European Commission website. Retrieved June 30, 2015, from http://ec.europa.eu/growth/sectors/social-economy/cooperatives/index_en.htm

Fonteyne, W. (2007). *Cooperative banks in Europe-policy issues* (IMF WP/07/159). Washington, DC: International Monetary Fund.

Fornasari, M., & Zamagni, V. (1997). *Il movimento cooperativo in Italia. Un profilo storico-economico (1854–1992)*. Firenze: Vallecchi.

Goglio, S., & Alexopoulos, Y. (2013). *Financial co-operatives and local development*. London: Routledge Studies in Development Economics.

Goglio, S., & Leonardi, A. (2012). The motivations of economic behavior: The case of cooperative credit. *Journal of Entrepreneurial and Organisational Diversity, 1*, 65–84.

Granovetter, M. (1985). Economic action and social structure: The problem of embeddedness. *American Journal of Sociology, 91*(3), 481–510.

Groeneveld, J. M. (2011, August 24–27). *The value of European co-operative banks for the future financial system*. Paper presented at the ICA Global Research Conference, Mikkeli, Finland. Retrieved June 30, 2015, from http://www.helsinki.fi/ruralia/materiaalit/ICA2011/Groeneveld.pdf

Groeneveld, J. M. (2014). Features, facts and figures of European co-operative banking groups over recent business cycles. *Journal of Entrepreneurial and Organisational Diversity, 3*(1), 11–33.

Groeneveld, J. M., & de Vries, B. (2009). European co-operative banks: First lessons from the subprime crisis. *International Journal of Co-operative Management, 4*, 8–22.

Guinnane, T. W. (2013). Zwischen Selbsthilfe und Staatshilfe: die Anfänge genossenschaftlicher Zentralbanken in Deutschland (1864–1914). In C. H. Beck Verlag (Ed.), *Die Geschichte der DZ BANK. Das genossenschaftliche Zentralbankwesen vom 19. Jahrhundert bis heute* (pp. 36–92). München: Beck.

Ianes, A. (2013). *Introduzione alla storia della cooperazione in Italia (1854–2011): Profilo storico-economico e interpretazione*. Soveria Mannelli: Rubbettino.

International Co-operative Alliance (ICA). (1995). Statutes, revised by the General Assembly, 20 November 2009 (pp. 1–11).

International Monetary Fund. (2015, April). *Global Financial Stability Report: Navigating monetary policy challenges and managing risks*. Washington, DC: Author.

Jassaud, N. (2014). *Reforming the corporate governance of Italian banks* (IMF WP/14/181). Washington, DC: International Monetary Fund.

Jassaud, N., & Kang, K. (2015). *A strategy for developing a market for nonperforming loans in Italy* (IMF WP/15/24). Washington, DC: International Monetary Fund.

Kay, J. (2006, April 26). The mutual interest in building trust still remains. *Financial Times*.

Klein, M. (1997). *Leben, werk und nachwirkung des genossenschaftsgründers Friedrich Wilhelm Raiffeisen*. Köln: Rheinland Verlag.

Leogrande, A. (2012). *Co-operative banks vs financial crisis: An application of the STV vs. SHV debate* (Working Paper). Retrieved June 30, 2015, from https://www.academia.edu/8404544/Cooperative_Banks_vs_Financial_Crisis

Leonardi, A. (2000). Dalla beneficenza al mutualismo solidale: l'esperienza cooperativa di F. W. Raiffeisen ed i suoi primi riflessi in Italia. In V. Zamagni (Ed.), *Povertà e innovazioni istituzionali in Italia* (pp. 551–583). Dal Medioevo ad oggi, Bologna: Il Mulino.

Leonardi, A. (2011). Istituzioni autonomistiche e sviluppo territoriale. In A. Leonardi (Ed.), *Istituzioni ed economia* (pp. 19–41). Bari: Cacucci.

Leonardi, A. (2012). Italian credit cooperatives from 1918 to 1945. *The Journal of European Economic History, XLI*(2), 51–86.

Merler, S., & Wolff, G. B. (2013, December). Ending uncertainty: Recapitalisation under European Central Bank supervision. *Bruegel Policy Contribution*, Issue 2013/18.

Oliver Wyman. (2014). *Cooperative banking: Leveraging the co-operative difference to adapt to a new environment* (Financial Services Report).

Rossi, A. (1895, November). *Personal archive of Senator Alessandro Rossi (1819–1898)*, fasc. 59, doc. 3. Schio: Civic Library "Renato Bortoli."

Sapelli, G. (1998). *La cooperazione: Impresa e movimento sociale*. Roma: Edizioni Lavoro.

Schulze Delitzsch, H. (1987). *Schulze-Delitzsch—Ein lebenswerk für generationen*. Wiesbaden: Deutscher Genossenschaftsverband.

Stickdorn, M. (2004). *Kooperation in staat und wirtschaft: Raiffeisenbanken, genossenschaftsbanken. Formen und wirkungen von geld*. Norderstedt: Grin Verlag.

Stiglitz, J. (1999). Formal and informal institutions. In P. Dasgupta & I. Serageldin (Eds.), *Social capital: A multifaceted perspective* (pp. 59–68). Washington, DC: World Bank.

Weber, O., & Remer, S. (2011). Social banking: Introduction. In O. Weber & S. Remer (Eds.), *Social banks and the future of sustainable finance* (pp. 1–14). London, UK: Routledge.

Weisser, G., & Engelhardt, W. W. (Eds.). (1968). *Genossenschaften und genossenschaftsforschung: Strukturelle und ablaufanalytische, historische und systematische aspekte der genossenschaften des 19. und 20. jahrhunderts*. Festschrift zum 65. Geburtstag von Georg Draheim. Göttingen: Vandenhoeck & Ruprecht.

Werner, W. (1988). *Raiffeisenbriefe erzählen genossenschaftsgeschichte: Die frühzeit der Raiffeisen-organisation an hand der briefe von Raiffeisen an marchet (1872–1884)*. Wien: Österreichischer Agrarverlag.

Zaninelli, S. (Ed.). (1996). *Mezzo secolo di ricerca storica sulla cooperazione bianca. Risultati e prospettive* (voll. 4). Verona: Valdonega.

31

THE RECENT DEVELOPMENT AND PERFORMANCE OF ETHICAL INVESTMENTS

Philippe Gillet and Julie Salaber-Ayton

The development of faith-based funds and socially responsible funds challenges modern portfolio theory as some investors move away from the risk-return paradigm by constraining their portfolios to "ethical" investments. This type of investment attempts to balance the regard for morality of a firm's activities and the regard for return on investment. Such ethical investors will shun companies whose behaviors they condemn, or focus on companies that represent values in which they believe. Hence, in addition to maximizing return and/or minimizing risk, they integrate non-pecuniary preferences into their investment decisions (Gillet, 2009). Ethical investments include a wide range of mutual funds, unit trusts, and equity indices that can be classified into Socially Responsible Investment (following so-called Environmental, Social, and Governance criteria) and faith-based investment (following for instance Christian or Islamic principles). Socially responsible and Islamic funds have grown considerably in the last 20 years, both in volume and in value (Hoepner, Rammal, & Rezec, 2011; Renneboog, Ter Horst, & Zhang, 2012). On the one side, the characteristics and performance of socially responsible funds and indices have been subject to many empirical studies which offer conflicting evidence (Leite & Cortez, 2014; Renneboog, Ter Horst, & Zhang, 2008). On the other side, the Islamic financial system survived the 2007–2008 financial crisis, and several reasons might explain the resistance of Islamic funds; for example, the fact that they comply with Islamic moral and ethical standards or that they exclude equities from the traditional financial sector (Jouini & Pastré, 2009).

Since ethical funds differ from traditional funds in terms of diversification and systematic risk, it is important to assess their risk-adjusted long-term performance relative to other forms of investments. This chapter proposes to investigate the recent development and performance of ethical investment funds around the world by answering the following questions: What exactly are these extra financial criteria? Are they similar across all types of ethical investments? Are they similar across regions and countries? Have they evolved over time? What is the impact of such constraint on investment risk and return? Do ethical funds represent a good investment opportunity in times of crisis?

Background

Ethical investment has largely evolved from its premises back in the 17th century, when the Quakers refused to profit from the weapons and slaves trade as they settled in North America.

The founder of Methodism, John Wesley, stated that people should not engage in sinful trade or profit from exploiting others. Later, the Methodist Church in the UK avoided investing in sinful companies, for example companies involved in alcohol, tobacco, and gambling, when they began investing in the stock market in the 1920s. The first ever ethical (faith-based) investment fund was the Pioneer Fund (then Fidelity Mutual Trust) launched in 1928. It is now the third oldest mutual fund in the United States.

Islamic funds appeared in South East Asia in the 1960s. The world's first Islamic fund, Lembaga Tabung Haji (Pilgrims Fund Board), was created in 1963 by the Malaysian government to help Muslims save for their pilgrimage to Mecca. Since then, many Islamic funds have been launched in Muslim countries as well as several European countries such as the UK, Switzerland, France, and the Netherlands. Based on the teachings of the Koran and its interpretations, these funds avoid investing in companies involved in pork production, pornography, and gambling, as well as in interest-based financial institutions.

In the 1970s, ethical funds in the United States started to refocus their strategy by integrating Environmental, Social, and Governance (ESG) screening criteria. Indeed, a series of social campaigns (e.g., anti-war and anti-racist movements) have made investors concerned about the social consequences of their investments. The first modern socially responsible mutual fund, the Pax World Fund, was founded in 1971 in the United States. Created for investors opposed to the Vietnam War, the fund avoided investing in weapons contractors. The same year, representatives from 270 Protestant denominations joined together to form the Interfaith Center on Corporate Responsibility (ICCR) in order to challenge the role of banks and companies in Apartheid South Africa. Nowadays, the ICCR aims at influencing corporate decision making on environmental and social issues. Similar organizations have been created in Europe such as the Association Ethique et Investissement (1983) in France and the Ecumenical Council for Corporate Responsibility (1989) in the UK.

Socially responsible funds have then largely surpassed faith-based funds—both in volume and in value (see the next section for the current market size of ethical funds). Although their number and assets are constantly growing, they still represent a niche relative to the total assets under management. Among faith-based investment funds, Islamic funds have seen a rapid development in the last 15 years, especially since the 2007–2008 financial crisis.

Besides Islamic funds, we find other investment funds following specific religious denominations such as Lutheran (Lutheran Brotherhood Funds), Presbyterian (New Covenant Funds), Mennonite (Mennonite Mutual Aid–Praxis Funds and Meritas), Catholic (Ave Maria Mutual Funds, Catholic Values, and Aquinas Funds), Conservative Christian (Timothy Plan and Noah Fund), and Jewish (Jewish Community Investment Fund).

Many stock exchanges and index companies also provide ethical indices. KLD launched the Domini 400 Social Index (now MSCI KLD 400 Social Index) in 1990 and the Catholic Values 400 Index (now MSCI USA Catholic Values Index) in 1998. In 1999, Dow Jones created the Dow Jones Islamic Market Index, and Kuala Lumpur stock exchange introduced the KLSE Shariah Index in Malaysia. Nowadays, all big index companies provide families of socially responsible funds (e.g., STOXX Europe Sustain 40), Islamic funds (e.g., S&P500 Shariah, STOXX Europe Islamic), and Christian funds (STOXX Europe Christian).

Current market for ethical funds

We provide in this section statistics on the evolution of the ethical investment industry in terms of number of funds and assets under management. Comprehensive data are available only for the two main categories of ethical funds: socially responsible and Islamic funds. Moreover, these statistics are not easy to collect and to compare because of the large variety of sources and methods used to define and measure these markets.

Socially responsible funds

The definition of Socially Responsible Investment varies widely from one country to another (Salaber, 2010); hence it is impossible to produce an estimation of the global market for SRI. The US SIF (Forum for Sustainable and Responsible Investment) provides statistics and trends for the US market, which are summarized in Figure 31.1. Vigeo provides similar data for the European market (focusing on retail funds only), and the trend is reproduced in Figure 31.2. The number of socially responsible funds and their assets under management are constantly

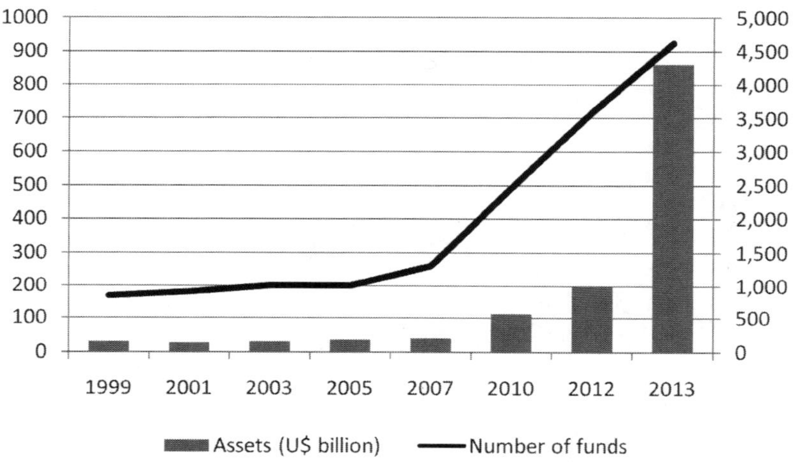

Figure 31.1 Evolution of the US SRI funds market

Source: Based on US SIF 2014 Report (US SIF 2014 Report).

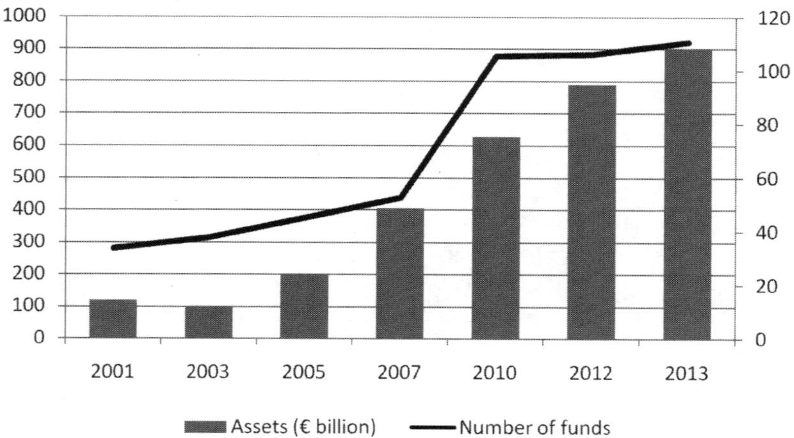

Figure 31.2 Evolution of the European SRI funds market

Source: Based on Vigeo 2014 Report (Vigeo 2014 Report).

growing, although they still represent a niche relative to the total market. Indeed Vigeo calculated that the market share of SR funds in the total European fund industry was 1.7 percent in 2013. Still, in both markets, there has been an unprecedented growth of Socially Responsible Investments since the financial crisis. The growth has been much more spectacular in the United States in recent years.

Islamic funds

The evolution of Islamic funds in terms of number and assets is presented in Figure 31.3. The number of Islamic funds around the world has multiplied tenfold from 105 funds in 2000 to 1,070 in 2013. However, in terms of assets under management, Islamic funds still represent a niche in the market, with a global market share varying from 0.17 percent in 2004 to 0.24 percent in 2013 (with a peak at 0.27 percent in 2008). We acknowledge that using several sources to estimate the trend in the global Islamic funds market might introduce a bias, but we are confident that the definition of Islamic investments is standard over time and across regions.

Other faith-based funds

As stated above, there are no statistics available for other types of faith-based investment funds, not even Christian funds. The popularity, and therefore market size, of each type of faith-based funds depends on the primary religion of each country and the importance of religion for individuals (see the next section for the ethical preferences of different investors in different countries). For instance, Catholic funds are not very popular in Belgium, France, Italy, and Spain, even though Catholicism is the main religion in these countries. As a matter of fact, religious sentiment is not very strong in Europe, and Europeans are not used to giving or investing money in charities. Indeed most Christian funds are located in the United States, whether they are "all Christian" or more specifically denominated (e.g., Lutheran, Presbyterian, and Mennonite funds). Israel has several Jewish funds, such as Calvert funds or AMIDEX35 Israel Fund, although the distinction between faith-based funds and patriotic funds is not very clear; for example, AMIDEX35 is the only mutual fund investing exclusively in Israeli companies. Finally, some Buddhist funds have been set up but they remain marginal.

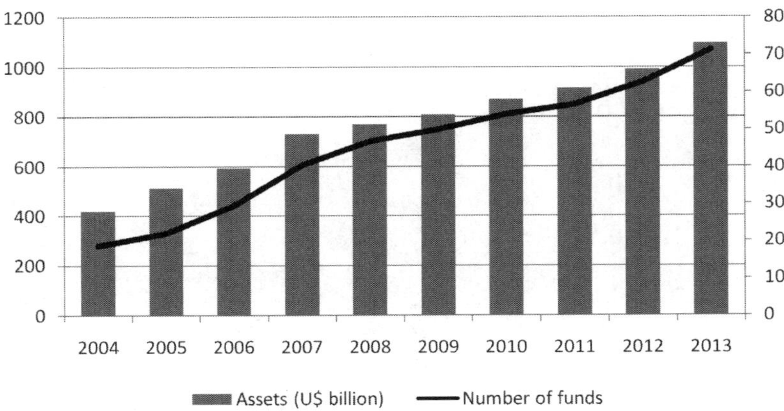

Figure 31.3 Evolution of the global Islamic funds market

Source: Based on MFIC Insight Report 2014, Eurekahedge, KFH Research Limited, and EFMA Report.

Ethical screening process

All ethical equity funds (whether socially responsible or faith-based) follow the same two-step process: ethical screening and financial filtering. First, the fund manager screens companies based on the ethical values (social or personal) of her targeted group of investors. This can be a simple exclusion (alcohol, tobacco, and gambling) or a selection (positive and/or negative) based on specific ESG criteria (e.g., environmental protection, gender equality, and Corporate Social Responsibility). The Eurosif (European Sustainable Investment Forum) categorizes these ethical screening strategies into three groups: exclusions (sector-based or product-based negative screening), norms-based screening (exclusion based on international ethical standards and principles), and best in class selection (positive ESG screening). Second, the fund manager selects companies according to her judgment regarding certain financial ratios as well as the orientation of the fund (e.g., value vs. growth). It is worth noting that ethical indices are subject to the same screening process as ethical funds. In practice, the process varies widely across and within categories of funds. We describe below the screening process of Islamic, Christian, and socially responsible funds.

As shown in Figure 31.4, the ethical screening of Islamic funds is quite complex and is usually supervised by an independent Shariah Board which controls the compliance of the fund to Islamic law. Islamic or Shariah law prohibits sinful activities (Haram), interest earnings or usury (Riba), speculation and gambling (Maisir), and uncertainty (Gharar). However, Islamic scholars agree that it is very difficult to find companies that are completely Shariah compliant, and hence have developed general cumulative tolerance criteria to govern Shariah-compliant equity investments. These screening criteria are applied at the product level and at the financial structure level. First, fund managers exclude all financial institutions operating on interest (conventional banks and insurance companies), as well as all companies deriving more than 5 percent of their revenues from manufacturing, selling, or offering alcohol, tobacco, gambling, pornography, weapons, pork products, non-halal food, and beverages. Second, the manager

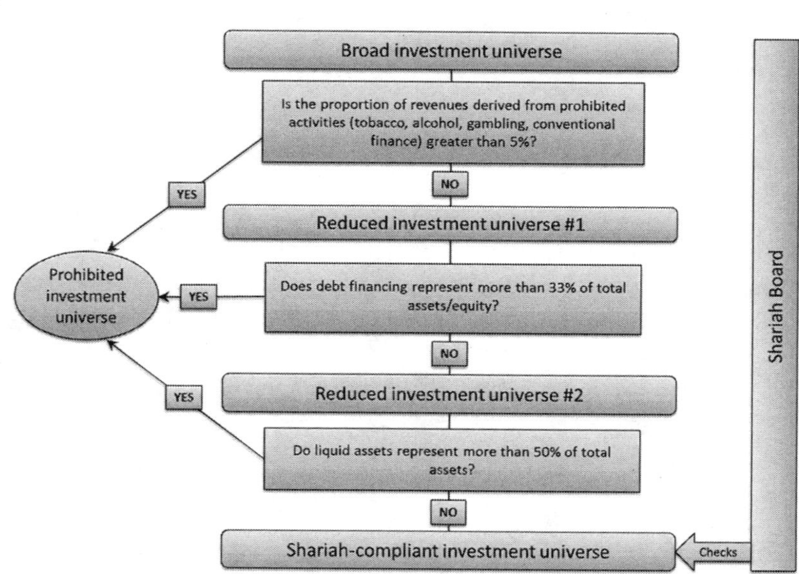

Figure 31.4 Ethical screening process of Islamic funds

eliminates stocks of companies that depend heavily on interest-based debt financing (debt to assets ratio >33 percent or debt to equity ratio >33 percent). Third, companies whose cash and cash equivalents divided by their total assets exceeds 50 percent are prohibited. Fourth, companies whose interest-bearing cash and short-term investments divided by their market capitalization exceeds 30 percent will not be considered as Shariah compliant. Finally, it is suggested that the proportion of interest income in the dividend paid to shareholders must be given to charity. Similarly, the portion of non-compliant revenues (up to 5 percent) has to be purified. Shariah Boards exist at the country level (e.g., the Shariah Advisory Councils in Hong Kong and Malaysia) or at the investment company level (e.g., the Dow Jones Islamic Market Shariah Supervisory Board). Hence, thresholds for financial ratios might differ from one Sharia Board to another, and we present here the most commonly used thresholds.

Other faith-based funds have less screening criteria than Islamic funds. In the case of Christian funds, the investment process is not as sophisticated or standardized. By analyzing many fund prospectuses, we have identified two main categories of Christian screening. The first one, illustrated in Figure 31.5, is a simple exclusion of companies whose products and/or policies are counter to Biblical principles, such as: respecting the human person, promoting the family, respecting work and the worker, pursuing peace, and caring for the poor. For instance, the Ave Maria Catholic Values Fund states that the screening process would in general avoid two categories of companies: those involved in the practice of abortion and those whose policies are judged to be anti-family (e.g., companies that distribute pornographic material). Another fund family, Timothy Plan, explicitly excludes stocks of companies involved in the production or distribution of alcohol, tobacco, and gambling, or involved in abortion and pornography. Sometimes a Christian Advisory Board, equivalent to the Sharia-Board, helps fund managers in their investment decisions by setting the criteria for screening out companies based on religious principles. For instance, the MSCI USA Catholic Values Index follows the United States Conference of Catholic Bishops' Socially Responsible Investment Guidelines, excluding companies involved in abortion, contraceptives, stem cells, and adult entertainment. The Ave Maria fund family has its own Catholic Advisory Board which is "loyal to the Magisterium of the Roman Catholic Church."

Hence the ethical screening criteria are not standardized and the allowance depends on the existence and rigor of compliance boards. As a shortcut, some fund managers select companies from existing faith-based indices. For example, the Liga Pax Cattolico Union Fund invests exclusively in the shares of companies that are listed in the Ethical Index Global Return, combining both Christian values and ESG criteria.

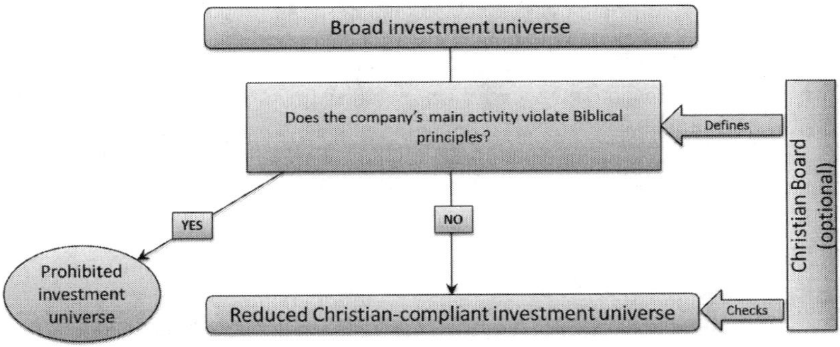

Figure 31.5 Ethical screening process of Christian funds—Simple screening

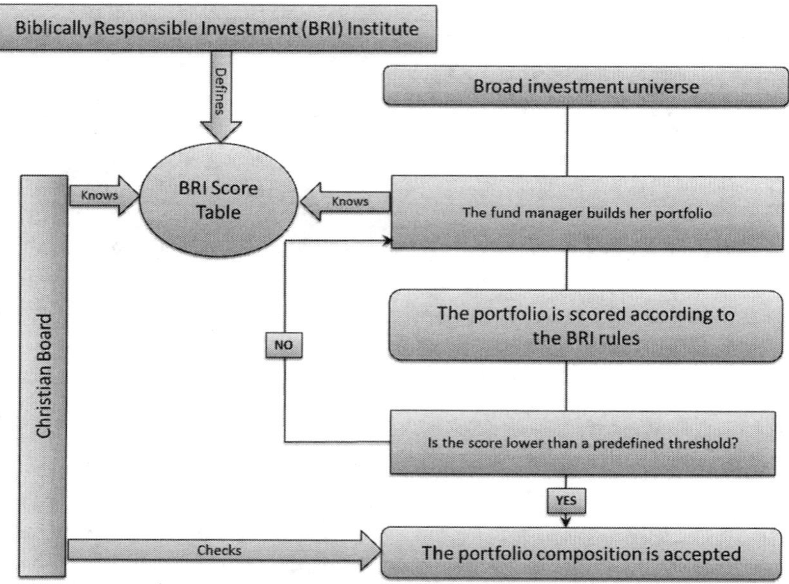

Figure 31.6 Ethical screening process of Christian funds—BRI screening

The second, more rigorous, Christian screening process is based upon investment rules provided by the Biblically Responsible Investment Institute (BRII). The BRII rates public companies—in the United States and abroad—based on their involvement in unethical activities (abortion, alcohol, anti-family issues, bioethics, gambling, human rights, low-income financial services, non-married lifestyles, pornography, and tobacco); and calculates an overall company score to help assess its suitability for investment (the higher the score, the more unethical the company). A maximum score is defined by the relevant board, and the fund manager is not allowed to exceed this threshold, as shown in Figure 31.6. Investment funds using Biblically Responsible Investing (BRI) practices are growing, reaching $13 billion in 2012 (Smith, 2013).

Socially responsible funds around the world use a variety of investment criteria that represent the values of particular groups of populations (Salaber, 2010). For instance, socially responsible funds in the United States favor product-based exclusions of alcohol, tobacco, weapons, and gambling companies (SIF, 2007), whereas funds in Belgium, France, and Switzerland follow a combined approach of positive screening (best in class) and norms-based screening (Eurosif, 2008, 2012). Even within Europe there is no consensus on a unified definition of socially responsible (or sustainable) investment. For instance, the exclusion of alcohol companies from ethical funds is popular in Denmark, Spain, and Sweden but not in Austria, France, and Germany. Similarly, nuclear power plants are excluded from most socially responsible funds in Austria, Germany, and Spain but are not automatically screened out in other European countries. Such product-based exclusions are more popular in Continental Europe than in the UK where they are mostly used by Church, charity, and private investors (Eurosif, 2012). Finally, norms-based exclusions, especially related to human rights and environmental issues, are very popular in Nordic countries. International norms include, among others, the UN Global Compact, OECD Guidelines for multinational enterprises, and ILO Conventions.

Table 31.1 summarizes all ethical screening criteria used by various types of funds. There are different levels of screening: X corresponds to total exclusion (by all funds in the category);

Table 31.1 Screening criteria used by different ethical funds around the world

Screening criteria	*Socially responsible funds*	*Christian funds*	*Conservative Christian funds*	*Islamic funds*	*Jewish funds*	*Hindu funds*	*Buddhist funds*
Product-based exclusions							
Alcohol	P	P	P	X	NA	NA	NA
Tobacco	X	X	X	X	NA	P	P
Gambling	X	X	X	X	X	P	P
Pornography	X	X	X	X	X	P	P
Weapons	P	P	P	X	X	X	X
Nuclear	P	P	P	NA	NA	NA	NA
Animal testing	P	NA	NA	NA	NA	X	X
Violence	NA	NA	NA	NA	NA	X	X
Stem cells	NA	P	X	NA	NA	NA	NA
Abortion/non-marital	NA	P	X	NA	NA	NA	NA
Non-kosher products	NA	NA	NA	NA	X	NA	NA
Pork-related products	NA	NA	NA	X	X	NA	NA
Conventional banking and insurance	NA	NA	NA	X	NA	NA	NA
Interest-based products	NA	NA	P	R	NA	NA	NA
Financial ratios							
Leverage ratio	NA	NA	NA	R	NA	NA	NA
Liquidity ratio	NA	NA	NA	R	NA	NA	NA
Interest income	NA	NA	NA	R	NA	NA	NA
ESG screening (positive/negative)							
Environmental/ ecological standards	I/X	I/X	I/X	NA	NA	NA	NA
Business practices	I/X	I/X	I/X	NA	NA	NA	NA
Human rights	I/X	I/X	I/X	NA	NA	NA	NA
Labor relations and diversity	I/X	I/X	I/X	NA	NA	NA	NA
Community	I	I	I	NA	NA	NA	NA
Corporate governance	I/X	I/X	I/X	NA	NA	NA	NA
Businesses open on Shabbat	NA	NA	NA	NA	X	NA	NA

P represents partial exclusion, that is, by some funds in the category; R indicates threshold-based restriction; and I corresponds to positive screening (inclusion) such as best in class approach. NA means that the fund category doesn't screen this particular criterion. This table was created from various sources, including Ghoul and Karam (2007), Renneboog, Ter Hoost and Zhang (2012), the Pew Research Center, the Eurosif, and the France and United States Conferences of Catholic Bishops. Between 2008 and 2013, 84 countries around the world have ratified the Dublin Convention on Cluster Munitions which prohibits the use, production, transfer, and stockpiling of cluster munitions. Among them, Australia, Japan, and most European countries are States Parties, but not the United States. This has an important implication for screening strategies, as ethical fund managers in these countries now systematically exclude companies that produce, sell, or distribute cluster bombs. Hence, the negative screening of controversial weapons recently became the most common screening strategy used by European ethical funds.

Apart from this particular exclusion, only two industries (gambling and pornography) are negatively screened by all categories of funds. Next is the tobacco industry, negatively screened by almost all categories. It's worth noting that Christian funds and socially responsible funds have very similar screening criteria due to the fact that socially responsible funds originated from Christian funds. Moreover, even though Islamic funds have universal rules in terms of ethical screening, other categories of funds have their own investment processes which can differ widely across funds. More particularly, positive screening is very subjective, and often fund managers will orientate their investments in accordance with the personal values of their targeted customers.

Characteristics of ethical funds

By definition, integrating non-financial criteria in the investment decision, that is, restraining the investment universe, implies under-diversification. All categories of funds employ some kind of negative screening of particular sectors (e.g., tobacco, gambling, pornography, and defense), which means that they are under-represented in these sectors. Figure 31.7 shows the sector breakdown of four indices: a conventional index, a socially responsible index, a Catholic index, and an Islamic index. The strongest industrial bias is acknowledged by Islamic funds which completely discard the (traditional) financial sector because of interest-based activities, and consequently overweight low-levered industries such as IT, health care, and energy (Hussein & Omran, 2005). Indeed, it is argued that Islamic funds have survived the recent crisis precisely because they shun financial institutions (Jouini & Pastré, 2009). Catholic funds and indices also show some level of industrial bias, the most obvious being the under-representation of health care companies. Indeed most Catholic funds do not invest in firms involved in the abortion industry in the production of contraceptives. Recently, both socially responsible and Catholic funds/indices have discarded energy companies because of concerns toward nuclear energy. However, due to the subjective nature of their screening process, socially responsible funds and indices don't exhibit the same level of under-diversification. Although some socially responsible funds have a higher exposure to IT and telecommunication sectors (Benson, Brailsford, & Humphrey, 2006; Statman, 2006), the portfolio allocation of US socially responsible and conventional funds does not significantly differ (Benson et al., 2006; Hawken, 2004).

Regarding the market risk of ethical funds, extant literature finds that, on average, they exhibit betas close to one (Girard & Hassan, 2008; Ferruz, Muñoz, & Vargas, 2012; Liston & Soydemir, 2010; Nofsinger & Varma, 2014; Boasson, Boasson, & Cheng, 2006). In some countries, betas are lower than one for Islamic funds (Hayat & Kraeussl, 2011; Hoepner et al., 2011; Walkshäusl & Lobe, 2012) and socially responsible funds (Leite & Cortez, 2014; Cortez, Silva, & Areal, 2012). Regarding the exposure of ethical funds to size and value, extant literature offers conflicting results. Some studies report a significant small cap bias for socially responsible funds (Areal, Cortez, & Silva, 2010, 2012; Bauer, Otten, & Rad, 2006; Gregory, Matatko, & Luther, 1997; Gregory & Whittaker, 2007) and faith-based funds (Areal et al., 2010; Girard & Hassan, 2008; Hoepner et al., 2011; Liston & Soydemir, 2010). Other studies find that ethical funds mostly invest in large companies (Bauer, Koedijk, & Otten, 2005; Nofsinger & Varma, 2014; Renneboog et al., 2008; Schroder, 2004; Walkshäusl & Lobe, 2012). Similarly, the value premium on ethical funds has been found to be positive (Ferruz et al., 2012), negative (Cortez, Silva, & Areal, 2012; Hoepner et al., 2011; Gregory & Whittaker, 2007), or not significant (Areal et al., 2010, 2012), depending on the country and methodology used.

Hayat and Kraeussl (2011) emphasize other risks specific to Islamic funds that could impact their performance: risk of changes in Islamic law, high exposure to companies that might be sub-optimally leveraged, and companies with low working capital.

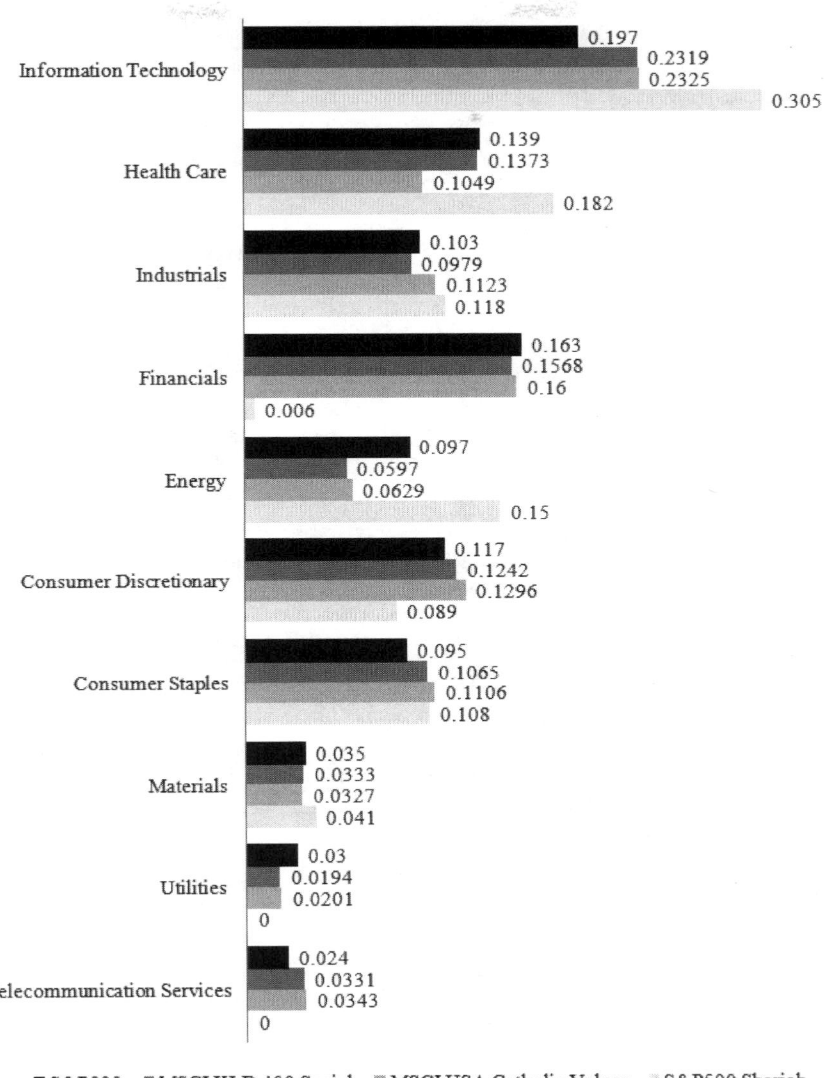

Figure 31.7 Sector breakdown of different indices

Source: Based on prospectus of each index (September 2014).

Performance of different ethical funds

There are two competing hypotheses regarding the performance of ethical funds relative to conventional funds. According to modern portfolio theory, under-diversification should imply under-performance (for a given level of risk). According to Corporate Social Responsibility and stakeholder theory, the ethical screening process generates value-relevant information and helps select securities that are better performing than average. Renneboog et al. (2008) test these two hypotheses over a sample of 440 ethical funds (both socially responsible and faith-based) across 17 countries between 1991 and 2003. Even though ethical funds seem to earn negative risk-adjusted returns (four factor alphas) in some countries, they perform the same as conventional funds in most countries (e.g., Australia, the United States, Canada, the UK, Germany, and Malaysia). Other pre-crisis studies concentrate on one type of ethical funds in individual countries and find similar results. Overall, ethical funds perform similarly or slightly worse than traditional funds, whether they are socially responsible (Bauer, Derwall, & Otten, 2007; Bauer et al., 2006; Girard, Rahman, & Stone, 2007; Gregory & Whittaker, 2007; Statman, 2000) or Islamic funds (BinMahfouz & Hassan, 2012; Mansor & Bhatti, 2011). Abdullah, Hassan, and Mohamad (2007) analyze the risk-adjusted performance of Malaysian funds over 1992–2001 and find that Islamic funds outperformed (under-performed) conventional funds during bear (bull) markets. On the contrary, it seems that Islamic indices outperform in bull markets and under-perform in bear markets (Hussein, 2004, 2007; Hussein & Omran, 2005).

More and more studies compare the performance of socially responsible, faith-based, and conventional investments. Overall, the risk-adjusted performance is similar across all types of funds (Adams & Ahmed, 2012; Abdelsalam, Duygun, Matallín-Sáez, & Tortosa-Ausina, 2014). Results for equity indices in the United States are conflicting: Beer, Estes, and Munte (2011) show that the Islamic index (DJIM) outperforms the socially responsible index (KLD Domini 400 Social), which outperforms the conventional index (S&P500); whereas Albaity and Ahmad (2011) do not find any significant difference across indices. More recent results, including the post-crisis period, provide similar evidence. The performance of ethical funds is not statistically different (or slightly lower) than the performance of conventional funds, both for socially responsible (Leite & Cortez, 2014) and faith-based funds (Ferruz et al., 2012; Adams & Ahmed, 2012). Within faith-based funds, Adams & Ahmed (2012) report that Islamic funds significantly outperformed Christian funds over 1998–2009. Hoepner et al. (2011) study the performance of 265 Islamic funds around the world over the period 1990–2009. Using a conditional 12-factor model (four risk factors across three geographical levels), they find that Islamic funds located in Muslim countries (GCC) perform slightly better than their conventional benchmarks, whereas Islamic funds located in non-Muslim countries (e.g., Germany, the UK, and the United States) significantly under-perform their benchmarks (no significant difference was found in Malaysia). Finally, Nofsinger and Varma (2014) investigate the performance of US ethical funds during crisis and non-crisis periods over 2000–2011. On average, ethical funds outperform conventional funds during crisis periods (2000–2002 and 2007–2009) but under-perform during non-crisis periods. These findings are driven by the performance of socially responsible funds (using ESG criteria), as faith-based funds do not exhibit any significant out- or under-performance over crisis and non-crisis years.

Based on existing literature and conflicting evidence across countries and types of funds, we conduct a performance analysis on a sample of ethical funds and indices to assess their behavior before and after the financial crisis. Since it is very difficult to collect extensive data on international funds, and for comparison purposes, we focus on the performance of US funds and indices denominated in US dollars. We collected data from the DataStream daily stock market for five ethical funds and indices, including four faith-based and one socially responsible. We also collected data for the S&P500 Composite Index, which is used as a benchmark. Our sample period runs from January 2003 to July 2014 and includes the whole period of financial crisis and following recession. The list of funds with their characteristics is presented in Table 31.2.

Figure 31.8 shows the evolution of each fund/index over the 2003–2014 period. Consistent with Table 31.2, the Islamic Index has the highest holding period return, and the New Covenant Fund has the lowest. The Ave Maria Catholic Values Fund has done relatively well in periods of bull markets, especially before the financial crisis. The KLD 400 Social Index did relatively poorly through 2003–2011 but considerably improved in the last 3 years of the sample. Annualized average returns and standard deviation of returns are shown in Figure 31.9 for each fund/index. The two Islamic indices seem to have the best risk-return profile, at least compared

Table 31.2 Sample description and characteristics (authors' calculations)

	Ave Maria Catholic Values Fund	*New Covenant Growth*	*DJ Islamic US*	*DJ Islamic World Developed*	*KLD 400 Social*	*S&P500*
Inception date	7/19/2001	6/28/2000	1/1/1996	1/1/1996	4/30/1990	12/31/1963
Currency	US$	US$	US$	US$	US$	US$
Type	Fund	Fund	Index	Index	Index	Index
Focus country	United States	United States	United States	World	United States	United States
Characteristics	Catholic	Presbyterian Church	Islamic	Islamic	Socially Responsible	General
Number of observations	2,995	2,995	2,995	2,995	2,995	2,995
Total holding period return	180%	145%	200%	193%	172%	178%
Average daily return	0.04%	0.04%	0.04%	0.04%	0.04%	0.04%
Average annual return	10.70%	9.27%	11.01%	10.39%	10.29%	10.50%
Daily standard dev.	1.27%	1.16%	1.18%	1.05%	1.22%	1.23%
Annualized standard dev.	20.14%	18.47%	18.79%	16.62%	19.33%	19.50%
Skewness	−0.2315	−0.1688	0.0844	−0.2341	0.0046	−0.0714
Kurtosis	7.9395	10.2112	11.9587	10.6398	10.5444	11.641
Shapiro–Wilk Test	0.9055	0.8934	0.8935	0.8976	0.8868	0.8775
Jarque–Bera Test	6,996.57	11,912	16,173.28	12,633.66	12,464.83	15,111.67
Normality	Rejected	Rejected	Rejected	Rejected	Rejected	Rejected
Risk-free rate benchmark	5-year US bond yield	5-year US bond yield	5-year US bond yield	5-year US bond yield	5-year US bond yield	5-year US bond yield

to the S&P500 and the KLD 400 Social. Even though Ave Maria's returns were high on average, they were also very volatile, making this fund the most risky investment of our sample.

For our performance analysis, we have calculated a series of risk-adjusted measures of performance over the whole period, as well as over three sub-periods corresponding to pre-crisis (January 2003–June 2007), crisis (July 2007–June 2009), and post-crisis (July 2009–July 2014). The Sharpe ratio (Sharpe, 1966) and Treynor ratio (Treynor, 1965) are well-known measures of portfolio performance where the portfolio risk premium $R_p - R_f$ (average portfolio return in excess of the risk-free rate) is calculated per unit of risk taken. The Sharpe ratio (*S*) considers the total portfolio risk σ_p (standard deviation of returns):

$$S = \frac{R_p - R_f}{\sigma_p}$$

whereas the Treynor ratio (*T*) only considers the portfolio's systematic or market risk, measured by its beta coefficient (β_p):

$$T = \frac{R_p - R_f}{\beta_p}$$

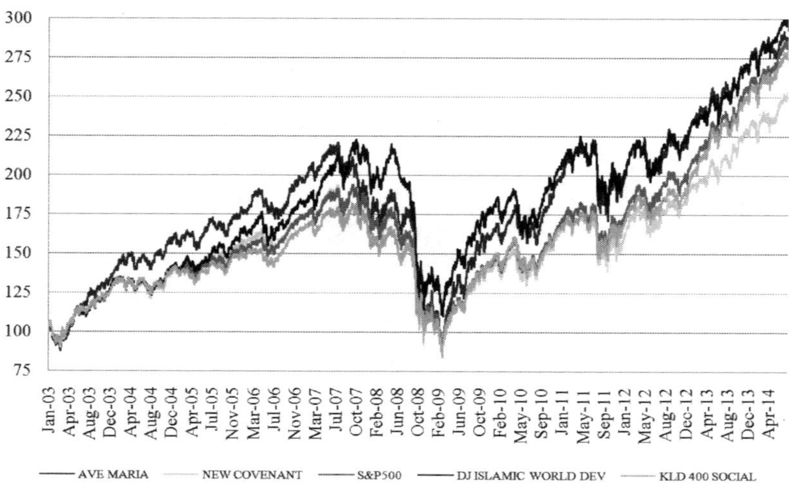

Figure 31.8 Daily price indices, 2003–2014 (100 = January 2003)

Source: Based on DataStream (2014).

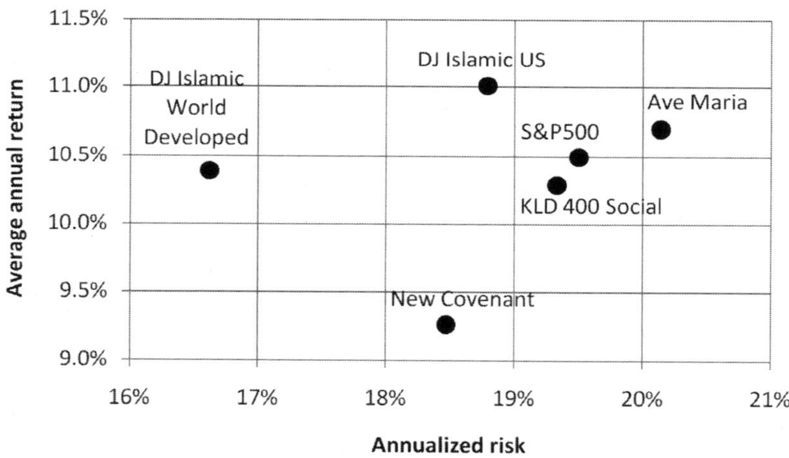

Figure 31.9 Mean-variance graph

We also calculated Jensen's alpha (α_p) based on the Capital Asset Pricing Model (Jensen, 1968). α_p represents the average abnormal return on a portfolio over and above its expected risk-adjusted return and is calculated as follows:

$$\alpha_p = R_p - \left[R_f + \beta_p \left(R_M - R_f\right)\right]$$

Results are presented in Table 31.3. Over the whole period, the Islamic indices have the best risk-adjusted performance measured by the Sharpe and Treynor ratios, as well as Jensen's alpha. The New Covenant Growth Fund is still doing poorly on a risk-adjusted basis. During the crisis period, all funds/indices lost 10–20 percent of their value, and all earned a negative Sharpe ratio

Table 31.3 Risk-adjusted performance (authors' calculations)

	Ave Maria Catholic Values Fund	*New Covenant Growth*	*DJ Islamic US*	*DJ Islamic World Developed*	*KLD 400 Social*	*S&P500*
Whole period						
Average annual return	10.70%	9.27%	11.01%	10.39%	10.29%	10.50%
Annualized standard dev.	20.14%	18.47%	18.79%	16.62%	19.33%	19.50%
Sharpe ratio	0.399	0.358	0.444	0.465	0.395	0.402
Beta (vs S&P500)	0.982	0.933	0.945	0.768	0.984	NA
Bull beta (vs S&P500)	0.956	0.906	0.933	0.728	0.994	NA
Bear beta (vs S&P500)	0.983	0.936	0.921	0.794	0.963	NA
Jensen's alpha (annualized)	0.34%	−0.71%	0.94%	1.70%	−0.09%	NA
Information ratio (vs S&P500)	0.513	−5.707	2.103	−0.215	−1.398	NA
Tracking error (vs S&P500)	0.0039	0.0022	0.0024	0.0054	0.0015	NA
Treynor ratio	0.082	0.071	0.088	0.101	0.078	NA
Pre-crisis period						
Average annual return	17.33%	14.27%	13.98%	16.19%	12.80%	14.12%
Annualized standard dev.	12.06%	11.80%	12.80%	10.79%	12.41%	12.16%
Sharpe ratio	1.115	0.881	0.789	1.141	0.719	0.842
Beta (vs S&P500)	0.884	0.947	1.028	0.788	1.008	NA
Bull beta (vs S&P500)	0.839	0.921	1.010	0.770	1.031	NA
Bear beta (vs S&P500)	0.840	0.966	1.007	0.811	0.984	NA
Jensen's alpha (annualized)	4.40%	0.70%	−0.42%	4.25%	−1.40%	NA
Information ratio (vs S&P500)	8.994	0.924	−0.795	5.868	−10.753	NA
Tracking error (vs S&P500)	0.0036	0.0017	0.0018	0.0035	0.0012	NA
Treynor ratio	0.152	0.110	0.098	0.156	0.089	NA
Crisis period						
Average annual return	−18.54%	−17.70%	−9.39%	−12.56%	−13.23%	−15.67%
Annualized standard dev.	35.59%	31.61%	32.00%	27.63%	34.45%	34.73%
Sharpe ratio	−0.604	−0.653	−0.385	−0.561	−0.469	−0.536
Beta (vs S&P500)	0.982	0.901	0.904	0.709	0.986	NA
Bull beta (vs S&P500)	0.941	0.885	0.911	0.687	0.996	NA
Bear beta (vs S&P500)	0.959	0.926	0.914	0.807	0.955	NA
Jensen's alpha (annualized)	−3.20%	−3.87%	4.50%	−2.30%	2.18%	NA
Information ratio (vs S&P500)	−4.470	−5.688	14.036	3.068	9.972	NA
Tracking error (vs S&P500)	0.0064	0.0036	0.0045	0.0102	0.0024	NA
Treynor ratio	−0.219	−0.229	−0.136	−0.219	−0.164	NA
Post-crisis period						
Average annual return	16.31%	15.41%	16.38%	14.25%	17.29%	17.57%
Annualized standard dev.	17.21%	16.13%	16.02%	15.01%	15.76%	16.14%
Sharpe ratio	0.862	0.865	0.931	0.851	1.004	0.998
Beta (vs S&P500)	1.031	0.984	0.980	0.866	0.969	NA
Bull beta (vs S&P500)	1.009	0.972	0.980	0.863	0.966	NA
Bear beta (vs S&P500)	1.031	0.978	0.971	0.872	0.960	NA
Jensen's alpha (annualized)	−1.74%	−1.89%	−0.87%	−1.16%	0.22%	NA
Information ratio (vs S&P500)	−4.452	−12.123	−7.450	−8.918	−2.224	NA
Tracking error (vs S&P500)	0.0028	0.0018	0.0016	0.0037	0.0012	NA
Treynor ratio	0.144	0.142	0.152	0.148	0.163	NA

and Treynor ratio. Still, it seems that the DJ Islamic US Index and the KLD 400 Social Index did better than other investments on a risk-adjusted basis (they earned positive alphas). This outperformance during the crisis extended to the post-crisis period, when the KLD 400 earned the best risk-adjusted performance. In terms of alpha, although most funds/indices performed worst during the crisis than before/after the crisis, the DJ Islamic US Index and the KLD 400 Social Index actually performed better during the crisis. Gillet and Salaber (2015) provide a comprehensive performance analysis of various ethical funds over the 2007–2008 financial crisis.

Conclusion

Although still a niche, ethical investment has developed rapidly in the last 15 years, even more so since the 2007–2008 financial crisis. Ethical investment vehicles include both socially responsible and faith-based (mainly Islamic and Christian) funds and indices. All these ethical funds and indices adopt different screening processes depending on the type of fund and its country of origin. We have tried in this chapter to present the wide variety of ethical funds and their screening criteria, in order to understand their performance over the recent financial crisis and beyond. Using a sample of US funds and indices over the period 2003–2014, and various risk-adjusted measures of performance, we show that overall, and more specifically during the crisis, Islamic and socially responsible indices have slightly outperformed conventional and Catholic funds/indices. This outperformance may be driven by the fact that they avoid investing in some sectors, such as the financial sector, which has been mostly hit by the recent crisis. Hence, the under-diversification of ethical funds has played in their favor for the last 15 years.

Overall, our results have various implications. First, the number and assets under management of ethical funds are growing sharply, even though ethical investments remain a niche. From a theoretical perspective, this observation challenges the portfolio theory analysis framework which is based on return maximization under risk constraint. Indeed, new constraints such as ethical values also have to be taken into account. Second, there is no financial penalty for investing in faith-based and/or socially responsible funds. Return and risk characteristics of ethical funds are very similar to those of traditional funds. As a matter of fact, several authors have raised the question of whether SRI funds are "conventional funds in disguise" (Bauer et al., 2006; Benson et al., 2006; Hawken, 2004). Cortez et al. (2012) recently refuted this hypothesis, showing that SRI funds have a significantly higher ethical ranking than standard funds. In some cases, such as during the 2007–2008 crisis, ethical funds can appear as a shield for investors, although it is very difficult to generalize to other types of crises.

Hence, several factors lead us to believe that ethical investments will continue to grow in the future. Interestingly, several authors have been talking about the convergence of different types of ethical funds, such as environmental-focused funds, human rights-focused funds, and Christian and Islamic funds (Jaufeerally, 2011; Novethic, 2009), as all share commonalities and complementarities in their screening processes. These studies suggest, for instance, that Islamic Finance must upgrade from mere Shariah compliance to becoming Shariah-based SRI, integrating for instance best in class screening approaches. Similarly, authors have suggested that SRI screening methodology could be improved in order to truly make a difference, that is, influence and encourage companies to improve their ethical, social, and environmental performance (De Colle & York, 2009). Overall, although there are still controversies about the true purpose of ethical investments, the good news is that investors can make a difference while making money, and the range and diversity of investment funds offered to ethical investors keep increasing around the world.

References

Abdelsalam, O., Duygun, M., Matallín-Sáez, J. C., & Tortosa-Ausina, E. (2014). Do ethics imply persistence? The case of Islamic and socially responsible funds. *Journal of Banking & Finance, 40*, 182–194.

Abdullah, F., Hassan, T., & Mohamad, S. (2007). Investigation of performance of Malaysian Islamic unit trust funds: Comparison with conventional unit trust funds. *Managerial Finance, 33*(2), 142–153.

Adams, J. C., & Ahmed, P. (2012). The performance of faith-based funds. *Journal of Investing, 22*(4), 83–92.

Albaity, M., & Ahmad, R. (2011). Return performance and leverage effect in Islamic and socially responsible stock indices: Evidence from Dow Jones (DJ) and Financial Times Stock Exchange (FTSE). *African Journal of Business Management, 5*(16), 6927–6939.

Areal, N., Cortez, M. C., & Silva, F. (2010, September 13). Investing in mutual funds: Does it pay to be a sinner or a saint in times of crisis? *University of Minho*. doi:10.2139/ssrn.1676391

Bauer, R., Derwall, J., & Otten, R. (2007). The ethical mutual fund performance debate: New evidence from Canada. *Journal of Business Ethics, 70*(2), 111–124.

Bauer, R., Koedijk, K., & Otten, R. (2005). International evidence on ethical mutual fund performance and investment style. *Journal of Banking and Finance, 29*(7), 1751–1767.

Bauer, R., Otten, R., & Rad, A. T. (2006). Ethical investing in Australia: Is there a financial penalty? *Pacific-Basin Finance Journal, 14*(1), 33–48.

Beer, F. M., Estes, J. P., & Munte, H. J. (2011). The performance of the faith and ethical investment products: An empirical investigation of the last decade. *The Journal of the Academy of Business and Economics, 30*, 101–124.

Benson, K. L., Brailsford, T. J., & Humphrey, J. E. (2006). Do socially responsible fund managers really invest differently? *Journal of Business Ethics, 65*(4), 337–357.

BinMahfouz, S., & Hassan, M. K. (2012). A comparative study between the investment characteristics of Islamic and conventional equity mutual funds in Saudi Arabia. *The Journal of Investing, 21*(4), 128–143.

Boasson, E., Boasson, V., & Cheng, J. (2006). Investment principles and strategies of faith-based funds. *Managerial Finance, 32*, 837–845.

Cortez, M. C., Silva, F., & Areal, N. (2012). Socially responsible investing in the global market: The performance of US and European funds. *International Journal of Finance & Economics, 17*(3), 254–271.

De Colle, S., & York, J. G. (2009). Why wine is not glue? The unresolved problem of negative screening in socially responsible investing. *Journal of Business Ethics, 85*(1), 83–95.

Eurosif. (2008). *European SRI study*. Paris: Eurosif.

Eurosif. (2012). *European SRI Study*. Paris: Eurosif.

Ferruz, L., Muñoz, F., & Vargas, M. (2012). Managerial abilities: Evidence from religious mutual fund managers. *Journal of Business Ethics, 105*(4), 503–517.

Ghoul, W., & Karam, P. (2007). MRI and SRI mutual funds: A comparison of Christian, Islamic (morally responsible investing), and socially responsible investing (SRI) mutual funds. *The Journal of Investing, 16*(2), 96–102.

Gillet, P. (2009). La mesure de performance des fonds éthiques et vicieux. In Bernard Pras (Ed.), *Management, enjeux de demain* (pp. 280–294). Paris: Vuibert.

Gillet, P., & Salaber, J. (2015). *Are ethical funds more resistant to crisis than conventional funds?* Working Paper, University of Westminster, London, UK.

Girard, E. C., & Hassan, M. K. (2008). Is there a cost to faith-based investing: Evidence from FTSE Islamic indices. *The Journal of Investing, 17*(4), 112–121.

Girard, E. C., Rahman, H., & Stone, B. A. (2007). Socially responsible investments: Goody-two-shoes or bad to the bone? *Journal of Investing, 16*(1), 96–110.

Gregory, A., Matatko, J., & Luther, R. (1997). Ethical unit trust financial performance: Small company effects and fund size effects. *Journal of Business Finance & Accounting, 24*(5), 705–725.

Gregory, A., & Whittaker, J. (2007). Performance and performance persistence of ethical unit trusts in the UK. *Journal of Business Finance & Accounting, 34*(7–8), 1327–1344.

Hawken, P. (2004). *Socially responsible investing: How the SRI industry has failed to respond to people who want to invest with conscience and what can be done to change it*. Sausalito, CA: Natural Capital Institute.

Hayat, R., & Kraeussl, R. (2011). Risk and return characteristics of Islamic equity funds. *Emerging Markets Review, 12*(2), 189–203.

Hoepner, A. G. F., Rammal, H. G., & Rezec, M. (2011). Islamic mutual funds' financial performance and international investment style: Evidence from 20 countries. *The European Journal of Finance, 17*(9–10), 829–850.

Hussein, K. (2004). Ethical investment: Empirical evidence from FTSE Islamic index. *Islamic Economic Studies, 12*(1), 21–40.

Hussein, K. (2007, November 21–24). *Islamic investment: Evidence from Dow Jones and FTSE indices.* Paper presented at the 6th International Conference on Islamic Economics and Finance, Jakarta, Indonesia.

Hussein, K., & Omran, M. (2005). Ethical investment revisited: Evidence from Dow Jones Islamic indexes. *The Journal of Investing, 14*(3), 105–126.

Jaufeerally, R. Z. (2011). Islamic banking and responsible investment: Is a fusion possible? In W. Vandekerckhove, J. Leys, K. Alm, B. Scholtens, S. Signori, & H. Schafer (Eds.), *Responsible investment in times of turmoil* (pp. 151–163). Dordrecht, the Netherlands: Springer.

Jensen, M. C. (1968). The performance of mutual funds in the period 1945–1964. *The Journal of Finance, 23*(2), 389–416.

Jouini, E., & Pastré, O. (2009). *La Finance Islamique—Une solution à la crise?* Paris: Economica.

Leite, P., & Cortez, M. C. (2014). Style and performance of international socially responsible funds in Europe. *Research in International Business and Finance, 30*, 248–267.

Liston, D. P., & Soydemir, G. (2010). Faith-based and sin portfolios: An empirical inquiry into norm-neglect vs norm-conforming investor behavior. *Managerial Finance, 36*(10), 876–885.

Mansor, F., & Bhatti, M. I. (2011). Risk and return analysis on performance of the Islamic mutual funds: Evidence from Malaysia. *Global Economy and Finance Journal, 4*(1), 19–31.

Nofsinger, J., & Varma, A. (2014). Socially responsible funds and market crises. *Journal of Banking & Finance, 48*, 180–193.

Novethic. (2009). *Finance islamique et ISR: Convergence possible?* Retrieved February 26, 2015, from Novethic, http://ribh.files.wordpress.com/2009/06/novethic-finance-islamique-et-isr.pdf

Renneboog, L., Ter Horst, J., & Zhang, C. (2008). The price of ethics and stakeholder governance: Performance of socially responsible mutual funds. *Journal of Corporate Finance, 14*, 302–322.

Renneboog, L., Ter Horst, J., & Zhang, C. (2012). Money-flows of socially responsible investment funds around the world. In H. K. Baker & J. R. Nofsinger (Eds.), *Socially responsible finance and investing: Financial institutions, corporations, investors, and activists* (pp. 455–477): Wiley.

Salaber, J. (2010). *Ethique et Toc: Promesses et Performances de l'Investissement Socialement Responsable.* Editions Universitaires Européennes.

Schroder, M. (2004). The performance of socially responsible investments: Investment funds and indices. *Financial Markets and Portfolio Management, 18*(2), 122–142.

Sharpe, W. F. (1966). Mutual fund performance. *Journal of Business, 39*(1), 119–138.

SIF. (2007). *Report on socially responsible investing trends in the United States.* Retrieved February 26, 2015, from Social Investment Forum, http://www.socialinvest.org

Smith, W. C. (2013, June 15). Investing your values. *World Magazine.*

Statman, M. (2000). Socially responsible mutual funds. *Financial Analysts Journal, 56*(3), 30–39.

Statman, M. (2006). Socially responsible indexes: Composition, performance and tracking error. *Journal of Portfolio Management, 32*(3), 100–109.

Treynor, J. L. (1965). How to rate management of investment funds. *Harvard Business Review, 43*(1), 63–75.

Walkshäusl, C., & Lobe, S. (2012). Islamic investing. *Review of Financial Economics, 21*, 53–62.

32

THE EVOLUTION OF REGULATIONS IN BANKING

A cycle-based approach

Mehmet Hasan Eken, Suleyman Kale, and Hüseyin Selimler

The academic discussion regarding the specialness of banks is closely linked to the developments and evolution of bank regulations. It is argued that, as delegated monitors, banks are special for the fact that they transform risk, maturity, and liquidity for generating investment (liabilities) and funding (assets) instruments that meet the needs of a wide range of individuals and corporations. Due to information asymmetry, it is in favor of individuals to delegate banks as their agencies dealing with risky operations that they are not capable of managing effectively. Corrigan (1982, 2000) discusses that what make banks special are (1) they offer transaction accounts, (2) they are sources of liquidity for all other institutions, and (3) they are a transmission belt for monetary policy. He continues to justify the regulations imposed upon banks as a result of their unique roles in economies. Calomiris and Gorton (1990) also state that banks are unique due to the services that they provide on each side of their balance sheets. Similarly, Diamond and Dybvig (1986) state that banks are special due to the fact that they offer transformation services that enable them to convert illiquid assets into liquid assets, that is, creating liquidity.

The reliability of banks as the protectors of households' deposits and/or savings is another issue that governments and regulators try to assure. The reaction toward this issue is twofold. Academics who have a complete trust in the market economy are against regulating banks for the fact that banks are just like other profit-seeking firms that are subject to market rules that will eventually make a distinction between reliable and unreliable banks. For example, Fama (1980), quoting from Tobin (1963), argues that the specialness of banks derives from regulations rather than the business they do or the functions they perform. It is claimed that if banks are left to function in a market free of regulations, their equilibrium would be determined by the market rules, just like it is the case for other industries. Ferrera (1990) also discussed that the heavy regulation wall had to fall due to the fact that it was no longer possible to keep banks separated from other activities such as investment banking and even owning non-financial subsidiaries. Additionally, Barth, Caprio, and Levine (2012) state that tightening capital requirements or increasing supervisory powers had no positive impact on the financial sector, and in fact increased supervision was found to be positively related to corruption in banking. They further argue that strengthening private monitoring was found to be associated with deeper, more efficient, and less corrupt financial systems, but not with greater financial stability.

The regulations imposed upon banks are justified for different reasons. Blinder (2009) specifies that government intervention in markets is justified for the following purposes: (1) to create and enforce the rules of the game and keep the system honest; (2) to guard against undue concentration, thus keeping markets competitive; (3) to redistribute income, for example, through the tax-and-transfer system; (4) to correct externalities or other market failures, for example those due to asymmetric information; and (5) to protect the interests of taxpayers, for example in cases in which public money is being spent or put at risk. He further underlines that, by implementing regulations, governments attempt to protect consumers and taxpayers and ensure financial and economic stability both locally and internationally.

Another issue about bank regulations is the cost of preventing and/or combating financial crises. Calomiris and Gorton (1990) state that while private bank coalitions are effective in monitoring banks and mitigating the effects of banking panics, governments eliminate banking panics through costs of deposit insurance and reserve requirements. They also underlined that a private self-regulation system could be effective when combined with some government policies.

Currently banks are the most heavily regulated firms. The evolution of regulations, in line with the expanding businesses and functions of banks and experienced financial crises, causes regulations to become more and more complicated. However, regulations are intended to be designed in line with the market rules, and whenever possible direct controls on banks' operations are to be avoided such as interest rate controls applied in the past. After underlining that safety nets could produce a suboptimal market by inflating banks' incentives to take risk, Stevens (2000) suggests banking regulation and supervision to replace safety nets by market discipline. The third pillar of Basel II, called Market Discipline, is aimed to increase the level of private monitoring in bank regulations that will reduce the level of government intervention in future regulations. Thus, in order to minimize government involvement, it can be observed that regulations are to be made consistent with market rules.

Another issue regarding the regulations is about the internationalization of them throughout the world. Regulations that were initially imposed upon banks were nationally based, and after the internationalization of banking businesses, the current regulations contain international dimensions, and it was aimed to harmonize them throughout the world after the foundation of the Basel Committee in 1975. Despite the fact that it is not compulsory to adapt to the regulations developed by the Basel Committee, it has been the duty of the IMF and the Word Bank to spread these rules among almost all countries in the world.

Another dimension of regulations is related to product innovation and technology. As stated by Markham (2010), banks became financial supermarkets, and this makes their balance sheets even more complicated for regulators to identify risks coherent to their balance sheets and take the necessary measures to control them. Similarly, DeYoung (2007) states that during the 1980s it became increasingly difficult to maintain a regulatory environment that could protect the banking industry from competition while, at the same time, ensuring a vibrant and healthy banking industry. He then suggests that changes in market conditions and financial and technological innovation necessitated changes in the regulatory regimes too.

Although there might be some other features of regulations, they are not discussed here. In the remaining parts of this chapter, the evolution of bank regulations will be analyzed from different perspectives with a specific focus on the relationship between financial crises and regulations. Regulations regarding the scope of banking in the first part, regulations regarding capital requirements in the second part, and finally regulations regarding deposit insurance will be investigated with a historical-based literature review.

The evolution of regulations regarding the scope of banking activities

The scope of banking, as widely accepted, can be divided into two main pillars, namely commercial banking and investment banking. Although there are other banking activities such as private banking, consumer banking, and international banking that are a part of current banking businesses, from the regulatory point of view they are not considered as being completely different from either of the two main sections mentioned. These banking businesses can be a part of either investment banking or commercial banking.

The main distinction between a commercial bank and an investment bank is that a commercial bank accepts deposits from households and transfers these funds mainly to traders in the form of self-liquidating loans. On the other hand, investment banks do not have licenses to accept deposits and thus they are free to get involved in risky businesses such as stock market operations, underwriting activities, etc.

In the United States, the regulation cycle regarding scope of banking started during colonial times when banks were provided with a charter to operate. Apart from providing commercial banking activities, charter banks provided services to the government as the underwriters of their bonds. However, after seeing that the charter banking system caused corruption and instability in the US banking system, due to creating a monopoly, these regulations were repealed and it was followed by an era of free banking. McCarthy (March/April 1984) underlines that charter regulations were criticized as being against the free spirit of US civil institutions. Thus, new regulations were designed to assure that anyone who could meet the minimum legal capital requirements was entitled to own a bank. After the establishment of the free banking system in the United States, many banks were established to offer commercial banking services to their customers. They were also assisting the government in raising revenue by purchasing and depositing state bonds for guaranteeing the convertibility and circulation of their own banknotes.

As indicated by McCarthy (March/April 1984), due to heterogeneous bank notes and the exploitation of the free banking system by the so-called "wildcat banks,"[1] many bank failures were witnessed, and that necessitated the reorganization of the banking system in the United States, which led to the national banking system.

The national banking system was established after the enactment of the National Currency Act by the US Congress in 1863. McCarthy (March/April 1984) outlines that the Act imposed a number of restrictions on bank activities in order to enhance bank soundness and stability. Alongside minimum capital requirements, these new regulations were: (1) reserve requirements, (2) restrictions on the scope of operations primarily to accepting deposits and making short-term, self-liquidating loans to businesses, and (3) a requirement to provide periodic reports of conditions to the Comptroller.

After the establishment of the national banking system, commercial banks were not allowed to be a part of capital market operations and they were encouraged to serve trade activities and invest their funds mainly in so-called self-liquidating loans. However, they were allowed to broker securities for their customers. As indicated by Markham (2010), the Office of Comptroller of Currency prevented this in 1902. Nonetheless, this did not last for a long period of time. As emphasized by McCarthy (March/April 1984), the entering of the United States into World War I accelerated the integration of commercial and investment banking activities and that enabled banks to finance the government's war expenditures. Therefore, the involvement of commercial banks in investment banking activities continued to grow and the commercial lending of banks declined significantly.

By the time of the Great Depression of 1929, many commercial banks went bankrupt just because they were heavily involved in investment banking operations. Therefore, the economic crisis of 1929 led to two new banking regulations with the enactment of the Banking Act of 1933 and the Glass-Steagall Act (GSA) in the United States. The first regulation was related to the separation of investment banking from commercial banking, and the second was the prohibition of paying interest on demand deposits and setting an interest rate ceiling on various types of deposits. These two regulations were enacted because, during the global crisis of 1929, banks were heavily involved in investment banking that swallowed almost all of their deposit borrowings from households. Thus, the aim of these regulations were to push banks into traditional banking activities, that is, borrowing deposits and lending self-liquidating short-term commercial loans. On the other hand, interest rate-related regulations were enacted to prevent banks from unjustified interest rate competition.

The GSA remained in force until 1999 when the enactment of the Gramm-Leach-Bliley Act (GLBA) in 1999 repealed it and enabled commercial banks to convert themselves into financial holding companies that could provide not only commercial banking services but also investment banking services alongside many other modern financial services. However, as stated by Blinder (2009), it is believed that the repeal of the GSA led to the 2008 global financial crisis and it is suggested that it would be wise to reenact the GSA, which provided a half-century of financial crisis-free banking in the United States. On the other hand, DeYoung (2007) states that from the early 1980s through the early 1990s, approximately 10 percent of US commercial banks failed, in contrast to the period 1940–1980 when only 237 banks failed. However, he discusses the fact that the appearance of safety and soundness during those years of the GSA is deceptive because the financial regulations and industry structure present at the time were themselves the root cause of the bank insolvencies of the 1980s and 1990s.

Despite the fact that the GSA reshaped banks in the United States, that is, banks had to separate their commercial banking and investment banking activities, as indicated by Ferrera (1990), in mainland Europe banks were formed under the name of universal banking that enabled commercial banks to provide not only investment banking services but also own industrial companies. This was the case in Japan and Turkey as well. Gruson and Nikowitz (1988) indicate that the Second Banking Directive of the European Economic Community counted securities and derivatives trading as a part of European banks' activities.

These different types of bank structures in Europe and the United States were the center of debates for a long period of time. Before the repeal of the GSA, Shull and White (1998) suggested that both the holding company affiliate arrangement and the operating subsidiary structure appear to be safer than the universal banking for non-traditional activities that are not examinable and supervisable by bank regulators. They were suggesting that US banks be converted into bank holding companies rather than universal banks in order to effectively compete with banks outside of the United States. Jeannot (May 2000) states that the dismantlement of the GSA was inevitable due to the fact that the deregulation of banking industries in developed countries (mainly in Europe) had potentially placed US banks in a disadvantageous environment and left them uncompetitive. On the other hand, as indicated by Macey (2000), the GSA was dead even before the GLBA because federal regulators, particularly the Federal Reserve Board and the Comptroller, had already eviscerated the "Maginot Line" between commercial and investment banking through liberal regulatory interpretations of the statute long before the Act was passed. Thus Congress, in passing the Act, merely gave formal recognition to the changes that had been taking place in the marketplace over the past years. Markham (2010) also supports the statement of Macey (2000) regarding the legal disintegration of the GSA as being a result of the developments in the markets that practically dismantled the GSA. In other words, bankers were able to exploit and/or create loopholes in the GSA in order to allow themselves to provide investment banking services alongside the traditional banking activities. As they were doing this, the regulators were not preventing them, due to the fact that not only the financial system but also the banking system was getting more and more complicated following the invention of new financial instruments such as certificates of deposits in the 1960s, securitization in the 1980s, credit default swaps in the 1990s, and other revolutionary and complex instruments. Indeed regulators needed time to understand and then regulate these issues.

It is obvious that the cycle of regulations regarding the scope of banking has two extremities: the unity of commercial and investment banking on one extreme side and their separation on the other. The cycle started with the free banking era in the United States when these two banking services were unified, and later the cycle continued with the separation of these two banking facilities during the national banking era. After that, regulators were forced by the market players to unify them despite the existence of the regulations preventing it. Nonetheless, banks were providing both types of banking services in the market after being encouraged by the federal government for its own financing purposes. Having continued until 1929, banks found themselves exposed to market risks empowered by the global depression. The cycle kept continuing with the enactment of the GSA that banned again the unification of these two types of banking facilities at extreme sides. Nonetheless, the market forces gradually succeeded to dismantle the GSA over time, especially with the help of new financial instruments and technology that resulted in intense competition in the banking industry alongside creating complex balance sheets and risk structures that finally caused the legal repeal of the GSA in 1999.

After the global financial crisis of 2008, some have argued that the GSA should be reenacted in order to prevent future financial crises. Some also argue that the restoration of the GSA is impossible. Kregel (2010) discusses the fact that the GSA provided unregulated investment banks with a monopoly over securities market activities that were functionally equivalent to the deposit business and liquidity creation of regulated banks. He then adds that due to the complexity of financial markets in comparison to the time of the inauguration of the GSA, it will not be possible to reenact the GSA. Nonetheless, he suggests that the banking definition be widened so as to include investment banking activities under the regulatory umbrella of today's commercial banks. However, Carpenter and Murphy (June 2010) indicate that, after the 2008 financial crisis, a new regulation, named the "Volcker Rule" and enacted in the United States, already limits the ability of commercial banking institutions and their affiliated companies and subsidiaries to engage in trading unrelated to their customer needs and investing in and sponsoring hedge funds or private equity funds.

After stating five reasons behind the global financial crisis of 2008—(1) firing the chairman of FED in 1987 who opposed deregulation processes, (2) tearing down the walls separating banks' investment banking activities from their commercial banking operations, (3) application of leeches such as tax cuts in the United States, (4) faking the numbers that caused the enactment of Sarbanes-Oxley to combat operational risk, and (5) letting it bleed (veering from one course of action to another)—Stiglitz (2009) criticizes the belief that markets are self-adjusting and that the role of government should be minimal. On the other hand, Calomiris and Gorton (1990) state that the history of US banking regulation can be written largely as a history of government and private responses to banking panics.

In which direction is the cycle going to continue—the separation or unification of the scope of banking? Building upon the latest core banking regulations of the Basel Committee, aka Basel III, it can be said that banks will continue to get involved in investment banking activities due to the fact that capital regulations are heavily related to complex synthetic instruments and the calculation of their risk weights. Nonetheless, the debates over the separation and unification of commercial banking and investment banking activities will remain unsolved. Within the borders of the cycle defined, the degree of separation and/or unification will change depending on market conditions, geography, tradition, and bankers' lobbying power.

Having gone through a brief history of regulations regarding the scope of banking, it is easy to recognize that regulations are introduced following financial crises. Thus, the structure of new regulations is extremely affected by the last crisis lived. Accordingly, new regulations are designed and implemented for combating financial crises similar to the latest crisis that crashed markets and influenced the content of new regulations. However, new regulations which are designed to prevent a specific crash usually do not have a complete perspective to cover and/or to combat new types of crises to be witnessed in the future. Also the regulations introduced after financial crises soon become the shooting target of the market players for the changes that will allow them to freely act in the markets in order to maximize their market value and/or profitability. And the cycle goes on indefinitely.

Nonetheless, the Basel Committee's new and comprehensive regulations, called Basel III, seem to be designed with a broader and longer vision so as to ensure that banking systems around the globe will be sound and stable for upcoming potential crises in the markets.

The evolution of regulations regarding capital adequacy

In present times the main regulatory body of capital regulations and also bank regulations is the set of regulations that has been developed by the Basel Committee since 1975 when the committee was established. Before moving into the details of the present capital regulations, Basel III, looking at the historical developments of the capital requirements will help to better understand the capital adequacy issue and its evolving directions.

As outlined in FDIC (2003), prior to the Basel regulations regarding capital requirements, US regulators stressed factors such as managerial capability and loan portfolio quality and largely downplayed capital ratios. Supervisors did try to make use of a variety of capital adequacy measures as early as 1864, when the National Banking Act set static minimum capital requirements based on the population of each bank's service area, but most early attempts at quantifying the notion of capital adequacy were controversial and unsuccessful. In the 1930s and 1940s, state and federal regulators began to look at the ratios of capital-to-total deposits and capital-to-total assets, but both were dismissed as ineffective tests of true capital adequacy. Tarullo (2011) states that it was after the recognition of the effects of losses that occurred on banks' loans to foreign sovereigns that US regulators started to reimpose minimum capital ratios upon banks.

As stated in FDIC (2003), various studies related to the ways of adjusting assets for risk and creating capital-to-risk assets ratios were undertaken in the 1950s, but none were universally accepted at that time. Therefore, a judgment-based, subjective, bank-by-bank approach to assessing capital adequacy remained effective in the United States until the failure of many banks during the 1981 recession. After that, the federal banking agencies introduced explicit numerical regulatory capital requirements. The standards adapted employed a leverage ratio of primary capital (which consisted mainly of equity and loan loss reserves) to average total assets. It was this capital regulation that resulted in the first comprehensive capital regulations developed by the Basel Committee in 1988 that combined a risk-based capital approach named Basel I.

The analysis of banking crises in different countries showed that bank failures could be classified in many ways, including by risk type, the type of shock that precipitated the failures or crisis, the state of the banking system, what portion of the banking system was affected, how the crisis was resolved, and whether the failures resulted in regulatory changes (Basel Committee, 2004, p. 67).

While each country's experience has unique characteristics, the common element in the crises that they lived is similar. Spain, Norway, Sweden, and the US had very similar experiences when they liberalized their financial systems. Credit risk, particularly real estate lending, led to widespread banking problems in Switzerland, Spain, the United Kingdom, Norway, Sweden, Japan, and the US. Market risk was the principal cause of failure in the isolated failure of Herstatt (Germany) and also caused the first stage of the US Savings and Loans failures. Financial liberalization (deregulation) was a common feature of major banking crises, often combined with supervisory systems that were inadequately prepared for the change. It is also stated that banking problems are more severe and/or more difficult to resolve when they hit weakly capitalized institutions (Basel Committee, 2004, p. 68).

These crises affecting a variety of countries all around the world have helped the regulators of these countries to agree upon internationally accepted bank regulations around the world. Legislative and regulatory changes followed three main lines. First, supervisors tried to improve the risk adequacy of regulation. Second, legislators and supervisors tried to strengthen market and supervisory discipline. Finally, some countries revised legislation with a view to more efficient resolution. While considerable efforts to improve banking regulation and ongoing supervision were taken on a national level, national authorities have also pooled their experience within the revision of international capital standards under the guidance of the Basel Committee on Banking Supervision (Basel Committee, 2004, p. 69).

As a matter of fact following banking crises in different countries, regulators were encouraged to redefine the capital adequacy ratio and related body of regulations. The Basel Criteria that were initially introduced in the form of the Cooke Ratio basically converted the previously used simple shareholders' funds over assets ratio into regulatory capital over risky assets. It was hoped that, by recognizing the different risk structures of individual banks, it would help regulators to better control banks with proper recognition of each bank's financial statements. However, the definition of risky assets was initially limited to credit risk only and missing other risks such as interest rate risk, liquidity risk, foreign exchange rate risk, operational risk, and others. Nonetheless, having witnessed bank failures due these above-mentioned risks, the remaining risks (in the form of market risk and operational risk) were included in the calculation of capital adequacy ratios in order to complete the risk-based regulations regarding the capital requirements.

Soon after the capital adequacy formula had been finalized, the bankers started to complain about the calculation process—that it did not take into consideration the management skills of individual banks and that it was providing the same standard calculating procedure for all banks alike. The Basel Committee decided to allow banks to calculate their own risk-weighted assets based on the internal models developed by them and approved by the local regulatory authorities. This initiative given to banks allowed them to measure their riskiness using their internal models and provided them with an opportunity to reduce their risk-weighted assets by improving their risk management skills. The better the risks are managed, the lower the risk-weighted assets are to be calculated by their own internal models. This tradeoff between risk management skills and risk-weighted assets allowed banks, while increasing the total sizes of their balance sheets, to keep their risk-weighted assets under control without violating the existing capital rules.

This helped banks to keep their risk-based capital ratios well above the required ratios, also with the help of asset sales through securitization and other structured facilities. As discussed by Eken (2006), these activities left banks with high leverage ratios but still well-sufficient risk-based capital adequacy ratios. Recognizing this, the Basel Committee amended a new condition to Basel III regarding the leverage level of banks free of their risk-based capital adequacy ratios in order to assure the soundness of banks alongside the comprehensive capital adequacy ratios imposed upon them.

Similar to the cycle of regulations regarding banking scope, capital adequacy regulations also move between two extremities—the basic "shareholders' funds over assets" ratio and the complicated "regulatory capital over risk-weighted assets" ratio. The global financial crisis of 2008 has caused regulators to restructure the capital-related regulations as converting Basel II regulations into Basel III. Although the calculation of the capital adequacy ratio was left very much similar, some new amendments were introduced for the strengthening of the capital adequacy levels of banks. As specified by the Basel Committee (2011), aka Basel III, alongside additional increases in the minimum capital ratios specified in Basel II, banks will be forced to maintain additional 2.5 percent Tier 1 capital-to-risk-weighted assets. Besides this, a maximum leverage multiplier is introduced. Three percent Tier 1 capital-to-on-balance-sheet assets plus the off-balance-sheet items, multiplied with the suitable credit conversion factors, is going to be tested during the period January 1, 2013–January 1, 2017.

These new regulations have bound banks with tighter restrictions that will eventually be the shooting target of professional bankers soon. It is also mentioned in Basel III that especially the leverage ratio will be tested in the future, leaving both regulators and supervisors with an option to abolish it after a certain period is passed free of shocks. And the cycle will probably continue with the easing of regulations and then continue again by tighter regulations after banks are hit by a new crisis.

Within the extremities of this cycle, it is apparent that for the safety and soundness of banking systems and for the protection of depositors initially, tight capital requirement ratios are implemented. Following that, modification is in line with the demands of bankers and developments in the markets that looser regulations over time take place in the future. Finally, after a strike by a financial crisis, the regulations are restructured or reshaped in order to combat the problems that occurred.

The evolution of regulations regarding deposit insurance

The main idea behind the establishment of deposit insurance is to protect households' savings that will keep public confidence restored and eventually ensure a stable banking industry. A Safety Fund was in place during the free banking era in the United States that was criticized for two reasons: The first was the cost of participating in the fund, and the second was that the cost was calculated with a flat rate for all banks that meant that low-risk banks subsidized bankers with high-risk preferences. McCarthy (1984) stated that similar to the establishment of the safety fund system in the 1820s the Federal Deposit Insurance Corporation (FDIC) was established to restore public confidence in the banking industry following the great depression of 1929. Calomiris and White (1994) indicated that, until the great depression of 1929, it would be very unlikely to adopt deposit insurance in the United States. That was because prior to 1933 when, by the enactment of the GSA, FDIC was established, eight state-level deposit insurance systems had been created since 1908, and in the 1920s all had collapsed under the weight of excessive risk taking and fraud, encouraged by the protection of deposit insurance.

Following the establishment of FDIC, deposit insurance has been widely included in banking regulations around the world. For example, it was after the collapse of Herstatt in 1974 that German authorities decided to set up a deposit protection system in 1976 (Basel Committee, 2004, p. 6). Following the bankers' crisis, a crisis occurred after the liberalization of the financial markets that alongside traditional banks allowed so-called bankers—individuals authorized to accept deposits—to compete for deposits by offering higher interest rates in the early 1980s.

This competition ended with the collapse of many bankers that forced the Turkish authorities to set up a deposit insurance system in 1983 in order to restore public confidence.

As stated by Santos (2000), government-backed deposit insurance has proven very successful in protecting banks from runs, but at a cost as it leads to moral hazard, which has been underlined by many other academics. Diamond and Dybvig (1986) state that banks are subject to runs mainly due to the transformation services they offer. However, they indicate that any regulation to prevent bank runs must not simultaneously prevent banks from producing liquidity which will eventually prevent banks from doing their businesses. Nonetheless, Diamond and Dybvig suggest that introducing deposit insurance is crucial to keep banks out of risky businesses that may eventually cause their failures.

Mishkin (2006) states that policymakers' pledge not to engage in a bailout of large banks is not time-consistent: when a large bank is about to fail, policymakers will want to renege on their pledge because they want to avoid the systemic risk that the failure of the bank would entail. At the beginning of the 1994 banking crisis in Turkey, deposit insurance coverage increased to 100 percent of deposits, and it was widened to include all banks' borrowings after the crisis of 2000 and 2001 when almost all failed banks were taken over by the government. However, after the restoration of public confidence, the coverage range was limited to savings deposits and its level was dropped to only 50,000 Turkish lira. Similar examples are seen in almost every country.

Basically when there is a tension in the markets, deposit insurance becomes an important tool for the restoration of public confidence in almost every country. However, after the tension is over, the coverage of deposit insurance is narrowed for the sake of not causing moral hazard. Nonetheless, when markets are hit by another shock, the coverage range and limit of deposit insurance is widened again. And this movement between two extremities keeps repeating itself, similar to the cycles of other regulations.

Conclusion

As indicated by academics, there is a strong connection between regulations imposed upon banks and the financial crises lived. On the one hand, in order not to interfere with free market rules, regulators want to avoid imposing heavy or tight regulations upon banks. On the other hand, in order to prevent any costs occurred during financial crises to be imposed upon taxpayers, for the protection of savers and for a sustainable public confidence they aim to have some minimum regulations in place. Nonetheless, during financial crises, the cost is almost all the time imposed upon taxpayers by the governments. Alongside imposing costs upon taxpayers, some heavy regulations are introduced in order to restore public confidence in the system. After it is achieved, the new regulations undergo severe criticisms directed by market professionals and free market advocates that generally end up with major corrections of the regulations imposed, if they are not abolished completely. It is argued that it is probably this process that plants the seeds for new crises to follow.

The process of imposing and abolishing regulations that continues to go this way has not preserved banks and/financial systems from market shocks so far. In other words, the indecisive character of regulations, that is, differentiating regulations in line with market expectations and in line with market shocks, introduce the regulations themselves with a variation or volatility that eventually could cause the ineffectiveness of regulations at all. Always-changing regulations make it difficult to adapt to for banks and make it difficult for the regulators to pursue. Of course, it is evident that as time passes market conditions change and technology and the product range evolve, and that requires them to be converged with the regulations. This can be done either by the way that regulations could be loosened to allow markets to develop new products, or products that are to be developed could be formed taking into consideration the existing rules and regulations. Whichever way is preferred, it is better to be decisive. No matter whether regulations are tight or loose, it is a matter to have regulations stable at a certain level and at least for a certain period of time that will help banks and regulators with a clearer vision for the future.

However, as mentioned earlier, regulations are not stable, and they change over time for different reasons, such as covering new instruments, including contemporary developments and similar issues. On the one hand, it is justified that by doing this regulations are structured to cover any developments that might possibly cause disturbances. On the other hand, it is justified that this ensures that the regulations are not in conflict with the market rules. This seems to be a strong part of the regulatory structure so as to keep regulations vivid and elastic. However, this also causes regulations to have a volatile feature that makes it difficult to adapt to easily and on a timely basis.

There are always inventions in the financial markets regarding new instruments, products, and structures. It takes time for regulators to recognize, understand, and finally include them within the coverage of the existing regulations. In other words, there is always a time lag between innovations in the market and their inclusion within the coverage of regulations. After allowing the market players time for adaptation to the changes in regulations, the time lag between innovations and the implementation of the regulations becomes even wider. By the time this gap is narrowed, some new innovations appear to take place in the markets and the gap becomes wider again.

Apart from this time lag between regulations and innovations, regulators aim to ease regulations in order to be in harmonization with free market rules. To do that, amendments to the existing set of regulations are introduced, together with an adaptation period for the harmonization of the new rules. Sometimes even before adapting to the changes, some new rules are introduced that are also followed by newer changes, and it goes on this way until there is a shock in the market. Following the new crisis, the existing and loosened regulations are tightened again in order to restore confidence in the system.

This cycle can be witnessed in almost every country and regarding any type of regulation. The movements between the two extremities of the cycle diminish the targeted effects of regulations. The initial tight regulations basically prevent banks from getting involved in risky and/or complex activities so as to keep their balance sheets sound and stable that would eventually result in sound and stable financial markets. Nonetheless, the loosening of regulations in line with market professionals' demand and in line with the idea of converging regulations with the market rules results in ineffective regulations by the time of financial crises. In other words, it makes no difference between having regulations and having no regulations. Then tight regulations are put in place in order to restore public confidence. Therefore, instead of having regulations that move between two extremities, it would be better to have regulations that are stable at a predetermined level for a certain period of time. This sustainability in the level of regulations will help the market to find its equilibrium in line with the stable level of regulations. Otherwise the market equilibrium will also change in line with the changing regulations.

Acknowledgments

With permission to reprint by ACRN Oxford.

Article previously published as: Eken, M. H., Kale, S., & Selimler, H. (2013). The evolution of regulations in banking: A cycle based approach. *ACRN Journal of Finance and Risk Perspectives, 2*(2), 15–26.

Note

1 For a definition of wildcat banks, see, for example, Gianni and Vannini (2010, p. 413).

References

Barth, J. R., Caprio, G., Jr., & Levine, R. (2012). *The evolution and impact of bank regulations* (Policy Research Working Paper 6288). Washington, DC: The World Bank.

Basel Committee on Banking Supervision. (2004, April). *Bank failures in mature economies* (Working Paper 13). Basel, Switzerland: Bank for International Settlement.

Basel Committee on Banking Supervision. (2011, June). *Basel III: A global regulatory framework for more resilient banks and banking systems*. Basel, Switzerland: Bank for International Settlement.

Blinder, A. S. (2009, October 23). *It's broke, let's fix it: Rethinking financial regulation*. Paper presented at the Federal Reserve Bank of Boston Conference, Chatham, MA.

Calomiris, C. W., & Gorton, G. (1990, March 22–24). *The origins of banking panics: Models, facts and policy implications*. Paper presented at the National Bureau of Economic Research's Conference on Financial Crises, Key Biscayne, FL.

Calomiris, C. W., & White, E. N. (1994, May 20–21). *The origins of federal deposit insurance*. Paper presented at the National Bureau of Economic Research's Conference on *The Regulated Economy: A Historical Approach to Political Economy*, 1993, in volume edited by Claudia Goldin and Gary D. Libecap, published by the University of Chicago.

Carpenter, D. H., & Murphy, M. M. (2010, June). *The "Volcker Rule": Proposals to limit "speculative" proprietary trading by banks*. Washington, DC: Congressional Research Service.

Corrigan, E. G. (1982). *Are banks special?* (Annual Report, pp. 1–12). Minneapolis: Federal Reserve Bank of Minneapolis.

Corrigan, E. G. (2000). *Are banks special? A re-visitation* (The Region, Special Issue, 1–4). Minneapolis: Federal Reserve Bank of Minneapolis.

DeYoung, R. (2007). Safety, soundness and the evolution of the US banking industry. *Economic Review*, Federal Reserve Bank of Atlanta, First and Second Quarters, 41–66.

Diamond, D. W., & Dybvig, P. H. (1986). Banking theory, deposit insurance, and bank regulation. *The Journal of Business, 59*(1), 55–68.

Eken, M. H. (2006, May). *The effects of Basel II on banks' credit pricing activities and implications for Turkish banks*. Paper presented at the conference organized by Marmara University and the University of Vienna, titled Financial Sector Integration: Review and Steps Ahead, Proceedings, 235–244.

Fama, E. F. (1980). Banking in the theory of finance. *Journal of Monetary Economics, 6*, 39–57.

FDIC. (2003, January 14). *Basel and the evolution of capital regulation: Moving forward, looking back*. Retrieved May 13, 2013, from http://www.fdic.gov/bank/analytical/fyi/2003/011403fyi.html

Ferrera, P. J. (1990, Fall). International trends in the combination of banking, securities and commerce. *Cato Journal, 10*(2), 329–346.

Gianni, L., & Vannini, R. (2010). Toward an evolutionary theory of banking regulation: The United States and Italy in comparison. *Review of Banking and Financial Law, 29*, 405–439.

Gruson, M., & Nikowitz, W. (1988). The second banking directive of the European Economic Community and its importance for non-EEC banks. *Fordham International Law Journal, 12*(2), 206–241.

Jeannot, J. M. (2000, May). An international perspective on domestic banking reform: Could the European Union's second banking directive revolutionize the way the United States regulates its own financial services industry? *American University International Law Review, 14*(6), 1715–1760.

Kregel, J. (2010). *No going back: Why we cannot restore Glass-Steagall's segregation of banking and finance*. Public Policy Brief No. 107, Levy's Economics Institute of Bard College, 4–17.

Macey, J. R. (2000). *The business of banking: Before and after Gramm-Leach-Bliley*. Yale Law School, Faculty Scholarship Series, Paper 1412.

Markham, J. W. (2010). The subprime crisis—A test-match for the bankers: Glass-Steagall vs. Gramm-Leach-Bliley. *University of Pennsylvania Journal of Business Law, 12*(4), 1081–1134.

McCarthy, F. W. (1984, March/April). The evolution of the bank regulatory structure: A reappraisal. *FRB Richmond Economic Review, 70*(2), 3–21.

Mishkin, F. S. (2006). How big a problem is too big to fail? A review of Gary Stern and Ron Feldman's too big to fail: The hazards of bank bailouts. *Journal of Economic Literature, XLIV*, 988–1004.

Santos, J. A. C. (2000, September). *Bank capital regulation in contemporary banking theory: A review of the literature* (BIS Working Paper No. 90). Basel, Switzerland: Bank for International Settlements.

Shull, B., & White, L. J. (1998). Of firewalls and subsidiaries: The right stuff for expanded bank activities. *Journal of Banking Law, 115*(May), 446–476.

Stevens, E. (2000, March 1). Evolution in banking supervision. *Federal Reserve Bank of Cleveland.*

Stiglitz, J. E. (2009, January). Capitalist fools. *Vanity Fair.*

Tarullo, D. K. (2011, November 9). *The evolution of capital regulation.* Paper presented at the Clearing House Business Meeting and Conference, New York, NY.

Tobin, J. (1963). Commercial banks as creators of money. In D. Carson (Ed.), *Banking and monetary studies* (pp. 408–419). Homewood, IL: Irwin.

33

EVOLVING ROLES OF REGULATORS IN THE IMPLEMENTATION OF ENVIRONMENTAL AND SOCIAL GOVERNANCE IN THE FINANCIAL INSTITUTIONS OF EMERGING MARKETS

Adeboye Oyegunle

Sustainable finance is becoming increasingly popular within the global financial sector. This is due to an increase in the integration of environmental and social (E&S) considerations into the activities of financial institutions. In the past, most financial institutions, especially banks, were non-committal to incorporating sustainability standards into their business decision processes and client relationship management (Jeucken, 2010). This is because banks perceived E&S concerns as secondary to their business, believing that such responsibilities are primarily the role of government (European Commission, 1997; Weber, 2014; Weber & Acheta, 2014). But as this practice grows, a greater number of banks are now adopting and integrating E&S considerations into their internal and credit decision processes.

Historically, sustainable finance development in the banking sector was fueled by the global drive toward sustainability, the impact of global sustainability codes, increasing stakeholder pressure, and the need to protect customers' funds (Mcgeachie, Kiernan, & Kirzner, 2005; OECD, 2010; Stampe, 2014). These factors have contributed to increasing the pressure on banks to incorporate E&S risk management into their businesses.

Events in the last few decades have also influenced this change as financial institutions come to realize that their business can be affected by the risks their clients are exposed to. Ultimately, banks are the pillar upon which the economy rests, and every client's decision has an indirect impact that exposes financial institutions to risks that could impact the safety of their funds. It thus became apparent to banks that they are not totally buffered from the negative impact of externalities, such as climate risks or other factors that could affect their business. This reality is increasingly becoming a source of institutional and regulatory concern as depositors' funds are at risk. In addition, the impact of new environmental legislation which makes banks liable and obliged to pay remediation costs exposes them to risk in the event of environmental pollution as a result of third-party activities (Wijen, Zoeteman, Pieters, & Seters, 2012).

Due to the potential effect on the safety of bank funds, the E&S implications of clients' activities, as well as environmental remediation legislation (e.g., CERCLA Law in the United States), banks in developed economies were compelled to develop internal voluntary E&S initiatives, codes, and governance structures (Azapagic & Perdan, 2000; UNEP Inquiry, 2014; Wijen et al., 2012). In time, these voluntary individual codes developed into collaborations among leading financial institutions and other organizations, which gave birth to environmental governance frameworks and organizations such as the Equators Principles (Oyegunle & Weber, 2015; UNEP Inquiry, 2014; Wright & Rwabizambuga, 2006).

Need for regulatory drive

The above scenario laid the foundation for the establishment of sustainable finance standards by banks in developed economies. It places responsibilities on financial institutions, particularly as it concerns their relationship with clients, the adoption of internal sustainable practices, and the expansion of credit risk management frameworks. In addition, it also presents a departure from traditional banking operations as it expands the definition of risk to include all aspects of uncertainties—financial and non-financial, and internal and external. This increased the interest of banks in the environmental implications of their business decisions, as well as in financial risks arising from E&S issues.

Beyond the environmental impact, these changes introduced a new dimension of social considerations, such as labor practices, ethics, and sustainable products and services, into the management of business relationships with clients. This compelled financial institutions to have a more robust lending decision-making process and forced them to take into consideration both financial and non-financial concerns while undertaking credit assessments. As a result, there has been an evolution in sustainable finance principles and standards, which has begun to challenge traditional banking practices. Banks responded to these challenges by including E&S considerations as an important part of their product portfolios, such as financial inclusion, female empowerment, and social financing. These developments were largely driven by collaborations between individual financial institutions in a bid to limit the environmental impact of economic growth on their business rather than rely on governments, which are often bogged down with bureaucracies (Thistlethwaite, 2014).

While these changes were relatively successful in developed economies, research has shown that the process is often purely institutionally driven with little or no regulatory input. This was exacerbated by the lack of clear global or national laws to help drive sustainable finance processes in leading economies (UNEP Inquiry, 2014, 2015a). Though government and regionally owned development banks are some of the institutions championing sustainable finance globally, regulatory acts are either totally non-existent or ineffective within developed countries. At the international level, the financial system is guided by a host of "soft law" agreements, standards, and principles, which are implemented at the national level and monitored through a variety of international mechanisms with little or no enforcement and control (Cotter, 2014; UNEP Inquiry, 2014). This lack of oversight has left individual institutions with the responsibility of leading and implementing sustainable finance systems.

Since standards are formulated by the banks themselves, they are non-uniform. Unfortunately, financial regulators do not see the need to integrate sustainable finance frameworks into existing financial regulations. Without effective regulation, addressing E&S issues is left to the discretion of banks, with no compliance mechanism, incentives, or standardization. As the driving force of an economy, the financial system's value lies in its ability to enable a dynamic and efficient sustainable system, which delivers inclusive sustainable development (UNEP Inquiry, 2015a). This responsibility expands the expectations from banks with regard to E&S issues and the need for regulatory guidance in its goal of supporting a sustainable economy.

Though the adoption of sustainable finance systems grew quickly in developed economies, it is sometimes implemented for no purpose other than "greenwashing." Compliance is often weak or non-existent, and as a result, challenges emerge in monitoring and evaluation, verification of claims, reliability of reports, and implementation of sustainability goals, while individual banks define sustainable objectives in ways that suit them and their businesses. This creates room for manipulation, as business and profit arguments often supersede environmental concerns. It also poses a challenge to those truly interested in making sustainable impacts, as there is no level playing field and expectations are left to the discretion of the implementing bank on the level of compliance required. Consequently, experts have argued that "to effectively shift to Sustainable Banking practices, banks require an enabling regulatory context that ensures a level playing field and provides the right economic incentives" (IFC, 2014). It could be said that despite the achievements of voluntary codes, there is still a need for legislative backing and states' involvement to positively influence attitudes of institutions, help enhance the sustainable economy, and build a stable financial system.

Evolving regulatory approach

The scenario described above is a challenge in the establishment of sustainable finance policies globally. Though it can be argued that voluntary approaches to sustainability have been relatively successful in driving sustainable finance approaches in Europe, North America, and other developed economies (Amalric, 2005), regulatory interest and enforcement has been low, while the expected role of banks and expectations in this domain have never been clearly defined (Busch, Bauer, & Orlitzky, 2015). Recently, there have been arguments regarding the need for regulatory intervention in financial sectors with respect to E&S issues (IFC, 2014; OECD, 2010; UNEP Inquiry, 2015b). The need for this intervention becomes more critical when considering that financial policymakers rarely incorporate the implications of green economy outcomes on financial performance and accountability while monitoring the efficient functioning of the financial system. This could be explained by the fact that the interpretations of macro-prudential roles do not incorporate sustainability challenges into the assessment and management of systemic risks (UNEP Inquiry, 2014). Stampe (2014) reaffirmed this assertion while arguing that the banking sector needs to significantly change its attitudes and actions to promote more responsible and sustainable business practices. Surprisingly, there is a growing trend in challenging this approach to sustainable finance management within the developing economies of Africa, Asia, and Latin America.

In recent years, regulators, banking associations, environment ministries, and central banks in emerging markets are taking up more environmental responsibilities by establishing sustainable finance policies. This development is aimed at enhancing banks' corporate social and environmental performance, increasing their capacity to strengthen the financial system, and helping to enhance the real economy. It is also changing the outlook in the adoption of sustainable finance practices among emerging economies (Cheung, Tan, Ahn, & Zhang, 2010; Hu & Scholtens, 2012). The involvement of regulators, which is a departure from practices in developed economies, is creating a new approach to sustainable development standards in the banking sector.

Contrary to the system in developed economies where individual institutions are leading the charge, regulators in emerging economies are taking up leading roles in the formulation of sustainability guidelines in the financial and banking sectors (Oyegunle & Weber, 2015). In most of the countries researched, it was discovered that not only are regulators leading the way, but there is obvious evidence of collaborations between banks and regulators. In one of the cases studied by Oyegunle and Weber (2015), the banks themselves actually invited the central bank to lead the process to ensure compliance. More importantly, the practice is gradually becoming a Sustainable Banking model that is fast-growing in emerging markets, which is a deviation from the voluntary system being practiced in more developed nations.

This raises questions on the ability of central banks and other bodies saddled with regulating the financial industry to combine sustainable finance management with other fiscal and regulatory responsibilities. Considering that this is essentially an unchartered territory, what lessons are there to learn from this evolving process? Could this have an effect on a hitherto untested operational model as regulatory bodies and apex banks take on more responsibilities in driving environmental and social governance in the financial sector?

Sustainable Banking regulations

Since China undertook the first environmental regulatory policy for its financial sector in 2007 (Aizawa & Chaofei, 2010; Bai, Faure, & Liu, 2013), there has been a series of developments in which more countries are adopting the process. Between early 2011 and April 2015, eight additional countries adopted sustainable guidance policies for their financial sector. Meanwhile, the two early adopters, China (2007) and Brazil (2008), have improved on the initial regulations, expanded their frameworks, or, in the case of Brazil, moved from a voluntary protocol to a more regulatory-driven policy.

The interesting issue here is that all the countries in this pool are emerging economies. Table 33.1 shows countries with established Sustainable Banking regulations. Also there are a number of countries that are currently in the process of developing their own sustainable finance regulations. This list is expected to keep increasing and changing as more developing countries implement this practice.

Below is a description of the regulations in three of the ten countries listed in Table 33.1. This will help provide some insights into the content and motivation of the Chinese, Bangladeshi, and Nigerian regulations.

Table 33.1 Countries with existing financial sustainability regulations

Country	*Region*	*Year of adoption*
Bangladesh	Asia	2011
Brazil	South America	2008/2009 (2014)
China	Asia	2007 (2014)
Colombia	Latin America	2011
Indonesia	Asia	2015
Kenya	Africa	2015
Mongolia	Asia	2014
Nigeria	Africa	2011
Peru	Latin America	2015
Vietnam	Asia	2015

Source: Based on IFC Sustainable Banking Network (IFC, 2015).

The Chinese regulation focuses on flexible interest rates for environmentally friendly and polluting industries (Zhao & Xu, 2012). Banks have to implement assessment and pricing systems for the environmental impacts of their clients and consequently vary the interest rates based on their compliance. Second, Chinese banks are obliged to reduce the amount of loans to polluting industries in their portfolio by assessing new businesses and terminating businesses with clients that are non-compliant to environmental regulations. Current challenges are in the assessment of environmental risks (Jin & Mengqi, 2011). However, these challenges were addressed recently by introducing new guidelines. The guidelines have two goals: to reduce the environmental impacts of industries, which is not something central banks usually deal with, and to help address financial risks for the financial sector arising from environmental concerns.

The Bangladeshi guideline is mandatory for all banks in the country. The guideline mandates banks to train their staff and raise their awareness on E&S issues, formulate their own E&S risk management framework, introduce sector-specific policies, and start reporting on E&S issues. The policy includes the classification of investments into high, medium, and low-risk E&S categories, and division into sector-specific aspects to complement the general due diligence guidelines. It also focuses on strengthening the banks' ability to evaluate environmental risks as part of lending and investment activities. Furthermore, the Central Bank of Bangladesh introduced some refinance schemes for commercial banks to finance environmentally sustainable projects, such as solar power, biomass plants, effluent treatment plants, and energy-efficient kilns. The interest rate for these schemes is lower than the market rate and therefore could be an effective means for improving the environmental standard in Bangladesh. Similar to China, the regulator tries to manage the financial sector's sustainability (Bangladesh Bank, 2011; Islam & Das, 2013; Kamruzzaman, 2012).

The Nigerian regulation consists of nine principles that cover E&S risk management, E&S footprint, human rights, women's economic empowerment, financial inclusion, E&S governance, capacity building, collaborative partnerships, and reporting (Central Bank of Nigeria, 2012). Nigeria's central bank mandated full adoption and implementation of these principles and guidelines by the financial institutions and promised to provide incentives for compliance. It also requires a quarterly report of progress from all banks with the expectation that all banks in Nigeria would have fully implemented and integrated the principles at the latest by December 2015. The reason why the Nigerian central bank introduced these guidelines was to guarantee access for their banks to foreign investments, protect core industries, and ensure a level playing field among banks. Financial institutions such as the Dutch FMO and German DEG which have investment in some of the banks in the country also require information about how sustainability is addressed by their investees.

To put this into perspective, central banks in developing countries have a relatively strong impact on the financial sector. A focus on the industry helps to enforce E&S regulations through financial incentives and control mechanisms aimed at creating a stable financial system. The reasons for establishing these regulations in developing countries could be (1) the financial sector in these countries is easier to control than in developed countries, (2) regulations are easier to enforce in one sector than in a number of different sectors with environmental impacts, and (3) external financiers influence regulators to guarantee the sustainable investment of foreign financial capital. Research is needed to analyze the presence, absence, and impact of these motivations in different countries.

Growing trend and need for intervention

Figure 33.1 gives an insight into the regional spread of countries that have adopted sustainable finance guidelines in the financial sector.

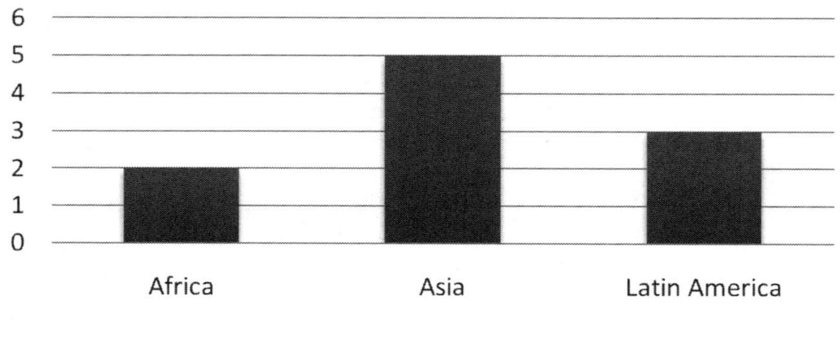

Figure 33.1 Country by region

This raises the question of why this process is growing in Latin America, Africa, and Asia, but is less popular in the developed economies of Europe and North America. While the main focus of this chapter is not to delve critically into this question, several factors bothering socio-political and economic interests wield substantial influence on the banking industry since financial institutions play a prominent role in the market evolution process. It is important to note that the development of a sustainable finance management system that is policy driven can help play this part, since it could ensure a positive impact on E&S behaviors, while playing a fundamental role that is critical to the activities of businesses with regards to sustainability expectations (Bernstein & Cashore, 2007).

This chapter observes that the influence of banks on businesses is an important platform through which developing economies derive capacity to help manage specific sectors and other social, environmental, and economic interests. An analysis of the structure of these policies indicates clear overarching principles for specific sectors of the respective economies, aimed at protecting those sectors. These could be creating standards for the lending process in key sectors of the economy (Bangladesh, Brazil, Mongolia, and Nigeria are good examples), focused on encouraging further growth and planning for the future (Indonesia, Vietnam), or aimed at protecting and encouraging environmental responsibility (Bangladesh, China, Brazil).

Despite the presence of respective guidelines for individual sectors in these policies, their importance and overall influence on the financial system cannot be undermined. They provide a platform for implementing sustainable finance frameworks, and direction for banks in the developing economies. This is what the soft laws of the voluntary global codes and individually driven sustainability initiatives of the developed economies have not been able to achieve. This is where the regulators come in. The challenge with most voluntary codes as they presently exist is that they are basically process or risk focused, rather than being outcome-based (Weber & Acheta, 2014). Also due to the diverse nature of sustainability, no singular principle, code, or process has been able to provide the necessary balance that will ensure compliance at all levels for businesses. This has resulted in weak enforcement and monitoring mechanisms as there are no compliance requirements to help guarantee adherence to standards (Missbach, 2004; O'Sullivan & O'Dwyer, 2009).

Guaranteeing a balanced field of play for those implementing and adhering to good environmental standards and their competition within the same markets is also one of the core reasons why regulatory influences are necessary. More importantly, there is the need for compliance, monitoring, and control to actualize the goals of providing sustainable finance with a positive impact on the social, environmental, and economic landscape of their constituencies. There is also the need to encourage and incentivize banks and support proactive environmental policies. Considering these needs and their importance, it is very obvious that allowing financial institutions to drive the process by themselves may leave them unable to achieve E&S goals in the long run. This could be detrimental to achieving a sustainable financial system. In its present format, the voluntary system can only encourage and enhance competition, but cannot enforce this process due to a lack of control. The fact is that the compliance and regulatory procedure may not only aid the implementation of E&S considerations, but can also contribute to ensuring sound E&S practices amongst borrowers of bank funds.

These realities have necessitated a need for regulators to be more involved in the creation of national enabling frameworks for sustainable banking. It has also created an emerging trend in which regulators are involved in banks' adoption of E&S practices, which is fast evolving and gradually expanding the responsibilities of regulators in the financial sector (UNEP Inquiry, 2015b). This chapter argues that banks can have a significant impact on the way economies and businesses conduct themselves in the near future in relation to climate change management and may provide a hint on what is to come in the future of sustainable finance governance. This is why the involvement of central banks, bankers associations, environment ministries, and other regulatory bodies is important. However, further research is needed to determine the impact of this participation, and whether or not it will produce a positive influence on the global banking sector.

Sustainable Banking process drivers

Having assessed the impact and evolving roles of regulators' participation in developing sustainable finance, one key point of discussion is why financial regulators engage in sustainability issues, and the main drivers of the process. The need to understand this is critical to the goal of examining the evolving roles of regulators with regards to the management of sustainable finance processes.

When implementing E&S practices, there is often no singular driver for the process across different climes. One notable factor in integrating sustainability issues is the existence of different incentives and drivers for respective central banks and regulatory agencies taking up this role. As described above, motivating factors differ between nations, as they act as the business case for integrating ESG at different places. While some countries are committed to this process for the purpose of managing their exposure to specific industries and sectors (e.g., China, Bangladesh), others are interested in its capacity to help the financial sector capitalize on opportunities, such as socio-economic and environmental support provided by development finance institutions (DFIs) (e.g., Nigeria).

One interesting observation is the role played by some of the banks themselves, such as FEBRABAN—the Brazilian Federation of Banks, the main representative body of the Brazilian banking sector, which championed the process in Brazil; the Bankers Committee in Nigeria, which led the process of adoption for the Nigerian Sustainable Banking principles; the Kenya Bankers Association (KBA); the Colombian Banking Association—ASOBANCARIA; and the Mongolian Bankers Association (MBA) (IFC, 2015). These associations not only contributed significantly to the establishment of the process, but in some instances invited regulators to take the lead and ensure compliance of their self-developed rules (Central Bank of Nigeria, 2012; FEBRABAN, 2012). The clear driver here is the need to align with global best practice and ensure adherence of their members to emerging global standards in the financial sector. Though the social, economic, and political climates are different from what is present in developed countries, by ensuring regulatory influence these groups have been able to ensure control and take the sustainability governance of the sector beyond self-governance, thus increasing influence among their members.

Attracting foreign investment and the need to protect business interests in some of the fastest-growing economies in the world may be another factor for implementing sustainable finance regulations in these countries. Despite their promising economic prospects, the business environment of emerging economies comes with inherent risk and lack of infrastructure, which no concerned regulator or apex bank will allow. The E&S implications of these risks are often too high, while weak regulation will have an adverse effect on the banking system. One way to mitigate these risks is to address the basic reasons for their existence, which can be accomplished through the provision of a sustainable financial system that ensures the environmental, social, and economic needs of society are addressed. This partly explains why the leading DFIs and the World Bank's IFC are promoting this process across different countries (Goodland, 2005; Grigoryeva, Morrison, Mason, & Gardiner, 2007).

What does the future hold?

One recurring question is to determine if regulators' participation in the sustainable finance process will catalyze any significant change for the financial sector. Unfortunately, sustainable finance adoption is still in its infancy, and it cannot be said for certain what effects the introduction of regulations will have on the banking industry and the emerging markets economy. This point is crucial considering the fact that this is an evolving process with little or no research into its function, implementation, or impacts across adopting countries. The current wave is less than a decade old, though quickly gaining popularity, which makes it more difficult to predict its effects.

Despite this uncertainty, the biggest economies in Africa, Asia, and Latin America have taken the lead with regards to the implementation of regulatory-driven E&S governance in the financial sector. The growth pattern of these economies in the last decade could be evident of a new trend toward consolidating current economic successes by strengthening social and environmental behaviors through the banking system. The rate at which other developing countries are also embedding this approach for their financial sector could also be an indicator as to what lies ahead. While this leaves room for optimism, the question of whether or not developing countries will take the lead in this space from the originator of the process remains unanswered. In other words, there is a need to determine whether the approach of these countries could help drive a regulator-led integration of sustainable systems in financial institutions globally, while encouraging leading economies to join the process. If this evolves, E&S considerations can be strengthened through legislation, which could help ensure that climate targets are met much faster, sustainable finance and products are promoted, social investment is increased, and businesses adhere to more responsible practices.

As discussed earlier in this chapter, there is also the need to address issues surrounding governance and socio-political concerns in developing economies. If not dealt with, it could be a hindrance to the progress made with regards to sustainable finance implementation in these countries. Despite these weaknesses, developing countries are showing remarkable progress while implementing this practice at their individual levels. For example, China's transition from guiding policies to full regulation between 2007 and 2014, as well as Brazil's progress from a voluntary code system to a regulatory-driven and sector-based compliance process between 2008 and 2014, shows a willingness to improve. Also, Indonesia's medium to long-term plans and Nigeria's ongoing implementation process, despite a change of government, demonstrate these countries' commitment to E&S management in the banking sector.

However, there is still a need for proper delineation of the regulated and regulator roles in ensuring effective implementation of the whole process. There needs to be defined roles that the established regulations, policies, and guidelines will play in this transition. This will go a long way in determining the adoptability of the process beyond its present implementation, and help determine if this is unique to emerging countries due to the nature of its operating environment, or if there are lessons that can be learnt with regards to regulatory requirements for driving sustainable finance practices in other spheres.

Beyond the enforcement and compliance push that regulators bring to the table, it also provides a platform for demonstrating governments' commitment to the E&S cause, particularly in the banking sector. This chapter has observed that these policies are easily adaptable to fit the respective country's needs. For instance, no two countries have the same guidelines or policy, regardless of similar structures (Nigeria and Mongolia; Colombia and Brazil (Protocol Verde)). Yet individual countries have developed their policies to suit their respective challenges, by addressing peculiar sustainability issues as need be. Through this approach, individual countries can develop focused policies and guidelines to help drive the process within their domain in line with their desired sustainable finance needs. Within developed economies, there is also hope that this practice will expand, considering the European Commission's December 2014 request for top organizations to provide non-financial reports and Turkey's sustainable finance principles, which have the commitment of the bankers association for voluntary adoption (Banks Association of Turkey, 2014; European Commission, October 22, 2014). Overall, this practice is still in its infancy and it will be interesting to see what difference it will make in the financial sector's impact on the E&S behaviors of businesses in the countries already implementing the process and whether or not others will adopt it in the near future.

References

Aizawa, M., & Chaofei, Y. (2010). Green credit, green stimulus, green revolution? China's mobilization of banks for environmental clean-up. *The Journal of Environment & Development, 19*(2), 119–114.

Amalric, F. (2005). *The equator principles: A step towards sustainability?* (CCRS Working Paper No. 01/05). Künstlergasse, Zurich, Switzerland: University of Zurich.

Azapagic, A., & Perdan, S. (2000). Indicators of sustainable development for industry: A general framework. *Process Safety and Environmental Protection, 78*(4), 243–261.

Bai, Y., Faure, M., & Liu, J. (2013). The role of China's banking sector in providing green finance. *Duke Environmental Law and Policy Forum, 24*, 89–279.

Bangladesh Bank. (2011). *Environmental Risk Management (ERM) guidelines for banks and financial institutions in Bangladesh*. Dhaka, Bangladesh: Bangladesh Bank.

Banks Association of Turkey (BAT). (2014). *Sustainability guidelines for the banking sector*. Retrieved August 20, 2015, from http://www.tbb.org.tr/en/Content/Upload/Dokuman/137/Sustainability-Guidelines-for-The-Banking-Sector.pdf

Bernstein, S., & Cashore, B. (2007). Can non-state global governance be legitimate? An analytical framework. *Regulation & Governance, 1*(4), 347–371.

Busch, T., Bauer, R., & Orlitzky, M. (2015). Sustainable development and financial markets: Old paths and new avenues. *Business & Society, 55*(3), 303–329.

Central Bank of Nigeria. (2012). *Nigerian sustainable banking principles*. Abuja, Nigeria: Central Bank of Nigeria.

Cheung, Y., Tan, W., Ahn, H.-J., & Zhang, Z. (2010). Does corporate social responsibility matter in Asian emerging markets? *Journal of Business Ethics, 92*(3), 401–413.

Cotter, L. (2014). *Incorporating sustainability in the principles of the financial regulatory system* (Internal Working Paper for the UNEP Inquiry).

European Commission. (1997). *The role of financial institutions in achieving sustainable development* (Report to the European Commission). London, UK: Delphi International LDT in Association with Ecologic GMBH.

European Commission. (2014, October 22). Directive 2014/95/EU of the European parliament and of the council of amending Directive 2013/34/EU as regards disclosure of non-financial and diversity information by certain large undertakings and groups.

FEBRABAN. (2012). FEBRABAN and the Brazilian banking sector support the United Nations conference on sustainable development (Rio +20).

Goodland, R. (2005). Strategic environmental assessment and the World Bank group. *International Journal of Sustainable Development and World Ecology, 12*(3), 245–255.

Grigoryeva, E., Morrison, N., Mason, C. H. J., & Gardiner, L. (2007). *Banking on sustainability: Financing environmental and social opportunities in emerging markets*. Washington, DC: World Bank.

Hu, V., & Scholtens, B. (2012). Corporate social responsibility policies of commercial banks in developing countries. *Sustainable Development, 22*(4), 276–288.

International Finance Corporation (IFC). (2014, March 2–4). *Sustainable banking network 2nd international sustainable banking forum*. Lagos, Nigeria (Conference Report). Washington, DC: IFC.

IFC. (2015). *Sustainable banking guidance from SBN members*. Retrieved August 15, 2015, from http://www.ifc.org/wps/wcm/connect/Topics_Ext_Content/IFC_External_Corporate_Site/IFC+Sustainability/Partnerships/Sustainable+Banking+Network/SB+Guidance+from+SBN+Members

Islam, M. S., & Das, P. C. (2013). Green banking practices in Bangladesh: A study on some selected commercial banks. *IOSR Journal of Business and Management (IOSR-JBM), 8*(3), 39–44.

Jeucken, M. (2010). *Sustainable finance and banking: The financial sector and the future of the planet*. Sterling, VA: Routledge.

Jin, D., & Mengqi, N. (2011). The paradox of green credit in China. *Energy Procedia, 5*, 1979–1986.

Kamruzzaman, M. (2012, October 21). *Corporate sustainability in the Bangladeshi banking sector: An overview*. Rochester, NY: Social Science Research Network.

Mcgeachie, S., Kiernan, M., & Kirzner, E. (2005). *Finance and the environment in North America: The state of play on the integration of environmental issues into financial research*. Canada: Risk Management Institute, University of Toronto, and Innovest Strategic Value Advisors.

Missbach, A. (2004). The equator principles: Drawing the line for socially responsible banks? An interim review from an NGO perspective. *Development, 47*(3), 78–84.

OECD. (2010). *Regulatory policy and the road to sustainable growth*. Paris: Organisation for Economic Co-operation and Development.

O'Sullivan, N., & O'Dwyer, B. (2009). Stakeholder perspectives on a financial sector legitimation process. *Accounting, Auditing & Accountability Journal, 22*(4), 553–587.

Oyegunle, A., & Weber, O. (2015). *Development of sustainability and green banking regulations—Existing codes and practices* (CIGI Papers Series No. 65). Waterloo, ON: CIGI.

Stampe, J. (2014). *Environmental, social and governance integration for banks: A guide to starting implementation*. Gland, Switzerland: WWF—World Wide Fund for Nature (formerly World Wildlife Fund).

Thistlethwaite, J. (2014). Private governance and sustainable finance. *Journal of Sustainable Finance & Investment, 4*(1), 61–75.

UNEP Inquiry. (2014). *Aligning the financial system with sustainable development—Insights from practice* (The Inquiry into the Design of a Sustainable Financial System, 2nd Update Briefing). Geneva, Switzerland: UNEP.

UNEP Inquiry. (2015a). *Aligning the financial system with sustainable development—Pathways to scale* (The Inquiry into the Design of a Sustainable Financial System, 3rd Progress Report). Geneva, Switzerland: UNEP.

UNEP Inquiry. (2015b). *Aligning the financial system with sustainable development—The coming financial climate* (The Inquiry into the Design of a Sustainable Financial System, 4th Progress Report). Geneva, Switzerland: UNEP.

Weber, O. (2014). The financial sector's impact on sustainable development. *Journal of Sustainable Finance & Investment, 4*(1), 1–8.

Weber, O., & Acheta, E. (2014). *The equator principles: Ten teenage years of implementation and a search for outcome* (CIGI Papers Series No. 24). Waterloo, ON: CIGI.

Wijen, F., Zoeteman, K., Pieters, J., & Seters, P. V. (Eds.). (2012). *A handbook of globalisation and environmental policy: National government interventions in a global arena* (2nd ed.). Cheltenham, UK: Edward Elgar Publishing.

Wright, C., & Rwabizambuga, A. (2006). Institutional pressures, corporate reputation, and voluntary codes of conduct: An examination of the equator principles. *Business and Society Review, 111*(1), 89–117.

Zhao, N., & Xu, X.-J. (2012). Analysis on green credit in China. *Advances in Applied Economics and Finance (AAEF), 3*(21), 501–506.

III.2
Trading the Environment

34

TRADING UNDER UNCERTAINTY

An investigation of the Australia emissions market

Deborah Cotton and Marija Buzevska

The Renewable Energy Target (RET) scheme was established as a direct response to the government's commitment to facilitate a smoother transition into a clean energy future for Australia through the reduction of emissions of harmful greenhouse gases (GHGs) from electricity generation. Specifically, the scheme aims to ensure that the equivalent of at least 20 percent of electricity is produced from renewable sources by 2020. Since its inception in 2001, the RET scheme has been the subject of constant review and policy restructure. Despite the long-run operation of the scheme, trading on the market is light and a far reach from operating as a developed financial market. In particular, with respect to liquidity, the market displays potential issues regarding a low frequency of trade, with only as few as 113,023 certificates traded on a weekly basis. This study aims to determine whether an elevated ambiguity surrounding the RET scheme is an explanatory factor for these issues. Principally, the research centers on answering the question—"Are observed inefficiencies in the RET in Australia attributable to a presence of elevated ambiguity in the market?"

This chapter considers various factors regarding the nature of the RET market and its participants. The primary research focus is deconstructed into three distinct objectives tailored to successfully answer this question. First, this chapter considers the presence of ambiguity in the RET. The aim is to determine whether there exists a level of ambiguity in this market that is greater than the uncertainty presented in other market trading. Second, the study distinguishes the principal indicators and determinants of ambiguity in the emissions market. With regard to these factors, the focus then draws in on analyzing the association between the level of ambiguity in the RET and the low-frequency trading in this market. We investigate investors' behavior in this market given the evidence for the prevailing level of uncertainty in the Australian emissions market.

Existing literature examining the effects of ambiguity in a financial market proposes that it negatively affects trading involvement particularly regarding volume and frequency of trade. Easley and O'Hara in their 2009 study determine that rational investors have a higher propensity to discontinue trading on the market in order to avoid ambiguity. Routledge and Zin (2009) also arrive at a similar conclusion and state in their study that the presence of ambiguity not only reduces the willingness of participants to trade on the market but also reduces the overall effectiveness of the market.

The empirical study on which this chapter is based differs from many others in this field of research which observe the effects of ambiguity in a controlled experiment setting. This study employs a primary data collection approach and presents empirical evidence of the ambiguity concept in a currently operating market. An online questionnaire aimed at the participants in the RET is used as the fundamental research method, alongside supplementary exploratory forms of research in the form of structured interviews and a focus group.

The concluding findings of this chapter are aligned with current literature surrounding the matter. Cotton and Michayluk (2014) used trading volume and the bid-ask spread in the RET market to measure levels of ambiguity. They found that information in the market increased volume and reduced the bid-ask spread, indicating that it improves effectiveness and reduces the level of ambiguity. This indicates that in the RET there is an elevated degree of ambiguity for market participants particularly concerning the future state of the market. This chapter aims to determine the major cause/s of this ambiguity through surveying the market participants.

This chapter is structured as follows:

- Contextual basis
- Overview of past literature on ambiguity in financial markets and the mechanisms of the Australian emissions market
- Methodology and data
- Presentation and interpretation of the results
- Concluding remarks to the research findings.

The Renewable Energy Target

The primary purpose of the RET is to reduce GHGs by instigating a greater level of renewable energy technology in electricity generation and ensuring that renewable energy sourcing is ecologically sustainable. This objective is addressed through a set target that guarantees that the equivalent of at least 20 percent of electricity is produced from renewable sources by 2020.

The RET scheme (initially established as the Mandatory Renewable Energy Scheme under the "Renewable Energy (Electricity) Act 2000") commenced in April 2001, prior to Phase I of the European Emissions Trading Scheme (EU ETS). In 2011, the RET scheme was subdivided into two core components that make up the overall scheme but operate as separate and distinct markets. These are the Large-scale Renewable Energy Target (LRET) sector and the Small-scale Renewable Energy Scheme (SRES) sector. The decision to divide the RET was guided by a concern that a rapid uptake of small-scale mechanisms in the market would have a crowding-out effect of investments in large-scale renewable energy systems.

The RET operates comparably to a cap-and-trade scheme, in which tradable Renewable Energy Certificates (RECs) are issued and exchanged on an over-the-counter basis. One REC is a contract representative of 1 megawatt hour of renewable electricity produced. Creation of certificates in the RET market arises from the generation of renewable energy by an eligible power station (or creator). Permits are created for generation that lies above the required baseline volume for firms. Firms may also have a signed power purchase agreement (PPA) that entitles liable entities to a set quantity of permits that are produced by a renewable energy project or station.

Participating companies in the RET market may at times also simultaneously take the role of liable entity to purchase as well as a creator to sell REC. Both the LRET and SRES markets also encompass voluntary investors that create further demand for renewable energy permits over the mandated requirement. The trade system is designed with the intention of establishing a market that provides ease-of-transfer and financial incentives to both large-scale renewable power stations and the owners of small-scale systems.

In 2014 the RET was undergoing key policy reviews and changes, making the time of this survey of particular interest when discussing possible improvements to the efficiency and effectiveness of the scheme. A topical adjustment to the marketplace in recent times has also been the repeal of "The Clean Energy Legislation (Carbon Tax Repeal) Act 2014," which abolishes the carbon pricing mechanism from July 1, 2014, after only 3 years in operation. This occurred due to a change in the party in power in the federal government in Australia. Despite the revoked legislation not having direct implications on firms until the following financial year, it presents an example of some of the radical changes driven by the change of government and the consistency in changes with the election of a new government. Jotzo, Jordan, and Fabian (2012) studied the uncertainty surrounding the carbon tax, stating that the primary reason for uncertainty surrounding the future of the carbon market is the lack of bipartisan political support.

An added measure of revision to the scheme is the proposal to establish a full two-way link between the RET scheme and the EU ETS which would see Australia sharing a portion of its REC. The arrangement to expand the exchange transparency of both systems is proposed to start from July 2018 and would allow entities to access international carbon markets, including the EU ETS and eligible Kyoto units that are generated by renewable energy projects or sequestration activities under the Kyoto Protocol. It is uncertain if this will occur due to the aforementioned change in federal government.

The future outlook of the market displays a pronounced dependency on the actions of the government in power. In more recent developments, the Abbott government announced support to scale back the RET from the current 41,000 GWh to approximately 26,000 hours by 2020. It appears that the scheme faces an elevated level of uncertainty of its future not only through the economic risks of climate change but also through the inconsistencies and variability of decisions taken by the government about the most effective ways in which Australia can combat global warming.

Literature review

Ambiguity in financial markets

Knight (1921) theorized that known odds or measurable risk could be defined as "risk" and unknown odds or immeasurable and unquantifiable risk as "uncertainty." Ellsberg (1961) implemented this idea and provided an alternate way of observing subjective preferential behavior. He tested the effects of ambiguity and uncertainty on the choice behavior of individuals through his notable experiment, the Ellsberg Paradox. Ellsberg conducted a controlled experiment in which he observed the behavioral preferences of individuals in an uncertain or ambiguity-driven context. The study implies that subjects do not display a preference for one particular object over the other as may be understood under the Savage (1954) theory; rather they prefer definite to indefinite information or, in this case, known over unknown probability of outcomes. His study furthers the notion that investors avoid uncertainty or ambiguity in probabilities and thus can be classified as ambiguity-averse individuals.

More recent papers regarding the uncertainty concept have instead focused their efforts on studying how ambiguity affects the behavior of agents by determining the change in their trading practices, frequency, and volume of trade and other observable characteristics. Studies such as Easley and O'Hara (2010) have also looked at the consequent changes in the micro and macro structure of the market. By testing the effects of ambiguity and risk on investors in a controlled experiment setting, Easley and O'Hara repeatedly arrive at the same conclusion, that is, "non-participation arises from the rational decision by some traders to avoid ambiguity" (Easley & O'Hara, 2009, p. 1840). Routledge and Zin (2009) suggest that ambiguity reduces the desirability to trade, adding that this market ambiguity also has a negative effect on the overall effectiveness of the market. An earlier study by Easley, Hvidkjaer, and O'Hara (2005) states that mispricing (as a flow-on effect from uncertainty about the true value of an asset) can also lead to non-participation by traders in the market. Caskey (2009) also studied mispricing induced by ambiguity aversion in the marketplace, as well as developing a model that shows that aggregate information can reduce the impact of ambiguity aversion on the equity premium and non-participation in these stock markets. Sarin and Weber (1993) have studied this non-involvement effect and illustrate that ambiguous assets induce a sense of psychological discomfort for decision-makers, varying with the level of ambiguity aversion they display. Bossaerts, Ghirardato, Guarnaschelli, and Zame (2010) find that the presence of ambiguity and consequently ambiguity-averse investors indirectly affect prices in the market by increasing the per capita amount of risk that is to be shared among the marginal investors. Ohn (2013) examines the effect of elevated levels of ambiguity during the global financial crisis and concludes that the uncertainty surrounding the payoffs of assets following the crash reduced the liquidity in asset markets. Consequently, a "no trade region" emerges in which strategic and value traders cannot agree on a price to clear the market. Easley and O'Hara (2010) propose a similar argument of a "trading freeze," which they find occurs despite the active positing of bid-and-ask offers, albeit at largely different prices. Easley and O'Hara (2005) extend the analysis of ambiguity effects in financial markets by stating that uncertainty is amplified in developing and new financial markets. Grossman and Stiglitz (1980) similarly find that the value of information is higher in ambiguous markets than in markets with or without minimal ambiguity. This finding is of particular importance in the study of the RET scheme due to the nature of the market itself despite its long-running term.

Our analysis of the RET scheme centers on observing inefficiencies and specifically uncertainty measures through macro-structural characteristics and features of the market. Consequently, the research is not concerned so much with the probability distribution regarding specific asset payoffs but rather the overall behavioral effects of uncertainty and ambiguity on trader behavior. However, we do make a distinction between measures of risk and measures of uncertainty by recognizing that in a seemingly underdeveloped market such as the RET, traded assets seemingly display unknown and ambiguous probabilities of payoffs due to the lack of complete knowledge on the assets' cost-and-benefit structure. Hence, for the purpose of the study, we examine the aggregate presence of ambiguity in the RET and subsequently observe the overall effects on investors' behavior. The terms "ambiguity" and "uncertainty" will be representative of a unified concept describing an environment in which there is an absence of complete knowledge.

Emissions trading markets and the RET

The Australian emissions market has received little attention, with the predominant portion of environmental markets research directing efforts on investigating the EU ETS and its micro-structural characteristics. Cotton and Trück (2013) provide a detailed review of the RET scheme in Australia as the central emissions trading market amongst a few smaller statewide schemes. Jotzo et al. (2012) also examine the role of the carbon tax in Australia, through a survey on experts directly involved in decision making on carbon-intensive investments.

They find that even these experts do not have reliable information about the policy outlook and future market developments, signifying that policy instability, due to a lack of cross-party political support, is the primary reason. A further significant finding states that investors benefit from ceasing to enter the market when experiencing an absence of complete and reliable information. Hence the value in waiting for better information may be greater than the potential cost savings from entering the carbon market.

When testing the efficiency of newer and developing markets such as the EU ETS and the RET schemes, research on ambiguity effects in markets by Easley and O'Hara (2005, 2009, 2010) has been the central theme for a growing number of studies. In particular Easley and O'Hara (2010) identify an amplified effect of ambiguity in markets that are newly established and developing. Despite the long-running operation of the RET in Australia, constant reviews and regime amendments to the schemes additional to an indicated low volume of trade categorize this scheme as an undeveloped financial market.

Grubb and Neuhoff (2006) contribute to the research on structural and behavioral characteristics of emissions trading markets and find that firms choose to delay investment until they gain more knowledge about the future prices and allocation levels and are able to make more informed decisions. Jotzo and Pezzey (2007) develop the idea further by concluding that a primary obstacle for commitment to full participation in emissions reductions is uncertainty in the market and of future outcomes and payoffs. In a parallel tone, Pinkse (2007) explores the intentions of multinational firms to participate in emissions trading and in its infancy stages of development through a solicited questionnaire. Findings from the survey indicate a tendency for companies to refrain from participation on the market, and those that participated did so due to industry pressure.

Method and data

Survey design

This chapter utilizes a questionnaire for the attainment of unique market data from the RET scheme that contributes to the level of information in this market. Moreover, measures of uncertainty and market ambiguity have not been particularly well defined in past literature—hence a case study analysis of a variety of market features and the behaviors of its participants paints a more complete picture of the market situation. Preliminary groundwork in the evaluation and assessment of past RET documentation and publications was the first step undertaken to gather knowledge about the state of the market at the time of writing. As the first step in the primary data component of the research, we developed a pilot survey to examine factors of interest surrounding the trading practices of participants, their knowledge of market rules and regulations, and the future outlook of the market. This initial version formed the basis for the final distributed questionnaire. Two structured interviews were held with brokerage firms who trade in this market. We conducted further exploratory research within a small focus group setting with a participating trading firm in the market. This was then circulated to a group of academics from the Finance and Marketing Faculties at the University of Technology Sydney for revision on areas of content, design, and execution.

The final version of the questionnaire consists of 34 questions and takes an approximate 10 minutes to complete.[1] The complete survey was administered online with promotion and distribution assistance by the Australian Financial Markets Association (AFMA) and the brokerage company Next Generation Energy (NGES), over the period of June–September 2014. The sampling method is therefore dependent on the clientele of the administrating firms, so can accordingly be classified as a combination of random and convenience sampling. The research and distribution methods comply with the directives set forth by the UTS Human Research Ethics Committee (HREC)[2] to maintain anonymity amongst survey respondents and de-identification of individuals in the survey process.

The concluding usable sample of data comprises 32 unique firm responses. The quality of the information gained from the questionnaire regarding the consistency and reliability of responses is maintained upon a number of factors. The distributing parties, that is, AFMA and NGES, assisted in lifting the credibility of the questionnaire with clients as well as providing a trusted client base for the sample. Anonymity of responses further ensured that participants are less inclined to refrain from providing firm-specific information about trading that may be considered sensitive, and helped to maintain the completeness of information collected.

The entirety of the emissions trading market in Australia involves an estimated 370 firms. The largest sections of participants are liable entities creating or purchasing permits in the REC market under the National Greenhouse and Energy Reporting Act (NGER). Our study captures 8.64 percent of this market, which is on par with the rate of return of similar-type studies utilizing questionnaires as the primary mode for data collection (Bancel & Mittoo, 2004; Brounen, De Jong, & Koedijk, 2004; Graham & Harvey, 2002).

The survey itself is arranged in four sections addressing: (1) the trading practices of participants, (2) the trading procedures of participants, (3) participants' knowledge of market rules and regulations, and (4) participants' future outlook of the market.

In deciding the structural standpoint and content of the survey more closely, we drew on notable findings about microstructure and the effects of ambiguity by Easley and O'Hara (2010). The chapter notes that when considering the determinants of non-participation in the financial marketplace, trading practices, trading procedures, and market rules all play an influential role in the removal of "worst case" distributions for investors and in turn allow for market participation that may otherwise not occur. With regard to the above findings, this particular questionnaire specifically examines the trading practices of participants, the trading procedures of participants, and participants' knowledge of market rules and regulations as three distinct and potentially influential aspects. The predominant focus with the use of this finding is to uncover their influence on the level and type of uncertainty in the Australian emissions market and see their potential effects on trading.

The fourth section of the survey follows an approach by Anderson, Ghysels, and Juergens (2009) which proposes the use of disagreement among forecasters to measure ambiguity at a macroeconomic level. The questionnaire examines investors' view on the future outlook of the market with the aim of determining overall market sentiment on whether uncertainty or ambiguity play a significant role in influencing current and upcoming trade volumes and practices. This section broadly supports the previous three sections in shedding light on not only the presence or lack thereof of ambiguity or uncertainty in the market but also the type or rather the source of this uncertainty and ambiguity. The analysis is extended to detect investors' level of confidence in the future of the market by asking them to estimate the potential price movement of LGC and STC certificates in 1 year. The survey also obtains the demographic firm characteristics of the participants.

Data

The data collected by the questionnaire predominantly measures the categorical variables of a dichotomous, nominal, or ordinal nature through the use of open and closed format questions. Hence non-parametric measures are the center of the analysis. Supplementary to a regression analysis, a number of qualitative and descriptive measures such as frequency plots, coefficient of variation, and text and clustering analysis methods were also employed. Tackling the research question by taking a case study approach aids a process through which we encompass both quantitative methods and extract meaning from qualitative responses for a greater understanding of the dynamics within single settings (Eisenhardt, 1989).

In the context of this study we aim to explore the ambiguity present at a market level rather than a firm level—hence our study draws from papers like Anderson et al. (2009). These emphasize aggregate measures of disagreement of investors' forecasts and use this as a measure of ambiguity about the future movements of markets. We follow and adapt this approach and subsequently make an assessment about the heterogeneity of beliefs of agents and its flow on effects on trading in the market. Specifically, our study employs a forward-looking measure that captures the perceptions of decision makers in the market and measures the coefficient of variation in the dispersion of this response. This is accomplished through questioning respondents to estimate the future movements in price of both LGC and STC.

Ambiguity in the RET is also observed qualitatively through clustering and subsequent deconstruction of open text data. Directive questioning on the inadequacies in the market also aids the process of identifying whether additive uncertainty surrounding particular market factors plays a role in elevating the overall degree of ambiguity in the market. Through use of the same process, the survey also extracts the primary indicators of this state of the market or, rather, the uncertainty in the current and future state of the RET.

With respect to the observed indicators of increased ambiguity in the RET, the succeeding analysis focuses on the effects of these indicators on investor behavior in this market. One way in which this relationship is explored is through the use of a robust least square regression to test whether there exists a causal impact of indicators of ambiguity or proposed "ambiguity proxies" on trading in the LRET and the SRES. Specifically, we use the number of certificates traded in the 2013/2014 financial year as a reasonable proxy for level of involvement or participation in the market. Given this analysis, we are able to make reference and principally test previous theories proposed by Caskey (2009), Easley and O'Hara (2009), and Routledge and Zin (2009), which state that ambiguity reduces the desirability to trade. Proposed measures or proxies for ambiguity are a combination of recognized ambiguity proxies in existing literature (Anderson et al., 2009) and an adaptation of these findings based on the survey data collected. Moreover, indicators and determinants of this uncertainty in the RET identified in the previous section are incorporated into the empirical analysis. The two regression models vary only by the dependent variables, that is, the same variables for ambiguity as well as controls are used. Model measures and proxies are presented in Table 34.1.

Quantitative analysis on the causal impact of certain ambiguity proxies forms only a part of a more detailed study of the overall influence of these proxies on investor behavior and on market effectiveness. In his review of case study research, Mitchell (1983) states that case studies such as the one studied in this chapter are not based on statistical inference but rather the inference of the theoretical links among the features in the case study. He further states that validity of this kind of analysis is based not upon the typicality or representativeness of the case but on the power of the theoretical reasoning. Thus, we are cautious in making strong inferences of the effects of ambiguity and extend our analysis further, to incorporate a more inclusive and correct view of how the market is influenced. To achieve this, the questionnaire designates directive questioning and open text analysis.

The complete sample of 32 participating firms is described in Tables 34.2 and 34.3. The average Surrendered Eligible Emissions Units for both markets collectively is 836,458 units.

Table 34.1 Description of the variables used in the empirical model

Variables	*Description*	*Mean*	*S.D.*
Y_1	Log LGC certificates turnover in the last financial year	10.2354	4.5728
Y_2	Log STC certificates turnover in the last financial year	11.7411	3.5863
Complexity	1 if participant indicated "increased complexity of market restructure" following market split		
Information transparency	1 if indicated "strongly agree" to the statement: "The environmental authority (the Clean Energy Regulator) has helped firms understand the rules behind the trading process and to trade emissions"		
Rule clarity	1 if participant ranked "market rules are not clear" first as a negative effect on the efficiency of the market		
Climate change	1 if participant indicated that the scheme has been "effective in tackling climate change"		
Comparative risk	1 if participant indicated this market as "higher risk" than other developed financial markets		
Price discovery	1 if participant indicated that the role of price discovery is ineffective		
Firm size (employees)	Firm size measured by the number of employees		
PPA[a]	1 if the firm has an existing PPA		

a Power purchase agreement (PPA) is a contract between a liable entity and a power generator that sets the commercial terms for the sale of electricity between the two parties.

Table 34.2 Sample demographics

Industry type	*N*	*%*
Utilities	16	57.1
Manufacturing/industrials	3	10.7
Financial services	3	10.7
Mining	3	10.7
Other	3	10.7
Firm size (employees)		
Micro (<4)	4	14.29
Small (5–19)	1	3.57
Medium (20–199)	8	28.57
Large (>200)	15	53.57
Total	28	100.0

Note: Missing values accounting for n = 4 have been excluded from the table.

This number is closely aligned with the figure reported by the Clean Energy Regulator for the past year, which stands at 748,384 units on average (CER, 2014). Utility firms are naturally both a creator of renewable energy and an emitter of GHGs and thus are liable participants of both markets. Sole trading in the LRET and SRES markets attracts a more specialized caliber of participants such as individuals or households trading STC permits for solar energy production.

Table 34.3 Large-scale Renewable Energy Target and Small-scale Renewable Energy Scheme market characteristics and segmentation

			Large-scale Renewable Energy Certificates		*Small-scale Renewable Energy Certificates*	
		%[a]	*Mean*	*S.D.*	*Mean*	*S.D.*
Type of market participation	*Liable entity*	34.40%	695,189	618,746	1,286,735	1,281,520
	Creator of certificates	31.30%	129,979	248,293	280,452	386,349
	Both liable and a creator	25.00%	859,375	1,330,517	1,341,250	1,598,029
	Voluntary	6.30%	1,348,698	1,062,502	1,038,510	52,341
	Non-participant	3.10%	n.a.	n.a.	n.a.	n.a.
Trading approach	*Active*	84.60%	448,047	298,698	537,760	620,952
	Passive	15.40%	597,396	900,043	986,235	1,241,933
Purchase power agreement	*Yes*	35.70%	1,056,079	1,111,562	1,444,504	1,393,668
	No	64.30%	361,749	608,797	696,390	1,027,638
Industry	*Utilities*	59.40%	350,674	736,125	249,563	421,219
	Manufacturing and industrials	9.40%	876,386	1,041,661	1,576,371	1,425,553
	Financial services	9.40%	407,431	329,030	379,507	602,771
	Mining	9.40%	5,000	5,000	230,000	194,679
	Other	12.50%	443,597	266,387	765,014	537,814

a Percentage proportions are based on full sample (n = 32).

Results

Presence of additive ambiguity on a market level

With consideration of the aforesaid methodologies on ambiguity measures[3] outlined in the empirical design of the study, our chapter utilizes the dispersion amongst the market attitudes of respondents in the LGC and STC as an acceptable factor measuring ambiguity presence in the RET. We measure the coefficient of a variation of answers about the efficiency of price discovery in the current and future states of the market, valued on a five-point Likert scale. When questioned about the price fairness of the markets, we observe a large disparity in opinions. The LGC market is more consistently specified as being priced at a more fair value by participants (77.2 percent). This result is not anticipated due to the lower frequency of trade and thus liquidity of market in comparison to the SRES. However, we note a very high variability of attitudes in the newly established SRES (97.6 percent). This is a possible indication that the market remains in the development stages—thus there is an amplified effect of ambiguity (dispersion amongst participants, attitudes). This particular point is observable as evidence for the amplified effects of ambiguity on investors (Easley & O'Hara, 2009).

Concurrently, respondents were asked to provide an estimation of the future price movements of the schemes. The results shown in Table 34.4 display a higher variability of opinion in the future of the LRET market in comparison to the SRES market. This is in contrast to the current price discovery discussed above.

The perception of the future outlook of the scheme was further examined on a macro policy level across both markets. A clustering analysis of these perceptions reveals that the stability of the current government and the volatility of their proposed future actions are of primary concern for investors. Additional evidence of indicated inefficiencies saw participants

Table 34.4 The direction the respondents see the price of LGCs and STCs changing over the course of the next year

	LRET	*SRES*
Mean-centered COV	44.1%	31.0%
Median-centered COV	45.3%	37.0%

expressing a stronger view towards the repeal of two schemes and the re-establishment of a unified Renewable Energy Certificates market. Respondents stated: "The willingness and even possibility of governments changing the legislation and regulations is a significant uncertainty and increases volatility" (RET Survey, 2014).

Indicators and determinants of ambiguity

Descriptive analysis of the questionnaire data reveals the general consensus amongst respondents is that the level of risk associated with trading renewable energy certificates is perceived to be much higher when compared to risks encountered when trading well-recognized financial instruments in a more transparent market. Respondents attributed this factor primarily to the uncertainty stemming from the volatility of regulatory changes as well as the insufficient transparency of the market. Current state uncertainty and future uncertainty identify as the two prime indicators of this view.

By far the most prevalent and recurring argument throughout the survey is the idea that there is an elevated uncertainty as an effect of constant and volatile changes to the scheme by the governing body. The structural reform of the scheme such as the aforementioned split into two distinct targets (the LGC and the STC) in 2011 is observed as a pivotal point of adjustment in this market. In particular, consistent contingent claims such as that of the government review of the efficiency of the scheme, the set target, and changes to the trading rules in the market are essential in gaining a complete understanding of the possible indicators of ambiguity for these investors. A lack of cross-party political support is seen as a fundamental portion of the regulatory uncertainty surrounding the market. The data collected indicates 88 percent of responses indicate that regulatory risk is the leading negative contributor to the effectiveness and efficiency of the scheme compared with 12 percent indicating illiquidity as the main contributor.

Moreover, respondents who scaled the average level of market uncertainty in the RET as higher than that contained within other financial markets attributed this characteristic to the constant regulatory changes by the governing body. A predominant portion of reactions point to an unforeseeable policy regime and the unpredictability of these regime changes as the main concerns regarding the uncertainty of the future of the market—"Other markets face regulatory uncertainty hurdles; perhaps the main issues for RET is that the uncertainties are not well flagged in advance and the terms of reference that create the uncertainties are too broad" (RET Survey, 2014). Others believe that the government is overstepping its governing position and is instead imposing constant changes to the scheme that are driven by political and not by economic principles: "Government needs to stop reviewing the scheme and let the market work" (RET Survey, 2014). Remaining participants indicated that inefficiency in the liquidity of the market was the primary basis for the level of uncertainty for investors. Additional evidence for this view depicts that the consistent regulatory reforms by the government are a significant contributor to the issue of efficiency in this market. Figure 34.1 presents this.

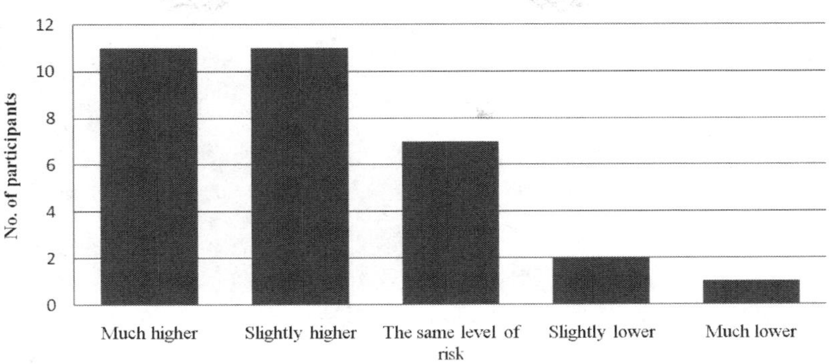

Figure 34.1 The level of risk of the REC market in comparison to other financial markets

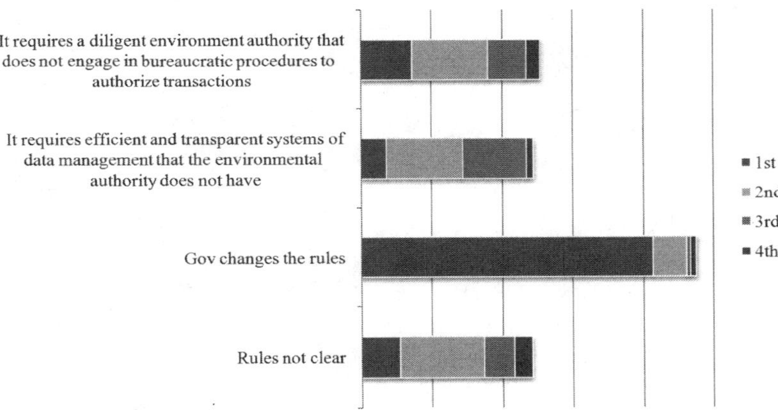

Figure 34.2 Ranking of the most significant elements that negatively affect the efficiency of the scheme

> The true value of the asset is unknown so that makes it slightly more difficult to deal in compared to known markets (the risk lies with the fact that you don't really know the value of the asset you're trading).
>
> *(RET Survey, 2014)*

When asked to rank the main elements negatively affecting performance, changes in the rules was clearly top, as shown in Figure 34.2.

This result is particularly illustrative of the theory proposed by Easley and O'Hara (2009), which demonstrates that regulation of unlikely events can induce stability in the market and intensify participation by decreasing the effects of ambiguity. In this particular context, the ambiguity effects are amplified—hence the regulatory risk may be perceived to be greater than that during times of certainty and stability of the future market outlook.

Despite the long-term operation of the RET scheme since 2001, there seems to remain an uncertainty surrounding the value of the assets traded. We observed this as further evidence of the scheme's shortcomings seen through the observation of investors' perceptions of the primary benefits for trading in this market. Over half (67 percent and 53 percent respectively) of the participants indicate that an obligatory rather than financially beneficial motive is the primary intention behind trading in the LRET and the SRES. The results are presented in Figures 34.3 and 34.4. Additionally, we observed responses such as:

> The true value of the asset is unknown so that makes it slightly more difficult to deal in compared to known markets (the risk lies with the fact that you don't really know the value of the asset you're trading).
>
> *(RET Survey, 2014)*

The issue of transparency in the market was looked at, with respondents asked to indicate whether they agreed with the following statement: "The environmental authority (the Clean Energy Regulator) has helped firms understand the rules behind the trading process and to trade emissions." We found 62.5 percent indicated they agree with the statement, with 21.9 percent of respondents indicating a "neutral" response. A significant proportion of people who use brokerage firms for trading also believe that these brokerage firms increase the level of transparency in the market. We find that participants indicate a lack of confidence about the benefits of trading and hence the true value of the asset, as has been shown above. Conversely, a significant portion of respondents (50 percent) strongly agreed that the scheme is efficient when it comes to its effectiveness in tackling climate change. This may be simply indicating the scheme is effective despite its observed inefficiencies.

Despite a negligible number of the subsample of passive participants in the market, it is interesting to note that 75 percent of these types of participating firms indicated that they are

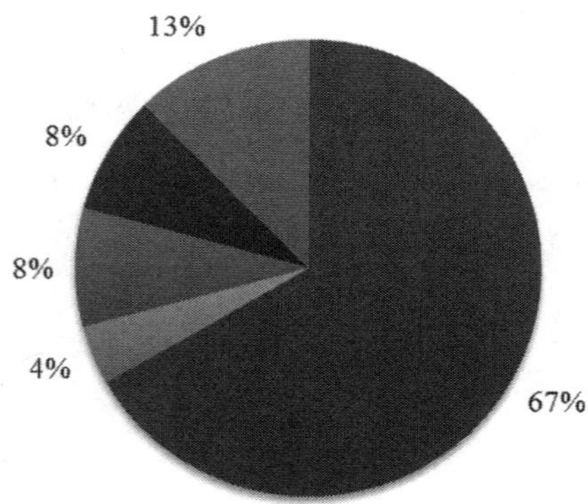

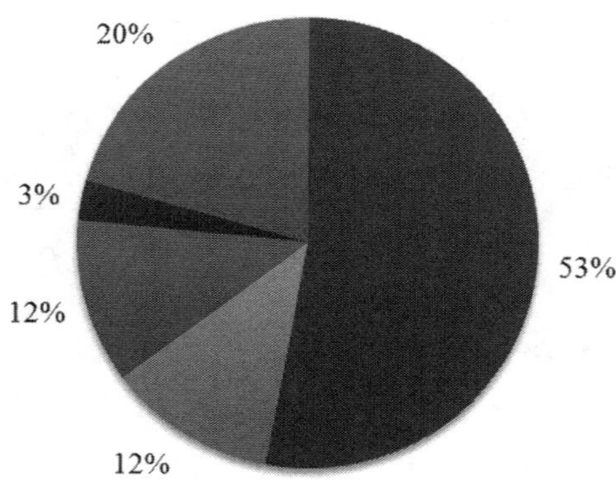

Figures 34.3 and 34.4 The indicated primary benefits of trading in the LRET and SRES

in fact not considering voluntarily entering the market when asked whether they would consider doing so in the near future. Lack of market qualities such as a strong market liquidity, potential profitability, and hedging benefits were signified as the primary reasons for this stance within the portion of non-active participants. Although the minimal size of the result is not a representative sample of non-participating stakeholder firms in the Australian emissions market, it contributes to the argument about the inefficiency of the scheme as a completely financially sound and beneficial trade for institutional investors.

Effects of ambiguity on trading

The respondents were questioned on the impact of the scheme split on the frequency of trade, to which 68.75 percent indicated a difference in trade frequency. This segment of participants was further asked to identify the primary sources of change within this period. The results are displayed in Figure 34.5.

A Spearman statistical test on the relationship of these variables reveals a significantly positive correlation between respondents who specified a "decreased frequency of trading" following the REC market split and respondents who indicated that the primary reason for this shift in trading as "increased uncertainty in the outlook and future of the industry." Interpretation of this result modestly serves as a basis for further investigation into the relationship between these variables.

Again utilizing the Spearman correlation test of analysis of the association between non-parametric categorical variables, we have found that there is a significant negative relationship between the amount of certificates traded in the LGC market and the indicator variable "Rules not clear" in Figure 34.2. Referring back to our classification of ambiguity, this result can be seen as possible evidence for the negative relationship between ambiguity and the level of trading in the market. Additional to this we observe a significant relationship (99 percent confidence level) between the respondents who feel that "the governing body changes the rules constantly" and those respondents who have indicated, "It requires a diligent environment authority that does not engage in bureaucratic procedures to authorize transactions." This result may be indicative

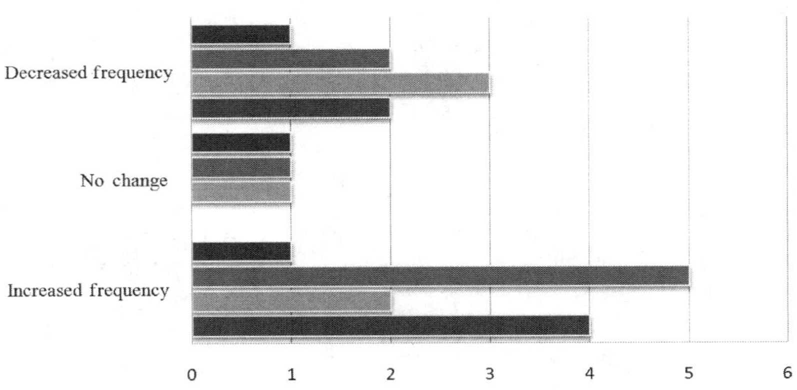

Figure 34.5 Reasons for change in trade frequency following the scheme split in 2011

Table 34.5 Parameter estimates and p-values; for variable names, see Table 34.1

Variable	*Y_1 (LGC turnover)*			*Y_2 (STC turnover)*		
	Coeff.	*S.E.*	*P-value*	*Coeff.*	*S.E.*	*P-value*
Constant	7.7747	1.5964	0.0000	10.5034	1.3408	0.0000
Complexity	2.7764	1.4029	0.0478	1.1505	1.1679	0.3246
Info transparency	−2.1333	1.6261	0.1895	1.3094	1.3788	0.3423
Rule clarity	−1.9384	1.4666	0.1863	−0.4683	1.2751	0.7134
Climate change	−1.2380	1.6433	0.4512	−0.2041	1.0190	0.8412
Comparative risk	5.0042	1.5963	0.0017**	0.2444	1.3504	0.8564
Price discovery	−4.5017	1.8296	0.0139**	0.1721	1.2350	0.8892
Firm size	0.0000	0.0000	0.4257	0.0000	0.0000	0.7385
PPA	1.5475	1.4763	0.2946	1.4470	1.2671	0.2534

$R^2 = 0.365446$; $R^2 = 0.113804$

* Significant at 10% critical level.

** Significant at 5% critical level.

of the view respondents have of the governing body in the market. In particular, it shows that these may be two determining variables for the trading in the LGC market. Additional evidence for this view is drawn from open text responses. Unlike the LGC market, the STC market does not show any significant correlations.

Firstly we ran a model testing the effects of the set ambiguity proxies on the volume of certificates in the LRET and then repeated the model to test for effects in the SRES market. Testing for normality was performed on the LGC and STC variables. Both present heteroscedasticity and are non-normally distributed—hence the choice to use a robust least square regression to attempt to mitigate these issues. Wu and Fuller (2005) proposed an estimation of regression coefficients with survey data with unequal probability samples. The study results show that the least squares method would obtain a biased estimator with unequal probability samples as the variance is not homogeneity. The model results are presented in Table 34.5.

Results of the model show some significant explanatory factors for the level of trading in the LRET and no significant explanatory factors for trading in the SRES. As an initial interpretation of this result, we can attribute this to the high variability of trading and the presence of a greater degree of ambiguity in the SRES when compared to the LRET. Hence, there appears to be no significant pattern of trading in the market. This result aids the argument that there is an elevated level of uncertainty in the RET market and thus a high dispersion of possibilities and influences on trading and other market features.

One of the primary explanatory factors of trading permits in the LRET is the efficiency of price discovery in the market. We observe a significant negative effect on the level of trading of LGC when respondents indicate that there is a lack of efficiency in price discovery on the market. Hence, the greater the uncertainty surrounding the price discovery of the market—or, rather, the true value of the assets traded—the lower the permits freely traded in the LRET. From this result it is inferred that price discovery, as a type of proposed ambiguity measure, negatively affects trading in the market. The finding aligns with existing literature of the ambiguity about price information in the market. Jotzo et al. (2012) showed that market participants cease trading when faced with this type of uncertainty. The model also presents an unexpected result, stating that the level of relative risk of the RET to developed financial markets has a positive effect on trading in the LRET. Simply, it states that trading increases when participants indicate that the RET market is more risky in comparison to other financial markets.

The quantitative models seem to provide inconclusive evidence about the causal effects of ambiguity on trading when testing the RET market in Australia. However, an overall analysis of the scheme through a case study approach reveals that ambiguity proxies do have some influence on activity in the market.

Conclusion

Efficient emission markets should ultimately reflect a stable and credible policy focusing on the effective reduction of GHGs in a way that is politically and economically beneficial for involved parties. A case study analysis of the RET in Australia shows that this is not the case for this market. This study achieves the objective of presenting a comprehensive analysis of the RET scheme and more importantly establishes clearly that an elevated degree of uncertainty prevails in this market. A full assessment of the current situation of the RET through the means of qualitative and quantitative research is undertaken and indicates that the primary determinants of ambiguity in this scheme are regulatory uncertainty, uncertainty surrounding the efficiency of price discovery, as well as a lack of information transparency between the governing body and the participants in the market. Investors are seemingly not viewing certificates as sound and fairly priced assets from which they can benefit financially. Rather the market lacks a transparency of information regarding the benefits and costs of trading for firms. This chapter finds some preliminary evidence for the negative effects of the perceived ambiguity on the level of trading in this market. Given the context of the analysis and the current and impending changes of the scheme, such as the abolishment of the carbon pricing mechanism as well as the proposed changes to the LRET target by the government, it is plausible to state that the effects of future ambiguity on investors may be amplified. However reasonable this may seem, this study is cautious in making strong inferences over the effects of ambiguity in this market. The chapter does however state clearly that this market is plagued with a high level of uncertainty especially surrounding government policy changes, price discovery, and transparency of information. The implications from the results lie with future policy reforms and reviews of the scheme by government from a political and economic perspective. With reference to the primary result of the analysis, that inefficient and unstable government policies are primary indicators for greater uncertainty in the market, we can recommend that careful planning leads to programs that are proactive and preventative rather than to activities that are reactive and remedial. Thus, a greater focus on aligning political party support in order to maintain stability in the scheme is crucial in the improved sustainment of the scheme. Stern (2006, p. 324) states: "To reap the benefits of emissions trading, deep and liquid markets and well designed rules are important … hence broadening the scope of schemes will tend to lower costs and reduce volatility."

Notes

1 A copy of this survey may be obtained by contacting the authors of this chapter.
2 Application number: UTS HREC 2014000044.
3 See Zhang (2006), Anderson et al. (2009), and Barron, Stanford, and Yong (2009) for a description of ambiguity measures.

References

Anderson, E. W., Ghysels, E., & Juergens, J. L. (2009). The impact of risk and uncertainty on expected returns. *Journal of Financial Economics, 94*, 233–263.

Bancel, F., & Mittoo, U. (2004). Cross-country determinants of capital structure choice: A survey of European firms. *Financial Management, 33*, 103–133.

Barron, B. E., Stanford, M. H., & Yong, Y. (2009). Further evidence on the relation between analysts' forecast dispersion and stock returns. *Contemporary Accounting Research, 26*, 329–357.

Bossaerts, P., Ghirardato, P., Guarnaschelli, S., & Zame, W. (2010). Ambiguity in asset markets: Theory and experiment. *Review of Financial Studies, 23*(4), 1325–1359.

Brounen, D., De Jong, A., & Koedijk, K. (2004). Corporate finance in Europe: Confronting theory with practice. *Financial Management, 33*(4), 71–101.

Caskey, J. A. (2009). Information in equity markets with ambiguity-averse investors. *The Review of Financial Studies, 22*, 3595–3627.

Clean Energy Legislation (Carbon Tax Repeal) Act, 2014 (Cth).

Clean Energy Regulator (CER). (2014). About the renewable energy target, in the Department of the Environment, ed. (Commonwealth of Australia).

Cotton, D., & Michayluk, D. (2014). Ambiguity in markets: A test in an Australian emissions market. *ACRN Journal of Finance and Risk Perspectives, 3*, 99–119.

Cotton, D., & Trück, S. (2013). Emissions mitigation schemes in Australia—The past, present and future. *Low Carbon Economy, 4*, 80–94.

Easley, D., Hvidkjaer, S., & O'Hara, M. (2005). *Factoring information into returns* (Working Paper Series). New York, NY: Cornell University.

Easley, D., & O'Hara, M. (2005). Information and the cost of capital. *The Journal of Finance, 59*(4), 1553–1583.

Easley, D., & O'Hara, M. (2009). Ambiguity and nonparticipation: The role of regulation. *The Review of Financial Studies, 22*(5), 1817–1843.

Easley, D., & O'Hara, M. (2010). Microstructure and ambiguity. *Journal of Finance, 65*, 1817–1846.

Eisenhardt, K. M. (1989). Building theories from case study research. *Academy of Management Review, 14*, 532–550.

Ellsberg, D. (1961). Ambiguity and Savage axioms. *The Quarterly Journal of Economics, 75*, 643–669.

Graham, J., & Harvey, C. (2002). How do CFOs make capital budgeting and capital structure decisions? *Journal of Applied Corporate Finance, 15*, 8–23.

Grossman, S. J., & Stiglitz, J. E. (1980). On the impossibility of informationally efficient markets. *The American Economic Review, 70*, 393–408.

Grubb, M., & Neuhoff, K. (2006). Allocation and competitiveness in the EU emissions trading scheme: Policy overview. *Climate Policy, 6*, 7–30.

Jotzo, F., Jordan, T., & Fabian, N. (2012). Policy uncertainty about Australia's carbon price: Expert survey results and implications for investment. *Australian Economic Review, 45*(4), 395–409.

Jotzo, F., & Pezzey, J. C. V. (2007). Optimal intensity targets for greenhouse gas emissions trading under uncertainty. *Environmental and Resource Economics, 98*, 259–284.

Knight, F. H. (1921). *Risk, uncertainty and profit*. Boston, MA: Houghton Mifflin Company.

Mitchell, J. C. (1983). Case and situation analysis. *Sociology Review, 51*, 187–211.

Ohn, J. Y. J. (2013). Ambiguity aversion, funding liquidity and liquidity dynamics. *Journal of Financial Markets, 18*, 49–76.

Pinkse, J. (2007). Corporate intentions to participate in emissions trading. *Business Strategy and the Environment, 16*, 12–25.

Routledge, B. R., & Zin, S. E. (2009). Model uncertainty and liquidity. *Review of Economic Dynamics, 12*, 543–566.

Sarin, R. K., & Weber, M. (1993). Effects of ambiguity in market experiments. *Management Science, 39*(5), 602–615.

Savage, L. J. (1954). *The foundations of statistics*. New York, NY: John Wiley and Sons.

Stern, N. (2006). *The Stern review of the economics of climate change*. Cambridge: Cambridge University Press.

Wu, Y., & Fuller, W. (2005). Preliminary testing procedures for regression with survey samples. In *Proceedings of the Section on Survey Research Methods*. American Statistical Association, 3892–3688.

Zhang, X. F. (2006). Information uncertainty and stock returns. *Journal of Finance, 61*, 105–137.

35

CREDIT RISK AND ECOSYSTEM SERVICES

A review of small-scale emission-certified agroforestry

Emmanuel Olatunbosun Benjamin and Gertrud Buchenrieder

Innovative smallholder agricultural credit instruments used by financial intermediaries (both conventional commercial and microfinance intermediaries) must acknowledge the presence of climate change and environmental degradation, both of which threaten food production and food security in parts of Sub-Saharan Africa (Schrieder, 1997). Smallholder farmers usually source funds in order to smooth consumption, thereby preserving farm resources as well as investing in the farming business. Thus, access to credit instruments may also be linked to environmental resource management (Anderson, Locker, & Nugent, 2002). Despite certain improvements in the last three decades, total lending volume to smallholder farmers, especially female farmers, in Sub-Saharan Africa remains low (Kiptot & Franzel, 2012). Financially constrained smallholders without universal land property rights have been observed to exhibit adverse behaviors which are reflected in their improper natural resources and sustainability management strategies (Barrett, 2008; Johnston & Morduch, 2007). These behaviors point to motives and circumstances beyond those of just coping with consumption risks. The major challenges confronting agricultural lending in parts of Sub-Saharan Africa stem from issues related to imperfect credit markets. These cause high transaction costs and a lack of adequate and eligible collateral, often due to restricted land property rights (Havemann, 2011; Rodrigues de Aquino, Aasrud, & Guimarães, 2011). The lack of information on the character and business qualities of smallholder farmers in Sub-Saharan Africa is a hindrance to the credit evaluation process of financial intermediaries, which is reflected in the extremely high market transaction costs experienced by conventional lenders. Furthermore, assets which may minimize losses in the case of smallholder loan default usually have no value because they lack a market. To overcome today's credit constraints faced by smallholder farmers, certain questions have to be raised. For instance, which instruments are available to financial intermediaries for identifying creditworthy smallholder farmers based on sustainable and environmental criteria in order to ensure business quality? Are there sustainable income schemes that guarantee smallholder farmers a long-term cash flow or physical collateral? This chapter explores whether small-scale emission-certified agroforestry could be the next innovation in smallholder lending instruments improving, among other issues, access to credit for smallholders and reducing transaction costs for lenders.

Agroforestry is perceived as an alternative cropping system which, in the presence of climate change, can preserve and improve productivity compared to conventional farming practices (Challinor, Wheeler, Garforth, Craufurd, & Kassam, 2007; Garrity, 2004). Agroforestry is a strong alternative system because the trees are better able to withstand climate shocks, decrease soil erosion, and increase soil fertility through nitrogen fixing, all while providing additional income through sales of timber and non-timber products (Thorlakson & Neufeldt, 2012). Moreover, certain types of agroforestry also provide ecosystem services; for instance, cultivated trees are able to sequestrate (capture and store) carbon, thereby reducing the amount of CO_2 in the atmosphere.

Wunder (2006, p. 2) defines ecosystem services as

> a voluntary transaction in which a well-defined environmental service (ES), or a land use likely to secure that service, is being "bought" by at least one ES buyer from at least one ES provider if, and only if, the ES provider secures ES provision, i.e., conditionality.

Carbon sequestrated via agroforestry generates carbon credits which are traded under diverse emission schemes, resulting in payment for ecosystem services (PES). The Center for International Forestry Research argues that agroforestry carbon sequestration may reduce poverty through increases in income and capital accumulation among smallholder farmers (Smith & Scherr, 2002). To a large extent, agroforestry PES schemes offer diverse training and farm-level demonstrations to smallholder farmers, thereby expanding their human and social capital as well as bringing about internal and external organizational innovation in a rural context (Benjamin, 2015; Shames et al., 2012). Furthermore, PES contracts signed by smallholder farmers have led to systematic welfare gains among these farmers (Wunder, 2008). It is estimated that by 2030 around 25–50 million smallholder farmers in developing countries may have benefited immensely from participation in emission-certified agroforestry programs (Milder, Scherr, & Bracer, 2010).

This chapter reviews the potential of emission-certified agroforestry programs and the corresponding PES to improve smallholder farmers' access to credit. This assumes that potential lenders are more willing to contract with borrowers enjoying a stable form of on-farm cash flow in the form of PES because this might serve as eligible collateral to fulfill financial contract requirements. Furthermore, the presence of PES contracts reduces the information asymmetry vis-à-vis the potential lender and subsequently lowers transaction costs. Around the globe, financial intermediaries, including microfinance intermediaries, are increasingly adopting standardized risk management strategies, which require informational inputs in order to assess the creditworthiness of potential borrowers. Restricted lending by formal financial intermediaries, such as commercial banks or credit unions, to enterprises in emerging markets may be attributed to credit market imperfections, notably information asymmetry, expressing itself in high transaction costs on the side of the lender (Benjamin, 2013; IFAD, 2003; IFC, 2013). Collateral requirements are a result of information asymmetry and serve to mitigate losses in cases of borrower default. Less risky borrowers are willing to pledge more valuable collateral, thus enjoying lower interest rates, effectively reducing adverse selection problems, and possibly improving the profitability of financial intermediaries (Jimenez & Saurina, 2004). However, smallholder farmers often lack the high value and marketable collateral demanded by formal financial intermediaries (Jama & Pizarro, 2008; Johnston & Morduch, 2007). The inability of smallholder farmers in developing countries to secure loans to purchase improved inputs and to adapt to the effects of climate change may contribute to cementing the poverty trap. In the tropical and sub-tropical developing countries in particular, the issue of poverty traps is complex and often linked to resource degradation, not only due to population pressure but also due to the above-mentioned issues: restricted land property rights, which inhibit their use as collateral, and the subsequent inability to borrow and finance productivity-increasing and environmentally sound investments (Barrett, 2008). Therefore, it is important to analyze innovative mechanisms which address the aforementioned imbalances. Credit market imperfections may be addressed if evaluations of borrowers are based on criteria which also consider environmental and socioeconomic benefits (Benjamin, 2015).

We aim to establish a basis for the benefits of emission-certified agroforestry programs accrued to participating smallholder farmers beyond the obvious. Instruments which provide information about a smallholder farmer's business enterprise and future cash flow may potentially reduce information asymmetry on the side of the potential lender, easing credit constraints and improving credit terms. It is hypothesized that emission-certified agroforestry programs improve smallholder farmers' agricultural financing by impacting on financial intermediaries' risk management strategies. We therefore review topics relating to smallholder agroforestry, PES, and agriculture financing.

Formal financial intermediation and small-scale agriculture

The volume of credit allocated to small-scale agriculture by formal financial intermediaries in Sub-Saharan Africa remains low. The Food and Agriculture Organization (FAO) (2012) states that small-scale agriculture lending as a percentage of commercial banks' total credit portfolio was less than 10 percent in developing countries. This is in line with the results of Benjamin (2015) which show that commercial bank lending to agricultural small and medium enterprises in Kenya was 6 percent of the total credit portfolio. However, Jama and Pizarro (2008) argue that for Sub-Saharan Africa to witness a green revolution (i.e., higher productivity, increased food security, and poverty reduction), investments in soil fertility, innovative farm inputs, and access to credit and new markets are required. Remember that the growing population will require an increase in global feed and food production of 70 percent by 2050 (FAO, 2009). Information asymmetry, lack of eligible collateral, and inadequate capabilities for the appraisal of small-scale agriculture are some of the factors which limit smallholders' credit accessibility and investment in Sub-Saharan Africa (Anderson & Khambata, 1985; Fernando, 2008; Onumah, 2003). Hoff and Stiglitz (1990) identified three hurdles confronting rural credit markets in developing countries: screening, incentives, and enforcement. All these hurdles contribute to transaction costs, which can thus become prohibitively high. Screening is the process of determining a borrower's likelihood of default with the awareness that borrowers differ in the level of risk they pose. Incentives ascertain that borrowers are investing in business ventures which ensure adequate returns to cover principal and interest. Enforcement involves obligatory repayment instruments such as legal entities. Screening and incentives are related to information asymmetry which can impose immense monitoring costs on lenders in a smallholder context. These hurdles have also been identified in the study by Benjamin (2015) as some of the reasons for the limited advancement of credit to the agriculture sector (see Figure 35.1) in parts of rural Kenya even though agriculture is one of the main drivers of the region's economy.

Hoff and Stiglitz (1990) therefore argue that formal financial intermediaries in rural credit markets in developing countries usually depend heavily on collateral due to the limited availability of adequate instruments capable of directly screening and monitoring borrowers' activities. Information asymmetry remains a challenge for financial intermediaries in developed and, especially, developing countries, as national standardized regulations require risk management based

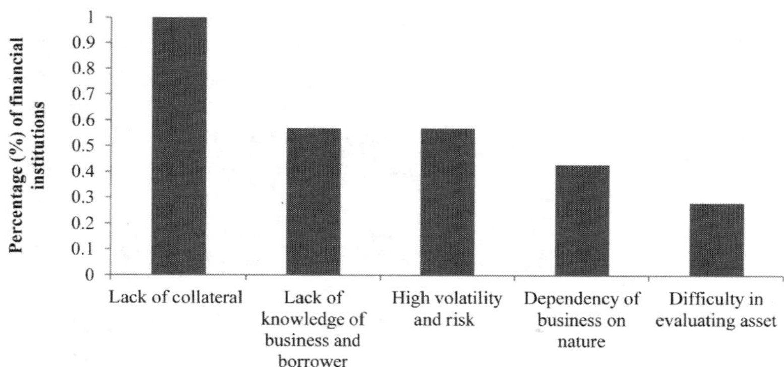

Figure 35.1 Reasons for low-level commercial bank lending in rural Kenya (Meru, Embu and Nanyuki)
Source: Benjamin (2015).

on screening, incentives, and enforcement (Fernando, 2008; Swinnen & Gow, 1999). Formal financial intermediaries in rural areas are therefore less likely to advance credit to borrowers perceived as risky, such as smallholder farmers. Onumah (2003) argues that formal financial intermediaries are becoming increasingly risk-averse, limiting their exposure to agriculture and the rural economy in Sub-Saharan Africa. This may worsen the credit situation of smallholder farmers in parts of rural Sub-Saharan Africa, further limiting agriculture financing.

Traditionally, farmers in developing countries had no choice but to rely on the informal financial market for loans, even though interest rates outside of self-help group lending initiatives could reach usurious heights. Informal entities such as moneylenders might charge annual interest rates that sometimes exceeded 100 percent to mitigate their risks, given the limited collateral requirements at the time of lending (Benjamin, 2015). Obviously, interest rates in this instance play the role of loan pricing as well as acting as a risk strategy measure for the lender while no significant transaction costs occur on the side of the borrower. The interest rates in the formal financial market are normally more modest than in the informal market despite the fact that formal financial intermediaries are increasingly turning to risk-based pricing of interest rates when allocating (consumer) loans (Edelberg, 2006). According to Edelberg (2006), risk-based pricing of interest rates is using estimates of default risk to price individual loans, which was the usual practice of financial lenders in the mid-1990s. However, other factors such as documentation requirements, etc., that resulted in high transaction costs kept smallholder farmers and, to some extent, formal financial intermediaries away from agriculture credit. The evaluation of a borrower's tangible and intangible assets (e.g., reputation) has also been shown to flow into the calculation of the interest rate (Benjamin, 2013). On the contrary, Stiglitz and Weiss (1981) argue that formal financial intermediaries usually charge an optimal interest rate, while credit rationing is not necessarily based on evaluation of the borrower given their likelihood of default, especially during excess demand for credit. One critical point acknowledged by Stiglitz and Weiss is that, considering a multiple period, borrowers who are "good" may end up paying a lower interest rate and investing in safe projects. This is in line with the paper by Dell'Ariccia and Marquez (2004) which argues that credit markets with high information asymmetry may charge higher interest rates while banking policies may restrict lending to creditworthy borrowers. Therefore, certain borrower characteristics have the potential to reduce the transaction costs on the side of the formal lender, thus maintaining the comparably lower interest rate. Formal lenders may even stand to gain a comparative advantage by lending at a reasonable rate to smallholder farmers investing in ventures that increase productivity (Jama & Pizarro, 2008).

The process of calculating risk-based pricing of interest rates as stated above also takes the borrower's collateral (asset) evaluation into consideration. The borrower's collateral is therefore an important element in financial risk management since its evaluation is essential in determining the probability of default (Benjamin, 2013; Johnston & Morduch, 2007). Jimenez and Saurina (2004) provide evidence that, in the absence of a banking relationship, collateralized loans had a lower probability of default compared to loans without collateralization. It is argued by Wette (1983) that collateral requirements are set by formal financial intermediaries at a level optimal in limiting adverse selection which can reduce the returns of lenders. Other eligible instruments that may be used to screen and monitor borrowers within the rural credit market are linkages to (new) markets and warehouse receipts (Hoff & Stiglitz, 1990). These are in essence nothing other than a form of guaranteed cash flow or physical collateral.

Emission-certified agroforestry in a smallholder context

Small-scale agroforestry is not a new concept for smallholder farmers in parts of Sub-Saharan Africa since it has been utilized in a number of ways and has passed down from generation to generation. Trees are vital to the farm economy in Sub-Saharan Africa since they serve as a substitute for on-farm employment and can stabilize household income during periods of environmental and economic stress (Dewees, 1992). Trees planted on farmland, apart from providing shade for sensitive cash crops such as coffee and cacao, may be a source of supplementary soil nutrients and may supply food and medicine—so-called non-timber products. Kiptot and Franzel (2012) indicated that smallholder farmers in several areas in Kenya and Uganda who use agroforestry practices involving *Calliandra calothyrsus* as fodder or a supplement in dairy nutrition have increased milk production, thus increasing *net* annual total farm revenue by US$ 62–US$ 122. *Calliandra calothyrsus* is a multi-purpose small tree which grows in the tropics and is able to adapt to poor soil conditions. It is also a suitable feed supplement for stable animals and poultry. This corresponds to between 5 and 10 percent of total annual farm income. Sales of agroforestry products also help diversify household on-farm income, while reforestation may increase the value of the land and act as a "savings account" for the coming generation (Thacher, Lee, & Schelhas, 1997). The agroforestry production of *G. africanum* (e.g., leaves, kernel), which is available year round, as well as other indigenous fruit trees, contributes on average between US$ 1,300 and US$ 2,629 per annum to smallholder farmers' incomes in Tanzania and Cameroon (Kiptot & Franzel, 2012). The few countries in Sub-Saharan Africa that have incorporated agroforestry into their so-called national poverty reduction strategy papers (PRSPs) (designed to monitor the millennium or sustainable development goals) have had promising results (Garrity, 2004). Given the vulnerability of many regions in Sub-Saharan Africa to climate change, the use of trees as a mitigation effort has gained increasing attention. Atmospheric CO_2 captured and stored in trees (depending on species) can either be measured during their lifetime or estimated over a tree's projected lifetime (Wunder, 2006). In Kenya, emission-certified agroforestry programs are part of climate smart agriculture, delivering triple benefits (higher yields, crop drought resilience, and increased carbon storage) to smallholder farmers. These benefits move farmers in the direction of sustainable and environmental resource management (World Bank, 2011). In the presence of information asymmetry between smallholder farmers and project developers, it is argued that agricultural investment in ecosystem land use is likely to result in welfare losses for PES recipients who have committed themselves via contract to a project which, in some cases, may run for more than 25 years. However, the limited number of tropical PES projects involving smallholder farmers has been observed to lead to welfare gains—implying information symmetry between smallholder farmers and project developers (Wunder, 2008).

Emission-certified agroforestry programs bring together different stakeholders, including: smallholder farmers; local, regional, and international authorities; organizations; and carbon developers. A carbon developer is responsible for compiling documents such as the project idea note (PIN) and project design document (PDD) under all carbon offset projects. These documents provide information relating to participating smallholder characteristics, farm bio-physical properties, and agribusinesses which are relevant for the "*additionality clause*" prescribed in most carbon offset projects. For instance, environmental *additionality* of agroforestry is based on *ex ante* and *ex post* farm productivity data, which may account for improved soil fertility within a project. These data also identify barriers to project implementation relating to institutional, financial, and environmental constraints (Valatin, 2011). This implies the likelihood that information on smallholder farming activities is available prior to their participation in the emission-certified agroforestry program. This information symmetry associated within carbon offset projects has broad implications for smallholder farmers, especially in terms of potentially debt-financed agricultural investments.

The low level of formally secured property rights among smallholder farmers in rural Sub-Saharan Africa has been identified as a barrier to land use or agroforestry carbon offset projects (Benjamin, 2015; Luedeling, Sileshi, Beedy, & Dietz, 2011; Pagiola, Arcenas, & Platais, 2005). Land tenure security would therefore reduce the risk exposure of investors investing in land use or agroforestry carbon offset projects. Secured land tenure, which is a prerequisite for emission offset investments, is likely to be the reason why Sub-Saharan African forestry projects account for just 1 percent of compliance emission schemes (Rodrigues de Aquino et al., 2011). However, land tenure improvements may be a spinoff effect within carbon offset projects due to local authority involvement and negotiations (Milder et al., 2010; Rodrigues de Aquino et al., 2011; Wunder, 2006). Emission-certified agroforestry in Niger and Kenya has been observed to secure the land tenure rights of smallholder farmers given the involvement of local and national stakeholders (Rodrigues de Aquino et al., 2011). Consequently, smallholder farmers who in the past cultivated land but did not possess legal rights to that land now have some form of land rights as a result of carbon offset. Again, this development has broad implications for agricultural financing through the establishment of legalized collateral.

The reward for environmental services is based on the premise that smallholder farmers providing these services derive higher non-financial and, to a certain extent, financial compensation compared to the alternative land use, that is, lower opportunity cost. Part of the financial incentive accruable to smallholders comes from emission schemes based on either market-driven mechanisms, that is, the buying and selling of emissions on the carbon market, or some form of compensation. For the latter, smallholders receive a PES depending on their bargaining power and ability to reach a fair price for each ton of carbon. A carbon market with a price of US$ 50 per ton of carbon dioxide equivalent (tCO_2e) could generate income between US$ 20 and US$ 30 billion per year (Milder et al., 2010). According to Milder et al. (2010) this additional income would improve the livelihoods of smallholder farmers immensely. However, based on 2013 prices and depending on the carbon market, one ton of CO_2e ranges between US$ 0.50 and US$ 10 tCO_2e (Benjamin, 2013). Wunder (2008) found that PES-like schemes on biodiversity conservation and landscape beautification in Bolivia resulted in annual income gains of between US$ 77 and US$ 640 per household. Smallholder emission-certified agroforestry, depending on the size of the farm, has the potential to sequestrate about three tons CO_2e per hectare per year, resulting in revenues of between US$ 1.50 and US$ 30 per hectare per year (Benjamin, 2013; Luedeling et al., 2011). This PES revenue is somewhat comparable to the revenues from PES watershed schemes observed in Bolivia of between US$ 3.50 and US$ 7 per hectare per year, with the relatively minimal opportunity costs resulting in positive per capita gains (Wunder, 2008). This diversification of on-farm income, especially PES, under a well-designed carbon offset program has been argued to lead to relatively stable forms of cash flow (Pagiola et al., 2005; Wunder, 2006). The existence of PES schemes and the subsequent income streams may serve as a form of eligible collateral in agricultural financing. Although in some cases PES is less than the opportunity costs, it may however account for around 10 percent to above 50 percent of future household income (Milder et al., 2010; Pagiola et al., 2005). If the low PES observed in developing countries persists, a direct impact on the livelihoods of smallholder farmers most in need is unlikely (Wunder, Dung The, & Ibarra, 2005). Despite the low remuneration from PES, other direct benefits of agroforestry such as increased soil fertility, erosion control, and tree products may translate into financial gains through increased productivity of smallholder farmers.

Agroforestry PES and the link to formal credit

The broader impacts of agroforestry PES on smallholder farmer credit in developing countries, especially Sub-Saharan Africa, remain relatively unknown due to the sparse literature addressing this topic and the limited number of projects that have been undertaken. The implementation of projects that offer PES to smallholder farmers may result in not only positive social and cultural capital gains but also increased access to some form of credit facility if the PES scheme serves as a substitute for conventional credit collateral (Benjamin, Blum, & Punt, 2015; Pagiola et al., 2005). Benjamin et al. (2015) provide theoretical and empirical evidence that PES may, to a certain extent, improve the credit accessibility of farmers in South Africa and Kenya. Thacher et al. (1997) argue that there may be a correlation between farmers who have access to formal credit, that is, financial management expertise, and participation in reforestation programs. Although one may argue that *reversible causal* relationships exist (an argument which is beyond the scope of this chapter), the fact remains that a correlation has been observed or is anticipated between formal credit and participation in reforestation programs. It is for these reasons and other observational benefits of agroforestry to smallholder farmers that this study hypothesizes that carbon offset projects may lead to access to formal credit among smallholders while improving their livelihoods and contributing to rural development.

The rural agriculture credit market consists of supply and demand sides comprising formal financial intermediaries and smallholder farmers, respectively. It appears that some sort of disequilibrium is currently prevailing in the rural credit market. This market imperfection may be a result of the conventional risk management strategy of financial intermediaries who ration the supply of formal credit to rural agriculture. As illustrated in Figure 35.2, the conventional risk management strategies of the credit supply side weigh up or evaluate potential borrowers based on their level of risk, and prescribe certain collateral requirements. Smallholder farmers are exposed to a somewhat identical (covariant) risk and are likely to be incapable of providing adequate business information or collateral. This increases both the cost of information gathering for financial intermediaries and supply side risk exposure. Therefore, financial intermediaries prefer to lend to other sectors of the economy, with lower transaction costs and risk, rather than the agricultural sector. This may result in an agricultural credit market with excess demand, whereby farmers who are unable to secure working capital (the so-called unbankable) source funds from informal financial entities such as relatives, self-help groups, and money lenders. On the one hand, financial intermediaries, who treat the demand side of the agricultural credit market as a homogenous entity and thus employ conventional risk management strategies, may ignore the climate-related dynamics of the demand side such as sustainable agricultural practices. On the other hand, ongoing trends relating to climate change mitigation and sustainable

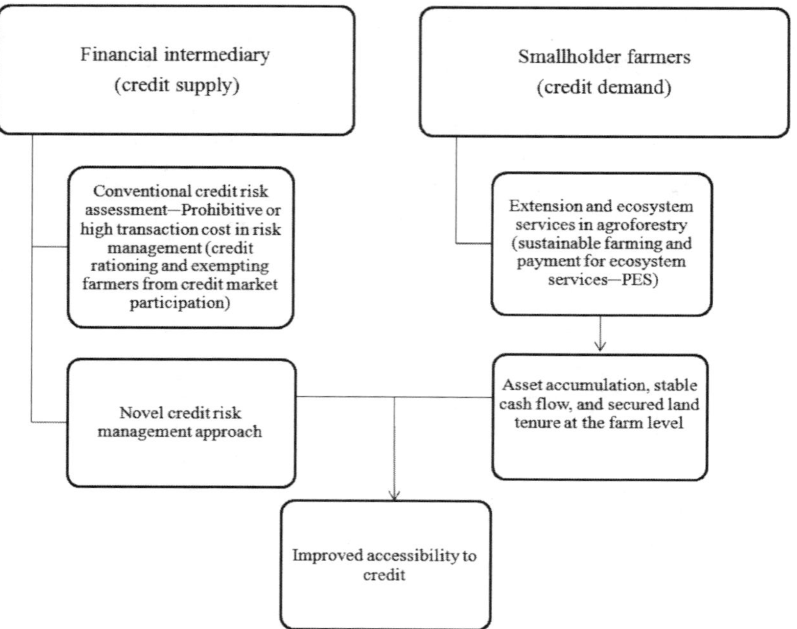

Figure 35.2 The impact of the smallholder farmer ecosystem and extension service on agricultural credit

agriculture, for example climate smart agriculture among rural smallholders, may render conventional risk management strategies redundant. Extension services which emphasize climate smart agriculture and its corresponding PES, although still in their infancy, may create a new form of profitable and sustainable farming enterprise. For instance, PES from small-scale agroforestry is a stable long-term cash flow which, depending on emission prices, may help smallholder farmers acquire innovations that increase productivity and contribute to household capital accumulation. Furthermore, the use of agroforestry practices, especially in areas that lack secure land tenure, may be an innovative instrument in land right policy. While acknowledging other benefits of certain types of agroforestry, such as increased soil fertility, control of erosion, etc., the aforementioned PES and land rights may be rather important to the supply side of the agricultural credit market. As efforts increase to globally incorporate environmental and sustainable indices into the operations of financial intermediaries, a new form of financial market risk management is emerging. This novel risk management strategy of financial intermediaries (supply side) based on the environmental, sustainable, and (social) capital accumulation index of smallholders (demand side) results in a new credit market equilibrium, which may increase the volume of credit made available to smallholder agriculture. The effects of the attributes of agroforestry PES on formal credit in rural areas is further elaborated below.

Information (accessibility and availability) is a determinant in the adoption of agroforestry PES programs in agriculture (Garbach, Lubell, & DeClerck, 2012). Information symmetry and experience has generally been found to reduce the risk involved in smallholder loans in developing countries, as lenders are able to distinguish between high- and low-risk borrowers (Anderson & Khambata, 1985). Therefore, the information symmetry associated with emission-certified agroforestry programs may help smallholder farmers to access loans, especially microfinance loans which, in certain cases, are uncollateralized in the traditional way (i.e., assets with universal property rights). Any instrument or intermediary that enables smallholder farmers to manage and reduce exposure to diverse risks further diminishes the general perception that these farmers are high-risk clients (Onumah, 2003). This intermediary, similar to the Zambian warehouse model or the warehouse receipt as prescribed by Onumah (2003), may improve lender–borrower (principal agent) relationships. According to Onumah (2003, p. 3), warehouse receipts are defined as

> documents issued by warehouse operators as evidence that specified commodities, of stated quantity and quality, have been deposited at particular locations by named depositors. The system will help formalize their trade transactions, enabling a database on their activities to be generated. This will help overcome the problem of lack of track record, and enable banks to screen borrowers more effectively and with minimum delay.

Onumah (2003) further argues that, given a sustainable and regulated information system with no entry barrier, it is more likely that formal financial intermediaries will readily supply loans to smallholders otherwise considered as *unbankable* (on this issue see also Theesfeld & Buchenrieder, 2000). Agroforestry PES programs which operate similarly to those of a warehouse receipt system should reduce the instances of lack of a track record and improve smallholder cash flow, allowing banks to screen borrowers more effectively and without delay.

Smallholder farmers in parts of Sub-Saharan Africa do not usually have formal or customary rights to conventional assets, such as the farmland they cultivate. The absence of effective legal/registration systems renders not only the evaluation but also the commercialization of such assets almost impossible, thereby increasing the risk of borrower default, affecting lenders' returns (Fernando, 2008). Although smallholders may lack rights to assets *prior* to the implementation of an emission-certified agroforestry program, this situation may change *post* implementation since land right security is a minimum requirement for carbon offset projects. Formal financial intermediaries in developing countries were observed not to secure loans (including agricultural lending) based on risk management which evaluates repayment ability rather than the quantity and quality of collateral (Anderson & Khambata, 1985). Although formal lenders in developing countries may gradually be shifting attention away from *conventional* or *classical* collateral (such as land) to other eligible forms of collateral, it is obvious that collateral requirements will continue to dominate risk management strategies. Furthermore, loans to smallholders which potentially improve their assets' accumulation may reduce the inherent risks associated with agricultural financing (Fernando, 2008). Benjamin (2013) identifies asset evaluation as a basis for estimating risk indicators within the framework of the international banking regulation standard (Basel Accord).

Using only net revenue from agriculture as the decision criterion in agricultural credit evaluation and ignoring all other sources of farm income may hinder credit allocation, given the high volatility in crop prices as well as exposure to losses due to natural disasters. Agricultural credit evaluation by certain formal financial intermediaries and microfinance intermediaries in developing countries increasingly focuses on overall *net* cash flow as an *eligible form of collateral* instead of net revenue from the loan-financed investment (Fernando, 2008). This practice based on overall *net* cash flow, although an exception rather than the rule, may have a positive implication for smallholder farmers participating in a well-designed emission-certified agroforestry program. The contribution of PES to household income in a smallholder context may be substantial despite the low level of payment and often low carbon prices. PES received by participating smallholder farmers provides relatively stable cash flow when compared to other on-farm revenues, despite the periodic re-evaluation which might affect the pricing of emission units (Pagiola et al., 2005; Wunder, 2006). Moreover, a PES, given a fair price for carbon, presents a new form of asset accumulation for smallholders and reduces smallholders' probability of default as well as interest rates (Benjamin, 2013).

Despite the critical views on the *ex ante* analysis of the impact of agroforestry PES on the livelihoods of smallholder farmers in the tropics, the limited available evidence does support the further implementation of such programs (Wunder, 2006). Pagiola et al. (2005), Benjamin et al. (2015), and Wunder (2008) have highlighted the potential of PES programs to alleviate poverty and build assets including the easing of the credit constraint of smallholder farmers in developing countries, especially Sub-Saharan Africa. Regarding the latter (credit accessibility), it may be the case that the number of studies has so far been limited by the modest direct contribution of agroforestry PES to the livelihoods of smallholder farmers due to the low market prices for carbon units. Wunder (2008) argues that the per capita income gains provided by environmental services were usually low as a result of the prices negotiated by the buyers of environmental services. At a price of less than US$ 10 per Megagram (Mg) CO_2e, the carbon stored through an agroforestry system in Sub-Saharan Africa would contribute a small fraction of US$ 30 per hectare per year to annual farm income (Luedeling et al., 2011). This revenue might not cover the transaction costs associated with the monitoring, verifying, and reporting of carbon offset projects (Luedeling et al., 2011).

Conclusion

The potential of emission-certified agroforestry programs and corresponding PES to positively influence employment and reduce poverty in rural areas in developing countries has been identified by Wunder (2008) and Luedeling et al. (2011). Agroforestry may increase farm revenues in a number of ways, ranging from cost-saving measures and the market sale of timber and non-timber products to improved labor supply. However, limited research has been conducted on the impact of emission-certified agroforestry programs on agricultural financing. Proof that agroforestry and ecosystem services may improve agricultural financing could strengthen the argument for formal financial intermediaries and smallholder farmer participation in sustainable development partnerships. A study by Benjamin (2013) provides a theoretical argument for the contribution of PES to the appreciation of conventional or classical assets, for example farmland, which implies the lower probability of farmers with a PES to default on loans. The tenure security prerequisite of emission-certified agroforestry investments has been observed to improve the weak tenure structure among smallholder farmers in parts of rural Sub-Saharan Africa and also has an implication for formal credit accessibility. This subsequent development in smallholder land rights and titling may increase the availability of eligible collateral and enforcement ability, the lack of which is usually lamented by formal lenders, resulting in limited loans and investment in rural agriculture. Neglecting *net* farm revenue and instead focusing on *net* loan-financed investment in the evaluation of creditworthiness, as practiced by numerous formal financial intermediaries in developing countries, may not improve the situation in formal agricultural lending. Overlooking the contribution of agroforestry practices to farm revenues may bias the creditworthiness analysis of rural formal financial intermediaries, potentially leading to the exclusion of certain smallholders and the likelihood of adverse selection. Emission-certified agroforestry programs may improve the level of agricultural loans and investment by formal financial intermediaries in smallholder enterprises if adequately designed and implemented with a pro-poor smallholder approach. Some of the necessary steps include: providing a secured land tenure system; finding a fair value for the social cost of carbon within national and international policy; strengthening the bargaining power of providers of environmental services; and increasing the adoption of conservation among smallholder farmers. Further research on the benefits of the incentives of agroforestry ecosystem services on the livelihoods of smallholder farmers in the tropics needs to be conducted with respect to agricultural financing. In-depth research on this novel approach agricultural financing would enhance and strengthen our knowledge on the benefits of PES and contribute to the existing literature.

References

Anderson, C. L., Locker, L., & Nugent, R. (2002). Microcredit, social capital, and common pool resources. *World Development, 30*(1), 95–105.

Anderson, D., & Khambata, F. (1985). Financing small-scale industry and agriculture in developing countries: The merits and limitations of "commercial" policies. *Economic Development and Cultural Change, 33*(2), 349–371.

Barrett, B. C. (2008). Poverty traps and resource dynamics in smallholder agrarian systems. In A. Ruijs & R. Dellink (Eds.), *Economics of poverty, environment and natural resource use* (pp. 17–40). Dordrecht, the Netherlands: Springer.

Benjamin, O. E. (2013). Credit risk modeling and sustainable agriculture: Asset evaluation and rural carbon revenue. *Journal of Sustainable Finance & Investment, 3*(1), 57–69. doi:10.1080/20430795.2013.765382

Benjamin, O. E. (2015). *Financial institutions and trends in sustainable agriculture: Synergy in rural Sub-Saharan Africa* (e-published doctoral dissertation). Bergische University of Wuppertal, Germany. Retrieved February 15, 2015, from http://elpub.bib.uni-wuppertal.de/edocs/dokumente/fbb/wirtschaftswissenschaft/diss 2015/benjamin

Benjamin, O. E., Blum, M., & Punt, M. (2015). The impact of extension and ecosystem services on smallholders' credit constraint. *Journal of Developing Areas, 50*(1), 333–350.

Challinor, A., Wheeler, T., Garforth, C., Craufurd, P., & Kassam, A. (2007). Assessing the vulnerability of food crop systems in Africa to climate change. *Climate Change, 83*(3), 381–399.

Dell'Ariccia, G., & Marquez, R. (2004). Information and bank credit allocation. *Journal of Financial Economics, 72*(1), 185–214.

Dewees, A. P. (1992). *Social and economic incentives for smallholder tree growing: A case study from Muranga District, Kenya*. Community Forestry Case Study Series No. 5. Rome: Food and Agriculture Organization.

Edelberg, W. (2006). Risk-based pricing of interest rates for consumer loans. *Journal of Monetary Economics, 53*(8), 2283–2298.

Fernando, A. N. (2008). Managing microfinance risks: Some observations and suggestions. *Asian Journal of Agriculture and Development, 4*(2), 1–22.

Food and Agriculture Organization (FAO). (2009). *High-level expert forum on how to feed the world in 2050*. Retrieved October 11, 2014, from http://www.fao.org/fileadmin/templates/wsfs/docs/expert_paper/How_to_Feed_the_World_in_2050.pdf; http://www.fao.org/wsfs/forum2050/wsfs-background-documents/hlef-issues-briefs/en/

Food and Agriculture Organization (FAO). (2012). *Part 1—The setting. People and demography*. Retrieved February 21, 2014, from http://www.fao.org/docrep/015/i2490e/i2490e01a.pdf

Garbach, K., Lubell, M., & DeClerck, F. A. J. (2012). Payment for ecosystem services: The roles of positive incentives and information sharing in stimulating adoption of silvopastoral conservation practices. *Agriculture, Ecosystems and Environment, 156*(1), 27–36.

Garrity, P. D. (2004). Agroforestry and the achievement of the Millennium Development Goals. *Agroforestry Systems, 61–62*(1–3), 5–17.

Havemann, T. (2011). *Financing mitigation in smallholder agricultural systems: Issues and opportunities* (CCAFS Working Paper No. 6). CGIAR Research Program on Climate Change, Agriculture and Food Security (CCAFS), Copenhagen, Denmark.

Hoff, K., & Stiglitz, J. E. (1990). Imperfect information and rural credit markets—Puzzles and policy perspectives. *World Bank Economic Review, 4*(3), 235–250.

IFAD. (2003). *Agricultural marketing companies as sources of smallholder credit in Eastern and Southern Africa: Experiences, insights and potential donor role*. The International Fund for Agricultural Development. Retrieved September 15, 2014, from http://www.ifad.org/ruralfinance/policy/pf.pdf

IFC. (2007). *Banking on sustainability: Financing environmental and social opportunities in emerging markets*. International Finance Corporation. Retrieved June 22, 2014, from http://firstforsustainability.org/media/IFC%20Banking%20on%20Sustainability.pdf

IFC. (2013). *Leverage in IFC's climate—Related investments*. Retrieved June 22, 2014, from http://www.ifc.org/wps/wcm/connect/f69ea30041ca447993599700caa2aa08/Leverage+in+IFC's+Climate-Related+Investments.pdf?MOD=AJPERES

Jama, B., & Pizarro, G. (2008). Agriculture in Africa: Strategies to improve and sustain smallholder production systems. *Annals of the New York Academy of Sciences, 1136*, 218–232.

Jimenez, G., & Saurina, J. (2004). Collateral, type of lender and relationship banking as determinants of credit risk. *Journal of Banking and Finance, 28*(9), 2191–2212.

Johnston, D., Jr., & Morduch, J. (2007). The unbanked: Evidence from Indonesia. *World Bank Economic Review, 22*(3), 517–537.

Kiptot, E., & Franzel, S. (2012). Gender and agroforestry in Africa: Who benefits? In N. Ramachandran & D. Garrity (Eds.), *Agroforestry—The future of global land use*. Dordrecht, the Netherlands: Springer.

Luedeling, E., Sileshi, G., Beedy, T., & Dietz, J. (2011). Carbon sequestration potential of agroforestry systems in Africa. In B. M. Kumar & N. P. K. Ramachandran (Eds.), *Carbon sequestration potential of agroforestry systems: Opportunities and challenges* (pp. 61–83). Dordrecht, the Netherlands: Springer.

Milder, C. J., Scherr, S. J., & Bracer, C. (2010). Trends and future potential of payment for ecosystem services to alleviate rural poverty in developing countries. *Ecology and Society, 15*(2), 1–19.

Onumah, E. G. (2003, June 2–4). *Improving access to rural finance through regulated warehouse receipt systems*. Paper presented at international conference on Best Practices: Paving the Way Forward for Rural Finance, Washington, DC.

Pagiola, S., Arcenas, A., & Platais, G. (2005). Can payments for environmental services help reduce poverty? An exploration of the issues and the evidence to date. *World Development, 33*(2), 237–253.

Rodrigues de Aquino, A., Aasrud, A., & Guimarães, L. (2011). Can forest carbon finance influence land tenure security in project areas? Preliminary lessons from projects in Niger and Kenya. In B. M. Kumar & N. P. K. Ramachandran (Eds.), *Carbon sequestration potential of agroforestry systems: Opportunities and challenges* (pp. 231–246). Dordrecht, the Netherlands: Springer.

Schrieder, G. (1997). Financial innovations combat food insecurity of the rural poor: The case of Cameroon. In F. Heidhues & A. Fadani (Eds.), *Food security and innovations: Successes and lessons learned* (pp. 331–345). Frankfurt: Peter Lang Publishers.

Shames, S., Wollenberg, E., Buck, L. E., Kristjanson, P., Masiga, M., & Biryahaho, B. (2012). *Institutional innovations in African smallholder carbon projects*. Climate Change, Agriculture and Food Security (CCAFS) Report No. 8. Retrieved March 7, 2016, from http://ecoagriculture.org/wp-content/uploads/2015/08/InstitutionalInnovationsforAfrican.pdf

Smith, J., & Scherr, S. J. (2002). *Forest carbon and local livelihoods: Assessment of opportunities and policy recommendations* (CIFOR Occasional Paper, 37). Jakarta: CIFOR.

Stiglitz, J. E., & Weiss, A. (1981). Credit rationing in markets with imperfect information. *American Economic Review, 71*(3), 393–410.

Swinnen, F. M. J., & Gow, H. R. (1999). Agricultural credit problems and policies during the transition to a market economy in Central and Eastern Europe. *Food Policy, 24*(1), 21–47.

Thacher, A. T., Lee, D. R., & Schelhas, J. W. (1997). Farmer participation in government sponsored reforestation incentive programs in Costa Rica. *Agroforestry Systems, 35*(3), 269–289.

Theesfeld, I., & Buchenrieder, G. (2000). Improving bankability of small farmers in northern Vietnam. *Savings and Development, 14*(4), 385–403.

Thorlakson, T., & Neufeldt, H. (2012). Reducing subsistence farmers' vulnerability to climate change: Evaluating the potential contributions of agroforestry in western Kenya. *Agriculture & Food Security, 1*(15), 1–13.

Valatin, G. (2011). *Forests and carbon: A review of additionality* (Forestry Commission Research Report; pp. i–vi + 1–22). Edinburgh: Forestry Commission. Retrieved August 10, 2014, from http://www.forestry.gov.uk/pdf/FCRP013.pdf/$FILE/FCRP013.pdf

Wette, H. (1983). Collateral in credit rationing in markets with imperfect information: Note. *American Economic Review, 73*(3), 442–445.

World Bank. (2011). *Triple win of climate-smart agriculture put into practice*. Retrieved April 27, 2014, from http://web.worldbank.org/WBSITE/EXTERNAL/TOPICS/EXTSDNET/0,,contentMDK:22842518~menuPK:64885113~pagePK:7278667~piPK:64911824~theSitePK:5929282,00.html

Wunder, S. (2006). Are direct payments for environmental services spelling doom for sustainable forest management in the tropics? *Ecology and Society, 11*(2), 23.

Wunder, S. (2008). Payments for environmental services and the poor: Concepts and preliminary evidence. *Environment and Development Economics, 13*(3), 279–297.

Wunder, S., Dung The, B., & Ibarra, E. (2005). *Payment is good, control is better: Why payments for environmental services so far have remained incipient in Vietnam*. Bogor: CIFOR.

36

EVOLUTION OF THE EU EMISSIONS TRADING SYSTEM

A new emphasis on distributional and scaling-up dimensions

Noriko Fujiwara

Markets and institutions can provide enabling settings for sustainable finance. North (1990) defines "institutions" as "the rules of the game in a society" or, more formally, "the humanly devised constraints that shape human interaction" which in consequence "structure incentives in human exchange, whether political, social, or economic." In this context, environmental regulations impose various constraints on economic activities, be they performance standards, limits on the volume of emissions, or levies and taxes. Based on the above background, this chapter will examine how non-traditional mechanisms and instruments can address distributional and scaling-up issues and, in doing so, how markets and institutions can contribute to sustainable finance.

To answer these questions, this chapter will focus on examples of carbon markets, especially the EU emissions trading system (EU ETS), the world's biggest carbon market to date, up and running since 2005. At present, the EU ETS covers around 45 percent of total greenhouse gas (GHG) emissions from more than 11,000 heavy-energy-using installations in power generation and industry sectors and from aviation activities in 28 EU member states and three non-EU countries in European Economic Areas (Iceland, Liechtenstein, and Norway).[1] The enquiry will start with a brief observation on how the EU ETS addresses effectiveness and sustainability challenges.

Effectiveness and sustainability

The EU ETS was established to reduce EU GHG emissions in a long-term and cost-effective manner by allowing companies to purchase or sell allowances. European economic recessions triggered by the financial crisis have undermined the effectiveness of the EU ETS. As outputs of European economic activities declined and GHG emissions from the so-called ETS sector fell, compliance buyers had less demands for allowances to meet the caps on emissions. Some ETS-covered installations could sell unused allowances which were allocated free during Phase II (2008–2012).

Consequently, the system has experienced a structural imbalance between the supply and demand of allowances, with an accumulated surplus of up to 2.1 billion allowances by the end of 2013. The EU carbon price (European Union Allowance [EUA] price) has fallen from 30€/tCO_2 in mid-2008 to less than 5€/tCO_2 in mid-2013 (Koch, Fuss, Grosjean, & Edenhofer, 2014). Koch et al. (2014) conclude that variations in economic activities are robust in explaining the EUA price dynamics, while the inflow of international credits generated through the Clean Development Mechanism and renewable policy had moderate impacts on EUA prices. The low price has weakened the incentives for long-term investments in the technologies and measures that could deliver significant GHG emission reductions.

It is projected that such a structural surplus will likely stay at around two billion allowances during most of Phase III. This challenge prompted the EU to propose both short-term and long-term measures. Accordingly, the EU has decided to reschedule the auctioning timetable for 900 million allowances in ETS Phase III ("back loading") in order to rebalance the demand and supply of allowances in the short term. Moreover, as a sustainable solution to the surplus in the long term, the European Commission proposed the establishment of a Market Stability Reserve (MSR) for the ETS (European Commission, 2014a, 2014b). The objectives of this reserve are to tackle the surplus of emission allowances that has built up and to improve the system's resilience to external shocks by adjusting the supply of allowances to be auctioned. The MSR would function by triggering adjustments to annual auction volumes in situations where the total number of allowances in circulation is outside a certain predefined range (price corridor) (European Commission, 2014a, 2014b; see also Gilbert et al., 2014). In practice, this is how the system of a price corridor would work with the aim of mitigating market instability: adding allowances to the reserve by deducting them from future auction volumes due to a large temporary surplus in the EU ETS if the total surplus is above 833 million allowances; and releasing allowances from the reserve and adding them to future auction volumes due to a large temporary deficit in the EU ETS if the total surplus is below 400 million allowances (European Commission, 2014a).

The lower carbon price has further implications for the revenue side. The lower carbon price would reduce the size of EU member states' potential revenues from the auctioning of a predetermined number of allowances. The reduction of potential revenues would constrain member states' capacity to not only implement domestic policies and measures for climate change objectives within their jurisdiction, but also help developing countries implement climate change policies and measures. A potential price rise to be expected from the back-loading decision could increase the size of auctioning revenues available in the short term. Moreover, a more stable pricing system could contribute to a sustainable supply of finance.

The next three sections will examine the evolution of the ETS and its design elements over three phases with a view to drawing lessons for the role of markets and institutions in sustainable finance.

Single market rules and flexible institutional designs

The EU ETS is based on the cap-and-trade model which sets a cap on emissions, allocates allowances ex ante, and allows trade of these allowances to meet the cap. Under ETS Phase II (2008–2012), which was set to coincide with the first commitment period of the Kyoto Protocol, national caps were tightened so that the EU and committed member states can meet the Kyoto Protocol targets. Phase III (2013–2020) introduced an EU-wide single cap with a linear factor that decreases the cap annually so that the EU can meet the target to reduce GHG emissions by 20 percent compared with 1990 levels by 2020. From 2021 the linear factor would be raised from 1.74 percent to 2.2 percent in order to meet the EU's target to reduce GHG emissions by at least 40 percent compared with 1990 levels by 2030

(Council of the EU, 2014). This approach would ensure both cost effective and long-term solutions to distribute mitigation efforts ex ante to the ETS sector.

The EU ETS started with free allocation to operators while gradually increasing the share of member states' auctioning from 5 percent in Phase I (2005–2007) to 10 percent in Phase II (2008–2012). In Phase III (2013–2020), however, electricity generators are required to make a transition from free allocation to auctioning. It was agreed in the final phase of negotiation in the context of derogation to start the auctioning rate at 30 percent in 2013 and then gradually raise it to 100 percent in 2020 (Council of the EU, 2008; see also Article 10a, the EU ETS Directive; European Union, 2009). This decision is aligned with the EU's long-term ambition embodied in the low-carbon economy roadmap which aims at reducing GHG emissions by 80–95 percent compared with 1990 levels and de-carbonizing the electricity sector by 2050.

While applying the same rules to all the covered operators in a harmonized way, the EU ETS Directive allows limited differentiation in its application to member states, taking into account variance in their circumstances and capacities. The impact assessment for the amendment of the ETS Directive before Phase III (European Commission, 2008) identifies cost effectiveness and fairness among other key principles. By "cost effectiveness," the European Commission suggests that achieving the agreed objectives can have significant economic impacts, and therefore the implementation of cost effective policy instruments is crucial. By "fairness," the Commission refers to the European Council's recognition that it is necessary to take into account member states' different circumstances and the reality that differing levels of prosperity have an impact on member states' capacity to invest (European Commission, 2008).

In the impact assessment the European Commission acknowledged the need to share the effort in a fair and equitable way, as agreed by the EU heads of states and governments (European Commission, 2008). The impact assessment assumed that the overall relative direct costs would still be significantly high in a number of member states with a relatively low GDP/capita compared to the richer ones. A cost effective distribution of the effort among member states would result in higher direct costs for member states with lower GDP per capita and hence the smaller capacity to invest in GHG mitigation and renewable energy. Distribution of auctioning rights was expected to address this challenge and to reinforce the fairness criterion (European Commission, 2008). The beneficiaries include Bulgaria (53 percent), Cyprus (20 percent), Czech Republic (31 percent), Estonia (42 percent), Hungary (28 percent), Latvia (56 percent), Lithuania (46 percent), Malta (23 percent), Poland (39 percent), Romania (53 percent), Slovakia (41 percent) and, Slovenia (20 percent). Although some EU-15 countries also benefited from the redistribution, their average share is below 20 percent: Belgium (10 percent), Greece (17 percent), Italy (2 percent), Luxembourg (10 percent), Portugal (16 percent), Spain (13 percent), and Sweden (10 percent) (European Union, 2009).

In addition to the fairness criterion, new member states mostly in Central and Eastern Europe were temporarily exempted from stricter requirements for efforts and/or granted extra allowances in specific provisions. For example, it was agreed in the final phase of negotiation that some member states would have options for transitional-free allocation to installations until 2020 for modernization of electricity generation (Council of the EU, 2008, Annex IV; see also Article 10c, the EU ETS Directive; European Union, 2009).

Another example is (re-)distribution of auctioning allowances for solidarity and growth within the community: 10 percent of allowances to the least wealthy member states in terms of GDP per capita as an additional source of revenue (European Commission, 2014c; see also Council of the EU, 2008 and Article 10.2(b), the EU ETS Directive; European Union, 2009).

The third example is (re-)distribution of auctioning revenues for early efforts to reduce GHG emissions: the remaining 2 percent are distributed as *a bonus* to nine member states which have outperformed 2005 by at least a 20 percent reduction in GHG emissions compared with the reference year set by the Kyoto Protocol (Council of the EU, 2008, Article 10.2(c), EU ETS Directive; European Union, 2009). The beneficiaries are Bulgaria (15 percent), Czech Republic (4 percent), Estonia (6 percent), Hungary (5 percent), Latvia (4 percent), Lithuania (7 percent), Poland (27 percent), Romania (29 percent), and Slovakia (3 percent). The majority (88 percent) of allowances are distributed for auctioning to member states based on their share of emissions in 2005 (Article 10.2(a), the EU ETS Directive; European Union, 2009).

These design elements are expected to secure wider participation of member states with variance in their capacities (both disadvantaged operators and over-performing ones) in the EU-wide system without undermining the integrity of the system rules.

The European Commission's progress report (2012) shows that in effect economic recessions resulted in reducing the cost of the ETS implementation compared with what was originally envisaged for all member states and that the reductions were greater in member states with lower income. As the costs have fallen for all member states, the advantages given to certain member states would be less significant than was originally foreseen. Nevertheless, the Commission confirms that (re-)distribution of auctioning revenues could contribute to a more equitable distribution of efforts among member states (European Commission, 2012).

In principle the latest impact assessment for the 2030 climate and energy policy framework (European Commission, 2014c) maintains the assumption that efforts in lower-income member states are relatively larger than those in higher-income countries because of higher energy system costs compared to GDP and higher additional investment needs. Consequently, the existing provisions linked to modernization, solidarity, and over-performance (Articles 10c, 10.2(b), and 10.2(c), EU ETS Directive; European Union, 2009) would remain in place and could continue up to 2030. Member states with a GDP per capita *below 60 percent of the EU average* may opt to continue to give free allowances to the energy sector up to 2030. The maximum amount which the member state hands out for free after 2020 should be no more than 40 percent of the allowances allocated for auctioning (Council of the EU, 2014). This is intended to produce more equitable outcomes through (re-)distribution of ETS auctioning revenues (European Commission, 2014c). Other options to meet the equity objective are differentiation of GHG targets for non-ETS sectors and renewable energy targets, and leveraging private investment flows through smart and innovative financial instruments (European Commission, 2014c). However, the (re-)distribution of auctioning revenues as a compensatory measure has been emphasized only to the extent that it would not decrease the overall cost effectiveness.

Based on this background, the European heads of state and government agreed to establish a new fund, the "modernization fund." A new reserve of 2 percent of the allowances will be set aside and auctioned to address particularly high additional investment needs in low-income member states (GDP per capita below 60 percent of the EU average). The fund based on the proceeds from the reserve aims at improving energy efficiency and modernizing the energy systems of these member states, so as to provide their citizens with cleaner, secure, and affordable energy. Until 2030 the distribution of the fund will be based evenly on the verified emissions (50 percent) and the GDP criteria (50 percent). In addition, for the purposes of solidarity, growth, and interconnections, 10 percent of the allowances to be auctioned by the member states will be distributed among low-income member states (GDP per capita does not exceed 90 percent of the EU average) (Council of the EU, 2014).

More recently, in the final stage of the negotiation between the Council of the EU and the European Parliament for the MSR, it was agreed among other issues that the above solidarity component would be temporarily exempted from deduction of allowances into the reserve until

2025, that is, lower-income member states will be granted temporary exemption from contribution to the reserve in 2021–2025. However, they will be subject to the same rule from 2026 onwards. Other main features of the agreement are the following: the MSR will be established in 2018 and start operation from January 1, 2019; back-loaded allowances will be placed in the reserve; unallocated allowances will be placed in the reserve in 2020; and the forthcoming ETS review will consider possible use of the unallocated allowances, and a limited number of allowances to supplement existing resources to support CCS, renewables, and low-carbon industrial innovation projects.[2]

The trilogue agreement on the MSR also includes a provision that in any year a corresponding number of allowances will be released from the reserve to member states, then to the market via auctioning, in the same proportions and order as applied at the time of their placement in the reserve. Although higher-income member states will be expected to make a larger contribution to the reserve than the former, in particular in 2021–2025, they will likely benefit earlier and more from the potential rise in the allowance price at the time of release. It is possible that there will be uneven impacts of MSR implementation across member states.

This is the first lesson learned from the experiences of the EU ETS for the roles of markets and institutions in sustainable finance: the application of the single market rules and the flexible institutional designs are not mutually exclusive but complementary to each other. Their main challenge would be to balance different policy objectives: the cost effectiveness of the European carbon market, the long-term perspective of the EU climate policy reflected in its cap setting, and the equitable and fair distribution of efforts through its allocation procedures.

Centralization with member states' discretion

From Phase II (2008–2012) to Phase III (2013–2020) the EU ETS has made a transition from a relatively decentralized system to a more centralized system. One example is, as mentioned above, a move from national cap setting to EU-wide cap setting. Another example is a shift from national allocation to sectoral allocation across the EU. The third example is the establishment of an EU new entrant reserve of 300 million allowances ("NER300") to support innovative renewable energy technologies and capture and geological storage of CO_2 (CCS) in the EU (Article 10a(8) in the EU ETS Directive; European Union, 2009; see next section for further discussion).

On the other hand, the EU ETS retains member states' discretion in its implementation: member states continue to play a central role in the implementation of the system, in particular where fiscal policies matter, for example in auctioning. The ETS Directive states that at least 50 percent of member states' revenues from auctioning should be dedicated to climate and energy-related purposes: for example, research, development, and demonstration, renewable energies, energy efficiency, forestry sequestration, and low-emission public transport (Article 10a(3) in the EU ETS Directive; European Union, 2009). In relation to the focus of this chapter on the distributional dimensions of the EU ETS, it is important to note that auctioning revenues could also provide financial support for tackling fuel poverty in lower- and middle-income households by improving energy efficiency (see Article 10.3(h) in the EU ETS Directive; European Union, 2009).

The first progress report shows that EU member states will use or plan to use for climate and energy-related purposes up to €3 billion out of the total €3.6 billion raised by auctioning in 2013, with 87 percent on average, far above the required 50 percent of the revenues spent for these objectives. Moreover, 11 member states, that is, Germany, the United Kingdom, Spain, France, Greece, the Netherlands, Portugal, Slovakia, Ireland, Lithuania, and Latvia, reported that they would spend 100 percent of the revenues for climate and energy-related purposes (European Commission, 2014d). The above results support EU member states' strong commitments to climate-related activities.

The EU ETS Directive further specifies the list of activities including not only financing European projects to meet climate change objectives, but also supporting developing countries in measures for mitigation and adaptation (e.g., avoiding deforestation, increasing afforestation and reforestation, transferring technologies, facilitating adaptation to the adverse effects) and contributing to global initiatives for such supports (e.g., the Global Energy Efficiency and Renewable Energy Fund, the Adaptation Fund) (Article 10.3(a)(c)(e) in the EU ETS Directive; European Union, 2009). Although the EU ETS Directive is aimed at installations and operators within the EU for climate change mitigation, its institutional design with fiscal implications would have a wider impact on mitigation and adaptation measures on a global scale.

It is up to each member state to determine how to allocate the revenues between different objectives and between domestic and external programs. For example, the 40 million emissions allowances sold in 2008 (each for one ton of CO_2 equivalent emissions) by the German government brought a revenue of roughly €1 billion. Of that income, €400 million was allocated to a comprehensive climate change program focused on domestic measures, which included €120 million for a cooperation program in developing countries (Konukiewitz, 2009). In this way the ETS auctioning enables each member state to set their priorities in the implementation of the support program and to ensure annual flows of finance sourced from auctioning.

The focus on the revenues of the ETS auctioning leads to the second lesson for the roles of markets and institutions in sustainable finance. Designing a more centralized system and decentralized implementation of auctioning could work together. The latter could enhance the perceived effectiveness and sustainability in revenue distribution, thereby contributing to member states' support for the former.

Scaling up climate finance

There is an increasing expectation for the potential role of smart and innovative financing instruments to leverage private investment flows with relatively small public funding. While the EU faces significant long-term investment needs identified in the 2030 climate and energy policy framework, the economic crisis has imposed additional constraints in the short term on member states' and businesses' abilities to pay for the associated costs of compliance and finance-necessary investments across sectors. Smart and innovative financial instruments are expected to provide governments, businesses, and households with access to long-term financing. The EU provides a wide range of innovative financing instruments: for example, European Investment Bank Bonds, the Project Bonds Initiative, Refinancing Guarantees, and Public–Private Risk Sharing Arrangements. The choice of the instruments depends on how to alleviate the different capabilities of member states to finance long-term investments (European Commission, 2014c).

One of these instruments for co-financing is NER300 in the EU ETS. The innovative financing scheme, NER300, sets aside a New Entrants' Reserve of an extra 300 million EUAs under the EU ETS that are earmarked for supporting CCS and renewable energy projects (Article 10a(8) in the EU ETS Directive; European Union, 2009). There is a cap on the maximum amount of receipt at 15 percent of the total number of allowances available. At least one but no more than three projects (CCS and renewable in total) will be funded in each member state. The NER300 finances up to 50 percent of the construction and operational costs of the projects. Project developers and/or member states will have to provide the rest of the funding.

The 300 million EUAs were sold in two tranches, in 2013 and 2014. The first call of the NER300 awarded a total €1.2 billion, the revenue from selling 200 million EUAs, to 20 renewable energy projects, which is estimated to have leveraged additional funding of over €2 billion from private sources.[3] The awarded projects will be implemented in 16 member states: Austria, Belgium, Cyprus, Finland, France, Germany, Greece, Hungary, Ireland, Italy, the Netherlands, Poland, Portugal, Spain, Sweden, and the United Kingdom.[4]

The second call of the NER300 awarded a total of €1 billion, the revenue from selling the remaining 100 million EUAs and unspent funds from the first call to 18 renewable energy projects and one carbon capture and storage project. This amount is estimated to have leveraged additional funding of over €860 million from private sources.[5] The awarded projects will be implemented in 12 member states: Croatia, Cyprus, Denmark, Estonia, France, Ireland, Italy, Latvia, Portugal, Spain, Sweden, and the United Kingdom.[6]

In the remaining period of EU ETS Phase III (2013–2020), there will be no more funding available through NER300. It has been decided by the EU heads of state and government that in Phase IV up to 2030, the existing NER300 facility will be renewed, including support for CCS and renewable energy, with the scope extended to low-carbon innovation in industrial sectors. For this purpose, a new fund will be established, that is, *the innovation fund*, with its initial endowment of up to 400 million EUAs (to be called "NER400") (Council of the EU, 2014). In addition, the final round of the negotiations for the MSR resulted in an agreement between the Council and the European Parliament that the forthcoming ETS review will consider before 2021 a possible use of a limited number of the allowances (up to 50 million) to supplement existing resources to promote those projects under the scope of NER300 and low-carbon industrial innovation projects (European Parliament, 2015).

The NER300 adheres to the cost effectiveness principle. In the NER300 procedure, an initial list of demonstration projects is ranked by cost-per-unit performance, that is, for renewable energy projects, cost per unit of clean energy produced, and for CCS projects, cost per ton of CO_2 stored. Despite the limit on the receipt of a grant and the number of projects per country, the two call results suggest that more projects will be hosted in relatively wealthy member states: Cyprus, France, Ireland, Italy, Portugal, Spain, Sweden, and the United Kingdom.

The third lesson can be drawn from EU-level auctioning in the form of the NER300 under the EU ETS: the centralized implementation of auctioning might reinforce the cost effectiveness of the single market rather than take into account the effects of project distribution based on equity. This is inevitable, provided that innovative financial instruments such as NER300 rely on co-financing between the host government and the private sector.

Concluding remarks: Equity in the long term

The example of the EU ETS highlights the EU's difficulties with disparity in member states' capacities and its efforts to achieve balance on three dimensions: between single market rules and flexible institutional designs; between the centralized system and decentralized implementation of auctioning; and between the centralized implementation of auctioning and its possible consequence on the distribution of project finance. In doing so, it also illustrates the versatility of the market and institutional designs that could be adapted to address both EU-wide long-term common goals and short-term constraints on the capabilities of individual member states. Such versatility enables the evolutionary development of the ETS.

Addressing distributional and scaling-up issues through the EU ETS and associated financing instruments respectively, the EU seeks to meet the fairness or equity challenges in the long term. The ambition of equity, however, might be reconciled by the cost effectiveness principle. The leveraging effects of smart financial instruments appear to strengthen the cost effectiveness principle at first sight. How such instruments could also attract new investments for deployment of low-carbon technologies and innovation in lower-income member states remains to be seen.

Notes

1 Retrieved July 24, 2015, from http://ec.europa.eu/clima/policies/ets/index_en.htm
2 Retrieved July 24, 2015, from http://www.consilium.europa.eu/en/press/press-releases/2015/05/13-market-stability-reserve and https://eu2015.lv/news/media-releases/1703-member-states-adopt-market-stability-reserve-file-to-fight-against-climate-change
3 Retrieved July 24, 2015, from http://ec.europa.eu/clima/policies/lowcarbon/ner300/index_en.htm
4 Retrieved July 24, 2015, from http://europa.eu/rapid/press-release_MEMO-12-999_en.htm
5 Retrieved July 24, 2015, from http://ec.europa.eu/clima/policies/lowcarbon/ner300/index_en.htm
6 Retrieved July 24, 2015, from http://europa.eu/rapid/press-release_MEMO-14-465_en.htm

References

Council of the European Union. (2008, December 12). *Energy and climate change: Elements of the final compromise*. EU Document No. 17215/08, Brussels.

Council of the European Union. (2014, October 24). *European Council conclusions*. EUCO 169/14, Brussels.

European Commission. (2008). *Impact assessment: Document accompanying the package of implementation measures for the EU's objectives on climate change and renewable energy for 2020*. Commission Staff Working Document, SEC (2008) 85/3. Brussels: Author.

European Commission. (2012). *Analysis of options beyond 20% GHG emission reductions: Member state results*. Commission Staff Working Paper, SWD (2012) 5 final. Brussels: Author.

European Commission. (2014a). *Proposal for a decision of the European Parliament and of the Council concerning the establishment and operation of a market stability reserve for the Union greenhouse gas emission trading scheme and amending Directive 2003/87/EC*. COM (2014) 20 final. Brussels: Author.

European Commission. (2014b). *Impact assessment accompanying the document, proposal for a decision of the European Parliament and the Council concerning the establishment and operation of a market stability reserve for the Union greenhouse gas emission trading scheme and amending Directive 2003/87/EC*. SWD (2014) 17 final. Brussels: Author.

European Commission. (2014c). *Impact assessment accompanying the Communication from the Commission to the European Parliament, the Council, the European Economic and Social Committee and the Committee of the Regions: A policy framework for climate and energy in the period from 2020 up to 2030*. Commission Staff Working Document, SWD (2014) 15 final. Brussels: Author.

European Commission. (2014d). *Progress towards achieving the Kyoto and EU 2020 objectives: Annex to the report from the Commission to the European Parliament and the Council*. COM (2014) 689 final. Brussels: Author.

European Parliament. (2015, May 6). ETS market stability reserve: MEPs strike deal with Council. *European Parliament News*.

European Union. (2009). Directive 2009/29/EC of the European Parliament and of the Council of 23 April 2009 amending Directive 2003/87/EC so as to improve and extend the greenhouse gas emission allowance trading scheme of the Community. *Official Journal of the European Union, L 140*, 63–83.

Gilbert, A., Lam, L., Sachweh, C., Smith, M., Taschini, L., & Kollenberg, S. (2014). *Assessing design options for a market stability reserve in the EU ETS*. London, UK: ECOFYS.

Koch, N., Fuss, S., Grosjean, G., & Edenhofer, O. (2014). Causes of the EU ETS price drop: Recession, CDM, renewable policies or a bit of everything?—New evidence. *Energy Policy, 73*, 676–685.

Konukiewitz, M. (2009). Revenues from the carbon market. In *Innovative financing for development: The I-8 group, leading innovative financing for equity*. New York, NY: The United Nations.

North, D. (1990). *Institutions, institutional change and economic performance*. Cambridge, UK: Cambridge University Press.

37

CLIMATE CHANGE MITIGATION

Are carbon markets the "silver bullet" solution?

Scott J. Niblock and Jennifer L. Harrison

Global warming is considered to be one of the greatest market failures of all time. In particular, organizations have consistently failed to consider the full environmental and social costs of their production processes, simply passing the costs of their pollution on to society without penalty (Garner, 2006). Andrew (2008) states that:

> The environment is a "public good" in that it is not the exclusive property of any one person or group; thus, a large number of people enjoy the benefit of it even if they have not paid for it. Many people consume it without any need to compete with one another for the benefit and at nil or little cost to any of them. Because there is no cost and an apparent abundance of natural resources to consume there has been massive over consumption of the environment.
>
> *(p. 396)*

While climate change is a naturally occurring phenomenon, the Intergovernmental Panel on Climate Change (IPCC) (2014b) recently stated that "[w]arming of the climate system is unequivocal" (p. 1) and "[i]t is *extremely likely* that human influence has been the dominant cause of the observed warming since the mid-20th century" (p. 2). This process of warming has its basis in the earth receiving energy from the sun and radiating it back into the stratosphere, primarily as invisible infrared light. Long-lived gases, such as carbon dioxide (CO_2), reduce the outflow of this light, producing an energy imbalance known as the "greenhouse effect" (Garner, 2006). As such, the release of CO_2 from fossil fuels over the past century has increased an energy imbalance, resulting in significantly warmer temperatures (Victor & House, 2004). The consequences of increasing CO_2 and other greenhouse gas (GHG) concentrations will present significant future climatic risks and costs for society (Larson & Parks, 1999). Indeed, the outcomes of a "business-as-usual" approach to this issue seem likely to be irreversible, potentially resulting in calamitous events such as the extinction of many species, the disappearance of low-lying islands under rising oceans, floods, famine, increased deaths due to tropical diseases and heat stress, and mass human migration (Her Majesty's Treasury (HMT), 2006). Obviously, opportunities for economic prosperity can no longer be considered independent of environmental preservation (Garner, 2006).

The potential adverse effects of climate change are problematic for all nations because climate change is both global and long-term (MacGill, Outhred, & Nolles, 2004). Other issues include: appropriate policy development and maintenance; adverse economic impacts from global warming; and environmental and societal impacts (e.g., a shift from fossil fuels to cleaner alternatives, land use and resource management issues, energy security matters, and equity concerns) (MacGill et al., 2004). However, the body of scientific evidence and ever-increasing quantitative assessment of climate change risks are now sufficient to give strong guidance to policy makers in determining an appropriate economic response (HMT, 2006).

The mechanics of carbon markets

Governments and regulatory bodies are currently taking collective action to address climate change. However, global climate change policy positions to date have been ambiguous and non-binding—promoting economic benefits for polluting industries at a significant cost to society and the environment (Garnaut Review, 2008; Niblock & Harrison, 2013a). Recognizing the difficulty of successfully implementing broad policy measures, the United Nations Framework Convention on Climate Change (UNFCCC), with the backing of comprehensive economic analysis (Garnaut Review, 2008; HMT, 2006), indicated that to drive the GHG abatement necessary to reduce the effects of climate change, market-based instruments should be implemented. Economists generally uphold tradeable permits as a viable climate change policy alternative; however, the concept has been criticized at times due to previous environmental market failures (e.g., the failure of water quality permit schemes) (Ellerman, 2005).

Prominent economist Sir Nicholas Stern (HMT, 2006) asserts that instruments or "mechanisms" such as carbon trading can promote a price-based incentive for GHG abatement, economic efficiency, and flexibility. He also suggests that while there are substantial opportunities and risks involved with market-based GHG mitigation mechanisms, the cost of doing nothing about climate change is far greater than doing something. Similarly, Professor Ross Garnaut (Garnaut Review, 2008) claims that carbon trading stimulates economic growth and benefits, and drives investment.

The concept of carbon trading has been widely embraced by developed economies and has thus far been a compliance-driven market, where buyers engage in carbon transactions because of regulatory constraints at international or sub-national levels. The European Union (EU) successfully implemented the world's first mandatory multi-country, multi-sector cap-and-trade carbon trading scheme, namely the "EU Emissions Trading Scheme" (EU ETS). The significance of the scheme is that the EU economy is the first economy in the world to be carbon-constrained (Castellas, 2013; Taberner, Taubman, & Burns, 2005). Other international schemes that are currently operational or proposed have also been influenced heavily by the design of the EU ETS.

Having commenced operation on January, 2005, the EU ETS is a high-volume and liquid broad-based market whereby companies operating under the scheme can trade in carbon emissions (which are measured in tons). The gas concentration of these emissions (or equivalence of other gases) can be measured in the atmosphere or estimated directly from the energy source (e.g., the amount of electricity or fuel burnt). As energy usage is also measurable, carbon emissions can easily be translated into tons (HMT, 2006). Therefore, the trading "currency" of the EU ETS is the European Union Allowance (EUA), where one EUA equals the right to emit "one ton" of CO2-e during the specified period (World Bank, 2012).

Garner (2006) asserts that "[i]mplementation of this trading scheme constitutes an effective policy instrument, based on economic rationality in order to achieve the EU's commitment to reduce emissions under multi-lateral agreements such as the Kyoto Protocol" (p. 85). Essentially, the EU ETS forms an alternative to imposing absolute emission limits on individual companies, allowing for a more flexible determination on how and where emissions are reduced (Alberola, Chevallier, & Chèze, 2008; Ernst & Young, 2012).

The economic basis of carbon markets, like the EU ETS, lies in the ideas of Coase (1960) and involves putting a price on carbon emissions by creating limited property rights and then enabling organized markets for trading those rights (generally known as carbon allowances, permits, or credits). Thus, a market for carbon emissions is created and the market mechanism can do its work to efficiently allocate the limited rights to emit amongst emitters. A carbon trading scheme also generally requires that the government(s) and/or agency provide monitoring and enforcement to ensure that emission reduction targets are met (Thompson & Campbell-Watt, 2005). For instance, non-compliers usually pay a penalty and still have to buy the requisite number of allowances in the scheme over each successive period (World Bank, 2012).

Allowances for emissions reductions can be traded in mandatory or voluntary markets. In a mandatory cap-and-trade system, the property rights which create the market are based on determining maximum emissions levels over a certain time period(s), dividing that limit into allowances, and allocating those allowances (via sale, auction, or, more controversially, freely) to emitters ("the cap"). Scheme participants (emitters) who exceed the cap will need to purchase further allowances from other participants under the cap due to the use of less carbon-intensive energy sources or investment in new technologies ("the trade") (Ernst & Young, 2012; Pearce, 2005). Hence participants who can cut their emissions cheaply can sell their excess allowances to those participants who cannot (Tyrell, 2006). In theory, the net effect is the reduction of aggregate emissions at the lowest possible cost. In practice, there are significant barriers to creating an effective, efficient, and credible carbon market, as discussed in the remainder of this chapter. Despite this, carbon markets are seen as a key and even preferred mechanism for climate change mitigation (Stern, 2006; Tirole, 2008).

The investability of carbon markets

Having established the theoretical attractiveness of carbon trading from environmental and economic perspectives, we now consider its appeal from an investment perspective. This in part depends on whether carbon can be classed as an emerging asset market (e.g., a financial market that is small by capitalization but growing rapidly). If so, the development and investment potential of the carbon market is extremely high if carbon is indeed considered a global asset. To gain an understanding of this proposition, the current economic and investment environment needs to be outlined. The global financial crisis (GFC) of 2007–2008 triggered an economic recession in most developed economies, effectively driving investors to an aversion of risky assets. As a result, asset classes such as shares and corporate bonds became riskier and less favorable than traditionally expected (Ernst & Young, 2012). In light of this investment environment, market players sought a hedge against expectations of falling asset prices by investing in "tangible assets" (i.e., assets that have physical properties or a "store-of-value"). As such, less risky investment vehicles (like government bonds and cash instruments) and commodity assets (such as gold, metals, oil, agricultural, and environmental) became the focus of considerable interest to investors (particularly in the absence of high-yielding, low-risk investment alternatives) (World Bank, 2012).

Environmental commodities like "carbon" have become a new financial instrument in commodity trading markets, particularly in Europe. For example, carbon can be bought and sold like a barrel of oil or a ton of coal (Benz & Trück, 2006). Arguably, carbon is not a "tangible" commodity because, while carbon allowances can be owned and traded, there is no natural underlying carbon reduction asset (Blair, 1998; World Bank, 2012). However, like tangible commodities, carbon allowances are traded in markets at fair value based on supply (e.g., allowance allocation caps, allowance importation, and new scheme participants) and demand (e.g., weather, economic conditions, and renewable energy availability) (Andrew, 2008; Blair, 1998; Kemfert, Diekmann, & Ziesling, 2004).

While the carbon market is relatively new, it is growing in size and scope. For example, in addition to the EU ETS, there are more than 15 implemented carbon trading schemes, including the California Cap-and-Trade Program, the Regional Greenhouse Gas Initiative (RGGI) (covering several eastern states in the US), several sub-national pilot programs running in China, and other national or sub-national schemes in Switzerland, New Zealand, Canada, Kazakhstan, and Japan (World Bank, 2014). The value of carbon in these schemes totalled US$ 30 billion at the end of 2013 (World Bank, 2014). There are also several additional planned schemes including, importantly, a national carbon market in China, the world's largest emitter, reportedly to be implemented in 2016 (Chen & Reklev, 2014). This would create the largest carbon market in the world.

Non-emitters can also hedge, invest, or speculate in carbon allowances, opening up possibilities for changing price behavior and dynamics that increase the importance of these emerging markets in the financial system (Ernst & Young, 2012; Miclăus, Lupu, Dumitrescu, & Bobircă, 2008). In addition to the increasing size, scope, and potential liquidity of the carbon markets, their attractiveness to investors will depend on the potential for low correlations with other investment alternatives, thus providing diversification benefits (Abraham, 2007; Benz & Hengelbrock, 2008).

However, while emerging markets play an important role in the financial system, not all deliver the perceived investment benefits that are expected of them. Niblock and Harrison (2012, 2013b) show that European carbon markets have exhibited poor investability (e.g., low risk-adjusted returns) and minimal diversification benefits (e.g., high positive correlations with international equity markets) since their inception. They further claim that the poor returns and high risk associated with carbon assets to date suggest that investors may need to reduce their portfolio weightings and/or consider other alternative investments until carbon markets demonstrate better price return performance and less volatility. It is indeed a point of interest to observe how carbon performs under less volatile market conditions.

If emerging markets, like carbon, are statistically linked and consistently underperform other markets, the benefits of international diversification and investment appeal are reduced significantly. As emerging markets are expected to demonstrate negative to low positive correlations with more developed markets, this indeed raises questions about portfolio theory and its application. Ultimately, the influx of modern technology, removal of international borders, and ongoing financial crises suggests that emerging markets, like carbon, are now influenced similarly to developed markets and are becoming increasingly integrated into the global economy (Castellas, 2013).

Carbon market efficiency

Further reducing the investment potential of carbon markets is the uncertainty caused by the political machinations involved. Ongoing difficulties in developing mandatory international agreements, changes in policy (e.g., Australia), and failures to commit all dissuade investment and ultimately weaken the chances of achieving the overall objective (i.e., to mitigate the economic, social, and environmental effects of climate change). Furthermore, surplus allowances left in the aftermath of the GFC have depressed carbon prices, limiting even further carbon's potential as a "stand-alone" asset class. A raft of other criticisms have been voiced about the carbon market operational issues, ranging from allowance allocation problems to lack of monitoring and transparency, and even market manipulation (Egenhoffer, 2007; Taylor, 2007; Willis & Fitz-Gerald, 2007). Such operational issues have the potential to limit the efficiency of carbon markets. If this is the case, prices will be less reliable and may not send the correct signals to the market.

A lack of information or unequal access to information leads to incorrect pricing because it gives a false impression of the scarcity of a resource (i.e., the inability of a price to act as an appropriate signal to both consumers and producers). Market participants who have limited information will make poor decisions, thus reducing the efficiency of the market as an allocator of scarce resources (Andrew, 2008). So what are the implications for policy makers, businesses, investors, the economy, environment, and society in general, if carbon markets are *not* informationally efficient? Moreover, are these price signals allowing the efficient allocation of resources throughout the carbon economy? The answers to these questions are of paramount importance to carbon stakeholders for two reasons: (1) the primary aim of setting up carbon markets is to regulate polluting companies by facilitating environmental compliance in a cost-effective and economically optimal manner, an approach which implicitly demands that the market itself is *prima facie* informationally efficient (Abeysekera, 2001)—this concept of informational efficiency is consistent with Fama's (1970) efficient market hypothesis (EMH) that states that existing asset prices incorporate all available information, which means that asset prices always trade at equilibrium (or at fair value) and markets are efficient; and (2) understanding whether carbon markets are informationally efficient or otherwise will guide future policy design, influence regulation, highlight the investment strategies that market participants pursue, and determine whether carbon trading is the solution to GHG mitigation and climate change prevention (Albrecht, Verbeke, & De Clercq, 2006).

Despite being an essential assumption underlying one of the key abatement mechanisms advanced for global climate change mitigation, the informational efficiency of carbon markets has received only modest attention. Several research studies (e.g., Christiansen, Arvanitakis, Tangen, & Hasselknippe, 2005; Ellerman, 2005; Ellerman & Buchner, 2008; Ellerman, Joskow, & Harrison, 2003; McKibbin & Wilcoxen, 2006; Seifert, Uhrig-Homburg, & Wagner, 2008) have been published in the economics literature on the science, mechanisms, and policy implications of carbon markets, but little empirical research has been undertaken from a financial economic/investment perspective. In fact, the empirical literature is surprisingly limited given the recent emergence, explosive growth, and controversial nature of carbon markets. Of those empirical studies that have been undertaken, several of them (Alberola, 2006; Arouri, Jawadi, & Nguyen, 2012; Benz & Hengelbrock, 2008; Boutaba, 2009; Chevallier, 2010; Milunovich & Joyeux, 2007; Milunovich, Stegman, & Cotton, 2007; Uhrig-Homburg & Wagner, 2009) found short- and long-run dynamic relationships in EU ETS spot and forward markets, signifying joint price discovery and some level of informational efficiency. These results also suggest that carbon markets may be suitable for investment, hedging, and risk management. Charles, Darné, and Fouilloux (2013) also find that EUA futures contracts are co-integrated with spot prices and interest rates over several maturities. However, individual and joint tests reject the cost of carry hypothesis, inferring that market inefficiencies and arbitrage opportunities may be apparent in European carbon markets.

In a transnational study, Mizrach (2012) explores the market architecture and common factors of emission reduction instruments in Europe and the US. Mizrach finds that spot and futures prices across European exchanges are co-integrated, while uncertainty surrounding the clean development mechanism has kept EUA and Certified Emission Reduction (CER) prices from converging. Alternatively, RGGI allowances appear to share a common trend with EUAs.

Using econometric models with multiple stationary time series, Aatola, Ollikainen, and Toppinen (2013) find that the EUA forward price depends on German electricity, gas, and coal prices. Similarly, Lutz, Pigorsch, and Rotfub (2013) examine the nonlinear relationship between the EUA price and fundamentals such as energy prices, macroeconomic risk factors, and weather conditions. Using a Markov regime switching model, they find that the relationship between the EUA price and its fundamentals varies over time. The most important EUA price drivers are stock market and energy price changes, while gas, oil, and coal prices also demonstrate a positive impact.

Numerous studies have also been carried out on the random walk properties of carbon markets. For instance, Lu and Wang (2010) explore informational efficiency, applying daily European Union allowances prices (spot and forward) in Phase I (2005–2007) and Phase II (2008–2010). The results suggest that Phase II allowances demonstrate weaker rejection against the random walk hypothesis (RWH) than Phase I allowances. Upon dividing Phase I and Phase II into two sub-periods, respectively, they further reveal that the latter half of Phase I allowances (after the EU ETS allowance over allocation announcement on April 26, 2006) showed considerably less robust rejection against the RWH. Lu and Wang conclude that European carbon markets are developing and demonstrating an increasingly higher informational efficiency status as they develop.

Similarly, Montagnoli and de Vries (2010) investigate the EMH by employing daily spot EU ETS price data for Phase I (2005–2007) and Phase II (2008–2009). The results indicate that Phase I was informationally inefficient, whereas Phase II confirms signs of improved market efficiency. Charles, Darné, and Fouilloux (2011) also examine the martingale difference hypothesis using daily and weekly European Union allowances prices (spot and forward) over the 2005–2009 period. Phase I results show price return predictability, suggesting that speculative trading could have resulted in abnormally large returns, while Phase II findings reveal that spot and forward price changes are random. Charles et al. (2011) conclude that European markets have become more informationally efficient.

Niblock and Harrison (2013a) also examine the efficiency status of the European carbon market over periods of sustained volatility, uncertainty, complexity, and ambiguity (VUCA) (i.e., 2008–2012). Niblock and Harrison suggest that emerging carbon markets may be as efficient as their developed counterparts, particularly when employing simple technical trading rules that take into consideration the effects of transaction costs. They further infer that despite ongoing market VUCA and global climate change policy ambiguity, it appears that European carbon markets are becoming more informationally efficient over time.

Conversely, Daskalakis and Markellos (2008) use daily Phase I EU ETS price data (spot and forward) from 2005 to 2006 to examine informational efficiency. They find that Phase I spot and forward European carbon returns are non-random and that basic technical trading strategies can be used to make substantial risk-adjusted profits. Daskalakis and Markellos conclude that European carbon market returns may be predictable and are *not* consistent with the behavior that is expected from an informationally efficient market. Notably, their findings directly challenge the EMH. If carbon markets are informationally inefficient and remain so, this implies that the carbon abatement mechanism is ineffective, thus resulting in market failure and uncertain outcomes for the global economy and environment in the long run.

In a more recent study, Daskalakis (2013) employs simple technical analysis rules and naïve forecasts to establish whether European emission allowance futures markets are efficient. Daskalakis shows that the European carbon market has become weaker-form efficient from 2010 onwards and is gradually attaining a state of maturity. Bredin, Hyde, and Muckley (2014) also assess the efficiency of the EU ETS. Employing intra daily data, they reveal that significant developments in the carbon market are consistent with sequential information arrival. Further,

EUAs demonstrate a negative contemporaneous relationship between volume and volatility, indicating that liquidity traders dominate any role played by informed traders. On the other hand, Crossland, Li, and Roca (2013) test whether the EU ETS exhibits return predictability in terms of momentum and overreaction. They reveal robust short-term momentum and medium-term overreaction in the EU ETS. Also, trading strategies appear to generate excess returns (after taking into account transaction costs), suggesting that the EU ETS may *not* be informationally efficient.

Based on the above-mentioned research, the sole use of market-based mechanisms to address climate change must surely be questioned. Essentially, informational constraints result in incorrect pricing and the misallocation of resources, preventing markets from operating efficiently and achieving their primary objective. In the case of the carbon market, an incorrect pricing mechanism will obstruct the allocation of carbon resources (via the non-fluent trading of GHG emission allowances) and promote systemic market risks (such as price crashes) similar to those experienced in Phase I of the EU ETS. If carbon markets fail as a result of informational inefficiencies, it is envisaged that the international climate change movement will suffer a significant setback. For instance, policy makers and environmental economists (Garnaut Review, 2008; HMT, 2006) have primarily promoted carbon trading as the global "silver bullet" for preventing climate change, placing considerably less emphasis on other policy devices (such as carbon taxes, abatement purchasing, and other complementary environmental legislation).

A potential carbon market failure further substantiates the notion that market-based mechanisms may not be the best approach to reduce GHG emissions. More specifically, a carbon market collapse would confirm the broader market failure literature, demonstrating that financial markets left to their own devices (e.g., poor or "non-existent" regulation during the GFC resulted in market manipulation, fraud, greed, and lack of market transparency, morality, and integrity) or being the product of unnecessary government intervention (e.g., bad policy, political agendas, "red tape," and bureaucracies) simply do not function effectively. Therefore, sole reliance on traditional economic philosophies to solve complex, global problems simply may not be the panacea, and policy alternatives to market-based mechanisms should be considered collectively.

Also, the effect market behavior or "psychology" has on carbon market participants is uncertain. If carbon markets are informationally constrained, are they inefficient because of poor policy, regulation, and other economic fundamentals or are they inefficient because of the way international investors and market participants traded them? If the latter is deemed to be the appropriate answer, this has great significance for the behavioral finance discipline. Essentially, an efficient carbon market may have become inefficient by the panic selling and other irrational investment decisions that were associated with policy mishaps (i.e., Phase I price crash) and GFC, respectively. In other words, do emotional investment and trading behaviors become predictable during crises and, if so, does emotional behavior drive market inefficiency or does market inefficiency drive emotional behavior, or both?

Opportunities and challenges for carbon markets

Carbon markets clearly present significant opportunities and challenges for the global economy. Given the threat of climate change, the carbon market could become the world's largest commodity market (Castellas, 2013; Pearce, 2005; Tyrell, 2006). However, carbon trading is but one of a number of policy instruments available to address climate change; it is not the "silver bullet" (Niblock & Harrison, 2013b). If carbon markets are informationally inefficient, this holds numerous implications for policy makers, market participants, society, and the environment. First, international carbon trading schemes (both current and proposed) have been designed largely around the EU ETS model, paying close attention to the lessons learnt from past mistakes and building on them. However, the notion has been consistently criticized on geopolitical, social, and environmental issues.

Non-binding international climate change agreements and poor regulation have compromised the integrity of market-based mechanisms, resulting in carbon investment skepticism and prolonged uncertainty across the globe. From a social perspective, large polluters have been accused of reaping windfall profits from manipulative or "creative carbon accounting" activities, simply passing trading costs on to the consumer without reducing their GHG emissions. Furthermore, low GHG targets and weak trading caps have placed downward pressure on carbon prices and investment, prevented viable clean energy alternatives (such as solar, wind, nuclear, geothermal, bio fuel, and tidal energy) from competing with the carbon intensive polluters, and reduced GHG emissions less than anticipated (Garnaut Review, 2008; World Bank, 2012). Overall, these criticisms have led to somewhat of a public relations crisis for carbon markets and about policy makers' ability to deal with the complex problems associated with them, as reflected in headlines such as "ETS, RIP?" (The Economist, 2013).

The above-mentioned issues and the alleged informational inefficiencies highlighted pose potential problems for international, national, and sub-national schemes that adopt similar market-based mechanisms for their own climate change policy agendas. Notably, future start dates for other schemes will depend on how quickly policy makers can resolve the alleged design flaws of "cap-and-trade" schemes like the EU ETS. However, the complexities and controversial nature of these issues are not unique to Europe. Climate change policy disputes are occurring across the globe and are undermining efforts both domestically and internationally. For example, Australia has ruled out a domestic emissions trading scheme and the Swiss have delayed planned integration of their carbon market with the EU ETS. Moreover, how carbon trading is implemented at the national level will be vital to its effectiveness as a global environmental policy tool (Castellas, 2013; Stevens & Rose, 2002).

One of the main disparagements of carbon trading schemes to date has been that they discourage rather than encourage investment in new and low carbon fuels and technologies in the long term. This may be partly a result of international regulatory indecision, which in turn reduces predictability and, hence, the lack of investment certainty (Egenhoffer, 2007; IPCC, 2014a). Ultimate certainty will only be achieved once a truly global and comprehensible framework with a long horizon (to match the long-term investment decision-making needs of low carbon technologies) involving all major emitters has been agreed upon, and an international carbon price signal exists (Garnaut Review, 2008; Tirole, 2008). Until this eventuates, governments, market participants, investors, and society will continue to be faced with a considerable degree of uncertainty regarding carbon trading, low carbon investments, and climate change (Egenhoffer, 2007; Ernst & Young, 2012).

Arguably, the carbon market's major risks are related to poor policy, inefficient regulation, a lack of international cooperation/agreement, and the absence of market continuity and planned investment. However, if the global goal is to meet science-based mitigation targets, dealing with these issues will be necessary even if carbon markets are only one part of the solution. In particular, cooperation will be necessary. The United Nations Environment Programme (UNEP) (2013) indicates that there is a significant gap between the emissions cuts needed to limit temperature increases to 2°C and those likely under current policies. Closing this gap will require a significant and speedy increase in the scale and scope of action to reduce emissions, and cooperation will be essential to achieving this outcome at reasonable cost (World Bank, 2014). A step towards this cooperation will involve linking emissions trading programs, for example between California and Quebec, thus "converting fragmented initiatives into internationally integrated carbon pricing approaches" (World Bank, 2014, p. 19). Such cooperation has many benefits, for example preventing carbon leakage (e.g., industries in a mandatory carbon trading scheme that shift their operations overseas to avoid paying for pollution allowances) (Garnaut Review, 2008), and providing more coherent price signals than under the current state of affairs where carbon prices per ton vary significantly across emissions trading schemes, ranging from under US$1 (New Zealand) to US$95 (Japan) in 2013 (World Bank, 2014). Price signals from carbon taxes are similarly varied (World Bank, 2014). Furthermore, efficiency needs to be encouraged, transaction costs reduced, and unnecessary duplication avoided (HMT, 2006; World Bank, 2012).

The carbon market also needs to be supported with other policy mechanisms to stimulate low carbon investment. For example, governments (unilaterally or collectively) should encourage the development of alternative market-based instruments, taxes, and/or direct action plans that can be used to stimulate low carbon investment by either decreasing investment costs or improving risk-adjusted returns (IPCC, 2014a). Overall, the rules of the game must be clear: markets must adhere to a "goldilocks" regulatory scenario (i.e., somewhere between being left to their own devices and being driven wholly by regulators/governments); markets should be liquid; trading is to be encouraged to deliver a clear price signal (including, for example, no fixed prices, no price safety valves (i.e., a cap or floor on tradeable market prices), and auctioning of allowances); and everyone needs be educated about their climatic footprints and responsibilities (World Bank, 2012).

Ultimately, the success of further reform depends upon the degree to which policy makers and regulators are committed to increasing market transparency, and on their overall ability to remove the uncertainty surrounding carbon trading. The removal of obstructive policies and regulations and the development of more appropriate legislation will ultimately create a more conducive and liquid investing environment in both spot and forward carbon markets, therefore creating more optimal conditions for carbon market efficiency. If policy makers desire these outcomes, they should implement decisive reform(s) to address the informational constraints (including over-allocation of allowances, loose emissions targets and caps, market manipulation, market opacity, lax reporting standards, and restrictive access to information and education) facing carbon trading schemes. Policy makers may also have to reconsider the sole use of carbon trading or its cousin, carbon taxes, as the preferred global GHG mitigation play, and instead flank market-based mechanisms with a diverse range of flexible, cost effective policy alternatives and instruments that can be scaffolded and policed across international borders. Moreover, a less distorted long-term carbon price is needed to inform market participants about carbon risks and opportunities and to guide their future investment decisions (Castellas, 2013; Egenhoffer, 2007).

The question remains whether policy makers can actually promote certainty in carbon markets, and if so, will better market conditions and operability increase informational efficiency in the long run? What is abundantly clear is that an efficient, global price on carbon must be established in a timely manner if international trading is the chosen GHG abatement mechanism, economic growth is to be maintained, and environmental preservation is deemed a priority.

Conclusion

With the IPCC's (2014b) unequivocal conclusion on global warming and the UNEP's (2013) estimate that current policy initiatives will not be enough to limit that warming to 2°C, the importance of climate change mitigation cannot be underestimated. Anthropogenic global warming has been intensified by growing populations, abundantly cheap natural resources (e.g., energy, food, and water sources), and the failure of international policy makers and polluting businesses to address growing GHG emissions over time. Furthermore, corporate profits have been fuelled at the expense of environmental conservation and sustainability, and this behavior is likely to continue if the "business-as-usual" mentality is maintained. Acknowledging this dilemma, international policy makers and economists have recently popularized market-based abatement mechanisms (such as carbon trading schemes and taxes) as the "silver bullet" solution for curbing GHG emissions and enforcing environmental protection.

However, carbon trading schemes and their associated policies to date have been criticized regarding their appropriateness, lack of transparency, accessibility, complexity, poor regulation, manipulation, inter-operability, stability, innovation, and inflexibility. While carbon markets have the potential to rival previous investment booms (such as the "dot.com" technology boom), it is the above-mentioned criticisms, along with a lack of international policy certainty, that threaten to derail the climate change movement.

International climate change politics have faltered due to disagreements over emerging and developed country GHG abatement commitments and responsibilities. Global pessimism and short-termism due to the GFC (and the limited debt/equity financing available to market participants) have reduced opportunities and increased risks in carbon markets. Domestic climate change politics have been sidelined to protect primary industry and corporate/political interests during recent economic uncertainty. Finally, a lack of certainty on green investment payback due to directionless global climate change policy has deterred investment in clean fuels and technologies, and reduced the popularity of carbon trading/markets in general.

Upon consideration of these controversial issues, it is possible that information is being constrained and that the effective allocation of scarce natural resources is not occurring in carbon markets. Furthermore, such behavior could lead to market inefficiencies or failure over time, thus preventing carbon markets from fulfilling their primary objective/s (namely, to reduce global GHG emissions and preserve the environment for future generations). If informational inefficiencies are evident in carbon markets, it is questionable whether market-based GHG abatement mechanisms are the solution for climate change mitigation in the long run. Investigation of carbon market informational efficiency is therefore an obvious imperative for the economic and finance disciplines. However, the informational efficiency literature indicates that researchers have neglected to examine informational efficiency in carbon markets with the scrutiny it deserves. The problem is, while researchers have investigated informational efficiency issues extensively in emerging capital markets, little is known about the informational efficiency of emerging carbon markets. As mentioned previously, uncertainties surrounding the operational effectiveness of carbon trading schemes, the potential role of carbon markets in the successful abatement of GHG emissions, and the impact of the GFC have further exacerbated the problem.

The need for further carbon market research is underpinned by the significant risks of global warming and their potential negative impact on humankind. Further research will undoubtedly contribute to developing more effective global warming policies that combine economic growth with a more robust environment for future generations. Clearly, humankind is reaching the limits of its natural resources and requires a more sustainable approach. Furthermore, the GFC has highlighted the need for international economies to be re-designed around people and the environment, not "profit driven" corporations and individuals. While the GFC has had serious economic ramifications for society, it may be a relatively insignificant event, particularly in a future where money could be the least of the planet's concerns. Tackling global warming with full commitment is a matter of the planet's very survival.

> We are playing Russian roulette with features of the planet's atmosphere that will profoundly impact generations to come. How long are we willing to gamble?
>
> *(Dr David Suzuki (Department of Energy and Environmental Protection (DEEP), 2010, p. 1)*

References

Aatola, P., Ollikainen, M., & Toppinen, A. (2013). Price determination in the EU ETS market: Theory and econometric analysis with market fundamentals. *Energy Economics, 36*, 380–395.

Abeysekera, S. P. (2001). Efficient markets hypothesis and the emerging capital market in Sri Lanka: Evidence from the Colombo stock exchange—A note. *Journal of Business Finance and Accounting, 28*(1–2), 249–261.

Abraham, A. (2007). Is carbon the new asset class? *Infinance, 121*, 7–39.

Alberola, E. (2006). *The informational efficiency of the EU ETS: An empirical evaluation on the spot and futures prices*. Working Paper, University of Paris, Paris, France.

Alberola, E., Chevallier, J., & Chèze, B. (2008). Price drivers and structural breaks in European carbon prices 2005–2007. *Energy Policy, 36*(2), 787–797.

Albrecht, J., Verbeke, T., & De Clercq, M. (2006). Informational efficiency of the US SO_2 permit market. *Environmental Modelling and Software, 21*(10), 1471–1478.

Andrew, B. (2008). Market failure, government failure and externalities in climate change mitigation: The case for a carbon tax. *Public Administration and Development, 28*(5), 393–401.

Arouri, M. E. H., Jawadi, F., & Nguyen, D. K. (2012). Nonlinearities in carbon spot-futures price relationships during Phase II of the EU ETS. *Economic Modelling, 29*(3), 884–892.

Benz, E., & Hengelbrock, J. (2008, December 16–18). *Liquidity and price discovery in the European CO_2 futures market: An intraday analysis*. Paper presented at the 21st Australasian Finance and Banking Conference, The University of New South Wales, Sydney, Australia.

Benz, E., & Trück, S. (2006). *Specifying and pricing a new class of assets: CO_2 emission allowances*. Working Paper, University of Bonn, Bonn, Germany.

Blair, R. (1998, May 14–15). Trading in carbon rights—Legal issues. *Australian Forest Grower*.

Boutaba, M. A. (2009). Dynamic linkages among European carbon markets. *Economics Bulletin, 29*(2), 499–511.

Bredin, D., Hyde, S., & Muckley, C. (2014). A microstructure analysis of the carbon finance market. *International Review of Financial Analysis, 34*, 222–234.

Castellas, P. (2013). *Where's the world going on carbon trading?* Retrieved September 29, 2013, from http://www.businessspectator.com.au/article/2013/6/7/carbon-markets/wheres-world-going-carbon-trading

Charles, A., Darné, O., & Fouilloux, J. (2011). Testing the martingale difference hypothesis in CO2 emission allowances. *Economic Modelling, 28*(1–2), 27–35.

Charles, A., Darné, O., & Fouilloux, J. (2013). Market efficiency in the European carbon markets. *Energy Policy, 60*, 785–792.

Chen, K., & Reklev, S. (2014). *China's national carbon market to start in 2016—Official*. Retrieved August 31, 2014,fromhttp://uk.reuters.com/article/2014/08/31/china-carbontrading-idUKL3N0R107420140831

Chevallier, J. (2010). A note on cointegrating and vector autoregressive relationships between CO_2 allowances spot and futures prices. *Economics Bulletin, 30*(2), 1564–1584.

Christiansen, A. C., Arvanitakis, A., Tangen, K., & Hasselknippe, H. (2005). Price determinants in the EU emissions trading scheme. *Climate Policy, 5*(1), 15–30.

Coase, R. H. (1960). The problem of social cost. *The Journal of Law and Economics, 3*, 1–44.

Crossland, J., Li, B., & Roca, E. (2013). Is the European Union Emissions Trading Scheme (EU ETS) informationally efficient? Evidence from momentum-based trading strategies. *Applied Energy, 109*, 10–23.

Daskalakis, G. (2013). On the efficiency of the European carbon market: New evidence from Phase II. *Energy Policy, 54*, 369–375.

Daskalakis, G., & Markellos, R. (2008). Are the European carbon markets efficient? *Review of Futures Markets, 17*(2), 103–128.

Department of Energy and Environmental Protection (DEEP). (2010). *Climate change and waste*. Retrieved September 21, 2010, from http://www.ct.gov/dep/cwp/view.asp?a=2714&q=432260&depNAV_GID=1645

Egenhoffer, C. (2007). The making of the EU ETS: Status, prospects and implications for business. *European Management Journal, 25*(6), 453–463.

Ellerman, D. A. (2005). A note on tradable permits. *Environmental and Resource Economics, 31*(2), 123–131.

Ellerman, D. A., & Buchner, B. K. (2008). Over-allocation or abatement? A preliminary analysis of the EU ETS based on the 2005–2006 emissions data. *Environmental and Resource Economics, 41*(2), 267–287.

Ellerman, D. A., Joskow, P. L., & Harrison, D., Jr. (2003). *Emissions trading in the US: Experience, lessons, and considerations for greenhouse gases*. Washington, DC: Pew Center on Global Climate Change.

Ernst & Young. (2012). *The future of global carbon markets: The prospect of an international agreement and its impact on business*. Retrieved September 29, 2013, from http://www.ey.com/GL/en/Services/Specialty-Services/Climate-Change-and-Sustainability-Services/The-future-of-global-carbon-markets_Prospect-of-an-international-agreement-business-impact

Fama, E. F. (1970). Efficient capital markets: A review of theory and empirical work. *Journal of Finance, 25*(2), 383–417.

Garnaut Review. (2008). *Garnaut climate change review "final report."* Retrieved March 10, 2016, from http://www.garnautreview.org.au/index.htm

Garner, R. (2006). Regulating a national emissions trading system within Australia: Constitutional limitations. *Macquarie Journal of International and Comparative Environmental Law, 3*(1), 83–112.

Her Majesty's Treasury (HMT). (2006). *Stern review on the economics of climate change*. Retrieved July 24, 2008, from http://webarchive.nationalarchives.gov.uk/+/http:/www.hm-treasury.gov.uk/independent_reviews/stern_review_economics_climate_change/stern_review_report.cfm

Intergovernmental Panel on Climate Change (IPCC). (2014a). *Climate Change 2014: Mitigation of climate change*. Working Group III Contribution to the IPCC 5th Assessment Report, Cambridge University Press, Cambridge, UK.

Intergovernmental Panel on Climate Change (IPCC). (2014b). Headlines statements from the summary for policymakers. *Climate Change 2013: The physical science basis*. Retrieved September 30, 2014, from http://www.ipcc.ch/news_and_events/docs/ar5/ar5_wg1_headlines.pdf

Kemfert, C., Diekmann, J., & Ziesling, H. J. (2004). Emissions trading in Europe: Effective tool or flight of fancy? *Intereconomics, 39*(3), 119–121.

Larson, D., & Parks, P. (1999). *Risks, lessons learned, and secondary markets for greenhouse gas reductions*. Washington, DC: World Bank Development Research Group.

Lu, W., & Wang, W. (2010). Weak-form efficiency of European Union emission trading scheme: Evidence from variance ratio tests. *International Journal of Green Economics, 4*(2), 183–196.

Lutz, B. J., Pigorsch, U., & Rotfub, W. (2013). Nonlinearity in cap-and-trade systems: The EUA price and its fundamentals. *Energy Economics, 40*, 222–232.

MacGill, I., Outhred, H., & Nolles, K. (2004). National emissions trading for Australia: Key design issues and complementary policies for promoting energy efficiency, infrastructure investment and innovation. *Australasian Journal of Environmental Management, 11*, 78–87.

McKibbin, W. J., & Wilcoxen, P. J. (2006). *A credible foundation for long term international cooperation on climate change*. Brookings Discussion Paper in International Economics, Washington, DC.

Miclăus, P. G., Lupu, R., Dumitrescu, S. A., & Bobircă, A. (2008). Testing the efficiency of the European carbon futures market using event-study methodology. *International Journal of Energy and Environment, 2*(2), 121–128.

Milunovich, G., & Joyeux, R. (2007). *Market efficiency and price discovery in the EU carbon futures market?* Discussion Paper, Division of Economic and Financial Studies, Macquarie University, Sydney, Australia.

Milunovich, G., Stegman, A., & Cotton, D. (2007). Carbon trading: Theory and practice. *JASSA: The FINSIA Journal of Applied Finance, 3*, 3–9.

Mizrach, B. (2012). Integration of the global carbon markets. *Energy Economics, 34*(1), 335–349.

Montagnoli, A., & de Vries, F. P. (2010). Carbon trading thickness and market efficiency. *Energy Economics, 32*(6), 1331–1336.

Niblock, S. J., & Harrison, J. L. (2012). Do dynamic linkages exist among European carbon markets? *International Business and Economics Research Journal, 11*(1), 33–44.

Niblock, S. J., & Harrison, J. L. (2013a). Carbon markets in times of VUCA: A weak-form efficiency investigation of the phase II EU ETS. *Journal of Sustainable Finance and Investment, 3*(1), 38–56.

Niblock, S. J., & Harrison, J. L. (2013b). Investability of the European Union emissions trading scheme: An empirical investigation under economic uncertainty. *International Journal of Green Economics*, 7(3), 226–240.

Pearce, F. (2005). A most precious commodity. *New Scientist, 185*(2481), 6–7.

Seifert, J., Uhrig-Homburg, M., & Wagner, M. W. (2008). Dynamic behaviour of CO_2 spot prices. *Journal of Environmental Economics and Management, 56*(2), 180–194.

Stern, N. (2006). What is the economics of climate change? *World Economics*, 7(2), 1–10.

Stevens, B., & Rose, A. (2002). A dynamic analysis of the marketable permits approach to global warming policy: A comparison of spatial and temporal flexibility. *Journal of Environmental Economics and Management, 44*(1), 45–69.

Taberner, J., Taubman, A., & Burns, S. (2005). European Union emissions trading scheme. *Australian Environment Review, 20*, 3–5.

Taylor, R. (2007). Catching up with the new carbon cycle. *ECOS, 138*, 12–15.

The Economist. (2013, April 20). *ETS, RIP? The failure to reform Europe's carbon market will reverberate round the world.* Retrieved April 20, 2014, from http://www.economist.com/news/finance-and-economics/21576388-failure-reform-europes-carbon-market-will-reverberate-round-world-ets

Thompson, A. G., & Campbell-Watt, R. (2005). Australia and an emissions trading market—Opportunities, costs and legal frameworks. *International Energy Law and Taxation Review, 4*, 79–89.

Tirole, J. (2008). Some economics of global warming. *Revista di Politica Economica, 98*(6), 9–41.

Tyrell, K. (2006). Linking the world with emissions trading. *ENDS Report, 380*, 34–37.

Uhrig-Homburg, M., & Wagner, M. W. (2009). Futures price dynamics of CO_2 emission certificates—An empirical analysis. *Journal of Derivatives, 17*(2), 73–88.

United Nations Environment Programme (UNEP). (2013). *The Emissions Gap Report 2013.* Retrieved December 11, 2013, from http://www.unep.org/pdf/UNEPEmissionsGapReport2013.pdf

Victor, D. F., & House, J. C. (2004). A new currency: Climate change and carbon credits. *Harvard International Review, 26*(2), 56–59.

Willis, M., & Fitz-Gerald, L. (2007). *Carbon credits: The new currency.* Retrieved April 21, 2008, from http://www.wme.com.au/categories/emissions/feb5_07.php

World Bank. (2012). *State and trends of the carbon market.* Washington, DC: World Bank Institute.

World Bank. (2014). *State and trends of the carbon market.* Washington, DC: World Bank Institute.

III.3
Country Specifics and Cases

38

THE LANDSCAPE OF SOCIAL AND SUSTAINABLE FINANCE IN VISEGRAD (V4) COUNTRIES

Daniela Majerčáková

Despite a growing interest in social enterprise, social entrepreneurship, and social innovation, there is limited understanding about the current state, size, scope, and funding of social enterprises in the Visegrad Group countries (also known as the "Visegrad Four" or simply "V4" countries). The Visegrad Group (V4) is an informal grouping of four central European countries—Slovakia, the Czech Republic, Hungary, and Poland. It is a living and informal regional structure composed of four Member States of the EU and NATO that adhere to shared values and have a common history, culture, and geographical situation. The V4 is a dynamic regional grouping of EU Member States, representing a platform for strengthening the coordination and consultation mechanism with a view to reaching common positions and opinions on topical issues of foreign and European policy, regional development, and economic and cultural cooperation.

The terms social enterprise, social entrepreneurship, and Social Entrepreneur are all connected to the concept of social innovation. There has been a major uptake in scholarship around these concepts in the last years; at least two journals have been created to deal with them explicitly. *The Social Enterprise Journal* and *The Journal of Social Entrepreneurship*. Similar to debates on social innovation, definitional questions have persisted because these are concepts with fuzzy boundaries and a couple of different interpretations. In particular, in V4 countries, social enterprises are still associated with employment creation or work insertion initiatives.

Research (e.g., Chell, 2007; Chell, Nicolopoulou, & Karatas-Özkan, 2010; Dees & Anderson, 2006; Nicholls, 2010; Shaw & de Bruin, 2013) has explored the role of social enterprises, third-sector organizations, and networks as agents of economic and social change, as well as their relationship to welfare systems. As opposed to stakeholder wealth, the most important drive for social entrepreneurship is the creation of social value (Noruzi, Westover, & Rahimi, 2010; Thake & Zadek, 1997). A common theme among all interpretations of social enterprise is the idea of the need to balance commercial and social objectives. This is seen as the distinctive feature of social enterprise and one of the reasons why it requires special analysis and research.

There are lots of definitions for the term "social innovation" (e.g., European Union, 2010; Mulgan, 2006; Mulgan, Tucker, Ali, & Sanders, 2007; Murray, Caulier-Grice, & Mulgan, 2009; Phills, Deiglmeier, & Miller, 2008; Pol & Ville, 2009; Westley & Antadze, 2010). Some definitions are specific and exclude many examples of social innovation, while others are so broad as they describe projects and organizations that are not particularly innovative, even if they are in some way social. This is partly because social innovation is a practice-led field—understandings, definitions, and meanings have emerged through people doing things in new ways rather than thinking about them in an academic way. For example, social innovation will take on a different form in rural Hungary than urban parts of the central Czech Republic or in eastern Slovakia as the social needs and the context will be different in different parts of V4 countries. We define social innovations as new ideas (products, services, and models) that simultaneously meet social needs (more effectively than alternatives) and create new social relationships or collaborations (European Union, 2010). In other words, they are innovations that are good both for society and to enhance society's capacity to act.

As one of the key elements of the new innovation paradigm, social innovation has become a global phenomenon, which responds to great challenges that our societies are facing. Social innovation research is just starting to become part of scientific discourse and international community building is still at an early stage. Although considerable research has been done into business innovation, social innovation remains relatively under-researched (Murray et al., 2009). With regards to their invention, development, and spread, social innovations are clearly distinct from technical innovations. Due to their specific process and product's dimensions, social innovations generally arise outside the realms of corporate and academic research divisions. The very beginning of research into social entrepreneurship and social innovation highlights the need to develop a common understanding not only of the term "social innovation" but also its links with social entrepreneurship (Philips, Lee, Ghobadian, O'Regan, & James, 2014). In V4 countries, there is a significant lack of research into the process of social innovation.

Social innovations are reliant on institutional support to help them address social needs. The potential opportunity for social innovation would be the possibility of the asset of private investments. Research done by Moore, Westley, and Nicholls (2012) suggests that commercial financial institutions and practices tend to marginalize social entrepreneurs, individuals, and communities benefiting from social innovations. We can observe a similar situation in V4 countries, where private financial institutions do not have a very strong interest in investing in social businesses and social innovation. Moreover, public authorities are becoming reluctant to invest in a project of social innovation; they do not perform their own duties in supporting the social business if the existing projects are financed by philanthropic organizations or private investors. Many social enterprises therefore fight with the possibilities of finding the investor or gaining the necessary capital for their innovation projects and ideas. If an organization is interested in commercial activities and is profitable, it is considered as a regular profit-making organization, where there is no possibility to be ranked and classified as a social business irrespective of the different character services offered and the profit usage. Private investors expect demonstrable social and economic return on investment, and this is the factor that forces public authorities to expect the same effect from their own investment. However, the added value is to be able to measure the social impact, because it can help to improve the services offered. Anyway, we are also facing the trend to show more performance and innovation character than to measure the real impact on services, individuals, or society.

In V4 countries, the concept of social business is developed more than the idea of social investments. In spite of some successful projects of social businesses and social innovations, the issue of not understanding the context of social business and project mismanagement in Slovakia in 2011 remains in the background. In general, there is a continuing tendency of establishing social businesses and successful innovation projects that have the character of social innovations from governmental, European, and private investments in all four V4 countries—Slovakia, the Czech Republic, Poland, and Hungary. Some impulses are based on the enhancement of the social services offered, bringing the innovation character toward the existing services and systems that function in the particular countries.

Only a few years ago, social entrepreneurship was an emerging phenomenon in V4 countries, and the situation has changed in the last few years with some positive changes occurring in the field of social entrepreneurship and in the strategies and tools to support it. The term "social enterprise" has become more familiar to academics and policy makers and also increasingly to the general public as a new innovative business model that meets both social and economic objectives and contributes to labor market integration, social inclusion, and economic development. The failure of neoliberalism to address the structural problems of poverty and social exclusion has led V4 governments to look closely into civil society initiatives as the potential solutions to these difficulties. Current and future trends are examined in critical areas for the development of social enterprises in V4 countries, such as institutional and legislative frameworks, financial environments, and support structures and tools.

Social enterprises in V4 countries are also local initiatives with the objective of combating exclusion and creating well-being for individuals and communities. They are generally understood as an innovative business model that meets both social and economic objectives contributing to labor market integration, social inclusion, and economic development. The organizational arrangements and legal forms that social enterprises adopt vary greatly across V4 countries. Current debate has widened the definition of social enterprise that includes cooperatives, non-profits, and community-based businesses that are integrated into social economy and community economic development strategies. These entrepreneurial organizations are driven by socio-economic objectives to benefit the community and to combine social and economic goals in an original way. The core of this chapter examines how they combine financial and non-financial resources and the current landscape of financial sources available to social enterprises in Slovakia, the Czech Republic, Hungary, and Poland.

Prior to the identification of the main sources of funding social enterprises and related factors in V4 countries, we first need to define the legal environment there. How a social enterprise is legally structured can greatly influence the types of funding available and the organization's operation and growth. As the different sources of funding often lead to disparities in social enterprises, the potential for sustainability, the legal entities, and the structures of the social organizations must be examined. The importance of gaining access to finances relates to the particular mode of creation and business model. Therefore, this chapter discusses at first the legal liabilities between related actors and social enterprises under an obligatory relationship.

Regulating social enterprises in V4 countries: Some key questions

Comparing national laws on social enterprises in V4 countries, which are influenced by the legal, social, and economic context of each country, some common features and some differences can be observed. Different models in Slovakia, the Czech Republic, Hungary, and Poland not only represent an indication of the various organizational types that social enterprises can adopt but also contribute to shape the entrepreneurial extent of their missions, as they result from various legal frameworks. These models allow different kinds of enterprises to become organized and recognized as social enterprises to meet the criteria identified by each national law.

In relation to the different functions of legislation surrounding social enterprises, it is also important to note that V4 legal systems promote social enterprises mainly using non-monetary incentives or by regulating organizational models, rather than providing direct monetary support. On the other side, the opposite is valid with respect to legislative systems surrounding non-profit organizations. Indeed, organizational models, which can adequately reflect the balance between its "social mission" and entrepreneurship, are what is missing fundamentally within traditional legislation for both traditional for-profit enterprises and non-profit organizations. Through a comparative analysis of V4 legislation that has been made in this field, the question of who should regulate social enterprises, whether public regulators, private organizations representing social enterprises, or entrepreneurs themselves, will also be discussed in this chapter.

With regards to this common framework, our results show that, while the choice of legal forms in V4 countries is a significant factor behind the governance structure and type of social enterprise, some features may be shared by different models regardless of the form. Indeed, a clear-cut polarization based on the adoption of specific legal forms is not easy to detect. Some common features in OECD countries were identified in Noya (2009), namely:

- The possibility of an entrepreneurial activity being the main activity of an organization with which to achieve social goals.
- A control mechanism over the social goals pursued by the organization, as defined at least by broad principles by law and specified in the by-laws of the organization. The enforcement of a positive (although not necessarily total) assets lock to ensure the achievement of social goals.
- The possibility for the social enterprise to sustain its own activity through remunerated financing.
- A certain degree of stakeholder representation within the governance of the enterprise, with specific but not necessarily exclusive representation with regard to beneficiaries and employees.
- The enforcement of a non-discrimination principle concerning the composition of membership.
- The enforcement of accountability of the governing bodies to allow pluralism, fair dialogue, and the restriction of controlling rights, unless they are in favor of non-profit organizations which share the social goals and democratic nature of the social enterprise.
- An adequate degree of information disclosure (also in favor of third parties) about the governance and activities of the social enterprise.

Of course, there are many differences among the legal systems within V4 countries. As we have seen, some differences may occur for reasons that are endogenous to such systems. For example, some reasons may include activism of the public sector within the sphere of social enterprises. On one side, success of the cooperative model as the main private factor in the social economy of a country; on the other side, a significant appreciation for volunteerism in another country which slows down the process of entrepreneuralization by limiting the amount of paid work that may be undertaken.

The most visible (but not necessarily dominant) activity of social enterprises in V4 countries can be identified as the work integration of disadvantaged groups. Beyond work integration itself, the majority of social enterprise services are to be found across the full spectrum of social welfare services or social services of general interest:

- Long-term care for the elderly and for people with disabilities,
- Early education and childcare,
- Employment and training services,
- Social housing,
- Social integration of the disadvantaged such as ex-offenders, migrants, drug addicts, etc.,
- Healthcare and medical services.

Poland

In Poland, there is no official definition of social enterprise and the term "social enterprise" is not very often used in this country. social enterprises are mostly perceived as an element of the "social economy," which is a broader concept that itself does not have an official or commonly accepted definition. For example, social cooperatives, employment cooperatives, the cooperatives of disabled and blind people, non-profit organizations such as foundations and associations, limited liability companies and corporations pursuing public benefit activities and not focusing on profit, social inclusion centers, and occupational therapy workshops belong to the so-called "social economy entities" in Poland.

An attempt to define a social enterprise has been made in the proposal of the "National Program for Social Economy Development"—KPRES (Annex to Resolution No. 164 of the Council of Ministry of 12 August 2015—Monitor Polski 2914, Item 811, Volume 1), where social enterprise is defined as an entity which carries out business activity with clear organizational boundaries and its own financial reporting. The objective of such business activity must be either the social and employment integration of people at risk of social exclusion or to provide public benefit services while at the same time fulfilling pro-employment objectives. Moreover, the distribution of profit or financial surplus among shareholders is forbidden and profits or financial surplus must be used for increasing company capital. KPRES envisages the adoption of a Legal Act on social enterprise which should introduce a social enterprise legal status to do the following (Wilkinson, 2014c):

- To define and legitimize social enterprises,
- To enable clear identification of entities that are the subject of specific public policies,
- To help relevant entities identify their position in the socio-economic systems of the country,
- To build public awareness on social enterprises, their role, and their service—both as providers of goods and services and as potential employers.

There are no official assessments of the number of social enterprises in Poland. The study by Wilkinson (2014c) estimates that there are approximately 5,200 entities in Poland that could be classified as social enterprises by applying the EU Operational Definition, employing around 70,000 people, who represent approximately 0.3 percent of all registered and active enterprises and around 0.4 percent of total employment in the Polish economy.

Hungary

In Hungary, a single and widely accepted definition for social enterprises does not exist. Certain ambiguity regarding the term "social enterprise" exists even among potential social entrepreneurs and Social Investors. The institutional form of social enterprise in Hungary exists under the label of social cooperative defined by the Legal Act on Cooperatives. The terminology in some of the newer publications (Borzaga et al., 2014) is based on the EU report (e.g., The Contribution of Social Capital in the Social Economy to Local Economic Development in Western Europe—CONSCISE, DG Research, April 2013), where social enterprises:

- Are not-for-profit organizations,
- Seek to meet social aims by engaging in economic and trading activities,
- Have legal structures which ensure that all assets and accumulated wealth are not in the ownership of individuals but are held in trust and for the benefit of those persons and/or areas that are the intended beneficiaries of the enterprise's social aims,

- Have organizational structures in which full participation of members is encouraged on a cooperative basis with equal rights accorded to all members,
- Encourage mutual cooperation.

Under such an interpretation, social enterprises can be not-for-profit organizations and also commercial institutions which use sustainable business models to carry out their basic social mission which may concern different objectives. One example is assistance to disabled people or the long-term unemployed excluded from the labor market, for instance through offering employment, such as sheltered workshops. However, the backbone of social enterprises in Hungary today is the host of non-profit organizations engaged in economic activities of some sort and also cooperatives, including primarily social cooperatives. These are complemented by a small number of social enterprises working under the classical for-profit organizational form without democratic decision-making. Many of these social enterprises are embedded in a network including associations and other non-profit organizations that support them with general advice or specialist services. There are also a number of entities operating under such forms which fulfill EU operational criteria and hence can be seen as a social enterprise.

There are no official estimations of the number of social enterprises in Hungary. The study by Wilkinson (2014b) estimates that based on the data published by the Hungarian Central Statistical Office there are around 3,000 social enterprises fulfilling the criteria of the EU Operational Definition.

Czech Republic

The Czech Republic is the country where the roots of the social economy can be identified back to the emergence of worker cooperatives, municipal savings banks, cooperative agricultural banks, associations of different types, and the non-profit sector developed under the Habsburg Empire in the middle of the 19th century. In the Czech Republic, social entrepreneurship is not defined in national legislation (its inclusion in national legislation is being discussed) and there is no specific policy document or public body that is officially designed to prepare and deal with it. However, the legal form of a social cooperative has been included in the legislation (Commercial Corporations Act No. 90/2012).

The framework for the identification of social enterprises serves the initiative called the "Thematic Network of Social Economy" (TESSEA), which has developed a definition of social enterprise that is generally accepted, including the Czech Ministry of Labour and Social Affairs, the Agency for Social Integration, and the Association of Czech and Moravian cooperatives. TESSEA was founded in 2009 and currently includes over 350 legal and physical persons from business.

TESSEA defines the broader concepts of social economy and social entrepreneurship in the following ways (Wilkinson, 2014a):

- The social economy is a sum of activities undertaken by social economy entities, the purpose of which is to increase employment in local conditions or to fulfill other requirements and objectives of the community in the field of economic, social-cultural, and environmental development.
- Social economy entities are social enterprises, financial, consulting, and training institutions that support social entrepreneurship, and non-governmental non-profit organizations that carry on economic activities in order to secure work for their clients or gain additional financing for their mission.

- Social economy entities share common values, which are the fulfillment of a publicly beneficial objective, democratic decision-making, supporting citizens' initiatives, independence from public or private institutions, a different way of using profits, taking into account environmental considerations, and prioritizing local needs and local resources.
- Social entrepreneurship entails enterprise activities benefiting society and the environment.
- Social entrepreneurship plays an important role in local development and often creates jobs for the disabled or the socially or culturally disadvantaged.
- The majority of profits are used for the further development of the social enterprise.
- Achieving profit is equally important for social enterprises as increasing public benefit.

In the Czech Republic, we can follow some developments in national legislation that should lead to significant changes. In the legislative plan of the Czech government for the first quarter of 2015, social entrepreneurship has been included. This means that there is a possibility to introduce the concept of social enterprise into Czech legislation and could be a first step to a more systematic support of social enterprises.

It is estimated (Wilkinson, 2014a) that in the Czech Republic there are up to 300 organizations fulfilling the criteria of the EU Operational Definition of social enterprises.

Slovakia

Like the Czech Republic, one of the early manifestations of the social economy in Slovakia was the cooperation and mutual movement that started to emerge in the territory of the Habsburg Empire in the middle of the 19th century. Since this time different types of cooperatives and mutual unions have emerged such as saving unions, credit unions, commodity cooperatives, and purchase cooperatives that can be seen as predecessors of social enterprises. In 1845, in Sobotište in Western Slovakia, one of the first cooperative-like organizations was established not just in the territory of the Habsburg Empire but also in continental Europe by one of the pioneers of the cooperative movement in Slovakia, the teacher Samuel Jurkovič.

Unlike in other V4 countries, the legal definition of social enterprise exists in Slovakia. The definition of social enterprise was introduced into legislation in September 2008 by an amendment of the Legal Act 5/2004 on Employment Services. Social enterprise is defined as a physical or legal person who does the following (Wilkinson, 2014d):

- Employs workers that were disadvantaged jobseekers prior to the employment,
- Has at least 30 percent disadvantaged jobseekers in his workforce,
- Supports employed disadvantaged jobseekers in finding employment on the free labor market,
- Re-invests at least 30 percent of financial resources gained from one's own activities that remain after paying all costs associated with one's own activities into the creation of new job positions or into improving working conditions,
- Is listed in the register of social enterprises.

The physical or legal person must fulfill these conditions to be accepted onto the register of social enterprises and gain a status of a social enterprise. However, if a social enterprise does not satisfy these conditions for at least 12 consecutive months, it will lose its status. Meeting these criteria is checked through an annual activity report submitted to the Central Office of Jobs, Social Affairs and Family. This office holds an authority to issue a certificate of social enterprise to a requesting entity. The status of social enterprise may be awarded also to protected workplaces and sheltered workshops.

It is important to note that, when compared with other V4 countries (where, as we have seen, the definitions of a social enterprise are very broad and not unique), legislation in Slovakia has narrowed down the understanding of the social enterprise to only one type of organization whose main purpose is to prepare disadvantaged persons to enter the labor market.

It seems that Slovakia has trapped itself into a legalistic vision of the social economy. As of 2014, there were only 96 organizations using the status of social enterprise as defined by the Legal Act 5/2004 on Employment Services. However, the study by Wilkinson (2014d) estimates there are around 900 organizations in Slovakia that could potentially be regarded as social enterprises as defined by EU criteria.

Financial landscape of social enterprises in V4 countries

While social enterprises continue to emerge in various activity sectors across V4 countries, the identification and access to various forms of financing funds represent an important element for them to thrive and to consolidate their activities. For social enterprises to emerge and to consolidate their activities, they must have access to capital. New innovative financial instruments for social enterprises are appearing in these countries, and also the investment market has transformed during the last few years to respond to the capital needs of social enterprises, together with the growing public demand for new Socially Responsible Investment opportunities.

In addition to governments as essential stakeholders (community-based investment, program-related investment, and Venture Philanthropy), traditional financial providers (philanthropy, financial institutions, and public financing) are seeing themselves playing an important role in this process. All these financial sources generate an added value instead of an exclusive financial return, and need to be measured by emerging measurement tools such as social accounting and social return on investment.

Common to all V4 countries is the recognition that new financial tools and instruments that combine financial and social returns require the investment of both private and public actors. Besides the products that correspond to the growing proactive investment attitude in V4 countries, the following five are of special interest for the financing of social enterprises:

1 Solidarity finance;
2 Venture Philanthropy;
3 Institutional investment;
4 Individual investment;
5 Different forms of equity instruments.

Moreover, the experience of many countries where social entrepreneurship is much more developed has shown that enabling legal and institutional frameworks are the pillars upon which this activity can emerge and grow. Governments and parliaments in V4 countries are trying to support some specific policy and legislative measures—for example:

- Offering fiscal incentives to attract investors into social enterprises;
- Offering different forms of credit enhancement;
- Offering support services, financial advice, and labor market training for employees;
- Developing legislative innovation based on multi-stakeholder consultation;
- Offering support and training systems specifically for emerging social finance intermediaries.

However, a mere transposition of financial tools and instruments from countries with developed financial markets to V4 countries will not suffice, because the specifics of these economies must be taken into consideration. Common to Slovakia, the Czech Republic, Poland, and Hungary is the recognition that innovative financial tools and instruments that combine financial and social returns require investment from both private and public institutions. In the still-evolving environment in which social enterprises in V4 countries have emerged, the traditional roles assigned to the public, private, and third sector are transforming. The specific nature of these enterprises has called for financial innovations, for a customized financial sector that is not a mere replication or extension of existing financial products and instruments.

The need for financial innovation complements the traditional sources of funding which include government, communities, philanthropy, and financial institutions (especially commercial banks), as well as individual investors. In all V4 countries a relatively well-developed micro-credit financial market that provides access to loan capital for marginalized groups and individuals "red-lined" by commercial banks already exists. The role of governments is important in facilitating this type of investment activity and has taken different forms, including legislation to establish special financial intermediaries to reduce the perceived risk often associated with investing in social enterprises. Moreover, these financial intermediaries increase the capacity to attract investment capital from EU funds.

The importance of gaining access to finance social enterprises relates to the particular mode of creation and business model. As business models in V4 countries move toward greater levels of earned income, so the evidence suggests that, like any other enterprise, social enterprises need external finance to start up and scale their activities. Similarly, in common with any start-up, social enterprises face problems of access to finance due to their track record and lender transaction costs. However, given their specific characteristics, accessing finance from traditional sources is particularly problematic for social enterprises. Conventional investors and lenders do not typically understand the dual-purpose business models of social enterprises and financial intermediaries, and innovative financial instruments are currently underdeveloped in V4 countries. Given that social investment markets are currently underdeveloped in these countries, governments must play a key role in designing dedicated financial innovations.

Social investment markets in Poland are underdeveloped and there are no specialist investors or financial intermediaries investing in or offering financial products to social enterprises in Poland. Theoretically, social enterprises in this country may borrow with the same conditions as the so-called mainstream enterprises, but in practice demand for financing is very limited and so is access. Consequently, social enterprises find it difficult to access finance from external sources. There are no specialist social banks which, often in close cooperation with their clients and shareholders, explicitly strive to address pressing societal challenges and thus contribute to a more sustainable development. Philanthropic investment probably exists in Poland, but no data is officially available that would enable one to assess the importance of this segment.

Grant funding is available to social economy entities from structural funds programs. In 2005 the so-called Citizens' Initiatives Fund was established. Its main objective is the strengthening of non-government organizations including their financial strength and increasing their participation in the development of social society. The program was extended to the 2014–2020 period with an unchanged annual allocation of around EUR 12 million.

There are a limited number of financial instruments specifically targeting social economy entities in Poland, such as:

- The Polish-American Community Assistance Fund (PAFPIO);
- Towarzystwo Inwestycji Społeczno-Ekonomicznych SA (TISE);
- Fund for Social Economy in Malopolska (Malopolski Fundusz Ekonomii Spolecznej).

The Polish-American Community Assistance Fund (Polsko-Amerykański Fundusz Pożyczkowy Inicjatyw Obywatelskich) was created in 1999. The fund offers loans to non-governmental organizations and other not-for-profit initiatives. Associations and foundations constitute a significant majority among the PAFPIO's borrowers. However, there are also some commercial law companies allocating their commercial profit to their statutory goals (such as TBS—Social Building Associations). As a rule, the fund does not lend money to finance political or religious activity. Since its beginning, the fund has extended loans to 570 institutions for a total amount exceeding more than PLN 176 million.

Social and economic investment company TISE SA has more than 20 years of business history. It was established in 1991 by the BISE Bank, the Social and Economic Investment Fund, and the French investment fund SIDI. Today it is owned by the French bank Credit Cooperatif, which has financed social economy projects for over 120 years. Initially TISE was in the business of project financing for small and medium enterprises through venture capital, granting credit guarantees, and subordinated loans.

In 2002 TISE joined the European Federation of Ethical and Alternative Banks—FEBEA, formed by 22 institutions financing social and ethical projects. TISE still remains the only Polish representative in FEBEA. Since 2006 TISE has been the administrator of the European capital fund Coopest, which supports social economy entities.

Since 2008 TISE has been actively granting loans to NGOs, microenterprises, and SMEs. Funds for this purpose are partly derived from TISE's own funds, that is, the company's 5 million EUR share capital. Since 2012 TISE's operations have been funded by Bank Gospodarstwa Krajowego (National Economy Bank) under agreements with the European Union, namely the Operational Program "Development of Eastern Poland" and the Jeremie initiative, with funds equivalent to EUR 20 million.

TISE is also a partner of Bank Gospodarstwa Krajowego in the pilot project co-financed by the European Social Fund under Measure 1.4, "Support to financial engineering for the development of social economy." The ES Fund that was established as part of the program is endowed with PLN 25 million destined for loans to social economy entities with a preferential interest rate of up to 1.37 percent p.a. maximum today! The clients are labor cooperatives, cooperatives of the disabled and the blind, social cooperatives, NGOs, non-profit companies, and ecclesiastical legal bodies. Hitherto TISE has already granted 740 loans totaling EUR 34 million. Four hundred and ninety-five loans have been granted out of TISE's own funds and 245 from funds provided by Bank Gospodarstwa Krajowego.

The Fund for Social Economy in Malopolska (Malopolski Fundusz Ekonomii Spolecznej) was established in 2009 by private and public entities and specializes in the provision of credit guarantees for social enterprises. In over 5 years of its existence, it has provided more than 100 guarantees and small loans totaling around EUR 1.2 million, contributing to the creation of more than 30 social cooperatives and around 40 microenterprises.

In addition to these initiatives, we can find a couple of examples of small local initiatives such as microloan and guarantee funds and social venture capital funds. For example, the Centre for Economic Development in Paslek (Stowarzyszenie "Centrum Rozwoju Ekonomicznego Pasłęka") is to develop and test a model of venture capital support in vocational integration with support from EU funds. The project will consist of the preparation of people to lead social enterprises, with a focus on return on capital along with the profit generated by the social enterprises. Charity and social aid, including families and individuals facing difficult situations, belong to the additional fields of activities of this center, ensuring equal opportunities, supporting economic and entrepreneurship development, promoting employment and activation of the unemployed and of individuals threatened with job loss, promoting volunteer work, etc.

The social investment market in Hungary is underdeveloped. There is only a small group of private investors and limited amounts of public financing, in some cases combined with EU funds. Funding of actors in the "social economy" comes mostly from the national government (through co-financed operational programs) and municipalities, and only a small part from private investors. The only actual participant in the social investment market is the US social enterprise support organization NESsT (National Eagle Staffing Solutions Team) which entered the country in 2001.

NESsT works to solve critical problems in emerging market countries by developing and supporting social enterprises that strengthen civil society organizations' financial sustainability and maximize their social impact. NESsT achieves its mission by combining the tools and strategies of business entrepreneurship with the mission and values of non-profit entrepreneurship to support the development of social enterprises in emerging democracies worldwide. NESsT receives its capital from individuals and foundations, and the capacity-building services offered include pre-start and investment readiness support, general and specialist consultancy services, and networking.

At the end of 2012, the total value of all financing outstanding (live projects) of NESsT in Hungary was around USD 580,000, of which 78 percent was in the form of grants, loans accounted for 15 percent, and guarantees were 6.5 percent. The value of NESsT loans supplied ranged from 6,600 to 55,000 USD, with duration from 6 months to 6 years.

A community bank (MagNet Bank), considering itself an "ethical bank" and owned by Hungarian companies and citizens, has recently started operations in Hungary, offering special conditions to SMEs, social enterprises, and non-profit organizations. Depositors are included in management decisions and together decide which projects the bank should finance with its money and who they should give loans to, as well as agreeing on decisions about the bank's philanthropy activities. Some other banks (Erste Bank and UniCredit) occasionally publish small-scale tenders providing a modest grant to non-profit organizations or social enterprises.

In the Czech Republic, there is no systematic policy support for financing social entrepreneurship at national and regional policy levels. Possible sources of financing involve European Union financing, financing from international development programs, government funds, and other sources (banking institutions, multinational companies, endowment funds, and foundations). Public support tends to be characterized by one-off project grants, for example OPHRE (Operating Programme Human Resources and Employment) and IOP (Integrated Operational Programme) grant schemes. The only systematic support is received by WISE (Work Integration Social Enterprises), employing people with health disabilities who claim financial contributions from the Czech Labour Office. Social investment markets are underdeveloped and offer a very limited supply of finance.

Since 2009, in the Czech Republic, there have been three public grant schemes initiated and supported by the Czech Ministry of Labour and Social Affairs (MoLSA):

1 Grant call no. 30: "Social Economy" within the OPHRE;
2 IOP grant call no. 1: "Investment support of social economy;"
3 IOP grant call no. 8: "Investment support of social economy."

These three schemes focus exclusively on WISE, and one of the main eligibility conditions is that at least 40 percent of the workforce of the potential applicants must come from the following target groups (Wilkinson, 2014a):

- People with health disabilities;
- Youth threatened by socially pathological influences;

- The homeless;
- Care and prison leavers;
- Victims of criminal activities;
- Carers for relatives at risk;
- People with experience of substance misuse;
- Long-term unemployed;
- Other people at risk of social exclusion or the socially excluded.

In total, these public support schemes supported approximately 150 social enterprises and focused on the support of new entrepreneurship activities. Successful applicants received non-investment financial support, that covered 100 percent of the eligible costs of the project (grant call no. 30), or investment support covering 80 percent of eligible project costs (IOP grants). At the moment, there are no financial schemes in the Czech Republic supporting social enterprises on a comparable scale.

A few smaller projects supporting social entrepreneurship are currently being financed from OPHRE, such as a project called "Support of social entrepreneurship in the Czech Republic" (its primary objective is to test the support of social enterprises by creating a national network of 10 local consultants and 5 experts) and a project called "Innovative establishment of social entrepreneurship" which aims to raise awareness about social entrepreneurship. OPHRE also supports TESSEA in cooperation and experience sharing with foreign stakeholders involved in social entrepreneurship.

In the Czech Republic, there are some non-publicly funded support services for social enterprises with a fractured and non-standardized structure. This kind of support depends on individual organizations and it is not coordinated at the national level. Some programs that provide consultancy and training support for social enterprises are funded by banks:

- The program "Better Business: Support for Social Entrepreneurship" is financed by the Unicredit VIA Foundation and is supporting start-ups and new entrepreneurship activities (amount of funding EUR 65,000),
- The program "Academy of Social Entrepreneurship" (source of funding is available from Ceska Sporitelna) supports already-existing social enterprises and aims to make them more efficient,
- "Good.bee" is an initiative of Erste Group Bank to provide microfinance to social enterprises and the support is aimed at co-working spaces and work integration services (amount of financial support is EUR 130,000),
- The program "Stabilization of Social Enterprises" is financed by CSOB Bank and aims to support already-existing social enterprises and make them more efficient.

Other organizations providing financial and business support for social enterprises include the following (Wilkinson, 2014a):

- Czech Labour Office, that provides a financial contribution to the creation of positions for people with health disabilities and to employers who employ at least one employee with a health disability per healthy employee;
- Agency for Social Integration, that promotes social entrepreneurship as a means for resolving employment issues;
- People, Planet and Profit, that provides services for social enterprises;
- Union of Czech and Moravian Worker Cooperatives, that was actively involved in the development of the TESSEA definition and indicators. It also carried out two projects; currently it offers support for cooperatives in starting up social enterprises;

- Fokus Praha, that initiated the "Platform for Social Firms" and published the "Standards for Social Firms;"
- HUB Prague, that provides shared workplace and consultancy for social enterprises;
- Social Economy Centre, that provides consultancy on the legal, financial, grant, and marketing aspects of social enterprise in Prague.

These examples give an idea of how little financial funds are currently available in the Czech Republic for both the start-up and scaling-up of social enterprises. Existing social enterprises clearly feel a lack of external financing options.

In Slovakia, there is no social investment market in the strict sense and also a limited number of investors who are ready to invest in the social projects. Only sporadically some socially oriented investors can be identified. This is the consequence of the fact that in Slovakia awareness about the concept of social enterprises and the social economy is still very low. The major sources of financing for social enterprises are the state, municipalities, tax assignation by individuals and legal persons (the Slovak legislative framework stipulates that an individual can devote up to 2 percent of his/her income tax while a legal person can devote up to 1.5 percent to a civil society organization, and tax assignation from individuals and legal persons is the greatest source of revenue for them), and especially EU funds. The most common instruments are grants and subsidies, whilst loans from financial institutions are rarely offered and accessible.

In the past there were several projects co-founded from the European Social Fund, some of them co-managed by the United Nations Development Programme (UNDP) Slovakia. In fact, UNDP Slovakia was the very first organization conducting research on the social enterprise sector in Slovakia, which has implemented one large-scale publically funded project supporting business capacities (unfortunately, the project was never completed due to lack of available funding). However, the UNDP Regional Centre in Bratislava has ended its activities there and moved its seat to Istanbul as of July 1, 2014.

The aim of the UniCredit Provida Foundation is to strengthen the entrepreneurial capacities of social organizations in Slovakia by rewarding innovative businesses that have measurable social impact and supporting them with grants and consulting and training activities. The idea that inspires this project is that the creation of an enterprise's social value should have an impact not only on itself or its stakeholders but also on the community within which it operates. Provida offers grants of up to EUR 12,000 for start-up or early stage projects for a selected number of the most promising applicants. In parallel, Provida also runs an incubator in order to strengthen the capacity of organizations or individual Social Entrepreneurs who receive consultancy support in the form of the conceptualization of business plans or market analysis.

Furthermore, another non-public organization providing support to social enterprises in Slovakia is NESsT Slovakia, which has been operating in the country since the year 2001. NESsT Slovakia has evaluated over 90 social enterprise ideas. Through rigorous tailored capacity support, it has helped over 70 organizations and entrepreneurs to develop sustainable business plans and has provided them with start-up and incubation support. At the moment, it has no office in Slovakia and support is provided only through ad hoc consultancy delivered by its members who reside in other countries in Central and Eastern Europe. The closure of the permanent office in Slovakia was preceded by an internal evaluation that took into account the potential of the social enterprise sector: the evaluation concluded that the relative development of the social economy sector in Slovakia and its potential was fairly low, and the resources of NESsT were shifted to other countries of the region.

EU funds are a very important source for social enterprises in Slovakia. State funding during the time period 2007–2013 was co-financed with funding from the "Employment and Social

Inclusion Operational Programme" and EU funding was also obtained by private applicants who did not rely on any public support. Yet, although certain social service organizations relied on EU funds, before 2014 there was not a specific theme under the European Social Fund devoted to social enterprise organizations (during the new programming period 2014–2020 this situation is changing).

The participation of commercial banks which are active in the financial markets of Slovakia is almost non-existent. Only a very few exceptional examples can be mentioned, for example Erste Group Bank, which invested in one social entity and has also analyzed this sector. Citi Bank Slovakia has provided limited support within its CSR (Corporate Social Responsibility) activities. However, there are no specialized products for social enterprises or organizations defined as part of the social economy in the Slovakian banking sector. There are no social banks or so-called "business angels" supporting social enterprises.

The results of the analysis of the sector which has been done by Erste Group Bank indicates that social economy organization and social enterprises in Slovakia more specifically are perceived as very risky investments primarily due to relatively weak business models, lower management standards, lack of sufficient assets as collateral, and very limited capacity to generate enough cash inflows from the private market. As a consequence, social enterprises and social economy organizations are undercapitalized. Generally, we can say that the weak investment readiness of Slovak social enterprises belongs to the most important barriers for the development of the sector. Moreover, some negative connotations of social enterprises in Slovakia stem from the unsuccessful pilot phase during the year 2009.

Conclusion

Social enterprises in V4 countries have to face a number of barriers which generally relate to:

- The lack of legal recognition and poor understanding of the concept of social enterprise;
- The difficulties of accessing finance from external sources; financial intermediaries, banks, and lenders do not understand the dual purpose and specific business models of social enterprises;
- Specialist investors that are currently either non-existent or underdeveloped;
- Specialist support (e.g., pre-starts, start-ups, incubators, mentoring, training schemes, etc.) that is either absent or limited;
- The limitation of measuring and reporting the social impact of social enterprises.

To grasp the landscape of Social and Sustainable Finance in V4 countries, a list of criteria has been developed which includes: the national legal framework, the fulfillment of the EU operational definition of social enterprise, the estimates of the number of social enterprises, the existence of public support schemes targeting social enterprises, the role of European Structural Funds, and the current status of social investment markets.

The most visible activity of social enterprises in V4 countries can be identified as Work Integration Social Enterprises (WISE).

Unlike in the other V4 countries, the legal definition of social enterprise exists in Slovakia. On the other hand, organizations fulfilling the EU operational definition of social enterprise can be found in all V4 countries.

Estimates of the numbers of organizations that meet all of the criteria set by the EU operational definition used in our study have been difficult to establish. We conjecture that the regional pattern of numbers of social enterprises is also likely to mask significant differences in their characteristics both across and within V4 countries. The crucial point is that the estimate

Table 38.1 The landscape of social innovation in V4 countries

	Slovakia	*Czech Republic*	*Hungary*	*Poland*
National legal framework	The definition of a social enterprise was introduced in Act No. 5/2004 on employment services	No legal definition of social enterprise (social cooperative defined by Commercial Act No. 90/2012)	No legal definition of social enterprise (social cooperative defined by Act No. X of 2006)	No legal definition of social enterprise (social cooperative defined by the Act of April 24, 2006)
National law narrowly focuses on Work Integration social enterprises (WISE)	yes	no	no	yes
EU operational definition of social enterprise fulfilled	yes	yes	yes	yes
Estimates of the number of social enterprises (social enterprises by applying the EU operational definition)	96 (900 organizations could potentially be regarded as social cooperatives)	1,000	3,000	5,200
Public support schemes targeting social enterprises	limited but dominant source of income	limited but dominant source of income	limited but dominant source of income	limited but dominant source of income
WISE activities do constitute the dominant form of social enterprise	yes	yes	yes	yes
European Structural Funds (ERDF and ESF) play an important role in raising funds	yes	yes	yes	yes
Income derived from market sources (e.g., the sale of goods and services)	≤50%	≥50%	≤50%	≤50%
Current status of the social investment markets	underdeveloped	underdeveloped	underdeveloped	underdeveloped
Dedicated financial instruments	no	no	no	no
social impact reporting system	Social purpose company has to produce an annual report on how it acted on the established social goals	voluntary	voluntary	voluntary

Source: Based on country reports by Charu Wilkinson (2014a, 2014b, 2014c, 2014d).

of total numbers of social enterprises is likely to vary considerably depending on the definitions and key assumptions made in the calculation.

There is a lack of appropriate capital going toward social enterprises in V4 countries, social investment markets are currently non-existent or underdeveloped, and the majority of funding comes from the public sector. In raising funds, European Structural Funds (ERDF and ESF) play an important role, too. The amount of capital currently present in the social investment market is difficult to calculate exactly.

Summary

The key contribution that this chapter has made is to identify the main sources of funding social enterprises and related actors in V4 countries. Through a comparative analysis of legal frameworks our results show that the choice of legal forms is also a significant factor. In V4 countries, the concept of social enterprises evolved under different forms, where the legal personality is recognized under various laws and acts. Presently a number of local cooperatives, foundations, associations, non-government organizations, church organizations, and voluntary organizations fulfill functions that are compatible with those of the social economy.

The potential of social enterprises funding is still far from being fully harnessed in V4 countries. The allocation of capital is challenged by a lack of efficient intermediation, the investment infrastructure is fragmented, and social enterprises still have a lack of sufficient absorptive capacity. This chapter generates important insights, and highlights that the majority of social enterprises in V4 countries diversify their funding structure and that the main actors of social investment can be grouped into the following primary types: public sector, private sector, and EU funds.

This chapter offers an overview of the social enterprise landscape in the countries studied. However, in order to fully understand the specific characteristics of social enterprises and Social Investors in V4 countries, as well as their impact, further research is required. Prioritizing this research, particularly at the national level, would help to account for social activity and impact in order to understand and recognize better the efforts and accomplishments of the landscape, as well as to providing visibility in the sector. In addition, comparative studies of V4 and developed economies could illustrate the diversity across countries, as well as patterns and similarities in the social enterprise landscape.

References

Borzaga, C., Bodini, R., Carini, C., Depedri, S., Galera, G., & Salvatori, G. (2014). *Europe in transition: The role of social cooperatives and social enterprises* (Euricse Working Papers No. 69/14). Rochester, NY: Social Science Research Network.

Chell, E. (2007). Social enterprise and entrepreneurship: Towards a convergent theory of the entrepreneurial process. *International Small Business Journal, 25*, 5–26.

Chell, E., Nicolopoulou, K., & Karatas-Özkan, M. (2010). Social entrepreneurship and enterprise: International and innovation perspectives. *Entrepreneurship & Regional Development, 22*(6), 485–493.

Dees, J. G., & Anderson, B. B. (2006). Framing a theory of social entrepreneurship: Building on two schools of practice and thought. In R. Mosher-Williams (Ed.), *Research on social entrepreneurship: Understanding and contributing to an emerging field* (ARNOVA Occasional Paper Series, 1(3), 39–66).

European Union. (2010). *This is European social innovation*. Brussels: European Union. doi:10.2769/825

Jedlička, J., Kotian, J., & Münz, R. (2014). *Visegrad Four—10 years of EU membership*. Erste Group Research: CEE Special Report/Fixed Income/CEE.

Moore, M., Westley, F. R., & Nicholls, A. (2012). The social finance and social innovation nexus. *Journal of Social Entrepreneurship, 3*, 115–132.

Mulgan, G. (2006). The process of social innovation. *Innovations, 1*(2), 145–162.
Mulgan, G., Tucker, S., Ali, R., & Sanders, B. (2007). *Social innovation: What it is, why it matters, how it can be accelerated*. Oxford, UK: Skoll Centre for Social Entrepreneurship.
Murray, R., Caulier-Grice, J., & Mulgan, G. (2009). *Social venturing* (The Social Innovator Series). London, England: Nesta.
Nicholls, A. (2010, July). The legitimacy of social entrepreneurship: Reflexive isomorphism in a pre-paradigmatic field. *Entrepreneurship Theory & Practice*, 611–633.
Noruzi, M. R., Westover, J. R., & Rahimi, G. R. (2010). An exploration of social entrepreneurship in the entrepreneurship era. *Asian Social Science, 6*(6), 4–10.
Noya, A. (Ed.). (2009). *The changing boundaries of social enterprises*. OECD Local Economic and Employment Development (LEED). OECD Publishing, Corrigenda.
Pčolinská, L. (2013). *Social economy, its perception and possibilities of its development in conditions of the Slovak Republic*. Retrieved October 12, 2014, from http://www.ciriec-ua-conference.org/theme-3-laws-on-social-economy-legal-statutes-and-types-of-undertaking1
Philips, W., Lee, H., Ghobadian, A., O'Regan, N., & James, P. (2014). Social innovation and social entrepreneurship: A systematic review. *Group & Organization Management*. Retrieved February 20, 2015, from http://gom.sagepub.com/content/early/2014/12/05/1059601114560063.full.pdf+html
Phills, J. A., Deiglmeier, K., & Miller, D. T. (2008). Rediscovering social innovation. *Stanford Social Innovation Review, 6*, 34–43.
Pol, E., & Ville, S. (2009). Social innovation: Buzz word or enduring term? *Journal of Socio-Economics, 38*, 878–885.
Shaw, E., & de Bruin, A. (2013). Reconsidering capitalism: The promise of social innovation and social entrepreneurship? *International Small Business Journal, 31*(7), 737–746.
Thake, S., & Zadek, S. (1997). *Practical people, noble causes: How to support community social entrepreneurs*. London, England: New Economics Foundation.
Westley, F., & Antadze, N. (2010). Making a difference: Strategies for scaling social innovation for greater impact. *The Innovation Journal: The Public Sector Innovation Journal, 15*, 3–20.
Wilkinson, C. (2014a). *A map of social enterprises and their eco-systems in Europe. Country report: Czech Republic*. European Commission.
Wilkinson, C. (2014b). *A map of social enterprises and their eco-systems in Europe. Country report: Hungary*. European Commission.
Wilkinson, C. (2014c). *A map of social enterprises and their eco-systems in Europe. Country report: Poland*. European Commission.
Wilkinson, C. (2014d). *A map of social enterprises and their eco-systems in Europe. Country report: Slovakia*. European Commission.

39

GOVERNMENT-SPONSORED VENTURE PHILANTHROPY AND SOCIAL ENTREPRENEURSHIP IN CHINA

An exploratory study

Qihai Cai

Social entrepreneurship has been introduced as a potentially promising strategy to provide innovative and sustainable solutions to the world's most pressing social problems, such as poverty, health, education, unemployment, and social exclusion (Dees, 2007; Borzaga & Defourny, 2001; Nicholls, 2006). The Grameen Bank in Bangladesh and the Work Integration Social Enterprises (WISEs) in Europe are two prominent examples of social entrepreneurship. The Grameen Bank provides microfinance to impoverished people to help them establish financial self-sufficiency and fight against poverty. The WISEs provide training and employment for people with disadvantages and disabilities to help them back into the labor market, and thus address the issue of social exclusion. By empowering the previously excluded groups, microfinance and WISEs are exemplified as innovative, sustainable, and effective solutions to poverty and social exclusion which have been perceived as "wicked problems" for government.

Given the promising features of social entrepreneurship, it is not surprising that governments around the world implement supportive policies for social entrepreneurship, which include legal recognition, financial support, and managerial assistance. For example, the UK government created a Social Enterprise Unit within the Department of Trade and Industry in 2001 which was later incorporated into the Office for the Third Sector within the Cabinet Office in 2006 to support the development of social entrepreneurship; in South Korea, the social enterprise Promotion Law was enacted in 2006 to facilitate the launch of social enterprises and create an enabling environment that is favorable for these entities; in the United States, the White House Office of Social Innovation and Civic Participation was established in 2009 to support social entrepreneurship; and in the same year, the Shanghai Municipal Government in China launched an annual policy, "Shanghai Community Venture Philanthropy" (SCVP), to support social entrepreneurship.

Although the institutional experimentations to stimulate social entrepreneurship are still ongoing and their effects are to be measured, Venture Philanthropy stands out as a noteworthy and viable alternative because of its synergetic effects on social entrepreneurship (John, 2006). Venture Philanthropy applies the techniques of venture capitalism to philanthropy by emphasizing stakeholder involvement, organizational capacity building, performance measurement, and exit strategy (Frumkin, 2003; Letts, Ryan, & Allen, 1997; Moody, 2008). Admittedly, some features of Venture Philanthropy are either keys to success in social entrepreneurship (e.g., organizational capacity building), or compatible with social entrepreneurship (e.g., sustainability and innovation). However, current research has tended to "investigate social entrepreneurship and Venture Philanthropy as separate and often unrelated concepts" (Van Slyke & Newman, 2006). Neglecting the linkage between Venture Philanthropy and social entrepreneurship may risk losing the opportunity to create greater benefits for the whole society. This study responds to this call and seeks to contribute to filling up the lack of analysis on the relationship between Venture Philanthropy and social entrepreneurship, and raises the following questions: *What* is the theoretical and empirical relationship between Venture Philanthropy and social entrepreneurship? *How* does the combination of Venture Philanthropy and social entrepreneurship contribute to sustainable social finance? These questions are worth exploring since the combination has already shown its potential in providing innovative and sustainable social services (see John, 2006; Van Slyke & Newman, 2006).

Government-sponsored Venture Philanthropy has been a popular policy for local governments in China. Following Shanghai, Shenzhen (in 2009), Dongguan (in 2011), Suzhou (in 2011), Kunshan (in 2012), Shunde (in 2012), Wuxi (in 2013), Hangzhou (in 2014), and Guangzhou (in 2014) Municipal Governments had also implemented similar government-sponsored Venture Philanthropy to support the development of social entrepreneurship in the local community. This policy requires the non-profit organizations to design and implement community-based Social Entrepreneurial programs to tackle social problems. The community-based Social Entrepreneurial programs address pressing social problems in innovative and sustainable ways, but they do not necessarily constitute separate organizations that can be identified as social enterprises per se. In return, local governments provide start-up funds and managerial assistance for the selected programs. Perhaps it is not coincident that local governments in China enthusiastically embrace this policy due to the increasing gap between the demand and supply of social service. As the first government-sponsored Venture Philanthropy practice in China, the "SCVP" is an excellent case for empirical examination.

The exploration of this topic proceeds in four steps. First, this chapter reviews the current literature on Venture Philanthropy and social entrepreneurship, and discusses the origins, definitions, and implications of these two concepts. Second, this chapter explores whether Venture Philanthropy and social entrepreneurship, as two important actors in the social economy, are theoretically compatible. A social catalyst model is proposed to capture the dynamics of the combination of Venture Philanthropy and social entrepreneurship. Third, drawing from the empirical study of government-sponsored Venture Philanthropy in China, this chapter examines the social catalyst model. Empirical evidence suggests that the powerful combination of Venture Philanthropy and social entrepreneurship helps Social Entrepreneurs develop organizational infrastructure, stimulates innovative and sustainable solutions to social problems, and ameliorates resource efficiency by facilitating collaborations between different sectors. Last, this chapter concludes with the implications for future research and practice of sustainable social finance.

Venture Philanthropy

Four interrelated factors in the 1990s contributed to the proliferation of Venture Philanthropy. First, the 1990s dot-com boom created abundant wealth which provided new resources for philanthropy. Second, the new fortune holders—the new philanthropists—were desperate to find out about more effective ways of philanthropy to replace the old-fashioned grant mode. Furthermore, the success of venture capitalists at that time provided both mature techniques and confidence for Venture Philanthropy. Last, the prevalence of neoliberalism, which was accompanied by the triumph of the market economy and government retrenchment, played an important role in the development of Venture Philanthropy. In other words, its compatibility with the political and economic climates in the 1990s made Venture Philanthropy prevalent at that time. Although the boom years of Venture Philanthropy have passed, its influence on philanthropy remains (Morino & Shore, 2004).

In their benchmarked article in *Harvard Business Review*, Letts et al. (1997) address the question of why non-profit programs that began with high hopes and great promise often ended up with limited impact and uncertain prospects. They suggest that traditional philanthropy often neglects non-profit organizational capacity building which is crucial for program implementation. In this respect, foundations should adopt the techniques from venture capitalists to build up non-profit organizational capacity for greater social impact. Due to the close relation with venture capitalism, this approach was labeled as "Venture Philanthropy." Actually, Letts et al. did not use the term "Venture Philanthropy," and their following research indicates they prefer "high engagement philanthropy" instead (Letts & Ryan, 2003). However, their 1997 article is widely recognized as the first one to provide the framework of Venture Philanthropy (Moody, 2008; Sievers, 2001; Van Slyke & Newman, 2006). This study uses "Venture Philanthropy" and "high engagement philanthropy" interchangeably. Built on the Venture Philanthropy literature (Cobb, 2002; Frumkin, 2003; Gemelli, 2010; Letts & Ryan, 2003; Letts et al., 1997; Moody, 2008), Venture Philanthropy in this study is defined as:

> A funding strategy that adopts techniques from the venture capital funding model, including risk management, consultative engagement, long-term relationship between grantor and grantee, performance measurement, and exit strategy. Venture Philanthropy seeks to build non-profit organizational capacity to address social problems and improve the effectiveness of philanthropy.

This definition emphasizes both the means and the ends of Venture Philanthropy. By adopting high engagement partnership, organizational capacity development, and performance measurement, Venture Philanthropy seeks to address the ineffectiveness of traditional philanthropy (Frumkin, 2003). Venture Philanthropy emphasizes the long-term partnership between granters and grantees to provide consultative assistance and stable financial resources for program implementation. The techniques of venture capitalism are important means to build organizational capacity. However, neither Social Return on Investment (SROI) nor Balanced Scorecard authentically solves the problem of performance measurement (Frumkin, 2003; John, 2006; Sievers, 2001). Although the real impact of Venture Philanthropy remains to be measured, an undeniable fact is that it has influenced philanthropic practices in both the United States and European countries (John, 2006).

Due to its close link with market principles, Venture Philanthropy is facing many challenges. Sievers (2001) uses "flying pig" as a metaphor to describe the illusionary optimism towards the applicability of venture capitalism in the philanthropic world. He argues that the four fundamental assumptions of venture capitalism, namely bottom line, going to scale, funder control, and exit strategy, will become problematic in philanthropy. First, non-profit activity has a range of intangible goals which cannot be simply measured and quantified. Besides, going to scale will infringe non-profit organizations' ability to mobilize the local community's resources. Moreover, control and exit strategy may incline the non-profit world into market forces, and thus distort its original goals. Moody (2008) discusses the potential hazard of the "business–non-profit culture clash," which occurs when the culture of venture capitalism is brought into the non-profit world. The lack of mutual understanding will raise the problem of asymmetric expectations. This mutual culture shock not only infringes civil society, but also affects Venture Philanthropy's effectiveness. Indeed, the appropriateness of applying the business model to the non-profit sector does remain questionable, and the non-profit organization should examine this carefully before applying Venture Philanthropy. Moreover, the attainment of the merits of Venture Philanthropy is by no means automatic, nor easy. For example, funders in Venture Philanthropy have to invest not only money, but also time and personnel, to meet the requirements of their new roles, which may cause extra burdens.

In sum, Venture Philanthropy's "greatest lasting effect may be to reinforce a few basic principles of effective philanthropy that were already emerging" (Kramer, 2002), and thus to pull the wagon of philanthropy that carries tremendous resources onto the right track. The emphases on partnership between grantor and grantee, organizational capacity development, and performance measurement have already enlivened the philanthropic world (Frumkin, 2003), offered a different lens with a changed set of priorities (Cobb, 2002), and provided a healthy critical perspective to challenge philanthropic goals, operating principles, and results (Sievers, 2001). Although the real impact is still unfolding, Venture Philanthropy is aspiring to change the philanthropic world toward effectiveness and sustainability. Venture Philanthropy will "influence the grant making practices of traditional capital providers and bring in new funders and skills for growing entrepreneurial social purpose organizations" (John, 2006). After illustrating Venture Philanthropy, we now move to the other major theme—social entrepreneurship.

Social entrepreneurship

Defining social entrepreneurship is difficult, partly because this term has been used in a very broad sense which ranges from voluntary activism to Corporate Social Responsibility (CSR) (Nicholls, 2006). social entrepreneurship means "different things to different people" (Dees, 1998), and the definition of social entrepreneurship is "anything but clear" (Martin & Osberg, 2007). The current literature suggests at least three different debates with increasing intensity.

The first debate focuses on the essence of social entrepreneurship. social entrepreneurship has long been related to business approach operations. In this perspective, social entrepreneurship means non-profits adopting revenue generation strategies or market-type mechanisms for a social impact. Boschee and McClurg (2003) argue that "unless a non-profit organization is generating earned revenue from its activities, it is not acting in an entrepreneurial manner." In contrast, Dees (2003) suggests that thinking of social entrepreneurship only as non-profits generating earned income is a dangerously narrow view that "shifts attention away from the ultimate goal of creating social impact to one particular method of generating resources." social entrepreneurship should be able to leverage economic, political, and cultural transformation rather than merely revenue generation (Alvord, Brown, & Letts, 2004). The key point of this debate lies in the different understandings of entrepreneurship. Although the term entrepreneurship is closely related to market-oriented mechanisms, it also means discovering the neglected opportunities to create sustainable social value and continuous innovation (Drucker, 1985; Schumpeter, 1980). Therefore, earned income is only one important instrument to achieve social betterment, and it is "not always the best means" (Dees, 2003).

The second debate surrounds the scale of social entrepreneurship. Should social entrepreneurship contain all social entrepreneurial activities or should it only care about activities which create large-scale changes? The inclusive view committed that social entrepreneurship ranges from a variety of social entrepreneurial activities from voluntary activism to CSR (Defourny & Develtere, 2009; Nicholls, 2006). On the contrary, Martin and Osberg (2007) argue that social entrepreneurship should forge "a new, stable equilibrium" to ensure a better future for targeted people and even society at large. Social entrepreneurship is thus reserved for large-scale change in a prevailing social equilibrium (Light, 2008). The rationale of adopting the exclusive account of social entrepreneurship is that without a well-established boundary to prevent resources from pouring into "non-entrepreneurial" activities, the significance and benefits of social entrepreneurship will be undermined. However, there are two risks when focusing only on the large-scale change. First, many social entrepreneurial activities which have great potential for social transformation but start with a small change will be stifled in the cradle. Moreover, one of the most important merits of social entrepreneurship is the characteristic of social experimentation. Experimenting with new ideas through social entrepreneurship will provide society with more opportunities to learn with less risk (Dees, 2007). It will be very difficult, if not impossible, to provide fertile soil for experimenting with social innovation under such an exclusive setting.

The third debate is whether social entrepreneurship should be regarded as a process or as an outcome. Dees (1998) conceives social entrepreneurship as a process in which Social Entrepreneurs

> adopt a mission to create and sustain social value; recognize and relentlessly pursue new opportunities to serve that mission; engage in a process of continuous innovation, adaptation, and learning; act boldly without being limited by resources in hand; exhibit heightened accountability to the constituencies served and for the outcomes created.

In this respect, social entrepreneurship is a process of how Social Entrepreneurs use unique entrepreneurial skills to fulfill social missions. While others, as we have elaborated in previous debates, emphasize that only if either a new social equilibrium (Martin & Osberg, 2007) or a pattern-breaking change (Light, 2006) is created can the activity be termed as "social entrepreneurship."

Drawing from the above review and analysis, my working definition of social entrepreneurship mainly consolidates from the EMES (Borzaga & Defourny, 2001) and Nicholls (2006), and it is defined as follows:

> Social entrepreneurship is a process by which individuals, groups, and organizations catalyze and hybridize diverse resources (e.g., sales or fees, public subsidies, donations and volunteering, and social capital) to provide innovative, sustainable, and effective solutions to social problems, and thus create social values for target groups.

The purpose of social entrepreneurship is to create innovative, sustainable, and effective ways for social betterment, either by catalyzing new resources or by hybridizing existing resources. These resources include sales or fees, public subsidies, donations and volunteering, and social capital. Therefore, social entrepreneurship here focuses on social entrepreneurial activities rather than on social enterprises that have already been labeled as specific kinds of institutions.

As Light (2008) points out: "There may still be strong disagreements on the underlying assumptions about social entrepreneurship, but not on its basic goal." Social entrepreneurship aims to change the unjust social equilibrium for social betterment. However, social entrepreneurship often lacks an effective and supportive infrastructure to function in reality (Dees, 2007; Light, 2009). A vicious circle emerges: Insufficient support prevents social entrepreneurship from fully exerting its potential benefits; and society starts to question the real impact of social entrepreneurship, which results in the reluctance to provide further resources. This quagmire of social entrepreneurship has been noted, and Dees (2007) advocates creating an enabling environment for social entrepreneurship by providing essential resources, formulating public policies that support and enable Social Entrepreneurs to innovate and experiment, and changing the culture of the social sector to emphasize impact and performance. In this regard, the combination of Venture Philanthropy and social entrepreneurship could foster an enabling environment for them both. This combination is explored from a theoretical perspective in the next section.

A marriage made in heaven?

The possible combination of Venture Philanthropy and social entrepreneurship has been examined under a case study of the East Lake Community Development Program in the United States. Van Slyke and Newman (2006) suggest that "high engagement philanthropy coupled with the entrepreneurial vision and action directed toward social need, community change, and poverty reduction would be more likely to achieve positive results." Based on the study of Venture Philanthropy across Europe, John (2006) describes the relationship between Venture Philanthropy and social entrepreneurship as "two strands of DNA": "[They are] two social sector capital market actors, representing capital supply and demand, equally in need of each other, to express sustainable social benefit." Although these two studies open the window to exploring the collaboration between Venture Philanthropy and social entrepreneurship, the relationship has not yet been analyzed theoretically or beyond a single case study. This section connects this missing link and aims to build a theoretical framework of the combination of Venture Philanthropy and social entrepreneurship.

First, rooted from the themes of venture capitalism and entrepreneurship, both Venture Philanthropy and social entrepreneurship can be regarded as "the marketization of the nonprofit sector" (Eikenberry & Kluver, 2004). Adopting the languages and principles from the market sector, both Venture Philanthropy and social entrepreneurship emphasize sustainable resource streams, greater efficiency, and innovation. Although the marketization of the nonprofit sector has the potential to substantively improve the efficiency of the third sector, it may also infringe the role of the non-profit sector in building a strong civil society. Though the effects of marketization in the third sector are still mixed, the similar origins and goals make the collaboration between Venture Philanthropy and social entrepreneurship possible.

Second, there are both demand and supply forces at work. The current predicament of social entrepreneurship is caused due to the fact that sufficient supports have not yet been rendered to this young but ambitious field. Social entrepreneurship often lacks financial resources and organizational capacity to function and succeed. Putting high expectations on social entrepreneurship to solve the imperative social problems, however, without deliberately building an enabling environment for it to function, is over-optimistic at best and illusory at worst. Venture Philanthropy invests not only financial resources but also managerial assistance to build the grantee's organizational capacity with the goal of making a broad and significant social impact. From the demand-supply perspective, the development of organizational capacity from Venture Philanthropy considerably benefits Social Entrepreneurs to achieve their social agenda. Besides, the sustainability and great social impact generated by successful social entrepreneurship corresponds well with the preference of Venture Philanthropy. The complementarity provides a solid foundation on which a strategic alliance between Venture Philanthropy and social entrepreneurship can be achieved.

Last, resource dependence theory proposes that organizations are not capable themselves of providing all the resources needed for their survival and are thus dependent on external resources and a continuous transaction process with other actors in their environment (Salanick & Pfeffer, 1978; Sander, 1990). The term "resource" here means almost anything that is perceived as valuable—from building contracts, to press exposure, to control over systems and analysis (Pfeffer, 1992). The underlying logic of resource dependence is that each sector has its own distinctive advantages and resources. Only by collaboration can we exert these advantages and resources to create synergy between different sectors. Social entrepreneurship, understood as a process of hybridization of diverse resources from different sectors, is the catalyst of collaborations between different sectors to address social problems. However, the synergy that could emerge in the collaboration is by no means automatic, and this provides substantive room for Venture Philanthropy to function. By providing start-up funds and organizational capacity building, Venture Philanthropy seeks to leverage resources from other sectors to generate sustainable social impact. Venture Philanthropy—either government-sponsored or market-funded—triggers social entrepreneurship. In this respect, Venture Philanthropy and social entrepreneurship can benefit from each other in a compatible way.

Building from the above analysis, this study proposes a social catalyst model to demonstrate the dynamics between different sectors in the process of collaboration (see Figure 39.1). In the form of Venture Philanthropy, governments and corporations offer start-up funds and managerial assistance to facilitate and support social entrepreneurship. In return, social entrepreneurship provides an imperative social service to the target groups. Meanwhile, corporations could fulfill their CSR to improve public relations by continuously funding social service programs or by providing other supports. Citizens could participate in the process as service recipients, volunteers, or even as Social Entrepreneurs. The participation of different actors in the co-productive work not only ameliorates resource efficiency by exerting the distinctive advantages and resources of each actor, but also enhances social innovation by cutting across organizational and sectoral boundaries (Mulgan, Tucker, Ali, & Sanders, 2007). For example, more and more social services are now provided by non-profit organizations through government contracts and grants (Salamon, 1995; Smith & Lipsky, 1993; Van Slyke, 2007). Non-profit organizations

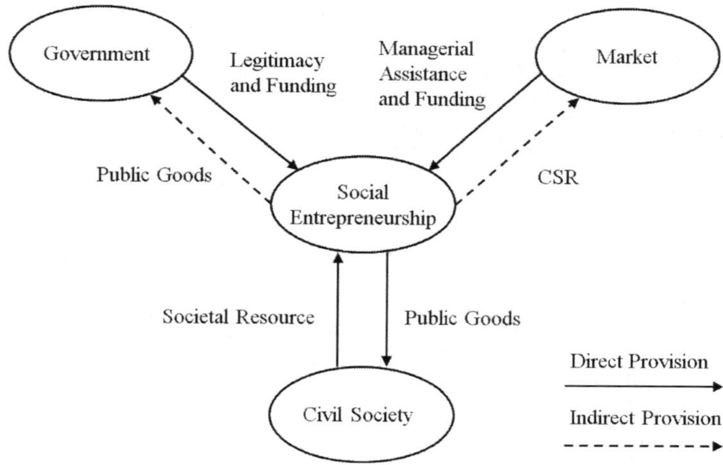

Figure 39.1 Social catalyst model

are believed to reduce the transaction costs of social service delivery not only by understanding the needs of the target groups and thus identifying potential solutions but also by mobilizing the local community resources and volunteer workforce. Compared to the traditional form of service delivery that was directly designed and provided by the government, the social catalyst model stimulates social exchanges between different actors to co-produce a public service (Alford, 2002), which reduces the burdens that each of them would undertake when undertaking the enterprise alone.

This section has explored a theoretical framework to explain the combination of Venture Philanthropy and social entrepreneurship. Standing alone, they are two major actors in the social economy; combined together, they catalyze collaborations between different sectors to co-produce a public service. This approach of social service provision resonates with the current political and economic climates. Due to the economic downturn, we are now facing a political quagmire: the demand for public goods is increasing; however, governments lack the ability and resources to deliver them all. Sustainable and effective solutions for pressing social problems are desperately needed. To this end, the combination of Venture Philanthropy and social entrepreneurship is proving to be a rewarding option for government. The next section will now examine the empirical evidence from government-sponsored Venture Philanthropy in China.

Government-sponsored Venture Philanthropy in China

Data and methods

The SCVP, as the first government-sponsored Venture Philanthropy practice in China, provides a good opportunity for examination. This policy was initiated by the Shanghai Municipal Bureau of Civil Affairs and administered by the Non-Profit Incubator (NPI) in 2009. Established in 2006, the NPI is a non-profit organization which aims to provide support to newly established and small-sized non-profit organizations. A total amount of 1.55 million USD was appropriated from the Welfare Lottery Funds to support this policy. Non-profit organizations were required to design community-based social entrepreneurial programs under seven themes, namely community development, family and children, elderly care, disability, women, migrant workers, and teenagers. Each selected program was granted one-year financial support of up to 46,000 USD for program operation. In order to prevent corruption, management expense including the employee payroll was limited to 10 percent of total funding. Besides this, the funding did not support fixed asset investment. The selection criteria were innovation and sustainability: innovation means the program should adopt a new and effective approach to address social problems; sustainability is regarded as a requirement that the program should be self-sustaining after the one-year financial grant, either by self-generated revenues or by being funded by the market. After the competition, 59 programs stood out. On behalf of the Shanghai Municipal Bureau of Civil Affairs, the NPI offered organizational capacity training programs for funded organizations and evaluated all programs.

As a government-sponsored Venture Philanthropy practice, the SCVP partly adopts the idea of Venture Philanthropy while maintaining many characteristics of the traditional grant model. Despite the fact that the funding is only for one year, the SCVP emphasizes organizational capacity building and the innovation and sustainability of the social service program. All selected programs are devoted to addressing the seven pressing social problems in innovative and sustainable ways, which can be regarded as social entrepreneurial activities. Therefore, the appropriateness of using this case to examine the relationship between Venture Philanthropy and social entrepreneurship is warranted.

This study employs qualitative methods for investigation. The data were collected from November 2009 to February 2010. First, we conducted several semi-structured interviews with the officials administrating the SCVP. Besides this, we collected all 59 program plans of the 2009 SCVP for document analysis. Most importantly, eight sponsored programs were selected for conducting in-depth participant observation by eight trained researchers from the Collaborative Governance Research Center at Fudan University. Accordingly, primary data were gathered through document analysis, semi-structured personal interviews, and in-depth participant observation. In what follows, I present and discuss the findings of the empirical study.

Findings and discussion

The first finding is that this policy helps the non-profit organizations to develop organization infrastructure. Organization infrastructures are mainly regarded here as large amounts of seed capital, organizational capacity building, and professional networks. Based on the information we gathered from the study, the SCVP contributes to ameliorate organization infrastructure in four different ways. First, the provision of seed capital of up to 46,000 USD not only eases capital shortage urgency in the early stage of the non-profit organizations but also provides them with opportunities to experiment with new ideas (e.g., the development of a community culture center for migrant workers). Starting with small-scale experimentation, the SCVP reduces the risk for both government and Social Entrepreneurs. One of the Social Entrepreneurs (personal communication, January 26, 2009) told us:

> The support from government really helps us to try to see whether the theoretically promising projects are feasible in reality. We are sharing the risks together. If the program did not work out, the information gathered from its failure may still be helpful.

Second, the SCVP improves the funded organization's capacity (e.g., human resource management, financial management, and volunteer management) through the associated training programs. "NPI will ask us to participate in seminars such as human resources management and financial management for non-profit organizations. The lecturers they invited were both experienced and excellent. We do learn a lot from the seminars," one organizational leader (personal communication, January 19, 2010) was quoted as saying. Third, the SCVP builds a platform for Social Entrepreneurs to facilitate their interactions and collaborations. The organizational networks make not only an exchange of experiences, but also future collaborations between different organizations for possible joint ventures. Last, the SCVP provides some Social Entrepreneurs with access to premises for their working place, which reduces their operational costs. As one Social Entrepreneur (personal communication, March 23, 2010) told us, "The office they provided is just awesome … we can work with other organizations to learn from them, to seek for a future joint program, and more importantly, finding a working place is really a time-consuming activity and very costly for us."

Admittedly, the SCVP cannot be regarded as pure Venture Philanthropy because of the provision of short-term funding and the subsequent forced exit strategy. However, the applications of the principles of Venture Philanthropy that focus on organizational capacity building still have positive effects. One important indicator to demonstrate that Venture Philanthropy promotes social entrepreneurship is the extent to which new organizations are partly funded by Venture Philanthropy. The distribution of organizational age (see Table 39.1) shows that 28 out of 57 funded organizations (49.1 percent) were established three years or less prior to or even after the inauguration of the SCVP in 2009. This point is important because the capital

Table 39.1 Age of the funded organizations in the 2009 SCVP

Organizational age (N, year)	*Number of organizations**	*Percentage*
N<1	21	36.8
1≤N<3	7	12.3
3≤N<5	10	17.5
5≤N<7	11	19.3
7≤N	8	14.1
Total	57	100

Source: Based on analysis of the project plans of funded organizations in the 2009 SCVP.

* Two organizations were both awarded two independent programs in the 2009 SCVP, so therefore only 57 organizations are counted here.

shortage problem is even more severe for a new organization. Another interesting observation from Table 39.1 is that 21 out of 59 funded organizations (36.8 percent) were established during 2009. This large portion of new organizations benefits a lot from the provision of seed capital and capacity-building programs because new Social Entrepreneurs desperately need funds and capacities for implementing their new ideas. Moreover, according to interviews and participant observations, the social service programs that these new Social Entrepreneurs designed to compete in the SCVP were their first attempts to utilize the relevant information concerning the problems focused on by their proposed target groups to formulate potential solutions. In other words, the SCVP provides opportunities for social experimentation. The provision of seed capital, capacity-building programs, and office facilities, plus the establishment of organizational networks, creates an enabling environment for Social Entrepreneurs.

The second finding is that the adoption of selection criteria and exit strategy stimulates an innovative and sustainable social service design. To win the grant from government, Social Entrepreneurs have to use their information from the field to seek any ignored opportunities for social improvement, and develop innovative and sustainable solutions. Furthermore, the exit strategy encourages, if not forces, Social Entrepreneurs to establish financial self-sufficiency. The purpose of the exit strategy is to reduce dependence on government, so that after the one-year financial support the program should be self-sustaining by self-generated revenue. Therefore, Social Entrepreneurs have to seek inter-organizational collaborations to ensure stable resource streams for sustainability at the stage of program design. The "exit strategy" of the SCVP is very controversial—because it simply means that the funding to each recipient will expire after one year of financial support. It thus adopts the time span as the exit standard rather than the establishment of financial self-sufficiency that the original Venture Philanthropy practice proposes. Admittedly, a common problem of supportive policies for social entrepreneurship is when to stop the financial aid. An appropriate exit strategy is difficult to develop, and this is one of the most prominent criticisms that Venture Philanthropy is receiving. Taking the "Enhancing Self-Reliance through District Partnership Program" in Hong Kong for example, the original funded period of no more than two years has been prolonged to no more than three years in response to a need to sustain financial support during the difficult start-up period. Along with the criticisms, the adoption of selection criteria and exit strategy still provides incentives for Social Entrepreneurs to become innovative and to find a sustainable solution.

The third finding is that this policy improves resource efficiency by facilitating collaborations between different sectors. The program "Be Your Eyes" (BYE) is used as an example to elaborate on this. This program was designed to deal with the shortage of Braille paper for the blind. In the first year, BYE produced about 10,000 Charity Calendars, which were made from Braille paper, and they were exchanged with citizens for used ordinary calendars. The recycled calendars were re-produced as new Braille paper and distributed to the blind to write on. In the next few years, BYE will contact corporations to purchase Charity Calendars to sustain the project's operations. In return, corporations could print logos and slogans on Charity Calendars for advertisements. After the first year, because the Charity Calendars are made from Braille paper, the recycled ones can be directly distributed to the blind to use the blank back pages without further processing. This program successfully mobilizes resources from different actors: BYE used its information about the needs of the blind and existing resources such as volunteers and connections with the local community to design this program; the government provided the seed capital and organizational capacity building for the program; and corporations took part in the program by providing continuous funding to fulfill their CSR. Resource efficiency is ameliorated because this program effectively addresses the problem of the shortage of Braille paper, reduces operational costs through the use of a volunteer workforce, establishes sustainability through exerting resources from different sectors, and makes the best use of old calendars to become environmentally friendly.

The matching grant mode in "Dongguan Venture Philanthropy" is another example to show how collaborations between different actors could improve resource efficiency. Dongguan Municipal Government adopts a matching grant to encourage non-profit organizations to raise funds from society. The matching ratio is 1:2, and the maximum size of the matching grant for each program is 80,000 USD. In other words, within the maximum limit of 80,000 USD, with each dollar the non-profit organization raises, Dongguan Municipal Government will grant an additional two dollars for its program operation. Considering the difficulty of fundraising, Dongguan Municipal Government will still compensate the programs that cannot reach the minimum operational cost of 48,000 USD after the matching. As a result, nearly 250,000 USD is raised from society, which accounts for about 11 percent of total government spending (i.e., 2.24 million USD) in this policy. The matching grant mode enables the government to identify capable non-profit organizations in terms of fundraising. Fundraising capacity is a crucial indicator of program sustainability. Besides this, the due diligence from the donated corporation helps the government to reduce the evaluation cost of each program. Risk sharing between different actors enables the collaborative endeavor to be possible.

The emergence of government-sponsored Venture Philanthropy is path breaking in stimulating and catalyzing social entrepreneurship in China. This policy has the potential to increase the responsiveness of social service provision by bridging between the government and the community. However, the future success of government-sponsored Venture Philanthropy is highly contingent on the government's perception of the non-profit organizations (Jing & Gong, 2012).

Conclusion

Among the diverse studies and practices of Venture Philanthropy and social entrepreneurship, there is increasing interest in the potential of collaboration between these two important actors in the social economy. This chapter has shed light on the interplay between government-sponsored Venture Philanthropy and social entrepreneurship in providing an innovative and sustainable social service. The empirical analysis suggests that the powerful combination of Venture Philanthropy and social entrepreneurship helps Social Entrepreneurs develop an organizational infrastructure, stimulates innovative and sustainable solutions to social problems, and ameliorates resource efficiency by facilitating collaborations between different sectors. Organizational infrastructure, social innovation, and collaborations between different sectors all contribute to sustainable social finance. As shown in the social catalyst mode, the collaborations between different sectors not only secure the sustainable resource stream but also improve resource efficiency by bringing to the fore the distinctive advantages of each actor.

This chapter makes two important contributions to the literature. First, although the synergistic effects between Venture Philanthropy and social entrepreneurship have been noted, systematic analysis has yet to emerge. Building from the empirical study of government-sponsored Venture Philanthropy in China, this chapter proposes the social catalyst mode to understand the dynamics of the collaboration between Venture Philanthropy and social entrepreneurship. Second, we still know little about social finance in China, or more broadly, the actors, impetus, and constraints of social finance practice in developing countries. In fear of the potential political challenges proposed by mobilized societal resources, developing countries often adopt stringent regulations to suppress grassroots mobilization. However, this chapter shows that the municipal governments in China actively engage in promoting social finance to find innovative and sustainable solutions for imperative social problems. With the gap between the supply and demand of social services increasing, the room for the development of social finance continues to grow. Investigating the different practices in these countries is essential if we are to fully comprehend the impact of social finance on modern society.

Perhaps the most compelling implication of this chapter is the possible policy transfer of government-sponsored Venture Philanthropy to develop social entrepreneurship in other countries. This policy might be appropriate for developing countries where the institutional environments for non-profit sector development are relatively immature. Under such circumstances, public grant becomes the most important source of funding to trigger social finance. However, the socioeconomic context and the unique histories of each different region will affect social entrepreneurship (Kerlin, 2010). Therefore, the replicability of this policy needs further examination.

An inevitable limitation of this exploratory study concerns data availability. The empirical findings are mainly based on the available data of the 2009 SCVP. To measure the real impact of government-sponsored Venture Philanthropy on entrepreneurial activities that solve social problems, some important indicators, such as the success rate of entrepreneurial social service projects after one year's financial support, need to be developed and tested through future research and examination. In this regard, future efforts which are dedicated to investigating what factors are imperative for the successful combination of Venture Philanthropy and social entrepreneurship will be rewarding. Understanding the dynamics and factors that influence success can provide recommendations and suggestions for practitioners in social finance.

References

Alford, J. (2002). Defining the client in the public sector: A social-exchange perspective. *Public Administration Review, 62*(3), 337–346.

Alvord, S., Brown, L., & Letts, C. (2004). Social entrepreneurship and societal transformation: An exploratory study. *The Journal of Applied Behavioral Science, 40*(3), 260–282.

Borzaga, C., & Defourny, J. (2001). Conclusions. Social enterprises in Europe: A diversity of initiatives and prospects. In C. Borzaga & J. Defourny (Eds.), *The emergence of social enterprise* (pp. 350–370). London: Routledge.

Boschee, J., & McClurg, J. (2003). *Toward a better understanding of social entrepreneurship: Some important distinctions*. Retrieved March 10, 2016, from http://www.caledonia.org.uk/papers/Social-Entrepreneurship.pdf

Cobb, N. K. (2002). The new philanthropy: Its impact on funding arts and culture. *The Journal of Arts Management, Law, and Society, 32*(2), 125–143.

Dees, J. G. (1998). *The meaning of social entrepreneurship*. Retrieved March 10, 2016, from http://e145.stanford.edu/upload/articles/dees_SE.pdf

Dees, J. G. (2003). Social entrepreneurship is about innovation and impact, not income. *Social Edge Online*, 1–4.

Dees, J. G. (2007). Taking social entrepreneurship seriously. *Society, 44*(3), 24–31.

Defourny, J., & Develtere, P. (2009). The social economy: The worldwide making of a third sector. In D. Jacques, D. Patrick, F. Bénédicte, & N. Marthe (Eds.), *The worldwide making of the social economy: Innovations and changes* (pp. 15–40). Leuven: ACCO.

Drucker, P. (1985). *Innovation and entrepreneurship*. London: Harper-Business.

Eikenberry, A. M., & Kluver, J. D. (2004). The marketization of the nonprofit sector: Civil society at risk. *Public Administration Review, 64*(2), 132–140.

Frumkin, P. (2003). Inside venture philanthropy. *Society, 40*(4), 7–15.

Gemelli, G. (2010). Venture philanthropy. In H. Anheier & S. Toepler (Eds.), *International encyclopedia of civil society* (pp. 1604–1608). New York: Springer-Verlag.

Jing, Y., & Gong, T. (2012). Managed social innovation: The case of government-sponsored venture philanthropy in Shanghai. *Australian Journal of Public Administration, 71*(2), 233–245.

John, R. (2006). *Venture philanthropy: The evolution of high engagement philanthropy in Europe*. Working paper, Skoll Centre for Social Entrepreneurship, University of Oxford, UK.

Kerlin, J. A. (2010). A comparative analysis of the global emergence of social enterprise. *Voluntas, 21*(2), 162–179.

Kramer, M. R. (2002, May). Will venture philanthropy leave a lasting mark on charitable giving? *The Chronicle of Philanthropy*, 2.

Letts, C., & Ryan, W. (2003). Filling the performance gap: High-engagement philanthropy. *Stanford Social Innovation Review, 1*(1), 26–33.

Letts, C., Ryan, W., & Allen, A. (1997). Virtuous capital: What foundations can learn from venture capitalists. *Harvard Business Review, 75*, 36–42.

Light, P. (2006). Reshaping social entrepreneurship. *Stanford Social Innovation Review, 4*(3), 47–51.

Light, P. (2008). *The search for social entrepreneurship*. Washington, DC: Brookings Institution Press.

Light, P. (2009). Social entrepreneurship revisited. *Stanford Social Innovation Review,* 7(3), 21–22.

Martin, R., & Osberg, S. (2007). Social entrepreneurship: The case of definition. *Stanford Social Innovation Review, 5*(2), 29–39.

Moody, M. (2008). Building a culture: The construction and evolution of venture philanthropy as a new organizational field. *Nonprofit and Voluntary Sector Quarterly, 37*(2), 324–352.

Morino, M., & Shore, B. (2004). *High-engagement philanthropy: A bridge to a more effective social sector*. Reston, VA: Venture Philanthropy Partners and Community Wealth Ventures. Retrieved March 10, 2016, from http://www.vppartners.org/sites/default/files/reports/report2004.pdf

Mulgan, G., Tucker, S., Ali, R., & Sanders, B. (2007). *Social innovation: What it is, why it matters and how it can be accelerated*. Working paper, Skoll Centre for Social Entrepreneurship, University of Oxford, UK.

Nicholls, A. (2006). Introduction. In A. Nicholls (Ed.), *Social entrepreneurship: New models for sustainable change* (pp. 1–30). Oxford: Oxford University Press.

Pfeffer, J. (1992). *Managing with power: Politics and influence in organizations*. Boston: Harvard Business Press.

Salamon, L. M. (1995). *Partners in public service: Government-nonprofit relations in the modern welfare state*. Baltimore: Johns Hopkins University Press.

Salancik, G. R., & Pfeffer, J. (1978). A social information processing approach to job attitudes and task design. *Administrative Science Quarterly, 23*, 224–253.

Sander, K. (1990). *Prozesse der Macht*. Berlin: Springer.

Schumpeter, J. (1980). *Theory of economic development*. London: Transaction Publishing.

Sievers, B. (2001, November 16). *If pigs had wings: The appeals and limits of venture philanthropy*. Address to the Waldemar A. Nielsen Issues in Philanthropy Seminar, Georgetown University, Washington, DC.

Smith, S. R., & Lipsky, M. (1993). *Nonprofits for hire: The welfare state in the age of contracting*. Cambridge, MA: Harvard University Press.

Van Slyke, D. M. (2007). Agents or stewards: Using theory to understand the government-nonprofit social service contracting relationship. *Journal of Public Administration Research and Theory, 17*(2), 157–187.

Van Slyke, D. M., & Newman, H. (2006). Venture philanthropy and social entrepreneurship in community redevelopment. *Nonprofit Management & Leadership, 16*(3), 345–368.

40
THE ROLE OF SOCIAL INVESTORS IN DEVELOPING AND EMERGING ECONOMIES

Lisa M. Hanley, Aline Margaux Laucke, and Tim Weiss

Social investments, understood as financial and technical support provided for social enterprises, have increased in size and amount over the last decades (Nicholls, 2010a; Saltuk, Bouri, & Leung, 2011). Social enterprises, in this chapter, will be understood in a wide sense to encompass all organizations that receive support from Social Investors and thus seek to use market-driven and entrepreneurial approaches to address social problems. Particularly in emerging markets, where many social problems remain unresolved, market-based development approaches that claim to be more efficient and more effective than traditional development aid (McMullen, 2011) have spurred significant interest among scholars and practitioners. For philanthropists and aid donors, social investments promise to be a financially sustainable alternative to traditional charitable funding or a more business-like way of deploying their funds. In contrast to grants or donations that are given to organizations for a specific service delivery, social investments relate to efforts that "start up, sustain, or grow individual, group, organizational, or sectoral action, and which generate a return appropriate to the initial outlay, taking into account risk" (Nicholls, 2010a, p. 72); investors expect to generate social impact alongside financial returns, and governments see it as a helpful complement to their activities, particularly in times of stretched budgets (Emerson & Bugg-Levine, 2011; Koh, Karamchandani, & Katz, 2012). Despite this growing excitement, information regarding the field of social investments in emerging and developing economies remains scarce. Various types of actors including development agencies, commercial investors, foundations, and high-net-worth individuals have entered the field, where they co-exist, compete, and collaborate, with varying intentions and interests. Altogether they form a nascent and pre-paradigmatic ecosystem, in which common definitions and practices are currently being developed. This chapter uses Nicholls' (2010a) conceptualization of social investment as a "socially constructed space within which different investment logics and investor rationalities are currently in play" (p. 70), and focuses on social investment approaches that explicitly seek to foster social and economic development in developing and emerging economies.

We argue that, in order to understand the role and potential of social investments in emerging and developing markets, the practices that are currently in play need to be understood in the context of the development aid arena. Foreign aid, be it commercially or socially oriented, has had a tremendous impact on developing and emerging economies today (Buira, 2002; Henisz, Zelner, & Guillén, 2005). Decades of reforms in the global south fostered market liberalization, deregulation, and privatization. Services moved from the public realm to the private sphere and left a range of unmet basic needs. This in turn created new opportunities for alternative forms of service delivery that have the potential to be both more innovative and efficient than the public sector (Savas, 1987). In addition, significant changes to the landscape of traditional development aid have occurred, as other types of financial flows have increased and therefore the relative importance of, for example, non-repayable financial support has decreased. Countries of the global south therefore present new opportunity spaces for investments, as basic needs, that is, the minimum consumption needs of a family which include adequate food, shelter, and clothing, as well as essentials such as safe water, sanitation, public transport, health care, education, and cultural facilities (International Labour Organization, 1977), go unmet and privatization reforms persist. Development approaches have shifted from perspectives that traditionally funded non-profit and non-governmental organizations to increasingly market-oriented approaches that have legitimized for-profit organizations providing basic goods and services. Given both the need for basic needs service delivery and opportunities for new approaches to development, Social Investors have seized these spaces as new terrains in an attempt to combine both social and financial value creation. Investments that seek a double bottom-line or blended value creation are instances of this trend (Emerson, 2003).

Based on exploratory data collected from Social Investors in Colombia, Mexico, Kenya, and South Africa, this chapter aims to provide a first step toward contextualizing social investments in the development aid arena. The field of social investment keeps growing and gaining importance as a legitimate approach to foster development in developing and emerging economies. However, it is believed that actual practices need to be juxtaposed with the high expectations that are projected on Social Investors if the development impact of social investment is to be maximized. Questions including who Social Investors are and what the focus of their activities is in developing and emerging economies need to be answered in order to allow for an integration of social investments into the development arena and an increase of their contribution to social and economic development.

The chapter will be structured as follows. First, the current trends in the development arena as well as the opportunity spaces that have emerged for social investments will be introduced. Second, the literature on social investment will be reviewed. And finally, the study's empirical data will be presented. Given that social investment is a weakly institutionalized field in which actors co-exist, compete, and collaborate without any supervision or common mandate, the empirical section first locates social investment in the current trend toward market orientation that takes place in the development aid arena. For this purpose, it will display social investment networking behavior—more precisely co-investment patterns and perceptions of competition. The chapter then elaborates on Social Investors' role and intentions in promoting economic development. It examines the target group that Social Investors focus on, the type of organizations that receive support, and the financing vehicles that Social Investors use to pursue their objectives.

New opportunity spaces in developing and emerging economies

New opportunity spaces—that is, spaces where traditional development aid or local public agencies have either failed to successfully deliver basic needs and services or their role has been reduced in recent years—for investment in basic needs and services in emerging markets have materialized in recent decades primarily due to two trends. First, opportunity spaces in the global south have opened as a result of market liberalization, which entails a reduction of state-delivered services, an acceptance of privately delivered basic goods and services, as well as an increased legitimacy of involving for-profit (Peck, 2001; Savas, 1987) actors. This legitimacy of for-profit organizations working in the basic needs sector comes along with a second trend, where actors from the global north seek new, untapped markets. These twin trends have led to the emergence of opportunity spaces, where Social Investors including actors from various backgrounds co-exist, compete, and collaborate. As the next sections will describe, Social Investors may hold a key advantage to working in these new opportunity spaces, as traditional commercial investors find the market too risky and unattractive and traditional development actors are not yet prepared to seize the opportunities that have arisen.

Market liberalization

In the last decades, developing and emerging economies increasingly transitioned into liberalized economies, a step that involved deregulation and privatization (Henisz et al., 2005). Structural adjustment programs carried out by the International Monetary Fund (IMF) and the World Bank (WB) left many countries in the global south with no alternative to the course of deregulation, marketization, privatization, and sale of public assets in an effort to promote the functioning of free markets, as well as competitiveness and economic self-sufficiency (Peck, 2001; Rhodes, 1994). This shift has resulted in a penetration of market mechanisms to deliver services or goods in almost all aspects of life (Fine & Hall, 2012), and a changing role for the state. At the supranational level, states are encouraged to create good business environments and flexible labor markets, and instigate entrepreneurship, which have not necessarily minimized the role of the state. Today, the public sector encourages the leveraging of third parties such as non-profit and for-profit organizations and seeks to network their capabilities to create solutions to social problems (Salamon, 2002). The state still plays an active role, but the role has changed from the provider of services to an enabler role; the enabler role entails significant state intervention, but mostly on behalf of the business environment (Peck, 2001). In this context, the role of the state has not disappeared with regard to the provision of basic needs and services, but rather exerts a different power.

As posited by many scholars (e.g., Jessop, 1999), this new orientation toward market liberalization has far-reaching implications for social redistribution, citizenship rights, and access to services. In practice, concerns about service quality, social equity, and employment conditions raise questions about the benefits of privatization and market-oriented service provision (Bel, Fageda, & Warner, 2010; McDonald & Ruiters, 2012). On the flip side, progressive, grassroots movements that concern mobilizing social economies and deepening as well as democratizing local capacities and countermovements are possible (Amin, 1999; Warner & Clifton, 2013). Empirical studies provide conflicting evidence on the costs and benefits of privatization. However, the growing legitimacy of for-profit partners coupled with public perception and pressure for improved government efficiency has kept privatization on the government and international development agenda.

Development landscape and financing

The last decades have also seen significant changes in the composition of capital inflows to developing and emerging economies, as well as to the overall structure of the international development finance system, which includes bilateral and multilateral donors on the public side and NGOs, private philanthropy, and the commercial sector on the private side.

While "Official Development Aid" (ODA), defined as those flows to countries and territories and to multilateral development institutions, has increased significantly in absolute terms, its share of total developing country inflows has decreased remarkably, as flows such as remittances, commercial loans, and equity investments have become more important (OECD, 2008). While ODA constituted around 35 percent of total capital inflows in 1990, it accounted for less than 15 percent in 2007 (OECD, 2007). Furthermore, the last decades have demonstrated that funding from traditional development organizations, that is, government aid distributed through bilateral and multilateral organizations, is insufficient to solve the problems faced by the people living at the so-called bottom of the pyramid (BoP) (Prahalad & Hart, 1999). Although significant progress has been made in reducing poverty, significant work still remains, as can be witnessed through the measurement of Millennium Development Goals (MDG). Although significant progress has been made, the MDG's target of 2015 has fallen short in many categories, and there is a need for a post-2015 agenda, as poverty has not been eradicated (United Nations, 2010). Consequently, the traditional players in development have begun to explore alternative approaches to encourage innovative—particularly collaborative—forms of service delivery and consequently of development finance (Jackson, 2013). This can be witnessed through programs at the United Nations, World Bank, and Inter-American Development Bank, as well as priorities within bilateral aid and other philanthropic organizations for the delivery of basic needs. In addition, new actors such as Social Investors and social enterprises are appearing, which has changed the landscape of traditional development aid to an interdependent system of complementing and competing organizations. The public, the third, and the private sectors increasingly engage in partnerships that blur the lines between sector boundaries (Dees, 2003). Understanding these new financial flows and instruments as well as new forms of collaborating can provide insights into the new development landscape, and the organizations and policies that contribute to fighting poverty.

In sum, a new landscape of development aid has thus emerged, in which social and commercial objectives start to blur and which emphasizes reciprocity in aid relationships (Easterly, 2010). Non-profits and local government, once the default intermediary partner for development programs, have seen their role diminish as preferences for market-oriented approaches increase—supported by social investments which embody this new development paradigm. And given both the need for service delivery and opportunities for new approaches to development, they have seized these spaces as new terrains in an attempt to combine both social and financial return expectations.

New opportunity spaces

Given the trend of marketization coupled with the declining influence of traditional development aid, new opportunity spaces for investments have emerged, followed by new actors in the development arena. As the poor and marginalized in the global south struggle to gain access to basic goods and services, the clarity of who is in charge and how goods and services should be provided has been converted into a complex network of actors. Social Investors have thrived in these new spaces and seized the opportunity to adopt new approaches to economic and social development that capitalize on the insufficient provision of basic goods and services.

The ability of the Social Investor to emerge is grounded in the fundamental belief that market competition in the private sector is a more efficient way to provide these services and allows for greater citizen choice (Savas, 1987). This tendency toward market-oriented approaches of both financing organizations and service delivering organizations reflects a fundamental change in ideology and culture with regard to meeting social needs (Dart, 2004). This ideology has been institutionalized by supranational organizations not only through former privatization reforms, but currently by the increasing development of market-oriented policies, and a proliferation of for-profit organizations as legitimate service providers.

As markets in the North become increasingly saturated with diminishing returns, financial flows service new geographic terrain or, more simply, the global south. However, traditional commercial investors may find investments in these areas too risky and insufficiently profitable. At the same time, non-profits have not yet adapted to meet the demands of the new market-oriented development ideology. Social enterprises attempt to fill this void, by developing innovative business models that often combine both social and financial objectives. Consequently, they have raised the interest of Social Investors, who blend practices from "well-established institutional traditions based in civil society and mainstream capital management" (Nicholls, 2010a, p. 75f), thereby creating innovative development finance vehicles. However, the role and practices of Social Investors in emerging markets remain largely unexplored.

Given this new landscape, in which organizations can capitalize on these new opportunity spaces, a crucial point for research is whether social enterprises and Social Investors know that their provision of basic needs and services does not fall under the same critique as privatization. Up until approximately the 1980s, it was accepted that the preferable provider of many basic needs was government or non-profit organizations, rather than private, profit-seeking companies (Clifton, Comín, & Fuentes, 2003). It is precisely through the increasing emphasis on markets and private ownership that basic goods and services are commodified. And this, commodification can have a significant impact on both the properties and provision. As critics of privatization caution, it can result in an adjustment of the quality and quantity of services to the purchasing power of customers instead of providing the best possible services for all users or clients—that is, rich and poor, rural and urban, to name just a few. For example, health care is a basic need that is often delivered with varying quantity and quality; however, the difference in quality can often result in life and death situations (Hermann, 2009). Traditional commercial approaches have therefore flourished in health services for upper-income levels that have the purchasing power to pay for high quality. Low-income populations, however, have largely been left for the often chronically underfinanced and dysfunctional public or third sector as well as a large informal sector.

Traditional commercial investors may lack incentives to provide inclusive services. Although BoP approaches are based on the idea that large companies can find significant new business opportunities when serving the needs of low-income markets (Prahalad & Hart, 1999), the contribution of BoP approaches to fighting poverty has been contested. However, Social Investors with their double bottom-line do. Yet, questions remain with regard to the issues that Social Investors address. What is their role and their intention in the development arena? How can Social Investors be integrated into the development arena in order to maximize their development impact?

In conclusion, basic goods and services do not necessarily have to be provided by the state. A variety of actors can and increasingly do contribute to their provision, including social enterprises and Social Investors. Recognizing this fact, however, as we argue, requires a deeper understanding of the contemporary delivery of basic goods and services, which is critical to ensuring that these goods remain accessible and of universal quality and do not rely on an ability-to-pay model.

An overview on social investments

The institutionalization of the field of social investment is currently taking place. While new social investment funds with the aim to achieve both social and financial return on their investments in emerging markets open up regularly, umbrella organizations such as the Aspen Network of Development Entrepreneurs (ANDE), the Global Impact Investor Network (GIIN), or the European Venture Philanthropy Association (EVPA) keep growing. Furthermore, an increasing amount of tools are being developed to foster standardization in social investment practices, such as the Impact Reporting and Investment Standards (IRIS) as well as the Global Impact Investing Rating System (GIIRS). Both instruments were initiated in a collaborative effort by the Rockefeller Foundation, Acumen Fund, and B Lab.

The size of the social investment field is difficult to measure. A study on Impact Investment conducted by JP Morgan in 2011 counts 2,200 transactions totaling over USD 4 billion of investment. Of this investment amount, 44 percent was placed in emerging markets (Saltuk et al., 2011). As a study conducted by JP Morgan from 2010 found, return expectations in emerging markets are higher for both debt and equity investments when compared to return expectations in developed markets (O'Donohoe, Leijonhufvud, Saltuk, Bugg-Levine, & Brandenburg, 2010). Monitor furthermore estimated that until 2021 Impact Investment alone could grow to represent 1 percent of all assets that are managed—this would amount to approximately USD 500 billion (Freireich & Fulton, 2009). Yet, due to the fuzzy boundaries and the lack of exhaustive monitoring possibilities, these figures remain rough estimations that strongly depend on the definitional boundaries that are set. Nicholls (2010a), for instance, who applies a much broader lens on social investment, estimates that globally social investments amount to 6.8 trillion USD—including more established funding approaches such as mainstream philanthropy and clean energy investments.

In other words, the institutionalization takes place at the practice level and is accompanied by an increasing amount of practitioner-oriented research, but little academic attention has been dedicated to investigating social investments—even less so in developing and emerging economies. Furthermore, practitioner-oriented studies are oftentimes limited to a specific concept within the wider field of social investment. Most publications focus on Impact Investment defined as "investments made into companies, organizations, and funds with the intention to generate social and environmental impact alongside a financial return" (Global Impact Investing Network, n.d., para. 1), which is by far the most institutionalized field of action. And few concentrate on Venture Philanthropy, which doesn't necessarily expect a financial return, but still applies an investment discipline when providing financial and technical support to social organizations. Yet, the social investment spectrum is much larger, and clear categorizations of investment approaches are often difficult to realize. Many foundations and philanthropic organizations for instance deploy mission-related investment (MRI), defined as program-related investment "capitalized with assets from the endowment of a foundation that seeks to create social impact as well as typically market-rate, risk adjusted financial return" (O'Donohoe et al., 2010, p. 78), to further their philanthropic goals while seeking a market rate or below-market financial return. MRI can therefore be classified as Impact Investments; however, it also fits the definition of Venture Philanthropy. Figure 40.1 presents a simplified overview of the main concepts and terms that are currently used to classify existing investment approaches on the spectrum of social to financial value generation. The graph is based on a conceptualization of the European Venture Philanthropy Association (EVPA) (Hehenberg & Harling, 2013); however, it has been adapted by the authors with regard to two aspects. First, it now includes Venture Philanthropy and Impact Investing, as both concepts are prevalent in the context of social investment approaches that explicitly seek to foster social and economic development, and are therefore considered in the empirical approach underlying this chapter. Second, it extends the scope of potential investees to include traditional businesses (represented by the dashed lines in Figure 40.1). As opposed to social investment in more developed economies, traditional businesses in emerging and developing economies present an attractive investment opportunity for Social Investors both from socially and commercially oriented backgrounds. Small and medium-sized businesses as well as entrepreneurship are nowadays both considered important drivers of

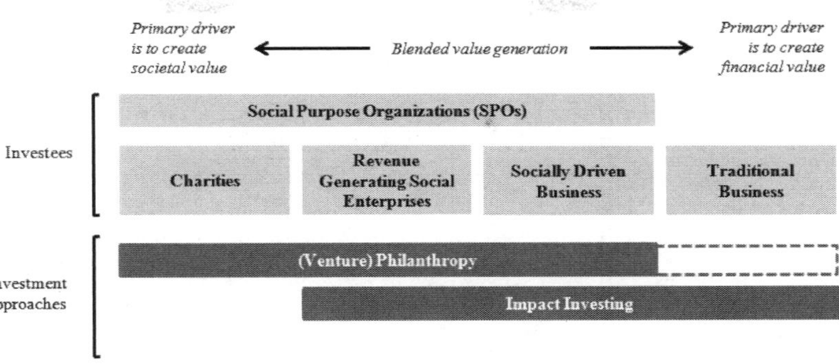

Figure 40.1 Social investment spectrum

Source: Adapted from Hehenberg and Harling (2013, p. 22).

growth and prosperity. Foundations as well as development organizations that primarily and explicitly pursue social objectives have therefore increasingly channeled grant funding toward traditional businesses in developing and emerging economies.

Corresponding to the wide range of investment approaches that are being employed in social investment, the field is also populated by a variety of actors. Development agencies and banks have launched programs that try to account for the specific financing requirements of market-based development approaches. With a program called "Opportunities for the majorities," the Inter-American Development Bank, for instance, provides loans, guarantees, and technical cooperation for "market-based, sustainable business models that engage private sector companies, local governments and communities in the development and delivery of quality products and services for the base of the pyramid in Latin America and the Caribbean" (Inter-American Development Bank, n.d., para. 1). And specific social impact funds, exclusively dedicated to promoting the idea of blended value creation (Emerson, 2003), that is, investments with social and financial return expectations, have furthermore started to emerge globally—attracting funds from a variety of actors including high-net-worth individuals, institutional investors, foundations, and development agencies. Examples of such funds are Bamboo Finance, Acumen Fund, Gray Ghost Ventures, or Vox Capital.

Another distinction is commonly made between so-called "Financial First Investors" and "Impact First Investors," which Lyons and Kickul (2013) define as follows:

1 Financial First Investors seek to optimize financial returns with a floor for social/environmental impact. This group tends to consist of commercial investors who search for sub-sectors that offer market-rate returns while yielding some social/environmental good. [...]
2 Impact First Investors seek to optimize social or environmental returns with a financial floor. This group uses social/environmental good as a primary objective and may accept a range of returns, from principal to market rate. This group is able to take a lower than market rate of return in order to seed new investment funds that may be perceived as higher risk or to reach tougher social/environmental goals that cannot be achieved in combination with market-rates of return. (p. 152)

Yet, some investors also emphasize that they have no clear prioritization of financial versus impact goals. While some claim that they pursue balanced goals of social and financial value creation, others emphasize the need to overcome the assumption that social and financial value creation trades off (Emerson, 2003)—an assumption that is implied in the above-mentioned distinction between financial vs. impact first investors.

Achleitner, Heinecke, Noble, Schöning, and Spiess-Knafl (2011) explain that "the social finance sector emerged with the goal of reducing transaction costs and helping to allocate capital more efficiently in the social enterprise space" (p. 44). Still, the variety of actors who co-exist, compete, and collaborate in this space lack a common mandate as well as a clear task division when it comes to the targeted support of social enterprises in emerging markets. The existing literature provides indications and first explanations for this argument.

For instance, recent publications have repeatedly described the existence of a so-called "pioneer gap," referring to the unwillingness of most investors to fund early stage ventures that haven't proven their model yet and therefore yield higher investment risks (Dichter, Katz, Koh, & Karamchandani, 2013). Experts and scholars have therefore called for mechanisms that coordinate "impact capital"—referring to the capital deployed in Impact Investing—along a social enterprise's life cycle (Kohler, Kreiner, & Sawhney, 2011) and highlighted the role of philanthropy in closing the pioneer gap (Koh et al., 2012). In contrast to commercial investors, philanthropic actors and organizations such as foundations have no obligation to generate financial returns on their investments. Hence, their capital is arguably ideal to fund pioneering ventures and help them to achieve investment readiness. Yet, so far only limited focus is given on "risk-taking expansion capital" (Lyons & Kickul, 2013, p. 151). Social investments therefore don't represent "a suitable solution for every social enterprise at every stage of growth" (Achleitner et al., 2011, p. 42). To date social investments mainly target social enterprises that have already proven their concept and have clear plans on how to scale them to the next level.

Finally, as Koh and colleagues (2012) argue, the market has been "structured around a history of bifurcation between philanthropy and investment" (p. 4). Trying to shape the institutionalization of social investment, actors from both philanthropic and commercial backgrounds combine individually selected aspects from philanthropic and financial investment strategies to make sense of their own social investment approach (Miller & Wesley II, 2010). This eclectic nature of the social investment field challenges research efforts that try to derive generable conclusions and boundaries around what social investment is and what it is not. As we argue in the next section, a self-referential approach to the empirical investigation of social investment helps to detect and interpret current trends with regard to Social Investors' contribution to development goals.

Exploring social investment in emerging and developing markets

The field of social investments is a socially constructed space in which a variety of actors with different rationalities co-exist, collaborate, and compete. In order to empirically investigate the field of social investment, we gathered information from social investment organizations that explicitly seek to support market-based development approaches, such as social enterprises, double bottom-line organizations, or small and growing businesses in developing and emerging economies. Social Investors therefore target both for-profit and non-profit organizations while utilizing both gift giving and investment strategies (Lyons & Kickul, 2013). In other words, Social Investors draw on both the logic of mainstream capital markets and philanthropy. These markets differ substantially with regard to their objectives, values, mechanisms, and practices (Miller & Wesley II, 2010). Yet, academic research has only recently started to investigate Social Investors' rationalities and practices—so far with limited focus on emerging economies.

Drawing on data collected through the International Research Network on Social Economic Empowerment (IRENE I SEE), this section will elaborate on exploratory data about Social Investors in four specific developing and emerging economies, namely Colombia, Mexico, Kenya, and South Africa. Social Investors were identified through membership organizations such as the Aspen Network of Development Entrepreneurs (ANDE) or the Global Impact Investor Network (GIIN), as well as through snowball sampling, expert consultation, and the personal knowledge of the authors. Social Investors were included in the sample when they defined themselves as Social Investors or were defined as such by others and when they explicitly committed themselves to contributing to social and economic development. Social Investors—including organizations that provide financial as well as technical resources—were therefore filtered by using keywords such as "Impact Investing," "social investing," "blended value," "market-based development," "base of the pyramid," or "Venture Philanthropy." The sample does not include investment approaches that produce social or economic impact as a side effect, such as Socially Responsible Investing where generally investors only apply a negative screening to avoid investing in harmful companies. With this self-referential empirical approach, the data focus on organizations that are endorsed as Social Investors by resourceful or powerful organizations and thus socially legitimized as being actors within the field of social investment (Deephouse & Suchman, 2008). The resulting Social Investor sample included 148 organizations that provide support to social enterprises in Colombia, Mexico, Kenya, and South Africa. These Social Investors were relatively evenly distributed across the countries, with Kenya accounting for the largest share of Social Investors (31 percent) and Mexico the second largest (28 percent). With 20 percent, the smallest share of the sample refers to investors who focus on Colombia, and the second smallest to South Africa (21 percent).

A screening of the Social Investor sample furthermore provided information on their type of organization. As Figure 40.2 illustrates, self-declared Social Impact Investors represent the largest share with 32 percent, followed by accelerators or incubators (16 percent) and foundations (15 percent).

Data was collected through an online survey. In total, 36 Social Investors completed the survey (24 percent) and another 12 Social Investors partially answered the questionnaire. Data was also collected from 286 social enterprises in Colombia, Mexico, Kenya, and South Africa

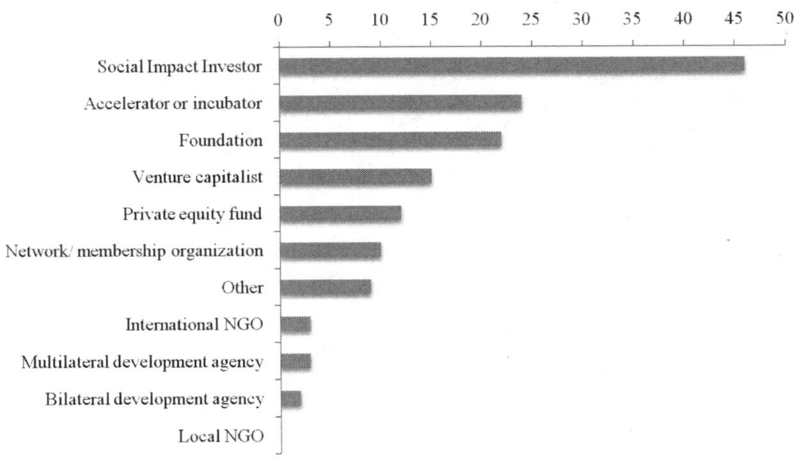

Figure 40.2 Structure of initial Social Investor sample (n = 148)

(Hanley, Wachner, & Weiss, 2015). Wherever useful, the presented results will furthermore be triangulated with data collected from social enterprises that these Social Investors supported or invested in.

The aim of the chapter is to provide exploratory data on Social Investors who harness opportunity spaces in emerging and developing economies by means of investing in social enterprises that explicitly seek to promote social or economic development. The next sections will present and interpret results with a focus on (1) co-investment patterns and (2) Social Investors' main competitors as an indication for Social Investors' networking behavior. The chapter furthermore seeks to explore Social Investors' role and intentions in promoting economic development. It will examine (3) the social target group that Social Investors focus on, (4) the type of organizations that receive support, (5) the financing vehicles that they use to pursue their objectives, and (6) the tools they use to measure their social impact.

Co-investments

The social investment market is in a nascent or pre-paradigmatic stage (Nicholls, 2010b) in which transaction costs to find a suitable investment target are high and intra-organizational investment templates to facilitate the investment process yet developing. Newly emerged opportunity spaces to provide basic goods or services in low-income settings experience a founding wave of organizations that yield both financial and social returns in filling these spaces. Despite the acknowledged potential of social investments and the rising interest of various actors to get involved in the field, investments in organizations that address basic needs and services remain risky, albeit with market potential.

As high-quality information that investors require during the due diligence process is costly, Social Investors tend to pool their resources and syndicate their investment. A common strategy is the identification of a lead investor who prepares term sheets and agrees on investment conditions for all parties involved. The pre-investment process is time-consuming; however, investors are able to mitigate risks and acquire experience in a nascent market together. Cooperation seems pivotal in making sense of the environment, as only 2.4 percent of the surveyed Social Investors stated that they do not co-invest. For the resting Social Investors, Figure 40.3 provides an overview of co-investment patterns, showing that across all types of Social Investors, popular co-investment partners are foundations and philanthropists, social impact funds, development agencies, and institutional investors. The local public sector, accelerators and incubators, banks, and private companies are servicing the end of the list. Furthermore, the figure shows that Social Investors do not necessarily seek relationships outside their sector—foundations, for instance, mainly co-invest with other foundations and philanthropists. Social impact funds, in contrast, seem to enter co-investment partnerships with actors from all backgrounds. In this respect, the proposition that blended value-creating approaches blur sector boundaries proves to be only fulfilled by certain actors.

The finding that incubators and accelerators are actors with whom co-investment rarely occurs resonates with the already-mentioned "pioneer gap" that experts from the field have described repeatedly. A report presented by ANDE and Village Capital, for instance, finds that Impact Investors remain hesitant in entering formal partnerships with accelerators (Baird, Bowles, & Lall, 2013)—thereby inhibiting the coordination of social investments along social enterprises' life cycle. A possible explanation, however, may be that incubators and accelerators are insignificant partners for larger investment funds to work with on larger deals. They may cultivate the investment value chain from the bottom up; however, they become insignificant to co-invest with in later stages that require higher amounts.

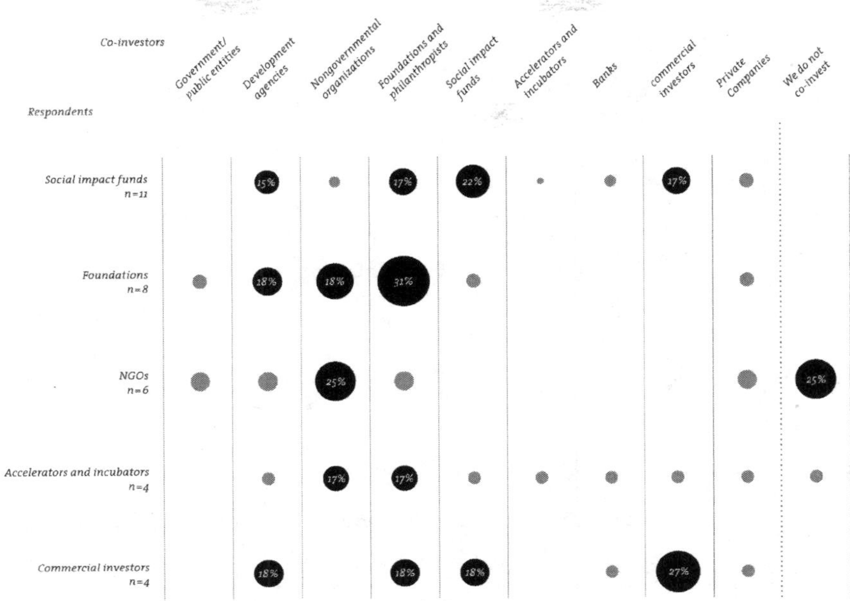

Figure 40.3 With whom Social Investors co-invest (n = 36)

Overall, the data show that co-investment and therewith cooperation is a cornerstone of the nascent social investment market. However, for most types of Social Investors, co-investments mainly occur within and not across sectors, reinforcing rather than reducing sector barriers.

Competition in social investment

Especially in nascent ecosystems and industry clusters, competition and cooperation among actors co-exist (Saxenian, Saxenian, & Societies, 1996). It is accelerators and incubators, foundations and philanthropists, as well as development agencies and social impact funds, that compete with each other over deals—a dynamic that requires further research attention. These actors compete with each other over investment targets; however, they offer different financial products. Some offer grants; others focus on loans or equity as a financing vehicle. This severely influences market dynamics and the behavior of social enterprises—a phenomenon that is yet to be understood.

As Figure 40.4 shows, the largest share of the surveyed respondents (38 percent) indicates that they do not have any competitors. This may be explained in two ways. First, investable organizations are scarce and cooperation may be the only way to find and close deals—particularly for new entrants. Second, many investors build up sector-specific expertise in order to have a competitive advantage in finding deals and providing resources (knowledge and networks) to their portfolio companies. The prevalence of such sector-specific strategies may result in little to no direct competition. In other words, the nascent social investment space can be characterized as being competitive and collaborative at the same time. Some investors may seek a collaboration strategy, and others may identify market niches, preventing them from having any direct competitors. The diverse picture the chart paints reflects the nascent nature of the social investment landscape, which still seeks clear behavioral patterns that are worth imitating.

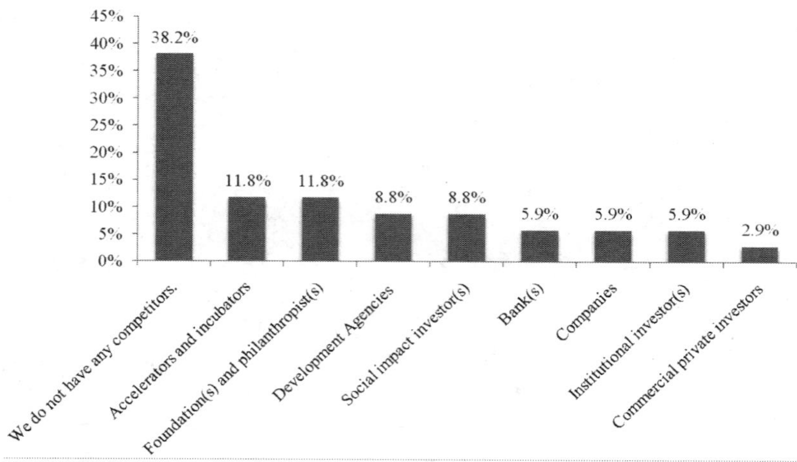

Figure 40.4 "Thinking back to your last investments, who was your organization's main competitor?" (n = 34)

Social target group

Social Investors often claim to invest in organizations that apply market-based approaches to serve or integrate people living at the so-called "base of the pyramid" (Prahalad, 2004) into fair and competitive markets. Traditionally, domestic governments, local and international NGOs, and development agencies have provided services to the low-income population of developing and emerging economies. With the emergence of new opportunity spaces, it is now market-based approaches that increasingly service the poorest of the poor.

However, it remains unclear if all income levels can be serviced with market-based approaches, as the possibility to reach profitability might be severely limited, especially when targeting people living on <2 USD. As repeatedly argued in academic and practitioner-oriented research, only a few social enterprises have so far been able to develop financially sustainable or even profitable business models that reach the poorest of the poor (Simanis, 2012). However, as our results show, most Social Investors target people living on <2 USD per day, that is, people living in extreme and moderate poverty as defined by the World Bank (see Figure 40.5). This suggests that many Social Investors are indeed willing to sacrifice short-term financial return expectations for social impact generation. However, the results from the IRENE SEE study about the social enterprises that have received support from these Social Investors (Hanley, Wachner, & Weiss, 2015) provide a different explanation. Particularly, for-profit social enterprises tend to focus on low- to middle-income people and less on those living at the very "bottom." In other words, both surveys provide contrasting results, which reveals a mismatch between Social Investors' intentions and their investees' actual practices. Further research is needed to shed light on this mismatch.

In order to resolve the challenge of operating profitably when serving the poorest of the poor, the social investment field could lean on the experience of and collaborate with development organizations that have put forth various approaches to subsidize the consumption of low-income people. Such subsidization strategies may help to provide affordable services and products to people living on less than two dollars a day. Governments, NGOs, development agencies, and also the commercial sector can furthermore act as partners to subsidize prices and lower costs substantially up to a point where services can be provided for free.

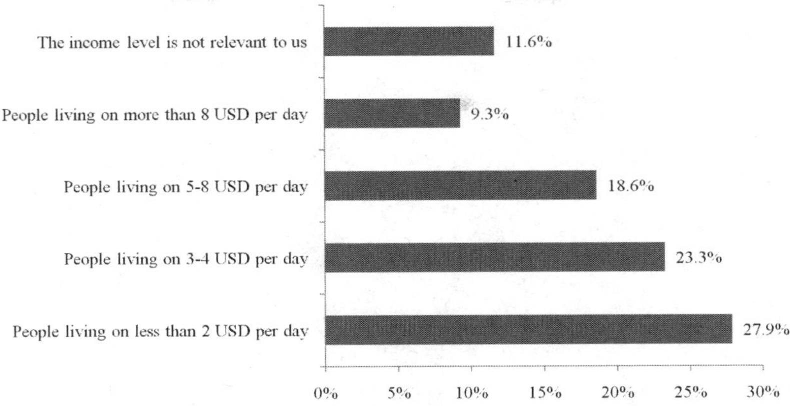

Figure 40.5 "What is the predominant income level of your portfolio organizations' target group?" (n = 25)

Targeted investee organizations

Traditionally, service provision and goods delivery for the low-income population in emerging and developing economies has largely been undertaken by the public sector, the third sector, as well as a large informal private sector. The first two were the primary vehicle for international development agencies to reach important developmental goals such as the MDGs. A shift toward market-based approaches changed the landscape. This is reflected in Social Investors' preferable funding route (see Figure 40.6). In fact, only 8 percent purely fund NGOs. It is the for-profit, organizations that have claimed Social Investors' attention. Sixty-two percent purely invest in for-profit, and 30 percent would invest in both organizational forms.

Studying Social Investors' portfolio companies reveals a similarly striking picture. For-profit organizations are on the rise and make up the majority of an investor's portfolios nowadays. In addition, dual-structured social enterprises are a recent phenomenon, referring to organizational constructs where social enterprises simultaneously operate a for-profit and non-profit venture. These organizational constructs allow one to exploit funding opportunities along the full spectrum of grants, loans, and equity.

Financing vehicles

Social Investors are equipped with a variety of financing products that are ideally tailored to the needs of the social enterprise. As they stretch at one end from purely socially driven investors who adhere mostly to grant giving, it is on the other end of the spectrum that equity capital becomes an important product offered by financially driven Social Investors. In between the two extremes, innovative blends such as convertible debts or forgivable loans apply. Both products operate on the basis of pre-agreed milestones. If the milestones are met, a convertible debt turns into an equity investment and a forgivable loan turns into a grant. If milestones are not achieved, a convertible debt and a forgivable loan both turn into a standard loan with a priori agreed terms that have to be paid back. Another important product is quasi-equity which refers mostly to a revenue participation model in which the risk and therewith a share of future revenue streams is shared. This wide spectrum in funding possibilities reflects the dynamic and eclectic environment social enterprises are embedded in.

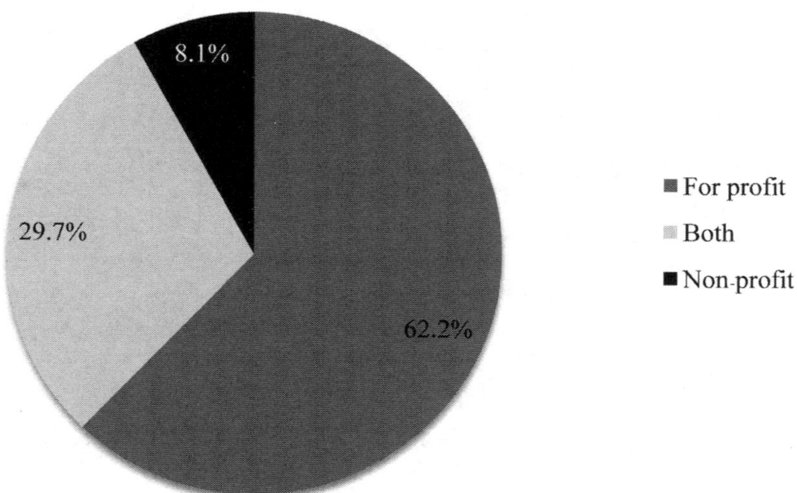

Figure 40.6 "On which type of organization does your organization focus?" (n = 37)

The surveyed Social Investors reflect the diversity in financial products (see Figure 40.7) with an emphasis on equity capital (22 percent), convertible debt (16 percent), grants (12 percent), and quasi-equity (12 percent). The importance of equity capital illustrates the increasing focus on for-profit organizations. As opposed to equity investments in the commercial sector, equity capital in the social investment landscape is often referred to as patient capital. Investors recognize a longer investment process that might take up to 10 years in order to grow a social enterprise so that an exit can be realized. However, with few exits realized, it is yet to be seen whether this financial product is an adequate catalyzer for social change. In contrast, the rise of innovative products such as convertible debts and quasi-equity demonstrates the need for tailor-made financial products which take into account the financing needs of social enterprises in developing and emerging economies and the limited predictability of the market environment and therewith future cash flows. Grants therefore remain at play. They are, for instance, much needed in dual-structured social enterprises to finance non-financially sustainable activities such as awareness creation or capacity building of target groups. In addition, Social Investors deploy grants strategically. They may accompany an equity investment with a grant component. The grant can serve as a vital resource to build capacity within social enterprises, for example the accounting department, or it can be used as a credit enhancement tool, for example in "catalytic first loss capital" programs where an investor agrees to bear first losses in an investment in order to catalyze the participation of co-investors that otherwise would not have entered the deal (Global Impact Investing Network, 2013).

Impact measurement

A pivotal dimension of social investments is data on the social impact that investments generate. It has proven difficult to track the data as the environmental conditions social enterprises operate in vary considerably, making a comparison challenging. Yet, organizations such as ANDE and GIIN push the use of standardized tools in order to allow cross-sector and within-sector comparability. In addition, the Impact Measurement Working Group of the Social Impact Investment

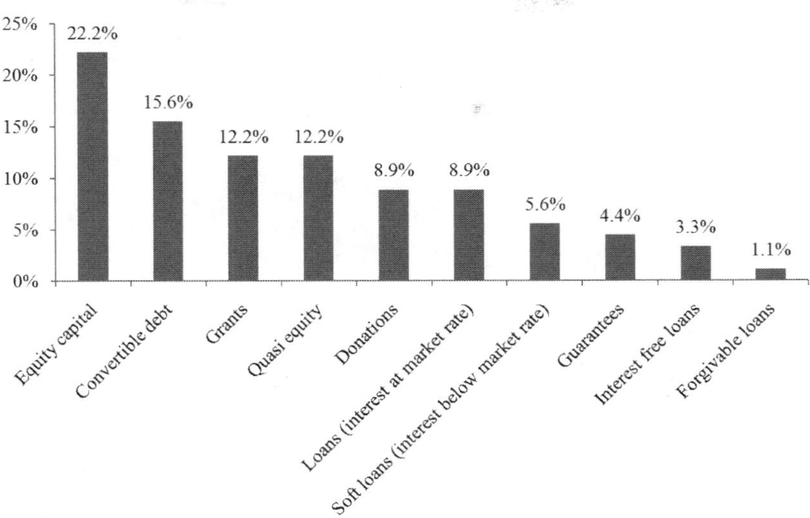

Figure 40.7 "What type of financial product(s) does your organization provide?" (n = 38)

Taskforce fosters and encourages measurement as a way to clarify investor intent and justify the industry (Impact Measurement Working Group, 2013a, 2013b).

In order to monitor the work of social enterprises, Social Investors use social as well as financial indicators as performance measurement tools. As mentioned previously, there is not yet a globally accepted and applicable performance or impact measurement method for social investment. Figure 40.8 shows that the topic of performance measurement remains largely defined on a case-by-case basis, as 33.3 percent of the Social Investors indicated that they jointly define the indicators together with the investees. However, 21.1 percent of Social Investors claim to use commonly accepted standards such as IRIS, which increases comparability and longitudinal approaches in performance measurement. And 10 percent allow social enterprises to define their indicators on their own. This shows that there is room for innovative measurement tools, where standards may be adopted to local circumstances. After all, agreeing on indicators together may reduce principal agent problems. Also, to allow comparability across the portfolio, 10 percent of Social Investors define the indicators on behalf of Social Entrepreneurs. In sum, different techniques to measure social impact are at play. Studying the portfolio organizations of Social Investors reveals a similar picture. However, with a follow-up question, the authors sought to understand whether or not social impact data is useful for the social enterprises' decision making. Thirty-two percent indicated that indeed they are useful and only 5 percent marked that they are not. The great majority (63 percent of 258 surveyed organizations) skipped the question. This demonstrates the ambiguous nature of social impact measurement tools and therewith points to a key challenge that the ecosystem needs to resolve. Establishing standards that not only allow for a comparison of organizations' social impact but also assist them in making better decisions remains crucial.

In contrast to development organizations, which often use fragmented tools across countries and organizations, the social investment field has initiated first steps to establish industry-wide measurement tools. However, to date, it remains unclear to what extent the impact of Social Investors and social enterprises contributes to development goals.

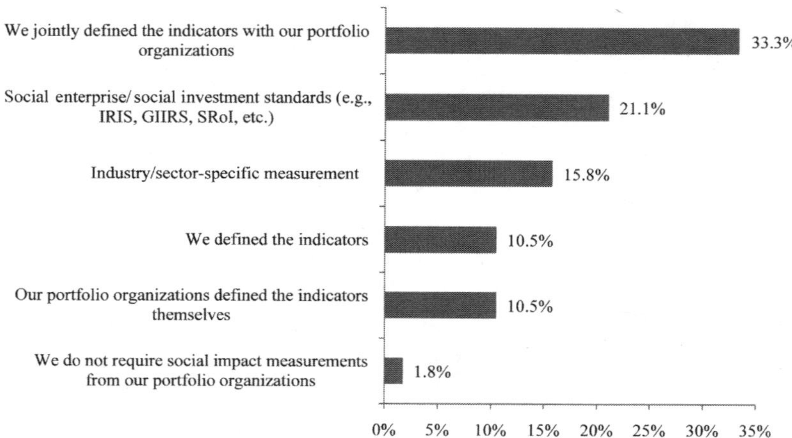

Figure 40.8 "What tools does your organization expect its portfolio organizations to use in order to evaluate social impact?" (n = 36)

Conclusion

Despite their fuzzy boundaries, market-based development approaches form a growing field in practice—and so do social investments. An increasing variety of actors, including development agencies, commercial investors, foundations, and high-net-worth individuals, keep entering the field, with varying intentions and interests. They co-exist, compete, and collaborate—but without any supervision or common mandate to promote social and economic developments.

The global processes described in this chapter—which challenges the traditional role of the state and promotes market-oriented approaches to solve social problems in developing and emerging economies—have created an environment suitable for the proliferation of social investment. In a broader sense, the reduction of the public sector has contributed to the strengthening of third sectors as well as private sector roles in the satisfaction of public goods and services. New organizations such as Social Investors and social enterprises are becoming the latest trend in development policy as they raise the expectation to blur the boundaries between the public, the third, and the private sectors and thus to leverage their respective strengths in solving societal problems—hence the question of how well social investment can contribute to achieving development goals. More specifically: Who are Social Investors? What do they support and how? And what can we expect from social investment as a development approach? This chapter has provided the first answers to these complex questions.

Data collected through the International Research Network on Social Economic Empowerment (IRENE SEE) suggests that Social Investors are indeed collaborative actors but with a prevailing hesitance of certain types of Social Investors to enter cross-sector partnerships. Furthermore, the lack of coordination in the social investment space, as well as the heterogeneity and individuality of Social Investors' intentions, remain considerable challenges in directing social investment toward a systematic contribution to development goals. This is also reflected in the diversity and ambiguity of impact measurement tools. The role of umbrella organizations such as ANDE, GIIN, and EVPA is paramount in this regard as they have considerable possibilities to shape the institutionalization of social investment by bringing together the wide range of actors involved.

The data furthermore suggest a mismatch between Social Investors' professed goals to serve the poor in a financially sustainable or even profitable way and the actual practice of social enterprises. The BoP proposition has raised considerable interest by suggesting that poverty alleviation can occur in financially attractive ways (Prahalad & Hart, 1999). However, to date social enterprises and similar types of organizations are still experimenting with various business models in order to prove the BoP proposition in sectors other than microfinance. It has to be noted, however, that microfinance also remains a contested field. While some scholars and practitioners emphasize the social impact of microfinance (Yunus, 2004), others caution that empirical evidence about this social impact remains ambiguous (Khavul, 2010; Nega & Schneider, 2014). Evidence suggests that financially successful social enterprises that are also succeeding in keeping their focus on the poorest of the poor are limited (Simanis, 2012). Many social enterprises at the BoP that seek financial sustainability are pushed up toward middle-income customer segments where they can generate financial gain. Meeting basic needs and services at any level of the BoP is a significant contribution to fighting poverty. However, finding ways to encourage social investments that help meet the needs of the poorest of the poor, but at the same time remain financially sustainable or even profitable, remains a challenge.

Acknowledgments

The funding for the research of this chapter was provided by Siemens Stiftung as part of the International Research Network for Social Economic Empowerment (IRENE I SEE). The research network was coordinated by Zeppelin University, launched in 2011, and concluded in early 2015. The aim of the project was to research organizational approaches that foster "Social Economic Empowerment"—understood, in this context, as the process of economic self-empowerment through professional assistance. The main focus was on entrepreneurial solutions to social problems such as social enterprises, which in the last decades have increasingly been discussed as a promising complement to traditional development cooperation.

References

Achleitner, A.-K., Heinecke, A., Noble, A., Schöning, M., & Spiess-Knafl, W. (2011). Unlocking the mystery: An introduction to social investment. *Innovations: Technology, Governance, Globalization, 6*(3), 145–154.

Amin, A. (1999). An institutionalist perspective on regional economic development. *International Journal of Urban and Regional Research, 23*(2), 365–378.

Baird, R., Bowles, L., & Lall, S. (2013). Bridging the "Pioneer Gap": The role of accelerators in launching high-impact enterprises. *A report by the Aspen Network of Development Entrepreneurs and Village Capital.* Retrieved January 30, 2015, from http://www.aspeninstitute.org/sites/default/files/content/docs/ande/Bridging%20the%20Pioneer%20Gap%20The%20Role%20of%20Accelerators%20in%20Launching%20High%20Impact%20Enterprises%20.pdf

Bel, G., Fageda, X., & Warner, M. E. (2010). Is private production of public services cheaper than public production? A meta-regression analysis of solid waste and water services. *Journal of Policy Analysis and Management, 29*(3), 553–577.

Buira, A. (2002, August). *An analysis of IMF conditionality* (G-25 Discussion Paper Series, No. 22, Research Papers for the Intergovernmental Group of Twenty-Four on International Monetary Affairs). New York and Geneva: United Nations.

Clifton, J., Comín, F., & Fuentes, D. D. (2003). *Privatisation in the European Union: Public enterprises and integration.* Dordrecht: Springer Science + Business Media.

Dart, R. (2004). The legitimacy of social enterprise. *Nonprofit Management & Leadership, 14*(4), 411–424.

Deephouse, D. L., & Suchman, M. C. (2008). Legitimacy in organizational institutionalism. In R. Greenwood, C. Oliver, K. Sahlin, & R. Suddaby (Eds.), *The SAGE handbook of organizational institutionalism* (pp. 49–77). London: Sage.

Dees, G. (2003). Sector-bending: Blurring lines between nonprofit and for-profit. *Society, 40*(4), 16–23.

Dichter, S., Katz, R., Koh, H., & Karamchandani, A. (2013, Winter). Closing the pioneer gap. *Stanford Social Innovation Review, 2013*, 36–43.

Easterly, W. (2010). Democratic accountability in development: The double standard. *Social Research, 77*(4), 1075–1104.

Emerson, J. (2003). The blended value proposition: Integrating social and financial returns. *California Management Review, 45*(4), 35–51.

Emerson, J., & Bugg-Levine, A. (2011). *Impact investing: Transforming how we make money while making a difference* (1st ed.). San Francisco, CA: Jossey-Bass.

Fine, B., & Hall, D. (2012). Terrains of neoliberalism: Constraints and opportunities for alternative models of service delivery. In D. McDonald & G. Ruiters (Eds.), *Alternatives to privatization: Public options for essential services in the global south* (pp. 45–70). London: Routledge.

Freireich, J., & Fulton, K. (2009). *Investing for social and environmental impact.* New York: Monitor Group.

Global Impact Investing Network. (2013, October). *Catalytic first-loss capital* (Issue Brief). New York: A. Bouri & A. Mudaliar.

Global Impact Investing Network. (n.d.). *About impact investing.* Retrieved January 28, 2015, from http://www.thegiin.org/cgi-bin/iowa/resources/about/index.html

Hanley, L. M., Wachner, A. M., & Weiss, T. (2015). *Taking the pulse of the social enterprise landscape in developing and emerging economies.* Retrieved May 20, 2015, from http://issuu.com/siemensstiftung/docs/taking_the_pulse_2015

Hehenberg, L., & Harling, A.-M. (2013). *European venture philanthropy and social investment 2011/2012—The EVPA Survey.* Brussels: European Venture Philanthropy Association.

Henisz, W. J., Zelner, B. A., & Guillén, M. F. (2005). The worldwide diffusion of market-oriented infrastructure reform, 1977–1999. *American Sociological Review, 70*(6), 871–897.

Hermann, C. (2009). The marketisation of health care in Europe. In L. Panich & C. Leys (Eds.), *Socialist register 2010* (pp. 125–144). London: Merlin Press.

Impact Measurement Working Group. (2013a). Impact measurement guidelines in practice: Five case studies. In *Social Impact Investment Taskforce.* Retrieved March 25, 2015, from http://www.thinknpc.org/wp-content/uploads/2014/09/IMWG_Case_Studies.pdf

Impact Measurement Working Group. (2013b). Measuring impact: Guidelines for good impact practice. In *Social Impact Investment Taskforce.* Retrieved March 25, 2015, from http://apsocialfinance.com/wp-content/uploads/2014/11/GIIN_impact_measurement_guidelines.pdf

Inter-American Development Bank. (n.d.). *Opportunities for the majority: Market-based solutions for the base of the pyramid.* Retrieved January 28, 2015, from http://www.iadb.org/en/topics/opportunities-for-the-majority/idb-opportunities-for-the-majority-serving-the-base-of-the-pyramid-in-latin-america,1377.html

International Labour Organization. (1977). *The basic needs approach to development.* Geneva: International Labour Organization.

Jackson, E. T. (2013). Interrogating the theory of change: Evaluating impact investing where it matters most. *Journal of Sustainable Finance & Investment, 3*(2), 95–110.

Jessop, B. (1999). Narrating the future of the national economy and the national state: Remarks on remapping regulation and reinventing governance. In G. Steinmetz (Ed.), *State/culture: State-formation after the cultural turn* (pp. 378–405). New York: Cornell University Press.

Khavul, S. (2010). Microfinance: Creating opportunities for the poor? *Academy of Management Perspectives, 24*(3), 58–72.

Koh, H., Karamchandani, A., & Katz, R. (2012). *From blueprint to scale: The case for philanthropy in impact investing.* Mumbai: Monitor Group.

Kohler, J., Kreiner, T., & Sawhney, J. (2011). *Coordinating impact capital: A new approach to investing in small and growing businesses—An examination of impact investors and phased investing for the launch and growth of social enterprises.* Santa Clara: Santa Clara University & Aspen Network of Development Entrepreneurs.

Lyons, T. S., & Kickul, J. R. (2013). The social enterprise financing landscape: The lay of the land and new research on the horizon. *Entrepreneurship Research Journal, 3*(2), 147–159.

McDonald, D. A., & Ruiters, G. (Eds.). (2012). *Alternatives to privatization: Public options for essential services in the global south* (1st ed.). New York: Routledge.

McMullen, J. S. (2011). Delineating the domain of development entrepreneurship: A market-based approach to facilitating inclusive economic growth. *Entrepreneurship Theory and Practice, 35*(1), 185–193.

Miller, T. L., & Wesley II, C. L. (2010). Assessing mission and resources for social change: An organizational identity perspective on social venture capitalists' decision criteria. *Entrepreneurship Theory and Practice, 34*(4), 705–733.

Nega, B., & Schneider, G. (2014). Social entrepreneurship, microfinance, and economic development in Africa. *Journal of Economic Issues, 48*(2), 367–376.

Nicholls, A. (2010a). The institutionalization of social investment: The interplay of investment logics and investor rationalities. *Journal of Social Entrepreneurship, 1*(1), 70–100.

Nicholls, A. (2010b). The legitimacy of social entrepreneurship: Reflexive isomorphism in a pre-paradigmatic field. *Entrepreneurship Theory and Practice, 34*(4), 611–633.

O'Donohoe, N., Leijonhufvud, C., Saltuk, Y., Bugg-Levine, A., & Brandenburg, M. (2010). *Impact investments: An emerging asset class*. New York: JP Morgan Global Research.

OECD. (2007). *Development Centre perspectives. Financing development: Aid and beyond*. Paris: OECD Publications.

OECD. (2008, November). *Is it ODA?* Retrieved January 28, 2015, from http://www.oecd.org/dac/stats/34086975.pdf

Peck, J. (2001). Neoliberalizing states: Thin policies/hard outcomes. *Progress in Human Geography, 25*(3), 445–455.

Prahalad, C. K. (2004). *The fortune at the bottom of the pyramid: Eradicating poverty through profits*. Philadelphia, PA: Wharton School Publishing.

Prahalad, C. K., & Hart, S. L. (1999). The fortune at the bottom of the pyramid. *Harvard Business Review, 86*(6), 53–57.

Rhodes, R. A. W. (1994). The hollowing out of the state: The changing nature of the public service in Britain. *The Political Quarterly, 65*(2), 138–151.

Salamon, L. M. (2002). The new governance and the tools of public action: An introduction. In L. M. Salamon (Ed.), *The tools of government: A guide to the new governance* (pp. 1–47). Oxford: Oxford University Press.

Saltuk, Y., Bouri, A., & Leung, G. (2011, December 14). Insights into the impact investment market—An in-depth analysis of investor perspectives and over 2,200 transactions. *Social Finance Research*. Retrieved January 28, 2015, from http://www.jpmorganchase.com/corporate/socialfinance/document/Insight_into_the_Impact_Investment_Market.pdf

Savas, E. S. (1987). *Privatization: The key to better government*. Chatham, NJ: Chatham House Publishers.

Saxenian, A. L., Saxenian, A., & Societies, A. C. (1996). *Regional advantage: Culture and competition in Silicon Valley and Route 128* (Rev. ed.). Cambridge, MA: Harvard University Press.

Simanis, E. (2012, June). Reality check at the bottom of the pyramid. *Harvard Business Review*. Retrieved January 21, 2015, from https://hbr.org/2012/06/reality-check-at-the-bottom-of-the-pyramid

United Nations. (2010). *Keeping the promise: A forward-looking review to promote an agreed action agenda to achieve the Millennium Development Goals by 2015*. Retrieved January 21, 2015, from http://www.un.org/ga/search/view_doc.asp?symbol=A/64/665

Warner, M. E., & Clifton, J. (2013). Marketisation, public services and the city: The potential for Polanyian counter movements. *Cambridge Journal of Regions, Economy and Society*. doi:10.1093/cjres/rst028

Yunus, M. (2004). *Banker to the poor: Micro-lending and the battle against world poverty* (Rev. ed.). New York: Perseus Books.

41

BUILDING THE IMPACT INVESTING MARKET

Drivers of demand and the ecosystem conditioning supply

Maximilian Martin

The financial crisis called into question business as usual and whether global capital markets effectively fulfilled their role of pricing risk and allocating capital. The notion of safe assets is now gone. The USD 600 trillion in financial assets globally in 2010 represented claims against a nominal global GDP of roughly USD 63 trillion. In Japan alone (i.e., the world's third largest economy), USD 8.5 trillion sits in commercial banks as cash deposits. There will be an estimated USD 900 trillion in financial assets by 2020, representing claims against about USD 90 trillion/year of global GDP. The figures in the world of global finance are so large that even transformational initiatives in relatively large developing countries, such as the total estimated USD 75–79 billion cost of Ethiopia's Growth and Transformation Plan (GTP) currently underway, can seem like small change. The challenge, though, has been to orient the world of finance toward consistently adding value to the real economy in ways that are noticeable to average citizens.

There is good news on the horizon, however: we are currently witnessing the early days of the next transformation of the global economy. At the core of this development is a very powerful idea. The simultaneous and intentional creation of economic and social or environmental value by all sectors of the economy and society is powered by innovative ways to access and allocate capital and incentives in order to achieve financial and extra financial performance that can simultaneously benefit shareholders and stakeholders.

Next to the technology revolution underway, a key theater of this transformation is the world of investments. The quest for holistic value opens the path to use capital much more efficiently to fund solutions to social and environmental challenges. The market for so-called Impact Investments—investments made with the intention to generate measurable social and environmental impact alongside a financial return—holds great promise as a tool to grow the economy and fund the provision of public goods (Global Impact Investing Network, 2014). As measured by the cumulative investments' outstanding made by the members of GIIN, the practice of Impact Investing has grown into a USD 46 billion market since the inception of the foundational term "Impact Investment" in 2007—with USD 4.3 billion worth of Impact Investments made in 2011 almost doubling to USD 8 billion in 2012, a USD 10.6 billion committed in 2013, and a planned USD 12.7 billion in 2014 (Saltuk, El Idrissi, Bouri, Mudaliar, & Schiff, 2014, p. 21). There is an estimated potential to advance the overall pool of assets invested for impact to USD 400–1,000 billion by 2020 (GIIN, 2013). Delivering on this potential will most certainly require reaching outside the current networks of self-identified Impact Investors (given their current pace of building scale) so that Impact Investments become a part of standard asset allocations in investor portfolios, as well as other supporting measures to establish a functioning large-scale impact capital market.

Taking Impact Investing to a critical mass where it can make a noticeable contribution in the development trajectories of countries—the focus of this chapter—requires unlocking and financing the innovations that are now needed to drive social progress and inclusive growth at a scale that matters in the big scheme of things. Based on the progress made around the world in investing for social impact and financial returns alike over the past decade, we can now design financial instruments that embed incentives to drive micro-level social improvements that touch lives, and economic incentives that boost competitiveness. After the 2008–2009 Great Recession, fresh solutions are needed to ensure opportunity for all. In the mainstream of the economy, innovative financial instruments are similarly needed to fund the upgrading and reactivation of the key industries within a country by linking financial incentives to the continuous improvement of social outcomes and total resource productivity. Making smart use of the combination of different sources of capital, and rewarding risk taking appropriately, is a necessity to achieve this.

This chapter argues that Impact Investing can add up to big change and drive both the modernization of public good provision and private sector value creation on an unprecedented scale. But to deliver on capital formation, business opportunities and new jobs, social inclusion, and effective operational implementation, impact needs to be made investable first. This requires understanding the factors that drive demand as well as those conditioning supply. Necessary conditions for a functioning impact capital market are a sound Impact Investment ecosystem composed of investors, investees, and intermediaries; a generally competitive social sector; and a supportive national policy agenda. The cheapest and fastest way to build such a capital market is collaborative, systemic action. The chapter covers the lessons of a number of examples of market building around the world, including the pioneering lessons from the UK experience. The findings are derived from well over a decade of work in the sector, including the author taking part in the original meeting in Bellagio, Italy, where the term was collectively coined, as well as several research activities, including a screening of almost 200 Impact Investment-related reports in the major languages of the G8, a dedicated online survey distributed to over 250 market players from around the world, and a media search of 26 terms (translated across the languages of the G8, covering roughly 50 percent of global GDP) related to "Impact Investment." Commissioned by the UK Cabinet Office, an earlier version of this chapter was circulated to participants of the first-ever G8 conference on social investment held in 2013 under the UK presidency of the G8 in that year, as a companion to the in-depth report "Making Impact Investible" published by the investment and strategy firm Impact Economy (Martin, 2013b, 2013c).

The chapter first describes the landscape of Impact Investing and defines the term. It then places Impact Investing in the broader context of four megatrends identified through the research: massive pent-up demand at the "bottom of the pyramid," the need for radical resource efficiency and green growth enabling a circular economy, new approaches to the provision of public services, and leveraging the innovation capacity stemming from the virtuous consumer segment. The chapter finishes by looking at the role different groups of capital providers play in the market, ranging from philanthropic investors such as foundations, angel and venture stage capital providers, private and institutional capital providers, financial services institutions, and government. Last but not least, it concludes by highlighting some of the core barriers that still need to be overcome in terms of developing a more effective Impact Investment marketplace.

At a time when the reputation of mainstream finance has been called into question, Impact Investing provides a major opportunity to demonstrate a new role for finance and financial innovation. This new role will be fundamental to the emerging imperative for sustainable growth and to the stewardship of society's assets in the twenty-first century (The Task Force for Global Health, 2012). The sheer breadth, depth, and speed of progress makes a compelling case for the emerging Impact Investing industry as an innovation in finance whose time has come, especially after the financial crisis. The challenge now is to calibrate efforts and manage expectations. This chapter aims to help the reader master the key terms and mechanics, as well as point to core challenges and opportunities.

Definitions, landscape, and opportunities

Impact Investing is based on the principle that private capital can intentionally create positive environmental and social outcomes as well as financial returns. The idea is straightforward, but today Impact Investing is still a nascent market. Evidence suggests that we are on the verge of a very significant movement, however. The Impact Investing market is expected to grow to USD 400–1,000 billion by 2020 (O'Donohoe, Leijonhufvud, Saltuk, Bugg-Levine, & Brandenburg, 2010). Notwithstanding, this would amount to only about 0.1 percent of all financial assets by the end of the decade, which are estimated to reach USD 900 trillion (Bain & Company, 2012, pp. 3 and 7).

The opportunity for Impact Investing to drive the renewal of capital markets and positive social outcomes might nevertheless be much larger than suggested by these figures. Increasing economic demand at the poorest levels of society, climate change, and a growing population coinciding with a strained welfare state may expand the potential of the market. Impact Investing has the potential to play a catalytic role in the myriad of challenges facing education, health care, unemployment, and the environment—leveraging innovative entrepreneurs, trillions of dollars in public and private capital, and financial innovation to benefit society at large.

To get a sense of the magnitude of the opportunity, consider just one theater: the gap in public funding. A 2012 study by Accenture and Oxford Economics projected a public services expenditure gap between expected demand for services and the ability to pay through the year 2025 (Accenture, 2012, p. 4). The results were startling. The expenditure gap was USD 90 billion for Canada; USD 100 billion for France; USD 80 billion for Germany; USD 30 billion for Italy; USD 170 billion for the UK; and USD 940 billion for the US. This is not small change, and private capital will be critical to addressing this emerging gap. Intentionally investing for both social impact and financial return provides a way to systematically engage that capital.

What is Impact Investing?

The term "Impact Investing" was coined in 2007 and is defined by GIIN (2014) as "investments made into companies, organizations, and funds with the intention to generate measurable social and environmental impact alongside a financial return." The word "intention" differentiates these investments from Socially Responsible Investments, which aim to *avoid* social or environmental harm, while still pursuing a single bottom line of profit (this chapter uses "Impact Investment" as coterminous with "Social Impact Investment," unless otherwise specified).

An Impact Investment can be made in both developed and emerging countries and seeks below-market or market rate returns. This characteristic makes it different from a grant, which is simply a donation of funds with no expectation of financial return. Specific variations within these classifications include program-related investment (PRI) and mission-related investment (MRI), which are types of Impact Investments made by charitable foundations (Levitt, 2011).

The Impact Investing market today is still small compared to mainstream capital markets, but growing fast. Approximately 2,200 Impact Investments worth USD 4.3 billion were made in 2011. Two years later, investments made grew to USD 10.6 billion in 2013, with more than double the transactions (i.e., 4,914 executed deals), whereby the median investor was allocating USD 13 million across six transactions in that year; 6,419 deals were planned for 2014 (Martin, 2013b, p. 5). By the end of 2013, the total market as captured by the stock of investments outstanding made by members of the Global Impact Investing Network had advanced to USD 46 billion, of which 70 percent was invested in emerging markets and 30 percent in developed markets. Interestingly, development finance institutions had 42 percent of total assets under management, followed by fund managers managing 34 percent of total assets (Saltuk, El Idrissi, Bouri, Mudaliar, & Schiff, 2014).

The potential financial returns of Impact Investments in emerging markets are compelling. A 2010 study by JP Morgan, based on a survey of Impact Investors, found the expected returns of many existing Impact Investments in emerging markets fall largely in the 8–11.9 percent bracket for debt investments, and the 20–24.9 percent bracket for equity. This compares to developed market return expectations of 5–7.9 percent for Impact Investments and 15–19.9 percent in debt and equity, respectively (Carmody, McCarron, Blinch, Prevatt, & Arosio, 2011).

Historically, private foundations through grants, program-related investments, and mission-related investments have played an important role in building the Impact Investment market to the current size, as have high-net-worth individuals and families. Apart from a few champions, large financial institutions including banks and pension funds are only gradually beginning to join the effort. Next to a way to allocate capital, Impact Investing is also a powerful idea for reconciling the world of investment with the greater public good. It draws much more significant media attention than the size of the market alone would suggest, and has triggered an inflow of talent from mainstream finance and other industries.

Thus far, professional investors, specialized funds, and government have been the main capital providers for Impact Investing. Their motivations are diverse, ranging from (a) an interest in segments of the market uncorrelated with mainstream global benchmarks, (b) sector orientation (such as education, health care, housing, or water), or (c) achieving social or environmental objectives more efficiently via investments rather than grants. Depending on whether the financial or social impact objective takes precedence, investors have been characterized as "finance first" or "impact first" investors (Monitor Institute, 2009, p. 31). Given that high-impact and market rate returns need not be at odds with each other, this may be to some extent a false dichotomy. Impact Investing actors can be categorized in at least three different ways as per their contribution to market building. According to their impact in growing an industry sector, Omidyar Network distinguishes between (a) "market innovators," or entrepreneurs, who believe in a product or service before its profit potential is identified by established investors; (b) "market scalers," who enhance sector growth by scaling as individual firms; and (c) "market infrastructure" players, who address the collective needs shared between a number of industry players and thereby contribute to the extension of a supportive ecosystem for entrepreneurial innovation (Bannick & Goldman, 2012). Next to capital providers and capital recipients, the Impact Investment market also involves intermediaries, government, and professional service providers (Jackson & Associates Ltd, 2012, p. 9).

A final market component includes those entities creating demand for Impact Investments—such as small and medium-sized businesses, entrepreneurial non-profits with an earned income, and cooperatives. In many cases, these entities are referred to as "social enterprises." Rather than their legal form, the common denominator is typically that these entities work under the premise of attaining both a financial and a social impact. However, some governments are also exploring various legal forms that could help to better enable the creation of social enterprises.

This demand side of the market is also growing. For example, in the UK, the RBS social enterprise 100 (SE100) Index is now in its fourth year, with the goal of tracking the success of social enterprises across the UK. The SE100 Index has not only shown high average growth, but the growth in revenue by index entrants is thus far impressive when compared with both the FTSE100 and the SME sector (social enterprise, 2011).

Challenges and opportunities

Growth in the Impact Investment market has been impressive, but significant challenges remain. Impact Investing is a work in progress. In the survey conducted for this chapter, market players pointed to the lack of a track record of successful investments as the main concern, followed by too few established players active in Impact Investing; no universally accepted ratings of Impact Investments; a lack of appropriate products; as well as performance concerns and a lack of Impact Investment opportunities. These findings are broadly aligned with other studies (Simon & Barmeier, 2010, p. 3).

Megatrends

Why can we nevertheless be optimistic about the potential and what then drives the supply of and demand for Impact Investments? Our research into Impact Investing identified four megatrends that will shape the global market. These include (a) pent-up demand at the "bottom of the pyramid," (b) the need for increased resource efficiency, (c) new approaches to the provision of public services, and (d) the building out and leveraging of the virtuous consumer segment (Martin, 2014a).

Pent-up demand at the "bottom of the pyramid"

The term "bottom of the pyramid" (also referred to as "base of the pyramid," with the identical acronym BoP) was coined in the 1930s but has since evolved to describe the 4 billion people from mostly developing countries that live on less than USD 2 per day. The efforts by the World Bank, donor nations, aid agencies, and others to eradicate the persistent problems of the BoP—such as those related to health, finance, and housing—have so far not provided adequate solutions (Prahalad, 2010).

Private enterprise may be able to complement existing efforts and bring innovative, market-based solutions to these challenges. Unlocking the approximate USD 5 trillion in latent BoP demand may have the added advantage of providing new sources of growth (Murphy, 2012). Part of the funding to encourage innovation solutions at the BoP will come from traditional capital markets and established forms of public–private partnerships. An example of this kind of partnership in action is Electricité de France (EDF), the French electricity provider. In 2002, EDF created a public–private partnership to bring renewable energy to the nearly 10 percent of Moroccan citizens who, because of prohibitive costs, lacked access to electricity. By virtue of its presence in this market, EDF has gained important insight into developing country market dynamics, which will pay dividends as it strives to bring solutions to energy challenges, and others, faced by the BoP (Hockerts & Morsing, 2008). Another illustration is health care for the BoP. Globally, 39 million people are blind and approximately 285 million people have serious visual impairment (World Health Organization, 2013). Of those, 90 percent live in the developing world, and 1–2 million people lose their sight each year. Impact Investments can help scale solutions to treat cataracts, the leading cause of preventable blindness. To finance expanding eye care in developing countries to include services to the poor, established Deutsche Bank the Eye Fund in 2010, a USD 14.5 million fund launched in partnership with a collection of non-profit organizations (Deutsche Bank, 2010). Commercial investors receive a market rate of return, while US foundations making program-related investments receive lower returns, but achieve their mission by mobilizing new, non-grant capital for health outcomes.

Resource efficiency and green growth

The percentage reduction in carbon emissions needed to limit global warming is 4.8 percent per year (PricewaterhouseCoopers, 2011, p. 4). The World Economic Forum and Bloomberg New Energy Finance (as cited in PwC, 2011) estimates that this shift will require USD 500 billion per year of funding to carbon reducing projects by 2020. The investment gap is substantial: actual investment in this sector in 2010 was estimated at USD 243 billion (ibid., p. 12). Given the investment objective of achieving financial as well as environmental outcomes, this field holds enormous potential to invest for impact.

The needs of a global population estimated to reach 9 billion by 2050 will stretch the limits of natural resource and require investments in new infrastructure as well as radical resource efficiency. Investments in energy efficiency can produce cost savings and promote job growth. In Europe, one million jobs could be created from a 20 percent cut in present energy consumption, the equivalent of EUR 60 billion annually (European Commission, 2010, p. 13). Layered investment structures and public–private non-profit partnerships are often crucial to mobilizing new capital and achieving viable investments (Martin, 2010). Partnerships for social impact in the green economy offer a way forward, and designing appropriate investment instruments to resource them provides another. Partnerships with corporations, investors, non-profit organizations, and governments can help ensure robust green financing.

New approaches to the provision of public services

The proportion of workers contributing to those benefiting from the welfare system peaked for the advanced economies of North America, Europe, and East Asia between 2000 and 2010 (Bloom & Canning, 2011). Other challenges, such as poverty and recidivism, also remain costly to national exchequers. Fortunately, new social impact financing mechanisms are emerging to address these challenges. The UK, like many countries, struggles with the issue of recidivism: about half of all crime is committed by people who have already been through the criminal justice system. The cost to the UK taxpayer of reoffending is estimated to be GBP 9.5 to GBP 13 billion per year (Home Office, Ministry of Justice, & Andrew Selous MP, 2014). One potential solution for these challenges are so-called “Social Impact Bonds” (SIBS)—a public–private partnership where private investors finance service delivery upfront, and government ensures a financial return if a non-profit service provider can achieve certain outcomes over a set time period. The UK has pioneered this model to decrease recidivism rates, and at least six US states are also exploring the approach (Martin, 2011b, pp. 29–33; Ragin & Palandjian, 2013). After 2010, which saw the start of the first Social Impact Bond pilot in the UK—focusing on reducing recidivism rates among former inmates associated with a particular English prison—the idea of SIBs caught on. Time will tell if this particular instrument of capital allocation will help drive significant social progress or not; there are currently more than 100 pilots underway around the world. But the underlying idea of linking financial returns to the achievement of social goals as per a predefined metric is very powerful. Attempts are now also being made to apply the contingent return idea to social issues in developing countries, resulting in a series of so-called "Development Impact Bond" pilots or "DIBs" (Center for Global Development & Social Finance, 2013). Pilot applications include funding measures to reduce sleeping sickness in Uganda, antiretroviral treatments to prevent HIV and TB in Swaziland, as well as access to education in Pakistan and Uganda (Center for Global Development & Social Finance, 2013).

SIBs can help to increase the efficacy of social programs and allow governments and donors to do more with less because they offload risk to private investors, provide incentives for continuous improvement, and create greater transparency about the link between inputs and outcomes. This structure creates win–win situations for government agencies or development donors seeking to reduce costs, and private investors wanting to invest with impact. Provided the first batch of pilot implementations is successful, designing bespoke financial instruments that value externalities and innovation has the potential to significantly change how social programs are funded and carried out.

However, with respect to the original SIB pilot in the UK—Peterborough prison—enthusiasm has been recently called into question. First, the Peterborough pilot is to be replaced by 2015 via a new UK government program seeking to transform rehabilitation in 21 parts of the UK, including Peterborough, by having private contractors run rehabilitation services, signaling the sensitivity of new financial solutions to shifting policy environments (Cahalane, 2014). This means that the SIB pilot provided good "R&D" input for government planners, but it will not be possible to comprehensively assess its long-term viability as an Impact Investment instrument. Second, released in August 2014, the reduction in reoffending rates by 8.4 percent over the national average of the first cohort is an acceptable but not a superb result. The cohort consists of roughly 1,000 offenders. The good news is that the success rate achieved was better than the minimum requirement the SIB had to meet. To keep the possibility that investors into the SIB would recoup their investment, interventions needed to reduce the number of reconvictions (i.e., the number of times an offender is convicted of a follow-up offense at court within 1 year) by 7.5 percent over the course of two cohorts, and this was achieved regarding the first cohort. The pilot however failed to meet another criterion that would have triggered immediate repayment to Impact Investors: achieving a 10 percent threshold over either one of the cohorts, which—if it had already been met in the first cohort—would have led to a success payment for Impact Investors right away (Ministry of Justice & Grayling, 2014).

The noteworthy contribution here to building the Impact Investment market is that governments and the world of development aid are now experimenting with new mechanisms to support social innovation. In order to facilitate this new approach to investing and to coordinate across the necessary agencies and sectors, several governments have developed initiatives to support social innovation markets. The US White House Office of Social Innovation and Civic Participation (SICP) promotes service and volunteerism, increases investment in new solutions that demonstrate outcomes, and encourages innovative partnership models (The White House, 2014). In the UK, Big Society Capital (BSC) supports the development of social investment finance intermediaries and works to increase awareness of and confidence in social investment by promoting best practices, sharing information, and improving links between social investment and mainstream financial markets (Big Society Capital, 2014). In Canada, the Community Economic Development Investment Funds (CEDIFs) were created to surmount financial hurdles facing local entrepreneurs and to generate economic development in Nova Scotia (Nova Scotia Canada, 2014). In Australia, Impact Investing was covered for the first time at the government level in 2014 in the country's first Financial System Inquiry since 1997; the 2014 FSI Interim

Report included the investment style (and Social Impact Bonds) under Section 3 (Funding), mentioning examples such as the GoodStart syndicate. GoodStart raised AUD 165 million for 650 ABC Learning day care centers, which it now runs on a not-for-profit basis; mentioned also was the Government of New South Wales' launching of Australia's first two Social Impact Bond pilot programs in 2011 (Financial System Inquiry, 2014). The SIB pilots raised AUD 7 million in capital for UnitingCare Burnside to support families in facilitating their child's return from foster care, and AUD 10 million for the Benevolent Society to prevent family breakdowns. The potential roles that government could play in these and other areas include the provision of risk capital, the creation of a dedicated Social Impact Investment bank, as well as tax incentives, all of which are covered in the FSI Interim Report and provide a good example of early steps a government can take to encourage the development of the Impact Investing market. The advocacy non-profit Impact Investing Australia accordingly considered the FSI coverage to be "a pivot point for Impact Investing in Australia" (Bowden, 2014). Countries that recently went through a major economic adjustment following the Great Recession such as Portugal are similarly seeking for new ways to reactivate their economies and are looking to Impact Investing as one potential lever (Martin, 2014b).

The rise of the "lifestyles of health and sustainability" (LOHAS) consumers

Similar to 2013, respondents to the 2014 JP Morgan/GIIN Impact Investor survey (Saltuk, El Idrissi, Bouri, Mudaliar, & Schiff, 2014) identified the "lack of appropriate capital across the risk/return spectrum" (p. 5) and the "shortage of high quality investment opportunities with track record" (p. 6) as the currently most limiting characteristics of the Impact Investing market. In fact, only 11 percent, or USD 5 billion, of the capital invested by the 125 respondents was committed to start-ups and venture stage businesses. This is less than one-sixth of the capital invested by global companies in start-ups via corporate venturing over the same period, which amounted to USD 29.4 billion in 3,995 deals (Saltuk et al., 2014); the question is, which additional avenues can be located to build out the early stage Impact Investing market (Martin, 2014c)?

One promising avenue is investing for impact in the so-called "LOHAS" segment. While the concept of healthy and sustainable living is certainly not new, the acronym "LOHAS" originated around the time we ushered in the new millennium and has proven to be a unifying term for consumers who, individually, want their products to reflect their personal values and, collectively, aspire to positively influence society with their purchases (Horler, 2011). LOHAS consumers can be found across a broad array of industries, such as food, fashion, real estate, and transportation. Consumer demand in the US has enabled a LOHAS market of over USD 300 billion and growth at a clip of better than 10 percent per annum (ONE Media, n.d.). More than 80 percent of US adults are somehow engaged in sustainability, whether they are consciously part of the LOHAS movement or not (Roberts, 2010, p. 12). While the US consumer has traditionally been viewed as the driver of global growth, change is already occurring. By 2025, consumption in emerging markets is forecast to have grown by 150 percent from 2010 levels, while in developed markets it will have grown just 31 percent. Emerging markets will be nearly on par with developed markets in trillions of consumption dollars. To remain relevant, companies from developed countries will have to learn how to tap into this growth, which has so far proven to be a tall order: McKinsey surveyed 100 leading companies from developed countries and found that 83 percent of revenues came from developed markets despite the fact that the share of global gross GDP of emerging markets has nearly doubled from 19 percent to 36 percent in just two decades (McKinsey & Company, 2012).

Predictions suggest that emerging markets will drive global middle-class consumption and that the nature of consumers from these countries is different. For example, individuals are five times wealthier than they were just a decade ago. Much of this wealth is simply sitting in savings, ready to be deployed for products and services in line with their goals and values (Brandes Investment Partners, 2012). Unlike US consumers who are among the most sensitive to the sometimes higher prices of green products and services, emerging market consumers are not (Roberts, 2010, p. 13). Some data suggest that approximately 84 percent of consumers from emerging market players like China, India, Malaysia, and Singapore would pay a premium for environmentally friendly products, compared to just 50 percent for consumers from the US, Japan, France, and Germany (Accenture, 2010). The proliferation of the sustainable consumer in these emerging markets is supposedly so strong that a study by Edelman labels them "Purpose Bull Markets" (Edelman, 2012). Accenture (2011) warns, though, that "with the exception of products and services that are niche, clearly offering added value or representing genuine innovation, the market for purposely designed sustainable alternatives will not likely command premium prices in the long run" (p. 7).

Looking at the fundamentals of building supply to meet demand, Impact Investing and the LOHAS segment thus appear to be a natural fit. Numerous such investment deals are transacted in international Impact Investor networks such as Toniic (2014), who often back early and growth stage venture capital investments. Established LOHAS topics are organic food, fair trade, and health, with large players such as the publicly listed Wholefoods Market, with over 50,000 employees and almost USD 10 billion in turnover (Wholefoods Market, 2014). In fact, Impact Investors now invest in the cohort of potential future Wholefoods comprising pretty much anything deemed sustainable, ranging from sustainable jeans to sustainable seafood. LOHAS businesses typically produce responsibly along the entire supply chain, and some turn a mainstream product such as shoes or glasses into a LOHAS product by building charity into brand and product offerings. For example, TOMS—a US for-profit company recently invested in by Bain Capital, with a non-profit subsidiary, Friends of TOMS—has pioneered the one-for-one model (De La Merced, 2014). Founded in 2006, it designs and sells shoes and eyewear (TOMS, 2014). For every pair of shoes sold, a pair of shoes is given to an impoverished child; and for every pair of eyewear sold, part of the profit is donated to help restore the eyesight to people in developing countries.

Sustainable products are likely to become the new normal in due course. Companies unwilling to adjust their supply chains or reconfigure their business offerings to prepare for this changing market paradigm are, at best, missing out on an enormous growth opportunity and, at worst, sealing their fates. The logical step is for companies themselves to engage in corporate Impact Investing: as sustainability increasingly influences value creation, assessing joint opportunities for financial and social returns is the way forward to build future business. Consider the case of IKEA, the world's largest furniture retailer, which plans to almost double its revenues to EUR 45–50 billion in turnover by 2020 (Martin, 2014a). The firm faces growing consumer demand, rising raw material prices, as well as more stringent ecological pressures resulting from growth and changing consumer expectations. Encouraging current suppliers to move from compliance-driven to shared value-based social and environmental performance is only one component of the strategy. The other element is to include engaging in venture capital investments that combine impact and profitability to get to the fresh products and services needed to execute on the strategy (i.e., to engage in Impact Investing). Investments made by IKEA's corporate venture GreenTech AB into green technology companies help the company "go renewable" in its core activities. Addressing energy, materials, water, and waste issues are just some of the examples of investments on a massive scale that are planned. Corporate Impact

Investing is especially promising because deep industry expertise enables large corporations to perceive many trends and business ideas first.

As strategist Michael Porter points out, government can be instrumental in the continued competitiveness of these companies:

> On the one hand, firms and the private sector are the ultimate engines of innovation. On the other hand, the innovative activities of firms within a country are strongly influenced by national policy and the presence and vitality of public institutions. In other words, innovation intensity depends on an interaction between private sector strategies and public sector policies and institutions.
>
> *(Porter & Stern, n.d.)*

To enhance competitiveness, the public and private sectors together need to jointly promote a favorable environment for innovation, and Impact Investing can be the pathway to allocate the necessary capital.

The Impact Investor ecosystem

The fundamental supply and demand drivers for Impact Investments have the potential to enable an investment market that is even larger than the USD 1 trillion forecast by 2020. Let us now turn to the key aspects of the Impact Investor ecosystem needed to actualize this potential. Relevant for making the ecosystem work is not so much who the different players are, but which kind of capital they can provide in terms of their ability to take risk, the financial return expectations, liquidity needs, investment time horizon, ticket size, and need for prior track record to invest at all.

Philanthropic capital providers

Much of the work to develop the Impact Investing market has been pioneered by foundations. This includes grant funding with a zero financial return expectation for the development of Impact Investment infrastructure (e.g., pilots, studies, technical support, and intermediaries) and engaging in program-related investing. Philanthropic capital providers, such as foundations, have the privilege to allocate capital to an investment thesis or theory of change without any track record. This turns them into potential first movers. Most foundations are however risk averse and do not act on this privilege.

In the US, foundations typically use PRIs to invest in seed or early stage social enterprises. However, due to cost and complexity, these are rarely used (Ford Foundation, 2014). For example, in 2009, only five one-hundredths of 1 percent of US foundation capital deployed went to equity PRIs (Bannick & Goldman, 2012). As the market matures, foundations can be expected to continue to play an important role by disseminating knowledge on best practices and capacity building to support deal flow and reduce transaction costs (Salamon & Burckart, 2014). In countries where such philanthropic investors are not present, their absence holds back market development. Philanthropic subsidies also play an enabling role in kick starting investible social businesses and taking them through the proof-of-concept phase so as to close what has been termed the "pioneer gap" via hybrid financing (Koh, Karamchandani, & Katz, 2012; Martin, 2011a). There is a whole spectrum of approaches for funders interested in supporting social businesses, ranging from classical enterprise philanthropy in developing countries to grant funding aimed at the extension of certain ecosystems or markets by supporting the development of complementary business models. Their common denominator is the ability to forego risk-adjusted market rate financial returns and to take a medium- and long-term perspective; however, the size of this capital pool is limited, and ticket sizes are typically insufficient to support investees who reach the capital stage.

Next to seeding Impact Investing infrastructure, philanthropic investors can also have a relevant demonstration effect in their own peer group. For example, tracking the conversion to Impact Investing of the portfolio of the KL Felicitas Foundation in the United States in a detailed report highlights how a 100 percent Impact Investment asset strategy can be achieved with a USD 10 million portfolio (Lai, Morgan, Newman, & Pomares, 2013). Its founder, IT entrepreneur-turned-Impact Investor Charly Kleissner, believes that the methodology deployed in his foundation and the associated asset allocation can serve as a blueprint to invest USD 5 to 500 million for total impact (Moehrle, 2014).

Angel and early stage capital

In the US and Europe, angel capital providers have served as a reliable source of early financing for high growth companies. Although venture capital draws the majority of attention from policy makers, angel investment is actually the primary supply of external seed and early stage equity financing in many countries. Angel investors also tend to be less sensitive to market cycles than venture capitalists (OECD, 2011). While the ticket sizes are typically small, their focus on the seed stage is very valuable to enable the creation of more investable social businesses. In taking a company from seed to growth stage, angel investors can do much more than just provide money. For example, they bring expertise in assessing deals. The strength of angel investor networks is one driver of early stage Impact Investment market development. If super returns on specific investments—compensating for losses on other investments that have to be written off—are not part of the business model of Impact Investing, however, it is less clear how angel capital can earn its expected return on capital so as to engage in Impact Investing on a larger scale.

Professional investor capital

Professional investors increasingly want both to "do good" and "do well" with a part of their portfolio. This can be achieved through ethical funds (i.e., "Socially Responsible Investments" or SRI), which are estimated at about USD 3.74 trillion worldwide, and Impact Investments (Chamberlain, 2013; US SIF Foundation, 2012, p. 11). In a world where safe assets no longer exist, the unusual risk-return combination offered by Impact Investments has begun to look more attractive. Their ability to absorb risk, invest with a longer time horizon, and defer liquidity with a portion of their portfolio renders professional investors a promising group to stimulate market development. Some professional investors look for risk-adjusted financial returns in their Impact Investment capital allocation, whereas others are willing to trade financial return for social impact to some extent. For billionaire investors, ticket sizes can reach the double-digit million-dollar category.

Policy makers can best stimulate professional investor engagement by facilitating Impact Investing products with clear risk-return characteristics, product quality, and tax transparency. For example, the EU's new EuSEF law provides a designation for funds that allocate at least 70 percent of their capital towards "social undertakings." However, it is key not to raise the barriers to entry so much that innovation is stifled.

Institutional investors

Institutional investors are gradually entering the Impact Investment market. They are the potential game changers of the Impact Investment market, but also a group that is prone to herding, and one which invests in a fairly scripted fashion. Potentially large ticket sizes need to earn a risk-adjusted financial return and remain relatively liquid or—where a longer term investment horizon is intentionally chosen—offer a clear divestment strategy.

However, public pressure on institutional investors to invest for impact is building up. A recent UK survey of 4.5 million pension holders revealed that 47 percent of all respondents expected to have some form of Impact Investments in their portfolio within the next 2 years (Social Finance, 2012, p. 4). Notwithstanding, many investment managers feel discomfort both in pursuing something other than the highest risk-adjusted financial return, as well as the lack of track record of Impact Investments (Social Finance, 2012). A key limiting factor is the prevailing interpretation of fiduciary duty. A World Economic Forum study found that two key requirements must be met for pension funds to engage in Impact Investing: (a) products must meet the long-term needs of the fund and (b) they must undergo a reliable evaluation of their long-term effects on fund portfolios (Wood, 2013). In spite of alignment with their mandate to store wealth and create value over the long term and the public's growing interest, Impact Investing is to date perceived as a rather unconventional field for pension funds, which is hardly surprising given the small current market size.

One way forward involves Impact Investing practitioners who aim to attract pension funds dealing directly with the theory and practice of fiduciary duty, thus attempting to reconsider the conventional interpretations that can lead to herding when making investment decisions (ibid.). Collaboration with large asset owners to develop systems that evaluate promising new sectors for Impact Investment, link long-term performance to social and environmental considerations, and identify performance measurement systems that do not favor short-term herding are essential to drive market growth (ibid.). How long it will take to gain critical mass and reach a tipping point is hard to predict, a point the sudden advent of the recent financial crisis helped to demonstrate.

Private sector capital and corporate impact venturing

To build out the Impact Investing ecosystem, an avalanche of new products and services that achieve both profitability and positive social impact is needed. In practice, however, most start-ups struggle in bringing their business to market, as established customers are wary to adopt products and services from unproven and young companies, and sales cycles can be lengthy (Martin, 2013a).

Corporate Impact Investors have the potential to play an important role in enabling the market, because their investment requirements and capabilities are complementary to those of the other providers of capital discussed above. From the investee perspective,

> a partnership with a large corporation can deliver immediate and significant benefits for any type of start-up, whether socially focused or not. Not only can the partnering corporation be a client and first customer, but it can also open doors for the start-up with other corporations, reducing the sales cycle. Often enough, the start-up can tap additional resources such as advice, resources, and sometimes executives from the corporation. The company is subsequently a potential buyer for the start-up.
>
> *(Martin, 2013a, p. 18)*

From the vantage point of large companies, engaging in Impact Investing can also be beneficial. In spite of their prowess, corporations often find it difficult to bring innovations to market. Next to classical in-house R&D, corporations began to make strategic investments in the 1960s in firms with intellectual property that could be turned into products—the Corporate Venture Capital (CVC) model was born in the process. Corporations can write large tickets, be medium to long-term investors if the investment carries the prospect to significantly enhance the core business or open new markets, and subordinate financial return expectations to strategic business development considerations. Prior track record of the investee is not strictly needed if value-creating elements such as intellectual property are present.

In practice, new market segments, such as poor consumers at the BoP and virtuous consumers in emerging middle classes around the world, are now blurring the boundaries between corporate responsibility and opportunity, and consequently inviting an adjustment of the corporate venturing model: rather than a primary focus on technological innovation, these new segments require a combination of technical and business model innovation. Unsurprisingly, the new metric for measuring success includes a combination of profitability and social and environmental impacts. Well suited to the structural changes in the operating environments of business is a new approach called Corporate Impact Venturing (CIV) (Martin, 2014a). The mechanics are comparable to Corporate Venture Capital. When a company invests in start-ups or spin-offs, it has three options: (a) setting up an internal corporate venturing group that invests off balance sheet, (b) creating a dedicated external corporate venturing fund, or (c) becoming a limited partner in one or several venture funds that follow investment strategies that are relevant to the corporation. The success metric is typically a combination of financial return and a "strategic" contribution to the parent's business innovation goals, which can be hard to quantify. To this, Corporate Impact Venturing adds the metric of social impact, wedding the logic of investments and impact. This provides a powerful blueprint for corporate Impact Investing, creating a complementary pool of capital for overall market development.

Financial services industry

Leading financial institutions are now starting to offer more Impact Investment products; private banks are important aggregators of client capital; and investment banks have the merger and acquisition expertise needed to build a fully functioning market. The Impact Investment market presents an attractive opportunity for profit over the long term and offers a response to consumers looking to align investments with personal values. The challenge though is making the equation work in the short term. Examples of large banks entering the Impact Investing space are the JP Morgan Social Finance Unit launched in 2007 to service the growing market for Impact Investments and the Morgan Stanley "Investing with Impact Platform" launched in April 2012. This latter platform has been designed to allow investors to have access to a range of investment products that have been evaluated for financial risk and return potential as well as societal impact (JP Morgan Chase & Co, 2014; Morgan Stanley, 2014).

Financial institutions have played a pioneering role in market building since the mid-2000s, when firms such as UBS, JP Morgan, and LGT Venture Philanthropy first initiated their activities in the Impact Investing space. They were initially partially subsidized by central company budgets so as to engage in effective product and market building while reaping a reputational return for the respective bank, and are now gearing up to start offering a profitable business line in its own right to the parent company.

Government

Government plays an important role in creating the framework conditions and stimulating the Impact Investment market: it can provide capital and writes the rules. There are three primary ways that government can "invest in" or support the Impact Investment industry, including: stimulating supply, directing capital, and regulating demand. Government can use supply development policies in order to increase the amount of Impact Investment capital supplied. These policies can take the form of incentives to invest through co-investing or risk sharing with the government, creating investor requirements for Impact Investing, or directly providing funding for Impact Investments or the intermediaries that invest in them.

Seeding intermediaries in particular is an important early step to enable a liquid domestic Impact Investment market to get off the ground. Alternatively, government can direct how capital is used and can better leverage its own investments and expenditures for social impact, for example through its own procurement, privatization, and investment policies. These policies change the risk and return features of Impact Investments by adjusting market prices, and improving transaction efficiency and market information, such as harmonizing impact measurement standards. Lastly, by stimulating the demand for Impact Investment and promoting investment readiness, government can further encourage the growth of the market. Demand development policies increase the demand for Impact Investment by building the capacity of Impact Investment recipients to absorb capital (Thornley, Wood, Grace, & Sullivant, 2011).

Government can moreover create completely new markets for public good provision, for example by fostering "contingent return" models that link a financial return to achieving a social or environmental goal and engage in financial product innovation on a broad front. This is not only a risk mitigation strategy in the event a specific product solution backed by government may not work in scale, but a broader approach linking social outcomes to financial metrics to unlock fresh capital, as has been argued for almost a decade, providing the conceptual framework for product innovations such as the Social Impact Bond at the time (Wood & Martin, 2006). To make innovation efficient and keep costs down, government can also help to internationalize Impact Investment markets by collaborating on shared standards that will facilitate cross-border investment and overall growth of the Impact Investing industry nationally and internationally.

It is worth remembering that while government cannot build a viable Impact Investment ecosystem alone, it is safe to say that without a constructive government role, other players' efforts are doomed. Unfortunately, in spite of the declared intention of a number of governments to enable the Impact Investing market, governments are also creating fresh constraints. For example, the EU's Markets in Financial Instruments Directive 2004/39EC ("MiFID") and Alternative Investment Fund Managers Directive ("AIFMD") require fund managers who want to sell their products in the European Union to register in all countries in which they want to sell their financial product, and in some cases to possibly have representatives in the EU country in question (European Commission, 2004, 2011). The logic of consumer protection intends to protect the investor, but this simultaneously raises the cost of compliance and risks pricing small, innovative first-time funds investing abroad out of the game. Worse, in 2014, several aspects concerning the implementation of the EU regulations were not yet clear to the financial community, adding a further layer of cost to the fund manager's operations associated with uncertainty.

Conclusion

The concept of Impact Investing has managed to generate significant attention in a short amount of time. This provides an interesting counterpoint to the reputation of mainstream finance, which has been called into question around the world in the aftermath of the financial crisis. Interestingly, Impact Investing provides a major opportunity to demonstrate how financial innovation is fundamental to making finance work for the long-term viability of the real economy and society, showing a way forward for the stewardship of society's assets in the emerging sustainability imperative of the early twenty-first century (The Task Force for Global Health, 2012).

Enabling transformational impact

The litmus test for Impact Investing though is its ability to enable transformational impact: will it be able to make a decisive contribution to the long-term viability of advanced economies and sustainable development in emerging and frontier markets? Put differently, is the capital catalytic? Reflecting on its investing of over USD 630 million over 9 years into Impact Investments, the Omidyar Network argues that the critical question concerns whether an investment is catalytic financially *and* strategically. Such "catalytic capital" enables investors to operate in markets they otherwise would not consider worth an investment; moreover, authors of the report "Impact Investing 2.0" encourage investors to re-think their motivations, collaborate with mission and strategy-driven peer investors, and create groups of structural innovators (Clark, Emerson, & Thornley, 2013).

In a world where politics takes center stage, the success of markets and Impact Investing is not a given. Africa, for example, is considered by many to be the next big thing and where some progress is already happening without significant Impact Investment volumes thus far. In 2008, Africa had one billion people with USD 1.6 trillion GDP and USD 860 billion in combined consumer spending; foreign direct investment in 2010 was USD 55 billion (Roxburgh et al., 2010). The 2020 forecast is for a GDP of USD 2.6 trillion, and roughly USD 1.4 trillion in combined consumer spending; and in 2040, when Europe and China will have grayed, we can expect 1.1 billion Africans of working age (Roxburgh et al., 2010).

Today, consumer-facing industries on the continent already grow two to three times faster than in the OECD. For Eastern and Western companies, early entry into African economies can provide opportunities to create markets, establish brands, shape industries, influence consumer preferences, and foster long-term relationships. Yet, fully seizing the opportunity will mean empowering people on a large scale and ensuring inclusive growth, in addition to the massive capital investment needed. Africa will play an increasingly important role in the global economy if current trends continue. The continent could be an important beneficiary of the changes underway in the world of finance as well, provided the continent offers an attractive operating and financing environment. Pent-up demand will drive growth in Africa for decades to come. Only 15.6 percent of the African population has access to the Internet and only 41.8 percent to electricity (Internet World Stats, 2012). With abundant resources and fast-growing market opportunities, the continent's potential is undisputed. Devising solutions that simultaneously respond to nonlinear challenges, such as global warming, will be key for driving long-term prosperity. Significant progress in education, health, and living standards is needed in order to ultimately overcome multidimensional poverty, and this can only be achieved on the back of a modernizing and competitive economy.

The opportunities are enormous, but so are the challenges. To take advantage of the underlying opportunities and innovations underway in capital markets, the time has come to find ways to initiate the transition from a state-led development model to one where the private sector plays a larger role. Investors who want to make a profit while building the Africa of the future are becoming more numerous, and one can see how "impact light" (i.e., a focus on a handful of extra financial indicators next to financial performance that are good predictors of a positive contribution to development and modernization) could both bring more long-term-oriented and responsible capital investment to the table, as well as shaping the future of capital markets via the investment track record it creates (Martin, 2014d). But transformational impact will not truly happen until we identify and execute on the biggest opportunities in this dawning age of impact and create the corresponding policy environments and product innovations now needed.

Core barriers to overcome

Barriers to developing a more effective marketplace of Impact Investment persist. There are a number of steps that policy-makers could take that would serve to help harmonize the field, leverage the megatrends discussed earlier, define the roles of investors and corporations, and increase transparency and harmonization. These recommendations include the long-term creation of more strategic commitments to stimulating, directing, or otherwise regulating the market, as well as more immediate and tactical repositioning, amending, or otherwise changing existing government policies.

Typically, the discussion on barriers to Impact Investing focuses on four dimensions where progress is needed: (a) optimizing existing policies and creating new tools (such as the Social Impact Bond); (b) clarifying legal structures and fiduciary responsibility, and—where needed—combining legal structures or creating new ones altogether; (c) leveraging the private sector to access more capital and functional knowledge on, for example, currency and credit risk, or structuring new products; and (d) creating smart, market-enabling regulation (Martin, 2013b, pp. 29–31).

These are all valuable points. But let us make no mistake: to go mainstream, Impact Investing will ultimately have to deliver on several core requirements. (a) One key problem is that in a world facing pervasive "manufactured" (manmade) risk and volatility, making a qualified statement on commensurate risk taking is not possible if we do not work harder at understanding the risks in the first place, for example by seeking to differentiate between the "known" risks, "unknowns," and "unknowables" ("KUU"), with the goal of grasping what is known, unknown, and unknowable relating to possible events affecting the outcome of an investment (Martin, 2008). A more suitable approach to defining risk taking is essential to unlock the potential of Impact Investing. (b) Similarly, building a path to much greater liquidity for Impact Investments is a must; (c) as is bringing costs under control by graduating from a subscale investment approach that would for the most part not be viable without subsidies from governments, foundations, and banks who can cross-subsidize their Impact Investing activities based on accruing reputation benefits from engaging. (d) Finally, we need to assess whether the path to mainstreaming should really rely heavily on new legal structures. After all, these need to be introduced to the investor and reporting community in a lengthy process first, and thereby risk turning Impact Investing into a "niche of niche" phenomenon, rather than building a path to rendering Impact Investing the standard way to invest over the medium term. The potential is massive and we have every reason to be ambitious and bullish—but if these obstacles remain unaddressed, the constraints they imply are likely to short change the inherent possibilities.

Alternatives to success

Interestingly, in *Finance and the Good Society*, Robert Schiller, one of the few experts to actually predict the financial crisis, makes the case that what is needed now is more financial innovation, not less. He states, "The financial crisis was not due simply to greed or dishonesty of players in the world of finance; it was ultimately due to fundamental structural shortcomings in our financial institutions" (Schiller, 2012, p. 18). The irony, as Schiller emphasizes, is that "better financial instruments, not less activity in finance, is what we need to reduce the probability of financial crises in the future" (2012, p. 17). Intermediation will be a key feature of the ability to grow the Impact Investment market, as it has been in traditional theaters of finance, and a deeper review by government of "the requirements of obtaining licenses and registration that could be modified to recognize that many of the potential players may come from backgrounds other than financial services and will be performing only limited activities typically associated with a financial professional" (Simon & Barmeier, 2010, p. 5). The challenge for policy-makers is determining how to best enable the Impact Investing industry; investors and their advisors similarly need to determine how to optimally engage in this new market.

If Impact Investment asserts itself as an investment style rather than an asset class, the ramifications of this USD 46 billion industry for the overall competitiveness, prosperity, and sustainability of the world's market economies and beyond could well exceed the estimate of an asset class that reaches 0.1 percent of all financial assets by 2020. This is a good thing given the work that lies ahead in building strong, inclusive economies in the OECD and the developing world. The stakes are high. The current rise of extremist social movements and forms of governance in the Middle East and elsewhere reminds us that if we fail in financing the construction of inclusive and competitive economies and societies around the world, we may end up in a divided, unsustainable world. Today, thinking about advanced military robots combating hordes of extremists to protect the remaining spheres of prosperity sounds like science fiction. As our technological capabilities keep advancing, let us make sure it stays that way. Financing and building an inclusive, sustainable world is a better and safer outcome.

References

Accenture. (2010, January 8). *Mobility takes center stage: The 2010 Accenture consumer electronics products and services usage report.* Retrieved August 17, 2014, from http://www.ilsole24ore.com/fc?cmd=document&file=/art/SoleOnLine4/Tecnologia%20e%20Business/2010/02/AccentureConsumerTech2010.pdf?cmd=art

Accenture. (2011). *Long-term growth, short-term differentiation and profits from sustainable products and services: A global survey of business executives.* Retrieved August 17, 2014, from http://www.ddline.fr/wp-content/uploads/2012/12/Accenture-Long-Term-Growth-Short-Term-Differentiation-and-Profits-from-Sustainable-Products-and-Services1.pdf

Accenture. (2012). *Delivering public service for the future: Navigating the shifts.* Retrieved July 17, 2014, from https://www.accenture.com/t20150527T210823__w__/ca-fr/_acnmedia/Accenture/Conversion-Assets/DotCom/Documents/Local/fr-ca/PDF/Accenture-Delivering-Public-Service-for-the-Future-112712.pdf

Bain & Company. (2012). *World awash in money: Capital trends through 2020.* Retrieved July 16, 2014, from http://www.bain.com/Images/BAIN_REPORT_A_world_awash_in_money.pdf

Bannick, M., & Goldman, P. (2012). *Priming the pump: The case for a sector-based approach to impact investing.* Omidyar Network. Retrieved August 20, 2014, from http://boundlessimpact.net/wp-content/uploads/Omidyar-Network-Priming-the-Pump.pdf

Big Society Capital. (2014). *Transforming social investment.* Retrieved August 15, 2014, from http://www.bigsocietycapital.com

Bloom, D. E., & Canning, D. (2011). *Demographics and development policy.* Harvard School of Public Health, Program on the Global Demography of Aging. Retrieved August 13, 2014, from http://www.hsph.harvard.edu/pgda/wp-content/uploads/sites/1288/2013/10/PGDA_WP_66.pdf

Bowden, A. (2014, July 16). Australian financial system inquiry flags impact investing for consideration. *Impact Investing Australia News and Events.* Retrieved August 15, 2014, from http://impactinvestingaustralia.com/social-impact-bonds/australian-financial-system-inquiry-flags-impact-investing-for-consideration

Brandes Investment Partners. (2012). *Five compelling reasons to allocate to emerging markets*. Retrieved August 16, 2014, from http://www.brandes.com/Documents/Publications/Five%20Compelling%20Reasons%20to%20Allocate%20to%20EM.pdf

Cahalane, C. (2014, May 1). Social impact bonds: Is the dream over? *The Guardian*. Retrieved August 12, 2014, from http://www.theguardian.com/voluntary-sector-network/2014/may/01/social-impact-bonds-funding-model-sibs-future

Carmody, L., McCarron, B., Blinch, J., Prevatt, A., & Arosio, M. (2011). Impact investing in emerging markets. *Responsible Research*. Retrieved July 22, 2014, from http://www.thegiin.org/binary-data/RESOURCE/download_file/000/000/252-1.pdf

Center for Global Development & Social Finance. (2013). *Investing in social outcomes: Development impact bonds*. Center for Global Development. Retrieved August 12, 2014, from http://www.cgdev.org/sites/default/files/investing-in-social-outcomes-development-impact-bonds.pdf

Chamberlain, M. (2013, April 24). Socially responsible investing: What you need to know. *Forbes*. Retrieved August 18, 2014, from http://www.forbes.com/sites/feeonlyplanner/2013/04/24/socially-responsible-investing-what-you-need-to-know

Clark, C., Emerson, J., & Thornley, B. (2013). *Impact Investing 2.0: The way forward—Insight from 12 outstanding funds*. Pacific Community Ventures, Impact Assets, and Duke's Center for the Advancement of Social Entrepreneurship. Retrieved August 20, 2014, from http://www.pacificcommunityventures.org/impinv2/wp-content/uploads/2013/11/2013FullReport_sngpg.v8.pdf

Community and Economic Development. (2013, May 16). *Program-related investments (PRIs): A potential funding source for community economic development?* UNC School of Government. Retrieved August 18, 2014, from http://ced.sog.unc.edu/?p=4515

De La Merced, M. J. (2014, August 20). After sale to Bain, Toms's chief wants to expand global reach. *New York Times*. Retrieved August 21, 2014, from http://dealbook.nytimes.com/2014/08/20/toms-sells-half-of-itself-to-bain-capital/?_php=true&_type=blogs&emc=eta1&_r=0

Deutsche Bank. (2010). *Eye Fund finances eye care for the poor*. Deutsche Bank Corporate Social Responsibility. Retrieved August 7, 2014, from https://www.db.com/usa/docs/Eye_Fund_I_Profile(1).pdf

Edelman. (2012). *Edelman Good Purpose 2012: Global consumer survey*. Edelman INSIGHTS. Retrieved August 19, 2014, from http://www.slideshare.net/secret/4FBiBICpOiDK3r

European Commission. (2004). *Markets in Financial Instruments Directive (MiFID) 2004/39/EC. Official Journal of the European Union, L 145*. Retrieved September 4, 2014, from http://ec.europa.eu/yqol/index.cfm?fuseaction=legislation.show&lexId=1&pageNum=2

European Commission. (2010). *Europe 2020: A European strategy for smart, sustainable, and inclusive growth*. Retrieved August 9, 2014, from http://ec.europa.eu/eu2020/pdf/COMPLET%20EN%20BARROSO%20%20%20007%20-%20Europe%202020%20-%20EN%20version.pdf

European Commission. (2011). *Alternative Investment Fund Managers Directive 2011/61/EU. Official Journal of the European Union, L 174/1*. Retrieved September 4, 2014, from http://ec.europa.eu/yqol/index.cfm?fuseaction=legislation.show&lexId=9

Financial System Inquiry. (2014). *Impact investment and social impact bonds: Financial system inquiry*. Government of Australia. Retrieved August 15, 2014, from http://fsi.gov.au/publications/interim-report/03-funding/impact-investment

Ford Foundation. (2014). *Program-related investment*. Retrieved August 17, 2014, from http://www.fordfoundation.org/grants/program-related-investment

Global Impact Investing Network (GIIN). (2013). *Perspectives on progress: The impact investor survey*. Retrieved July 11, 2014, from http://www.thegiin.org/cgi-bin/iowa/resources/research/489.html

GIIN. (2014). *About impact investing*. Retrieved July 11, 2014, from http://www.thegiin.org/cgi-bin/iowa/resources/about/index.html

Hockerts, K., & Morsing, M. (2008). *A literature review on corporate social responsibility in the innovation process*. Copenhagen Business School (CBS), Centre for Corporate Social Responsibility. Retrieved August 7, 2014, from http://www.samfundsansvar.dk/file/318819/a_literature_review_corporate_social_responsibility_innovation_process_september_2008.pdf

Home Office, Ministry of Justice, & Andrew Selous MP. (2014). *Reducing reoffending and improving rehabilitation*. UK Government. Retrieved August 11, 2014, from https://www.gov.uk/government/policies/reducing-reoffending-and-improving-rehabilitation

Horler, A. (2011, March 11). LOHAS: A new era of green consumption? *ecopoint.asia*. Retrieved August 16, 2014, from http://www.ecopoint.asia/2011/03/11/%E2%80%9Clohas%E2%80%9D-a-new-era-of-green-consumption

Internet World Stats. (2012). Measuring progress towards energy for all: Power to the people? *World Energy Outlook 2012*. Retrieved August 21, 2014, from http://www.worldenergyoutlook.org/media/weowebsite/energydevelopment/2012updates/measuringprogresstowardsenergyforall_weo2012.pdf

Jackson, E. T., & Associates Ltd. (2012). *Accelerating impact: Achievements, challenges and what's next in building the impact investing industry*. New York: Rockefeller Foundation. Retrieved July 29, 2014, from https://assets.rockefellerfoundation.org/app/uploads/20120707215852/Accelerating-Impact-Full-Summary.pdf

JP Morgan Chase & Co. (2014). *Social finance*. Retrieved August 19, 2014, from http://www.jpmorganchase.com/corporate/socialfinance/social-finance.htm

Koh, H., Karamchandani, A., & Katz, R. (2012). *From blueprint to scale: The case for philanthropy in impact investing*. Monitor Group and Acumen Fund. Retrieved August 20, 2014, from http://acumen.org/content/uploads/2013/03/From-Blueprint-to-Scale-Case-for-Philanthropy-in-Impact-Investing_Full-report.pdf

Lai, J., Morgan, W., Newman, J., & Pomares, R. (2013). *Evolution of an impact portfolio: From implementation to results*. Sonen Capital. Retrieved August 20, 2014, from http://www.sonencapital.com/evolution-of-impact.php

Levitt, D. A. (2011). Investing in the future: Mission-related and program-related investments for private foundations. *The Practical Tax Lawyer*. Retrieved July 19, 2014, from http://www.adlercolvin.com/pdf/PTXL1105_Levitt.pdf

Martin, M. (2008). *E4C—ecosystems for change: Environmental philanthropy—Catalyzing sustainability*. UBS Philanthropy Services, 4–8. Retrieved September 9, 2014, from http://papers.ssrn.com/sol3/papers.cfm?abstract_id=1322392

Martin, M. (2010). After Copenhagen: Perspectives on energy. *Viewpoint*, 54–65. Retrieved August 9, 2014, from http://ssrn.com/abstract=1532825

Martin, M. (2011a). *Understanding the true potential of hybrid financing strategies for social entrepreneurs*. Impact Economy Working Papers, 3. Retrieved August 20, 2014, from http://impacteconomy.com/papers/IE_WP2_EN.pdf

Martin, M. (2011b). *Four revolutions in global philanthropy*. Impact Economy Working Papers, 1. Retrieved August 12, 2014, from http://www.impacteconomy.com/papers/IE_WP1_EN.pdf

Martin, M. (2013a). *CSR's new deal: A blueprint for your first hundred days in the world of impact economy*. Impact Economy Working Papers, 3. Retrieved August 18, 2014, from http://www.impacteconomy.com/de/wp3.php

Martin, M. (2013b). *Making impact investible*. Impact Economy. Retrieved July 11, 2014, from http://www.impacteconomy.com/press/PR_MII_EN.pdf

Martin, M. (2013c). *Status of the social impact investing market: A primer*. Impact Economy. Retrieved July 11, 2014, from http://www.impacteconomy.com/de/primer1.php

Martin, M. (2014a). *Driving innovation through corporate impact venturing: A primer on business transformation*. Impact Economy. Retrieved August 19, 2014, from http://www.impacteconomy.com/en/primer3.php

Martin, M. (2014b). *Fazer do Impacto um Investimento*. Documentos de trabalho da Impact Economy, 4. Retrieved August 15, 2014, from http://www.impacteconomy.com/en/wp4.php

Martin, M. (2014c, June 10). Corporate impact venturing: Building the pipeline of later-stage opportunities for impact investors. *Alliance Magazine*. Retrieved August 15, 2014, from http://www.alliancemagazine.org/blog/corporate-impact-venturing-building-the-pipeline-of-later-stage-opportunities-for-impact-investors/

Martin, M. (2014d, September). Time for a total-sector perspective on impact investing. *Alliance Magazine*. Retrieved August 15, 2014, from http://www.alliancemagazine.org/opinion/time-for-a-total-sector-perspective-on-impact-investing

McKinsey & Company. (2012). *Winning the $30 trillion decathlon*. McKinsey & Company. Retrieved August 16, 2014, from http://www.mckinsey.com/features/30_trillion_decathlon

Ministry of Justice & Grayling, C. (2014, August 7). *Payment-by-results pilots on track for success*. UK Government. Retrieved August 13, 2014, from https://www.gov.uk/government/news/payment-by-results-pilots-on-track-for-success

Moehrle, C. (2014, August 14). *Inbegriff dessen, wie wir leben wollen*. CFO World. Retrieved August 20, 2014, from http://www.cfoworld.de/inbegriff-dessen-wie-wir-leben-wollen

Monitor Institute. (2009). *Investing for social & environmental impact: A design for catalyzing an emerging industry*. Retrieved July 23, 2014, from http://www.monitorinstitute.com/downloads/what-we-think/impact-investing/Impact_Investing.pdf

Morgan Stanley. (2014). *Sustainability: Investing with impact*. Retrieved August 19, 2014, from http://www.morganstanley.com/globalcitizen/investing-impact.html

Murphy, R. M. (2012, July 9). What will the global 500 look like in 2021? *CNN Money*. Retrieved August 5, 2014, from http://www.money.cnn.es/galleries/2012/news/companies/1207/gallery.global-500-future.fortune/index.html

Nova Scotia Canada. (2014). *Community economic development investment funds*. Retrieved August 15, 2014, from http://www.gov.ns.ca/econ/cedif

O'Donohoe, N., Leijonhufvud, C., Saltuk, Y., Bugg-Levine, A., & Brandenburg, M. (2010). *Impact investments: An emerging asset class*. JP Morgan Global Research. Retrieved July 15, 2014, from https://assets.rockefellerfoundation.org/app/uploads/20101129131310/Impact-Investments-An-Emerging-Asset-Class.pdf

OECD. (2011). *Financing high-growth firms: The role of angel investors*. Retrieved August 18, 2014, from http://www.eban.org/wp-content/uploads/2013/03/OECD-Angel-Financing-Publication.pdf

ONE Media. (n.d.). *The LOHAS market*. Retrieved August 16, 2014, from http://www.effectpartners.com/onelifetour/the-lohas-market

Porter, M. E., & Stern, S. (n.d.). *National innovative capacity*. Harvard Business School. Retrieved August 17, 2014, from http://www.hbs.edu/faculty/Publication%20Files/Innov_9211_610334c1-4b37-497d-a51a-ce18bbcfd435.pdf

Prahalad, C. K. (2010). *The fortune at the bottom of the pyramid: Eradicating poverty through profits*. New Jersey: Pearson Education.

PricewaterhouseCoopers (PwC). (2011). *Counting the cost of carbon: Low Carbon Economy Index 2011*. Retrieved August 7, 2014, from https://www.pwc.com/en_GX/gx/sustainability/publications/low-carbon-economy-index/assets/low-carbon-economy-Index-2011.pdf

Ragin, L., & Palandjian, T. (2013). *Social impact bonds: Using impact investment to expand effective social programs*. Federal Reserve Bank of San Francisco. Retrieved August 11, 2014, from http://www.frbsf.org/publications/community/review/vol9_issue1/social-impact-bonds-impact-investment-expand-effective-social-programs.pdf

Roberts, J. M. (2010). *LOHAS consumers around the world*. Natural Marketing Institute. Retrieved August 16, 2014, from http://www.lohas.com/sites/default/files/lohasconsumers.pdf

Roxburgh, C., Dörr, N., Leke, A., Tazi-Riffi, A., van Wamelen, A., Lund, S., . . . Zeino-Mahmalat, T. (2010). *Lions on the move: The progress and potential of African economies*. McKinsey Global Institute. Retrieved August 21, 2014, from http://www.mckinsey.com/insights/africa/lions_on_the_move

Salamon, L. M., & Burckart, M. (2014). Foundations as philanthropic banks. In L. M. Salamon (Ed.), *New frontiers of philanthropy* (pp. 165–208). New York: Oxford University Press.

Saltuk, Y., El Idrissi, A., Bouri, A., Mudaliar, A., & Schiff, H. (2014, May). *Global social finance. Spotlight on the market: The Impact Investor Survey*. JP Morgan & the Global Impact Investing Network. Retrieved July 19, 2014, from http://www.jpmorganchase.com/corporate/socialfinance/document/140502-Spotlight_on_the_market-FINAL.pdf

Schiller, R. (2012). *Finance and the good society*. New Jersey: Princeton University Press.

Simon, J., & Barmeier, J. (2010). *More than money: Impact investment for development*. Center for Global Development. Retrieved August 10, 2014, from http://www.cgdev.org/sites/default/files/1424593_file_More_than_Money_FINAL_web.pdf

Social Enterprise. (2011). *The RBS SE100 Data Report 2011: Charting the growth of the UK's top social businesses*. Social Enterprise and RBS Community Banking. Retrieved July 29, 2014, from http://www.socialenterpriselive.com/section/se100/management/20110711/vibrant-sector-defies-downturn-powerful-growth

Social Finance. (2012). *Microfinance, impact investing, and pension fund investment policy survey*. Retrieved August 18, 2014, from http://www.socialfinance.org.uk/microfinance-impact-investing-and-pension-fund-investment-policy-survey

The Task Force for Global Health. (2012). *Collaborate and innovate to transform global health: 2012 annual chapter*. Retrieved July 15, 2014, from http://www.taskforce.org/sites/default/files/final_tfgh_ar12updated.pdf

The White House. (2014). *Office of Social Innovation and Civic Participation*. Retrieved August 13, 2014, from http://www.whitehouse.gov/administration/eop/sicp

Thornley, B., Wood, D., Grace, K., & Sullivant, S. (2011). *Impact investing: A framework for policy design and analysis*. Insight at Pacific Community Ventures & The Initiative for Responsible Investment at Harvard University. Retrieved August 19, 2014, from http://www.pacificcommunityventures.org/uploads/reports-and-publications/Impact_Investing_Policy_Full_Report.pdf

TOMS. (2014). Retrieved August 17, 2014, from http://www.toms.com

Toniic. (2014). Retrieved August 21, 2014, from http://www.toniic.com

US SIF Foundation. (2012). *Chapter on sustainable and responsible investing trends in the United States*. US SIF Foundation: The Forum for Sustainable and Responsible Investment. Retrieved August 18, 2014, from http://www.ussif.org/files/Publications/12_Trends_Exec_Summary.pdf

Wholefoods Market. (2014). Retrieved August 17, 2014, from http://www.wholefoodsmarket.com

Wood, A., & Martin, M. (2006). Market based solutions for financing philanthropy. *Viewpoints*, 58–63. Retrieved August 21, 2014, from http://ssrn.com/abstract=980097

Wood, D. (2013). The current limits and potential role of institutional investment culture and fiduciary responsibility. In World Economic Forum Investors Industries. *From ideas to practice, pilots to strategy: Practical solutions and actionable insights on how to do impact investing* (pp. 15–17). World Economic Forum. Retrieved August 20, 2014, from http://www3.weforum.org/docs/WEF_II_SolutionsInsights_ImpactInvesting_Report_2013.pdf

World Health Organization (WHO). (2013). *Universal eye health: A global action plan 2014–2019*. Retrieved August 19, 2014, from http://www.who.int/blindness/AP2014_19_English.pdf?ua=1

42

FORMATIVE DYNAMICS IN THE UK SOCIAL INVESTMENT MARKET, 2000–2015

An "organization rich" agenda on how markets form

Guillermo Casasnovas and Marc J. Ventresca

Market formation has been a topic of great interest for economic sociologists for a long time, with lively current debates and competing arguments. Research on the sociology of markets (Fligstein, 2001; Granovetter, 1985; White, 1981) has been key to understanding markets not as the idealized assumptions of neoclassical economics but as the messier, more complex, socially constructed spaces that we find in real life (Beckert, 2009; Biggart & Delbridge, 2004; Hirsch, Michaels, & Friedman, 1987; Munir, 2005). Available arguments have been developed in the last few decades and highlight three well-developed streams on markets as politics, markets from culture, and the network origins of markets (Fligstein, 1996; Fourcade, 2007; Padgett & Powell, 2012; Santos & Eisenhardt, 2009; Thornton, 2004).

Insights from this literature can help us understand the development of the social investment market in the UK (Casasnovas, forthcoming). But apart from that, a close observation of how the social investment space has been framed and constructed can grant us further learnings about how markets are formed more generally. This is because of the particularities of this sector: on the one hand, it is an "extreme case" of market formation in a complex context, due to the interaction of different sectors and conflicting institutional logics (Nicholls, 2010); on the other hand, it can be representative of other incumbent value chains where business and financial practices are being challenged by external actors advocating institutional alternatives, such as crowdfunding, social entrepreneurship, or microfinance. We use these particular features of the UK social investment market dynamics to develop more general arguments for a research agenda.

As with other nascent markets, the challenge is that the same features that make the social investment space an interesting research context—ambiguity, unsettled boundaries, contestation—also make it more difficult to study with standard tools and theories. Or, in other words, we cannot study it as an industry with its clearly defined actors, relations, and institutions. Instead, we need to take an exploratory approach and look at how organizations cross the boundaries of adjacent fields, how actors struggle to dominate critical activities, who defines the rules of the game and how this occurs, and how plural discourses about value, market actors, and purpose conflict, align, and persist in tension over time.

With this research, we re-animate the now standard concerns of economic sociology approaches with an "organization rich" focus, one that borrows from organizational and institutional theory to specify a research agenda that can leverage the features of the social investment context. We start by summarizing the research design of our exploratory study of the social investment space in the UK and initial findings. Then we develop six themes relevant for understanding the development of social investment markets and make use of them to discuss how to reframe and move forward theories of market formation. We conclude with a general discussion to revitalize the sociology of markets with this organization rich approach.

Social investment in the UK

How to approach the study of a market in formation? We are using the term UK social investment market to reference a broad range of activities, institutional relationships, conventions, and actors that have been visible since the early 2000s. The fact of these activities is well documented and well known, and the UK is regularly referenced as a global leader in this space. But beyond this broad general point, there is no single "market" to see; instead, there are many initiatives that over time are threaded into more and more linked activities.

We approached this study trying to cope with the variation of initiatives and perspectives around investing with the purpose of financial and social returns, without preconceptions from our part about what should or should not be included in the category. We have collected extensive data on the emerging UK social investment space, including interviews with over 30 industry insiders and observers, from which we use some illustrative quotes throughout the chapter (the list of interviewees can be found in the Appendix). We have also coded over 80 industry and policy reports spanning almost two decades, carried out field observation, and collected online text sources. For details on these source data and the research, please refer to our other work (Casasnovas, 2015; Casasnovas & Ventresca, 2015).

The practice of investing "with the intention to generate social and environmental impact alongside a financial return" (Global Impact Investing Network, 2015) is not something new, as we can find individuals and organizations that have been concerned about the impact of their investments since the very beginnings of investing practices (Nicholls, 2010). However, there is evidence that discourse and practice around this issue have increased substantially in the UK since the early 2000s, partly alongside the rising interest in the role of social enterprises in the economy and policy agenda (Sepulveda, 2014). As a manager of a trade association in the field said:

> [With] the Social Investment Task Force (...) there was a recognition, I think, publically and politically, in a way for the first time, of the problems associated with lack of credit and lack of access to good, quality, financial products (...) And so, in a way, that was when the concept of social investment was really formed.
>
> *(Interviewee #16)*

Since then, social investment has become a common term used by policymakers, social sector organizations, and some niches of the financial industry, especially after 2010. The period between 2000 and 2015 has seen multiple direct and varied initiatives to stabilize the idea and practice of social investment, hence becoming a window to understand processes of market formation in this space.

It is useful at this point to highlight the main actors in this field of activity: investors, investees, intermediaries, and regulators. Among the investors, we mainly find the government (through national bodies and local administrations), charitable trusts and foundations, high-net-worth individuals (like the so-called "social business angels"), and commercial banks. Investees are also diverse, from organizations which fall under the category of VCSE (Voluntary, Community, and social enterprises) to for-profit companies with a social purpose. In terms of legal form, they range from charities to companies limited by shares or guarantee, and from cooperatives or associations to community interest companies (CICs). However, some investors or intermediaries limit their scope to certain types of organizations or sectors, and for others the very definition of "social investment" is restricted to specific niches of that broad market. Intermediary organizations include managers of social investment funds, brokers or advisors, trade associations, and other platforms. Different government agencies also play an important role as investors, regulators, or market champions. Finally, a special mention is needed for Big Society Capital (BSC), an organization that was founded and funded by the government as a response to the recommendation of the Commission on Unclaimed Assets, and which has played a central role in the market since its establishment in 2012 as a wholesaler of capital for the social sector.

While the mentioned organizations are considered by many as being part of the social investment market, several others might be up for discussion about whether they too belong to the circle. Also among those studying social enterprises, which are the main recipients of social investment, there are different definitions and hence ambiguity when a new survey or research is presented (Lyon & Sepulveda, 2009). For this reason, most reports of the social investment market, in the UK and elsewhere, start by defining the scope of their analysis in terms of what investors and investees they are focusing on. However, this ambiguity is not uncommon in the early stages of market formation, when products, meanings, and boundaries are not yet well established (Fligstein, 2001; Hajek, Ventresca, Scriven, & Castro, 2011).

During our thorough exploration of the social investment market, we have been constantly iterating between the data collected and the claims from theories of market formation, innovation, organizations, and institutions. Based on this work, we have identified six themes that are central to understanding the development of social investment in the UK and which directly address our dual purpose: leveraging existing market formation theories to make sense of the social investment space, and extracting learnings from this context to enhance existing theoretical frameworks. In the following subsections, we describe each of these themes, which are summarized in Table 42.1.

Ambiguity and innovation in nascent markets

The intention of achieving a social mission whilst applying business methods to generate sustainable financial flows and reduce external dependencies is not new (Sepulveda, 2014), nor is the idea of investing with a specific social motivation (Nicholls, 2010). There is, however, evidence that activity and discourse around social investment in the UK has increased and changed in focus and intensity since the turn of the millennium (Nicholls, 2010; Sepulveda, 2014). Our findings suggest that this period of experimentation, which paves the way for building a robust social investment market, is ongoing without many signs that that experimentation is reduced.

We see experimentation in financial products, in business models, and in policy. Experimentation takes place in the different financial products employed by social investment organizations. Social finance, for example, pioneered the work on Social Impact Bonds; platforms like Ethex or the Social Stock Exchange believe in the power of public stock markets; Bridges Ventures and other social investment fund managers directly apply private equity tools; Charity Bank and Triodos Bank operate as traditional retail banks with a social mission; ClearlySo promotes the role of angel investors, and so on.

Table 42.1 Summary of main learnings and insights for future research

Theme	*Learnings from economic sociology*	*Insights for future research*
Ambiguity and innovation in nascent markets	Early stages of market formation are full of ambiguity, experimentation, and contestation. These generative and innovative periods then lead to temporary settlements, which may redraw future boundary struggles.	The processes from market emergence to (provisional) stabilities are not singular or linear; we propose a focus on the changing configurations of ambiguities, context, and actors by looking at how networks, meanings, and institutions are built.
Discourse and logics	Early or pre-market discourses typically engage different institutional logics that contend over the features of basic market elements such as actors, boundaries, governance, or valuation strategies.	Discourses in these early moments reflect and also refract myriad local ambiguities in all basic market elements and provide a way to link empirical actors and frames to efforts to settle this complexity at multiple levels.
Role of the state	State actors are complex organizational actors that play diverse roles in early markets, most visibly as regulators but also across many value-creating activities.	Too often we study "states" only in terms of regulatory impact. There is a need to study the knowledge regimes that structure mechanisms and provide content for policymaking, as well as the effects of different government interventions such as legislation, taxation, or direct investment, and toward purposes that include capacity building, authorization, and value theorizing.
Intermediation in nascent markets	Intermediaries can play critical roles in processes of valuation and shaping market boundaries, distinct from the conventional roles of market intermediaries.	Intermediary organizations play an important role in converting the ambiguity of early moments into stable networks, routines, and the cultural and institutional elements that support new market assembly and definition.
System-building strategies	Some public and private actors play especially consequential roles in bringing together the networks, meanings, resources, norms, and practices of which large systems are formed. These can have intended and unintended consequences.	Studying system-building processes and organizational actors alerts us to the range of available strategies, legacy systems, and alternatives "unbuilt" or closed down, and the longer-term nature of their work.
Markets from interstitial spaces	Interstitial spaces are especially fertile grounds for processes of market emergence and innovation.	Origins of actors and resources involved in early market formation processes provide cues about market development over time.

Partially derived from innovation in social investment products, there is experimentation with new business models. We find platforms that connect conscious retail investors with stock markets, fund managers leveraging money both from grants and from commercial origins, foundations using part of their endowment for social investment, or the government setting up different funds and organizations to build capacity and market infrastructure. Connected to this last point, we see experimentation in policymaking with different regulations and more or less direct government action in the social investment market during the last 15 years.

Ambiguity is most evident in the wealth of terms, definitions, and understanding around what social investment is and is not. First, people speak about social investment, social finance, impact investment, community finance, responsible investment, builder capital, and positive investment, as well as different combinations of them, when referring to the market where money is exchanged with the promise of delivering both financial returns and social impact. The variety of words captures distinct communities, strategies, and conceptions of purpose and control. This ambiguity is reinforced because some organizations are active in different market niches, and also because the role of the government in promoting the market is sometimes seen as an effort to strengthen the social sector but sometimes as having other political agendas.

Contestation is also present in the social investment space, over rules of the game, alternative pathways and forms, and strategies. The UK social investment market is full, with many diverse institutional, organizational, and individual actors; these actors take various positions with regard to emerging conventions and social investment approaches that are becoming mainstream. Some actors propose and keep alive different alternatives, and there is not a settled agreement on the features, forms, and focus of the different actors and market segments. Most of the critiques are targeted at the government and some of its interventions, like the way in which the substantial resources from BSC are being channeled into the sector. Other examples of contestation refer to different approaches in the social investment market, mostly between those who support the idea of targeting "market level" financial returns and those who think that that is not compatible with a model that works well for social sector organizations.

Another important finding is the persistence of substantial diversity in key forms, features, and processes, even after the dominant order that resulted after the founding of BSC and other government interventions. The reality is that experimentation, ambiguity, and contestation still abound. If we take a look at recent developments in the field, we see that many features are not yet settled. For example, as recently as November 2014, different actors from the social enterprise, social investment, non-profit, and academic sectors set up the Alternative Commission on social investment

> to investigate what's wrong with the UK social investment market and to make practical suggestions for how the market can be made more accessible and relevant to a wider range of charities, social enterprises and citizens working to bring about positive social change.
>
> (*The Alternative Commission on Social Investment, 2015*)

Other signs of experimentation and ambiguity are the new platforms, such as Impact Investor, that are being launched to tap into the retail investor market; the recent changes in the delivery of the Investment and Contract Readiness Fund; the general sense that there are still many different views as to what social investment is; or the fact that new regulations are still in their infancy—it was not until November 2014 that the first investor benefited from Social Investment Tax Relief.

We have portrayed the UK social investment space as a nascent market, full of experimentation, ambiguity, and contestation. Similarly, Santos and Eisenhardt (2009, p. 644) defined nascent markets as "business environments in an early stage of formation," characterized by an undefined industry structure, unclear product definitions, and lack of a dominant logic. Given that these characteristics are still present in the social investment market 15 years after its first steps in the early 2000s, one conclusion is that it takes time for markets to become established and have a dominant design (Utterback & Abernathy, 1975), especially when the "technology" in place is not a technical feature but a set of meanings, values, resources, and tools that can be combined in multiple ways. Insights from the literature on the technology life cycle (Tushman & Anderson, 1986; Utterback & Abernathy, 1975) and the early moments of new industries (Geroski, 2003) prompt us to look at processes of market formation as going from "ferment" to "dominant design," similar to the takings from economic sociology and research on organizational fields that talk about "emergence" or "variation" on one side and "settlement" or "stability" on the other (Fligstein & McAdam, 2012; Padgett & Powell, 2012). These perspectives remind us that experimentation, either in the form of new products, new entries and exits of organizations, new policies, or new tools, usually takes place for relatively long periods of time until the market reaches a certain necessary level of agreement and efficiency that allows for scaling and maturing.

Mapping this imagery onto the social investment market, we can specify paths to market development and variation in strategies in this period of ferment, one that is still full of financial, organizational, and political innovation. From the point of view of innovation, such variety is positive, while the push from certain actors to standardize the tools and definitions of the market can be in detriment for fertile innovative activity. If the goal is instead to promote a specific understanding of what social investment is or should be, then establishing the necessary institutions and path dependencies might ensure the viability of that perspective as the "dominant design," a well-understood anchor for market building.

These developments in the UK social investment market can help us raise some questions that arise when forcing a dialogue between the literature on new technologies and innovation economics and research on the formation of new markets and fields. A relevant one is about whether the rise of a dominant order (driven by the state or other actors) reduces the ambiguity of the market and hence takes it to a period of settlement and stabilization (DiMaggio & Powell, 1983; Stinchcombe, 2001). We might expect different outcomes (in terms of speed, resilience, legitimacy, and opposition) depending on whether the efforts to resolve ambiguity are top-down or bottom-up, as well as on whether it is a market with a strong component of technological innovation, an emphasis on social norms, a more salient role of the government, etc. Another set of questions would be around how to encourage sustained experimentation in a certain market, both in terms of strategies by public and private actors and regarding what organizations or constituencies benefit more or less from that continued innovation.

Discourse and logics

If we look at some of the reports published in the early 2000s and compare them to more recent documents, the market appears to have experienced a change in focus. For example, the reports from the Social Investment Task Force (in 2000, 2003, and 2005) were labeled "Enterprising Communities: Wealth Beyond Welfare"; the first fund financed by the government (in 2001) was called the Community Development Venture Fund, and it was managed by then-called Bridges Community Ventures; and a report from the Bank of England was about the financing needs of social enterprises (Bank of England, 2003). On the contrary, if we look at current documents, we see titles such as "Growing the Social Investment Market" (Cabinet Office UK, 2011; City of London, 2013), "The First Billion" (Brown & Swersky, 2012), or "Investor Perspectives on social enterprise Financing" (ClearlySo, 2011).

This suggests that there has been a shift, at least in discourse, from a sector centered in the local communities and the needs of the social enterprises, to pivoting around Social Investors and how they can achieve financial and social returns. For example, BSC has the mission of "growing the social investment market," which seems to be focused on the means (social investment as a sector) rather than on the ends (increasing social impact). This shift in the language—from social investment being a means to being an end in itself—is arguably a reflection of broader changes in the market (in legitimacy, in power imbalances, in resource allocation, in boundary struggles, etc.), and it may be the cause of the increased contestation against some practices or organizations in the last few years.

The shift has not only been around the meaning of the term social investment, but also the use of other similar terms. If early on one would hear more often the language of "community development," after 2010—and partly because of the influence of the United States ("The Americans didn't want it to be called social investing" (Interviewee #28))—the term "impact investment" has become more central in the discourse. As a social investment fund manager stated, when the investors are at the center, language is often different: "If I'm talking to an investor (...) the word 'social' doesn't get the conversation started" (Interviewee #9). And, as one of our interviewees from a social investment platform said, even if they are similar concepts, "Impact Investing has more of a connotation around market rates of return" (Interviewee #16).

These struggles between different discourses links to recent trends of studying institutional logics and institutional complexity (Greenwood, Raynard, Kodeih, Micelotta, & Lounsbury, 2011; Thornton, Ocasio, & Lounsbury, 2012), as one of its focal points has been on how organizational fields experience a shift over time from one logic to another (Haveman & Rao, 1997; Reay & Hinings, 2005). In this sense, an important contribution to this type of research will be around the interplay among multiple logics in nascent markets or organizational fields. If institutional logics are understood as stable systems of meaning and practice, to what extent are they present in the early stages of development of a new field? Those early struggles over meaning and power might be the consequence of product and service ambiguity and contestation, rather than a reflection of conflicts among broader institutional orders.

As we have seen, the exploration of archival material and current discourse developments suggest that the public discourse around social investment has shifted from being centered in the local communities and social enterprises to the concerns of the investors and the financial intermediaries. In this case, a longitudinal exploration of industry documents via topic modeling or network text analysis can help us identify changes in how the market is conceptualized. If we then can link that to generalized changes in practices, values, and strategies, we will be able to portray those logic struggles and investigate the origins of this logic shift.

Linking nascent markets, institutional logics, and discourse analysis opens important questions about how different actors influence (or try to influence) public discourse, whether institutional logics are identifiable in the early stages of market formation, what textual sources can be more accurate to study the evolution of public discourse over a period of time, or how logics "travel" from adjacent sectors to the new markets in formation.

Role of the state

The case of social investment in the UK provides a paradigmatic example of a government that has committed considerable financial and organizational resources to drive the growth of the market. The government's two main roles have been as a regulator and as a funder. As the former, it passed the measure Community Investment Tax Relief in 2002, the regulation for CICs in 2004, the Dormant Bank and Building Society Accounts Act in 2008, the measure Social Investment Tax Relief in 2013, and other regulations involving public procurement like the Social Value Act or the Social Outcomes Fund, both in 2012. As an investor, the government has financed social sector organizations through its own funds (e.g., Futurebuilders in 2004), through private funds (e.g., Bridges Ventures in 2002), and more recently through the establishment of an independent wholesaler fund—BSC in 2012.

However, the government has also acted as a convener and as an innovator. It has brought together social investment actors and consulted with them on many occasions, especially via the Social Investment Task Force that sparked the field in 2000, and the G-8 Social Impact Investing Task Force in 2013, which addressed the global challenges of the sector, was an opportunity to share best practices among different countries, and portrayed the UK as a leader in this space. In terms of innovation, the UK government has the credit for commissioning the first Social Impact Bond in 2010 and expanding this financial instrument through the Department of Work and Pensions (DWP), the Department for Communities and Local Government (DCLG), and the Ministry of Justice (MoJ). Furthermore, the government is responsible for innovating with regulations that have been pioneering worldwide, such as the CICs or the establishment of BSC.

The government can hence be labeled as a market champion, because of its interest in this market to grow and succeed. The reasons behind this interest can be diverse, and there are probably differences between the political agendas of the former Labour administration and the Coalition Government (between the Conservatives and Liberal Democrats) that took over in 2010. However, the driving role of the government has been constant since the early 2000s, a position that becomes clear in the following statement from Prime Minister David Cameron in 2010: "[We will] create a Big Society Bank to help finance social enterprises, charities and voluntary groups through intermediaries, [which will be] established using every penny of dormant bank and building society account money allocated to England."

This dominant stance of the government has gained some criticisms, as put by a social investment advisor: "One of the things that is going wrong in the social finance market in the UK is the issues being very heavily influenced by a government and the Cabinet Office" (Interviewee #22). But its role in driving the market forward is hard not to notice, as commented by another Social Investor regarding the government's establishment of BSC: "Undoubtedly it had the effect that they wanted it to have, which was to stimulate the market" (Interviewee #14).

Even though states are not homogenous entities but rather a collection of coalitions and interests (Skocpol, 1985), researchers have already shown that they can play an important role in determining the fate of markets and organizational fields (Fligstein, 1996). It is not infrequent that "state regulation of economic activities changes the balance of power in a market" (Fligstein, 1996, p. 664), and it is generally the role of governments to regulate the flow of resources, for example via taxation or direct investment, as they are responsible for designing, passing, and enforcing legislation. However, research has often focused on the state's role as regulator, omitting its capacity to build markets by shaping its meanings, building the necessary networks, and developing other tools and skills.

Therefore, two main questions arise when investigating the dominant role of the UK government in the social investment context. First, about the mechanisms by which these interventions shape the market for social investment. We will need to take into account legitimacy, networks, risks, and resource dependencies in order to determine the effects of the policies over the organizational field. And second, about the origins of those government interventions. The role of interests, ideologies, social movements, and translation of international practices is probably crucial to explaining how ideas travel from different sectors to political discourse and then to specific policy regimes (Campbell, 2002). To study this we need to take a close look at the early days of social investment or other markets and analyze how different epistemic communities (the social sector, the private equity industry, Socially Responsible Investors, community finance organizations, etc.) interacted, shared their ideas, and influenced the government. In this sense, it is also worth comparing different countries and analyzing how different origins have resulted in different policy regimes (Campbell & Pedersen, 2014).

With this focus on the role of the state in the formation of new markets, we can ask questions about how organizations or communities influence the government in its understanding of a nascent market and the regulation needed, the effects of the different kinds of government interventions (legislation, direct investment, founding of agencies, endorsement, etc.) on the processes of market formation, the extent to which the pace of market formation is dependent on those different interventions, or the influence of similar policies in other countries.

Intermediation in nascent markets

One of the mantras of the social investment sector in the last few years has been the need to build a range of intermediary organizations that would enable the growth of the market. These include the so-called SIFIs (social investment financial intermediaries), but also brokers, platforms, incubators and accelerators, or trade associations. They are all organizations involved in matching, channeling, or aggregating financial and organizational resources in the social investment space. Apart from investors, investees, and regulators, we can consider most of the other organizations in the market as mediating between those three sets of actors. social investment fund managers like Bridges Ventures, Big Issue Invest, or Resonance are raising capital from public and private institutions and investing it in social enterprises or other social-purpose organizations; ClearlySo or Social Finance UK help frontline organizations raise funding from their networks of business angels and other investors; CDFA or the Social Investment Forum bring actors together to learn from each other and plan their collective action; and Ethex or the Social Stock Exchange provide platforms to find investment opportunities.

Recent industry reports have highlighted the importance of these organizations (Shanmugalingam, Graham, Tucker, & Mulgan, 2011), some of which "are leading the way in product innovation" (City of London, 2013, p. 6). This has certainly been the government's strategy, as they often state that they "want to see new social finance intermediaries enter the market" (Cabinet Office UK, 2011, p. 8), and they have promoted that by specifying BSC's role as financing intermediary organizations. But what is the role of these intermediaries?

On the one hand, they have a cultural influence by shaping the language, the meanings, and the information of the market. They drive the language used in the field by naming themselves according to different connotations around social investment (e.g., Social Finance UK, Social Investment Business Group, Impact Investor, Community Development Finance Association, Social Investment Forum) and by pushing for specific definitions or practices, as stated by an interviewee from a social investment platform: "What I was trying to do is (…) to say that responsible investing is investing in listed social impact businesses" (Interviewee #17). They also produce and disseminate information, like the reports published by many of these intermediaries, the annual surveys from the Community Development Finance Association, or the extensive information provided by BSC on its website. All this information is very important to set the track records, standards, and best practices that will have much influence on other market actors, especially in the early stages of market development.

On the other hand, they influence the formal and informal institutions of the market by lobbying for certain regulations and coming with new tools and practices. Many of these intermediaries were members of the G-8 Social Impact Investment Task Force, and hence having a say in what the state of the market is and where it should be heading to, and they were also consulted by the government before passing different regulations. A senior executive from a social investment fund even mentioned that "one of us is in the Cabinet Office every week" (Interviewee #8). Another social investment broker described their advisory role with the government in the following terms:

> Initially our government advisory work was mainly around Social Impact Bonds and helping them to understand and think through where they could create (...) social value (…) We've been asked to undertake an increasing amount of (...) advisory work more broadly.
>
> *(Interviewee #12)*

Their influence in more informal institutions such as the metrics or financial instruments used has also been important, because of their capacity to innovate and to bridge between investors and investees.

Economic theories have traditionally focused on intermediaries as decreasing transaction costs and hence increasing the efficiency of financial markets (Allen & Santomero, 1998; Gurley & Shaw, 1960). From this perspective, their main task is to reduce information asymmetries, build trust between the seller and the buyer, and create economies of scale (Yanelle, 1989; Zucker, 1986). Network theories complement this perspective by taking into consideration the broader networks in which financial transactions (and economic action more generally) are embedded in sets of individual and organizational relations (Granovetter, 1985). In this sense, intermediaries' role is seen as connecting different nodes and networks, often by bridging structural holes, and therefore providing valuable resources and information to the connected parties (Burt, 1992; Fernandez & Gould, 1994).

However, what we see in the social investment market in the UK is that intermediary organizations perform an important role that goes beyond reducing transaction costs or leveraging their structural position. We see that these organizations are also promoting certain metrics and standards; they are lobbying for specific regulation; and they are developing the discourses that dominate the sector; they are innovating with new financial instruments; and they are, in the end, building the market by shaping its boundaries and its main features and conventions. Through their interactions with the other organizations in the field, they are a vital set of actors in the formation and development of its institutions.

This perspective links with organization theory that looks at the role of certain organizations in shaping and building markets: how technology entrepreneurs claim, demarcate, and control their markets (Santos & Eisenhardt, 2009), how market information regimes constrain or expand available categories (Anand & Peterson, 2000), how rankings define what is valued in a certain market (Espeland & Sauder, 2007), how trade associations enable cohesion through field-level events (Mair & Hehenberger, 2013), or how NGOs can redefine market architecture and legitimate market actors (Mair, Martí, & Ventresca, 2012).

This perspective on cultural and institutional intermediation helps us put emphasis on important processes such as how the patterns of innovation are affected by the degree of intermediation, how the role of intermediaries changes across the different stages of market formation, whether highly mediated markets develop faster or slower than other markets, or to what extent intermediaries can buffer or reinforce institutional pressures.

System-building strategies

If we look at the social investment space in the UK in the last few years, BSC stands out as a major player. The first seed for its creation was planted by the Social Investment Task Force that took place in 2000: The task force concluded that more funding needed to be channeled to the social sector with the government playing a central role. However, it was not until the Commission on Unclaimed Assets in 2007 that talk about a "social investment bank" became more widespread. The recommendation of that commission—the creation of a "wholesaler of capital working through existing and new financial intermediaries" (Commission on Unclaimed Assets, 2007)—was taken by the government through the Dormant Bank and Building Society Accounts Act in 2008, and finally BSC started its operations as an independent organization in 2012. Its £600 million of funding come from those dormant bank accounts (£400 m) and from the major UK banks (£200 m).

BSC's mission, as identified on their corporate website, is "to help grow the social investment market" (BSC, 2015), both as an investor—supporting social investment intermediaries—and as a market champion—increasing awareness, promoting best practices, and sharing information. BSC has invested in many of the main social investment funds of the sector, including funds from Bridges Ventures, Big Issue Invest, Resonance, FSE Group, Social Investment Scotland, and Nesta impact investments, among others. It has also invested in crowdfunding platforms, in the Social Stock Exchange, or in developing the charity bond market via Investing for Good. As a market champion, it has established a Social Investment Research Council with other organizations, it has helped the government think about the most appropriate regulations for the market, it has developed a matrix for impact measurement that is being used by many actors in the sector, and it is always present in social investment events.

This activity has brought much praise, and also some criticism. As BSC's CEO Nick O'Donohoe wrote recently, "The good news [of being such a central organization] is, you get all of the attention. The bad news is, you get all of the attention" (O'Donohoe, 2015). Detractors say that BSC was designed with too many constraints, which limit their ability to address the needs of the social sector. As an interviewee from a trade association put it, "I have quite a lot of sympathy with BSC, it kind of has its hands tied behind its back, in the way that it's structured" (Interviewee #28). It is true that its funding has been slow in reaching frontline organizations, and that many of them need smaller amounts at cheaper interest rates compared to what BSC is able to offer. Despite these shortcomings, it seems clear that since 2012 BSC has played a main role in building the social investment ecosystem and defining what it looks like.

Although it is not rare to find this kind of system-building actor in other markets or fields (Mair et al., 2012; Morgan, 2008), BSC has certain characteristics—vast resources and close connections to the financial, public, and social sectors—that make it specially capable of doing it. Building systems is usually a collective effort, but some individuals and organizations can play special roles (Hughes, 1983) at different points in time. Sometimes researchers have highlighted the purposeful action of these actors in building new institutions, and have labeled them as institutional entrepreneurs (Battilana, Leca, & Boxenbaum, 2009; Maguire, Hardy, & Lawrence, 2004). However, the concept of system building puts more emphasis on coordination among the loosely coupled components of those emerging systems, which need different resources and leaderships at different stages (Hughes, 1983, 1987).

By studying how these market-building efforts have taken place in the social investment space, we can learn about the different strategies available for governments and other actors when they want to stimulate the creation or development of a certain market. Looking at BSC's experience, some of the issues to take into account are the flexibility of the organization, resources according to the size and stage of the market, strong ties to different sectors, wide political legitimacy (not seen as the project of one party), leveraging resources from other organizations, and the different forms of capital needed—not only financial but also social, human, cultural, and political.

The essence of an ecosystem is the connections among actors, but also its shared meanings, resources, norms, and practices. They are usually the result of different organizations pushing at once in different directions, especially in its early stages, but there are often actors who play a special role in making the system coalesce. The case of the UK social investment market prompts us to think about whether different types of organizations (public vs private, big vs small, new vs old) build systems in different ways, the range of available strategies for system building, the nature of these system builders (individuals, organizations, groups of organizations), and to what extent some parts of the system need to be in place before other parts are built.

Markets from interstitial spaces

The UK social investment market is an exemplar case of a market born at the intersection of three different sectors, in this case the social sector, the public sector, and the financial sector. Furthermore, we see organizations actively bringing in different kinds of resources—financial, social, human, and cultural capital—in order to build a new market.

For example, the Social Stock Exchange, a platform offering impact investment opportunities to investors, has attracted financial capital from the public sector through BSC and from the social sector through Panahpur Foundation's Venture Fund and the Joseph Rowntree Charitable Trust. Whilst these funds have been used to cover the operations at the Social Stock Exchange, the CDFA (Community Development Finance Association) has brought investment from different sources in order to distribute it to social enterprises and financially excluded individuals and organizations. They are managing a fund fueled by £30 million from the UK government's Regional Growth Fund and £30 million from two social banks. Similarly, the social investment fund manager Resonance has received funding from social sector agencies such as Esmée Fairbairn Foundation—and from the public sector through BSC and Nesta, organizations acting "at arm's length" from the government. Interestingly, Resonance also taps different sources of capital (individuals, foundations, public authorities) for the funds that it manages, which are focused on affordable housing in the UK.

Other organizations that have sourced financial capital from different sectors are Bridges Ventures (government, private investors, and foundations), social finance's first Social Impact Bond (17 different investors from different backgrounds), BSC (government and commercial banks), FSE Group (government and foundations), Investing for Good (government and foundations), and Nesta impact investments (government and Social Investors).

However, a market needs more than money to be developed. It needs actors making use of that funding, individuals with certain skills, regulation and norms of conduct, standards, relationships, information, and so on. As Bourdieu said, "it is in fact impossible to account for the structure and functioning of the social world unless one reintroduces capital in all its forms" (1986, p. 241). It is hence a worthy opportunity to learn about capital sources in diverse ways (financial, social, human, political) and in fact different forms of capital mix in a new field—to what impacts and how the origins of capital can influence the future development of the market.

One example is social capital, usually defined as "the goodwill available to individuals and groups" (Adler & Kwon, 2002) that comes from the benefits of bonding within a collective or bridging across networks. Intermediary organizations, because their activities lie at the intersection of different sectors and organizations, are especially suitable for bringing in social capital to a new market. For example, organizations like Resonance, ClearlySo, and social finance have their own networks of investors or business angels, to whom they present investment opportunities that are not available to the general public. Similarly, Bridges Ventures benefits from its close connections to the private equity and venture capital industries, while intermediaries like CAF Venturesome or Big Issue Invest have brought information and resources from the social sector thanks to the role of their parent organizations (CAF and Big Issue) in the world of charities.

Schumpeter (1942) said that entrepreneurship is about the recombination of existing resources to create new products and hence disrupting existing industries. This recombination activity, which is well acknowledged at the individual and organizational levels, can also take place in the birth of new markets and fields (Abernathy & Clark, 1985). As we know from the study of the early stages of market development, these nascent markets often borrow or are built from ideas and innovations in other adjacent fields (Clark, 1985).

The formation of a new market is hence a complex and multifaceted process. In the case of social investment, we have seen that organizations leverage different forms of capital from different sectors, so it is worth understanding the effects of this variety of resources in the subsequent features of the social investment market. Also analyzing whether the new activity is actually at the intersection of the different adjacent fields, or instead is closer to one field that provides most of the material resources and legitimacy, will help us understand current boundaries and characteristics of the market.

Interstitial spaces are especially fertile ground for innovation (Funari, 2014; Hargadon & Sutton, 1997), and therefore it is not surprising that they see the birth of new markets. Early activity in these contexts (in terms of the actors and resources involved) can explain much of the field's future development, so it is good to raise questions around the origin of resources (financial, human, social, cultural) in the early days of new markets, the influence of adjacent sectors in setting the standards of the new field, the characteristics of the different kinds of interstitial spaces (discursive, physical, relational, organizational, etc.), or what kinds of actors thrive in these interstitial spaces and which ones find more difficulties for survival or success.

Discussion

The purpose of this chapter has been to lay out a research agenda that stems from looking at the UK social investment market with the lens of the sociology of markets. Questions of how new markets and fields emerge are timely and relevant (Fligstein & McAdam, 2012; Padgett & Powell, 2012), especially when we go past economic theories of supply and demand and we focus on processes that involve the active role of networks, power, and culture: the production and diffusion of information and knowledge regimes (Anand & Peterson, 2000; Campbell & Pedersen, 2014), the development of a particular language (Grodal, 2007), the origins of innovation (Powell, Koput, & Smith-Doerr, 1996), agreements over certain standards and metrics (Espeland & Sauder, 2007), or the articulation of supply and demand (Geroski, 2003; Porac, Thomas, & Baden-Fuller, 1989; White, 1981).

The social investment market provides an exemplar context to study these issues. It has the characteristics of a nascent market (experimentation, ambiguity, contestation), but there is already a history of 15 years to look at what has happened so far. We have plenty of industry reports and other documents, and the pioneers of the field are still actively involved. It is driven by different logics (Nicholls, 2010) and sectors (public, social, financial), which increases its complexity, and therefore highlights the different mechanisms that take place in the process of market formation.

Our close observation of this market has enabled us to identify six themes that provide a fresh perspective on questions of market formation: the timeframe of experimentation and innovation; the relation between discourse and shifts in field-level logics; the templates for active government intervention; the institutional role of intermediary organizations; the strategies available for system builders; and the rise of interstitial communities as a locus of activity. These observations also give us some clues as to what methods and approaches to use when studying early stage markets.

First, they highlight the importance of looking at the origins and early moments of industries. Furthermore, when we focus on those periods of ferment, we need to use research methods that enable us to capture the variation that is present in the market at that point. For this reason, instead of using pre-established definitions of how the market is conceptualized, it is worth looking at the struggles over market boundaries that take place at those early stages (Santos & Eisenhardt, 2009). This way we will also be able to identify those plausible markets or niches that never took place because of the fights over meaning and resources that happened before a "dominant design" appeared.

Second, we have seen that actors cannot be analyzed independently. Interactions between them matter, as they all need to be aware of each other to make sense of what the market demands (White, 1981). This also implies putting special emphasis on interstitial spaces as contexts of fertile market activity, and on intermediaries as drivers of market formation.

Third, we need to acknowledge the ambiguity that characterizes these early markets. In this sense, although the institutional logics perspective (Thornton et al., 2012) is very useful to understand institutional pressures in stable markets or fields, it may be less so in contexts where the institutions are not settled yet. In these cases, the demands that we would otherwise assume are coming from certain logics are often mixed up, and market actors do not have a clear view on what pressures they need to respond to.

Finally, and more generally, we can learn about the complex processes by which new institutional contexts arise. Despite the central role of the government, of organizations like BSC, and of individuals such as Sir Ronald Cohen, we cannot tell the story of social investment as if one or some of them are the "institutional entrepreneurs" building the field from scratch. Instead of being "built," institutions are more likely to "arise" from the interactions and dynamics among a variety of actors and sectors. Predicting how these processes will wind up during a period of two or three decades is a difficult task, but understanding the mechanisms that have taken place in a specific context will help managers and policy makers design their organizations and institutions so that they can nudge and incubate new markets and fields in their desired direction.

Acknowledgments

We are grateful for comments from Silvia Dorado, Matthew Grimes, Suntae Kim, Alex Nicholls, and Tracy Thompson, as well as the editor Othmar Lehner, one anonymous reviewer, and the attendees to the Social and Sustainable Finance and Impact Investing Conference 2015. We also acknowledge financial support from the Skoll Centre for Social Entrepreneurship Small Grants Programme, University of Oxford, and a productive, congenial research stay at the Center for Philanthropy and Civil Society (PACS), Stanford University.

References

Abernathy, W., & Clark, K. (1985). Innovation—Mapping the winds of creative destruction. *Research Policy, 14*(1), 3–22. http://doi.org/10.1016/0048-7333(85)90021-6

Adler, P. S., & Kwon, S.-W. (2002). Social capital: Prospects for a new concept. *The Academy of Management Review, 27*(1), 17–40.

Allen, F., & Santomero, A. M. (1998). The theory of financial intermediation. *Journal of Banking & Finance, 21*(11–12), 1461–1485. http://doi.org/10.1016/S0378-4266(97)00032-0

Anand, N., & Peterson, R. A. (2000). When market information constitutes fields: Sensemaking of markets in the commercial music industry. *Organization Science, 11*(3), 270–284.

Bank of England. (2003). *The financing of social enterprises.* London: Bank of England Domestic Finance Division.

Battilana, J., Leca, B., & Boxenbaum, E. (2009). How actors change institutions: Towards a theory of institutional entrepreneurship. *The Academy of Management Annals, 3*(1), 65–107.

Beckert, J. (2009). The social order of markets. *Theory and Society, 38*(3), 245–269.

Biggart, N. W., & Delbridge, R. (2004). Systems of exchange. *Academy of Management Review, 29*(1), 28–49.

Big Society Capital (BSC). (2015). *What we do: Making social investment available to charities & social enterprises.* Retrieved August 24, 2015, from http://www.bigsocietycapital.com/about-big-society-capital

Brown, A., & Swersky, A. (2012). *The first billion: A forecast of social investment demand.* London: Boston Consulting Group/Big Society Capital.

Bourdieu, P. (1986). The forms of capital. In J. G. Richardson (Ed.), *Handbook of theory and research for the sociology of education* (pp. 241–258). New York: Greenwood Press.

Burt, R. (1992). *Structural holes: The social structure of competition.* Cambridge, MA: Harvard University Press.

Cabinet Office UK. (2011). *Growing the social investment market: A vision and a strategy.* London: Cabinet Office UK.

Campbell, J. L. (2002). Ideas, politics, and public policy. *Annual Review of Sociology, 28*(1), 21–38.

Campbell, J. L., & Pedersen, O. K. (2014). *The national origins of policy ideas: Knowledge regimes in the United States, France, Germany, and Denmark.* Princeton, NJ: Princeton University Press.

Casasnovas, G. (forthcoming). *How markets form: Ambiguity and intermediation in the early moments of the UK social investment market.* Doctoral thesis University of Oxford.

Casasnovas, G., & Ventresca, M. (2015). Building a robust social investment market. *Stanford Social Innovation Review.* Retrieved March 10, 2016, from http://www.ssireview.org/blog/entry/building_a_robust_social_investment_market

City of London. (2013). *Growing the social investment market: Landscape and economic impact.* London: City of London.

Clark, K. B. (1985). The interaction of design hierarchies and market concepts in technological evolution. *Research Policy, 14*(5), 235–251.

ClearlySo. (2011, July). *Investor perspectives on social enterprise financing.* Report prepared for the City of London Corporation, City Bridge Trust, and the Big Lottery Fund, London.

Commission on Unclaimed Assets (CUA). (2007, March). *The Social Investment Bank: Its organisation and role in driving development of the third sector.* London: CUA.

DiMaggio, P. J., & Powell, W. W. (1983). The iron cage revisited: Institutional isomorphism and collective rationality in organizational fields. *American Sociological Review, 48*(2), 147–160.

Espeland, W. N., & Sauder, M. (2007). Rankings and reactivity: How public measures recreate social worlds. *American Journal of Sociology, 113*(1), 1–40.

Fernandez, R. M., & Gould, R. V. (1994). A dilemma of state power: Brokerage and influence in the national health policy domain. *American Journal of Sociology, 99*(6), 1455–1491.

Fligstein, N. (1996). Markets as politics: A political-cultural approach to market institutions. *American Sociological Review, 61*(4), 656–673.

Fligstein, N. (2001). *The architecture of markets: An economic sociology of twenty-first-century capitalist societies.* Princeton, NJ: Princeton University Press.

Fligstein, N., & McAdam, D. (2012). *A theory of fields.* New York: Oxford University Press.

Fourcade, M. (2007). Theories of markets and theories of society. *American Behavioral Scientist, 50*(8), 1015–1034.

Furnari, S. (2014). Interstitial spaces: Microinteraction settings and the genesis of new practices between institutional fields. *Academy of Management Review, 39*(4), 439–462.

Geroski, P. (2003). *The evolution of new markets.* Oxford and New York: Oxford University Press.

Global Impact Investing Network (GIIN). (2015). *About impact investing.* Retrieved August 24, 2015, from http://www.thegiin.org/cgi-bin/iowa/home/index.html

Granovetter, M. (1985). Economic action and social structure: The problem of embeddedness. *American Journal of Sociology, 91*(3), 481–510.

Greenwood, R., Raynard, M., Kodeih, F., Micelotta, E. R., & Lounsbury, M. (2011). Institutional complexity and organizational responses. *Academy of Management Annals, 5*(1), 317–371.

Grodal, S. (2007). *The emergence of a new organizational field—Labels, meaning and emotions in nanotechnology* (Unpublished dissertation). Stanford University, Stanford, CA.

Gurley, J. G., & Shaw, E. S. (1960). *Money in a theory of finance.* Washington, DC: Brookings Institution.

Hajek, F., Ventresca, M. J., Scriven, J., & Castro, A. (2011). Regime-building for REDD+: Evidence from a cluster of local initiatives in south-eastern Peru. *Governing and Implementing REDD+, 14*(2), 201–215.

Hargadon, A., & Sutton, R. I. (1997). Technology brokering and innovation in a product development firm. *Administrative Science Quarterly, 42*(4), 716–749.

Haveman, H. A., & Rao, H. (1997). Structuring a theory of moral sentiments: Institutional and organizational coevolution in the early thrift industry. *American Journal of Sociology, 102*(6), 1606.

Hirsch, P., Michaels, S., & Friedman, R. (1987). "Dirty hands" versus "clean models." *Theory and Society, 16*(3), 317–336.

Hughes, T. (1983). *Networks of power: Electrification in Western society, 1880–1930.* Baltimore: Johns Hopkins University Press.

Hughes, T. (1987). The evolution of large technological systems. In W. E. Bijker, T. P. Hughes, & T. Pinch (Eds.), *The social construction of technological systems: New directions in the sociology and history of technology* (pp. 51–82). Cambridge, MA: MIT Press.

Lyon, F., & Sepulveda, L. (2009). Mapping social enterprises: Past approaches, challenges and future directions. *Social Enterprise Journal, 5*(1), 83–94.

Maguire, S., Hardy, C., & Lawrence, T. B. (2004). Institutional entrepreneurship in emerging fields: HIV/AIDS treatment advocacy in Canada. *Academy of Management Journal, 47*(5), 657–679.

Mair, J., & Hehenberger, L. (2013). Front stage and back stage convening: The transition from opposition to mutualistic co-existence in organizational philanthropy. *Academy of Management Journal.* doi:amj.2012.0305

Mair, J., Martí, I., & Ventresca, M. J. (2012). Building inclusive markets in rural Bangladesh: How intermediaries work institutional voids. *Academy of Management Journal, 55*(4), 819–850.

Morgan, G. (2008). Market formation and governance in international financial markets: The case of OTC derivatives. *Human Relations, 61*(5), 637–660.

Munir, K. A. (2005). The social construction of events: A study of institutional change in the photographic field. *Organization Studies, 26*(1), 93–112.

Nicholls, A. (2010). The institutionalization of social investment: The interplay of investment logics and investor rationalities. *Journal of Social Entrepreneurship, 1*(1), 70–100.

O'Donohoe, N. (2015). *Big Society Capital's blog: Brothers and sisters—Access launches.* Retrieved March 10, 2016, from http://www.bigsocietycapital.com/blog/brothers-and-sisters-access-launches

Padgett, J. F., & Powell, W. W. (2012). *The emergence of organizations and markets.* Princeton, NJ: Princeton University Press.

Porac, J. F., Thomas, H., & Baden-Fuller, C. (1989). Competitive groups as cognitive communities: The case of Scottish knitwear manufacturers. *Journal of Management Studies, 26*(4), 397–416.

Powell, W. W., Koput, K. W., & Smith-Doerr, L. (1996). Interorganizational collaboration and the locus of innovation: Networks of learning in biotechnology. *Administrative Science Quarterly, 41*(1), 116–145.

Reay, T., & Hinings, C. R. (Bob). (2005). The recomposition of an organizational field: Health care in Alberta. *Organization Studies, 26*(3), 351–384.

Santos, F. M., & Eisenhardt, K. M. (2009). Constructing markets and shaping boundaries: Entrepreneurial power in nascent fields. *Academy of Management Journal, 52*(4), 643–671.

Schumpeter, J. A. (1942). *Capitalism, socialism and democracy.* New York: Harper & Brothers.

Sepulveda, L. (2014). Social enterprise—A new phenomenon in the field of economic and social welfare? *Social Policy & Administration.* doi:10.1111/spol.12106

Shanmugalingam, C., Graham, J., Tucker, S., & Mulgan, G. (2011). *Growing social ventures—The role of intermediaries and investors: Who they are, what they do, and what they could become.* NESTA/The Young Foundation.

Skocpol, T. (1985). Bringing the state back in: Strategies of analysis in current research. In P. Evans, D. Rueschemeyer, & T. Skocpol (Eds.), *Bringing the state back in.* Cambridge: Cambridge University Press.

Stinchcombe, A. L. (2001). *When formality works: Authority and abstraction in law and organizations.* Chicago, IL: University of Chicago Press.

The Alternative Commission on social investment. (2015). *Making social investment more social.* Retrieved August 24, 2015, from http://socinvalternativecommission.org.uk/

Thornton, P. H. (2004). *Markets from culture: Institutional logics and organizational decisions in higher education publishing.* Stanford, CA: Stanford University Press.

Thornton, P. H., Ocasio, W., & Lounsbury, M. (2012). *The institutional logics perspective: A new approach to culture, structure, and process.* Oxford: Oxford University Press.

Tushman, M. L., & Anderson, P. (1986). Technological discontinuities and organizational environments. *Administrative Science Quarterly, 31*(3), 439–465.

Utterback, J. M., & Abernathy, W. J. (1975). A dynamic model of process and product innovation. *Omega, 3*(6), 639–656.

White, H. C. (1981). Where do markets come from? *American Journal of Sociology, 87*(3), 517–547.

Yanelle, M.-O. (1989). The strategic analysis of intermediation. *European Economic Review, 33*(2–3), 294–301.

Zucker, L. G. (1986). Production of trust: Institutional sources of economic structure, 1840–1920. *Research in Organizational Behavior, 8*, 53–111.

Appendix A

List of interviews

#	*Date*	*Type of interview*	*Type of organization*	*Role of interviewee*	*Country*
1	Dec-12	Exploratory	Social Inv. Fund Manager	Former Associate	UK
2	Dec-12	Exploratory	Social Inv. Fund Manager	CEO	UK
3	Feb-14	Exploratory	Media	Social Entrepreneur	USA
4	Feb-14	Exploratory	Investor	Founder	UK
5	Apr-14	Exploratory	Advisor	CEO	UK
6	Apr-14	In-Depth	Wholesale Bank	Investment Associate	UK
7	May-14	Exploratory	Advisor	Analyst	UK
8	May-14	In-Depth	Social Inv. Fund Manager	Partner	UK
9	May-14	In-Depth	Social Inv. Fund Manager	CEO	UK
10	May-14	In-Depth	Advisor	Capital Raising	UK
11	May-14	In-Depth	Advisor	CEO	USA
12	May-14	In-Depth	Advisor	Director	UK
13	Jun-14	In-Depth	Investor	Investment Manager	UK
14	Jun-14	In-Depth	Social Inv. Fund Manager	CEO	UK
15	Jun-14	In-Depth	Industry Association	CEO	UK
16	Jun-14	In-Depth	Platform	Founder	UK
17	Jun-14	In-Depth	Platform	Founder	UK
18	Sep-14	In-Depth	Industry Association	Project Manager	USA
19	Sep-14	In-Depth	Government	Social Inv. Team	UK
20	Oct-14	In-Depth	Industry Association	Project Manager	USA
21	Nov-14	In-Depth	Social Enterprise	Founder and CEO	UK
22	Dec-14	In-Depth	Research Org.	Founder	UK
23	Dec-14	In-Depth	Government	Director	UK
24	Dec-14	In-Depth	Social Enterprise	Founder and CEO	UK
25	Mar-15	In-Depth	Social Inv. Fund Manager	Investment Executive	UK
26	Mar-15	In-Depth	Foundation	Investment Associate	UK
27	Mar-15	In-Depth	Social Inv. Fund Manager	Investment Director	UK
28	Mar-15	In-Depth	Industry Association	Deputy CEO	UK
29	Mar-15	In-Depth	Foundation	Director of Policy and Strategy	UK
30	Mar-15	In-Depth	Social Inv. Fund Manager	Director of Business Development	UK
31	Mar-15	In-Depth	Social Ent. Incubator	Research and Evaluation Manager	UK
32	Mar-15	In-Depth	Social Inv. Fund Manager	CEO	UK
33	Apr-15	In-Depth	Social Inv. Fund Manager	CEO	UK
34	Apr-15	In-Depth	Legal Advisor	Partner	UK
35	Apr-15	In-Depth	Legal Advisor	Partner	UK

43

REGIONAL IMPACT INVESTING FOR INSTITUTIONAL INVESTORS

The Bay Area Impact Investing Initiative

Lauryn Agnew

The San Francisco Bay Area is a robust, diversified regional economy, recently ranked as the nineteenth largest in the world (Randolph, 2012). We are a center of innovation, academia, medicine, finance, and scenic beauty. However, we are also in need of more investments in our community. We know our infrastructure is crumbling. Our housing stock is inadequate to meet the needs of our residents across all economic levels. Transportation is more problematic each year. We must address water, power, and technology infrastructure upgrades for our region to thrive. We need to invest more in our own backyard if we want to preserve our leadership positions and maintain a superior quality of life for everyone in the Bay Area. At the same time, the Bay Area is awash in money. We can channel some of those assets to local investments to promote sustainable and resilient prosperity in the Bay Area.

Background on Impact Investing

Traditionally, Socially Responsible Investing (SRI) strategies were based on actively excluding the stocks of companies whose products or activities were contrary to an organization's mission or beliefs. These types of SRI strategies are primarily limited to public equities. However, the field has expanded considerably over the last 20 years and now accounts for over 10 percent of global institutional equity assets (US SIF, 2014). This includes a large number of options and different screening strategies or investment foci (e.g., faith-based issues or green funds).

Impact Investing is a proactive, intentional strategy and—like SRI, more recently referred to as Sustainable and Responsible Investing—seeks to find investments that offer both a strong financial return and a positive social and/or environmental impact or mission alignment. (Many investors use "SRI" and "Impact Investing" synonymously; others often associate Impact Investing primarily with private investments.) Impact Investing strategies can be implemented across all asset classes in a variety of investment vehicles, with varying degrees of liquidity, performance expectations, risk, and impact. Equity investors that seek impact can identify relevant Environmental, Social, and Governance (ESG) factors for research and analysis to build portfolios of companies that are aligned with a particular mission or goal. Equity investors can also have an impact on corporate behavior through direct engagement, shareholder activism, and proxy voting. Fixed income investors can identify impact more directly than equity investors, particularly through the community development and affordable housing bond markets, which are some of the earliest, largest, and most successful examples of Impact Investing. Long-term investments in infrastructure would have alignment with many missions for healthy and diverse communities and economic development. Real estate and private equity/venture capital can have some of the greatest impact-creating companies and jobs through direct investment of private equity and private debt, but often with less liquidity and transparency. Global Impact Investment opportunities in all asset classes can have a significant impact on the "bottom of the pyramid," the poorest and most vulnerable in our world, while also delivering strong financial returns, as shown by the success of micro-finance and international micro-lending.

Regional Impact Investments for place-based missions can be effective as well as prudent and provide an opportunity to track impact locally. Taking a whole portfolio approach, as directed by ERISA, UPMIFA, and prudent investor standards, fiduciaries of institutional assets can build impact into any or all parts of a portfolio with the appropriate intention, due diligence, and oversight, as this chapter will show. A regional Impact Investing intermediary can be a clearinghouse for financial partnerships that cut across silos and connects capital with opportunity.

Fiduciary duty

For many reasons, most fiduciaries of institutional funds (public-defined benefit plans, endowment funds, and quasi private/public foundations) have been reluctant to adopt Impact Investing, Socially and Sustainably Responsible Investing, or ESG factors in their investment policies and philosophies. The main objection to these investing practices revolves around the belief that these strategies will reduce the investor's overall financial performance and, in so doing, would be contrary to one's fiduciary duty to maximize (risk-adjusted) returns. Other objections include the perceptions that there are costly due diligence issues, confusing investment structures, lack of track records and expertise in the area, and impact-tracking challenges. On the other hand, one can argue that ESG factors ought to be critical to the investment processes and policies of fiduciaries of long-term, sustainable intergenerational asset pools (Johnson, 2014). This research study will implement due diligence processes with the expectation of using traditional market benchmarks in each asset class and will seek managers in each asset class who have a competitive expected return when compared to traditional investment opportunities and benchmarks.

Building the Bay Area Impact Investing Initiative portfolios

In designing model asset class portfolios and using other financial tools to mitigate a variety of risks, we can identify investment opportunities that meet both financial and impact goals. We understand that each asset class portfolio has its own risk, return, liquidity, and impact profile, as shown in Figure 43.1.

Our investment beliefs are reflected as criteria for developing the Bay Area Impact Investing Initiative (BAIII) model portfolios:

- Multi-manager structures can reduce specific manager risk and style risk, and each manager would be expected to have institutional experience and proven track records.
- Collaborating with other investors for many communal investments can reduce risks that come with single choice investments. Size and scale can help diversification and fee negotiation.

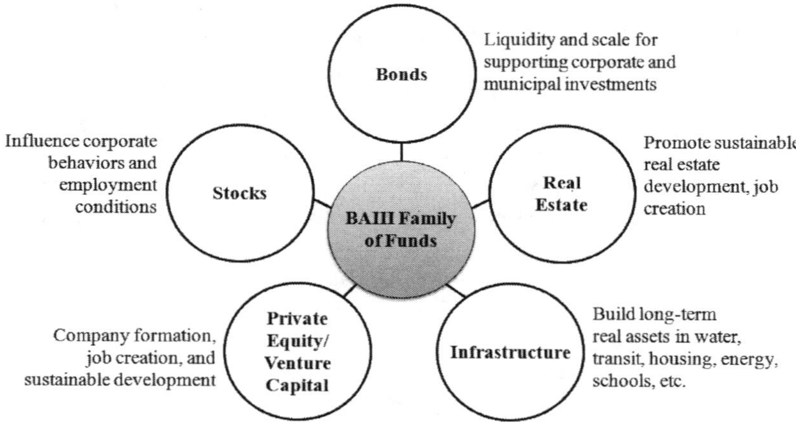

Figure 43.1 Intentional impact across asset classes

- Centralized and shared due diligence and monitoring is more efficient and cost-effective for small allocations than doing the research separately for many small investments.
- Collective and coordinated investments are likely to have more impact and voice than single-sourced smaller investments.
- Geographic focus and ESG criteria can be included in the investment process so long as traditional fiduciary standards are upheld (that the risk and reward expectations between a traditional investment opportunity and one that also includes some impact would be economically indistinguishable).
- Impact is unique to each asset class and can be tracked and disclosed.

Each of the five asset class model portfolios would engage a mission-aligned Community Development Financial Institution (CDFI) or community bank and three to four registered investment advisory firms. Each of the investment advisory firms will have demonstrated their investment strategies to have qualified people, strong investment processes, evidence of competitive financial performance against standard and traditional institutional portfolios and benchmarks, and have exhibited some positive local impact.

The BAIII multi-manager public equity portfolio is modeled using three investment strategies in addition to the CDFI's cash position: the original research initiated at the United Way of the Bay Area (Agnew, 2012), which is a custom-enhanced index-like portfolio aligned with a mission to reduce poverty in the Bay Area; an active ESG-integrated stock picking approach; and a broad, market-based index fund with active corporate engagement.

The BAIII multi-manager fixed income portfolio models four fixed income management firms: the CRA-qualified fixed income fund of a CDFI focusing primarily in government-related housing subsectors; a building and jobs investment fund; an active research strategy in sustainable bonds; and a direct lender to small and medium-sized companies.

The BAIII multi-manager real estate model portfolio would invest in a variety of complementary real estate managers and strategies: a Bay Area-based CDFI real estate lender, a registered investment advisor with a liquid REIT strategy with ESG integration, and real estate investment managers who are building affordable housing and mixed-use properties in the Bay Area, creating jobs, and using sustainable environmental practices in building processes while delivering strong investment returns.

The BAIII multi-manager private investment model portfolio would expect to provide a broad approach to targeted private investments for new business formation, growth, and job creation through the market and business cycle: short-term loans through the community bank and green bond fund, early-stage funding and mentoring, and private equity and/or debt financing using experienced private equity firms that are specialized in double bottom-line investing locally for many years. Access to funds and their liquidity is limited in private equity, with lock-up periods usually longer than 10 years. Returns can be elusive in the early years, as the investments take time to develop profitability and achieve some exit such as an IPO or acquisition, yet those returns can be significant.

The BAIII infrastructure model portfolio would consider energy development and distribution, including renewable energies and energy efficiency improvements, water, telecommunications and technology, roads and other sources of transit, and housing. Infrastructure is often funded through public–private partnerships, using complex capital stacks that can combine private capital, public funds and subsidies, taxes and fees, low-interest-rate loans, risk capital, and grant capital. BAIII has identified several opportunities around the Bay Area in infrastructure or clean/green technology funds, projects needing senior capital in project finance relationships, and other investors with whom we could partner to fund infrastructure projects through public–private partnerships.

BAIII multi-manager family of funds

This research has modeled five multi-manager funds, where we have confidence in the structures and investment advisors to be a reasonable prudent institutional investment, *and* we can have an ancillary benefit for our local economy. The funds and the managers' details are included at the end of this chapter.

In Figure 43.2 we illustrate the BAIII ecosystem. Like-minded, regional institutional asset owners would agree to collaborate to have a larger voice together, a more positive impact on the regional economy and environment, and address fiduciary and community needs and requirements, presuming the same risk and return profiles as traditional investments. In most cases, a small 1 percent of a portfolio would have very little impact, for any investor in any asset class. But in the Bay Area, with its hundreds of millions of dollars of wealth pools, combining a small 1 percent slice of all the institutional assets (community foundations, endowments, family foundations, corporate and public retirement funds, etc.) could exceed $1 billion. With this amount we can move the needle on bringing more Impact Investing dollars to reinvigorate our communities.

As Figure 43.2 shows, the BAIII intermediary would consolidate the 1 percent slices, and allocate the dollars to the designated asset class funds. Investors could choose the fund or combination of funds that meet their investment policies and goals. Small funds may prefer the liquidity offered from the stock and bond portfolios. Long-term investors and larger institutions may choose an allocation to the more illiquid assets like real estate, infrastructure, and private equity. Investors can choose to allocate their 1 percent by their own overall portfolio asset allocation target, like 60 percent stocks/40 percent bonds, or equal weight across all five funds for a balanced 20 percent each weighting, or any combination suitable to the investor. Fiduciaries understand the risk, return, and liquidity characteristics of each asset class and how each can contribute to the success of their overall portfolio. Allocating to a geographically (but not exclusively) focused fund may seem to be adding an additional level of risk. The BAIII strategies, at a 1 percent allocation, would not be a material change in the geographic concentration of a global portfolio. By way of comparison, 19 percent of the Russell 3000 index is headquartered

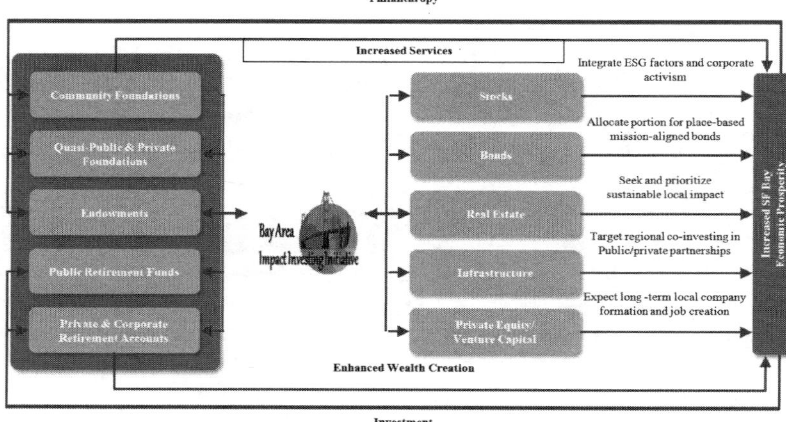

Figure 43.2 BAIII ecosystem: Collaborate with 1 percent

in the San Francisco Bay Area (Bloomberg). The 1 percent additional intentional allocation, not all of which need be in any one asset class, is not likely to increase the overall risk profile of the underlying global portfolio.

Each of the five asset classes as seen in Figure 43.2 represent the pooled funds, which would be distributed among the appropriate managers in each fund. Some placements would depend on who is open for new investments at any given period. Different flows into different asset classes can also affect the return patterns. Some benchmarks are not investable, but serve as market indicators.

Risk mitigators: A de-risking toolkit

In a recent article by Bridges Ventures/B of A Merrill Lynch, "Shifting the Lens: A De-risking Toolkit for Impact Investment," the various risks that come with financial and Impact Investments were discussed and "unpacked" (Bridges Ventures, 2014). Once these risks are analyzed, risk mitigators can be identified so that the expectations of risks and returns can be clarified and access to Impact Investments can be understood.

In their De-risking Toolkit framework and through the best practices we already use as institutional investors, we can address five broad risks: capital loss risk, unquantifiable risk, transaction cost risk, exit risk, and impact risk. The BAIII fund structures aim to incorporate as many de-risking tools as possible and would track the impacts unique to each asset class.

Capital (loss) risk can be mitigated by proper structuring of the portfolios so that the managed BAIII fund in each asset class would be designed to closely follow its benchmark and have no more inherent risk to a capital investment loss than the market portfolio or benchmark. In the BAIII approach for institutional investors, the relative performance to a benchmark, particularly underperforming that benchmark, is the more common risk than absolute loss of capital. Thus, the portfolios are designed for market-like risk and returns in each asset class using registered investment advisors with complementary but different strategies in their specialty. Liquidity risk, or exit risk, also must align with the liquidity parameters of each asset class. Providing standard liquidity expectations would enable fair comparison to similar choices, with or without intentional impact. Stocks and bonds are liquid; real estate, private equity, and infrastructure are less so.

In addition, there is an unquantifiable risk, "what we don't know we don't know," which can be addressed in Impact Investing with comprehensive investment manager due diligence, and standard institutional investors risk mitigation tools. We seek investment managers with the appropriate experience, background, and track records, who can demonstrate expertise in the areas we target. The managers identified for the BAIII strategies have a large institutional presence and can also customize portfolios. These specialists often provide ongoing technical assistance to their investees, particularly in the long-term investments like real estate, infrastructure, and private equity, as well as to the funds' intermediaries regarding distribution and placement systems in place.

Transaction costs are one risk cited by many investors who do not have the staff for undertaking the specialized due diligence and managing the collaborative efforts needed to structure some of these special local Impact Investments. Often there is a mismatch between the size of the investment desired, the capital interested in investment, and the requirements of diversification. The BAIII intermediary would provide the due diligence (as evidenced by the model portfolios), create the financial structures in each asset class that could attract capital from many sources, redistribute that capital to a broad number of investment opportunities across all asset classes, and continuously monitor the financial and impact metrics. This collective investing, or bundling, can be more cost efficient with larger assets. Costs and fees could be driven down and scale could be achieved through well-crafted designs and collaboration.

As Impact Investors, we will work to identify and measure impact in terms of outputs and outcomes over what sometimes are long periods of time. Impact measurement is evolving. Several initiatives, like IRIS (Impact Reporting & Investment Standards), a project of the GIIN (Global Impact Investing Network), are working on metrics that we can use across many categories and industries. Integrating ESG factors into the investment process makes sense even if the outputs or outcomes are sometimes difficult to quantify. Understanding how investment management firms incorporate risk assessments relating to ESG factors is important for controlling and mitigating future costs related to those risks. For our purposes, the BAIII would work to identify and share any new positive ancillary impacts from our investments that add to sustainable prosperity for the San Francisco Bay Area. One non-profit CDFI has developed an impact calculator which we could use in our later research into public–private partnerships—The Low Income Investment Fund's impact calculator: http://www.liifund.org/calculator

Give local! Buy local! Eat local! The BAIII theme: What about invest local?!

With the enormous pools of wealth in the Bay Area (creating millionaires by the minute), and the wealth we have accumulated over the past few decades in our unique region, we could intentionally invest in our own backyard to protect, preserve, strategically optimize, and build our future. Collectively, a small portion (1–2 percent) of our trusts, retirement plans, savings accounts, estates, foundations, and endowments of our portfolios could have tremendous impact when combined and invested locally.

This chapter illustrates examples of prudent portfolios in real estate, infrastructure, and private capital, as well as model equity and fixed income funds, all with an intentional positive impact on the San Francisco Bay Area and its sustainable economic prosperity.

Using the BAIII asset class portfolios as building blocks, an investor can build a unique investment plan according to its goals for return, risk, and impact. For example, a conservative (risk-averse) investor might seek a low volatility combination made of the bond, real estate, and infrastructure portfolios, which represent the more stable, income-oriented, capital preservation-oriented strategies. A moderately risky portfolio could be a combination of all five asset classes in a unique asset allocation (such as 40 percent equity, 30 percent fixed income, 10 percent real estate, 10 percent infrastructure, and 10 percent private equity, or a fixed mix of 20 percent each, for example). A more risk-tolerant investor with a goal of higher returns could build a strategy dominated by the public equity and private equity portfolios.

Similarly, an investor who seeks housing as an impact focus could concentrate their Impact Investing in the real estate, bond, and infrastructure portfolios. A different investor, whose impact goals center on job creation, would overweight public and private equity as job creators and could also include the real estate and infrastructure investments that create jobs.

Extremely risk-averse and high Impact Investors could invest in a short-term investment fund using a diversified group of select CDFIs and community banks that would provide stable, positive returns through community loans to non-profits and small businesses and participate in developing financing for public–private partnerships. A "Community Short-Term Investment" fund using the various CDFIs we have included in our asset class portfolios would provide a range of impact outcomes through their different missions at a very low risk.

The public–private partnership and the complex capital stack

When redevelopment agencies were active in California, public agencies routinely arranged community development financing for everyday impact/community improvement goals. Through BAIII, we create a replacement for the redevelopment agency's financing role in the form of a regional Impact Investing intermediary. We can build a financial intermediary that can leverage the public and private resources of the region and develop investable opportunities to address housing, transit and mobility, and job creation and resiliency in our communities.

The Regional Impact Investing Intermediary would act as a regional clearinghouse. The intermediary, as an asset manager for these fiduciary (market return) assets, would be in position to catalog the various capital sources in its region, following along the inventory developed by the California Financial Opportunities Roundtable (2012). The recent work of the California Economic Summit (http://www.caeconomy.org) has suggested that access to capital across California's various and unique regions is a challenge, which represents opportunity. Each region has a unique set of resources as well as needs. The Bay Area's resources and needs will be vastly different from those of more rural regions, like Northern California or the Inland Empire. Developing a regional map of the financial resources would enable change makers on the ground to align with capital that can catalyze that change. A financial navigator tool could be created to align mission with assets, investors with investable opportunities, and achieve more diversification within a region and more collective impact. The regional clearinghouse can work with the asset owners and develop partnerships for investing in financial vehicles that create impact and financial returns. Some investors also have philanthropic goals where grants, Mission-Related Investments (MRIs) and Program-Related Investments (PRIs) can be partnered to leverage public and community development dollars, as Figure 43.3 shows.

Bringing many types of capital to the regional table could result in faster implementation of impact ideas and goals. A few examples are presented below.

Social Impact Bonds (SIBs) are a new tool for regional players to advance the financing for a common social goal that has (perhaps) more social than financial return. Not a true bond, this form of pay-for-success (PFS) contract would arrange for private funding to support a program or intervention that would improve societal outcomes in the future. Public health, inmate recidivism, and early childhood education are areas where PFS contracts have been tested. Over time, they are expected to reduce future costs to society by establishing better programs with higher, long-term

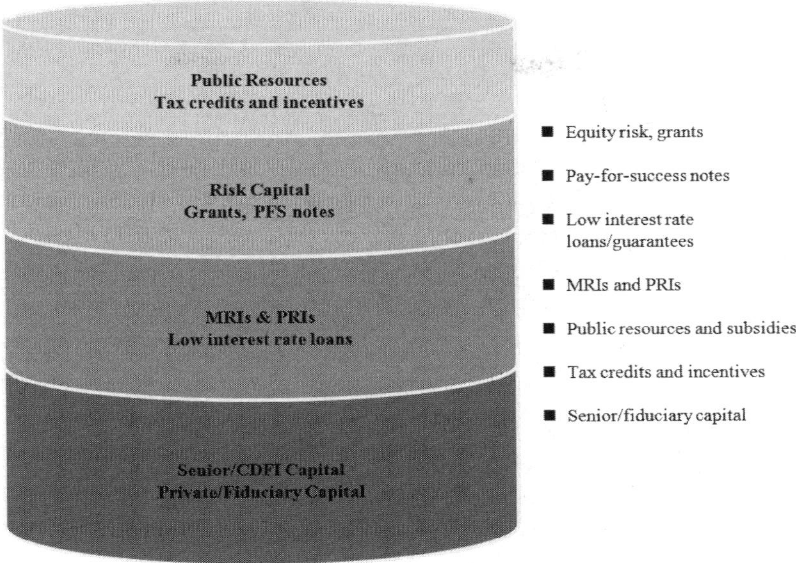

Figure 43.3 Getting out of silos and into public–private partnerships

success rates, resulting in lower future expenses. For example, early childhood education—pre-school—has been targeted for PFS contracts because it can be shown to be effective at cutting future costs dramatically: $1 invested in pre-school provides up to an estimated $7 return of future cost savings by reducing the need for special education services, lower juvenile delinquency rates, lower future incarceration and criminal costs, better graduation rates, and better long-term employment opportunities (Heckman, 2012). Similarly, public health intervention programs are ripe for PFS contracts: early intervention at the family and community level for asthma or diabetes can show significant future savings for public health providers with limited resources. Keeping children out of the emergency room with better asthma management and intervention can save thousands of dollars per visit per child (Hernandez & Genser, 2014).

A regional Impact Investing intermediary is also positioned to serve its region's unique employment needs. Understanding the members of the community, including small, medium, and large businesses and the skills they seek in their employees, can be a starting point for developing regional education-to-employment programs. Regionally, industries are often clustered and their employment needs can result in a precise plan for training and placing employees with specific skills as determined by the marketplace. One attractive Impact Investment could be a public–private partnership that aligns regional resources to develop training, education, certification, and placement programs unique to the needs of the employers in the area. In the Bay Area we see many jobs unfilled for lack of proper training and placement. A model is being created in the Bay Area with industry associations, corporations, and community colleges for developing custom curricula for many of California's employment needs and gaps.

It remains to be determined what the structure of a regional Impact Investing intermediary would be. It could be a non-profit developed for a specific purpose, like the Bay Area Transit Oriented Affordable Housing Development fund (TOAHD; http://www.bayareatod.org). Alternatively, it could be a public–private partnership that leverages the resources of the public agencies, private capital, and philanthropic organizations. As an asset manager, it could be a revenue generator, financed by grants, early-stage private capital, or even Social Impact "Bonds" whose potential return could be based on profitability and success metrics. The early investors and participants will influence the structure and ownership of the intermediary, subject to financial regulations and public impact goals.

The BAIII can evolve further with the contributions of various partners around the Bay Area. We can catalyze significant assets to work for the benefit of our communities, our environment, and our people while we earn strong returns on our investments.

The BAIII model portfolios

Table 43.1 and the following discussions on each asset class portfolio illustrate the variety of investment strategies we uncovered that complement each other within our model portfolios and are expected to deliver strong financial returns and local environmental or social impact. This list is not a recommendation for investment or a guarantee of any future returns. The managers listed here are believed to be effective examples of institutional investment management firms who can execute their investment strategy as mandated and have a Bay Area presence. Further information can be found on each firm's website.

Table 43.1 Model portfolios' manager rosters

BAIII model funds managers	*Possible BAIII structure*	*Investment style or strategy*	*Benchmark and return expectations*	*Impact*	*Risk/fees*
BAIII Public Equity					
New Resource Bank Aperio Group HIP 100 BlackRock R3000	Mutual fund, daily liquidity	Deposits/loans Enhanced, ESG index, active and passive	Track or exceed Russell 3000	Proxy votes: employment conditions, corporate engagement	Volatile asset class
BAIII Fixed Income					
Community Capital Management AFL-CIO Housing Investment Trust Breckinridge Cap White Oak Global	Mutual fund, daily liquidity	Regional and specialty bonds, direct lending, housing bonds	Track or exceed Barclays Agg	Financing, scale, patient capital	Geographic focus, community-oriented lending
BAIII Real Estate					
NorCal Community Loan Fund American Realty HIP Investor REIT Gerding Edlen	REIT/ co-mingled trust	Sustainable real estate lending and development	Current income plus appreciation	Sustainable building, affordable housing	Possibly less liquid, quarterly liquidity?
BAIII Infrastructure					
The Bay Area TOAHD The California I-Bank Mosaic Solar Other candidates	Public–private partnerships + projects	Transit, power energy, IT, water, housing	Long-term income, inflation hedge	Jobs, transit, community development, environmental solutions	Long-term lock-up

BAIII Private Equity					
Community Bank of the Bay: BAGF Bay Area Council Equity Fund 3 Pacific Community Ventures SAIL DBL Investors	Limited partnership Long-term lock-up	Venture capital, TA, innovative technologies, green + small business loans	High return potential, long-term lock-up	Company + job formation in LMI communities	Higher fee, illiquid

BAIII multi-manager public equity model portfolio

The public equity space has often been the largest asset class in institutional portfolios. It provides investors with liquidity, growth (inflation protection), and transparency in pricing. Public equities may be less efficient at being measured for direct impact, but because we as shareholders get to *vote* for our proxies, shareholder activism can be a powerful force for change in corporate behavior. Many large shareholders, like CalPERS (California Public Employees Retirement System), participate in shareholder activism and direct corporate engagement: voting proxies, submitting resolutions, and working with management for long-term positive change and sustainable shareholder value (http://www.calpers.ca.gov).

The BAIII multi-manager public equity portfolio is modeled using three complementary strategies (a custom-enhanced index-like portfolio, an active ESG-integrated strategy and a passive index fund with corporate engagement) and a cash position at a local, publicly held community bank. The custom investment strategy was developed in the original equity portfolio research initiated at the United Way of the Bay Area (UWBA) and published by the Federal Reserve Bank of San Francisco: "Impact Investing for Small, Place-Based Fiduciaries: The Research Study Initiated by the United Way of the Bay Area" (Agnew, 2012). The research resulted in a custom-enhanced index-like portfolio aligned with a mission to reduce poverty in the Bay Area. (The United Way of the Bay Area was the initial seed ground of this study. It has not endorsed and does not support any particular investment strategy at this time.)

When we were developing the equity portfolio research for UWBA, we determined that we must achieve several characteristics to assure our fiduciary standards were upheld: (1) have low/reasonable fees, (2) use a rules-based and objective process, (3) be implemented through professional (conflict-free) registered investment advisors, (4) be monitored through a prudent, standard due diligence process based on traditional benchmarks, and (5) expect market-like returns. This original UWBA research study was key to understanding how to assess and identify factors that are aligned with the mission of alleviating poverty in the Bay Area. This process was transferable to the current BAIII research, whose broad mission is to promote sustainable prosperity in the Bay Area economy.

UWBA/Aperio Group—BAIII custom public equity strategy

With the expertise of the Aperio Group, a Bay Area investment firm that builds custom portfolios, we developed an enhanced/ESG-integrated/Bay Area-focused custom strategy for an endowment fund whose mission is to reduce poverty in the Bay Area. The model equity portfolio was screened for ESG factors that were deemed proxies for a poverty alleviation mission as well as for a geographic focus on the San Francisco Bay Area. Two dominant themes were identified for reducing poverty: having a good job and having an affordable place to live.

The Bay Area-focused public equity model portfolio was developed from a unique universe dominated (75 percent) by companies headquartered in the Bay Area. As discussed in the original research, we chose Bay Area employers as the significant geographic factor and used screens for ESG factors that are aligned with a poverty alleviation mission, such as having a good job. We believed that a good job with a good company that offered good salaries and benefits, had good labor relations, and transparent and diverse management and governance structures contributed to poverty reduction through steady employment. The Bloomberg Bay Area Index, created by *Bloomberg* and the *San Francisco Chronicle* in 2003, provided the underlying universe of companies headquartered in the Bay Area (symbol: BBACAX). The custom universe was analyzed and a portfolio of equities was optimized against the Russell 3000 that would balance the goal of maximizing the ESG score while minimizing the tracking error to the benchmark. These companies represent those who have positive employee relations, good benefits, transparent and diverse management, strong environmental policies, etc., as detailed in the chapter. A broad impact of this portfolio includes monitoring and encouraging good corporate citizenship through active proxy voting and corporate engagement.

Portfolio construction

Portfolio optimization builds portfolios with sector weightings similar to the benchmark. Except for Telecommunications Services, all major industries are represented in the Bay Area. Compared to the overall market, the Bay Area is over-weighted in Information Technology, Financials, and Health Care and underweighted in Industrials and Materials. Our surprisingly diverse and remarkably robust region is the 19th largest economy in the world, and is home to the second largest concentration of Fortune 500 companies in the world. In order to reduce tracking error and more closely represent some of the largest employers and missing sectors in the Bay Area, about 15 extra companies were added to our custom universe of Bay Area employers.

ESG integration

The next step in creating our custom portfolio was to determine a series of social criteria (see Table 43.2) that would be proxies for identifying companies that could be classified as being "good employers" (S), having "good management" (G), and behaving as "good environmental

Table 43.2 UWBA custom ESG factors

Criteria	*Data elements*	*Importance*	*Weighting*	*% of total*
Labor Relations	Evaluation of Relationships with Organized Labor	High	4	22%
Recognition	Workplace and Diversity	High	4	22%
Diversity	Total Workforce and Management	Medium	2	11%
Sexual Orientation	Non-discrimination Statement Same Sex Benefits	Medium	2	11%
Environmental	Toxic Release Information and Spills	Medium	2	11%
Human Rights	Global Sullivan and Global Compact	Medium	2	11%
Corporate Governance	Governance Metrics Grades	Medium	2	11%

stewards" (E) in the Bay Area. We ranked those criteria and used objective data sources to identify companies who rated well in these ESG criteria to create a custom score for each company in the universe. By identifying only the top handful of criteria that are relevant to a poverty alleviation mission, we did not dilute the screening intentions with too many factors.

Balancing ESG and tracking error

Developing weightings for those factors, through a consensus voting process by the committee and staff, we created a custom scoring system unique to UWBA's mission. Each company/stock in the universe would be evaluated on its custom ESG score as well as for its fit in the portfolio structure as measured by its contribution to diversification and minimizing tracking error. Using computer-driven portfolio optimization programs at the Aperio Group we developed a series of portfolios with varying levels of custom ESG scores and tracking error to the Russell 3000. The goal was to create a model portfolio of stocks that would maximize the aggregate custom ESG score while minimizing the tracking error to the Russell 3000, thereby balancing idealism with pragmatism. We also tested three different underlying universes of stocks, since we could see that the tracking error resulting from the geographic focus was much greater than the tracking error resulting from the ESG screens. As shown in Table 43.3, the three universes varied by the degree to which the companies in the universe were headquartered in the Bay Area or not: 100 percent, 75 percent, or 50 percent.

Graphing the various portfolios that demonstrated the trade-off between tracking error and high to low ESG scores, over the three universes, resulted in three "frontiers." The resulting "middle" equity portfolio (see Figure 43.4) appears to balance the desire for a highly rated ESG portfolio with the desire to minimize tracking error to the benchmark. In this portfolio, the equity holdings, of which 75 percent are headquartered in the Bay Area, give us a 4× overweighting to the Bay Area versus the Russell 3000, where just 19 percent of the companies are headquartered here in the Bay Area.

This model portfolio is tilted towards the companies whose practices were aligned with positive employee relationships, good governance, and good environmental practices. Being optimized against our benchmark, the portfolio is expected to exhibit sector weightings, risk, and performance expectations similar to the Russell 3000, with a tracking error of 1.64 percent. The screens used in the custom ESG scoring system improved from the basic ESG score for the Russell 3000 of 46 to the model portfolio's ESG score of 60, a 30 percent improvement for ESG criteria at a small (<2 percent) cost to tracking the benchmark.

This custom model portfolio is now more aligned with the core mission of regional poverty alleviation and can be expected to earn market levels of return and experience similar risks as its benchmarks. The historical performance of the model equity portfolio was within range of the projected tracking error, with the model portfolio outperforming its Russell 3000 benchmark for the 4-year period ending December 31, 2014: 17.49 percent versus 15.27 percent annualized. In Table 43.4, the strategy presented is the custom model portfolio and does not include fees.

The second public equity investment strategy is an active stock selection approach with ESG integration and a proprietary fundamental analysis of human capital factors to score companies on five key criteria: health, wealth, earth, equality, and trust. The third strategy is a passive Russell 3000 index fund with active corporate engagement and shareholder voting using a formal process to frame and understand issues, analyze this, engage management on identifying and mitigating key risk factors, and help to protect long-term shareholder value.

Combining these three strategies, the custom ESG/optimized enhanced index portfolio with its 4× overweighting in Bay Area publicly traded employers/companies, the active ESG integrated

Table 43.3 Sample portfolios

Screened portfolio version	*R3000 Index*	*1*	*4*	*8*	*10*	*13*	*7*	*11*
Percent Headquartered in Bay Area	19%	100%	100%	75%	75%	75%	50%	50%
Benchmark	R3000	R3000	R3000	R3000	R3000	R3000	R3000	R3000
Model Universes	R3000 Index	BBACAX+15	BBACAX+15	BBACAX+15 + 25% other	BBACAX+15 + 25% other	BBACAX+15 + 25% other	BBACAX+15 + 50% other	BBACAX+15 + 50% other
Universe—Holdings	2,940	252	252	1,982	1,982	1,982	1,982	1,982
Standard Deviation	20.43	20.57	20.65	20.48	20.52	20.49	20.44	20.47
Tracking Error vs. Benchmark, %	0.00	2.41	3.02	1.36	1.95	1.64	0.67	1.32
Model UWBA Social Score	*46*	*51*	*65*	*50*	*65*	*60*	*49*	*65*
Bay Area Weight %	19	100	100	75	75	75	50	50
Number of Holdings	2,940	126	99	264	178	210	450	294
Average Market Capitalization, $ Billions	87.9	80.0	93.2	89.0	89.0	89.5	89.8	91.6

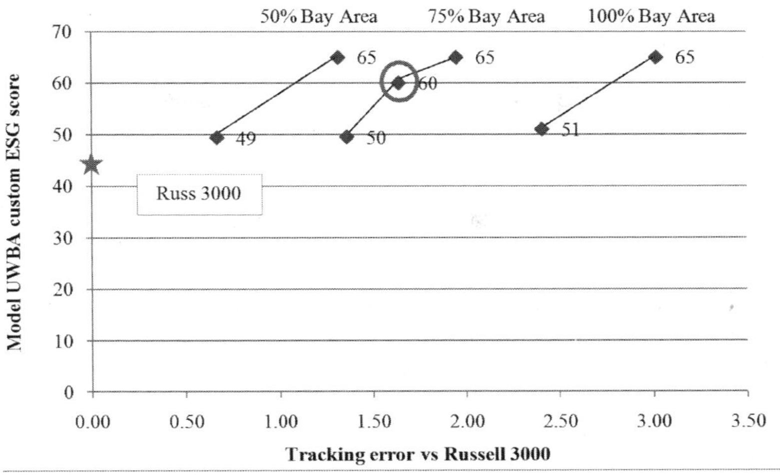

Figure 43.4 Mapping ESG scoring with tracking error

Table 43.4 Custom portfolio performance January 1, 2011 through December 31, 2014

Month	*Russell 3000*	*Aperio/UWBA custom*
CY 2011	1.01%	1.56%
CY 2012	16.37%	20.95%
CY 2013	33.46%	33.38%
CY 2014	12.54%	16.29%
Inception cumulative	76.54%	90.53%
Inception annualized	15.27%	17.49%

Table 43.5 Public equity portfolio managers

BAIII public equity	
New Resource Bank	https://www.newresourcebank.com
Aperio Group	https://www.aperiogroup.com
HIP Investor—HIP 100	http://www.hipinvestor.com
BlackRock R3000	http://www.blackrock.com

portfolio, and the passive index fund with corporate engagement, we can be fairly confident that we would achieve market levels of risk and return over a market cycle and longer term as well (the public equity portfolio managers are listed in Table 43.5).

BAIII multi-manager fixed income model portfolio

Fixed income is usually a big portion of our institutional portfolios. Until recently, there were limited opportunities to use fixed income assets to make a social impact. Now there are an increasing number of bonds that provide the attractive aspects of owning fixed income securities, such as the promised coupon (yield), a specific time frame (maturity), and an understandable,

Table 43.6 Fixed income portfolio managers

BAIII fixed income	
Community Capital Management	http://www.ccmfixedincome.com
AFL-CIO Housing Investment Trust	http://www.aflcio-hit.com
Breckinridge Cap	http://www.breckinridge.com
White Oak Global	http://www.whiteoaksf.com

quantifiable risk level (default risk) with the added benefit of some positive impact. A certain number of these impact-oriented fixed income investments provide liquidity directly to specific projects, like affordable housing, micro-investing/micro-lending, or global green projects. Investors are more likely to get better metrics from our fixed income investments about impact (like the number of affordable housing units or clean water systems built) than in public equities.

The terms of these impact bonds in the portfolio will show where these investments can fit in the asset allocation (short or long duration, domestic or global, investment grade or high yield). These assets can continue to act as a diversifier and lower the risk of the entire portfolio because they have low correlation to and less volatility than equities. Understanding these attributes within the whole portfolio context is part of the necessary due diligence process. When we monitor the portfolio and performance against its benchmarks over time, we can track the impact as well.

As shown in Table 43.6, the BAIII multi-manager fixed income portfolio models four fixed income management firms: a CRA qualified fixed income fund focused primarily in government-related housing subsectors, a building and jobs investment fund, an actively researched strategy in sustainable bonds, and a direct lender to small and medium-sized companies. Each portfolio would own bonds with a Bay Area impact.

Alternative Impact Investments

Sustainable/Impact/ESG Investment strategies can be integrated into real estate, private equity funds, loan funds, hedge funds, venture capital, infrastructure, and other funds of funds vehicles. It can sometimes be easier to identify impact in the alternative investment space than in publicly traded markets. We can often see the direct benefit of the capital investment, such as R&D for vaccines, green and clean tech development like solar energy or electric cars, and community outreach programs and providers. Collaboration between private and public investors may also yield different investment structures with different risk characteristics that achieve common goals, like a community development public/private partnership that could combine affordable housing, transit, economic development, and open space acquisition and protection goals.

Many alternative investments are generally not as liquid and as available to all investors as are mutual funds of stocks and bonds. The following model portfolios suggest a variety of managers, each of whose liquidity, style, and vehicle is unique. We offer the following investment advisory firms as evidence that there are reliable investment strategies that do provide the institutional investor positive impacts and market-like returns, and can pass the regular due diligence requirements.

BAIII multi-manager real estate model portfolio

Real estate is an asset class used in institutional portfolios to diversify the equity and fixed income holdings with a different, less correlated return pattern. It can serve as an income generator and

Table 43.7 Real estate portfolio managers

BAIII real estate	
NorCal Community Loan Fund	www.ncclf.org
American Realty	www.americanreal.com
HIP Investor REIT	www.hipinvestor.com
Gerding Edlin	www.gerdingedlin.com

inflation hedge in long-term portfolios. The BAIII Multi-Manager Real Estate portfolio would invest in a variety of complementary real estate managers and strategies: a Bay Area based CDFI real estate lender, a registered investment advisor with a liquid REIT strategy with ESG integration, and real estate investment managers who are building affordable housing and mixed use properties in the Bay Area, creating jobs, and using sustainable environmental practices in the Bay Area. As shown in Table 43.7, these real estate investment strategies could be combined to produce a unique multi-manager real estate portfolio, with an extra focus on the San Francisco Bay Area.

BAIII multi-manager private equity fund

Private equity/venture capital is an asset class suitable for larger, long-term-oriented investors. These investments often fund start-up companies or provide capital for small companies to grow, create jobs, and build wealth. Private investments are generally managed by specialists in limited partnership structures with a 10–year-plus time horizon for return of capital and appreciation. Proven venture capital firms, particularly in the Bay Area, have funded disruptive and transformative technologies for decades, like Apple, Google, Facebook, and eBay. The unique ecosystem of the Bay Area, in combining the academic expertise of our world-class universities with the entrepreneurial mindset that Silicon Valley has embraced, has lifted the Bay Area private equity industry to global leadership. In Table 43.8 we have identified a few private equity managers who have had proven success in delivering both strong financial returns and a positive local impact on our economy and residents, whose strategies' descriptions follow and whose financial performance was in the top quartile of its peer group (Cambridge Associates; www.cambridgeassociates.com). Implementing the private equity portfolios would be contingent on which fund manager is accepting new investors when we may be ready to invest, what sectors and locations are available, the state of the overall market and economy, and other factors. Liquidity is limited in private equity, with lock-up periods usually 10 or more years. Returns can be elusive in the early years as the investments take time to develop profitability and achieve some exit such as an IPO or acquisition, but those returns can be significant. By using various investing opportunities, the BAIII multi-manager private investment model portfolio would expect to provide a broad approach through the market cycle: short-term loans, working capital, private equity, or debt financing using experienced venture investing firms in the Bay Area.

Table 43.8 Private equity portfolio managers

BAIII private equity	
Community Bank of the Bay: BAGF	www.bankcbb.com
Bay Area Council Equity Fund 3	www.bayareacouncil.org
Pacific Community Ventures SAIL	www.pacificcommunityventures.org
DBL Investors	www.dblinvestors.com

Regional private equity double bottom-line/Impact Investing in the San Francisco was pioneered by the Bay Area Council in 2002 with its private equity and real estate funds. A new fund is being developed by the Bay Area Council for local private investment into low and moderate income neighborhoods and double bottom-line results. Combining these private equity/Impact Investing firms can provide complementary strategies over the capital and growth cycle, as shown in Table 43.8.

BAIII multi-manager infrastructure fund

Infrastructure can be a valuable asset class and impact provider for long-term investors, offering results often tied to inflation through long-term leases or power purchase agreements, providing attractive current cash flow, inflation protection, and real asset appreciation. There are many types of infrastructure investments: energy development and distribution, including renewable energy and energy efficiency improvements, water, telecommunications and technology, roads and other sources of transit, and housing. Infrastructure is often funded through public–private partnerships, using complex capital stacks that combine private capital, public funds and subsidies, taxes and fees, low interest rate loans, risk capital, and philanthropic capital.

Building an infrastructure portfolio will involve ongoing research and due diligence. We have identified several advisors and funds around the Bay Area in infrastructure or clean/green technology funds, as well as projects that are examples of senior capital needs in project finance as well as relationships and other investors that we could partner with to fund projects. At the State of California, new policy proposals are being developed to provide more efficient financing of local infrastructure projects through Enhanced Infrastructure Financing Districts (EIFDs) and collective choice energy partnerships (www.caeconomy.org). A regional or statewide clearinghouse of infrastructure opportunities, such as the California I Bank will likely provide more opportunities. Specialty fund managers investing in energy efficiency and renewable energy and water systems are also likely candidates, as shown in Table 43.9.

With the enormous pools of wealth in the Bay Area (creating millionaires by the minute), combined with the wealth we have accumulated over the past few decades in our unique region, we could think about intentionally investing in our own backyard to protect, preserve, strategically optimize, and build our future. Collectively investing our trusts, retirement plans, savings accounts, estates, foundations, and endowments—even just 1–2 percent of our portfolios, when combined and invested right here in our own backyard—would have tremendous impact.

The BAIII is dedicated to building these model portfolios and sharing the solutions and potential impacts across our community of investors, students, citizens, and policy makers. We have developed and shared examples of prudent and impactful portfolios in real estate, infrastructure, and private capital, as well as model equity and fixed income funds, all with an intentional positive impact on the San Francisco Bay Area and its sustainable economic prosperity.

Table 43.9 Infrastructure portfolio managers

BAIII infrastructure	
The Bay Area TOAHD	www.bayareatod.org
The California I-Bank	www.ibank.ca.gov
Mosaic Solar	www.joinmosaic.com
Other candidates	www.calcef.org

We ask: If you could invest where you live, to help it retain its strengths, remedy its weaknesses, and recycle some of this region's wealth for you and your mission, achieving both strong financial returns and positive local impact, would you?

The BAIII can evolve further with the contributions of various partners around the Bay Area. We can catalyze significant assets to work for the benefit of our communities, our environment, and our people while we earn strong returns on our investments. We welcome more partners to the regional table to determine how to proceed.

Acknowledgments

With permission to reprint by the publisher: Agnew, L. (2012). Impact investing for small, place-based fiduciaries: The research study initiated by the United Way of the Bay Area. *Federal Reserve Bank of San Francisco Working Paper* (2012–05).

References

Agnew, L. (2012). *Impact investing for small, place-based fiduciaries: The research study initiated by the United Way of the Bay Area*. Retrieved August 31, 2015, from http://www.frbsf.org/community-development/files/wp2012-05.pdf

Bridges Ventures. (2014). *Shifting the lens: A de-risking toolkit for impact investing*. Retrieved March 14, 2016, from http://www.trilincglobal.com/wp-content/uploads/2014/01/BV_BoA_de-risking_report_FINAL-2.pdf

California Financial Opportunities Roundtable. (2012). *Access to capital*. Retrieved August 31, 2015, from http://www.rd.usda.gov/files/CA-CalFOR.pdf

Heckman, J. (2012). *Invest in early childhood development: Reduce deficits, strengthen economy*. Retrieved August 31, 2015, from http://heckmanequation.org/content/resource/invest-early-childhood-development-reduce-deficits-strengthen-economy

Hernandez, M., & Genser, J. (2014). *Social impact bonds and community foundations: Making pay-for-success initiatives accessible*. Retrieved March 14, 2016, from https://www.missioninvestors.org/system/files/tools/social-impact-bonds-article-antony-bugg-levine-richmond-cf-oct-2014.pdf

Johnson, K. (2014). Introduction to institutional investor fiduciary duties. *International Institute for Sustainable Development Report, 44*. Retrieved March 14, 2016, from https://www.iisd.org/sites/default/files/publications/fiduciary_duties_en.pdf

Randolph, S. (2012, March 18). Bay Area must work hard to maintain economic edge. *San Francisco Chronicle*. Retrieved March 18, 2012, from http://www.sfgate.com

US National Advisory Board on Impact Investing. (2014). *Private capital and public good: How smart federal policy can galvanize impact investing and why it's urgent*. Retrieved August 31, 2015, from http://www.socialimpactinvestment.org/reports/US%20REPORT%20FINAL%20250614.pdf

US SIF (2014). *2014 report on US sustainable, responsible and impact investing trends*. Retrieved March 14, 2016, from http://www.ussif.org/store_product.asp?prodid=19

INDEX